HARDPRESS .NET

ISBN: 9781314125122

Published by:
HardPress Publishing
8345 NW 66TH ST #2561
MIAMI FL 33166-2626

Email: info@hardpress.net
Web: http://www.hardpress.net

Coimisiún Láimhscríbhinní na hÉireann

REFLEX PROCESS FACSIMILES

III

THE ANNALS OF LOCH CÉ

Reproduced at the Ordnance Survey
Dublin

DUBLIN
PUBLISHED BY THE STATIONERY OFFICE

To be purchased directly from the
Government Publications Sale Office, 3—4 College Street, Dublin
or through any Bookseller

1939
Price Fifteen Shillings

THE

ANNALS OF LOCH CÉ

THE

ANNALS OF LOCH CÉ.

A CHRONICLE OF IRISH AFFAIRS

FROM A.D. 1014 TO A.D. 1590.

EDITED, WITH A TRANSLATION,

BY

WILLIAM M. HENNESSY, M.R.I.A.

PUBLISHED BY THE AUTHORITY OF THE LORDS COMMISSIONERS OF HER MAJESTY'S
TREASURY, UNDER THE DIRECTION OF THE MASTER OF THE ROLLS.

VOL. II.

LONDON:
LONGMAN & Co., AND TRÜBNER & Co., PATERNOSTER ROW
ALSO BY PARKER & Co., OXFORD;
MACMILLAN & Co., CAMBRIDGE;
A. & C. BLACK, EDINBURGH; AND A. THOM, DUBLIN

1871

Printed by
ALEXANDER THOM, 87 & 88 Abbey-street. Dublin.
For Her Majesty's Stationery Office.

CONTENTS.

CORRIGENDA.

VOL. I.

Page 123, line 4, *for* the king of Eile, *read* another king.

„ 240, note ², *for* typographical, *read* topographical.

„ 515, last line but two, *for* Mac Oirechtaigh, *read* Mac Raghnaill.

„ 527, line 7, *for* Mac Flannchchaidh, *read* Mac Flannchaidh.

VOL. II.

Page 72, note ¹. *for* Mor ahon (in parenthesis), *read* Mahon.

„ 273, line 18, *for* O'.Neill, *read* O'Domhnaill.

αnnαlα lochα cé.

ANNALS OF LOCH CÉ.

ꞇnnꞑlꞑ lochꞑ cé.

[MS. defective. Text supplied from " Annals of Connacht."]

Iꞇ. Enꞇiꞃ ꞃoꞃ Ꝺaꞃꝺꞇoin, ocuꞃ cecꞁꞃe uꞇchꞇꝺ ꞃuiꞃꞃi ; M°.ccc°.xl°.ix. ; bliꞇꝺꞇin ꞇoꞃꞇꞓ noiꝺecꝺꞇ i ; [ꞃecunꝺo] anno inꝺicꞇioniꞃ ; xxii. cicli ꞃolaꞃiꞃ. Ꝃillꞇ na naem Uꞇ hUcinn moꞃꞇuiꞃ eꞃꞇ. Maiꝺin ꝺo chaꝃaiꞃꞇ ꝺꞀeꝺ .h.Ruꞇi ꞃe aꞃꝼlaꞇꞁꞇꞃꞇach.h.Ruꞇiꞃe ocuꞃ aꞃ Ꝺonꝺchaꝺ .h.nꝺomnaill, ocuꞃ aꞃ Ꝺaꞃꞇꞃꞇiꞃib, ocuꞃ Ꝗꞃ Mac ꝼlanꞃchꞇꝺ, ꞇꞇiꞃéch Ꝺaꞃꞇꞃꞇiꞃi, ꝺo maꞃꝃaꝺ anꝺ, ocuꞃ Ꝗillꞇ na naem Maꞃ ꝼlanꞃchaꝺ, ocuꞃ Lochlainn mac Anꝺiliꞃ .h.bꞇiꞃill, eꞇ alii mulꞇi nobileꞃ. Mac mic anꝺ Iꞇꞃlꞇ ꝺo ꞇeachꞇ a Connachꞇaib ocuꞃ cꞃeach ꝺo ꞃaꝃail ꝺó, ocuꞃ mac Uilliam buꞃc ocuꞃ Mac ꝼeoꞃaiꞃ ꝺo bꞃeicꞁ aiꞃ, ocuꞃ maiꝺm aꝺꝃal ꝺo chaꝃaiꞃꞇ aiꞃ, ocuꞃ mac mic inꝺ Iꞇꞃlꞇ ꝺo ꞃaꝃail anꞃ, ocuꞃ moꞃan ꝺo Chloinn Ricaiꞃꝺ ꝺo ꞃaꝃail ocuꞃ ꝺo maꞃꝃaꝺ anꝺ boꞃ. Cocaꝺ moꞃ eꞇiꞃ ꝼeꞃꞃal Mac nꝺiaꞃmaꝺa ocuꞃ Ruaiꝺꞃi mac Caꞇhail, ocuꞃ Ꝗaill ocuꞃ Ꝗaiꝺeal Connachꞇ ꝺo ꞇinol ꝺo Mac Ꝺiaꞃmaꝺa, ocuꞃ Cenel Conaill aꞃuꞃ Clann Muiꞃcheaꞃꞇaiꞃ, ꞃuꞃ chuiꞃeꝺaꞃ mac Caꞇhail ꞃꞇ cloinn ꝼeꞃumoiꞃi, ocuꞃ niꞃ ꝼeoꞃaꝺ ni ꝺo, cuꞃ imꞃoꝺaꞃ cen ꞃiall can eiꝺiꞃe, aꞃuꞃ cuꞃ loiꞃc ocuꞃ cuꞃ aiꞃcc mac Caꞇhail uꞃmoꞃ Moiꞃi Luiꞃꞃ iaꞃom. Plaꞃ moꞃ immoiꞃ Luiꞃc ocuꞃ an Eꞃinꝺ ulꞇ in hoc anno. Maꞇha mac Caꞇhail.h.Ruaiꞃe ꝺecc

---

1 *Alii.* aⲗi, B and C.

2 *Cathal*; i.e. Cathal, son of Domhnall O'Conchobhair. See under the year 1348, where another war is mentioned as having occurred between this same Ruaidhri, son of Cathal, and Ferghal Mac Diarmada, or Farrell Mac Dermot.

ANNALS OF LOCH CÉ.

THE kalends of January on Thursday, and the fourth of the moon; Mº.cccº.xlº.ix. It was the first year of the Nineteen; [secundo] anno Indictionis; xxv. cycli solaris. Gilla-na-naemh O'hUiginn mortuus est. A victory was gained by Aedh O'Ruairc over Flaithbhertach O'Ruairc, and over Donnchadh O'Domhnaill, and over the Dartraighe; and Aedh Mac Flannchaidh, chieftain of Dartraighe, was slain there, and Gilla-na-naemh Mac Flannchaidh, and Lochlainn, the son of Andiles O'Baighill, et alii[1] multi nobiles. The Earl's grandson went into Connacht, and took a prey; and Mac William Burk and Mac Feorais overtook him, and inflicted a great defeat on him; and the Earl's grandson was taken prisoner there; and a great number of the Clann-Rickard were, moreover, captured and slain there. A great war between Ferghal Mac Diarmada and Ruaidhri, son of Cathal;[2] and the Foreigners and Gaeidhel of Connacht were assembled by Mac Diarmada, together with the Cenel-Conaill and Clann-Muirchertaigh; and they drove the son of Cathal towards Clann-Fernmhaighe, but were unable to do him any injury; and they returned without pledge or hostage.[3] And the son of Cathal afterwards burned and plundered the greater part of Magh-Luirg. A great plague in Magh-Luirg, and in all Erinn, in hoc[4] anno. Matthew, son of Cathal O'Ruairc, died of this

---

[3] *Hostage.* eiτιηε, C. oιτιηε, B. | [4] *Hoc.* oc, B.

ᴅon plaıᵹ pın. Ϻac mıc an ıapla ᴅo écc. Rıpᴅepᴅ
.h.Raıᵹıllıᴆ, pí na ᴮpeıpne ᴛoıp, ᴅo éccaıᴆ. ᴅonᴅ-
chaᴆ pıaᴆach, mac Ϻaelechlaınn chappaıᵹ Ϻıc
ᴅıapmaᴅa, ᴅo ᵹaᴆaıl ᴅo Copmac boᴆap Ϻac ᴅıapmaᴅa, ocup a ᴮpeıᴆ leıp a nᴄᴄıpᴛech, ocup a ᵐapᴆaᴆ
a pıll ᴅo mac ᵹılla Cpıopᴅ mıc ᴛaıchlıᴆ acup ᴅo Ua
Cepnaıᵹ.ıappın. ᵹıllıbepᴅ.h.plannacan, ᴛaıpech ᴛuaıᴆı
páᴛha, ᴅo ᵐapᴆaᴆ ᴅo macaıᴆ ᴮpıaın.h.plannacan.
Ϻuıpᴄeapᴛach píaᵹanach Ϻaᵹ ᴄᴄenᵹupa ᴅo mapᴆaᴆ
ᴅıa ᴮpaıᴆpıᴆ peın.

ᴋᴄᴛ. ᴇnaıp pop ᴄᴄıne, ocup coıceᴆ .x. puıppı ; Ϻ°.ccc°.ᴌ. ;
an ᴅapa blıaᴆaın ᴅon cıcıl naeᴅecᴅo í, ocup ın ᴛpep
blıaᵹaın ᴅon cıcıl ınᴅıcᴛıonıp ; xxuı. cıclı polapıp
pepᵹal mac Ualᵹapᵹ.h.Ruaıpc ᴅo mapᴆaᴆ ᴅo mac
Caᴛhaıl clepıᵹ Ϻıc ᴅonᴅochaıᴆ. ᴮpıan Ϻac ᴅıapmaᴅa, ᴅaᵐına pıᵹ Ϻoıᵹı.luıpc, ᴅo mapᴆaᴆ ıpRop
Comman ᴅo muınnᴛıp an eppoıcc .h. pınnachᴛa, ᴅaen
upchop ᴛpoıᵹᴛı co ᴛubaıpᴛech, ocup ın pep ap ap cuıpeᴅ
anᴛ opᴄᴜıp .ı. Ruaıᴆpı ınᴛ peompa .h.ᴅonᴅochaᴆa, ᴅo
mapᴆaᴆ ocup ᴅo chıppᴆaᴆ ann. ᴮpıan, mac ᴅoᵐınaıll
mıc ᴮpıaın puaıᴆ .h.ᴮpıaın, ᴅo mapᴆaᴆ a pıll ᴅo
ınacaıᴆ lopcan Ϻec Ceoᴛhach, uᴛ ᴅıxıᴛ poeᴛa

ᴛpuaᵹ aen mac ᴅoᵐnaıll ᴅala,
ᴛpuaᵹ oıᵹıp ᴮpıaın ᴮopámha,
ᴛpuaᵹ a ᴅol map nap paıleᴆ,
ᴛpuaᵹ clann Ceoch ᴅa coᵐmaıᴆeᵐ.

ᴛoıppᴅhealbach acc .h.ᴮpıaın ᴅo mapᴆaᴆ pe ᴛıp nᴅecc
ᴅo clann Ceoch, ocup a cpoᴅ ocup a pepanᴅ ᴅo ᴆuaın
ᴅıᴆ beopp. ᴄᴄeᴅ.mac ᴄᴄeᴅa ᴮpeıpnıᵹ .h. Conchoᴆaıp,

---

1 *Earl's grandson.* The Four Mast.
call him "the Earl's son"; but Mageoghegan, who adds that he died of
the plague just mentioned, states that
he was "the Earl of Ulster's grand-
child."

² *Breifne in the East*; i.e. Eastern
Breifne, Breifne O'Reilly, or the present county of Cavan.

³ *By O'Cernaigh.* So in C. B reads
ᴅo Connachᴛaıb, "by Connachtmen"; but the reading of C is apparently the more correct, as it agrees
with the expression in the Four Mast.

⁴ *Kalends.* The Dom. Letter (C)
is added in the margin in B.

⁵ *Cycle of Nineteen*; i.e. the Lunar
Cycle.

plague. The Earl's grandson[1] died. Richard O'Raighil-   A.D.
ligh, king of Breifne in the East,[2] died. Donnchadh   [1349.]
Riabhach, the son of Maelechlainn Carrach Mac Diarmada, was taken prisoner by Cormac Bodhar Mac Diarmada, who took him with him to Airtech, where he was
afterwards slain, in treachery, by the son of Gilla-Christ
Mac Taichligh, and by O'Cernaigh.[3] Gilbert O'Flannagain,
chieftain of Tuath-ratha, was slain by the sons of Brian
O'Flannagain. Muirchertach Riaganach Mac Aenghusa
was slain by his own brothers.

The kalends[4] of January on Friday, and the fifteenth   [1350.]
of the moon. M°.ccc°.l. It was the second year of the
cycle of Nineteen ;[5] and the third year of the cycle of the
Indiction ; xxvi. cycli solaris. Ferghal, son of Ualgharg O'Ruairc, was killed by the son of Cathal Clerech
Mac Donnchaidh. Brian Mac Diarmada, royal heir of
Magh-Luirg, was unfortunately[6] killed in Ros-Coniain,
by the Bishop O'Finnachta's people, with one discharge
of an arrow ; and the man who was convicted of the shot,
i.e. Ruaidhri-int-seomra[7] O'Donnchadha, was slain and
mangled there. Brian, son of Domhnall, son of Brian
Ruadh O'Briain, was killed, in treachery, by the sons of
Lorcan Mac Ceothach, ut dixit poeta—

     " Pity ! the only son of Domhnall of the assembly ;
     Pity ! the heir of Brian Borumha ;
     Pity ! his going as was not expected ;
     Pity the Clann-Ceoch[8] should triumph over him."

Toirdhelbhach Og O'Briain killed sixteen men of the
Clann-Ceoch, who were deprived, moreover, of their stock
and land. Aedh, son of Aedh Breifnech O'Conchobhair,

---

[6] *Unfortunately.* co cubaircech,
C. co cubaipech, B.
[7] *Ruaidhri-int-seomra ;* literally,
" Ruaidhri of the chamber."
[8] *Clann-Ceoch.* Written " Claun-

Ceothach " in the prose account. The
Four Mast. write the last word of the
name " Ceoach," and " Ceoch." See
Dr. O'Donovan's note, Four Masters,
ad an.

[MS. defective. Text supplied from "Annals of Connacht."]

ris iarti .h. Conchoḃair Breifnech, do marḃaḋ la hAeḋ .h. Ruairc a moig Engaiti in hoc anno. Ruaiḋri, mac Cathail mic Domnaill .h. Conchubair, do marḃaḋ a fill do cloinn Fergail Mic Donnchaḋa, tria forgall Aeda mic Toirrdhealḃaiġ. Muirgius mac Donnchaid do ecc in hoc anno. Aeḋ mac Toirrdhealḃaiġ do athriġaḋ do ṁac Uilliam Burcc agus do thuathaiḃ Connacht, ocus Aed mac Feiḋlimiḋ do riġaḋ doibh ina aḋaiġ. Aengus .h. hEoḋusa mortuus est. Aengus ruaḋ .h. Dalaiġ, sai Erend re dán, quieuit. Cuchoigriche mor mag Eochacan, dux cenel Fiachaiḋ, quieuit. Uilliam espcop Ua Dubda, .i. espcop Cille hAlaid, quieuit.

Kl. Enair for Sathairnn, ocus ui.xx. fuirri; M°.ccc°.l. primo; tertio anno cicli lunaris; iiii. annus indictionis; xxuii. cicli solaris. Pilip Mag Uidir mortuus est. Aed mac Toirrdhealbaiġ do theaċt is tír, ocus braiġdi Connacht do thaḃach dó, ocus mac Feiḋlimiḋ dinnarbaḋ re bliaḋain do iar sin. Aed .h. Ruairc do gaḃail ic teacht o Cruaich Padruic, do mac Pilpin mic Uilliam Burcc, ocus Fergal mac Diarmada do ergi tríd an ngaḃail sin, ocus cur fás cocaḋ coitchend hi Connachtaiḃ uile, ocus Maġ Luirg do lomarcain trit sin. Gairm coitchend do thabairt dUilliam mac Donnchaiḋ Muimnigh .h. Cellaiġ, im notlaicc na garma, do dáiṁscolaiḃ Erend uili, ocus a teaċt lán buidech uile etir uasal ocus isel. Mathgamain Mac Consnama do marḃaḋ do cloinn Donnchaid Mic Consnama. Eogan Mac Suibne do marbaḋ la Magnus .h. nDomhnaill isin bliadhain cedna sin. Enna .h. Flannacan, taiseċ Tuaithe ratha, mortuus est.

---

1 *Hoc.* hocc, B and C.

2 *Tuatha*; i.e. the people of the "Three Tuatha;" districts in the north-east of the county of Roscommon. See O'Donovan's *Four Masters*, A.D. 1189, note d.

3 *Quievit.* This entry is not in C.

4 *Mac Udhir*; or Maguire. The Four Mast. add that he was chieftain of Muinter-Pheodachain, a district in the county of Fermanagh.

A.D.

[1350.]

[1351.]

who was usually called O'Conchobhair Breifnech, was slain by Aedh O'Ruairc, in Magh-Enghaiti, in hoc anno. Ruaidhri, son of Cathal, son of Domhnall O'Conchobhair, was killed, in treachery, by the sons of Ferghal Mac Donnchadha, at the instigation of Aedh, son of Toirdhelbhach. Maurice Mac Donnchaidh died in hoc[1] anno. Aedh, son of Toirdhelbhach, was deposed by Mac William Burk and by the Tuatha[2] of Connacht ; and Aedh, son of Fedhlimidh, was inaugurated by them in opposition to him. Aenghus O'hEodhusa mortuus est. Aenghus Ruadh O'Dalaigh, the most eminent poet in Erinn, quievit. Cucoicriche Mor Mac Eochagain, dux of Cenel-Fiachaidh, quievit. Bishop William O'Dubhda, i.e. bishop of Cill-Alaidh, quievit.[3]

The kalends of January on Saturday, and the twenty-sixth of the moon ; tertio anno cycli lunaris ; iiii. annus indictionis; xxvii. cycli solaris. Philip Mac Udhir[4] mortuus est. Aedh, the son of Toirdhelbhach, came into the country, and the hostages of Connacht were taken by him ; and the son of Fedhlimidh was afterwards exiled by him for the space of one year. Aedh O'Ruairc was taken prisoner by Mac Philpin Mac William Burk, whilst coming from Cruach-Patraic; and Ferghal Mac Diarmada rebelled in consequence of this capture, so that a general war[5] broke out in all Connacht, through which Magh-Luirg was wasted. A general invitation was given by William, son of Donnchaidh Muimhnech[6] O'Cellaigh, about "Christmas of the invitation," to all the learned of Erinn, and they all returned fully grateful, both[7] high and low. Mathghamhain Mac Consnamha was slain by the sons of Donnchadh Mac Consnamha. Eoghan Mac Suibhne was slain by Maghnus O'Domhnaill in the same year. Enna O'Flannagain, chieftain of Tuath-ratha, mortuus est.

---

[5] *War.* cocaó ; repeated in C.
[6] *Muimhnech.* This is an epithet signifying " Momonian," applied to Donnchadh O'Cellaigh from his having been fostered in Mumha, or Munster.
[7] *Both.* eciŋ (lit. " inter "), ß. eaŋuaŋ, C.

[*MS. defective. Text supplied from " Annals of Connacht."*]

Ict. Enaiр ꝛoр Ooṁnaċ, ocuꝛ ꝛechcmaḃ uachaḃ ꝛuiꝛꝛi ; M.ccc.L.ꝛecunꝺo ; 1111. anno cicli Lunaꝛiꝛ ; [u.] anno 1nꝺiccioniꝛ ; ꭓꭓu111. anno cicli ꝛolaꝛiꝛ. CCeḃ mac Coiꝛꝛꝺhealḃaiᵹ ꝺo ᵹaḃail ꝛiᵹi Connachc aꝛ ecin caꝛ ᵹallaiḃ ocuꝛ caꝛ ᵹaiḃealaiḃ. CCeḃ .h.maelḃꝛenainn ocuꝛ a ꝺá mac ꝺo maꝛḃaḃ La hCCeꝺ mac ꝛeiḃlimiḃ .h. Conchoḃaiꝛ. CCeḃ .h.Ruaiꝛc, ꝛi ḃꝛeiꝛne, ꝺo maꝛḃaꝺ ꝺo Chachal mac CCeḃa ḃꝛeiꝛniᵹ .h.Conchoḃaiꝛ ocuꝛ ꝺo cloinn Muiꝛḃeaꝛcaiᵹ aꝛchena, ocuꝛ áꝛ ᵹalloclaechaiḃ cloinne Suḃne inaꝛoen ꝛiꝛ. CCenᵹuꝛ O · Ooṁnaill, ꝛi ciꝛi Conaill, ꝺo maꝛḃaḃ La Maᵹnuꝛ .h.nOoṁnaill peꝛ ꝺolum. Oaḃáce, Oilmain mac Uilliuc Umaill, cenn ceiḋiꝛne Connachc, ꝺo ecc in hoc anno. ꝛlaichḃeaꝛcach .h.Ruaiꝛc, ꝛi ḃꝛeiꝛne, ꝺo ecc in hoc anno. macha maᵹ [O]oꝛchaiḃ ꝺo maꝛḃaḃ La Cloinn Muiꝛcheaꝛcaiᵹ. Commach ḃaili in ꝺuin La hCCeꝺ mac Coiꝛꝛꝺhealḃaiᵹ, ocuꝛ ꝺich ḃo ocuꝛ caeꝛach ann. Conchuḃaꝛ mac Muiꝛᵹioꝛa mic Oonꝺchaiḃ ꝺo hecc in hoc anno. Nuala, inᵹen mic Oiaꝛmaꝺa, ꝺo hecc in hoc anno. Comaꝛ Maᵹ Raᵹnaill moꝛcuuꝛ eꝛc. Caꝺcc mac Siaccuꝛa hi Cellaiᵹ ꝺo ec in hoc anno.

Ict. Enaiꝛ ꝛoꝛ Maiꝛc, occuꝛ ochcmaḃ ꝺecc ꝛuiꝛꝛi ; quinco anno cicli Lunaꝛiꝛ; ui. anno 1nꝺiccioniꝛ; pꝛimuꝛ annuꝛ ꝛolaꝛiꝛ cicli ; anno Oomini M°.ccc°.L.ꝛeꝛcio. CCeḃ mac Ruaiḃꝛi hi Neill moꝛcuuꝛ eꝛc. Caꝺᵹ Maᵹ Raᵹnaill, caiꝛeḋ Muinuciꝛe hⒺolaiꝛ, ꝺo maꝛḃaḃ ꝺo chloinꝺ cSeaꝛꝛaiḃ Meᵹ Raᵹnaill. CCeḃ mac Coiꝛꝛꝺhealḃaiᵹ ꝺo achꝛiᵹaḃ, ocuꝛ mac ḃꝛanainn ꝺia caḃaiꝛc iꝛ ciꝛ. ᵹoꝛmlaich inᵹean hi Ooṁnaill, ḃen hi Neill, in Cꝛiꝛco quieuic. machᵹaṁuin mac ᵹilla na naeṁ hi ꝛheꝛᵹail moꝛcuuꝛ eꝛc.

---

1 *Cycli.* cĩm, B.

2 *Anno.* Omitted in B.

3 *Toirdhelbhach* ; i.e. Toirdhelbhach O'Conchobhair, or Turlough O'Conor.

4 *Galloivglasses.* ᵹallaiḃ, i.e. Foreigners, B.

5 *Dilmhain.* This is the Irish form of the name " Dillon."

The kalends of January on Sunday, and the seventh of the moon ; M.ccc.l.secundo ; iiii. anno cycli[1] lunaris ; [v.] anno Indictionis ; xxviii. anno[2] cycli solaris. Aedh, son of Toirdhelbhach,[3] assumed the sovereignty of Connacht by force, in spite of Foreigners and Gaeidhel. Aedh O'Maelbhrenainn and his two sons. were slain by Aedh, son of Fedhlimidh O'Conchobhair. Aedh O'Ruairc, king of Breifne, was killed by Cathal, son of Aedh Breifnech O'Conchobhair, and by the Clann-Muirchertaigh likewise. and a slaughter of the Clann-Suibhne's gallowglasses along with him. Aenghus O'Domhnaill, king of Tir-Conaill, was killed by Maghnus O'Domhnaill, per dolum. Dabac Dilinhain,[5] son of Ulick of Umhall, head of the kerns of Connacht, died in hoc[6] anno. Flaithbhertach O'Ruairc, king of Breifne, died in hoc anno. Matthew Mac [D]orchaidh was killed by the Clann-Muirchertaigh. Demolition of Baile-in-duin by Aedh, son of Toirdhelbhach ; and a destruction of .cows and sheep *was committed* there. Conchobhar, son of Maurice Mac Donnchaidh, died in hoc anno. Nuala, daughter of Mac Diarmada, died in hoc anno. Thomas Mac Raghnaill mortuus est. Tadhg, son of Siacus[7] O'Cellaigh, died in hoc anno.

The kalends[8] of January on Tuesday, and the eighteenth of the moon ; quinto anno cycli lunaris ; vi. anno Indictionis ; primus annus solaris cycli ; anno Domini M°.ccc°.l.tertio. Aedh, son of Ruaidhri O'Neill, mortuus est. Tadhg Mac Raghnaill, chieftain[9] of Muinter-Eolais, was slain by the sons of Jeffrey Mac Raghnaill. Aedh, son of Toirdhelbhach, was deposed, and Mac Branan brought him into the country.[10] Gormlaith, daughter of O'Domhnaill, wife of O'Neill, in Christo quievit. Mathghamhain, son of Gilla-na-naemh O'Ferghail, mortuus est.

---

[6] Hoc. oc., B.

[7] *Siacus.* Jacques.

[8] *Kalends.* The Dom. Letter (F) is added in the margin.

[9] *Chieftain.* ᴛᴀɼᴄʜ, B.

[10] *Into the country;* i.e., into Mac Branan's country, Corca-Achlann, in the co. of Roscommon.

[MS. defective. Text supplied from " Annals of Connacht."]

·Ⰽⱦ. Ɇⱃⱥⱦ ⱎⱁⱃ Cⱦⱦⱥⱦⱃ, ⱥⰷⱳⱃ .ⱦⱦ. ⱎⱦⱍⱦⰽ ⱎⱳⱦⱃⱃⱦ ;
Ⱦ. cccc. ⰽ. ⱳⱦⱥⱃⱦⱃⱅⱁ ; ⱳⱦ. ⱥⱃⱃⱁ ⱦⱦⱦⰽ ⱡⱳⱃⱥⱎⱦⱃ ; ⱳⱦⱦ. ⱥⱃⱃⱁ
ⱦⱃⰱⱦⱦⱅⱦⱁⱃⱦⱎ ; ⱦⱦ· ⱥⱃⱃⱁ ⱎⱁⱡⱥⱎⱦⱃ ⱦⰽⱡⱦ. Ȼⱃⱦⱥⱃ Ⱳⱥ Ⰰⱳⰱⰴⱥ,
ⱎⱦⰷ Ⱳⱥ ⱎⱦⱥⱍⱎⱥⱍ, ⱞⱁⱎⱅⱳⱳⱎ ⱦⱎⱅ. Ⱨⱳⰱⱎⱥⱦⰷ Ⱳⱥ Ⱞⱁⱎⰱⱥ,
ⱎⱦⰷ ⱡⱥⱦⰷⱎⱃ, ⱞⱁⱎⱅⱳⱳⱎ ⱦⱎⱅ. Ȿⱦⱅⱎⱦⱳⱁ Ⱞⱥⰷ Ȿⱥⱞⱎⱥⰴⱥⱦⱃ
ⱞⱁⱎⱅⱳⱳⱎ ⱦⱎⱅ. Ȿⱦⱎⰱⱎⱁⱎⰷⱥⱦⱡⱡ ⱦⱃⰷⱦⱥⱃ ⱨⱦ Chⱁⱃⱍⱁⰱⱥⱦⱎ
ⱞⱁⱎⱅⱳⱥ ⱦⱎⱅ. Ȿⱦⱎⱎⱎⱥⱦⰱ Ⱞⱥⰷ Ⱨⱥⰷⱃⱥⱦⱡⱡ ⱞⱁⱎⱅⱳⱳⱎ ⱦⱎⱅ.
Ȼⱥⰱⰷ Ⱞⱥⱍ Ȿⱦⱃⱡⱥⱦⱍ ⱞⱁⱎⱅⱳⱳⱎ ⱦⱎⱅ. Ȿⱦⱥⱥⱃ Ⱳⱥ Ɑⱦⱃⱃⱥⱍⱅⱥ,
ⱦⱎⱎⱳⱍ ⱁⱦⱡⱦⱎⱦⱁ, ⱦⱃ Cⱎⱦⱎⱅⱁ ⱳⱦⱎⱦⱦⱦⱅ. Ɑⱦⰱ. ⱞⱥⱍ Cⱁⱎⱞⱥⱦⱍ
ⰱⱳⱦⰱⱦⱎ ⱅⱁ ⱞⱥⱎⰱⱥⰱ ⱅⱁ ⱞⱥⱍⱳⱦⰱ Ⰰⱁⱃⱃⱍⱥⱦⰱ ⱎⱦⱥⰱⱥⱦⰷ. Ⱁ
ⱡⱥⱍⱎⱅⱃⱥⱃ, ⱦⱎⱎⱳⱍ Cⱁⱃⱃⱥⱍⱎⱅ, ⱦⱃ Cⱎⱦⱎⱅⱁ ⱳⱦⱦⱦⱦⱅ. Ⱞⱥⱍ
Ⱞⱳⱎⱍⱎⱥⰱⱥ ⱅⱁ ⱅⱥⱎⱎⱳⱦⱃⰷ ⱅⱁ Ȿⱥⱡⱡⱥⱦⰱ, ⱁⱍⱳⱎ ⱍⱁⱍⱍⱥⰱ ⱞⱁⱎ
ⱦⱍⱦⱎ Ȿⱥⱡⱡⱥⱦⰱ ⱁⱍⱳⱎ Ȿⱥⱦⰱⱦⱡⱥⱦⰱ ⱅⱎⱦⱅ ⱎⱦⱃ. Ɑⱦⰱ Ⱞⱥⱍ
Ȿⱥⱞⱎⱥⰴⱥⱦⱃ ⱅⱁ ⰴⱳⱡ ⰴⱦⱍⱍ ⰴⱦⱥ ⰷⱁⱃⱥⱦⰱ. ⰱⱎⱦⱥⱃ ⱞⱥⱍ Ɑⱦⰱⱥ
ⱞⱁⱦⱎ ⱨⱦ Ⱨⱦⱦⱡⱡ ⱞⱁⱎⱅⱳⱳⱎ ⱦⱎⱅ. Ⱎⱦⱦⰱⱡⱦⱞ ⱞⱥⱍ Cⱥⱅⱍⱥⱦⱡ ⱦ
Cⱁⱃⱍⱁⰱⱥⱦⱎ ⰴⱦⱍⱍ ⱦⱎⱦⱃ ⰱⱡⱦⱥⰱⱥⱦⱃ cⱦⰴⱃⱥ ⱎⱦⱃ. Cⱥⱅⱍⱥⱡ ⱞⱥⱍ
Ⱨⱦⱦⱡⱡ ⱨⱦ Ⱨⱳⱥⱦⱎⱍ ⱅⱁ ⱨⱦⱍ. Ⱞⱥⱦⰱⱞ ⱞⱁⱎ ⱅⱁ ⱅⱍⱥⰱⱥⱎⱅ ⱅⱁ
ⱍⱍⱁⱦⱃⰴ Ɑⱍⰱⱥ ⰱⱳⱦⰴⱦ ⱁⱍⱳⱎ ⱅⱁ Ȿⱥⱡⱡⱥⱦⰱ Ⰰⱳⱦⱃⱦ Ⰰⱦⱡⱍⱥⱃ ⱥⱎ
Ɑⱦⰱ Ⱳ Ⱨⱦⱦⱡⱡ· ⰴⱍⱳⱎ ⱥⱎ ⱞⰴⱎ ⱅⱁ ⱍⱍⱳⱎ ⱥⱃⱃ. ⰱⱁⱦⰱⱦⱎⱅ
ⱥ ⰱⱳⱎⱍ ⱅⱁ ⱍⱦⰴⰴ ⱦⱃ ⱍⱁⱍ ⱥⱃⱃⱁ. Ⱨⱳⱥⱦⰴⱎⱦ ⱞⱥⱍ Ȿⱦⱁⱍⱎ
Ⱞⱦⰷ Ⱞⱥⱍⰷⱥⱞⱍⱃⱥ ⱅⱁ ⱞⱥⱎⰱⱥⰴ ⱦⱡⱡⱁⱃⰷⱎⱁⱎⱅ Ⱞⱦⰷ Ⱞⱥⱍⱍ-
ⰷⱥⱞⱍⱃⱥ.

Ⰽⱦⱅ. Ɇⱃⱥⱦⱎ ⱎⱁⱎ Ⰰⱥⱎⱁⱥⱁⱦⱃ, ⱁⱍⱳⱎ ⱍ. ⱳⱥⱍⱍⱥⰴ ⱎⱳⱎⱎⱎⱦ ;
Ⱞ.ccc.ⱡⱳ ; ⱳⱦⱦ. ⱥⱃⱃⱁ ⱦⰽⱡⱦ ⱡⱳⱃⱥⱎⱎⱎ; ⱁⱍⱅⱥⱳⱁ ⱥⱃⱃⱁ ⱦⱃⰴⱦⱍ-
ⱅⱦⱁⱃⱎⱎ ; ⱦⱦⱦ. ⱥⱃⱃⱁ ⱦⰽⱡⱦ ⱎⱁⱡⱥⱎⱳⱎ. Ȿⱦⱎ Ⱞⱳⱦⱎⱳⱎ Ⱎⱦⱅⱁⱞⱥⱎ,
ⰷⱦⱳⱎⱎⱁⱦⱎ ⱃⱥ ⱨⱦⱎⱦⱃⰴ ⱁⱍⱳⱎ ⱦⱥⱎⱡⱥ Ⰰⱦⱎⱞⱳⱞⱥⱃ, ⱅⱁ ⱦⱍⱍ ⱦⱎⱦⱃ
ⰱⱦⱦⰴⱥⱦⱃ ⱎⱦⱃ. Ⰰⱁⱞⱃⱥⱡⱡ ⱞⱥⱍ Ⱎⱦⱁⱥⱃ .ⱨ. ⱎⱦⱎⰷⱥⱦⱡ, ⱅⱥⱦⱎⱦⱍ
ⱞⱳⱦⱃⱃⱅⱦⱎⱦ ⱨⱭⱃⰷⱥⱡⱦ, ⱅⱁ ⱦⱍⱍ, ⱁⱍⱳⱎ ⱥ ⱥⰴⱃⱥⱍⱥⱡ ⱥ ⱡⱦⱅⱎⱥⱍⱍ.
Cⱁⱃⱍⱳⰱⱥⱎ Ⱞⱥⱍ Cⱁⱃⱎⱃⱥⱞⱍⱥ, ⱦⱎⱎⱁⱍⱍ ⱃⱥ ⰱⱎⱦⱦⱎⱃⱦ, ⱦⱃ Cⱎⱦⱎⱅⱁ
ⱳⱦⱦⱦⱦⱅ. Ⰰⱦⱥⱎⱞⱥⱦⰴ .ⱨ.Ⱞⱥⱦⱡⱞⱦⱥⰴⱥⱦⰷ, ⱅⱥⱦⱎⱦⱍⱍ ⱞⱳⱦⱃⱅⱦⱎⱥ
Cⱦⱎⰱⱥⱡⱡⱥⱃ, ⱅⱁ ⱞⱥⱎⰱⱥⰴ ⱅⱁ Ⱞⱳⱦⱃⱅⱦⱎ ⰱⱦⱎⱃ, ⱁⱍⱳⱎ ⱞⱁⱎⱥⱃ
ⱅⱁ Ⱞⱳⱦⱃⱅⱦⱎ Ɇⱁⱡⱥⱦⱎ ⱞⱥⱎⱁⱦⱃ ⱎⱦⱎ. Ⱞⱥⱦⰱⱞ ⱅⱁ ⱍⱍⱥⰱⱥⱦⱎⱅ

---

¹ *Kalends.* The Dom. Letter (E) is added in the marg. in B.
² *Cormac Bodhar;* i.e. Cormac the Deaf [Mac Diarmada].
³ *Donnchadh Riabhach.* " Donnchadh the Swarthy," son of Melachlin Carragh Mac Diarmada, or Mac Dermot.

A.D.
[1354.]

The kalends[1] of January on Wednesday, and the twenty-ninth of the moon; M.ccc.l.quarto; vi. anno cycli lunaris; vii. anno Indictionis; ii. anno solaris cycli. Brian O'Dubhda, king of Ui-Fiachrach, mortuus est. Rudhraighe O'Mordha, king of Laighis, mortuus est. Sitric Mac Samhradhain mortuus est. Derbforgaill, daughter of O'Conchobhair, mortua est. Jeffrey Mac Raghnaill mortuus est. Tadhg Mac Senlaigh mortuus est. John O'Finnachta, bishop of Oilfinn, in Christo quievit. Aedh, son of Cormac Bodhar,[2] was slain by the sons of Donnchadh Riabhach.[3] O'Lachtnain, bishop of Connacht, in Christo quievit. Mac Murchadha was torn asunder[4] by Foreigners, through which a great war occurred between[5] Foreigners and Gaeidhel. Aedh Mac Samhradhain died of his wounds. Brian, son of Aedh Mor O'Neill, mortuus est. Fedhlim, son of Cathal O'Conchobhair, died in the same year. Cathal, son of Niall O'Ruairc, died. A great defeat was given by the Clann-Aedha-Buidhe and the Foreigners of Dun-Delgan to Aedh O'Neill, in which a great slaughter was committed. Hubert Burk died in hoc anno. Ruaidhri, son of John Mac Mathghamhna, was slain in Mac Mathghamhna's fortress.

[1355.]

The kalends of January on Thursday, and the tenth of the moon; M°. ccc°. lv.; vii. anno cycli lunaris; octavo anno Indictionis; iii. anno cycli solaris. Sir Maurice Fitz-Thomas, Justiciary of Erinn, and Earl of Des-Mumha, died in this year. Domhnall, son of John O'Ferghail, chieftain of Muinter-Anghaile, died, and was buried in Lethrath.[6] Conchobhar Mac Consnamha, bishop of the Breifne,[7] in Christo quievit. Diarmaid O'Maelmiadhaigh, chieftain of Muinter-Cerbhallain, was killed by Muinter-Birn, and a great number of the Muinter-Eolais along with him. A defeat was given by the

---

[4] *Torn asunder.* vo ταιιιαιης; lit. "was drawn."
[5] *Between.* ιτιη, B. eαvaη, C.
[6] *And was buried in Lethrath.*

ocuη α αὸnacal laeηιιαch. This clause is not in C.
[7] *Bishop of the Breifne;* i.e. Bishop of Kilmore.

[MS. defective.
Text supplied
from " Annals
of Connacht."]

ᴅo ʒallaiʙ iapʈhaip Connachʈ ap mac Uilliam ʙupc,
ocup mopan ᴅo mapʙaʙ ann.　Caʈhal.h.Cuinn, ʈaipech
Muinnʈipe ʒilizain, occipup epʈ, azup coicep ᴅa ʙpaiʈ-
piʙ mapoen pip, ᴅo cloinᴅ ɑeʙa azup ʈ8eaain
.h.pepzail.　Copmac Maz Raznaill, ʈaipech muinʈipe
heolaip, ᴅo mapʙaʙ ᴅo cloinn Imhaip Mez Raznaill.
Maiᴅm ᴅo ʈhaʙaipʈ ᴅo ʒaiʙelaiʙ laizin ap ʒallaiʙ
ɑʈa cliaʈh.　Emann mac Uilliam mic Ricaipᴅ ᴅo
mapʙaʙ le pil nɑnmcnaʈa.　Maiᴅm mop ᴅo ʈhaʙaipʈ
le Ricapᴅ occ ap luchʈ ʈizi mic Uilliam, .i. Emanᴅ a
ʙupcc, azup ap ʈpil nɑnmchaʈa, ᴅap mapʙaʙ Sciaṁna
Mac Siupᴅan azup ᴐnpi mac pilbin, azup pe meic piz
ᴅéc ᴅo ʈpil nɑnmchaʈa.　Caʈh ᴅo ʈnaʙaipʈ ᴅo ṁac
piz-Saxan azup ᴅo piz ppanc.　Ri ppancc azup a ṁac
ᴅo zaʙail anᴅ, azup ap móp ᴅo ʈhaʙaipʈ poppo.　Tuaim
ᴅa zualanᴅ ᴅo lopcaʙ ᴅo Caʈhal ócc, ocup ᴅo mac
Uilliam ʙupc.　Niall Maz Maʈhzamna ᴅo mapʙaʙ
ᴅo cloinn ʈ8eoain Mez Maʈhzamna.　Mupchaʙ mac
Caʈhail.h.pepzail mopʈuup epʈ.　Mac Caʈhail, .i. abb
Spuʈhpa, in Cpipʈo quieuiʈ in hoc anno.　ɑᴅᴅucc Mac
Uzilin ᴅo mapʙaʙ le hopʈhepaiʙ.　ᴅeich nuain ᴅo
bpeiʈh ᴅo en chaipiz in hoc anno.　ᴅonnchaʙ.h.
ᴅoṁnaill ᴅo mapʙaʙ az bpeiʈh inzine Mez Uʙip ap
ecin lep.　Taʙcc Mac ɑeʙacan mopʈuup epʈ.　Mac
ʒallzaiʙil, abb na Tpinioiʈʈi, in Cpipʈo quieuiʈ.
pepzal, mac pepzail, mic Muipcheapʈaiz moip, mic
Conzalaz Mez ᴇochacan, ʈaipech ceneil piachaiʙ mic
Neill .ix. ziallaz, ᴅo ecc in quapʈo iᴅup pepʈimbep.
ᴅepbopzaill inzen .h.pepzail mopʈua epʈ.

---

[1] *The sons of Aedh and John.* The
descendants of these two members of
the family of O'Ferghail were distinguished by the tribe names of Clann-
Aedha (or Clann-Hugh), and Clann-
Seain (or Clann-Shane). The possessions of the Clann-Hugh, who were
seated in the barony and county
of Longford, are described in an
Inquisition taken at Ardagh on
the 4th of April, in the tenth year
of James I.

[2] *Cathal Og;* i.e. Cathal the
Younger [O'Conor]. He was the son

A.D.
[1355.]

Foreigners of the West of Connacht to Mac William Burk, when a great number were slain. Cathal O'Cuinn, chieftain of Muinter-Gillgan, occisus est, and five of his brothers along with him, by the sons of Aedh and John[1] O'Ferghail. Cormac Mac Raghnaill, chieftain of Muinter-Eolais, was slain by the sons of Imhar Mac Raghnaill. A defeat was given by the Gaeidhel of Laighen to the Foreigners of Ath-cliath. Edmond, the son of William, son of Richard *Burk*, was slain by the Sil-Anmchadha. A great overthrow was given by Richard Og to the household of Mac William (i.e. Edmond Burk), and to the Sil-Anmchadha, on which occasion Stephen Mac Jordan, Henry Mac Philbin, and sixteen princes of the Sil-Anmchadha, were slain. A battle was fought by the son of the King of the Saxons and the King of France. The King of France and his son were taken prisoners there, and a great slaughter was inflicted on them. Tuaim-da-ghualann was burned by Cathal Og[2], and by Mac William Burk. Niall Mac Mathghamhna was slain by the sons of John Mac Mathghamhna. Murchadh, son of Cathal O'Ferghail, mortuus est. Mac Cathail, i.e. the abbot of Sruthair, in Christo quievit in hoc anno. Adduc Mac Ugilin was slain by the Oirthera. Ten lambs were brought forth by one sheep in hoc anno. Donnchadh O'Domhnaill was slain whilst forcibly carrying off Mac Udhir's daughter. Tadhg Mac Aedhagain mortuus est. Mac Gallgaeidhel, abbot of the Trinity,[3] in Christo quievit. Ferghal, son of Ferghal, son of Muirchertach Mor, son of Conghalach Mac Eochagain, chieftain of the descendants of Fiachadh[4] son of Niall-nai-ghiallach, died in quarto idus Septembris. Derbhorgaill, daughter of O'Ferghail, mortua est.

---

of O'Conor Sligo, and the most valiant man of his race at this time.

[3] *The Trinity.* The monastery of the Blessed Trinity in Loch-Cé, county of Roscommon. This entry precedes the obit of Tadhg Mac Aedhagain in C.

[4] *Descendants of Fiachadh.* The Cenel-Fiachaidh, or Kenaliaghe. See note 4, p. 556, vol. i.

[MS. defective.
Text supplied
from "Annals
of Connacht."]

Ict. Ɵnαιρ ϝορ Cιne, αʒυϝ .xxι. ϝυιρρe; m.ccc.luι;
occαυο αnno cιclι Lunαριϝ; ιx. αnno ιnοιccιoniϝ; quαρcο
αnno cιclι ϝolαριϝ. Cɵɓ mαc Τοιρρɓhεαlbαιʒ .ɧ. Conchoɓαιρ, ριʒ Connαchc, οο mαρɓαɓ α mbαιlι Lochα
Dεcαιρ lε Donnchαɓ cαρραɓ .ɧ. Cεllαιʒ αʒυϝ lε clαιnn
αn ɓαιρο, αρ ϝορʒαll mαιnεch, αnοιʒαlcαρ ιnʒιne
8εοιnιn α ɓυρc, .ι. ben .ɧ. Cεllαιʒ, οο bρειɓ οο mαc
Τοιρρɓhεαlbαιʒ lειϝ αρ αιchεɓ αʒυϝ αρ ειοɓ; αʒυϝ Cɵɓ
mαc ϝειɓlιmιɓ .ɧ. Conchuɓαιρ οο ʒαɓαιl lαn ριʒε Connαchc ιαραm. Conchóbαρ mαcc Ταιοc .ɧ. Cεllαιʒ οο
mαρɓαɓ οο Ταοc mαc Dιαρmαοα .ɧ. Cεllαιʒ. ϝερchαρ
.ɧ.ϝαllαmαιn, cαοιϝεɓ Cloιnne hUαοαɓ, mορcυυϝ εϝc.
Τοιρρɓhεαlbαɓ ιnαc Cɵɓα ɓρειϝnιʒ.ɧ.Conchoɓαιρ οο
mαρɓαɓ οο ɓloιnn nDonnɓαιɓ. Dιαρmαιο mαʒ Cαρρ-
chαιʒ αʒυϝ α mαc οο mαρɓαɓ lα hιb 8υιllεαɓαn, .ι.
Donοchαɓ mαc Dιαρmαοα. mορ, ιnʒεαn.ɧ.Concho-
bαιρ, ben .ɧ.ϝερʒαιl, οο hεʒ ιn hoc αnno. Rυαιɓρι mαc
Cɵɓα .ɧ.Chonchoɓαιρ mορcυυϝ εϝc. mυιρchεαρcαch
mαc 8εοαιn .ɧ.Nειll οο mαρɓαɓ lα ριlιρ mαʒ Uɓιρ ιn
hoc αnno. ʒιιιϝcιϝ Cchα clιαch mορcυυϝ εϝc. mαc
ϝεοραιϝ οο mαρɓαɓ lα ʒαllαιɓ ιn hoc αnno. Dubʒαll
mαc 8υιɓne οο mαρɓαɓ lα Domnαll.ɧ.Conchoɓαιρ ιn
hoc αnno. Donοchαɓ mαc Conmαρα, mαc cαιριʒ ρob
ϝεαρρ nα αιmριρ, occιϝυϝ εϝc. Domnαll mαc Cɵɓα
ɓρειϝnιʒ.ɧ.Conchoɓαιρ mορcυυϝ εϝc. 11ιcol mαʒ Cαch-
υϝαιʒ, εϝρocc Οιρʒιαll, ιn Cριϝcο quιευιc. 8olαm
.ɧ.mεllαιn, mαεϝ ɓlυιcc ιnο ιοαchcα, ϝειchεm coιc-
chεαnn οο chlιαραιɓ Ɵρεnο, mορcυυϝ εϝc. Donnchαɓ
ρροιϝcεch οο mαρɓαο οο οιϝ οα mυιnncιρ ϝειn ρεϝ
οolum. ʒεροοιn Τριεl οο chαρραιnʒ οο οuɓ ʒαllαιɓ

---

[1] *Kalends.* A marginal note indicates C II as the Dom. Letters for the
year.

[2] *Clann-in-bhaird.* The tribe name
of a sept of the Sodhans in Hy-Many,
otherwise called Mac-an-Ward, and
Mac Ward.

[3] *Was slain by.* οο mαρɓαɓ οο, C.

B reads oc. 2 αϝϝ o, for "occisus est
a suia o (by)."

[4] *The Justiciary;* i.e. Thomas de
Rokeby, appointed Justiciary, for the
second time, on the death of Maurice
Fitz-Thomas, Earl of Desmond, in
1355.

[5] *Occisus.* oɓ ριϝυϝ, B and C.

A.D.
[1356.]

The kalends[1] of January on Friday, and the twenty-first of the moon; M.ccc.lvi. ; octavo anno cycli lunaris; ix. anno Indictionis ; quarto anno cycli solaris. Aedh, son of Toirdhelbhach O'Conchobhair, king of Connacht, was killed in Baile-Locha-Dechair by Donnchadh Carrach O'Cellaigh, and by Clann-in-bhaird,[2] at the instigation of the Ui-Maine, in revenge for Seonin Burk's daughter, i.e. O'Cellaigh's wife, whom Toirdhelbhach's son had carried off privately and clandestinely ; and Aedh, the son of Fedhlimidh O'Conchobhair, afterwards assumed the full sovereignty of Connacht. Conchobhar, son of Tadhg O'Cellaigh, was slain by Tadhg, son of Diarmaid O'Cellaigh. Ferchar O'Fallamhain, chieftain of Clann-Uadach, mortuus est. Toirdhelbhach, son of Aedh Breifnech O'Conchobhair, was slain by[3] the Clann-Donnchaidh. Diarmaid Mac Carthaigh and his son, i.e. Donnchadh, son of Diarmaid, were slain by the Ui-Suillebhain. Mor, daughter of O'Conchobhair, wife of O'Ferghail, died in hoc anno. Ruaidhri, son of Aedh O'Conchobhair, mortuus est. Muirchertach, son of John O'Neill, was killed by Philip Mac Udhir in hoc anno. The Justiciary[4] of Ath-cliath mortuus est. Mac Feorais was slain by Foreigners in hoc anno. Dubhgall Mac Suibhne was slain by Domhnall O'Conchobhair in hoc anno. Donnchadh Mac Conmara, the best son of a chieftain in his time, occisus[5] est. Domhnall, son of Aedh Breifnech O'Conchobhair, mortuus est. Nicholas Mac Cathusaigh, bishop of Oirghiall, in Christo quievit. Solomon O'Mellain, steward of clog-ind-idachta,[6] the general patron of the learned of Erinn, mortuus est. Donnchadh Proistech was slain by two of his own people, per dolum. Gerodin[7] Tyrrell was torn asunder by Black

---

[6] Clog-ind-idachta ; lit. "the bell of the testament ;" so called from having been bequeathed by St. Patrick to one of his disciples, as alleged. See Reeves's Adamnan, pp. 323, 326, and

329. Instead of ιnτ ι∂αchτα, C has ιnτ ι∂αchτα (for αnτιαchτα), which is incorrect.

[7] Gerodin. This is a diminut. form of the name "Geroid," or Garrett

[MS. defective.
Text supplied
from "Annals
of Connacht."]

ap paichči Ccha cliach. Mupchač mac Opiain .h. Neill
mopcuup epc.

Kt. Enaip pop Domnač, aʒup aili uachao puippi;
m°. ccc°. luii.; ix. anno cicli Lunapip; x. anno inoiccionip;
u. anno cicli polapip. Maʒnup Maʒ Machʒamna,
pi Oipʒiall, mopcuup epc. Lochlainn mac Muipcheap-
caiʒ .h. Chonchobaip mopcuup epc. Iapla Oepmuman
oemeppup epc ac ool caiiip. Peiðlim .h. Oomnaill ocup
a mac, .i. Raʒnall, oo mapbað illaini la Seoan .h.
nOominaill. Pepʒal Muininech .h. Ouiðʒennan, ollam
Conmaicne ocup cloinne Maelpuanaiʒ cip ocup cuap,
mopcuup epc. Macha mac Comaip .h. Ruaipcc, ceno
ʒaipcið na Opeipne, mopcuup epc. Macpaich maʒ
Eppaiʒ, pai coiccheno, mopcuup epc. Oonnpleiði
Mac Cepbáll, pai pe peinm, mopcuup epc. Opian
mac ʒilla Cpiopo .h. Ruaipc, ocup Maʒnup buiðe Maʒ
Sampaðan, oo mapbað ap puca mic Uʒilin la hCceð
.h. Neill in hoc anno. Clemenc .h. Ouiðʒennan, bicaip
Cille Ronain, in Cpurco quieuic. Sich coiccheann ecip
in oa Cachal in hoc anno, .i. Cachal mac Cceða
Opeipniʒ, acup Cachal oc mac Cachail mic Oominaill.

Kt. Enaip pop Luan, aʒup cpep .x. puippi; m°. ccc°. luii.;
x. anno cicli Lunapip; xi. anno inoiccionip; ui. anno cicli
polapip. Oominall .h. hEʒpa, pi Luiʒne, oo heʒ po
caip in hoc anno. Maʒnup Maʒ Uoip oo mapbað oo
cloinn Cachmail in hoc anno. Conchubap .h. hCcnliʒi,
oux Cenel Tobcha mic Ccenʒupa, oo ecc iap mbpeiч
buača o oeinan aʒup o ooinan in hoc anno. Maiom
mop oo chabaipc le hCceð .h. Neill ap Ccpʒiallaið aʒup

---

1 *Kalends.* The Dom. Letter (A)
is added in the margin.

2 *Demersus.* oimeppup, C.

3 *Going across*; i.e. passing over to
England.

4 *Muimhnech.* This epithet signifies the "Momonian."

5 *Lower and Upper.* "The Lower
Clann-Mulrony were the Mac Donoughs, who were seated in the barony
of Tirerrill, in the county of Sligo;
and the Upper Clann-Mulrony were
the Mac Dermots of Moylurg."—
O'Donovan's note, Four Mast., A.D.
1357, note P.

Foreigners on the green of Ath-cliath. Murchadh, son of Brian O'Neill, mortuus est.

The kalends[1] of January on Sunday, and the second of the moon ; M°.ccc°. lvii. ; ix. anno cycli lunaris ; x. anno Indictionis; v. anno cycli solaris. Maghnus Mac Mathghamhna, King of Oirghiall, mortuus est. Lochlainn, son of Muirchertach O'Conchobhair, mortuus est. The Earl of Des-Mumha demersus[2] est in going across.[3] Fedhlimidh O'Domhnaill and his son, i.e. Raghnall, were slain in confinement by John O'Domhnaill. Ferghal Muimhnech[4] O'Duibhgennain, ollamh of the Conmaicne, and of Clann-Maelruanaigh Lower and Upper,[5] mortuus est. Matthew, son of Thomas O'Ruairc, head of valour of the Breifne, mortuus est. Macraith Mac Erraigh, an eminent man in general, mortuus est. Donnsleibhe Mac Cerbhaill, an eminent musician, mortuus est. Brian, son of Gilla-Christ O'Ruairc, and Maghnus Buidhe[6] Mac Samhradhain, were killed in Ruta-Mic-Ugilin, by Aedh O'Neill, in hoc anno. Clement O'Duibhgennain, vicar of Cill-Ronain, in Christo quievit. A general peace between[7] the two Cathals in hoc anno, viz., Cathal, son of Aedh Breifnech, and Cathal Og, son of Cathal, son of Domhnall.

The kalends[8] of January on Monday, and the thirteenth of the moon ; M°.ccc°.lviii. ; x. anno cycli lunaris ; xi. anno Indictionis ; vi. anno cycli solaris. Domhnall O'hEghra, king of Luighne, died about Easter in hoc anno. Maghnus Mac Udhir was slain by the Clann-Cathmhail in hoc anno. Conchobhar O'hAinlighe, dux of Cenel-Dobhtha-mic-Aenghusa,[9] died after triumphing over the devil and the world, in hoc anno. A great defeat was given by Aedh O'Neill to

---

[5] *Maghnus Buidhe ;* i.e. "Maghnus (or Manus) the Yellow."

[7] *Between.* ecip, B. eaoap, C.

[8] *Kalends.* The Dom. Letter (G) is added in the marg. in B.

[9] *Cenel-Dobhtha-mic-Aenghusa ;* i.e. "the descendants of Dobhath, son of Aenghus"; the tribe name of the O'Hanlys of Roscommon. See O'Donovan's ed. of the Ann. Four Mast., A.D. 1189, note [d].

[MS. defective.
Text supplied
f om "Annals
of Connacht."]

αρ ρεραιϐ Manach, ϭυ αρ marϐαϐ Ccéϭ mac Caba αξυρ
mac an erpuic .h.Ϭuϐϭα. Cιτh móρ ϭo ρερτhαιn hι
Carρρι ιριnτ ραιṁραϐ, αξυρ nιρ mó ριαϐ uϐαll nα cach
cloιch ϭon chιch ριn ιιlι. Ɱαιϭm moρ ϭo τhαϐαιρτ ϭΙΙ
Ɱορϭα ρορ ξαllαιϐ Ccéα clιατh, αξυρ ϭα .xx. αρ ϭα ceϭ
ϭo marϐαϐ αnn. Ϭριαn mαc Cατhmαιl, erpocc Ccρξιαll,
quιeuιτ. Senιcιn Ɱαc Uξιlιn morτuuρ erτ ιn hoc αnno.
Ɱαc Ccnϭριι mιc Ƒeoραιρ morτuuρ erτ.

ɫct. Ɛnαιρ ρορ Ɱαιρτ, αξυρ cετhαρ ρ̇ιchet ρ̇uιρρι ;
Ɱ°.ccc°.L.ιx. ; xι. αnno cιclι lunαριρ ; xιι. αnno ιnϭιc-
τιonιρ ; uιι. αnno cιclι rolαριρ· Coρmαc mαξ Carρτhαιξ,
ρí Ϭermuṁαn, morτuuρ erτ. Ɱαιϭm moρ ϭo τhαϐαιρτ
ϭo Chατhαl oc .h.Conchoϐαιρ ρα beol Ccéα Senαιξ ρορ
Conαllchαιϐ, ocuρ Seoαn .h.Ϭochαρταιξ, ταιρech Ccρϭα
Ɱιϭαιρ, αξυρ Ɛoξαn Connαchταch, αξυρ Τοιρρϭheαl-
bαch Ɱαc Sιιϐne ϭo ξαϐαιl αnϭ beorr, αξυρ αρ moρ ϭo
τhαϐαιρτ αnϭ. Ɱατhα mαc Sαmhραϐαn, αϭϐαρ ταιρξ
Chellαιξ Ɛchαch, ϭo loτ αn lá ριn, αξυρ α ecc ϭon loτ
ριn oc α τιξ. Ιn Cατhαl ceαϭnα ριn ϭo ϭol αρ ρluαξαϐ α
Τιρ Conαιll, αξυρ α ṁιιnτιρ ϭo ϭol α cριch.h.ξαιρm-
leαϐαιξ, αξυρ Cατhαl boϭαρ .h.Ruαιρc ϭo marϐαϐ lα
Ɱαιlρechlαιnϭ .h.ξαιρmleαϐαιξ, αξυρ Ɱαelρechlαιnϭ
ϭo marϐαϐ αρ ιι lατhαιρ ceαϭnα ριn lα Τιξernαn .h.
Ruαιρcc. Ɱuιρ̇ceαρταch mαc Τomαιρ .h.Ƒlοιnn Líne,
ϭαṁnα ριξ .h.Τuιρτρι, ϭo ṁαρbhαϐ ρερ ϭolum lα hCceϐ
mαc Ϭριαιn .h.Neιll .ι. mαc Ϭριαιn mιc Ccéϭα buιϭe.
Ɱuρchαϐ oc mαc Ɱατhξαṁnα, ϭαṁnα ριξ Corcα Ϭαρ-
cιnn, ϭo marbhαϐ lα ριl mϐρíαιn. Ɱαξnuρ .h.Ϭuϐϭα,
mαc ριξ .h.Ƒιαchραch, morτuuρ erτ. Ϭριαn Ɱαc

---

1 Son. The Four Masters call him
Maoileachlainn, i.e. Malachi.

2 Senicin. . This name would be
Anglicised "Jenkin."

3 Kalends. The Dom. Letter (F)
is added in the margin in B and C.

4 Mac Suibhne. Mac Sweeny, or
MacSwiney. mαc Subne, B.

5 Heir to the Chieftaincy. αϭϐαρ
ταιρech [rectè ταιρξ] ; lit. "materies principis," B. ταοιριξ, C.

6 Tellach-Echach. Now Tullyhaw,

the Airghialla and the Feara-Manach, in which Aedh Mac
Caba, and the son[1] of the bishop O'Dubhda, were slain. A
great shower *of hail* fell in Cairbre in the summer, and
a wild apple was not larger than each stone of this shower.
A great defeat was given by O'Mordha to the Foreigners
of Ath-cliath, and two hundred and forty were slain there.
Brian Mac Cathmhail, bishop of Airghiall, quievit. Senicin[2]
Mac Ugilin mortuus est in hoc anno. The son of
Andrew Mac Feorais mortuus est.

The kalends[3] of January on Tuesday, and the twenty-
fourth of the moon; M°.ccc".lix.; xi. anno cycli lunaris; xii.
anno Indictionis ; vii. anno cycli solaris. Cormac Mac Carthaigh, king of Des-Mumha, mortuus est. A great defeat was given by Cathal Og O'Conchobhair to the Cenel-
Conaill, near Bel-Atha-Senaigh, and John O'Dochartaigh,
chieftain of Ard-Midhair, and Eoghan Connachtach, and
Toirdhelbhach Mac Suibhne,[4] were moreover taken pri-
oners there ; and a great slaughter was committed there.
Matthew Mac Samhradhain, heir to the chieftancy[5] of
Tellach-Echach,[6] was wounded that day, and died at home
of that wound. The same Cathal went on a hosting to
Tir-Conaill ; and his people went into O'Gairmledhaigh's
territory, and Cathal Bodhar O'Ruairc was slain by
Maelsechlainn O'Gairmledhaigh ; and Maelsechlainn was
killed on the same spot by Tighernan O'Ruairc. Muir-
chertach, son of Thomas O'Floinn Líne, royal heir of Ui-
Tuirtre,[7] was slain per dolum by Aedh, the son of Brian
O'Neill, i.e. the son of Brian, son of Aedh Buidhe. Murchadh Og Mac Mathghamhna, royal heir of Corca-
Bhaiscinn, was killed by Sil-Briain.[8] Maghnus O'Dubhda,
son of the king of Ui-Fiachrach, mortuus est. Brian Mac

---

the name of a barony in the county
of Cavan. C has Ⱅheallaċ
Ǝchach ; but B reads Ⱅhell
Ǝchach (for Ⱅhellaⱷ Ǝchach),
the correct genit. form.

VOL. II.

[7] *Ui-Tuirtre.* The word Tuirtre is
omitted in C.

[8] *Sil-Briain ;* i.e. "the seed of
Brian," or sept of O'Brien.

C 2

[MS. defective.
Text supplied
from "Annals
of Connacht."]

Oonnchaib, abbap puᵹ cine hOilella, vo manbaᵹ vo
mac Sencha voipeacht .h.ᵹabpae. Enpi mac Uillec
mic Ricaipv mopcuup epc. Oomnall mac Caibᵹ .h.
Machᵹamne occipup epc. Ceᵹ mae Conchobaip Mic
Cebacain vo ecc in hoc anno.

Kct. Enaip pop Cevain, aᵹup coiceᵹ uachav puippi;
M.ccc.lx. Mac puᵹ Saxan vo ceacht a nEpinn, aᵹup
loipcti mopa ipin bliaᵹain pin .i. Rop Coman ocup
Oamuip, aᵹup Sliceᵹ, aᵹup manipcep Lepa ᵹabail,
aᵹup Pionach, aᵹup Opuim liap. Oiapmaiv mac
Oonnchaiᵹ piabaiᵹ Mic Oiapmava vo manbaᵹ la
Cachal occ. Oiapmaiv .h.Opuain vo achpiᵹaᵹ vo mac
bpachap a achap pein. Maelpuanaiᵹ mac an ᵹilla
muinelaiᵹ .h.baiᵹill mopcuup epc. Sip Robepv Sabaip
vo ecc in hoc anno. Cimlaiᵹ mac Seppaiv Meᵹ Raᵹnaill occipup epc. Seoan mac ᵹilla Cpiopv .h.Ruaipc
occipup epc o Ceᵹ Maᵹ [O]opchaiᵹ. Oiapmaiv .h.
hCcnliᵹe mopcuup epc. Cuachal .h.Pinnacca mopcuup
epc in hoc anno. Ppimpaiᵹ Cpva Macha in Cpipco
quievic. Pepᵹal mac Seppaiᵹ meᵹ Raᵹnaill mopcuup
epc in hoc anno. Cachal mac an caich Meᵹ Raᵹnaill
occipup epc in hoc anno. In ᵹilla vuᵹ Maᵹ builichan
mopcuup epc. Seoan mac Simaᵹ Mic Uᵹilin occipup
epc. Inᵹen Coippvhealbaiᵹ .h.Conchubaip, ben Pepᵹal
.h.Raiᵹilliᵹ, vo manbaᵹ vepcup in hoc anno. ᵹilla
na naem Ua Conmaiᵹ, ollam Cuaᵹmuman pe peinm,
mopcuup epc. Uilliam mac comapba Caillin occipup
epc. Naemacc .h.Ouibᵹennan mopcuup epc.

---

1 *Richard;* i.e. Richard Burk.

2 *Hoc.* hocc, B.

3 *Kalends.* The Dom. Letters (ED)
are added in the margin in B.

4 *Son.* Lionel, Duke of Clarence.

5 *Cathal Og.* Cathal (or Charles)
the Younger [O'Conor Sligo].

6 *Gilla-Muineiach.* This is a
sobriquet signifying "the [wry-]
necked fellow."

Occisus. oᵹ cipup, B and C.

7 *Hoc.* hocc, B and C.

9 *The Primate.* ppimpaiᵹ, B and
C. This word properly means "chief
prophet." See note 5, p. 148, vol. i.
The Primate referred to was Richard
Fitz-Ralph, whose death is entered in
the Ann. Four Mast. under the year
1356, where the entry is mixed up
with the obit of "Ferghal, son of Jeffrey MacRaghnall," in such a manner
as to convey the impression that the

Donnchaidh, royal heir of Tir-Oilella, was slain by Mac Sencha of the sept of O'Gadhra. Henry, son of Ulick, son of Richard,[1] mortuus est. Domhnall, son of Tadhg O'Mathghamhna, occisus est. Aedh, son of Conchobhar Mac Aedhagain, died in hoc[2] anno.

A.D. [1859.]

The kalends[3] of January on Wednesday, and the fifth of the moon ; M.ccc.lx. The son[4] of the king of the Saxons came to Erinn ; and great burnings were committed in this year, viz., Ros-Comain, Daimhinis, Sligech, the monastery of Lis-gabhail, and Fidhnach, and Druim-lias were burned. Diarmaid, son of Donnchadh Riabhach Mac Diarmada, was killed by Cathal Og[5]. Diarmaid O'Briain was deposed by the son of his own father's brother. Maelruanaidh, son of the Gilla-Muinelach[6] O'Baighill, mortuus est. Sir Robert Savage died in hoc anno. Amhlaibh, son of Jeffrey Mac Raghnaill, occisus[7] est. John, son of Gilla-Christ O'Ruairc, occisus est by Aedh Mac [D]orchaidh. Diarmaid O'hAinlighe mortuus est. Tuathal O'Finnachta mortuus est in hoc[8] anno. The Primate[9] of Ard-Macha in Christo quievit. Ferghal, son of Jeffrey Mac Raghnaill, mortuus est in[10] hoc anno. Cathal, son of the Caech Mac Raghnaill, occisus est in hoc anno. The Gilla-dubh Mac Builichan mortuus est. John, son of Simag[11] Mac Ugilin, occisus est. The daughter of Toirdhelbhach O'Conchobhair, wife of Ferghal O'Raighilligh, was killed by a fall in[10] hoc anno. Gilla-na-naemh O'Conmhaigh, ollamh[12] of Tuadh-Mumha in music, mortuus est. William, son of the comarb of Caillin,[13] occisus est. Naemhag O'Duibhgennain mortuus est.

[1860.]

---

primate's name was Ferghal Mac Raghnaill.

[10] In. en, B.

[11] Simag. This is probably a mistake for Senicin, or Jenkin.

[12] Ollamh (pron. ollave); i.e. chief professor, or doctor.

[13] Comarb of Caillin. St. Caillin

was the founder of the church of Fidhnacha, now Fenagh, in the county of Leitrim, the comarbs of which were of the family of O'Rodaigh, or O'Rody. See the pedigree of the family printed by Rev. Dr. Todd, Miscel. of the Irish Archæol. Soc., Vol. 1., p. 113.

[MS. defective.
Text supplied
from "Annals
of Connacht."]

·Kt. Enαιρ ρορ Cine, αγυρ υι.x. ρυιρρι ; M.ccc.lxı. ;
xιιιı. anno cιclı lunαριρ; xιιιı. anno ινοιcτιονιρ ; ıx.
anno cιclı ρolαριρ. Cρττ Mac Muρchαοα, ρι Lαιϩhen,
αγυρ Ooṁnall ριαοach, αοοαρ ρι Lαιϩen, οο ϩαοαιl
ρερ οolum οο mαc ριϩ Sαxan ına τιϩ ρειn, αγυρ α necc
αιϩe. beneοechτ .h. Mochan, αιρcıοeachαın Cıllı Cthραchτα, mορτuur eρτ.. Oonοchαο Uα Lochlαınn, ριϩ
Cορcα Mοορuαιο, mορτuur eρτ. Sıρ Emανο α buρc
mορτuur eρτ. Cluıτı αn ριϩ αn Eρινο ulı co ρορlechan,
αγυρ Rıροαρο Sαοαιρ οecc οe. Remann mαc buρcαιϩ
an Muıne mορτuur eρτ. Cαthαl αγυρ Muıρcheαρτach, οα mαc Cεοα mıc Eoϩαιn, mορτuı ρunτ. Uατερ
Sτονοun mορτuur eρτ. Cuαthαl .h. Mαılle mορıτuρ.
Comαρ Mαϩ Cıϩeαρnan, ταιρech Cellαιϩ Ouncɦαοα,
mορıτuρ. Nıcol .h. ρınnachτα mορτuur eρτ. ϩıllıberτ
mαc Mαılıρ mορτuur eρτ ın hoc anno.

Kt. Enαιρ ρορ Sαthαρn, αγυρ ρechτmαο .xx. ρυιρρι;
anno Oomını M°.ccc°.lxıı.; xιιιı. cιclı lunαριρ; xu. anno
ınοιcτιονιρ; x. anno cιclı ρolαριρ. Eoϩαn ρινο .h.Conchuοαιρ, mαc ριϩ Connachτ, οο ecc ın hoc anno. Nıαll
Mαϩ Sαṁραοαιn, οux Cellαιϩh Echοach, quıeuıτ.
Mαelρuanαιϩ .h. Ouοα αγυρ α οen, .ı. ınϩean Mıc
Oonοchαο, mορτuı ρunτ. Cαthαl occ αγυρ mαc ρειολımıο .h. Conchobαιρ οο ϩαοαιl bαιlı ın τobαιρ bρıϩτı.
Sluαϩαο αοοαl mορ lα Cαthαl oc O Conchobαιρ αγυρ·
lα mαc ρειολımıο .h.Concoοαιρ,ρι Connachτ, ıρın Mıοe,
cuρ lοıρcρıτ co hαthαιρ Mıοe, αγυρ ceτhρe τempoıll

---

¹ *Kalends.* The Dom. Letter (C)
is added in the margin in B.

² *With him* ; i. e. whilst in his power.
αιϩe, C. αcee, B.

³ *Corca-Modhruaidh.* Cορcαιϩ m.
for Cορcαιϩ Mοορuαιο, gen. of
Cορcach Mοορuαιο, C. Cορ̄c, B.
The proper form is " Corca-Modhruaidh," i. e. the descendants of
Modh-ruadh. See O'Donovan's ed.

of *O'Huidhrin's Topograph. Poem,*
Appendix, p. lxxii, note 639.

⁴ *Cluithi-an-righ;* i.e. "the King's
game." Some epidemic which in
Ware's Annals is said to have consumed "many men, but few women,"
in England and Ireland.

⁵ *Meyler.* Probably Meyler Mac
Goisdelbh, or MacCostello, in which
family the Christian names Gilbert
and Meyler were much used.

The kalends[1] of January on Friday, and the sixteenth of
the moon; M.ccc.lxi.; xiii. anno cycli lunaris; xiiii. anno
Indictionis; ix. anno cycli solaris. Art Mac Murchadha,
king of Laighen, and Domhnall Riabhach, royal heir of
Laighen, were taken prisoners by the son of the king of the
Saxons, per dolum, in his own house; and they died with
him.[2] Benedict O'Mochain, archdeacon of Cill-Athrachta,
mortuus est. Donnchadh O'Lochlainn, king of Corca-
Modbruaidh,[3] mortuus est. Sir Edmond Burk mortuus
est. Cluithi-an-righ[4] throughout all Erinn, and Richard
Savage died of it. Redmond, son of Burk of the Muine,
mortuus est. Cathal and Muirchertach, two sons of Aedh,
son of Eoghan, mortui sunt. Walter Staunton mortuus
est. Tuathal O'Maille moritur. Thomas Mac Tighernain,
chieftain of Tellach-Dunchadha, moritur. Nicholas O'Fin-
naghta mortuus est. Gilbert, son of Meyler,[5] mortuus est
in hoc anno.

The kalends[6] of January on Saturday, and the twenty-
seventh of the moon; anno Domini M°.ccc°.lxii.; xiiii.
cycli lunaris; xv. anno[7] Indictionis; x. anno cycli solaris.
Eoghan Finn[8] O'Conchobhair, son of the king of Connacht, died in hoc anno. Niall Mac Samhradhain,
dux of Tellach-Echach, quievit. Maelruanaidh O'Dubhda,
and his wife, i.e. the daughter of Mac Donnchaidh, mortui sunt[9]. Cathal Og, and the son of
Fedhlimidh O'Conchobhair, took possession of Baile-in-
tobair-Brighde[10] A great hosting by Cathal Og O'Conchobhair, and by the son of Fedhlimidh[11] O'Conchobhair,
King of Connacht, into Midhe, when they triumphantly

---

[6] *Kalends.* The Dom. Letter (B)
is added in the margin in B.

[7] *Anno.* Omitted in B.

[8] *Eoghan Finn*; i.e. "Eoghan the
Fair."

[9] *Mortui sunt.* m. 2, for moṗċuuṗ
eṗċ, B and C.

[10] *Baile-in-tobair-Brighde.* "The town
of Brigid's well," now Ballintober, in
the barony of the same name, and
county of Roscommon. The letters
N.B. (*nota bene*) are added in the
margin in B.

[11] *The Son of Fedhlimidh*; i.e. Aedh
(or Hugh) O'Conor.

[MS. defective. Text supplied from "Annals of Connacht."]

oec aguṙ Cell Caınnıg oo loṙcaṫ ooıṫ ; aguṙ nı báṫ uṗuṙa a áṗeıṁ na a ṗıṁ aṙ mılleṫ oın Mıṫe ın tan ṙın ; aguṙ a teacht ṙlan oa tıgıṫ ıaṙaṁ. Coṙmac ballach .h.Maılechlaınn, ṙı Mıṫe, moṙıtuṙ. Taocc mac Conċuṫaıṙ mıc Toıṙṙohealḃaıg .h.ḃṙaın oo maṙḃaṫ oo Cloınn Culeın. Caṫal occ .h.Conchoḃaıṙ, ant aen mac ṙıg oo ba mó clu aguṙ cıuoe, aguṙ alla aguṙ aṙo noṙ, neaṙt aguṙ mıachaṙ oo ḃı a naeṅ aımṙıṙ ṙıṙ, oo heg oon ṗlaıgh ı Slıcech ın tṙeaṙ la ıaṙ Saṁaın. Oıaṙmaıo mac Seaṅ.h.Ṗeṙgaıl, taıṙech Muınntıṙe hⱰngaıle, moṙtuuṙ eṙt. Ooṁnall mac Ruaıṫṙı .h.Cellaıṫ moṙtuuṙ eṙt. Caṙṙṙı.h.Cuıno, taıṙech Muınntıṙe gıllgaın, moṙtuuṙ eṙt. Tomaṙ.h.ḃıṙn moṙtuuṙ eṙt. Muıṙcheaṙtach ᴅono Mag Oṙeaċtaıg quıeuıt. Ɒenguṙ Mac ıno oclaıg, aıpcıoeochaın Cılle hⱰıpıo, ın Cṙıṙto quıeuıt. Muıṙchaṫ manach mac Taıog quıeuıt. Eogan .h. Maıllı ocuṙ a ṁac, .ı. Oıaṙmaıo, moṙtuı ṙunt. Cucoıgcṙıche mac Oıaṙmaoa Meg Eochacan, acuṙ Muıṙıṙ mac Muıṙcheaṙtaıg Meg Eochacan, moṙtuı ṙunt.

ⰓⱵt. Enaıṙ ṙoṙ Ooṁnaċ, ocuṙ ochtmaṫ uathaṫ ṙuıṙṙı ; M.ccc.Lx ııı. ; ⱴu. cıclı lunaṙuṙ ; ı. anno ınoıctıonıṙ ; ⱦı. anno cıclı ṙolaṙıṙ. Magnuṙ Eoganach .h.Ooṁnaıll oo ecc ın hoc anno. Ɒeṫ Mag Uṫıṙ, ṙı ṙeṙ Manach, oo ecc ın hoc anno. Muıṙcheaṙtach ṙuaṫ, mac Ooṁnaıll ıṙṙuıṙ.h.Conchoḃaıṙ, oo ṁaṙḃaṫ oo Magnuṙ mac Caṫaıl.h.Choncoḃaıṙ. Taocc Mac Conṙnaṁa, taıṙech Muınntıṙe Cınaıth, oo loc accuṙ ᴅo gaḃaıl le Caṫal mac Ɒeṫa.h.Conchubaıṙ, aguṙ a eg ıṙın lamoıchaṙ ṙın. Catıṙṙına, ıṅgean .h.Ṗeṙgaıl, ben .h.Raıgıllıg, oo écc. Caṫal Mac Oonnchaıṫ oo maṙḃaṫ oo lucht Moıgı Luıṙg. gaeth móṙ ın hoc

---

1 _Cill-Cainnigh._ Kilkenny West, in the barony of the same name, and co. of Westmeath.

2 _Afterwards._ ıaṙaṁ. Omitted in B.

3 _Archdeacon._ The Four M. say aıṙchınoeaċ, i.e. Erenagh, or Herenach.

4 _Murchadh Manach;_ i.e. Murchadh (or Murrough) the Monk.

burned Midhe ; and fourteen churches, and Cill-Cainnigh,[1] were burned by them ; and it would not be easy to enumerate or count all that was then destroyed of Midhe. And they afterwards[2] returned home safely. Cormac Ballach O'Maelechlainn, king of Midhe, moritur. Tadhg, son of Conchobhar, son of Toirdhelbhach O'Briain, was killed by the Clann-Cuilen. Cathal Og O'Conchobhair, the king's son of greatest fame, and generosity, and renown, and politeness, strength, and heroism in his own time, died of the plague in Sligech, the third day after Allhallowtide. Diarmaid, son of John O'Ferghail, chieftain of Muinter-Anghaile, mortuus est. Domhnall, son of Ruaidhri O'Cellaigh, mortuus est. Cairbre O'Cuinn, chieftain of Muinter-Gillgan, mortuus est. Thomas O'Birn mortuus est. Muirchertach Donn Mac Oirechtaigh quievit. Aenghus Mac-ind-oglaich, archdeacon[3] of Cill-airidh, in Christo quievit. Murchadh Manach[4] Mac Taidhg quievit. Eoghan O'Maille and his son, i.e. Diarmaid, mortui sunt. Cucoicriche, son of Diarmaid Mac Eochagain, and Maurice, son of Muirchertach Mac Eochagain, mortui sunt.

The kalends of January on Sunday, and the eighth of the moon ; M.ccc.lxiii. ; xv. cycli lunaris ; i. anno Indictionis ; xi. anno cycli solaris. Maghnus Eoghanach[5] O'Domhnaill died in hoc anno. Aedh Mac Udhir, king of Feara-Manach, died in hoc anno. Muirchertach Ruadh, son of Domhnall Irruis O'Conchobhair, was slain by Maghnus, son of Cathal O'Conchobhair. Tadhg Mac Consnamha, chieftain of Muinter-Cinaith, was wounded and taken prisoner by Cathal, son of Aedh O'Conchobhair ; and he died in this confinement. Catherine[6], daughter of O'Ferghail, wife of O'Raighilligh, died. Cathal Mac Donnchaidh was slain by the people of Magh-Luirg. Great wind in

---

[5] *Eoghanach.* This is a sobriquet signifying " of ['Tir-]Eoghain", or Tyrone, applied to Maghnus from his having been fostered in that district.

[6] *Catherine* Ceirrina for Cairrina, B and C. The Four Mast. write the name Lairainriona (pron. Lassa-rina).

[MS. defective.
Text supplied
from "Annals
of Connacht."]

anno cup bpír cempaill αξup cιξι, αξυp cup báιθ lonξα
αξυp apτpaιξι imõaι. bebιnn inξen Mec Θochaξaιn,
uxop Uulpιp, quιeuιc.

Κt. Θnaιp fop luan, αξup .ιx. õecc fuιppι; M.ccc.
lx. quapτo; xιιι. cιclι lunapιp; ιι. anno ιnõιccιonιp;
.xιι. anno cιclι folapιp. Αeθ .h. Neιll, pι coιcιθ
Ulaθ, ιnc aen pí ιp feпp caιιιcc ιna aιmpιp feιn, õo
écc ιap mbpeιch bυaθa o õeιñan αξυp o õoñan.
Õιapmaιõ .h. bpιaιn, pí Cυaõmuñan, õo ecc ιn hoc
anno. Maelpechlaιnõ, mac Mupchaιθ, mιc Ζιolla
na naeñ, mιc Αeõho, mιc Αñlaιθ, mopcuup epc.
Ζιolla na naeñ mac Ζoõanõ na pcel, paι penchupa,
mopcuup epc. Õoñnall mac Ruaιõpι .h. Cellaιξ,
õañna pιξ .h. Mane, quιeuιc. Mapξpec, ιnξean Uacep
a bupcc, ben mιc Feιõlιmιθ, quιeuιc. Ζιolla na
naeñ .h. Õυιbõaõopenn, ollañ Copcumpuaθ pe bpeιθ-
eañnup, õo hecc ιn hoc anno. Õonchaθ .h. hUιξιnn,
paι penchaιθ, mopcuup epc. bpan .h. bpaιn, paι cιm-
panaιξ, quιeuιc.

Κt. Θnaιp fop Ceõaoιn, αξup .ιx.xx. fuιppι;
M.ccc.lx.u.; xuιι. cιclι lunapιp; ιιι. anno ιnõιccιonιp;
xιιι. cιclι folapιp. Ruaιõpι mac Õoñnaιll .h. Neιll
õo mapõaθ õo Mhaιlpechlaιnõ mac ιn ξιpp Mac
Cachñaιl õo oen opchup cpoιξõι. Comap Mac
Mupchaθa .h. Fepξaιl õo ecc ιn hoc anno. 1nõpaιξιθ
õo õenañ õo Cloιnn Ζopõelb· ap lυιξnιchaιθ, õap
mapõaõ uι.ep mac pιξ fo Chopbmac .h. nΘξpa, .ι. aθõap
pιξ lυξnι ιn Copbmac pιn. 1nõpaιξιθ elι le hΑeθ mac
n'Õιapmaõa fop muιnncιp Θolaιp· Cealξa mopa αξup

---

1 *Churches,* cempaιll, B.　cem-
poll, C.
2 *Vulpis.* Ulpιp, B and C. This
is, of course, a Latinization of the
Irish name "Sinnach," or "Fox."
For the curious origin of this name see
Miscel. Irish Archæol. Soc., pp. 187–8.

3 *Kalends.* The Dom. Letters for
the year (GF) are added in the marg.
in B.
4 *Amhlaibh.* Αñlaιõ, B. Αñᴄ.,
C. He was of the family of O'Ferghail, or O'Farrell.
5 *Mortuus est.* Omitted in B.

hoc anno, which demolished churches[1] and houses, and sank numerous ships and boats. Bebhinn, daughter of Mac Eochagain, uxor Vulpis,[2] quievit.

The kalends[3] of January on Monday, and the nineteenth of the moon ; M.ccc.lx. quarto ; xvi. cycli lunaris ; ii. anno Indictionis; xii. anno cycli solaris. Aedh O'Neill, king of the province of Uladh, the best king that came in his own time, died after triumphing over the devil and the world. Diarmaid O'Briain, king of Tuadh-Mumha, died in hoc anno. Maelsechlainn, son of Murchadh, son of Gilla-na-naemh, son of Aedh, son of Amhlaibh,[4] mortuus est.[5] Gilla-na-naemh Mac Gobhann-na-sgél,[6] a most eminent historian, mortuus est. Domhnall, son of Ruaidhri O'Cellaigh, royal heir of Ui-Maine, quievit. Margaret, daughter of Walter Burk, wife of the son of Fedhlimidh,[7] quievit. Gilla-na-naemh O'Dubhdabhorenn, chief brehon of Corcumruaidh, died in hoc anno. Donnchadh O'hUiginn,[8] an eminent historian, mortuus est. Bran O'Brain, a celebrated harper,[9] quievit.

The kalends of January on Wednesday, and the twenty-ninth of the moon ; M.ccc.lxv. ; xvii. cycli lunaris ; iii. anno Indictionis; xiii. cycli solaris. Ruaidhri, son of Domhnall O'Neill, was killed by Maelsechlainn Mac-in-ghirr Mac Cathmhail, with one shot of an arrow. Thomas, son of Murchadh O'Ferghail, died in hoc anno. An attack was made by the Clann-Goisdelbh on the Luighne, on which occasion six sons of kings were slain, along with Cormac O'hEghra ; (i.e. this Cormac was heir to the sovereignty of Luighne). Another attack was made by Aedh Mac Diarmada on Muinter-Eolais. Great treacheries and im-

---

6 *Mac Gobhann-na-sgél*; i.e. "Mac Gobhann (Mac Gowan) of the tales (or stories)." "Mac Gabhann-na-sgel," C.

7 *The son of Fedhlimidh.* Aedh (or Hugh) O'Conor.

8 *O'hUiginn.* h.hUiginn, C. Ui

hUiginn, B. ; which is wrong, as Ui is the gen. sing, and nom. pl. form of Ua, or O'.

9 *Celebrated harper.* ται timpanaig. Mageoghegan (Ann. Clonmacnois) translates these words " insignis Cytharædus."

[MS. defective.
Text supplied
from "Annals
of Connacht."]

cpeacha αιϭϭλι το τεηαṁ απ Muιηητιπ ηϭολαιπ τοη
chup pιη, αȝυρ nochap cpecha cιη τιȝαιλ ηα cpeaϭa
pιη, απ τιαιȝ το mapϭaϭ αηηπϭe Copbmac Mac
Διαπmaτα puaϭ, αȝυρ τα mαcc Coιηαλταιȝ .h.bιpη .ι.
Maeleachlaιηη cáech αȝυρ ȝιλλα Cpιοpτ; αȝυρ το
ȝαϭαϭ αητ beupp Διαπmαιτ Mac Διαπmaτα αȝυρ
Maelpuαηαιȝ mac Dοητchαϭα pιαϭαιȝ; αȝυρ mαιϭm
ηα mαcαṁ αιηm ιη mαϭmα pιṅ οpιη ιλλε. Ϝeϭλιmιϭ
αη εηιȝ, mac Dοṁηαιλλ.h.Conchuϭαιp Copcumpuaϭ,
pí Copcumτpuaϭ, το ecc. bpιαη mac Maτha Meȝ
Cιȝeαpηαη, ταιρech Cελλαιȝ Dunchαϭα, pep το po mo
cλú το bhpειppηechαιϭ, mopτuup epτ, uτ τιcιτup—

> bpιαη Mαȝ Cιȝeαpηαη ηα τpep;
> Re α enech ηιp cóιp commep;
> Ro λeη cιη pιch τοη peλι;
> bαϭ nem cpιch α cαchpeme.

bpιαη mac Αεϭα Meȝ Mατhȝαmhηα το ȝαϭαιλ pιȝe
ηOpȝιαλλ, αcυρ cleαṁηαρ το τεηαṁ τó pe 8οṁαιρλε
mac Eοιη τυιϭ Mιc Dοmhηαιλλ, απτ conpταpλα cοιcιϭ
Uλαϭ, αȝυρ co τucc pαιp ιηȝεη .h.Rαιȝιλλιȝ το lecan
αȝυρ α ιηȝεη pειη το chaϭaιpτ; αȝυρ ηιp po cιαη απ
α hαιchλι pιη co τucc chuιcι απ cuιpeϭ τól píηα
mαp bαϭ eϭ; αȝυρ ιpe cuιpeϭ puαιp o ηα chλιαṁαιη ιη
ταη pιη α ȝαϭαιλ αȝυρ α chengαλ αȝυρ α chup ι loch
τα polach. bpιαη pειη το ιητapba τpιαpαη ηȝηιοṁ
pιη. Cuconnαchτ .h.Rαιȝιλλιȝ το τολ ιητ οpτ ιη hoc
αηηο. Αεϭ mac Neιλλ .h.Dοmηαιλλ το mapϭaϭ lα
Dοṁηαλλ mac Muιpcheαpταιȝ .h.Conchobαιp. Cατc
mac Mαȝηupα .h.Conchoϭαιp το ϭpειch απ Dοṁηαλλ

---

¹ *Maelechlainn Caech.* Maelechlainn
the one-eyed. Instead of "Caech,"
B. has cecup for "cæcus."

² *Donnchadh Riabhach;* i.e. Donnchadh the Swarthy [Mac Diarmada].

³ *Fedhlimidh - an - einigh.* Fedhlimidh "of the *einech* (or hospitality)."

⁴ *Ut dicitur.* C adds απ τó po
páιτεατ, i.e. "of him was said."
The word "pαηη" ("a stanza") is
also added in the margin in C.

⁵ *To conceal him.* τα polach.
Mageoghegan, who represents Somhairle (or Sorley) as the person that

mense depredations were committed on Muinter-Eolais on this occasion ; but these depredations were not depredations without retaliation, for Cormac Mac Diarmada Ruadh, and the two sons of Tomaltach O'Birn, viz., Maelechlainn Caech[1] and Gilla-Christ, were slain there ; and Diarmaid Mac Diarmada, and Maelruanaidh, son of Donnchadh Riabhach,[2] were moreover taken prisoners there ; and "the defeat of the youths" is the name of that defeat from that day to this. Fedhlimidh-an-einigh,[3] son of Domhnall O'Conchobhair of Corcumruaidh, king of Corcumruaidh, died. Brian, son of Matthew Mac Tighernain, chieftain of Tellach-Dunchadha, the most famous man of the Breifnians, mortuus est, ut dicitur[4]—

A.D.
[1365.]

> Brian Mac Tighernain of the conflicts—
> With his hospitality comparison was not just—
> He followed generosity without hatred ;
> Heaven was the end of his battle-career.

Brian, son of Aedh Mac Mathghamhna, assumed the sovereignty of Oirghiall, and contracted a marriage alliance with Somhairle, son of John Dubh Mac Domhnaill, high constable of the province of Uladh, who induced him to put away O'Raighilligh's daughter, and wed his own daughter. And it was not long after that until he (*Brian*) invited him to a feast, to drink wine as it were ; and the feast which his son-in-law then gave him was, to apprehend him, and bind him, and put him in a lake to conceal him.[5] Brian himself was banished through this deed. Cuchonnacht O'Raighilligh entered the Order[6] in hoc anno. Aedh, son of Niall O'Domhnaill, was slain by Domhnall, son of Muirchertach O'Conchobhair. Tadhg, son of Maghnus O'Conchobhair, came

---

acted traitorously towards his son-in-law, states (Ann. Clonmacnois, ad an.) that MacMahon was committed "to a strong place on a lough to bee kept." The Ann. Ult. and the Four Mast. represent Mac Mahon as the perpe-

trator of the deed; and the latter Annalists add that Somhairle was drowned on the occasion.

[6] *The Order.* The Four Mast. say ꞇꞅ ꝺꞟꞇ ꞃ̇ꞃꞑꞟ ᵬꞃꞙꞇꞃꞟᵬ, lit. "went into the Friars."

[MS. defective. Text supplied from "Annals of Connacht."]

αn lα ceαonα, αʒυr α ċυρ αρ ρıbαl ın lα ceαonα. ¹ρın, αʒυr oρonʒ oα mυınnτıρ oo mαρϐαo rα αeϐ mαc Conchυϐαıρ mıc Tαoc. pılıp .ḣ.Rαıʒıllıʒ oo ρıʒαϐ ıno ınαo Conchonnαchτ .ḣ.Rαıʒıllıϐ. Mαc Uατın ϐαρeτ, .ı. Roϐeρo, moρτυυr eρτ. Mαc ρıʒ Sαxαn oo rαcbαıl Eρeαnn ın hoc αnno.

Ḳl. ¹enαıρ roρ Oαρoαoın, αʒυr αenmαo .x. rυıρρı; αnno Oomını M.ccc. Lxuı. ; xuııı. cıclı Lυnαρıρ; ıııı. αnno ınoıcτıonır ; xıııı. cıclı rolαρıρ. Cατhαl mαc αeϐα ϐρeırnıʒ mıc Cατhαıl ρυαıϐ, αʒυr α ṁαc .ı. Mαʒnυr occ, oo mαρϐαo α rıll lα pılıp Mαc Uϐıρ, ρıʒ reρ Mαnαch, αʒυr lαρın rαıρchıoeochαın Mαʒ Uϐıρ, ınα nαıρechταr reın, αʒυr cρechα αıϐϐlı oo oenαṁ αρ Cloınn Mυıρċeαρταıʒ ıαραṁ, αʒυr ρıτh oo oenαṁ oo Mυınnτıρ Rυαıρc αʒυr oreαραıϐ Mαnαch ρe chele. Cατhαl Mαʒ Flαnnchαıϐ, ταıρech Oαρτραıʒı, oo mαρϐαo lα Cloınn Mυıρċeαρταıʒ. ıαρρın. Coρmαc oono Mαʒ Cαρρτhαıʒ, ρı .ḣ.Cαρρρı αʒυr .ḣ.nechαċ Mυṁαn, oo mαρϐαo α rell lα mαc α oeρϐρατhαρ bυoeın .ı. lα mαc Oomnαıll nα nOoṁnαll. Conchυϐαρ .ḣ.Conchυϐαıρ, ρı Cıαρραıʒe Lυαchρα, oo mαρϐαo oo ϐραnαchαıϐ. Seoαn Mαc Goroelb, τıʒeαρnα Sleıϐı Lυʒα, oo ecc. Rυαϐρı mαc Mυıρċeαρταıʒ.ḣ.Conchoϐαıρ oo bαϐαo αρ Sınαıno. Mαıϐm moρ le Tαoc mαc Mαʒnυrα .ḣ.Conchoϐαıρ αρ Seoαn .ḣ.nOoṁnαıll conα ʒαlloclαϐαıϐ, ocυr Mαc Sυbne oo ʒαϐαıl αno, αʒυr ϐραıʒoı ımoα mαılle ρır, αʒυr oαıne ımϐα oo mαρϐαo αno beoρ. Mαc Conmαρα, ταıρech Cloınne Culen, moρτυυr eρτ. Mαıʒırτıρ Floρınτ Mαc ıno oclαıʒ oo ecc ırın blıαϐαın rın. Coıṁτınol cocαıϐ

---

¹ *Defeated him.* α ċυρ αρ ρıbαl; lit. " sent him walking."

² *Tadhg;* i.e. Tadhg O'Conor.

³ *Kalends.* The Dom. Letter (D) is added in the marg. in B and C.

⁴ *Cathal Ruadh.* "Cathal the Red [O'Conor]."

⁵ *Archdeacon.* The MSS. have rαıρchıoeochαın, as if "parochiæ diaconus" was meant, instead of "archidiaconus."

⁶ *Assembly,* αıρechταr. The Four Mast. say "at Srath-Feara-Luirg," for the probable situation of which see O'Donovan's note, Ann. Four Mast., A.D. 1366, note ᵃ.

up with Domhnall. the same day, and defeated him,[1]
and killed a number of his people, including Aedh, the [1365.]
son of Conchobhar, son of Tadhg.[2] Philip O'Raighilligh
was made king in the place of Cuchonnacht O'Raighilligh.
Mac Wattin Barrett, i.e. Robert, mortuus est. The son
of the king of the Saxons left Erinn in hoc anno.

The kalends[3] of January on Thursday, and the eleventh [1366.]
of the moon ; anno Domini M.ccc. lxvi. ; xviii. cycli lunaris ;
iiii. anno Indictionis ; xiiii. cycli solaris. Cathal, son of
Aedh Breifnech, son of Cathal Ruadh,[4] and his son, i.e.
Maghnus Og, were slain in treachery by Philip Mac
Udhir, king of Feara-Manach, and by the Archdeacon[5]
Mac Udhir, in their own assembly[6] ; and prodigious depredations were afterwards committed on the Clann-
Muirchertagh ; and peace was concluded by Muinter-Ruairc
and the Feara-Manach with each other.[7] Cathal Mac
Flannchaidh, chieftain of Dartraighe, was after that
slain by the Clann-Muirchertaigh. Cormac Donn Mac
Carthaigh, king of Ui-Cairbre and Ui-Echach-Mumhan,
was slain in treachery by his own brother's son, i.e. by
the son of Domhnall-na-nDomhnall.[8] Conchobhar O'Conchobhair, king of Ciarraighe-Luachra, was slain[9] by the
Branachs.[10] John Mac Goisdelbh, lord of Sliabh-Lugha,
died. Ruaidhri, son of Muirchertach O'Conchobhair,
was drowned in the Sinainn. A great victory by
Tadhg, son of Maghnus O'Conchobhair, over John
O'Domhnaill with his gallowglasses ; and Mac Suibhne
was captured there, and many other captives along
with him ; and many persons were also slain there.
Mac Conmara, chieftain of Clann-Cuilen, mortuus est.
Master Flórence Mac-ind-oglaich died in this year.

---

[7] *Each other.* The Four Mast. state
that this peace was concluded
through hatred of the Clann-Muirchertaigh.

[8] *Domhnall-na-nDomhnall.* "Domhnall of the Domhnalls." Instead of

the gen. pl. art. ꞃa, as in B, C incorrectly reads ua.

[9] *Was slain.* ᴅo maꞃbaᴅ. Repeated in C.

[10] *The Branachs.* A neighbouring
English family.

[MS defective.
Text supplied
from "Annals
of Connacht."]

do Domnall .h.Néill dindraigid Néill.h.Néill, agus
Mac Cáthmail do dichur ar a duthaig amach doib,
agus breit doib ar deped na nimircech ; agus Ragnall
mac Alaxandair, oigri cloinne Alaxandair, do teacht
a hInrib Gall ron am rin dochum Néill.h.Néill, agus
cethern galloglach ag gach cuid dib .i. int athair do
chaeb agus in mac agus in brathair don taeb araill ;
Toirrdelbach an brathair, agus Alaxandar an mac.
Agus cuirir Ragnall teachta da iarraid orra dibli-
naib in onoir a rinnrireachta can teacht. air ; agus
nir dechrad do, acht ro indraigrit co hobann dochum
atha an imiricc ina agaib, ara racadar Raghnall,
agus tutrat troit agus tachar anmin da cheli ann
rin ; agus do marbad ann mac Ragnaill, agus do
gabad Alaxandar mac Domnaill and ; agus nir leg
Ragnall da muinntir a marbad, agus aduairt
Ragnall nach bed erbad a brathar agus a mic air ;
agus do marbad moran do muintir Domnaill .h.Neill
annrin. Cocad mor etir Gallaib Connacht .i. Mac
Uilliam agus Mac Muiri. Clann Muiri dinnarbad
la mac Uilliam Burc, agus a cur a clann Ricaird
don cur rin. Muircheartach mag Ragnaill, mec
Ragnaill Meg Ragnaill, do marbad a rill le
Maeleaclainn Mag Ragnaill, taireach Muinntire
hEolair. Maileaclainn rein do ecc a cinn da mir iar
rin.

Kł. Enair for Aine, agus aili .xx. fuirri ; anno
Domini M.ccc.lx.uii. ; xix. cicli lunarir : quinto anno
indictionir ; xu. cicli rolarir. Int erbacc .h.Fergail,
.i. erpog Ard achaid, in Crirto quieuit. Sitriuc mac
ind airchinnig Meg Tigearnan mortuur ert. Cathal
mac Imair meg Tigearnain mortuur ert. Imirci do

---

1 *Ford of battle.* ath an imiricc (Ath-an-imiricc). This is
probably a proper name; but if so,
it has become obsolete. At least the
Editor does not know any place at
present so called.

A warlike muster by Domhnall O'Neill, to attack
Niall O'Neill; and Mac Cathmhail was expelled from
his country by them; and they overtook the rere of the
emigrating body. And Raghnall, son of Alexander, the
heir of the Clann-Alexander, came from Innsi-Gall at
this time to Niall O'Neill; and each party had a band
of gallowglasses, viz., the father on the one side, and
the son and kinsman on the other side : (Toirdhelbhach
was the kinsman, and Alexander the son). And Raghnall
sent messengers requesting them both, in honour of his
seniority, not to oppose him; and they regarded him
not, but they advanced quickly towards the ford of
battle,[1] where they saw Raghnall; and they then delivered a fierce battle and conflict to each other. And the
son of Raghnall was slain there; and Alexander Mac
Domhnaill was taken prisoner there; and Raghnall did
not permit his people to kill him, for Raghnall said
that he would not lose both his kinsman and his son.
And a great number of Domhnall O'Neill's people were
slain there. A great war between the Foreigners of
Connacht, viz., Mac William and Mac Maurice. The Clann-
Maurice were expelled by Mac William Burk, and he
(*Mac Maurice*) was driven into Clann-Rickard on that
occasion. Muirchertach Mac Raghnaill, son of Raghnall
Mac Raghnaill, was slain in treachery by Maelechlainn
Mac Raghnaill, chieftain of Muinter-Eolais. Maelech-
lainn himself died in two months afterwards.

The kalends[2] of January on Friday, and the twenty-
second of the moon ; anno Domini M.ccc.lxvii. ; xix.
cycli lunaris; quinto anno Indictionis ; xv. cycli solaris.
The Bishop O'Ferghail, i.e. Bishop of Ard-achadh, in
Christo quievit. Sitric, son of the Airchinnech Mac
Tighernain, mortuus est. Cathal, son of Imhar Mac
Tighernain, mortuus est. A migratory excursion was

---

[2] *Kalends.* The Dom. Letter (C) is added in the margin.
VOL. II.   D

[MS. defective. Text supplied from " Annals of Connacht."]

oenaṁ oo Cloınn Muıɼcheaɼtaı̌g ı Moı̌g Nıɼı ın hoc anno, aʒuɼ toıɼc oo oenaṁ ooıᵬ ımmoı̌g Luıɼg .ı. Taoc mac Ruaıᵭɼı .ḣ. Conchoᵭaıɼ acuɼ Feɼʒal Maʒ Tıʒeaɼnan, oux Tellaı̌g Ɗunchaᵭa, aʒuɼ Ɗıaɼmaıo Maʒ Raʒnaıll, oux Muıntıɼe hⴹolaıɼ, aʒuɼ ʒalloclaechaıᵬ maɼaen ɼıu ; aʒuɼ Lonʒphoɼt Αeᵭa Mıcc Ɗıaɼmaoa oo Loɼcaᵬ leo. Feɼʒal Mac Ɗıaɼmaoa, ɼı Moıʒı Luıɼʒ, oo bɼeıch ɼoɼɼa, aʒuɼ Αeᵭ Mac Ɗıaɼmaoa, aʒuɼ tachaɼ oo chaᵭaıɼt ooıᵬ, acuɼ oaıne oa muınntıɼ oo maɼᵭaᵭ. Cuconnacht .ḣ. Raıʒıllıʒh, ɼı na Ƀɼeıfne no ʒuɼ ᵭɼeıcc hı aɼ Ɗhıa, moɼtuuɼ eɼt. Maıᵭm moɼ oo chaᵭaıɼt la Ɗoṁnall mac Muıɼceaɼtaı̌g .ḣ. Chonĉoᵭaıɼ, aʒuɼ la Muınntıɼ Ruaıɼc aʒuɼ le Cloınn Ɗonochaıᵭ, aʒuɼ le Teboıt a Ƀuɼcc cona cethıɼnn conʒᵭala, aɼ Taoc mac Maʒnuɼa .ḣ. Conchoᵭaıɼ, aʒuɼ bɼeıᵭ ɼoɼɼo aʒ tɼaıʒ ⴹothuıle ınt ɼaıɼ, aʒuɼ ʒalloclaechaıᵬ mıc Maʒnuɼa oo maɼᵭaᵭ ann tılı .ı. .x. aʒuɼ ιιι.xx., ɼa Ɗoṁnall mac 8oṁaıɼle aʒuɼ, ɼa Ɗoṁnall oc a ṁac, aʒuɼ oa mac Mıc 8ubne, aʒuɼ, ɼa mac an eɼɼoıcc .ḣ. Ɗuᵭoa, aʒuɼ ɼa Uıllıam Mac 8ıchıᵭ. Ɗeɼᵭaıl ınʒean Maelɼuanaı̌g moıɼ Mıc Ɗıaɼmaoa, ben Ualʒaıɼʒ .ḣ. Ruaıɼc, oo maɼᵭaᵭ la Cloınn Muıɼcheaɼtaı̌g. Αenʒuɼ mac an oeacanaı̌g Mıc 8aṁɼaᵭan, quıeuıt. Taoc Mac 8aṁɼaᵭaın moɼtuuɼ eɼt. Maeleaĉlaınn mac 8eɼɼaıᵭ mıc ʒılla Paoɼuıc, ocuɼ oɼeam oa ṁuınntıɼ, oo maɼbhaᵭ la ʒallaıᵭ a ɼıll. Maelmuıɼe oʒ Maʒ Cɼaıch oo ecc ın hoc anno. Taoc ocuɼ Lochlaıno, oa mac Αenʒuɼa ɼuaıᵭ .ḣ. Ɗálaıʒ, moɼtuı ɼunt. Mac Muıɼıɼ na mⴹɼıʒ moɼtuuɼ eɼt. ⴹoʒan mac Ruaıᵭɼı .ḣ. Cellaı̌g moɼtuuɼ eɼt. Muıɼcheaɼtach

---

¹ For . . . God. aɼ Ɗhıa, C. Omittted in B.

² Kern reainers. cethıɼnn conʒᵭala ; lit. " retaining (or maintaining) kerns."

³ Traigh-Eothuile-int-sair. " The strand of Eethuil the carpenter"; Trawohelly, a well-known strand near Ballysadare, in the co. of Sligo.

⁴ Son of the Bishop O'Dubhda. Cos-

made by the Clann-Muirchertaigh to Magh-Nise in hoc
anno, and they went on an expedition into Magh-Luirg,
viz., Tadhg, son of Ruaidhri O'Conchobhair, and Ferghal Mac Tighernain, dux of Tellach-Dunchadha, and
Diarmaid Mac Raghnaill, dux of Muinter-Eolais, accompanied by gallowglasses. And they burned Aedh Mac
Diarmada's fortress. Ferghal Mac Diarmada, king
of Magh-Luirg, and Aedh Mac Diarmada, overtook
them, and gave them batt'e, and killed some of their
people. Cuchonnacht O'Raighilligh, king of the Breifne
until he resigned it for *the sake of* God,[1] mortuus est.
A great defeat was given by Domhnall, son of Muirchertach O'Conchobhair, and by Muinter-Ruairc, and the
Clann-Donnchaidh, and Tibbot Burk with his kern
retainers,[2] to Tadhg son of Maghnus O'Conchobhair :
they overtook them at Traigh-Eothuile-int-sair,[3] and the
gallowglasses of the son of Maghnus were all slain there,
viz., one hundred and fifty, along with Domhnall, son of
Somhairle, and Domhnall Og, his son, and the two sons
of Mac Suibhne, and the son of the Bishop O'Dubhda,[4]
and William Mac Sithidh. Derbhail, daughter of Maelruanaidh Mor Mac Diarmada, wife of Ualgharg O'Ruairc,
was slain by the Clann-Muirchertaigh. Aenghus, son
of the Dean Mac Samhradhain, quievit. Tadhg Mac
Samhradhain mortuus est. Maelechlainn, son of Jeffrey
Mac Gilla-Patraic, and a number of his people, were
slain by Foreigners in treachery. Maelmuire Og Mac
Craith died in hoc anno. Tadhg and Lochlainn, the
two sons of Aenghus Ruadh O'Dalaigh, mortui sunt.
Mac Maurice na-mBrigh[5] mortuus est. Eoghan, son of
Ruaidhri O'Cellaigh, mortuus est. Muirchertach, son of

---

namhach, son of William O'Dubhda
(or O'Dowda), bishop of Killala. See
Harris's ed. of *Ware*, vol. i., p. 650,
and O'Donovan's *Hy-Fiachrach*, p.
117, note c.

VOL. II.

[5] *Mac Maurice na-mBrigh.* Mac
Maurice of "the Brees," or "Bryze," a
castle in the parish of Mayo, barony of
Clanmorris, and county of Mayo.

D 2

mac Muincheantaiᵹ .h.Chonchoḃain moncuun enc.
ḃeḃinn, inᵹean Ualᵹaince .h.Ruaince, ben Tomulcaiᵹ
Mic Donochaḃa, moncua enc. Ainciᵭeochan Cⱃᵹiall,
.i. Malacin Maᵹ Uᵭin, in Cⱃincto ᵪuieuic.

Kt. Enain ⱃoⱃ Sacthuⱃⱃn, ocuⱃ cⱃeaⱃ huacthaᵭ ⱃuiⱥⱥⱥu;
anno Domini M°.ccc°.Lⱥⱥⱥⱥ.; ⱥⱥⱥⱥⱥⱥ annuⱥ cicli Lunaⱥⱥⱥ;
ui. anno inᵭiccionⱥ; ⱥⱥⱥ. anno cicli ⱥolaⱥⱥⱥ·. Ceᵭh
mac Feiᵭlimiᵭ.h.Conchoḃain, ⱥⱥ Connacht, cenᵭ ᵹaile
ocuⱥ ᵹaⱥⱥⱥᵭ na nᵹaⱥᵭel, ocuⱥ Luᵹaⱥᵭ Laⱦⱥaᵭa Leⱥthe
Cuⱥnᵭ inᵭaᵭaⱥᵹ ᵹall ocuⱥ ᵹaⱥᵭel ᵭⱥⱥⱥ ⱥna aᵭaⱥᵹ, ᵭo
ⱦeᵹ ⱥaⱥ mⱥuaⱥᵭ naⱥchⱥⱥᵹe ⱥⱥᵷoⱥ Cumman, ⱥaⱥ na ᵭeⱥⱥh
ᵭa ⱥⱥⱥaᵹaⱥⱥ ᵭecc ⱥⱥⱥⱥᵹe Connacht amal aⱥⱥeⱥc an
ⱥⱥle—

> Da ḃⱥⱥaᵭaⱥⱥ ᵭec ᵭeoch mⱥᵭaⱥᵹ
> D'Ceᵭ a nⱥnaᵭ a cuⱥᵹⱥᵭaⱥᵹ;
> Cⱥⱥm ⱥa ceᵭ ᵭo chuⱥⱥ na ᵭoⱥⱥ,
> ᵹe ᵭo ⱥⱥuaⱥⱥ ecc ⱥⱥ haᵭoⱥc.

Cⱥⱥch Caⱥⱥⱥⱥe ᵭo ⱥoⱥⱥᵭ aⱥ ᵭó eⱥᵭⱥⱥ mac Maᵹnuⱥa
.h.Conchoḃaⱥⱥ ocuⱥ Doⱦⱥall mac Muⱥⱥcheaⱥⱥaⱥᵹ.
Feⱥᵹal Mac Diaⱥmaᵭa, ⱥⱥ Muⱥᵹe Luⱥⱥᵹ, moⱥcuuⱥ
eⱥc. Tⱥᵹeⱥⱥan mac Cachaⱥl .h. Ruaⱥⱥc moⱥcuuⱥ eⱥc.
Coⱥⱦac occ Mac Diaⱥmaᵭa, ᵭeᵹ aᵭᵭaⱥ ⱥⱥᵹ aⱥ a
ᵭucthaⱥᵭ ⱥeⱥⱥ, moⱥcuuⱥ eⱥc. Diaⱥmaᵭ mac Coⱥⱦaⱥc
ᵭuⱥⱥᵭ Meᵹ Caⱥⱥⱥthaⱥᵹ ᵭo ᵹaᵭaⱥl le Maᵹ Caⱥⱥⱥthaⱥᵹ
Caⱥⱥⱥⱥeach, ocuⱥ a ⱥᵭⱥacal ᵭo ᵹallaⱥᵭ, ocuⱥ a ⱦⱥlleᵭ
ⱥaⱥ ⱥⱥⱥ. Daⱥⱥᵭ O Tuaⱥhaⱥl ᵭo maⱥⱥaᵭ ᵭo ᵹallaⱥᵭ
Cctha clⱥacth. Seaaⱥ Ua Doⱦⱥallaⱥⱥ moⱥcuuⱥ eⱥc.
Uⱥllⱥaⱥ Saⱥⱥanach mac ⱥⱥ Eⱥⱥaⱥⱥ a ᵭuⱥc, .i. oⱥᵹⱥⱥ na
nUⱥllⱥaⱥaⱥ, ᵭo hecc ᵭon ᵹalaⱥ ⱥⱥecc an Iⱥⱥⱥ Cua.

---

¹ Of the Gaeidhel. na nᵹaⱥᵭel, B. ᵹaⱥᵭel Eⱥⱥenn, the Gaeidhel of Erinn, C.

² Lughaidh Lamhfhada. "Lughaidh of the long hand," a personage whose valour and exploits furnished the theme of many compositions of the Irish bards. O'Flaherty represents him as having flourished A.M. 2764. See Ogygia, cap. 13, p. 177.

³ The son. ᵭa mac, "the two sons," B.

⁴ Muirchertach; i.e. Muirchertach O'Conchobhair (Murtough O'Conor).

Muirchertach O'Conchobhair, mortuus est. Bebhinn,
daughter of Ualgharg O'Ruairc, wife of Tomaltach Mac
Donnchadha, mortua est. The archdeacon of Airghiall,
i.e. Malachi Mac Udhir, in Christo quievit.

The kalends of January on Saturday, and the third
of the moon; anno Domini M°.ccc°.lxviii.; primus annus
cycli lunaris; vi. anno Indictionis; xvi. anno cycli
solaris. Aedh, son of Fedhlimidh O'Conchobhair, king
of Connacht, head of the valour and bravery of the
Gaeidhel,[1] and the Lughaidh Lamhfhada[2] of Leth-Chuinn
against the Foreigners and Gaeidhel who were opposed
to him, died after the victory of penance, in Ros-Comain,
after having been twelve years in the sovereignty of
Connacht, as the poet said :—

> Twelve lasting, prosperous years
> Was Aedh in the place of his provincial king;
> His body was pierced by weapons one hundred times;
> Nevertheless, he died on his pillow.

The territory of Cairbre was divided into two parts
between the son[3] of Maghnus O'Conchobhair and Domhnall, the son of Muirchertach.[4] Ferghal Mac Diarmada,
king of Magh-Luirg, mortuus est. Tighernan, son of
Cathal O'Ruairc, mortuus est. Cormac Og Mac Diarmada, the good material of a king over his own country,
mortuus est. Diarmaid, son of Cormac Donn Mac
Carthaigh, was taken prisoner by Mac Carthaigh Cairbrech; and he was surrendered to the Foreigners, and
afterwards slain. David O'Tuathail was slain by the
Foreigners of Ath-cliath. John O'Domhnallain mortuus
est. William Saxanach, son of Sir Edmond[5] Burk, i.e.
the heir of the Mac Williams, died of the small pox[6] in

---

[5] Sir Edmond. B has ſiſſ Remann,
as if for "Sir Redmond," which is the
form of the name in Mageoghegan's
translation of the so-called Annals of
Clonmacnois, where the disease of

which he died is called "the little
pox."

[6] Small pox. ᵹaƚaſſ bſſecc, B.
ᵹaƚaſſ bſſeac, C. The literal meaning is "speckled disease."

Tomoltach occ mac ₱eₙȝail Mic Oiaₙmaoa, τánaiₙτe
Moiȝi Luiₙȝ, oo ecc oon ȝalaₙ bₙec. Laiₙeach mac
Oaiio 1 Moₙᵬa moₙτuiiₙ eₙτ. Sluaȝaᵬ aᵬᵬal moₙ
la Niall Ua Néill, ₱i cóiciᵬ Ulaᵬ, an Oiₙȝiallaibh,
oₙoₙbáiₙ aₙ ᵬhₙian Maȝ Maτhȝaᵯna, ocuₙ Lonȝₚoₙτ
oo ȝaᵬail oo a mieoᵬon an τiₙe, ocuₙ cuᵯaᵬa moₙa
oo τhaiₙcₙin oó o ᵬhₙian Maȝ Maτhȝaᵯna, .i. leᵬ
Oₙȝiall oo τhaᵬaiₙτ oo Niall mac Muₙchaiᵬ mic
ᵬₙiain na coiliȝ oiₙₙino, .i. oon ₱iȝ oo bói ₱emhe
₱oₙₙan τiₙ, acuₙ coᵯaoae moₙa eli oO Néill ino eₙic
Mic Ooᵯnaill ; ocuₙ .h. Neill oa naenτuȝaᵬ ₱in. Ocuₙ
coᵯaiₙli aili oo oenaᵯ oo mac Muₙchaiᵬ Meȝ Maτhȝaᵯna, ocuₙ oCClaₙanoaₙ oc Mac Ooᵯnaill, oo τiȝ-
eaₙna na nȝalloȝlaᵬ, ocuₙ ȝluaₙachτ ooiᵬ oiblinaiᵬ
can ceτ can comaiₙle oO Neill, τₙi coₙaiȝᵬi seaoₙa-
ᵬacha coᵯmoₙa, oinoₙaiȝiᵬ Meȝ Maτhȝaᵯna, ocuₙ
ammuₙ Lonȝₚoiₙτ oo τhaᵬaiₙτ ooiᵬ ₱aiₙ; ocuₙ Maȝ
Maτhȝamna an lin oo bái oo eₙȝi ina naȝhaiᵬ, aȝuₙ
maiᵬm oo τhaᵬaiₙτ oó aₙ in ₱lúaȝ ₱in, ocuₙ mac
Muₙchaiᵬ Mec Maτhȝaᵯna, oiȝₙi Oₙȝiall, oo maₙ-
ᵬaᵬ annₙin, ocuₙ CClaₙanoaₙ ócc mac Toiₙₙohelbaiȝ
Mic Ooᵯhnaill, conₙabla na nȝalloȝlach ocuₙ oiȝₙi
Cloinne Ooᵯnaill, oo ᵯaₙᵬaᵬ, ocuₙ Eoȝan mac Toiₙₙ-
ohelbaiȝh mic Maelₙechlainn.h. Ooᵯnaill oo maₙ-
ᵬaᵬ ann, eτ alii mulτi nobileₙ eτ iȝnobileₙ. Tomaₙ
.h. ₱loinn, ₱i.h. Tuiₙτₙi, ₱ai Eiₙeann aₙ enech ocuₙ
aₙ enȝnaᵯ ocuₙ aₙ uaiₙli, oo ecc in hoc anno. Taoc,
mac Maȝnuₙa, mic Caτhail, mic Ooᵯnaill.h. Concho-
ᵬaiₙ, oo ȝaᵬail ₱eₙ oolum oo Ruaiᵬₙi.h. Chonchobaiₙ,
oo ₱iȝ Connachτ, ina Lonȝₚhoₙτ ₱éin an CCₙo in choil-
lin, iaₙ na ᵬₙeiτh leiₙ oo Choₙmac Mac Oonochaiᵬ
ȝo τech.h. Conchuᵬaiₙ; ocuₙ iₛ ₱ₙia ₱in ₱o ₱amalτi

---

1 *Into Oirghiall.* CCn Oiₙȝial-
láibh, C. an Oₙȝiall, B.
2 *Brian - na - cailigh - oifrinn;* i.e.
"Brian of the mass chalice."

3 *As an eric.* ino eₙ.ecc, C. ʼino
icc,.lit. "in payment," B.
4 *Mac Domhnaill.* Apparently
Somhairle Mac Domhnaill, or Sorley

A D.

[1368]

Inis-Cua. Tomaltach Og, son of Ferghal Mac Diarmada, tanist of Magh-Luirg, died of the small pox. Laisech, son of David O'Mordha, mortuus est. A prodigious hosting by Niall O'Neill, king of Uladh, into Oirghiall,[1] to attack Brian Mac Mathghamhna ; and he pitched his camp in the centre of the territory ; and Brian Mac Mathghamhna offered him large terms, viz., to give the half of Oirghiall to Niall, the son of Murchadh, son of Brian-na-cailigh-oifrinn,[2] i.e. the king who was before him over the territory, and other large conditions to O'Neill as an eric[3] *for the death* of Mac Domhnaill.[4] And O'Neill accepted these. But another resolution was adopted by the son of Murchadh Mac Mathghamhna, and by Alexander Og Mac Domhnaill, lord of the gallowglasses, both of whom marched, without the permission or consent of O'Neill, with a force of three united great battalions, against Mac Mathghamhna, and attacked his fortress ; and Mac Mathghamhna opposed them with all the force he had, and defeated this army ; and the son of Murchadh Mac Mathghamhna, heir of Oirghiall, was slain there; and Alexander Og, the son of Toirdhelbhach Mac Domhnaill, constable of the gallowglasses, and heir of the Clann-Domhnaill, was slain ; and Eoghan, son of Toirdhelbhach, son of Maelechlainn O'Domhnaill, was slain there, et alii multi nobiles et ignobiles. Thomas O'Floinn, king of Ui-Tuirtre, the most eminent man in Erinn for hospitality, prowess, and nobility, died in hoc anno. Tadhg, son of Maghnus, son of Cathal, son of Domhnall O'Conchobhair, was taken prisoner, per dolum, by Ruaidhri O'Conchobhair, king of Connacht, in his own fortress in Ard-in-choillin, after he had been taken to O'Conchobhair's house by Cormac Mac Donnchaidh ; and it is to this that every evil was usually compared,

---

Mac Donnell, put to death Brian Mac Mahon, as recorded above, under the year 1365. See note [5], p. 28.

Dig

[MS. defectire.
Text supplied
from " Annals
of Connacht."]

cech olc ; ocuʃ ni ʀo ʀamlaᵭ olcc ʃʀiʃ, .i. ní meʀa ᵹaᵭail maic Maᵹuuʀa; ocuʃ ní baᵭ meʀa ina ʀin ᴅo ᴅenaṁ
ʀiʃ aʀ cʀill, .i. a ᴛiᵭnacal ᴅo 'Ooṁnall mac Muiʀ-
cheaʀᴛaiᵹ .h. Chonchoᵭaiʀ, ocuʃ a ṁilleᵭ ʀa ᵭeoiᵹ la
'Ooṁnall i caiʀlen ᴛ8licciᵹ ; cuʀ ʀáʀ coccaᵭ moʀ i
Connachᴛaiᵭ uili ᴛʀiaʀan nᵹmoṁ ʀin, .i. eiᴅiʀ mac
Uilliam ocuʃ .h. Concoᵭaiʀ, ocuʃ Mac 'Oiaʀmaᴅa.
Ruaiᵭʀi mac 8eoṅacc Mec Eochacan, ʀai na hEʀenᴅ
uli cin imʀiʀain a nenech ocuʃ a nenᵹnaṁ, ᴅo eᵹ i
quinᴅiᴅ Ƈᴛ. Enaiʀ in hoc anno.

Ƈᴛ. Enaiʀ ʀoʀ Luan, ocuʃ cechaʀ ᴅec ʃuiʀʀi ; anno
'Oomini M.°ccc.°Ιxix. ; ii. annuʃ cicli lunaʀiʃ ; uii. annuʃ
inᴅicᴛioniʃ ; xuii. annuʃ cicli ʃolaʀiʃ. Piliʀ .h. Raiᵹil-
liᵭ ᴅo ᵹaᵭail ᴅa ᵭʀaiᵭʀiᵭ ʃein, ocuʃ a ċuʀ a cloich
Locha huachᴛaiʀ, ocuʃ ʀiᵹe ᴅo ᵹaᵭail ᴅo Maᵹnuʃ
.h. Raiᵹilliᵹ ina inaᴛ ; ocuʃ cocaᵭ ʀo móʀ ᴅo eʀᵹi iʀin
ᵭhʀeiʃne ᴛʀiaʀan nᵹaᵭail ʃin, ocuʃ ʃluaᵹ moʀ ᴅo
ᴛinol la hαnnaᵭ .h. Raiᵹilliᵹ, .i. mac Riʃᴅaʀᴅ, .i. Maᵹ
Maᴛhᵹaṁna ocuʃ Oiʀᵹallaiᵭ aʀcheana, ᴅo ᴛhaᵭach
Philib .h. Raiᵹilliᵹ aʀ Maᵹnuʃ ; ocuʃ maiᵭm moʀ ᴅo
ᴛhaᵭaiʀᴛ aʀ Maᵹnuʃ a mᵭlen cuʀa ᴅo Maᵹ Maᴛhᵹaṁna ocuʃ ᴅo Chloinn Caʀa, inaʀ maʀᵭaᵭ ᴛʀi meic
Coʀmuic .h. ʃeʀᵹail, 8eonin ocuʃ Maeleaċlainn occuʃ
ʃeʀᵹuʃ, ocuʃ ʃeᵭlimiᵭ mac αeᵭa in cleiᴛín .h. Chonchoᵭaiʀ, ocuʃ ᴅa mac ʃlaiᵭᵭeaʀᴛaiᵹ muiʀ Mic Con-
ʀuba .i. 'Oonn ocuʃ ᵭʀian, ocuʃ 8iᴛʀecc na ᵹʀona Mac
an maiᵹiʃᴛiʀ. ᵹeʀalᴛ Caeṁanach, aᵭᵭaʀ aiʀᴅʀiᵹ
Laiᵹean, ᴅo maʀᵭaᵭ ᴅon ʀiᴅiʀe ᴅuᵭ. Ƈiᵹeaʀnan
.h. Ruaiʀc ᴅo ᴅol ʃoʀ cʀeich i Luʀᵹ, ocuʃ a ᴛaᵭaiʀᴛ

---

[1] *Most eminent.* ʃai. Mageoghegan
says of this Ruaidhri, "though mine
Author maketh this great account of
this Rowrie, that he extolleth him
beyond reason, yett his Issue now,
and for a long time past, are of the
meanest of their own name."

[2] *Fifth.* B and C have quinᴛiᴅ;

as if quinᴛ iᴅ (fifth of the ides) was
first intended, and the characters
Ƈᴛ (for Kalends) afterwards added.

[3] *Kalends.* The Dom. Letter for
the year (G) is added in the marg. in B.

[4] *Cloch-Locha-Uachtair* ; i.e. the
stone keep of Loch·Uachtar. See
note *, p. 260, vol. i.

(but no evil was equal to it): i.e. "the taking of the son of Maghnus was not worse." But a worse deed was committed against him after a while; i.e., he was surrendered to Domhnall, son of Muirchertach O'Conchobhair, and was ultimately killed by Domhnall in the castle of Sligech. And a great war arose in all Connacht through this deed, viz., between Mac William, and O'Conchobhair, and Mac Diarmada. Ruaidhri, son of Seonac Mac Eochagain, the most eminent[1] man in Erinn, without dispute, for bounty and prowess, died on the fifth[2] of the kalends of January in hoc anno.

The kalends[3] of January on Monday, and the fourteenth of the moon; anno Domini M.ccc.lxix.; ii. annus cycli lunaris; vii. annus Indictionis; xvii. annus cycli solaris. Philip O'Raighilligh was taken prisoner by his own brethren, and put into Cloch-Locha-Uachtair;[4] and the sovereignty was assumed in his place by Maghnus O'Raighilligh. And a very great war occurred in the Breifne through this capture; and a great army was assembled by Annadh O'Raighilligh, i.e. the son of Richard, (viz., Mac Mathghamhna, and the rest of the Airghialla), to rescue Philip O'Raighilligh from Maghnus. And a great defeat was inflicted on Maghnus, at Blencupa, by Mac Mathghamhna and the Clann-Caba, in which were slain the three sons of Cormac O'Ferghail, viz., Seonin, Maelechlainn, and Fergus; and Fedhlimidh, son of Aedh-an-chleitín[5] O'Conchobhair; and the two sons of Flaithbhertach Mor Mac Conrubha, viz., Donn and Brian; and Sitric-na-srona[6] Mac-in-Maighistir. Gerald Caemhanach, heir to the chief sovereignty of Laighen, was slain by the Black Knight.[7] Tighernan O'Ruairc went to take a prey in Lurg, and brought it with him;

---

[5] *Aedh-an-chleitín.* "Hugh of the little sword."

[6] *Sitric-na-srona.* "Sitric of the nose."

[7] *The Black Knight.* In a marginal note in the MS. vol. of the Four Masters preserved in Trin. Coll., Dublin, (class H. 2–11), Roderick O'Flaherty remarks that this Black Knight was one of the English of Dublin.

[MS. defective.
Text supplied
from "Annals
of Connacht."]

Leṗ ; ocuṗ Ɑeḃ occ mac Ɑeḃα Uı Ruαıṗc ᴅo mαṗḃαḃ
ᴅO Mαelαᴅuın Luıṗʓ ın ıαṗmαıṗeαċṫ nα cṗeıċı. Oıαṗ-
mαıᴅ Lαıṁᴅeṗʓ Mαc Muṗchαᴅα, αıṗᴅṗıʓ Lαıʓen, ᴅo
ḃeıċh α Lαıṁ ṗαᴅα αʓ ʓαllαıḃ Ɑṫhα clıαṫ, ıαṗ nα
ʓαḃαıl α ṗıll ᴅon ṗıᴅıṗı ᴅαḃ, ocuṗ α ċhαṗṗαınʓ ṗαᴅeoıḃ
ᴅoıḃ ; ʓnıoṁ ıṗ mo ᴅo ṗonnαḃ ınᴅ Eṗınn α nᴅeṗeḃ
αınṗıṗe. Mαċhʓαṁαın Mαenmαıʓı .h. Ḃṗıαın, ṗı Ṫuαḃ-
muṁαn, αn ʓαıḃeαl ıṗ ṗeṗṗ ocuṗ ıṗ αıṗeʓᴅo ᴅo ḃı ınα
αınṗıṗ ṗeın, ᴅo eʓ ınα Lonʓḃuṗṫ ıαṗ mbuαıḃ nαıċhṗıʓe,
ocuṗ Ḃṗıαn occ .h. Ḃṗıαın ᴅo ʓαḃαıl ṗıʓe ınα ınαṫ ıαṗ
ṗın. Uα Mαelαᴅuın Luıṗʓ ᴅo mαṗḃαḃ α ṗıll ᴅo ṁαcαıḃ
Neıll .h. Ooṁnαıll, ocuṗ Ṗılıp Mαʓ Uḋıṗ ᴅo ᴅol
Lonʓuṗ moṗ ᴅo ᴅıʓuıl α oclαoıch αṗ mαcαıḃ .h. Ooṁnαıll, ocuṗ Nıαll occ .h. Ooṁnαıll ᴅo mαṗḃαḃ Leıṗ
Ḃṗıαn mαc Ɑeḃα buıḃe hı Neıll, αḋḃαṗ ṗıʓ Eṗenn,
moṗċuuṗ eṗc. Eṗpuc Oᴅo O Néıll, .ı. eṗpuc Oıṗʓıαll,
ın Cṗıṗᴅo quıeuıṫ. Rıcαṗᴅ .h. Rαıʓıllıʓ, eṗpuc nα
Ḃṗeıṗne, ın Cṗıṗᴅo quıeuıṫ. Mαıḃın moṗ ᴅo ċhαḃαıṗṫ
Lα Ḃṗıαn .h. mḂṗıαın, ṗı Ṫuαḃṁuṁαn, ınαṗ ʓαḃαḃ
ʓeṗoıṫ ıαṗlα ocuṗ ʓoıll moṗα nα Muṁαn αṗchenα ;
ocuṗ nı meınıc ᴅo ċuıṫ αṗ αon Lαṫhαıṗ ṗıαṁ uṗᴅuıl αṗ
ċuıṫ ᴅo ᴅoınıḃ αnnṗın. Luımnech ᴅo Loṗcαḃ ᴅon ṫuṗuṗ
ṗın ; ocuṗ ᴅo ṗonṗαᴅ ʓıαllαḃ ᴅU Ḃṗıαın ; ocuṗ Sıᴅα
occ mαc ınʓıne .h. Ouḃᴅıṗ ᴅo ʓαḃαıl bαṗṗᴅαċṫα αn
bαıle ıαṗ ṗın. Ṫoıṗc Loınʓṗı ᴅo ᴅenαṁ ᴅo Ṗılıp Mαʓ
Uḋıṗ co Loch Uαchᴅαıṗ, ocuṗ cloch .h. Rαıʓıllıʓ ᴅo
ʓαḃαıl ᴅo ; ocuṗ Ṗılıp .h. Rαıʓıllıḃ, ṗı Ḃṗeṗne, ᴅo
ḃı α Lαıṁ ınᴅı ᴅo ċhαḃαıṗṫ eṗᴅı ; ocuṗ α ṗıʓe ṗeın ᴅo
ċhαḃαıṗṫ ᴅo αṗıṗ ıαṗ ṗın.

Ḳᴅ. Enαıṗ ṗoṗ Mαıṗᴅ, ocuṗ coıceḃ .xx. ṗuıṗṗı ;
M.ccc.Lxx. ; ııı. αınuṗ cıclı Lunαṗıṗ ; uııı. αnnuṗ

---

¹ *In the pursuit of the prey.* ın ıαṗ-
mαıṗeċṫ nα cṗeıċı. Omitted in B.

² *The Black Knight.* See note ⁷,
last page.

³ *Torn asunder.* At horses' tails. The
Four Masters say ᴅo ḃαṗúʓαḃ, "was
put to death."

⁴ *Bishop of Oirghiall;* i.e. bishop of
Clogher.

⁵ *Breifne.* The bishopric of the
Breifne is now the diocese of Kilmore.

⁶ *Often.* meınıc, C. ıııneıc, B.

⁷ *They;* i.e. the people of Luimnech,
or Limerick.

and Aedh Og, son of Aedh O'Ruairc, was slain by O'Maeladuin of Lurg in the pursuit of the prey.[1] Diarmaid Lamhderg Mac Murchadha, chief king of Laighen, was a long time confined by the Foreigners of Ath-cliath, after having been taken prisoner, in treachery, by the Black Knight,[2] and was at last torn asunder[3] by them : the greatest deed committed in Erinn in later times. Mathghamhain Maenmaighe O'Briain, king of Tuadh-Mumha, the best, and most illustrious Gaeidhel that was in his own time, died in his own fortress, after the victory of penitence ; and Brian Og O'Briain assumed the sovereignty in his place. O'Maelduin of Lurg was slain, in treachery, by the sons of Niall O'Domhnaill ; and Philip Mac Udhir went with a great fleet, to avenge his vassal on the sons of O'Domhnaill, and Niall Og O'Domhnaill was slain by him. Brian, son of Aedh Buidhe O'Neill, one qualified to be king of Erinn, mortuus est. Bishop Odo O'Neill, i.e. the bishop of Oirghiall,[4] in Christo quievit. Richard O'Raighilligh, i.e. bishop of the Breifne,[5] in Christo quievit. A great defeat was given by Brian O'Briain, king of Tuadh-Mumha, in which Earl Garrett and the other great Foreigners of Mumha were taken prisoners ; and not often[6] before did as many persons fall in one spot as fell there. Luimnech was burned on this expedition, and they[7] gave hostages to O'Briain ; and Sida Og,[8] son of O'Duibhidhir's daughter, assumed the wardenship of the town afterwards. A naval expedition was made by Philip Mac Udhir to Loch-Uachtar, and Cloch-Ui-Raighilligh was taken by him ; and Philip O'Raighilligh, king of Breifne, who was imprisoned therein, was taken out of it, and his own sovereignty was afterwards again given to him.

The kalends[9] of January on Tuesday, and the twenty-fifth of the moon ; M.ccc.lxx. ; iii. annus cycli lunaris ;

---

[8] *Sida Og.* Sid the Younger (Mac Commara, or Mac Namara).

[9] *Kalends.* The Dom. Letter (F) is added in the margin in B.

[MS. defective.
Text supplied
from "Annals
of Connacht."]

ınoıctıonıр; xuı11. cıclı рolaрıр. 'Oořhnall .ħ. Néıll oo
chaбaıрt tıξeрnaıр ocuр брaıξoı oo Nıall .ħ. Néıll.
бре
ocuр moрan oo бáthaб ocuр oo mılleaб ano. Cocaб
moр eıoıр Clann Mhuıрcheaрtaıξ ocuр Muınntıр
Raıξıllıξ ın hoc anno. ħ. Raıξıllıξ ocuр .ħ. Ϝeрξaıl,
ocuр Maξ Uбıр, ocuр .ħ. Conchoбaıр oo eрξe anaбaıξ
Cloınne Muıрcheaрtaıξ, aξuр a cuр a Muınntıр
Θolaıр рe neaрt na рıξ рın, ocuр a nool aррıбe
oochum mıc Uıllıam бuрcc, aξuр Maξ Tıξeaрnaın oo
ool Leo annрıoe. Clann Œeбa Mıc Cathmaıl oo
maрбaб Ƶılla Paoрuıc Mıc Cathmaıl, рıξhthaoıрıξ
Cenel Ϝeрaбaıξ, рeр oolum, ocuр Conulaб Mıc Cathmaıl, ocuр a řhıc ocuр a řhna..ı. ınξean Maξnuрa Meξ
Mathξařhna. Muрchaб a бeрбрathaıр ına ınatt ıaр
рın. Muıрĉeaрtach Sınnach, рex рeр Tethba, quıeuıt
xıx. n. Ϝeбraб. Cathal .ħ. Conchoбaıр, aббaр рıξ
.ħ. Ϝalξı, ocuр Muıрĉeaрtach .ħ. Moрбa oo toıtım
aр cрeıch La Ƶallaıб Laıξen.

]ct. Θnaıр рoр Ceoaın, ocuр .uı. uathao рuıррı;
M.ccc.Lxxı.; quaрtuр annuр cıclı Lunaрıр; ıx. annuр
ınoıctıonıр; xıx. cıclı рolaрıр. Ϝeрξal Maξ Cochlan
oo eξ ıllaıřh ac .ħ. Cenoeoıξ ın hoc anno. Ϝeрξal
Maξ Θochaξan quıeuıt hı .u. ıo Septımрeр. Muрchaб .ħ. Maoaoan, рeıcheam coıttcheann oϝeрaıбΘрeno,
oo maрбaб ooen oрchoр tрoıξoı ın hoc anno. Taoc
occ mac Maξnuрa .ħ. Conchoбaıр oo maрбaб a ϝıll oo
'Oořhnall mac Muıрĉeaрtaıξ .ħ. Conchoбaıр oa Lařhaıб
рeın, ı caıрlen Slıcıξ, ıaр na бeıб рaoa ıllaıřh ı cuıбрech
aıξe; aξuр nı meınıcc oo рonnaб a nΘрınn рıařh maрбaб
baб meрa ına рın. 'Oonnchaб .ħ. бıрn quıeuıt. брıan
.ħ. Cennetıξ, рı Uрřhuřhan, oo řhaрбaб LaƵallaıб. Œıрo-
eррoξ Tuama, ceno enıξ na hΘрeno, ın Cрıрto quıeuıt.

---

¹ From thence. aррıбe, C. aрр
рıбe, B.
² Kalends. The Dom. Letter (E)
is added in the marg. in B.

³ Of Erinn. Θрeno, B. Θıрeann,
C.
⁴ In chains. ı qıбрech, for ı cuıбрech, B. hı ccuıбрeać, C.

viii. annus Indictionis ; xviii. cycli solaris. Domhnall A.D.
O'Neill gave lordship and hostages to Niall O'Neill. [1370.]
Niall gave an overthrow to Brian Mac Mathghamhna,
when a great many were drowned and killed. A great
war between the Clann-Muirchertaigh and Muinter-
Raighilligh in hoc anno. O'Raighilligh, and O'Ferghail,
and Mac Udhir, and O'Conchobhair rose against the
Clann-Muirchertaigh, who were driven into Muinter-
Eolais through the power of these kings ; and they went
from thence[1] unto Mac William Burk ; and Mac Tighernain went along with them. The sons of Aedh Mac
Cathmhail killed Gilla-Patraic Mac Cathmhail, king-
chieftain of Cenel-Feradhaigh, per dolum, and Cu-
Uladh Mac Cathmhail, and his son, and his wife, i.e.
the daughter of Maghnus Mac Mathghamhna. His
brother Murchadh *was appointed* afterwards in his
place. Muirchertach Sinnach, rex of Feara-Tethbha,
quievit on the 19th of February. Cathal O'Conchobhair,
royal heir of Ui-Failghe, and Muirchertach O'Mordha fell
on a foray by the Foreigners of Laighen.

The kalends[2] of January on Wednesday, and the sixth [1371.]
of the moon ; M.ccc.lxxi. ; quartus annus cycli lunaris ;
ix. annus Indictionis ; xix. cycli solaris. Ferghal Mac
Cochlan died whilst in the hands of O'Cennedigh in
hoc anno. Ferghal Mac Eochagain quievit on the 5th
of the ides of September. Murchadh O'Madadhain,
general patron of the men of Erinn,[3] was killed by one
shot of an arrow in hoc anno. Tadhg Og, son of Maghnus
O'Conchobhair, was slain in treachery by Domhnall, son
of Muirchertach O'Conchobhair, with his own hands, in
the castle of Sligech, after having been a long time confined in chains[4] by him ; and not often before had a
worse homicide been committed in Erinn than this.
Donnchadh O'Birn quievit. Brian O'Cennedigh, king of
Ur-Mumha, was slain by Foreigners. The Archbishop of
Tuaim,[5] head of the bounty of Erinn, in Christo quievit.

---

[5] *Archbishop of Tuaim* ; i.e. John O'Grada.

[M.S. defective.
Text supplied
from "Annals
of Connacht."]

Ct. Ɛnαιꞃ ꞃoꞃ Ɗαꞃⱱαιn, ocuꞃ uιι.x. ꝼuιꞃꞃι;
ⱦ°.ccc".lxxιι.; u. αnno cιclι lunαꞃιꞃ; x. αnno ιnⱱιc-
ⱴιoιιιꞃ; xⱴ. αιιno cιclι ꞃolαꞃιꞃ. Ꞃꞃιαn moꞃ ⱦαᵹ
ⱦαⱦᵹαmnα, αꞃⱱꞃιᵹ Oꞃᵹιαll, ꞃeꞃ ιꞃ mo ⱱo mαꞃⱱ ⱱo
Ᵹαllαιⱱ ocuꞃ ⱱo ᵹⱨαιⱱelαιⱱ ιnα αιmꞃιꞃ ꞃeιn αn Ɛꞃιnⱱ,
ⱱo ⱴoιⱴιm le ᵹαllocłαc ⱱα ⱦuιnnⱴιꞃ ꞃeιn α ꝼιll ιn hoc
αnno. Ꞃeααn moꞃ Uα Ɗuⱱαᵹαιn, ꞃαι ꞃe ꞃenchαꞃ ocuꞃ
ollαmⱨ .h. ⱦαιne, ⱱo hecc ιn hoc αnno. ⱦuιꞃcheαꞃ-
ⱴαch ⱦuιⱦneαch·mαc ⱦuιꞃceαꞃⱴαιᵹ moιꞃ ⱦeᵹ Ɛochι-
αcαn, ⱴαιꞃech Cenel ꝼιαchαιⱱ mιc Neιll, quιeuιⱴ ι
Ct. Ocⱴιmⱱeꞃ. Uιllιαⱦ mαc Uιllιc, cenn ꞃuαꞃcuꞃα
Ɛꞃenn ulι, quιeuιⱴ. Uιllιαm occ .h.Cellαιᵹ, αⱱⱱαꞃ ꞃιᵹ
.h.ⱦαιne, quιeuιⱴ.

Ct. Ɛnαιꞃ ꞃoꞃ Ꞃαⱴhαꞃnn, ocuꞃ ochⱴmαⱱ .xx. ꝼuιꞃꞃι;
ⱦ.ccc.lxxιιι.; uι. αnno cιclι lunαꞃιꞃ; xι. αnno ιnⱱιc-
ⱴιoιιιꞃ; xxι. αnno cιclι ꞃolαꞃιꞃ. Inⱱꞃαιᵹιⱱ ⱱo ⱱenαⱦ
ⱱo Ᵹαllαιⱱ nα ⱦιⱱe ιꞃιn Cnᵹαιle, ocuꞃ Ruαιⱱꞃι mαc
Cαⱴhαιl .h. ꝼeꞃᵹαιl ocuꞃ α ⱦαc ⱱo nιαꞃⱱαⱱ ⱱoιⱱ, ocuꞃ
moꞃαn ⱱα muιnnⱴιꞃ mαιlle ꞃιu; ocuꞃ Ɗonⱱochαⱱ .h.ꝼeꞃ-
ᵹαιl ⱱα lenⱦαιn, ocuꞃ moꞃαn ⱱo mαꞃⱱαⱱ leꞃ ⱱιⱱ; ocuꞃ
α ⱦαꞃⱱαⱱ ꞃeιn ⱱo én oꞃchαꞃ ⱴꞃoιᵹⱴι ꞃα ⱱeoιⱱ. Uιllιαm
Ɗαlαⱴun, ꞃeꞃꞃαⱦ nα ⱦιⱱe, ⱱo ⱦαꞃⱱαⱱ le Cenel
ꝼιαchαιⱱ occuꞃ lα .h.ⱦαιlechlαιnⱱ. Cⱱαιm .h.Cιαnαn,
ꞃαι ꞃenchαⱱα, ⱱo ecc α lιꞃ ᵹαⱱαιl ιnα chαnαnαch.
ⱦαc αn ꞃeꞃꞃun ⱦιc ꝼeoꞃαιꞃ ⱱo mαꞃⱱαⱱ lα ⱴoιꞃꞃ-
ⱱheαlⱱαch ꞃuαⱱ .h.Concⱨoⱱαιꞃ ⱱo en ⱱuιlle cloιⱱιⱦ hι
Conⱦαιcne Ɗunα moιꞃ, ⱱeꞃ ꝼιll ⱱo ⱱenαmⱨ ꞃαιꞃ ⱱoιⱱ,
ocuꞃ ꞃe αᵹ ⱴeαchⱴ α Conmαιcne Cúιlι; ocuꞃ ⱴeαchⱴ ⱱo
ꞃeιn αꞃ loꞃ α lαιⱦe lαιⱱιꞃι αꞃ ocuꞃ ꞃe ⱱeoloιⱴι; ocuꞃ
Cnⱱꞃιαꞃ ⱦαc Cιnαιⱴh ⱱo mαꞃⱱαⱱ ⱱoιⱱ ⱱeꞃ ⱴoιꞃꞃ-
ⱱhelⱱαιᵹ ꞃuαιⱱ ⱱα ⱴαιꞃⱱeιꞃⱴ ⱱoιⱱ α nᵹιll ꞃe α nιⱱꞃeιⱴ

---

1 **Kalends.** The Dom. Letters for
the year (D C) are added in the
marg. in B.

2 **Ollamh;** pron. *ollave*; i.e. chief
professor. This John Mor O'Dubhagain was the author of the curious
Topographical Poem edited by Dr.
O'Donovan for the Irish Archaeol.
and Celt. Soc.; Dublin, 1862.

3 **Ulick;** i.e. Ulick Burk.

The kalends[1] of January on Thursday, and the seven-teenth of the moon ; M°.ccc°.lxxii. ; v. anno cycli lunaris ; x. anno Indictionis ; xx. anno cycli solaris. Brian Mor Mac Mathghamhna, chief king of Orghiall, the man who slew most of Foreigners and Gaeidhel in his own time in Erinn, fell by a gallowglass of his own people, in treachery, in hoc anno. John Mor O'Dubhagain, a most eminent historian, and ollamh[2] of Ui-Maine, died in hoc anno. Muirchertach Muimhnech, son of Muirchertach Mor Mac Eochagain, chieftain of Cenel-Fiachaidh-mic-Neill, quievit on the kalends of October. William, the son of Ulick,[3] head of the gaiety of all Erinn, quievit. William Og O'Cellaigh, royal heir of Ui-Maine, quievit.

The kalends[4] of January on Saturday, and the twenty-eighth of the moon ; M.ccc.lxxiii. ; vi. anno cycli lunaris ; xi. anno Indictionis ; xxi. anno cycli solaris. An incur-sion was made by the Foreigners of Midhe into the Anghaile, and Ruaidhri, son of Cathal O'Ferghail, and his son, were slain by them, and several of their people along with them. And Donnchadh O'Ferghail pur-sued them, and many of them were slain by him ; but he himself was ultimately killed by one shot of an arrow. William Dalton, the sheriff of Midhe, was slain by the Cenel-Fiachaidh, and by O'Maelechlainn. Adam O'Cianan, an eminent historian, died a canon at Lis-gabhail. Mac-an-persun Mac Feorais was killed by Toirdhelbhach Ruadh O'Conchobhair, with one stroke of a sword, in Conmaicne-Duna-moir, after they (*Mac Feorais's people*) had acted treacherously towards him, whilst coming from Conmaicne-Cuile ; and he himself escaped through the power of his strong arm, but severely wounded. And Andrias Mac Cinaith was killed by them, after having been delivered[5] to them by Toirdhelbhach Ruadh, as a hostage from whom they might obtain their

---

[4] *Kalends.* The Dom. Letter for the year (B) is added in the margin.   [5] *Delivered.* ᴅᴀ ᴛᴀɪɲϐeɪɲᴄ, C. ᴅᴀ ᴄʜᴀϐᴀɪɲᴄ, B.

[*MS. defective. Text supplied from "Annals of Connacht."*]

fein dfaġḃail doiḃ ar. Barrdub ingen .h. Ruairc, ben Doṁnaill Meg Tiġearnan, quieuit. Gaeth ro ṁor in hoc anno, ler briseḋ móran do themplaibh.

Kl. Enair for Domnach, ocus noemaḋ uathaḋ fuirri; M.ccc.lxx.quarto; uii. anno cicli lunaris; xii. anno indictionis; xxii. anno cicli solaris. Senicin Sabais do marḃaḋ la Mag Aengusa. Doṁnall occ .h. Dochartaiġ do ecc in hoc anno. Cuchoigcriche occ Mac Eochacain, dux Cenel Fiachaiḋ mic Neill, do marḃaḋ a fill hi coiṁteacht an espaig Faltaig, do laiṁ ant Sindaig mic Meran, hi sex Kl. Septimbris; ocus in Sinnach fein do tarraing ocus baill do denaṁ de iar sin. Teboit a Burcc, oiġri Mic Uilliam, do marḃaḋ la hiḃ Maine. Tiġearnan mac Briain Meg Tiġearnain, deġ mac tairiġ, quieuit. Maidm mor la Niall .h. Neill for Gallaiḃ, inar tuit in ritiri Rotrich ocus Bocsa na Cairrci, agus an Santalach, ocus in Burcach, ocus Uilliam Baili dalad cenn ansfeli Ereann. Maileachlaind mac Diarmada .h. Fergail mortuus est. Tadc og Mag Ragnaill mortuus est. Tadcc mac Ruaiḋri mic Cathail ruaiḋ .h. Conchoḃair, daġ ṁac riġ, do ec in hoc anno.

Kl. Enair for Luan, ocus ficheḋ fuirri; M°.ccc°.lxx°.u.; uiii. anno cicli lunaris; xiii. anno indictionis; xxiii. anno cicli solaris. Mathġaṁain mac Maġnusa .h. Conchuḃair quieuit. Caislen Rosa Coman do thaḃairt do Toirrdhealbach ruaḋ .h. Conchoḃair do Ruaiḋri .h. Conchobair, ocus baile in tobair dfagbail ar, ocus comtha imḃa nach airmthear sunda.

---

1 *Kalends.* The Dom. Letter (A) is added in the marg. in B.

2 *Indictionis.* indus, B.

3 *Senicin.* Jenkin.

4 *Cenel-Fiachaidh-mic-Neill.* "Descendants of Fiachadh, son of Niall." See note 4, p. 556, vol. i.

5 *Faltach.* This is an attempt at writing the name of De Valle, or Wale (Stephen), bishop of Meath from 1369 to 1379. See Harris's ed. of *Ware*, vol. 1, p. 147.

6 *The Sinnach Mac Merain;* i.e. "the Fox Mac Merain."

own award. Barrdubh, daughter of O'Ruairc, wife of Domhnall Mac Tighernain, quievit. Very great wind in hoc anno, by which several churches were broken down.

The kalends[1] of January on Sunday, and the ninth of the moon; M.ccc.lxx.quarto; vii. anno cycli lunaris; xii. anno Indictionis;[2] xxii. anno cycli solaris. Senicin[3] Savage was slain by Mac Aenghusa. Domhnall Og O'Dochartaigh died in hoc anno. Cuchocriche Og Mac Eochagain, dux of Cenel-Fiachaidh-mic-Neill,[4] was slain in treachery, in the company of the Bishop Faltach,[5] by the hand of the Sinnach Mac Merain,[6] on the sixth of the kalends of September; and the Sinnach himself was afterwards drawn, and cut to pieces. Tibbot Burk, heir of Mac William, was slain by the Ui-Maine. Tighernan, son of Brian Mac Tighernain, a good son of a chieftain, quievit. A great victory by Niall O'Neill over Foreigners, in which the knight Roche, and Bocsa-na-Cairrge,[7] and the Sandal, and the Burk, and William of Baile-dalad, head of the inhospitality of Erinn, were slain. Maelechlainn, son of Diarmaid O'Ferghail, mortuus est.[8] Tadhg Og Mac Raghnaill mortuus est. Tadhg, son of Ruaidhri, son of Cathal Ruadh O'Conchobhair, a good son of a king, died in hoc[9] anno.

The kalends of January on Monday, and the twentieth of the moon; M°.ccc°.lxx°.v.; viii. anno cycli lunaris; xiii. anno Indictionis; xxiii. anno cycli solaris. Mathghamhain, son of Maghnus O'Conchobhair, quievit. The castle of Ros-Comain was given by Toirdhelbhach Ruadh O'Conchobhair to Ruaidhri O'Conchobhair,[10] and Baile-in-tobair was obtained from him, besides several other

---

[7] *Bocsa-na-Cairrge.* Bocsa of the Rock [i.e. of Fergus, or Carrickfergus].

[8] *Mortuus est.* The Four Mast. say that he was slain in battle with the English.

[9] *Hoc.* occ, B and C.

VOL. II.

[10] *To Ruaidhri O'Conchobhair.* The corresponding words are omitted in C, in which the note "malaipt Rora Coman ap baile an tobaip," i.e. "exchange of Ros-Comain for Baile-an-tobair," is added in the margin.

E

[MS. defective.
Text supplied
from "Annals
of Connacht."]

Mac αrten, uppa. Cenel Fαʒupταʒ, do mapδαδ α Fill
do mac ʒilli Ʈepnαind. Mαiδm mop do chαδαipʈ αp
ʒαllαiδ Dúin dα Leʒ ʒlαp inαp mαpbhαoh pip Sémup
bαile αthα ʈiδ, Fep inαiʈ piʒ Sαxαn, αʒup αn δupcαch
Camlinne, eʈ αlii mulʈi. Cu Ulαδ Mαʒ Mαthʒαṁnα
do dol dheʒ do cuipƚinn. αpʈ Mac Uδip quieuiʈ.
Donδchαδ Cαeṁαnach Mac Mupchαδα, piʒ Lαiʒen,
do mapδαδ do ʒαlloiδ α Fill. Diαpmαid Mαʒ
Rαʒnαill do dol αp inopαiʒiδ dochom Copmαic
.h.δipn, ocup Donδchαδ mαc Conchoδαip αn copαn
do mapδαδ αnn, ocup dαine imδα αili; ocup mopαn
édαlα do chαδαipʈ Leó. Toipcc do chuαdαp dα ṁαc
Meʒ Ʈiʒeαpnαn dochom ʒαll, .i. Cαipbpe ocup Eoʒαn,
ocup Fep dα muinnʈip Fein do Fell Foppo ocup dα peic
pe ʒαllαiδ do chinn indmupα, ocup ʒαill do ʈinol inα
ʈimchell, ocup cóicep αp .xx. do mapδαδ αnn, ocup α
ndichennαδ Fα dα mαc Meʒ Ʈiʒeαpnαn. Sip Emαnd
αlpαnαch .i. mac Uilliαm δupc, mopʈuup epʈ iαp
nbuαiδ nαithpiʒe ocup nonʒchα, ocup α ṁαc inα inαd
.i. Tomαp. Mαeleαċlαinn .h. Doṁnαllαin, deʒ Fep
dαnα, do ecc don Filun. Cαthαl mαc Cαthαil oicc
do Clαinn Ricαipd mopʈuup epʈ. Mac Feopαip αthα
nα piʒ mopʈuup epʈ. Opcup mαc αipʈ meʒ Uδip do
mapδαδ do cloinn Donδchαδ meʒ Uδip. Seppαiδ
mαc ʒillα nα nαeṁ .h. Fepʒαil, deαʒ αδδαp ʈαipiʒh
nα hαllʒαile, in Cpipʈo quieuiʈ.

Jcᴛ. Enαip Fop Mαipʈ, ocup αen uαthαδ Fuippi;
M°.ccc°.Lxxui.; ix. αnno cicli Lunαpip; xiiii. indicʈionip;

---

1 Not enumerated. nαch αipmʈep,
B. nαch αipṁiʒʈep, C.

2 Gilla-Ternain. Another member
of the family of Mac Artan, or Mac
Cartan.

3 Baile - atha - tidh. This is the
Irish form of the name of Malahide,
near Dublin, the seat of the Talbot
family; but it is a mistake to say
that a Sir James Talbot was Lord

Deputy of Ireland at the time referred
to.

4 Alii. αli, B and C.

5 Conchobhar-an-chopain; i.e. "Conor
of the Cup."

6 Sold them. dα peic, C. dα
cpecc, i.e. purchased them, B.

7 The "Alun." A disease of the
glands.

considerations not enumerated[1] here. Mac Artan, chieftain of Cenel-Faghartaigh, was slain, in treachery, by
the son of Gilla-Ternain.[2] A great defeat was given to
the Foreigners of Dun-da-lethglas, in which Sir James
of Baile-atha-tidh,[3] the king of the Saxons' Deputy, and
Burk of Camlinn, et alii[4] multi, were slain. Cu-Uladh
Mac Mathghamhna died of *the opening of* a vein. Art
Mac Udhir quievit. Donnchadh Caemhanach Mac Murchadha, king of Laighen, was slain by Foreigners in
treachery. Diarmaid Mac Raghnaill went on an expedition against Cormac O'Birn ; and Donnchadh, son of
Conchobhar-an-chopain,[5] was slain there, and many other
persons ; and they brought great spoils with them. The
two sons of Mac Tighernain, viz., Cairbre and Eoghan,
went on an expedition against the Foreigners ; and a man
of their own people betrayed them, and sold[6] them to
the Foreigners for the sake of wealth ; and the Foreigners
assembled around them, and five and twenty were slain
there, and beheaded, along with the two sons of Mac
Tighernain. Sir Edmond Albanach, i.e. Mac William
Burk, mortuus est after the triumph of penance and
unction ; and his son, i.e. Thomas, *was appointed* in his
place. Maelechlainn O'Domhnallain, a good poet, died of
the "filun."[7] Cathal, son of Cathal Og of the Clann-
Rickard, mortuus est.[8] Mac Feorais of Ath-na-righ
mortuus est. Oscur, son of Art Mac Udhir, was slain
by the sons of Donnchadh Mac Udhir. Jeffrey, son of
Gilla-na-naemh O'Ferghail,[9] a good[10] heir to the chieftaincy of the Anghaile, in Christo quievit.

The kalends of January on Tuesday, and the first
of the moon ; M°.ccc°.lxxvi. ; ix. anno cycli lunaris ; xiiii.

[1376.]

---

[8] *Mortuus est.* This entry is quite
wrong. The Four Masters say that
" Cathal Og, son of Cathal Mor, son
of Domhnall O'Conchobhair, was slain
by the Clann-Rickard," which seems
more correct.

[9] *O'Ferghail.* The clause ending
with this name is erroneously repeated in C.

[10] *Good.* ᵐᵃⁱᵗ, C. ᵗᵉⁿᵈ (i.e.
"stout"), B.

xxiiii. anno cicli ꞃolaꞃiꞃ. Ταυc.h.Ruaiꞃc ꞃi bꞃeiꞃne
moꞃtuuꞃ eꞃt, ocuꞃ Τiᵹheaꞃnan.h.Ruaiꞃc υo ᵹaбail
ꞃiᵹe υa éiꞃe. Ꙅonnchaб Ⅿac Ꝼiꞃбiꞃiᵹ quieuit.
Cuaiꞃne .h. Conchuбaiꞃ Ꝼalᵹi, mac ꞃiᵹ ꞃo ṁaith,
quieuit. Ruaꞃcan .h. hꞀꞵυmaill, ollam.h.Ꞁnluain,
quieuit. Θoin.h.Ruanaбa, ollaṁ Ⅿeᵹ Ꞁenᵹuꞃa,
quieuit. Ⅿailechlainυ.h.Ⅿailmena, ollaṁ.h.Cathan,
moꞃtuuꞃ eꞃt. Ꞁeб .h.Τuathail, ꞃi .h.Ⅿail, υo
maꞃбaб la Ꙅalloiб in hoc anno. Ꙅalbach mac Ⅿail-
eaċlainn.h.bꞃain, mac ꞃiᵹ ꞃo maith, υo ᵹuin υa ꞃꞃoꞃ
ꞃein, ocuꞃ a· ecc υe. Conchobaꞃ.h.bechan, ꞃai ꞃe
ꞃenchaꞃ, quieuit. Cellach Ⅿac Cꞃuitin, ollaṁ
Τúaбṁuṁan ꞃe ꞃenchaꞃ, quieuit. Roibeꞃυ.h.Ꝼeꞃᵹail
quieuit. bebinn inᵹean Ꙅoiṁnaill .h.Ꙅhuinn, ben
.h.Ꙅimuꞃaiᵹ, quieuit. Ꞁeб mac Seoan .h. Ꝼeꞃᵹail
moꞃtuuꞃ eꞃt.

Kt. Θnaiꞃ ꞃoꞃ Ꙅaꞃυain, ocuꞃ aili .x. ꞃuiꞃꞃi; Ⅿ°.ccc°.
lxxuii.; x. anno cicli lunaꞃiꞃ; xii. inυictioniꞃ; xxii. anno
cicli ꞃolaꞃiꞃ. Uaceꞃ mac ꞃiꞃ Ꙅabiυ a buꞃc moꞃtuuꞃ
eꞃt. Seꞃꞃaiб .h.Ꝼlannacan, taiꞃech Cloinne Cathail,
moꞃtuuꞃ eꞃt. Ⅿaiυm υo thaбaiꞃt le Ⅿac CoꞀmaꞃa
.i. CuꞀaꞃa, ocuꞃ le cloinn Culén aꞃchena, ꞃoꞃ cloinn
Ricaiꞃυ, inaꞃ· maꞃбaб Τeboit mac Uillic, cenυ na
cethiꞃne moꞃi, ocuꞃ tꞃi meic .h.Θoin; ocuꞃ moꞃan
υo maithiб cloinne Ricaiꞃυ υo ṁaꞃбaб ócuꞃ υo ᵹaбail
ann ꞃoꞃ. bꞃian.h.Ꝼlaithбeaꞃtaiᵹ moꞃtuuꞃ eꞃt. Seaan
.h.Roυacꞁan, coṁoꞃba Caillin, ꞃai Θiꞃenn, moꞃtuuꞃ
eꞃt. Int eꞃꞃocc Ua Cellaiᵹ, eꞃꞃocc chluana ꞃeꞃta
bꞃenainυ, quieinc. Socaб moꞃ eiυiꞃ Ruaiбꞃi .h.Con-
chuбaiꞃ ocuꞃ Ⅿac Ꙅiaꞃmaυa, ocuꞃ Ⅿaᵹ Luiꞃᵹ υo
loꞃcaб eiυiꞃ ꞃoꞃcneṁ ocuꞃ aꞃбaꞃ, ocuꞃ υaine υo

---

1 *Tighernan O'Ruairc.* He is called
Tighernan Mor (Tighernan the Great)
in a marg. note in B and C. The
remainder of the entry, together with
the name "Donnchadh" in the next
entry, is omitted in B.

² *Ollamh;* pronounced *ollave.* The
title of *ollamh* was usually applied to
the chief doctor or professor of any
art or science.

³ *By Foreigners.* la Ꙅalloiб, B.
υo Ꙇhalloiб, C.

Indictionis; xxiiii. anno cycli solaris. Tadhg O'Ruairc, king of Breifne, mortuus est, and Tighernan O'Ruairc[1] assumed the sovereignty after him. Donnchadh Mac Firbisigh quievit. Cuaifne O'Conchobhair Failghe, a very good son of a king, quievit. Ruarcan O'hAdhmaill, O'hAnluain's ollamh,[2] quievit. John O'Ruanadha, Mac Aenghusa's ollamh, quievit. Maelechlainn O'Maelmhena, O'Cathain's ollamh, mortuus est. Aedh O'Tuathail, king of Ui-Mail, was killed by Foreigners[3] in hoc anno. Dalbhach, son of Maelechlainn O'Brain, a very good son of a king, was wounded by his own spur, and died in consequence. Conchobhar O'Bechan, an eminent historian, quievit. Cellach Mac Cruitin, chief historian[4] of Tuadh-Mumha, quievit. Robert O'Ferghail quievit. Bebhinn, daughter of Domhnall O'Duinn, wife of O'Dimusaigh, quievit. Aedh, son of John O'Ferghail, mortuus est.

The kalends[5] of January on Thursday, and the twelfth of the moon; M°.ccc°.lxxvii.; x. anno cycli lunaris; xv. Indictionis; xxv. anno cycli solaris. Walter, son of Sir David Burk, mortuus est. Jeffrey O'Flannagain, chieftain of Clann-Cathail, mortuus est. A defeat was given by Mac Conmara, i.e. Cumara, and by the rest of the Clann-Cuilen, to the Clann-Rickard, in which Tibbot, son of Ulick, head of the great band of kerns, and the three sons of O'hEdhin, were slain; and several of the chiefs of the Clann-Rickard were also slain or taken prisoners there. Brian O'Flaithbhertaigh mortuus est. John O'Rodachan, comarb of Caillin,[6] the sage of Erinn, mortuus est. The Bishop O'Cellaigh, bishop of Cluain-fertaBrenainn, quievit. A great war between Ruaidhri O'Conchobhair and Mac Diarmada, and Magh-Luirg was burned, both buildings and corn, and people were killed

---

[4] *Chief historian.* ollaṁ -... . . ṅe ṙenchaṙ, "chief professor in history." The word ṙenchaṙ is omitted in C.

[5] *Kalends.* The Dom. Letter for the year (D) is added in the margin in B and C.

[6] *Caillin.* See note [11], p. 21, *supra*.

[MS. defective.
Text supplied
from " Annals
of Connacht."]

mapꞇaꞇ eaꞇoppa; ocuꞃ ꞃíꞇh ꞇo ꝺenamh eaꞇoppa ꞃa
ꝺeoiꞇ, ocuꞃ cnꞇaꝺa ꞇopa ꝺꞃaꞇꞇail ꞇo ꞇꞇac ꞇhiap-
maꝺa ꞇn a ꞇiꞇꞇail ꞇo chꞇnꝺ ꞃꞇꝺa. ꞇellꞇm ꞇoꞃa
Coman la ꞇuaꞇꝺꞃ.h.Cꞇnchobaꞃ ꞃoꞃ mac ꞇꞇlliam
ꞇuꞃce, ocuꞃ ꞃoꞃ ꞇꞇaꞇeaꞇlanꞇ.h.Cellaꞇꞇ, ꞃꞇ .h.ꞇaꞇne,
ꞇaꞃ mapꞇaꞇ ꞇꞃꝺeaꞃꝺ a ꞇuꞃe, aꞇꞃ ꞇoꞇnall mac
Caꞇhal oꞇce, ocuꞃ ꞇaꝺc oc mac ꞇaꞇꝺc.h.Cellaꞇꞇ, ocuꞃ
.h.ꞇaꞇnnín, ꞃaꞇ ꝺeꞇ enꞇ ꝺaenꞇachꞇach, ocuꞃ ꞇꞇac
ꞇuꞇꞇaꞇll ꞇallocclach, ocuꞃ mac ꞇeꞇll chaꞇm, eꞇ clꞇꞇ
mulꞇꞇ nobꞇleꞃ eꞇ ꞇꞇnobꞇleꞃ. ꞇꞇnꞇaꞃꝺ ꞃꞇ ꞇaꞇan quꞇeuꞇ
ꞇn Cꞃꞇꞇꞇo. ꞇonꝺchaꞇ mac ꞇꞇllꞇam alaꞇnꝺ.h.Ceꞃ-
ꞇaꞇll, ꞃꞇꞇ ꞇlꞇ, quꞇeuꞇ. ꞇꞇaꞃmaꞇꝺ loꞃc mac ꞇꞃanan,
ꝺuꞇ Coꞃca ꞇꞇhꞇlaꞇꝺh, quꞇeuꞇ ꞃꞇnꝺ ꞇóꞇꞇ. ꞇachꞇna
mac ꞇaꞇꝺ.h.ꞇoꞃꝺa, aꞇꞇaꞃ ꞃꞇꞇ laꞇꞇꞃꞇ, quꞇeuꞇ. Caꞇꞃ-
len lꞇꞃ aꞇꝺ abla ꝺo ꝺenaꞇ la ꞇeoaꞇ.h.ꞃeꞃꞇaꞇl ꞇn
hoc anno. ꞇanꞇꞃceꞇꞃ ꞇꞃa ꞃuaꞇꞇ ꞇo loꞃcaꞇ ꞇn hoc
anno. ꞇoꞇꞃaꞇꞇ mac ꞇnnaꞇꞇ .h.ꞃaꞇꞇꞇllꞇꞇ occꞇꞃuꞃ eꞇ
o cloꞇnn ꞇn Chaꞇch. ꞇn ꞇecanach ꞇꞇac ꞇuꞇꞃꞇꞇoꞃa ꞇn
Cꞃꞇꞇꞇo quꞇeuꞇ.

ꞇꞇ. ꞇnaꞃ ꞃoꞃ ꞇꞇne, ocuꞃ ꞇꞃeaꞃ ꞃꞇcheaꞇ ꞃuꞇꞃꞇꞇ;
ꞇꞇ°.ccc°.lꞇꞇ.uꞇꞇꞇ.; ꞇꞇ. anno cꞇclꞇ lunaꞃꞇꞃ; ꞃꞃꞇmuꞃ annuꞃ
ꞇnꝺꞇcꞇꞇonꞇꞃ; ꞇꞃꞇꞇ. anno cꞇclꞇ ꞃolaꞃꞇꞃ. ꞇoꞇꞃꞃꞇealꞇach
ꞇꞇac ꞇuꞇꞇne áꞃꝺ ꞇonꞃꞇabla Chonnaꞇꞇ,

* * * * * * *
* * * * * * *
* * * * * * *
* * * * * * *
* * * * * * *

<hr>

1 *Richard Burk.* The Four Mast. state that he was the brother of Mac William.

2 *Cathal Og;* i.e. Cathal the younger [O'Conor].

3 *Mac Dubhgaill Galloglach.* "Mac Dubhgall the gallowglass.

4 *Niall Cam;* i.e. Niall the Crooked [Mac Neill]. See note 7, p. 649, vol. 1.

5 *Alii.* alꞇ, B.

6 *Alainn;* i.e. the beautiful, or magnificent.

7 *Diarmaid Losc.* Diarmaid the Lame. The order of this entry and the preceding one is reversed in C.

8 *lxxviii.* lxxxviii., B.

9 *High Constable of Connacht.* áꞃꝺ ꞇonꞃꞇabla Chonnaꞇꞇ. Here a defect commences which extends to the year 1384. The word áꞃꝺ in the

between them ; and peace was ultimately concluded
between them ; and great conditions were obtained by
Mac Diarmada for his injuries, in consideration of peace.
The battle of Ros-Comain *was gained* by Ruaidhri
O'Conchobhair over Mac William Burk, and over Mael-
echlainn O'Cellaigh, king of Ui-Maine, in which were
slain Richard Burk[1], and Domhnall, son of Cathal Og ;[2]
and Tadhg Og, son of Tadhg O'Cellaigh ; and O'Mainnin,
an eminently generous and humane man ; and Mac
Dubhgaill Galloglach,[3] and the son of Niall Cam ;[4] et
alii[5] multi nobiles et ignobiles. Edward, king of the
Saxons, quievit in Christo. Donnchadh, son of William
Alainn[6] O'Cerbhaill, king of Eli, quievit. Diarmaid
Losc[7] Mac Branan, dux of Corca-Achlann, quievit in
Rome. Fachtna, son of David O'Mordha, royal heir of
Laighis, quievit. The castle of Lis-ard-abhla was built
by John O'Ferghail in hoc anno. The monastery of
Es-Ruaidh was burned in hoc anno. Godfrey, son of
Annadh O'Raighilligh, occisus est by the Clann-in-
Chaich. The Dean Mac Morrissy in Christo quievit.

The kalends of January on Friday, and the twenty-
third of the moon ; M°.ccc°.lxxviii.;[8] xi. anno cycli lunaris ;
primus annus Indictionis ; xxvi. anno cycli solaris.
Toirdhelbhach Mac Suibhne, high constable of Connacht,[9]
died.

---

foregoing clause is the last word of
the entry in B, in which (p. 168) the
note "desunt fere octo anni " occurs.
The following memorandum has been
written by the late Theophilus O'Flan-
agan in the MS.C. :—"N.B. The remainder of this Annal, together with
the years 1379, 1380, 1381, 1382,
1383, 1384, are wanting in the
Annals of Connaght, all to the following fragment of the year 1384 ; but
they may be filled from the Four
Masters, who have transcribed the
above Annals."

*　*　*　*　*　*
*　*　*　*　*　*

Seon mac Ζιollά Coιpceli, maιξιpτιp, aιpchιnυeač ocυp peappún Αιpιξ δροpca, υéξ. Ruaιδpι mac Τοιppδeal-δaιξ Uι Chončυδaιp, pι Connaέτ, υeξ υon ρlaιξ čéαυna oιυclι pelι Caιτpíona banoιξι ιpιn ξeṁpιuδ, ιap caιtheaṁ .uι. mblιaδan .x. ocυp paιche hι lάn pιξι Connachτ, aṁaιl poιpξlep an pιlι, .ι. Maιlιn .h. Maιlčonaιpe, a nυuaιn ιn peme pιξpaιυhe :

　　　ρuaιp Ruaιδpι pιξδa an pnaιτι
　　　Α pé υéaξ ιp υeξ pachι,
　　　Αp Chpuachan Αι ξan ιpξaιl,
　　　Mac τachap δoρb Τοιppδealδaιδ.

Υa pι υo υenaṁ ιna ιnaτ ιap pιn .ι. Τοιppδelδach puaδ mac Αeδa meιc ρeιδlιmιδ υo pιξaδ υo Mac Υιapmaυa ocυp υo čloιnn Mυιpčeapτaιξh Mυιṁnιξ, ocυp υo čaιpeċaιδ Connachτ apchena, .ι. υo čaιpeċaιδ pιla Mυιpeυaιξ; ocυp Τοιppυhelbach occ mac Αeδa mιc Τοιppυhelbaιξ υo pιξaδ υO Chellaιξ ocυp υo Chloιnn Rιcaιpυ ocυp υo Υoṁnall mac Mυιpcheapτaιξ .h. Conchobaιp, ocυp υo chloιnn Υonυchaιδ ; cυp páp coccaδ coιτchenυ hι Conυachτaιδ uιlι ιap pιn, ocυp conυepnpaτap uιlcc ιmδa ocυp upτha acυp aιpcne υoaιpneιp υa epι pιn. ριlιp .h. Raιξιllιξ quιeuιτ. Maιlιp a δupcc υo mapδaδ υo epcυp. Εoξan .h. Maιlle ocυp Copmac .h. Maιllι eτ alιι mulτι υo mapδaδ υo ṁuιnnτιp ρlaιτhδeapτaιξ. Υaιδι a δupc quιeuιτ. Maelmopδa .h. Υuιδξιnnan quιeuιτ. ρol Maξ Τethechan, comopba Cluanι ιn Cpιpτo quιeuιτ. Uιllιam mac pιpp Εmaιnn a δupcc quιeuιτ. Seppaιδ .h. ρepξaιl

---

[1] *Plague.* A terrible plague referred to in all the Irish Annals. See Wilde's Table of *Cosmical Phenomena*, Census of Ireland for 1851, part v., vol. 1.

[2] *Night.* oιυchι. The hiatus in B terminates with this word.

[3] *Of Catherine.* Cατpιch pιna, B. The festival of St. Catherine the

Virgin occurs on the 25th of November.

[4] *In the poem.* anυuaιn, C. anυ ιn υuaιn, B. The composer of this poem is elsewhere called Donn Losg O'Maelchonaire. See p. 483, vol. 1.

[5] *Made king.* A marginal note in the following words occurs in C, viz.,

*　*　*　*　*　*
*　*　*　*　*　*

John Mac Gillachoisceli, master, erenagh, and parson of Airech-Brosca, died. Ruaidhri, son of Toirdhelbhach O'Conchobhair, king of Connacht, died of the same plague[1] on the night[2] of the festival of Catherine[3] the Virgin, in the winter, after spending sixteen years and a quarter in the full sovereignty of Connacht, as the poet, i.e. Mailin O'Maelchonaire, testifies in the poem[4] of the " Reim Righraidhe."

> Ruaidhri the royal obtained the reins
> For sixteen years and a quarter,
> On Cruachan Ai, without contention—
> The battle-fierce son of Toirdhelbhach.

Two kings were afterwards appointed in his place, viz., Toirdhelbhach Ruadh, son of Aedh, son of Fedhlimidh, was made king[5] by Mac Diarmada, and by the Clann-Muirchertaigh-Muimhnigh, and by the chieftains of Connacht also, viz., the chieftains of Sil-Muiredhaigh ; and Toirdhelbhach Og, son of Aedh, son of Toirdhelbhach, was made king by O'Cellaigh, and by the Clann-Rickard, and by Domhnall, son of Muirchertach O'Conchobhair, and the Clann-Donnchaidh. And a general war subsequently broke out in all Connacht ; and they committed numerous injuries, and indescribable[6] burnings and plunders, after that. Philip O'Raighilligh quievit. Meyler Burk was killed by a fall. Eoghan O'Maille, and Cormac O'Maille, et alii multi, were slain by Muinter-Flaithbhertaigh. David Burk quievit. Maelmordha O'Duibhgennain quievit. Paul Mac Tethechan, comarb of Cluain,[7] in Christo quievit. William, son of Sir Edmond Burk, quievit. Jeffrey O'Ferghaill

---

eavarrgarað agur coimearcc ſiol gConcubair on mbliagain 1384, i.e. "separation and confusion of the Sil-Conchobhair from the year 1384."

[6] *Indescribable.* vocairneir ; omitted in B.

[7] *Cluain ;* i.e. Cluain-Conmaicne, or Cloon, in the barony of Mohill, and county of Leitrim.

[MS. defective.
Text supplied
from "Annals
of Connacht."]

quıeuıc. Maʒ Raʒnaıll ɒuḃ .ı. Ɖıaρmaıɒ mac
Maıleaċlaınn, ın ʒáρ ꞇaıρeach, ρaı an eneaċ ocuρ
an enʒnaṁ, ɒo maρḃaɒ ρeρ ɒolum ɒo ċloınn Raʒnaıll
Meʒ Raʒnaıll, a nɒoρaρ ꞇıʒı Rıρɒaρɒ Meʒ Raʒnaıll.
Muıρcheaρꞇach .h. Conchoḃaıρ, ρı .h. Ƒaılʒı, ɒo écc
ına ρenoıρ. Ꞇomulꞇaċ Maʒ [Ɖ]oρċhaıḃ, ɒux Cenel Lua-
chaın, ɒo maρḃaɒ ɒa ρcın ρeın ocuρ ρe aʒ cuρ cρu.
Cuċonnachꞇ.h.Ƒeρʒaıl; ꞇıʒeaρna Maıʒı Ꞇρeʒa, quıeuıc.
Ɖonnchaɒ .h. Ɖuɒɒa quıeuıc. Cceḃ .h. Cellaıʒ ocuρ
Ƒeρaḃach .h. Cellaıʒ ɒo écc ɒon ṗláıʒ an aen ρechꞇ-
maın. Ualʒaρʒ Ua Ruaıρc, aḃḃaρ ρıʒ Ḃρeıρne, ɒo
ḃaꞇhaɒ aρ Loch Ʒamna. Ɖoṁnall mac Ƒlaıꞇḃeaρ-
ꞇaıʒ Uı Ruaıρc quıeuıc. Rıcaρɒ mac Maıɒıucc mıc
Ꞇomın ḃaρeꞇ, ρeıcheaɒ coıꞇchenɒ clú móρ ɒo clıaρaıḃ
Eρenɒ, ɒo écc ıaρ mbuaıɒ naıꞇhρıʒe. Uʒuıρꞇín
.h.Ɖuıḃʒınnan, ollaṁ Conmaıcne ρe ρenchaρ, quıeuıc.
8eaan a ḃuρc ɒo écc ɒon ṗlaıʒ ın hoc anno.

Kꞇ. Enaıρ ρoρ Ɖoṁnach, ocuρ x. maɒ uaꞇhaɒ ρuıρρı;
m.ccc.lxxx.u.; xuııı. anno cıclı lunaρıρ; ocꞇauo anno
ınɒıcꞇıonıρ; u. anno cıclı ρolaρıρ. Cρꞇ mac Cıρꞇ
ṁoıρ Uı Maıleaċlaınn quıeuıc ı ρρıḃ callaın Maı.
8luaʒaɒ la Mac Ɖonnchaıɒ ocuρ le hUa Ruaıρc cona
ρochρaıꞇı ʒalloʒlach maρaen ρıu a Maʒ Luıρʒ, cuρ
loıρceɒ leó Lonʒphuρꞇ Mıc Ɖıaρmaɒa ocuρ ın chρıch
uılı, ocuρ cuρ maρḃaɒ leo a ꞇóρaıʒheaċꞇ anꞇ ρluaıʒ
ρın Mac 8eoan .h. heʒxaı, ocuρ a ḃρaꞇhaıρ elı ɒo
ʒaḃaıl. Inɒρaıʒıɒ la cloınn mıc Ƒeıɒlımıɒ aρ Maʒ
Oρeaċꞇaıʒ, ocuρ ın baılı ɒo loρcaɒ leó, ocuρ ɒaıne ɒo
maρḃaɒ ann, ocuρ Maʒ Oρéachꞇaıʒ ρeın ɒo ʒaḃaıl
ɒoıḃ ıaρ ρın. Ɖaıɒıɒ mac Emaınn mıc hoıbeρɒ ɒo
ʒaḃaıl la hCceḃ .h. Conchoḃaıρ, aʒuρ a ecc a mḃalı
ın ꞇobaıρ ıρın laıṁɒıchaρ ρın. Inɒρaıʒıɒ la Ƒeıɒlımıɒ

---

1 *Eminent for bounty.* ρaı an
eneaċ, C. B has ρaıɒρ̄ an ēech,
which is corrupt.

2 *Richard.* ρıρɒeɒɒ, B; ρıρɒaρɒ,
C, which is the more usual form.

3 *Tomin.* Ꞇomı, B. Ɖoṁnaıll
(of Domhnall), C.

4 *The grandsons of Fedhlimidh.*
Toirdhelbhach Ruadh O'Conor, and
his brothers.

quievit. Mac Raghnaill Dubh, i.e. Diarmaid, son of Maelechlainn, the noble chieftain, eminent for bounty[1] and prowess, was slain per dolum by the sons of Raghnall Mac Raghnaill, in the doorway of Richard[2] Mac Raghnaill's house. Muirchertach O'Conchobhair, king of Ui-Failghe, died a senior. Tomaltach Mac [D]orchaidh, dux of Cenel-Luachain, was killed by his own knife while he was shoeing *a horse.* Cuchonnacht O'Ferghail, lord of Magh-Tregha, quievit. Donnchadh O'Dubhda quievit. Aedh O'Cellaigh and Feradach O'Cellaigh died of the plague in the same week. Ualgharg O'Ruairc, heir to the sovereignty of the Breifne, was drowned on Loch-Gamhna. Domhnall, son of Flaithbhertach O'Ruairc, quievit. Richard, the son of Maidiuc, son of Tomin[3] Barrett, renowned general patron of the learned of Erinn, died after the victory of penitence. Augustin O'Duibhgennain, chief historian of Conmaicne, quievit. John Burk died of the plague in hoc anno.

The kalends of January on Sunday, and the tenth of the moon; M.ccc.lxxxv.; xviii. anno cycli lunaris; octavo anno Indictionis; v. anno cycli solaris. Art, son of Art Mor O'Maelechlainn, quievit the day before the kalends of May. A hosting by Mac Donnchaidh and O'Ruairc, with their force of gallowglasses, into Magh-Luirg, when Mac Diarmada's fortress, and the entire district, were burned by them; and the son of John O'hEghra was slain whilst in pursuit of the army, and his other brother was taken prisoner. An attack was made by the grandsons of Fedhlimidh[4] on Mac Oirechtaigh, and the town[5] was burned by them, and people were slain there; and Mac Oirechtaigh was afterwards taken prisoner by them. David, son of Edmond, son of Hubert,[6] was taken prisoner by Aedh O'Conchobhair; and he died in Baile-in-tobair in this captivity. An incur-

---

⁵ *The town;* i.e. Mac Oirechtaigh's residence.

⁶ *Hubert.* Hubert Burk.

[MS. defective. Text supplied from "Annals of Connacht."]

cléipeač .h. Conchoḃaip ocuṗ la Conchoḃaṗ occ Mac Diaṗmaoa, α ṫip Oiliella, aḃuṗ ṗabṫi iomḃa oo ool ṗompα ocuṗ oṗcill oo ḃeiṫ aṗ α cinn, ocuṗ ḃṗeṗ oo oenaṁ ooiḃ, ocuṗ ceiṫhiṗnn ocuṗ maṗc ṗlúaḃ nα ṗoṗaiṗe oa ṗṗeaḃṗa, ocuṗ ṗiaṫ oc maṗḃaḃ bó ocuṗ oáine, ocuṗ Caṫhal Caiṗbṗech Mac Donochaiḃ oo maṗḃaḃ annṗin, ocuṗ Conchuḃaṗ Mac Diaṗmaoa oo ḃaḃail, ocuṗ Ṗeiolimiḃ .h. Conchuḃaiṗ oo loṫṫ anoṗin. Inoṗaiḃiḃ aili la Muiṗcheaṗṫach mac Caṫhail, ocuṗ le Coṗmac mac Ruaiḃṗi, ocuṗ la Taoc Mac nDiaṗmaoa, ocuṗ le Caṫhal Mac nDiaṗmaoa, ṗoṗ Maḃ Raḃnaill ṗuaḃ ocuṗ aṗ Aeḃ .h. Conchoḃaiṗ, ocuṗ α nḃaḃail oiḃlinaiḃ, ocuṗ α mbṗeiṫh aṗ chaṗṗaiḃ Lochα Céoa comeo. Caṫhal .h. Ṗeṗḃail, oaḃ aḃḃaṗ ṫaoiṗiḃ nα hAnḃaile, quieuiṫ. Cumuiḃi Ua Caṫhan, ṗi Oiṗeaċṫa .h. Caṫhan, quieuiṫ ṗo ṗino naiṗṁe. Moṗ inoṗaiḃiḃ le hUa Conchoḃaṗ ṗuaḃ ocuṗ le Macc nDiaṗmaoa, ocuṗ le cloinn Muiṗcheaṗṫaiḃ, ocuṗ le ṫaiṗechaiḃ Connachṫ, aṗ mac Emaino .h. Cellaiḃ, ocuṗ baile mic Emaino oo loṗcaḃ ooiḃ, ocuṗ moṗan oo ṁilleaḃ ooiḃ; aḃuṗ Uilliam buioi Ua Neachṫain oo maṗḃaḃ ooiḃ. Ḃṗeiṗniḃ ocuṗ Oileallaiḃ oo ṫeachṫ i conne .h. Conchoḃaiṗ ouinn, ocuṗ Coṗca Aċclann oo loṗcaḃ ooiḃ, ocuṗ α ḃuiṗṫ oo ḃeṗṗaḃ uile. Tiṗ Ṗiachṗach oo loṗcaḃ le mac Uilliam Ḃuṗc, ocuṗ α ool aṗṗiḃe co Sliccech, ocuṗ Caiṗbṗi ṗoṗ oo loṗcaḃ leo, ocuṗ Sliceč; ocuṗ Maioecc mael oo maṗḃaḃ ime ocuṗ bṗaiḃoi oo ḃaḃail imme. Tiṗ Aṁalḃaiḃ oo loṗcaoh le Domhnall mac Muiṗčeṗṫaiḃ, ocuṗ oaine oo maṗḃaḃ, ocuṗ bṗaiḃoi oo ṫaḃaiṗṫ laiṗ ocuṗ eoala moṗa.

---

1 *Cathal;* i.e. Cathal O'Conor.

2 *Ruaidhri.* Also a member of the O'Conor family.

3 *Of a chieftain.* ṫaoiṗiḃ, C. ṫaiṗech (which is the nom. form), B.

4 *Summit of renown.* ṗino náiṗṁe, C. ṗinoo naṗe, B.

5 *Men of Breifne.* Ḃṗeiṗniḃ, B. Ḃṗeiṗniḃ, C.

6 *Corca-Achlann.* Coṗc aṫhcḃ, B. See note 10, p. 596, vol. 1.

sion *was made* by Fedhlimidh Cleirech O'Conchobhair, and by Conchobhar Og Mac Diarmada, into Tir-Oililla; but many forewarnings had preceded them, and a force was in readiness to meet them; and they made an attack, and the kerns and cavalry of the watching party responded to them whilst they were killing cows and people; and Cathal Cairbrech Mac Donnchaidh was slain there; and Conchobhar Mac Diarmada was taken prisoner, and Fedhlimidh O'Conchobhair was wounded there. Another incursion *was made* by Muirchertach, son of Cathal,[1] Cormac, son of Ruaidhri,[2] Tadhg Mac Diarmada, and Cathal Mac Diarmada, against Mac Raghnaill Ruadh and Aedh O'Conchobhair, who were both captured and taken to the Rock of Loch-Cé to be imprisoned. Cathal O'Ferghail, the good material of a chieftain[3] of the Anghaile, quievit. Cumhuighe O'Cathain, king of Oirecht-Ui-Chathain, quievit at the summit of renown.[4] A great incursion *was made* by O'Conchobhair Ruadh, Mac Diarmada, the Clann-Muirchertaigh, and the chieftains of Connacht, against the son of Edmond O'Cellaigh, and the son of Edmond's town was burned by them, and much was destroyed by them; and William Buidhe O'Nechtain was slain by them. The men of Breifne[5] and [Tir-]Oilella went to meet O'Conchobhar Donn; and Corca-Achlann[6] was burned by them, and its cornfields were all cut down. Tir-Fiachrach was burned by Mac William Burk, who went from thence to Sligech; and Cairbre also[7] was burned by them, and Sligech; and Maideg Mael[8] was killed in his company, and prisoners were taken about him. Tir-Amhalgaidh was burned by Domhnall, the son of Muirchertach;[9] and men were slain, and captives were carried off by him,

---

[7] *Also.* ꝼoꞃ, C. aꞃoꞃ, B ·

[8] *Maideg Mael;* i.e. Maideg the Bald. The Four Masters say that he

was "one of the chieftains" of Mac William's people.

[9] *Muirchertach;* i.e. Muirchertach (or Murtough) O'Conor Sligo.

[MS. defective.
Text supplied
from " Annals
of Connacht."]

maɪᴐm moɲ La mupchaᴆ .h. Conchoᵬaɪp, ɲɪ .h. ꝼaɪlᵹɪ,
ocuɲ La Cenel ꝼɪachaɪᴆ mɪc lleɪll, ꝼoɲ ᵹalloɪᵬ na
mɪᴆe hɪ ᴛochaɲ Cɲuachan ᵬɲɪ eli, ɪnaɲ maɲᵬaᴆ ɪn
8eompach ocuɲ a ɯac, ocuɲ ɪnᴛ Uɪnᴐɲɪonnach na
mɪᴆe, eᴛ alɪɪ mulᴛɪ nobɪleɲ eᴛ ɪᵹnobɪleɲ. Ɀanaɪᴐe
Ua maelchonaɪɲe, ollaɯ ɲɪla muɪɲeᴆaɪᵹ muɪlle-
chaɪn ɲe ɲenᴄuɲ ocuɲ ɲe ꝼɪlɪᴆeachᴛ, ocuɲ ɪnᴛɪ ᴐo ᵬo
ᴛɲeɪɲ aɲ a ollaɯnachᴛ ꝼéɪn ᴐo ᵬɪ an eɲɪnᴐ ana aɪmɲɪɲ
ꝼeɪn, ᴐo ecc ɪna ᴛɪᵹ ꝼeɪn ɪaɲ mbuaɪᴐh onᵹᴛha ocuɲ
aɪᴛhɲɪᵹe ꝼo Luᵹhnaɲa, ocuɲ a aᴆlacaᴆ a Cluaɪn
Caɲɲᴄɪ. eoɪn mac eoᵹaɪn mɪc ᵹɪlla ꝵeᴐaɪɲ ᴐo maɲᵬaᴆ La Caᴛhal .h. Conchobaɪɲ aɲ ᵹɲeɪɲ ɪ mbaɪle
.h. ᴐoɯnallaɪn. 8ɪᴛh ᴐo ᴐenaɯ ᴐo Chonnachᴛaɪᵬ
ɪaɲaɯ, ocuɲ 8ɪl muɪɲeᴆaɪᵹ ᴐo ɲoɪnᴐ aɲ ᴐó eɪᴐɪɲ ɪn
ᴐá .h. Conchoᵬaɪɲ ɲɪn, ocuɲ Ꮯcᴆ .h. Conchoᵬaɪɲ ocuɲ
Conchoᵬaɪɲ mac ᴐɪaɲmaᴐa ᴐo Lecen amach. ᴐeɲ-
boɲᵹall, ɪnᵹean Chaᴛhaɪl óɪcc, ben .h. Chonchoᵬaɪɲ
ɲuaɪᴆ, quɪeuɪᴛ ᴐo Lamnaᴐ. ᵬenmɪᴐɪ ɪnᵹean meᵹ
maᴛhᵹaɯna, bean .h. lleɪll, quɪeuɪᴛ.

ʞᴛ. enaɪɲ ꝼoɲ Luan, ocuɲ aen ꝼɪchɪᴛ ꝼuɪɲɲɪ;
m°. ccc°. Lxxuɪ. ; xɪx. anno cɪclɪ Lunaɲɪɲ ; ɪx. anno
ɪnᴐɪᴛɪonɪɲ; ɪɪɪ. anno cɪclɪ ꝼolaɲɪɲ. Ꮯɪne, ɪnᵹean
Ɀaɪᴆᵹ mɪc ᴐonnchaɪᴆ, uxoɲ Ɀɪᵹeaɲnaɪn .h. Ruaɪɲc,
ɲɪ bɲeɪꝼne, aen ɲoᵹa ban leɪᴛhe Cuɪnᴐ, ᴐo écc a Ɀúaɪm
8enchaɪᴐ oc Loch ꝼɪnᴐmaɪᵹɪ, ocuɲ a haᴆlacaᴆ a 8lɪ-
cech ɪaɲ ɲɪn. Caɲbɲɪ mac bɲɪaɪn mɪc muɲchaɪᴆ
.h. ꝼeɲᵹaɪl, ᴛɪᵹheaɲna chalaɪᴆ na hᏌenᵹaɪle, moɲᴛuuɲ
eɲᴛ. lliall mac Conchocɲuche oɪcc mec eochacaɪn
ᴐo maɲᵬaᴆ La ᴐalaᴛunchaɪᵬ ɪn .xuɪɪ. ʞᴛ. maɪ ; ocuɲ

---

1 *Muiredhach Muillethan.* "Muiredhach (or Murrough) of the flat head."
The epithet "Muillethan" is omitted
in C. See note 2, p. 550, vol. 1.

2 *Into t wo parts.* A marginal note
in B. reads ᴛaᵬaɪɲ ꝼɪn ꝼoᴐeaɲ [a],
i.e. "observe this."

3 *Those two O'Conchobhairs;* i.e.

the two Toirdhelbhachs, or Turloughs,
referred to under A.D. 1384.

4 *Kalends.* The Dom. Letter (G)
is added in the margin in B. and C.

5 *Indictionis.* The year of the Indiction is omitted in C., which gives
the year of the Solar cycle as ix., instead of vi.

and great spoils. A great victory by Murchadh O'Conchobhair, king of Ui-Failghe, and by the Cenel-Fiachaidh-
mic-Neill, over the Foreigners of Midhe, at Tochar-
Cruachan-Bri-Ele, in which were slain the Chambers and
his son, and the Nugent of Midhe, et alii multi nobiles et
ignobiles. Tanaidhe O'Maelchonaire, chief professor of
the race of Muiredhach Muillethan[1] in history and
poetry, and the person who was most powerful in his
own art in Erinn in his own time, died in his own
house, after the victory of unction and penitence, about
Lammas, and was interred in Cluain-Coirpthe. John,
son of Eoghan Mac Gilla-Petair, was slain by Cathal
O'Conchobhair, in an assault, in Baile-Ui-Domhnallain.
Peace was afterwards made by the Connachtmen, and
Sil-Muiredhaigh was divided into two parts[2] between
those two O'Conchobhairs[3] ; and Aedh O'Conchobhair
and Conchobhar Mac Diarmada were set at liberty.
Derbhorgaill, daughter of Cathal Og, wife of O'Conchobhair Ruadh, quievit in childbirth. Benmidhe, daughter
of Mac Mathghamhna, wife of O'Neill, quievit.

The kalends[4] of January on Monday, and the twenty-
first of the moon; $M^{o}.ccc^{o}.lxxxvi.$; xix. anno cycli lunaris ;
ix. anno Indictionis ;[5] vi. anno cycli solaris. Aine, daughter of Tadhg Mac Donnchaidh, uxor of Tighernan
O'Ruairc, king of Breifne, the choicest of the women of
Leth-Chuinn, died in Tuaim-Senchaidh at Loch-Finnmhaighe, and was afterwards buried[6] in Sligech. Cairbre,
son of Brian, son of Murchadh O'Ferghail, lord of Caladh-
na-hAnghaile,[7] mortuus est. Niall, son of Cucocriche Og[8]
Mac Eochagain, was killed by the Daltons on the seven-
teenth of the kalends of May ; and this man was well

---

[6] *Buried.* α haòlacaò, B. α
haònacal, C.

   Caladh-na-hAnghaile ; i.e. the
Callow (or Strath) of the Anghaile, in
the county Longford. See O'Donovan's note F. M., A.D. 1411, note *.

[8] *Son of Cucocriche.* mac Concho-
cpiche, B. C incorrectly reads mac
Conèuòaip, "son of Conchobhar."
The name Cucocriche (lit. border-
hound, from *cu*, a hound, and *co-crich*,
border), is Anglicised "Peregrine."

[MS. defectiv. Text supplied from "Annals of Connacht."]

ꝺo bo ꝺeʒ aꝺꝗap ꞇaıpıʒ pop a ꝺuꞇhaıʒ peıꞃ ın ꞃep
ꞃıꞃ. Maʒꞃup mac Ceꝺa Mıc Ꝺıapmaꝺa ꝺo mapꝗaꝺ
laꞃ ın muıꞃꞇıp ceaꝺꞃa ꞃıꞃ. Ua Conchoꝗaıp puaꝺ ꝺo
ꝺoɫ ꝺo ꞇunʒꞃaṁ la mac Uıɫɫıam ꝗupc, ocuꞃ a puaıp
ꝺo Chonꞃacuꞇaıꝗ leıꞃ, aꞃaꝺaıʒ Ꝺoṁꞃaıɫɫ mıc Muıp-
cheapꞇaıʒ ocuꞃ cɫoıꞃne Ꝺoꞃꝺchaıꝗ, ocuꞃ cpecha mopa
ꝺo ꞇhaꝗaıpꞇ a ꞇıp ꝉ̇achpaꞇ Muaıꝱe, ocuꞃ ꝺoɫ ꝺoıꝗ
ıaꞃ ꞃıꞃ a cpıch cɫoıꞃne Rıcaıpꝺ pop cpeachpꞃaꞇhap,
ocuꞃ ꞃɫuaʒ ꝺıapmıꝱe ꝺo bpeıꞇh poꞃpa ꞃa .h. ꞃıꝷpꞃaıꞃ
ocuꞃ ım mac Uıɫɫıam cɫoıꞃne Rıcaıpꝺ. Ua Conchoꝗaıp
puaꝺ ꝺo ımpoꝺ ppıꝷ, ocuꞃ maıꝱm ꝺo ꞇhaꝗaıpꞇ poppo,
ocuꞃ Conchoꝗaꞃ mac Ꞇaıꝱc mıc Conchoꝗaıp .h. ꝷhpꞃaıꞃ
ꝺo mapꝗaꝺ anꞃ, eꞇ aɫıꞃ muɫꞇı.

Ꞁꞇ. Θꞃaıp pop Maıpꞇ, aıɫı uaꞇhaꝺ ꞃuıppı ; M.ccc.
ɫxxx.ꞇꞇꞇ. ; ꞃpımuꞃ aꞃꞃuꞃ cıcɫı Luꞃapıp ; x. ıꞃꝺıcꞇıoꞃıꞃ ;
ꞇꞇꞇ. aꞃꞃuꞃ cıcɫı pоɫapıꞃ. Saꝺꝗ, ıꞃʒen Ceꝺa Uı Neıɫɫ,
ben mıc Θoıꞃ ꝷıpeꝺ, ocuꞃ ben ꝺob peꞃp ap ꞃɫıochꞇ
Neıɫɫ naı ʒıaɫɫaıʒ, ın Cpıꞃꞇo quıeuıꞇ. Mac Uıɫɫıam
cɫoıꞃne Rıcaıpꝺ .ı. Rıcapꝺ occ, quıeuıꞇ. Ruaıꝱpı .h.
Cıanan, oɫɫaṁ Opʒıaɫɫ ꞃe ꞃenchaꞃ, mopꞇuuꞃ epꞇ.
Conchuꝗap mac ꝷpꞃaıꞃ chappaıʒ .h. Neıɫɫ ꝺo ṁapꝗaꝺ
la muıꞃꞇıp ınꞇ Spáꞇbaıɫe. Uıɫɫıam mac Ꝺıapmaꝺa
Meʒ Ruʒꞃaıɫɫ, aꝺꝗap ꞇaoıꞃıʒ Muıꞃꞇıpe hΘoɫaıp, ꝺo
mapꝗaꝺ la muıꞃꞇıp ꝷıpꞃꞃ.

Ꞁꞇ. Θꞃaıp pop Ceaꝺaıꞃ, ocuꞃ ꞇpeaꞃ ꝺeʒ ꞃuıppı ;
M°.ccc°.ɫxxx.ꞇꞇꞇꞇ. Copmac Mac Ꝺoꞃꝺchaıꝗ, pıʒꝺaṁna
Ꞇıpe hOıɫeɫɫa, ꝺo ꝺoɫ pop cpeıch oıꝺchı ı Maʒh
Luıpʒ, ocuꞃ cpeacha mopa ꝺo ʒaꝗaıɫ ꝺo, ocuꞃ a cop
a noíꞇın ꝺó ; ocuꞃ .h. Conchoꝗaıp púaꝺ ocuꞃ cɫaꞃꞃ
mıc ꝉeıꝱɫımıꝱ, ocuꞃ cɫann Caꞇhaıɫ oıcc .h. Conchoꝗaıp,
ocuꞃ cɫann Ceꝺa Mıcc Ꝺıapmaꝺa .ı. Caꞇhaɫ occuꞃ
Copmac, ocuꞃ mopan ꝺo ɫuchꞇ an ꞇıpe o ꞃın amach

---

¹ Against. aꞃaꝺaıʒ, C. aꞃꝺaʒ, B.

² Kalends. The Dom. Letter (F) is added in the margin in C.

³ Srat-baile. More usually called "Srat-baile Duna-Delgan," i.e. the "street-town of Dun-Delgan (or Dundalk).

fitted to be chieftain over his own country. Maghnus, son of Aedh Mac Diarmada, was slain by the same
people. O'Conchobhair Ruadh, together with all the
Connachtmen he got *to join him*, went to assist Mac
William Burk against[1] Domhnall, the son of Muirchertach,
and the Clann-Donnchaidh ; and they carried off great
preys from Tir-Fiachrach-Muaidhe. And they went afterwards into the territory of Clann-Rickard on a predatory
incursion, when they were overtaken by an innumerable
army, including O'Briain and Mac William of Clann-
Rickard. O'Conchobhair Ruadh turned upon them, and
routed them ; and Conchobhar, son of Tadhg, son of
Conchobhar O'Briain, was slain there, et alii multi.

The kalends[2] of January on Tuesday, the second of the
moon ; M.ccc.lxxxvii. ; primus annus cycli lunaris ; x. Indictionis ; vii. annus cycli solaris. Sadhbh, daughter of
Aedh O'Neill, wife of the son of John Bisset, and the best
woman of the descendants of Niall of the Nine Hostages,
in Christo quievit. Mac William of Clann-Rickard, i.e.
Richard Og, quievit. Ruaidhri O'Cianain, chief historian
of Oirghiall, mortuus est. Conchobhar, son of Brian Carrach O'Neill, was killed by the people of the Srat-baile.[3]
William, the son of Diarmaid Mac Raghnaill, heir to
the chieftaincy of Muinter-Eolais, was killed by
Muinter-Birn.

The kalends[4] of January on Wednesday, and the thirteenth of the moon ; M°. ccc°. lxxxviii. Cormac Mac
Donnchaidh, lord of Tir-Oilella, went on a nocturnal
foray into Magh-Luirg, and captured great preys, which
he put into a place of security ; and O'Conchobhair
Ruadh, and the grandsons of Fedhlimidh, and the sons
of Cathal Og O'Conchobhair, and the sons of Aedh Mac
Diarmada, (viz., Cathal and Cormac), and several of the
people of the district besides, followed him in pursuit of

---

[4] *Kalends.* The Dom. Letters (E D) are added in the margin.

[MS. defective.
Text supplied
from "Annals
of Connacht."]

ꝺα lenṁαιn hι τόραιξecht nα cреαch, ocuр Cормαc
ꝺо ξαϐαιl ꝺeрιϐ α ṁuιnτιрu рeιn, ocuр nαр ξαϐ αnαcαl
uατhαιb cор bo hecen α ṁαрϐαϐ рα ϐeoιϐ; αξuр Con-
chobαр mαc ꝺоnꝛchαιϐ, ocuр muрchαϐ mαc Cормαιc
.mιc ꝺоnnčαιϐ, ocuр mαc ꝺιαрmαꝺα рuαϐ ꝺо ξαϐαιl
αnꝺ; ocuр ꝛιр mо écht mιc рιξ ꝺα nꝺeрnαϐ αn Eрιnn
uιle ιnα рιn. Cξuр .h. Conchoϐαιр рuαϐ ꝺα lenṁαιn
ꝺαр рlιαϐ рíр, ocuр Clαnn ꝺоnꝺchαιϐ ꝺо τeιcheαϐ рα
Cúl mαιl ocuр ро ιchταр Tιрe hOιlιоllα. muιр-
cheαрταch mαc ꝺоṁnαιll .h. Conchuϐαιр ꝺо ꝺоl рα
рорlоnξϐuрτ .h. ꝺоṁnαιll α mαnιрτeιр Eрα Ruαιϐ,
ocuр ꝺαιnе ιmꝺαι ꝺо mαрϐαϐ αnꝺ рα chloιnn .h. bαιξιll,
αξuр рα Uα nξαllčuϐαιр conα bрαιϐрιϐ. Eιch ocuр
ꝺαιnе ꝺо τhαϐαιрτ ꝺо leιр, ocuр mαc 8uϐnе ocuр α
ṁαc ꝺо ξαϐαιl αnꝺ. Seααn рuαϐ .h. Tuατhαιl, рι
.h. muιрeϐαιξ, рeξι enιξ ocuр enξnαṁα Eрenn ιnα
αιmрιр рeιn, ꝺо mαрϐαϐ ꝺо ϐоꝺαch ιnα čιξ рeιn, ocuр
αn bоꝺαch рeιn ꝺо ṁαрϐαϐ ꝺорαṁ ιαрαṁ. 8ιξрαιϐ
Uα Cuрnín ocuр Cαιррре .h. Cuιрnín ꝺо ṁαрϐαϐ ꝺо
ξαllαιϐ lαιξeαn. Cреαchα mора ꝺо ꝺenαṁ ꝺO Chon-
chuϐαр рuαϐ αр .h. Conchoϐαιр nꝺоnn, ocuр coccαϐ
mόр cотchenꝺ ꝺо eрξι hι Connαchταιϐ uιlι τрιτ рιn.
Cucoιccрιche Uα mαιlmuαιϐ, рιξ рeр Cell, quιeuιτ
ιn рeрτιmо]{αlenꝺαр mαрτι. Tιnnрcnα cocαιϐ eιꝺιр
.h. Ruαιрc ocuр Clαnn ꝺоnꝺchαιꝺh ιn hoc αnno.

]{t. Enαιр рор Cιnе, ocuр cethрαmαꝺ .xx. рuιррι;

---

1 *From them;* i.c. from the pursuers.
This event is more fully related by
the Four Masters, who state that the
pursuers had orders not to kill Mac
Donnchaidh (Mac Donough) if he
submitted to be taken prisoner; but
he refused, and was consequently
slain.

² *Conchobhar.* Conchoū, B. Con-
chuр, C:

³ *Murchadh son of Cormac Mac
Donnchaidh.* Omitted in B.

⁴ *Feat of a king's son.* écht mιc
рιξ. The translation is literal, but
does not convey the express idea intended to be conveyed by the chronicler, who meant to say that the fate
of Cormac Mac Donnchaidh was as
grievous a calamity as had happened
to any king's son in Erinn.

⁵ *The mountain.* рlιαϐ; i.e. Sliabh-
Seghsa, or the Curlieu Mountains,
between the counties of Roscommon
and Sligo.

the preys; and Cormac placed himself in the rere of his own people, and would not accept quarter from them,[1] so that it was necessary ultimately to kill him; and Conchobhar[2] Mac Donnchaidh, and Murchadh son of Cormac Mac Donnchaidh,[3] and Mac Diarmada Ruadh, were taken prisoners there. And there was no greater "feat of a king's son"[4] committed in all Erin than this. And O'Conchobhair Ruadh followed them down beyond the mountain,[5] and the Clann-Donnchadh fled towards Cul-Maile and the lower part of Tir-Oilella. Muirchertach, son of Domhnall O'Conchobhair, attacked O'Domhnaill's[6] camp in the monastery[7] of Es-Ruaidh, and killed many persons there, including the sons of O'Baighill, and O'Gallchubhair[8] with his brothers. Horses and men were carried off by him; and Mac Suibhne and his son were taken prisoners there. John Ruadh O'Tuathail, king of Ui-Muiredhaigh, pillar of the bounty and prowess of Erinn in his own time, was killed by a clown in his own house; and the clown himself was afterwards killed by him.[9] Sigraidh O'Cuirnin, and Cairbre O'Cuirnin, were slain by the Foreigners of Laighen. Great depredations were committed by O'Conchobhair Ruadh upon O'Conchobhair Donn; and a great general war broke out in all Connacht through this. Cucocriche O'Maelmhuaidh, king of Feara-Cell, quievit in[10] septimo kalendas[11] Martii. Commencement of a war between O'Ruaire and the Clann-Donnchaidh in hoc anno.

The kalends of January on Friday, and the twenty-

---

[6] *O'Domhnaill's.* 11. Oomhnaill, C. Tom., B.

[7] *In the monastery.* The Four Masters say that O'Domhnaill's camp was " near the monastery," which is more correct.

[8] *O'Gallchubhair.* O'Gallagher. Ua nṠallcuṗ, C. nṠall., B.

[9] *By him.* The chronicler has here

committed a very characteristic blunder, in making O'Tuathail kill the person who *had slain* himself. The fact is, probably, that although the wound received by O'Tuathail in the encounter was mortal, he lived long enough to kill his assailant.

[10] *In.* an, B and C.

[11] *Kalendas.* Calainnar, B.

[MS. defective.
Text supplied
from "Annals
of Connacht."]

ᴍ.ccc.ʟxxx.ıx. ; ııı. anno cıclı lunaꝛıꝛ ; [xıı.] anno
ınꝺıcᴛıonıꝛ ; ıx. anno cıclı ꝛolaꝛıꝛ. Ua Ruaıꝛc ꝺo
ᴛhaᵬaıꝛᴛ cloınne Caᴛhaıl óıcc čuıcı ıaꝛ ꝛın, ocuꝛ ın
cocaᵬ ꝺo eꝛᵹı co haꝛꝛachᴛa ıaꝛ ꝛın. Eoᵹan .h. Ruaıꝛc
ocuꝛ clann Chaᴛhaıl óıcc ꝺo ꝺol co Caıꝛlen ın nuaᵬaıꝛ,
ocuꝛ maꝛcꝼluaᵹ Muınᴛıꝛe hEılıᵬe ꝺeꝛᵹe ꝺoıᵬ, ocuꝛ
ꝛuaıᵹ ꝺo ᴛhaᵬaıꝛᴛ ꝼoꝛꝛo, ocuꝛ mac O nEılıᵬı ꝺo
maꝛᵬaᵬ ꝺoıᵬ ım Maᵹnuꝛ O nEılıᵬe. Cꝛecha Muınᴛıꝛe hEılıᵬı ꝺo ꝺenaṁ ꝺU Ruaıꝛc ocuꝛ ꝺo chloınn
Chaᴛhaıl óıcc. Muıꝛcheaꝛᴛach O hEılıᵬı ꝺo maꝛᵬaᵬ
aꝛ ın cocaᵬ ꝛın. Maᵹnuꝛ Ua Ruaıꝛc ꝺo ᵹaᵬaıl ꝼeꝛ
ꝺolum ꝺo Choꝛmac O Ꝼheꝛᵹaıl. Sıᴛh ꝺo ꝺenam ꝺU
Ruaıꝛc aᵹuꝛ ꝺo Ꝺoṁnall mac Muıꝛčeaꝛᴛaıᵹ, ocuꝛ ꝺo
Chloınn Ꝺonnchaıꝺ ꝺıᵬlınaıᵬ. Sıᴛh elı ꝺo ꝺenaṁ ꝺo
Chloınn Ꝺonnchaıꝺh occuꝛ ꝺo Mac Ꝺıaꝛmaꝺa. Con-
choᵬaꝛ Mac Ꝺonꝺchaıᵬ ocuꝛ Muꝛchaꝺ mac Coꝛmac
ꝺo leıᵹean amach ıaꝛ ꝛın. Maıleačlaınn cam O Loch-
laınꝺ, ꝛı Choꝛcumꝺꝛúaꝺh, ꝺo maꝛᵬaᵬ ꝺa ᵬꝛaıᴛꝛıᵬ
ꝼeın a ꝛıll. Caᴛhal Mac Ꝺıaꝛmaꝺa ꝺo ᵹaᵬaıl ꝺo
Mhac Ꝺonꝺchaıᵬ, ocuꝛ coꝛ Chaᴛhaıl ꝺo ᵬꝛıꝛeᵬ, ocuꝛ
a leıccın amach a coṁꝼuaꝛlacaᵬ ıꝛınᴛ ꝛıᵬ ꝛın. Muıꝛıꝛ
maol Ua Conchoᵬaıꝛ Ꝼhaılᵹı ꝺo maꝛᵬaᵬ ꝺuꝛchuꝛ
ᴛꝛoıᵹꝺe le ꝼeꝛ ꝺıᵬ Cellaıᵹ Leıᵹe. Mac Neıll .h. Ruaıꝛc
quıeuıᴛ. Cꝛeacha Muınᴛıꝛe Ꝺuıꝛnın ꝺo ꝺenaṁ
ꝺo Mac Enꝛı ı Neıll aꝛ monᴛeach Moıᵹı henı ın hoc
anno. Cꝛeacha Tıꝛe Conaıll ꝺo ꝺenaṁ ꝺo Ꝺoṁnall mac
Muıꝛčeaꝛᴛaıᵹh. Raᵹnall maᵹ Ruaıꝛc, ꝼlaıᴛh ᴛellaıᵹ
Conmuꝛa, quıeuıᴛ ın Cꝛıꝛᴛo. Ꝅꝛıan mac Ꝺoṁnaıll
oıcc .h. Ruaıꝛc ꝺo ṁaꝛᵬaᵬ ꝺo cloınn Mhuıꝛčeaꝛᴛuıᵹ.
Nıall occ O Neıll ꝺo ᵹaᵬaıl la Ᵹallaıᵬ ın hoc anno.

---

1 *Lunaris.* The criteria for this
year are very inaccurately given in
C.

2 *Subsequently;* i.e. after the break-
ing out of the war referred to in the
last entry under the previous year.

3 *Son of Cormac;* i.e. son of Cormac
Mac Donnchaidh.

4 *Liberated.* The persons here stated
to have been liberated had been taken
prisoners in the preceding year.

5 *Son of Muirchertach;* i.e. of Muir-

fourth of the moon ; M.ccc.lxxxix.; iii. anno cycli lunaris;[1] [xii.] anno Indictionis; ix. anno cycli solaris. O'Ruairc subsequently[2] brought the sons of Cathal Og to him, and the war grew fierce after that. Eoghan O'Ruairc and the sons of Cathal Og went to Caislen-in-nuabhair, when the cavalry of Muinter-hElidhe opposed them, and made an attack on them ; and the son of O'hElidhe was killed by them, together with Maghnus O'hElidhe. Muinter-hElidhe were plundered by O'Ruairc, and by the sons of Cathal Og. Muirchertach O'hElidhe was slain in this war. Maghnus O'Ruairc was taken prisoner, per dolum, by Cormac O'Ferghail. Peace was concluded by O'Ruairc, and by Domhnall son of Muirchertach, and by the Clann-Donnchaidh, respectively. Another peace was concluded by the Clann-Donnchaidh and Mac Diarmada. Conchobhar Mac Donnchaidh, and Murchadh son of Cormac,[3] were afterwards liberated.[4] Maelechlainn Cam O'Lochlainn, king of Corcumruaidh, was killed by his own brothers in treachery. Cathal Mac Diarmada was taken prisoner by Mac Donnchaidh ; and Cathal's leg was broken ; and he was liberated in exchange for another, in *pursuance of* that peace. Maurice Mael O'Conchobhair Failghe was killed by a shot of an arrow, by a man of the Ui-Cellaigh of Legh. The son of Niall O'Ruairc quievit. Muinter-Duirnin were plundered by the son of Henry O'Neill, on Montech-Maighe-Heni, in hoc anno. Tir-Conaill was plundered by Domhnall, the son of Muirchertach.[5] Raghnall Mac Ruairc, chief of Tellach-Conmusa,[6] quievit in Christo. Brian, son of Domhnall Og O'Ruairc, was slain by the Clann-Muirchertaigh.[7] Niall Og O'Neill was taken prisoner by the Foreigners in hoc anno.

---

chertach (or Murtough) O'Conor, of the family of O'Conor Sligo.

[6] *Of Tellach-Conmusa.* Ꞇeʟʟach Conmuᵽa, B and C. But Ꞇeʟʟach is the nom. form ; gen. Ꞇeʟʟaich.

[7] *Clann-Muirchertaigh.* Apparently theClann-Muirchertaigh-Muimhnigh, or descendants of Muirchertach Muimhnech (i.e. Murtough the Momonian) O'Conor.

[MS. defective. Text supplied from "Annals of Connacht."]

Kt. Enαιp pop Sαchαpnn, ocup peιpιδ.uαchαδ puιppι; m.ccc.xc.; ιιιι. αnno cιclι lunαpιp; xιιι. αnno ιnδιc-
τιonιp; x. αnno cιclι polαpιp. Coccαδ móp eιδιp Uα
Ruαιpc ocup Uα Rαιξιllιδ, ocup Ccnξαιlιξ ocup Eolup-
αιξ, ocup Tellαch Ounchαδα, ocup clαnn mhuιpcheαpταιξ δο τeαchτ po τoξαιpm αn τoξαιδ pιn τpe
peolαδ Oomnαιll mιc mhuιpcheαpταιξ occup To-
molταιξ mιc Ounδchαιδ. mαξnup .h. Ruαιpc δο δι
αξ .h. Rαιξιllιδ α cloιch Lochα huαchταιp, éloδ δο
epτι, ocup δοl co cαιplen Lochα ιn pcuιp, ocup clαnn
muιpδeαpταιξ δpαξδαιl bpαιch αιp, ocup α mαpδαδ
δοιδ αξ τeαchτ αp α δοιτι. Upιαn mαc Uιllιαm
mιc Upαnαn occιpup epτ .u. οιδchι pια pαmpuιn. Sιδ
δο δenαm δO Ruαιpc ocup δUα Rαιξιllιξ, ocup comτhα
mopα δpαξbαιl δO Rαιξιllιξ o .h. Ruαιpc δο chιnn
α námιαδ αccup α epcαpαδ δο τpeccαδ δO Rαιξιllιξ,
ocup διnnαpbαδ uαδα; ocup Eoξαn Uα Ruαιpc ocup
mαc Cαthαιl pιαδαιξ δο τhαδαιpτ α nξell pιu pιn. Clαnn
muιpcheαpταιξ ocup τellαch Ounchαδα δο δenαm
ιmιpcι noιpτ αp· muιnτιp Ruαιpc pα Pιδ nα pιnnoιξe,
ocup pα Slιαδ Choppαn, ocup pα chenel Luαchαιn;
ocup α pιp pιn δpαξδαιl δO Ruαιpc ocup pe α nξlιnn
ξαδlι, ocup α ιmιpcechα δο δpeιch lep po bαpp chenel
Luαchαιn, ocup ιnnpαιξhιδ epoδα δupcupαch δο δenαm
δO Ruαιpce αp nα pιξ cuδpιnnαιδ pιn, ocup mαιδm δο
τhαδαιpτ poppιo, ocup mαpδαδ δο δeδ αp αn ellαιξιδ
o δeol αthα δαιpι Oubthαιξ co múllαδ nα τulαιξιb
mUpeιppnech. Tomαp mαc mαthξαmnα .h. Rαιξιllιξ
quιeuιτ ιpιn poξmαp δα epι. Pepξαl .h. hEξpα, pι
Luξne, mopτuup epτ. Seαn Uα Rαιξιllιδ δο pιξαδ.

---

1 *Kalends.* The Dom. Letter (B) is added in the margin.
2 *To join in that war.* Instead of po τo-ξαιpm αn τoξαιδ pιn (lit. at the call of that war), as in C, B has α Con-nαchταιb "into (or from) Connacht."
3 *From it.* epτι, B. οιpτιξ, C.
4 *Fidh - na - finnoige* "the crow's wood," C. B has pιδ.h.Pιnnoιce "the wood of O'Finnoc," which seems incorrect, although the Four Masters also write the name thus.

The kalends[1] of January on Saturday, and the sixth of the moon; M.ccc.xc.; iiii. anno cycli lunaris; xiii. anno Indictionis; x. anno cycli solaris. A great war between O'Ruairc and O'Raighilligh; and the people of Anghaile, and Muinter-Eolais, the Tellach-Dunchadha, and the Clann-Muirchertaigh come to join in that war,[2] under the direction of Domhnall, the son of Muirchertach, and of Tomaltach Mac Donnchaidh. Maghnus O'Ruairc, who had been *imprisoned* by O'Raighilligh in Cloch-Locha-uachtair, escaped from it[3] and went to the castle of Loch-in-scuir; but the Clann-Muirchertaigh obtained secret intelligence of this, and he was slain by them when coming out of his cot. Brian, son of William Mac Branan, occisus est five nights before Allhallowtide. Peace was concluded by O'Ruairc and O'Raighilligh, and O'Raighilligh obtained liberal rewards from O'Ruairc in consideration of O'Raighilligh forsaking and banishing his (*O'Ruairc's*) enemies and adversaries; and Eoghan O'Ruairc, and the son of Cathal Riabhach, were given as pledges for *the payment of* these rewards. The Clann-Muirchertaigh and Tellach-Dunchadha emigrated in despite of Muinter-Ruairc, towards Fidh-na-finnoige,[4] Sliabh-Corran, and Cenel-Luachain; and O'Ruairc obtained intelligence of this whilst he was in Glenn-Gaibhlc; and he brought his bands to the upper part of Cenel-Luachain; and a brave, destructive assault was made by O'Ruairc on these royal divisions, who were routed; and the killing of their flocks continued from Bel-atha-doire-Dubhthaigh[5] to the summit of the Breif-nian hills.[6] Thomas, son of Mathghamhain O'Raighilligh, quievit in the succeeding harvest. Ferghal O'hEghra, king[7] of Luighne, mortuus est. John O'Raighilligh was

---

[3] *Bel-atha-doire-Dubhthaigh;* lit. "the mouth of the ford of Dubhthach's oak wood." The name is now obsolete.

[6] *Hills.* ꞇulaiᵹib, for ꞇulaċ, the proper gen. pl., C. ꞇul., B.

[7] *King.* ꞃi, C. ꞃiᵹ, B.

[MS. defective. Text supplied from "Annals of Connacht."]

Caiꞃlen Chille ḃaꞃꞃꞃinne ꝺo ḃꞃiꞅeḃ le ꝺoṁnall mac MuiꞃċeaꞃꞄaiᵹ. ḃꞃian mac Ccꝺacan, ollaṁ ḃꞃeiꞄeman na ḃꞃeiꞃne, moꞃꞄuuꞅ eꞃꞄ. Seαn oiꞃiꞃꞄel mac Ccꝺacan, ꞃeꞃ a inaiꞄꞄ ꞃein ꝺoḃ ꞃeꞃꞃ ina aimꞅiꞃ, ꝺo maꞃ ḃaꝺ ceiꞄhꞃe hoiꝺċi ꞃia noꝺluicc; ocuꞃ ni ꞃeiꝺiꞃ cia ꞃoꞃ maꞃ ḃ. ꝺiaꞃmaiꝺ maᵹ Caꞃmaicc occiꞃuꞃ eꞃꞄ. ꝺuiḃᵹinn Ua ꝺuiḃᵹinnaii, ollaṁ Conmaicne ꞃe ꞃenchuꞃ, quieuiꞄ.

Kt. Enaiꞃ ꞃoꞃ ꝺoṁnach, ocuꞃ .ui.x. ꞃuiꞃꞃi; M.°ccc.°xc. ꞃꞃimo; u. anno cicli lunaꞃiꞅ; xiiii. inꝺicꞄioniꞃ; xi. cicli ꞃolaꞃiꞃ. ꝺiaꞃmaiꝺ mac ꝺonꝺchaiꝺ mic MuiꞃcheaꞃꞄaiᵹh moiꞃ Mec Eochacan, ꝺux Cenel Fiachaiꝺ mic Neill, quieuiꞄ a ꞃꞃiꝺ io Enaiꞃ. Siꝺ ꝺo ꝺenaṁ ꝺlla Ruaiꞃc ocuꞃ ꝺO Raiᵹilliꝺ, ocuꞃ Ua Ruaiꞃc ꝺo ꝺol co ꝺꞃuim leꞄan i coinne Ui Raiᵹilliꝺ becan ꝺa luꞄꞄ Ꞅiᵹi buꝺein, ocuꞃ coiᵹeꞃ aꞃ Ꞅꞃi ꞃichiꞄ ꝺo ċloinn MuiꞃcheaꞃꞄaiᵹ ꝺo ꝺol ꞃemhe aꞃ belach, ocuꞃ Ua Ruaiꞃc ꝺinꝺꞃaiᵹiꝺ an ḃelaᵹ, ocuꞃ Seαn móꞃ mac mic na banꞃꞃoiᵹiꝺe ꝺo ꝺol i coinne .h. Ruaiꞃc le buille ꞃleᵹi, ocuꞃ .h. Ruaiꞃc ꝺo ꝺol ꝺa ꞃꞃeaꞃꝺal ocuꞃ ꝺa ꞃꞃichalaꝺ, ocuꞃ a ṁaꞃ ḃaꝺ co hollaṁ aꞄloṁ ꝺaen builli ꞃleᵹi, ocuꞃ buille aile ꝺo ꞄhaḃaiꞃꞄ ꝺó aꞃ ꝺonꝺchaꝺ mac Ccꝺha in cleꞄiᵹ, ocuꞃ a ṁaꞃ ḃaꝺ beoꞅ; ocuꞃ Comaꞃ O ꝽaiꞄhin ꝺo ċoṁmaiꝺeṁ leiꞃ beoꞅ; ocuꞃ a imꞄeachꞄ ꞃéin imꞃlan cona ṁuinnꞄiꞃ co cꞃoꝺa coꞃcuꞃach, iaꞃ coṁmaiꝺeṁ ceꞄhꞃaiꞃ ꝺon cheꞄhiꞃn. ꝺoṁnall maᵹ CaꞃꞄhaiᵹh, ꞃi ꝺeꞃmuṁan, ꝺo éᵹ iaꞃ naiꞄhꞃiᵹhe. Mac ᵹilla Muiꞃe, ꞃi Ua nꝺeꞃca Cein, occiꞃuꞃ eꞃꞄ a ꞃuiꞃ. Ua hCcnluain, ꞃi na nOꞃꞄheꞃ, ꝺo

---

1 *Made king.* In succession to Thomas, son of Mathghamhain O'Raighilligh (Mor ahon O'Reilly), whose death has just before been noticed.

2 *Muirchertach;* i.e. Muirchertach (Murtough) O'Conor Sligo.

3 *John Oifistel;* i.e. John the Official.

4 *Ollamh;* pron. *ollave,* "professor," or "doctor."

5 *Kalends.* The Dom. Letter for the year (A) is added in the margin in B.

6 *Cenel-Fiachaidh-mic-Neill.* See note 4, p. 556, vol. i.

7 *Five.* coiᵹeꞃ, C. coceꞃ, B.

8 *Before.* ꞃemhe, B. ꞃoiṁe, C.

made king.[1] The castle of Cill-Barrfhinne was demolished by Domhnall, son of Muirchertach.[2] Brian Mac Aedhagain, chief brehon of the Breifne, mortuus est. John Oifistel[3] Mac Aedhagain, the best man of his own position in his time, was slain four nights before Christmas; and it is not known who killed him. Diarmaid Mac Carmaic occisus est. Duibhginn O'Duibhgennan, ollamh[4] of Commaicne in history, quievit.

A.D.
[1390.]

The kalends[5] of January on Sunday, and the sixteenth of the moon; M.°ccc.°xc. primo; v. anno cycli lunaris; xiiii. Indictionis; xi. cycli solaris. Diarmaid, son of Donnchadh, son of Muirchertach Mor Mac Eochagain, dux of Cenel-Fiachaidh-mic-Neill,[6] quievit the day before the ides of January. Peace was concluded by O'Ruairc and O'Raighilligh, and O'Ruairc went to Druim-lethan to meet O'Raighilligh, with a few of his own household; and sixty-five[7] of the Clann-Muirchertaigh went before[8] him on a pass[9]; and O'Ruairc advanced towards the pass, and John Mor,[10] grandson of the ban-fidhighe,[11] met O'Ruairc with a lance thrust, and O'Ruairc proceeded to attend and meet him, and readily, quickly, killed him with one lance thrust; and he delivered another thrust to Donnchadh, son of Aedh-an-cletigh, whom he also killed; and Thomas O'Gaithin was likewise slain by him; and he himself departed safely with his people, bravely, enriched with spoils, after slaying four of the band. Domhnall Mac Carthaigh, king of Des-Mumha, died after penitence. Mac Gilla-Muire,[12] king of Ui-nErca-Chein, occisus est a suis. O'hAnluain, king of the Oirthera,

[1391.]

9 *A pass.* The Four Masters call it beaḷaċ an ċṗionaıᵹ "the pass of the withered trees (or brambles)," which Dr. O'Donovan states (note ʲ, ad an.) was the old name of the road, or pass, leading from the monastery of Drumlane, in the county of Cavan, into West Breifny, or the county of Leitrim.

10 *John Mor.* He was the son of Mathghamhain O'Conor, and belonged to the sept of the Clann-Muirchertaigh-Muimhnigh.

11 *The ban-fidhighe;* i. e. "the weaveress."

12 *Mac Gilla-Muire;* i.e. the son of Gilla-Muire. The Four Masters call him Cu-Uladh O'Morna.

[MS. defective.
Text supplied
from "Annals
of Connacht."]

ṁaṗḃaᴅ ṗeṗ ᴅoluṁ o α ḃṗaiṫṗiḃ ṗéin. Cαḃc mαc
Ꝉillα Choluim Ꝉi Uiꝁinᴅ, ocuṗ ḃebinn inꝁeαn Ꝉi
Mαilchonαiṗe, ollαṁ ᴅinꝁḃαlα ṗe ᴅán ocuṗ ṗe ᴅαen-
nαċᴅ, ᴅo eꝁ iαṗ nαiṫṗiꝁe móiṗ.

Ꝃᴅ. enαiṗ ṗoṗ Luαn, ocuṗ ṗechᴅ .xx. ṗuiṗṗi;
ṁ.°ccc.°xcii.; ṗexᴅo αnno cicli Lunαṗiṗ; ᴅu. αnno
inᴅicᴅioniṗ; xii. αnno cicli ṗolαṗiṗ. Ꝃᴅᴅeṗṗoꝁ Connαchᴅ .i. Ꝃṗiꝁoiṗ Uα Mochαn, ṗαi cṗαiḃḃeαċ cleṗ-
cheṁuil, quieuiᴅ in Cṗiṗᴅo. enṗi αṁṗeiᴅ, ṗeṗ αnᴅi-
phṗαṗim, mαc Néill ṁóiṗ .h. Neill, ṗiꝁḃαṁhnα héṗenᴅ
ᴅe iuṗe, ocuṗ αḃḃαṗ ṗiꝁ Ulαḃ cαn αṁuṗαṗ ᴅiα mαiṗeḃ,
ocuṗ ṗeṗ ᴅo bα mo ᴅuαṗ ocuṗ ᴅiḃnucαl ocuṗ ᴅαṗḃeαṗ-
ᴅuṗ ᴅαiniec αṗ ṗlichᴅ Neill mic echαiḃ Muiꝁmeαḃoin,
ocuṗ ṗeṗ ṗo ṗo inꝁαnᴅα ocuṗ ṗo bo ᴅṗαeḃnoṗαiḃe
eineċ uαiṗ eli, moṗᴅuuṗ eṗᴅ in bono ṗine im ṗeil
ḃṗenαinᴅ. Cunᴅαiṗ ᴅeṗmuṁαn .i. inꝁαiṗ iαṗlα Uṗ-
ṁuṁαn, ben ᴅéṗceαċ ᴅeꝁ einich, quieuiᴅ. ᴅonnchαᴅh
Uα ᴅimuṗαiꝁ quieuiᴅ. Moṗṗluαꝁαḃ lα Uα Conchuḃ-
αiṗ nᴅonn ocuṗ lα huṗṁoṗ Connαchᴅ lαiṗ, α niḃ
Mαine, ocuṗ in cṗich ᴅo Loṗcαḃ Leó, ocuṗ Cαᴅhαl mαc
Ꝃeᴅα .h. Ruαiṗc ᴅo ṗαꝁḃαil co hαnoṗᴅαiꝁᴅe αṗ ᴅeiṗeαḃ
αnᴅ ṗluαiꝁ, ocuṗ α ꝁαḃαil le hUα Conchoḃαiṗ ṗuαḃ,
ocuṗ αṗαile ᴅo mαṗḃαḃ ᴅiḃ. ᴅoṁnαli mαc enṗi Ui
Néill ᴅo ꝁαḃαil le Coiṗṗᴅhealbach Uα nᴅoṁnáill,
ocuṗ cṗeαchα αiḃble ocuṗ uṗᴅhα ᴅo ᴅénαṁ ᴅó αn lα
céαᴅnα αiṗ mαc enṗi. Moṗṗluαꝁαḃ lα Niαll .h. Néill
ṗoṗ Ꝃαllαiḃ αnᴅ Spαᴅḃαile, αꝁuṗ Seṗín ṗαiᴅ ᴅo mαṗḃαḃ αnn ᴅon ᴅolα ṗin. Coiṗṗḃealḃαċ mαc ḃṗiαin
Uα Cuαnαch moṗᴅuuṗ eṗᴅ. Ꝃinᴅꝁuαlα inꝁeαn Mαꝁ-
nuṗα iic Cαᴅαil .h. Chonċuḃαiṗ quieuiᴅ. Ruαiᴅṗi
mαc ᴅonᴅchαiḃ .h. Cheṗḃαill, ṗiꝁᴅαṁhnα eli, quieuiᴅ.

---

1 *Kalends.* The Dom. Letters (G
F) are added in the margin in B.
2 *Pious.* cṗαiḃḃeαċ, C. cṗαiḃḃ,
for cṗαiḃḃech, B.
3 *Amhreidh;* i.e. the Unquiet.

4 *Per antiphrasim.* Because he
was peaceably disposed. C reads
ṗ αnᴅṗiṗicim.
5 *If he had lived.* ᴅiα mαṗṗeḃ, C.
ᴅiα mαṗmαᴅ, B.

was slain per dolum by his own kinsmen. Tadhg, son of Gilla-Coluim O'hUiginn, a worthy doctor in poetry and humanity, and Bebinn, daughter of O'Maelconaire, died after great penitence.

The kalends[1] of January on Monday, and the twenty-seventh of the moon; M.°ccc.°xcii.; sexto anno cycli lunaris; xv. anno Indictionis; xii. anno cycli solaris. The arch-bishop of Connacht, i.e. Gregory O'Mochain, an eminently pious,[2] clerical man, quievit in Christo. Henry, *surnamed* Amhreidh,[3] per antiphrasim,[4] son of Niall Mór O'Neill, royal heir of Erinn de jure, and who would have been king of Uladh, without doubt, if he had lived;[5] and the greatest man for bestowing rewards, gifts and presents, that came of the race of Niall, son of Eochaidh Muigh-medhoin, and at other times the most wonderful and famous man for hospitality, mortuus est in bono fine, about the festival of Brenainn. The countess of Des-Mumha, i.e., the daughter of the Earl of Ur-Mumha, a charitable, bountiful woman, quievit. Donnchadh O'Dimusaigh quievit. A great hosting by O'Concho-bhair Donn, accompanied by the greater part of Connacht, into Ui-Maine, and the country was burned by them. And Cathal, son of Aedh O'Ruairc, was negligently left in the rear of the army, and was taken prisoner by O'Conchobhair Ruadh; and some others of them were slain. Domhnall, son of Henry O'Neill, was taken prisoner by Toirdhelbhach O'Domhnaill, who on the same day committed great depredations and ravages upon the son of Henry. A great hosting by Niall O'Neill against the Foreigners of the Srat-baile, and Seffin White[6] was slain there on that occasion. Toirdhelbhach Mac Briain of Ui-Cuanach mortuus est. Finnghuala, daughter of Maghnus, the son of Cathal O'Conchobhair, quievit. Ruaidhri, son of Donnchadh O'Cerbhaill, royal

---

⁶ *White.* Ⲣⲁⲓⲧ, B. Ⲣⲁⲟⲓⲧ, C.

[MS. defective. Text supplied from "Annals of Connacht."]

Θταιn ιnξean Sερραιᵭ .h. Ϝlannacan, uxoρ .Uιlliam mιc Ḃρanan, quιeuιτ ιm ϝeιl Cρορ.

ǀCᵭ. Θnaιρ ϝορ Ceᵭaιn, ocuρ ochᵭmaᵭ uaᵭhaᵭ ϝuιρρι; ᴜᴵᴵ.ccc°.xcιιι°.; uιι. cιclι lunaριρ; ι. anno ιnᴠιcᴛιonιρ; xιιι. anno cιclι ϝolaριρ. Œeᴠh mac Conchuᴅaιρ Ⅿιc Ởιαρmαᴠα, ρι Ⅿoιξι Luιρξ, ϝeρ lan ᴠo cech uιlι maιch, ᴠo ecc ιαρ mbuaιᵭ naιᴛhριξhe, ocuρ α ṁac .ι. Caᴛhal Ⅿac Ởιαρmaᴠα, ᴠo baᴛhaᵭ aρ Loch Ởoιρι ιαραṁ. Θmann mac Ⅿaιlechlaιnn Ⅿeξ Raᴠnaιll, ᴠαṁnα ᴛαoιριξ Ⅿuιnᴛιρe hΘolaιρ, moρᴛuuρ eᵴᴛ. Ⅿaelρuanaιᵭ mac Ϝeρξαιl Ⅿιc Ởιαρmaᴠα ᴠo ριξaᵭ ϝoρ Ⅿaξ Luιρξ le neaρᴛ Tomalᴛαιξ Ⅿιc Ởonᴠchaιᵭ, ocuρ ιnᴠραιξιᵭ ᴠo ᴠénaṁ ᴠo cloιnn Œeᴅa Ⅿιc Ởιαρmaᴠα co cluaιn .h. Coιnᴠen ιριn calaᵭ Lochae Ởeιcheᴛ, αρ Ⅿac nᴓιαρmaᴠα, ocuρ bualaᵭ ᴠo ᴛhaᴅaιρᴛ ᴠoιᵭ ᴠιαραιlι; ocuρ bριᴵρeaᵭ aρ cloιnn Œeᴅa annριn, ocuρ Tomulᴛach ᴠuᵭ mac Ởιαρmaᴠα ᴠo ṁαρᴅαᵭ ann ριn, ocuρ Conchuᴅaρ mac Ởιαρmaᴠα, ocuρ Ruaιᴅρι a ᴅραᴛaιρ ᴠo ξαᴅαιl ann, ocuρ Ϝeρξal mac Ởonᴠᴄaᵭ ριαᴅαιξ ᴠo ξαᴅαιl anᴠ, αξuρ α éloᵭ ιαραṁ; ocuρ moραn elι ᴠo ξαᴅαιl ann. Ḃριαn .h. Cellaιᴠh, ριξᴠαṁnα Ua Ⅿaιne, moρᴛuuρ eᵴᴛ ιριn eρραch ceᴠna ριn. Ϝeρξal maξ Saṁραᴅαιn, ᴠux ᴛellaιch Θchᴛach, ocuρ ϝeρ ᴠo coṁmolaᴠh le clιαραιᵭ Θιρeann ocuρ le cρoρanaιᵭ ιn ϝeρ ριn, eιᴠιρ chaιρᴛ αξuρ belᴛaιne. Seaan mac Seρραιᵭ Uι Raιξιllιᵭ, eaρρocc na Ḃρeιϝne, ιn Cριᴵᴛo quιeuιᴛ. Sιᴛh ᴠo ᴠenaṁ ᴠo luchᴛ Ⅿoιξι Luιρξ ιριnᴛ ραṁραᵭ ριn ϝα ρoιnᴠ ᴛιρe ocuρ coṁϝuαρlαcαᵭ bραξαᴛ. Raξnaιlᴛ, ιnξean mιc Ϝeιᴠlιmιᵭ .h. Conchoᴅαιρ, quιeuιᴛ. Ởubᴠαρα Ua Ⅿaιllι moρᴛuuρ eᵴᴛ. Ⅿaξnuρ Ua

---

1 *Etain.* Θᴛᴛαoιn, C. This name is now represented by " Edwina."

² *Kalends.* The Dom. Letter (E) is added in the margin in B.

³ *Loch-Doire.* In the Annals of Ulster (Dublin copy) it is stated that

Cathal Mac Diarmada was drowned at Inis-Daighre, now Inisterry, in Loch-Cé, county of Roscommon.

⁴ *Donnchadh Riabhach.* Donough the Swarthy [Mac Dermot].

⁵ *Of the Breifne.* na Ḃρeιϝne, B.

heir of Eli, quievit. Etain,[1] daughter of Jeffrey O'Flan- A.D.
nagain, uxor of William Mac Branan, quievit about the [1392.]
festival of the Cross.

The kalends[2] of January on Wednesday, and the eighth [1393.]
of the moon; M°.ccc°.xciii.; vii. cycli lunaris; i. anno
Indictionis; xiii. anno cycli solaris. Aedh, son of Conchobhar Mac Diarmada, king of Magh-Luirg, a man full
of all good, died after the triumph of penitence; and his
son, i.e. Cathal Mac Diarmada, was afterwards drowned
in Loch-Doire.[3] Edmond, son of Maelechlainn Mac Raghnaill, intended chieftain of Muinter-Eolais, mortuus est.
Maelruanaidh, son of Ferghal Mac Diarmada, was made
king over Magh-Luirg by the power of Tomaltach Mac
Donnchaidh; and an incursion was made by the sons of
Aedh Mac Diarmada to Cluain-O'Coinden, in the callow
of Loch-Techet, against Mac Diarmada; and they
attacked each other, when the sons of Aedh were routed,
and Tomaltach Dubh Mac Diarmada was slain; and Conchobhar Mac Diarmada, and his brother Ruaidhri, were
taken prisoners there; and Ferghal, son of Donnchadh
Riabhach,[4] was taken prisoner there, and escaped afterwards; and several others were taken prisoners there.
Brian O'Cellaigh, royal heir of Ui-Maine, mortuus est in
the same spring. Ferghal Mac Samhradhain, dux of Tellach-Echach, (and a man who was equally praised by the
poets and satirists of Erinn), *died* between Easter and
May-day. John, son of Jeffrey O'Raighilligh, bishop of the
Breifne,[5] in Christo quievit. A peace was concluded by
the people of Magh-Luirg, in this summer, regarding the
division of land and the mutual release of hostages.[6]
Raghnailt, daughter of the son[7] of Fedhlimidh O'Conchobhair, quievit. Dubhdara O'Maille mortuus est. Maghnus

---

The bishoprick of the Breifne, or of
Triburnia, as it was sometimes called,
is now represented by the diocese of
Kilmore.

[6] *Of hostages.* bpaiṡoi, C. bṙac,
for bṙaṡac, B.

[7] *The son.* Aedh (or Hugh)
O'Conor, who died in 1368.

[MS. defective. Text supplied from "Annals of Connacht."]

hEġra, aḋḃar riġ Luiġne, quieuit. Mac Emainn Ui Cellaiġ quieuit. Muirir cam mac Ruaiḋri meġ Eochacan mortuus est in Noiuimber, ocus Brian macc Uilliam oicc meġ Eochacan mortuus est; in .ui. nonas Octobris quieuit. Edaoin ingean Chaṫail oiġ Ui Chonchuḃair, bean Bhriain mic Maileaċlainn Ui Chealllaiḋ, Domnall ocus Emann, da ṁac Maoileaċlainn Ui Cheallaiġ, ocus Diarmaid Ua Flannagan, áḋḃar taoisiċ Tuaiṫe ráṫha, do ecc. Mainistir Chille hAchaiḋ in easpucoideacht Chille dara do ḋeanaṁ do ḃraiṫriḃ san Fransias la hUa Concuḃair bFhailġe.

* * * * *

* * * *

* * * * *

* * * *

* * * * *

Tomas mac Muirġeasa mic Donnchaiḋ, epscop Achaiḋ Conaire, do ecc. Coġaḋ mór do eirġiḋ eidir Ua Néill .i. Niall óg, ocus O Doṁnaill, Toirrḋealḃaċ; ocus a ṫáoiseaċaiḃ ocus a oireacht do ṫréigeḋ Ui Dhoṁnaill, go mbúi a ccuṁga ṁóir ag cloinn Enri Ui Neill, ag cloinn tSeain Ui Dhoṁnaill, ag Ua nDoċartaiġ, ocus ag cloinn tSuiḃne. Do chóiḋ mac Ui Dhoṁnaill, Niall garḃ, ocus clann Doṁnaill mic Néill Ui Domnaill, for ionnsaiġiḋ i Fánaiṫ, gurro gaḃadh leo Eoin mac Maolmuire mic Suiḃne, ocus condéarnsat orgain. Goill ocus Gaoiḋeal cóigiḋ Ulaḋ do ḋol i teach Ui Neill, ocus braiġde ocus umla do thaḃairt dó cenmothá O Doṁnaill a aenar.

Morsluaġaḋ la Niall occ .h. Neill, airdri coiceḋ

[1] *Quievit.* quieuerunt, B and C. The remaining entries for this year are wanting in B, but are given in C, into which they seem to have been copied from the Annals of the Four Masters. The transcriber of MS. B has added the note "desunt fere sex anni." The entries for the years 1394, 1395, 1396, 1397, and a part of 1398, are wanting in both B and C.

[2] *O'Conchobhair Failghe.* The transcriber of MS. C has added the following note: "N.B.—The years 1394, 1395, 1396, and 1397, are

O'hEghra, intended king of Luighne, quievit. The son of Edmond O'Cellaigh quievit. Maurice Cam, son of Ruaidhri Mac Eochagain, mortuus est in November; and Brian, son of William Og Mac Eochagain, mortuus est; in vi. nonas Octobris quievit.[1] Etain, daughter of Cathal Og O'Conchobhair, wife of Brian, son of Maelechlainn O'Cellaigh; Domhnall and Edmond, two sons of Maelechlainn O'Cellaigh; and Diarmaid O'Flannagain, heir to the lordship of Tuath-ratha, died. The monastery of Cill-achaidh in the bishopric of Cill-dara was built for the Brothers of Saint Francis by O'Conchobhair Failghe.[2]

*　　*　　*　　*　　*

*　　*　　*　　*

*　　*　　*　　*　　*

*　　*　　*　　*

Thomas, son of Maurice Mac Donnchaidh, Bishop of Achadh-Conaire, died. A great war broke out between O'Neill, i.e. Niall Og, and O'Domhnaill, i.e. Toirdhelbhach; and his chieftains and his tribe abandoned O'Domhnaill, so that he was reduced to great straits by the sons of Henry O'Neill, by the sons of John O'Domhnaill, by O'Dochartaigh, and by the Clann-Suibhne. O'Domhnaill's son, (Niall Garbh), and the sons of Domhnall, son of Niall O'Domhnaill, went upon an excursion into Fanat, when John, the son of Maelmuire Mac Suibhne, was captured by them, and they committed a depredation. The Foreigners and Gaeidhel of the province of Uladh went into O'Neill's house, and gave him hostages and submission, with the exception of O'Domhnaill alone.

A great hosting[3] by Niall Og[4] O'Neill, chief king of

---

wanting in the original, but may be filled from the Four Masters." The four first entries for the year 1398 appear to have been so filled in C.

[3] *Great hosting.* mop ṙluaġaḋ.

The text re-commences with these words in B, the four preceding entries being given only in C. See last note.

[4] *Og.* occ, B.; óg occ, C.

[MS. defective.
Text supplied
from "Annals
of Connacht."]

Conchuɓaıp, a ꞇıp Conaıⱡⱡ Ʒuⱡbaın mıc Neıⱡⱡ, co pan-
caꝺap a ꞃꞃꞇhı co ꞃꞇ Œeꝺa uap ep Ꞃuaıꝺ mıc ɓaꝺaıpn,
ocup ꞃo aıꞃcıꝺap manıꞃꞇıp Eꞃa Ꞃuaıꝺ ꞃo na huıⱡe
ınnmuꞃ ꝺon ꞇuꞃap ꞃın, ocup ꝺꞃonƷ ꝺo ṁuınnꞇıp .h.
Ꝺoṁnaıⱡⱡ ꝺo ꞇhaɓaıꞃꞇ ꞇachaıꞃ ꝺonꞇ ꞃⱡuaƷ, ocup ꝺaıne
ꝺo ṁapɓaꝺ ocup ꝺo ɓapcaꝺ ann ꞃın; acuꞃ Œeꝺ mac
mıc Ꝑepʒaıⱡ ꞃuaıꝺ ꝺo Ʒabhaıⱡ ⱡa hEoʒanchaıꝺ, ocuꞃ
a nımꞇeachꞇ ꞃeın ꞃⱡan ꝺıa ꞇıʒıꝺ.

Sⱡuaıʒeꝺ ⱡa Ꞇomaꞃ a ɓupc, ꞇıʒeapna Ʒaⱡⱡ Con-
naꞯꞇ, ocuꞃ ⱡa Ꞇoıꞃꞃꝺheaⱡbach ꞃuaꝺ .h. Conchuɓaıꞃ,
ꞇıʒeapna Ʒaıꝺeⱡ Connachꞇ, ocuꞃ ⱡa Ꝑeıꝺⱡımıꝺ mac
Caꞇhaıⱡ oıcꞇ .h. Conꞯuɓaıꞃ cona ɓꞃaıꞇꞃıꞯaıꝺ, ocuꞃ ⱡa
Ꞃuaıꝺꞃı Ua nꝺuꝺꝺa cona ɓꞃaıꞇꞃeꞯaıꝺ, ocuꞃ ⱡa Ꞇaꝺʒ
Ua neꞯꞃa cona ꞯoıṁꞇınoⱡ ocuꞃ cona ɓꞃaıꞇhꞃechaıꝺ, a
ꞇıꞃ nOıⱡıoⱡⱡa, cuꞃ mıⱡⱡeꝺ ⱡeo an ꞇıꞃ uıⱡe eıꝺıꞃ ꞃép
ocuꞃ apꝺaꞃ, eıꝺıꞃ ⱡoch ocuꞃ cıⱡⱡ, ocuꞃ ꝺunꞇıꝺ ocuꞃ
ꝺınnʒnaıꝺ ocuꞃ ꝺꞃoɓeⱡaıꝺ ꞃꞇ. Conchuɓaꞃ occ mac
Œeꝺa mıc Ꝺıapmaꝺa ocuꞃ a ɓꞃaıꞇꞃıꞯaıꝺ ꝺo ꞇeaꞯꞇ a
Maʒ ⱡuıꞃʒ; aʒuꞃ Maeⱡꞃuanaıʒ Mac Ꝺıapmaꝺa,
ꞃex Moıʒı ⱡuıꞃʒ, ꝺo ꝺoⱡ an oıꝺchı ꞃın co manıꞃꞇıꞃ
na ɓuıⱡⱡe, ocuꞃ a ꞃuaıꞃ ꞃe ꝺo ɓıaꝺ a maınıꞃꞇeꞃ na
ɓuıⱡⱡe ꝺo choꞃ aꞃ caꞃꞃuıc ⱡocha Cé ꝺó. Œʒuꞃ ⱡoꞃʒ
na ꞃeꝺna ꞃın ꝺꞃaʒɓaıⱡ ꝺó Chonchoɓaꞃ cona ṁuınꞇıꞃ,
ocuꞃ an ⱡoꞃʒ ꝺo ⱡeanṁaın ꝺoıꝺ co hEchꝺꞃuım mıc
nŒeꝺa a ꞇıꞃ Ua mɓꞃıuın na Sınna, ocuꞃ ꞇempoⱡⱡ
Echꝺꞃoma ꝺo ⱡoꞃcaꝺ ꞃoꞃꞃa, ocuꞃ Conchobaꞃ mac Ꝑeꞃ-
ʒaıⱡ Mıc Ꝺıapmaꝺa ꝺo mapɓaꝺ ann, ocuꞃ Maeⱡ-
ꞃuanaıꝺ Mac Ꝺıapmaꝺa ꝺo ʒabaıⱡ ann, ocuꞃ moꞃan
ꝺa ṁuınꞇıꞃ ꝺo mapɓaꝺ ann; ocuꞃ a neıch ocuꞃ a
neꞇıꝺ ꝺo beın ꝺıꝺ.

---

¹ *Coiced-Conchobhair* ; i.e. "the
fifth (or province) of Conchobbar"
[Mac Nessa], a bardic name for Ulster.

² *Tir - Conaill - Gulban - mic - Neill.*
The territory of Conall Gulban, son
of Niall of the Nine Hostages, called
Tir-Conaill, or Tirconnell, a district

co-extensive with the present county
of Donegal.

³ *Es-Ruaidh-mic-Badhuirn.* The cataract of [Aedh] Ruadh, son of Badhurn; now the Salmon Leap at Assa-
roe, near Ballyshannon, in the county
of Donegal.

⁴ *Its.* na, omitted in B.

A.D.
[1398.]

Coiced-Conchobhair,[1] into Tir-Conaill-Gulban-mic-Neill,[2] so that his scouts arrived at Sidh-Aedha over Es-Ruaidh-mic-Badhuirn;[3] and they plundered the monastery of Es-Ruaidh of all its[4] riches on this expedition; and a party of O'Domhnaill's people gave battle to the army, and men were slain and injured there; and Aedh, grandson of Ferghal Ruadh,[5] was taken prisoner by the Eoghanachs; who themselves went home safely.

A hosting by Thomas Burk, lord of the Foreigners of Connacht, and by Toirdhelbhach Ruadh O'Conchobhair, lord of the Gaeidhel of Connacht, and by Fedhlimidh son of Cathal Og O'Conchobhair, with his kinsmen, and by Ruaidhri O'Dubhda, with his kinsmen, and by Tadhg O'hEghra, with his muster, and with his kinsmen, into Tir-Oilella, when the entire country was destroyed by them, both[6] grass and corn, lake[7] and church, forts, fastnesses, and strongholds, &c. Conchobhar Og, son of Aedh Mac Diarmada, and his kinsmen, came to Magh-Luirg; and Maelruanaidh[8] Mac Diarmada, rex of Magh-Luirg, went that night to the monastery of the Buill, and all the food that he found in the monastery of the Buill was transferred to the Rock of Loch-Cé by him. And the track of this party was discovered by Conchobhar[9] with his people, who pursued them as far as Echdruim-mic-nAedha in Tir-Ua-Briuin-na-Sinna; and the church of Echdruim was burned over them, and Conchobhar, son of Ferghal Mac Diarmada, was slain there, and Maelruanaidh Mac Diarmada was captured there; and several of his people were killed there; and their horses and armour were taken from them.

---

[5] *Ferghal Ruadh.* Ferghal the Red. The Four Masters call him Aedh, son of Ferghal O'Ruairc.

[6] *Both.* eioip (lit. between), B. eaoap, C.

[7] *Lake.* The chronicler meant to convey that the islands and structures of the lakes were destroyed.

[8] *Maelruanaidh.* The Four Masters write the name Ferghal (or Farrell); but Mageoghegan, in his version of the Annals of Clonmacnoise, calls him "Mollronie Mac Fierall Mac Dermott."

[9] *Conchobhar;* i.e. Conchobhar Og, son of Aedh Mac Diarmada.

[MS. defective.
Text supplied
from " Annals
of Connacht."]

Sluaxaꝺ la Muircheaꞃtach mac nꝺoṁnaill .h.
Conchubhaiꞃ ı τıꞃ αeꝺa ꞃuaıꝺ mıc ꝺaꝺuıꞃnn ꝺochum
.h. ꝺoṁnaıll, ocuꞃ nı ꞃucꞅaτ aꞃ eꝺáıl ann, ocuꞃ a
nımꞃoꝺ ıaꞃ ꞃın. αxuꞃ αeꝺ Ua ꝺuıꞃnın ꝺa lenṁaın
a τoꞃaıxeaϲꞇ, ocuꞃ ımꞃúaxaꝺ ꝺo τhaꝺaıꞃꞇ ꝺoıꝺ a
mbeol αϲha Senaıx, ocuꞃ ech αeꝺa ꝺo loꞇ ocuꞃ a
eꞃcaꞃ ꞃeın ꝺı, ocuꞃ τıux anꞇ ꞃluaıx ꝺo loıxı aıꞃ, ocuꞃ
a ṁaꞃꝺaꝺ la cloınn ꝺonꝺchaıꝺ ; ocuꞃ Seon mac
Muıꞃeꝺaıx ꞃuaıꝺ ꝺo ṁaꞃꝺaꝺ aꞃ ın τóꞃaıxeachꞇ ꞃın.
Loch ꞅaꞃbach ꝺo xaꝺaıl la Ruaıꝺꞃı mac αeꝺa mıc
ꝺıaꞃmaꝺa, la ꞃıxꝺaṁna Moıxı Luıꞃx, ocuꞃ nı ꝺeochaıꝺ
a coṁaıꞃeṁ a ꞃꞃıϲh ꝺéꝺaıl aıꞃ. Muꞃchaꝺ bán mac
Seaın mıc ꝺoṁnaıll .h. ꞅeꞃxaıl, an mac ꞃıx τaıꞃıx ıꞃ
ꞃeꞃꞃ ꝺoı an ꞓıꞃınn ına aımꞃıꞃ ꞃeın, moꞃτuuꞃ eꞇ mı
ꞃıa noꝺluıcc móꞃ, ꝺo ꝺáꞃ ola ocuꞃ onxϲha ocuꞃ aıϲhꞃıxhe, eꞇ ꞃeꞃulꞇuꞃ eꞇ a manıꞃτıꞃ leaϲhꞃaϲha a
leꝺaıꝺ a αϲhaꞃ ocuꞃ a ꞃeanaϲhaꞃ. Muıꞃıꞃ mac
Pıaꞃꞃuıꞃ ꝺalaτun occıꞃuꞃ eꞇ la Muıꞃcheaꞃτach
occ mac ꞓochacan, ocuꞃ la ꝺꞃıan mac .h. Chonchoꝺaıꞃ
ꞃaılxı. Xlenꝺ ꝺa locha ꝺo loꞃcaꝺ la Saxanchaıꝺ
ocuꞃ le xallaıꝺ hꞓıꞃenꝺ ıꞃınꞇ ꞃaṁꞃaꝺ ꞃın aꞃꝺꝺıꞃe.
ꝺoṁnall .h. Nuallan occıꞃuꞃ eꞇ o xalloıꝺ ın hoc
anno. Ua ꝺꞃıaın mael moꞃτuuꞃ eꞇ. Pılıp mac
Maϲhxaṁna ꝺuınn .h. Cenneꝺıx moꞃτuuꞃ eꞇ. Semuꞃ
mac ꞓmaınꝺ .h. Cenꝺeꝺıx quıeuıꞇ. Mac ꝺıaꞃmaꝺa
ꞃeıꞃꝺ ı ꝺꞃıaın moꞃτuuꞃ eꞇ. Uaꞇeꞃ mac ꝺaıꝺıꝺ a
ꝺuꞃcc ꝺo maꞃꝺaꝺ la xallaıꝺ na Muṁan. xeꞃalꞇ
.h. ꝺꞃaın, ꞃı Ua ꞃaelan, quıeuıꞇ. Maelechlaınꝺ Ua
Moꞃꝺa, ꞃı laıxꞃı, moꞃτuuꞃ eꞇ. τomaꞃ mac Caϲhaıl,
mıc Muꞃchaꝺa .h. ꞅeꞃxaıl, ꝺo maꞃꝺaꝺ la xallaıꝺ

---

1 *Tir-Aedha-Ruadh-mic-Badhuirn*;
i.e. the country of Aedh Ruadh, son of
Badhurn; now the barony of Tirhugh,
co. Donegal.

2 *Son of Muiredhach Ruadh.* Mageoghegan, in his version of the Annals of Clonmacnoise, says "John
Mac Jelpine Roe."

3 *After.* The clause ꝺo ꝺáꞃ ola
ocuꞃ onxϲha ocuꞃ aıϲhꞃıxhe, literally translated, would read "of a
death of oil, unction, and penitence."

4 *O'Cennedigh.* .h. Chınꝺeꝺıx, C.

5 *Mortuus est.* So in B. quıeuıꞇ,
C.

A hosting by Muirchertach, son of Domhnall O'Con-chobhair, into Tir-Aedha-Ruaidh-mic-Badhuirn,[1] against O'Domhnaill; and they captured no spoils there; and they turned back afterwards. And Aedh O'Duirnin fol-lowed them in pursuit, and they attacked one another at Bel-Atha-Senaigh; and Aedh's horse was wounded, and he himself was unhorsed; and the throng of the army pressed upon him, and he was slain by the Clann-Donnchaidh. And John, son of Muiredhach Ruadh,[2] was killed in this pursuit. Loch-Fharbhach was taken by Ruaidhri, son of Aedh Mac Diarmada, royal heir of Magh-Luirg; and countless spoils were found in it. Murchadh Bán, son of John, son of Domhnall O'Ferghail, the best son of a king-chieftain that was in Erinn in his own time, mortuus est a month before Great Christmas, after[3] unction and penitence; et sepultus est in the monastery of Leth-ratha, in the tomb of his father and grandfather. Maurice, son of Piers Dalton, occisus est by Muirchertach Og Mac Eochagain, and by Brian, the son of O'Conchobhair Failghe. Glenn-da-locha was again burned in this summer by the Saxons and Fo-reigners of Erinn. Domhnall O'Nuallan occisus est by Foreigners in hoc anno. O'Briain Mael mortuus est. Philip, the son of Mathghamhain Donn O'Cennedigh,[4] mortuus est.[5] James, the son of Edmond O'Cennedigh, quievit. The son of Diarmaid Serbh[6] O'Briain mortuus est. Walter Mac David[7] Burk was slain by the Foreigners of Mumha. Gerald O'Brain,[8] king of Ui-Faelain, quievit. Maelechlainn O'Mordha, king[9] of Laighis, mortuus est. Thomas, the son of Cathal, son of Murchadh O'Ferghail, was killed by the Foreigners

---

[6] *Serbh*; i.c. "the Sour."

[7] *Mac David.* mac Oaibi, C. mac ꝏ, B.

[8] *O'Brain.* h. bꝛ, C. h.bꝛiain, B, which is a mistake for h. bꝛain,

VOL. II.

the Irish form of the name of O'Byrne. The death of Gerald O'Broin, son of Tadhg, is given by the Four M. at the year 1399.

[9] *King.* ꝛi, C. ꝛig, B.

G 2

[MS. defective. Text supplied from "Annals of Connacht."]

ṅα Mιꞅe ιꞃιn Chαιllιn ꞓꞃubαch, ocuꞅ ꞇo ꞇhαꞬαιll αn Ꞇomαꞅ ꞅιn ꞇιᵹeαꞃnαꞅ nα hⱭnᵹαιle ι nαᵹαιꞌ ꞇ8eoαιn mιc Ꞃꞃιαιn mιc Muꞃchαιꞌ, cen coꞅ cóιꞃ ꞇol α nαᵹαιꞌ αnꞇ ꞅιnꞅιꞃ Ꞃꞃαꞇαꞃ mαιꞇh. Mαιꞌm moꞃ lα Mαᵹ Cαꞃꞃꞇhαιᵹ Cαιꞃꞃꞃech ꞅoꞃ Uιꞌ 8úιllιꞬαn, ocuꞅ Uα 8uιllιꞬαn cαlbuꞅ ꞇo mαꞃꞬαꞌ αnn, ocuꞅ ꞇá mαc .ḣ. 8uιllιꞬαn moιꞃ .ι. Ꞡoᵹαn ocuꞅ Conchoꞃαn buιꞌe, eꞇ αlιι mulꞇι. Muιꞃcheαꞃꞇαch occ mαᵹ Ⱨenᵹuꞅα occιꞅuꞅ eꞃꞇ o α Ꞃꞃαιꞇꞃechαιꞌ buꞌéιn. Moꞃ ιnꞇꞃαιᵹιꞌ lα mαc Uιllιαm Ꞃuꞃc ocuꞅ lα cloιnn Chαꞇhαιl oιcc ꞅoꞃ 8lιᵹech, ocuꞅ ιn bαιle ꞇo loꞅcαꞌ ocuꞅ ꞇo lomαꞃᵹαιn ꞇoιꞌ. Cιnᵹ Rιꞅꞇeꞃꞇ, ꞃι 8αꞗαn, ꞇo ꞇeαchꞇ α nꞖꞃιnꞇ ιn hoc αnno, ocuꞅ Ⱥꞃꞇ Mαc Muꞃchαꞌα, ꞃí Lαιᵹen, ꞇo Ꞌeιꞇ α nαṁneαꞃꞇ moꞃ on ꞃιᵹ ocuꞅ o 8αꞗαnchαιꞌ αꞃcheαnα. Mαc Muꞃchαꞌα ꞇo ꞇol αꞃ ιnꞇꞃαιᵹιꞌ, ocuꞅ ᵹαιll Lαιᵹen ocuꞅ nα Mιꞌe ꞇo bꞃeιꞇh ꞅαιꞃ, αᵹuꞅ móꞃαn ꞇo ꞅluαᵹ 8αꞗαn occuꞅ ceιꞇheꞃnα conᵹꞗαlα Mιc Muꞃchαꞌα ꞇo mαꞃꞬαꞌ αnn, ιm clαιnn Ꞇonnchαꞌα .ḣ. Ꞌuιnn .ι. CeꞃꞬαll ocuꞅ Ꞡoᵹán, co mαιꞇhιꞌ α muιnꞇιꞃe mαιlle ꞅιu, ocuꞅ Uιllιαm mαc CeꞃꞬαιll mιc Ꞡιllα Ꞃαꞇꞃuιcc, ocuꞅ mαc Ꞌιαꞃmαꞇα ꞃuαιꞌ Mιc Ꞡιllα Ꞃαꞇꞃuιcc, ꞇo mαꞃꞬαꞌ αnn beoꞅꞅ.

8luαᵹαꞌ lα .ḣ. Conchoꞗαιꞃ ꞃuαꞌ, ocuꞅ lα Conchuꞗαꞃ Mαc nꞌιαꞃmαꞇα, ꞃι Moιᵹι Luιꞃᵹ, ι Ꞇíꞃ nOιlellα, co ꞃαncαꞇαꞃ α ꞅceṁeαlꞇα co Mαᵹ Ꞇuιꞃeꞌ nα ꞅoṁoꞃαch; ocuꞅ αιꞃᵹnι moꞃα ꞇo ᵹαꞬαιl ꞇoιꞌ; ocuꞅ α ꞇαꞗαꞃꞇ ꞅo choιllꞇιꞌ Conchuꞗαιꞃ, ocuꞅ α ceꞇhιꞃn conᵹꞗαlα ocuꞅ ᵹlαꞃꞅlαιꞇι ꞇo ιmꞇeαꞓꞇ le nα neꞇαlαιꞌ, ocuꞅ

---

1 *Cairbrech.* Cαιꞃꞃꞃech, C. Cαꞃꞃꞃuch, B.

2 *Buidhe;* i.e. "the Yellow." This word, and the addition eꞇ αlιι mulꞇι, are omitted in B. Mageoghegan says "O'Sullevan Bearrie."

3 *His.* α. Omitted in B.

4 *Cathal Og.* Cathal Og (or Charles the Younger) O'Conor.

5 *King.* ꞃι, C. ꞃιᵹ, B. King

Richard II. came to Ireland in 1899, not 1898.

6 *Came.* ꞇo ꞇeαchꞇ, C. ꞇo ꞇoꞅ, for ꞇo ꞇochꞇ, B.

7 *On an expedition.* αꞃ ιnꞇꞅꞌ, B. αꞃ ιonnꞅαιᵹιꞌ, C.

8 *Diarmaid Ruadh Mac Gilla-Patraic.* The Christian name, Diarmaid, is alone given in C.

9 *Magh-Tuiredh-na-Fomorach;* i.e.

of Midhe in the Caillin-crubach; and this Thomas had sought the sovereignty of the Anghaile in opposition to John, the son of Brian, son of Murchadh, although it was not right to oppose the senior, noble kinsman. A great victory by Mac Carthaigh Cairbrech[1] over the Ui-Suillebhain, and O'Suillebhain Calvus was slain there, and the two sons of O'Suillebhain Mór, viz., Eoghan and Conchobhar Buidhe,[2] et alii multi. Muirchertach Og Mac Aenghusa occisus est by his[3] own brothers. A great attack by Mac William Burk and the sons of Cathal Og[4] on Sligech, when the town was burned and entirely plundered by them. King Richard, king[5] of the Saxons, came[6] to Erinn in hoc anno, and Art Mac Murchadha, king[5] of Laighen, was much weakened by the king and the other Saxons. Mac Murchadha went on an expedition,[7] and the Foreigners of Laighen and Midhe overtook him; and a great number of the Saxon army, and the kerne retainers of Mac Murchadha, were slain there, including the sons of Donnchadh O'Duinn, viz., Cerbhall and Eoghan, together with the nobles of their people; and William, the son of Cerbhall Mac Gilla-Patraic, and the son of Diarmaid Ruadh Mac Gilla-Patraic,[8] were also slain there.

A hosting by O'Conchobhair Ruadh, and by Conchobhar Mac Diarmada, king of Magh-Luirg, into Tir-Oilella, so that their scouts reached Magh-Tuiredh-na-Fomorach;[9] and great spoils were obtained by them, which they carried towards Coillte-Conchobhair;[10] and their kerne retainers and young recruits departed with their spoils, and

---

"Magh-Tuiredh of the Fomorians," the name of a plain in the county of Sligo, celebrated as the scene of a great battle alleged to have been fought there, A.M. 2764, between the Firbolgs and Fomorians. The name of Magh-Tuiredh is still preserved in those of two townlands called Moytirra east, and Moytirra west, in the parish of Kilmactranny, barony of Tirerrill, and county of Sligo; and some remarkable traces of a battle are yet to be seen there.

[20] Coillte-Conchobhair. "Conchobhar's woods." This was the name of a woody district in the north-east of the present barony of Boyle, and county of Roscommon.

[MS. defective.
Text supplied
from "Annals
of Connacht."]

.h.Conchobaiṗ ocuṗ Mac Ơiaṗmaơa, ocuṗ Soṁaiṗle buiơe mac Maṗcuṗa mic Ơoṁnaill, conṗabla Mic Ơiaṗmaơa, ơo ṗacơail ơa muinnṫiṗ ṗein inơ uaṫhaơ ṗlúaiẋ. Muiṗcheaṗṫach mac Ơomnaill, ocuṗ Mael-ṗuanaiơ Mac Ơonnchaiơ, ṗi ṫíṗe hOilella, ơo bṗeiṫ ṗoṗṗo cona ṗochṗaiơi ơiơlinaiơ i Cnucc in cṗomai, ocuṗ a maơmachaơ annṗiơe, ocuṗ Soṁaiṗle buiơe cona ṁuinnṫiṗ ơo maṗơaơ i Cnucc in cṗoma, ocuṗ laṁ ơeṗ .h. Conchoơaiṗ ơo chṗeaċṫnuẋaơ co móṗ ơaiṫiuṗ aen oṗchuiṗ ṗoṗ in ṗluaẋaơ ṗin. Mac Muiṗiṗ buiơe .h. Moṗơa, ơpocheơ ơáṁ ocuṗ ơeoṗaiơ Eṗenơ, ṫiẋh-eaṗṅa Sleiơe Maiṗẋ, moṗṫuuṗ eṗṫ. Cϲṗṫ cam Ua ṗaelan quieuiṫ. Ingen Ḃṗiain .h. ṗeṗẋail, uɀoṗ Uulṗiṗ, quieuiṫ. ṗinơẋuala inẋean Caṫail Ui Maơaơan, moṗṫua eṗṫ. Ṗláẋ móṗ in hoc anno.

Ƙϲt. Enaiṗ ṗoṗ Ceơaoin ocuṗ ceṫhaṗ .ɀ. ṗuiṗṗi ; M°.ccc°.ɀc.iɀ.; ɀiii. anno cicli lunaṗiṗ; ųii.inơicṫioniṗ ; ɀiɀ. cicli ṗolaṗiṗ. Ḃṗian.h.ḃṗiain, ṗi Ṫuaơmuṁan, ṫuile oṗơain ocuṗ aiṗechaiṗ na hEṗenơ uile, ơo ecc iaṗ mḃṗeiṫh buaơa o ơoman ocuṗ o ơeṁan in hoc anno ; aẋuṗ Ṫoiṗṗơealơach mac Muṗchaiơ.h.ḃṗiain, leṫṗo-man Ṫuaơmuṁan, ơo eẋ. Cϲeơ.h.Ơonơchaơa, ṗi Eoẋan-achṫa Locha Lein, quieuiṫ. Ẓilla na naeṁ Mac Cϲeơ-acan, ollaṁ oiṗṫheaṗ Muṁan ṗe bṗeiṫheaṁnaṗ, ocuṗ ·ḃaeṫhẋalach Mac Cϲeơacan,ollaṁ bṗeiṫeṁan.h.ṗiaṫh-ṗach ocuṗ .h. nCϲṁalẋaiơ, moṗṫui ṗunṫ. Ṫoiṗṗ-ơhealbach mac Mailmuiṗe mic Suiơne, ṫiẋheaṗṅa ṗanaṫṫ, quieuiṫ. Cu Ulaơ Ua Neill .i. mac Neill .h. Neill, ṗeicheaơ coiṫchenơ ơecṗiơ Eṗenơ, quieuiṫ.

1 Buidhe; i.e. "the Yellow."

² Domhnall; i.e. Domhnall O'Con-chobhair, or Daniel O'Conor [Sligo].

³ Supporter. ơpocheơ; literally "bridge," B and C.

⁴ Sliabh-Mairge. A mountain in the Queen's county, giving name to the barony of Slewmargy, or Slieve-maraguе, in the same county. Both the mountain and barony, or district, were comprised in the ancient territory of Laighis, or Leix, the chieftains of which (the O'Mores) were sometimes called "lords of Sliabh-Mairge," by way of distinction.

⁵ Art Cam; i.e. Art the Crooked.

O'Conchobhair, and Mac Diarmada, and Somhairle Buidhe,[1] the son of Marcus Mac Domhnaill, Mac Diarmada's constable, were left by their own people with a few companions. Muirchertach, son of Domhnall,[2] and Maelruanaidh Mac Donnchaidh, king of Tir-Oilella, with their respective armies, overtook them at Cnoc-in-croma, where they were routed; and Somhairle Buidhé,[1] with his people, was slain at Cnoc-in-croma; and O'Conchobhair's right hand was greatly wounded from the effect of one shot on that hosting. The son of Maurice Buidhe[1] O'Mordha, supporter[3] of the learned and destitute of Erinn, lord of Sliabh-Mairge,[4] mortuus est. Art Cam[5] O'Faelain quievit. The daughter[6] of Brian O'Ferghail, uxor Vulpis,[7] quievit. Finnghuala, daughter of Cathal O'Madadhain, mortua est. A great plague in hoc anno.

The kalends of January[8] on Wednesday, and the fourteenth of the moon; M°.ccc°.xcix.; xiii. anno cycli lunaris; vii. Indictionis; xix. cycli solaris. Brian O'Briain, king of Tuadh-Mumha, flood of the dignity and nobility of all Erinn,[9] died after[10] triumphing over the world and the devil, in hoc anno; and Toirdhelbhach, son of Murchadh O'Briain, bulwark of Tuadh-Mumha, died. Aedh O'Donnchadha, king of Eoghanacht Locha-Lein, quievit. Gilla-na-naemh Mac Aedhagain, ollamh of the East of Mumha in judicature, and Baethghalach[11] Mac Aedhagain, ollamh-brehon of Ui-Fiachrach and Ui-Amhalghaidh, mortui sunt.[12] Toirdhelbhach, son of Maelmuire Mac Suibhne, lord of Fanad, quievit. Cu-Uladh O'Neill, i.e., the son of Niall O'Neill, general protector of the learned of Erinn,

---

[6] *Daughter.* ıngen, B. ıngheαn, C.

[7] *Uxor Vulpis;* i.e. wife of the Sinnach, or Fox, chief of Muinter-Tadhgain. See note [2], p. 26, *supra.* Ulpıſ, B.

[8] *Of January.* Θnαıſ; omitted in B, in which the Dom. Letter (E) is added in the margin.

[9] *Of all Erinn.* nα hΘſεnꝺ uıłε, B. Θıſεαnn uıłε, C.

[10] *After.* αſ, B. ıαſ, C.

[11] *Baethghalach.* This name is usually Latinized Boethius.

[12] *Mortui sunt.* m. 2, for moſṫuuſ eſⱦ, B.

[MS. defective.
Text supplied
from "Annals
of Connacht."]

Ƒeιɓlιmιɓ mac Cαϲhαιl .h. Conchuɓαιρ, ριɡɓαṁnα .h. Ƒαlɡι, mορϲuuρ eρϲ. ꝰeeαn mᾰc Ƀριαιn mιc Muρchαɓ .h. Ƒeρɣαιl, ϲαοιρeαch nα hᾼnɡαιle, ꝺο ecc, αccuρ ꝺοṁnαll mac ꝰeαιn .h. Ƒeρɣαιl ιnα ιnαϲ. hαnρι meρ mac Uαϲιn, ϲιɣeαρnα Ϲιρe hᾼṁαlɡαιɓ, qυιeuιϲ ιn Cριϲϲο. ꝺοṁnαll mac Ɉιllα 1ρα ρuαιɓ Uι Rαιɣιllιɓ qυιeuιϲ. ꝺιαρmαιꝺ mac ᾼeɓα mιc Ƒeɓlιmιɓ .h. Conchoɓαιρ, ꝺeɣ αɓɓαρ ριɣ Connαchϲ, qυιeuιϲ. Mαc Eochαɓα eolαch, ollαṁ nα Cαeṁαnαch ρe ꝺαn, ocuρ ρeιcheɓ coιϲchenꝺ ꝺρeραιɓ Eρenꝺ, ꝺο ecc ιαρ mbuαιɓ nαιϲhριɣe. Ρριṁƒαιɓ ᾼρꝺα Mαchα, .ι. ιn Colϲunαch, ιn Cριϲϲο qυιeuιϲ. Ϲαꝺc .h. Ceρɓαιll, ρι Elι, ꝺο ɡαɓαιl lα hιαρlα Uρṁuṁαn ιn hoc αnno. Coρmαc Uα Cuρnιn, αɓɓαρ ollαṁαn nα Ƀρeιƒne, ꝺο ecc ιn hoc αnno. ꝺοṁnαll ρuαɓ mac Ꝙιɡραιɣ .h. Cuρnιn, αɓɓαρ ollαṁαn nα Ƀρeιƒne, ꝺο ecc ꝺon ρlαιɣ ιn hoc αnno. Moρρluαɣαɓ lα mac Uιllιαm Ƀuρc ocuρ le cloιnn Cαϲhαιl οιcc, ocuρ le cloιnn .h. Cellαιɓ, α Cαιρρρι, αcuρ Ruαιɓρι mac ꝺοṁnαιll mιc Ƒlαιϲɓeαρϲαιɣ .h. Ruαιρc ꝺο mαρɓαɓ leo ꝺon ϲuραρ ριn, ocuρ echϲα ιmꝺα elι nαch αριmϲheρ ρunn.

Ⱪϲ. [Enαιρ] ρορ ꝺαρꝺαιn, ocuρ cuιcιꝺ ριcheαϲ ƒuιρρι; M°.cccc°. ; xιιι. cιclι Lunαριρ; uιϲιꝺ, xx. αnno cιclι ρolαριρ. ᾼeɓ .h. Mαιlmuαιɓ, ρex ρeρ Cell, qυιeuιϲ xιιιι. Ⱪϲ. Ƒeɓρα. Lαιɣnech mac Ƒeρɣαιl ρuαιɓ mιc ꝺonnchαιɓ meɣ Eochαcαιn qυιeuιϲ α ϲeιρϲ ιꝺ ꝰeρϲιmbιρ. Rιρꝺαρꝺ mac Ƒeoραιρ cum αlιιρ ꝺο mαρɓαɓ α ƒιll α ϲιɣ eρροιcc nα Mιɓe .ιx. cαllαιnꝺ Iuιl.

---

[1] *Cathal.* The name is "Cathair" in the Annals of Ulster, and also in the Annals of the Four Masters. Both names (*Cathal* and *Cathair*) are now Anglicised Charles.

[2] *Mac Eochdha Eolach.* "Mac Eochadha (or Mac Keogh) the learned." The word eoȴach is not in C.

[3] *Primate.* ρριṁƒαιɓ. This word properly signifies "chief prophet." See note [3], p. 148, vol. i.

[4] *The Coltunach.* John Colton, or De Colton, Archbishop of Armagh. His "quievit" is misplaced above, as he died in the year 1404. See Dr. Reeves's ed. of *Colton's Visitation;* Introduction, p. ii.

[5] *Several other deeds.* euchϲα ιοmɓα eιle, C.

quievit. Feidhlimidh, son of Cathal[1] O'Conchobhair, royal heir of Ui-Failghe, mortuus est. John, son of Brian, son of Murchadh O'Ferghail, chieftain of the An-ghaile, died; and Domhnall, son of John O'Ferghail, *was appointed* in his place. Henry Mer Mac Wattin, lord of Tir-Amhalghaidh, quievit in Christo. Domhnall, son of Gilla-Isa Ruadh O'Raighilligh, quievit. Diarmaid, son of Aedh, son of Feidhlimidh O'Conchobhair, who was well qualified to be king of Connacht, quievit. Mac Eochadha Eolach,[2] chief poet of the Caemhanachs, and general protector to the men of Erinn, died after the victory of penitence. The primate[3] of Ard-Macha, i.e. the Coltunach,[4] in Christo quievit. Tadhg O'Cerbhaill, king of Eli, was taken prisoner by the Earl of Ur-Mumha in hoc anno. Cormac O'Cuirnin, intended ollamh of the Breifne, died in hoc anno. Domhnall Ruadh, son of Sigradh O'Cuirnin, intended ollamh of the Breifne, died of the plague in hoc anno. A great hosting by Mac William Burk, and by the sons of Cathal Og, and the sons of O'Cellaigh, into Cairbre; and Ruaidhri, son of Domhnall, son of Flaithbhertach O'Ruaire, was slain by them on this expedition; and several other deeds[5] *were committed by them* that are not enumerated here.

The kalends [of January][6] on Thursday, and the twenty-fifth of the moon; M°.cccc°.; xiiii. cycli lunaris; viii. Indictionis;[7] xx. anno cycli solaris. Aedh O'Maelmhuaidh, rex of Feara-Cell, quievit the 14th[8] of the kalends of Feb-ruary. Laighnech, son of Ferghal Ruadh, son of Donnchadh Mac Eochagain, quievit on the 3rd of the ides of September. Richard Mac Feorais, cum aliis,[9] was slain, in treachery, in the house of the Bishop of Midhe,[10] on the ninth of the

---

6 [*Of January*]. Omitted in both B and C, in each of which the Dom. Letters (D C) are added in the margin.

7 *Indictionis*. The number of the Indiction is represented by uıcıꝺ, instead of uııı. ıꝺ, in B and C.

8 *The* 14*th*. xıııı., C. xuıı. (17th), B.

9 *Aliis.* aᷱlı, C. aſ, B.

10 *Of Midhe* (Meath). na Mıꝺe, C. na Mıꝺee, B.

[MS. defective.
Text supplied
from " Annals
of Connacht."]

Donōčað Sinnach, tiȝeapna muintire Tarocain, ocur pi
ȝer Teċhða de iupe, quieuit. Diarmaio ocur Ọrian,
ọa mac . h. Caċharnaiȝ mic ant Sinnaiȝ, quieuerunt
i]callainn Ccuȝurt. Cairlen Ọuin Imọain ọo ȝaðail
ọo mac an abaið .h. Conchuðair, ocur ̇obero mac
Ọmainọ mic ̇obero a ðuṗr ọo ̇marðað ann, ocur
mac mic Ọmainọ .h. Cellaȝ ọo ̇i a Larḣọechur anọ
ọo Lecen ar ọó. Ȝrizoir mac Tanaiðe .h. Maelchonaire,
aððar ollaḣan trila Muireðaiȝ muillethain, ocur
rai roirðči ina cheiro buðéin, ọo marðaọh ȝo tubair-
teċh ọo en ðuille ȝai ọo Laimh Uilliam ȝairbh mic
Daiðio ror tochar Ọuin Imọain anọ aḣricht, ocur
tucað re ba aȝur ui. xxit bo ina erirc. Saðð inȝeȝn
Taiọc mic Donọchaið quieuit. Ruaiọri mac Ccirt
Meȝ Ccenȝura ọo marðað le cloinn Conulaọh .h. ̇eill,
ocur la Caċharr maȝ Ccenȝura in hoc anno. Simon
.h. Treðair, airchiọechan Cille rorȝa, quieuit. Tomar
O Curnin, ollaḣ rer mỌreirne, quieuit. Creach mor
la cloinn rir Daiðio ror Niall mor .h. nUiȝinn, ocur
Ọia ọo ọenaḣ inọiȝti rorra inọ oiọchi rin .i. ár
aððal ọo chaðairt rorra o huachọ na haiọchi. Seaan
.h. Raiȝillið .i. mac Pilip .h. Raiȝillið, ri na ọreirne
čoir, quieuit ọo biọcc. Domnall aro .h. Ọuððir ọo
marðað la Ȝallaið in hoc anno. Coȝað mór eiọir
clainn tSeaain .h. Ọomnaill ocur .h. Ọomnaill rein.

---

1 O'Catharnaigh. O'Kearney. See
next note.

2 Son of the Sinnach. The name Sinnach (i.e. Fox), originally a sobriquet
of the chieftains of the family of
O'Catharnaigh (or O'Kearney) of
Teffia, ultimately became the surname
of a branch of the same family. For
the origin of the name Fox, see the
Miscell. of the Irish Archæol. Soc., pp.
187–188; the Chron. Scotorum. A.D.
1022; and vol. i. of this work, p.
27 (A.D. 1024). Instead of the clause
"h. Caċharnaiȝ mic ant Sinnaiȝ,"

as in the text, the Four Masters have
"mac Caċharnaiȝ mic ant Sinnaiȝ," which Dr. O'Donovan translates "sons of Catharnach Mac-ant-
Sinnaigh," as if he considered Mac-
ant-Sinnaigh a proper surname.

3 Mac-an-abaidh; i.e. the son of
the Abbot.

4 In confinement. a Larḣọechur,
B. a Larḣọeačar, C.

5 Was let. ọo Lecen, B. ọo
Léiȝean, C.

6 Sil-Muiredhaigh-Muillethain; i.e.
" the race of Muiredhach Muille-

A.D.
[1400.]

kalends of July. Donnchadh Sinnach, lord of Muinter-Tadhgain, and king, de jure, of Feara-Tethbha, quievit. Diarmaid and Brian, two sons of O'Catharnaigh[1] son of the Sinnach,[2] quieverunt on the kalends of August. The castle of Dun-Imdhain was taken by Mac-an-abaidh[3] O'Conchobhair; and Hubert, the son of Edmond, son of Hubert Burk, was slain there; and the grandson of Edmond O'Cellaigh, who was in confinement[4] there, was let[5] out of it by him. Gregory, son of Tanaidhe O'Mael-chonaire, intended ollamh of Sil-Muiredhaigh-Muillethain,[6] and a man perfect in his own art, was unfortunately[7] killed in mistake, by one cast of a spear from the hand of William Garbh Mac David,[8] on the causeway[9] of Dun-Imdhain; and six score and six cows were given as eric[10] for him. Sadhbh, daughter of Tadhg Mac Donnchaidh, quievit. Ruaidhri, son of Art Mac Aenghusa, was slain by the sons of Cu-Uladh O'Neill. and by Cathbharr Mac Aenghusa, in hoc anno. Simon O'Trebhair, archdeacon of Cill-Forga, quievit. Thomas O'Cuirnin, ollamh of the men of Breifne, quievit. A great depredation *was committed* by the sons of Sir David[11] upon Niall Mor O'hUiginn; and God inflicted punishment on them that night,[12] viz., a great destruction was brought upon them by the cold of the night. John O'Raighilligh, i.e., the son of Philip O'Raighilligh, king of East Breifne, quievit of a sudden fit. Domhnall Ard[13] O'Duibhidhir was slain by Foreigners in hoc anno. A great war between[14] the sons of John O'Domhnaill and O'Domhnaill himself.

---

than," the tribe name of the O'Conors of Connacht, and their correlatives.

[7] *Unfortunately.* co τuβuρech, B. co τubu:ρeαch, C.

[8] *William Garbh Mac David;* i.e. William the Rough Mac David [Burk].

[9] *Causeway.* τochαρ, C. τuch, for τachαρ, B.

[10] *Eric.* eιριc, C. eριcc, B. Eric denoted the fine, or compensation, paid for offences involving death or injury to persons.

[11] *Sir David;* i.e. Sir David Burk.

[12] *Night.* oιρochι, B. oιcho, C.

[13] *Ard;* i.e. the high, or tall; omitted in B.

[14] *Between.* eιoιρ, B. eαoαρ, C.

[MS. defective. Text supplied from "Annals of Connacht."]

Sluagaḋ mor la Niall .h. Neill a tir Conaill, cor ṁill mor dárbar an tíre. Eich ocus daine do ḃuain de. Clann Flaiṫḃeartaiġ .h. Ruairc do indarbaḋ asin Bhreifne amach. Gilla Isa mac Anrig do rigaḋ isin Breifne, ocus a ecc a cinn mís. Mac rig Saxan do ṫeaċt an Erind in hoc anno. Muiris mac mic Iarla Dermuṁan do ecc don pláiġ. Tadc .h. Cerḃaill do eloḋ on iarla a Belach Gaḃrain. Mac Mic in milid, tiġearna na Stondunach, occisus est o Uilliam a Burcc. Mac Maġnusa meg Uidir, bruġaiḋ dferaiḃ Erenn, do ecc do bidcc. Mailechlaind mac an airdepoicc .h.Cellaiġ do ecc don galar brecc. Crech mor do denaṁ do ċlainn Flaiṫḃeartaiġ ar Ua Ruairc. Creach do denaṁ do Tiġearnan .h. Ruairc ar Ua Maeladuin Luirg, occus .h. Doṁnaill do breith fair, ocus in creach do thaḃairt uaḋa ar ecin. Finnguala, ingen Chathail mic Aeḋa Breifniġ, ben Mic Suiḃne Fanat, quieuit. Diarmaid mac Muircheartaiġ ruaiḋ .h. Birn obiit .uii. idus Mai.

Kl. Enair for Sathairnn, ocus ui.eḋ uathaḋ fuirri; M.cccc.primo; xu. cicli lunaris; ix. anno indictionis; xxi. cicli solaris. Maelechlainn .h. Cellaiḋ, ri .h. Maine, fer lan denech, ocus dengnuṁ, ocus do ṫréidiḃ in tiġearnais, do ecc iar mbreith buadha o deman ocus o doṁan. Tomas mac Emaind Albanaiċ .i. mac Uilliam Burc, tiġearna Gall Connacht ocus moran da Gaiḋelaiḃ, mortuus est in hoc anno. Conchuḃar .h. Maileaċlainn, rex

---

1 *So that.* cor (for co ro), B. gur, C.

2 *Son of Henry;* i.e. of Henry O'Reilly.

3 *In hoc anno.* This entry should be given under 1401, in which year Thomas Duke of Lancaster, son of King Henry IV., arrived in Ireland.

4 *The Earl;* i.e. the Earl of Ur-Mumha, or Ormond.

5 *Brughaidh to the men of Erinn.* dfearaiḃ Eirionn, C. The term "brughaidh" was applied to an opulent farmer of great influence and authority.

6 *Suddenly.* do bidcc, B. do ḃiodg, C.

7 *Galar brec;* i.e. "the speckled disease," or small-pox.

A great hosting by Niall O'Neill to Tir-Conaill, so that[1] he
destroyed much of the corn of the country. Horses and men were taken from him. The sons of Flaithbhertach O'Ruairc were banished out of the Breifne. Gilla-Isa, son of Henry,[2] was made king in the Breifne, and died before the end of a month. The son of the king of the Saxons came to Erinn in hoc anno.[3] Maurice, grandson of the Earl of Des-Mumha, died of the plague. Tadhg O'Cerbhaill escaped from the Earl,[4] from Belach-Gabhrain. The son of Mac-in-mhilidh, lord of the Stauntons, occisus est by William Burk. The son of Maghnus Mac Uidhir, brughaidh to the men of Erinn,[5] died suddenly.[6] Maelechlainn, son of the Archbishop O'Cellaigh, died of the galar brec.[7] A great depredation was committed by the sons of Flaithbhertach[8] upon O'Ruairc. A depredation was committed by Tighernan O'Ruairc upon O'Maeladuin of Lurg; and O'Domhnaill overtook him, and the prey was taken from him by force. Finnghuala, daughter of Cathal, son of Aedh Breifnech,[9] wife of Mac Suibhne of Fanad, quievit. Diarmaid, son of Muirchertach Ruadh O'Birn, obiit vii. idus Maii.[10]

The kalends[11] of January on Saturday, and the sixth of the moon; M.cccc. primo; xv. cycli lunaris; ix. anno Indictionis; xxi. cycli solaris. Maelechlainn O'Cellaigh, king of Ui-Maine, a man full of bounty[12] and valour,[13] and of the wealth of the sovereignty, died after obtaining triumph over the devil and the world. Thomas, son of Edmond Albanach, i.e. Mac William Burk, lord of the Foreigners of Connacht, and of many of its Gaeidhel, mortuus est in hoc anno. Conchobhar O'Maelechlainn,

---

[8] *Sons of Flaithbhertach*. Flaithbhertach (or Flaherty) O'Ruairc.

[9] *Aedh Breifnech*. Aedh, or Hugh, the Breifnian (O'Conor); so called, doubtless, from having been fostered in the Breifne.

[10] *Maii.* ᵐⱥı, B and C.

[11] *Kalends.* The Dom. Letter (B) is added in the margin in B.

[12] *Of bounty.* ꝺᵉneċ, for ꝺo eneċ, B. ꝺenᵹnaċ, C.

[13] *Of valour.* ꝺenᵹnuṁ, for ꝺo enᵹnuṁ, C. ꝺeᵹnaṁ. C.

[MS. defective. Text supplied from "Annals of Connacht."]

Mroie ve iupe, quieuit a ceipt callainn Appil irin Let-
innre Muigi hElli in bona pine. Muircheaptac occ
mac Muirceartaigh móir meg Eochacan, vo marbav
i ceipt noin Octimbir i mbeol Atha impir vo en
urchur gai, la Geroitt mac Robert Valatun, i
comerciir orochi, ver a muintiri vo chur uav ar
invraigiv irin mbrenav muinntiri Gillgan. Voiïn-
nall mac Teboit .h. Mailmuav, avvar riz rer Cell,
interrectur ert in Almain Laigen o Galloiv, in privie
rour Man. Gilla na naeiï mac Aevacan, ollaïn
breiteaïnan .h. railgi ocur cenel Piachaiv, quieuit.
Teboiv buivi .h. Mailmuav vo marbav i cill
Crumchir Piachrach i ceipt callainv Octobir la
clainn Airt .h. Mailechlainv. Cathal ruav mag
Ragnaill, vux muinntire hEolair, vo marbav a
nVruim cubra le Serrav mac Maileachlainv meg
Ragnaill, hi cinv mír verrach .i. hi quint noin
Martai. Maelruanaig mac Cathail ruav meg
Ragnaill vo marbav la cloinv Maeleaclainn meg
Ragnaill in bliavain cevna, ä lurg a chreiche. Va
inac Uilliam vo venaïn tapéir Tomair a burc .i.
mac Uilliam vo venaïn vUillec mac Ricairv oicc,
ocur mac Uilliam eli vo venaïn vo Uater mac
Tomair a burc, ocur a crevemain vo mac Uilliam
cloinne Ricairv ar rnvrirrecht. Conchovar anabaiv
Ua Cellaig vo rigav a ninat a athar féin. Voiïnall
Ua Maille, ri Uïnaill, vo ecc in hoc anno. Cormac
mac Viarmava mic branan occirur ert rer volum

---

1 Midiæ. Mevie, B and C.

2 The Leth-inse of Magh-hElli. The name of the plain of Magh-hElli is still preserved in that of the townland of Moyally, parish of Kilmanaghan, barony of Kilcoursey, and King's County. Leth-inse, or Lehinch, is a townland in the parish of Kilbride, in the same barony and county.

3 Bel-atha-Impir; i.e. "the mouth of the ford of Imper." This seems to have been the name of a ford over the river Blackwater, near Emper, a townland in the present parish of Kilmacnevin, barony of Moygoish, and county of Westmeath. The words i mbeol, "in Bel—," are omitted in B.

rex Midiæ[1] de jure, quievit on the third of the kalends
of April, in the Leth-inse of Magh-hElli,[2] in bona fine.
Muirchertach Og, son of Muirchertach Mor Mac Eochagain,
was killed on the third of the nones of October, in Bel-
atha-Lmpir,[3] with one cast of a spear, by Garrett son of
Robert Dalton, in a nocturnal encounter, after he had
sent away his people on an incursion into the Brenadh of
Muinter-Gillgan. Domhnall, son of Tibbot O'Maelmhuaidh, heir to the sovereignty of Feara-Cell, interfectus
est in Almha of Laighen, by Foreigners, in pridie idus
Maii. Gilla-na-naemh Mac Aedhagain, ollamh-brehon of
Ui-Failghe and Cenel-Fiachaidh, quievit. Tibbot Buidhe
O'Maelmhuaidh was slain in Cill-Cruimthir-Fiachrach,[4]
on the third of the kalends of October, by the sons of
Art O'Maelechlainn. Cathal Ruadh Mac Raghnaill, dux
of Muinter-Eolais, was slain in Druim-cubhra by Jeffrey,
son of Maelechlainn Mac Raghnaill, before the end of a
month of spring, i.e. on the fifth of the nones of March.
Maelruanaidh, son of Cathal Ruadh Mac Raghnaill, was
slain by the sons of Maelechlainn Mac Raghnaill, in the
same year, whilst pursuing his prey.[5] Two Mac Williams
were made after[6] *the death of* Thomas Burk, viz., Ulick,
the son of Richard Og, was made the Mac William; and
Walter, son of Thomas Burk, was made another Mac
William; but he submitted to Mac William of Clann-
Rickard in consequence of his seniority. Conchobhar
Anabaidh[7] O'Cellaigh was made king in the place of his
own father. Domhnall O'Maille, king of Umhall, died in
hoc anno. Cormac, son of Diarmaid Mac Branan, occisus

---

[4] *Cill-Cruimther-Fiachrach.* "The
church of Cruimther (or presbyter)
Fiachra;" probably a mistake for
Cill-Cruimther-Fraich, or church of
Cruimther Fraech, now Kilcumreragh,
barony of Moycashel, co. Westmeath.

[5] *Pursuing his prey;* i.e. whilst
pursuing a prey that had been taken

from him by the sons of Maelechlainn
Mac Raghnaill.

[6] *After.* ταρέιτ, C. ναρετ, B.
[7] *Conchobhar Anabaidh;* i.e. "Conchobhar (or Conor) the Unripe," or
the Abortive; so called, as it would
appear, from having been born prematurely.

[MS defective. Text supplied from "Annals of Connacht."]

la Conchobap mac Seain mic bpanan. Ap vimop la hApt mac Aipt, pi Laigen, pop cunvae Lochai Zapman in hoc anno; acup a cumain pin la Zallaib Atha cliath pop Zaivelaibh Laigen, ocup mopan vo ceithepnaib congbala na Muman pa Thavg .h. Meachaip vo mapbav ann. Peptelencia magna hi Conmaicnib Cuili, ocup i Clainn Ricaipv. Pilib Apal vo ecc von plaig pin. Uilliac mac Ricaipv, vo clainn Ricaipv, pubmeppup ept pop Tuplach mop .h. Piachpach in hoc anno. Mopp .h. Plannacan Eli in hoc anno. Palgi mac Eogain Ui Conchobaip palgi vo mapbav vatheyp aen upchuip vo poigit gipp in hoc anno. Uilliam occ .h. hUicinn occipup ept o cloinn Cathail na mbanpigec meg Planchaib eivip va abainv, in hoc anno. Mac gilla Brigti na Muigi vo mapbav vo ercup. Cpeacha vo venam vo cloinn Domnaill mic Muipcheaptaig ap Mac n'Diapmava in hoc anno. Cappaic Locha Cé vo gabail vo cloinn Pepgail Mic Diapmava, ocup vaine imva vo mapbav ocup vo bathav ina timchell, ocup luct a coimeva va tinvlacab vo chinv cumav. Peivlimib mac Cathail oicc .h. Conchubaip vo mapbav vo mac .h. Conchubaip vuinv. Zper an Chabain vo venam la cloinn .h. Ruaipc, .i. Tigeapnan occ ocup Aeb bubi ocup Tavg, ocup vo cloinn Meg Sampavan, pop Maelmorva Ua Raigillig, occup poplongpopt ag muintip Mailmorva ap a neip, ocup ni hupupa a apim ap milleb

---

[1] *Under Tadhg O'Meachair.* pa Thavg .h. Meachaip. Repeated in B.

[2] *Turloch-mor of Ui-Fiachrach;* i.e. "the great pool of Ui-Fiachrach-[Aidhne]," now probably Turlough-Keeloge, in the parish of Kinvarra-doorus, barony of Kiltartan, and county of Galway.

[3] *O'Flannagain of Eli.* The sept of O'Flannagain of Eli were also known as the Cenel-Farga, or Kinel-arga, and occupied a district co-extensive with the present barony of Bally-brit, King's County. See O'Donovan's ed. of *O'Huidhrin's Topog. Poem;* Appendix, p. lxxxiv.

[4] *Cathal-na-mbanfigech.* "Cathal (or Charles) of the weaving women." This appears to have been an op-

A.D.
[1401.]

est per dolum by Conchobhar, son of John Mac Branan. A great slaughter *was committed* by Art, son of Art, king of Laighen, in the county of Loch-Garman, in hoc anno; and retaliation for this was committed by the Foreigners of Ath-cliath on the Gaeidhel of Laighen, and a great many of the retained kerns of Mumha, under Tadhg O'Meachair,[1] were slain there. Pestilentia magna in Con-maicne-Cuile, and in Clann-Rickard. Philip Afal died of this plague. Ulick, son of Richard, of the Clann-Rickard, submersus est in Turloch-mor of Ui-Fiachrach,[2] in hoc anno. Mors of O'Flannagain of Eli[3] in hoc anno. Failghe, son of Eoghan O'Conchobhair Failghe, was killed from the effect of one shot of a short arrow in hoc anno. William Og O'hUiginn occisus est by the sons of Cathal-na-mbanfigech[4] Mac Flannchaidh, between[5] two rivers, in hoc anno. Mac Gilla-Brighdi, of the Magh,[6] was killed by a fall. Depredations were committed by the sons of Domhnall, son of Muirchertach,[7] upon Mac Diarmada in hoc anno. The Rock of Loch-Cé was taken by the sons of Ferghal Mac Diarmada, and many persons were slain and drowned around it; and its ward surrendered it for the sake of a bribe. Fedhlimidh, son of Cathal Og O'Concho-bhair, was killed by the son of O'Conchobhair Donn. The attack of the Cabhan was made by the sons of O'Ruairc—viz., Tighernan Og, and Aedh Buidhe, and Tadhg, and by the sons of Mac Samhradhain, on Mael-mordha O'Raighilligh; and Muinter-Maelmordha had an encampment after them; and it is not easy to count the

---

probrious epithet, for the art of weaving was of all trades "of greatest reproach amongst the Irishrye," as Mageoghegan says (Ann. Clonmacnoise, A.D. 1391).

[5] *Between.* erroir, B. earoar, C. Possibly erroir va avainv may be some territorial designation.   -.

[6] *The Magh.* "The Plain;" i.e. Mgah-Finn, otherwise called the

Bredach, and "Keogh's Country," a district in the barony of Athlone, and county of Roscommon. See *Miscell. Irish Archæol. Soc.*, vol. i., p. 77, note[x], and O'Donovan's ed. of *O'Dubhagain's Topog. Poem*; Appendix, p. xlvi.

[7] *Son of Muirchertach.* Muircher-tach O'Conor.

[MS. defective.
Text supplied
from " Annals
of Connacht."]

anoṁoe oo oainiḃ ocuṛ mainiḃ, ocuṛ oo Loiṛceḃ
.xx. beaṛc eciḃ ann ṛa mac in biacaiḃ cainicc oo
conṡnaṁ la muinnciṛ Raiṡilliḃ, ocuṛ oo benaḃ oa
xx'c ech oiḃ beoṛ. Soccaḃ aḃuaċṁaṛ oo eṛṡi
eioiṛ Toiṛṛohelbach mac Neill ṡaiṛḃ mic Ceḃa
.h. Ohoṁnaill, ocuṛ ṛiṡoaṁna na nEoṡanach .i. bṛian
mac Eṇṛi aṁṛeiḃ Ui Neill, ocuṛ ṛoṛlonṡṗuṛc
cloinne Oalaiṡ, ocuṛ Toiṛṛohelbaich mic Neill
ṡaiṛḃ ciṡeaṛna na Conallach, oo innṛaiṡiḃ co oṛoch-
ċoṁaiṛlech oimṛach la mac Eṇṛi, ocuṛ ṛṛaenmaiḃṁ
ṛechṛanach oo ḃen aṛca oo cuṛ lai co láioiṛ
lanchalma. Ocuṛ maṛ nach ceio olc cin inoicheo
na oal can oiṡalcuṛ, ni oechaoaṛ na oala ṛin ṡan
oiṡalcuṛ ṡo oeṡċaṛaiḃ o chenel Conaill; ocuṛ iṛ
aṁlaiḃ oo ṛalaoaṛ na oala ṛin ooiḃ .i. mac Ui
Neill oṛaṡḃail in huachaḃ ṛluaiṡ oeooli, ocuṛ
cṛech Eṇṛi .h. ṡaiṛṁleaḃaiṡ ṛemhe, ocuṛ ṛo benaic
na cṛeacha ṛin oeṛiṁ la Cenel Moan, ocuṛ ṛob e
ṛin anc aicheṛ con anaicheṛ oo Chenel Moan; aṛ ṛo
ṁaṛḃṛam mac .h. ṡaiṛṁleaṡaiḃ ooen ḃuille cloiḃiṁ;
ocuṛ aṛa haichle ṛin oo iaoṛao Cenel Conaill uile
a cimchioll in cṛén ṁilioh, ocuṛ oo maiḃeoh
in móṛ echc ṛin la Toiṛṛoealbhach Ua n'Ooṁnaill; occuṛ oo maṛḃaḃ Niall mac Neill ṡaiṛḃh
.h. Ooṁnaill, ocuṛ Maelṛechlaino mac Ḟlaich-
ḃeaṛcaiṡ .h. Riuaiṛc cuṛ an lai ṛin la hEoṡanċaiḃ;
ocuṛ oo bo lan ṁóṛ a neṛḃaḃa oṛin amach, achc nach
ṛoich a naiṛemh uli aṛ oman a nemilciuṛ.

---

¹ Broke out between. oo eṛṡi eioiṛ;
lit. "arose between," B. oo eiṛṡiḃ
eaoaṛ, C.

² Henry Amhreidh; i.e. "Henry the
Unquiet," or "Uneasy."

³ Clann-Dálaigh. This was the
tribe name of the O'Donnells of Tir-
Conaill, derived from their progenitor,
Dalach, who died in 868.

⁴ Assaulted. oinoṛaiṡiḃ, B. oo
innṛaiṡiḃ, C.

⁵ Completely routed. The literal
translation of the clause ṛṛaenmaiḃṁ
ṛechṛanach oo ḃen aṛca, as in B,
would be "a broken scattering
rout was taken out of them." C reads
ṛṛaenṁaiḃṁ ṛeachṛanaċ oo ḃain
aṛcuḃ.

A.D.
[1401.]

people and valuables that were destroyed there; and twenty loads of clothing were burned there, along with the biatach's son, who came to assist Muinter-Raighilligh; and two score horses were taken from them besides. A horrible war broke out between[1] Toirdhelbhach, the son of Niall Garbh, son of Aedh O'Domhnaill, and the royal heir of the Eoghanachs, i.e. Brian, son of Henry Amhreidh[2] O'Neill; and the fortress of the Clann-Dalaigh,[3] and of Toirdhelbhach, son of Niall Garbh, lord of the Conallians, was ill-advisedly, haughtily, assaulted[4] by the son of Henry, and they were powerfully, bravely, and completely routed,[5] at the beginning of the day. And as no evil goes unrevenged,[6] nor offence unpunished, these transactions did not pass without being promptly avenged by the Cenel-Conaill. And thus it was that these things happened to them, viz. :—the son of O'Neill was left with a small company at the close of the day, and Henry O'Gairmledhaigh's prey before him; and these preys were taken from him by the Cenel-Moan. And this was the joy with sorrow to the Cenel-Moan, for he (*Brian*) killed the son of O'Gairmledhaigh[7] with one stroke of his sword. And immediately afterwards the Cenel-Conaill all closed around[8] the powerful hero, and the great feat was performed[9] by Toirdhelbach O'Domhnaill. And Niall, son of Niall Garbh O'Domhnaill, and Maelsechlainn, son of Flaithbhertach O'Ruairc, were slain in the beginning of that day by the Eoghanachs;[10] and their losses besides were very great; but the enumeration of all cannot be attempted for fear of prolixity.

---

[6] *Unrevenged.* cin inoich, for cin inoicheo (lit. without revenge), B. ᵹan oiᵹailc, C.

[7] *The son of O'Gairmledhaigh.* The Four Mast. call him Henry O'Gairmledhaigh. The name is now written O'Gormley, or Gormley, without the O'.

[8] *Around.* a cimcioll, C. a cimchall, B.

[9] *The great feat was performed;* i.e. the killing of Brian O'Neill. oa maroeoh in mon echc, B. oa maoroiorh an mon euchc, C.

[10] *The Eoghanachs;* i.e. the Cenel-Eoghain, or followers of O'Neill.

[MS. defective. Text supplied from "Annals of Connacht."]

Ɩcɩ. εɴαɩρ ρορ Ɖoṁɴach, ocuρ .xuɩɩ. ꝼuɩρρɩ; Ṁ.cccc.ɩɩ.; xuɩ. cɩcʟɩ ʟuɴαρɩꝼ; x. αɴɴo ɩɴɔɩccɩoɴɩꝼ; xxɩɩ. cɩcʟɩ ꝼoʟαρɩꝼ. Cocαɓ αɓɓαʟ móρ εɩɔɩρ Ɩαρʟα Uρṁuṁαɴ ocuꝼ Ɩαρʟα Ɖeρṁuṁαɴ, ocuꝼ ɩɴ ɔα mαc Uɩʟʟɩαm ɔo ɔoʟ ɔɩbʟɩɴαɓ ɔo ꝼuρcαchc Ɩαρʟα Uρṁuṁαɴ. Ꝼeρɣαʟ mαc Ccеɓα .h. Ꞃuαɩρcc, mαc ρɩ̄ᵹ Ḃρeɩꝼɴe, ocuꝼ αɓɓαρ ρɩ̄ᵹ Uα mḂρɩuɩɴ, ɩɴcερꝼεccuꝼ εꝛc ɩɴα cɩᵹ buɔeɩɴ ʟα ʟochʟαɩɴɴ coʟαch mαc Cαbα peρ ɔoʟum, cαɩccɩᵹɩꝼ ꝼɩα Cαɩρcc, ocuꝼ α αɓʟαcαɓ α mαɴɩꝼcɩρ cᵹʟɩᵹɩ̄ᵹ. Cαρραɩc ʟochα Ce ɔo ᵹαɓαɩʟ ɩcερum ʟα Cochuɓαρ occ mαc Ccеɓα Ṁɩc Ɖɩαρmαɔα co hαρραchcα ɩɴceꝼ̄ ρoρ cʟoɩɴɴ Ꝼερᵹαɩʟ Ṁɩc Ɖɩαρmαɔα. Ɲɩαʟʟ oᵹ, mαc Ɲeɩʟʟ moɩρ, mɩc Ccеɓα moɩρ .h. Ɲeɩʟʟ, αɩρɔρɩ coɩcɩɓ Uʟαɓ, ɔo εcc α ꝼoᵹ̄ṁαρ ɴα bʟɩαɓɴα ꝼα ɩαρ mḃρeɩch bάɩρɩ αρ ɩɴ ꝼαεᵹuʟ ꝼα, ɔo čʟu ocuꝼ ɔeɴech ocuꝼ ɔαρɔɴóρ, o ʟuchc αɴ ɓeαčαɓ ꝼρεcɴαɩꝼc; ocuꝼ cuρρo αɩρchɩꝼɩ Ɖɩα ɔɩα αɴmαɩɴ, ocuꝼ ꝼαcραɩcc. Ṁuɩρcheαρcαch mαc Ɖoɴɔchαɩɓ .h. Ɖuɓɔα, ꝼeρ ɴαρ éρ ɔuɩɴe ꝼɩαṁ ɩm ɴí αρ ɔoṁαɴ, ocuꝼ α ɓeɩɓ αɩce, ɔo εcc ɩɴ boɴo ꝼɩɴe α ꝼαṁραɓ ɴα bʟɩαɓɴα ꝼo, εc ꝼερuʟcuꝼ εꝛc α ɴCcρɔ ɴα ꝼɩαɔ. Ꝑɩʟɩb mαc Ḃρɩαɩɴ ṁóɩρ mεᵹ Ṁαchᵹαṁɴα, αρɔ ꝼɩ Oρᵹɩαʟʟ, ɔo εcc ɩɴ bεɴo ꝼɩɴe, ocuꝼ Ccρɔᵹαʟ mαc Ḃρɩαɩɴ ɴα ɩɴαɔ ɩαραṁ. Cuchoɴɴαchc mαc Ṁαᵹɴuρα mɩc Coɴchoɴɔαchc .h. Ꞃαɩᵹɩʟʟɩ̄ᵹ, ρɩᵹɔαṁɴα Ḃρeɩꝼɴe, ocuꝼ αeɴ ṁαc Uɴα ɩɴᵹɩɴe Coɩρρɔheαʟbαɩᵹ .h. Choɴchoɓαɩρ, ɔo εcc α ɴαɩmρɩρ ρoᵹ̄ṁαɩρ. Ḃρɩαɴ mαc Ɖoṁɴαɩʟʟ .h. Ꝼʟαɩchɓeαρcαɩᵹ, ρɩɔαṁɴα Cαɩρɴ ᵹecαɩɴ, quɩεuɩc ɩɴ Cρɩꝼco. Ṁoρρ Comαɩꝼ mɩc Ꞩeααɩɴ ɴα cuαɩche. Ɩɴραɩᵹɩɓ ʟα cʟoɩɴɴ Coρmαɩc mɩc Ɖoɴɴchαɩɓ mεᵹ Cαρρchαɩᵹ ρoρ

---

1 *Kalends.* The Dom. Letter (A) is added in the margin in B. .

2 *Went.* ɔoɔoʟ, repeated in B and C.

3 *Lochlainn Colach;* i.e. "Lochlainn the Sinful." Instead of coʟαch, as in B, C has εoʟαch, "the Learned."

4 *Mór;* i.e. "the Great." αɴ oɩρ, "of the gold," B.

5 *High King.* αρɔ ρɩ, B. αɩρɔ ρɩᵹ, C.

6 *Of Carn-Gecain.* Cαɩρɴ ᵹεcŭ, B and C. O'Donovan prints this name Cαɩρɴ ᵹεccαɩᵹ, "of Carn-Gegach" (*Four Mast.*, ad an.), and refers to the "Annals of Connacht," where, he says, "this place is called

The kalends[1] of January on Sunday, and the seven-teenth of the moon; M.cccc.ii.; xvi. cycli lunaris; x. anno Indictionis.; xxii. cycli solaris. A terrible war between the Earl of Ur-Mumha and the Earl of Des-Mumha; and the two Mac Williams went[2] together to the assistance of the Earl of Ur-Mumha. Ferghal, son of Aedh O'Ruairc, son of the king of Breifne, and royal heir of the Ui-Briuin, interfectus est in his own house by Lochlainn Colach[3] Mac Caba, per dolum, a fortnight before Easter, and was interred in the monastery of Sligech. The Rock of Loch-Cé was bravely, powerfully taken iterum by Conchobhar Og, son of Aedh Mac Diarmada, against the sons of Ferghal Mac Diarmada. Niall Og, the son of Niall Mor, son of Aedh Mor O'Neill, high king of the province of Uladh, died in the harvest of this year, after bearing the palm in this world for fame, bounty, and excellence, from the people of the present life; and may God and Patrick be merciful to his soul. Muirchertach, son of Donnchadh O'Dubhda, a man who never refused a person regarding anything in the world, if he had it, died in bono fine in the summer of this year, et sepultus est in Ard-na-riadh. Philip, son of Brian Mór[4] Mac Mathghamhna, high king[5] of Oirghiall, died in bono fine; and Ardghal, son of Brian, *was appointed* in his place afterwards. Cuchonnacht, son of Maghnus, son of Cuchon-nacht O'Raighilligh, the royal heir of Breifne, and only son of Una, daughter of Toirdhelbhach O'Conchobhair, died in harvest time. Brian, son of Domhnall O'Flaith-bhertaigh, royal heir of Carn-Gecain,[6] quievit in Christo. Mors of Thomas, son of John-na-tuaithe.[7] The sons of Cormac, son of Donnchadh Mac Carthaigh, attacked the

---

Gno-beg." But this is a mistake, for, although Gno-beg was the name of the southern part of the present barony of Moycullen, in the county of Galway, which was at this time possessed by the O'Flahertys, it is not that by which the territory of the

chieftain of the sept is called in either of the Dublin copies of the "Annals of Connacht."

[7] *John-na-tuaithe;* i.e. "John of the tuath," or territory. His actual name, family, or sept, has not been identified.

[MS. defective. Text supplied from "Annals of Connacht."]

bαροιϑechαιϑ, ocuρ mαιϑni ϑo chαϑαιρτ ρορρο ϑo bαροιϑechαιϑ, ocuρ mαc mιc ϑonϑchαιϑ meϑ Cαρρchαιϑ ϑo ϑαϑαιl αnϑ, ocuρ moραιι ϑα ṁuιιιnτιρ mαιlle ριρ; ocuρ Αρτ .h. Cαοιṁ ϑo ιιαρϑαϑ αnn beoρρ. mαc Cιnαιch αn Τριυchα ϑo mαρϑαϑ ϑα ϑραιϑριϑ ρειn περ ϑolum. ρειϑlιμιϑ mαc Cατhαιl ϑιcc ϑo leccen αρ α lαṁϑechαρ. bριαn mαc Ἡειll οιcc .h. Ἡειll quιeuιτ ιn Cριρτo αρ ράlαιϑ α ατhαρ. muιρcheαρταch Uα ρlαnnαcαn, ραρcιϑeochαn Οlιριnn, quιeuιτ.

κt. θnαιρ ρορ Luαn, ocuρ ochτmαϑ .xx. ρuιρρι; m°.cccc°. τερϑιο; xιιι. cιclι Lunαριρ; xι. αnno ιnϑιc- τιονιρ; xxιιι. cιclι ρolαριρ. mαϑnuρ mαc Conmuιϑι nα cαιlleαϑ, ρι Cιαnαchτα, ṁορτuuρ eρτ. Ƈαϑc mαc Cατhαιl ϑιcc .h. Conchuϑαιρ occιρuρ eρτ lα clοιnn Τοιρρϑheαlbαιϑ οιcc .h. Chonċuϑαιρ, ocuρ lα hθοϑαn mαc ιnϑ αραιϑ .h. Conchoϑαιρ, ρορ mαchαιρe nα nοι- leαϑ, ιn hoc αnno, ρο ρειl bριϑιϑι, eτ ρεριlτuρ eρτ ιllebαιϑ Cατhαιl mιc ϑoṁnαιll, α ρειιατhαρ. Conchu- ϑαρ αnαbαιϑ Uα Cellαιϑ, ρι .h. mαιne, nατhαιρ neṁe nα nϑαιϑeι αρ ϑeoϑαchτ ocuρ cρeαchαραchτ, ϑo ecc ιαρ nonϑαϑ ocuρ ιαρ nαιchριϑe, eτ ρεριlτuρ eρτ α mαnιρτειρ θοιn bαρτι hι τιρ mαne .ι. mαnιρτιρ αρ αρ ṁορ α cummαιn buϑeιn. Cατhαl .h. ϑιμuραιϑ, ριϑ- ϑαṁnα clοιnne mαιluϑρα, occιρuρ eρτ lα ϑαllαιϑ; ocuρ αιchριριϑ αn ριαllαιϑ ϑαnα cuρ mαιch α enech ocuρ α enϑnαṁ. bρίαn .h. ϑιμuράιϑ, α ϑερϑρατhαιρ, ϑo ṁαρϑαϑ ϑo ϑαllαιϑ ι cιnϑ mιρ ιαρριι. ρeϑlιμιϑ Uα ϑιμuραιϑ ϑo mαρϑαϑ lα ϑαllαιϑ beoρ. ρινϑ- ϑuαlα, ιnϑeαn Τοιρρϑheαlbαιϑ .h. Chonċuϑαιρ, uxoρ

---

1 *Mac Cinaith of the Triucha.* Mac Kenna of Trough, in the county of Monaghan.

2 *Cathal Og;* i.e. Cathal Og ("the younger") O'Conor, son of Cathal O'Conor, king of Connacht in 1324.

3 *Immediately after.* αρ ράτ (for αρ ράlαιϑ; lit. "at the heels").

4 *Archdeacon.* ραρcιϑeochαn, as if for "parochiæ diaconus," B and C.

5 *Kalends.* The Dom. Letter (G) is added in the margin in B.

6 *Cumaighe-na-cailledh;* i.e. "Cumaighe (canis campi) of the wood;" Cumaighe O'Cathain, otherwise Cooey O'Kane.

A.D.
[1402.]

Barretts, but were defeated by the Barretts, and the grandson of Donnchadh Mac Carthaigh was captured there, and a great number of his people along with him ; and Art O'Caimh was furthermore slain there. Mac Cinaith of the Triucha[1] was slain by his own brothers per dolum. Fedhlimidh, son of Cathal Og,[2] was released from his captivity. Brian, son of Niall Og O'Neill, quievit in Christo immediately after[3] his father. Muirchertach O'Flannagain, archdeacon[4] of Oilfinn, quievit.

[1403.]

The kalends[5] of January on Monday, and the twenty-eighth of the moon; M°.cccc°. tertio ; xvii. cycli lunaris ; xi. anno Indictionis ; xxiii. cycli solaris. Maghnus, son of Cumaighe-na-cailledh,[6] king of Cianachta, mortuus est. Tadhg, son of Cathal Og O'Conchobhair, occisus est by the sons of Toirdhelbhach Og O'Conchobhair Donn, and by Eoghan Mac-in-abaid[7] O'Conchobhair on Machaire-nan-oilech, in hoc anno, about the festival of Brighid, et sepultus est in the tomb of Cathal, the son of Domhnall, his grandfather.[8] Conchobhar Anabaidh[9] O'Cellaigh, king of Ui-Maine, the poisonous serpent of the Gaeidhel for vigour and depredation, died after unction and after penitence, et sepultus est in the monastery of John the Baptist[10] in Tir-Maine, i.e. a monastery to which his own munificence was great. Cathal O'Dimusaigh, royal heir of Clann-Maelughra, occisus est by Foreigners ; and the people report that his bounty and prowess were great. Brian O'Dimusaigh, his brother, was slain by Foreigners before the end of a month afterwards. Fedhlimidh O'Dimusaigh was also slain by Foreigners. Finnghuala, the daughter of Toirdhelbhach O'Conchobhair, uxor of

---

[7] *Mac-in-abaid;* i.e. "the son of the Abbot."

[8] *His grandfather.* α ⟨enαⱦαⱞ, B. α αⱦαⱨ, C.

[9] *Conchobhar Anabaidh;* i.e. " Conchobhar the Unripe;" so called, apparently, from having been prematurely

born. See him already mentioned above under the year 1401.

[10] *Monastery of John the Baptist.* This monastery was situated at Rindown, or Saint John's, in the barony of Athlone, and county of Roscommon.

[MS. defective. Text supplied from "Annals of Connacht."]

Ⅿαιʟecɦʟαιɴꝺ .ɦ. Ceʟʟαιɫ ꝛι Uα Ⅿɑιɴe, αɴ ḃeɴ ꝛοḃꝛeꝛꝛ
cʟú ꝺο bι α ɴαeɴ αιⅿꝛιꝛ ꝛꝛιαꝛι ιɴꝺ Єιꝛιɴɴ uʟι, ꝗuιeuιϲ.
8ʟuαɫαḃ αḃḃαʟ ⅿόꝛ ʟα Uα Coɴcɦοḃαιꝛ ɴꝺοɴɴ, οcuꝛ
ʟα Ⅿuιꝛcɦeαꝛϲαcɦ ⅿbαcαcɦ ⅿαc ꝺοṁɴαιʟʟ, ϲιɫeαꝛꝛɴα
8ʟιccιḃ, ιɴ uαcɦϲαꝛ Coɴɴαϲϲ, οcuꝛ ϲιɫeαꝛꝛuꝛ Єοɫαιɴ
.ɦ.Ⅿαꝺαḃαɴ ⅿιc Ⅿuꝛcɦαιḃ ꝺο ɫαḃαιʟ ꝺοιḃ ꝺοɴ ꝺuʟαḃ
ꝛιɴ; οcuꝛ ꝺοʟ ꝺοιḃ α cʟαιɴꝺ Rιcαιꝛꝺ ιαꝛαṁ ꝺο coɴɫ-
ɴαṁ ʟα ɦUιʟʟeαc ⅿαc Rιcαιꝛꝺ ιɴ αḃαιɫ Ⅿαιɴecɦαιꝛꝺ;
οcuꝛ ꝺο ɫαḃαꝺαꝛ ϲꝛeɴ ꝺοɴ ϲuꝛαꝛ ꝛιɴ αꝛ Ⅿαιɴecɦαιḃ,
ꝗcuꝛ ϲαɴcαϲαꝛ cάɴ ϲοbeιⅿ cαɴ ϲubαιꝛϲ ꝺια ϲιɫιḃ
ιαꝛꝛιɴ. Ⅿuιꝛcɦeαꝛϲαcɦ bαcαcɦ, ⅿαc ꝺοṁɴαιʟʟ, ⅿιc
Ⅿuιꝛcɦeαꝛϲαιɫ .ɦ. Cɦοɴcɦuḃαιꝛ, ϲιɫeαꝛɴα ιοcɦϲαιꝛ
Coɴɴαcɦϲ, ꝺο écc ιαꝛ ⅿḃꝛeιϲ bαꝛι αꝛ α ḃιḃḃαḃαιḃ ιɴ
cecɦ αιꝛꝺ ꝺeꝛιɴɴ uιʟe, ιɴ αιɴe ιαꝛ ꝛeιʟ Ⅿιcɦeιʟ.
Ⅿuιꝛcɦeαꝛϲαcɦ cʟeꝛeϲ Uα ꝺuḃꝺα, ϲοɫα eꝛꝛuιc cɦιʟʟe
ɦαʟʟαιḃ, ꝗuιeuιϲ. Coccαḃ ⅿόꝛ ꝺο ꝛάꝛ eιꝺιꝛ ḃꝛeιꝛ-
ɴecɦαιḃ οcuꝛ Cʟαɴɴ ꝺοɴɴcɦαιḃ ιɴ ɦοc αɴɴο, ꝺαꝛ ⅿαꝛ-
ḃαḃ ꝺαιɴe ⅿαιϲɦe, .ι. Ϲοⅿόʟϲαcɦ όcc ⅿαc Ϲοⅿuʟϲαιɫ
ⅿeɫ ꝺοꝛcɦαιḃ, ꝺeοḃꝛʟαιϲɦ cɦeɴeʟ ʟuαcɦαιɴ, ꝺο ⅿαꝛ-
ḃαꝺɦ eαϲοꝛꝛα, οcuꝛ Ⅿuιꝛcɦeαꝛϲαcɦ οɫ .ɦ. ɦeιʟιḃι,
bꝛuɫαιḃ ceαꝺαcɦ coɴαιcɦ, ꝺο ṁαꝛḃαḃ αꝛ ιɴ coccαḃ
ꝛιɴ. Ⅿαeʟⅿοꝛḃα, ⅿαc Coɴcoɴɴαϲϲ ⅿιc ɫιʟʟα 1ꝛα
ꝛuαιḃ, ꝺο ɫαḃαιʟ ϲιɫeαꝛɴαιꝛ ⅿuιɴϲιꝛe Ⅿαιʟιⅿοꝛḃα ιɴ
ɦοc αɴɴο. Єοɫαɴ ⅿαc 8eοαιɴ .ɦ. Ruαιꝛc ꝺο ɫαḃαιʟ ʟα
Ⅿαeʟeαϲʟαιɴɴ .ɦ. Ruαιꝛc; αɫuꝛ 8eααɴ ⅿαc Ϲαιḃɫ ⅿιc
Uαʟɫαꝛɫ .ɦ. Ruαιꝛc ꝺο ɫαḃαιʟ οcuꝛ ꝺο ʟοϲ ʟα ⅿuιɴϲιꝛ
Ⅿαιʟⅿοꝛḃα; οcuꝛ coccαḃ ꝺο eꝛɫι αꝛꝛιꝺe eιꝺιꝛ ṁuιɴɴ-
ϲιꝛ Rαιɫιʟʟιɫ οcuꝛ ⅿuιɴϲιꝛ Ruαιꝛc; οcuꝛ Ⅿαϲɫαṁαιɴ
ⅿαc ɫιʟʟα Cꝛιοꝛꝺ ⅿιc ꝼʟαιϲɦḃeαꝛϲαιɫ Ⅿιc Cάbα ꝺο
ʟοϲ ιɴ ʟά ꝛιɴ ʟα ⅿuιɴɴϲιꝛ .ɦ. Ruαιꝛc, οcuꝛ αꝛ αɴꝛꝺ

---

1 *Best reputation.* ꝛοḃ ꝛeαꝛꝛ cʟú,
C. ꝛοbe ꝛeꝛꝛ cʟú οcuꝛ cʟ., B.

2 *All.* uʟι, B. uιʟe, C.

3 *Son of Domhnall;* i.e. the son of
Domhnall O'Conor Sligo, who was
the son of Muirchertach.

4 *Against.* ιɴ αḃαιɫ, B. αɴαɫαιꝺ,
C.

5 *After triumphing.* ιαꝛ ⅿḃꝛeιϲ
bαꝛι, B. ιαꝛ ⅿḃꝛeιϲ bάιꝛe, C.

6 *O'hElidhe.* This name is written
ɦ.ɦeʟιꝺι in B, and ɦ. ɦeιʟιꝺe in

Maelechlainn O'Cellaigh, king of Ui-Maine, the woman of best reputation[1] in her time in all[2] Erinn, quievit. A very great hosting by O'Conchobhair Donn, and by Muirchertach Bacach, son of Domhnall,[3] lord of Sligech, into Upper Connacht, and the lordship of Eoghan O'Ma-dadhain, the son of Murchadh, was seized by them on this occasion. And they afterwards went into Clann-Rickard, to assist Ulick, the son of Rickard, against[4] the Ui-Maine ; and they obtained sway over the Ui-Maine on this expedition, and returned home subsequently without blemish or mischance. Muirchertach Bacach, son of Domhnall, son of Muirchertach O'Conchobhair, lord of Lower Connacht, died, after triumphing[5] over his enemies in every part of all Erinn, the Friday after the festival of Michael. Muirchertach Clerech O'Dubhda, bishop-elect of Cill-Alaidh, quievit. A great war arose between the Breifnians and the Clann-Donnchaidh in hoc anno, when noble men were slain; viz., Tomaltach Og, son of Tomaltach Mac Dorchaidh, the last chief of Cenel-Luachain, was killed between them ; and Muir-chertach Og O'hElidhe,[6] a wealthy brughaidh-cedach,[7] was killed in that war. Maelmordha, the son of Cucon-nacht, son of Gilla-Isa Ruadh,[8] assumed the lordship of Muinter-Maelmordha in hoc anno. Eoghan, son of John O'Ruairc, was taken prisoner by Maelechlainn O'Ruairc, and John, the son of Tadhg, son of Ualgharg O'Ruairc, was taken prisoner, and wounded, by Muinter-Mael-mordha ; and a war arose[9] out of this between Muinter-Raighilligh and Muinter-Ruairc; and Mathghamhain, son of Gilla-Christ, son of Flaithbhertach Mac Caba,[10] was wounded on that day by O'Ruairc's people : and it was

---

C. It is now written O'Healy, or Healy, without the O'.

[7] *Brughaidh-ceduch.* The Brugh-aidh-cedach was an opulent farmer of great influence and authority.

[8] *Gilla-Isa Ruadh.* Gilla-Isa Ruadh (Gelasius the Red) O'Reilly.

[9] *Arose.* ꝺo eꞃᵹı, B. ꝺo eıꞃᵹıꝺ, C.

[10] *Mac Caba.* Mac Cabe. mc Cábα, C. mc Cαpα, B.

[MS. defective. Text supplied from "Annals of Connacht."]

το ponnaꝺ ꝼꞃeꞃ an Chaꝺain aṁail a ꝺuꝺꞃamaꞃ ꞃo-ṁainꝺ, maꝺ iaꞃ napaili liuꝺaꞃ. Muiꞃcheaꞃtach ꝼaꞃꝺ Ua Sechnuꞃaiꝼ, ꞃiꝼꝺaṁna Ua Ꝑiachꞃach Cιꝺne, το maꞃꝺaꝺ la Mainechaibh. Seaan buꝺe mac Seoiꞃꞃꞃ a ꝺuꞃc occiꞃuꞃ eꞃꞇ o clannmaicne Θοꝶain .h. Cellaiꝼ, ocuꞃ o cloiꞃꞃ hobeꞃꝺ Ꝺalaꞇun.

Κt. Θnaiꞃ ꝼoꞃ Maꞃꞇ, ocuꞃ naeṁaꝺ uaꞇhaꝺ ꝼuiꞃꞃι ; Mᵒ.ccccᵒ.iꞃꞃ. ; xuꞃꞃ. cicli lunaꞃiꞃ ; xꞃ. ιꞃꝺιcꞇιoniꞃ ; xxιιꞃ. cicli ꞃolaꞃiꞃ. Comaꞃ Ꝺaꞃeꝺ, eaꞃꞃocc Oliꝼιꞃꝺ, ꞃaι Θꞃeꞃꝺ, ιꞃ Cꞃιꞃꞇo quιeuιꞇ a neꞃꞃach na bliaꝺna ꞃo, eꞇ ꞃepulꞇuꞃ eꞃꞇ ι nꝏiꞃeṁ Lοcha Con. Moꞃꞃ Maιl-eaꞇlaιꞃꞃ meꝶ Oꞃechꞇaiꝼ, ꝺux muιncꞃι Raꝺuιꝺ, ιꞃιꞃ ꝺoṁnach meoꝺanach ꝺon chaꞃoccuꞃ, eꞇ ꞃepulꞇuꞃ eꞃꞇ aꞃRuꞃ Comman. Conchuꝺaꞃ occ mac Ccꝺa mιc Ꝺiaꞃιnaꝺa, ꞃι Moιꝶι Luιꞃꝶ, ocuꞃ beιꞇιꞃ aꞃ beoꞇ-achꞇ, το ecc eιꝺιꞃ ꝼeιl Mιcheιl ocuꞃ ꞃamhaιn ; ocuꞃ Caꝺꝶ mac Ccꝺa ιneιc Ꝺiaꞃmaꝺa το ꞃιꝶaꝺ ιꞃa ιꞃaꝺ cιmchell na ꞃaιꞃlιꞃa ιaꞃꞃιꞃ. Coꞃmac Mac Ꝺiaꞃmaꝺa το maꞃꝺaꝺ aꞃ ιꞃꞃuaꝶaꝺ a claιꞃꞃ Rιcaιꞃꝺ la maꞃc-ꞃluaꝼ cloιꞃꞃe Rιcaιꞃꝺ ocuꞃ Cuaꝺmuṁaꞃ aꞃchena, ι cιꞃꝺ míꞃ ꝺon ꞃοꝶmaꞃ ceaꝺna ꞃιꞃ ; ocuꞃ ꝺob e ꞃιꞃ an baιnne ꞃιa ꝼꞃaιꞃ το Moιꝶ Luιꞃꝶ .ι. Caꞇhal ꞃιa Conchuꝺaꞃ Iꞃꝶen .h. Chonchuꝺaiꞃ ꞃaιlꝶι .ι. ben ꝶιlla Ꝑaꝺꞃuιcc .h. Moꞃꝺa, quιeuιꞇ. Caꞇhal mac Ꝺonꝺchaιꝺ moꞃꞇuuꞃ eꞃꞇ ι Ꝑuꞃꞇ ιꞃoꞃι ιꞃa loꞃꝶꞃuꞃꞇ ꝼeιꞃ, ιaꞃ ιꞃbuaιꝺ naιꞇh-ꞃιꝶhe ; eꞇ ꞃepulꞇuꞃ eꞃꞇ ι Cιll mιc Callaιꞃ. Ꝺoṁnall

---

[1] *The attack of the Cabhan.* The battle, or attack, of Cavan, referred to above under the year 1401.

[2] *The Clannmaicne-Eoghain O'Cellaigh;* i.e. the descendants of Eoghan O'Cellaigh (or Owen O'Kelly), who was the son of Domhnall Mór, son of Tadhg Taillten O'Kelly, sl. 1180. The name of Clannmaicne-Eoghain is preserved in that of the barony of Clonmacnowen in the county of Galway, which is erroneously printed "Clonmacoow" in Beaufort's "Civil and Ecclesiastical map of Ireland."

[3] *Tuesday.* The Dom. Letters (F E) are added in the margin in B.

[4] *In Airemh-Locha-Con.* ιꞃ Ꝏiꞃeṁ Lοcha Con, C. ιꞃꝺ Ꝏꞃem Lοcha Cū, B. Airemh-Locha-Con (Airemh of Loch-Con), now called Errew, is a peninsula extending into Loch-Con, in the parish of Crossmolina, barony of Tirawley, and county of Mayo. The Four Mast. write the name Airech-Locha-Con.

[5] *Between.* eιꝺιꞃ, B. eaꝺaꞃ, C.

[6] *About.* cιmchell, B. cιmcιoll, C.

on this occasion, according to other books, the attack of the Cabhan[1] was made, as we have related above. Muirchertach Garbh O'Sechnusaigh, royal heir of Ui-Fiachrach-Aidhne, was killed by the Ui-Maine. John Buidhe, son of Seoinin Burk, occisus est by the Clann-maicne-Eoghain O'Cellaigh,[2] and by the sons of Hubert Dalton.

The kalends of January on Tuesday,[3] and the ninth of the moon; M°.cccc°. iiii.; xviii. cycli lunaris; xii. Indictionis; xxiiii. cycli solaris. Thomas Barrett, bishop of Oilfinn, the most eminent man in Erinn, in Christo quievit in the spring of this year, et sepultus est in Airemh-Locha-Con.[4] Mors of Maelechlainn Mac Oirechtaigh, dux of Muinter-Raduibh, on the middle Sunday of Lent, et sepultus est in Ros-Comain. Conchobhar Og, son of Aedh Mac Diarmada, king of Magh-Luirg, and a bear in vigour, died between[5] Michaelmas and Allhallowtide; and Tadhg, son of Aedh Mac Diarmada, was afterwards made king in his place, about[6] Allhallowtide. Cormac Mac Diarmada was slain in an onset in Clann-Rickard, by the cavalry of Clann-Rickard, and of Tuadh-Mumha besides, before the end of a month of the same harvest; and that[7] was the "drop before a shower"[8] for Magh-Luirg.[9] i.e. Cathal before Conchobhar.[10] The daughter of O'Conchobhair Failghe,[11] i.e. the wife of Gilla-Patraic O'Mordha, quievit. Cathal Mac Donnchaidh mortuus est in Port-insi, in his own fortress, after the victory of penitence; et sepultus est in Cill-mic-Callain.[12] Domhnall,

---

[7] *That.* eրin, C. eրein, B.

[8] *Drop before a shower.* For the meaning of this phrase, see vol. i., p. 417, note 6.

[9] *For Magh - Luirg.* ꝺo Nloiᵹ Luiⱄᵹ. B. ꝺo Níhoiᵹi Luiⱄᵹ, C.

[10] *Cathal before Conchobhar.* - The name Cathal is probably a mistake for that of Cormac, whose death was the "drop" that preceded the "shower"

of misfortune soon to follow with the death of Conchobhar Mac Diarmada.

[11] *Failghe.* ᚠⱥiłᵹi, C. ᚠⱥłᵹi, B.

[12] *Cill-mic-Caillin.* cill ᚋc caℓℓ., B and C. Apparently Cill-mic-Callain, or Kilmacallen, in the barony of Tirerrill, county of Sligo, a few miles to the north-east of Port-insi, or Portinch, where Cathal Mac Donnchaidh died.

[MS. defective.
Text supplied
from " Annals
of Connacht."]

mac Θnρι Uι Neill το ʒαϐαιl ριʒι ιn choιcιϐ. Οccιρυρ
ερτ mac Œenʒυρα mιc Ɗoṁnαll óιcc mιc Ɗoṁnαιll
lα Ɗonɗchαϐ Uα Cellαιʒ. ʒallρα ιmϐα ιnɗ Θριnn, ocuρ
ʒαlαρ nα lερταε co ρunɗραϐach, ιn hoc αnno. Mυρ-
chαϐ occ mac Conchobαιρ mιc Cαϐαιl mορτuuρ ερτ.
Οccιρυρ ερτ Τomαρ .h. Cenɗετιʒ, lετρι Uρṁuṁan, lα
Ɗoṁnαll mac Ριlιρ .h. Cenɗετιʒ. Mαιϐm Œchα ɗuιϐ
lα ʒιllα Ραɗρυιʒ.h.Morϐα, ρι Lαιʒρι, ρορ ʒallαιϐ, ocuρ
mοραn το mαρϐαϐ αnn, ocuρ eιch ιmϐα ocuρ αρm ocuρ
éɗeϐ το beιn τιϐ beoρ. Ɗonɗϐαϐ mac.h.Cenɗετιʒ ɗuιnn
το ecc hι lαṁɗιchuρ αc α ϐραιϐριϐ buϐeιn ιn hoc αnno.
Ιαρlα Uρṁuṁan, cenn cρoϐachτα nα hΘρenɗ, quιeuιτ.
Mac Cαthṁαιl, ɗux cenel Ϝeραϐαιʒ, ιnτeρρecτuρ ερτ.
Ɗonɗchαϐ ban .h. Mαιlchonαιρe, ollαṁ ριl Muιρeϐαιʒ
muιlleαϐαn ρe ρenchuρ, mορτuuρ ερτ. ʒιllα ɗubιn
mac Cρuιτιn, ollαmh Τuαϐṁuṁan ρe ρenchuρ, mορτuuρ ερτ. Ϝeιϐlιmιϐ .h. Τuαchαιl, ρι .h. Muιρeϐαιʒ,
mορτuuρ ερτ. Cerϐαll Uα Ɗαlαιʒ, ollαṁ ɗαnα Cor-
cumɗρuαϐ, quιeuιτ. Ϝιnʒen mac Θoʒαιn meʒ Cαρτhαιʒ
mορτuuρ ερτ. Mαcραιth .h. 8uιlleαϐαn mορτuuρ ερτ.
Ɗoṁnαll mac Ɗonɗchαϐ .h. Ɗαlαιʒ, .ι. bolʒ αn ɗαnα,
mορτuuρ ερτ. Ϝlαnn occ mac 8eoαn Uι [Ɗoṁnαllαιn,
ollαṁ ριl Muιρeαɗαιʒ ι nɗάn], mορτuuρ ερτ. Cormac,
mac Ueϐu, mιc Ϝeιϐlιmιϐ, mιc ʒιllα Ιρα ρuαιϐ .h.Rαι-
ʒιllιϐ, mορτuuρ ερτ. Cocαϐ ɗeρʒι eιɗιρ Maʒ Cαρρ-
thαιʒ ocuρ .h. 8uιlleαϐαn buϐι, ocuρ clαnn Ɗιαρmαɗα
Meʒ Cαρρτhαιʒ ; ocuρ Τoιρρɗhelbαch meιth mac
Mαthʒαṁnα ιnα lonʒρeoιρ αʒ Maʒ Cαρρτhαιʒ ιn ταn
ριn ; ocuρ bρeιth το αρ .h. 8uιlleαϐαn αρ ραιρρʒe ocuρ
αρ ϐlαιnn Ɗιαρmαɗα τιϐlιnαιϐ, ocuρ .h. 8uιlleϐαn το

---

[1] *Of the Province*; i.e. of Ulster.
ιn choιcιϐ, B. ιn cóιʒιϐ, C.

[2] *Especially the bed - distemper.*
ʒαlαρ nα lερταε co ρunɗιραϐach,
B. ʒαlαρ nα leαρϐα ʒo ρonραϐαϐ,
C. Probably some kind of ague.

[3] *Cathal*; i.e. Cathal O'Conchobhair.

[4] *Half-king.* leτρι, B. leιϐ ριʒ, C.

[5] *Race of Muiredhach Muillethan.*
See note [3], p. 550, vol. i.

[6] *In history.* ρe ρenchuρ; repeated
in B.

[7] *Bolg-an-dána*; i.e. "the budget
of song."

son of Henry O'Neill, assumed the sovereignty of the Province.[1] The son of Aenghus, son of Domhnall Og Mac Domhnaill, occisus est by Donnchadh O'Cellaigh. Numerous diseases in Erinn, and especially the bed distemper,[2] in hoc anno. Murchadh Og, son of Conchobar, son of Cathal,[3] mortuus est. Thomas O'Cennedigh, half-king[4] of Ur-Mumha, occisus est by Domhnall, son of Philip O'Cennedigh. The victory of Ath-dubh by Gilla-Patraic O'Mordha, king of Laighis, over Foreigners, where many were slain; and a great quantity of horses, arms, and clothing were moreover taken from them. Donnchadh, son of O'Cennedigh Donn, died whilst imprisoned by his own brothers in hoc anno. The Earl of Ur-Mumha, head of the prowess of Erinn, quievit. Mac Cathmhail, dux of Cenel-Feradhaigh, interfectus est. Donnchadh Ban O'Maelchonaire, professor in history of the race of Muiredhach Muillethan,[5] mortuus est. Gilla-Dubhin Mac Cruitin, professor of Tuadh-Mumha in history,[6] mortuus est. Fedhlimidh O'Tuathail, king of Ui-Muiredhaigh, mortuus est. Cerbhall O'Dalaigh, ollamh of poetry of Corcumruadh, quievit. Finghin, son of Eoghan Mac Carthaigh, mortuus est. Macraith O'Suillebhain mortuus est. Domhnall, son of Donnchadh O'Dalaigh, i.e. Bolg-an-dána,[7] mortuus est. Flann Og, son of John [O'Domhnallain, ollamh of Sil-Muiredhaigh in poetry],[8] mortuus est. Cormac, son of Aedh, son of Fedhlimidh, son of Gilla-Isa Ruadh O'Raighilligh, mortuus est.[9] A war arose between[10] Mac Carthaigh and O'Suillebhain Buidhe, and the sons of Diarmaid Mac Carthaigh; and Mac Carthaigh's naval officer at that time was Toirdhelbhach Meith[11] Mac Mathghamhna, who came up at sea with O'Suillebhain, and the sons of Diarmaid, together; and O'Suillebhain

---

[8] *In poetry.* The words enclosed within brackets in the text, omitted in B and C, are supplied from the Annals of the Four Masters.

[9] *Mortuus est.* Omitted in B.

[10] *A war arose between.* cocaó oen̄ɟı eivoıp, B. coɟaɗ ɗoıp̄ɟıɗ eaɗap, C.

[11] *Toirdhelbhach Meith;* i.e. Toirdhelbhach the Fat (or Gross).

[MS. defective.
Text supplied
from "Annals
of Connacht."]

Ḃaᴛhaᴅ, ocuʃ Ꝺonᴅchaḃ mac Ꝺiaʃmaᴅa ocuʃ Ꝺoṁnall
mac Eoʒain ᴅo ʒaḃail ᴅo ḃeoʃʃ. Ꝺnᴅʃuu ḃaʃoiᴅ ᴅo
ṁaʃḃaḃ la hiḃ Muʃchaᴅha. Eoʒan mac Muʃchaḃ
mic Caᴛhaiʃ .h. Conchoḃaiʃ ʃalʒiʒ ᴅo maʃḃaḃ la hiaʃla
Chille ᴅaʃa. Huala inʒhean Ꝺoṁnaill mic Muiʃ-
cheaʃᴛaiʒ .h. Conchoḃaiʃ, ben Ꝼeʃʒail mic Coʃmaic
mic Ꝺonnchaiḃ, quieuiᴛ. Uilliam .h. Ꝺeoʃain, ollaṁ
bʃeiᴛeaṁan na Caeṁanach, moʃᴛuuʃ eʃᴛ. Ꝼeʃʒal
mac Ceboiᴅ .h. Mailmuaiḃ moʃᴛuuʃ eʃᴛ. Ꝺonᴅca-
ᴛhaiʒ mac Muiʃeḃaiʒ meʒ Senlaoiḃ, bʃuʒaiḃ ceaᴅach
conaich ᴅo Coʃca aᴛhᴄ̈lann, ocuʃ lán ʃeʃ ʒʃaḃa ᴅo
Ruaiḃʃi .h. Conchuḃaiʃ, ᴅo ʃiʒ Conᴅaᴄ̈ᴛ, ocuʃ ʃeʃ ʃoʃ
aʃaḃi cach uile ʃonaʃ co a ḃaʃ, ocuʃ ʃuaiʃ loʒhaᴅh
a ṗeacaᴅh ʃa ᴅeoiḃ i cuiʃᴛ an ṗaʃa, quieuiᴛ an la
iaʃ ʃeil Micheil.

Ḳᴛ. Enaiʃ ʃoʃ Ꝺaʃᴅain, ocuʃ ʃicheᴅ ʃuiʃʃi; M°.cccc°.
u.; ɑɪɑ. cicli lunaʃiʃ; ɑiii. inᴅicᴛioniʃ; ɑɑu. cicli ʃolaʃiʃ.
Moʃʃ Ꝼeʃʒal mic Coʃmaic mic Ꝺonnchaiḃ, ʃiʒᴅaṁna
.h. nOiliella, in hoc anno. Riʃᴅeʃᴅ Ḃuᴛileʃ ʃuʃiʃaiᴛi
coʃ cʃuaiḃ ᴅo maʃḃaḃ la mac Ꝼachᴛna .h. Moʃᴅa.
Cocaḃ moʃ aʒ Mac Muʃchaᴅa ʃe ʒallaiḃ, co ᴛaiɴcc
cʃeaᴄ̈loʃcaḃ na cunᴅae miaḃcha; aʒuʃ Ceᴛhuʃlach ocuʃ
ᴅiʃiʃᴛ Ꝺiaʃmaᴅa ᴅo loʃcaḃ leiʃ. Caᴛhal mac Ꝺuinᴅ
meʒ Saṁʃaḃain moʃᴛuuʃ eʃᴛ in hoc anno. Ꝺonᴅchaḃ
cam .h. lochlainᴅ, ʃi Coʃcumʃuaḃ, occiʃuʃ eʃᴛ o
clainn Mailechlainᴅ .h. lochlainᴅ an eiʃic a naᴛhaʃ
ʃein. Riʃᴛaʃᴅ Maʒ Raʒnaill, aḃḃaʃ ᴛaiʃiḃ na

---

[1] Ui-Murchadha; i.e. the O'Murphys,
a family, or sept, located in the east of
the present county of Wexford, where
the name O'Murphy (or Murphy,
without the O') is still pretty numerous.

[2] The Caemhanachs. The Cavan-
aghs, or Kavanaghs. The Four Masters say ollaṁ Laiʒen, i.e. "ollamh
of Leinster," for the Kavanaghs were

at this time regarded by the Irish as
the principal family of Leinster.

[3] Brughaidh-cedach. See note [2],
p. 396, vol. i.; and note [7], p. 105 supra.

[4] Of Corca - Achlann. Coʃca
aᴛhᴄ̈laoiḃ, C. Coʃca aᴛhcᴛ̈, B.
See note [10], p. 596, vol. i.

[5] Thursday. The Dom. Letter (D)
is added in the margin.

[6] Cos-cruaidh; i.e. "hard-foot."

was drowned; and Donnchadh, son of Diarmaid, and Domhnall son of Eoghan, were furthermore captured by him. Andrew Barrott was slain by the Ui-Murchadha.[1] Eoghan, son of Murchadh, son of Cathair O'Conchobhair Failghe, was killed by the Earl of Cill-dara. Nuala, daughter of Domhnall, son of Muirchertach O'Conchobhair, wife of Ferghal, son of Cormac Mac Donnchaidh, quievit. William O'Deorain, ollamh-brehon of the Caeulhanachs,[2] mortuus est. Ferghal, son of Tibbot O'Maelmhuaidh, mortuus est. Donncathaigh, son of Muiredhach Mac Senlaich, a wealthy brughaidh-cedach[3] of Corca-Achlann,[4] and full servant of trust to Ruaidhri O'Conchobhair, king of Connacht, and a man who enjoyed every happiness up to his death, and who ultimately obtained remission of his sins in the Pope's court, quievit the day after the festival of Michael.

The kalends of January on Thursday,[5] and the twentieth of the moon; M°.cccc°.v.; xix. cycli lunaris; xiii. Indictionis; xxv. cycli solaris. Death of Ferghal, son of Cormac Mac Donnchaidh, royal heir of Ui-nOilella, in hoc anno. Richard Butler, who was usually called Coscruaidh,[6] was killed by the son of Fachtna O'Mordha. A great war *was waged* by Mac Murchadha with the Foreigners, from which resulted the burning of the Contae-riabhach;[7] and Cetharlach and Disert-Diarmada were burned by him. Cathal, son of Donn Mac Samhradhain, mortuus est in hoc anno. Donnchadh Cam O'Lochlainn, king of Corcumruadh, occisus est by the sons of Maelechlainn O'Lochlainn, in retaliation[8] for their own father.[9] Richard[10] Mac Raghnaill, heir to the

A.D. [1404.]

[1405.]

---

[7] *Of the Contae-riabhach.* Cunoae puabcha, C. The last word (puabhcha, gen. of riabhach), is omitted in B. The present county of Wexford was so called by the Irish speaking people in the fifteenth and sixteenth centuries.

[8] *In retaliation.* an eipic, C. an epaicc, B.
[9] *Their own father.* Maelechlainn Cam (the Crooked) O'Lochlainn, slain A.D. 1389, by his own brother.
[10] *Richard.* Ripcapo, C. Ripoeo, B.

[MS. defective.
Text supplied
from "Annals
of Connacht."]

neolurach, quieuic iar nól uirci becha ʒo himurcach,
ocur vob uircce marbca vo Rirvaro. Ⴀiarmaiv
mac Ⴀonvchaiỏ .h. Chončuỏair Ciarraiʒe vo marỏaỏ
la Mac Muirir Ciarraiʒe. Ⴀomnall occ .h. Ruaire
morcuur erc. Milir Ⴀalacun vo marỏaỏ lar na
Ⴀalacunacha, ocur la cloinn hobervo Ⴀálacun.
Cairlen nua .h. Finvacain vo bloỏaỏ la ỏranachaiỏ
in hoc anno. Inʒen Ⴀomnaill .h. ỏriain, ben Pilip
mic Macʒamna vuinv .h. Cenneviʒ, morcua erc.
Ʒilla na naem mac Ruaiỏri .h. Cianan, ollam ren-
chaỏa rer Manach, vo écc co hobanv a ciʒ mic Nevi
.h. mailconaire hi Cairrri ʒaỏra, ocur a aỏlacaỏ
a mainirceir Lecracha. Muirchearcach .h. Ⴀuiỏ-
ʒinvan quieuic. Sluaʒaỏ Ⴀrciʒ la Ⴀavʒ mac
nⴀiarmava, la riʒ Moiʒi Luirʒ, viarraỏ a ciʒ-
earnair ar cloinn Conchuỏair mic Ⴀaichliʒ ocur
ror luchc Ⴀrciʒ archena, amail roba vual vⴀir a
inaic vo ʒrer. Aʒur Mac Ⴀiarmava vo chur a
cumcach ac Loch Laban i crich Ⴀrciʒ uchcleỏain
mic Ⴀoiminicin, vU Conchobair vonv aʒur vo cloinn
Muirchearcaiʒ Muimniʒ .h. Conchoỏair, ocur vo cloinn
Ferʒail mic Ⴀiarmava, ocur vo luchc Ⴀrciʒ buvein,
ocur vo cloinn Cechernaiʒ, ocur vo cloinn Concubair;
ocur mar ruaracar imarcraỏ na nemhcharav Mac
Ⴀiarmava im baeʒal vo ỏoircrev rair cenv i cenv;
o ro bavar rein va orev no cri orev vo ỏainỏ re
Mac nⴀiarmava, vo chuirevar chuci viblinaiỏ, ocur
vo ỏorcrevar saerraiʒechv .h. Conchuỏair eivir choir
ocur ech ina chenv, ocur cucacar in rrairr vo ỏai
ir nabovaỏ aiỏ viaraile, ocur vo brireỏ le Mac

---

1 Heir to the chieftaincy. aỏỏar
cairic (lit. "materies principis"), B.
aỏỏar caoireac, C.

2 Uisce-betha. Usquebaugh, aqua
vitæ, or whiskey. This is the first
reference to this drink in the Irish
Annals.

3 Uisce-marbhtha; i.e. death-water.

4 By the Daltons. Leir na Ⴀalacunacha, C. Lar in Ⴀalacunacha, B.

5 The Branachs; i.e. the Byrnes.

6 Interred. a aỏlacaỏ, B. a
aỏnacal, C.

7 Airtech Uchtlethan. "Airtech of

A.D.
[1405.]

chieftaincy[1] of Muinter-Eolais, quievit after drinking uisce-betha[2] to excess; and it was uisce-marbhtha[3] to Richard. Diarmaid, son of Donnchadh O'Conchobhair Ciarraighe, was slain by Mac Maurice Ciarraighe. Domhnall Og O'Ruairc mortuus est. Miles Dalton was slain by the Daltons,[4] and by the sons of Hubert Dalton. Newcastle-O'Finnagain was demolished by the Branachs[5] in hoc anno. The daughter of Domhnall O'Briain, wife of Philip, son of Mathghamhain Donn O'Cennedigh, mortua est. Gilla-na-naemh, son of Ruaidhri O'Cianain, chief historian of Feara-Manach, died suddenly in the house of Neide O'Maelchonaire, in Cairbre-Gabhra, and was interred[6] in the monastery of Lethratha. Muirchertach O'Duibhgennain quievit. A hosting to Airtech by Tadhg Mac Diarmada, king of Magh-Luirg, to demand his chiefry from the descendants of Conchobhar, son of Taichlech *Mac Diarmada*, and from the other people of Airtech, as it was always due to the man in his station; and Mac Diarmada was put into straits at Loch-Laban, in the territory of Airtech Uchtlethan[7] son of Tomintin, by O'Conchobhair Donn, and by the Clann-Muirchertaigh-Muimhnigh O'Conchobhair, and by the sons of Ferghal Mac Diarmada, and by the people of Airtech themselves, and by the Clann-Cethernaigh and Clann-Conchobhair. And when the superior number of his enemies found Mac Diarmada exposed to danger, they poured down together upon him, for they had twice or thrice as many men as Mac Diarmada. They all attacked him; and O'Conchobhair's band, both[8] foot and horse, poured in upon him; and they delivered the shower *of arrows* that were in the bows at each other. And a defeat was inflicted by Mac Diarmada,

---

the wide bosom." This personage, from whom the name of Airtech (a district comprising the parish of Tibohine, in the county of Roscommon) is alleged to be derived, is stated to have

been the father of Ruadh, the wife of Dathi, monarch of Ireland, who died in the year 428. See Mac Firbis's Geneal. MS., R. I. Acad. copy, p. 261.

[8] *Both.* ероιη, B. eαoaη, C.

[MS. defective. Text supplied from " Annals of Connacht."]

nᵭιαρmαᵭα ɣoρρα, ocuɼ lα ᵭonᵭchαᵭ mαc nᵭoṁnαιll, conɼαρlα ṁιc ᵭιαρmαᵭα, ocuɼ lα Lochlαιnn colαch ṁαc Cαbα, ocuɼ lα ɢlαɼlαιch ṁoιꝝι Luιɼꝝ αρchenα, hι ᴛuɼ ιn lαι ɼoɼ ιn cummαɼcαᵭ ɼluαιꝝ ɼιn ocuɼ neṁchαραᵭ, ocuɼ ᵭo mαρᵭαᵭ bɼoᴛαɼɼαch moɼ ᵭo ɼoᵭαιnιᵭ lα muιnᴛιρ ṁιc ᵭιαρmαᵭα; ocuɼ cιᵭeᵭ ᵭob e ɼιn ιnᴛ αιᴛheɼ co nαnαιᴛheɼ ɼαᵭeoιᵭ ᵭo muιnᴛιρ ṁιc ᵭιαρmαᵭα, oιɼ ᵭoιꝝ αṁ ᴛuc ɼeɼ éιcιn ᵭon ᵭebαιᵭ ɼɼιᴛhɼoιɼc uɼchuιɼ ᵭuαιbɼech ᵭo ɼαιꝝιᴛ ɼon ṁιll moɼαᵭᵭαl ᵭo mαιᴛhιᵭ αn moɼɼluαιꝝ ᵭo bαι ιc ιmᵭιᴛιn ιnᵭ αɼᵭɼlαᴛhαι ocuɼ αcα αnαcαl αɼ oɼchoιᴛιᵭ nα hιɼꝝαιle, αcuɼ ᵭo ɼechnαιᴛ lαɼιn ɼoιꝝιᴛ ɼιn ᵭoeɼcuɼɼluαꝝ ᵭιmαιn ocuɼ ɼoᵭαoιne, ocuɼ ꝝαlꝝαᴛα ꝝαιɼcιᵭ ocuɼ ꝝαιᴛhlenꝝαιᵭ ιn ɼluαιꝝ αɼchenα; ocuɼ ᵭo ḃenαɼᴛαɼ nα ꝝoιᴛhne ᵭuᵭ ᵭιαᵭlαιꝝι ι coɼɼ bɼαꝝαᴛᴛ nα ɼlαᴛhα co ɼιαᵭhnαch. Ccht αᴛα nι nαmα, α hαιᴛhle nα huɼᵭαᵭα ɼιn cαn ɼoιɼιꝝᴛιn αꝝuɼ nα ᴛubuɼᴛι ɼιn cαn ᴛuɼᵭɼoᵭ ɼιlαɼαᵭαɼ ɼoeɼchlαnnα 8leᵭι 8eꝝɼα ocuɼ cuɼαιᵭ cnuιc ιn 8cαιl, occuɼ ᴛulchαιn ṁαᵭlɼuαnαιꝝ moιɼ ɼe nαᵭɼαᵭ cαch ꝝo coιᴛchenn αnoɼα, uᴛ ᵭιꝝιᴛ ιn ɼιle, .ι. ṁαc Coιɼι,

> Cnoc ιn ɼcαιl α αιnm αɼ ᴛuɼ,
> O ɼe ḃeɼα ɼα e αɼuɼ;
> Tulchαn ṁαᵭlɼuαnαιꝝ nα ɼenᵭ
> ḃɼᵭe α αιnm co ᴛι αn ɼoɼᵭenᵭ, ⁊ɼl.,

ᵭo ɼαccαιᵭɼeᴛ αn ᴛιɼ ιαɼɼιn, ocuɼ ᴛαncαᵭαɼ ᵭα ᴛιꝝιᵭ, ocuɼ ᴛucαᵭh Tαᵭcc ᵭα αᵭnαcαl α noᴛhαɼ lιꝝe α ɼhenɼιɼ; occuɼ α hαιᴛle αᵭnαιcᴛhe Tαιᵭcc ᵭo ɼιꝝɼαᴛ

---

¹ In the beginning of the day. hι ᴛuɼ ιn lαι, B. αᴛᴛuɼ αn lαι, C.
² Phalanx. mιll, for ιnιll, B and C.
³ Protecting. αꝝ ιmᵭιᵭeαn, C. ιc ιmᵭιᴛιn, B.
⁴ In fine. αchᴛ αᴛα nι nαmα; lit. "but there is a thing only."
⁵ Irreparable. cαn ɼoιɼιꝝᴛιn,

and by Donnchadh Mac Domhnaill, Mac Diarmada's constable. and by Lochlainn Colach Mac Caba, and the
recruits of Magh-Luirg, in the beginning of the day,[1] on
this mixed and hostile army ; and a great multitude of
inferior persons were slain by Mac Diarmada's people.
Nevertheless, this was at last the "joy with sorrow" to
Mac Diarmada's people, for some one of the combatants
directed a terrible return shot of an arrow at the immense phalanx[2] of chiefs of the great host who were
protecting[3] the high prince, and guarding him from the
dangers of the conflict ; and the worthless rabble and
inferior people, and the champions of valour and warriors
of the host besides, were avoided by this arrow, and the
point of the black, devilish dart entered plainly in the
prince's throat. In fine,[4] immediately after this irreparable[5] reverse, and irresistible mishap, experienced by
the nobles of Sliabh-Seghsa, and the heroes of Cnoc-
in-scail, and of Tulchan-Maelruanaidh-Moir[6] (of which
all in general now say, ut dixit the poet, i.e. Mac Coise,[7]

> Cnoc-in-scail was its name at first,
> From Nera's time,[8] whose abode it was ;
> Tulchan-Maelruanaidh of the weapons
> Shall be its name until comes the end, &c.),

they left the district subsequently, and went home ; and
Tadhg was brought to be interred in the tomb of his
ancestors. And soon after the burial of Tadhg they in-

---

this Maelruanaidh, the family name of
MacDiarmada, or MacDermot, is derived.

[7] *Mac Coise.* The death of Erard
(or Urard) MacCoise, "chief poet of
the Gaeidhel," and probably the person above referred to, is recorded in
the Chron. Scotorum under the year
988=990. The death of another
Erard MacCoise is given by the Four
Mast. at the year 1023, where he is

called "chief chronicler of the Gaeidhel." See Todd's *Irish Nennius*, p. 209,
note [7].

[8] *Nera's time.* The Nera here referred to was probably the person
whose adventures in the fairy residence of Cruachan (Rathcroghan, co.
Roscommon) form the subject of the
romantic tale called *Tain Be Ainghin*,
preserved in the MS. H. 2. 16, Trin.
Coll., Dublin.

[MS. defective.
Text supplied
from "Annals
of Connacht."]

Ruαıδρı mαc Cceδo mıc Oıαρmαoα; ocur oαρ mo
oebρoch nír bo cloch an ınαc uıʒı rın; ocur ro rel
cror oo ronαδ an roʒnıom rın αmαıl ınoırır ın
cronıcαe ouın. Mαʒnur mαc Cceδo Uı Uıcıno quıeuıc
Cceoh .h. hCClnlıδe, oux cenel Oobchα mıc CCenʒαır,
quıeuıc ın Crırco xuı. Κt. CCuʒurc, ec rerulcur erc
hı Cluαın cαırbeı ror bru Sınnα, ro coınne berαıʒ.
Mor, ınʒean mıc Ʒorrrαıδ .h. Rαıʒıllıʒ, quıeuıc ın
Crırco ıı. Κt. Mαrcıı. Iohαnner mαc Mαılmαrcαın,
uıcαrıur Uıllαe cemplı, [quıeuıc] .u. Καlenoαr Mαrcıı.
CCıne ınʒean Brıαın meʒ Tıʒeαrnαn quıeuıc xuııı. Κt.
Mαıı.

Κt. Θnαır ror CCıne, ocur αen uαchαıo rrıırrı;
M°.cccc°.uı°.; rrımur αnnur lunαrır cıclı; xıııı. ınoıc-
cıonır; xx. rexco cıclı rolαrır. Lαıʒrech .h. Nuαllán,
αδδαr rıʒ rochαrc, ocur CCeoh .h. Tuαchαıl αoδαr rıʒ
.h. Mαıl, ocur Brαn .h. Brαın oαmhnα rıʒ [.h.] Rαelαn,
ocur Oomnαll mαc Tomαır Mıc Murchαδα, morcuı
runc oon plαıʒ ın hoc αnno. Mαelruαnαıʒ mαc Tαıδʒ
mıc Oonochαıδ, rı .h. nCCılellα, oo écc ınα eıʒ reın ıαr
mbuαıδ nonʒchα ocur nαıchrıʒhe, ec rerulcur erc α
mαnırcır nα Bullı ın hoc. αnno. Mαıδm oermαr lα
Murchαδ .h. Conchuδαır, rı .h. Rαılʒı, conα clαınn
ocur co nα clαnnmαıcne buδeın mαroen rır, ocur
Cαchαl ouδ ocur Tαoc, oα mαc rıʒ Connαcc, buoen

---

1 *They inaugurated Ruaidhri.* oo
rıʒrαc Ruαıδrı, C. oo rıʒhrαcc
Ruαıohrıδ, B.

2 *By my word.* oαr mo oebροch.
An expression said to have been first
used by St. Patrick, and explained by
etymologists as signifying " By God
my Judge."

3 *The chronicle.* ın cronıcαe, C.
ın cncαe, for ın croncαe, B.

4 *In the hope of meeting Berach.* Ṝ
coıñe beῖ, for ro coınne berαıʒ
("towards meeting Berach"), B. St.

Berach was the founder of the church
of Cluain-Cairbthe, or Kilbarry (Cill-
Beraigh), in the parish of Termonbarry, barony of Ballintober North,
and co. of Roscommon.

5 *Godfrey.* Ʒorrrαıδ, C. Ʒαr-
rαıδ, B.

6 *Villa templi.* The word cemplı
is omitted in B. Villa templi would
be Anglicised "Ballintemple"; but
there are many places so called in
Ireland.

7 *Maii.* mαı, B and C.

augurated Ruaidhri,[1] son of Aedh Mac Diarmada ; and by my word[2] this was not "a stone in the place of an egg." And about the festival of the Cross that great deed was done, as the chronicle[3] tells us. Maghnus, son of Aedh O'hUiginn, quievit. Aedh O'hAnlidhe, dux of Cenel-Dobhtha-mic-Aenghais, quievit in Christo on the xvi. of the kalends of August, et sepultus est in Cluain-Cairbthe on the margin of the Sinainn, in the hope of meeting Berach.[4] Mor, daughter of the son of Godfrey[5] O'Raighilligh, quievit in Christo ii. kalendas Martii. Johannes Mac Maelmartain, vicarius Villæ templi,[6] [quievit] v. kalendas Martii. Aine, daughter of Brian Mac Tighernain, quievit xviii. kalendas Maii.[7]

The kalends[8] of January on Friday, and the first of the moon ; M°.cccc°.vi°. ; primus annus[9] lunaris cycli ; xiiii. Indictionis ; xx. sexto cycli[10] solaris. Laighsech O'Nuallain, royal heir of Fotharta ; and Aedh O'Tuathail,[11] royal heir of Ui-Mail ; and Bran O'Brain, royal heir of [Ui]-Faelain, and Domhnall, son of Thomas Mac Murchadha, mortui sunt of the plague in hoc anno. Maelruanaidh, son of Tadhg Mac Donnchaidh, king of Ui-nOilella, died in his own house after the victory of unction and penitence, et sepultus est in the monastery of the Buill, in hoc anno.[12] A great defeat *was inflicted* by Murchadh O'Conchobhair, king of Ui-Failghe, accompanied by his own sons and descendants, (and Cathal Dubh,[13] and Tadhg, two sons of the king of Connacht, who had just gone

---

[8] *Kalends.* The Dom. Letter (C) is added in the margin in B and C.

[9] *Annus.* anꝺuꞃ, B and C.

[10] *Cycli.* ciclo, B and C.

[11] *Aedh O'Tuathail;* Hugh O'Toole. Instead of .h. Tuaċail, B and C read .h. Maċh-. The note toiꞃiꞃh Laiꞃean ꞃunꝺ; i.e. "the chieftains of Leinster here," is added in the margin opposite to these names.

[12] *Anno.* Omitted in B.

[13] *Cathal Dubh.* Cathal (or Charles) the Black. A marg. note in C reads Caꞇal ꝺuḃ mac Ccoꝺha mic Ḟeꞃꝺlimiꝺ Ccꞇha na ꞃiꞃ ꞃ ꞃann Uι Choncoḃaιꞃ Ḟaιꞃe ꞃunn; i.e. "Cathal Dubh, son of Aedh, son of Fedhlimidh of Ath-narigh (Athenry), on the side of O'Conchobhair Failghe here."

[MS. defective.
Text supplied
from "Annals
of Connacht."]

becc marcach maroen pip beup, ap nool ap cuaipc voiỗ
a nlhỗ Luigi vochum .h. Conchoỗaip, pop Ʒallaỗ na
Mive ocup pop Eoʒan mac mo abaioh .h. Conchoỗaip,
ocup pop cethepnaỗ coizỗala Convachc maroen
pip. Conveoᵭavup na pluaiʒ pin oiỗlinaỗ mo
uachcaip Ʒopille, ocup comvcochaỗ mac mo abbaiỗ co
Cluain immoppuipp cona cepachaỗ buỗein, co buile in
Ʒilla buve mic Maelcoppa, ocup vap mo vebpoỗ po ba
pepp voiỗ na vechcaip, co puc poppa annpin in
Calỗach mac Mupchaiỗ .h. Conchuỗaip ocup Cathal
.h. Conchuỗaip, pepeap mapcach ; convuỗaipc in Ʒilla
buive, ocup aiʒin an Calỗaiʒ bai ap iapachc aiʒe aʒ
venaĩ lenna, ocup pe ap muin oclaiʒ vonc pluaʒ,
poʒpaim haiʒin vec a Chalỗaiỗ. Ʒaiỗim laip ap in
Calỗach. Do pav pep von topaiʒ opchop aitheapach
vo cloich cup ben ap coin an aiʒin, cup maiʒ vonc
pluaʒ apin pach pin, ocup cup mapỗaỗ mac iin apaiỗ
ap in monaio alla thuaiỗ von baile lupin ; ocup ni
heỗ aĩain, achc nip luʒa na cpi ceav vo voiiỗ an
spbaiỗ oca pin co Cluain Aine a Cpich na cévach, uc
auvimup o ᵭach co coiccheno ; uaip po bup aʒ cup an
aip hipin o Cluain immoppuip co Cluain Aine. Ocup vo
benav apv minvo Connachc uile viỗ in lá pin .i. in
buacach Paopaica vo bith an Oilpino. Sexto vup
luln apai laithi mip ʒpeine ; via Sathaipn, imoppo,
apai laiỗi pechcmaine, vo poncic na ʒiioĩa pin, .i. in
x. maỗ la vo mi luil epive. Caỗc mac Donnvchaiỗ
.h. bipn, vux cipe bpuum na Sinna, obiic quapco vup
Houmben apai laiỗi mip ʒpeine ; via Cevain imoppo
apai laithe pechcmaine, .i. in la pe péil Mapcain.
Coippỗealỗaᵭ ᵭcc mac Aeỗa mic Coippỗhealỗaiʒ, pi

---

¹ Word. See note ², p. 116, supra.

² For thee. The clause pocpaim
haʒan vec lit. means "I proclaim thy
cauldron for thee." The description
of this "defeat" is rather ludicrous.

³ By reason of which. The Four

Masters explain that the flight of the
party engaged in this plundering expedition was caused by the "noise
and sound" (puaim ocup pocpom)
produced by the stone striking against
the cauldron.

A.D.
[1406.]

gone on a visit into Ui-Failghe, to O'Conchobhair, with a small band of cavalry, were also with him), on the Foreigners of Midhe, and on Eoghan, son of the Abbot O'Conchobhair, and on the retained kerns of Connacht along with him. Both these armies went to the upper part of Geshill; and the Abbot's son went with his own band to Cluain-imorruis, to the town of Gilla Buidhe Mac Maelcorra, (and by my word[1] it were better for them that they had not gone), where the Calbhach, son of Murchadh O'Conchobhair, and Cathal O'Conchobhair, with six horsemen, overtook them. And the Gilla Buidhe said, (the Calbhach's cauldron, which he had as a loan whilst brewing ale, being on the back of a young man of the army), "there is thy cauldron for thee,[2] O Calbhach!" "I accept it," said the Calbhach. One of the pursuing party violently flung a stone which struck the bottom of the cauldron, by reason of which[3] the army took to flight; and the Abbot's son was killed in the bog to the north of the town; and not only this, but their loss was not less than three hundred men from thence to Cluain-Aine in Crich-na-cedach, ut audimus from all in general, for this slaughter was continued from Cluain-imorruis to Cluain-Aine. And the chief relic of all Connacht, i.e. the Buacach-Patraic,[4] which was usually kept in Oilfinn, was taken from them on that day. Sexto idus Julii as regards the day of the month—on Saturday, moreover, as regards the day of the week—these deeds were performed, i.e. the 10th day of the month of July. Tadhg, son of Donnchadh O'Birn, dux of Tir-Briuin-na-Sinna, obiit quarto idus of November, as regards the day of the month; on Wednesday, moreover, as regards the day of the week; i.e. the day before the festival of Martin. Toirdhelbhach Og,[5] son of Aedh, son of Toirdhelbhach,

---

[4] *Buacach-Patraic.* buacach Patraicc, C. buacach Pincce, B. The word *buacach* seems derived from *buac*, a cap. But the exact nature of the relic is not known to the Editor.

[5] *Toirdhelbhach Og.* .Toirdhelbhach the Younger [O'Conor Donn].

[MS. defective.
Text supplied
from "Annals
of Connacht."]

Conⱦachⱦ ⱃe ⱦa ⱦliaⱦain aⱃ .xx. hi coⱀⱃⱶlaiⱦioⱃ ocuⱃ
.h. Conchobaiⱃ ⱃuaⱦ, ⱃo maⱃⱦaⱦ la Caⱦhal ⱃuⱦ mac
.h. Conchuⱦaiⱃ ⱃuaⱦ, ocuⱃ le Seaan, mac hЄmainn,
mic hobeⱃⱦ, mic ⱃⱃ Ɗaⱦiⱃ a buⱃⱦce ocuⱃ mna Muⱀⱶan
ⱀᵹⱀe mic Feⱦlimiⱦ, aᵹuⱃ la Ɗiaⱃmaiⱃ .h. ⱦaⱀaⱃen
leⱃ cuⱦⱦⱦᵹeⱃ co miliⱦa ⱀ móⱃ ecⱀⱦ ⱃⱀ, a ⱦⱦᵹ Ɽⱦⱥaⱃⱃ
mic Seaan buⱦⱦe mⱦc Єmaⱦⱃ mⱦc hobeⱃⱃ, ⱀⱃ Cⱃⱥⱥaⱀ
ⱃe ⱦaeb Fⱃⱃⱦcen hⱦ cloⱀn Conⱦmⱥᵹ; aᵹuⱃ ⱦⱃⱃe ⱃⱀ ⱀ
ⱦⱃeⱃ ⱃⱦᵹ ⱃⱃ ⱃⱦᵹaⱦ Conⱦachⱦ ⱃo maⱃⱦaⱦ a cloⱀⱀ
Conⱦmⱥᵹ .ⱀ. Conchuⱦaⱃ ⱞaenmaⱦᵹⱦ mac Ruaⱦⱃⱃ mⱦc
ⱦoⱃⱃⱃⱦelⱦaⱦᵹ ⱞoⱃⱃ, ocuⱃ Ruaⱦⱃⱃ mac Caⱦhaⱦl ⱃⱥⱥⱦ,
mⱦc Conchuⱦaⱃ ⱃⱥⱥⱦ, mⱦc Ⱞⱥⱃⱃcheaⱃⱦaⱦᵹ ⱞⱥⱀⱀⱞⱥᵹ,
mⱦc ⱦoⱃⱃⱃⱦhealⱦaⱦᵹ ⱞoⱃⱃ, ⱃⱦ Єⱃeⱀⱦ; aᵹuⱃ ⱦoⱃⱃⱃⱦheal-
ⱦaⱦ occ mac ⱥceⱦa mⱦc ⱦoⱃⱃⱃⱦhealⱦaⱦᵹ oⱃcc, aⱞaⱦl
aⱃⱥⱦⱃⱥⱞaⱃ ⱃeⱞⱥⱦⱃⱦ; u. ⱃⱥⱥⱃ Ɗecⱦmⱦeⱃ aⱃⱥⱦ laⱦho
mⱦⱃ ᵹⱃeⱀⱦe; ⱃⱦa Ɗaⱃⱃaⱦn ⱦmoⱃⱃo aⱃⱥⱦ [laⱦ]
ⱃechⱦmaⱀⱦ, .ⱀ. ⱀ ⱀ.eⱦ lá ⱃéc anⱦe ⱃeⱃⱦuⱞ naⱦale
Ɗoⱞⱦⱀⱦ ⱀoⱃⱦⱃⱦ leⱃⱥ Cⱃⱃⱃⱦⱦ.

‖cⱦ. Єnaⱃ ⱃoⱃ Saⱦhaⱃⱃⱀ ocuⱃ aⱦlⱦ .x. ⱃⱥⱃⱃⱃⱃ;
ⱞ°.cccc°.uⱀⱦ; ⱃecⱥⱀⱃⱥⱃ anⱀⱥⱃ cⱦclⱦ lⱥⱀaⱃⱦⱃ; .xⱦⱦ. ⱞⱃⱦc-
ⱦⱦoⱀⱃ; xxⱀⱦ. cⱦclⱦ ⱃolaⱃⱃ. Caⱦhal mac .h.Conchⱥⱦaⱃ
Faⱦᵹⱦ ⱃo maⱃⱦaⱦ la cloⱀn Feoⱃaⱃⱃ, ⱀoⱀo ‖cⱦ.
Ⱞaⱃⱦⱦⱦ aⱃaⱦ láⱦhe mⱦⱃ ᵹⱃeⱀⱦe; ⱃⱦa Lⱥaⱀ, ⱦmoⱃⱃo,
aⱃaⱦ laⱦhe ⱃeachⱦmaⱀⱦ .ⱀ. aⱀⱦ aenⱞaⱦ la ⱃⱦcheⱃ
ⱃeⱃⱃach eⱃⱦⱃe ⱀ ⱃeⱃⱦaⱦ ⱦlⱦaⱦⱀa cⱦcⱦl ⱀ Conⱀⱃeⱦ,
aᵹuⱃ ⱦ ⱦoⱃach ⱦlⱦaⱦⱀa ⱀ cⱦcⱦl noⱦⱃⱦcⱃa; coⱀⱃ ⱃeⱦⱦo
ⱀⱦ annalaⱦ ⱦaⱃ cⱦcⱦl an ⱦⱦᵹeaⱃⱀa ocuⱃ ⱀⱀ. ⱦaⱃⱃⱀ
cⱦcⱦl noⱦⱃecⱃa. Seoan .mac ⱦaⱦⱃc .h. Ruaⱦⱃc, aⱦⱦaⱃ ⱃⱦᵹ
ⱦⱃeⱃⱃⱀe, ⱃo ecc ⱦ Ⱞⱥⱦᵹ Lⱥⱦⱃᵹ, ocuⱃ a aⱦⱀⱥcal a ⱀⱃⱃⱥⱦⱞ
leⱦan, ⱀ hoc aⱀⱀo. Ⱞac ⱦaⱦⱃc mⱦc Ⱞaⱦhᵹⱥⱞⱀa

---

¹ *Ben-Mumhan*; lit. "Woman of
Mumha (or Munster)."

² *Ruaidhri.* A marg. note in C
reads aⱀ Ruaⱦⱃⱃ mⱥc Caⱦⱥⱦl
ⱃⱥⱥⱦ ⱃⱀ a ᵹcaⱃⱞⱦⱦⱃ le Feⱃ-
lⱦmⱦⱃ Ⱥⱦa na ⱃⱦcch, ocuⱃ ᵹⱥⱃⱃ
ⱃⱦ Connachⱦ aⱦᵹⱦ aⱃ ⱃaⱃ ⱃé mⱦⱃa
ᵹⱥⱃ ⱞoⱃⱦaⱃ ⱞaⱃ ⱃeaⱃaⱃ 1316;

i.e. "this Ruaidhri, son of Cathal Ruadh, was in alternation with Fedhlimidh of Ath-na-righ, and had the
title of king of Connacht during the
space of six months, until he was
slain, as is related [under A.D.]
1316."

³ *Ante.* aⱀⱃ, B and C.

king of Connacht during twenty-two years in co-
sovereignty with O'Conchobhair Ruadh, was slain by
Cathal Dubh, the son of O'Conchobhair Ruadh, and by
John, the son of Edmond, son of Hubert, son of Sir
David Burk and of Ben-Mumhan,[1] grand-daughter of
Fedhlimidh, and by Diarmaid O'Tanaidheu, by whom
this great deed was bravely shared, in the house of
Rickard, son of John Buidhe, son of Edmond, son of
Hubert, in the Crecan, by the side of Fidhiceu in Clann-
Connmhaigh, (and he was the third king of the kings
of Connacht who were slain in Clann-Connmhaigh,
viz. :—Conchobhar Macmmaighe, son of Ruaidhri, son of
Toirdhelbhach Mor ; Ruaidhri,[2] son of Cathal Ruadh, son
of Conchobhar Ruadh, son of Muirchertach Muimhnech,
son of Toirdhelbhach Mor, king of Erinn ; and Toirdhelbhach Og, the son of Aedh, son of Toirdhelbhach Og, as
we said before), the fifth of the ides of December as regards the day of the month ; on Thursday, moreover, as
regards [the day] of the week ; i.e. the sixteenth day
ante[3] festum natale Domini nostri Jesu Christi.

The kalends of January on Saturday,[4] and the
twelfth of the moon ; M°.cccc°.vii. ; secundus annus cycli
lunaris ; xv. Indictionis ; xxvii. cycli solaris. Cathal, son
of O'Conchobhair Failghe, was killed by the Clann-
Feorais, nono 'kalendas Martii as regards the day of the
month ; on Monday, moreover, as regards the day of the
week : i.e. it was the twenty-first day of spring, in the end
of the year of the Lord's cycle, and the beginning of the
year of the Decennovenalian cycle ; so that the annal is
sexto[5] according to the cycle of the Lord, and the
seventh according to the Decennovenalian cycle. John,
son of Tadhg O'Ruairc, heir to the sovereignty of Breifne,
died in Magh-Luirg, and was interred in Druim-lethan,
in hoc anno. The son of Tadhg, son of Mathghamhain

---

[4] *Saturday.* The Dom. Letter (B) is added in the marg.

[5] *Sexto :* i.e. the sixth year after A.D. 1400.

[MS. defective.
Text supplied
from "Annals
of Connacht."]

ouinn .h. Cenneoiᵹ, ciᵹeapna Upṁumhan uaċcapaiᵹ,
oo mapᐁaᐁ la .h.Cepᐁaill. Maiᐁm mop la ᵹal-
laiᐁ, ocur le 8ᵹpub, ap ᵹaiᐁelaiᐁ Muṁan, ou inap
mapᐁaᐁ Caocc Ua Cepᐁaill, pi Eli, ocur peicheaᐁ coic-
chenᐁ oo chliapaiᐁ Epenᐁ ocur Clpan in Caoc hipin,
ocur coppo aipchipe Oia oia anmain. Muipcheapcach
h.Cellaiᵹ .i. apᐁerpocc Connachc, pai na hEpenn uile
inᐁ ecna ocur an ᐁepc ocur in ᐁoennachc, in Cpipco
quieuic i Cuaim oa ᵹualann, po peil Michil. Maiᐁm
la h.Conchoᐁaip puaᐁ ocur la .h.Cellaiᵹ, inap mapᐁaᐁ
opem oo cloinn Csichiᐁ, ocur ni pecappa a nanmann.
Maiᐁm Cille achaᐁ in hoc anno la .h.Conchoᐁaip
puaᐁ, ocur la macaiᐁ Maileaᐁlainn .h.Cellaiᵹ, ocur
la Ruaiᐁpi Mac Oiapmaoa, piᵹ Moiᵹi Luipᵹ, pop macc
Uilliam cloinne Ricaipᐁ, ocur pop Cathal mac
Ruaiᐁpi .h.Conchoᐁaip, oap ᵹapmeᐁ ᵹaipm piᵹ ᐁep
.h.Conchuᐁaip ouinn oo mapᐁaᐁ la Cathal ouᐁ mac
.h.Conchuᐁaip puaiᐁ, cup bpireᐁ pop cloinn Ricaipᐁ,
ocur pop Cathal mac Ruaiᐁpi, cup ᵹaᐁaᐁ ann Cathal
mac Ruaiᐁpi ocur Uilliam ᐁupcc annpioe, ocur cup
mapbhaᐁ ocur cup ᵹaᐁaᐁ mopan eli ann beop; ocur po
peil Iohain baicpi oo ponaic na mopᵹnioṁa pin.
Cuiplcn coᐁaip Culpci oo bpireᐁ pemepioe la ᐁpian
mac Ooṁnaill mic Muipcheapcaiᵹ .h. Conchuᐁaip,
ocur la cloinn Oonochaᐁ, ocur Cathal mac Ruaiᐁpi
oo chop ap Capnn Ppaich ᐁoiᐁ. Conmac .h.pepᵹail
morcuup erc oo ᐁap anabaiᐁ. Morcuur erc Eoᵹan
mac Cathail, mic Ceᐁa ᐁpeipniᵹ, mic Cathail puaiᐁ

---

1 *Of Upper.* uaċcapaiᵹ, C. uaċ-
capai, B.

2 *Scrope.* 8ᵹpub, B and C. Sir
Stephen le Scrope, Deputy to Thomas
Duke of Lancaster, Viceroy of Ireland,
and the Joshua of the Anglo-Irish
annalists. Ware (*Annals*), speaking
of this victory, says "it was averr'd
by many that the sun stood still for
a space that day, till the English-men
had rod 6 Miles, which was much
wondered at."

3 *Archbishop of Connacht*; i.e. of
Tuam.

4 *I know not.* ni pecappa, B.
ni peioippa, C.

Donn O'Cennedigh, lord of Upper[1] Ur-Mumha, was killed by O'Cerbhaill. A great victory by the Foreigners, and by Scrope,[2] over the Gaeidhel of Mumha, in which Tadhg O'Cerbhaill, king of Eli, was slain; and this Tadhg was general patron of the learned of Erinn and Alba; and may God have mercy on his soul. Muirchertach O'Cellaigh, archbishop of Connacht,[3] the most eminent man of all Erinn in wisdom, charity, and humanity, in Christo quievit in Tuaim-da-ghualann, about the feast of Michael. A victory by O'Conchobhair Ruadh, and by O'Cellaigh, in which a number of the Clann-Sithigh were slain; and I know not[4] their names. The victory of Cill-achaidh *was gained* in hoc anno by O'Conchobhair Ruadh, and by the sons of Maclechlainn O'Cellaigh, and by Ruaidhri Mac Diarmada, king of Magh-Luirg, over Mac William of Clann-Rickard, and over Cathal, the son of Ruaidhri O'Conchobhair, (who was proclaimed[5] king after O'Conchobhair Donn had been slain by Cathal Dubh, son of O'Conchobhair Ruadh); and the Clann-Rickard and Cathal, son of Ruaidhri, were defeated; and Cathal, son of Ruaidhri, and William Burk were captured there; and many more besides were slain and captured there. And about the festival of John the Baptist[6] these great deeds were performed. The Castle of Tobar-Tuilsce[7] was previously[8] broken down by Brian, son of Domhnall, son of Muirchertach O'Conchobhair, and by the Clann-Donnchaidh; and Cathal, son of Ruaidhri, was put upon Carn-Fraich[9] by them. Conmac O'Ferghail mortuus est of an immature death. Mortuus est Eoghan, son of Cathal, son of Aedh

---

[5] *Who was proclaimed.* oαη ζαη-meꝺ, B. oαη ζαιηmeαꝺ, C.

[6] *Of John the Baptist.* Ioīṅ. bαιϲ-ϝꞃ, B. Iohαnneꞃ bαιϝꝺι, C.

[7] *Tobar - Tuilsce.* "The well of Tuilsc," or Tulsk, a village in the barony and county of Roscommon. See O'Donovan's ed. of the Four Mast., A.D. 1407, note ᵐ.

[8] *Previously.* ꞃemeꞃꝺe (lit. before that), B. ꞃoιṁeꞃꝺe, C.

[9] *Put upon Carn-Fraich.* This is a conventional way of saying that Cathal, son of Ruaidhri [O'Conor], was inaugurated king of Connacht. The Carn-Fraich here referred to is the same as the Carn-Fraich-mic-Fidhaigh alluded to in note ¹, p. 554, vol. i.

[MS. defective.
Text supplied
from "Annals
of Connacht."]

.h.Conchuϑαιρ, ετ ρεριltur ερτ hι manιρτειρ na buιlle in hoc anno. Αϑam mac ζιllι Muιρe, ρι .h. nechach, το marϑaϑ lι hαceϑ mαζ αenζura, ocuρ la 8enιc oc. Maelmorϑa .h. Dιmuραιζ, ρι cloιnnι Maeluζρa, quιeuιτ ιn hoc anno. 8eoan mac Cathaιl mιc Cethep-naιζ morτuur ερτ. Morρ Lochlaιnn mιc Doṁnaιll la Feϑlιmιϑ mac Ruaιϑρι .h. Chonchoϑaιρ. Mac Uιllιam oιcc .h. Cellaιζ ocur mac Mathζaṁna .h. Neachτaιn το marϑaϑ la Feραϑach .h. Cellaιζ ρερ τolum. Doneητ ϑερmaρ ocur τιch morρ ρορ ιnϑιlιϑ ιn hoc anno.

ẛcτ. enaιρ ρορ Doṁnach, ocur τρer ρicheατ ρuιρρι; m°.cccc°.uιιι; τερτιur annur lunaριρ cιclι; ρριmuρ ιnϑιcτιonιρ; xxuιιι. cιclι ρolaριρ. αṁlaιϑ mαζ αṁal-ζαιϑ, τux Caιρaιϑe, morτuur ερτ, eτ ρεριltur ερτ an αch lúaιn. Tomar mac ριζ 8αxan το τochτ an eριnn ιn hoc anno, occur ιaρla Cιlle τaρa το ζαϑaιl leιr beur. 8luαζαϑ la mac ιn ριζ ι Laιζnaιϑ ιaρ ριn, acur hιτριn Dιuιτ το marϑaϑ ρορ anτ ρluαζαϑ ριn, ocur τοb anba an erϑατ ριn. Perτιlencιa mαζna ιριn mρϑe ιn hoc anno, ocur 8cρub ριϑιρe ρο croϑa, ocur ρερ ιnaιτ ρí 8αxan ιnτ eριnτ, το ec τon ϸlαιζ ριn. Cathal mac Cethepnaιζ ocur Conchuϑaρ mac Cethep-naιζ, ocur 8eóan macc 8eoan mιc Cethepnaιζ, ocur Tomulτach ocur Doṁnall meιc Fιnζeιn meιc Cethep-naιζ, occιρι ρunτ la cloιnn Muιρcheaρταιζ ιn hoc anno, ιn τιζalτuιρ Mαζnura mιc Muιρcheaρταιζ mιc Cathaιl το marϑaϑh a cloιnn Cethepnaιζ ρemhι ριn. Tomar, mac hoberτ, mιc emaιnn mιc hoberτ, το marϑaϑ το

---

1 *Adam Mac Gilla-Muire.* Ware (*Annals,* A.D. 1407) calls this person "Mac Adam Mac Gilmori", and states that he was never baptized, and was therefore called "Corbi." Under the year 1408, however, he writes the name Hugh Mac Gilmore.

2 *Senic Og.* Senic (or Senicin) the Younger. He was apparently the

son of Senicin (Jenkin) Savage who was slain in 1374, as above re-corded.

3 *Anno.* Omitted in B.

4 *Domhnall.* Probably Domhnall, son of Cathal Og O'Conor.

5 *Sunday.* The Dom. Letters (AG) are added in the marg. in B.

6 *Hitsin.* Conell Mageoghegan (in

Briefnech, son of Cathal Ruadh O'Conchobhair, et sepultus
est in the monastery of the Buill, in hoc anno. Adam
Mac Gilla-Muire,[1] king of Ui-Echach, was killed by Aedh
Mac Aenghusa, and by Senic[2] Og. Maelmordha O'Dimusaigh, king of Clann-Maelughra, quievit in hoc anno.[3]
John, the son of Cathal Mac Cethernaigh, mortuus est.
Mors of Lochlainn, son of Domhnall,[4] by Fedhlimidh, son
of Ruaidhri O'Conchobhair. The son of William Og
O'Cellaigh, and the son of Mathghamhain O'Nechtain,
were slain by Feradach O'Cellaigh per dolum. Very
inclement weather, and great destruction of cattle, in hoc
anno.

The kalends of January on Sunday,[5] and the twenty-
third of the moon; Mᶜ.ccccᵒ.viii.; tertius annus lunaris
cycli; primus Indictionis; xxviii. cycli solaris. Amhlaibh
Mac Amhalghaidh, dux of Calraidhe, mortuus est, et
sepultus est in Ath-Luain. Thomas, son of the king of
the Saxons, came to Erinn in hoc anno, and the Earl of
Cill-dara was taken prisoner by him. A hosting by the
king's son afterwards into Laighen; and Hitsin[6] Tuit
was slain on this hosting; and that was a great loss. Pestilentia magna in Midhe in hoc anno, and Scrope,[7] a very
valiant knight, and deputy of the king of the Saxons in
Erinn, died of this plague. Cathal Mac Cethernaigh, and
Conchobhar Mac Cethernaigh, and John, son of John
Mac Cethernaigh, and Tomaltach and Domhnall, sons of
Finghin Mac Cethernaigh, occisi sunt by the Clann-
Muirchertaigh in hoc anno, in revenge[8] of Maghnus, son
of Muirchertach, son of Cathal,[9] who was previously[10] slain
in Clann-Cethernaigh. Thomas, son of Hubert, son of

his version of the Annals of Clonmacnoise) writes this name "Hodgin."

[7] *Scrope.* Scꞃub, B and C. See
note [2], p. 122 *supra.*

[8] *In revenge.* in oiġalꞇuiꞃ, C.
inꝺġalꞇuꞃ, B.

[9] *Son of Cathal.* The Cathal here referred to was probably Cathal O'Conchobhair, usually called "Cathal of
Connacht."

[10] *Previously.* ꞃemhi ꞃin, B.
ꞃoiꞃhe ꞃin, C.

[MS. defective. Text supplied from "Annals of Connacht."]

oen upchup poᵹa la ᵹilla na naeṁ, mac Uilliam
ᵹallda .h. Ταιδc an ceᵹlaiᵬ. Cpeαcha mopα la
ꝼeᴅlimíᵬ mac Ruαiᵬpi .h.Conchobaip, ꝼop Eoᵹαn mαc
·h.Conchubaip puaiᵬ, ın hoc anno. Copmac .h. mαilli
occiꝼuꝑ eꝛc α ꝼpαcꝑe ꝑuo. maᵹnuꝑ maᵹ 8amhpαᴅan
ᴅo mαpᵬαᵬ ᴅon bαechan iilac ᵹilla puaiᵬ, ᴅopchop
chuαilli. milip Ὁαlαcun occiꝼuꝑ eꝛc α ꝼpαcpe ꝑuo,
ocuꝑ α chαꝑlen ᴅo bpiꝑeᵬ la ꝑliochc Cαchαil .h. ꝼeꝛᵹαil
ιαꝑcαin. Eoᵹαn .h. Ruαiꝑe occuꝑ clαnᴅ Ὁuinᴅ meiᵹ
8αmhpαᴅαin ᴅo ᴅol hi cip Chonαill ᴅo čoᵹαᵬ ꝼop
Ὁꝑeꝑneαčαiᵬ. ꝼeꝛᵹαl mac Conconᴅαchc Ui ꝼeꝛᵹαil
mopcuuꝑ eꝛc in hoc anno. Conchuᵬαp mac Iṁαip
.h. ϹϹnliᴅe occiꝼuꝑ eꝛc in hoc anno la Copcα ϹϹchchlαnn,
ocuꝑ la Cenel Ὁobčα buᵬein, ꝼop monα Cluαnα nα
cαilliᵬ .ı. lα nα mbꝑuαch iiᴅuᵬ, ocuꝑ ᴅo bo cꝑuαiᵬ in
lα ꝑin ᴅo Chαchαl ᴅuᵬ .h.Conchuᵬαip ocuꝑ ᴅo clαinn
Iṁαip .h. ϹϹnliᴅe ᴅiblinαiᵬ; ec ꝑepulcuꝑ eꝛc α
mαinꝑcip Roꝑα Commαn; coiꝑeαch in ᵹeṁpiᵬ in cαn
ꝑin. ϹϹeᵬ ꝑuαᵬ mac Ϲomαiꝑ .h. Ὁipn, ocuꝑ Ὁonᴅchαᵬ
α ṁαc, ocuꝑ Ὁpiαn buiᵬe mac ϹϹṁlαiᵬ puaiᵬ, occiꝑi
ꝑunc.

Κt. Enαiꝑ ꝼop mαiꝑc, ocuꝑ cechꝑe uαchαᵬ ꝼuiꝑꝑı;
mⁿ.cccc°.ıx°.; quαꝑcuꝑ αnnuꝑ lunαꝑiꝑ cicli; ꝑecunᴅuꝑ
inᴅiccioniꝑ; pꝑimuꝑ αnnuꝑ ꝑolαꝑiꝑ cicli. In luᵬꝑα ᴅo
ᵹαᵬαil ꝑıᵹ 8αxαn, ocuꝑ α chάꝑc ᴅo čeαchc α nEꝑinn,
ocuꝑ Ϲomαꝑ mac inᴅ ιαꝑlα ᴅo ꝑαᴅαil Eꝑenᴅ ꝑo chάꝑc
α αchαp, ιαꝑ lécαn ίαꝑlα Cille ᴅαꝑα αꝑ α ᵹeṁṅol ᴅó.

---

¹ *Hubert*; i.e. Hubert Burk.

² *With one cast.* ᴅo oen upchuꝑ,
B. ᴅoen upchoꝑ, C.

³ *William Gallda*; i.e. William the
Anglicised.

⁴ *O'Taidhg - an - teghluigh.* Otherwise written O'Taidhg, and now Anglicised Tighe. This name is derived
from Tadhg-an-teghlaigh, or "Tadhg
of the household," a Connacht prince,
who lived in the tenth century.

⁵ *Fratre.* ꝼꝛu, for ꝼpαcꝑı, B. C.

⁶ *To war*; i.e. to make inroads into
the territory of Breifne from the Tir-
Conaill side of the Erne river. ᴅo
čoᵹαᵬ, C. ᴅo cočαᴅ, B.

⁷ *Occisus est.* See the entry under
next year, where the chronicler ex-
presses a doubt as to whether the
death of Conchobhar O'hAinlidhe
should not be there recorded.

Edmond, son of Hubert,[1] was killed with one cast[2] of a javelin by Gilla-na-naemh, son of William Gallda[3] O'Taidhg-an-teghlaigh.[4] Great depredations *were committed* by Fedhlimidh, son of Ruaidhri O'Conchobhair, upon Eoghan, the son of O'Conchobhair Ruadh, in hoc anno. Cormac O'Maille occisus est a fratre suo. Maghnus Mac Samhradhain was killed by the Baethan Mac Gilla-ruaidh, with a cast of a pole. Miles Dalton occisus est a fratre[5] suo; and his castle was afterwards broken down by the descendants of Cathal O'Ferghail. Eoghan O'Ruairc, and the sons of Donn Mac Samhradhain, went into Tir-Conaill, to war[6] against the Breifnians. Ferghal, son of Cuchonnacht O'Ferghail, mortuus est in hoc anno. Conchobhar, son of Imhar O'hAinlidhe, occisus est[7] in hoc anno by the Corca-Achlann, and by the Cenel-Dobhtha[8] themselves, on the bog of Cluain-na-caillidh,[9] i.e. on Lá-na-mbruach-ndubh, (and that was a hard day both for Cathal Dubh O'Conchobhair, and for the sons of Imhar O'hAinlidhe), et sepultus est in the monastery of Ros-Comain. It was the beginning of winter at that time. Aedh Ruadh, son of Thomas O'Birn, and his son Donnchadh, and Brian Buidhe, son of Amhlaibh Ruadh,[10] occisi sunt.

The kalends of January on Tuesday,[11] and the fourth of the moon; M°.cccc°.ix°.; quartus annus lunaris cycli; secundus Indictionis; primus annus solaris cycli. The king of the Saxons was seized with leprosy; and the report reached Erinn, and Thomas, the Earl's son,[12] left Erinn at the report of his father's illness, after having liberated the Earl of Cill-dara from his bonds.[13]

---

[8] *Cenel-Dobhtha.* The tribe name of the O'Hanlys of Roscommon.

[9] *Cluain-na-caillidh*; i.e. "the hag's meadow." *Lá-na-mbruach-ndubh* means "the day of the black borders."

[10] *Amhlaibh Ruadh.* Amhlaibh "the Red" O'Birn.

[11] *Tuesday.* The Dom. Letter (F) is added in the marg. in B.

[12] *The Earl's son.* mac ino lapla, B and C. It should be mac ino ꞅuᵹ, "the king's son."

[13] *From his bonds.* aꞅ a ᵹeṁil, B. aꞅ a ᵹeiṁiol, C.

Maelᵱechlainᴅ mac Ḃᵱiain Meᵹ Ꞇiᵹeᵱnain moᵱꞇuuᵱ
eᵱꞇ in hoc anno. Cꞇꞇaiᵱech ᴅo ᴅenaṁ ᴅo Maelᵱechlainᴅ moᵱ Maᵹ Eochacan, ocuᵱ ᵱeᵱᵹal mac ᵱeᵱᵹail
ᵱuaiḃ Mec Eochacan, mec ᴅonᴅchaiḃ, ina maꞇ iaᵱᵱin.
Coᵱᵱ Riᵱᴅeᵱᴅ a Ḃuᵱcc ᴅo Ḃᵱiᵱeḃ le coin ᴅo Ḃai
na ᵱich, ocuᵱ a écc ᴅe ᵱin ᵹo ꞇuḃaiᵱᴅech. Cᵱeach
Ḃeoil leci la Ꞇiᵹeᵱnan Ua Ruaiᵱc aᵱ .h. nᴅoṁnaill,
ocuᵱ aᵱ Caꞇhal .h. Ruaiᵱc, ocuᵱ ᵱoᵱ Eoᵹan .h. Ruaiᵱc;
ocuᵱ .h. ᴅoṁnaill ocuᵱ cenel Conaill a ᵱoᵱlonᵹᵱoᵱꞇ
alla ꞇhall ᴅon eᵱᵱ, ocuᵱ Caꞇhal ocuᵱ Eoᵹan alla Ḃoᵱᵱ
ᴅon eᵱ ceaᴅna, ocuᵱ ꞇucc in cᵱeich uaḃaiḃ ᴅiḃlinaiḃ.
Sluaᵹaḃ la Ḃᵱian mac ᴅoṁnaill mic Muiᵱcheaᵱꞇaiᵹ
.h.Chonchoḃaiᵱ, ocuᵱ la Conchoḃaᵱ mac ᴅonᴅchaiḃ,
ᵱi Ꞇiᵱe hOiliella, ocuᵱ la clainn Ꞇiᵹeaᵱnain .h. Ruaiᵱc
in hoc anno, cuᵱ chuiᵱeꞇaᵱ lón ocuᵱ biaᴅ ᴅainᴅeoin
Conᴅaéꞇ o ᵱliaḃ ᵱuaᵱ uile, ocuᵱ ᵱiaᴅ ꞇinolꞇi aᵱ a chinᴅ
uli eiᴅiᵱ coiᵱ ocuᵱ ech ocuᵱ ᵹalloclaé, hi caᵱleu Roᵱa
Coman, in luan iaᵱ ᵱeil Micheil aᵱchainᵹiol ; acuᵱ ᴅo
ᵱaoileaᴅaᵱ o ᵱliaḃ ᵱíᵱ comḃéꞇiᵱ Clanᴅ Ricaiᵱᴅ ina
ᵱochaiᵱ ᵱéin aᵹ cuᵱ in Ḃiḃ ᵱin a caᵱleu Roᵱa Coman,
ocuᵱ ni ᵱaḃaꞇaᵱ, achꞇ mac Uilliam Ḃuᵱḃen becc
maᵱcaé ᴅo ꞇochꞇ co Ḃaile in ꞇoḃaiᵱ ina coinne ; accuᵱ
ᴅo ᵱuaḃᵱaꞇaᵱ locaḃ annᵱiḃe o nach ꞇancaꞇꞇaᵱ ᵱluaᵹha
cloinne Ricaiᵱᴅ chucꞇha aṁail ᵱo ᵹellᵱaᴅ ; ocuᵱ a
ᴅuḃaiᵱꞇ Mac ᴅonnchaiḃ naé locᵱaḃ no co ꞇuiꞇeᴅ, no
co cuiᵱeḃ biaᴅ iᵱin caᵱlen, ocuᵱ aᴅuḃaiᵱꞇ ᵱe mac
Uilliam anṁain anᴅᵱin o nach ᵱaiḃi lin ꞇᵱoᴅai no
ꞇeᵹṁala ᴅo ꞇhaḃaiᵱꞇ ᴅo Chonᴅachꞇaiḃ ; ocuᵱ ᴅa
maᵱbhꞇhaᵱ ᵱinne iᵱ maiꞇh linn ꞇuᵱa beó aᵹ aᵱ

---

¹ *Unluckily.* co ꞇuḃaiᵱᴅech, C.
co ꞇuḃaiᵱech, B.

² *Cascade.* eᵱᵱ. An *ess*, or cascade, on the river Erne, near Belleek,
in the county of Fermanagh.

³ *From the mountain upwards;* i.e.
the part of Connacht to the south of
the Curlieu mountains, on the borders

of the counties of Sligo and Roscommon. This entry is very loosely constructed in the original.

⁴ *From the mountain downwards;*
i.e. to the north of Sliabh-Seghsa, or
the Curlieu mountains.

⁵ *Expected.* ᴅo ᵱaoileaᴅaᵱ, C.
ᴅo ꞇᵱailiꞇiᵱ, B.

A.D.
[1409.]

Maelsechlainn, son of Brian Mac Tighernain, mortuus est in hoc anno. Maelsechlainn Mor Mac Eochagain was deposed from the chieftaincy; and Ferghal, son of Ferghal Ruadh Mac Eochagain, son of Donnchadh, *was appointed* afterwards in his place. Richard Burk's leg was broken by a greyhound which was running, and he died unluckily[1] in consequence. The plundering of Bel-lice was effected by Tighernan O'Ruairc against O'Domhnaill, and against Cathal O'Ruairc, and Eoghan O'Ruairc; and O'Domhnaill and the Cenel-Conaill were encamped on the opposite side of the cascade,[2] and Cathal and Eoghan on this (*i.e. the south*) side of the same cascade; and he brought the prey from them all. A hosting by Brian, son of Domhnall, son of Muirchertach O'Conchobhair, and by Conchobhar Mac Donnchaidh, king of Tir-Oilella, and by the sons of Tighernan O'Ruairc, in hoc anno; and they put stores and provisions into the castle of Ros-Comain, in despite of all *the men of* Connacht from the mountain upwards,[3] who were all assembled to oppose him, both foot and horse, and gallowglasses, on the Monday after the festival of Michael the Archangel. And those from the mountains downwards[4] expected[5] that the Clann-Rickard would have been with themselves when putting the provisions into the castle of Ros-Comain; and they were not; but Mac William himself, with a few horsemen, came to meet them to Baile-in-tobair. And they[6] endeavoured to stop there, since the armies of Clann-Rickard did not come to them as they had promised; but Mac Donnchaidh said that he would not stop, though he should fall, until he would put provisions into the castle. And he told Mac William to remain there, as he was not[7] strong enough to give battle or encounter to the Connachtmen; "for if we are slain," (*said he*), "it is agreeable to us that thou

---

[6] *They.* Apparently the forces of O'Conor Sligo and O'Ruairc. The phraseology of this entry is very loose and ungrammatical; and the words

"endeavoured to stop there" do not literally convey the meaning of the text.

[7] *As he was not.* o naċ ṗaıḃı, C. o nach ṗaḃa, B.

[MS. defective.
Text supplied
from " Annals
of Connacht."]

lenbaiʊ ιναρ nʊιαιξ ʊα coτhaξaʊ. Cιʊ τρα achτ, ʊo
ξluáιρ mac ʊονʊchaιʊ ιρρemτhuρ να ρʼlιξeʊ, ocuρ
ιιρ αν ρé ʊοιι ρéιιι ocuρ ʊoιι ρuaτhaρ ριιι no co
ραιιιcc co Roρ Comman; ocuρ ʊo chιιιρcτaρ lón ιριιι
caιρʼleιι; ocuρ ιιιρ maρʊaʊ achτ αeιι oclaech ʊιʊ, ocuρ
ρuccρaʊ ρeιιι α choρρ leó; ocuρ ιιι meιιιcc ʊo ριξιιeʊ αν
Θριιιι ριαιιι ριʊal ba cρoʊa ocuρ baʊ calma ιιια ιιι
ριʊal ριιι. mιιιιιτιρ Chιιιριιιιι ʊo maρʊaʊ α cheιle ιιι
hoc αιιιιo .ι. Seoαιι αξυρ Conla ʊo maρʊaʊ la Όιαρmaιτ
mac mιιιρcheaρταξ Uι Chιιιριιιιι, hι τιξ .h. Όuιʊξιιιιιαιι
baιle choιllτe ρoξαιρ; acuρ Όιαρmaιτ ρeιιι ʊo ʊol co
τech Conchoʊaιρ cριιιιιι mιc Ταιʊcc .h.Conchoʊaιρ, .ι.
α ʼιξeaρнα αξυρ α ʊeρʊcóмallτα, ocuρ Conchoʊaρ ʊa
ξαʊaιl ιιια ʼιξ buʊeιιι, occuρ α ʼιʊlacaʊ ʊo mιιιιιτιρ
Rнαιρc ocuρ ʊo mιιιιιτιρ Chιιιριιιιι; ocuρ α beιʓ τιιιl-
leaʊ ocuρ coιcτιξιρ ιllαιιιι, ocuρ α τoιτιm la mac Seaαιι
.h. Cιιιριιιιι ρα ʊéoιʊ. Caτhal mac ʊονʊchaιʊ moρτιιιρ eρτ ꜩιιιι. ꝭallαιιιιι Ocτobιρ; ocuρ ιιι ʊeмιιι lem
naʓ ι ρo blιaʊαιιι ιιι baʊ chóιρ Conchoʊaρ mac iмaιρ
.h. ꝋnlιʊe ʊó choρ ρίρ. mιιιρcheaρτach mac ꝏeʊa-
caιι, ollaιιι bρeιʓeaнαιι ρeρ Τeρτha, moρτιιιρ eρτ.

ꝭτ. Θναιρ ρoρ Ceʊαιιι, ocuρ ꜩu. ρuιρρι; anno
Όomιιιι M°.cccc°.ꜩ.; qιιιιτυρ αιιιιuρ [cιclι] lunaριρ;
τeρτιιιρ ιιιʊιcτιoιιιρ; ιι. αιιιιuρ cιclι ρolaριρ. Raξnall
маξ Raξнαιll, ʊuꜩ mιιιιιτιρι hΘolαιρ, moρτιιιρ eρτ
ιαρ nonξaʊh ocuρ αιτhιρξhe, ocuρ Cumρcρach маξ
Raξнαιll, ʊαρ ξαιρeaʊ маξ Raξнαιll ιιια ιιιατ, ʊo écc
ι cιιιι coιcτιξιρ ιαρ nξaʊaιl ταιριξheaʓτα ʊó, ocuρ ʊob
e ριιι ιιιτ eρcuρ ι мbeol αιρechταιρ. Ꝭeιʊlιмιʊ cleρeʓ,

---

1 Performed. ʊo ριξιιeʊ, B. ʊo
ριιιιιeaʊh, C.

2 Killed one another. ʊo maρʊaʊ
α cheιle. This is a loose way of
saying that some members of rival
septs of Muinter-Cuirnin were slain
in family disputes.

3 Baile - choillte - foghair. baιle
choιllʼ ρoʊ, for Baile-choillte-fobhair,
B. The name of this place is now

Anglicised Castlefore. It is a village
in the county of Leitrim.

4 Real foster-brother. ʊeρʊcóm-
alτα, C. ʊeρlchomomalτa, B.

5 That this is not. naʓ ι ρo, C.
naʓ ιρι ρo, B.

6 Conchobhar. See note 7, p. 126.

7 Wednesday. The Dom. Letter
(E) is added in the margin in B.

shouldst live for our children after us, to maintain them."
Mac Donnchaidh proceeded on in advance, therefore, and
desisted not from this career and onset until he arrived
at Ros-Comain ; and they put provisions into the castle;
and only one warrior of them was slain, whose body they
themselves carried with them : and not often before had
there been performed[1] in Erinn a braver and more mighty
expedition than that expedition. Muinter-Cuirnin killed
one another[2] in hoc anno, i.e. John and Conla were slain by
Diarmaid, son of Muirchertach O'Cuirnin, in the house of
O'Duibhgennain of Baile-choillte-foghair[3]; and Diarmaid
himself went to the house of Conchobhar Crom, the son of
Tadhg O'Conchobhair, i.e. his lord and real foster brother[4];
and Conchobhar apprehended him in his own house,
and delivered him up to Muinter-Ruairc and Muinter-
Cuirnin ; and he was more than a fortnight in confinement, and at last fell by the son of John O'Cuirnin.
Cathal Mac Donnchaidh mortuus est the fourteenth of the
kalends of October, (and I am not certain that this is
not[5] the year in which it would be right to set down
Conchobhar,[6] son of Imhar O'hAnlidhe). Muirchertach
Mac Aedhagain, ollamh-brehon of the men of Tebhtha,
mortuus est.

The kalends of January on Wednesday[7], and the fifteenth
of the moon; anno Domini M°.cccc°.x. ; quintus annus
[cycli] lunaris ; tertius Indictionis; ii. annus cycli solaris.
Raghnall Mag Raghnaill, dux of Muinter-Eolais, mortuus
est after unction and penitence; and Cumscrach Mag
Raghnaill, who was proclaimed Mag Raghnaill in his
place, died in the course of a fortnight after he had
assumed the chieftaincy; and that was the fall in presence of an assembly.[8] Fedhlimidh Clerech,[9] son of Aedh,

---

[8] *In presence of an assembly.*
mbŭoł αɲechcaɪɼ, B. ɪ mbeoł
aɲɲuchcaɪɼ, C. This is a proverb,
literally meaning "in the mouth of
an assembly," but conventionally signifying in the approach to, or rather

within view of, honour and distinction.

[9] *Fedhlimidh Clerech*; i.e. Fedhlimidh the Cleric. See the second
entry under the next year, where the
date of this obit is corrected.

[MS. defective.
Text supplied
from "Annals
of Connacht."]

mac. Ceóa mic ᵽeιólιmιó .h. Conchubaιp, ᴅo ecc
coιccιᵹιp pe ᵽeιl Ópιᵹᴅe ιn hoc anno. Ⅿac Ruaιóᵽι
óιcc .h. Chonchoóaιp ᴅo ecc ιn hoc anno; aᵹuᵽ Caᴅc
caᵽᵽaċ mac Coιppᴅhealbaιᵹ ᴅuιnn .h. Conchoóaιp ᴅo
écc beoᵽᵽ ιn hoc anno. Ⅿaeleaċlaιnn mac Eoᵹaιn
h. Ruaιᵽc occιᵽuᵽ eᵽc o Conallchaιó, ocuᵽ caιᵽlen
Duιn Cᵽιṁchanᴅaιn ᴅo bloᴅaó la Caιᵽbᵽeachaιó
aᵹuᵽ la Óᵽeιᵽpneachaιb ιaᵽᵽιιι. Doṁnall Ua ᵽlaιch-
ᵬeaᵽcaιᵹ, ᵽιᵹ ιaᵽchaιᵽ Conᴅachc, ᴅo maᵽᵬaó leᵽιn
nᵹιlla nᴅuᵬ Ua ᵽlaιᵬᵬeaᵽcaιᵹ, peᵽ ᴅolum. Doṁnall
Ua Neιll, ᵽι coιcιᵬ Ulaᵬ, ᴅo ᵹaᵬaιl ṁaᵽ ṅaᵽ cuᵬaιᵬ
la Óᵽιan maᵹ Ⅿachᵹamna. Comaᵽ mac Ⅿaιlmuιᵽe
meᵹ Cᵽaιch, ollaṁ Cuaᴅmuṁan, moᵽcuuᵽ eᵽc.
Donᴅchaᴅ Ua Duιᵽnιn moᵽcuuᵽ eᵽc. Saᴅᵬ ιnᵹean
Conchubaιᵽ .h. Óᵽιaιn, uxoᵽ Uaceᵽ a Óuᵽc, moᵽ-
cua eᵽc. Doṁnall mac Coᵽmuιc .h. eᵹᵽa, aᴅᵬaᵽ
ᵽιᵹ Luιᵹne, moᵽcuuᵽ eᵽc. Coᵽmac occ maᵹ Caᵽchaιᵹ
ᴅo ecc ι nᵹeιṁιol Ⅿeᵹ Caᵽᵽchaιᵹ moιᵽ. Eᵽᵬaιᵬ baᵬ
mo na cach eᵽᵬaιᵬ ᴅo ceaċc a nᴅeιᵽeᵬ na blιaᴅna ᵽo,
coιccιᵹιᵽ caᵽeᵽ na ᵽelι Ⅿιcheιl, .ι. Caᴅc .h. Cellaιᵬ,
ᵽι Ua Ⅿaιne, anc aen ᵹaιᵬel ᴅo ba mó cιnnlaιcċι ocuᵽ
caᵬaᵽcaᵽ ᴅo baι an Eᵽιnn ιna aιmᵽιᵽ, ocuᵽ an Alpaιn,
ᴅo écc ιaᵽ mbuaιᵬ onᵹcha ocuᵽ aιchᵽιᵹhe; aᵹuᵽ cuᵽ
aιᵽchιᵽι Dιa ᴅιa αnmaιn ιn ᵽecula ᵽeculoᵽum.
Emanᴅ mac Uιllecc ᴅo ecc ιn ᵽamhᵽaᴅ ᵽιa Caᴅc
.h. Cellaιᵹ, ocuᵽ Caᴅcc mac Uιllιam mιc Conchobaιᵽ
mιc Óᵽanan, ᴅux Coᵽca Achchlaιᵬ ᵽᵽι ᵽé naι
mblιaᴅan, ᴅo écc la ᵽamhιna caᵽeᵽ Caᴅc .h. Cellaιᵹ,
ιna cιᵹ ᵽeιn a coιlleᵬ moιᵽ Cluana Sencha, ιaᵽ nonᵹaᴅ
ocuᵽ aιchᵽιᵹhe nᴅιnᵹᵬala ᴅo Dιa caᵽeᵽ a chιnaᴅ ocuᵽ a
ᵬaᵽᵹaᵬala, ec ᵽepulcuᵽ eᵽc hι manιᵽcιᵽ Roᵽa Cumman
a nochaᵽlιᵹι a ᵽenachaᵽ ocuᵽ a achaᵽ. Eoᵹan mac

---

¹ *A fortnight.* coιcιᴅιᵽ, B. coιc-
ċιᵹιᵽ, C.
² *O'Flaithbhertaigh.* O'Flaherty.
Ua ᵽlaιᵬbeacaιᵹ. C.
³ *Luighne.* Luᵹnι, B. Luιᵹne, C.

⁴ *In captivity.* ι nᵹeιṁιol, C. ι
nᵹeιṁιl, B. The words ι nᵹeιṁιol
Ⅿeᵹ Caᵽᵽchaιᵹ moιᵽ literally
mean " in the gyves of Mac Carthaigh
Mor."

son of Fedhlimidh O'Conchobhair, died a fortnight[1] before the festival of Brighid in hoc anno. The son of Ruaidhri Og O'Conchobhair died in hoc anno; and Tadhg Carrach, the son of Toirdhelbhach Donn O'Conchobhair, died also in hoc anno. Maelechlainn, son of Eoghan O'Ruairc, occisus est by the Conallachs; and the castlo of Dun-Crimhthannain was afterwards demolished by the people of Cairbre and Breifne. Domhnall O'Flaithbhertaigh,[2] king of the West of Connacht, was slain by the Gilla-dubh O'Flaithbhertaigh, per dolum. Domhnall O'Neill, king of the province of Uladh, was taken prisoner, in an unbecoming manner, by Brian Mac Mathghamhna. Thomas, son of Maelmuire Mac Craith, ollamh of Tuadh-Mumha, mortuus est. Donnchadh O'Duirnin mortuus est. Sadhbh, daughter of Conchobhar O'Briain, uxor of Walter Burk, mortua est. Domhnall, son of Cormac O'hEghra, heir to the sovereignty of Luighne,[3] mortuus est. Cormac Og Mac Carthaigh died whilst detained in captivity[4] by Mac Carthaigh Mor. A loss greater[5] than every loss occurred[6] in the end of this year, a fortnight after Michaelmas, i.e. Tadhg O'Cellaigh, king of Ui-Maine, the greatest Gaeidhel of his time in Erinn, and in Alba, for distributing gifts and presents, died after the victory of unction and penitence; and may God be merciful to his soul in sæcula sæculorum. Edmond, son of Ulick, died the summer before Tadhg O'Cellaigh; and Tadhg, son of William, son of Conchobhar Mac Branan, dux of Corca-Achlann[7] during nine years, died on Allhallows Day after Tadhg O'Cellaigh, in his own house at Coillidh-mor of Cluain-Sencha, after unction, and after suitable penitence to God for his sins and transgressions, et sepultus est in the monastery of Ros-Comain, in the tomb of his grandfather and father. Eoghan, son of Murchadh

---

[5] *Greater.* baд mo, "which was greater," B; iɼ mo, "which is greater," C.

[6] *Occurred.* ɒo ceáċc; lit. "came."
[7] *Corca-Achlann.* B and C have *Corca Athchlaidh.*

[MS. defective.
Text supplied
from "Annals
of Connacht."]

Muɼċaιδ .h. Maδaδan, ɼι τɼιʟ nαɴmċaδa, ocuɼ
Cobτhach .h. Maδaδan, δamhna ɼιξ ocuɼ eɼɼoιcc,
moɼτuι ɼunτ. Ꝺonδchaδ .h. Ceʟʟaιξ, ι. mac Maιʟeaċ-
ʟaιnn, δo ɼιξaδ ɼoɼτ Taιδξ. Coιc ceaδ bo ʟa cʟoιnn
.h. Conchoδaιɼ δuιnn o muιnnτιɼ .h. Conchoδaιɼ ɼuaιδ,
o ɼaιch δɼenaιnn, ɼo bɼaιξιτ na 8amhna ιn hoc anno.
Muιɼcheaɼτach .h. Ꝺιmuɼaιξ moɼτuuɼ eɼτ ιn hoc anno.
Toιɼɼδeaʟδaċ ocuɼ Taδcc, δa mac hι Maιʟmuaιδ, ocuɼ
Ꝺoṁnaʟʟ mac mιc hoιbιcιn hι Maoιʟṁuaιδ, δo maɼδaδ
ʟa cʟoιnn Maoιʟuξɼa hι ɼex caʟʟaιnδ αuξuɼτ aɼaι
ʟaιche mιɼ ξɼeιne ; διa Ꝺoṁnaιξ ιmoɼɼo aɼaι ʟaιche
ɼechτmaιne. Muɼchaδ Ua Pʟaιchδeaɼτaιξ δo ɼιξaδ
τaɼeιɼ Ꝺomhnaιʟʟ .h. PꝪaιchδeaɼτaιξ δo maɼδaδ
ʟaιɼιn Ꝡιʟʟa nδuδ. Uιʟʟιam .h. Tomaʟτaιξ, ɼɼιoιɼ τιξι a
nαcτh ʟuaιn, quιeuιτ. Maeʟechʟaιnn moɼ, mac Peɼξaιʟ,
mιc Peɼξaιʟ, mιc Muιɼcheaɼτaιξ moιɼ meξ Eochacan,
δux ceneʟ Pιachaιδ mιc Heιʟʟ naι ξιaʟʟaιδ, moɼτuuɼ eɼτ
ι mιɼ Ꝺecembeɼ na bʟιaδna ɼa. Moɼιanuɼ Pιʟιuɼ
Taτhaι .h. bιɼn ɼubmeɼɼuɼ eɼτ .xιιιι. Kaʟʟaιnδ Ocτobιɼ.

Kt. Enaιɼ ɼoɼ Ꝺaɼδaιn, ocuɼ .xxuι. ɼuιɼɼι ;
M°.cccc°.xι. ; uι. annuɼ cιcʟι ʟunaɼιɼ ; quaɼτuɼ ιnδιc-
τιonιɼ ; τeɼτιuɼ cιcʟι ɼoʟaɼιɼ. 8ιδan ιnξean ιaɼʟa
Ꝺeɼṁuṁan, uxoɼ meξ Caɼτhaιξ moιɼ, moɼτua eɼτ.
αξ ɼo bʟιaδaιn chóιɼ Peιδʟιmιδ cʟéɼιξ ocuɼ mιc
Ruaιδɼι oιcc. Ꝺoṁnaʟʟ mac Conchoδaιɼ .h. bɼιaιn,
ɼιξδamhna Tuaδṁuṁan, δo maɼδaδ ʟaɼ an ṁbaɼɼach

---

1 *Intended king and bishop.* δamhna ɼιξ ocuɼ eɼɼoιcc ; lit. " materies
regis et episcopi." Roderick O'Flaherty states, in a marginal note in
the Trin. Coll. (Dublin) copy of the
Four Masters, at the year 1411, that
O'Madden was intended bishop of
Clonfert.

2 *At the approach of Allhallowtide.*
ɼo bɼaιξιτ na 8amhna. The words
ɼo bɼaιξιτ signify lit. " about the
neck," and correspond to the Lat.
gula in " *gula Augusti.*"

3 *Tadhg.* B has Taδc, which is
the genit. form.

4 *The day of the month.* ʟaιche
mιɼ ξɼeιne. This clause, together
with the three words following it, is
omitted in C.

5 *The Gilla-dubh;* i.e. the "Black
fellow." Another O'Flaherty. See
p. 133.

6 *Race of Fiachadh.* The Cenel-
Fiachaidh, or Kineleagh. See note 5,
p. 500, vol. i.

O'Madadhain, king of Sil-Anmchadha, and Cobhthach O'Madadhain, an intended king and bishop[1], mortui sunt. Donnchadh O'Cellaigh, i.e. the son of Maelechlainn, was made king after Tadhg. Five hundred cows *were carried off* by the sons of O'Conchobhair Donn from O'Conchobhair Ruadh's people, from Rath-Brenainn, at the approach of Allhallowtide,[2] in hoc anno. Muirchertach O'Dimusaigh mortuus est in hoc anno. Toirdhelbhach and Tadhg,[3] O'Maelmhuaidh's two sons, and Domhnall, grandson of Hobicin O'Maelmhuaidh, were slain by the Clann-Maelughra on the sixth of the kalends of August, as regards the day of the month;[4] on Sunday, moreover, as regards the day of the week. Murchadh O'Flaithbhertaigh was made king after Domhnall O'Flaithbhertaigh had been slain by the Gilla-dubh.[5] William O'Tomaltaigh, prior of a house at Ath-Luain, quievit. Maelechlainn Mor, the son of Ferghal, son of Ferghal, son of Muirchertach Mor Mac Eochagain, dux of the race of Fiachadh[6] the son of Niall-nai-ghiallach, mortuus est in the month of December of this year. Marianus filius Tathei O'Birn submersus est the fourteenth of the kalends of October.[7]

The kalends of January on Thursday,[8] and the twenty-sixth of the moon; M°.cccc°.xi.; vi. annus cycli lunaris; quartus Indictionis; tertius cycli solaris. Siblian, daughter of the Earl of Des-Mumha, uxor of Mac Carthaigh Mor, mortua est. This is the proper year[9] of Fedhlimidh Clerech, and of the son of Ruaidhri Og. Domhnall, son of Conchobhar O'Briain, royal heir of Tuadh-Mumha, was slain by the Barrach Mor.

---

[7] At the end of this entry the note Pacin qui repibric (sic) occurs in B and C. The identity of this Patin forms the subject of some observations in the Introduction.

[8] *Thursday.* The Dom. Letter (D) is added in the margin in B.

[9] *The proper year.* The chronicler means that this is the year in which the obits of Fedhlimidh Clerech O'Conchobhair, and the son of Ruaidhri Og O'Conchobhair, which have been entered above under 1410 (pp. 130-2), should be recorded.

[MS. defective.
That supplied
from "Annals
of Connacht."]

mop. Ua Suilleaban vo ċallaó via ḃpaiṫpiḃ buṫein
pep volum, ocup Conchuḃap mac ꝣilla Mochuva .ḣ.
Suilleaban occipup ept a ɼpaṫpe ɼuo pep volum.
Manipṫip Θnaiꝣ vúin vo Loɼcaó in hoc anno.
Doṁnall .ḣ. ḃechan, ɼai ɼenchaió, mopṫuup ept.
Diapmaiv, mac ꝣilla Ipa meꝣ Capṫhaiꝣ, ollaṁ
Tuaṫṁuṁan pe ván, mopṫuup ept. 8aóḃ inꝣean mic
Mupchaóa, uxop Mic ꝣilla Paṫpuic, mopṫua ept.
Muipcheapṫach mac Conulaó .ḣ. Neill mopṫuup ept.
Invpaiꝣió le hΘmann a ḃupcc ɼop cloinn 8eoan Ua
hΘꝣpa, ocup mopan von ṫip vo Loɼcaó Leip, ocup Αpṫ
mac Muipcheapṫaiꝣ .ḣ. eꝣpa vo mapḃaó la ɼoiꝣiv in
la ɼin. ḃenmuṁan inꝣen Αeóa .ḣ. Conchoḃaip, uxop
Mupchaió mic Copmaic mic Donnchaió, mopṫua ept.
Doṁnall mac Caṫail mic Αeóa .ḣ. Ruaipc mopṫuup
ept in hoc anno. Taichleaċ buve mac 8eain .ḣ. eꝣhpa
mopṫuup ept. Maióm mop le mac Doṁnaill na
hΑlpan ɼop ꝣallaḃ Αlpan, ocup mac ꝣilla Θoin vo
muinnṫip mic Doṁnaill vo mapḃaó hi ɼpiṫꝣuin an
maóma ɼin. Iapla Depmuṁan vo invapba la 8emup
mac ꝣepoiṫ, .i. a vepḃpaṫaip. Seppiam na Mióe vo
ꝣaḃail la .ḣ. Conchoḃaip Faiꝣi in hoc anno, ocup
ɼuaplacaó mop vo ḃein ap iappin. Ua Suilleaban
mop vo ꝣaḃail, ocup a mac vo mapḃaó, la Doṁnall
vuḃ .ḣ. Suilleaban pep volum. Caech na mochepꝣi,
mac Taióc, mic Diapmava meꝣ Capṫhaiꝣ, vo mapḃaó
pep volum la Feiólimió mac Diapmava meꝣ Capṫhaiꝣ.
Maꝣ Capṫhaiꝣ mop vo innapbaó la hUa Suilleaḃain
in hoc anno. Fepꝣal mac Maꝣnupa ṫiꝣeapna ṫipe
Tuaṫhail, ocup a mac Αeó, vo mapḃaó pep volum

---

¹ *Fratre.* ɼpi, for ɼpaṫpi, C.

² *Mac Carthaigh.* The Four Mas-
ters write the name Mag Craith, or
Magrath, which is certainly the proper form.

³ *Earl.* The Four Masters call him

"Thomas, the son of John." The
cause of his expulsion was a marriage
contracted with a girl of humble station. On this Moore has founded the
song, "By the Feale's wave be-
nighted."

⁴ *Brother.* Recté " Uncle."

O'Suillebhain was blinded by his own kinsmen per dolum; and Conchobhar, the son of Gilla-Mochuda O'Suillebhain, occisus est a fratre[1] suo, per dolum. The monastery of Euach-dúin was burned in hoc anno. Domhnall O'Bechan, an eminent historian, mortuus est. Diarmaid, son of Gilla-Isa Mac Carthaigh,[2] ollamh of Tuadh-Mumha in poetry, mortuus est. Sadhbh, daughter of Mac Murchadha, uxor of Mac Gilla-Patraic, mortua est. Muirchertach, son of Cu-Uladh O'Neill, mortuus est. An attack was made by Edmond Burk on the sons of John O'hEghra, and a great part of the country was burned by him; and Art, son of Muirchertach O'hEghra, was killed by an arrow that day. Benmumhan, daughter of Aedh O'Conchobhair, uxor of Murchadh, son of Cormac Mac Donnchaidh, mortua est. Domhnall, son of Cathal, son of Aedh O'Ruairc, mortuus est in hoc anno. Taichlech Buidhe, son of John O'hEghra, mortuus est. A great victory by Mac Domhnaill of Alba over the Foreigners of Alba; and Mac Gilla-Eoin of Mac Domhnaill's people was slain in the counter-wounding of that victory. The Earl[3] of Des-Mumha was expelled by James, son of Garrett, i.e. his brother.[4] The Sheriff of Midhe was taken prisoner by O'Conchobhair Failghe in hoc anno; and a great ransom was subsequently exacted from him. O'Suillebhain Mor was taken prisoner, and his son slain, by Domhnall Dubh O'Suillebhain, per dolum. Caech-na-mocherghi,[5] son of Tadhg, son of Diarmaid Mac Carthaigh,[6] was slain, per dolum, by Fedhlimidh son of Diarmaid Mac Carthaigh.[6] Mac Carthaigh Mor was expelled by O'Suillebhain in hoc anno. Ferghal Mac Maghnusa, lord of Tir-Tuathail, and his son Aedh,[7] were slain, per dolum, by the sons of

A.D. [1411.]

---

[5] *Caech-na-mocherghi*; lit. "the blind [man] of the early rising." The Four Masters say that his real name was Tadhg, and that he was the son, not the grandson, of Diarmaid, or Dermot.

[6] *Mac Carthaigh*. Mac Carthy. meᵹ Caṗṫha, B.

[7] *Aedh*; i.e. Hugh. B and C have Ꝺeḋa, which is the genitive form of the name.

[MS. defective.
Text supplied
from "Annals
of Connacht."]

ꝺo cloinn Ruaıꝺꞃı mıc Maᵹnuꞃa, .ı. Eoᵹan ocuꞅ
Muıꞃċeaꞃꞇać cam ; ocuꞅ ꞇıᵹeaꞃna ꝺo ꝺenaṁ ꝺEoᵹan
ıaꞃaṁ ꞃoꞃ ꞇıꞃ Ꞇuaċaıl. Caꞇhal .h. Cuıꞃnın, aꞃꝺꞗaꞃ
ollaṁan na Ḃꞃeıꞃne, quıeuıꞇ. Maᵹnuꞅ mac Ḃaeċh-
ᵹalaıᵹ mıc Cceꝺacan, pꞃıoıꞃ Slıcıᵹ, moꞃꞇuuꞅ eꞅꞇ.
Cꞃoch naeṁ. Raċa boċh ꝺo ꞇelccen ꞃola ꞇaꞃ a
cꞃechꞇaıꝺ ıꞃın blıaꝺaın ꞃın, ocuꞅ moꞃ ꝺo mıꞃꝺuılıꝺ
ꝺo ꝺenaṁ ꝺı, ocuꞅ ᵹalꞃa ocuꞅ ꞇeꝺmanna ımꝺa ꝺo
choꞃcc ꝺı. Maelmoꞃꝺa .h. Raıᵹıllıꝺ, ꞃı muıınꞇıꞃe
Maılmoꞃꝺa, moꞃꞇuuꞃ eꞅꞇ. Cuċonnachꞇ ꞃuaꝺ, mac
Pılıp mıc Ḃꞃıaın moıꞃ mec Maċhᵹaṁna, ꝺo maꞃꝺaꝺ
ꝺo cloınn ꞇ8eaın baılꞇ̃ mıc Ḃꞃıaın móıꞃ meᵹ
Maċhᵹaṁna, ılluꞃᵹaın Ꝕeꞃꞃmaıᵹe, ın eꞃꞃach na
blıaꝺna ꞃın. Roḃeꞃꝺ Munꞇan, eꞃꞃoᵹ na Mıꝺe, ın
Cꞃıꞃꞇo quıeuıꞇ. bellum Ḃeoıl na mıılleaꝺ la Conchoḃaꞃ mac 8eaın mıc Ḃꞃanaın, ꞃoꞃ cloınn Conchoḃaıꞃ
mıc Ḃꞃanan, ın ꞃamhꞃaꝺ ꝺeꞃ Ꞇaıꝺc mıc Ḃꞃanan, ıaꞃ
nᵹaıꞃın ꝺa ꞇıᵹeaꞃna aꞅa, .ı. Conn mac Cceꝺa, ocuꞅ
Conchoḃaꞃ mac 8eaaın mıc Echmaꞃcaıᵹ, ubı occıꞃı
ꞃıınꞇ Conn ocuꞅ Mane, ꝺa mac Cceꝺa mıc Conchuḃaıꞃ
mıc Ḃꞃanan, ocuꞅ Uıllıam ꞃınn mac Cuınn, eꞇ alıı ; ꝺıa
Lúaın aꞃaı laıċhe ꞃechꝺmaıne eꞃꝺe ; ocuꞅ ꞃuccaꝺ Conn
beoloıꞇıꝺe ꞃoꞃ ın nᵹꞃencha, ocuꞅ nı ꞃeꞇaꞃꞃa a aoıꝺıᵹ
oꞃın amaċ ; eꞇ ꞃeꞃuleꞃc̃ ı manıꞃꞇıꞃ na mḃꞃaċhaꞃ
ıꞃꞃuꞃ Coman ; mí ꞃıa Luᵹnaꞃaꝺ ꝺo ꞃonaıꞇ na ꞃoᵹınṁa
ꞃın, ocuꞅ ꝺo ꞃan an ꞇoıꞃıᵹeaċꞇ aᵹ Conchoḃaꞃ ıaꞃ ꞃın.
Caıꞇılın ınᵹean Ꞇomalꞇaıᵹ .h. Ꝑeꞃᵹaıl, uꝺoꞃ Maıleaċlaınn ṁoıꞃ meᵹ Eochacan, quıeuıꞇ a mıꞃ Ꝺecımbeꞃ
na blıaꝺna ꞃın. Ḃeanmúṁan, ınᵹean Cceꝺa mıc Ꝑeꝺ-
lımıꝺ .h. Chonchoḃaıꞃ, banꞇıᵹeaꞃna cloınne Connmaıᵹ

---

1 Tadhg ; i.e. Tadhg, the son of
William, son of Conchobhar Mac
Branan, whose death is recorded under
the previous year.

2 Occisi. occı, B and C.

3 Son of Conn ; i.e. of Conn Mac
Branan, sl. 1396, as above recorded.

4 To the Grencha. ꝼ ın nᵹncĥ.,
B. Omitted in C.

5 Sepulti sunt. ꞃeꞃuleꝓꞇ̃, apparently by mistake for ꞃeꞃulꞇı ꞃunꞇ,
B and C.

6 Caitilin ; i.e. Kathleen.

7 Benmumhan ; lit. "Woman of

Ruaidhri Mac Maghnusa, viz., Eoghan and Muirchertach
Cam; and Eoghan was afterwards made lord over
Tir-Tuathail. Cathal O'Cuirnin, intended ollamh of the
Briefne, quievit. Maghnus, son of Baethghalach Mac
Aedhagain, prior of Sligech, mortuus est. The Holy
Crucifix of Rath-both shed blood through its wounds in
this year; and a great many miracles were wrought by
it; and many distempers and diseases were checked by
it. Maelmordha O'Raighilligh, king of Muinter-Mael-
mordha, mortuus est. Cuchonnacht Ruadh, son of
Philip, son of Brian Mor Mac Mathghamhna, was killed
by the sons of John Balbh, son of Brian Mor Mac
Mathghamhna, in Lurgan of Fernmhagh, in the spring
of this year. Robert Montan, bishop of Midhe, in Christo
quievit. The battle of Bel-na-muilledh *was gained* by
Conchobhar, son of John Mac Branan, over the sons of
Conchobhar Mac Branan, the summer following *the death of*
Tadhg[1] Mac Branan—after two lords had been proclaimed
by them, viz., Conn, the son of Aedh, and Conchobhar,
the son of John, son of Echmarcach—ubi occisi[2] sunt
Conn and Maine, the two sons of Aedh, son of Conchobhar Mac Branan, and William Finn, son of Conn,[3]
et alii; (this was on Monday as regards the day of the
week; and Conchobhar was carried mortally wounded
to the Grencha,[4] and I know not his subsequent fate); et
sepulti sunt[5] in the Friars' monastery in Ros-Comain.
A month before Lammas these great deeds were performed; and the chieftainship remained afterwards with
Conchobhar. Caitilin,[6] daughter of Tomaltach O'Ferghail,
uxor of Maelechlainn Mor Mac Eochagain, quievit in the
month of December of this year. Benmumhan,[7] daughter
of Aedh, son of Fedhlimidh O'Conchobhair, lady of the

Munster." This entry is given as
follows in C:—Uenmurhan ınġeαn
Ccoda mıc Ƒeıdlımıd αtha na
ruech, ocur deırbƒur Toırr-
dhelbaıġ ruaıd, leıt rıġ Con-

nacht, banтıġeαrna, &c.; i.e.
"Benmumhan, daughter of Fedhlimidh of Ath-na-righ [sl. 1316], and
sister of Toirdhelbhach Ruadh, half-
king of Connacht, lady, &c."

[MS. defective.
Text supplied
from " Annals
of Connacht."]

ꝛe Linn ꞇꝛiꝛ ꞇiꝣheaꝛnaiꝣi, moꝛꞇua eꝛꞇ. Muiꝛcheaꝛ-
ꞇach Miꝺech mac Uꝛiain .h. Feꝛꝣail, ꞇiꝣeaꝛna in
ꞇalaꝺ na hⱭnꝣaile, ꝛeꝛ na himꝺeꝛꝣaꝺ ꝛiaṁ, ꝷuieuiꞇ
in Cꝛiꝛꞇo.

Ct. enaiꝛ ꝛoꝛ ⱭIne, ocuꝛ ꝛechꞇmaꝺ huaꞇhaꝺ
ꝛuiꝛꝛi ; M°.cccc°.ꭓii. ; uii. anno cicli lunaꝛiꝛ; ꝷuinꞇuꝛ
inꝺicꞇioniꝛ; ꝷuaꝛꞇuꝛ annuꝛ cicli ꝛolaꝛiꝛ. Ricaꝛꝺ
Uaꝛeꝺ ꝺo ꝺol ꝛoꝛ inꝺꝛaiꝣiꝺ i Cuil Ceꝛnaꝺa, ocuꝛ
maiꞇhe an ꞇiꝛe uile ꝺo bꝛeiꞇh ꝛaiꝛ ocuꝛ a chuꝛ
ꝺochóm na Muaiꝺe, ocuꝛ a baꞇhaꝺ ꝛuiꝛꝛi ; ocuꝛ ꝺꝛonꝣ
moꝛ ꝺa ṁuinnꞇiꝛ ꝺo ꝧaꞇaꝺ ocuꝛ ꝺo ꝣaꝧail ann beuꝛ.
Ꞇiꝣeaꝛnan oc mac Ꞇiꝣeaꝛnain mic Ualꝣaꝛꝣ .h. Ruaiꝛc,
.i. ꝺeꝡ aꝺꝧaꝛ ꝛiꝣ Uꝛeiꝛne, ꝺo ecc in hoc anno a
ꝛoiꝛchinꝺ a .ui. mbliaꝺan .ꭓꭓꭓ. eiꝺiꝛ chaiꝛc ocuꝛ bell-
ꞇaine. Feꝛꝣal .h. heꝣꝛa, aꝺꝧaꝛ ꝛiꝣ Luiꝣne, moꝛꞇuuꝛ
eꝛꞇ. Ꝺoṁnall mac Neill .h. Ꝺoṁnaill ꝺo ecc in hoc
anno. Coꝣaꝺ aꝣ .h. Feꝛꝣail ꝛe ꝣallaiꝧ, ocuꝛ Fabaꝛ ꝺo
loꝛcaꝺ Léo, ocuꝛ ꝺaine imꝺa ꝺo maꝛbhaꝺ ocuꝛ ꝺo
ꝣaꝧail Leo. Uaile na ꝣaillṁe ꝺo loꝛcaꝺ. Saꝺꝧ inꝣean
Ꞇiꝣeaꝛnan .h. Ruaiꝛc, uꭓoꝛ emainꝺ mic Ꞇomaiꝛ mic
Caꞇhail .h. Feꝛꝣail, moꝛꞇua eꝛꞇ. Coccaꝺ eiꝺiꝛ .h.
Caꞇhain ocuꝛ .h. Ꝺoṁnaill, ocuꝛ clann Seaain .h.
Ꝺoṁnaill ꝺo ꝧeiꞇ a ꝛann .h. Chaꞇan ; ocuꝛ Ua Caꞇhain
ocuꝛ an clann ꝛin ꝺo ꝺol ꝛoꝛ inꝺꝛaiꝣiꝺ ꝛoꝛ Ua
n'Ꝺoṁnaill, aꝣuꝛ ceꞇhꝛe ꝛiꝛ .ꭓ. ꝺo muinnꞇiꝛ .h.
Ꝺhoṁnaill ꝺo maꝛꝧaꝺ ꝺoiꝧ ꝛa mac Feiꝺlimiꝺ .h.
Ꝺoṁnaill, ocuꝛ ꝛo Caꞇhal mac Raꝣnaill .h. Uaiꝣill.
Ꝺonꝺchaꝺ maꝣ Uꝛaꝺaiꝣ, ꞇiꝣeaꝛna Cuili Uꝛiꝣꝺin,
moꝛꞇuuꝛ eꝛꞇ. Mac Lochlainꝺ .h. Ruaiꝛc, ꝛiꝛ aꝛaiꞇi
in ꝣiolla ballach, mic Ꝺonꝺchaiꝺ mic Lochlainꝺ, ꝛai
ꝛial oiꝛꝺeiꝛc aiꞇheaꝛach, móꝛꞇuuꝛ eꝛꞇ in hoc anno.

---

1 *Muirchertach Midhech*; i.e. Muirchertach (Murtough) the Meathian;
so called from having been fostered in
Midhe, or Meath.

2 *Friday.* The Dom. Letters (C
B) are added in the margin.

3 *Cuil-Cernadha.* Cuil Ceꝛnaꝺa, B. Cuil Ceaꝛnaꝺa, C. Now
called Coolcarney, a district in the
barony of Gallen and county of Mayo.

4 *Hoc.* hocc, B.

Clann-Connmhaigh during the time of three lords, mortua est. Muirchertach Midhech,[1] son of Brian O'Ferghail, lord of Caladh-na-hAnghaile, a man who had never been reproached, quievit in Christo.

The kalends of January on Friday,[2] and the seventh of the moon; Mº.ccccº.xii.; vii. anno cycli lunaris; quintus Indictionis; quartus annus cycli solaris. Richard Barrett went on an expedition to Cuil-Cernadha;[3] and the principal men of the country overtook him, and drove him to the Muaidh, in which he was drowned; and a great number of his people were furthermore drowned and captured there. Tighernan Og, son of Tighernan, son of Ualgharg O'Ruairc, i.e. a good heir to the sovereignty of Breifne, died in hoc[4] anno, at the termination of his thirty-sixth year, between Easter and May-day.[5] Ferghal O'hEghra, intended king of Luighne, mortuus est. Domhnall, son of Niall O'Domhnaill, died in hoc anno. A war was waged by O'Ferghail with Foreigners; and Fabhar was burned by them, and many persons were slain and captured by them. The town of the Gaillimh was burned. Sadhbh, daughter of Tighernan O'Ruairc, uxor of Edmond, son of Thomas, son of Cathal O'Ferghail, mortua est. A war between O'Cathain and[6] O'Domhnaill, and the sons of John O'Domhnaill were on the side of O'Cathain; and O'Cathain and these sons (of John) went on an expedition against O'Domhnaill, and fourteen men of O'Domhnaill's people were slain by them, including the son of Fedhlimidh O'Domhnaill, and Cathal, the son of Raghnall O'Baighill. Donnchadh Mac Bradaigh, lord of Cuil-Brighdin, mortuus est. The son of Lochlainn O'Ruairc,[7] who was usually called the Gilla Ballach, son of Donnchadh, son of Lochlainn, a generous, illustrious,[8] joyous, eminent[9] man, mortuus est in hoc

---

[5] *Between Easter and May-day.* eιδιη chαιρc οcuρ bellταιne, B. Not in C.

[6] *And.* οcuρ, C. comὸ, B.

[7] *O'Ruairc.* Uα Rαιξιllιξ, C.

[8] *Illustrious.* οιηὸειηc, C. uη-ὸαιηcc, B.

[9] *Eminent man.* ραι, C. ραn, B.

[MS. defective.
Text supplied
from "Annals
of Connacht."]

Oelḃ Muıre Catha trⱮım do ḋenaṁ mıorḃuılıḋ mór. Cúaḃa Maʒ Corman, ⱱer ʒⱮaḋa dO Ḃrıaın, mortuuⱮ erⱭ. CaıⱭⱱerⱱına, ınʒen Maıleaĕlaınn mıc MurʒıuⱮa mıc Oonoĥaıḋ, uxor Mıc ⱱⱮⱱⱮⱮʒh, do baⱭĥaḋ do tuıle ⱱeⱭĥa aʒ dol dociⱮum aⱮⱮⱮⱮ an doṁnaıʒ o a Ɑıʒ ⱱeⱮⱮ. Aeḋ mac EⱮⱮⱮ .h. ⱮⱮeⱮⱮ do eloḋ a hAⱭĥ cⱮⱮaⱭĥ o Ʒallaıḃ, ıaⱮ na ḃeⱮĥ deıĥ mbⱮⱮaḋna a laıṁ ⱮeṁerⱮḋe, ocuⱮ Ɑaʒ moⱮan bⱮaʒⱱⱭ aⱮ a mbⱮoⱭⱭ leⱮⱮ ⱮⱮ ⱭⱮⱮ ⱮⱮⱮ. Eⱱa a LeⱮⱮ ocuⱮ mac ⱮⱮⱮaⱮla CⱮⱮle daⱮa do ĥeʒmaⱮⱮ ⱱe ⱮⱮⱮⱮe a cⱮⱮⱮ MocelⱮoʒ, ocuⱮ a ⱱoⱮⱭⱮm ⱱe ⱮⱮⱮⱮe aⱮⱮⱮⱮⱮ. MoⱮⱮⱮⱮaʒaḋ la ḂrⱮⱮⱮ, mac DoṁⱮⱮaⱮⱮ mⱮc MⱮⱮⱮĥeaⱮⱭaⱮʒ .h. ChonchoⱮaⱮⱮ, ⱱo bⱮaʒⱮⱭⱭ na LⱮʒⱮaⱮⱮaḋ, conⱱeacⱮⱮaḋ a ⱮʒⱮⱮⱮeⱮʒⱮḋ aⱮ ⱱⱮⱮ, ocuⱮ aⱮⱮⱮḋe a CⱮⱮⱮⱮ CⱮⱮaⱮⱮ, ocuⱮ Ɱ CeⱮⱮa ocuⱮ hⱮ CⱮⱮⱮⱮaⱮcⱮe cⱮⱮⱮⱮⱮ ⱭⱮⱮaⱮʒ; ocuⱮ ⱮⱮⱮⱮⱮe leⱮⱮ cⱮⱮⱮⱮⱮ MⱮⱮⱮⱮⱮ ⱮⱮ mbⱮⱮʒ cona caeⱮaⱮʒeacⱮⱭ ⱮⱮⱮⱮ cⱮⱮⱮⱮⱮ ⱮⱮⱮ; aʒⱮⱮ do ⱱⱮⱮⱮⱮaⱱaⱮ cⱮⱮⱮⱮ UⱮⱮⱮⱮam ⱮⱮⱮⱮⱮe, Ua ⱮⱮⱮⱮⱮⱮeaⱮⱭaⱮʒ ocuⱮ mⱮⱮⱮ-ⱭⱮⱮ MaⱮⱮⱮe, ocuⱮ ⱮaⱮeⱱaⱮʒ, ocuⱮ ʒaⱮⱮeaⱮʒaⱮʒ, ocuⱮ ʒoⱮⱱeⱮⱮaⱮʒ ocuⱮ SⱭoⱮⱱⱮⱮaⱮʒ aⱮ a cⱮⱮⱱ, ocuⱮ ⱮⱮ ⱭⱮⱮⱮⱮaⱱ ⱮⱮⱮ ⱭⱮoⱮⱱ Ɱo ⱭacⱮaⱮ do; aʒⱮⱮ do LoⱮⱮe ḂⱮⱮⱮⱮ na cⱮⱮⱮⱮa ⱱa ⱮaⱮⱮⱮḋeoⱮⱮ, ocuⱮ do ⱮⱮⱮⱮ a ⱮʒⱮⱮⱮⱭ ⱮⱮⱮ, ocuⱮ do LoⱮⱮe a LoⱮʒⱱⱮⱮⱮ Ɱ. caⱮⱮⱮⱮen an ḂⱮaⱮⱮⱮaⱮʒ, ocuⱮ ⱮⱮ LeⱭⱮ ⱮⱮⱮⱮe ocuⱮ ⱱaⱮⱮe LocⱮa MeⱮⱮa. OcuⱮ do cⱮⱮⱮ cⱮaⱮⱮ MⱮⱮⱮⱮⱮ cona caeⱮaⱮʒeaⱱⱭ ⱮⱮaⱮ ⱱⱮ ⱭⱮʒⱮⱱ ⱮaⱮⱮⱮ; aʒⱮⱮ do ⱱeⱮ ⱮⱮⱱⱮ a ʒallaⱮⱱ ocuⱮ a ʒⱮⱮⱱeⱮⱮⱮⱱ ConⱮⱮacⱮⱭ don cⱮⱮⱮ ⱮⱮⱮ; ócⱮⱮ ⱭaⱮⱮⱮce ⱮeⱮⱮ ⱮⱮⱱⱮⱮⱮ ⱱa ⱱⱮʒ ⱮaⱮⱮⱮ. SⱮⱮaʒaḋ ⱮⱮⱮe Le hEⱮʒaⱮ mac DoṁⱮⱮaⱮⱮ ⱮⱮⱮ MⱮⱮⱮⱮeaⱮⱭaⱮʒ UⱮ ConchoⱮaⱮⱮ, Ɱo maⱱaⱮⱮe ConⱱacⱮⱭ, Ɱo ⱭⱮʒⱮaⱮⱮⱮ cⱮoⱮⱮⱮe

¹ *Miracles.* moⱮⱮⱮuⱮⱮḋ, C. mⱮⱮ-ⱮⱮaⱮⱮ (a miracle), B.

² *To O'Brian.* dO ḂⱮⱮaⱮⱮ, for do O ḂⱮⱮaⱮⱮ, B. dO ḂⱮⱮaⱮⱮ, C.

³ *After.* ⱮaⱮ, C. aⱮ, B.

⁴ *Eda Leis.* Eⱱa a LeⱮⱮ, B and C. His proper name was Hugh Lacy, or Hugo de Lacy. See O'Donovan's ed. of the Four Masters, A.D. 1412, note ᵇ.

⁵ *The son.* mac. C. a mac, "his son," B. He was Thomas, son of Maurice, fourth Earl of Kildare, wherefore Ware (Annals) calls him Thomas Fitz-Maurice.

⁶ *At the approach.* ⱱo bⱮaʒⱮⱭⱭ; lit "about the throat." See note ², p. 134.

⁷ *Bands.* caeⱮaⱮʒeacⱮⱭ. Bands of persons who accompanied the

anno. The Image of Mary of Ath-Truim wrought great miracles[1]. Cu-abha Mac Gormain, a man of trust to O'Briain,[2] mortuus est. Catherine, daughter of Maelechlainn, son of Maurice Mac Donnchaidh, uxor of Mac Firbisigh, was drowned by a rushing flood whilst going to Sunday-mass from her own house. Aedh, son of Henry O'Neill, escaped from Ath-cliath, from the Foreigners, after[3] having been ten years in confinement previously; and he brought many captives with him from their captivity on that occasion. Eda Leis[4] and the son[5] of the Earl of Cill-dara encountered one another in Cill-Mochellog, and fell by each other there. A great hosting by Brian, the son of Domhnall, son of Muirchertach O'Conchobhair, at the approach[6] of Lammas, when he went first into Gailenga, and from thence into Clann-Cuain, and into Cera, and into Conmaicne-Cuile-Tolaidh; and he brought the Clann-Maurice-na-mBrigh, with their bands,[7] into this territory. And the sons of William Burk, O'Flaithbhertaigh, Muinter-Maille, the Barretts, the people of Gailenga, the Goisdelbhas, and the Stauntons assembled against him; but they gave him neither conflict nor battle; and Brian burned the districts in despite[8] of them, and destroyed all their corn-fields, and burned their fortresses, viz., Caislen-an-Bharraigh, and the Leth-innse, and Baile-Locha-Mesca. And he sent the Clann-Maurice, with their bands, home safely afterwards. And he exacted[9] peace from the Foreigners and Gaeidhel of Connacht on that occasion, and came home quite safely[10] himself after that. Another hosting by Eoghan, son of Domhnall, son of Muirchertach O'Conchobhair, into[11] the plain of Connacht, at the call of the sons of Toirdhelbhach

---

predatory forces for the purpose of driving and guarding the preys, and who were well armed, and commanded by officers, were called *caeraighecht*.

[8] *In despite.* ᴅᴀ naimḃeoin, C. ᴅᴀ nanᴅeoin, B.

[9] *He exacted.* ᴅo ben, B. ᴅo baın, C.

[10] *Quite safely.* ımᵱlan, C. ᵱlan, B.

[11] *Into.* ᵱo would perhaps be better translated " through."

[MS. defective.
Text supplied
from " Annals
of Connacht."]

Coippᴅhealbaıᵹ .h. Conchobaıp, cup mıllpeᴅ cuıᴅ
cloınne mıc Peıᴅlımıᴅ ᴅon machaıpe, ocup puccpaᴅ
bu ocup bpaıᵹᴅı leo ıap pın. Emanᴅ αlamap mopᴅuup
epᴅ ın hoc anno. Ruaıᴅpı mac Caᴅhaıl .h. Pepᵹaıl
ᴅo mapᴅaᴅ a machaıpe Cuıpcne ᴅupchop ᴅpoıᵹᴅı].

Kt. ıanaıp; ᴅpı blıaᴅna .x. ocup .cccc. ocup mıle aıp
an Cıᵹepna. Concubap O Docapᴅaıᵹ, .ı. ᴅaıpech apᴅa
Mıᴅaıp, ocup ᴅıᵹepna ınnpe hEoᵹaın, ocup peap eınıᵹ
coıᴅceınn, ᴅec an blıaᴅaın pı. Cuaᴅhal O Maılle ᴅo
ᴅul a cınᵹeaᴅ Ulaᴅ ap buannachᴅ, ocup a beᴅ blıaᴅaın anᴅ; ocup ᴅeachᴅ ᴅo ᴅap aıp luchᴅ .uıı. lonᵹ, ocup
ᵹaoᴅ mop ᴅeıpᵹe ᴅoıb, ocup a mbpeᴅ buᴅ ᴅuaıᴅ laım
pe hαlpuın, ocup Donnchaᴅ mac Eoᵹaın Connachᴅaıᵹ
mıc ᴅSuıbne ᴅo beᴅ ann, ocup Domnall ballaᴅ mac
Suıᴅne ᵹıpp, ocup a mbaᴅhaᴅ uıle co na muınᴅep eᴅıp
mnaı ocup pep; ocup Cuaᴅhal peın ᴅo ᴅeachᴅ a ᴅıp
ap eıᵹın an αlbaın.

Kt. ıanaıp; ceıᴅpı blıaᴅna .x. ocup .cccc. ocup mıle
aıp ın Cıᵹepna.

Kt. ıanaıp; cuıᵹ blıaᴅna .x. ocup cccc. ocup mıle
aıp an Cıᵹepna. Saxanaᴅ ᴅo ᴅeachᴅ a nEıpınn an
blıaᴅaın pı .ı. loapᴅ Pupnamal, ocup ᴅo aıpᵹ pe mopan
ᴅoep ᴅana Eıpenn.

---

¹ *Alamar.* This name is at present
generally written Delamar, or Dela-
mer.

² *Arrow.* This concludes the hiatus
which begins at the year 1316 (vide
p. 584, vol. i., note ¹), and which,
for the reasons stated in the Introduction, it has been thought desirable to
supplement from the MSS. B and C.

³ *Kalends.* The text from this to
the year 1461, inclusive, is written on
seven leaves of paper (bound up
with the vellum), in the handwriting of Brian Mac Dermott, the
person for whom the rest of the MS.
was transcribed. The handwriting
is pretty legible, although the ink is
somewhat faded; but the orthography
is rude and incorrect. The entries
in this portion of the Chronicle
are unfortunately very meagre,
many years being simply represented by the usual chronological
criteria; and it would be a mat-
ter of doubt whether this fragment
should be at all considered as a por-

O'Conchobhair, when they destroyed the part of the plain belonging to the grandsons of Fedhlimidh; and they carried away cows and prisoners afterwards. Edmond Alamar[1] mortuus est in hoc anno. Ruaidhri, son of Cathal O'Ferghail, was killed in Machaire-Cuirene by a shot of an arrow[2]].

A.D.
[1412.]

The kalends[3] of January. The age of the Lord one thousand, four hundred, and thirteen years. Conchobhar O'Dochartaigh, i.e. chieftain of Ard-Midhair, and lord of Inis-Eoghain, and a man of universal bounty, died this year. Tuathal O'Maille went to the Province of Uladh, on military service, and was a year there. And he returned with a fleet of seven ships; and a great wind arose, and they were carried northwards near Alba; and Donnchadh, son of Eoghan Connachtach Mac Suibhne, was there, and Domhnall Ballach Mac Suibhne Gerr—who were drowned with all their people, both woman and man; and Tuathal himself landed with difficulty in Alba.

[1413.]

The kalends of January. The age of the Lord one thousand, four hundred, and fourteen years.[5]

[1414.]

The kalends of January. The age of the Lord one thousand, four hundred, and fifteen years. A Saxon came to Erinn this year, i.e. Lord Furnival; and he plundered many of the poets of Erinn.[6]

[1415.]

---

tion of the chronicle, if the so-called Annals of Connacht were not equally meagre at this period. The fragment is preceded by a transcript in the handwriting of the late Professor O'Curry.

[4] *Alba.* Here the scribe left a space of ten lines, of which some "Conall O'Ferall" has availed himself to scribble a few doggerel rhymes.

[5] *Years.* A space of some lines, left between this and the next entry, is also occupied by some rhymes, in Irish, one stanza of which was written by "Maelruanaidh, son of Aedh Mac Diarmada."

[6] *Erinn.* After this entry there is a note in very faded ink (apparently in the handwriting of the person who wrote the continuation of the "Chronicon Scotorum" in the MS. classed H. 1, 18, Trin. Coll., Dublin), to the following effect: τρι ουιℓℓεόσα ocuρ ρο ρίςεο ουιℓℓεος μεμρυιμ ατά ιριηℓεαϐυη ρο, ocuρ ρεαχττηονιℓ-ℓεοσα ραρειρ ιαρ ϐρίοη, i.e. "three leaves and six score leaves of vellum that are in this book, and seven leaves of paper, truly." The MS. at present consists of ninety-nine leaves of vellum, and seven of paper leaves.

ʃct. 1αnαιρ; ρο blιαοnα οhec ocυρ .cccc. ocυρ mιle αιρ
ιn Cιʒeρnα. Ʒορmlαιċ ιnʒen Neιll mοιρ 1 Ncιll, ben
τSeαιn 1 Oomnαιll, οec αn blιαοαιn ρι. Mαc Mατhunα, .ι. Ccροʒαl mαc Ƀριαιn mοιρ meʒ Mατhunα, οο
ουl οec, ocυρ α mαc .ι. Ƀριαn οο ριʒαο ꝼορ Oιρʒιαl-
lαιb ιnα ιnαο.

ʃct. 1αnαιρ; ρeαchτ mblιαοnα οhec ocυρ .cccc. ocυρ
mιle αιρ αn Cιʒeρnα. Mαc Mυρchαοα, .ι. ρι Lαιʒen,
.ι. Ccρτ mαc Ccιρτ Chαοιnαnαʒ, αn coιceοhαċ οob ꝼeρρ
ċιnech ocυρ enʒnυm ocυρ οeρc οο bι nα αιmριρ, οhec
nα Loυʒρορτ ρeαιn αn blιαοαιnρι, ιαρ mbυαιο οιʒċα
ocυρ αιċριʒe.

ʃct. 1αnαιρ; ochτ mblιαοnα .x. ocυρ .cccc. ocυρ mιle
αιρ αn Cιʒeρnα. Cιʒeρnαn mαc Uαlαιρʒ 1 Rυαιρc, .ι.
ριʒ Ƀρeꝼne, οhec αn blιαοαιn ρι. Ƀριαn bαllαch mαc
Ccοƀα mιc Ꝼeιlιm 1 Conchobαιρ, αƀƀαρ ριʒ Connαchτ,
οhec. Cαοʒ mαc Cατhαl mιc Cαιοʒ meʒ Ꝼhlαιnnchαιƀ,
ταιρech Oαρτραιʒe, οhec ιn blιαοαιn ρι. Θοʒαn mαc
Cιʒeρnαιn 1 Rυαιρc, .ι. αƀƀαρ ριʒ Ƀρeꝼne, οο bατhαο
αρ Loc Ꝼιnοmιιʒe αn blιαοαιn ρι. Ccοƀ bυιοhe .h.
Rυαιρc οο ʒαbαιl ριʒe nα Ƀρeꝼne αnοιαιƀ α αthαρ,
.ι. Cιʒeρnαιn mοιρ.

ʃct. 1αnαιρ; nαι mblιαοnα .x. ocυρ .cccc. ocυρ mιle
αιρ αn [Cιʒeρnα]. Coʒαο mορ eτιρ O Neιll, .ι. Oomnαll mαc Θαιρɼ 1 Neιll, ocυρ Θοʒαn mαc Neιll οιʒ
1 Neιll, ocυρ Θοʒαn αρ nοeαnαm cenʒαιl ριρ O nOom-
nαιll, .ι. Cοιρροheαlbαch, ocυρ O Oomnαιll αρ cορ
τρlυαιʒ mοιρ αnα ιnαο, ocυρ οοl α τιρ Θοʒαιn, ocυρ
αn τιρ υιle οο mιlleο οοιƀ; ocυρ O Ncιll, .ι. Oomnαll,
οο ιnοαρbαο αριn τιρ lα neαρτ Conαllαċ ocυρ Θοʒαιn
1 Neιll. Slοιʒeο mορ le Ƀριαn O Conchobαιρ οοn cυρ

---

1 *Mac Mathuna*. For Mac Mathghamhna, or Mac Mahon.
2 *Died*. οο ουl οec; lit. "went
to death." At the end of this entry
the scribe has added the note "Oeαρ-
οαοιn eιοιρ οα cαιρʒ αnιυ ƀαm

α ρορ Comαιn cnαc Ʋ Oιαρ-
mαοα;" lit. " Thursday between two
Easters [i.e. Easter Sunday and Low
Sunday] to-day; and I in Ros-
Comain . . . ."
3 *Loch - Fianmhaighe*. Garadice

The kalends of January ; the age of the Lord one thousand, four hundred, and sixteen years. Gormlaith, daughter of Niall Mór O'Neill, wife of John O'Domhnaill, died this year. Mac Mathuna,[1] i.e. Ardghal, son of Brian Mor Mac Mathuna, died ;[2] and his son, i.e. Brian, was made king over the Oirghialla in his place.

The kalends of January; the age of the Lord one thousand, four hundred, and seventeen years. Mac Murchadha, i.e. the king of Laighen, i.e. Art son of Art Caemhanach, the best provincialist that was in his time for hospitality, and prowess, and charity, died in his own fortress this year, after the triumph of unction and penitence.

The kalends of January ; the age of the Lord one thousand, four hundred, and eighteen years. Tighernan, son of Ualgharg O'Ruairc, i.e. the king of Breifne, died this year. Brian Ballach, son of Aedh, son of Felim O'Conchobhair, intended king of Connacht, died. Tadhg, son of Cathal, son of Tadhg Mac Flannchaidh, chieftain of Dartraighe, died this year. Eoghan, son of Tighernan O'Ruairc, i.e. the intended king of Breifne, was drowned on Loch-Finnmhaighe[3] this year. Aedh Buidhe O'Ruairc assumed the sovereignty of the Breifne in succession to his father, i.e. Tighernan Mór.

The kalends of January; the age of the [Lord] one thousand, four hundred, and nineteen years. A great war between O'Neill, i.e. Domhnall son of Henry O'Neill, and Eoghan the son of Niall Og O'Neill ; and Eoghan formed a league with O'Domhnaill, i.e. Toirdhelbhach. And O'Domhnaill collected a great army, and went into Tir-Eoghain, and the entire country was destroyed by them; and O'Neill, i.e. Domhnall, was expelled from the country through the power of the Conallachs and Eoghan O'Neill. A great hosting by Brian O'Conchobhair on

Lough, in the county of Leitrim. The Annals of the Four Masters, and also the Annals of Connacht, add that

Eoghan O'Ruairc was going from Inis-na-dtore, or Hog Island, to visit his father.

ŗιιι τo ċaoḃ ŗeolτα 1 Neill a τιŗ Ꮯoḃa, ocuŗ Muŗḃaċ
1 Ꭰomnaill, .ı. lonȝpoŗτ 1 Ꭰomnaill, τo loŗcuḃ leaıŗ,
ocuŗ τıŗ Ꮯoḃa τo milleτ. Ꮯomaŗ bacaċ, mac mıc
1aŗla Uŗmuman, τo τul τo conȝnam le ŗıȝ 8αxŗaıı
an blıaτaın ŗı, ocuŗ moŗan τuaıŗlıb Eŗeńn τo τul leıŗ
annŗa Ƒŗaınȝ aŗ an cocaτ ŗın. Ꮯn Calbaċ O Conchoḃaıŗ, ŗı O Ƒaılȝe, τo ȝabaıl a ŗeall le mac Líneḃeτ
a Ƒŗenτe, ocuŗ a ŗeıc τo ŗe ŗeŗ ınaıτ ŗıȝ 8αxαn, .ı.
loaŗτ Ƒuŗnamal, ocuŗ an τŗaċ τo ȝabaτ é, aıı τuıne
τo bí na ȝlaŗ τeloτ leıŗ τa τıȝ ŗeın. Ƒeŗceŗτ O hUı-
ȝınτ τhec, .ı. ŗaoı ŗe τan, ocuŗ ŗeŗ ċıȝe naıȝıτ coıτcenτ
τŗeŗaıb Eŗenn. Mac Muŗchaτa, .ı. ŗı Laıȝen, .ı. Ꭰonn-
chaτ Coemanach, τo ȝabaıl ŗe Ȝalloıb, ocuŗ [a] bŗeıċ
a 8[a]ŗanuıb an blıaτaın ŗı. Muıŗceŗτach mac Ḃŗıaıιι
1 Ƒhlaıċḃeŗτaıȝ, ŗı ıaŗċaıŗ Connachτ, τhec ın blıaτaın
ŗı, .ı. ŗeıċem. coıτcenτ τo clıaŗuıb ocuŗ τo τamaıḃ
Eıŗenn. 8ean mac Caċaıl meȝ Uıτıŗ τo maŗbaτ an
blıaτaın ŗı. 8luaȝ moŗ leaıŗ O Ceallaıȝ Maıne ocuŗ
le Uıllıam O Ceallaıȝ, ocuŗ le mac Uıllıam Ḃuŗc,
ocuŗ le Caċal nτuḃ O Conchoḃaıŗ, ocuŗ le Mac
Ꭰıaŗmaτa Muıȝe Luıŗȝ, .ı. Ꮯomalτach an ınıȝ, mac
Conchoḃaıŗ meıc Ꭰıaŗmaτa, ocuŗ Uıllıam ȝaŗb mac
Ꭰabuıċ, τıȝeŗna claınne Connmuıȝ; ocuŗ a ceıċeŗna
ȝallóclaeċ τo bŗeċ leo, .ı. Mac Ꭰuḃȝaıll ocuŗ Ꮯoıŗŗ-
τhelbach mac Ꭰomnaıll; ocuŗ a nτul τun τuŗuŗ ŗın
a claınn Rıcaıŗτ, τa milleτ, ocuŗ τınτaŗbaτ Mıc
Uıllıam a claınn Rıcaıŗτ amaċ. 8loıȝeτ moŗ eıle
τo ḃeaċ aȝ Mac Uıllıam aŗ a cınτ, .ı. Ꮯaτȝ O Ḃŗıaıιι
ocuŗ a bŗaċŗeaċa, ocuŗ Ꭰomnall mac 8uıḃne, .ı.
Ꭰomnall na maτman. Ꮯaŗlα, ımoŗŗo, an τa τŗluaȝ
ŗın τa ceıle a mbel Ꮯċa Lıȝen, ocuŗ τuȝaταŗ τŗoıτ

---

1 *Calbhach.* Caḃ, MS.

2 *Linebed Frende.* This is also the form in the Annals of Connacht. In the Ann. of Ulster the Christian name is written Libened, but Libener by the Four Masters. The name Frende (or Frene) is now usually written Freyne and Freney.

3 *O'Cellaigh.* In the Annals of Connacht he is described as the son of

that occasion, at the instigation of O'Neill, into Tir-
Aedha, and Murbhach-O'Domhnaill, i.e. O'Domhnaill's
fortress, was burned by him, and Tir-Aedha destroyed.
Thomas Bacach, grandson of the Earl of Ur-Mumha,
went this year to aid the king of the Saxons; and many of
the nobles of Erinn went with him to France on this war.
The Calbhach[1] O'Conchobhair, king of Ui-Failghe, was
captured in treachery by the son of Linebed Frende,[2] and
sold to the king of the Saxons' Deputy, i.e. Lord Furnival;
and when he was captured, the person who was confined
with him absconded with him to his own house. Fer-
cert O'hUiginn died, i.e. an eminent poet, and a man
who kept a general house of hospitality for the men of
Erinn. Mac Murchadha, i.e. the king of Laighen, i.e.
Donnchadh Caemhanach, was captured by Foreigners,
and taken to Saxonland, this year. Muirchertach, son
of Brian O'Flaithbhertaigh, king of the West of Connacht, died this year; i.e. the general protector of the professors and learned of Erinn. John, son of Cathal Mag
Uidhir, was slain this year. A great hosting by O'Cellaigh[3] of Ui-Maine, and by William O'Cellaigh, and by
Mac William Burk, and by Cathal Dubh O'Conchobhair,
and by Mac Diarmada of Magh-Luirg, (i.e. Tomaltach-
an-einigh, son of Conchobhar Mac Diarmada), and William Garbh Mac David, lord of Clann-Connmhaigh. And
they took with them their bands of gallowglasses, viz.,
Mac Dubhgaill, and Toirdhelbhach Mac Domhnaill,
and went on this occasion into Clann-Rickard, to
destroy it, and to expel Mac William from out of Clann-
Rickard. Mac William had another[4] great army to
meet them, viz., Tadhg O'Briain and his kinsmen, and
Domhnall Mac Suibhne, (i.e. Domhnall na madhman).[5]
These two armies met, moreover, at the mouth of

Maelechlainn O'Cellaigh, or Malachy
O'Kelly.

[4] *Another.* ᵉᵉ eɪᴸᵉ, MS.; the two
first letters (ee) being the abbrev.

for the word eɪᴸᵉ, subsequently written.

[5] *Domhnall - na - madhman;* i. e.
"Domhnall of the defeats."

τά ροιle αnnρίn, ocuρ το marbατ Mac Duḃҕoill αnn, ocuρ α ḃiρ mac, ocuρ α nҕαllóclaeḋ uile, ocuρ Toιρρτhelbach mac Doṁnaill ocuρ α mac το τul αρ in τροιτ ρin ρlαn ; ocuρ α muιnnτeρ το marbατ uile αnτ ; ocuρ το marbατ ιlumατ ταοιneaḋ αιρ in lαταιρ ρin ; ocuρ το ҕαbατ O Cellαιҕ ocuρ mac Dαbιḋ ; ocuρ Uilliαm O Cellαιҕ το τul nα oenαρ αρin mαιτm ρin ; ocuρ moραn το mαιτhib O Mαine το ҕαbαιl ocuρ το marbατ ραn αρ ρin. Ocuρ ni ρeaταρ cιnneτh nα coṁαιρeam αρ meατ αn mατmα ρin, no αρ meτ eαταlα clαinnι Ricαιρτ ocuρ nα Muιmneaḋ, τechαιb ocuρ τeιτeτh, ocuρ το bραιҕτιḃ mαιτhe ρt. Αcoḃ buιḃe O Ruαιρc, mac Tιҕeρnαιn, τhec αn blιαταιn ρι α τuρ α ρατα nα longρορτ ρein, ocuρ Tατҕ mac Tιҕeρnαιn το ριҕαḃ nα ιιαḃ αρ αn mḃρeaρne αn blιαταιn ρι.

Ƿt. Ιαnαιρ ; ρïe blιαταn ocuρ .cccc. ocuρ mιle αιρ αn Tιҕeρnα. Uilliαm mac Mαιlečlαιnn ι Cellαιҕ, .ı. αṫḃaρ ριҕ .h. Mαine, τhec αn blιαταn ρι.

Ƿt. Ιαnαιρ ; blιαταιn αρ .xx. ocuρ .cccc. ocuρ mιle αιρ αn Tιҕeρnα.

Ƿt. Ιαnαιρ ; τα blιαταιn αρ .xx., ocuρ ceιτρι ceτ ocuρ mιle, αιρ αn Tιҕeρnα.

Ƿt. Ιαnαιρ ; τρι blιατnα .xx. αρ ceιτρι ceτ αρ mιle αιρ αn Tιҕeρnα. Ḃαρ Toιρτealbαιҕ αn ḟιnα ι Domnαιll, ρι τιρe Conuιll ocuρ cιneoιl Mοαιn, ocuρ Inτρι hɛoҕαιn, neḋ buτ mo ρeαn, ocuρ τοb ρeaρρ uαιρle ιnα αιmριρ, το τul τhec αn αιbιτ mαnαιҕ α mαιιιρτιρ Eρα Ruαιḃ. Cαιρlen ḃeoιl ατα Senαιҕ το τιnnρcnα ιn blιαταιn ρι le Ιιιαll O nDomnαιll.

Ƿt. Ιαnαιρ ; ocuρ ceτρι blιατnα .xx. ocuρ ceτρι ceτ ocuρ mιle αιρ αn Tιҕeρnα.

---

1 *Defeat.* A note at the end of the entry read**s** Uιllec ρuατ mac Uιllec ιn ριonα τuҕ ιn mαοιτm. ριn Ατα Lιten; i. e. " Ulick Ruadh, son of Ulick-in-fiona, that gave this defeat of Ath-Lithen." The Four Masters have no mention of this battle.

1 *Son of Tighernan.* Tιҕeρūι, MS.

2 *Four.* cuιҕ, "five," MS.

Ath-Lighen; and they gave battle to one another there; and Mac Dubhgaill was slain there, and his two sons, and all their gallowglasses; and Toirdhelbhach Mac Domhnaill, and his son, escaped safely from this battle; and his people were all slain there. And a great many men were killed in that field; and O'Cellaigh and Mac David were taken prisoners, and William O'Cellaigh escaped alone from this rout; and a great many of the nobles of Ui-Maine were slain and captured in that slaughter. And the extent of this defeat,[1] or the amount of the spoils of the Clann-Rickard, and of the Momonians, in horses, armour, noble captives, &c., could not be determined or counted. Aedh Buidhe O'Ruairc, the son of Tighernan, died this year, in the beginning of his prosperity, in his own fortress; and Tadhg, son of Tighernan,[2] was made king over the Breifne, in his place, this year.

The kalends of January; the age of the Lord one thousand, four hundred, and twenty years. William, son of Maelechlainn O'Cellaigh, intended king of Ui-Maine, died this year. [1420.]

The kalends of January; the age of the Lord one thousand, four hundred, and twenty-one years. [1421.]

The kalends of January; the age of the Lord one thousand, four[3] hundred, and twenty-two years. [1422.]

The kalends of January; the age of the Lord one thousand, four hundred, and twenty-three years. Death of Toirdhelbhach-an-fhina O'Domhnaill, king of Tir-Conaill, and of Cenel-Moan, and Inis-Eoghain—the person of greatest prosperity and[4] best nobility in his time: he died in a monk's habit in the monastery[5] of Es-Ruaidh. The castle of Bel-atha-Senaigh was begun this year by Niall O'Domhnaill. [1423.]

The kalends of January; and the age of the Lord one thousand, four hundred, and twenty-four years. [1424.]

---

[4] *And.* The character (7) for *ocur* ("and") is repeated in the MS.

[5] *Monastery.* ınınırcıp, for maınırcıp, MS.

Ƈt. 1αnαιρ; ocuρ .u. blιατnα .xx., ceτρι cετ ocuρ mιle, αιρ ιn ƇιƷeρnα.

Ƈt. 1αnαιρ; ocuρ .uι. blιατnα .xx. ocuρ ceτρι cετ, ocuρ mιle, αιρ αn ƇιƷeρnα.

Ƈt. 1αnαιρ; ocuρ uιι. mblιατnα .xx., ceτρι cετ ocuρ mιle, αιρ αn ƇιƷeρnα.

Ƈt. 1αnαιρ; ocuρ ochτ mblιατnα .xx., ocuρ ceτρι cετ ocuρ mιle, αιρ αn ƇιƷeρnα. Ccoτ mαc Ƥιlιρ meƷ Uιτιρ το éƷ αƷ τοιƷechτ τια οιlιτρι o cαρραιc ραn Sem; α eƷ α Cιnn τραle, ocuρ α cτnαcαl α CoρcαιƷ, ιαρ mbuαιτ onƷτα ocuρ αιτριƷe. Ccoτ oƷ mαƷ Uιτιρ το mαρbατ le clαιnn τonnchατα bαllαιƷ MeƷαmραιn.

Ƈt. 1αnαιρ; ιx. mblιατnα .xx. ocuρ ceτρι cετ [ocuρ mιle] αιρ ιn ƇιƷeρnα. O ƑlαnnαƷαιn Ƈuαιτι ρατα το mαρbατ le clαιnn Ccoτα meƷ Uιτιρ, ρορ Ʒρειρ noιτce ιno τιƷ ρειn. Mαιτm Ccχαιτ cιlle moρe lα .h. Neιll, ocuρ lα .h. RαιƷαllαιƷ, ρορ Ʒαllαιτ. Ιρ αnτρα mblιατnιn ρο το ρuƷατ Cceτ ρuατ mαc Neιll Ʒαιρτ ι τomnαιll.

Ƈt. 1αnαιρ; ocuρ .x. mblιατnα .xx. ocuρ ceιτρι cετ ocuρ mιle αιρ ιn ƇιƷeρnα. MαƷ Uιτιρ, .ι. Ʒιllα τuτ mαc Ƥιlιρ nα τuαιƷe, [το éc] ιn blιαταιn ρι, ocuρ α mαc το ρuƷατ nα ιnατ.

Ƈt. 1αnαιρ; ocuρ en blιαταιn τhec αρ ριcheτ αρ ceιτρι cετ αρ mιle αιρ. ιn ƇιƷeρnα. Seααn mαc Con-connαchτ mιc Ƥιlιb meƷ Uιτιρ το mαρbατ le Ƈeαllαc nEαchαc α ρeαll. ƤlαιƷ moρ α ρeαρuιτ Mαnαc αn blιαταιn ρι. EoƷαn O Ƒιαlαιn τhec. τomnαll bαllαch mαc bριαιn τhec.

Ƈt. 1αnαιρ; ocuρ τα blιαταιn τhec αρ ριcheτ, αρ ceιτρι cετ αρ mιle, αιρ ιn ƇιƷeρnα. O Neιll, .ι. τomnαll bocc mαc Eαnρι αιmρειτ, το mαρbατ lα

---

¹ *Rock of St. James.* Saint James of Compostella, in Spain.

² *Gilla-dubh.* "The Black fellow." Ʒιαllα τuτ, MS.

The kalends of January; and the age of the Lord one thousand, four hundred, and twenty-five years.

The kalends of January; and the age of the Lord one thousand, four hundred, and twenty-six years.

The kalends of January; and the age of the Lord one thousand, four hundred, and twenty-seven years.

The kalends of January; and the age of the Lord one thousand, four hundred, and twenty-eight years. Aedh, son of Philip Mag Uidhir, died whilst coming from his pilgrimage, from the Rock of St. James.[1] He died at Cenn-saile, and was interred at Corcach, after the triumph of unction and penitence. Aedh Og Mag Uidhir was slain by the sons of Donnchadh Ballach Magamhrain.

The kalends of January; the age of the Lord [one thousand], four hundred, and twenty-nine years. O'Flannagain of Tuath-ratha was slain by the sons of Aedh Mag Uidhir, in a nocturnal assault, in his own house. The victory of Achadh-Cille-móire by O'Neill and O'Raighilligh, over Foreigners. It was in this year Aedh Ruadh, the son of Niall Garbh O'Domhnaill, was born.

The kalends of January; and the age of the Lord one thousand, four hundred, and thirty years. Mag Uidhir, i.e. Gilla-dubh,[2] son of Philip-na-tuaighe, [died] this year; and his son was made king in his place.[3]

The kalends of January; and the age of the Lord one thousand, four hundred, and thirty-one years. John, son of Cuchonnacht, son of Philip Mag Uidhir, was slain by the Tellach-Echach in treachery. A great plague in Feara-Manach this year. Eoghan O'Fialain died. Domhnall Ballach, son of Brian,[4] died.

The kalends of January; and the age of the Lord one thousand, four hundred, and thirty-two years. O'Neill, i.e. Domhnall Bog the son of Henry Amhreidh,

---

[1] *Place.* The entries for the three following years (1431-2-3) are wanting in the Dublin copies of the Annals of Connacht, in which the note " desunt tres anni" occurs after the last entry for 1430.

[4] *Brian.* Brian Mac Maghnusa.

Cαϧhαnchαιϧ α nⲈαnαch, ocυρ Ϲρϲ Ϻαc Cαⲉmαoιl, eαρρυc Clocαιρ, ϧo ϧυl ϧhec ιn hoc αnno. Ⲉoξαn mαc Ⲙeιll óιξ l Ⲙeιll ϧo ριξαϧ ϝoρ Ϲιρ nⲈoξαιn. lnξnαϧ moρ ϧραξραιn α ϝoραιϧ Ϻαnαⲉ αn blιαϧαιn ριn, .ι. mυc ϧo bρeιⲉ υαιn ξιl. Uαϲeρ α bυρc, .ι. mαc mιc lαρlα Ulαϧ, ϧhéc. O Ϧυιϧξennαιn Chιlle Ꝛonαιn .ι. Ϻαⲉα ξlαϝ ϧhec; ϝαι ρe ρenchυρ ocυρ ϝeρ ϲιξι αιϧeϧ coιϲ-cιnn αρ ϝeρυιϧ Ⲉρenn.

Ϳcϲ. lαnαιρ; ocυρ ϲρι blιαϧnα ϧhec αρ .xx. αρ .cccc. αρ mιle. Ϻαc Ϻαξnυιρ meξ Uιϧιρ, .ι. Cαϧhαl mαc ξιllαραϧραιξ, ϧhec lα ϝeιlι Ϻιceιl, ocυρ α mαc nα ιnαϧ, .ι. Cαϧhαl oc. Ⲉιξneⲉαn O Ϧomnαιll ϧo ϧυl αρ cρeιⲉ αρ [α] bραⲉαιρ ϝeιn .ι. αρ Ϧonnchαϧ. Ϧonnchαϧ ϧo ϧυl α ϲoραιξechϲ nα cρeⲉe, ocυρ Ⲉιξneαchαn ϧo ϻαρϧαϧ ϧo. Sαmραϧ ξoρϲαⲉ αn ϝαmραϧ ϝo, ocυρ ϝαmραϧ nα meρ αιⲉne ϧo ξoρⲉαι ϧe.

Ϳcϲ. lαnαιρ; ocυρ ceιϲρι blιαϧnα ϧhec αρ ϝιcheϧ, αρ ceιϲρι ceϧ αρ mιle, αιρ ιn Ϲιξeρnα. O Ϧomnαιll, .ι. Ⲙιαll ξαρb mαc Ϲoιρϧeαlbαιξ αn ϝιnα, ϧo ϧυl αρ ϝlυαιξeϧ ϝα Ϻιϧe, ocυρ bρeⲉ αιρ ocυρ αρ beξαn bυιϧne ϲαmαll onϲ ϝlυαιξ, ocυρ α ξαbαιl ϝe ξαlloιb, ocυρ α cυρ co Ϻαnαιιϧ ϧα coιmeϧ; ocυρ αρ mbeⲉ αϲhαιϧ α ηϧρoⲉ bραιξϧeαnυρ αnn ριn bαρ ϧραξαιl ϧo, αρ mbeⲉ en blιαϧαιn ϧec α ϲιξeρnυρ ϲιρe Conαιll ocυρ ιchϲαιρ Connαchϲ; ocυρ Ϲoιρϧeαlbαch mαc Ⲙeιll l Ϧoϻnαιll ϧo mαρbαϧ αn lα ceϧnα. Sιoc moρ αnnρα blιαϧαιn ρ .ι. ρeαchϲ. ρeαchϲϻυιne ρe noϧlυιc, ocυρ ρeαchϲ ρeαchϲmυιne nα ϧιαιϧ. O Ꝛυαιρc ϧhec, .ι. Ϲαϧξ. Cαϧhαl boξυρ O Ꝛυαιρc ϧec.

Ϳcϲ. lαnαιρ; ocυρ .υ. blιαϧnα ϧhec αρ .xx., ocυρ ceιϲρι ceϧ ocυρ mιle, αιρ ιn Ϲιξeρnα. Ϻαιϧm ϲSlebι ϲρυιm leαρ O Ⲙeιll, .ι. Ⲉoξαn, αρ bριαn óc .h. Ⲙeιll

---

was slain by the Cathanachs[1] in Enagh; and Art Mac Cathmhail, bishop of Clochar, died in hoc[2] anno. Eoghan, son of Niall Og O'Neill, was made king over Tir-Eoghain. A great prodigy was observed in Feara-Manach this year, viz., a pig gave birth to a white lamb. Walter Burk, i.e. the grandson of the Earl of Ulster, died. O'Duibhgennain of Cill-Ronain, i.e. Matthew Glas, a professor of history, and keeper of a general house of hospitality for the men of Erinn, died.

The kalends of January; and one thousand, four hundred, and thirty-three years. Mac Maghnuis Mag Uidhir. i.e. Cathal the son of Gilla-Patraic, died the day of Michael's festival; and his son, i.e. Cathal Og, was appointed in his place. Egnechan O'Domhnaill went on a predatory expedition against his own brother, i.e. against Donnchadh. Donnchadh went in pursuit of the prey, and Egnechan was killed by him. This summer was a summer of dearth, and "the summer of the quick acquaintance" it was usually called.

The kalends of January; and the age of the Lord one thousand, four hundred, and thirty-four years. O'Domhnaill, i.e. Niall Garbh, son of Toirdhelbhach-an-fhina, went on a hosting into Midhe; and he was overtaken, with a few companions, a little distance from the army, and was taken prisoner by the Foreigners, and sent to Manann to be detained. And he died after he had been some time in severe confinement there, having been eleven years in the soverignty of Tir-Conaill and Lower-Connacht. And Toirdhelbhach, son of Niall O'Domhnaill, was slain the same day.[3] Great frost in this year, viz., seven weeks before Christmas, and seven weeks after it. O'Ruairc died, i.e. Tadhg. Cathal Bodhar O'Ruairc died.

The kalends of January; and the age of the Lord one thousand, four hundred, and thirty-five years. The victory of Sliabh-truim by O'Neill, i.e. Eoghan, over

oċuꞃ αꞃ Conαllċαıb, oċuꞃ ꞃċαċαꝺ Ḃꞃıαın oıc co
ʒoıꞃıꝺ nα ꝺıαıꝺ ꞃın αn blıαꝺαın ꞃı ; oċuꞃ Mαc Conmıꝺe,
.ı. Conċαḃαꞃ ꞃuαꝺ, ꝺo ṫeαċꞇ ʒo Connαċꞇα ꞃo αn
ꞃċαċαꝺ ꞃın Ḃꞃıαın 1 Neıll ın hoc αnno.. 11ıαll mαc
[Θoʒαın] 1 Neıll ꝺo mαꞃbαꝺ le cloınꝺ Cḣınαċ αꞃ ʒꞃeıꞃ.
Ꝺonnċαꝺ mαc Conconnαċꞇ mıc Ꝑılıb nα ꞇuαıꝺe·
ꝺhec.. Ꝣlαıꞃne mαc Conċuḃαꞃ 1 Rαıʒıllıʒ ꝺhec.

|ɔꞇ. 1αnαıꞃ; ꞃe blıαꝺnα ꝺhec αꞃ .xx. αꞃ .cccc. αꞃ
mıle. Conċuḃαꞃ mαc Seαm 1 Rαʒıllıʒ ꝺhec.

|ɔꞇ. 1αnαıꞃ; ꞃeαċꞇ mblıαꝺnα ꝺhec αꞃ .xx. αꞃ cccc.
αꞃ mıle.

|ɔꞇ. 1αnαıꞃ; oċꞇ mblıαꝺnα ꝺhec αꞃ .xx. αꞃ .cccc. αꞃ
mıle. Ꝑılıb mαc Ꞇomαıꞃ meʒ Uıꝺıꞃ ꝺo ʒαbαıl le nα
bꞃαṫꞃαıb ꞃeın, .ı. Ꞇomαꞃ oċuꞃ Ꝺomnαll oċuꞃ Ruαꝺꞃı.

|ɔꞇ. 1αnαıꞃ; oċuꞃ nαoı mblıαꝺnα ꝺhec αꞃ .xx. αꞃ
.cccc. αꞃ mıle. Mαʒ Uıꝺıꞃ ꝺo ʒαbαıl ıꞃın mblıαꝺαın ꞃo lα Ꝺomnαll mbαllαċ, oċuꞃ Ꝑılıb ꝺo leıʒeαn
αmαċ αn lα ceꝺnα. Mαʒ Uıꝺıꞃ ꝺo leıʒeαn [αmαċ] αn
blıαꝺαın ceꝺnα. O Ꝺomnαıll ꝺo ec ınα lαımꝺeċuꞃ α
Mαnαınꝺ ıꞃın mblıαꝺαın ꞃı, .ı. Nıαll ʒαꞃb, oċuꞃ
Neċꞇαın ꝺo ꞃıʒαꝺ ꞃoꞃ ꞇıꞃ Conαıll. Ꞃeꞃαꝺαċ, mαc
Ꝺuınn mıc Conconnαċꞇ Meʒ Uıꝺıꞃ, ꝺo mαꞃbαꝺ le
hOıꞃʒıαllαıḃ.

|ɔꞇ. 1αnαıꞃ; oċuꞃ ꝺα .xx. blıαꝺαn oċuꞃ .cccc. oċuꞃ
mıle αıꞃ ın Ꞇıʒeꞃnα. Ḃꞃıαn mαc Ꝺomnαıll mıc
Mhuıꞃceꞃꞇαıʒ 1 Conċobαıꞃ, ꞇıʒeꞃnα Slıʒıʒ, ꝺo ꝺul
ꝺhec; oċuꞃ ıꞃ ꞇeαꞃc mα ꝺo ḃı ꝺo ʒαoıꝺeαlαıḃ Ǝꞃenn
ꞃʒeαl buꝺ [mo] nα ꞃın. Mαʒnuꞃ Θoʒαnαċ mαʒ Uıꝺıꞃ

---

1 *Mutilated.* ꞃċαċαꝺ Ḃꞃıαın,
i.e. "mutilation of Brian," MS. The
expression in the Annals of Connacht
is α cıꞃꞃbαꝺ, which means the same
thing. The Four Masters state that
his hand and leg were cut off.

2 *Went to Connacht.* This clause of
the entry, which follows the obit of
Donnchadh Mag Uidhir in the MS.,
is added in a handwriting different

from that of Brian Mac Dermot. It
appears from the Annals of Connacht
that Brian O'Neill was under the
guarantee of the poet Mac Conmidhe,
who retired to Connaught, from
whence he satirized Eoghan O'Neill
and his associates with great bitter-
ness.

3 *Anno.* αꞇ, MS.

4 *Philip-na-tuaidhe;* "Philip of the

Brian Og O'Neill and the Conallachs; and Brian Og was mutilated[1] soon after that in this year; and Mac Con-midhe, i.e. Conchobhar Ruadh, went to Connacht[2] on account of this mutilation of .Brian O'Neill in hoc anno.[3] Niall, son of [Eoghan] O'Neill, was killed by the Clann-Cinaith in a conflict. Donnchadh, son of Cuchonnacht, son of Philip-na-tuaidhe,[4] died. Glaisne, son of Concho-bhar O'Raighilligh, died. [1435.]

The kalends of January; one thousand, four hun-dred, and thirty-six years. Conchobhar, son of John O'Raighilligh, died. [1436.]

The kalends of January; one thousand, four hundred, and thirty-seven years. [1427.]

The kalends of January; one thousand, four hun-dred, and thirty-eight years. Philip, son of Thomas Mag Uidhir, was taken prisoner by his own brothers, viz., Thomas, Domhnall, and Ruaidhri. [1438.]

The kalends of January; and one thousand, four hundred, and thirty-nine years. Mag Uidhir was taken prisoner in this year by Domhnall Ballach, and Philip[5] was liberated the same day. Mag Uidhir was liberated the same year. O'Domhnaill, i.e. Niall Garbh, died in his captivity[6] in Manann in this year; and Nechtan was made king over Tir-Conaill. Feradach, the son of Donn, son of Cuchonnacht Mag Uidhir, was killed by Oirghialla.[7] [1439.]

The kalends of January; and the age of the Lord one thousand, four hundred, and forty years. Brian, son of Domhnall, son of Muirchertach O'Conchobhair, lord of Sligech,[8] died; and it is doubtful if there was of the Gaeidhel of Erinn a [greater] calamity than that. Maghnus[9] Eoghanach Mag Uidhir died. Maghnus,[9] son [1440.]

---

hatchet." His name was Mag Uidhir, or Maguire.

[5] *Philip.* Philip, son of Thomas Mag Uidhir, taken prisoner the pre-vious year.

[6] *Captivity.* Niall Garbh O'Domh-naill was captured by the English of Meath in 1434, as recorded above.

[7] *Oirghialla.* Some entries belong-ing to the year 1591 are here added, in a hand different from that of Brian Mac Dermot.

[8] *Lord of Sligech.* The Four Mas-ters, and the Annals of Connacht, style him "lord of Lower Counacht."

[9] *Maghnus.* Maᵹup, Mˢ.

ᴠhec. Maᵹnuſ mac ᴅoṁnaill meic Coiſḃealḃaiᵹ an
ſina ᴅo maſḃaᴠ. ᴅomnall O ḃſeiſlen ᴠhec.

Ct. Ianaiſ; bliaᴠain ocuſ ᴠa .xx. ocuſ .cccc. ocuſ
mile aiſ in Ciᵹeſna.

Ct. Ianaiſ; ᴠa bliaᴠain ocuſ ᴠa .xx. ocuſ .cccc.
ocuſ mile aiſ in Ciᵹeſna. ḃſian mac Cſᴠᵹail meᵹ
Maᴛhᵹhamna, ſí Oiſᵹiall, ᴠo ᴠul ᴠhec.

Ct. Ianaiſ; ᴛſi bliaᴠna ocuſ ᴠa .xx. ocuſ .cccc.
ocuſ mile aiſ in Ciᵹeſna. Maᵹnuſ mac Cſᴠᵹail meᵹ
Maᴛhᵹhumna ᴠhec. eimeaſ maᵹ Maᴛhᵹhamna ᴠo
maſḃaᴠ leiſ O Neill, .ı. eoᵹan.

Ct. Ianaiſ; ceᴛſi bliaᴠna aſ ᴠa .xx. aſ. cccc. aſ
mile aiſ in Ciᵹeſna. C_oᴆ buiᴆe mac ḃſíain ballaiᵹ
1 Neill, ᴛuiſ einiᵹ ocuſ enᵹnuma Ulaᴠ ana cimſiſ,
ocuſ ſeſ einiᵹ coiᴛcenn ᴠa ᵹach aon, [ᴠo ṁaſḃaᴆ ᴠoen
oſchoſ ſoᵹa aſ ᴠeiſeᴆ cſeiche a cſich meᵹ Cenᵹuſa],
in hoc anno.

Ct. Ianaiſ; ú. bliaᴠna aſ ᴠa .xx., aſ .cccc. aſ mile,
aoiſ in Ciᵹeſna. Ruaiᴠſi mac Comaiſ meᵹ Uiᴠiſ
ᴠhec ᴠo bſóᵹ. Caiſeaᴄ Muinᴛiſe ſeoᴠaᴄain ᴠhec .ı.
ḃſian. Mac ᵹaſſaᴠa ſuaiᴆ [meᵹ Uiᴠiſ] ᴠhec, .ı. Cſᴠᵹal.

Ct. Ianaiſ; ſe bliaᴠna aſ ᴠa .xx. aſ .cccc. aſ mile.
Maᵹ Maᴛhᵹamna ᴠhec iſin mbliaᴠain ſo, .ı. Ruᵹſaiᴠhe
mac Cſᴠᵹail.

Ct. Ianaiſ; ſeachᴛ mbliaᴠna aſ ᴠa .xx. aſ .cccc.
aſ mile. O hUiccinn .ı. Caᴠᵹ óᵹ, ſái ſe ᴠan ocuſ cenᴠ
ſᵹoile eſenn na cimſiſ ſein, ᴠo ᴠul ᴠeᵹ an bliaᴠin
ſı. ᴅomnall ballach maᵹ Uiᴠiſ ᴠo maſḃaᴆ le
macuiᴆ Cſiᴛ meᵹ Uiᴠiſ, ocuſ le macaiᴆ [mec]
Oiſᵹiallᴛaiᵹh. Mac Caſa ᴠhec, Coſmac mac ᵹilla
Cſiſᴛ. ſeiᴠlim mac Seain mic ſilip 1 Raiᵹilliᵹ ᴠo
ᵹaḃail a ſill le ſeſ inaiᴛ ſiᵹ Saxan a nCᴄᴈ Cſuim,
ocuſ a eᵹ ᴠon ſlaiᵹ iaſᴠain.

---

1 *Maghnus.* Maᵹuſ, MS.
ª *Hoc.* hocc, MS. The clause
within brackets, omitted in the MS.,
has been supplied from the Annals of
Connacht.

3 *Brian;* i.e. Brian Mac Gillafinnen.
4 [*Mac*]. mec. Supplied from Annals of Four Masters.
5 *Gilla-Christ.* ᵹialla Cſᴛ, MS.
6 *Saxons'.* Saᵹan, for Saᵹſan, MS.

of Domhnall, son of Toirdelbhach-an-fhina, was slain. Domhnall O'Breislen died.

The kalends of January ; the age of the Lord one thousand, four hundred, and forty-one years.

The kalends of January ; the age of the Lord one thousand, four hundred, and forty-two years. Brian, son of Ardghal Mac Mathghamhna, king of Oirghiall, died.

The kalends of January ; the age of the Lord one thousand, four hundred, and forty-three years. Maghnus,[1] son of Ardghal Mac Mathghamhna, died. Emher Mac Mathghamhna was killed by O'Neill, i.e. Eoghan.

The kalends of January ; the age of the Lord one thousand, four hundred, and forty-four years. Aedh Buidhe, son of Brian Ballach O'Neill, pillar of the hospitality and prowess of Uladh in his time, and a man of general bounty to everyone, [was slain with one cast of a spear, whilst in the rear of a preying party in Mac Aenghusa's territory], in hoc[2] anno.

The kalends of January ; the age of the Lord one thousand, four hundred, and forty-five years. Ruaidhri, son of Thomas Mag Uidhir, died suddenly. The chieftain of Muinter-Pheodachain died, i.e. Brian.[3] The son of Goffraidh Ruadh [Mag Uidhir] died, i.e. Ardghal.

The kalends of January ; one thousand, four hundred, and forty-six years. Mac Mathghamhna died this year, i.e. Rughraidhe, the son of Ardghal.

The kalends of January ; one thousand, four hundred, and forty-seven years. O'hUiginn, i.e. Tadhg Og, a most eminent poet, and head of the schools of Erinn in his own time, died this year. Domhnall Ballach Mag Uidhir was slain by the sons of Art Mag Uidhir, and by the sons of [Mac]'Oirghiallaigh. Mac Caba died, i.e. Cormac, the son of Gilla-Christ.[5] Fedhlim, son of John, son of Philip O'Raighilligh, was treacherously taken prisoner by the king of the Saxons'[6] deputy, in Ath-truim, and died of the plague afterwards.

Ict. Ιαɴαɪρ; ochτ mbliaᴅɴα αρ ᴅα .xx. αρ .cccc.
[αρ] mile αɪρ αɴ Τɪʒερɴα.

Ict. Ιαɴαɪρ; ɴαοɪ mbliaᴅɴα αρ ᴅá .xx. αρ. cccc. αρ
mile αɪρ αɴ Τɪʒερɴα. Ο Raʒilliʒ, .ɪ. mac Seaɪɴ ᴅα
ɴʒορταɪ Εοʒαɴ ɴα ɍεροʒɪ, ᴅhec. Ϧριαɴ óʒ Ο Νeill ᴅhec.

Ict. Ιαɴαɪρ; ᴅeɪc mbliaᴅɴα αρ ᴅá .xx. αρ .cccc. αρ
mile αɪρ αɴ Τɪʒερɴα. Ϻαʒ Uɪᴅɪρ, .ɪ. Τοmαɪρ óʒ mac
Τοmαɪρ ele, ᴅο ᴅul ᴅοčum ɴα Roma ᴅο ραɪč α αɴɪɴα.
Cαthαl, mac Τοmαɪρ mɪc Τοmαɪρ ɪɴeʒ Uɪᴅɪρ, ᴅο mαρ-
bαᴅ le Ꝺοɴɴchαᴅ ɴꝊuɴcαčαč ɾɴαc Τοmαɪρ moɪρ ɪɴeʒ
Uɪᴅɪρ, α ɍɪll. Ꝺοɴᴅchαᴅ Ꝺuɴčαᴅαč ᴅο ɾʒαϲhαᴅ lα
hΕmαɴᴅ mac Τοmαɪρ ɪɴeʒ Uɪᴅɪρ αɴ bliaᴅαɪɴ ceᴅɴα,
Εαɍροʒ Clοčαɪρ ᴅhec, .ɪ. Ϸɪαρɾαρ mαʒ Uɪᴅɪρ.

Ict. Ιαɴαɪρ; eɴ bliaᴅαɪɴ ᴅhec αρ ᴅá .xx. αρ .cccc. αρ
mile αɪρ αɴ Τɪʒερɴα. Ϻαʒ Uɪᴅɪρ ᴅο čοɪʒechτ οɴ
Roɪɴ. Ϻαɪρʒρeʒ ɪɴʒeɴ Ι Cερbαɪll, beαɴ Ι Conchobαɪρ
ɍαɪlʒe, .ɪ. αɴ Cαlbαč, ᴅhec. Ϻαɪɴɪɾτɪρ αɴ Chαbαɪɴ ᴅο
lοɾcαᴅ leɪɾ αɴ mbɾαϲhαɪρ Ο Ϻοčlαɪɴ.

Ict. Ιαɴαɪρ; ᴅα bliaᴅαɪɴ ᴅhec αρ ᴅα ɍɪcheᴅ, αρ .cccc.
αρ mile, αɪρ αɴ Τɪʒερɴα. Ο Ꝺοmɴαɪll, .ɪ. Νeachταɪɴ
mac Τοɪρɾᴅhealbαɪʒ αɴ ɍɪɴα, τɪʒερɴα čɪρe Conαɪll
οcuɾ ceɴel Ϻuαɪɴ, οcuɾ Ιɴɴɪɾɪ hΕοʒαɪɴ, ɍeρ cροᴅα
cοɾαɴταč οcuɾ cɪɴɴlɪτɪρ cοʒαɪᴅ οcuɾ ɾɪče αɴ τuαɪɾcɪɾτ,
οcuɾ ᴅο čuɪρ mοɾαɴ cοɪcɾɪč ɍα ɴα čɪɪɴachταɪᴅ, ᴅο
mαρbαᴅ le clαɪɴɴ Νeill Ι Ꝺοɪɴɴαɪll, α ᴅeρbραčαɪρ
ɍeɪɴ, α ɴᴅubραɪl οɪᴅčɪ ɾeɪle Ϧρeɴαɪɴɴ ᴅο τɾοɴραᴅ,
αρ mbeč οchτ mbliaᴅɴα ᴅhec α τɪʒερɴuɾ τɪρe Conαɪll
ɍα buαɪᴅ cοɴαɪč οcuɾ cοɾɾcαɪρ.

Ict. Ιαɴαɪρ; τρɪ bliaᴅɴα ᴅhec αρ ᴅα .xx., αρ. cccc.
[αρ] mile, αɪρ αɴ Τɪʒερɴα. Ϻαʒ Ϻαϲhʒαmɴα ᴅhec, .ɪ.

---

1 *Eoghan-na-fesogi*; i.e. "Eoghan
(Owen) of the beard."

2 *Cathal.* Ict Cαl., MS., the letter Ict
being an abbrev. for Cαth.

3 *Dunchadhach.* This is an epithet
applied to Donnchadh Mag Uidhir

(Maguire), from his having been
fostered in the territory of Tellach-
Dunchadha, now Tullyhunco, a barony in the co. of Cavan.

4 *Cabhan.* Cavan. Cαɓ, MS.
Cαɓaɪ, for Cαɓαɪɴ, Ann. Ult.

5 *The sons.* The MS. has Τ, for

The kalends of January; the age of the Lord one thousand, four hundred, and forty-eight years.

The kalends of January; the age of the Lord one thousand, four hundred, and forty-nine years. O'Raighilligh, i.e. John's son, who was usually called Eoghan-na-fesogi,[1] died. Brian Og O'Neill died.

The kalends of January; the age of the Lord one thousand, four hundred, and fifty years. Mag Uidhir, i.e. Thomas Og, son of another Thomas, went to Rome for the good of his soul. Cathal,[2] son of Thomas, son of Thomas Mag Uidhir, was slain by Donnchadh Dunchadhach,[3] son of Thomas Mór Mag Uidhir, in treachery. Donnchadh Dunchadhach was mutilated by Edmond, son of Thomas Mag Uidhir, the same year. The bishop of Clochar died, i.e. Piers Mag Uidhir.

The kalends of January; the age of the Lord one thousand, four hundred, and fifty-one years. Mag Uidhir came from Rome. Margaret, daughter of O'Cerbháill, wife of O'Conchobhair Failghe, i.e. the Calbhach, died. The monastery of Cabhan[4] was burned by the Friar O'Mothlain.

The kalends of January; the age of the Lord one thousand, four hundred, and fifty-two years. O'Domhnaill, i.e. Nechtan, the son of Toirdhelbhach-an-fhina, lord of Tir-Conaill, and of Cenel-Moain, and Inis-Eoghain, a brave, protecting man, and the arbiter of war and peace of the North, and who had brought many neighbouring territories under his power, was slain by the sons[5] of Niall O'Domhnaill, his own brother, in the darkness of night, on the festival of Brenainn exactly, after having been eighteen years in the lordship of Tir-Conaill with the palm of wealth and victory.

The kalends of January; the age of the Lord one thousand, four hundred, and fifty-three years. Mac

---

cℓ, the usual abbrev. for cℓainn, "proles." The Four Masters give | the names of the sons of Niall as "Aedh" and "Domhnall."

Ccoḃ ρuαꝺ mαc Ruʒραιꝺe, ocuρ ſeιꝺlιm mαc ḃριαιη
mεʒ mαchʒαmηα ꝺo ριʒαꝺ ſoρ Oιρʒιαll.

ḱt. 1αηαιρ; ocuρ cεtρι blιαꝺηα ꝺhec αρ ꝺα .xx.,
αρ .cccc. αρ mιle, αιρ αη Cιʒερηα. Ruʒραιꝺe mαc
Ηeαchtαιη 1 ꝺomηαιll ꝺo ṁαρbαꝺ co mιραċmαρ,
ꝺeαη uρċαρ ꝺo cloιch α cαιρlεη 1ηηρι αmαċ, ꝺo
ꝺomηαll mαc Ηeαchtαιη 1 ꝺoṁηαιll, αρ mbeċ ꝺα
blιαꝺαιη α cιʒερηuρ Cιρe Coηαιll ꝺo Ruʒραιꝺe
ρoιme ριη. ḃριαη mαc Coηcubαιρ 1 Ɍαιʒιllιʒ ꝺhec.

ḱt. 1αηαιρ; u.blιαꝺηα ꝺhec αρ ꝺά .xx. [αρ] .cccc.
αρ mιle. O Ηeιll ꝺo ριʒαꝺ ſoρ Cιρ ηCoʒαιη, .ι. Cηρι
mαc Coʒαιη mιc Ηeιll oιʒ.

ḱt. 1αηαιρ; ρe blιαꝺηα ꝺhec αρ ꝺά .xx., αρ .cccc. αρ
mιle, αιρ αη Cιʒερηα. OꝺoṁηαιLL, .ι. ꝺomηαll mαc
Ηeιll 1 ꝺomηαιll, ꝺo mαρbαꝺ le clαιηη Ηechtαιη
1 ꝺoṁηαιll α cιʒ ḃuιꝺιη αη blιαꝺαιη ρι, αρ mbeτh ꝺα
blιαꝺαιη α cιʒερηuρ Cιρe Coηuιll ρα buαιꝺ ρmαchtα
ocuρ ριαʒlα, ocuρ Ccoḃ ρuαꝺ mαc Ηeιll 1 ꝺomηαιll
ꝺo ʒαḃαιl αη blιαꝺαιη ρι, ocuρ ριʒ ꝺo ʒαιρm ꝺo
Coιρꝺeαlbαċ Cαιρbρeċ mαc Ηeαchtαιη. O Ηeιll ꝺhec .ι.
Coʒαη mαc Ηeιll.

ḱt. 1αηαιρ; ρeαcht mblιαꝺηα ꝺeʒ αρ ꝺά .xx.
αρ .cccc. αρ mιle αιρ αη Cιʒeρηα. O Coηchobαιρ
ſhαιlʒe, .ι. αη Cαlbαch, αη mαc ʒαοιꝺeαl ꝺob ſeρρ
eιηeαċ ocuρ uαιρle, ocuρ ſα cρeιſρι αρ ʒαlloιb ocuρ αρ
ʒαοιꝺeolαιꝺ ꝺo ḃιċ α ηCριηη, ocuρ ιρ mo ꝺo mιll
umρu αη αοη αιmſιρ ρuρ, ꝺo ꝺul ꝺhec. mαc 8αmραꝺαιη
.ι. Comαρ ꝺhec. O Ruαιρc .ι. Lochlαιηη ꝺhec. Ccρt
mαc Coʒαιη 1 Ηeιll ꝺhec. mαιꝺm ηα ʒραιηe ꝺo
ċαꝺαιρt ꝺo mαʒ Uιꝺιρ ſoρ Loċlαιηη mαc Cαιꝺʒ
1 Ruαιρc, .ι. O Ruαιρc.

---

1 *Rule.* ριαlα, for ριαʒlα, gen.
sg. of ριαʒαιl＝regula, MS.
2 *Aedh.* (Coꝺα (the gen. form), MS.
3 *Gaeidhel.* mαc ʒαοιꝺeαl; lit.
"son of a Gaeidhel," MS.

4 *Thomas.* Comſ, MS.
5 *O'Ruaire*; i. e. *the* O'Ruaiſe,
the chief of his name and sept. The
defeat so briefly recorded here is
more fully described in the Annals of

Mathghamhna died, i.e. Aedh Ruadh, son of Rughraidhe; and Fedhlim, son of Brian Mac Mathghamhna, was made king over Oirghiall.

The kalends of January; and the age of the Lord one thousand, four hundred, and fifty-four years. Rughraihde, son of Nechtan O'Domhnaill, was unfortunately killed with one cast of a stone flung out from the castle of Inis, by Domhnall, son of Nechtan O'Domhnaill, after Rughraidhe had previously been two years in the sovereignty of Tir-Conaill. Brian, son of Conchobhar O'Raighilligh, died.

The kalends of January; one thousand, four hundred, and fifty-five years. O'Neill was made king over Tir-Eoghain, i.e. Henry, son of Eoghan, son of Niall Og.

The kalends of January; the age of the Lord one thousand, four hundred, and fifty-six years. O'Domhnaill, i.e. Domhnall, son of Niall O'Domhnaill, was slain by the sons of Nechtan O'Domhnaill, at Tech-Baithin, this year, after having been two years in the lordship of Tir-Conaill with the palm of authority and rule;[1] and Aedh[2] Ruadh, the son of Niall O'Domhnaill, was taken prisoner this year; and Toirdhelbhach Cairbrech, son of Nechtan, was proclaimed king. O'Neill died, i.e. Eoghan the son of Niall.

The kalends of January; the age of the Lord one thousand, four hundred, and fifty-seven years. O'Conchobhair Failghe, i.e. the Calbhach, the Gaeidhel[3] of greatest bounty. and nobility, and the most powerful against Foreigners and Gaeidhel in Erinn, and who destroyed most about them in his time, died. Mac Samhradhain, i.e. Thomas,[4] died. O'Ruairc, i.e. Lochlainn, died. Art, son of Eoghan O'Neill, died. The victory of the Graine was gained by Mag Uidhir over Lochlainn, the son of Tadhg O'Ruairc, i.e. O'Ruairc.[5]

Ulster, from which O'Donovan has extracted the substance of a long note | in his ed. of the Four Masters (under A.D. 1457, note ᵛ).

Ⅎct. ιαnαιρ; ocht mbℓιαδnα δhec αρ δα ρícheδ,
αρ .cccc. αρ mιℓe, αιρ αn Cιʒeρnα. Mαc Uιℓℓιαm ϋuρc
δhec, .ι. Emαnn. ϋαρun Ɔeαℓϋnα δhec, .ι. Semuρ
Nuιnnριnn. Mαc Ɔιαρmαδα Mυιʒe ℓuιρʒ, .ι. Comαℓ-
tαch mαc Conchobαιρ mιc Ccoδα, δαρ ċoṁαιnm Comαℓ-
tαch αn eιnιʒ, ρoʒα ʒαoιδeαℓ Eρenn, δhec; .ι. αn ρeρ
nααρ διuℓt δαιm nα δeoραʒ δo ℓeιϋ α ċuιℓ nα hoιʒϋe
ριαm ιn ʒceιn δo ṁαιρ; beαnnαcht ℓαιρ.

Ⅎct. ιαnαιρ; nαeι mbℓιαδnα δhec αρ δα .xx., αρ .cccc.
αρ mιℓe, αιρ αn Cιʒeρnα. O ϋριαιn, ριʒ Cuαδmumαn,
δhec. ʒℓαιρne mαc Chonċuϋαιρ 1 Rαʒιℓℓιʒ δo mαρbαδ
ℓα cℓαιnn Ruʒραιδe meʒ Mαchʒαmnα.

Ⅎct. ιαnαιρ; tρι ρίϋιδ bℓιαδαn αρ .cccc. αρ mιℓe αιρ
αn Cιʒeρnα. Ccoδ ρuαδ O'Ɔomnαιℓℓ, ριʒδαṁnα Ceneℓ
Conuιℓℓ, δo ℓeιʒeαn αρ α ℓαιmδeċoρ. Mαʒ Sαmραʒαn
δhec .ι. Eoʒαn.

Ⅎct. ιαnαιρ; bℓιαδαιn αρ tρι xxιt, αρ .cccc. αρ mιℓe, αιρ
αn Cιʒeρnα. Mαιϋm moρ δo ċαϋαιρt α Cιnδ mαʒαιρ
αn bℓιαδαιn ρι αρ .h. nɔomnαιℓℓ .ι. Coιρρδheαℓbαch
cαιρbρech, δo cℓαιnn Neιℓℓ 1 Ɔomnαιℓℓ, ocuρ O'Ɔomnαιℓℓ δo ʒαbαιℓ αnδ, ocuρ α ρcαthαδ nα διαιϋ ριn ; ocuρ
Ccoδ ρuαδ mαc Neιℓℓ ʒαιρb δo ριʒαϋ nα ιnαϋ δo
ċomαιρℓe Ɔe ocuρ δαoιneαϋ. Ⅎeιϋℓιm mαc Eoʒαιn 1 Neιℓℓ
δhec. O Conchobαιρ δonn δhec, .ι.Ccoϋ. Cαϋʒ, mαc
Coρmαιc mιc Ɔιαρmαδα mec [C]αρρthαιʒ, δhec. Ccon-
ʒuρ Mαcραιϋ δhec. Mαc Cαϋmαιℓ δhec, .ι. ϋριαn.

Ⅎct. ιαnαιρ; δα bℓιαδαιn αρ tρι .xx. αρ .cccc. αρ mιℓe
αιρ αn Cιʒeρnα. ϋριαn mαc ϸιℓιρ meʒ Uιδιρ δo mαρbαδ ρe ceneℓ Eoʒhαιn αn bℓιαδαιn ριn. Mαιnιρδιρ ρραϋαρ ṁιonuρ δo tιonnρʒnαδ α Mυιneαċαn ιn hoc αnno.

Ⅎct. ιαnαιρ; ocuρ tρι bℓιαδnα αρ tρι ρícheδ αρ
.cccc. αρ mιℓe αιρ αn Cιʒeρnα. ιαρℓα Ɔeρmumhαn, .ι.
Semuρ, ceιnnℓιtιρ ʒαℓℓ αn δeιρceρt, ocuρ comραιρ

---

1 *Kalends.* The contents of the   2 *Friars.* ρραϋαρ, for bραϋαρ,
MS. from this to the end are written   MS.
on vellum, but by various scribes.   3 *In.* α, for αn or ιn, MS.

The kalends of January ; the age of the Lord one thousand, four hundred, and fifty-eight years. Mac William Burk, i.e. Edmond, died. The Baron of Dealbhna, i.e. James Nugent, died. Mac Diarmada of Magh-Luirg, i.e. Tomaltach, son of Conchobhar, son of Aedh, (who was named Tomaltach-an-einigh), the choice of the Gaeidhel of Erinn, died : i.e. the man who never refused a guest or stranger for a night's entertainment, whilst he lived. A blessing with him.

The kalends of January ; the age of the Lord one thousand, four hundred, and fifty-nine years. O'Briain, King of Tuadh-Mumha, died. Glaisne, son of Conchobhar O'Raighilligh, was slain by the sons of Rughraidhe Mac Mathghamhna.

The kalends of January ; the age of the Lord one thousand, four hundred, and sixty years. Aedh Ruadh O'Domhnaill, royal heir of Cenel-Conaill, was liberated from his captivity. Mac Samhradhain died, i.e. Eoghan.

The kalends of January ; the age of the Lord one thousand, four hundred, and sixty-one years. A great defeat was inflicted at Cenn-Maghair, this year, on O'Domhnaill, i.e. Toirdhelbhach Cairbrech, by the sons of Niall O'Domhnaill ; and O'Domhnaill was captured there, and was afterwards mutilated ; and Aedh Ruadh, son of Niall Garbh, was made king in his place by the counsel of God and men. Fedhlim, son of Eoghan O'Neill, died. O'Conchobhair Donn died, i.e. Aedh. Tadhg, son of Cormac, son of Diarmaid Mac [C]arthaigh, died. Aenghus Macraith died. Mac Cathmhail died, i.e. Brian.

The kalends[1] of January ; the age of the Lord one thousand, four hundred, and sixty-two years. Brian, son of Philip Mag Uidhir, was killed by the Cenel-Eoghain this year. A monastery for Friars[2] Minor was commenced in Monaghan in[3] hoc anno.

The kalends of January ; and the age of the Lord one thousand, four hundred, and sixty-three years. The Earl of Des-Mumha, i.e. James, head of the Foreigners

einiξ ocur ξairξió na nξeralcach, óhec in hoc anno.
Ταόξ mac Θοghain 1 Conchobair óhec an bliαóain ri.
ΙΠαc Ὀοnnchαόα cire hOilella, .ι. Ταός mac Τοmαlcαιξ
moir, [morcuur erc]. Θnri mac Peróhlim 1 Rαιξιllιξ
óo marbαó óo Ὀοnnchαó maξ Uióir.

Ict. ιenair; ceιcri bliαξna ar cri richeó, ar .cccc.
ar ṁιle, αoιr an Τιξerna. Conn mac Ịleill 1
Ὀhoṁnιιll, rιοόαṁna cincil Conuill, ocur CConξuir
mac Ịleιll 1 Ὀhoṁnιιll óo ṁarbαó le hΘιξnechαn
.h. nὈοιṁnιιll α ύrιnn úruιm. Ταόξ mac Τοιrrόeal-
bαιξ rιαιό 1 Chončubaιr, leιú rι Connachc, óéξ .ι.
óuιno óo bά cuιξre ccreιξe α ξConnachcαιύ ιona αιmrιr
reιn.

Ict. ιenair; čúιξ úlιαξna ar cri richeó ar ceιcri
ceó ar ṁιle αoιr an Τιξerna. 1r ΙΠαξrαnιιll, .ι. mac
Cαčιιl rιαιό, [morcuur erc] in hoc anno. ξormᵘ
lαιύ Chaoṁanαč ιnξen ṁeιc ΙΠιrčαόα, bean 1 Ịleιll .ι.
Θιnrι ṁeιc Θοξιιn 1 Ịleιll, óéξ. ΙΠαc Ịlιύ̈ertaιξ óéξ
.ι. Cúchonnachc.

Ict. ιenair. 8é bliαξna ar ύrí rιčιc ar čeιύrι ceó
ar ṁιle αoιr an Τιξerna. Rι Τυαξṁuṁun, .ι. Ταός
O úrιαιn, coιnneal ξαιrξιό ocur eιξnuṁα leιύe ΙΠόξα,
[morcuur erc] in hoc anno. ΙΠαιóm ar ξhallnιύ lα
O Cončuύaιr Phαιlξe, .ι. Conn mac an Chαlbαιξ, ιοnαr
marbαó Seαóun mac ṁeιc Τοmαιr ocur morαn eιle.
Rιξ Oιrξιαll óéξ, .ι. Perólιm mac úrιαιn ṁeξ ΙΠhαčunα.

Ict. ιenair. Seαchc mblιαξna ar cri .αχ. ar .cccc.
ar ṁιle, αoιr an Τιξerna. 1arlα Ὀeαrṁuṁun, .ι. Τοmαr
mac Sémuιr ṁeιc ξeróιó ιarlα, óo ṁιlleó α nὈroιčeαc
CCύα leιr an nξιιrcιr nṁαó. ΙΠαc Ὀοnnchαόα cire
hOilella, .ι. Rιαιόrι mac Cončuύuιr ṁeιc Ὀοnnchαόα,
[morcuur erc] in hoc anno. ΙΠαξ Rαnιιll, .ι. Cαčul οξ

---

1 *Mac Ribhertaigh.* In the Ann.
Ulft., where the name is written Mac
Rithbhertaigh, he is called Maguire's
ollamh, or chief poet.

2 *John.* Incorrectly written Seaᵘ
óun in the MS

3 *Mac Mathghamhna.* Mac Mahon.
This name is written mac ΙΠhačunα

of the South, and the shrine of the hospitality and valour of the Geraldines, died in hoc anno. Tadhg, son of Eoghan O'Conchobhair, died this year. Mac Donnchadha of Tir-Oilella, i.e. Tadhg son of Tomaltach Mor, [mortuus est]. Henry, the son of Fedhlim O'Raighilligh, was slain by Donnchadh Mag Uidhir.

The kalends of January ; the age of the Lord one thousand, four hundred, and sixty-four years. Conn, son of Niall O'Domhnaill, royal heir of Cenel-Conaill, and Aenghus the son of Niall O'Domhnaill, were slain by Egnechan O'Domhnaill in Finn-druim. Tadhg, the son of Toirdhelbhach Ruadh O'Conchobhair, half-king of Connacht died, i.e. the most intelligent, learned man in Connacht in his own time.

The kalends of January ; the age of the Lord one thousand, four hundred, and sixty-five years. Ir Mag Rannaill, i.e. the son of Cathal Ruadh, [mortuus est] in hoc anno. Gormlaith Caemhanach, daughter of Mac Murchadha, wife of O'Neill, i.e. of Henry the son of Eoghan O'Neill, died. Mac Ribhertaigh[1] died, i.e. Cuchonnacht.

The kalends of January. The age of the Lord one thousand, four hundred, and sixty-six years. The king of Tuadh-Mumha, i.e. Tadhg O'Briain, the torch of valour and prowess of Leth-Mogha, [mortuus est] in hoc anno. A victory over the Foreigners by O'Conchobhair Failghe, i.e. Conn, the son of the Calbhach, in which John[2] the son of Fitz-Thomas, and many more, were slain. The King of Oirghiall died, i.e. Fedhlim, son of Brian Mac Mathghamhna.[3]

The kalends of January. The age of the Lord one thousand, four hundred, and sixty-seven years. The Earl of Des-Mumha, i.e. Thomas, the son of James, son of Earl Garrett, was killed in Droichet-atha by the new[4] Justiciary. Mac Donnchadha of Tir-Oilella, i.e. Ruaidhri, son of Conchobhar Mac Donnchadha, [mortuus

---

in the MS; but this is a very corrupt form. See note 1. p. 146 *supra*.

[4] *New.* ꞃúaᵭ ("red"), for núaᵭ, MS.

mac Catuil puaiv, [moptuuʃ eʃt] in hoc anno. O Cathain
.i. Maxnuʃ aʃ an mbliaxuin ceona. O Ruaipc .i.
Tixeʃnan, cinnlitiʃ ocuʃ coiṁevaix tʃlechta Ccova
ʃinn, [moptuuʃ eʃt] in hoc anno. Cn xilla vuṁ mac
Coʃmuic vallaix vo ṁaʃbav le Maoilʃeacluinn mac
Taivx ṁeic Ḃʃiain ṁeic Donnchava. Mac Conmaʃa,
tixeʃna cloinne Cuilen, .i. Seavun mac Meiccon ṁeic
Siova, moptuuʃ eʃt. Catul mac Cathail puaiv Mex-
xʃannill [moptuuʃ eʃt] in hoc anno. Doṁnull
O Moʃʃva, pix Laoivipi, moptuuʃ eʃt. O Cinneivix
vonn, .i. Seavun mac Tomaiʃ, leiṫ pi Uʃṁuṁun,
moptuuʃ eʃt. O Maille, .i. Tavx mac Diaʃmava,
[moptuuʃ eʃt] in hoc anno. O Maolconuipe, .i. Toʃna
mac Maoilin, moptuuʃ eʃt. Ri Oipxiall vex, .i.
Eoxun mac Ruxpuive. Maivm Cʃoiʃi ṁuixe Cʃoinn
la mac Uilliam cloinne Riocuipv, .i. Uilliox puav mac
Uilliox an ʃiona, aiʃ O Cheallaix ocuʃ aʃ Riocupv a
buʃc, vu aʃ ṫoitevuʃ iomaʃcav vaoineṁ. O Ceallaix
Maine vex, .i. Ccov mac Ḃʃiain. O Raixllix vex, .i.
Catul mac Eoxuin, caivcíʃ pia novluix.

Jct. ienaiʃ; ocht mbliaxna aʃ ṫʃi .xx., aʃ.cccc. aʃ
ṁile, aoiʃ an Tixeʃna. Max Caʃʃtuiṫ moʃ, .i.
Doṁnull mac Taivx ṁeic Doṁnaill oix, [moptuuʃ
eʃt] in hoc anno. Ḃean an ʃiʃ ceona, .i. Savṁ inxen
Uillic ṁeic Riocuipv oix, vʃaxuil Ḃaiʃ. O Ceallaix
tixeʃna O Maine, .i. Ccov mac Uilliaim meic Mhaoil-
ʃeacluinn, [vo éc]. Iaʃla Deaʃṁuṁun, .i. Tomaʃ mac
Sémuiʃ ṁeic xeʃóiv, vo viṫceannuv a n'Opoiceat áta.
Mac Donnchava ṫipe hOilella vex, .i. Ruaivʃi mac
Conĉuḃuiʃ. Maxʃanill .i. Catul vex. baile i Raixllix ocuʃ mainiptiʃ an Chaḃáin vo loʃxuv le xal-

---

1 *Aedh Finn.* "Hugh the Fair;"
the progenitor of the families of
O'Ruairc, Mac Tighernain, and their
correlatives.

2 *Ballagh;* i.e. "the speckled," or
"freckled." The Four Masters have
buivhe, "the yellow." They also
state that Gilla-dubh died.

3 *John.* Incorrectly written Seavun in the MS.

4 *Mortuus est.* In the Annals of
Connacht it is added that he died in
his own house at "Lis-Ferbain, or
Lis-Gerbain."

5 *Rughraighe;* i.e. Rughraighe (or
Rury) Mac Mahon.

est] in hoc anno. Mag Rannaill, i.e. Cathal Og, son of Cathal Ruadh, [mortuus est] in hoc anno. O'Cathain, i.e. Maghnus, *died* in the same year. O'Ruairc, i.e. Tighernan, the head and guardian of the race of Aedh Finn,[1] [mortuus est] in hoc anno. The Gilla-dubh, son of Cormac Ballach,[2] was killed by Maelsechlainn, the son of Tadhg, son of Brian Mac Donnchadha. Mac Conmara, lord of Clann-Cuilen, i.e. John[3] son of Maccon, son of Sida, mortuus est. Cathal, son of Cathal Ruadh Mag Rannaill, [mortuus est] in hoc anno. Domhnall O'Mordha, King of Laighis, mortuus est. O'Cennedigh Donn, i.e. John[3] son of Thomas, half-king of Ur-Mumha, mortuus est. O'Maille, i.e. Tadhg son of Diarmaid, [mortuus est] in hoc anno. O'Maelchonaire, i.e. Torna the son of Mailin, mortuus est.[4] The King of Oirghiall died, i.e. Eoghan, son of Rughraidhe.[5] The victory of Cros-Maighe-Croinn by Mac William of Clann-Rickard, i.e. Ulick Ruadh, son of Ulick-an-fhina, over O'Cellaigh, and over Richard Burk, in which a great many persons fell. O'Cellaigh of Ui-Maine died, i.e. Aedh the son of Brian. O'Raighilligh, i.e. Cathal, son of Eoghan, died a fortnight before Christmas.

The kalends of January; the age of the Lord one thousand, four hundred, and sixty-eight[6] years. MacCarthaigh Mór, i.e. Domhnall, son of Tadhg, son of Domhnall Og, [mortuus est] in hoc anno. The same man's wife, i.e. Sadhbh, daughter of Ulick, son of Rickard Og, died. O'Cellaigh, lord of Ui-Maine, i.e. Aedh, son of William, son of Maelsechlainn, [died]. The Earl of Des-Mumha, i.e. Thomas son of James, son of Garrett, was beheaded in Droichet-atha.[7] Mac Donnchadha of Tir-Oilella died, i.e. Ruaidhri son of Conchobhar. Mag Rannaill, i.e. Cathal, died. O'Raighilligh's town,[8] and the monastery of the

---

[6] *Eight*. The MS. has ꞔnoꞔ, "nine."

[7] *Droichet-atha*. Drogheda. The Annals of Connacht say at Traigh-Li mic Deadad, "the strand of Li the son of Dedad," now the town of Tralee, in the county of Kerry. This entry is merely a repetition of the one under the year 1467, which is the correct date.

[8] *O'Raighilligh's town;* or O'Reilly's residence; the town of Cavan, in the co. of Cavan.

loiḃ. Torna O Mháolċonuire déġ. O Caṫan déġ, .i. Maġnus.

Kalluinn Ienair; naoi mbliaġna ar ṫrí .xx., ar .cccc. ar ṁile, aois an Tiġerna. O Cerbuill .i. Donncuḋ mac Taiḋg ṁeic Taiḋg ṁeic Ruaiḋri mortuus est. Brian Maineaċ mac Donnċuiḋ ṁeic Aoḋa Meġ Uiḋir do ṁarḃuḋ la Emunn mag Uiḋir agus le cloinn Pilib ṁeg Uiḋir. Eogun mac Aoḋa ṁeg Uiḋir do ṁarḃuḋ la cloinn Pilib ċéḋna. Sluaiġeaḋ lá O nDoṁnuill, .i. Aoḋ ruaḋ, a nIochtar Chonnacht, ocus a mbráiġde do ġaḃail dó; ocus sluaiġ iochtuir Chonnacht do ḃreiṫ lais a gcenn mic Uilliam Burc, ocus a ndul assin a gCloinn Riocuird, ocus an Maċuire riaḃaċ, ocus baile an ċláir, .i. baile ṁeic Uilliam, do losguḋ léo. Mac Uilliam ocus O Briain do ḃreiṫ orrṫu, ocus mac I Chonċuḃuir Chorcumrúaḋ do ṁarbuḋ leo; ocus O Doṁnuill do ṫeacht da ṫiġ sa ḃuaiḋ. O Gaḋra déġ .i. Eoġun ṁac Tomultaiġ, ocus Eogan óg a mac déġ.

Kl. Ianair; deic mbliadna ar tri .xx., ar .cccc. ar mile, aeis in Tigerna. Mac I Conchobair Failge, .i. Tadg mac in Chalbaiġ mic Murchada, do ḋul dhec obann. O Conchobair Corcumruad, .i. Conchobar mac Briain oig, do marbad isin Leṫ moir co ḋroċ comairleċ le clainn a derbrathar fein, .i. le clainn Donnchada I Conchobair. Pilip mac Tomais mic Pilip Meg Uidir dheg. Ruaḋri bacaċ O Neill do marbad a Tobran le cloinn Airt agus le cloinn Bhriain óig. Maiḋm do ṫaḃuirt do ċloinn I Neill, .i. clann Einri, ar ċloinn Airt agus ar ċloinn Bhriain óig, ion[ar] marḃuḋ Einri mac Airt; ocus bí Art I Neill ocus

---

1 *Died.* These seem to be repetitions of entries under last year.

2 *O'Cerbhaill.* O'Carroll. Roderick O'Flaherty has written the name "O'Domhnaill" in the margin, by way of emendation.

3 *Brian Mainech;* i.e. "Brian the Mainean;" so called from having been fostered in Hy-Maine, or O'Kelly's country.

4 *Killed.* The text of this year's entries down to the word here trans-

Cabhan, were burned by Foreigners. Torna O'Maelchonaire died.[1] O'Cathain died,[1] i.e. Maghnus.

The kalends of January ; the age of the Lord one thousand, four hundred, and sixty-nine years. O'Cerbhaill,[2]
i.e. Donnchadh, son of Tadhg, son of Tadhg, son of
Ruaidhri, mortuus est. Brian Mainech,[3] son of Donnchadh,
son of Aedh Mag Uidhir, was killed by Edmond MagUidhir,
and by the sons of Philip Mag Uidhir. Eoghan, the son
of Aedh Mag Uidhir, was slain by the sons of the same
Philip. A hosting by O'Domhnaill, i.e. Aedh Ruadh, into
Lower Connacht, and their hostages were received by him ;
and he took the army of Lower Connacht with him towards
Mac William Burk ; and they all went from thence to
Clann-Rickard, and the Machaire-riabhach, and Baile-an-
chláir, i.e. Mac William's town, were burned by them.
Mac William and O'Briain came up with them, and the
son of O'Conchobhair of Corcumruaidh was slain by them ;
and O'Domhnaill went home with triumph. O'Gadhra
died, i.e. Eoghan, the son of Tomaltach ; and Eoghan Og,
his son, died.

The kalends of January ; the age of the Lord one
thousand, four hundred, and seventy years. The son of
O'Conchobhair Failghe, i.e. Tadhg, the son of the Calbhach, son of Murchadh, died suddenly. O'Conchobhair of
Corcumruaidh, i.e. Conchobhar, the son of Brian Og, was
ill-advisedly killed in the Leth-innsi, by the sons of his
own brother, viz., by the sons of Donnchadh O'Conchobhair. Philip, son of Thomas, son of Philip Mag Uidhir,
died. Ruaidhri Bacach O'Neill was killed[4] at Tobran, by
the sons of Art, and the sons of Brian Og. A defeat was
given by the sons of O'Neill, i.e. the sons of Henry,[5] to
the sons of Art, and the sons of Brian Og, in which
Henry, the son of Art, was slain, and Art O'Neill, and
Toirdhelbach Ruadh, son of Brian Og, were wounded.

---

lated is in the handwriting of Brian
Mac Dermott.

[5] *Henry*; i.e. Henry Amhreidh, or
Henry the Unquiet ; ob. 1392.

Τοιρρ̇δealbać ρυαδ mac Ḃριαιη όιϛ. Mac Ⅾοnnchaιὃ
an Choρuιnn ⅾο mαρbuὃ, .ı. Ḃρίαn mac Ταὃϛ, la mac
Ⅾοnnċuιὃ τίρε hⅯιlella, .ı. Ταὃϛ mac Ḃριαιn.

Ḱτ. Ιαnαιρ; aen bliαⅾαιη ⅾeϛ αρ τρι .ːⅹ. αρ .cccc.
αρ mιle αιρ an Τιϛeρna. Ταὃϛ mac Τοιρδealbαιϛ
mıc Muρċαⅾα na ραιέnιϛε, τιϛeρna Ⅽραὃ, ⅾeϛ.
Cαιρlen na hⅯϛmαιὃı ⅾο ϛαὃαιl leıρ O Ⅿeıll, .ı. Єnρı
mac Ⴆοϛαιn, ocuρ ρlιchτ Ⅽιρτ ⅾο ċuρ a Τıρ Conαιll.
Ɍuαⅾρı mac Ⅾοnnchαιὃ mıc Ⅽeὃa meϛ Ⅱıⅾıρ ⅾο
ṁαρbαⅾ le Colla mac Ⅽοⅾα meϛ Ⅱıⅾıρ. Ⅾοnnchαⅾ
όϛ mac Ⅾοnnchαıⅾ mıc Ⅽοⅾa ⅾο lenmuın Collα, ocuρ
Colla ocuρ a mac ⅾο mαρbαⅾ. Ⅽοὃ, mac Ḃριαιn mıc
Ρılıρ na τuαιϛε meϛ Ⅱıⅾıρ, ⅾhec.

Ḱτ. Ιαnαιρ; ⅾa bliαⅾαιη ⅾeϛ αρ τρι .ⅹⅹ. αρ. cccc. αρ
mıle αειρ an Τιϛeρna. O Cαέαn, .ı. Ɍuαⅾρı mac
Mαϛnαıρ 1 Cαċαın, ⅾhec. Mac 8uıὃne Ραnαⅾ ⅾο
mαρbαⅾ a mαιⅾm an Ταραὃαın, .ı. Maolmuıρe. Clann
meϛ Ɍαὃnαιll, .ı. Concubaρ ocuρ Maelρeċlαınn ocuρ
Cαċal oϛ, ⅾhec. Ⴅορραιὃ O Cαċan αϛuρ Coρmac
mac Ⅱıὃılın, ocuρ Ɍuϛραιⅾhe mac Ⅱıὃılın, ⅾhec.
O hⴹıⅾıρρϛeoıl mορ, .ı. Ρınϛean, ⅾο ⅾul ⅾeϛ na τıϛ ρeın
ıαρ nⅾenαṁ οıleὃρı ραn 8eam, ocuρ a mac .ı. Ταⅾϛ
mac Ρınϛeın ⅾhec co hαιτıρech ρıα cınⅾ ṁıρ ıαρ mbαρ
[a] αέαρ, ıαρ τeachτ on οιleὃρı ceⅾna. Ḃαıle na
Ⴅαıllmı ⅾο loρϛuὃ. Mac Ρeoραıρ ⅾhec, .ı. Τomαρ.
Mαınıρτıρ na mbραċαρ mınϛρ ⅾο τınnⅾρcnam a Ⅾun
na nϛαll ın blıαⅾαιη c[eⅾna].

Ḱτ. Ιεnαıρ; τρı blıαϛna ⅾéuϛ αρ τρı .ⅹⅹ. αρ .cccc. αρ
ṁıle άοıρ ın Τιϛeρna. Ⅾοnnchaⅾ mac Ⅽοⅾα Mαϛ
Ⅱıⅾıρ ⅾο ὃol ⅾéϛ. Ɍuαιⅾρı mac Ⅽıρτ 1 Ⅿeıll ⅾéϛ

---

1 _Kalends._ The entries for this
year and the next are in the handwriting of Brian Mac Dermott.

2 _Murchadh-na-raithnigh._ "Murchadh of the Fern." He was of the
family of O'Brien.

3 _Tapadhcn._ The Ann. Ult. say
at "_Bel átha in chaislen mhaoil_," "the
mouth of the ford of _Castle maol_," now
Castle-Moyle, in the parish of West
Longfield, barony of Omagh, and co.
of Tyrone.

Mac Donnchaidh of the Corann, i.e. Brian son of Tadhg, was killed by Mac Donnchaidh of Tir-Oilella, i.e. Tadhg son of Brian.

The kalends[1] of January; the age of the Lord one thousand, four hundred, and seventy-one years. Tadhg, son of Toirdhelbhach, son of Murchadh-na-raithnigh,[2] lord of Aradh, died. The castle of Oghmagh, was taken by O'Neill, i.e. Henry the son of Eoghan, who drove the descendants of Art to Tir-Conaill. Ruaidhri, the son of Donnchadh, son of Aedh Mag Uidhir, was slain by Colla, son of Aedh Mag Uidhir. Donnchadh Og, son of Donnchadh, son of Aedh, pursued Colla, and slew Colla and his son. Aedh, son of Brian, son of Philip-na-tuaighe Mag Uidhir, died.

The kalends of January ; the age of the Lord one thousand, four hundred, and seventy-two years. O'Cathain, i.e. Ruaidhri, the son of Maghnus O'Cathain, died. Mac Suibhne of Fanad, i.e. Maemluire, was killed in the defeat of the Tapadhan.[3] The sons of Mag Raghnaill, viz.; Conchobhar, and Maelsechlainn, and Cathal Og, died. Godfrey O'Cathain, and Cormac Mac Uibhilin, and Rughraidhe Mac Uibhilin, died. O'hEidirsceoil Mór, i.e. Finghin, died in his own house, after performing the pilgrimage of St. James ;[4] and his son, i.e. Tadhg the son of Finghin, died penitently before the end of a month after [his] father's death, after returning from the same pilgrimage. The town of Gaillimh was burned.[5] Mac Feorais died, i.e. Thomas. The monastery of the Friars Minors in Dun-na-ngall was begun the same year.

The kalends of January; the age of the Lord one thousand, four hundred, and seventy-three years. Donnchadh, son of Aedh Mag Uidhir, died. Ruaidhri, the son of Art O'Neill, died this year; and the harvest of

---

[4] *St. James.* Saint James of Compostella, in Spain.
[5] *Burned.* The Annals of Connacht (A.D. 1473) say that Gaillimh (the town of Galway) was burned by "*tene daith*," i.e. lightning.

αn ϐλιαξuιn ϻι, οϲuϻ ϻοξϻαϻ αn λαοι ϐuιϐ. Ο Ϲιnneιϑιξ
.ι. Ϲιαϻμαιϲ μαϲ ϻειϲ Ϲαϐξ, ϲιξεϻnα Uϻϻuϻαn
uαϲηϲαϻαιξε, ϑϻαξuιλ [ϐαιϻ]. Ϻαξ Θοϲαξαn, .ι. Ϲύ-
ϲοιξϻιϲε, ϲιξεαϻnα ϲειnιλ ϻιαϲηαιϐ, ϑο μαϻϐuϐ le
ϲλοιnn ϻηεϻξuιλ. Ϻαϲξαϻαιn, μαϲ Ϲοιϻϻϑεαλϐαιξ
μειϲ ϐϻιαιn ι ϐηϻιαιn, ϑϻαξuιλ ϐαιϻ αn ϐλιαξuιn ϻι ϻ
ϻιοϐαϻnα Ϲuαξϻuϻαn. Ο Ϲοnϲuϐuιϻ ϻηαιλξε .ι. Ϲοnn
μαϲ αn Ϲηαλϐαιξ μειϲ Ϻuϻϲηαιϐ, uαϲηϲαϻαn ειnιϲ
οϲuϻ εnξnαϻα ξαοιϐεαλ λαιξεαn, ϑϻαξαιλ ϐαιϻ ιοnα
λοnξϻϻοϻϲ ϻέιn. Ο Ϻαϲξαϻnα αn ϻuιnn ιαϻϲαϻuιξ, .ι.
Ϲοnϲuϐαϻ, μαϲ Ϲιαϻμαϑα, μειϲ Ϲοϻnαιλλ, μειϲ ϻιnξιn
μειϲ Ϲιαϻμαϑα μόιϻ, ϑο ϐuλ ϑέξ ξu ηαιϲϻιξεαϲ ιοnα
λοnξϻϻοϻϲ ϻειn α nΟϻϑ αn ϲεnnαιλ. Ϻαϲ ι Θιϑιϻϻξεοιλ
ϻοιϻ, .ι. Ϲιαϻμαιϲ, ϑϻαξαιλ [ϐαιϻ]. Ϻαϲ ϻεξ Ϲαϻϻ-
ϐuιξ μόιϻ, .ι. Ϲοϻμαϲ μαϲ Ϲαϐξ ϻηειϲ Ϲοϻnαιλλ όιξ,
ϲαnuιϻϲε Ϲεϻϻuϻαn, ϑϻαξuιλ ϐαιϻ αn ϐλιαξuιn ϻι.
Ϻαϲ ϻηειϲ Ϲοϻnuιλλ nα ηΟϲλϐun .ι. ξιλλα εϻϐuιξ μαϲ
Ϲλuϻϲϻαιnn ϻηειϲ Ϲοϻnuιλλ ϻηειϲ Θοιn nα ηιλε, [ϑο εϲ]
ιn ηοϲ αnnο. Ο Ϲοnϲuϐαιϻ Ϲοnnαϲηϲ ϑϻαξuιλ ϐαιϻ αn
ϐλιαξαιn ϻι, .ι. ϻειλιμ μαϲ Ϲοιϻϻϑηεαλϐαιξ όιξ,
λειϲϻι Ο Ϻuιϻεϑηαιξ, ϑο ϲuιϲιμ λέ ϻιολ ξϹεαλλαιξ Οϲα
λιαξ.

ϳϲαλλuιnn ιεnαιϻ; ϲειϲϻε ϐλιαξnα ϑέξ αϻ ϲϻι ϻιϲηεϑ
αϻ .ϲϲϲϲ. αϻ ϻηιλε άοιϻ αn Ϲιξεϻnα. Ο Ϻαϑαξαn .ι.
Ϻuϻϲηαϑ μαϲ Θοξuιn, ϲιξεαϻnα ϻιλ nΟϲnμϲηαϑα,
ϑϻαξuιλ ϐαιϻ αn ϐλιαξuιn ϻι. Ϻαϲ ι ϐηϻιαιn .ι. Ϲαϐξ
μαϲ Ϲοnϲuϐuιϻ, αξuϻ Ϲιαϻμuιϑ ϻηαϲ αn εαϻϐuιξ
ι ϐηϻιαιn, ϑο ϲεξϻαιλ α ξϲοιμεαϻξuϻ ϻε ϲειλε, αξuϻ
Ϲαϐξ ϑο ϲuϻ λαιϻε α nϹιαϻμuιϑ ϑα ξαϐαιλ, οϲuϻ
ϲuξ Ϲιαϻμαιϑ ϐuιλλεϐ ϑο ϲλοιϐεαϻ ϑο Ϲηαϐξ ξuϻ
λιϲ α ιnϲιnn αμαϲ αn αιϲ αn ϐuιλλιϐ. ξαϐuιϻ Ϲαϐξ
ειϻειn αξuϻ αιnϲιοϻ nα ϐιαιξ ϻιn έ, οϲuϻ ϐειϻιϻ λειϻ α

---

1 *Black day.* An annular eclipse of the sun is recorded to have occurred on the 27th of April in this year (*Art de Verif. les Dates*); but there is no mention of an eclipse of the sun in harvest, although such an event must be intended by the " black day."

the black day.[1] O'Cennedigh, i.e. Diarmaid, grandson of Tadhg, lord of Upper Ur-Mumha, died. Mag Eochagain, i.e. Cucocriche, lord of Cenel-Fiachaidh, was slain by the sons of Ferghal.[2] Mathghamhain, son of Toirdhelbhach, son of Brian O'Briain, royal heir of Tuadh-Mumha, died this year. O'Conchobhair Failghe, i.e. Conn, son of the Calbhach, son of Murchadh, head of the bounty and prowess of the Gaeidhel of Laighen, died in his own fortress. O'Mathghamhna of the Fonn-iartharach, i.e. Conchobhar, son of Diarmaid, son of Domhnall, son of Finghin, son of Diarmaid Mor, died penitently in his own fortress in Ard-an-tennail.[3] The son of O'hEdirsceoil Mór, i.e. Diarmaid, died. The son of Mac Carthaigh Mor, i.e. Cormac, son of Tadhg, son of Domhnall Og, tanist of Des-Mumha, died this year. The son of Mac Domhnaill of Alba, i.e. Gilla-esbuig, son of Alexander, son of Domhnall, son of John of Ilay, [died] in hoc anno. O'Conchobhair of Connacht died this year, i.e. Felim, son of Toirdhelbhach Og, half-king of Ui-Muiredhaigh, who fell[4] by the Sil-Cellaigh of Ath-liag.

The kalends of January; the age of the Lord one thousand, four hundred, and seventy-four years. O'Mad-adhain, i.e. Murchadh, the son of Eoghan, lord of Sil-Anmchadha, died this year. The son of O'Briain, i.e. Tadhg son of Conchobhar, and Diarmaid, son of the Bishop O'Briain, encountered one another; and Tadhg laid his hand on Diarmaid, to apprehend him, and Diarmaid struck Tadhg with a sword, so that his brain protruded from the wound. Tadhg apprehended him, and afterwards protected him, and bore him off a

[1474.]

---

[2] *Ferghal*; i.e. Ferghal Mag Eochagain, or Farrell Mageoghegan.

[3] *Ard-an-tennail*; "bonfire height;" now written Ardintenant, the name of a townland in the parish of Skull, barony of West Carbery, and co. of Cork.

[4] *Fell.* This entry is rather loosely written in the text. The Four Masters (under the year 1474) give a more detailed account of the death of Felim O'Conor, from which it appears that he was wounded by the O'Kellys at a conference, and died subsequently of his wounds.

Laiṁ é, ocur τearṿa Τaóᵹ iaṗum, ocur cṗoċuiṗ O Ḃṗiαin
Ṿiαṗmαiṿ α ᵹcionαiṫ mαṗbḟα α meic; ocuṗ ṽo bα ṽo
ṁóiṗṗcéluiṫ Ṿαl ᵹCαiṗ αn ṽiṗ ṗin τoṗċαiṗ. Θαṗbuᵹ
Ṿαiṗe ṽéᵹ, .1. ṗαiṗ Niocol.

Ḱt. 1enαiṗ; cuiᵹ bliαᵹnα ṽéᵹ αṗ ḟṗí .xx. αṗ .cccc. αṗ
mile áoiṗ αn Τiᵹeṗnα. Ccαoṫ mαc Neαchταin 1
Ṿhoṁnuill, ṗioṫαṁnα ċineoil ᵹConαill, ṽo Ḃαċuτ
α ᵹcoiτe αṗ Ḃun Ḃhαnnα. Ccoṫ mαc Θoᵹuin 1 Neill ṽo
ṫul ṽéᵹ αn Ṿliαᵹuin ṗi. Mαc Muṗchαṽα, ṗí Lαiᵹeαn,
.1. Ṿoṁnαll ṗiαḂαċ ṁαc ᵹeṗuilτ, ṽṗαᵹuil eαṗᵹαiṗ ṽαṗ
bṗiṗiuṫ α ċoṗ, αᵹuṗ α Ḃáṗ ṽo ċeαchτ ṽe ṗin. O Ḟeṗᵹuil
ṽeuᵹ, .1. Seαṫun mαc Ṿoṁnuill.

Ḱt. Θnαiṗ; ṗé bliαṽnαe .x. αṗ τṗi .xx.ᵗ αṗ ceṫṗi ceṽ
αṗ mile áiṗṗ αn Τiᵹeṗnαi. O hUiccinn, .1. Ḃṗíαn mαc
Ḟeṗᵹαil ṗuαiṽ, cenṽ ṗcoile Θṗenn ocuṗ Cclbαn, ṽo ṽol
ṽhec αn bliαṽαin ṗi. O heᵹṗα ṗiαḂαch, .1. Uilliαm
mαc αn eṗbuicc, [ṽhéc in bliαṽαin ṗi].

Ḱt. Θnαiṗ. Seαchτ mbliαṽnαi .x. αṗ τṗi .xx.ᵗ αṗ .cccc.
αṗ mile oeiṗṗ in Τiᵹeṗnαi. Sluαiᵹeṽ Lα hUα Neill
α τiṗ nOeṫαi, [ocuṗ] αn τíṗ ṽo milleṽ ocuṗ ṽo Loṗcαṫ
Lαiṗ. Oeṫ mαc Ṿonnchαṽα mic Τomαiṗṗ méᵹ Uiṫiṗ
ṽhec. Ḃṗien mαc Concoṗαiṗ óic mic Concoṗαiṗ ṗuαiṽ
mecc Uiṫiṗ ṽhec αiᵹċhe noṽlαcc. Ṗláᵹ moṗ ṽo τeαchτ
α cuαn Θṗṗαi ṗúαiṽ, ṽα nṽechαiṽ moṗαn ṽoene α τiṗ
Conαill, ocuṗ co hαiṗiᵹi Mαc αn Ḃαiṗṽ.

Ḱt. Θnαiṗ; ochτ mblieṽnαi .x. αṗ τṗi .xx.ᵗ αṗ .cccc.
αṗ mile oeiṗṗ in Τiᵹeṗnαi. Coṗbmαc mαᵹ Cαṗthαiᵹ ṽo
ṗpochαṽ ṗe cloinn Ṿieṗmαṽαi αn ṽúnαiṫ. Mαc αn
bαiṗṽ τiṗi Conuill, .1. ᵹoṗṗαiṽ, ṽo ṽol ṽécc αn bliαṽαin

---

1 *Nicholas.* Nicholas Weston. Ware
(Bishops) states that he died in 1484,
under which year his death is also
recorded *infra.*

² *Head of the schools.* In the Annals
of Ulster he is said to have been a
ṗαi ṗiṗṽαnα, or most eminent poet.

³ *Year.* The words within brack-

ets, being omitted in the text, are
supplied from the Annals of Ulster.
The scribe seems to have intended
adding some other entries, as a blank
space of ten lines ià left in the MS.

⁴ *Plague.* ṗliαᵹ. See next note.

⁵ *Went.* ṽαnṽech, for ṽαn
ṽechαiṽ, "of which went," or ṽαn

prisoner. And Tadhg died afterwards; and O'Briain A.D.
hanged Diarmaid for the crime of his son's death; and [1474.]
these two who fell were much deplored by the Dal-Cais.
The Bishop of Daire, i.e. Sir Nicholas,[1] died.

The kalends of January; the age of the Lord one [1475.]
thousand, four hundred, and seventy-five years. Aedh,
son of Nechtan O'Domhnaill, royal heir of Cenel-
Conaill, was drowned in a cot at the mouth of the Banna.
Aedh, son of Eoghan O'Neill, died this year. Mac
Murchadha, King of Laighen, i.e. Domhnall Riabhach son
of Gerald, received a fall by which his leg was broken;
and his death ensued therefrom. O'Ferghail died, i.e.
John, the son of Domhnall.

The kalends of January; the age of the Lord one thou- [1476.]
sand, four hundred, and seventy-six years. O'hUiginn,
i.e. Brian, son of Ferghal Ruadh, head of the schools[2] of
Erinn and Alba, died this year. O'hEghra Riabhach,
i.e. William, son of the Bishop, [died this year].[3]

The kalends of January. The age of the Lord one [1477.]
thousand, four hundred, and seventy-seven years. A
hosting by O'Neill into Tir-Aedha, [and] the country
was destroyed and burned by him. Aedh, son of
Donnchadh, son of Thomas Mag Uidhir, died. Brian,
son of Conchobhar Og, son of Conchobhar Ruadh Mag
Uidhir, died on Christmas night. A great plague[4] came
into the harbour of Es-Ruaidh, on which occasion many
persons went[5] into Tir-Conaill, and especially Mac-an-
bhaird.

The kalends of January; the age of the Lord one [1478.]
thousand, four hundred, and seventy-eight years. Cormac Mac Carthaigh was emasculated by the sons of
Diarmaid-an-dunaidh. Mac-an-bhaird of Tir-Conaill, i.e.

ᴅᴇᴄʜɑɪᴅ ᴅᴇᴄ, "of which went to death
[i.e. died"]. The Four Masters, who
have the occurrence under 1478, more
correctly say that a plague was
brought by a ship into the harbour of

Es-Ruaidh (Ballyshannon), of which
Mac-an-bhaird (or Mac Ward) of Tir-
Conaill died. Mac-an-bhaird's death
is also recorded in the next entry in
this chronicle.

ɼɪɴ ᴅoɴ ᵽɦɫáɪᵬ. Cƈɴ ɓαɼúɴ ᴅeɫᵬɴαɪ ᴅéc ᴅoɴ ᴘɫαɪᵬ.
ᴣoeɕ moɼ ɪɼɪɴ ɓɫɪαᴅαɪɴ ɼɪ co ᴣαɼ ᴅᵬɴ ɴoᴅɫuɪcc ɴα
ᴅíeɪᵹ. Ϻαc Rɪᵬᵬeɼɕαɪᵹ, .ɪ. Cɪɕɦɼuαᴅ, ᴅéᵹ. O Coɓᵬαɪᵹ
ᴅɦec, .ɪ. Ϻuɪɼceɼɕαcɦ ɓαᴅαᵬ. Eαɼɼαoɴɕα ɱóɼ ᴅo ᵽáɼɼ
eɕɪɼ ᵬɫoɪɴɴ Ϻαoɫɼuαɴαɪᵬ ocuɼ Ϻαᵹ ɫuɪɼc co ɦuɪɫɪᵬe.
Ϻαc ᴅɪαɼmαᴅα, .ɪ. Conchobαɼ mαc Conchobαɪɼ mɪc
ᴅɦɪαɼmαᴅα, ocuɼ α ɓɼαɪɕɼɪ ɼeɪɼɼɪɴ, .ɪ. ɼɫɪcɦɕ Concho-
ɓαɪɼ mɪc ᴅɦɪαɼmαᴅα, ocuɼ Ruαɪᴅɼɪ óᵹ mαc Ruαɪᴅɼɪ
ᵬαoɪᵬ mɪc ᴅɦɪαɼmαᴅα .ɪ. ɕαɴαɪɼᴅe Ϻɦoɪᵹe ɫuɪɼᵹ αɴ
ɕαɴ ɼɪɴ, ᴅo éɪɼᵹe α ɴαᴣɦαɪᴅ α ᵬéɫɪ, ocuɼ αɴ ɕíɼ ᴅoɓ
ɼeɼɼ ᴅo ᵬí αɴ Eɼɪɴɴ αɼ α méɪᴅ ɼéɪɴ ᴅo ɱɪɫɫeᴅ ᵬóɪᵬ
ᴅɪᵬɫíɴαɪᵬ. Ϻαc ᴅɪαɼmαᴅα coɴα ɓɼαɪɕɼɪᵬ ᴅo ᵬαɼɼuɪɴᵹ
mɪc Uɪɫɫíαm ɓúɼc .ɪ. Rɪcαɼᴅ O Cɦuαɪɼɼcɪᵬ αɼ ᵬuɪᴅ
Ruαɪᴅɼɪ mɪc ᴅɪαɼmαᴅα ᴅoɴ ɕíɼ, ocuɼ ᴣαɴ αɴɱuɪɴ α
cóɼαɪᵬ ɴα α ɕomɕɼom ɼɪɼ. Cƈɴ ɕíɼ ᴅo ɱɪɫɫeᵬ ᴅo Ϻαc
Uɪɫɫɪαm eɕɪɼ ᵬɪɫɫ ocuɼ ɕuαɪᵬ, ocuɼ ᴣαɴ ᴅo ɱαɪᵬ ᴅo
ᵬéɴum ᵬó ɪɼɪɴ ɕíɼ αcɦɕ α mɪɫɫeᵬ, ocuɼ α ɓᵽáᵹɓáɪɫ
αɪɱɼéɪᵬ αᵹ ɪmᵬeαcɦɕ ᵬó. Sɫɪᵹecɦ ᴅo ᴣαᵬáɪɫ ᴅo Ϻαc
Uɪɫɫíαm ᴅoɴ cɦuɼ ɼɪɴ, ocuɼ α mαc ᴅᵽáᵹɓáɪɫ ɴα
ɓαɼᴅαcɦɕ ᴅó. ɪαɼ ɴɪmᵬecɦɕ mɪc Uɪɫɫíαm, ɪmoɼɼo, αɼ
Ϻαᵹ ɫuɪɼᵹ, ocuɼ ɪαɼ mɓeᵬ ɕɼɪ hoɪᵬᵬe αɴ Cƈɼᴅ ɫαoᵬαcɦ
αᵹ cɴám ocuɼ αᵹ coɪmmɪɫɫeᴅ eᵹɫuɼe ocuɼ αoɪɼ eαɫαᴅαɴ
mɪc ᴅɦɪαɼmαᴅα, ɕαɴɪc Ruαɪᴅɼɪ mαc ᴅɪαɼmαᴅα ᴅoɴ
ɕíɼ, ᴅocuɼ ɼo ɼuɪᴅɪᵬ α cαoɼαɪᵹecɦɕ ɪɴ Cƈɼᴅ Cɦαɼɴα, ocuɼ
αɼɼɪɴ co ɓúɪɫɫ αɼ ᴣαcɦ ɕαoɪᵬ, ocuɼ ɕéɪᴅ ɼeɪɴ αɼ
Cɼuαᵬáɴ ocuɼ ɼo ᴣoɪɼeᴅ ɕɪᵹeɼɴα ᴅe αɼ ɓeoɫαɪᵬ
Conchobαɪɼ mɪc Conchobαɪɼ mɪc ᴅɪαɼmαᴅα. Ocuɼ ɼo
ᴣαɓαᴅ αɴ ᵬαɼɼuɪc ɫeɪɼ ɪαɼɼɪɴ; ocuɼ ɼo ᵬóɪ α ɕɼéɴ ɴα
ɕíɼe oɼɪɴ αmαᵬ. Ocuɼ ɼo mαɼɓαᴅ, ɪmoɼɼo, αoɴ mαc
ɱɪc ᴅɪαɼmαᴅα αɼ αɴ cαɼɼuɪc ᴅoɴ cɦuɼ ɼɪɴ, .ɪ. Ϲαᵬc
mαc Conchobαɪɼ mɪc ᴅɪαɼmαᴅα, ᴅuɼcɦoɼ ᴅo ɼóɪᵹɪᴅ.

Ƈт. Eɴαɪɼ; ɴoɪ.mɓɫɪeᵬɴαɪ .x. αɼ ɕɼɪ ɼɪcɦɪɕ αɼ .cccc.
αɼ mɪɫe óɪɼɼ ɪɴ Ϲɪᵹeɼɴαɪ.

---

¹ *Was destroyed.* ᴅo ɱɪɫɫeᴅ. Repeated in the MS.

² *The Rock.* The Rock of Loch
Cé, co. Roscommon.

¹ *Years.* The Annals of Connacht
have no events under this year;
and the record of the Four Masters is
very meagre.

Godfrey, died of the plague this year. The Baron of A.D.
Delbhna died of the plague. Great wind in this year, [1478.]
soon after Christmas. Mac Rithbhertaigh, i.e. Cithruadh,
died. O'Cobhthaigh, i.e. Muirchertach Bacach, died.
Great dissension grew up between the Clann-Maelruanaidh and all Magh-Luirg. Mac Diarmada, i.e. Conchobhar,
the son of Conchobhar Mac Diarmada, and his own
kinsmen, i.e. the family of Conchobhar Mac Diarmada,
and Ruaidhri Og, son of Ruaidhri Caech Mac Diarmada,
i.e. tanist of Magh-Luirg at that time, rose against each
other; and the best territory in Erinn of its own size was
destroyed by them respectively. Mac Diarmada and his
kinsmen brought Mac William Burk, i.e. Rickard O'Cuair-
scidh, upon Ruaidhri Mac Diarmada's part of the country,
and observed neither covenant nor equality towards him.
The country was destroyed[1] by Mac William, both church
and territory; and he did no good in the country; but he
destroyed it, and left it unquiet on his departure.
Sligech was occupied on this occasion by Mac William,
who left his son in its wardship. After the departure of
Mac William out of Magh-Luirg, however, and after he
had been three nights at Ard-Laodhach, wasting and
plundering the churches and the artisans of Mac Diarmada, Ruaidhri Mac Diarmada came into the country,
and placed his creaghts around Ard-Carna, and from
thence to Buill on every side; and he himself went upon
Cruachan, and was proclaimed lord in the face of Conchobhar, son of Conchobhar Mac Diarmada. And the
Rock[2] was afterwards taken by him; and he was in the
government of the country from thenceforth. And Mac
Diarmada's only son, i.e. Tadhg, the son of Conchobhar
Mac Diarmada, was killed on the Rock, moreover, on this
occasion, by a shot of an arrow.

The kalends of January; the age of the Lord one [1479.]
thousand, four hundred, and seventy-nine years.[3]

VOL. II.

N 2

Kɫ. Enaiɲ; ceʈɲi ɲichiʈ bliaɗan aɲ .cccc. aɲ mile
oeiɲɼ in Ciɣeɲnai. Eoɣhan mac Hell 1 Ɗoṁnuill,
ɗaṁnai ɲiɣ ʈiɲi Conaill, ɗo maɲbaɗ ɲe hEccnechán
mac Neachʈain Ui Ɗomnaill, a ccluain loeɠ an
bliaɗain ɲin, i ɲɲell. Mac Maɠnuɲɼai inʈ Senaiɗ
ɗhec, .i. Caʈhal oɠ. Ruɗɲaiɗe, mac Ruɗɲaiɗe mic
Neachʈuin Ui [Ɗomnaill], ɗo maɲbaɗ la clainn Nell
Ui Ɗomnaill. Ɲeɲɠal mac Eochaɗa ɗhec. Eoɠan
mac mic Ɑiɲʈ ɗhec.

Kɫ. Enaiɲ; bliaɗain aɲ ceʈɲae .xxⁱᶜ, aɲ .cccc. aɲ
mile, oeiɲɼ an Ciɣeɲnai. Coiɲɲɗhelbach maɠ Uiɗiɲ
ɗo maɲbaɗ a ɲɲell ɲe cloinn Ɗonnchaiɗ óicc mic
Ɗoɲɲchaiɗ meɠ Uiɗhiɲ. Ua Neill .i. Conn ɗo ɠaɗail
an bliaɗain ɲo. Mac Conmiɗe, .i. Concobaɲ ɲuaɗ, ɲái
ɲe ɗán, ɗo ɗol ɗhec an bliaɗain ɲoin. Bɲien mac Ɲelim
Ui Raiɠilliɠ ɗhec. Slaine inɣen Ui Bɲiain, ben mic
Uilliam clainni Ricaiɲɗ, .i. Uilleɠ ɲuaɗ mic Uillec in
ɲinae, .i. ɲeiʈhem coiʈcenɗ ɗo ɗámhaib ocuɲ ɗo
ɗeoɲaɗhaib Eɲenn, ɗhec.

Kɫ. Ienaiɲ; ɗa bliaɗain aɲ ceiʈɲi ɲichiʈ, aɲ .cccc.
aɲ mile, aiɲ an Ciɣeɲna. Conn mac Ɑoɗa buiɗe
mic Bɲiain ballaɠ i Neill, ɲuċoinneall oiniɠ ocuɲ
ɗaennachʈa, ʈinnlaicʈe ocuɲ ʈabaɲʈaiɲ an ʈuaiɲceɲʈ
uile, ɗɲaɠail baiɲ an bliaɗain ɲe. Ɗiaɲmaiɗ mac
Uilliam mic an eaɲɲuiɠ i Eaɗɲa ɗo maɲbaɗ le clainn
i Eaɗɲa buiɗe. Ɗonnchaɗ óɠ maɠ Uiɗiɲ ɗo maɲbaɗ
ɗuɲcoɲ ɲoiɠɗi.

Kɫ. Ienaiɲ; ʈɲi bliaɗna ocuɲ ceiʈɲi ɲichiʈ, ocuɲ
.cccc. ocuɲ mile, aoiɲ in Ciɣeɲna. Eaɲɲoɠ Clochaiɲ
ɗhec, .i. Roɲɲa mac Comaiɲ óiɠ meɠ Uiɗiɲ. O Ɲialan
ɗhec, .i. Seaan mac Eoɠain. O Cianan ɗhec, .i. Ruaiɗɲi
mac Caiɗɠ. O Ɗomnaill, .i. Ɑoɗh ɲuaɗh, ɗo ɗul
ɲluaɠ a maċaiɲe Oiɲɠiall, ocuɲ Ɑoɗ óɠ mac Ɑoɗa

---

1 O'Domhnaill. The member of the
name within the brackets, omitted in
the MS., has been supplied from the | Annals of Connacht, the contents of
which agree here with the text of this
chronicle.

The kalends of January; the age of the Lord one
thousand, four hundred, and eighty years. Eoghan, son
of Niall O'Domhnaill, royal heir of Tir-Conaill, was
killed this year by Egnechán, son of Nechtan O'Domhnaill, in Cluain-Laegh, in treachery. Mac Maghnusa of
the Senadh, i.e. Cathal Og, died. Rudhraidhe, son of
Rudhraidhe, son of Nechtan O'[Domhnaill],[1] was slain by
the sons of Niall O'Domhnaill. Ferghal Mac Eochadha
died. Eoghan, grandson of Art,[2] died.

The kalends of January ; the age of the Lord one [1481.]
thousand, four hundred, and eighty-one years. Toirdhelbhach Mag Uidhir was slain, in treachery, by the sons of
Donnchadh Og, son of Donnchadh Mag Uidhir. O'Neill,
i.e. Conn, was taken prisoner this year. Mac Conmidhe,
i.e. Conchobhar Ruadh, an eminent poet, died this year.
Brian, son of Felim O'Raighilligh, died. Slaine, daughter
of O'Briain, wife of Mac William of Clann-Rickard, i.e. of
Ulick Ruadh, son of Ulick-an-fhiona, the general patroness
of the learned and destitute of Erinn, died.

The kalends[3] of January ; the age of the Lord one [1482.]
thousand, four hundred, and eighty-two years. Conn, son
of Aedh Buidhe, son of Brian Ballach O'Neill, royal
torch of the hospitality and humanity, liberality and generosity, of the entire North, died this year. Diarmaid,
son of William, son of the Bishop O'hEghra, was killed by
the sons of O'hEghra Buidhe. Donnchadh Og Mag Uidhir
was killed by a shot of an arrow.

The kalends of January ; the age of the Lord one [1483.]
thousand, four hundred, and eighty-three years. The
bishop of Clochar died, i.e. Rossa, son of Thomas Og Mag
Uidhir. O'Fialain died, i.e. John, the son of Eoghan.
O'Cianain died, i.e. Ruaidhri son of Tadhg. O'Domhnaill, i.e. Aedh Ruadh, went with an army into Machaire-
Oirghiall, and Aedh Og, son of Aedh Buidhe, went there

---

[2] *Art*; i.e. Art O'Neill.
[3] *Kalends.* The entries for this and the two succeeding years are in the handwriting of Brian Mac Dermot.

buiᵭe ᴅo ᴅuʟ ṙʟuaᵹ eʟe ann; ocuṙ an 8ṙaᵭbaiʟe ᴅo
ʟoṙᵹaᵭ ʟeo, ocuṙ O 'Domnaiʟʟ ᴅo ᴄeacʜᴄ ṙʟan ᴅα ᴄiᵹ.

ḳᴄ. 1enaiṙ; ceiᴄṙi bʟiaᴅna. ocuṙ ceiᴄṙi ṙicʜeᴅ, ocuṙ
.cccc. ocuṙ miʟe, aiṙ [in] Ʒiᵹeṙna. Maiᵭm Mona
ʟaᵹṙaᵭi iṙin mbʟiaᴅain ṙo. Mαᵹ Maᴄʜᵹaṁna, [.1.]
Remann mac Ruᵹṙaiᵭe meic Ccṙoᵹaiʟ moiṙ, ᴅʜec a
n'Oṙoiᴄeᵭ Ccᴄα α mbṙaᴄiᴅenuṙ ṙaᴅa. Muṙcʜaᴅ mac 1
Concʜobaiṙ ṙaiʟᵹe, .1. mac Caᴄaiṙ, ᴅo maṙbaᴅ ᴅuṙᴄaṙ
ᴅo ᴄṙuiᵹiᴅ. Eaṙṙaᵹ 'Daiṙe ᴅʜeᵹ, .1. ṙaṙ N1coʟ.

ḳᴄ. Enaiṙ; cúicc bʟiaᴅnae aᵹuṙ ceᴄʜṙi ṙicʜiᴅ, aᵹuṙ
.cccc. ocuṙ miʟe, óeiṙṙ an Ʒiᵹeṙna. Ccᴅʜ ócc mac
Oeᵭa buiᴅi Uí Neiʟʟ, ṙiᴅáṁiae ṙʟecʜᴄae Oṙiain
baʟʟaiᵹ, ᴅʜec. R1 8aᵶan, .1. Cinᵹ Riṙᴅeṙᴅ, ᴅo maṙbaᴅ
a caᴄ, ócuṙ cúicc ceᴅ .x. ᴅo maṙbaᴅ himaiʟʟe ṙṙiṙ.
Maiᵭm na Muaiᵭe ᴅo ᴄaṙaiṙᴄ ᴅʟʟa 'Domnaiʟʟ, .1.
Oeᵭ ṙuaᴅh, ṙoṙ ᵹaʟʟoib ocuṙ ᵹoeᵭeʟaiᵭ cuiceᴅ
Connacʜᴄ. ᵹiʟʟaṙaᴄṙaic Ua hUiccinᴅ moṙᴄuuṙ eṙᴄ.
Mac Uiʟʟiam buṙc, no cʟainni Ricaiṙᴅ, ᴅʜec iṙin
bʟiaᴅain ṙo, .1. Uiʟʟec. Ccn baṙṙacʜ ᴅʜec. O 8uiʟʟea-
baìn beṙṙe ᴅʜec. O Daiᵹiʟʟ ᴅo ᴄuṙ a ᴄiᵹeṙnaṙ ᴅe, ocuṙ
a mac ᴅo ᴄuṙ ina inaᵭ, .1. Niaʟʟ mac Coiṙṙᴅeʟ-
baiᵹ. Ccṙᴄ a[n] boᵹain O Concʜobaiṙ ᴅo maṙbaᴅ ᴅa
ᴅeṙᵭṙaᴄʜaiṙ ṙeṙin, .1. ᴅo Cʜaᴄaiṙ.

ḳᴄ. Enaiṙ; ṙe bʟiaᴅnae aᵹuṙ ceᴄṙi ṙicʜeᴅ aᵹuṙ
.cccc. aᵹuṙ miʟe. Mac 'Diaṙmaᴅa Muiᵹi ʟuiṙᵹ, .1.
Ruaiᴅṙi óᵹ mac Ruaiᴅṙi caicʜ mic Oeᴅhai, ᴅʜec .1. ṙeṙ
moṙ ᴅoeinecʜ moṙ caicʜmeᴄ moṙ conaiᵹ, ᴅʜec aṙ an

---

1 *Srad-baile*; lit. "street-town,"
the old name of the town of Dundalk.

2 *Nicholas.* Nicholas Weston. See
note 1, p. 176. After this entry the
following note occurs: maʟʟacʜᴄ
oṙᴄ a Nicoʟaiṙ 1 8iṙiᴅain, ᴄuᵹ
oṙam mo ʟeaᴅaṙ ᴅo ṁiʟʟiuᴅ ṙe
ᴅṙóé ʟiᴄiṙ. Meṙi Oṙian mac
'Diaṙmaᴅa, ocuṙ ᴄaᴅṙaᴅ ᵹaᴄ
aon ʟeṙeṙ benᴅacʜᴄ aṙ manaim;
i.e. "a curse on thee, O Nicholas

O'Sheridan, who induced me to spoll
my book through a bad letter [i.e.
handwriting]. I am Brian Mac Diarmada; and let every one who
reads [this] utter a prayer for my
soul." A piece has been cut out
of the lower part of the leaf, and
another piece rudely stitched in its
place. This note is not referred to
in the Dublin copies of the Annals
of Connacht, the contents of which

with another army; and the Srad-baile[1] was burned by them; and O'Domhnaill reached home safely.

The kalends of January; the age of [the] Lord one thousand, four hundred, and eighty-four years. The defeat of Moin-Laghradhi in this year. Mac Mathghamhna, [i.e.] Redmond, the son of Rudhraidhe, son of Ardghal Mor, died in Droichet-atha, after long captivity. Murchadh, son of O'Conchobhair Failghe, i.e. the son of Cathair, was killed by a shot of an arrow. The Bishop of Daire died, i.e. Sir Nicholas.[2]

The kalends of January; the age of the Lord one thousand, four hundred, and eighty-five years. Aedh Og, son of Aedh Buidhe O'Neill, royal heir of the descandants of Brian Ballach, died.[3] The King of the Saxons, i.e. King Richard, was slain in battle; and fifteen hundred were slain along with him. The defeat of the Muaidh was given by O'Domhnaill, i.e. Aedh Ruadh, to the Foreigners and Gaeidhel of the province of Connacht. Gilla-Patraic O'hUiginn mortuus est. Mac William Burk, or *Mac William* of Clann-Rickard, i.e. Ulick, died this year. The Barrach died. O'Suillebhain Berre died. O'Baighill resigned his lordship, and his son, i.e. Niall the son of Toirdhelbhach, was appointed in his place. Art-an-bhogain O'Conchobhair[4] was slain by his own brother, i.e. by Cathair.

The kalends of January; one thousand, four hundred, and eighty-six years. Mac Diarmada of Magh-Luirg, i.e. Ruaidhri Og, the son of Ruaidhri Caech, son of Aedh, i.e. a man of great bounty, great expenditure, and great wealth, died[5] on the Rock;[6] and Conchobhar,

---

are otherwise here in agreement with the text.

[2] *Died.* The Four Masters state that he was killed by a cast of a javelin, whilst on a predatory incursion in Leth-Cathail, or Lecale, in the present county of Down. The entries for this and the two following years, which are almost the same as in the Annals

of Connacht, are in the handwriting of the scribe who wrote the entries for the years 1479, 1480, and 1481.

[4] *O'Conchobhair;* i.e. O'Conchobhair (or O'Conor) Failghe.

[5] *Died.* ⁊hec. This word, in its abbrev. form ⁊h, occurs a second time in the same entry.

[6] *The Rock;* the Rock of Loch-Cé.

ccαρραιce; αξυρ Concobαρ mαc Coρbmαιc mιc Comal-
ταιξ αꞃ οιꞃιξ ꝺo ριξhαꝺ nα ιꞃαꝺh. Mαξ RαꝺnuιLL, .ι.
Cαꝺξ mαc Cαṫαιl, ꝺhec. Moειleαꞔlαιnn ocuρ Rυαιꝺρι,
ꝺα mαc Mιc ꝺonnchαꝺα τιρe hOιLeLLαe, ꝺo mαρbαꝺ lα·
clαιnn ꝺomnuιLL ꞔαιm mιc Mιc ꝺonnchαꝺα. Seαn
bnιꝺι mαc Eoξhαιn mιc NeLL óιξ Uí NeLL ꝺhec.
ꝺomnαLL óξ mαc Cαρταιn, ράι noιnιξ, moρτuuρ eρτ.
Cꞁꞃ bαρραch moρ ꝺo mαρbhαꝺ.

Ḟɭ. ιenαιρ; ρeαchτ mbLιαꝺnαe αξuρ ceτρι ꝼιcheꝺ,
αξuρ .cccc. αξuρ mιle, oειρ αn Cιξeρnαι. Uα RαιξιLLιξ,
.ι. Coιρꝺeαlbαꞔ mαc Seαιn mιc Eoξhαιn Uι RαιξιLLιξ,
ꝺhec. bꞃιen mαc bꞃιαιn bαLLαιch, mιc Oeꝺhαe mιc
Ḟelιm Uι Concobαιρ, ꝺhec. Uα Moelconuιρι, .ι. Sιξραꝺ
mαc Seαιn ρúαιꝺ, ꝺhec. O Moelρechluιnn, .ι. Lαιξnech
mαc Cuιρc mιc Coρbmαιc bαLLαιξ, ꝺo mαρbαꝺ lα Conn
mαc Cιρτ mιc Cuιnn mιc Coρbmαιc bαιLLαιξ Uí
Moeιlechluιnn. bꞃιen mαc Eoξαιn mιc NeLL oιcc Uí
NeLL ꝺhec. Seαn mαc Conchobαιρ mιc Oeꝺuξαιn ꝺhec.
Cαꝺ mαc bꞃιαιn mιc ꝼeρξhαιl ρuαιꝺ Uí Uιξιnn ꝺhec.
Mαc ξoιρꝺelꝺ, .ι. Seαn, ꝺhec. Cꞁꞃ ꝺαlατúnαch, .ι.
Emuꞃn mαc Pιeρuιρρ, ꝺhec.

Ḟɭ. ιenαιρ; ochτ mbLιαξnα αξuρ ceτρe ꝼιcheꝺ, αξuρ
.cccc. αξuρ mιle, áoιρ αn Cιξeρnα. ꝺoṁnαLL mαc
ꝺoṁꞃnuιLL ιnειc NeιLL ꞁ ꝺhoṁnαιLL ꝺo ꞔρocαꝺ le hCꞁoꝺ
mαc Cꞁoꝺα ρuαιꝺ αn ꝺLιαξuιꞃꝼe. Mαolmuιρe mαc
Cαιꝺξ óιcc ꞁ Uιξιnn, ρáoι ρe ꝺáꞃ, ꝺꞃαξuιl ꝺáιρ αn
ꝺLιαξαιꞃꝼe. ꝺomnαLL ξoρm, mαc Cꞁuꝼτρuιnn ṁειc
ṁειc ꝺoṁnαιLL, ꝺo ṁαρbαꝺ ρé cloιnꞃ αn αbα ṁειc
Cꞁuꝼτρuιnn. O CeαLLuιξ ꝺéξ, .ι. Mαοιlρeαꞔluιnn mαc
Cꞁoꝺα ṁειc bꞃιαιn. O ꝼlαnnαξαn Cuατhα ρατhα, eꝺon
Coιρρꝺeαlbαꞔ mαc ξιLlα ιoρα, ꝺéξ. O Cúαꞔuιl .ι.
Eumαnn ꝺo mαρbuꝺ le cloιnn Cαιꝺξ ꞁ CheαρꝺuιLL.
Cαꝺξ mαc Cꞁoꝺα ṁειc Coιρρꝺeαlbuιξ ꞔáρρuιξ ꞁ
Chonꞔuꝺuιρ ꝺéξ. Mαξ Uιꝺιρ ꝺéξ, .ι. Eumαnn mαc

---

¹ *Tomaltach-an-oinigh*; i.e. "Tomaltach of the *oinech* (or hospitality)."

² *Aedh Ruadh.* Aedh Ruadh (Hugh
Roe) O'Domhnaill. The events of

son of Cormac, son of Tomaltach-an-oinigh,[1] was made king in his place. Mag Raghnaill, i.e. Tadhg the son of Cathal, died. Maelechlainn and Ruaidhri, the two sons of Mac Donnchadha of Tir-Oilella, were slain by the sons of Domhnall Cam, the son of Mac Donnchadha. John Buidhe, son of Eoghan, son of Niall Og O'Neill, died. Domhnall Og Mac Cartain, a most hospitable man, mortuus est. The Barrach Mór was killed.

The kalends of January; the age of the Lord one thousand, four hundred, and eighty-seven years. O'Raighilligh, i.e. Toirdhelbhach, the son of John, son of Eoghan O'Raighilligh, died. Brian, the son of Brian Ballach, son of Oedh, son of Felim O'Conchobhair, died. O'Maelconaire, i.e. Sigradh, son of John Ruadh, died. O'Maelsechlainn, i.e. Laighnech, son of Corc, son of Cormac Ballach, was killed by Conn, the son of Art, son of Conn, son of Cormac Ballach O'Maelechlainn. Brian, son of Eoghan, son of Niall Og O'Neill, died. John, son of Conchobhar Mac Aedhagain, died. Aedh, son of Brian, son of Ferghal Ruadh O'hUiginn, died. Mac Goisdelbh, i.e. John, died. The Dalton, i.e. Edmond, son of Piers, died.

The kalends of January; the age of the Lord one thousand, four hundred, and eighty-eight years. Domhnall, son of Domhnall, son of Niall O'Domhnaill, was hanged by Aedh, son of Aedh Ruadh,[2] this year. Maelmuire, son of Tadhg Og O'hUiginn, an eminent poet, died this year. Domhnall Gorm, son of Alexander, son of Mac Domhnaill, was slain by the sons of the Abbot, son of Alexander. O'Cellaigh died, i.e. Maelsechlainn, the son of Aedh, son of Brian. O'Flannagain of Tuath-ratha, i.e. Toirdhelbhach, the son of Gilla-Iosa,[3] died. O'Tuathail, i.e. Edmond, was killed by the sons of Tadhg O'Cerbhaill. Tadhg, the son of Aedh, son of Toirdhelbhach Carragh O'Conchobhair, died. Mag Uidhir died, i.e. Edmond, son of

---

this year are in the handwriting of the scribe who copied the entries for 1466, 7, 8, 9, and parts of 1470-5.

[3] *Gilla-Iosa.* Ꞡɩllα αoᵽα, MS. This name has been Latinized Gelasius.

Comáir óiʒ. Riʒ Cclbun, .ı. Sémur Sciobarb, bo ṁarbub a ʒcaṫ le na mac rein, .ı. Sémur óʒ. Orian mac Ccoba buıbe 1 Neıll béʒ bon ʒalur Oreac. Mac an bhaırb Oırʒeall béʒ, .ı. Núaba.

|Ct. 1enaır; naı mblıabnae ocur cecrı rıcheb, ocur .cccc. ocur mılı, oeırr ın Cıʒernaı. O Nell, .ı. Enrı mac Eoʒaın, bı bol bhéc. O Oaıʒhıll, .ı. Coırrbhealbach mac Nell ruaıb, morcuur erc. Ua Fıaláın, .ı. Eoʒan ócc, ocur Ccıchırne O hEoʒura, bhéc. Mac Uıbılín, .ı. Sınıcín rúab, bo marbab la Ualcaır mac Uıbılın. Seṫraıʒh mac ʒıllaracraıc, rí Orraıbhe, bécc. Ua Cerbaıll, .ı. Sean mac Moelroanaıb, bhec. Mac Uı Conchobaır ruaıb, .ı. Coırrbhealbach mac Felım rınb, .ı. rer a oerraı ar rerr bo buı ba čınec, bo marbab le claınn Ruaıbrı oıʒ mıc Ruaıbrı caoıch, .ı. re Caoʒ ocur re Corbmac, accaırʒín rıebuch claınnı Faʒharcaıʒ. Ccn Calbhach mac Uı Domnuıll bhec. Dıermuıcc, mac Caıoʒ mıc Domnuıll oıc meıʒ Carchaıʒ, bo marbab le hıerlaı nDermuman, .ı. Muırır mac Semuır. Ua Fıaláın, .ı. Eoʒan óʒ mac Eoʒaın, bhec.

|Ct. 1enaır, ocur beıch mblıabna ocur cecrı .xxıc ocur .cccc. ocur mıle aoırr ın Cıʒernaı. Coırrbealbach mac Coırrbealbuıʒ Uı Oaıʒhıll braʒhaıl baırr ıer na erccor ın blıabaın rın. Mac Domnuıll na hCclban, .ı. ın cıʒerna ócc, anc oen buınıu bob rerr ınb Erınn na ınb Cclbaın a comaımrır rrırr, bo marbab co mírachmar le rer cécc Erennach ınba reomraı rein, .ı. Dıermaıb Caırbrech. 1n Dılmuınıoch, .ı. Emanb mac Commaırr mıc ʒeroıc, bhec. Ua Concubaır ruab, .ı.

---

1 *Galar breac*; the small-pox, or "speckled disease."

² *Sethraigh*. The Four Mast. call him Sefraidh, or Jeffrey.

³ *Ruaidhri Og*. "Ruaidhri the Younger [Mac Dermot]."

⁴ *Cairgin-riabhach*; lit. "the swarthy little rock." The Four Mast. say

"Caislen-riabhach," now Castlerea, in the county of Mayo.

⁵ *Died*. This is a repetition, the obit of Eoghan Og O'Fialain, or O'Phelan, being the third entry under this year. The same repetition occurs in the Annals of Connacht, the contents of which agree

Thomas Og. The King of Alba, i.e. James Stewart, was killed in battle by his own son, i.e. young James. Brian, son of Aedh Buidhe O'Neill, died of the "galar breac."[1] Mac-an-bhaird of Oirghiall died, i.e. Nuadha. [1488.]

The kalends of January; the age of the Lord one thousand, four hundred, and eighty-nine years. O'Neill, i.e. Henry, the son of Eoghan, died. O'Baighill, i.e. Toirdhelbhach, the son of Niall Ruadh, mortuus est. O'Fialain i.e. Eoghan Og, and Aithirne O'hEoghusa, died. Mac Uibhilin, i.e. Senicin Ruadh, was killed by Walter Mac Uibhilin. Sethraigh[2] Mac Gilla-Patraic, King of Osraidhe, died. O'Cerbhaill, i.e. John, son of Maelruanaidh, died. The son of O'Conchobhair Ruadh, i.e. Toirdhelbhach, the son of Felim Finn, of his years the best man of his tribe, was killed by the sons of Ruaidhri Og,[3] son of Ruaidhri Caech, viz., by Tadhg and Cormac, in Cairgin-riabhach[4] of Clann-Faghartaigh. The Calbhach, son of O'Domhnaill, died. Diarmaid, son of Tadhg, son of Domhnall Og Mac Carthaigh, was slain by the Earl of Des-Mumha, i.e. Maurice, the son of James. O'Fialain, i.e. Eoghan Og, the son of Eoghan, died.[5] [1489.]

The kalends of January; and the age of the Lord one thousand, four hundred, and ninety years. Toirdhelbhach, son of Toirdhelbhach O'Baighill, died this year, after having been thrown *from a horse*. Mac Domhnaill[6] of.Alba, i.e. the young Lord, the best man in Erinn, or in Alba, in his time, was unfortunately slain by an Irish harper,[7] i.e. Diarmaid Cairbrech, in his own chamber. The Dillon, i.e. Edmond, son of Thomas, son of Garrett, died. O'Conchobhair Ruadh, i.e. Fedhlim [1490.]

very closely here with the text of this chronicle.

[6] *Mac Domhnaill.* The Ann. Ult. say " Aenghus Mac Domhnaill."

[7] *Irish harper.* ꞃeꞃ ꞇéeꞇ Eꞃennꞃach. The word Eꞃꞇꞃch, for Eꞃennꞃach, has been apparently

erased in the MS.; but it occurs in the Annals of Connacht, and Ann. Ult., in which latter chronicle the harper's name is given as Diarmait O'Cairpri; and it is added that the deed was committed at ꞁꞁꞃeꞃ Nꞇꞃ, or Inverness.

Feoḋlim finn mac Taoḋg Uí Conċubaiṙ, feṙ coġtaċ caṫaṙḋai comtimaṙcctech cṙechlinmaṙ, ḋec in bliaḋain ceḋnai. O Caṫáin, .i. 8ean mac Ḋiaṙmaḋai mic Ꭺibne, ḋo ġaḃail le luing tanic a hᎯlbain.

Ꝁt. 1enaiṙ, ocuṙ aon bliaḋain ḋhec ocuṙ cetṙi ṙicheḋ, ocuṙ .cccc. ocuṙ mile, aoiṙ an Tiġeṙna. Feiḋlim mac Ꭺoḋa mic Eoġain 1 Néill ḋo ṁaṙḃaḋ le Ḃṙian mac Remainḋ mic Ruġṙaiḋhe Meġ Mattġamna. O Raiġilliġ ḋhec inṙambliaḋain ṙi, .i. 8ean mac Toiṙḃealḃaiġ, ocuṙ O Raiġilliġ ḋo ġaiṙm ḋo 8heaċan mac Caṫail.

Ꝁt. 1enaiṙ; aġuṙ ḋa bliaġuin ḋéġ aġuṙ ceitṙe ṙicheḋ .cccc. aġuṙ mile áoiṙ an Tiġeaṙna. Ḃaṙun Sláine ḋéġ ḋo fṙlaiḋ alluiṙ, .i. 8émuṙ Plemeann. Cuiḋ ḋo ċṙann na cṙoiċe naoṁta ḋṙaġuil iṙin Roiṁ aḋlaicḋe a ḋtalaṁ, .i. an ċláṙ báoi oṙ ceann na cṙoiċe iona ṙaiḋe ṙgṙioḋta Ieṙuṙ Naȝaṙenuṙ Rex Iuḋeoṙum; ocuṙ ḋo fṙiṫ ṙgṙioḋta ṙan ionaḋ ċeḋna ġuṙuḃ i Elena ṙo ṫolaiġ é. Ceann na ṙleiġe léṙ loit Longinuṙ coṙṙ Cṙiṙt ḋo ċuṙ ċum na Roṁa iṙin mbliaġainṙe ḋo ṫiġeaṙna na ḋTuṙcaċ. Finġin O Mattúna ḋéġ. Mac Ġilla Fhinnen ḋhec, .i. Toiṙḋhealḃaċ mac Ḃṙiain. Maġṙaiḋ, coṁaṙba teṙmainḋ Ḋaḃeoġ, .i. Ḋiaṙmaiḋ mac Maṙcaiṙ mic Muiṙiṙ meic Nicoil mic Ꭺnḋṙiaṙ, ḋhec. Taḋġ cam O Cleiṙiġ, ṙencuiḋh cineil Conall, ḋhec. Ꭺonġuṙ mac an Ulltaiġ, bṙaṫaiṙ minuṙ, ḋhec. Mac Conmaṙa, .i. Cuṁeḋha mac 8eaain, ḋhec. Ꭺn Calḃaċ mac 1 Conchoḃaiṙ Fhailġe, .i. mac Caṫaiṙ, ḋo ṁaṙḃaḋ le maiṙtiṙ ġaṙt. 8eaan buiḋe mac Eoġain meġ Maṫġamna ḋhec. Ġoffaiġ O Caṫain ḋo maṙḃaḋ le Ḃaltaṙ mac Uiḃelin. Coṙmac mac

---

1 *Cathal.* The events of this year are in the handwriting of Brian Mac Dermot, who has added the following note : Meṙi Ḃṙian ḋo ṙgṙiḃ ṙin ġo holc, ocuṙ mallaċht oṙt a Nicolaiṙ, oiṙ tuġ tu oṙam mo leaḃuṙ ḋo ṁilleaḋ; i.e. "I am Brian who wrote that badly; and a curse on you, Nicholas; for you induced me to spoil my book."

2 *Plemenn;* i.e. Fleming.

3 *O'Mathúna.* A corrupt way of writing the name O'Mathghamhna, or O'Mahony. The first three entries

A.D.

Finn, the son of Tadhg O'Conchobhair, a warlike, martial, corrective man, possessed of numerous preys, died the [1490.] same year. O'Cathain, i.e. John, the son of Diarmaid, son of Aibhne, was captured by a ship that came from Alba.

The kalends of January; and the age of the Lord one [1491.] thousand, four hundred, and ninety-one years. Fedhlim, son of Aedh, son of Eoghan O'Neill, was killed by Brian, son of Redmond, son of Rudhraidhe Mac Mathghamhna. O'Raighilligh died this year, i.e. John, the son of Toirdhelbhach; and John, the son of Cathal,[1] was proclaimed O'Raighilligh.

The kalends of January; and the age of the Lord [1492.] one thousand, four hundred, and ninety-two years. The Baron of Slaine, i.e. James Plemenn,[2] died of a sweating plague. A portion of the wood of the Holy Cross was found in Rome, buried in the ground, i.e. the board that was over the head of the Cross, on which was written "Jesus Nazarenus rex Judæorum"; and it was found written in the same place that it was Helena who had buried it. The head of the lance with which Longinus wounded the body of Christ was sent to Rome, in this year, by the sovereign of the Turks. Finghin O'Mathúna[3] died. Mac Gillafinnen died, i.e. Toirdhelbhach, the son of Brian. Magraith, comarb of Termon-Dabheog, i.e. Diarmaid, the son of Marcus, son of Maurice, son of Nicholas, son of Andrias, died. Tadhg Cam O'Cleirigh, historian of Cenel-Conaill, died. Aenghus Mac-an-Ultaigh, a Friar Minor, died. Mac Conmara, i.e. Cumhedha, the son of John, died. The Calbhach, son of O'Conchobhair Failghe, i.e. son of Cathair, was killed by Master Gart.[4] John Buidhe, son of Eoghan Mac Mathghamhna, died. Godfrey O'Cathain was killed by Walter Mac Uibhilin. Cormac,[5]

under this year are in the handwriting of the scribe who copied the contents of the years 1469-72, &c.; and the remainder in that of Brian Mac Dermot.

[4] *Master Gart.* "One of the Earl of Ormond's people," the Four Masters say.

[5] *Cormac.* Cormac Mac Diarmada, or Mac Dermot.

'Oιαρmαⱱα meιc Rυαιⱱρι cαoιč, ocυρ 'Oιαρmαιⱱ ριαbαch
α mαc, ⱱo mαρbαⱱ le clαιnn Rυαιⱱρι oιᵹ mιc Rυαιⱱρι
cαoιč mιc Ccoⱱα, α nᵹαρᵹα nα coιlleαⱱ αmhρειⱱe.

Ⱪct. ιenαιρ, ocυρ τρí blιαⱱnα ⱱéᵹ αᵹυρ ceιτρe ριcheⱱ,
αᵹυρ .cccc. αᵹυρ mιle, áoιρ αn Τιᵹeρnα. O Ⱶéιll, .ι.
Conn mαc θιnρí, ⱱo ḿαρⱱυⱱ le nα ⱱeαρⱱρáčυιρ ρéιn, .ι.
θυnρí ócc, αᵹυρ θιnρí óᵹ ⱱo ᵹαⱱαιl τιᵹeρnτυιρ číρe
hθoᵹυιn. Ƥιnnᵹυαlα ιnᵹen αn Chαlⱱυιᵹ 1 Choнčυⱱυιρ,
beαn ⱱéρcαč ⱱαonnαchταč ρα mó clú nα hαιmριᵹ ⱱo
ⱱol ⱱéᵹ αn Ⱶlιαᵹυιn ριn. mαc Coιnmιⱱe, .ι. Ταⱱᵹ,
moρτυυρ eρτ. Ⱶριαn, mαc Ⱶeιll ᵹαlτα ḿeιc Ⱶριαιn
ⱷαllαιᵹ 1 Ⱶeιll, ⱱo ḿαρⱱυⱱ lé Ⱶριαn ḿαc Mυιρceαρ-
ταιᵹ ḿeuᵹ Ccoнᵹυρα, α nⱱιoᵹυιl α αčαρ.

Ⱪct. ιenαιρ; ceιτρe blιαᵹnα ⱱéᵹ αᵹυρ ceιτρe ριcheⱱ,
αᵹυρ .cccc. αᵹυρ mιle, áoιρ αn Τιᵹeρnα. Ⱶnᵹen 1
'Ohoḿnυιll, .ι. αn ιnᵹen ⱱυⱱ, beαn Ⱶéιll ḿeιc Cυιnn,
ⱱραᵹαιl ⱷαιρ αn Ⱶlιαᵹαιn ρe. [ⱷeαn mαc θoᵹαιn mιc
Ⱶeιll ᵹαιρⱱ hí 'Oomnαιll], ράoι ⱱυιne υαρυιl αρ α
čυlαⱱ ρéιn, ⱱo ᵹαⱱαιl le ρlιochτ 'Oonnchαⱱα 1 ⱷαllcυ-
ⱱυιρ, αᵹυρ α čαιρⱱeαρτ ⱱo Conn ḿαc Ccoⱱα ρυαιⱱ,
αᵹυρ α čρoⱱαⱱ ᵹαn čαιρⱱe le Conn. 'Ooḿnαll mαc
θoᵹhαιn 1 Choнčυⱱυιρ, τιᵹeαρnα Slιᵹιᵹ αᵹυρ ó ρlιαⱱ
αnúαρ, ⱱo mαρbαⱱ lα cloιnn Rυαιⱱρι ḿeιc Τοιρρⱱeαl-
bυιᵹ 1 Choнčυⱱυιρ α mbαⱱυn čαιρleιn Ⱶhυαnα ριnne.
O Ƥeρᵹυιl ⱱéᵹ, .ι. Conḿαc mαc Seαⱱυιn. θoιn beαρnαč
mαc mαolḿυιρe meιc Sυιⱱne ⱱo mαρⱱυⱱ lα Ταⱱᵹ mαc
Cυιnn ḿeιc 'Ooḿnυιll 1 Ⱶéιll. mαc ḿeιc Uιllιαm
bυρc ⱱo ḿαρⱱυⱱ ρα čαιρlén Slιᵹιᵹ αn blιαᵹυιnρe, .ι.
Uιllιαm ḿαc Rιocυιρⱱ ḿeιc θυmυιnn ḿeιc Τomαιρ α
Ⱶυρc.

---

1 *Garrdha-na-coilledh-amhreidhe.*
This name signifies "the garden of
the uneven wood." It is now obsolete.

2 *Kalends.* The entries for this
and the two following years are in
the handwriting of the scribe who
copied the annals for 1469–1472, &c.

3 *John.* The clause within brackets, omitted in the MS., has been supplied from the Annals of Connacht.

4 *From the mountain down;* i.e. the
territory to the north of the mountains
called Sliabh-Seghsa, or the Curlieu
hills, on the confines of the counties of

son of Diarmaid, son of Ruaidhri Caech, and his son
Diarmaid Riabhach, were slain by the sons of Ruaidhri
Og, son of Ruaidhri Caech, in Gardha-na-coilledh-
amhreidhe.[1]

The kalends[2] of January; and the age of the Lord one
thousand, four hundred, and ninety-three years. O'Neill,
i.e. Conn, the son of Henry, was killed by his own brother,
i.e. Henry Og; and Henry Og assumed the sovereignty of
Tir-Eoghain. Finnghuala, daughter of the Calbhach O'Conchobhair, a charitable, humane woman, of the greatest reputation in her time, died this year. Mac Conmidhe, i.e.
Tadhg, mortuus est. Brian, son of Niall Gallda, son of
Brian Ballach O'Neill, was slain by Brian, the son of
Muirchertach Mag Aenghusa, in retaliation for his father.

The kalends of January; the age of the Lord one
thousand, four hundred, and ninety-four years. O'Domhnaill's daughter, i.e. the Inghen-dubh, the wife of Niall,
son of Conn, died this year. [John,[3] son of Eoghan,
son of Niall Garbh O'Domhnaill], a most eminent gentleman in his own capacity, was taken prisoner by the descendants of Donnchadh O'Gallchubhair, and surrendered
to Conn, son of Aedh Ruadh; and he was hanged without
delay by Conn. Domhnall, son of Eoghan O'Conchobhair,
lord of Sligech, and from the mountain down,[4] was
killed by the sons of Ruaidhri, son of Toirdhelbhach
O'Conchobhair, in the bawn[5] of the castle of Bun-finne.
O'Ferghail died, i.e. Conmac, the son of John. Owen
Bernach, the son of Maelmuire Mac Suibhne, was killed
by Tadhg, the son of Conn, son of Domhnall O'Neill.
The son of Mac William Burk was slain this year near[6]
the castle of Sligech, i.e. William, son of Rickard, son of
Edmond, son of Thomas Burk.

Roscommon and Sligo. The expression anuar, "down from," would
imply that the entry was originally
written to the north of (or "below")
the Curlieu-hills.

[5] Bawn, baoun; lit. "cow fort."

[6] Near. The MS. has pa, which
properly means "about," "around,"
"under," or "concerning."

ḃt. Θnαıp; .u. ḃlıαᵹnα ⅾéuᵹ αᵹuꞃ ceıꞇꞃı ꞃıcheⅾ, αᵹuꞃ .cccc. ocuꞃ Mıle, αoıꞃ αn Cıᵹeꞃnα. Mαıⷠm αn Cheıⷱıᵹ ⷠꞃαoınıᵹ ⅾo ⷲαⷠuıꞃꞇ αꞃ ⷠıᵹeαꞃnα Ṡlıᵹıᵹ, .ı. αꞃ Ⴔheılım mαc Mαᵹnuıꞃ 1 Choncuⷠuıꞃ, ꞃıꞃ Ɉ n'Ɉoⷯnuıll, .ı. ꞃé hƆƆoⷠ ꞃuαⷠ. Mαc Ɉonchαⷠα ⷠıꞃı hɈıleαllα, .ı. Ⴀαⷠᵹ mαc Ꞃꞃıαın meıc Conⷲuⷠuıꞃ, ⅾo ⷯαꞃⷠαⷠ leıꞃ Ɉ n'Ɉoⷯnuıll, .ı. ƆƆoⷠ ꞃuαⷠ ⷯαc Neıll ᵹαıꞃⷠ, α mⷠel αn ⅾꞃoıⷲıꞇ. Ɉ 'Ɉuⷠⅾα, .ı. Θoᵹun cαoⷲ ⷯαc Ꞃuαıⷠꞃı, ⅾo mαꞃⷠuⷠ αnn ꞃóꞃ; αᵹuꞃ Ꞃꞃıαn cαoⷲ ⷯαc Ⴀαıⷠᵹ ⷯeıc Θoᵹuın 1 Choncuⷠuıꞃ, αᵹuꞃ Ⴀαⷠᵹ ⷯαc 'Ɉoⷯnuıll ⷯeıc Θoᵹhαın ⅾo mαꞃⷠαⷠ αnn ꞃóꞃ. Ɉ ᵹαⷠꞃα ⅾo ᵹαⷠαıl αnn, .ı. 'Ɉıαꞃmuıⅾ ⷯαc Θoᵹhαın. Moꞃán ⅾo ⷯαꞃⷠuⷠ αᵹuꞃ ⅾo ⷠαⷲhαⷠ αnn ⅾo ⷠeαᵹ ⷠáoınıⷠ ıochꞇuıꞃ Chonnαchꞇ o ꞃın αmαⷲ. Mαc Uıllıαm ⷲloınne Ꞃıocuıꞃⅾ ⅾo ⷲeαchꞇ α nıochꞇuꞃ Chonnαchꞇ, αᵹuꞃ αn ⷯéıⅾ náꞃ ⷯıll Ɉ 'Ɉoⷯnuıll ꞃoıⷯe ꞃın ⅾo ⷯılleⷠ ⅾo uıle. Ⴀomulꞇαⷲ ⷯαc Coꞃmuıc Ꞃαllαıᵹ ⅾéᵹ. Uα 'Ɉuıⷠᵹıoⷠnán Chıllı Ꞃónαn, .ı. 'Ɉuⷠꞇαⷲ mαc Mhαoıleαⷲluınn ⷯeıc Mhαꞇα ᵹlαıꞃ, ꞃáoı ꞃe ꞃeαnⷲuꞃ αᵹuꞃ ꞃe ꞃılıᵹechꞇ, ⅾéᵹ. Ɉ 'Ɉoⷯnuıll ⅾo ⷠul ᵹu ꞇeαⷲ ꞃıᵹ ƆƆlbun αn blıαⅾαın ꞃın. Mαc Ꞩαⷯꞃαᵹαın, .ı. Ⴔeıⷠlım, ⅾo ⷠαⷲhαⷠ, αᵹuꞃ Mαc Ꞩαⷯꞃαᵹαın ⅾo ᵹαıꞃm ıonα ıonαⷠ ⅾo 'Ɉhoⷯnαll ⷠeꞃnαⷲ. Mαc αn bαıꞃⅾ .ı. ƆƆoⷠ ⅾhec.

ḃt. ıenαıꞃ; ꞃe blıαᵹnα ⅾéᵹ αᵹuꞃ ceıꞇꞃı ꞃıⷲıꞇ, αᵹuꞃ .cccc. αᵹuꞃ Mıle, áoıꞃ αn Cıᵹeꞃnα. Máᵹ Uıⷠıꞃ, .ı. Ꞩeαⷠαn, ⅾo ᵹαⷠαıl α ⅾꞇeαꞃmonn Mheuᵹꞃαⷲ le Conn ⷯαc ƆƆoⷠα ꞃuαıⷠ 1 'Ɉhóⷯnuıll, αᵹuꞃ α lán ⅾeαchαıb ocuꞃ ⅾéⅾáıl ⅾo ⷠúαın αƆƆoⷠ .h. 'Ɉhoⷯnuıll αᵹuꞃ ⅾo Máᵹ Uıⷠıꞃ ⅾon ⷠꞃeıꞃım ꞃın. Ɉ Mαⷠᵹαⷯnα αn ꞃuınn

---

¹ *Ceidech-drainech.* This name, correctly written *Ceidech-draighnech*, signifies the "thorny hillocks;" now Keadydrinagh, in the barony of Carbury, and county of Sligo.

² *Bel-an-droichit*; i.e. "the mouth of the bridge;" now Ballindrehid, a little to the north of Ballysadare,

co. Sligo, on the road leading from that place to the town of Sligo.

³ *Cormac Ballach.* "Cormac the Freckled [Mac Donough]."

⁴ *O'Duibhgennain.* Corruptly written Uα 'Ɉuıⷠᵹıoⷠnán in the MS.; a way in which no intelligent member of the family would have written it.

The kalends of January; the age of the Lord one thousand, four hundred, and ninety-five years. The [1495.] defeat of the Ceidech-drainech[1] was given to the lord of Sligech, i.e. to Felim, the son of Maghnus O'Concho-bhair, by O'Domhnaill, i.e. by Aedh Ruadh. Mac Donnchadha of Tir-Oilella, i.e. Tadhg, the son of Brian, son of Conchobhar, was killed by O'Domhnaill, i.e. Aedh Ruadh, son of Niall Garbh, at Bel-an-droichit.[2] O'Dubhda, i.e. Eoghan Caech, son of Ruaidhri, was also killed there; and Brian Caech, son of Tadhg, son of Eoghan O'Concho-bhair, and Tadhg, son of Domhnall, son of Eoghan, were furthermore slain there. O'Gadhra was taken prisoner there, i.e. Diarmaid, the son of Eoghan. A great many besides of the nobles of Lower Connacht were killed and drowned there. Mac William of Clann-Rickard went into Lower Connacht, and all that O'Domhnaill had not previously destroyed was entirely destroyed by him. Tomaltach, the son of Cormac Ballach,[3] died. O'Duibh-gennain[4] of Cill-Ronain, i.e. Dubhtach, son of Maelechlainn, son of Matthew Glas, a most eminent historian and poet, died. O'Domhnaill went this year[5] to the king of Alba's house. Mac Samhradhain, i.e. Fedhlim, was drowned; and Domhnall Bernach[6] was proclaimed Mac Samhradhain in his place. Mac-an-bhaird, i.e. Aedh, died.[7]

The kalends of January; the age of the Lord one [1496.] thousand, four hundred, and ninety-six years. Mag Uidhir, i.e. John, was taken prisoner in Termon-Magraith by Conn, the son of Aedh Ruadh O'Domhnaill; and a great many horses and spoils were taken from Aedh O'Domhnaill and Mag Uidhir in this defeat. O'Math-ghamhna of the Fonn-iartharach, i.e. Finghen, general

---

[5] *This year.* If the events of each year were arranged in chronological order, this entry would be mis-placed, as according to other authori-ties O'Domhnaill returned from Scot-land in time to participate in the battle above recorded.

[6] *Domhnall Bernach;* i.e. Domhnall (or Daniel) of the "gapped" teeth.

[7] *Died.* This obit, which is not given in the Annals of Connacht, is added in Brian Mac Dermott's hand-writing.

ιαρċαρυιξ, .ι. Ρ̇ιηϛιη, ρειċεαṁ coιċċeαηη ϻαοηηαċτα αϛυρ οιηιξ ιαρċυιρ Ṁhυṁυη, οϛυρ αη ρεαρ ρα τρειḃιξε α Lαιϻιη αϛυρ α mbéυρλα α ϛcoṁαṁρ̇ιρ ρ̇ιρ̇, ϻο ḃυl ϻéϛ αη ḃλιαξυιηρ̇. Ϛλαιρηe, mαc Rcmαηη ṁειc Rυξρυιḃe ṁeξ Ṁατhξαṁηα, ϻο ṁαρḃυḃ lα Ϛιλλαρα-ϻρυιc ṁαc Ccϻα όιϛ ṁειc Ccϻα ρυαιḃ, αϛ cαρ̇léη Ṁυιηεαċάιη. Ο Ϻυḃϻα ϻυḃ, .ι. Uιλλιαm mαc Ϻοṁηυιll Ḃαλλαιξ, [ϻο ecc]. Ο ₣λαηηαξάη Τυαιċe ραċα ϻéυξ, .ι. Ϛιλλιḃερτ mαc Cορṁυιc ṁειc Ϛιλλα ιορα. Ṁαc Sαṁ-ραḃάιη, .ι. Ϻοṁηυλl ḃερηαċ mαc Τοmάιρ̇ ṁειc ₣ερξυιl,. ϻο ṁαρḃαḃ αḃ̇εαλl. Ṁαc Sυιḃηε τιρe ḃοξαιηe, .ι. Ṁαολmυιρι, ϻéϛ. Ṁαc Sαορ Εϻḃαρϻ luρ̇ταρ̇ ϻéϛ, .ι. Rolαη. Ο ₣ερξυιl ϻéϛ, .ι. Rυξρυιḃe ṁαc Cαċυιl. Ο ₣ερξυιl ϻο ξαιρm ϻο Chéϻαċ.

Ƙcτλ. Εηαιρ ρορ ḃοṁηαch. ᵏeαchτ mbλιαϻηα ϻhec οcυρ ceιτρι ρ̇ċιτ, .cccc. οcυρ mιle, αοιρ αη Τιϛερηα. Ειϛηεchάη mαc Ηεchταιη hι Ϻhomηαιll, ρ̇ϻαṁηα cιηεοιl Coηαιll, οcυρ̇ αη ρερ ιρ̇ mó ρυαιρ̇ ϻο ḃochυρ̇ α ḃύċhαιϻe leċ ρe ceηϻυρ̇ ρεḃηα, οcυρ̇ ιρ̇ mó léρ̇ τυιτ ϻά ηαιmϻιḃ, ϻο mαρḃαḃ le Coηη mαc Ccϻα ρυαιḃ hι Ϻhomηαιll α ḃ̇ορλοηξρορτ hι Ϻhomηαιll ρειη. Ccϻ ρυαιḃ .h. Ϻοṁηαιll ϻο ċυρ̇ α. τιϛερηυιρ̇ ϻe τρé ḃυαιḃρ̇ιυϻ α ċloιηηe ρ̇éιη. Coηη mαc Ccϻα ρυαιḃ ϻο ξαḃάιl τιϛερηυιρ̇ τιρe Coηαιll α ηιοηαḃ α αthαρ. Sloιϛεϻ lάηmορ̇ lα .h. ηϺomηαιll, .ι. Coηη, α ϛCoη-ηαchταιḃ, ϛο mαιċιḃ Coηαλϻαch mαιlle ρ̇ρ̇ιρ̇; αchτ cheηα ρo eιρ̇ιξρετ ρ̇lιchτ Ḃρ̇ιαιη Lαιξηιξ ϛο hυιlιϻe lcó ταρ̇ Coρρ̇ρ̇λιαḃ ηα Sεξρ̇α, οcυρ̇ α Ṁαξ Luιρ̇ξ ιη Ϻάξḃα. Ιρ̇ αηηρ̇ιη ρo ċ̇ηόιl Ṁαc Ϻιαρmαϻα, .ι. Ταḃ̇ 'mαc Rυαιϻρι mιc Ϻιαρmαϻα, α ċιηεϻh οcυρ̇ α clαηη mαιcηe ρ̇ειη αρ̇ ϛαch αιρϻ ϻά ιηηρ̇οιξεϻ, οcυρ̇ αη ṁειϻ ρυαιρ̇ ϻο ρ̇íl Ṁυιρ̇εξhαιξ, οcυρ̇ ϻο ċoειρ̇ρ̇εchαιḃ τhυατh Coṁ-ηαchτ, ιοηηυρ̇ ϛοmbόι οchτ ϛcóιρ̇ιξċ̇ι ϻhéc ϻο ḃεξ

---

¹ *Died.* ϻο ecc. Omitted in MS., and also in the Annals of Connacht.   ² *Kalends.* This entry begins with the handwriting of the "Philip" who

supporter of the humanity and hospitality of the West of
Mumha, and the most learned man of his time in Latin [1496.]
and English, died this year. Glaisne, son of Redmond, son
of Rughraidhe Mac Mathghamhna, was slain by Gilla-
Patraic, the son of Aedh Og, son of Aedh Ruadh, at the
castle of Muincchán. O'Dubhda Dubh, i.e. William, the
son of Domhnall Ballach, [died].[1] O'Flannagain of Tuath-
ratha died, i.e. Gilbert, son of Cormac, son of Gilla-Isa.
Mac Samhradhain, i.e. Domhnall Bernach, son of Thomas,
son of Ferghal, was killed in treachery. Mac Suibhne of
Tir-Boghaine, i.e. Maelmuire, died. The son of Sir
Edward Eustace died, i.e. Roland. O'Ferghail died, i.e.
Rughraidhe, the son of Cathal. Cedach was proclaimed
O'Ferghail.

The kalends[2] of January on Sunday. The age of the [1497.]
Lord one thousand, four hundred, and ninety-seven
years. Egnechan, the son of Nechtan O'Domhnaill, royal
heir of Cenel-Conaill, the man who experienced the
most of his country's adversity, in connexion with
the chief command, and by whom his enemies fell in
greatest number, was killed by Conn, the son of Aedh
Ruadh O'Domhnaill, in O'Domhnaill's own fortress. Aedh
Ruadh O'Domhnaill resigned his sovereignty, through
the dissensions of his own sons. Conn, the son of Aedh
Ruadh, assumed the lordship of Tir-Conaill in the place
of his father. A very great hosting by O'Domhnaill, i.e.
Conn, accompanied by the Conallian chiefs, into Connacht.
All the race of Brian Laighnech, moreover, went with
them across Corrsliabh-na-Seghsa, and into Magh-luirg-
in-Daghda. Then it was that Mac Diarmada, i.e. Tadhg,
son of Ruaidhri Mac Diarmada, assembled his kindred
and his own sons from all quarters, and as many as he got
to join him of the Sil-Muiredhaigh, and of the chiefs of
the Tuatha of Connacht, so that there were eighteen corps

transcribed the earlier part of the
chronicle, and who added the memor-

andum at the end of the year 1061,
printed in note 4, p. 58, vol. i.

VOL. II.

O 2

ſʟúαʒυιꞫ ꝺο αοn ϲoṁαιƿlе; оϲυſ ϲιαξυιꝺ αſ ϲιɳɳ hι Ꝺhоṁnαιll α ʒϹоιſſſʲlеιꞫ. ССϲhϲ ϲhеnα níſ ϲonʒυιꞫ αn ϲoιṁēɳól ϲαlmα ϲαꞫ ſʟúαʒαϲh ſιɳ О Ꝺоmnαιll. Iſ αɳɳſιɳ ſо ιɳſſαιξſеϲ ιn ꝺά αſꝺ ſоϲſαιꝺе ſιn α ϲ̆еlι ιm СhоιſſſʲléιꞫ, оϲυſ ní ſʒυϲhαꝺ ó ϲ̆еlι ꝺо ſóbαιſſеϲ nо ʒоɳꝺоſϲhαιſ ιl ιоmαꝺ ꝺά nάɳſαꝺαιꞫ оϲυſ ꝺά nάоſ ʒαιſϲιꝺ ιſιɳ nʒlеó ſιn. ССϲhϲ ϲhеnα ſо bſιſſеꞫ αſ .h. nꝺоmnαιll ꝺоn ꝺυl ſιn, ʒυſſо mαſbαꞫ оϲhϲ ϲеꝺ nо ɳι bυꞫ mó ꝺια ṁυιnϲеſ, оϲυſ ʒυſſо ʒαbαꞫ αnn Гéιꝺlιm mαϲ Mαξnυſα hι Сhоnϲ̆оbαιſ, .ι. lеιꞫ ſí Соɳɳαϲhϲ ó СhоιſſſlιαꞫ ʒо ꝹſоꞫαоιſ; оϲυſ ſо ʒαbαꝺ αɳɳ αn ꝺά Mαϲ ShυιꞫnе, оϲυſ ɳι hеιϲιſ α ſιоṁ ιɳά ſó αιſеm αſ bеnαꞫ ꝺéꝺάlυιꞫ αιſm оϲυſ еϲh оϲυſ éιꝺιξ, оϲυſ ꝺά ʒαϲh ϲιɳél αιſm оϲυſ еſſαιꞫ оſιn αmαϲh ꝺоn ꝺυl ſιn; оϲυſ ſо ιmϲ̆ιξ .h. Ꝺоmnαιll ſеιn αſ ϲоſαꞫ α еιſιоmυιl оϲυſ ꝺо nеſϲ α lαιmе αſſ αn mαιꞫm ſιn. Оϲυſ ſυξ Mαϲ Ϲιαſmαꝺα α bſάιξꝺе оϲυſ α Ɜυαn éꝺαιl lαιſ ιαſ mbυαιꞫ ʒϲоſʒαιſ; оϲυſ ιſſе ſυαſlυϲαꝺ ſо Ɜеn Mαϲ Ϲιαſmαꝺα αſ Геιlιm mαϲ Mαξnυſα hι Сhоnϲhоbαιſ, .ι. ϲυιꝺ ϲ̆lαιɳι MhαоlſυαnαιꞫ ꝺо ϲ̆óιϲеꝺ ϲ̆υαn Slιʒιξ, оϲυſ ϲlαɳɳ ϹαιꞫʒ mιϲ Ɜſιαιɳ mιϲ ꝹhоɳɳϲhαꞫα ιnα nυſſαιξιꞫ αιʒе ſſιſſιn ꝺо ϲоmαll ꝺó α ſéιn ſé ſϲ̆ιϲ lоιlʒеϲh. Оϲυſ ſά ϲ̆еnꝺ αιꞫξιſſе ιnα ꞫιαιꞫ ſιn .h. Néιll, .ι. Θnſí óʒ .h. Nеιll, ꝺо ϲ̆оιξеϲhϲ α ϲιſ Сhоnαιll ſʟυαιʒ ꝺιάſſιṁ, оϲυſ αn ϲιſ ꝺо ṁιllеꞫ ʒо hυιlιꞫе lαιſ; оϲυſ О Ꝺоmnαιll ꝺо bſеιꞫ оſſα, оϲυſ mαιꞫɳι Ɜél άꞫα Ꝺоιſе ꝺо ϲ̆αbαιſϲ αſ .h. nꝺоmnαιll, оϲυſ é ſéιn .ι. Соɳɳ ꝺо ϲ̆υιϲιn αɳɳ, оϲυſ mоſάn еlι mαιllе ſſιſ, оϲυſ ϲlαɳɳ hι Ꝺоmnαιll ꝺо ξαbάιl, .ι. Ꝺоmnαll оϲυſ Nιαll ʒαſꞫ, оϲυſ Nιαll ꝺſαʒαιl Ɜάιſ αɳɳſαn ʒlαſ; оϲυſ

---

1 *Defeat.* In some authorities this battle is called the battle of the Belach-buidhe, or the "yellow pass," now Ballaghboy, in the parish of Agha-nagh, barony of Tirerrill, and county of Sligo.

2 *Cuan-Sligigh.* This name signi-

fies "the harbour of Sligech," and was perhaps the name by which that part of the barony of Carbury bordering on Sligo harbour was familiarly known.

3 *Domhnall and Niall.* Brothers of Conn, and sons of Aedh Ruadh (or Hugh Roe) O'Domhnaill.

of good troops of one accord. And they proceed to meet O'Domhnaill in Corr-sliabh ; but this powerful, battle-numerous, multitude did not restrain O'Domhnaill. Then it was that these two great armies advanced towards each other about Corr-sliabh ; and they attempted not to separate from each other until a great number of their heroes and warriors fell in that fight. O'Domhnaill was defeated on this occasion, however, and eight hundred of his people, or more, were slain; and Fedhlim, the son of Maghnus O'Conchobhair, i.e. half-king of Connacht from Corr-sliabh to Drobhais, was taken prisoner there ; and the two Mac Suibhnes were taken prisoners there. And the quantity of spoils of arms, horses, clothing, and all kinds of weapons and battle-dresses besides, that were captured there on this occasion, cannot be calculated or over-reckoned. And O'Domhnaill himself escaped from this defeat,[1] through the effect of his courage, and the strength of his arm. And Mac Diarmada carried off his captives, and his numerous spoils, after gaining triumph. And the ransom which Mac Diarmada exacted from Felim, the son of Maghnus O'Conchobhair, was, viz., the Clann-Maelruanaidh's share of the fifth of Cuan-Sligigh,[2] and the sons of Tadhg, son of Brian Mac Donnchadha, as sureties for the fulfilment of this, on pain of *the forfeiture of* six score milch cows. And in a short time afterwards O'Neill, i.e. Henry Og O'Neill, went into Tir-Conaill with an innumerable host, and the country was entirely destroyed by him. And O'Domhnaill came up with him ; and the defeat of Bél-átha-doire was given to O'Domhnaill, and he himself, i.e. Conn, fell there, and a great many more along with him : and the sons of O'Domhnaill, viz., Domhnall and Niall[3] Garbh, were taken prisoners ; and Niall died in captivity;[4] and Aedh Ruadh

---

[4] *Died in captivity.* The corresponding words in the text, oṗaġail báiṙ annṛan ġLaṙ, (lit. "died in the lock"), are written over the word ṫoṛṫóiṙi ("again"), which has not been erased.

Ccoʝ ʁuaʝ .h. Ꝺomnaıʟʟ ꝺo ̵ʒabáıʟ a ̌cıʒeʁnuıʁ ʁeın
ın ꝺaʁna ʁeachc ꝺo coıʟ Ꝺé ocuʁ ꝺaoınıʝ. ⸆Ccoʝ mac
Ccoʝa ʁuaıʝ ꝺo ʟeıʒıon aʁʁ a bʁaı̵ʒꝺenuʁ an ̌ʟíaꝺaın
ʁın. Mac Ꝺıaʁmaꝺa Mhoı̵ʒe ʟuıʁ̵ʒ, .ı. Cončobaʁ mac
Coʁmaıc mıc Comaʟcaı̵ʒ an eını̵ʒ, ꝺo maʁbaʝ ʟa cʟaınn
Ruaıʝʁı mıc Ꝺıaʁmaꝺa a̵ʒ Cuıʁʁech O n̵ʒuanʁaʝ.
Mac Ꝺonnchaꝺa an Choʁuınn, .ı. ̵bʁıan mac Mhaoʟ-
ʁuanaıʝ mıc Comaʟcaı̵ʒ, ꝺhéc. ̵ʒoʁca ṁóʁ aʁ ʁeꝺh
eʁenn ın hoc anno. Ccıʟıonoʁa ın̵ʒen ıaʁʟa Cıʟʟe
ꝺaʁa, .ı. ben hı Heıʟʟ .ı. Chuınn mıc euʁí mıc eo̵ʒaın,
ꝺhéc. Ꝺomnaʟʟ mac Ccoʝa óı̵ʒ mıc Ccoʝa buıꝺé ꝺo
ṁaʁbaʝ ʟá Sean nꝺııʝ mac nꝺomnaıʟʟ.

‖ctt. enáıʁ; ochc mbʟıaꝺna ꝺhéc ocuʁ ceıʈʁe xxıc,
ocuʁ .cccc. ocuʁ mıʟe, aıʁ [ın Cı̵ʒeʁna]. h. Neıʟʟ, .ı.
euʁí ó̵ʒ mac euʁı mıc eo̵ʒaın, cı̵ʒeʁna ̌čeneıʟ eo̵ʒaın,
ocuʁ ʁeʁ ʟán ꝺo uaıʁ'ʟe ocuʁ ꝺaʁꝺ ʁaʈ, ꝺo maʁbaꝺ a
nꝺoıʁín ın ʁıaʝa ʟe cʟaınn Chuınn hı Heıʟʟ, anꝺı̵ʒaıʟ
ı nachaʁ. h. Cačaın, .ı. Sean mac Ccıꝺne, ʁeʁ eını̵ʒ
coıččınn ꝺeı̵ʒʁıʝ ocuʁ ꝺaoıʁ eaʟaꝺna eʁenn, ꝺhéc ın
hoc anno. Ꝺomnaʟʟ ṁac Hechcaın hı Ꝺomnaıʟʟ ꝺhéc
ꝺon ̵ʒaʟaʁ ̌bʁec. h. ̵bʁıaın, .ı. an ̵ʒıʟʟa ꝺuʝ O ̵bʁıaın,
ꝺhéc. Maꝺ̃m na Cʁoı̵ʁʁı Caıꝺénaꝺ̵ʒe aʁ .h. Heıʟʟ .ı.
Ꝺomnaʟʟ mác euʁí mıc eo̵ʒaın, ocuʁ Ƥeıꝺʟım mac euʁı
óı̵ʒ ꝺo ̌cuıcım a bʁʁı̵ʒ̵ʒuın an maꝺ̃ma ʁın. O Cúıʁnín,
.ı. oʟʟam ʁeʁ mbʁeıʁʁʁne ꝺhéc, Cončobaʁ caʁʁach, [.ı.
aʁꝺ oʟʟam .h. Ruaıʁc ocuʁ na Ra̵ʒaʟʟač].

‖ctt. enaıʁ; noı mbʟıaꝺna ꝺhéc ocuʁ ceıʈʁı ʁčıc
ocuʁ ceıʈʁı ceꝺ ocuʁ mıʟe aıʁ an Cı̵ʒeʁna. ̵ʒnım moʁ
ꝺo ̵ʒenum ʟé ʁı̵ʒ Ccʟban ꝺáʁ ̌bó comaınm Sémuʁ
Sꝺıꝺaʁꝺ, .ı. eoın móʁ mac Ꝺomnaıʟʟ, ʁı ınꝺʁı ̵ʒaʟʟ,

---

¹ *Aedh Bridhe.* "Hugh the Yellow [O'Neill]".

² *Domhnall.* Domhnall Cael (or "Daniel the Slender") O'Neill.

³ *Doirin-in-fiadha;* lit. "the little oak-wood of the deer." This name would be pronounced "Derrynauea." The Four Mast. say that Henry Og O'Neill was killed in Art O'Neill's house in Tuath-Eachadha, or Tonghie, a district comprised in the present barony and county of Armagh.

O'Domhnaill assumed his own sovereignty the second time, by the will of God and men. Aedh, the son of Aedh Ruadh, was released from captivity this year. Mac Diarmada of Magh-Luirg, i.e. Conchobhar, son of Cormac, son of Tomaltach-an-einigh, was killed by the sons of Ruaidhri Mac Diarmada, at Cuirrech-O'Guanradh. Mac Donnchadha of the Corann, i.e. Brian, the son of Mael-ruanaidh, son of Tomaltach, died. Great famine throughout Erinn in hoc anno. Ailinora, daughter of the Earl of Cill-dara, i.e. the wife of O'Neill, i.e. Conn, the son of Henry, son of Eoghan, died. Domhnall, son of Aedh Og, son of Aedh Buidhe,[1] was killed by John Dubh, son of Domhnall.[2]

A.D.
[1497.]

The kalends of January; the age [of the Lord] one thousand, four hundred, and ninety-eight years. O'Neill, i.e. Henry Og, the son of Henry, son of Eoghan, lord of Cenel-Eoghain, a man full of dignity and high prosperity, was slain in Doirín-in-fiadha[3] by the sons of Conn O'Neill, in revenge of their father. O'Cathain, i.e. John son of Aibhne, a man of general hospitality towards the poets and learned men of Erinn, died in hoc anno. Domhnall, son of Nechtan O'Domhnaill, died of the galar brec.[4] O'Briain, i.e. the Gilla-dubh O'Briain, died. The victory of Cross-Caibhenaigh over O'Neill, i.e. Domhnall, son of Henry, son of Eoghan; and Feidhlim, the son of Henry Og, fell in the counter-wounding of that victory. O'Cuirnin, i.e. the ollamh of the men of Breifne, Conchobhar Carrach, [i.e. the chief poet of the O'Ruaircs and O'Raighilighs],[5] died.

[1498.]

The kalends of January; the age of the Lord one thousand, four hundred, and ninety-nine years. A great deed was committed by the King of Alba whose name was James Stuart, viz.:—he hanged John Mór

[1499.]

---

[4] *Galar brec;* i.e. the small-pox; literally, "speckled disease."

[5] *O'Raighilighs.* The clause within brackets has been added by another

scribe, who has also written at the top of the page the memorandum, or apostrophe to his pen, cionnus ṁ a ṗeiṁ. "how is that. pen"?

ocuꞃ Ɇoɩɴ Caṫáɴacḣ, ocuꞃ Ⱥluꞃꝺaꞃ ꝑallaċ ꝺo ꞃɩaᵹḣaꝺ
ɩɴɴ aoɴ cꞃoɩċ. Ɱac Ꝺɩaꞃmaꝺa Ɱḣoɩᵹe Luɩꞃᵹ, .ɩ.
Taꝺᵹ mac Ruaɩꝺꞃɩ óɩᵹ mɩc Ruaɩꝺꞃɩ ċaoɩċ, .ɩ. ꝼeꞃ
coꞃꞃaɴꞇa clú a aꞃꝺaɩcꞇe ꝼeɩɴ ꝺuaɩꞃle ocuꞃ ꝺoɩɴecɦ
ocuꞃ ꝺoɩꞃꝺeꞃcuꞃ, ocuꞃ ɩmꝺíꝺɴɩᵹṫeoꞃ ꞃɩol Ɱuɩꞃ-
eᵹḣaɩᵹ ocuꞃ ꝼeꞃ ᵹCoɴɴacɦꞇ, ꝺḣéc ɩaꞃ mꝑꞃeɩṫ ꝺuaꝺa ó
ṫomuɴ ocuꞃ o ṫemuɴ. Coꞃmac mac Ꝺomɴaɩll mɩc
ꝑꞃɩaɩɴ Ꝉ Ⱡɩᵹɩɴɴ ꝺo maꞃꝑaꝺ ᵹo ꞇɩmpeɩꞃꝺecɦ ꝺeɴ
uꞃcḣuꞃ ꝺo ꝼoɩᵹɩꝺ lá claɩɴɴ Ꝑḣeoꞃuɩꞃ ɩɴ ꝑlɩaꝺaɩɴ ꞃɩɴ.
Rɩcaꞃꝺ óᵹ mac Rɩcaɩꝺ ḣɩ Cḣuaɩꞃꞃceɩṫ ꝺo ṁaꞃꝑaꝺ
ɩꞃɩɴ ló ceꝺɴa, .ɩ. aɴ ceꝺaoɩɴ ɩaꞃ ᵹcɩɴcɩꞃ.

Ⱪcꞇꞇ. Ɇɴáɩꞃ; cuɩᵹ ceꝺ ocuꞃ mɩle ꝑlɩaꝺaɴ aoɩꞃ aɴ
Ꞇɩᵹeꞃɴa. O Ruaɩꞃc, .ɩ. Ꝼelɩm, ꝺo ṫul ꝺḣéc ɩɴ hoc
aɴɴo. Ꞇomáꞃꞃ mac ꝑꞃɩaɩɴ mɩc Ꝼɩlɩp ɴa ꞇuaɩꝺe
Ɱḣéᵹ Uɩꝺɩꞃ ꝺo maꞃꝑaꝺ la claɩɴɴ Ꞇomáɩꞃ óɩᵹ mɩc
Ꞇḣómáɩꞃ óɩᵹ mɩc Ꞇomaɩꞃ ṁóɩꞃ Ɱḣéᵹ Uɩꝺɩꞃ. O ꝑꞃoɩɴ
Láɩᵹɩꞃɩ ꝺo ṁaꞃꝑaꝺ .ɩ. Caṫáꞃ mac Ꝺúɴlaɩɴᵹ. Ⱥɴ
ꝑaꞃꞃacɦ móꞃ ꝺo ṁaꞃꝑaꝺ le ɴa ꝺeꞃꝑꞃáꞇḣaɩꞃ ꝼeɩɴ, .ɩ.
ꝹáɩꞒɩṫ ꝑaꞃꞃa. Ɇꞃpuc Ꝺoɩꞃe ꝺḣec, .ɩ. Ꝺomɴall .ḣ.
Ꝼallamaɩɴ, ocuꞃ ꝑꞃaꞇḣaɩꞃ mɩɴúꞃ.

Ⱪcꞇꞇ. Ɇɴaɩꞃ; ꝑlɩaꝺaɩɴ aꞃ .u. ceꝺ aꞃ mɩle. Ɱaɩꝺm
Sleɩꝺ ꝑeꞇḣa la hⱰloꝺ mac Rémaɩɴɴ ṁéᵹ Ɱḣaꞇᵹaṁɴa,
ɩɴaꞃ maꞃꝑaꝺ Ꞇomáꞃ óᵹ mac Ꞇomaɩꞃ óɩᵹ mḣeᵹ Uɩꝺɩꞃ
co ɴáꞃ ꝺíaɩꞃṁe ꞇɩme. Ruᵹꞃaɩꝺe mac Caṫaɩꞃ mɩc
Cuɩɴɴ mɩc ɩɴ Calꝑaɩᵹ, .ɩ. mac ḣɩ Cḣoɴcḣoꝑaɩꞃ ꞃaɩlᵹe,
ꝺḣéc. Nɩall mac Ⱥɩꞃꞇ ḣɩ Neɩll ꝺḣéc. Caɩꞃléɴ Slɩᵹɩᵹ
ꝺo ᵹaꝑáɩl le ꝺꞃeɩmɩꞃe, .ɩ. le claɩɴɴ Ruaɩꝺꞃɩ mɩc Ꞇoɩꞃꞃ-
ꝺelꝺaɩᵹ ċaꞃꞃaɩᵹ ḣɩ Coɴcḣoꝑaɩꞃ; ocuꞃ aɴ Calꝑacɦ
caoċ mac Ꝺomɴaɩll mɩc Ɇoᵹaɩɴ ꝺo maꞃꝑaꝺ aɴɴ, ocuꞃ
Seaɴ mac Ruaɩꝺꞃɩ mɩc Ꞇoɩꞃꞃꝺelꝑaɩᵹ ꝺo ꞇuɩꞇɩm leɩꞃ

---

¹ *John Cathánach.* The Ann. Ult.
say that he was the son of John Mór
Mac Domhnaill. The sobriquet "Cathánach" was given to him from his
intimate connexion with the O'Ca-
thains (O'Kanes) of Cianachta, or
Keenaght, amongst whom he seems to
have been fostered.

² *Alexander.* Ⱥluꞃꝺaꞃ. The
Annal. Ult. call him Domhnall.

³ *Son of Brian.* The Four Mast.
say "son of Aedh, son of Brian."

Mac Domhnaill, king of Innsi-Gall, and John Cathánach,[1] and Alexander[2] Ballagh, on the same gallows. Mac Diarmada of Magh-Luirg, i.e. Tadhg, son of Ruaidhri Og, son of Ruaidhri Caech, the guardian of the fame of his own high family for nobility, and hospitality, and dignity, and the protector of the Sil-Muiredhaigh and men of Connacht, died after triumphing over the world and the devil. Cormac, son of Domhnall, son of Brian O'hUiginn, was violently killed with one shot of an arrow by the Clann-Feorais this year. Richard Og, son of Richard O'Cuairsceith, was killed on the same day, i.e. the Wednesday after Whitsuntide.

The kalends of January; the age of the Lord one thousand five hundred years. O'Ruairc, i.e. Felim, died in hoc anno. Thomas, the son of Brian,[3] son of Philip-na-tuaidhe[4] Mag Uidhir, was slain by the sons of Thomas Og, son of Thomas Og, son of Thomas Mór Mag Uidhir. O'Brain of Laighis[5] was killed; i.e. Cathair, the son of Dunlang. The Barry Mór was killed by his own brother, i.e. David Barry. The bishop of Doire died, i.e. Domhnall O'Fallamhain, a friar minor.

The kalends of January; one thousand, five hundred and one years. The victory of Sliabh-Betha by Aedh, son of Redmond Mac Mathghamhna, in which Thomas Og, the son of Thomas Og Mag Uidhir, was killed, with an innumerable slaughter about him. Rughraidhe, son of Cathair, son of Conn, son of the Calbhach, i.e. son of O'Conchobhair Failghe, died. Niall, son of Art O'Neill, died. The Castle of Sligech was taken by *means of* a ladder, i.e. by the sons of Ruaidhri, son of Toirdhelbhach Carragh O'Conchobhair; and the Calbhach Caech, son of Domhnall, son of Eoghan, was killed there; and John, the son of Ruaidhri, son of Toirdhelbhach, fell that night by the

---

[4] *Philip-na-tuaidhe*; i.e. "Philip of the battle-axe."

[5] *Laighis.* Leix, in the Queen's county. But Laighis was properly O'More's country. The Four Masters say that he was O'Brain (O'Byrne) of Laighen (Leinster), which is more correct.

ιn ʒCαlbαč αn οιȯče ριn. Ціȯne mαc hι Chαȼáιn ᴅo
mαρbαᴅ lα ḃριαn ριnn O Cαȼáιn. Ϲoιρṗȯelbαch mαc
Cuιnn mιc Єnρí mιc Єoʒαιn hι Иeιll ᴅo ṁαρbαᴅ lα
Mαʒ Mαȼȝαmnα, .ι. Ρορρα mαc Mαȝuρα.

Ϳϲtt. Єnáιρ; ᴅα blιαᴅαιn αρ .u. ceᴅ αρ mιle. Mαιȯm
nα Ϲulčα ριnne ᴅo ȼαbαιρt lα clαιnn Иeιll hι ḃhαιȝιll
αρ.h. mḃáιȝιll. O ḃáιȝιll ṗéιn, .ι. Иιαll, ocuρ α ȯιαρ
mαc, .ι. Ruȝραιȯe ocuρ Ꝺoṁnαll bαllαč, ocuρ ᴅρonʒ
moρ ᴅια muιntιρ ᴅo mαρbαᴅ αnn. Ꝺá αb ᴅo ȼí
α nιmρeρραιn ṗá αbȯαιne Єρρα Ruαιȯ, .ι. Ціρt O
ʒαllčubαιρ ocuρ Єoιn O Loιρᴅe, ᴅṗαȝαιl ȼáιρ ṗá αon
ló con oιȯche αn blιαᴅαιn ριn. Ꝺomnαll mαc ḃριαιn
hι Uιʒιnn, .ι. oιᴅe ρȝol Єρenn ρe ᴅán, ᴅhéc ιn hoc αnno.

Ϳϲtt. Єnáιρ; tρι blιαᴅnα αρ .u. ceᴅ αρ mιle. Mαc
hι Ꝺomnαιll, .ι. Ꝺonnchαᴅ mαc Ціoȼα ρuαιȯ, ᴅo
ρȝαȼαᴅ le nα ᴅeρbραȼhαιρ ṗéιn .ι. Ꝺomnαll, ᴅo čeᴅ
α αȼhαρ ṗeιn ocuρ ᴅá comαιρle. Mαc Uιllíαm ḃuρc,
.ι. Ϲeρóιᴅ mαc Uáιȼéιρ, ᴅhec. Mαιȯm ȯeoιl Ціȼα nα
nȝαρȯán le Rιcαρᴅ α ḃuρc co nα bρáιȼριȯ αρ Mαc
Uιllíαm ιochȼαιρ ocuρ αρ Mhαιnechαιȯ, ᴅú ιn ρo
mαρbαȯ Ruαιȯρι moρ mαc Ȿuιȯnι.

Ϳϲtt. Єnáιρ; ceιtρι blιαᴅnα αρ .u. ceᴅ αρ mιle.
Mαιȯm Chnuιc ȼhúαȝ ᴅo ȼαbαιρt αn ȯlιαᴅαιn ρι .ι.
ʒeρóιᴅ ιαρlα, ȝιúρᴅíρ nα hЄρenn, ᴅo ȼιnól ʒhαll ocuρ
ʒαoιᴅel čúιȝeᴅ Lαιȝen ocuρ leιȼι Cuιnn, ocuρ ȼeαchȼ α
ʒClαιnn Rιcαιρᴅ, ocuρ Mαc Uιllíαm clαιnnι Rιcαιρᴅ
ocuρ O ḃριαιn ᴅo ȼιnol ṗlúαιȝ ṁoιρ elι, ocuρ ȼeαchȼ
nα ʒcoιnne ʒo Cnoc ȼhúαȝ, ocuρ cαȼ ᴅo chuρ eȼoρρα
αnn ιnαρ mαρbαᴅ moρán ᴅo mαιȼιȯ ʒαll ocuρ ʒαoιᴅel,
co nαch ᴅȼucαȯ α commóρ ᴅo čαȼ ιριn αιmριρ ȯeιȝenαč
eȼιρ [ʒhαllαιȯ oȼuρ] ʒhαoιᴅeluιȯ. Mαȝnuρ mαc

---

1 *One day and night.* ṗá αon ló
con oιȯche, lit. "about one day with
a night"; i.e. within the space of
twenty-four hours. The entry in the
Annals of Connacht adds, ocuρ αᴅe-
ραιᴅ ʒuραb báρρ ᴅo luȼȝαιρ
ρuαιρ αn ρeαρ ᴅeιȝenαch ᴅιȯ:
"and they say that the latter died of
joy."

² *Anno.* αnᴅó, MS.

Calbhach. Aibhne, the son of O'Catháin, was killed by Brian Finn O'Catháin. Toirdhelbhach, the son of Conn, son of Henry, son of Eoghan O'Neill, was killed by Mac Mathghamhna, i.e. Rossa, the son of Maghnus. [1501.]

The kalends of January; one thousand, five hundred and two years. The defeat of Tulach-finn was given by the sons of Niall O'Baighill to O'Baighill. O'Baighill himself, i.e. Niall, and his two sons, viz., Rughraidhe and Domhnall Ballagh, and a great number of his people, were slain in it. Two abbots who were at issue regarding the abbacy of Es-Ruaidh, viz., Art O'Gallchubhair, and John O'Loisde, died this year during one day and night.[1] Domhnall, son of Brian O'hUiginn, tutor of the schools of Erinn in poetry, died in hoc anno.[2] [1502.]

The kalends of January ; one thousand, five hundred and three years. The son of O'Domhnaill, i.e. Donnchadh, son of Aedh Ruadh, was mutilated by his own brother, i.e. Domhnall, with the consent of his own father, and by his advice. Mac William Burk, i.e. Tibbot son of Walter, died. The defeat of Bel-atha-na-ngarbhán *was given* by Rickard Burk and his kinsmen to Mac William Iochtair and the Mainechs,[3] in which Ruaidhri Mor Mac Suibhne was slain. [1503.]

The kalends of January ; one thousand, five hundred, and four years. The overthrow of Cnoc-túagh was given this year ; viz., Earl Garrett, Justicary of Erinn, mustered the Foreigners and Gaeidhel of the province of Laighen, and of Leth-Chuinn, and advanced into Clann-Rickard ; and Mac William of Clann-Rickard, and O'Briain, assembled another great army, and came to Cnoc-túagh to meet them ; and a battle was fought there between them, in which a large number of chiefs of the Foreigners and Gaeidhel were slain ; so that no battle equal to it was fought in the late time between [Foreigners and][4] [1504.]

---

[3] *Mainechs*; i.e. the people of Ui-Maine, or O'Kelly's country.

[4] *Foreigners and.* Omitted in MS. Supplied from the Annals of Connacht.

bριαιn mιc Oonnchαoα, .ι. αb ṁαιnιρορeċ nα Τρίnoóιoe
αρ Loċ Cé; coṁραιρ ocuρ cιρoe coṁéτα eιnιᵹ ocuρ
enᵹnιmα nα hEρenn αn ρeρ ριn, ocuρ αnτ αon oιιne
ιρ mo oo τιōluιc ocuρ oo ċoιρōιρ oṗιleohαιb ocuρ
ooιρριoechαιb, ocuρ oo αoρ ᵹαchα ceρoα oά oτάιιιc
o Thomαlταch nα Cαιρρᵹe mιιαρρ, oo héc α ᵹCιll
Oιιōōúιn, eτ ρepυlτuρ eρτ αn oιlén nα Τριnoóιoe αρ
Loċ Cé; ocuρ ιρ buιlle oíċenoτα αρ αoιρ eαlαonα nα
hEρenn αnτ héc ριn mιc Mιc Oonnchαoα. Conċobαρ
mαc Rυαιoρι mιc Oιαρmαoα, .ι. ρυᵹoαmnα oιρροeρc
oιρbeρταch α αρo αιcιne .ι. αn mαc ριᵹ bά τρeιρρι ocuρ
bά τuαρυρcōάlαιᵹe τάιιιc ōά ōuthαιō ρe cιαn oαιmριρ,
oo mαρbαō lά ρᵘlιchτ Τomαlταιᵹ αn eιnιᵹ mιc Con
chobαιρ mιc Oιαρmαoα, α mōeαlαċ nα nuρṁoιιιτeċ.
Mαoιleċlαιṅ mαc Oonnchαoα mαc Mυρchαoα ohéc
ιn hoc αnno.

Κττ. Ɛnαιρ; u. blιαonα ocuρ .u. ceo ocuρ mιle. Ccō
ρuαō mαc Ϩeιll ᵹαιρb hι Oomnαιll, .ι. αnτ oen
ᵹαoιoel ιρ mo oo ᵹαō neρτ ocuρ τρeιρι ōά τάιιιc oo
ċṗlιchτ Ϩeιll .ιχ. ᵹιαllαιᵹ, ocuρ éρᵹα ιmmlάn eιnιᵹ
ōcuρ uαιρle αn τuαιρcιρτ, ρeρ ōάρ ᵹιαllρατ ριρ
Mhαnαch ocuρ Cenél Móαιn ocuρ ιochταιρ Chonnαchτ,
oo oul ohéc αn ōlιαoαιn ρι; ocuρ ιιι ρó lιnn ρe ραōα
nαch ραιōe ρe lιnn αn Ɛριnn Ϩαll nα Ϩαoιoeαl oo buō
τρeιρι αρ leιċ Cuιnn mάρρ; ocuρ τιιι ρeαchτṁuιne ρια
Luᵹnαρα ρuαιρ bάρρ oιᵹōα ocuρ αιτριᵹe α nOún nα
nᵹαll, ιαρ mbeιō ceιōρe blιαonα ocuρ oά ριċeτ α
τιᵹeριιuρ Τιρe Conαιll; ocuρ α mαc oo ρίᵹhαo nα
ιonαo, .ι. Ocō ouō mαc Oeōα ρuαιō. Ριnoᵹulα ιnᵹen
Rυαιoρι óιᵹ mιc Rυαιoρι ċoeιch, .ι. ben τ8heαιn mιc
Ταιōᵹ mιc bριαιn Mιc Oonnchαoα, ohéc. Mαᵹ
Cαρρτhαιᵹ ριαbαch, .ι. Ρίnᵹιn, ohéc. Cαιρbρι mαc

---

[1] *Shrine.* coṁnαιρ, MS., for coṁραιρ, as in the Annals of Connacht.

[2] *Tomaltach-na-Cairge.* "Tomaltach of the Rock," i.e. the Rock of
Loch-Cé, co. Roscommon.

[3] *Trinity-Island.* oιlen nα Τριnoóιoe, for oιlen nα Τριnóιoe, MS.

[4] *Tomaltach-an-enigh.* "Tomaltach of the Hospitality."

[5] *Bealach-nan-urmhointech.* "The

Gaeidhel. Maghnus, son of Brian Mac Donnchadha, i.e. abbot of the monastery of the Trinity on Loch-Cé, a man who was the preserving shrine[1] and casket of the bounty and prowess of Erinn, and the man who, of all that had come down from Tomaltach-na-Cairge[2], had given and presented most to poets and musicians, and to men of every craft, died at Cill-Duibhdhúin, et sepultus est in Trinity-Island[3] on Loch-Cé; and this death of Mac Donnchadha's son is a decapitating blow to the learned of Erinn. Conchobhar, the son of Ruaidhri Mac Diarmada, i.e. the illustrious, energetic royal-heir of his high sept, i.e. the most powerful and renowned prince that came of his nation for a long time, was slain by the descendants of Tomaltach-an-enigh,[4] the son of Conchobhar Mac Diarmada, in Bealach-nan-urmhointech.[5] Maelechlainn Mac Donnchadha, the son of Murchadh, died in hoc anno.

The kalends of January; one thousand, five hundred, and five years. Aedh Ruadh, son of Niall Garbh O'Domhnail, i.e. the Gaeidhel who obtained the greatest power and sway of all that came of the race of Niall-nai-ghiallagh, and full moon of hospitality and nobility of the North—a man to whom the Feara-Manach, and the Cenel-Moain, and Lower Connacht, gave hostages—died this year; and it is not too much to say that there was not in Erinn, during his time, any Foreigner or Gaeidhel more powerful over Leth-Chuinn than he. And three weeks before Lammas he died, after unction and penitence,[6] in Dun-na-nGall, after having been forty-four years in the sovereignty of Tir-Conaill; and his son was made king in his place, i.e. Aedh Dubh, son of Aedh Ruadh. Finnghuala, daughter of Ruaidhri Og, son of Ruaidhri Caech, i.e. the wife of John, son of Tadhg, son of Brian Mac Donnchadha, died. Mac Carthaigh Riabhach, i.e. Finghin, died. Cairbre,

---

pass of the wet bogs." The name is written "Bealach-nan-urbhrointech" in the Annals of Connacht, and also by the Four Masters.

[6] *Died, after unction and penitence;* literally, "received a death of unction and penitence."

Ḃμιαιn ɦı Uιʒınn ṽɦec ṽo ḃ ıoḃʒ. Αιnṽμιαμμ Ⅲɦáʒ
Cμαιᴄ ṽɦéc. 8eαan α ḃúμc ṽo ṁαμḃαṽ ɫe cɫαınn Uıɫɫıʒ
α ḃúμc.

ḳᴄᴄ. Ɵnαıμ. 8é ḃɫıανnα ocuμ .u. ceṽ ocuμ mıɫe αoıμ
αn Ⅽıʒeμnα. Ⅲαc Uıḃıɫín .ı. ḃɦαɫᴄαıμ, μeμ eınıʒ
čoıᴄčınn ocuμ ceṅṽ μeḃnα μo ṁαıᴄ, ṽo mαμḃαṽ αn
ḃɫıανnαın μı ɫα Ṽomnαɫɫ mαc 8eαın ɦı Cɦαᴄáın ocuμ ɫα
cɫoınn ḃɦɫoμcαıν. μáıνín .ɦ. Ⅲαoɫconαıμe .ı. μıᴄḃʒıμ
μeμ neμenn μe μıɫıḃecɦᴄ ocuμ μe μenčuμ, νμαʒαıɫ ḃáıμ
obuınn αn ḃɫıανnαın μın, .ı. ɫuıḃe μɫán αμ α ɫeαḃαıṽ ocuμ
α μαʒαıɫ mαμḃ αμ mαıνın. Ṽoṁnαɫɫ O Cμoıḃén, .ı.
cenναıʒe μαıṽḃeıμ ναonnαcɦᴄαcɦ, νμαʒαıɫ ḃáıμ obuınn
αn ḃɫıανnαın μı αʒ éıμνecɦᴄ αıμμμınn α mαınıμᴄıμ Ṽɦúın
nα nʒαɫɫ. Concɦoḃαμ mαc Ruαıṽμı mıc Ṽonncɦανnα
ṽo mαμḃαṽ ɫá ɦƟoʒαn mαc Ⅽıʒeμnáın ɦı Ruαıμc, α
mḃαıɫe αn Ṽúın αn ḃɫıανnαın μın.

ḳᴄᴄ. Ɵnαıμ. 8eαcɦᴄ mḃɫıανnα ocuμ .u. ceṽ ocuμ
mıɫe αoıμ αn Ⅽıʒeμnα. Ⅲαc Conmıṽe .ı. 8oɫαṁ, μóı
Ɵμenn μé νnán, ocuμ μeμ čıʒe αoıνeṽ coıᴄčınn ocuμ
čonάıʒ ṁóıμ, ṽo νuɫ ṽɦéc ın ɦoc αnno. Ⅲαınıμᴄıμ
ḃαıɫe ın Ṽúın ṽo čınnμcnα ɫα Ⅽomάμμ O ḃμeμʒαıɫ.
μéɫım mαʒ Uınnμıonnάın ṽɦéc. Ⅲάʒ Cμαıᴄ,.ı. Ⅽomάμμ
ṽɦéc. O Cuıɫɫ,.ı. Cenṽμαoɫα, ṽɦéc. O Ṽάɫαıʒ μınn,.ı.
ʒoμμμαıṽ, ṽɦéc. O Ṽάɫαıʒ Cαıμḃμecɦ,.ı. Oenʒuμ, ṽɦéc.
O ʒéμáın .ı. 8eαn : ɦı omneμ poeᴄαe ɦoc αnno ın Cμıμᴄo
ṽoμmıeμunᴄ.

ḳᴄᴄ. Ɵnάıμ. Ocɦᴄ mḃɫıανnα αμ .u. ceṽ αμ mıɫe αoıμ
ın Ⅽıʒeμnα. Cαıμɫén ınıμ 8ʒeıɫɫıonn ṽo ʒαḃάıɫ ṽo .ɦ.
Ṽɦomnαıɫɫ .ı. Oeṽ óʒ mαc αⱪoṽα μuαıṽ, ocuμ μɦıɫıp mαc
Ḃμıαın mɦéʒ Uıṽıμ ṽo ḃμıμμeṽ α čαıμɫéın μeın αμ eʒɫα
ɦı Ṽɦomnαıɫɫ. ʒoμμμαıṽ .ɦ. Cαᴄɦáın ṽo mαμḃαṽ ɫe

---

[1] *Domhnall.* The Four Mast. say that the person who slew Mac Uibhilín, or Mac Quillan, was Thomas, the son of Aibhne O'Catháin, or Evenew O'Kane.

[2] *Preceptor.* μıᴄḃʒıμ. The Annals of Connacht have μıᴄıμ, which is explained, "doctor," "teacher," by O'Reilly, and is used also in the same sense in Cormac's Glossary, vv. *gilldœ* and *lethech.* The Four Masters say that this O'Maelchonaire was the én

son of Brian O'hUiginn, died of a sudden fit. Andrias
Mag Craith died. John Burk was killed by the sons of
Ulick Burk.

The kalends of January. The age of the Lord one
thousand, five hundred, and six years. Mac Uibhilín, i.e.
Walter, a man of general hospitality, and an excellent
captain, was slain this year by Domhnall,[1] son of John
O'Catháin, and by the Clann-Bioscaidh. Páidín O'Maelchonaire, i.e. preceptor[2] of the men of Erinn in poetry and
history, died a sudden death this year—i.e. he lay down
on his bed quite well, and was found dead in the morning. Domhnall O'Croidhén, i.e. a rich, humane merchant,
died suddenly this year whilst hearing mass in the
monastery of Dun-na-nGall. Conchobhar, the son of
Ruaidhri Mac Donnchadha, was killed by Eoghan, son
of Tighernan O'Ruairc, in Baile-an-dúin, this year.

The kalends of January. The age of the Lord one
thousand, five hundred, and seven years. Mac Conmidhe,
i.e. Solomon, the most eminent poet in Erinn, keeper of a
general house of hospitality, and a man of great wealth,
died in hoc[3] anno. The monastery of Baile-an-dúin was
begun by Thomas O'Ferghail. Felim Mac Uinnsionnáin
died. Mag Craith, i.e. Thomas, died. O'Cuill, i.e. Cennfaeladh, died. O'Dalaigh Finn, i.e. Godfrey, died. O'Dalaigh Cairbrech, i.e. Aenghus, died. O'Gerain, i.e. John:
hi omnes poetæ[4] hoc[5] anno in Christo dormierunt.

The kalends of January. The age of the Lord one
thousand, five hundred, and eight years. The castle of
Inis-Sgeillionn[6] was captured by O'Domhnaill, i.e. Aedh
Og, son of Aedh Ruadh; and Philip, son of Brian Mag
Uidhir, broke down his own castle through fear of
O'Domhnaill. Godfrey O'Cathain was killed by the

---

roga ("one choice") of Erinn for
history and poetry.
[3] Hoc. 6c, MS.
[4] Poetæ. poeta, MS.

[5] Hoc. oc, MS.
[6] Inis-Sgeillionn. Enniskillen. More
usually, and correctly, written Inir
Ceitlionn.

ρlicht Maҳnuρα h1 Chaṫáin. Eρρuc Cċ Conaiρe ṽhéc
i. Comáρρ O Conҳaláin. Eρρuc Cluana mic Noiρ ṽhéc,
i. Uáiceρ a ḃhlac. Ciҳeρnán óҳ, mac Eoҳain mic
Ciҳeρnáin h1 Ruaiρc, ṽo maρḃaṽ le Sean mac Ciҳeρ-
náim ṗinn 1 Ruaiρc.

Ictt. Enaiρ; ix. mḃliaṽna aρ .u. ceṽ aρ mile aoiρ in
Ciҳeρna. O Néill, .i. Ṽomnall ρí ċiρe hEoҳain, ṽhéc
in hoc anno, ocuρ Ccρc mac Oeṽha h1 Neill ṽo ρiҳaṽ
na ionaṽ. O ḃaoiҳill, .i. Emon buiṽe mac Ileill h1
Ḃhaoiҳill, ṽo maρḃaṽ ṽén uρchuρ ṽo ҳa le Conċoḃaρ
óҳ O mḃáiҳill, a comeρcuρ oiṽċe a Luaċρuiρ ṽa ṗunnρaṽ.
Philip mac Ḃρiain mic Philip mhéҳ Uiṽiρ ṽhéc. Eoҳan
mac Cuinn mic Ccoṽa buiṽe ṽhec. Ccρc, mac Cuinn
mic Enρí mic Eoҳain h1 Ileill, ṽo ҳaḃail le hCciρc in
ċaiρléin mac Ileill mic Cciρc, ocuρ a ċaḃaiρc ṽO
Ṽhomnaill.

Ictl. Enáiρ; x. mḃliaṽna aρ .u. ceṽ aρ mile aoiρ in
Ciҳeρna. O ṗialáin, .i. Feρҳal mac Eoҳain, ρúi ρe ṽán,
ṽρaҳail ċáiρ. Eoҳan mac Ḃρiain h1 Uiҳinn, oiṽe ρeρ
nҳaoiṽel ρe ṽán, ṽhéҳ. O Ṽomnaill, .i. Oeṽh óҳ mac
Ccoṽa ρuaiṽ, ṽo ṽul aρ láρ a imṽe ocuρ a aoiρi ṽoċum
na Róṁa in hoc anno. Sloiҳeṽ lá ҳeρóiṽ Iaρla Chille
ṽaρa a cuiҳiṽ Muman, ҳo maiċliḃ Ҳall ocuρ Ҳaoiṽeal
Laiҳen laiρ, ṽaρ ċuṁṽaiҳ caiρlen ṽainṽeoin Ҳaoiṽel
Muman aҳ Caρρaiҳ Cícal. Lenuρ .h. Ṽomnaill é
beҳáin búiṽne cρíṽ an Miṽe, ocuρ aρρin ṽon Mhuman,
ocuρ ciaҳuiṽ aρ ρioḃal in Ealla, ocuρ ҳaḃuiṽ caiρlén
Chinn cuiρc, ocuρ aiρҳiṽ in cíρ; ocuρ ciaҳuiṽ a n'Oeρ-
mumain ṁóiρ ocuρ ҳaḃaiṽ caiρléin na Pailíρe, ocuρ
caiρlen choiρ Mhanҳe; ocuρ ceҳaṽ ρlán ṽaρ a naiρ a
ҳconṽáe Luimniҳ. Ṽo miaṽ aicinól ρlóiҳ iaρρin, ocuρ
cρainniҳiṽ Ҳeρalcaiҳ na Muman in Shémuρ mac Iaρla

---

1 *Achadh-Conaire.* "Conaire's field"
(Achonry, co. Sligo). Corruptly written Cċ Conaiρo ("Conaire's ford")
in the MS.

2 *Aedh Buidhe.* "Hugh the Yellow." See note 1, p. 198.

3 *In.* aρ; lit. "out of," M.S.

4 *Hoc.* óҳ, MS.

descendants of Maghnus O'Catháin. The bishop of Achadh-Conaire,[1] i.e. Thomas O'Conghaláin, died. The bishop of Cluain-mic-Nois, Walter Blac, died. Tighernan Og, son of Eoghan, son of Tighernan O'Ruairc, was killed by John, son of Tighernan Finn O'Ruairc.

The kalends of January ; the age of the Lord one thousand, five hundred, and nine years. O'Neill, i.e. Domhnall, king of Tir-Eoghain, died in hoc anno ; and Art, son of Aedh O'Neill, was made king in his place. O'Baighill, i.e. Edmond Buidhe, son of Niall O'Baighill, was killed with one cast of a spear by Conchobhar Og O'Baighill, in a nocturnal encounter, exactly in Luachrus. Philip, son of Brian, son of Philip Mag Uidhir, died. Eoghan, son of Conn, son of Aedh Buidhe,[2] died. Art, son of Conn, son of Henry, son of Eoghan O'Neill, was taken prisoner by Art-in-chaisléin, son of Niall, son of Art, and surrendered to O'Domhnaill.

The kalends of January ; the age of the Lord one thousand, five hundred, and ten years. O'Fialáin, i.e. Ferghal, son of Eoghan, a most eminent poet, died. Eoghan, son of Brian O'hUiginn, preceptor of the Gaeidhel in poetry, died. O'Domhnaill, i.e. Aedh Og, son of Aedh Ruadh, went to Rome in[3] the middle of his prosperity and age, in hoc[4] anno. A hosting into the province of Mumha by Garrett, Earl of Cill-dara, accompanied by the chiefs of the Foreigners and Gaeidhel of Laighen, on which occasion he erected a castle at Carraig-Cital, in spite of the Gaeidhel of Mumha. O'Domhnall follows him, with a small band, through Midhe, and from thence to Mumha ; and they march into Ealla, and take the castle of Cenn-tuirc, and plunder the district. And they proceed into great Des-Mumha, and take the castle of the Pailís, and the castle of Cois-Mainge ; and they return back safely into the county of Luimnech. They afterwards re-assemble an army, and collect the Geraldines of Mumha, with James, the son of the Earl of Des-Mumha, and

Oeϝϝṁuman, ocuϝ ʒoıʟʟ na ṁuman áıϝchena, ocuϝ
ṁáʒ Caϝϝchaıʒ ϝıabach, ocuϝ Coϝṁac óʒ mac Coϝṁaıc
mıc Chaıöʒ, ocuϝ ʒoıʟʟ ocuϝ ʒáıöheʟ ṁhıöe ocuϝ ʟaıʒen.
Cıaʒaıo ʒo ʟuımnech. Cınólaıö Coıϝϝöeaʟbach mac
Caıöʒ hı Òϝıaın ϝı Cuaʒṁuman, ocuϝ ṁac Conmaϝa,
ϝıʟ Oeöa ocuϝ cʟann Rıcaıϝo, moϝ ϝʟúaʒ eʟı ına naʒaıo,
ocuϝ ceıo ınc ıaϝʟa co na ϝʟuaıʒ cϝe öeaʟač na
ϝaöbaıoe, ocuϝ cϝé öeaʟač an ʒaṁna, ʒo ϝánıc oϝoıček
cϝaınn oo ϝıʒneö ʟé .h. mÒϝıaın aϝ 8ıonuınn; ocuϝ
bϝıϝϝoeϝ an oϝoıček ʟeó, ocuϝ anaıo a bϝoϝʟonʒϝoϝc
oıöče ıϝın cíϝ, ocuϝ oo ní .h. Òϝıaın ϝoϝʟonʒϝoϝc eʟe
ϝe na caoö ann. Cuıϝıϝ anc ıaϝʟa aϝ ná ṁáϝach a
cϝʟúaʒ a noϝougao, ocuϝ cuıϝıϝ ʒaıʟʟ ocuϝ ʒaoıoeʟ na
ṁuman a cúϝ, ocuϝ cuıϝıϝ ʒoıʟʟ na ṁıöe aϝ oeϝeö
a ϝʟúaıʒ. Cuıϝʟınʒıϝ .h. Oomnaıʟʟ an beʒán buıöne
oo öí a meϝc ʒaʟʟ, ocuϝ ʒaöuϝ an aıčʒıϝϝe cϝí ṁóın na
mbϝáchaϝ oočum ʟuımnıʒ; ocuϝ ıonnϝaıʒıc na ϝʟúaʒa
ϝın cϝíʟ mÒϝıaın na ϝʟóıʒ ϝın eʟe, ocuϝ maϝbcaϝ
ʟeo an baϝún Cınc, ocuϝ an Òéϝnṁáʟač, ocuϝ oaoıne
maıčı eʟı; ocuϝ ní ϝaıöe annϝın oo ʒaʟʟoıö ına oo
ʒaoıoeʟaıö én ouıne buo mó cʟu ʟaıme ná .h. Oomnaıʟʟ
aʒ cabaıϝc oeϝıö anc ϝʟúaıʒ ʒaʟʟ ϝın ʟaıϝ.

Ċcc. Enáıϝ; xı. aϝ .u. ceo aϝ mıʟe aıϝ ın Cıʒeϝna.
O Conchoöaıϝ Ƒhaıʟʒe, .ı. Cačaoıϝ mac Cuınn mıc ıı
chaʟbaıʒ, ϝéchem coıččeno öhécϝıö ocuϝ oaoıϝ eaʟaöna,
ocuϝ ceno ϝeöna ϝo ṁaıč ϝoϝ ʒaʟʟoıö ocuϝ ʒaoıoeʟaıö,
oo ṁaϝbaö ʟe cuıo oá čıneö ϝeın, .ı. ʟe cʟaınn Caıöʒ
hı Conchobaıϝ ocuϝ ʟe cʟaınn c8heaın öaʟʟaıʒ hı
Conchobaıϝ, ʟaım ϝe maınıϝcıϝ Ƒheoϝuıϝ. Ouöcach
mac Ouöcaıʒ hı Ouıöʒenoáın, ϝóı Eϝenn ϝe ϝenčuϝ,

---

1 _Wooden bridge._ The Four Mast.
say oϝoıček puıϝc cϝoıϝı, "the
bridge of Port-croisi," now Portcrusha,
in the parish of Stradbally, barony of
Clanwilliam, and county of Limerick.

² _Foreigners._ The Four Masters

have ʒaʟʟ αčα cʟıač ocuϝ mıöe,
"the Foreigners of Ath-cliath and
Midhe (Dublin and Meath)."

³ _Through._ cϝıo, for cϝı, MS.

⁴ _Cint._ _Rectè_ Kent.

⁵ _O'Duibhgennain._ A marginal note

the other Foreigners of Mumha; and Mac Carthaigh Riabhach, and Cormac Og, son of Cormac, son of Tadhg; and the Foreigners and Gaeidhel of Midhe and Laighen. They go to Luimnech. Toirdhelbhach, son of Tadhg O'Briain, king of Tuadh-Mumha, and Mac Conmara, the Sil-Aedha, and the Clann-Rickard, assemble another great army against them. And the Earl proceeds with his army through Bealach-na-fadhbaidhe, and through Bealach-an-gamhna, until he reached a wooden bridge[1] which had been made by O'Briain over the Sinainn; and the bridge is broken down by them; and they remain one night encamped in the country; and O'Briain establishes another camp close by them. The Earl puts his army into array on the morrow; and he places the Foreigners and Gaeidhel of Mumha in the front, and the Foreigners of Midhe in the rear of his army. He places O'Domhnaill, with the small band he had, amongst the Foreigners,[2] and takes the shortest way, through[3] Moinna-mbráthar, to Luimnech. And the armies of the Sil-Briain attack those other armies, and the Baron Cint,[4] and the Barnewall, and other nobles, are slain by them; and there was no man there of the Foreigners, or of the Gaeidhel, of greater fame for prowess than O'Domhnaill, in conducting the rear of this army of Foreigners.

The kalends of January; the age of the Lord one thousand, five hundred, and eleven *years.* O'Conchobhair Failghe, i.e. Cathair, son of Conn, son of the Calbhach, a general patron of poets and men of learning, and an excellent commander over Foreigners and Gaeidhel, was killed by some of his own kindred, i.e. by the sons of Tadhg O'Conchobhair, and the sons of John Ballagh O'Conchobhair, near Manister-Fheorais. Dubhtach, son of Dubhtach O'Duibhgennain,[5] the sage of Erinn in

in the MS., in the handwriting of Ròderick O'Flaherty, indicates that this O'Duibhgennain (or O'Duigenan) was one of the learned family of Cill-Ronain, or Kilronan, in the county of Roscommon.

VOL. II.

P 2

ocus fer saiḋḃris ṁóir, dhéc in ḃliadain si. Sloiged leis O Neill .i. Art mac Aeḋa a tír Chonaill, dár loisc Glenn ḟinne ocus ó tṡuiliġ anall; ocus benus braiġde dO Dhoċartaiġ. Cénel Feradaiġ do creachad le Máġnus O nDomnaill an bliadain si. Mac Donnchaḋa ṫíre hOilella, .i. Sean mac Taiḋg mic Briain mic Donnchada, coinneal ġaile ocus gaiscid ċlainni Mhaolruanaiḋ, ocus feichem coitċend congṁála dhecriḃ ocus daois ealadna leṫe Cuinn, dḟaġail ḃáis ina longport féin a mBaile an dúin; ocus ni himlán ro ċaiṫestar an ḃlíaduin sin a tigernus. Fergal mac Taiḋg mic Briain, .i. aḋḃar riġ O nOilella, do marbaḋ an ḃliadain cedna sin le clainn Ruaiḋri mic Diarmada. Espuc an dá Bhreiffne, .i. Tomárs mac Aindriú ṁéġ Bradaiġ. Clann Cathail mic Ruaidri mic Phéilimiḋ ċleiriġ do ṁarbaḋ a Tuillsge le clainn Taiḋg ḃuiḋe mic Cathail ruaiḋ, .i. Ruaiḋri ruaḋ ocus Brían, ocus Taḋg ocus Cathal.

Kal. Enáir; ḋá bliadain dhec ar .u. ced ar mile ais in Tigerna. O Domnaill do ṫeacht ón Róiṁ íar ḃforbaḋ a oilitri, ocus íar bḟaġail onóra móire for a ċuairt o rí Saxan. O Cléiriġ, .i. Taḋg mac Tuathail mic Taiḋg caim hI Chléiriġ, .i. sói re senċus ocus fer ṫiġe aoided coitċinn, dhéc iar nongad ocus naitriġe. Niall mac Cuinn, mic Aeḋa buiḋe mic Briain ḃallaiġ, tigerna trín Congail, ocus fer eniġ ċoitċinn, ocus méḋaiġṫe ord ocus egailsiḃ ocus gach maiṫessa áirchena, ocus ana oirrter Erenn, do ḋul dhéc in hoc anno. Sloiġeḋ lá Geróid Iarla Cille dara i. giúsdís na hErenn a trian Congail, dár ġaḃ caisslen

---

[1] *Hitherwards.* anall; i.e. to some point of the county of Donegal, south of the river Swilly, which flows through the valley of Glenswilly, in that county.

[2] *Died.* The entry of the death of Bishop Mac Bradaigh (or Mac Brady) is also left unfinished in the so-called Annals of Connacht.

[3] *Tadhg, and Cathal.* These were all members of the family of O'Conor Ruadh.

[4] *Tadhg.* Thaddeus. He is called Tuathal, the son of Tadhg Cam, in the

history, and a man of great wealth, died this year. A hosting by O'Neill i.e. Art, son of Aedh, into Tir-Conaill, on which occasion he burned Glenn-fhinne, and from Suiligh hitherwards ;[1] and he exacted hostages from O'Dochartaigh. Cenel-Feradhaigh was plundered by Maghnus O'Domhnaill this year. Mac Donnchadha of Tir-Oilella, i.e. John, son of Tadhg, son of Brian MacDonn-chadha, torch of valour and bravery of the Clann-Mael-ruanaidh, and general sustaining patron of the poets and men of learning of Leth-Chuinn, died in his own fortress in Baile-an-dúin ; and he did not spend that year entirely in the sovereignty. Ferghal, the son of Tadhg, son of Brian, i.e. the royal heir of Ui-Oilella, was slain the same year by the sons of Ruaidhri Mac Diarmada. The bishop of the two Breifnes, i.e. Thomas, son of Andrew Mac Bradaigh, died.[2] The sons of Cathal, son of Ruaidhri, son of Felimidh Clerech, were slain at Tuilsce by the sons of Tadhg Buidhe, son of Cathal Ruadh, viz., Ruaidhri Ruadh, and Brian, and Tadhg, and Cathal.[3]

The kalends of January ; the age of the Lord one thousand, five hundred, and twelve years. O'Domhnaill returned from Rome, after completing his pilgrimage, and after obtaining great honour from the king of the Saxons on his journey. O'Clerigh, i.e. Tadhg,[4] son[5] of Tuathal, son of Tadhg Cam O'Clerigh, i.e. a most eminent historian, and keeper of a general house for guests, died after unction and penitence. Niall, son of Conn, son of Aedh Buidhe, son of Brian Ballach,[6] lord of Trian-Congail, a man of general hospitality, and exalter of Orders and churches, and of every other good, and the opulence of the East of Erinn, died in hoc anno. A hosting by Garrett, Earl of Cill-dara, i.e. the Justiciary of Erinn, to Trian-Congail, on which occasion he took the castle of

---

Annals of Connacht, and also by the Four Masters.
[5] *Son.* mac ; interlined in MS.

[6] *Brian Ballach ;* i.e. Brian Ballach ("Brian the Freckled") O'Neill.

℧eoıl Ƒeꞃꞃꝺe, ocuꞃ ꝺáꞃ ḃꞃıꞃ caıꞃlén mıc Eoın, ocuꞃ ꝺáꞃ aıꞃʒ na Ʒlınne ocuꞃ móꞃán ꝺon cíꞃ; ocuꞃ cuc mac Neıll mıc Cuınn a mḃꞃaıʒꝺenuꞃ laıꞃ. Coʒaꝺ móꞃ eꝺıꞃ O n'Domnaıll .ı. Oeꝺh, ocuꞃ O Néıll .ı. Cꞃc mac Ccoḃa, ocuꞃ coʒaꝺ eꝺıꞃ O n'Domnaıll ocuꞃ Ⴖac Uıllıam ḃúꞃc, .ı. Emonn mac Rıcaıꞃꝺ; ocuꞃ ꞃoꞃꝺaıꞃ O 'Domnaıll .u. ceꝺ ꝺhéc cuaḃ a cíꞃ Chonaıll ocuꞃ a coıʒeꝺ Chonnacht, ocuꞃ a ḃꞃeꞃuıḃ Ⴖanach. Ʒluaıꞃıꞃ O 'Domnaıll ó 'Dhoıꞃe beʒan ꞃluaıʒ, ocuꞃ ʒaḃuꞃ caıꞃlén ḃeoıl ın člaıꞃ a ʒcocꞃıḃ Luıʒne ocuꞃ Ʒaılenʒ; ocuꞃ ꞃáʒḃuꞃ ḃaꞃꝺa ann, ocuꞃ ceıꝺ caꞃ aıꞃ a cíꞃ Ƒhıacꞃaḃ. Cꞃuınnıʒıꞃ mac Uıllıam ḃúꞃc, ocuꞃ ꞃuıꝺıꞃ ımón mḃaıle; ocuꞃ ıaꞃ na cloꞃ ꞃın ꝺO 'Dhomnaıll ıonnꞃaıʒıꞃ an baıle ꝺoꞃıꝺıꞃ, ocuꞃ ꞃáʒḃuꞃ mac Uıllıam ın baıle, ocuꞃ céıꝺ ꝺo chuꞃ lóın ocuꞃ ḃaꞃꝺa a ʒcaıꞃlen Eıꞃʒꞃech aḃann a cíꞃ Ƒhıacꞃach.

Ʞccc. Enaıꞃ; cꞃı blıaꝺna ꝺhec ocuꞃ .u. ceꝺ ocuꞃ mıle aıꞃ ın Cıʒeꞃna. Ⴖaıꞃʒꞃéʒ ınʒen Conchobaıꞃ hı Ḃꞃíaın, .ı. ben hı Ruaıꞃc, .ı. anc én ḃen ꝺob ꞃeꞃꞃ ꝺo čenꝺ ꝺáṁ ocuꞃ ꝺeoꞃaıꝺ ꝺá ꝺcánıc o Ḃꞃían Ḃhóꞃuma anuaꞃꞃ, ꝺo ḃul ꝺhec ıaꞃ nonʒaꝺ ocuꞃ naıcꞃıʒe. 'Donnchaꝺ mac Conchobaıꞃ hı Ḃꞃıaın, .ı. ın cenꝺ ꞃeḃna ꝺob ꞃeꞃꞃ ꝺo 'Dhál ʒCaıꞃ na comaımꞃıꞃ a leıḃ ꞃe laım ocuꞃ ꞃe huaıꞃle, ꝺo ṁaꞃḃaḃ a nʒꞃeıꞃ oıḃče le claınn Coıꞃꞃꝺhealḃaıʒ mıc Conchobaıꞃ hı Ḃꞃıaın. O 'Domnaıll .ı. Oeꝺh ꝺo ḃul aꞃ cuaıꞃc a ʒcenꝺ ꞃí Cclban an blıaꝺaın ꞃı. Roꞃꞃa mac Ⴖaʒnuꞃa .méʒ Ⴖhaḃʒamna, cıʒeꞃna Oıꞃʒıall, moꞃcuuꞃ eꞃc. Caꝺc mac Ⴖaoıleaclaınn ı Cheallaıʒ, cıʒeꞃna O Ⴖaıne, moꞃcuuꞃ eꞃc. Ⴖaıʒıꞃceꞃ Ⴖuıꞃıꞃ O Ƒıčeallaıʒ, ꝺocuıꞃ ꝺıaꝺachca, ocuꞃ ꞃe na aıꞃꝺeꞃꞃuıc a Cuaım, ocuꞃ an ꞃeꞃ ꝺo buꝺ mó clú cꞃaḃaꝺ ocuꞃ cléıꞃčeachca

---

1 *Mac Eoin*; lit. "son of John," or "Johnson"; the cognomen of the family of Bissett of the Glinns, in the county of Antrim. See Reeves's *Eccl. Antiqq.*, p. 325.

2 *Lays siege to the town.* The literal translation of the words ꞃuıꝺıꞃ ımón mḃaıle would be "sits about the place."

3 *Tir Fhiachrach.* This entry ap-

Bel-fersde, and broke down the castle of Mac Eoin,[1] and
plundered the Glinns, and a great part of the country;
and he carried off the son of Niall, son of Conn, in captivity.
A great war between O'Domhnaill, i.e. Aedh, and O'Neill,
i.e. Art, son of Aedh ; and a war between O'Domhnaill
and Mac William Burk, i.e. Edmond, son of Rickard.
O'Domhnaill retains fifteen hundred axes in Tir-Conaill,
and in the province of Connacht, and in Feara-Manach.
O'Domhnaill proceeds from Doire with a small band, and
takes the castle of Bel-in-chláir on the borders of Luighne
and Gaileng ; and he leaves warders in it, and goes back
into Tir-Fhiachrach. Mac William Burk musters *his
army*, and lays siege to the town.[2] And on hearing this
O'Domhnaill advances again towards the town ; and
Mac William leaves the place, and goes to put provisions
and warders into the castle of Eiscir-abhann in Tir-
Fhiachrach.[3]

The kalends of January; the age of the Lord one [1513.]
thousand, five hundred, and thirteen years. Margaret,
daughter of Conchobhar O'Briain, i.e. the wife of O'Ruairc,
i.e. the best woman towards guests and exiles that had
come from Brian Borumha down, died after unction and
penitence. Donnchadh, son of Conchobhar O'Briain, i.e.
the best captain of the Dal-Cais in his time, as regards
prowess and nobility, was killed in a nocturnal encounter
by the sons Toirdhelbhach, son of Conchobhar[4] O'Briain.
O'Domhnaill, i.e Aedh, went on a visit to the king of
Alba this year. Rossa, the son of Maghnus Mac Mathghamhna, lord of Oirghiall, mortuus est. Tadhg, son of
Maelechlainn O'Cellaigh, lord of Ui-Maine, mortuus est.
Master Maurice O'Fichellaigh, doctor of divinity, and
who was an archbishop in Tuaim, and the most distinguished man abroad or at home[5] for piety and clerkship,

pears unfinished both in this chronicle
and in the so-called Annals of Connacht. The Four Masters add some
other particulars.

[4] *Conchobhar.* Ꝋcch., MS. The
Four Masters say "Murchadh."

[5] *Abroad or at home.* τοιη ιná buη;
lit. "in the East, or here," MS.

ċoip má ḃaip. vo ʋul ʋhec an ḃliavan p¹. ʒepóiv.
lapla Chille vapa, .i. ʒiuipóíp na hEpenn, .i. anc oen
ʋuine pob pepp clú. ocup po buv mó nepc ocup oipp-
vepcup, ocup ip mo vo pʒ̃ne vo ʒaḃáltup ap ʒoeiḃelaiḃ,
ocup vo bpip vo cuiplenaiḃ na nʒaoivel, ocup vob
pepp pmachc ocup pechc ocup piaʒail, ocup ip mo cuc
va aipnéip pein a coipḃepcup vpepaiḃ Epenn came vo
ʒalloiḃ a nEpinn piam, vpaʒail ḃáip ola ocup onʒ̃a
ocup aicpiʒe a Cill vapa, ocup a ɱlucav a vcempul
Cpipc a mbaile ɑ̀ɑ cliaċ maille pe cuippi cpuim³
uphóip ʒall ocup ʒaeivel Epenn na ḃeoiḋ. ꙅlóiʒeḃ
mop la .h. Néill, .i. ɑpc mac Oeḃa, a cpian Conʒail,
váp loipe Maʒ Line, ocup váp epeaċ na ʒLinne; ocup
puʒ mac Neill mic Cuinn ocup mac Uiḃilín ap ċuiv
vonc plúaiʒ, ocup mapḃcap Oeʋh mac hi Neill von
cpoiv pin. Ceʒmav an plúaʒ ocup an cóip vá cele
iap na ɱápach, ocup mapḃcap mac Uiḃilín, .i. Ripvepv
mac Rúʒpaiḃe, ocup vponʒ ḃɑlbanchaiḃ, ocup ciʒ .h.
Néill cap aip iappin. ꙅlóiʒeḃ la pí Cɑlban ʒo maiċiḃ
Cɑlban nme vá paiḃe cpi .xx. mile pep conʒanca a
ʒcpiċ cShacan, ocup loippip an cpioċ ap ʒach caoḃ ḃe.
Cpuinniʒip loapv Seomaplin ocup a mac, ocup cliáp
cShacan ina naʒaiv, ocup cucaḃ caċ ecoppa, ocup
maiʒiv ap Cɑlbanchaiḃ, ocup mapḃcap pí Cɑlban, ocup
Mac ɑ̀ilín, ocup anc aipveppuc, .i. pancc Ciʋopíap,
ocup mopán vo ċiʒepnaċaiḃ Cɑlban, ocup mopan
vaoineaḃ eli. Cɑpc mac Cceḃa hi Neill, .i. ciʒepna
ċipe hEoʒain ʒan impeppain, bpaʒail ḃáip onʒ̃a ocup
aicpiʒe a nʋun ʒenainn. Cɑpc mac Cuinn hi Neill
vo piʒav ina ionav. Cɑpc mac Néill mic Cɑipc hi
Néill mopcuup epc. Caiplén ʋúinliʒp vo ʒabáil

---

¹ *The man.* anc oen ʋuine; lit. "the one man." The construction of this entry is rather involved.

² *Cill-dara.* Kildare. Ware (*Annals*, 1513) erroneously says that Earl Garrett died at Athy. The Four Mas-ters wrongly place his death under the year 1514.

³ *To the heavy grief.* maille ne cuippi cpuim; lit. "together with grief of weight."

died this year. Garrett, Earl of Cill-dara, i.e. the Justiciary of Erinn, i.e. the man[1] of greatest fame, greatest
power and dignity, (and who achieved the greatest con-
quests over the Gaeidhel, and broke down the greatest
number of the castles of the Gaeidhel—whose authority,
law, and rule were the best—and who gave the most of
his own property in presents to the men of Erinn), that
had ever come of the Foreigners in Erinn, died after
unction and penitence, in Cill-dara,[2] and was buried in
Christ-Church in the town of Ath-cliath, to the heavy
grief[3] of the majority of the Foreigners and Gaeidhel of
Erinn after him.   A great hosting by O'Neill, i.e. Art
son of Aedh, into Trian-Congail, on which occasion he
burned Magh-Line, and plundered the Glinns.   And the
son of Niall, son of Conn, and Mac Uibhilín, came up
with a part of the army, and Aedh, the son of O'Neill,
is slain in that encounter.   The army and the pursuers
meet each other on the morrow, and Mac Uibhilín, i.e.
Richard, son of Rughraidhe, and a number of the men
of Alba, are slain ; and O'Neill comes back afterwards.
A hosting by the king of Alba[4], accompanied by the
nobles of Alba, and sixty thousand auxiliaries, into the
Saxon territory ; and he burned the country on each
side of him.   Lord Seomarlin,[5] and his son, and the
Saxon troops, muster to oppose them ; and a battle
was fought between them ; and the men of Alba are
defeated, and the king of Alba, and Mac Ailin, and the
Archbishop, i.e. of Saint Andrews, and several of the
lords of Alba, and a great many other persons, are
slain there.   Art, son of Aedh O'Neill, i.e. lord of Inis-
Eoghain without dispute, died at Dun-Genainn after
unction and penitence.   Art, son of Conn O'Neill, was
made king in his place.   Art, son of Niall, son of Art
O'Neill, mortuus est.   The castle of Dún-lis was captured

---

[4] *King of Alba.* James IV., king of Scotland.

[5] *Seomarlin.* A rude attempt at writing the name of Surrey.

ρΙΙα Όhomnaιll αρ ċlaιnn Ʒεροίο mιc Uιɓιlίn, ocuρ α
ċαbαιρτ ɔo clαιnn Uαlταιρ mιc Uιɓιlίn. Ϸορlonʒϸορτ
ɔo ɔenum la .h. nΌomnαιll ιm 8hlιʒech o ϝειl ɓριʒɔe
ʒo cιncίρ, ocuρ ʒαn buαċαchαɔ ɓó αn uαιρριn. Θoʒαn
.h. Μάιlle ɔo mαρbαɔ luchτ τρι lonʒ α τίρ Uhóʒαιne
αn blιαɔαιn ριn. Θoʒαn ρuαɓ mαc 8uιɓne ɔo mαρbαɓ
le clαιnn α ɔερbρατhαρ ρéιn, ocuρ le Όonnchαɔ mαc
Τοιρρɔhealbαιʒ hι Ohαιʒιll. Νιαll mαc Cuιnn mιc
ιoɓα buιɓe ɔhéc lά cάρʒ ɔo ρunɔραɓ.

Jcll. Θnαιρ; ceτρα blιαɔnα ɔhec αρ .u. ceɔ αρ mιle
αιρ ιn Τιʒeρnα. Cαthαl óʒ, mαc Όomnαιll mιc Θoʒαιn
hι Conchobαιρ, ɔo mαρbαɓ α bριoll ʒράnnα ɔo mαc α
ατhαρ ρειn, .ι. Θoʒαn mαc Όomnαιll; ocuρ ιρρé αn
Cαthαl óʒ ριn mαc α αoρρα ιρ mó τuc ocuρ ρuαιρ
ταnιc ɔo τρlιchτ Uρίαιn lαιʒnιʒ mιc Τοιρρɔhealbαιʒ
moιρ; ocuρ nι hé ριn αmάιn ʒeαll ɔo beρmαoιρne ιnά
luchτ αρ ceρɔe ɓó, αchτ nαch τάιnc ɔo ċιneɔ Ʒάειɓιl
ʒlαιρ ιnα comαιmριρ ρéιn α commαιɓ αn uαιρle, αn
αιɓne, ocuρ αn eιnech, ocuρ ιρ ɔιllechτα τρuαʒ αn
eαlαɔαn ɔά éιρ ʒαn ρeρ α hιomċαιρ ιnά hαlτρuιm
mαρ Chαthαl αιce. Θoʒαn mαc Όomnαιll mιc Θoʒαιn
ɔo cρochαɔ leιρ .h.nΌomnαιll ρά ċeαnn τρι lά nα
ɓιαιɓ ριn. Μαc Uιllίαm Uúρc .ι. Θmon mαc Rιcαιρɔ
ɔo mαρbαɓ le clαιnn Uάιτeρ α Uúρc α bριoll ʒράnnα
α mαιnιρτιρ Rαċα Uραnɔuιɓ. Cαιρlén nα Cuιlenτραιʒe
ɔo bριρρeɓ, ocuρ αn ċoιll móρ ɔo ʒeρραɓ ocuρ ɔαρʒαιn,
ɔιαρlα Chιlle ɔαρα, .ι. Ʒεróιɔ mαc Ʒεróιɔ, αρ lαoιʒιρ
hι Μhóρɓα. Μαc Τοιρρɔhealbαιʒ óιʒ mιc Όomnαιll, conράρlα ʒαllóʒlαeċ, ɔo mαρbαɓ le lαoιʒιρ.
Cαιρlen Chúιle Rαċαιn ɔo bριρρeɔ lα .h. nΌomnαιll.
Cαιρlén nα hOʒmuιʒe ɔo bριρρeɓ lα .h. Νeιll ιn hoc
αnno. Μαιɓm ɔo ċαbαιρτ ɔΙΙα Νéιll αρ ċlαιnn

---

[1] *Craft.* The chronicler here speaks
of the profession of historian, or poet.
This clause is loosely expressed.

[2] *Gaeidhel Glas.* One of the alleged remote ancestors of the Gaeidhel,
from whom the name has been derived.
See Keating's History of Ireland, Hali-
day's ed., p. 229.

A.D.
[1513.]

by O'Domhnaill from the sons of Garrett Mac Uibhilín, and given to the sons of Walter Mac Uibhilín. A camp was pitched by O'Domhnaill around Sligech, from the festival of Brigid to Whitsuntide ; but he did not succeed on that·occasion. Eoghan O'Maille was slain this year in Tir-Boghaine, with the crews of three ships. Eoghan Ruadh Mac Suibhne was killed by the sons of his own brother, and by Donnchadh, the son of Toirdhelbhach O'Baighill. Niall, son of Conn, son of Aedh Buidhe, died on Easter day exactly

[1514.]

The kalends of January ; the age of the Lord one thousand, five hundred, and fourteen years. Cathal Og, son of Domhnall, son of Eoghan O'Conchobhair, was slain in ugly treachery by the son of his own father, i.e. Eoghan, son of Domhnall ; and this Cathal Og was the man who, of his age, had given and received most of all that came of the race of Brian Laighnech, son of Toirdhelbhach Mór. And that alone is not the character that we, or persons of our craft,[1] would give him ; but that there came not in his own time, of the race of Gaeidhel Glas,[2] his equal in nobility, intelligence, and hospitality : and science is a poor orphan after him, without a man to sustain or foster it like Cathal. Eoghan, son of Domhnall, son of Eoghan, was hanged by O'Domhnaill before the end of three days afterwards. Mac William Burk, i.e. Edmond, the son of Rickard, was killed by the sons of Walter Burk, in ugly treachery, in the monastery of Rath-Branduibh. The castle of Cuilen-tragh was broken down, and the Coill-mór[3] was cut down and destroyed, by the Earl of Cill-dara, i.e. Garrett, son of Garrett, against the Laighis-O'Mordha. The son of Toirdhelbhach Og Mac Domhnaill, constable of gallowglasses, was killed by the Laighis. The castle of Cul-Rathain was broken down by O'Domhnaill. The castle of the Oghmagh was broken down by O'Neill in hoc anno.[4] A defeat was given by O'Neill to

---

[3] *Coill-mór* ; i.e. the "Great Wood." | [4] *Hoc anno.* óg añó, MS.

'Oomnaill hī Neill ocur aρ clainn ακρτ hī Neill,
ocur moρán vechaib ocur vo éroeð ocur vo ðaoinið
vo ðuain víð. Slóigeð le Ʒeρóiv 1aρλα Chille vaρα
aρ .h. Raiʒilliʒ, ʒuρ bρir cairlen an Chabáin; ocur
O paiʒilliʒ vo matmachav leir; ocur ρo maρbat
O Raiʒilliʒ iρin maitm rin, Αοð mac Cathail 1
Raitilliʒ, ocur moρán vo maichib a muintiρe maille
rrir; ocur ρo ʒabat Mac Cába. Slóigeð la Semur
mac 1aρλα 'Ohermuman ocur leir Uá Coρðaill aρ
phiarρur buiтлéρ, ocur loircir an тρian metonach
ʒo himlán; ocur beριt Piarρur builteρ rair lion
a trlúaiʒ, ocur clann Tomáir mic 1aρλα Cille vaρa,
ocur ʒallóʒláoið ocur ʒaircevaiʒ, ocur ilimav maρc-
rlúaʒ vo muinteρ an 1aρλα maille riú oρρa, ocur
ρo imʒevaρ oρρa via naimðeoin. Cρecha móρα vo
ðenum ðO 'Ohomnaill a nʒaileng, vaρ loirʒ ocur
váρ aiρʒ an тir ʒo Cρuačán Ʒaileng; ocur maρðταρ
O Rúaán lair ann, ocur móρán eli maille. rrir.
Maitm lá .h. Neill aρ Αοð mac 'Oomnaill hī Neill,
ocur aρ Conn mac Neill mic ακρτ, vaρ maρð ocur váρ
ʒað moρán vá muinteρ, ocur vaρ ðen a neich ocur a
néiviʒ víð, innur ʒuρ an тiʒeρnur činéil Eoʒain ʒan
imρerrain aiʒe oρin amach. Coʒav ðéρʒe etiρ .h.
n'Oomnaill ocur .h. Neill, ocur moρan va. ðuannavhaib
vrarvóð aρ ʒach тaoið ðoið; ocur a mbeið a bra:v a
brorlonʒρορτ aρ aʒhaiv a čeli; ocur rið vo ðenum
voið, ocur тocht a ʒcenv a čéli aρ vroičet Αρva Sρata
ðoið, ocur cairver Cριorv vo ðenum ann. 1nir Eoʒain
ocur cénel Móáin ocur rera Manach vo leiʒen la .h.
Neill von vul rin, ocur a mac ρo. ðói ρe cian vaimrir
ρoime rin a laim aʒ .h. 'Oomnaill vo leiʒen amach
vinnrroiʒev hī Neill. Clann Ʒeróiv mic Uiðilín vo maρ-
ðav a brioll la clainn Ualtaiρ mic Uiðilín, ocur an тír

---

1 *Butler.* builтéρ, MS.

³ *Trian-medhonach;* the "middle
third," now the barony of Middlethird,.
co. Tipperary.

³ *O'Rúaán.* The correct form of
the name is "O'Ruadhain." It is at
present generally Anglicised Rowan,
without the O'.

the sons of Domhnall O'Neill, and the descendants of Art
O'Neill ; and he took from them a great quantity of
horses, armour, and men. A hosting by Garrett Earl of
Cill-dara against O'Raighilligh, when he broke down the
castle of the Cabhán ; and O'Raighilligh was routed by
him ; and O'Raighilligh *i.e.* Aedh, son of Cathal O'Raighilligh, was killed in that rout, and a great number of the
chiefs of his people along with him ; and Mac Caba was
taken prisoner. A hosting by James, son of the Earl of
Des-Mumha, and by O'Cerbhaill, against Piers Butler ;[1]
and he burns the Trian-medhonach[2] completely ; and
Piers Butler overtakes him with all his forces, and
the sons of Thomas, son of the Earl of Cill-dara, and
gallowglasses, and warriors, with an immense force of
cavalry of the Earl's people ; and they went away from
them in despite of them. Great depredations were committed by O'Domhnaill in Gailenga, on which occasion he
burned and plundered the country as far as Cruachan-
Gaileng ; and O'Rúáan[3] is killed there by him, and a
great many more along with him. A victory by O'Neill
over Aedh, son of Domhnall O'Neill, and over Conn, son of
Niall, son of Art, when he killed and captured a great
number of their people, and took their horses and apparel
from them ; so that the undisputed lordship of Cenel-
Eoghain remained with him from thenceforth. A war
arose between O'Domhnaill and O'Neill ; and a great
number of mercenaries were engaged by them on each
side ; and they were a long time encamped in presence of
each other. And they concluded peace, and came to meet
one another on the bridge of Ard-Sratha ; and they concluded gossipred there. Inis-Eoghain, and Cenel-Móáin,
and Feara-Manach, were left to O'Neill on that occasion ;
and his son, who had been for a long time previously in
O'Domhnaill's hands, was allowed to go to O'Neill. The
sons of Garrett Mac Uibhilín were slain, in treachery, by
the sons of Walter Mac Uibhilín ; and the country was

vo cpeachav ocuy vo loycuv vo mac Heill mc Cuinn
mc Oeva buive cpiv an ngnm yin. Sloigev la Zepoiv
Iapla Cille vapa iyin Mumain, vap loiyc hi Chonaill
ap mac Iapla Vhepmuman. Cpuinnigiy mac an Iapla
lin a cinoil, ocuy O Opiain go maichib Tuagmuman vo
congnim leiy, ocuy giveoh yo immchiv an yluag go
yenamail yiapyu yugyav inaic agallma aiy. Covlac
vo vavaib ocuy vo longuiv yaivi vo capyuing vO
Vhomnaill ap Loc Eiyne, ocuy veiv na comnaive a
byav ap Iniy Sgeillenv. Ccipgiy ocuy loiygiy oilen
Ciul na noiyep, ocuy vo ni yic na viaiv yin yu, ocuy
cig ylan va cig.

Kcc. Enaiy; u. bliavna vhec ap .u. cev ap mile aiy
an Tigepna. Cpeaca mopa vo venum vO Vhomnaill ap
clainn Viapmava yuaiv a nimell coillce Conchobaiy.
Sloigev la .h. Heill a gclainn Ccova buive, vap loiyc
ocuy vap cpeac ciiv moy von ciy, ocuy cig mac Heill
mc Cuinn a gcenn I Neill, ocuy gavuy cuayuyval uava;
ocuy invcoiy O Neill iayyin. Cpeca mopa vo venum
vO Vomnaill ap yliochc Opiain mheg Uioiy, ocuy a
mve uile aca pyein; ocuy yic vo venum yu aiy a
haicle. Caiylen Ccine vo gabail ap cShean mac Iapla
Vhepmuman vo cSemuy mac an Iapla; ocuy yuiviy
annyein ya caiylen Loc Zaiy, ocuy vo vi a cumgach
moy aige no guy cuiyevay yil mOpiain ocuy yil
gCepvaill ocuy cenel Ccova uava e. Oevh, mac Heill
mc Cuinn mc Ccova buive hi Neill, vo vul ap cpeic
von coill Ulltaig, ocuy cpec vo glacav vo anv. Lenuy
Niall mac Opiain mc Niall gallva a vcopaigechc e,
ocuy mapvcay Niall mac Opiain, ocuy aiygcey in coill
go hiomlan, ocuy anaig nepc cyin Congail uile ag

---

1 *Inis-Sgeillend.* Enniskillen, co.
Fermanagh. The more usual form
of the name is Inis-Ceithlenn; i.e.
"Ceithlenn's island."

2 *Son of Niall.* His Christian name
was Aedh (or Hugh).

3 *Foray.* cpv, for cpec, MS.

4 *The Coill-Ulltagh;* i.e. "the Ultonian wood;" Anglicised Killultagh,
the name of a district in the county
of Antrim.

5 *Coill.* The "wood." See last note.

preyed and burned by the son of Niall, son of Conn, son
of Aedh Buidhe, through that deed. A hosting by
Garrett, Earl of Cill-dara, into Mumha, on which occasion
he burned Ui-Conaill against the son of the Earl of Des-
Mumha. The son of the Earl assembles all his forces, and
O'Briain with the chiefs of Tuadh-Mumha assists him;
nevertheless, the host departed luckily before they
reached a place where they could confer with it. A fleet
of boats and long ships was launched by O'Domhnaill
on Loch-Erne, and he was a long time residing on Inis-
Sgeillend.[1] He plunders and burns the islands of Cuil-
na-noirer; and he makes peace with them afterwards,
and comes home safely.

The kalends of January; the age of the Lord one
thousand, five hundred, and fifteen years. Great depredations were committed by O'Domhnaill upon the Clann-
Diarmada Ruadh, on the border of Coillte-Conchobhair.
A hosting by O'Neill into Clann-Aedha-Buidhe, when
he preyed and burned a great part of the country; and
the son of Niall,[2] son of Conn, comes to meet O'Neill,
and accepts wages from him; and O'Neill turns back
afterwards. Great preys were taken by O'Domhnaill
from the descendants of Brian Mag Uidhir; and they
were all consumed amongst themselves; and he made
peace with them soon after. The castle of Aine was
captured from John, son the Earl of Des-Mumha, by
James, son of the Earl; and he then sits down before the
castle of Loch-Gair, which was in great straights by him
until the Sil-Briain, and the Sil-Cerbhaill, and the Cenel-
Aedha, sent him away from it. Aedh, the son of Niall,
son of Conn, son of Aedh Buidhe O'Neill, went on a foray[3]
to the Coill-Ulltagh,[4] where he took a prey. Niall, the
son of Brian, son of Niall Gallda, follows him in pursuit, and Niall son of Brian is killed, and the Coill[5]
is entirely plundered; and the power of all Trian-
Congail remains with Aedh, son of Niall, through that

Oeoh mac Neıll oonc ɼıobal ɼın. menma mháʒ
Caɼmaıc, ɼoɼeɼleıʒínn oo ʊí na eɼpuc a Ráĕ bhoĕ,
ın Cɼıɼoo quıeuıc. Oomnall mac Ccoĕa ɼuaıʊ hı
Ohoṁnaıll oo ṁaɼbaʊ la hCcoĕ mbuıʊe .h. nOoṁnaıll,
ɼa Tuaıĕ ʊlaohaıʊ, ın ʊlıaoaın ɼın.

Jctt. Enaıɼ ; ɼe blıaona ohéc aɼ .u. ceo aɼ mıle aıɼ
ın Tıʒeɼna. Caıɼlen 8lıʒıĕ oo ʒabáıl le .h. nOomnaıll,
ıaɼ mbeıĕ achaıo ɼaoa a coʒao ɼıɼ; ocuɼ ıɼ amlaıo
ɼo ʒabaʊ é .ı. ɼıoıɼe ɼɼancach táıııc oá oılıcɼı oocum
ɼuɼʒaoóɼa ɼacɼaıc, ocuɼ cuc O Oomnall onóıɼ ṁóɼ
ocuɼ cıʊlúıcĕe ʊó; ocuɼ oo ĕuıɼ an ɼıoıɼe lonʒ lán ooɼ-
oonáɼ, ocuɼ ʒunna móɼ bɼıɼoe caıɼléın uıɼɼĕı oocum
hı Ohomnaıll; ocuɼ ɼuıʊıɼ ɼán mbaıle, ocuɼ bɼıɼɼıɼ
an baıle ɼul ɼuaıɼ é, ocuɼ oo beɼ eınech oona ʊaɼoaıb.
Ocuɼ ceıo aɼɼın a cıɼ Oılella ocuɼ ʒaʊaıɼɼ caıɼlén Cúl
ṁáıle, ocuɼ cáıɼıol loĕa Oeɼʒáın, ocuɼ Oún na móna ;
ocuɼ ɼáʒbuɼ ʊaɼoa a ʒcuıo oíʊ, ocuɼ oo ʊeıɼ bɼaıʒoe
laıɼ ón ʒcuıo elı ; ocuɼ oo ʊí 8lıʒech cɼí blíaona ohéc
aʒ .h. Ohomnaıll oon oul ɼın no ʒuɼ ʒaʊ Taʊʒ óʒ mac
Taıʊc mıc Ccoĕa aıɼ é ıaɼɼın. mac Oonnchaoa an
Choɼuınn ocuɼ mac mıc Oonnchaoa oo ṁaɼbaʊ aʒ
ceachc a ʒceno cɼlúaıʒ hı Oomnaıll le Oonnchao mac
Toıɼɼohealbaıʒ hı ʊháıʒıll. Caıɼlén ı Ceɼʊaıll, .ı.
leım hı ʊhánáın, oo ʒabáıl lé hıaɼla Chılle oaɼa, .ı.
ʒeɼóıo ıaɼla, ıaɼ na ɼáɼuʒao ɼo a achaıɼ ; ocuɼ ní
huɼuɼa ʒo ocanıc ıɼın aımɼıɼ ɼın caıɼlen ɼó buo
cɼuaıʊe coɼnum ocuɼ conʒmáıl ınáɼɼ, no ʒuɼ bɼıɼ-
ɼeʊ cımchell na ʊaɼoa é. maıʊm moɼ oo ĕabaıɼc

---

¹ Quievit. ¹ o, MS.
    qeu'

² Year. The scribe of this part
of the work has here added the following note: "8ʒuıɼım ʊeɼo. ʒo
ocáuɼaıʊ Oía oɼeɼ ın leaʊ-
aıɼɼı ceachc ɼlan ó baıle Ccĕa
luoın .ı. Bɼıan mac Ruaıoɼı
mıc Oıaɼmaoa. mıɼı ɼılıp
ɼʒɼıɼɼıc (sic), 1588; lá ɼéıl

bɼenuınn oo ɼunnɼaʊ, 7 Clú-
aın hı Ohɼaoın mó loʒ ;" i.e. "I
desist from this. May God grant to
the man [owner] of this book to return safe from the town of Ath-Luain,
i.e. Brian, son of Ruaidhri Caech Mac
Diarmada. I am Philip [qui] scrip-
sit, 1588; the festival day of Brenainn exactly; and Cluain-Ui-Brain
is my place."

expedition. Menma Mac Carmaic, a distinguished lector, who was a bishop in Rath-Both, in Christo quievit.[1] Domhnall, son of Aedh Ruadh O'Domhnaill, was slain by Aedh Buidhe O'Domhnaill, in Tuath-Bladhaidh, in this year.[2]

The kalends of January; the age of the Lord one thousand, five hundred, and sixteen years. The castle of Sligech was taken by O'Domhnaill, after he had been a long time attacking it, and this is the way in which it was taken, viz.; a French knight came on his pilgrimage to Patrick's purgatory, and O'Domhnaill gave him great honour and presents. And the knight sent to O'Domhnaill a ship filled with ordnance, and containing a large castle-breaking gun. And he (O'Domhnaill) sits down before the castle, and demolishes the town before he obtained it; and he gave protection to the warders. And he goes from thence into Tir-Oilella, and takes the castle of Cúl-mhaile, and the cashel[3] of Loch-Dergan, and Dún-na-mona; and he leaves warders in some of them, and carried off prisoners from the rest. And O'Domhnaill held Sligech during thirteen years from this occasion, until Tadhg Og,[4] the son of Tadhg, son of Aedh, took it from him afterwards. Mac Donnchadha of the Corann, and the son of Mac Donnchadha, were slain whilst going to join O'Domhnaill's army, by Donnchadh, son of Toirdhelbhach O'Baighill. O'Cerbhaill's castle, i.e. Léim-Ui-Bhánáin, was taken by the Earl of Cill-dara, i.e. Earl Garrett, although his father failed in the attempt to do so; and it is not possible that there was[5] at that time a castle more bravely defended and maintained, until it was demolished about the warders. A great defeat was given by

---

[3] Cashel. caiрιοL. This is the Irish name for a stone wall, or maceria. The Four Mast. have caiрLen, "castle," which is probably correct, as a castle would be more likely to be destroyed by the big gun referred to than an Irish caisiol. The place referred to in the text is now called Castledergan,

VOL. II.

near Collooney, co. Sligo. The remains of a castle are still observable on a height overhanging the lake (Loch-Dergan).

[4] Tadhg Og ; i.e. Thaddeus the Younger [O'Conor Sligo].

[5] That there was. ро οcαnιc; lit. "that there came."

Q

Demonn mac Cómáιr buιτlér αn Phιαρur buιτlep,
ocur αn mac mιc Phιαρuιr, ocur mórán vá mιιnτer
ocur vα mbuαnnαvhαιb vo ḃávhαv ocur vo mαρbαv.
O Vočαρταιξ .ι. Conchobαr cαrραch O Vočαρταιξ mor-
τuιιr erτ. Cαιrlen mιc Shuιḃnι .ι. Rάč Mαolán vo
ἑuιτιm ιn hoc αnno. O Vomnαιll vo ḃul rά ḃó α τίr
Θoξαιn αr rloιξevh ιn ḃlιαvαιn rιn. Máξ Cαρρτhαιξ
mór, .ι. Cormαc lαξrαč mαc Cαιvξ, τιξernα Verḿumαn,
αn τe ιr rerr ruαιr α ἑιξernur ocur ιr mo ruαιr
vo ἑoξαv no ξo rαιḃe nα ἑιξernα ξαn ιmrerταιn, ocur
vob rerr vo čenv váṁ ocur veorαιv, ocur vob rerr
rechτ ocur rιαξαιl vo rιξrαιv Leιἑe Mαvα, vo ḃul
vhéc. Coιrrvheαlbαch mαc brιαιn uαιne hi Ξhαll-
čuḃαιr, comαrbα nα Cαιrrξe, morτuur erτ. Mαc
brιαιn čαoιč mιc Cαιvξ mιc Θoξαιn vo mαrbαv α brιoll
vo mαc Cαιvξ nα τuαιξe mιc Fhélιm mιc Θoξαιn, ocur
vo rlιochτ αn čerrbαιξ. ben hi Creαḃαιr .ι. Cαιτerínα
ιní Crιovαcáιn, ben vércech ḃαonnαchταch, morτuα erτ.
Uιllιαm mαc Vonnchαvα hi Fherξαιl, .ι. erruc nα
hαnξαιle, vhéc.

Jcττ. Θnαιr. Seαchτ mblιαvnα vhéc αr .u. cev αr
mιle αιr ιn Cιξernα. Vonnchαv mαc Coιrrvheαlbαιξ
hi Ḃhαιξιll vrαξαιl ḃáιr vuρurvιξ .ι. luchτ báιv vá
muιnτer ocur é reιn vo ḃul ξo Corαιch, ocur ξαoἑ
vια bruαvαch ron brαιrrξe rιαr, ocur nαch brríἑ en
rocul vá rξeluιḃ órιn αlle. Seαn mαc Cuιnn mιc Θnrí
mιc Θoξuιn hi Neιll vhéc. Phιlιp mαc Coιrrvheαlbαιξ Méξ Uιvιr vhec αoιne chάrξ vo runvrαv. bαrún
Sláιne vhéc α Sαχαnαιb, .ι. Crιrvóιr plemenn. αrτ
mαc αoḃα mιc Vomnαιll hi Neιll vo mαrbαv le Nιαll
mαc Cuιnn mιc Neιll mιc αιrτ. O Vuιḃξenvαιn Chιlle

---

1 *Butler.* This name is frequently written buιlτen in the MS.

2 *Hoc.* oc, MS.

3 *The Carraig.* See note 2, p. 245 infra.

4 *Eoghan.* The Four Masters call him Eoghan O'Conchobhair.

5 *Tadhg-na-tuaighe.* "Tadhg (or Thaddeus) of the Battle-axe."

6 *The Cerrbhach;* i.e. the Gambler.

A.D.
———
[1516.]

Edmond, the son of Thomas Butler,[1] to Piers Butler,[1] and to the grandson of Piers; and a great number of their people and mercenaries were drowned and killed. O'Dochartaigh, i.e. Conchobhar Carragh O'Dochartaigh, mortuus est. Mac Suibhne's castle, i.e. Rath-Maelain, fell in hoc[2] anno. O'Domhnaill went twice this year into Tir-Eoghain, on a hosting. Mac Carthaigh Mór, i.e. Cormac Ladhrach, son of Tadhg. lord of Des-Mumha, the man who best obtained his government, and who encountered the greatest hostility until he was undisputed lord, and who was the best protector of the learned and destitute, and whose law and rule were the best, of all the princes of Leth-Modha, died. Toirdhelbhach. son of Brian Uaine O'Gallchubhair, comarb of the Carraig,[3] mortuus est. The son of Brian Caech. son of Tadhg, son of Eoghan,[1] was treacherously slain by the son of Tadhg-na-tuaighe,[5] son of Felim, son of Eoghan, and by the descendants of the Cerrbhach.[6] O'Trebhair's wife, i.e. Catherine Ní Criodachain, a charitable, humane woman, mortua est. William, son of Donnchadh O'Ferghail, i.e. the bishop of the Anghaile,[7] died.

[1517.]

The kalends of January. The age of the Lord one thousand, five hundred, and seventeen years. Donnchadh, son of Toirdhelbhach O'Baighill. met with an unfortunate death, viz., a boat's crew of his people, and he himself, went to Torach, and the wind blew them westwards to sea, and no word of their fate was received from that time to this. John, son of Conn, son of Henry, son of Eoghan O'Neill, died. Philip, son of Toirdhelbhach Mag Uidhir, died on Easter Friday exactly. The Baron of Slaine, i.e. Christopher Fleming, died in Saxon-land. Art, the son of Aedh, son of Domhnall O'Neill, was killed by Niall, the son of Conn, son of Niall.[8] son of Art. O'Duibhgennain of

---

[7] *Bishop of the Anghaile* ; i.e. bishop of **Ardagh**, which diocese includes the ancient district of Anghaile. now the county of Longford.

[8] *Son of Niall.* This name is omitted in the pedigree of Niall, son of Conn. given in the Annals of Connacht. and by the Four Masters.

Rónαın, .ı. Mαžα ɣlαɾɾ mαc Oußčhαıɜ, ɔhéc ın hoc αnno.

Jctt. Ɵnαıɾ; ochc mblıαɔnα ɔhec αɾ .u. ceɔ αɾ mıLe αıɾ ın Cıɜeɾnα. Oeð bαlð, mαc Cuınn mıc Ɵnɾí mıc Ɵoɜαın hí ʼleıll, ɔhéc. Clαnn hí ʼleıll .ı. clαnn Oomnαıll mıc Ɵnɾí mıc Ɵoɜαın, ɔo ðul αɾ cɾeıč αɾ Ůɾíαn mαc Cuınn mıc Ɵnɾí, ocuɾ Ůɾıαn ɔo ðɾeıč oɾɾα αɜ Oomnαch αn eıch, ocuɾ mαıðm móɾ ɔo žαbαıɾc oɾɾα, ocuɾ Oeɔh mαc Oomnαıll ɔo ɣαbáıl αnɔ. Mαc Cαžmαoıl ocuɾ moɾán ɔo mαıžıbh čınél bɾeɾαɔhαıɜ ɔo mαɾbαɔ αnn. αn ɔeɜαnαch Mháɜ Uıɔıɾ, .ı. Oeð mαc Roɾɾα mıc Comáıɾ óıɜ .ı. mαc ın eɾɾuıc, ɔhec. Mαc 8uıðne ɾánαɔ ɔhéc, .ı. Ruαıɔɾı mαc Mαolmuıɾe, ım chαıɾc ɔo ɾunnɾαð. ɾélım mαc Ůɾıαın mıc Conchobαıɾ óıɜ Mhéɜ Uıɔıɾ ɔhéc.

Jctt. Ɵnáıɾ; ıx. mblıαɔnα ɔhéc αɾ .u. ceɔ αɾ mıLe αıɾ ın Cıɜeɾnα. ıuɾɔαıoıɾ nα hɵɾenn .ı. ɜeɾóıɔ ıαɾlα Chılle ɔαɾα, .ı. ɜeɾóıɔ óɜ mαc ɜeɾóıɔ, ɔo ðul ɾó žóɜαıɾm ɾıɜ 8αxαn ıαɾ nα žočuıɾeɔ ɾoıɾ cɾe ıonnlαčαıð ocuɾ cɾe eɔαɾčoɾɾαoıɔıð ɜαll Ɵɾenn ɾαıɾ; ocuɾ bá homnαch ımeɜlαč lá cáč α žuɾuɾ lα hıolαɾ nα nαımleıɾ ocuɾ nα nıomčoɾɾαoıɔıð. Ůeɾcılencıα mαɜnα ın hoc αnno, ocuɾ fuımeɾ moɾ ɔo ɣαlloıð αžo clıαž ɔo éɜ ɔon ceıðm ɾın. Roıbeɾɔ mαc Commαıɾ mıc ın ıαɾlα, .ı. ɾeɾ α αoıɾı ɾeın bα ɾeɾɾ αınm ocuɾ áıɾem ocuɾ uαıɾle ɔo ɜeɾαlcαchαıð Mıðe, ɔhéc ɔon ɣláıɜ ɾın. Mαc αnc 8hαð-ðαoıɾıɜ, .ı. Rαıðılín .ı. ɾeɾ ɾá mó oınech ocuɾ áɜ ɔo ɣαlloıb Ɵɾenn ınα αımɾıɾ ɾeın olčenα, ɔéɜ íαɾ ná žoɾɾonαɔ αɾ α ðužαıɔ lα cumhαchcαıð ıαɾlα Chılle ɔαɾα, ocuɾ lá ɾoɾɜαll ın ɾɾıóɾα Mhéɜ ααonɜuɾα; ocuɾ α žıɾ ɜo ɾeɾcuɾ ɾóınmech αɜ αn ɾɾıóıɾ ɔıα αımðeoın

---

1 *Aedh Balbh.* "Aedus Balbus," or "Hugh the Stammerer."

2 *Bishop.* Rossa (or Roger) Mag Uidhir, bishop of Clogher, who died in the year 1483.

3 *Pestilentia.* pᴢeLencıα, MS.

4 *In hoc.* αn 6c, MS.

5 *Robert.* Robert FitzGerald. Apparently the son of the celebrated Sir Thomas of Lackagh, who was the second son of Thomas, seventh Earl of Kildare.

Cill-Ronain, i.e. Matthew Glas, the son of Dubhthach,
died in hoc anno.

The kalends of January; the age of the Lord
one thousand, five hundred, and eighteen years. Aedh
Balbh,[1] son of Conn, son of Henry, son of Eoghan O'Neill,
died. The sons of O'Neill, viz., the sons of Domhnall,
son of Henry, son of Eoghan, went on a predatory
excursion against Brian, the son of Conn, son of Henry;
and Brian came up with them at Domnach-an-eich, and
gave them a great defeat; and Aedh, son of Domhnall,
was taken prisoner there. Mac Cathmhail, and many of
the chiefs of Cenel-Feradhaigh, were slain there. The
Dean Mag Uidhir, i.e. Aedh the son of Rossa, son of
Thomas Og, i.e. the son of the bishop,[2] died. Mac Suibhne
of Fánad, i.e. Ruaidhri, the son of Maelmuire, died
exactly at Easter. Felim, son of Brian, son of Conchobhar
Og Mag Uidhir, died.

The kalends of January; the age of the Lord one
thousand, five hundred, and nineteen years. The Justiciary
of Erinn, i.e. Garrett Earl of Cill-dara, i.e. Garrett Og,
the son of Garrett, went at the invitation of the King of
the Saxons,. after having been summoned eastwards
through the complaints and accusations of the Foreigners
of Erinn against him; and all persons were apprehensive
and fearful regarding his journey, in consequence of the
extent of the enmities and accusations. Pestilentia[3]
magna in hoc[4] anno; and a great number of the Foreigners
of Ath-cliath died of this plague. Robert,[5] son of Thomas,
son of the Earl, i.e. the best man in name, repute, and
nobility of the Geraldines of Midhe of his own age, died
of this plague. The son of the Savage, i.e. Raibhilin, the
man of greatest bounty and valour of all the Foreigners
of Erinn in his own time, died after having been expelled
from his patrimony by the power of the Earl of Cill-dara,
and the persuasion of the Prior Mag Aenghusa; and his
patrimony was quietly, prosperously, held by the Prior

ᵹo bᵹuaiṗ ṗum báṗ; ocuṗ ní buṫ maċtnaṽ ᵹe ᴨa
ᴅeolċaiṗe a ṫíṗe no ᵹébaṽ báṗṗ, .ı. tṗíċa ceṽ na ṗoillṗı.
Ǝmonn Taṫṫaoiṗ .ı. a mac ᴅo ṗíᵹhaᴅ ᴨa ıoᴨaṫ, ᵹeᴨ
ᵹo bᵹuaiṗ a ṫuċhaıᴅ ᵹo ṗéıṫ; ṗeṗ ṗéıᴨ ṗa mó ᴅaoᴨᴨaċt
ocuṗ ᴅaıᵹ eıᴨech ᴅo ᵹalloıṫ Ǝṗeᴨᴨ acht ᵹe ṗo beṗᴨaṫ
ṗó ᴨa ıᴨmechuṗ é. Ṗeıᴅlıᴨ mac Maᵹᴨuṗa hı Conchobaıṗ, tıᵹeṗᴨa ıochtaıṗ Connaċht, ṗeṗ ᴅéṗcech ᴅaoᴨ-
ᴨaċhtach ṗṗı ᴅamuıṫ ocuṗ ᴅeóṗaıᵹıṫ, ᴅo éᵹ ıᴨ hoc
anno. Mac Uıllıam claıᴨᴨı Rıcaıṗᴅ, .ı. Rıcaṗᴅ óᵹ
mac Uılléıᵹ a búṗc, .ı. ṗeṗ beoṫlaṗaċ buanċonáıᵹ,
moṗtuuṗ eṗt. Uıllıam mac Uıllıᵹ a búṗc ᴅo ṗíᵹhaᴅ
ᴅía éıṗ. ᴅonᴨchaᴅ caomáᴨach, ṗeṗ ṗaċmaṗ ṗo ċoᴨáıᵹ
ᴅo láᴨ ıṁaıṫıṫ Laıᵹeᴨ, ıᴨ hoc anno. Maoılíᴨ mac
Toṗᴨa hı Mhaılconaıṗe, ollam ṗíl Muıṗeᴅhaıᵹ, ṗeṗ
láᴨ ᴅo ṗaṫ ocuṗ ᴅéċṗı, ocuṗ ṗeṗ ᴅo ṫoᵹaᴅaṗ Ᵹoıll
Ᵹeṗaltach taṗ ollaṁᴨaıṫ Ǝṗeᴨᴨ, ṗeṗ ᴅo ᵹébaṫ ṗeoıᴅ
ocuṗ maoıᴨe o ᵹach aoᴨ ᴅuaıṗlıṫ Ǝṗeᴨᴨ ṗoṗ a ṗıṗeṫ,
ocuṗ ᴅo beṗeṫ ṗum ᵹo hanoıṗċeṗ aᴨ ní no ᵹeṫeṫ, a éᵹ a
maıᴨıṗtıṗ ᴅeṗᵹ a Teṫṫa. Ṗèṗceṗtne O Cuṗᴨíᴨ, ṗeṗ
ᵹṗáṫa Ǝoᵹaıᴨ hı Ruaıṗc, ocuṗ ceᴨᴅ eᵹᴨa ocuṗ éıxṗı a
ṗıᴨe ṗeıᴨ, moṗtuuṗ eṗt. ᴅoṁnall ᵹlaṗ O Cuṗᴨíᴨ
moṗtuuṗ eṗt. Comoṗbo ċlúano Conmaıcne, .ı. ceᴨᴅ
oıᴨıᵹ ocuṗ ᴅaoᴨᴨaċhta ocuṗ aoıᴅeṫchaıṗe cell Conmaıcne, ıaṗ bṗoṗbuṫ a óıṗı no ᴨíṗ uılle, quıeuıt ıᴨ
Cṗıṗto. O Neıll .ı. Ꝏꝛt óᵹ mac Cuıᴨᴨ hı Neıll moṗtuuṗ
eṗt. Coᴨᴨ mac Cuıᴨᴨ a ᴅeṗbṗathaıṗ ᴅo ṗıᵹhaᴅ ᴨa
ıoᴨaṫ; acht chena ᴨıṗ bo hıᴨaᴨᴨ mathaıṗ ṫóıṫ.
Taṽᵹ mac Ḃṗıaıᴨ mıc Toᴨaltaıᵹ hı Ḃıṗᴨ, taᴨuṗᴅe
.h. mḂṗıuıᴨ Shıonᴨa, moṗtuuṗ eṗt. Sámṗaṽ ocuṗ
ṗóᵹmaṗ ṗalcmaṗ ṗíṗ ṗlıuċ aᴨ ᵹlıaᴅaıᴨ ṗıᴨ; blıaᴅaıᴨ
ċalaᴅ ċeṗṗachtoṫ, acht ᵹeṗ ṫó ceṗᴨoᴅach teṫmaᴨᴅach
hí. Taṫc ṗuaṫ mac Maoıleċlaᴨᴨ hı Cheallaıᵹ, ṗṗıṗ
ıᴨ abaṗṫóı Taṫc ıᴨ ċalaᴅ, moṗtuuṗ eṗt. O Conchobaıṗ

---

1 *Tricha - ced - na - soillse.* "The
Tricha-ced (or cantred) of the light."
Lecale barony, co. Down.

2 *Hoc.* óc, MS.

3 *Manister-derg;* i.e. "the red ab-
bey;" now Abbeyderg, co. Longford.

4 *After completing his age;* i.e. after
completing the ordinary age of man.

in despite of him, until he died; and it would not be surprising if it was for grief on account of his territory, i.e. Tricha-ced-na-soillse,[1] that he died. Edmond Savage, i.e. his son, was inaugurated in his place, although he did not easily obtain his patrimony : the man of greatest humanity and bounty of all the Foreigners of Erinn, although he was injured regarding his property. Fedhlim, son of Maghnus O Conchobhair, lord of Lower Connacht, a charitable, humane man towards the learned and desti-tute, died in hoc[2] anno. Mac William of Clann-Rickard, i.e. Rickard Og, son of Ulick Burk, a very wealthy, opulent man, mortuus est. William, the son of Ulick Burk, was made king after him. Donnchadh Caemhan-ach, a prosperous, very wealthy man, one of the great chiefs of Laighen, died in hoc[2] anno. Mailín, son of Torna O'Maelchonaire, ollamh of Sil-Muiredhaigh, a man full of prosperity and learning ; a man whom the Geraldine Foreigners chose before the ollamhs of Erinn; a man who would obtain jewels and riches from every one of the nobles of Erinn from whom he would solicit them, and who would unsparingly give what he received, died in Manister-derg[3] in Tethbha. Ferceirtne O'Cuirnín, a favourite of Eoghan O'Ruairc, and head of the learning and poetry of his own tribe, mortuus est. Domhnall Glas O'Cuirnín mortuus est. The comarb of Cluain-Conmaicne, i.e. the head of the bounty, and humanity, and hospitality of the churches of Conmaicne, after completing his age,[4] or more, quievit in Christo. O'Neill, i.e. Art Og, son of Conn O'Neill, mortuus est. Conn, the son of Conn, his brother, was made king in his place ; but they had not the same mother. Tadhg, son of Brian, son of Tomaltach O'Birn, tanist of Ui-Briuin-Sionna, mortuus est. A rainy, truly wet, summer and harvest this year ; it was a hard, tormenting year, and a year of suffering and sickness. Tadhg Ruadh, son of Maelechlainn O'Cellaigh, who was usually called Tadhg-in-Chaladh, mortuus est.

ρuαꝺ, .1. Θoʒαn mαc Ϸeιlιmιꝺ ριnn, ρí ʒo bϥρeαϥαbϥα, ιn hoc αnno.

Ktt. Θnαιρ; ϥιče blιαꝺαn αρ .u. ceꝺ αρ mιle αιρ ιn Tιʒeρnα. Ϸlάιʒ ṁόρ α τoϥϥαch nα blιαꝺnα ϥα αn Θϥιnn. Ίuιϥꝺíϥ 8αxϥαnαch ιn Θϥιnn, ocuϥ ιαϥlα Chιlle ꝺαϥα α 8αχαnαιꝺ ꝺeόϥ. Mαc Uιllíαm člαιnnι Rιcαιϥꝺ .1. Uιllιαm buϥc ꝺhéc ιn hoc αnno. Rιcαϥꝺ α búϥc, .1. α ꝺeϥbϥαthαιρ el1, nα ιonαꝺ; clαnn ϥιeιn Uιllιʒ α buϥc ꝺιꝺlιnαιꝺ. Mαc Uιllιαm buϥc, .1. Mαoιlιρ mαc Teρόιꝺ, ꝺo ṁαϥbαꝺ ρeϥ ꝺolum lα clαιnn τ8heoιnín ṁoιρ mιc mιc 8heoιnín. Muιριρ mαc Tomαιρ mιc αn ιαϥlα, ϥoꝅα ʒαll nʒeϥαlταč uιle ꝺo ṁéιn ocuρ ꝺιnnϥoιꝅche, ꝺo mαϥbαꝺ lα Conn mαc Mhαoιlečlαιnn hι Mhoϥꝺα eτ αlιι mulτι. In ʒιllα ꝺuꝺ mαc Uιllíαm mιc Collα mιc Ỻuꝺʒάιll, conϥꝺάϥlα Mαιꝅe Luιϥʒ, moϥτuuϥ eϥτ. Uιllíαm mαc Uιllιαm Mιc 8ιuϥτάn moϥτuuϥ eϥτ. In ʒιllα ꝺub ṁάʒ Ϸιlιρ moϥτuuϥ eϥτ. Mάʒ ωonꝅuϥα, .1. ꝺomnαll mαc Oeꝺhα mιc ωιρτ, moϥτuuϥ eϥτ. Ϸélιm αn eιnιꝅ ṁάʒ Oenꝅuϥα, .1. α ꝺeϥbϥαthαιρ elι, ꝺo ϥιʒhαꝺ ιnα ιonαꝺ. Cαιϥbϥe, mαc Concobαιρ mιc Cαιϥbϥι mιc Coϥmαιc hι bιϥn, cόnϥαl ocuϥ cιnnlιτιρ mαιcne Mhuιϥeʒhαιꝅ, moϥιτủρ ιn hoc αnno. Mαιꝺm ꝺo ꝺαbαιϥτ αϥ ϥeϥoιꝺ Mαnαch le clαnn τ8heαιn mιc Cαταιl hι Rαιꝅιllιꝅ, ιnαϥ mαϥbαꝺ ocuϥ ιnαϥ bάιꝺheꝺ ꝺeιčnebαϥ αϥ ϥιchιτ ιm Ϸιlιρ mαc Θmuιnn mιc Tόmάιρ Mhéʒ Uιꝺιρ ocuϥ ιmon α mαc, ocuϥ ιm ʒhιllα ϥατϥαιc mαc Ϸιlιρ mιc Toιϥϥꝺheαlbαιꝅ conα bϥαιτϥιꝺ, .1. Θmonn ocuϥ Toιϥϥꝺelbαch ṁαc Ϸlαιčbeϥταιꝅ mιc Tόmάιρ όιʒ, ocuϥ mαc ʒιllα ϥuαιꝺ .1. ʒoϥϥϥαιꝅ, ocuϥ mόϥάn elι.

Ktt. Θnάιρ; blιαꝺαιn αϥ ϥčιτ αϥ .u. ceꝺ αϥ mιle αιϥ·

---

1 _Hoc._ όʒ, MS.

2 _Justiciary._ The Earl of Surrey, or "Earl O'Surrai," as he is called by some Irish chroniclers.

3 _Son of Thomas;_ i.e. son of Thomas of Lackagh, who was made Lord Chancellor of Ireland for life in a parliament held at Trim in 1484, but having espoused the cause of Lambert Simnel, was slain fighting for him in the battle of Stoke-upon-Trent in 1487. His son Maurice was appointed Lord Justice of Ireland in the year 1519.

O'Conchobhair Ruadh, i.e. Eoghan, son of Feilimidh Finn, a king whose title was disputed, *died* in hoc[1] anno.

The kalends of January; the age of the Lord one thousand, five hundred, and twenty years. A great plague in the beginning of this year in Erinn. A Saxon Justiciary[2] in Erinn, and the Earl of Cill-dara still in Saxon-land. Mac William of Clann-Rickard, i.e. William Burk, died in hoc anno. Rickard Burk, i.e. his other brother, *was appointed* in his place: both of these were the sons of Ulick Burk. Mac William Burk, i.e. Meiler the son of Tibbot, was killed per dolum by the sons of Seoinín Mor, son of Mac Seoinín. Maurice, son of Thomas,[3] son of the Earl, the choice of all the Geraldine Foreigners in disposition and valour, was slain by Conn, son of Maelechlainn O'Mordha, et alii multi.[4] The Gilla-dubh, son of William, son of Colla Mac Dubhgaill, constable of Magh-Luirg, mortuus est. William, son of William Mac Siurtán, mortuus est. The Gilla-dubh, son of Philip,[5] mortuus est. Mag Aenghusa, i.e. Domhnall, son of Aedh, son of Art, mortuus est. Felim-an-enigh[6] Mag Aenghusa, i.e. his other brother, was made king in his place. ·Cairbre, son of Conchobhar, son of Cairbre, son of Cormac O'Birn, the consul and leader of the descendants of Muiredhach,[7] moritur in hoc anno. A defeat was given to the Feara-Manach by the sons of John, son of Cathal O'Raighilligh, in which thirty persons were killed and drowned, along with Philip, the son of Edmond, son of Thomas Mag Uidhir, and his son; and Gilla-Patraic, son of Philip, son of Toirdbelbhach, with his kinsmen, viz., Edmond, and Toirdhelbhach son of Flaithbhertach, son of Thomas Og, and Mac Gilla-ruaidh, i.e. Godfrey, and many more.

The kalends of January; the age of the Lord one

---

[4] *Alii multi.* ໔ɪ muɪʟcɪ, MS.

[5] *Philip.* Philip Mag Uidhir (or Maguire).

[6] *Felim-an-enigh;* i.e. "Felim of the bounty," or "of the hospitality."

[7] *Muiredhach;* i.e. Muiredhach Muillethan ("Muiredhach of the broad crown"), the progenitor of the principal families of Connacht, including the family of O'Birn.

ιɴ Τιʒεριια. Μαιṫṁ mórp ɗo ṫαбαιp α τíp Mʜαιɴe
mιc Ϭcʜαcʜ αp .h. Concʜoбαιp ɴuαṫ, .ı. Ϲαṫʒ бuιṫe
mαc Ϲαṫʜαιʟ puαιṫ, ocup αp .h. Ϲeʟʟαιʒ .ı. Μαoιʟ-
eċʟαιnn mαc Uιʟʟιαm, ocup αp Μαc ɴ’Ɗuṫʒαιʟʟ .ı.
Ɗonncʜαɗ mαc Ϲoιppɗʜeʟбαιʒ α cónpαбαʟ ɗιṫʟíɴιṫ. Ιp
αmʟαιɗ popcαomnαʒαp pιn, .ı. ɗuʟ ɗóιṫ pop ιnɴpαιʒeɗ
αp pʟιcʜτ Ɗonncʜαɗα 1 Ϲʜeʟʟαιʒ, ocup cpeαċα ɗo
ʒαṫáιʟ ɗóιṫ, ocup pʟιcʜτ Ɗonncʜαɗα 1 Ϲʜeʟʟαιʒ coɴα
coιṁτιnóʟ ɗo бpeιṫ poppα. Ϲιṫ τpα αcʜτ po бpιppeṫ
poppα ιpιn Ιppepnαιʒ ɗo τṕιnnpαɗ. Ro ʒαбαṫ O Concʜoбαιp αnn, ocup po mαpбαɗ O Ϲeʟʟαιʒ ocup α mαc .ı.
Ϲαṫʒ. Ro mαpбαɗ Μαc Ɗuṫʒαιʟʟ αnn ɗno, ocup po
ʒαбαṫ α mαc .ı. αʟupɗαp, ocup po mαpбαɗ αnn
Conn cιτecʜ mαc Oeɗʜα mιc Ϭoʒαιn ʜ1 Concʜoбαιp; ocup nι ʜupupα α áιpeṁ ʒαcʜ αp ṫuιτ αnn
eɗιp ṁαpбαɗ ocup ʒαбáιʟ. Ιʟ ιmαɗ ecʜ ocup éιɗeṫ ocup
eppαṫ ɗo ṫéιn ɗιṫ ʒαn ατʒαṫáιʟ poppo. Μαʒ Oenʒupα
.ı. Ṕéʟιm αn enιʒ mαc Ααṫα mιc Αιpτ, ceɴɴ ɗαonnαcʜτα
pʟecʜτα Conαιʟʟ Ϲepnαιʒ, mopτuup epτ. Ϭmonn бuιṫe
mαc Ααṫα ɗo pιʒʜαɗ nα ιonαṫ. Ruʒnαιṫe mαc
Ϭιʒnecʜáιn ʜ1 Ɗomnαιʟʟ ɗo mαpбαɗ ʟα ʒαʟʟoιб αʒ Ɗún
Ɗeʟʒαιn, ocup é páṕé .h. Neιʟʟ .ı. Conn ṁαc Cuιnn.
Μαʒ Μʜαṫʒαmnα .ı. Remαnn mαc ʒʟαιpnι ɗʜéc. O
Ϲαṫʜán .ı. Ϲomápp mαc Ααṫne ɗʜéc. Μαoʟpuαnαιɗ
mαc Copmαιc Μιc Ɗιαpmαɗα ɗʜéc ιn ʜoc αnno.

Ι̇cττ. Ϭnαιp pop Ϲeɗαoιn; ɗá ṫʟιαɗαιn αp pιcʜιτ αp .u.
ceɗ αp mιʟe αιp ιn Ϲιʒepnα. Coʒαɗ mórp αp neιpʒe α
pαnn ιαpṫαpαcʜ nα ʜϬoppα αn ταn pιn eτιp ċιneṫ nα
ʒϹpιoρɗαιʒ, .ı. Róṁánαιʒ ocup Ϭɗáιʟʟιʒ ocup Ααʟmáιnnιʒ
ocup Ѕpαιnnιʒ ocup Ѕαxpαnαιʒ ɗén pαnn ocup ɗén
comαιpʟe, ιnαʒαιɗ pí Ϝpαnc α αonup αcʜτ Ααʟбαnαιʒ
αṁáιn ι pαnn pí Ϝpαnc, ocup mopán cαṫ ocup écʜτ ɗo
ιomʟuαɗ eτoppα; ocup ιp αmʟαιṫ puαpιomαp o ʟucʜτ

---

1 *Conn Ciṫech*; i.e. "Conn the left-
handed."
2 *Broke out.* The words of the text,

αp neιpʒe, lit. signify "after arising."
3 *Saxons*; i.e., the English.

thousand, five hundred, and twenty-one years. A great victory was gained in Tir-Maine-mic-Echach over O'Con-chobhair Ruadh, i.e. Tadhg Buidhe son of Cathal Ruadh, and over O'Cellaigh, i.e. Maelechlainn son of William, and over Mac Dubhgaill, i.e. Donnchadh son of Toirdhelbhach, the constable of both. The way it happened was thus, viz.; they went on an expedition against the descendants of Donnchadh O'Cellaigh, and seized preys; and the descendants of Donnchadh O'Cellaigh, with their muster, came up with them. They were defeated, moreover, in the Iffernagh exactly. O'Conchobhair was taken prisoner there, and O'Cellaigh and his son, i.e. Tadhg, were slain. Mac Dubhgaill was slain there also, and his son, i.e. Alexander, was taken prisoner; and Conn Citech,[1] the son of Aedh, son of Eoghan O'Conchobhair, was slain there. And it is not easy to enumerate all that fell there either by killing or capturing. A great quantity of horses, clothes, and battle dresses was taken from them, without any reprisal being made therefor. Mag Aenghusa, i.e. Felim-an-enigh, son of Aedh, son of Art, head of humanity of the race of Conall Cernach, mortuus est. Edmond Buidhe, the son of Aedh, was inaugurated in his place. Rughraidhe, son of Egnechán O'Domhnaill, was slain by Foreigners at Dun-Delgan, whilst he was in the company of O'Neill, i.e. Conn, the son of Conn. Mac Math-ghamhna, i.e. Redmond, son of Glaisne, died. O'Catháin, i.e. Thomas, son of Aibhne, died. Maelruanaidh, son of Cormac Mac Diarmada, died in hoc anno.

The kalends of January on Wednesday; the age of the Lord one thousand, five hundred, and twenty-two years. A great war broke out[2] in the western part of Europe, amongst the Christian races, viz., the Romans, Italians, Germans, Spaniards, and Saxons,[3] were of one part and counsel, against the king of France singly, except that the men of Alba alone were on the side of the king of France; and many battles and exploits took place between

ľʒαoıʟcı ľʒél ocuľ ċuαľcαıꝝċı cuαn ʒuľ αꞃ αʒ Fľαnc-
αċαıꝝ ꝺo ꝝí ꝝúαıꝺ αn ċoʒαıꝺ ľın αnαʒαıꝺ nα nuıle ċınél.
Coʒαꝺ αꝝꝝαıl αľ neıľʒe α nEľınn ꝼéın αn ꝝlıαꝺαın ľın,
ocuľ ʒo háıľıꝝċe ıľın cuαıľceľc .ı. ecıľ .h. ꞁeıll ocuľ
.h. ꝺomnαıll; ocuľ mαc Uıllıαm ċlαınnı Rıcαıľꝺ ocuľ
Ʒαıll ocuľ Ʒαıꝺel Chonnαċc, ocuľ ľíol mꝝľıαın ocuľ
ľíl ʒCeľꝝαıll αľ ʒcenʒαl ľıľ .h. ꞁeıll ꝺoċum ın ċoʒαıꝺ
ľın. O ꞁeıll ꝺo ċeαċc ľluαʒ móľ ʒo mαıċıꝝ Ulαꝝ,
ocuľ ľeċc Cclbαnαċ ocuľ móľán ꝺo ʒαlloıꝝ Mıꝝe,
ocuľ ʒαllóʒlαeċ ıαľlα Cılle ꝺαľα α cıľ Chonαıll,
ocuľ cαıľlén ꝝeoıl Ccα Senαıʒ ꝺo ʒαꝝαıl ꝺó, [ocuľ] bun
Ꝺľoꝝαoıľı ocuľ ꝝél Leıċıı ꝺo loľcuꝺ, ocuľ ımċeaċc
ľlán ꝺon ċuľ ľın; ocuľ ceαċc ľlúαʒ móľ ʒo ʒαľ nα
ꝝıαıꝝ ľın ꝺoľıꝝıľ α cíľ Chonαıll, ocuľ bľeıċ αľ cľeıċ
α Cınn mαʒαıľ, ocuľ α lán ꝺon cíľ ꝺo mıllec. O
Ꝺomnαıll ocuľ Mαʒnuľ .h. Ꝺomnαıll ꝺo cľuınnıuʒαꝺ
ľlúαıʒ móıľ αn αen áıc, ocuľ α nꝺul α cíľ Eoʒαın, ocuľ
cľeαċα moľα ocuľ mαľꝝċα ꝺo ꝺenum ꝝoıꝝ. O ꞁeıll
ꝺo cľuınnıuʒαꝺ ľlúαıʒ móıľ αn αoın ıonαꝺ, ocuľ mαc
Uıllıαm clαınne Rıcαıľꝺ .ı. Rıcαľꝺ mαc Uılleʒ mıc
Uıllıʒ mıc Uıllıʒ αn ꝼıonα, ocuľ Ʒoıll ocuľ Ʒαoıꝺel
Connαċc, ocuľ O Ceľꝝuıll ocuľ clαnn hı ꝝľıαın ꝺo
cľuınnıuʒαꝺ ınα comꝝáıl; ocuľ ľo ʒeαllαꝺαľ α ʒcoınne
α ċelı α cíľ Chonαıll; ocuľ cánıc αn ľluαʒ Connαċc-
αċ ľın ʒo 8lıʒeċ, ocuľ cánıc O ꞁeıll ʒo cınél Móáın
ocuľ ľeċc Cclbαnαċ αıʒe ľá mαc Mıc Ꝺhomnαıll, .ı.
Ccluľcαľ, ocuľ ľá. móľαn ꝺo ʒαlloıꝝ Mıꝝe ocuľ ꝺo
ʒαllóʒlαeċαıꝝ Lαıʒneċα. Ꝺαlα hı Ꝺomnαıll ocuľ
ċınel Conαıll, o nαċ ľαbαꝺαľ comcľom ꝺαoıneꝺ ľe
ceċcαľ ꝺon ꝺα cľlúαıʒ ľın, ıľľí comαıľle ꝺo ľınneꝺαľ
ınnľoıʒeꝺ oıꝺċe ꝺo ċαbαıľc αľ .h. ꞁeıll; ocuľ ꝺo
ľıʒneꝺαľ coıľıʒe ꝺα mαľcľlúαʒ mαılle ľe nα ʒcóıľıꝝċıꝝ.
Ocuľ ꝺo ꝝı O ꞁeıll α bꝼαľLonʒľoľc αʒ Cnoc αn ꝝoꝝα,

---

them; and as we learned from the distributors of news, and the frequenters of harbours, the French were victorious in that war against all the races. A terrible war broke out[1] in Erinn itself this year, and particularly in the North, i.e. between O'Neill and O'Domhnaill; and Mac William of Clann-Rickard, and the Foreigners and Gaeidhel of Connacht, and the Sil-Briain, and Sil-Cerbhaill, joined with O'Neill towards that war. O'Neill went into Tir-Conaill in great force, with the chieftains of Uladh, and an expeditionary force from Alba, and a great number of the Foreigners of Midhe, and of the Earl of Cill-dara's gallowglasses; and he took the castle of Bél-atha-Senaigh, [and] burned Bun-Drobhaise and Bél-leci; and he departed safely on that occasion. And he went again to Tir-Conaill, soon after that, with a large army, and caught a prey in Cenn-Maghair, and destroyed a great part of the country. O'Domhnaill, and Maghnus O'Domhnaill, mustered a large host to one place; and they went into Tir-Eoghain, and great depredations and homicides were committed by them. O'Neill assembled a large army to one place; and Mac William of Clann-Rickard, i.e. Rickard, the son of Ulick, son of Ulick, son of Ulick-an-fhiona,[2] and the Foreigners and Gaeidhel of Connacht, and O'Cerbhaill, and the descendants of O'Briain, came to join his muster; and they promised to meet one another in Tir-Conaill. And this Connacht army came to Sligech; and O'Neill came to Cenel-Móain, having an expeditionary force of Albanachs, along with the son of Mac Domhnaill, i.e. Alexander, and a great number of the Foreigners of Midhe, and of the Lagenian gallowglasses. As regards O'Domhnaill and the Cenel-Conaill, since they had not as many men as either of these two armies, the resolution they adopted[3] was to make a night attack on O'Neill; and they made infantry of their cavalry, along with their battalions. And O'Neill was encamped at Cnoc-an-Bhobha; and the Conallachs with one accord

ocuṛ ṗo ᵮinṛαiᵹeᴅαṛ Conαllαᵹ α hén comαiṗle iαᴅ ᵹαn
ċonᵹnum coiᵹcṛiċ αcα; ocuṛ ᴅo ḃṛiṡeᴅαṛ αṛ O Néill
αn oiᴅċe ṛin, ocuṛ ṗo mαṛḃαᴅ móṛαn ᴅá muinnᴛeṛ
eᴛiṛ cclbαnchαiḃ ocuṛ Eṗennchαiḃ, ocuṛ ᵹo háiṗiᵹéi
moṛαn ᴅo ᵹαlloiḃ Miᴅe ocuṛ ᴅo ᵹαllóᵹlαeċαiḃ
Lαiᵹnech, ocuṛ ᴅo ċlαinn ᴛ8híᴛhiᵹ; ocuṛ O Neill
ᴅimċechᴛ α ᵹcoiṛ ṁαᴅmα iαṛ nᴅiᴛuᵹαᴅ α ṁuinnᴛiṛe;
ocuṛ O ᴅomnαill ᴅṗilleᴅ iαṗ mḃúαiᴅ ᵹcoṛcαṗ mαille
ṗe hiomαᴅ éᴅαlαiḃ ech ocuṛ éiᴅiᵹ ocuṛ αiṗm; ocuṛ ᵹαn
comnαiᴅe ᴅo ᴅenum ᴅoiḃ no ᵹuṛ ᵹαḃαᴅαṛ ṗoṛlonᵹṗoṛᴛ
αᵹ ḃeinn Ᵹhulbαin; ocuṛ αn ᴅá mαc Uilliαm, ocuṛ αn
ᴅá O Conchobαiṛ, ocuṛ Mαc ᴅiαṗmαᴅα, ocuṛ O Ceṗ-
ḃαill ocuṛ clαnn hi ḃhṛíαin ᴅo ḃeiᴛ ṗluαᵹ ṗo ṁóṗ
αᴛimċell ᴛ8hliᵹiᵹ, ocuṛ mαṛ ṗuαṗαᴅαṛ ᴅeṗḃ ṛᵹélα αn
ṁαᴅmα ṛin ᴅo ċαḃαiṗᴛ αṛ O Néill, ᵹeṛ ṁóṗ culαᴅ
ocuṛ ᴅαoine αmḃói αnn, ṗo ᵶnᴛóᴅαṛ ᴛαṗ α nαiṗ ᴅíα
ᴛíṗiḃ; ocuṛ ní ṛeṗṛ ᴅO ᴅomnαill α nimᴛechᴛ no ᵹon-
ᴅeαċαᴅαṛ ᴛαṛ Coiṗṗṗliαḃ; ocuṛ ṗo ᴛuṗnαᴅ αn ċomḃáiḃ
ċoᵹαiᴅ ṛin ᴅon ᴅul ṛin. Rúᵹṛαiḃe mαc Ᵹoṗṗṗαᴅα mic
ccoᴅα ᵹαllᴅα, ocuṛ mαc ṁéᵹ Cellαiᵹ nα ḃṗeiṗṗne, ᴅo
mαṗḃαᴅ lé ṗluαᵹ hi Néill α nuchᴛ 8ᵹαiṗḃe iᴅóṗ iᴅ
ᵮṗαoiċ. Mαc 8uiḃne Ṫhíṗe ḃóᵹuine, .i. ḃṗíαn αn
ċoḃlαiᵹ, ocuṛ ᴅiαṗmαiᴅ mαc Ṫαiᴅᵹ cαim hi Chleiṗiᵹ,
ocuṛ ccoᴅ mαc Mic in ḃhαiṗᴅ, ocuṛ α lán eli ṗóṛ ᴅo
ṁαṗḃαᴅ α ᵹcαiṗlén ḃeoil αᴅα 8enαiᵹ le ṗlúαᵹ hi Néill.
ᴅomnαll mαc ᴅonnchαᴅα i Ruαiṗc, ṛói ḃuine uαṛṛαil
nα ᴅuᴛhαiᴅ ṛéin, ᴅo mαṗḃαᴅ le clαinn Ṗeilim hi
Ruαiṗc. ᴅomnαll mαc 8eαm hi Chαᴅáin, ṛαoṗmαc-
αom α ċineᴅ ṛéin ocuṛ ṛeṗ einiᵹ ċoiᴛċinn ᴅeicṛiḃ ocuṛ
ᴅαoiṗ elαḃnα, ᴅo mαṗḃαᴅ αn ḃliαᴅαin ṛ. Mαᵹ Coṗ-
mán .i. Mαoileċlαinn, αn ᴛé ᴅoḃ ṛeṗṗ ᴛuicṛi ocuṛ ᴛech

---

1 *Foreign.* coiᵹcṛiċ, *rectè* co-
cṛich, properly means "border," being
comp. of co (coṁ)=Lat. *con, com,*
and cṛich, *finis;* but it is also generally used to signify "foreign," "foreigner," and "stranger."

2 *Aedh Gallda;* i.e. "Aedh (or
Hugh) the Anglicised [O'Donnell]."
3 *In front.* α nuchᴛ; lit. "in the
breast." Instead of α nuchᴛ, the
Four Masters say ṗe ᴛαoḃ, "by the
side."

attacked them, without foreign[1] assistance ; and they defeated O'Neill that night; and a great number of his people were slain, both of the men of Alba and Eriun, and especially several of the Foreigners of Midhe, and of the Lagenian gallowglasses, and the Clann-Sithigh. And O'Neill retreated in disarray, after the destruction of his people, whilst O'Domhnaill returned triumphant, with a great quantity of spoils, horses, mail-armour, and weapons. And they (*O'Neill's forces*) rested not until they encamped at Benn-Gulbain. And the two Mac Williams, and the two O'Conchobhairs, and Mac Diarmada, and O'Cerbhaill, and the descendants of O'Briain, were around Sligech with a large army ; and when they received certain intelligence that this defeat had been given to O'Neill, though great the number of guards and men that were there, they turned back to their homes ; and O'Domhnaill did not know of their departure until they had crossed Corr-sliabh ; and that military alliance was humbled on that occasion. Rughraidhe, son of Godfrey, son of Aedh Gallda,[2] and the son of Mac Cellaigh of the Breifne, were killed by O'Neill's army in front[3] of Sgairbh-indsi-in-fraich.[4] Mac Suibhne of Tir-Boghaine, i.e. Brian-an-chobhlaigh,[5] and Diarmaid, the son of Tadhg Cam O'Cleirigh, and Aedh, son of Mac-an-bhaird, and many more besides, were slain in the castle of Bel-atha-Senaigh by O'Neill's army. Domhnall, the son of Donnchadh[6] O'Ruairc, a most excellent gentleman in his own country, was killed by the sons of Felim O'Ruairc. Domhnall, son of John O'Catháin, the noblest youth of his own tribe, and a man of general bounty towards poets and men of learning, was slain this year. Mag Corman, i.e. Maelechlainn, the best man for intelligence, and

---

[4] *Sgairbh-indsi-in-fraich.* "The scariff (or shallow ford) of the island of the heath." Not identified.

[5] *Brian-an-chobhlaigh.* "Brian of

the cobhlach (or fleet)." Ḃꞃian a ċoḃl, MS.

[6] *Donnchadh.* The Four Masters say "Domhnall."

naoıoheo oon aoṛ ṣṛáõa, ohéc ın hoc anno. Domnall
cleıṛech mac Seaın mıc Cuõne hı Chathaın, .ı. cenn
eınıʒ ocuṛ enʒnuma ın tuaıṛcıṛt a teıṛo ocuṛ a
tabaṛtuṛ, ocuṛ a tuaṛuṛcbáıl, oo ṁaṛbao la claınn
ʒılla ṗháoṛaıc mıc Mhaʒnuṛa hı Chatáın .ı. a
altṛonna ocuṛ a čaıṛoıṛṛıõe Cṛıoṛt. Ruʒṛaıõe
mac Cooa óıʒ mıc Cooa ṛuaıõ Mhéʒ Mhatʒamna
[ohec] ın hoc anno.

Ictt. Enáıṛ ṛoṛ õaṛoaoın. Tṛı blıaona ṛıčet aṛ .u.
ceo aṛ mıle aıṛ ın Tıʒeṛna. Doıneno ṁóṛ a túṛ na
blıaona ṛın, ocuṛ coʒao áõbaıl aṛ ṛeõ na hEoṛṛa aṛ
muıṛ ocuṛ aṛ tíṛ, ocuṛ ʒo háıṛıʒte etıṛ O Neıll ocuṛ
O n'Oomnaıll, ocuṛ O Doṁnaıll oo õeıt aṛ eoh an
eṛṛaıʒ ṛın a bṛoṛlonʒṛoṛt a nʒlıonn ṛınne, ocuṛ
Maʒnuṛ O Domnaıll oo õul ʒo hCClbaın, ocuṛ tocht
ṛlan ıaṛ cṛıočnuʒao a čuaṛta. O Domnaıll oo õul
ṛá õó a tıṛ Eoʒaın an Blıaoaın ṛın, ocuṛ tocht ṛlán
ıaṛ mılleõ ṁoṛáın, ocuṛ ṛıʒ oo õenum õóıõ oeṛeõ
blıaona, ocuṛ ʒan écht oıṛṛoeṛc oo õenum etoṛṛa
acht maṛ ṛın. O Catáın, .ı. Donnchao mac Seaın hı
Chathaın, an tí buõ mó clú eınıʒ ocuṛ uaıṛle oá
čıneoh ṛeın a comaımṛıṛ ṛıṛ ohéc, ocuṛ oá čıʒeṛna
oo ʒaıṛm anaʒhaıo a čélı na ıonao, .ı. Sean mac
Tomáıṛ hı Chathaın ocuṛ ʒoṛṛṛaıõ mac ʒoṛṛṛaõa hı
Chathaın, ocuṛ íao aṛaon a coʒao ocuṛ a nımṛeṛṛaın,
ocuṛ aʒ mılleo an tíṛe aṛ ʒach taoõ ṛan tıʒeṛnuṛ.
Mac hı Bṛıaın .ı. Taõʒ mac Toıṛṛohelbaıʒ, ṛeṛ a
aoṛṛa oob ṛeṛṛ enech ocuṛ uaıṛle ocuṛ ṛéṛ ṁó eʒla
a eṛcaṛao, ocuṛ oob ṛeṛṛ oo čeno oáṁ ocuṛ oeoṛaıõ,
ocuṛ ıṛ luʒa oo õıultṛeo ṛe oṛeıč n'ouıne um ní õá
nıaṛṛṛeo, oo maṛbao ʒo míṛatmaṛ oén uṛchoṛ oo
ʒunna leıṛın nʒıuıṛoíṛ .ı. Ṗıaṛṛuṛ ṛuao Buıtleṛ,

---

1 *Learned.* aoṛ ʒıaõa, i.e. persons eminent for learning and arts.
2 *Domhnall Clerech.* Domhnall
the Cleric. This is apparently a repetition of the second entry preceding. The Four Masters state that
Domhnall Clerech was slain by the
"Ruta," i.e. by the Mac Quillans of
the Route, a well-known district in
the county Antrim.

keeping a house of hospitality for the learned,[1] died in hoc anno. Domhnall Clerech,[2] son of John, son of Aibhne O'Catháin, i.e. the head of the hospitality and valour of the North in character, generosity, and reputation, was killed by the sons of Gilla-Patraic, son of Maghnus O'Catháin, i.e. his own fosterers and gossips. Rughraidhe, son of Aedh Og, son of Aedh Ruadh Mac Mathghamhna, [died] in hoc anno.

The kalends of January on Thursday ; the age of the Lord one thousand, five hundred, and twenty-three years. Great inclemency of weather in the beginning of this year, and a terrible war throughout Europe on sea and on land, and especially between O'Neill and O'Domhnaill ; and O'Domhnaill was during that spring encamped in Glenn-finne; and Maghnus O'Domhnaill went to Alba, and returned safely after terminating his visit. O'Domhnaill went twice this year into Tir-Eoghain, and returned safely after destroying much ; and peace was concluded by them at the end of the year;[3] and no great deed was committed between them except in that way. O'Catháin, i.e. Donnchadh, son of John O'Catháin, the person of greatest fame for hospitality and nobility of his own sept, in his time, died; and two lords were proclaimed in opposition to each other, in his place, viz., John the son of Thomas O'Catháin, and Godfrey, son of Godfrey O'Catháin ; and they were both at war and contention, and destroying the country on all sides, regarding the sovereignty. The son of O'Briain, i.e. Tadhg, son of Toirdhelbhach, the man of his age who was the best for hospitality and nobility, the most feared by his enemies, and the best protector of the learned and destitute, and who least would refuse a man anything that he would ask, was unluckily killed with one shot of a gun by the Justiciary, i.e. Piers

---

[3] *At the end of the year.* ɔeꞃeɔ bliaᴆona, MS. The Four Masters | more correctly say a nᴆeiꞃeɔ na bliaᴆona.

map ir ᵹnaŏ rói ᴅḟaᵹail anarc. Mac Ᵹilla Eain,
.ı. laċluinn mór mac Eċainn, ᴅo ṁaꞃbaŏ a bḟioll
leiꞃın pꞃoıꞃe mac Mıc Aılín a mbaıle ꞃíᵹ Alban ın
hoc anno. Máᵹ Ϲhıᵹeꞃnaın, .ı. Ᵽeꞃᵹal mac Ᵹilla
ıoꞃꞃa óıᵹ, mıc Ᵹilla Iꞃa mıc Ḃꞃıaın, ᴅux Ϲhellaıᵹ
ᵭhúnċaᴅa, ꞃeꞃ ᴅéꞃceċ ᴅaonnaċᴛaċ, ᴅḟaᵹail ḃáıꞃ
ına ḃaıle ꞃéın, ocur a ᴅeꞃbꞃaᴛhaıꞃ ᴅo ᵹaḃaıl a ıonaŏ
ŏá éıꞃ. Eoᵹan, mac Ᵽéŏlım mıc ᵭhonnċaᴅa óıᵹ mıc
Ϲhıᵹeꞃnaın óıᵹ hı Ruaıꞃc, ᴅo ḃáᴛhaᴅ aꞃ loċ Ᵹlenᴅa
éᴅa ın hoc anno. Roꞃꞃa, mac Ruaıᴅꞃı mıc Ḃꞃıaın mıc
Ᵽhélım mhéᵹ Uıᴅıꞃ, ᴅḟaᵹail ḃáıꞃ a mbꞃaıᵹᴅenuꞃ aᵹ an
ᵹcomaꞃba mháᵹ Uıᴅıꞃ, .ı. Cuconnaċᴛ. Aoŏ mac Aıꞃᴛ
hı Ϲhuaᴛhaıl, an mac a aoıꞃı buŏ mó clú enıᵹ ocur
uaıꞃle ᴅa ḟıne ꞃéın, ᴅo maꞃbaᴅ le Ḃꞃannaċaıb an
blıaᴅaın ꞃın. Mac Conmıŏe, .ı. Maoıleċlaınn mac
Ꞃeaın mıc Ꞃolaım, ollam hı Neıll, moꞃᴛuuꞃ erᴛ.
Ꞃloıᵹeaŏ aŏḃaıl la hıaꞃla Cılle ᴅaꞃa, .ı. Ᵹeꞃoıᴅ óᵹ
mac Ᵹeꞃóıᴅ, ocur la Ᵹalloıb Mıŏe, ocur la .h. Neıll,
.ı. Conn mac Cuınn mıc Enꞃı mıc Eoᵹaın, aꞃ .h. Con-
ċhobaıꞃ ꞃhaılᵹe ocur aꞃ Conall O Moꞃŏa, ocur aꞃ
Ᵹhaoıᴅelaıŏ laıᵹen. Na ᵹaıᴅel ꞃın uıle ᴅanmaın aꞃ
ꞃíᵹ hı Neıll eᴛoꞃꞃa ocur anᴛ ıaꞃla, ᴛaꞃeıꞃ áꞃnaıŏ
na nᵹaoıᴅel ꞃın ᴅo chuꞃ aꞃ laım hı Neıll, ocur O
Neıll ᴅo ċenᵹal na ꞃíŏe; ocur ᵹéıll ocur bꞃaıᵹᴅe
na nᵹaoıᴅel ꞃın ᴅḟaᵹaıl ᴅO Neıll na uꞃláıṁ, a nᵹeall
ꞃe ᵹach aᵹꞃa ᴅa noınᵹnaŏ anᴛ ıaꞃla oꞃꞃa ᴅo ṁolaŏ
hı Neıll, ocur a ꞃᵹaꞃᴛhaın ꞃeıŏ ꞃíᴛech ꞃe ċélı an ᴛan
ꞃın. O Máılle, .ı. Coꞃmac mac Eoᵹaın hı Mhaılle,
ꞃéıċem coıᴛċenᴅ enıᵹ ocur uaıꞃle ıaꞃᴛhaıꞃ Connaċᴛ,
moꞃᴛuuꞃ erᴛ. ᵭomnall mac Ϲomáıꞃ hı Maılle ᴅo
ᵹaḃáıl a ıonaŏ. Inᴅꞃoıᵹeᴅ le. h. nᵭomñaıll, ᵹo

---

¹ *Hero.* The orig. of this clause
stands in the MS. maꞃ ıꞃ ᵹnaŏ ꞃóı
ᴅḟaᵹ anaꞃc. It seems to be in the
nature of a proverb, which the Editor
has not met before, and of which he can
only venture a conjectural translation.

² *Brannachs.* The Byrnes, or
O'Byrnes, of Wicklow.

³ *O'Neill's peace;* i.e. the conditions
prescribed in the award, or decision, of
O'Neill.

Ruadh Butler, for it is usual to find an eminent man a hero.[1] Mac Gille-Eain, i.e. Lochlainn Mór, son of Echann, was killed in treachery by the knight, the son of Mac Ailin, in the king of Alba's town, in hoc anno. Mac Tighernain, i.e. Ferghal, son of Gilla-Isa Og, son of Gilla-Isa, son of Brian, dux of Tellach-Dunchadha, a charitable, humane man, died in his own town; and his brother assumed his place after him. Eoghan, son of Fedhlim, son of Donnchadh Og, son of Tighernan Og O'Ruairc, was drowned in the lake of Glenn-éda in hoc anno. Rossa, son of Ruaidhri, son of Brian, son of Felim Mag Uidhir, died whilst imprisoned by the comarb Mag Uidhir, i.e. Cuchonnacht. Aedh, son of Art O'Tuathail, the young man of his age who, of his own sept, was the most celebrated for hospitality and nobility, was slain by Brannachs[2] this year. Mac Conmidhe, i.e. Maelechlainn, son of John, son of Solomon, O'Neill's ollamh, mortuus est. A prodigious hosting by the Earl of Cill-dara, i.e. Garrett Og, the son of Garrett, and by the Foreigners of Midhe, and by O'Neill, i.e. Conn the son of Conn, son of Henry, son of Eoghan, against O'Conchobhair Failghe, and against Conall O'Mordha, and the Gaeidhel of Laighen. All these Gaeidhel abided by O'Neill's peace[3] between them and the Earl, after the interests of these Gaeidhel had been placed in O'Neill's hands; and O'Neill concluded the peace; and the pledges and hostages of these Gaeidhel were received by O'Neill into his power, as a guarantee for their granting every demand which the earl might advance through O'Neill's arbitration. And they then separated from each other in a quiet, peaceful manner. O'Maille, i.e. Cormac, son of Eoghan O'Maille, general supporter of the hospitality and nobility of the west of Connacht, mortuus est. Domhnall, son of Thomas O'Maille, assumed his place. An expedition by O'Domhnaill, with the accord of his

ʒcomαoɴτα ćíρe ocuρ ćoιʒcριce, ʒo Ḃρeιρρɴe hι Ruαιρc.
Ʒαch ɴech ꝛob ιɴɴρʟuαʒαꝛ ꝛá ραιꞃ ιριɴ ćíρ αρ α ćιɴɴ
ꝛo ćuαꝛαρ ʟe ɴα ʒcρeαchαιb α ɴꝛιαmραιꞃ ocuρ α
ɴιmmꝛoρchαιb ꝛá ɴιmćumꝛαch. O 'Domɴαιll ꝛιm-
ćeαchꞇ αɴ ćíρe ʒo huιlιꞃe, co ɴáρ ṗαʒuιꞃ ɴí αρ bιꞇ
ʒαɴ mιlleꝛ ꝛá bαιlꞇιꞃ ocuρ ꝛá hαρꞃoɴɴαιꞃ ꝛoɴ ꝛul ριɴ.

Ⱪll. Θɴáιρ ρoρ Ⱥιɴe, ocuρ bιρρeχ ρuιρρe; ceιꞇρι
blιαꝛɴα .χχ. αρ .u. ceꝛ αρ mιle αιρ ιɴ Tιʒeρɴα. 'Doιɴeɴꝛ
ṁóρ ocuρ áρ ρoρ ρbρéιꞃ α ꞇúρ ɴα blιαꝛɴu. 'Dιρ mαc
hι 'Dhomɴαιll, .ι. Nιαll ʒαρb ocuρ Θoʒαɴ, ꝛo ćeɴʒαl
combáχα ρe ćelι ιɴαʒhαιꝛ hι 'Dhomɴαιll, ocuρ α mbeꞇ
ꞇαmαll mαρ ριɴ αʒ buαιꞃρeꝛ αɴ ćíρe, ɴo ʒuρ cuιρeꝛ
ρuꞇhα ρeιɴ ꝛul ιɴαʒαιꝛ α ćelι, ocuρ Θoʒαɴ ꝛo ξαbáιl
ꞃαιle Neιll, .ι. cραɴɴóʒ Loċ ꞃeċhαꝛ, ocuρ hí αρ [α]
ιɴchαιb ρρéιɴ, ocuρ Nιαll ꝛρáʒbáιl αɴ ćíρe; ocuρ
ιɴɴραιξeꝛ ραꝛα ꝛo ćαbαιρꞇ αρ αɴ mbαιle ꞃó, ocuρ celʒ
ꝛo ꞃéɴum α ʒcomꞃoʒuρ ꝛó. Θoʒαɴ ꝛραʒαιl [α] ρeρρα
ριɴ, ocuρ Nιαll ꝛιɴɴροιʒeꝛ ꞃó; ocuρ α ɴꝛul ρá ćelι
αɴɴριɴ, ocuρ Θoʒαɴ ꝛo mαρbαꝛ ꝛoɴ láċhαιρ ριɴ, ocuρ
Nιαll ꝛo loꞇ, ocuρ α ꞃul ꝛhéc ꝛoɴ loꞇ ριɴ ρá ćeɴꝛ
αιmριρe ʒιρριe ɴα ꞃιαιꞃ ριɴ; ocuρ ɴι huρuρα α ραꞇα
ʒo ꞇáɴιc luchꞇ α ɴαoρα ꝛo ćeɴιul ʒConαιll buꞃ mo
ꝛéchꞇαιb ιɴα αɴ ꝛιαρ ριɴ. Ⱥɴ ceꝛ ṁí ꝛo ꞇṗαmραꝛ
ꝛo ριξɴeꝛ ɴα mαρbꞇα ριɴ. Sémuρ mαc Ḃριαιɴ uαιɴe
hι Ʒhαllćuꞃαιρ, αꞃbuρ coṁoρbα ɴα Cαιρρʒe, ꝛhec ιɴ
hoc αɴɴo. 'Dιαρmαιꝛ mαc αɴ Ʒιllα ꝛuιꞃ hι Ḃhρíαιɴ,
ρeρ α ćιʒeρρuιρ ρeιɴ ꝛob ρeρρ ɴα αιmριρ ꝛo ćeɴɴ ꝛáṁ
ocuρ ꝛeoραιꞃ, ocuρ ꝛo buꝛ mo muιρeρ ocuρ ꝛob ρíρ
áιꞃꞃle eɴech, ocuρ ꝛob ṗeρρ ꝛρeρ ρeιꞃιξꞇe cαραꝛ ocuρ
eρcαραꝛ, ocuρ ιρ mo ꝛo ραoιleꝛ ꝛαɴmαιɴ .ρe hιɴṁe α
ꞃuꞇhαιꞃe, ocuρ ιρ móꝛ ꝛo buꝛ compáɴαch coꞇćeɴꝛ ꝛoɴ
αoιρ eαlαꝛɴα, ꝛραʒhαιl ꞃαιρ oιʒꞇα ocuρ αιꞇριξe α

---

1 *Dark regions.* ιmmꝛoρchαιꞃ,
for ιmmꝛoρchαꝛαιꞃ, the more
correct form, and the dat. pl. of
ιmmꝛoρchαꝛ, a word comp. of the
intensive prefix ιm and ꝛoρchαꝛ,
or ꝛoρchαꞇu, a subst. derived from
the adjective ꝛoρchα = Eng. dark.

2 *The Carraig.* "The Rock." This
establishment would appear to have

country and neighbours, to Breifne-Ui-Ruairc. All who were fit to march of those that were in the country before him went with their preys into secret places, and dark regions,[1] to hide them. O'Domhnaill traversed all the country, so that he left nothing whatever of its towns and corn fields without destroying on this occasion.

The kalends of January on Friday, and a bissextile year; the age of the Lord one thousand, five hundred, and twenty-four years. Great inclemency of weather, and mortality of cattle, in the beginning of the year. O'Domhnaill's two sons. viz., Niall Garbh and Eoghan, made an alliance with each other against O'Domhnaill; and they were a while thus disturbing the country, until they themselves were induced to oppose one another; and Eoghan took Niall's town, i.e. the crannog of Loch-Bethadh, and it under his own protection. And Niall left the country; and he made a long expedition to attack the place, and lay in ambush in the neighbourhood. Eoghan obtained intelligence of this, and advanced against Niall; and they then encountered each other, and Eoghan was killed on the spot; and Niall was wounded, and he died of the wound in a short time after that; and it would not be easy to say that there came, of the Cenel-Conaill, any persons of their age who were greater losses than these two. The first month of summer these homicides were committed. James, son of Brian Uaine O'Gallchubhair, intended comarb of the Carraig,[2] died in hoc anno. Diarmaid, son of the Gilla-dubh O'Briain, the man of his means who was the best in his time towards the learned and destitute; who had the largest following, and the most truly prodigious hospitality; who was the best man for reconciling friends and enemies, and the most expected to live to enjoy the wealth of his inheritance, and who was in general the greatest companion of the

---

been in Donegal, where the sept of O'Gallaher was both numerous and influential; but it has not been iden-tified. There was a place called Carrig near the town of Donegal. See Four Mast., A.D. 1601.

mbaile mhég Ɗuɓɗa, ocuʃ bennacht laiʃ ɗocum nime.
Sloigeɗ lá .h. nƊomnaill a tiʃ Eogain, ɗaʃ loiʃc
ocuʃ ɗáʃ imthig in tíʃ, ocuʃ teacht ʃlán iaʃum.
Sloigeɗ leiʃin ngiuiʃɗíʃ, .i. Geʃóiɗ óg mac Geʃóiɗ
laʃla Chille ɗaʃa, ocuʃ leiʃ O Neill .i. Conn mac
Cuinn, a tiʃ Chonaill ɗoðum h1 Ɗomnaill a mí meɓóin
ʃógṁaiʃ, ocuʃ ʃlóigeɗ eli ag .h. Ɗomnaill na noiʃðill
ɗo coʃnum a cʃiðe ʃein, ocuʃ moʃan Ɑlbanach aʃ
teacht ðuige ʃón am ʃin, .i. clann Eoin Chaðánaig,
ocuʃ mac Ɗomnaill gallóglaeð, ocuʃ ɗaoine uaiʃle eli
aʃ Ɑlban. In giuʃɗíʃ ocuʃ .h. Néill ɗo gabáil ʃaʃʃ-
longʃuiʃt a poʃt na tʃi námaɗ, ocuʃ O Ɗomnaill co
na ʃlúaig ɗo ɓul go Ɗʃuim Ligen; ocuʃ geallaɗ
buailti ɗo ɓeith etoʃʃa aʃ na ṁáʃach. Magnuʃ .h.
Ɗomnaill ocuʃ Ɑlbanaig ɗo ɓul ɗo ðaitheɗ ʃlúaig
Ghall an oiɓðe ʃin, ocuʃ mac h1 Ɓʃuin ɗo ṁaʃbaɓ leó,
.i. an Calbach mac Ɓʃuin mic Thaiɓg, écht móʃ na
ɓúthaiɗ ʃein; ocuʃ cuinne tʃiðe ɗo ʃnaɓmaɓ etoʃʃa
aʃ na ṁáʃað, conɗeʃna an giúʃɗíʃ ʃiɓ eiɗiʃ .h. Néill
ocuʃ .h. Ɗomnaill, ocuʃ é ʃéin a ʃlanaibh etoʃʃa;
ocuʃ ɗo ʃígneɓ ʃiɓ ocuʃ caiʃɗeʃʃ Cʃiʃt maʃ an
ceɗna eiɗiʃ an ngiuʃɗíʃ ocuʃ .h. Ɗomnaill; ocuʃ iaʃ
bʃilleɗ ɗon giúʃɗíʃ ocuʃ ɗlla Néill ʃuaʃaɗaʃ Ɑoɓ
mac Neill mic Cuinn mic Ɑoɓa buiɓe, mic Ɓʃiain
ɓallaig h1 Neill, ʃlúag móʃ ag milleɗ tíʃe hEogain;
ocuʃ óɗ ðuala ʃiɓéin na ʃlúaga ʃin ele ɗo ɓeiɓ ðuige
ɗo cuiʃ a ðʃlúaig ʃein ʃoime lé na ðʃechaib ocuʃ lé na
néɗálaiɓ, ocuʃ ɗo an ʃéin a bʃaɗ na noiaiɓ aʃ begán
ɗaoineɓ, no go ʃug tʃom ant ʃluáig eli ʃaiʃ, ocuʃ guʃ
innʃaigeɗaʃ é iaʃ na ʃagail a mbaogal, guʃ maʃbaɓ
leó aʃ an lathaiʃ ʃin é; ocuʃ ní tánic ɗo ðinél Eogain
ʃe haimʃiʃ ʃaɗa a commaið a nuaiʃle ocuʃ a neinech,

---

1 Died an anointed, penitent death; lit. "obtained a death of unction and penitence."

2 O'Brain's son. mac h1 Ɓʃuin. Possibly the son of O'Brain (or O'Breen) of Brawny, a district now represented by the bar. of Brawny, co. Westmeath. The Four Masters say mac uí Ɓʃiain, son of O'Briain, or O'Brien.

learned, died an anointed, penitent death[1] in Baile-mic Dubhda; and a blessing be with him to Heaven. A hosting by O'Domhnaill into Tir-Eoghain, when he burned and overran the country ; and he afterwards returned safe. A hosting into Tir-Conaill against O'Domhnaill, by the Justiciary, i.e. Garrett Og, son of Garrett, Earl of Cill-dara, and by O'Neill, i.e. Conn, the son of Conn, in the middle month of harvest ; and another hosting by O'Domhnaill, to meet them, in defence of his own country. And a great number of Albanachs came to him about this time, viz., the sons of John Cathánach, and Mac Domhnaill Galloglaech, and other nobles out of Alba. The Justiciary and O'Neill fixed their camp at Port-na-tri-námhad ; and O'Domhnaill, with his army, went to Druim-Lighen ; and there was a promise of battle between them on the morrow. Maghnus O'Domhnaill and the Albanachs went to harass the army of the Foreigners that night, and O'Brain's son,[2] i.e. the Calbhach, son of Bran, son of Tadhg, a great loss in his own country, was slain by them. And a conference of peace was agreed to between them on the morrow, when the Justiciary made peace between O'Neill and O'Domhnaill, he himself being a guarantee between them ; and peace and gossipred were also concluded between the Justiciary and O'Domhnaill. And when the Justiciary and O'Neill were returning, they found Aedh, son of Niall, son of Conn, son of Aedh Buidhe, son of Brian Ballagh O'Neill, with a large host destroying Tir-Eoghain. And when he heard that these great armies were approaching him, he sent his own host on before him with his preys, and with their spoils ; and he himself remained a long way behind them, with a few men, until the entire mass of the other army overtook him. And they attacked him, on finding him exposed to danger ; and he was killed by them in that place. And there came not of the Cenel-Eoghain, during a long time, his equal in nobleness, in hospitality, and in reputation for defending his family,

ocuſ a ȝclú do čoſnum óſ cinn a člann ṁaicne, ocuſ iſ luȝa do léiȝ luiɖe ɖá eſcaiſdiɓ aiſ, ocuſ iſ ſeſſ do čoſſuin a cſíč ɖútħaid ſéin ȝuſ an uaiſ ſin. Oiſ dob eiſſiɖéin cinnliteſ a činiɓ ocuſ ſíſ čoſuſ na ſéli, ocuſ cend uiɖe an uiſd ſiliɓ, ocuſ ſélta tſoluſ tſoinenta tſlechta Oedħa buiɖe hi Neill; ocuſ ſóſſ ní ſoſbonn linn ſe ſaɖa naſ ſáȝuiɓ ſé an Eſinn duaiſliɓ ȝall ná ȝaoidel diȝbáil buɖ mó den aoiſ ealaɖna na ant Aoɖ ſin mac Néill mic Cuinn, et ſt. Mac Uiɖilín, .i. Coſmac, ocuſ mac Seain duiɓ Mic Domnaill, do lot ocuſ do ȝabáil a haičle an ṁaſɓča ſin le muinnteſ hi Néill. Inȝen hi Domnaill .i. ȝoſmlaič inȝen Aoɖa ſúaiɓ, ben Aoɖa mic Neill mic Cuinn, .i. ben einiȝ čoitčinn ocuſ clu tſaoȝalta do čoſnum, ocuſ do buɖ mó cumaoin aſ óſduiɓ ocuſ aſ aoiſ ealaɖna, do ɖul dħéc a mí ṁeɖóin eaſſaiȝ; ocuſ amail tucadaſ an lánſamuin ſin coimidechc daonnachta ocuſ clú ɖá čéli íſint ſaoȝal co haimſiſ a mbáiſ, ȝo dtucuid a naimanna coimidechc ȝlóiſe dá čéli a bſlaičiuſ Dé. Mac Donnchada tiſe hOilella, .i. Ruaiɖſi mac Tomaltaiȝ mic Bſiain, dſaȝail ɖáiſ, ocuſ coȝad móſ ediſ clainn n'Donnchada ſá čiȝeſnuſ an tiſe, ocuſ Mac Donnchada do ɖénum do Choſmac mac Taiɖȝ mic Bſiain. O Conchobaiſ Ciaſſaiɖ .i. Conchobaſ mac Conchobaiſ do ɖul aſ cſeich a ndútħaid Ealla, ocuſ Coſmac óȝ mac Coſmaic mic Tħaiɖc do bſeith ſaiſ, ocuſ bſiſſeɖ aſ .h. Conchobaiſ ocuſ é ſéin do lot ocuſ do ȝabáil ann; ocuſ Conchobaſ mac Diaſmada mic in ȝilla ɖuiɓ hi Bſiain do ṁaſbaɖ ann, ocuſ Diaſmaid mac Coſmaic hi Mháille, .i. échc móſ na ɖutħaid ſein, do maſbad ann ſóſ. Máȝ Caſſtħaiȝ ſiabach, .i. Domnall, mac Fínȝin mic

---

[1] *Greater loss.* The construction of this passage is peculiar. The chronicler meant to say that Aedh O'Neill left behind him no one of the Irish or English whose death could prove a greater calamity to men of science.

[2] *Couple.* lánſamuin. Usually written tanamuin. See Cormac's

A.D.
[1524.]

and one who less allowed his enemies to oppress him, and who better defended his own native territory up to that hour : for he was the leader of his sept, and the true fountain of generosity, and the head guardian of the poetic order, and the flashing light-star of the race of Aedh Buidhe O'Neill. And further, we don't think it superfluous to say that he did not leave in Erinn any one, of the nobles of the Foreigners or Gaeidhel, who was a greater loss[1] to the learned than this Aedh, son of Niall, son of Conn, et cetera. Mac Uibhilín, i.e. Cormac, and the son of John Dubh Mac Domhnaill, were wounded and taken prisoners, after this killing, by O'Neill's people. O'Domhnaill's daughter, i.e. Gormlaith, daughter of Aedh Ruadh, the wife of Aedh, son of Niall, son of Conn, i.e. a woman of general hospitality, and a protectress of worldly reputation, and the greatest benefactress to Orders and men of learning, died in the middle month of spring ; and as this couple[2] shared humanity and reputation with each other in the world, to the time of their decease, so may their souls share glory with each other in the kingdom of God. Mac Donnchadha of Tir-Oilella, i.e. Ruaidhri, son of Tomaltach, son of Brian, died ; and a great war *occurred* amongst the Clann-Donchadha regarding the sovereignty of the country ; and Cormac, son of Tadhg, son of Brian, was made Mac Donnchadha. O'Conchobhair Ciarraidhe, i.e. Conchobhar, son of Conchobhar, went on a foray into Duthaidh-Ealla ; and Cormac Og, son of Cormac, son of Tadhg,[3] overtook him, and O'Conchobhair was defeated, and he himself was wounded and taken prisoner there ; and Conchobhar, son of Diarmaid, son of the Gilla-dubh O'Briain, was slain there ; and Diarmaid, son of Cormac O'Maille, i.e. a great loss in his own country, was also slain there. Mac Carthaigh Riabhach, i.e. Domhnall, son of Finghin,

Glossary (O'Donovan's transl., ed. by Whitley Stokes, Calcutta, 1868, p. 102), where the word is explained lánṭhomaṁ, "full property of each other," from lán, "full," and ṭomaṁ, "property."

[3] *Tadhg* ; i.e. Tadhg (or Thaddeus) Mac Carthaigh.

Ɔιαρмαɔα, ɔo ɔul aр риoбαl cрeιčе a nᵹlιonn ḟleιрce,
ocuр бреιč co hαnoрɔαιᵹčι αιр αᵹ ра́ᵹба́ιl an ᵹlennα ;
ocuр é реιn ɔo ᵹαба́ιl, ocuр cuιɔ ɔа́ ᵹαιnιᵬ ɔo ᵬuαιn ɔe.
Mαᵹ Rαᵹnαιll .ι. Cαthαl óᵹ mαc Cαthαιl ɔo mαрбαɔ a
бḟιll aр раιčče a ᵬαιle реιn lα clαιnn ι Mhαoιlṁιαɔh-
αιᵹ. Mαc 8uιᵬne čιре Ꝺóᵹuιne, .ι. Ñιαll mαc Eoᵹαιn,
an cónрopul ɔoб реpр lа́ṁ ocuр ɔo бuɔ cрuαιᵬe coрcuр,
ocuр ɔoб реpр ᴛech aoιɔheɔ ocuр buᵬ mó muιреp ocuр
muιnᴛeр, ocuр ιр lια ᵬo бpιpᴛ ɔo бepnαᵬαιᵬ бαoᵹαιl
ɔа́ člαnnmαιcne реιn, ɔo ɔul ɔhéc ιαр nonᵹαɔ ocuр ιαр
nαιᴛpιᵹe nα cαιрlén réιn .ι. α Rαčαιn. ιnᵹen hι Ꝺhрíαιn .ι.
Móр ιnᵹen Ꞇoιррɔheαlбαιᵹ mιc Ꞇαιᵬᵹ hι Ꝺhрíαιn, ben
Ꝺonnchαɔα mιc Mhαčᵹαmnα hι Ꝺhрíαιn, ben ᴛιᵹe
αoιɔeɔ coιᴛčιnn, ɔo ɔul ɔhéc ιn hoc αnno. Ꝺιᵬιlιn
ιnᵹen рιɔιре ιn ᵹlennα, ben hι Conchoбαιр Chιαррαιᵬe,
ɔeιᵹᵬen ɔéрceαch ɔαonnαchᴛαch, ɔo ɔul ɔhéc. Ꞇoιрр-
ɔhelbαch mαc Ḟélιm buιᵬe hι Conchoбαιр ɔo mαрбαɔ
peр ɔolum lα Ꞇoιррɔhélбαch рuαᵬ, mαc Ꞇαιᵬᵹ ᵬuιᵬe
mιc Cαthαιl рuαιᵬ.

Ʞᴛᴛ. Enαιр роn Ꝺhomnαch ; u. ᵬlιαɔnα рιceᴛ aр .u.ceɔ
aр mιle αιр ιn Ꞇιᵹеpnα. h. Ꝺomnαιll .ι. Ꝺoᵬ mαc Oeɔhα
рuαιᵬ, ocuр .h. Neιll.ι. Conn mαc Cuιnn, ɔo ɔul ɔocum nα
comαιрle móιре a ᵹceɔɔ an ᵹιuрɔίр [α] ᴛúр nα blιαɔnα
рιn, ocuр éᵹnech ocuр ιomᴛαᵹрα ṁóр ɔo ᵬenum ɔóιᵬ ré
рoιle, ocuр рιlleᵬ ᵬóιᵬ αιmрéιɔ ɔαιmᵬeoιn a ᵹcαιɔoιᵬ
ᵹαll ocuр ᵹа́ιɔel vιᵬlínαιᵬ ; ocuр móра́n ɔo ṁιlleɔ
eᴛoррα ɔon čoᵹαɔ рιn. 8ιč ɔo ᵬenum ɔoιᵬ ιαррιn a
ᴛúр ро́ᵹṁαιр mαр αɔeрαɔ an ᵹιúрɔίр ocuр Mαᵹnuр O
Ꝺomnαιll ᵹnιm uαᴛṁαр ᵹраnnα ɔo ᵬenuṁ a nEрιnn
ιn ᵬlιαɔαιn рι .ι. eαрpuᵹ Leιᴛᵹlιnne ɔo mαрбαɔ a
meбαιl lα mαc an αбαιɔ Mαc Mhuрchαɔα, ocuр é

---

¹ *Cathal Ruadh.* " Cathal (or Charles) the Red [O'Conor]".

² *Council*; i.e. the Council at Dublin. This event is also entered under
the next year, which is the true date,
but in altered phraseology. A similar

repetition occurs in the Annals of the
Four Masters.

³ *Unreconciled.* αιmрeιɔ, lit.
" uneasy."

⁴ *Bishop of Lethghlinn.* Maurice
O'Doran. See the curious account of

son of Diarmaid, went on a predatory expedition to Glenn-
Fleisce; and he was overtaken in disarray when leaving
the glen, and he himself was taken prisoner, and some of
his people were captured from him. Mag Raghnaill, i.e.
Cathal·Og, son of Cathal, was slain in treachery on the
fair green of his own town, by the sons of O'Maelmhiadh-
aigh. Mac Suibhne of Tir-Boghuine, i.e. Niall, son of
Eoghan, the constable of best hand and·hardiest valour,
who was the best keeper of guest-houses, who had the most
troops and people, and who broke the greatest number
of "gaps of danger" for his own family, died after unction
and penitence, in his castle, i.e. in Rathain. O'Briain's
daughter, i.e. Mor, daughter of Toirdhelbhach,son of Tadhg
O'Briain, the wife of Donnchadh, son of Mathghamhain
O'Briain, a woman who kept a general house of hospitality,
died in hoc anno. Aibhilín, daughter of the Knight of the
Glenn, wife of O'Conchobhair Ciarraidhe, a good, chari-
table, humane woman, died. Toirdhelbhach, son of Felim
Buidhe O'Conchobhair, was killed per dolum by Toirdhel-
bhach Ruadh, son of Tadhg Buidhe, son of Cathal Ruadh.[1]

The kalends of January on Sunday; the age of the
Lord, one thousand, five hundred, and twenty-five years.
O'Domhnaill, i.e. Aedh son of Aedh Ruadh, and O'Neill,
i.e. Conn son of Conn, went to the great council[2] to meet
the Justiciary, [in] the beginning of this year; and they
made great complaints and accusations against each other;
and they returned unreconciled,[3] in despite of their friends
both Foreigners and Gaeidhel; and a great deal was
destroyed between them in this war. Peace was con-
cluded by them afterwards in the beginning of harvest,
according to the award of the Justiciary and Maghnus
O'Domhnaill. A horrid, ugly deed was committed in
Erinn this year, viz., the bishop of Lethghlinn[4] was killed
in treachery by Mac-an-abaid[5] Mac Murchadha, who was

---

this murder in Dowling's *Annals*
under the year 1522.
   [4] *Mac-an-abaid.* Lit. the "son of

the Abbot." Ware (*Annals*) calls him
"Maurice Cavanagh, Archdeacon of
Leghlin."

ḟaṙis féin maille ré grad mór ocus re síṫċáin, ocus an ċuid ar a rug Iarla Chille dara do lucht laṁaiġṫi an ġnioma sin, rug leis iad gur an áit a ndernad an droċ comairle sin, ocus tuc fódera a bḟendad beó ar túr, ocus a nabaiġe ocus a mionathar do ḃuain asda, ocus a loscad ina bḟiaḋnuse díḃlínaiḃ. H. Caṫáin .i. Sean mac Tomáis do marbad do ċuid dá ċineḋ fein .i. mac Ruaidri an Rútta hI Caṫáin ocus mac Goffraiġ hI Chaṫáin, oiḋċe lúġnusa do ṡunnrad. Easpuc Cille Dalúa .i. Toirrdhelḃach mac Maṫġaṁna hI Briain dhéc, .i. an Gaoidel is mó fuair ocus is ferr tuc uaḋ é diambui a comaimsir fris, ocus fer einiġ ċoitċinn comoirdere da gach oen ant esspuc sin, ocus fer ċosanta a ċóra a tír ocus a gcoicriċ do ḋeoin ocus do aimḋeoin, ocus fer slúaiġ ṁóir do chur a gcend a ċéle go minic do milled a escarad ocus do ċendsugad a ḃíḋḃad, conách raiḃe a gcomḟogus dó na ḋuthaid fein iná i ndúthaid eli na comḟogus mac Gaidel nar ġaḃ a ṫuillṁe ocus a ṫuarasdal uaḋ; ocus ní ele fós dob é ant esspuc sin .H. Briain ant écht ós gach echt ocus an esbud os gach esbuḋ da dtarla re healadán an én aimsir ris. An deganach mac Briain ruaiḋ Mic Conmiḋe, fer ṫiġe oeided coitċinn dá gach oen, ocus a mac .i. Cerḃall Mac Conmiḋe, dhéc in hoc anno. Ingen hI Dhuiḃgendain .i. Caiterḟina do ḋul dhéc iar nongad ocus iar naitriġe im ḟéil Columm Cille, ocus a hannlucad go honorach a mainistir Duin na nGall in hoc anno.

Kll. Enair for Luan. Sé bliadna .xx.et ar .u. ced ar mile air in Tigerna. Mac hI Ruairc .i. Taḋc mac Eogain do marbad a meabail lá muinter a derbráthar fein. O Néill .i. Conn ocus Maġnus O Domnaill

---

1 *Ruaidhri-an-Rúta.* "Ruaidhri of the Rúta (or Route)," a district in the county of Antrim.

2 *With or without consent.* do ḋeoin ocus do aimḋeoin; i.e. whether others would or not.

3 *Hoc.* 6c, MS.

4 *O'Duibhgennain.* The words Chille R[onain], "of Cill-Ronain," have been interlined after this name by Roderick O'Flaherty, the author of *Ogygia*.

A.D.
[1525.]

in his company, regarded with great love and friendship; and the Earl of Cill-dara carried off all whom he caught of those who had a hand in that deed, to the place where this evil counsel was adopted, and he commanded that they should be first flayed alive, and their bowels and entrails taken out of them, and burned respectively in their presence. O'Catháin, i.e. John, the son of Thomas, was killed by some of his own people, i.e. by the son of Ruaidhri-an-Rúta[1] O'Catháin, and by the son of Godfrey O'Catháin, on Lammas night exactly. The bishop of Cill-Dalua died, i.e. Toirdhelbhach, son of Mathghamhain O'Briain; i.e. the Gaeidhel who received the most, and dispensed it the best, of all who were in his time: and this bishop was a man of eminent general hospitality towards all; and a man for defending his right at home and abroad, with or without consent;[2] and a man for frequently setting large armies against each other, to destroy his enemies, and subdue his adversaries; so that there was not near him in his own country, nor in any neighbouring country, any son of a Gaeidhel who had not received his earnings and wages from him. And furthermore; this Bishop O'Briain was the calamity beyond all calamities, and the loss beyond all losses, that occurred in regard to learning in his time. The Dean, son of Brian Ruadh Mac Conmidhe, a man who kept a general house of hospitality for every one, and his son, i.e. Cerbhall Mac Conmidhe, died in hoc[3] anno. The daughter of O'Duibhgennain,[4] i.e. Catherine, died after unction and penitence, on the festival of Colum Cille, and was honourably interred in the monastery of Dun-na-nGall, in hoc[3] anno.

[1526.]

The kalends of January on Monday. The age of the Lord one thousand, five hundred, and twenty-six years. The son of O'Ruairc, i.e. Tadhg, the son of Eoghan, was killed in treachery by his own brother's people. O'Neill, i.e. Conn, and Maghnus O'Domhnaill went to meet the

oo ðul a ʒceno an ʒiúrðir oo ðenum ríte Conaloach
ocur Eoʒaɴach, ocur ιαρ ɛιɴól ṁóραιɴ oo ṁαιchιb
ʒαll ocur ʒαοιoel oα ríðuʒαo ɴíρ ðειoιρ α ríouʒαo
αɴɴrιɴ, ocur ɛαɴcooαρ αιmρειð oá ɛιʒιð. ̇ħ. Καιʒιllιʒ
.ι. Eoʒαɴ oo ðul ohéc, ocur coʒαo móρ εɛιρ α čɴιeð rá
ɛιʒeρɴur αɴ ɛιρe, ɴο ʒυρ ʒοιρeð . ħ. Καιʒιllιʒ oßeρʒαl
mαc Seαιɴ oo ṁοιαð αɴ ʒιúρðιρ· ocur ṁóρáιɴ oo ṁαιčιð
ʒαll ocur ʒαοιoel, ʒe ðo ðαoαρ oαοιɴe bu ríɴe ɴá hé
αʒ cur čυιʒe. Coʒαo móρ αρ ɴειρʒe α ɴιochɛαρ
Chοɴɴαchɛ αɴ ðlιαoαιɴ rιɴ, ocur α ɴυρṁóρ uιle oo
čeɴʒαl ρe čélι ιɴαʒhαιo hι Ohοmɴαιll, rα Uριαɴ mαc
ßélιm hι Conchobαιρ ocur rá mαc Cαɛhαιl óιʒ hι
Conchobαιρ, ocur rα ɛrlιochɛ Coρmαιc mιc Ooɴɴchαoα,
ocur ιochɛαρ Cαιρbρι oo cρeαchαo leo ; ocur O Oomɴαιll oo bριrreð ɴα ʒρáιɴριʒe, ocur oul α Mυιʒ Lυιρʒ
oo ɴα ðιαιð rιɴ ocur αɴ ɛíρ oo ṁιlleð ocur· oo loρcuo
lαιr. Αɛ ríl Conchobαιρ ocur αɴ člαɴɴ ɴOoɴɴchαðα
rιɴ oo ðí αρ αɴ ʒcoʒαo oo cρυιɴɴecħαð ocur ɛeαchɛ ʒo
Slιʒech ðóιð, ocur cuρ ʒo mαιð oočυm αɴ čαιréιɴ ɴο
ʒυρ mαρbαð oυιɴe mαιð oα mυιɴɛeρ .ι. Κυαιoρι bαllαč
mαc hι Αιρɛ. Ιmčeαchɛ oóιð αɴ lá rιɴ ocur cρυιɴɴeαch-
αo oοιð rá čeɴo ʒαιριo αρír, ocur ɛeαchɛ co Slιʒech
oo ṁιlleo ʒoρɛ ocur oo chυρɛ oočυm αɴ ðαιle, ocur O
Oomɴαιll oßαʒαιl rʒélα α mbeιð mαρ rιɴ, ocur α
ʒluαrrαchɛ čucu ocur bρeιð oρρα, ocur α mαðmuʒαo
lαιr, ocur cυιo ṁóρ rá ɴoáιɴeð oo ðυαιɴ oíð, ocur
eoáιl ṁóρ ech ocur αιρm ocur eιoιʒ. O Ηeιll.ι.Coɴɴ oo
čeαchɛ rlúαʒ móρ oo ɛοιρmeɛc oιρρι cαιréιɴ oo
čιɴɴrcυιɴ Mαʒɴυr O Oomɴαιll oo oeɴυm α ßυρɛ ɴα
ɛρι ɴαmαo, ocur Mαʒɴυr oo čeʒṁáιl re ɛúρ αɴɛ
rlúαιʒ, ocur mαc Seαιɴ hι Ηeιll.ι. Eɴρí oo ʒαbáιl leιr,
ocur O Ηeιll oυιɴčeαchɛ α ʒcoιρ ṁαðmα. O Cαɛáιɴ .ι.
ʒoßrαιʒ mαc ʒoßrαðα oo mαρbαo α ɴuchɛ ðeαlαιʒ

---

[1] *Between.* The original of this
clause, oo ðeɴυm ríte Conaloach
ocur Eoʒαɴach, signifies literally
"to make the peace of the Conallachs

and Eoghanachs," i.e. of the people of
Cenel-Conaill and Cenel-Eoghain.

[2] *Mail-armour.* eιoιʒ, gen. sg. of
eιoeč, lit. "clothing."

Justiciary, to make peace between[1] the Conallachs and Eoghanachs; and after several nobles of the Foreigners and Gaeidhel had assembled to pacify them, they could not be reconciled there ; and they went home unreconciled. O'Raighilligh, i.e. Eoghan, died ; and a great war *occurred* amongst his people regarding the sovereignty of the country, until Ferghal, son of John, was proclaimed the O'Raighilligh, by the decision of the Justiciary, and of many of the nobles of the Foreigners and Gaeidhel, although older men than he were claiming it. A great war broke out in Lower Connacht this year, and the majority of them all, including Brian, son of Felim O'Conchobhair, and the sons of Cathal Og O'Conchobhair, and the descendants of Cormac Mac Donnchadha, joined together against O'Domhnaill; and the lower part of Cairbre was pillaged by them. And O'Domhnaill demolished the Grainsech, and went afterwards to Magh-Luirg, and the country was destroyed and burned by him. Those of the Sil-Conchobhair and Clann-Donnchaidh who were engaged in that war assembled, and went to Sligech, and attacked the castle bravely, until a good man of their people, i.e. Ruaidhri Ballagh, son of O'hAirt, was slain. They departed on that day ; but they assembled again in a short time, and went to Sligech, to destroy corn-fields, and to attack the town. And O'Domhnaill received intelligence of their being thus engaged ; and he moved against them, and came up with them ; and they were defeated by him, and a great number of their men were captured from them, and a great spoil of horses, arms, and mail-armour.[2] O'Neill, i.e. Conn, went with a large army to prevent the construction of a castle which Maghnus O'Domhnaill had commenced to build at Port-na-tri-namhad ; and Maghnus met with the advance of the army, and the son of John O'Neill, i.e. Henry, was taken prisoner by him ; and O'Neill went off in broken array. O'Catháin, i.e. Godfrey, son of Godfrey, was killed

ιn čαmάιn Le mαc hι Néill .ι. Nιαll όჳ, αn ceⱱ ᵯí ⱱo
cŕάmⱤαᵭ, ocuⱤ Nιαll ŕéιn ⱱo ჳαⱱάιl ŕά čenⱱ αⱫჳαιⱤιⱱ
ιαⱤⱤιn LeιⱤ O Neill, ocuⱤ α ᵬeιᵭ nα čιmιᵬ. 8eαn
mαc Oeⱱhα mιc 'OιαⱤmαⱱα, αn ᵬeιᵭιⱤ ᵬeoᵭα ᵬιᵭ
oιⱤⱤⱱeⱤc, ⱱo mαⱤⱱαⱱ Le ⱤLιchc hι ConchoⱦαιⱤ Ɽuαιⱱ
ιαⱤ nά ŕαჳαιL α mⱦαoჳαL ŕoⱤ mullαč cⱤoιᵭe. 8lόιჳeαᵭ
Lά hιαⱤLα ChιLLe ⱱαⱤα ŕα mαchαιⱤe Chonnαchc αⱤ
ŕoⱤჳαLL hι ConchoⱦαιⱤ Ɽuαιⱱ, ჳuⱤ ჳαᵭuⱤcαⱤ ⱦαιLe
ᵭoⱤαιⱤ ⱦⱤίჳⱱι ocuⱤ cαιⱤLén Ɽιαⱦαch čLαιnnι ŕαჳαⱤ-
cαιჳ, ocuⱤ Ɽo ᵭίⱱLαιc ⱱO ChonchoⱦαιⱤ Ɽuαᵭ ιαⱱ.
LommαⱤჳαιn hι ConchoⱦαιⱤ Lα cLαnn RuαιⱱⱤι mιc
'OιαⱤmαⱱα αჳ CuιⱤⱤ ιn ⱱⱤoιčιc, ocuⱤ cúιჳⱤeⱤ no cŕeιⱤ-
ⱤeⱤ ⱱα muιnceⱤ ⱱŕάჳⱦάιL ⱱόιᵬⱤιom. αⱤჳαιn cŕLechcα
Cαιᵭc mιc ⱦⱤαnάιn ocuⱤ CuαᵭLα .h. ConchoⱦαιⱤ nα
čιnαᵭ. Ɽιéιn, ocuⱤ RuαιⱱⱤι mαc Cuιnn mιc ⱦⱤαnάιn ⱱo
ᵯαⱤⱦαᵭ Lα cLαιnn EαᵭᵯαⱤcαιჳ mιc ⱦⱤαnάιn. moⱤⱤ
mhéჳ αᵯαLჳαιᵭ Lα hUα mαoιLⱤechLαιnn, ⱱαⱤ ŕαⱤuჳαⱱ
αn ιαⱤLα. 8lόιჳeᵭ Lα ⱦⱤιαn O RuαιⱤc α muιnceⱤ
eoLuιⱤ, ჳuⱤ ჳαᵬ neⱤc ŕeⱤ ჳConmαιcne ocuⱤ čιnél
mⱦιᵭⱤαιჳ ⱱon ⱱuιL Ɽιn. mαc hι Chαchάιn .ι. ჳoⱤⱤⱤαιჳ
mαc 'Oonⱱchαⱱα, αᵭⱦαⱤ cιჳeⱤnα α čίⱤe ŕéιn, ⱱo ᵭuL αⱤ
ⱤιoⱦαL cⱤeιᵭe α nჳLenⱱ Choncαᵭuιn α mι eⱦάιⱤ ⱱo
ŕιⱱⱤⱤαᵭ, ocuⱤ é ŕeιn ⱱŕαჳⱦαιL, ocuⱤ nαch ⱦⱤⱤίᵭ én
ŕocuL ⱱά ⱤჳéLαιᵭ no ჳo ⱦⱤⱤίᵭ α čoⱤⱤ αnc ŕechcᵯuιn
ⱱéιჳenαch ⱱon čoⱤჳuⱤ αⱤ α čιnn ; ocuⱤ enⱤί mαc Neill
ᵯιc ⱦⱤιαιn, cιჳeⱤnα ⱦαιLe nα ⱦⱤάჳαⱱ ⱱo mαⱤⱦαⱱ αnn,
ocuⱤ mόⱤάn eLι ⱱo mαⱤⱦαᵭ ocuⱤ ⱱo Lechαⱱ αnn mαιLLe
Ɽιú ⱱά muιnceⱤ. mαιᵭm ⱱo ᵭαⱦαιⱤc ⱱo mαc mιc
ⱤιαⱤuιⱤ ⱦuιcιLéιⱤ αⱤ čLαιnn emuιnn ᵯιc ComάιⱤ
ⱦuιcιLeιⱤ, ⱱú ιnαⱤ mαⱤⱦαⱱ ConchoⱦαⱤ όჳ mαc ConchoⱦαιⱤ čoeιch hι 'OhomnαιLL, ⱱo ᵬí nα čόnⱤαⱦαL ჳαLLόჳLαeᵭ

---

1 *Sir.* The MS. has ᵳŕeιⱤⱤeⱤ, an
interesting, and rather unusual form,
of the numeral ⱤeιⱤeⱤ.

² *Of Tuathal.* The regular gen. of
the name CuαchαL is CuαchαιL,
not CuαᵭLα, as in the MS.

³ *In violation of the Earl;* i.e. in
violation of the guarantee of the Earl
(of Cill-dara, or Kildare) to protect
Mag Amhalgaidh (Magawley).

⁴ *Nothing was heard of him.* The
original, nach ⱦⱤⱤίᵭ én ŕocuL ⱱά

A.D.
[1526.]

in front of Bealach-an-chamáin, by the son of O'Neill, i.e. Niall Og, the first month of summer; and Niall himself was taken prisoner within a short time afterwards by O'Neill, and was *detained* a captive. John, son of Aedh Mac Diarmada, the ever-illustrious, vigorous bear, was killed by the descendants of O'Conchobhair Ruadh, on being found in a perilous position on Mullach-croiche. A hosting by the Earl of Cill-dara through Machaire-Connacht, at the instigation of O'Conchobhair Ruadh; and he took Baile-thobair-Brighde, and Caislen-riabhach of Clann-Foghartaigh, and gave them to O'Conchobhair Ruadh. Total plunder of O'Conchobhair by the sons of Ruaidhri Mac Diarmada, at Cur-in-droichit, where five or six[1] of their people were lost by them. The descendants of Tadhg Mac Branáin, and of Tuathal[2] O'Conchobhair, were plundered in retaliation therefor; and Ruaidhri, son of Conn Mac Branáin, was slain by the sons of Echmarcach Mac Branáin. Mors of Mag Amhalghaidh, by O'Maelechlainn, in violation of the Earl.[3] A hosting by Brian O'Ruairc into Muinter-Eolais, and he obtained sway over the Conmaicne and Cenel-Bibhsaigh on that occasion. The son of O'Catháin, i.e. Godfrey, the son of Donnchadh, heir to the sovereignty of his own country, went on a predatory march into Glenn-Concadhain, in the month of January exactly; and he himself was left behind, and nothing was heard of him[4] until his body was found the last week of the following Lent; and Henry, son of Niall, son of Brian,[5] lord of Baile-na-bràghad, was killed there, and many more of his people were killed and wounded there along with them. An overthrow was given by the grandson of Piers Butler to the sons of Edmond, son of Thomas Butler, in which Conchobhar Og, the son of Conchobhar Caech[6] O'Domhnaill, who was a constable of gallowglasses, and a good hand often, and especially

---

ᵁᵍᵉ́ᴸᵃᵢᵇ, literally rendered, is "not a word of his stories was obtained."

[5] *Brian*; i.e. Brian O'Neill.
[6] *Caech*; i.e. "the Blind."

!Glʰᵗ‑‑ ᵥ ᵥ   f

οcυρ να λάιṁ ιναιξ ɤο ιṁιΝιc, οcυρ ɤο hαιριξξι αΝ λά
ριΝ, οιρ Νιρ λειc α Νειρc οcυρ ιηéϑ α ιηεΝιηα οcυρ ρεϑυρ
α λαιṁε ϑó αΝαcαλ ϑο ξαϑάιλ ιαρ νά ξαιρcριΝ ϑó, οcυρ ϑο
ξυιξ ιιναξ ϑο ϑαοιΝιϑ ιηóρα ιναιξι ρα ιναιϑιη ριΝ ϑó
ιηαρcρλúαξαιϑ οcυρ ϑο ξαλλóξλαεcυιϑ. Ο Ϸοcάρξαιξ .ι.
Θchιηαρcαch, ξιξερΝα ιΝΝρι hΘοξαιΝ, ϑhéc α Νερρ α
αοιρρι ιΝ hοc αΝΝο, οcυρ cοξαϑ ιηορ εξιρ α čιΝεϑ ρά
ξιξερΝυι· αΝ ξίρε, οcυρ ξιξερΝα ϑο ϑεΝυιη ϑο ξεραλξ
ιναc Ϸοιηναιλλ ιηιc Ϸhéλιιη hι Ϸhοčαρξαιξ. Sλοιξεϑ λά
.h. ΝϷοιηΝαιλλ α ξίρ ιιιηαλξαιϑ ϑο čοιξΝυιη λé ρλιchξ
Ριcαιρϑ α ϑúρc, οcυρ CαορčαΝΝάΝ οcυρ Cρορ ιηhαοιλίΝα
ϑο ξαϑάιλ λειρ, οcυρ α ιηϑιρρεϑ ϑó, οcυρ ϑρáιξϑε οcυρ
éϑάλα ιιηϑα ϑο ξαϑαιρξ αρϑα ριΝ, οcυρ ρίξ ϑραξϑάιλ
εξιρ ρλιchξ Ριcαιρϑ α ϑúρc οcυρ ϑαιρéϑαchαιϑ ; οcυρ
ροιρλοΝξροριξ ϑο ϑéΝυιη ϑó αρ α ρίλλεϑ ρά čαιρλéΝ
Cúλιηαιλε, οcυρ ρίξ οcυρ ϑρáιξϑε ϑο ϑυαιΝ ϑο ξρλιοchξ
Cοριηαιc Ϻιc Ϸοννchαϑα αΝΝριΝ, εξ ρελιqυα.

Ϳcξξ. ΘΝάιρ ρορ ιηαιρξ. Sεαchξ ιηϑλιαϑΝα ριčεξ αρ
.υ. cεϑ αρ ιηιλε αιρ ιΝ ϹιξερΝα. Ϻαc ϷοΝΝchαϑα ξίρε
hΟιλελλα .ι. Cοριηαc ιναc Ϲαιϑξ ιηιc ϑρίαιΝ ϑο ϑυλ ϑhéc,
οcυρ cοξαϑ ιηóρ ιϑιρ čλαιΝΝ ΝϷοΝΝchαϑα ρά ξιξερΝυρ
αΝ ·ξίρε Να ϑιαιϑ, Νο ξυρ ξοιρεϑ Ϻαc ϷοΝΝchαϑα
ϑΘοξαΝ ιναc ϷοΝΝchαϑα Νιc Ϻυρchαϑα. ϑριαΝ ιναc
Ϸéλιιη ιηιc ϺαξΝυρα hι Conchobαιρ ϑhéc ίΝ hοc αΝΝο.
Ϸοιηναλλ ιναc Ϸéλιιη ιηιc Ϲhοιρρϑhελϑαιξ čαρραιξ hι
Conchobαιρ ιηορξυυρ ερξ. Ο Cλειριξ .ι. αΝ ξιλλα ριαϑαch
ιναc Ϲαιϑξ cαιιη, ρόι ρε hελαϑαιΝ οcυρ ρεΝ ραιϑϑυιρ ιηóιρ,
ϑραξαιλ ϑáιρ α Ναιϑίϑ ραΝ ϷρόιΝρéιρ α ιηί ιηεϑοιΝ ιΝ
ερραιξ. Ϸοιηναλλ ιναc αΝ ερρυιc hι Ϛhαλλčυϑαιρ ϑο
ιηαρϑαϑ λε cυιϑ ϑο ξρλιchξ ιιοΝξυιρ hι Ϛhαλλčυϑαιρ
αΝ ϑλιαϑαιΝ ρι. ιΝ Ϸοcξúιρ ιναc ΘοξαιΝ ι ϷυιΝΝρλειϑε,
ρόι ρε λειξερ οcυρ αΝΝρΝα hεαλαϑΝαιϑ ελι ϑυριηóρ,
οcυρ ρεΝ cονάιξ ιηóιρ οcυρ ξιξε αοιϑεϑ, ϑhéc αΝ ξρερρ

---

on that day, was slain ; for his strength, and the greatness of his mind, and the excellence of his hand, did not allow him to accept quarter after it had been offered to him ; and several great, good men, of the cavalry and gallowglasses, fell in that overthrow. O'Dochartaigh, i.e. Echmarcach, lord of Inis-Eoghain, died in the end¹ of his age in hoc anno ; and a great war *occurred* amongst his sept regarding the sovereignty of the country ; and Gerald, son of Domhnall, son of Felim O'Dochartaigh, was made lord. A hosting by O'Domhnaill to Tir-Amhalghaidh, to assist the descendants of Richard Burk ; and Caerthannán and Cros-Maeilína were taken by him, and broken down ; and he brought many captives and spoils out of these, and left peace betwixt the descendants of Richard Burk and the Barretts. And he encamped, on his return, before the castle of Cúl-mhaile, and exacted peace and hostages then from the descendants of Cormac Mac Donnchadha, &c.

The kalends of January on Tuesday. The age of the Lord one thousand, five hundred, and twenty-seven years. Mac Donnchadha of Tir-Oilella, i.e. Cormac, the son of Tadhg, son of Brian, died; and a great war *occurred* amongst the Clann-Donnchadha regarding the sovereignty of the country after him, until Eoghan, the son of Donnchadh, son of Murchadh, was proclaimed the Mac Donnchadha. Brian, son of Felim, son of Maghnus O'Conchobhair, died in hoc anno. Domhnall, the son of Felim, son of Toirdhelbhach Carragh O'Conchobhair, mortuus est. O'Clerigh, i.e. the Gilla-riabhach, son of Tadhg Cam, an adept in science, and a man of great wealth, died in the habit of Saint Francis, in the middle month of spring. Domhnall, son of the Bishop O'Gallchubhair, was killed this year by some of the descendants of Aenghus O'Gallchubhair. The Doctor, son of Eoghan O'Duinnshleibhe, an adept in medicine, and in most of the other sciences, and a man of great wealth, and one who kept a house of hospitality, died the third

lá ɲía bɲélɪ Ƒɲoɪnɲιaɲ·· maჯ Uιჰιɲ ᴅo ჰuʟ ᴅhéc an
ჰʟιaᴅaιn ɲι, ocuɲ cιჯeɲɲa ᴅo ჰenum ᴅon čoṁoɲba
mháჯ Uιᴅιɲ na ιonaჰ ·ι· ᴅo Chúconnachc mac Con-
connochc mιc Ủɲιaιn. Coιɲɲᴅheʟbach mac Eιჯnecháιn
ι ᵭhomnaιʟʟ moɲcuuɲ eɲc. Ƒéʟιm mac Ჯoɲɲaᴅa mιc
Seaιn ʟuιɲჯ hι ᵭomnaιʟʟ moɲcuuɲ eɲc. 8ʟoιჯeᴅ ʟeιɲ
O nᴅoṁnaιʟʟ a máჯ ʟuιɲჯ, ocuɲ an cιɲ ᴅo ṁιʟʟeᴅ ecιɲ
aɲჰaɲ ocuɲ Ƒoιɲჯnem, ocuɲ an caιɲʟén móɲ ocuɲ caιɲʟen
an Ủennaᴅa ᴅo ჯabáιʟ ᴅó, ocuɲ caιɲʟén an Chaʟaιჰ,
ocuɲ Ủaιʟe na huaṁa, ocuɲ an caιɲʟén ɲιabach ᴅo
ჯabáιʟ ᴅó; ocuɲ a mbɲιɲɲeᴅ ιaɲɲιn, ocuɲ maɲcach
maιჰ ᴅo ιιaɲbaᴅ ᴅo muιnceɲ hι ᵭomnaιʟʟ a nuchc an
ჰeʟaιჯ ჰuιჰe ·ι· Oeᴅ buιჰe mac an ᵭuჰaʟcaιჯ hι Ჯaʟʟ-
čuჰaιɲ. Caιɲʟen ʟιɲɲιɲ ᴅo čιnnɲcna ʟe maιჯnuɲ O
nᴅomnaιʟʟ ιn ceᴅoeιn ιaɲ bɲéιʟ Ủɲénaιnn, ocuɲ a
cɲιčnιჯaᴅ ʟe cuιᴅ ᴅonc Ƒaṁɲaᴅ ɲιn ecιɲ obaιɲ cɲaιnn
ocuɲ cʟoιče, ocuɲ coჯaᴅ hι Neιʟʟ ɲaιɲ. maჯnuɲ O
ᵭomnaιʟʟ ᴅo ჰuʟ aɲ ɲιubaʟ cɲeιčι a nჯʟιonn Ƒéιʟe aɲ
Oeᴅ mbuιჰe O nᴅomnaιʟʟ, ocuɲ cɲeač ᴅo čaბaιɲc ʟaιɲ,
ocuɲ ᴅιaɲ maɲcach ᴅá muιnceɲ ᴅo maɲbaᴅ ·ι· mac
ᵭomnaιʟʟ mιc Ƒhéʟιm mιc Œonჯuɲa óιჯ hι Ჯhaʟʟčuბaιɲ,
ocuɲ mac Ủɲιaιn čaoιč mιc ᵭomnaιʟʟ mιc·ιn ᴅeჯanaιჯ.
Commáɲ mac maჯnuɲa mhéჯჯ Uιᴅιɲ ᴅhéc ·ι· ɲoι
čʟéιɲιჯ ocuɲ ჰuιne čuιcɲιჯ cɲéιჯhιჯe ɲe ʟaιᴅιn ocuɲ ɲe
ჯaoιᴅιʟჯe, ocuɲ ᴅob Ƒeɲɲ cóιɲ ʟeabaɲ ʟaιᴅne ocuɲ
ჯaoιᴅιʟჯe a coṁჯaɲ ᴅó, ocuɲ ɲeɲ muιɲιɲ ṁóιɲ ᴅιomchuɲ
ocuɲ cιჯe aoιᴅheᴅ ᴅo čoιჯmáιʟ. Ruaιᴅɲι mac muɲ-
chaᴅa mιc c8huιჰne ᴅo maɲbaᴅ ᴅa bɲáιcɲιჰ ɲɲeιn ιn
hoc anno. Uιʟʟιam mac Œιnᴅɲιaɲɲ ṁéჯ Cɲaιჰ ·ι· ɲeɲ
ɲaιჰbɲιɲ ṁóιɲ ocuɲ bιacach maιჰ, ocuɲ a ჰen, ᴅhec an

---

1 *Francis.* Apparently St. Francis,
confessor, whose festival occurs on
October 4th. The Four Mast. state
that O'Duinnshleibhe (or O'Donlevy)
died on the 30th of September.

2 *John Luirg*; i.e. "John of Lurg;"
so called from having been fostered

by the O'Muldoons of Lurg, in the
north of the present county of Fermanagh.

3 *Caisl'n-mór*; i.e. the "great
castle," or Castlemore-Costelloe, now
Castlemore, in the barony of Costelloe, and county of Mayo.

day before the festival of Francis.[1] Mag Uidhir died this year; and the comarb Mag Uidhir, i.e. Cuconnacht, son of Cuconnacht, son of Brian, was made lord in his place. Toirdhelbhach, the son of Egnechán O'Domhnaill, mortuus est. Felim, son of Godfrey, son of John Luirg[2] O'Domhnaill, mortuus est. A hosting by O'Domhnaill to Magh-Luirg; and the country was destroyed, both corn and buildings; and the Caislén-mór,[3] and the castle of Bennada, were taken by him; and the castle of the Caladh, and Baile-na-huamha, and the Caislen-riabhach, were taken by him; and they were afterwards broken down. And a good horseman of O'Domhnaill's people, i.e. Aedh Buidhe, son of the Dubhaltach O'Gallchubhair, was killed in front of the Belach-buidhe. The castle of Liffer was begun by Maghnus O'Domhnaill the Wednesday after the festival of Brenainn,[4] and finished in the course of that summer, both timber and stone work, and O'Neill warring against him. Maghnus O'Domhnaill went on a predatory march into Glenn-fhéile, against Aedh Buidhe O'Domhnaill, and carried off a prey; and two horsemen of his people were slain, viz., the son of Domhnall, son of Felim, son of Aenghus Og O'Gallchubhair, and the son of Brian Caech, son of Domhnall Mac-an-decanaigh.[5] Thomas Mac Maghnusa Mag Uidhir died: i.e. a most eminent cleric, and an intelligent, learned man in Latin and Gaeidhilic, and who had the best copies of Latin and Gaeidhilic books of any in his neighbourhood; and a man who supported a large company, and kept a house of hospitality. Ruaidhri, son of Murchadh Mac Suibhne, was killed by his own kinsmen in hoc anno. William, son of Andrias Mag Craith, i.e. a man of great opulence, and a good biatach,[6] and his wife, died in one day and

A.D.

[1527.]

---

[4] *Brenainn.* St. Brendan of Clonfert, whose festival fell on the 16th of May.

[5] *Mac-an-decanaigh;* lit. "son of the Dean." This name is still borne by some families in Tyrone, under the forms Mac Digany, and Deane.

[6] *Biatach.* The title "*biatach*" was applied to a wealthy farmer of great influence and authority.

én ló con cιồcε ιn ồlιαồαιn ϝιn. Cαιcιlín ιnζεn Chuιnn
mιc. Oomnαιll hí Neιll, ben cϝαιồcεồ ồειζ εινιζ ồo ồí
αζ ϝεϝαιồ mαιồι.ι. αζ O Rαιζιllιζ αϝ cúϝ ocuϝ αζ O Ruαιϝc
nα ồιαιồ ϝιn, ồϝαζαιl ồáιϝ αn ồlíαồαιn ϝι ιαϝ nonζαồ
ocuϝ nαιồϝιζε. Ιαϝlα Chιlle ồαϝα ocuϝ mαc Ιαϝlα
Uϝϻumαn ồo ồul α Sαxαnαιồ cϝé ιmồnúồ ocuϝ cϝε
ιnnlαồ α ồéle, ocuϝ α ιnαồ ϝειn α nεϝιnn ồo ϝáζồáιl αζ
bαϝún Oelồnα, .ι. ζιυϝồíϝ nα hεϝεnn αn cαn ϝιn ιnc
Ιαϝlα ϝιn Cιlle ồαϝα. Oomnαll mαc Ϝεϝζαιl mιc
Oomnαιll hí ồιϝn, ồux ιn leιồe ϝíoϝ ồo ồιϝ ồϝιúιn,
ocuϝ α Sαιnồéle .ι. Ιαϝϝαιϝϝíonα ιnζεn cϩheαιn mιc ιn
ϝϝιεóϝα, moϝcuι ϝunc. Cαồζ mαc Cαιϝbϝι mιc ιn
ϝϝιεóϝα hí ồιϝn ồo ξαbáιl nα cαoιϝιζεchcα cαϝéιϝ
Oomnαιll αϝ bélαιb ϝιnnϝεϝ ϝ'lechcα Coϝmαιc hí ồιϝn,
αmαιl ιϝ ồú ồo ồεξ αιϝιlnιuồ, ocuϝ Mαoιlϝechluιnn O
ồιϝn α bϝαchαιϝ elι ồo ξαbáιl nα cαnαιϝồechcα. Moϝ
ιnζεn Mhαoιleồlαιnn Mhιc Cáϝα, uxoϝ hí αιnlιζε .ι.
αn ồεn ồob ϝεϝϝ cáιnιc α ζcenel Ooϝϝα mιc Oenξuϝα ϝε
cιαn ồαιmϝιϝ, buιme ồáϻ ocuϝ ồεoϝαιồ nα hεϝεnn,
αιồξιn Mhóιϝε Mumαn αϝ ồlú ocuϝ αϝ cϝαbαồ ocuϝ αϝ
ồαonồúồϝαchc, ben ιϝ mó cuc ồoϝϝáιl ocuϝ ồαlmϝαnαιồ
bíồ ocuϝ éồαιξ ồo ồochcαιồ ocuϝ ồαιồιlζnechαιồ αn
Choιmồιồ ocuϝ ồá ζαch αon no ϝιζεồ α leϝϝ α ϝαξαιl, α
héζ αϝ láϝ α Lonζϝuιϝc ϝéιn α ϝoϝc Loồα Leιϝι, εc
ϝεϝulcα εϝc α nOιlϝιnn ϝá ồιồen Oé ocuϝ Ϸháồϝαιc.
αn ϝϝιóιϝ óζ O Ϝεϝζαιl .ι. Comáϝϝ mαc Εmuιnn ϻιc
Roϝϝα, cιζεϝnα Chαlαιồ nα hαnξαιle, ocuϝ αn cúιζεồ
cuιồϝενồαch ồob ϝεϝϝ ồo ồóι ồo ồlαnnuιồ Ruζϝαιồε, ồo
mαϝbαồ lα clαιnn Εmuιnn hí Chellαιζ ocuϝ le ϝlιchc
Ϝélιm mιc Ζιllα nα nαom hí Ϝεϝζαιl, ocuϝ α cϝιuϝ mαc
mαιlle ϝϝιϝ ϝεϝ ồolum. Ϸoϝồuιϝε ồúιζ ϝεαchcϻuιneαồ
no αϝϝé lα clαιnn Ruαιồϝι mιc Oιαϝmαồα, ocuϝ lά
clαιnn Cαồζ mιc Ruαιồϝι mιc Oιαϝmαồα, ocuϝ lα
Mαc nOuồξαιll ocuϝ le ϝlιchc hí Conchobαιϝ ϝuαιồ,

---

1 *Married.* The original words,
ồo ồí αζ ϝεϝαιồ mαιồι, literally
rendered, would read "whom good
men owned."

2 *Sepulta.* ϝεϝulcuϝ, MS.

3 *Companion* cuιồϝενồαch; a
word deriv. from cuιồϝεnn, a share,
a portion. and also a company.

night this year. Caitilín, daughter of Conn, son of Domhnall O'Neill, a pious woman of good hospitality, who had been married[1] to good men, viz., to O'Raighilligh at first, and to O'Ruairc afterwards, died this year after unction and penitence. The Earl of Cill-dara, and the son of the Earl of Ur-Mumha, went to Saxon-land through mutual envy and complaints; and he left his own office in Erinn to the Baron of Delbhna, (i.e. this Earl of Cill-dara was Justiciary of Erinn at that time). Domhnall, the son of Ferghal, son of Domhnall O'Birn, dux of the lower half of Tir-Briúin, and his wife, i.e. Lasairfhína, daughter of John the Prior's son, mortui sunt. Tadhg, the son of Cairbre, son of the Prior O'Birn, assumed the chieftaincy after Domhnall, in preference to the senior of the descend- ants of Cormac O'Birn, as good merit deserves; and Maelsechlainn O'Birn, his other brother, assumed the tanistship. Mor, daughter of Maelechlainn Mac Caba, uxor of O'hAinlighe, i.e. the best woman that came into Cenel-Doffa-mic-Aenghusa for a long time; the nurse of the learned and destitute of Erinn; the equal of Mór Mumhan in reputation, piety, and good will; the woman who gave most in offerings and alms of food and clothing to the poor, and to the orphans of the Lord, and to every one who would require to receive them, died in the middle of her own residence, in Port-Locha-Leise, et sepulta[2] est in Oilfinn, under the protection of God and Patrick. The young Prior O'Ferghail, i.e. Thomas, the son of Edmond, son of Rossa, lord of Caladh-na-hAnghaile, and the fifth best companion[3] that was of the Clanna-Rughraidhe, was slain by the sons of Edmond O'Cellaigh, and by the sons of Felim, son of Gilla-na-naemh O'Fer-ghail, and his three sons along with him, per dolum. An investment of five weeks, or six, by the sons of Ruaidhri Mac Diarmada, and by the sons of Tadhg, son of Ruaidhri Mac Diarmada, and by Mac Dubhgaill, and the race of O'Conchobhair Ruadh, and the descendants of

ocuʃ ʃe ʃlιcℏτ Péℓιm ʃιηη, ocuʃ ℓe ʃlιcℏτ Ταιδʒ mιc
Uʃαηáιη, ʃοη čαιʃℓéη ʃιαbαcℏ člαιηⁿ Pαʒαʃταιʒ, ocuʃ
muc ιηʒηαδ cʃαιηη δο δεηυm čυιʒε δοιδ δο ℏʃαιℓʒιδ
δεʒ δαιηʒηε δαʃαčα, ocuʃ ʃαιℓʒε ʃαδα ʃíʃ ṁóʃα αʃ ℓuč
ʃúιčε. Dιαʃmαιδ mαc Ταιδʒ ʃυαιδ, ocuʃ mαʃcαcℏ
mαιč δο δυηαδ člαιηηε Μαοℓʃυηαιδ, δο ṁαʃbαδ αmαcℏ
αʃʃαη ʒcαιʃℓéη, ocuʃ αη ṁυc δο ʒεʃʃαδ ʃá δεοιδ ℓα
Τυαčℏαℓ ʃυαδ.

|cττ. Θηáιʃ ʃοʃ Cεδαοιη; bιʃʃεx ʃυιʃʃε. Ocℏτ
mblιαδηα ʃιcℏεδ ocuʃ .ιι. cεδ ocuʃ mιℓε αοιʃ αη Τιʒεʃηα.
Iηʒεη ℏι Uʃιαιη .ι. Pιηηʒυαℓα ιηʒεη Conchobαιʃ, αη δεη
ιʃ mó δο čοʃʃυιη δο člú α coιηαιmʃιʃ ʃíα δο čαοδ čυιʃʃ
ocuʃ αηmα, δο δυℓ δℏéc ιαʃ ʒcαιčℏεm α ℏαοιʃʃι ocuʃ α
ℏιηmε ʃε ℏοιηεcℏ ocuʃ ʃε δαοηηοcℏτ αʃ τúʃ, ocuʃ ιαʃ
ιηδειčℏ blιαδαιη αʃ ʃιčιτ α ηαιbíδ αη cʃεʃʃ υιʃδ αʒ
δεηυm cʃábαδ ocuʃ δαοηηαcℏτα ocuʃ δεʒ οιʃʃιʒčε δο
čαοδ Dℏé ocuʃ αητ ʃαοʒυιℓ. ℏ.Uʃíαιη .ι. Τοιʃʃδℏεlb-
αcℏ mαc Ταιδc, αη ʒαοιδεαℓ δοb ʃαιδε ʃε ℏυαιʃℓε ocuʃ
ʃε ℏεηεcℏ α ℓεč Μοδα υιℓε, ocuʃ οιʒʃι δίℓεʃ Uʃιαιη
Uοʃυmα αʃ čοηʒṁαιℓ čοʒαιδ ʃε ʒαℓℓοιb, δʃαʒαιℓ δáιʃ
ιαʃ ηοηʒαδ ocuʃ ιαʃ ηαιčʃιʒε, ocuʃ α mαc δο ʃιʒαδ ηα
ιοηαδ .ι. Conchobαʃ mαc Τοιʃʃδℏεαlbαιʒ. Μαc Dιαʃ-
mαδα ṁοιʒε ℓυιʃʒ .ι. Coʃmαc mαc Ruαιδʃí mιc Dιαʃ-
mαδα, ʃéιcℏεm coιτčεηη αʃ ειηεcℏ ocuʃ αʃ ʃéιℓε δαοιʃ
εαℓαδηα, ocuʃ míʃ cʃυαδα coʒαιδ ocuʃ εcčαιʒčι Con-
ηαcℏτ αη Coʃmαc ʃιη, ocuʃ ʃεʃ čοʃαητα α cʃιčε ʃειη
αʃ α ειʃʒcαιʃοιδ é, ocuʃ α éʒ ιαʃ ηοηʒαδ ocuʃ ιαʃ
ηαιčʃιʒε α ηεʃʃ α αοιʃʃι; ocuʃ α δεʃbʃáτℏαιʃ .ι.
Dιαʃmαιδ δο ʒαδáιℓ α ιοηαδ δια éιʃ· Conn mαc Νειℓℓ
mιc Ɑιʃτ ℏι Νειℓℓ, cειηʃεδηα mαιčℏ δο čιηéℓ Θοʒαιη,
δο ṁαʃbαδ ℓα mαc Ɑιʃτ óιʒ ℏι Νειℓℓ, ocuʃ δια[ʃ] mαc

---

1 *Engine.* muc; lit. "pig."

2 *Tuathal Ruadh.* In the Annals of
Connacht Tuathal is called mαc
Cuιηη, "the son of Conn [O'Don-
nell]," and it is added that the castle
was surrendered through famine.

3 *Third Order.* The third Order
of St. Francis.

4 *Hardy champion.* mιʃ cʃαδα,
M.S. The Four Masters and the
Annals of Connacht have also mιʃ

Felim Finn, and the descendants of Tadhg Mac Branáin, against Caislen-riabhach of Clann-Foghartaigh; and a wonderful wooden engine[1] for taking it was made by them of good, firm, oaken beams, and long, truly large beams supporting it. Diarmaid, son of Tadhg Ruadh, and a good horseman of the stock of Clann-Maelruanaidh, were killed from out of the castle; and the engine was at last cut to pieces by Tuathal Ruadh.[2]

The kalends of January on Wednesday; a bissextile; the age of the Lord one thousand, five hundred, and twenty-eight years. O'Briain's daughter, i.e. Finnghuala, daughter of Conchobhar, the woman who maintained the greatest reputation of all her contemporaries, as regards body and soul, died after spending her life and wealth at first in promoting hospitality and humanity, and after having been twenty-one years in the habit of the third Order,[3] performing devotion, clemency, and good works, on behalf of God and the world. O'Briain, i.e. Toirdhelbhach, the son of Tadhg, the Gaeidhel who had been longest identified with nobility and hospitality in all Leth-Modha, and the genuine heir of Brian Borumha in maintaining war with Foreigners, died after unction and penitence; and his son was made king in his place, i.e. Conchobhar, son of Toirdhelbhach. Mac Diarmada of Magh-Luirg, i.e. Cormac, son of Ruaidhri Mac Diarmada—(the general supporter of hospitality and bounty towards men of learning, and the hardy champion[4] of the warfare and defence of Connacht, was this Cormac, and the protector of his own territory against his enemies)—died after unction and penitence in the end[5] of his age; and his brother, i.e. Diarmaid, assumed his place after him. Conn, son of Niall, son of Art O'Neill, a good captain of the Cenel-Eoghain, was slain by the son of Art Og O'Neill; and O'Neill's two sons,[6]

---

cṙuaoa, which literally signifies "piece of steel." The construction of this entry is rather loose and inelegant.

[5] *The end.* α neṗṗ. See note [1], p. 258 *supra.*

[6] *O'Neill's two sons;* i.e. the two sons of Art Og O'Neill.

hı Neıll .ı. Eıṗí ocuṗ Coṗmac, ɒo ḃí a láıṁ aᵹ .h. Neıll
a ḃṗaɒ ṗoıme ṗın, ɒo ċaḃaıṗc ɒo claınn Cuınn mıc
Neıll, ocuṗ clann Cuınn ɒo cṗochaɒ na ɒeıṗı mac ṗíᵹ
ṗın. Caıṗlén Cúlṁaoıle ɒo ᵹaḃaıl aṗ Mac n'ɒonnchaɒa ɒa ᵹeṗḃṗachaıṗ ṗeın .ı. ɒo Muıṗceṗcach Mac
'ɒonnchaɒa mac Muṗchaɒa, ocuṗ Mac 'ɒonnchaɒa
ṗeın ocuṗ a mac .ı. Muṗchaɒ ɒo ᵹaḃaıl ṗá ċenɒ ᵹoıṗıɒ
na ᵹıaıḃ ṗın leıṗ O n'ɒuḃɒa, ocuṗ le Muıṗceṗcach
Mac n'ɒonnchaɒa, ocuṗ mac eıı ɒo Mac 'ɒonnchaɒa
ɒo ṁaṗḃaɒ ann .ı. 'ɒonnchaɒ. Sloıᵹeɒ leıṗ O n'ɒoṁ-
naıll maılle ṗe hᴁlbanchaıḃ móṗa ṗa ᴁluṗɒaṗ mıac
Eóın Chaċánaıᵹ a Muıᵹ luıṗᵹ, ocuṗ an bealaċ buıɒe
ɒo ᵹeṗṗaɒ ɒoıḃ, ocuṗ cíoṗ ocuṗ bṗáıᵹɒı ɒṗaᵹaıl on cíṗ,
ocuṗ ceachc ṗlán. O Ruaıṗe .ı. Eoᵹan mac Tıᵹeṗnáın,
cıᵹeṗna na ḃṗeıṗne, uṗṗa ċochaıᵹċe eınıᵹ ocuṗ uaıṗle
cṗleachca ᴁoɒa ṗınn, ɒṗaᵹaıl ḃáıṗ an ḃlıaɒaın
ṗın a naıḃíɒ ṗan Fṗoınṗéıṗ ıaṗ nonᵹaɒ ocuṗ ıaṗ
naıċṗıᵹe. Mac Suıɒne Fanaɒ .ı. 'ɒomnall óᵹ moṗcuuṗ
eṗc ıaṗ ᵹcuṗ aıḃíɒe an uıṗɒ Muıṗe uıme la ṗélı
Muıṗe ıṗın nᵹeıṁṗeɒ. ᵹaoċ ṁóṗ ıṗın mblıaɒaın ṗı
an aoıne ṗıa noɒlaıc, ıonnuṗ ᵹuṗ leᵹ móṗán ɒoıṗṗechaıḃ
cṗaınn ocuṗ cloıċe ocuṗ ıomaɒ ɒo cṗannuıḃ, ocuṗ ᵹo
háıṗıᵹċı ɒo bṗıṗ maınıṗcıṗ 'ɒhúın na nᵹall, ocuṗ ɒo
bṗıṗ ocuṗ ɒo ṗuaɒaıᵹ alán ɒaṗṗcṗoıᵹıḃ aṗ muıṗ ocuṗ
aṗ cíṗ. Muıṗıṗ mac 'ɒhonnchaɒa hı ḃıᵹleıᵹınɒ, ṗóı ṗe
leıᵹıuṗ, ɒṗaᵹaıl ḃáıṗ an ḃlıaɒaın ṗın. O Maoılṁıaɒh-
aıᵹ.ı.Cachal mac 'ɒomnaıll mıc Uaıċne ḃuıɒe, caıṗṗech
cheallaıᵹ Ceṗḃallaın, moṗcuuṗ eṗc.

Icc. Enaıṗ ṗoṗ ᴁoıne. Ilóı mblıaɒna ṗıcheɒ ocuṗ
.u. ceɒ ocuṗ mıle aıṗ ın Tıᵹeṗna. Conchoḃaṗ óᵹ O
baıᵹıll, canuṗɒe a ċalman ṗéın, ɒo ṁaṗḃaɒ lá claınn

---

[1] *Was killed.* ɒo ṁaṗḃaɒ. The
partic. ɒo has been erroneously repeated in the MS.

With a great many Albanachs. ṗe
hᴁlbanchaıḃ móṗa; lit. " with
great Albanacha," [i.e. men of Alba,
or Scotland].

[3] *John Cathánagh.* See note [1], p.
200 *supra.*

[4] *The Bealach-buidhe.* The " yellow
pass," now called Bothar-buidhe, or
Ballaghboy, bar. of Tirerrill, co. Sligo.

[5] *Aedh Finn.* " Hugh the Fair ;"
the ancestor of the O'Rorkes, O'Reillys,

A.D.

[1528.]

viz., Henry and Cormac, who had been detained in captivity by O'Neill for a long time previously, were surrendered to the sons of Conn, son of Niall ; and the sons of Conn hanged these two princes.   The castle of Cúl-mhaile was· taken against Mac. Donnchadha by his own brother, i.e. by Muirchertach Mac Donnchadha, the son of Murchadh ; and Mac Donnchadha himself, and his son, i.e. Murchadh, were captured in a short time after that by O'Dubhda, and by Muirchertach Mac Donnchadha ; and another son of Mac Donnchadha was killed[1] there, i.e. Donnchadh. A hosting by O'Domhnaill, with a great many Albanachs[2] under Alexander, the son of John Cathánagh,[3] to Magh-Luirg ; and the Bealach-buidhe[4] was cut down by them ; and they obtained rent and hostages from the country, and returned safely.   O'Ruairc, i.e. Eoghan, son of Tighernán, lord of the Breifne, the sustaining prop of the bounty and nobility of the race of Aedh Finn,[5] died this year in the habit of St. Francis, after unction and penitence.   Mac Suibhne of Fanad, i.e. Domhnall Og, mortuus est, after assuming the habit of the Order of Mary, on the day of the festival of Mary in winter.   Great wind in this year, the Friday before Christmas, which threw down a great many wooden and stone buildings, and several trees ; and it broke down, in particular, the monastery of Dún-na-nGall ; and it shattered and blew away a great number of boats on sea and land.   Maurice, son of Donnchadh O'Bigleighinn, an adept in medicine, died this year. O'Maelmhiadhaigh, i.e. Cathal, son of Domhnall, son of Uaithne Buidhe,[6] chief of Tellach-Cerbhallain, mortuus est.

[1529.]

The kalends of January on Friday ; the age of the Lord one thousand, five hundred, and twenty-nine years.   Concho-bhar Og O'Baighill, tanist of his own country, was slain

---

and their correlatives. The history of Aedh Finn is preserved in a curious Irish MS. called the *Book of Fenagh*, of which a translation will (it is hoped)

soon be given to the public by Denis H. Kelly, Esq., M.R.I.A.

[6] *Uaithne Buiahe*; "Yellow pillar;" in an English form, "Owney Boy."

h1 Óhaigill ɪn hoc anno. Iapla Oeppmuman, Semup, anc aon mac goill pá mo clú oɪnɪg ocuʐ uaɪple oo óɪ an Θpɪnn, ocuʐ oo óoɪ na uppaɪn cogaɪo pe galloɪb ocuʐ pe gaoɪóelaɪó, ocuʐ oob pepp oo čeno oáṁ ocuʐ oeopaɪo, ohéc a láp a aoɪpɪ ocuʐ a ɪnme oo galuʐ opann čpí noɪóče ɪm peɪl pan Seaɪn. Pélɪm mac·Conchobaɪp h1 Óháɪgɪll oo ṁapbao la claɪnn h1 Óhaɪgɪll ɪn hoc anno. mac mɪc Ohuógaɪll na hαlban oo ṁapbaó la hαoó mbuɪóe .h. n'Ooṁnaɪll a noopuʐ čaɪpléɪn Chúɪle ṁɪc an cpéɪn oén óúɪlle cloɪóem. Caɪplén Chúɪl mɪc an cpeɪn oo gabáɪl pá čeno gáɪpɪo na óɪaɪó pɪn le máʐnuʐ .h.n'Oomnaɪll, ocuʐ a bpɪppeó apʐ a haɪčle oo čopaó na comaɪple. O hUɪgɪnn .ɪ. Oomnall cam, paoɪ pe oán ocuʐ pe poʐluɪm, ohéc ɪn hoc anno. mac h1 Uɪgɪnn .ɪ. αoó mac glaɪpne, póɪ pe oáɪ, mopcuuʐ epc. Óʐɪan ballač mac Neɪll mɪc Cuɪnn oo ṁapbao le Copmac mac Uɪóɪlín, ocuʐ é ap ṁuɪnncepuʐ Óʐɪaɪn péɪn, ocuʐ píao·aʐ paʐbáɪl čaɪppʐe Pepʐuɪʐ. αn Copnamach mac Pepʐaɪl mɪc Oonnchaoa óuɪó mɪc αoóaʐáɪɪ, .ɪ. an pep pá huɪppoepca a bpeɪnechuʐ ocuʐ a bpɪlɪóechc pe bpeɪčemnuʐ cuaɪčɪ a cípɪó gaoɪoel, [mopcuuʐ epc] ec pepulcuʐ [epc] a nOɪlpɪnn. Oomnall mac Θoɪn mɪc Oomnaɪll mɪc Óɪppčagpa, aóbap olloman cuaɪpcepc Ulaó pe bépla peɪnechuɪʐ, mopcuuʐ epc ec pepulcuʐ [epc] a ʐcappaɪʐ Pepʐuɪʐ. Sémuʐ mac Ruaɪopɪ mɪc Óɪppčagpa, mac puɪpṁɪʐ a ealaona peɪn, mopcuuʐ epc. mac αɪlín .ɪ. Caɪlín mac gɪlle eppuɪʐ, én poʐa a noɪpɪʐ gaoɪóelaɪó uɪle ap enʐnum ocuʐ ap eɪnech, ohéc. Oomnall mac αoóa mɪc Oomnaɪll mɪc αoóaʐáɪn .ɪ.

---

1 *Hoc.* óc, MS.

2 *Council.* This event is more clearly related by the Four Masters, who state that ɪap ʐcʐúoaó a čoṁaɪple aʐeó oo cɪnneó laɪp an caɪplén no óʐɪpeó; i.e. "after scrutinizing his council, what he [Maghnus

O'Domhnaill] decided was to break it [the castle] down."

3 *In hoc.* an óc, MS.

4 *Fenechas;* i.e. the Irish Laws, or Brehon Laws.

5 *Lay Brehonship;* i.e. Civil Law.

6 *Bírla fenechais.* The *bírla* (or

by the sons of O'Baighill in hoc[1] anno. The Earl of Desmumha, James, the foreigner's son of greatest repute for bounty and nobility that was in Erinn, and who was a prop of battle against Foreigners and Gaeidhel, and the best protector of the learned and destitute, died in the middle of his age and prosperity, of a sudden illness of three nights, on the festival of Saint John. Felim, the son of Conchobhar O'Baighill, was killed by the sons of O'Baighill in hoc anno. The son of Mac Dubhgaill of Alba was killed by Aedh Buidhe O'Domhnaill, in the doorway of the castle of Cúl-mhic-an-tréin, with one stroke of a sword. The castle of Cúl-mhic-an-tréin was taken in the course of a short time after that by Maghnus O'Domhnaill; and it was broken down immediately in pursuance of the council.[2] O'hUiginn, i.e. Domhnall Cam, a doctor in poetry and learning, died in hoc[3] anno. The son of O'hUiginn, i.e. Aedh, son of Glaisne, a doctor in poetry, mortuus est. Brian Ballagh, son of Niall, son of Conn, was slain by Cormac Mac Uibhilín, who was in the friendship of Brian himself, as they were leaving Carraig-Ferghuis. The Cosnamhach, son of Ferghal, son of Donnchadh Dubh Mac Aedhagáin, the most eminent man in the lands of the Gaeidhel in fenechas,[4] and in poetry, with lay Brehonship,[5] [mortuus est], et sepultus [est] in Oilfinn. Domhnall, son of John, son of Domhnall Mac Birrthagra, intended professor of the North of Uladh in "bérla fenechais,"[6] mortuus est, et sepultus [est] in Carraig-Ferghuis. James, son of Ruaidhri Mac Birrthagra, a macfuirmigh[7] of his own art, mortuus est. Mac Ailín, i.e. Cailín, son of Gilla-espuig, the choice of all in Oirer-Gaeidhel for prowess and bounty, died. Domhnall, the son of Aedh, son of Domhnall Mac Aedhagáin, i.e. the Mac

---

language, of the *fenechas*, or Brehon Laws. . It was otherwise called *bérla Feine*. . See O'Donovan's Grammar, Introd., p. lxx.

[7] *Macfuirmigh*. "Son of composer."

This was the title of the sixth grade in the ancient classification of poets. See the *Book of Lecan*, fol. 157; and Ebel's ed. of Zeuss's *Gram. Celt.*, p. 27.

Mac Ccoᵯaᵹáın Uṗṁuman .ı. cenᴅ éıᵹᵲı leıᴄ̇e Moᴄ̇a aᵲ
eıᵹᵲı ocuᵱ aᵲ ꝼılıᴅeċᴄ, moᵲᴄuuᵲ eᵲᴄ. Mac Ḟeoᵲuıᵲ
Ꝺʰúın móıᵲ .ı. Macılıᵱ moᵲᴄuuᵲ eᵲᴄ. Muıᵲċeᵲᴄach
mac Maᵹnuᵲa Mıc Ꝺıaᵲmaᴅa ᵲuaıᵬ ocuᵱ Conchoᵬaᵲ
mac Ꝺ꜀olla Maᵲᵲᴄaın ᴅo maᵲᵬaᴅ an Oılꝼınᴅ, ocuᵱ
Ruaıᴅᵲı buıᴄ̇e mac Ꝺonnchaᴅa ᴄ̇uıᵬ ocuᵱ Emann mac
Ꝺuᵬᵹaıll ᴅo ᵹaᵬaıl ann leıᵲ O Conchoᵬaıᵲ ᵲuaᴅ.

Ⱪᴄᴄ. ꝺenaıᵲ ꝼoᵲ hꝼaᴄ̇aᵲn ; x. mᵬlıaᴅna xxᵉᴄ ocuᵱ .u.
ceᴅ ocuᵱ mıle aıᵲ ın Ꞇıᵹeᵲna. Caıᴄılín ınᵹen Muᵲ-
chaᴅa mıc ᴄ꜀huıᵬne, ben l Ꝺhoċaᵲᴄaıᵹ, moᵲᴄua eᵲᴄ.
Roıᵲᵲ ınᵹen hl Chaᴄ̇áın, ben Ḟhélım l Ꝺhoċaᵲᴄaıᵹ, ᴅo
ᴄ̇ul ᴅhéc ın hoc anno. 8lóıᵹeᴅ leıᵲ .ʜ. nꝺomnaıll a
mí ṁeᴅóın ᴄꝼaṁᵲaᴅ a coıᵹeᴅ Connachᴄ, ᴅáᵲ ᵹaᵬaᴄ̇
laıᵲ ᴄᵲıᴅ ċoıllᴄıᵬ Conchoᵬaıᵲ aᵲ ꝼaᴅ ocuᵱ aᵲᵲın a
nuáchᴄaᵲ ᴄ̇íᵲe, ocuᵱ ᴄaᵲ ᵬúıll buᴄ̇ᴅeᵲᵲ, ocuᵱ ᴄᵲíᴅ an
ᴄánuıᵲᴅechᴄ a Moıᵹ luıᵲᵹ, ocuᵱ ᴄaᵲ caᵲa Ꝺᵲomma
Ruıᵲc ᵲoıᵲ ᴅoᵲıᵬıᵲ ; ocuᵱ Muınᴄeᵲ Eoluıᵲ ᴅo ṁılleᴄ̇
ocuᵱ ᴅo loᵲcuᴅ laıᵲ, ocuᵱ cuıᴅ ᴅá ᴄ̇aoınıᵬ ᴅo buaın ᴅe
ım ċaıᵲlen lıaᴄ̇ᴅᵲomma .ı. Maᵹnuᵲ mac Ḟıᵲᵬoᵲᴄa
Mıc 8huıᵬne ocuᵱ mac Mıc Coılín .ı. Ꞇoıᵲᵲᴅelbach
ᴅuᵬ, ocuᵱ ᵹaᵬáıl aᵲᵲın aᵲıᵲᵲ ᴄaᵲ 8ınuınn ᵲıaᵲ, ocuᵱ ᴅo
ṁachaıᵲe Chonnachᴄ, ocuᵱ ᴅo ᴅᵲoıċeᴄ Ccᴄ̇a Moᴄ̇a ᴄaᵲ
8uca, ocuᵱ Clann Chıonnmaıᵹ ᴅo cᵲeachaᴅ ocuᵱ ᴅo
loᵲcuᴅ laıᵲ .ı. baılᴄı Mıc Ꝺáıᵬíᴄ̇ .ı. ᵹlınnᵲce ocuᵱ Cıll
Chᵲúáın, ocuᵱ éᴅála ımᵬa ᴅo ᴄ̇aᵬaıᵲᴄ aᵲᵲan ᴄíᵲ.
ᵬaıle an ᴄoᵲaıᵲ ᴅo ṁılleᴄ̇ ocuᵱ ᴅo loᵲcuᴅ ᴅon ᴅul ᵲın
laıᵲ, ocuᵱ cíoᵲᵲ coᵲᵲanᴄa ᴅꝼaᵹᵬáıl aᵲ .ʜ. Conchoᵬaıᵲ
ᵲuaᴅ .ı. ᵲé ᵱınᵹınᵲıe ıᵲın ᵹceᴄ̇ᵲomaın ᴅá ᴄ̇úᴄhaıᴅ ; ocuᵱ
ᵱılleᴅ ᴄaᵲaıᵲ ᴅon ᵬealaᵹ buıᴄ̇ı ıaᵲ mılleᴅ Muıᵹe
luıᵲᵹ, ocuᵱ ᵹan ᴅíᵹᵬaıl ᴅo ᴄ̇énum ᴅó. 8oᵲċa ınᵹen
Ccoᴄ̇a óıᵹ mıc Ccoᴄ̇a an eınıᵹ mıc Ⱶeıll mıc Cuınᴅ, uxoᵲ

---

1 *Donnchadh Dubh.* "Donough the Black." A member of the family of Mac Dermot, apparently. This entry is added in the handwriting of Brian Mac Dermot, to whom the MS. belonged, and is not in any other collection of Irish Annals accessible to the Editor.

2 *Hoc.* ᴏᴄ, MS.

3 *Cara-Droma-Ruisc*; i.e. "the weir

Aedhagáin of Ur-Mumha, i.e. head of the learned of Leth-Modha in knowledge and poetry, mortuus est. Mac Feoraisof Dún-mór, i.e. Meiler, mortuus est. Muirchertach, son of
Maghnus Mac Diarmada Ruadh, and Conchobhar Mac
Gilla-Martain, were slain in Oilfinn, and Ruaidhri Buidhe,
son of Donnchadh Dubh,[1] and Edmond Mac Dubhgaill,
were taken prisoners there by O'Conchobhair Ruadh.

The kalends of January on Saturday; the age of the Lord
one thousand, five hundred, and thirty years. Caitilín,
daughter of Murchadh Mac Suibhne, wife of O'Dochartaigh,
mortua est. Rose, daughter of O'Catháin, wife of Felim
O'Dochartaigh, died in hoc[2] anno. A hosting by O'Domhnaill into the province of Connacht, in the middle month
of summer, on which occasion he passed through Coillte-
Conchobhair, and from thence into Uachtar-thíre, and past
Buill southwards, and through the tanist's land into Magh-
Luirg, and eastwards again across Cara-Droma-Ruisc[3]; and
Muinter-Eolais was destroyed and burned by him. And
a number of his people were taken from him about the
castle of Liath-druim, viz., Maghnus, son of Ferdorcha
Mac Suibhne, and the son of Mac Cailín, i.e. Toirdhelbhach
Dubh. And he passed from thence westwards across the
Shannon again, and to Machaire-Connacht, and by the
bridge of Ath-Mogha, across the Suca. And Clann-Connmhaigh was plundered and burned by him, viz., Mac
David's towns, viz., Glinnsce and Cill-Crúain; and he carried off great spoils from the district. Baile-an-tobair was
destroyed and burned by him on this occasion; and he
imposed a defensive tribute[4] on O'Conchobhair Ruadh, i.e.
six pence on every quarter[5] of his country. And he
returned back to the Bealach-buidhe, after destroying
Magh-Luirg, no injury having been done to him. Sorcha,
daughter of Aedh Og, son of Aedh-an-enigh,[6] son of Niall,

A.D.

[1529.]

[1530.]

of Drum-Ruisc"; the old name of
Carrick-on-Shannon.

[4] *Defensive tribute;* i.e. a tribute
the payment of which secured the
protection of O'Donnell.

[5] *On every quarter;* i.e. on every
quarter (or cartron) of land.

[6] *Aedh-an-enigh;* i.e. "Aedh (or
Hugh) of the hospitality."

hi Neill .i. Cuinn mic Cuinn mic Enrí, mortua est. Mac Artáin dux ċineoil Ḟoġartaiġ mortuus est. Mac Domnaill gallóglaeċ .i. Colla mac Colla, consapal tire hEogain mic Neill, mortuus est. Cathal mac Ruaidri óig mic Ruaiḋri caoiċ Mic Ḋiarmada, sáoi ċinnfeḋna do ċrechairecht ocus do ċendsuġad a escarad ar gach taoiḃ ḋe, mortuus est. Cumsgraiċ mac Maolruanaiḋ mic Conchobair Mhéġ Ráġnaill mortuus est. Teaċ cranḋġaile dob ferr do ḃí an Erinn ag Mac Consnama ar Loċ Aillinne do loscud lais O nDomnaill, ocus an Ḃreifne uile ó tsḟliaḃ siar do ṁilleḋ ḋó. Creaċ ṁór do ḋénum dAoḋ Buiḋe O Ḋomnaill a nGailenġ. Sloiged eli leis .h. nDoṁnaill a mí ṁeḋóin an foġṁair ar mac Uilliam Búrc, dár milleḋ cuid don tír, ocus síṫ do ṡnaḋmad doib iarsin, ocus teacht slan acht óg ṁarcach maiṫ dont ṡlúaiġ .i. Aoḋ mac Conchobair riabaiċ hi Ḋuiḃiḋir. Ruġraiḋe, mac Eogain mic Aoḋa bailḃ mic tSheain hi Ḋoċartaiġ, écht mór na ḋuthaid féin, mortuus est. Mac Uilliam ċlainni Ricaird .i. Ricard mac Uilleg finn mic Uilleg ruaiḋ mic Uilleg an ḟína, cinnlitir Gall ocus Ġaoidel uachtair Connacht, ocus an té dob ferr oinech ocus uaisle, ocus buḋ daingne [recht] ocus riaġail tánic do tsliocht Uilliam Cuncúr re cian daimsir, dfaġail báis do ġalur aiṫġerr an ṁí déiġionach don errach. Caipidil na mbrathar mionúr a nDún na nGall an bliadain sin, ocus O Domnaill dá dtabairt amaċ uile ó ṫús co déreḋ ar a ċosdus fein maille re caithem mór ocus re soċraiḋecht aḋbail onorach. Espuc Oilefinn .i. ant espuc Grégech dfaġail báis, ocus ni hoilḃeim don

1 *Uxor.* uxar, MS.

2 *Mortua est.* moirti sunt, MS.

3 *From the mountain westwards*: i.e. all of the district of Breifne-O'Ruairc, or the present co. of Leitrim, to the west of Slieve-an-iarainn.

4 *Conchobhar Riabhach O'Duibhidhir*; or "Conor O'Dwyer the Swarthy." He was probably slain in the retreat homewards.

5 *Ulick-an-fhina*; i.e. "Ulick of the wine."

son of Conn, uxor[1] of O'Neill, i.e. Conn, son of Conn, son of Henry, mortua est.[2] Mac Artain, dux of Cenel-Foghartaigh, mortuus est. Mac Domhnaill Galloglaech, i.e. Colla, son of Colla, constable of Tir-Eoghain-mic-Neill, mortuus est. Cathal, son of Ruaidhri Og, son of Ruaidhri Caech Mac Diarmada, a most eminent captain for plundering and subduing his enemies on every side of him, mortuus est. Cumsgrach, son of Maelruanaidh, son of Conchobhar Mag Raghnaill, mortuus est. The best wooden house in all Erinn, which Mac Consnamha had on Loch-Ailinne, was burned by O'Domhnaill ; and all the Breifne from the mountain westward[3] was destroyed by him. A great depredation was committed by Aedh Buidhe O'Domhnaill in Gaileng. Another hosting by O'Domhnaill, in the middle month of harvest, against Mac William Burk, on which occasion a part of the district was destroyed. And peace was afterwards concluded by them ; and he (*O'Neill*) returned safely, with the exception of a good young horseman of the army, i.e. Aedh, son of Conchobhar Riabhach O'Duibhidhir.[4] Rudhraidhe, son of Eoghan, son of Aedh Balbh, son of John O'Dochartaigh, a great loss in his own country, mortuus est. Mac William of Clann-Rickard, i.e, Richard, son of Ulick Finn, son of Ulick Ruadh, son of Ulick-an-fhina,[5] head of the Foreigners and Gaeidhel of Upper Connacht, and the person of the best bounty and nobility, and of the firmest [law] and rule, that had come for a long time of the race of William the Conqueror,[6] died of a very brief illness in the last month of spring. A chapter of the Friars Minors in Dun-na-nGall this year ; and O'Domhnaill maintained them all from the commencement to the conclusion at his own cost, with great expenditure, and munificent, honourable hospitality. The Bishop of Oilfinn, i.e. the Greek bishop,[7]

---

[6] *William the Conqueror.* William Fitz Aldelm de Burgh.

[7] *Greek Bishop.* There is no account of this Bishop in any authority accessible to the Editor, nor does his name occur in the lists given by Ware and Harris.

ϱαοɴɴαcɧτ αɴτ éϛ αɴ εγρυιc ϛγέϛαιϛ. Coṁγοɲbα
Choʟυιɱ cιʟʟe α ɴϛʟιοɴɴ cιʟʟe .ι. Ϩοɴɴ ɱαϛ-Νιαʟʟυγγαιϛ
ɱοɲτυυγ εγτ. ιαγʟα Chιʟʟe ϱαγα .ι. ϛεγόιϱ ɱαc ϛεγόιϱ
ϱο ᵬí α ᵬαϱ γá γιαγϱ αϛ γιϛ Sαχαɴ ϱο τeαcɧτ α ɴЄγιɴɴ
οcυγ ϛιυιγϱιγ Sαχαɴαch ϱο τοcɧτ ʟειγ, οcυγ ιαϱ αϛ
ɱιʟʟeϱ ṁόγáιɴ γá ϛαοιᵬeαʟαιᵬ. Ο Rαιϛιʟʟιϛ ϱο ϛαbáιʟ
ϱόιᵬ οcυγ é αγ τeαcɧτ ɴα ϛceɴɴ γειɴ. ιɴϛeɴ Ϻιc ιɴ
ᵬɧαιγϱ .ι. Uɴα ϱɧec. ιɴϛeɴ ɦι ᵬɧαιϛιʟʟ .ι. Róιγ ιɴϛeɴ
Ϲοιγγϱɧeʟbαιϛ ɱιc Νeιʟʟ γυαιϱ, beɴ ϱéγcαch ϱειϛeɴιϛ,
ɱοɲτυα εγτ. Síʟe ιɴϛeɴ ɦι Ϝαʟʟαɱαιɴ υχογ Cαιγbγι
ɱιc ιɴ γγιόγα ɦι ᵬιγɴ, beɴ ϱéγcαch ᵬαοɴɴαcɧταch
ϱειϛ ϱeαʟᵬα ɴαγ ᵬιυʟτ ϱáṁ ɴα ϱeογαιϱ, ɱοɲτυα εγτ.

Ϳctt. Єɴáιγ γογ Ϩοɱɴαch ; eɴ bʟιαϱαɴ ϱéϛ αγ γιcɧιτ,
οcυγ cυιϛ ceϱ οcυγ ɱιʟe αιγ ιɴ Ϲιϛεγɴα. Ο Sιαϛαιʟ
οʟʟαɱ ʟειϛιγ ιɴɴγι ɦЄοϛαιɴ ɱοɲτυυγ εγτ. Cαιγʟeɴ
ᵬeοιʟ ʟειce ϱο ϛαbáιʟ ϱccοᵬ ᵬυιᵬe Ο Ϩɧοɱɴαιʟʟ, οcυγ
bυαιᵬγeϱ αɴ τíγe ϱο τeαcɧτ αγγ γιɴ ϛο ɱόγ. Ϩοɴɴ-
cɧαϱ ɱαc Ϲοιγγϱɧeʟbαιϛ ɱιc Ϲαιᵬc ɦι ᵬγιαιɴ,
τáɴυγϱe Ϲυαᵬṁυɱαɴ, ceɴɴγeᵬɴα ɱαιᵬ οcυγ γeγ
ϱéɴṁα ειɴιϛ οcυγ υαιγʟe, ϱɧéc ιɴ hoc αɴɴο. Ϻαϛ
Cαγγτɧαιϛ γιαbαch .ι. Ϩοɱɴαʟʟ ɱαc Ϝιɴϛιɴ ɱιc Ϩιαγ-
ɱαϱα, τιϛεγɴα όϛ Cαιγbγι, οcυγ γeγ ειɴιϛ cοιτᵭιɴɴ
ϱéιϛγιᵬ οcυγ ϱαοιγ eαʟϱɴα, οcυγ τιϛεγɴα ϱο bυ γο
ṁαιᵭ γeαcɧτ οcυγ γιαϛαʟ, οcυγ τυc ϛαιγɱ γcοιʟe
ϱγεγυιᵬ Єγeɴɴ, ϱο ᵬυʟ ϱɧéc ιɴ hoc αɴɴο. Ϻαc ɦι
Ϩɧοᵭαγταιϛ .ι. Νιαʟʟ ɱαc Coɴchοbαιγ ᵭαγγαιϛ ɱοɲτυυγ
εγτ. Ϩιαγɱαιϱ ɱαc Seαιɴ ɱιc Ͼcοᵬα ɱιc Ϻɧαοʟγυαɴ-
αιᵬ .ι. αɴᵭé ϱοb γeγγ υαιγʟe οcυγ ϱαοɴɴαcɧτ ϱία
ᵭοιγγϝιɴe γειɴ, ϱɧéc. Cοϛαϱ ɱόγ α τíγ Cοɴαιʟʟ αɴ
ᵬʟιαϱαιɴ γιɴ ιϱιγ Ο ɴϨοṁɴαιʟʟ οcυγ α ɱαc .ι. Ϻáϛɴυγ.
Ο Ϩοɱɴαιʟʟ ϱο cɧυγ τγʟúαιϛ ṁόιγ αɴ αοɴ áιτ οcυγ ϱυʟ

---

[1] *Glenn-Cille.* *Recte* Glenn-Coluim-
Cille (or Glencolumbkill), in the co.
of Donegal.

[2] *Donn Mac Niollusaigh.* In the
Annals of Connacht the Christian
name is Donnchadh, or Donough. The

surname Mac Niallusaigh is now written Mac Eneilis.

[3] *To meet themselves;* ɴα ϛceɴɴ
γειɴ; i.e. to meet them at their own
invitation.

[4] *Uxor.* υχαγ, MS.

died; and the death of the Greek bishop is no blemish to humanity. The comarb of Colum Cille in Glenn-Cille,[1] i.e. Donn Mac Niallusaigh,[2] mortuus est. The Earl of Cill-dara, i.e. Garrett son of Garrett, who had been a long time under arrest by the king of the Saxons, came to Erinn, and a Saxon Justiciary came with him; and they were destroying much against the Gaeidhel. O'Raighilligh was taken prisoner by them, after he had gone to meet themselves.[3] Mac-in-Bhaird's daughter, i.e. Una, died. O'Baighill's daughter, i.e. Rose, daughter of Toirdhelbhach, son of Niall Ruadh, a charitable, most bountiful woman, mortua est. Síle, daughter of O'Fallamhain, uxor[4] of Cairbre, son of the Prior O'Birn, a charitable, humane, beautiful woman, who refused neither guest nor stranger, mortua est.

The kalends of January on Sunday; the age of the [1531.] Lord one thousand, five hundred, and thirty-one years. O'Siaghail, chief physician of Inis-Eoghain, mortuus est. The castle of Bel-leice was taken by Aedh Buidhe O'Domhnaill; and the disturbance of the district resulted greatly from that event. Donnchadh, son of Toirdhelbhach, son of Tadhg O'Briain, tanist of Tuadh-Mumha, a good captain, and a man who practised hospitality and excellence, died in hoc anno. Mac Carthaigh Riabhach, i.e. Domhnall, son of Fínghin, son of Diarmaid, a young lord of Cairbre, and a man of general bounty to poets and men of learning—and a lord of most excellent law and rule, who had given a school invitation to the men of Erinn—died in hoc anno. The son of O'Dochartaigh, i.e. Niall, son of Conchobhar Carragh, mortuus est. Diarmaid, son of John, son of Aedh, son of Maelruanaidh, i.e. the most noble and humane person of his own kindred,[5] died. A great war in Tir-Conaill this year, between O'Domhnaill and his son, i.e. Maghnus. O'Domhnaill sent a large

---

[5] *His own kindred.* In the *Annals of Connacht* his sept is called *Síiocht Maelruanaidh,* or "descendants of Maelruanaidh," which was the tribe name of the Mac Donoughs of Corann, in the county of Sligo.

α nούchaιb Mhaᵹnuιp, ocup an cιp vo ṁιlleb bó; ocup
mac Oonnchava čoeιch Mhéᵹ Uιbιp, vuιne uappal
maιč vpepuιb Manach vo ṁapbab ap an plóιᵹev; ocup
Maᵹnup vo čeachc a cíp Ccoba ocup mopán vo ṁιlleb
ιnncι, ocup apaιle. Mac Mιc Uιbιlín .ι. Copmac, cenv
pebna ṁaιč ocup pep eιnιᵹ čoιcčιnn, vpaᵹaιl báιp co
hobann ιn hoc anno. 8loιᵹev leιpιn nᵹuιpvíp cpacpan-
ach .ι. Uιllíam 8ᵹemelcún a cíp Eoᵹaιn, ocup O Oomnaιll vo bul na ᵹconne, ocup caιplén Cιnnaιpv vo
bpιppeb ocup an cιp vo ṁιlleb; ocup Opían mac
Ločlιιnn mιc cShuιbne, conpapal ιapla Upṁuman, vo
ṁapbab a mbpuιᵹιn ap an ploιᵹev pιn peιn. ιollann
buιbe mac Mhaoιlečlaιnn mιc ιollaιnn Mιc ιn Leᵹa
puιaιb, póι na ealavaιn peιn, vhec an blιavaιn pιn.
8ιle ιnᵹen Chaιpbpe hI Oιpn, ben a haoppa péιn vob
pepp vo baιncoιppeachaιb píl Muιpeᵹhaιᵹh ιna coιmpé,
[vpaᵹbaιl báιp], ocup a hablucav a Ropp Chommáιn a
nočhupliᵹe a pιnnpep. Cuachal O Oomnalláιn ó
ṁuchaιpe Mhaonṁoιᵹe moptuup epc. ᵹιllapavpaιc
mac Ccbuιṁ Mιc ιn Ohaιpv moptuup epc.

ᵏCct. Enáιp pop Luan: bá blíavuιn vhéc ap pιčιc
ocup .u. cev ocup mιle. O Oomnaιll vo bul a ᵹcenv
an ᵹuιpvíp .ι. Uιllíam 8ᵹemelcún an blιavaιn pι, ocup
pann ocup cenᵹal vo benum pιp, ocup. an ᵹuιpvíp
8acpanach vo čochc a cíp Eoᵹaιn, ocup Oun ᵹenuιnn vo
bpιppeb bó, ocup an cιp vo ṁιlleb. ιapla Chιlle vapa
.ι. ᵹepóιv mac ᵹepóιv vo čochc app 8appanaιb ocup é na
ᵹuιpvíp ón pí. O Oomnaιll vo bul a Muιᵹ Luιpᵹ ocup
Mac Oomnaιll leιp .ι. Cclupvap mac Eoιn Chačánaιᵹ,
ocup cpeača ocup loιpčι vo benum boιb, ocup pιč vo
benum ᵹo luač na bιaιb pιn vóιb. Clann hI Neιll .ι.
clann Ccιpc óιᵹ .ι. Oomnall ocup Cuachal, vo bóι

---

[1] *Sᵹemelcín.* A rude way of writing the name of Skeffington.

[2] *Mac-in-Legha.* This name signifies "son of the Physician." Maelechlainn Mac-in-Legha, mentioned above
as the father of the person whose obit
is recorded, aided in the transcription,
in 1512, of an Irish medical MS. preserved in the King's Inns' Library,
Dublin. See Wilde's Report on *Table
of Deaths,* Census of Ireland for 1851,
part v., vol. i., p. 28.

army to one place, and went into Maghnus's country; and the district was destroyed by him. And the son of Donnchadh Caech Mag Uidhir, a good gentleman of the Feara-Manach, was killed on the hosting. And Maghnus went into Tir-Aedha, and destroyed much in it, &c. The son of Mac Uibhilín, i.e. Cormac, a good captain, and a man of general hospitality, died suddenly in hoc anno. A hosting by the Saxon Justiciary, i.e. William Sgemeltún,[1] to Tir-Eoghain ; and O'Domhnaill went to meet them; and they demolished the castle of Cennard, and destroyed the country. And Brian, son of Lochlainn Mac Suibhne, the Earl of Ur-Mumha's constable, was killed in a conflict on that same hosting. Illann Buidhe, son of Maelechlainn, son of Illann Mac-in-Legha[2] Ruadh, an eminent man in his own art,[3] died this year. Silè, daughter[4] of Cairbre O'Birn, the best woman of her own age of the ladies of Sil-Muiredhaigh in her time, [died], and was buried in Ros-Comain, in the tomb of her ancestors. Tuathal O'Domh-nallain, from Machaire-Maenmhaighe,[5] mortuus est. Gill-lapatraic, son of Adam Mac-in-Bhaird, mortuus est.

[1532.]

The kalends of January ; one thousand, five hundred, and thirty-two years. O'Domhnaill went this year to meet the Justiciary, i.e. William Sgemeltún,[1] and formed a friendship and compact with him; and the Saxon Justiciary went into Tir-Eoghain, and the castle of Dun-Genainn was demolished, and the country injured, by him. The Earl of Cill-dara, i.e. Garrett, son of Garrett, came from Saxon-land, as Justiciary from the king. O'Domhnaill went into Magh-Luirg; and Mac Domhnaill, i.e. Alexander, son of John Cathánach *was* with him ; and depredations and burnings were committed by them ; and peace was quickly after-wards made by them. The sons of O'Neill, viz., the sons of Art Og, viz., Domhnall and Tuathal, who had been

---

[3] *In his own art ;* i.e. in medicine.

[4] *Daughter;* ingen; probably a mistake for ben, "wife." See the last entry under 1530.

[5] *Machaire - Maenmhaighe.* The "plain of Maenmagh," a district in the county of Galway.

abḟad a mbraiġdenus ag O Néill, do crochad lais in hoc anno. Eoġan mac Thiġernain mic Eoġain hI Ruairc, sói ḋuine uassuil ar a ċulaiḋ fein, do ṁarbad le clainn I Mhaoilṁuadhaiġ a mbaile na mbráthar a nDruim ḋá eiṫiar. Mac Mhég Fhlannchaiḋ .i. Toirrdhelbach do ṁarbad dia ḋias derbráthar féin a ndorus baile Mhég Fhlannchaiḋ, ocus Brian O Ruairc do ṁilleḋ ṁorán a nDartraiġe tríssin. Inġen Mhic Shúiḃne Fhánad .i. Máire, .i. ben hI Dháiġill, dfaġail ḃáis go hobann .i. a hescur dá heaċ a ndorus a baile fein. O Maolconaire .i. Torna mac Torna mortuus est, ocus O Maolconaire do ġairm na ionad do Conchobar mac Domnaill ruaid hI Mhaoilconaire, ocus a ḋul dhéc go luaṫ na ḋiaiḋ sin. Caislén Aird na riaḋ do ġabáil le clainn hI Dhuḃda ar mac Seain a Búrc, ocus cogad etorra féin ocus sliocht Ricaird a Búrc, ocus mórán creaċ ocus marḃṫa do denum etorra in hoc anno. O Cerḃuill .i. Maolruanaiḋ, an Gaoidel dob uaisle ocus dob oirrderca a leṫ Moḋa, ocus is mó do ṁill fá ġalloiḃ ocus do lessaiġ fá ġaoidelaiḃ, dfaġail ḃáis in hoc anno. Comorba Fiḋnacha .i. Brian mortuus est. Mac Uiḋilín .i. Ualtar mac Geróid do ṁarbaḋ an egluis Dhúin bó, ocus Conchobar mac hI Chaṫáin, fer toictech tromċonáiġ, do loscud, ocus Mac Conulaḋ .i. Sémmus mac Airt Mic Conulaḋ do ġabail ann. Clann Doṁnaill ċleiriġ hI Chaṫáin do ríne na gníoma sin. Mac iarla Urṁuman .i. Tomás mac Piarais ruaid do marbad a nOssraiġe le Diarmaid mac Gillaṗádraic, aḋbar riġ Ossraiġe; ocus ní mór nar ḃé sin écht Mhaoilṁóire, daiġ nír ḃo cian iarsin gurro tairḃreṫ Diarmaid lé na derbráthair féin, .i. lá Mac Gillaṗadraic, don Iarla Urṁumnech, ocus ro cenglad

---

1 *In the Friars' town.* The Four Masters say "in the monastery."

2 "*Maelmor's feat.*" The Irish chronicles relate that Tuathal Maelgarbh, monarch of Ireland, was slain in the year 544, by a person named

A.D.
[1532.]

a long time imprisoned by O'Neill, were hanged by him in hoc anno. Eoghan, son of Tighernan, son of Eoghan O'Ruairc, a most excellent gentleman in his own position, was slain by the sons of O'Maelmhiadhaigh in the Friars' town,[1] in Druim-dhá-ethiar. The son of Mac Flann-chaidh, i.e. Toirdhelbhach, was slain by his own two brothers in the doorway of Mac Flannchaidh's resi-dence; and Brian O'Ruairc destroyed much in Dartraighe through that. The daughter of Mac Suibhne Fánad, i.e. Mary, O'Baighill's wife, died suddenly; i.e. she was thrown from her horse in the doorway of her own residence. O'Maelconaire, i.e. Torna, the son of Torna, mortuus est; and Conchobhar, son of Domhnall Ruadh O'Maelconaire, was proclaimed the O'Maelconaire in his place; and he died quickly after that. The castle of Ard-na-riadh was taken by the sons of O'Dubhda against the son of John Burk; and a war *broke out* between themselves and the descendants of Rickard Burk, and many depreda-tions and homicides were committed between them, in hoc anno. O'Cerbhaill, i.e. Maelruanaidh, the noblest and most illustrious Gaeidhel that was in Leth-Modha, and who destroyed most in regard to Foreigners, and im-proved most in regard to Gaeidhel, died in hoc anno. The comarb of Fídhnacha, i.e. Brian, died. Mac Uidhilín, i.e. Walter, son of Garrett, was killed in the church of Dún-bó; and Conchobhar, son of O'Catháin, a very rich, affluent man, was burned, and Mac Conuladh, i.e. James, the son of Art Mac Conuladh, was taken prisoner there. The sons of Domhnall Clerech O'Catháin committed those deeds. The son of the Earl of Ur-Mumha, i.e. Thomas, son of Piers Ruadh, was slain in Osraighe by Diarmaid Mac Gilla-Patraic, intended king of Osraighe. And this was very nearly " Maelmor's feat;"[2] for it was not long afterwards until Diarmaid was delivered by his own brother, i.e. by Mac Gilla-Patraic, to the Earl of

Maelmor, who was immediately killed himself in return. Hence the proverb "the fate of Maelmor" is used to ex- press sudden retaliation. See *Chron. Scotorum*, loc. cit.

Ɔιαρμαιɔ Láρ αn ιαρla ανɔιξuιl α ṁιc ocuρ ʒach uιlc
αιρċεnα ɔαιɔερnaɓ le Ɔιαρμαιɔ ροιme ριn ριαm.
Ɔuɓċαɓlαιʒ, ιnʒеn Conchobαιρ mιc Ruαιɔρι ɓuιɓι .ι.
ben Conchobαιρ óιʒ mιc Mուιρċеαρταιξ Mιc Ɔιαρmαɔα
ρúαιɔ, mορτuα еρτ.

Ictt. еnαιρ ɣορ Mαιρτ; τρι blιαɔnα ɔéʒ αρ xxιc αρ
.ιι. ceɔ αρ mιle αιρ ιn Tιʒеρnα. Mαс Ɔιαρmαɔα
ṁοιʒе Luιρʒ .ι. Ɔιαρmαιɔ αn еιnιʒ mαс Ruαιɔρι óιʒ
mιc Ruαιɔρι ċαοιċ Mιc Ɔιαρmαɔα, ɔο ṁαρɓαɓ ρеρ
ɔolum lα clαιnn Еοʒαιn mιc Thαιɓʒ mιc Ruαιɔρι Mιc
Ɔιαρmαɔα, .ι. bράιϑρе Mιc Ɔιαρmαɔα ρéιn, ocuρ ρά
móρ αnτ échτ ριn, óιρ ní ραιɓе α comαιmριρ ριρ α nꝋριnn
ρеρ α τιʒеρnuιρ ɔο buɓ mó οιnech ocuρ uαιρle, ocuρ
ɔob ρеρρ ɔο ceɔ ɔáṁ ocuρ ɔеoραιɓ, ocuρ αnn ʒach uιle
ιṅοɓ ɔuιne ṁαιɓ ιnáρρ; [ρеρ lán] ɔο αιἑnе ocuρ ɔеoluρ
ocuρ ɔеlαɔhαιn, ocuρ ɔα ʒach mαιɓ áιρchеnα; lá ρéιle
bρénuιnn ρορɔíἑеnɔαɔ α Lιορ Ccoɓáιn α cριċ Ccιρτιξ,
ocuρ Еοʒαn mαс Tαιɓʒ Mιc Ɔιαρmαɔα ɔο ριοξαɓ αρ
cριċ člαιnnι Mhαolρuαnαιɓ nα ɔιαιɓ. Cαιρlén 8lιʒιʒh
ɔο ξαɓáιl le Tαɓʒ óʒ mαс Tαιɓʒ mιc Ccoɓα hi Choncho-
bαιρ αρ ιnɔραιʒеɔ οιɓċе, íαρ ɓραξαιl ϑρеolτα ocuρ
ċuιρ αmαċ αιρ ó ċuιɔ ɔο luchτ coιméτα ιn ċαιρléιn
ρеιn. Cαιρlеn Ccιρɔ nα ριαɓ ɔο. ξαɓáιl lé clαιnn Tom-
máιρ α búρc αρ člαιnn hi Ɔhuɓɔα ραn οιɓċе muρ αn
ceɔnα. Cρеċ móρ ɔο ɓénum ɔO Ɔhomnαιll αρ .h.
nꝋρnα mbuιɓе ιɔιρ ɓá αɓuιnn. Nιαll mαс Muρchαɔα
Mιc 8huιɓnе ɔο ṁαρɓαɔ αρ ɔροιċеτ 8lιʒιʒh .ι. αnτ óʒ
mαсαοm ɔob ρеρρ ɔο τρlιochτ Ɔonnchαɔα ṁóιρ, ιn hoc
αnno. Muιρcеρταch mαс Ƒеιlιm mιc Tοιρρɔhеlbαιξ
ċαρραιξ ɔο ċρochαɔ lα .h. nƆoṁnαιll αρ ραιċτι cαιρlеιn

---

1 Diarmaid-an-einigh; i.e. "Diarmaid (or Dermot) of the hospitality."
2 Of his means. α τιʒеρnuιρ;
lit. "of his lordship;" (i.e. of equal
possessions).
3 Between the two rivers; i.e. the
rivers Owenmore and Coolaney, co.

Slige. But Idir-dhá-abhuinn may
have been an alias name for O'Hara
Buidhe's country.
4 Donnchadh Mór. The pedigree
of this Donnchadh Mór, from whom
the Mac Swineys are descended, is
given in Mac Firbis's genealogical

Ur-Mumha; and Diarmaid was manacled by the Earl in revenge of his son, and of every other evil which had been previously committed by Diarmaid. Dubhcabhlaigh, daughter of Conchobhar, son of Ruaidhri Buidhe, i.e. the wife of Conchobhar Og, son of Muirchertach Mac Diarmada Ruadh, mortua est.

The kalends of January on Tuesday; the age of the Lord one thousand, five hundred, and thirty-three years. Mac Diarmada of Magh-Luirg, i.e. Diarmaid-an-einigh,[1] son of Ruaidhri Og, son of Ruaidhri Caech Mac Diarmada, was killed per dolum by the sons of Eoghan, son of Tadhg, son of Ruaidhri Mac Diarmada, viz., Mac Diarmada's own kinsmen; and that was a great calamity, for there was not in his time in Erinn a man of his means[2] of greater hospitality and excellence, and a better protector of guests and strangers, and one more distinguished in every quality of a good man than he; [a man full] of knowledge, learning, and science, and of all good : on the day of Brenainn's festival he was beheaded in Lis-Aedhain, in the territory of Airtech; and Eoghan, son of Tadhg Mac Diarmada, was made king over the territory of the Clann-Maelruanaidh after him. The castle of Sligech was taken by Tadhg Og, son of Tadhg, son of Aedh O'Conchobhair, in a nocturnal assault, after he had obtained guidance, and an offer of its surrender, from some of the keepers of the castle themselves. The castle of Ard-na-riadh was taken by the sons of Thomas Burk from the sons of O'Dubhda, in the night, in like manner. A great depredation was committed by O'Domhnaill upon O'hEghra Buidhe, between the two rivers.[3] Niall, son of Murchadh Mac Suibhne, i.e. the best young man of the race of Donnchadh Mór,[4] was killed on the bridge of Sligech in hoc anno. Muirchertach son of Felim, son of Toirdhelbhach Carragh, was hanged by O'Domhnaill on the green of the castle of Enagh,

work (R. I. Acad. copy, p. 124), where he is said to have been the eleventh in | descent from Flaithbhertach O'Neill. who died in the year 1036.

Εναιξ, αρ νοιυιταο αn ϐαιle το ϭαϐαιρc αρρ οά ϭloinn
οcuρ οά ϐράιϭριϐ ρειn. Μαοιρuαnαιϐ óξ mαc Μhαοι-
ρuαnαιϐ 1 Cheρϐuιll οhéc ιn hoc αnno. Ο Μαοιrñuαιϐ
.ι. Οοmnαll cαοϭ mαc ιn ϭορnαmαιξ το rñαρϐαϐ α ϐριoll
le nα οeρϐράchαιρ ρειn, οcuρ le mαc α οeρϐράchαρ,
αρ ραιϭϯ Ιοιnn Εαlα, οcuρ Ο Μαοιrñuαιϐ το ξαιρm οά
ϭeρϐράchαιρ .ι. το Chαϭαοιρ. Εmonn mαc Cuιnn mιc
Νéιll το rñαρϐαϐ le clαιnn Μhéξ Uιϭιρ. Ϝειlιm bαcαϭ
mαc Νéιll mιc Cuιnn οhéc ιn hoc αnno.

Ϳctt. Εnáιρ ϝορ ϐαροαοιn; ceιτρι blιαοnα οεξ αρ
ριchιτ αρ .u. ceο αρ mιle αιρ ιn Cιξeρnα. Μαc Οιαρmαοα rñοιξe Ιuιρξ, .ι. Εοξαn mαc Cαιϭξ mιc Ruαιορι
Μιc Οιαρmαοα, οϝαξαιl ϐáιρ αn blιαοαιn ριn αρ
cαιρριξ Μιc Οhιαρmαοα ιαρ nοnξαο οcuρ nαιϭριξe,
οcuρ Ccοϐ mαc Cορmαιc mιc Ruαιϭρí Μιc Οιαρmαοα
το ξαϐáιl τιξeρnuιρ rñοιξe Ιuιρξ nα ϭιαιϐ, οcuρ é nα αb
α mαιnιροιρ nα ϐúιlle; οcuρ cαιρριξ Μιc Οhιαρmαοα
το ξαϐáιl le clαιnn Cαιϭξ mιc Ruαιορι Μιc Οιαρmαοα
αn uáιρ ριn .ι. το Ruαιορι οcuρ το Chomαlταch. Coξαο
οcuρ ιmρeρρuιn οϝáρ ιριn τíρ ϭe ριn. Μαc mιc
Εοchαοα .ι. Οοnnchαο mαc Μhαοlmuιρe mιc Εοchαοα,
αϭϐαρ οllαmαn Ιαιξen ξαn ιmmρeρuιn οcuρ ρeρ α
cϝαοchαιρ ρειn οοb ρeρρ αnn ξαch uιle ξné τοn
eαlαϐuιn, οcuρ οοb ρeρρ το ϭιξeρραch, το mαρbαο
ξο τuραιρτech οen uρchuρ το ξα le οeρϐραιϭριϐ α mαth-
αρ ρειn .ι. clαιnn [1] Cuαthαιl. Coιρροhelbαch ουϐ
Ο Οιmuραιξ το rñαρbαο α ϐριoll le nα ϐráchαιρ ρειn
.ι. le Μuιρceρταch óξ Ο nΟιοmuραιξ αρ ρlánuιϐ Οé
οcuρ Ειϐín nαοιm. Μuιρceρταch óξ ρειn το rñαρbαο
ξο luαϭ nα ϭιαιϐ ριn le .h. Μόρϐα τρe ϭumαchτuιϐ
Οé οcuρ Ειϐín. Εοξαn mαc Ccοϐα buιϐe mιc Νειll mιc
Cuιnn, αn mαc ριξ οοb ρeρρ το ϝlιοchτ Ccοϐα buιϐe, το

---

1 *Niall.* Ile was the son of Art
O'Neill, according to the Four Masters.

2 *Conn.* This Conn was probably

the person of the same name mentioned
in the preceding entry, as his grandson
Felim was, according to the *Annals of
Connacht,* the choice prince of the

after his own sons and kinsmen had refused to give the place for his ransom. Maelruanaidh Og, son of Maelruanaidh O'Cerbhaill, died in hoc anno. O'Mael-mhuaidh, i.e. Domhnall Caech, the son of the Cosnamh-ach, was killed in treachery by his own brother, and by his brother's son, on the green of Lann-Eala; and his brother, i.e. Cathair, was proclaimed O'Maelmhuaidh. Edmond, son of Conn, son of Niall,[1] was slain by the sons of Mag Uidhir. Felim Bacagh, son of Niall, son of Conn,[2] died in hoc anno.

The kalends of January on Thursday; the age of the Lord one thousand, five hundred, and thirty-four years. Mac Diarmada of Magh-Luirg, i.e. Eoghan, son of Tadhg, son of Ruaidhri Mac Diarmada, died this year on Mac Diarmada's Rock, after unction and penitence; and Aedh, son of Cormac, son of Ruaidhri Mac Diarmada, assumed the sovereignty of Magh-Luirg after him, and he an abbot in the monastery of the Buill; and Mac Diarmada's Rock was taken at that time by the sons of Tadhg, son of Ruaidhri Mac Diarmada, viz., by Ruaidhri and Tomaltach. War and dissensions grew in the country through this. The son of Mac Eochadha, i.e. Donnchadh, the son of Maelmuire Mac Eochadha, intended ollamh of Laighen, without dispute, and the best man of his own labour in every species of science, and the best house-keeper, was unhappily killed with one cast of a spear by his own mother's brothers, viz., the sons of O'Tuathail. Toirdhelbhach Dubh O'Dimusaigh was killed in treachery by his own relative, i.e. by Muirchertach Og O'Dimusaigh, whilst under the guarantees[3] of God and Saint Ebhin. Muirchertach Og himself was killed soon after that by O'Mordha, through the power of God and Ebhin. Eoghan, son of Aedh Buidhe, son of Niall, son of Conn, the best son of a king of the race of Aedh Buidhe, was killed by

[O'Neill sept called] Clann-Aedha-Buidhe (or Clannaboy).

[3] *Under the guarantees.* The person slain was apparently under the protection of an oath sworn by the names of God and Saint Ebhin.

ṁaṙbaḋ le hᴀlbanċaiḃ ḋen uṙċuṙ ḋo cṙoiġiḋ aṙ
Loċ Cuan. Iaṙla Ċille ḋaṙa, .i. ᵹeṙóiḋ mac ᵹeṙóiḋ
mic Ċómmaiṙ, ḋo ḃul a Saxuiḃ ṙá ċoᵹaiṙm ṙiᵹ
Saxṙan, ocuṙ anc Iaṙla ḋo chuṙ ḋoċum báiṙ .i. anc aon
mac ᵹoill ḋo buḋ mó ḋo ṙᵹél ḋo ḃí a nEṙinn na aimm-
ṙiṙ ṙéin; ocuṙ mac an Iaṙla .i. Comáṙṙ ḋo milleḋ
ṁuinnceṙi ṙiᵹ Saxṙan a nEṙinn le coᵹaḋ .i. ᵹach uile
ḋuine ḋá ṙaiḋe aᵹ muinechaḋ aṙṙ ṙi Saxṙan aṙ ṙeḋh
na Miḋe a mbailci ḋo bṙiṙṙeḋ ocuṙ a mbṙáiᵹḋe ḋo
ḃuain ḋíḃ; ocuṙ aiṙḋeṙṙṙacc ḃaile ᴀċa cliaċ ḋo maṙbaḋ
le mac an Iaṙla aṙ an coᵹaḋ ṙin. Ocuṙ ᵹuiṙḋíṙ Saṙ-
ṙanach ḋo ċeachc a nEṙinn on ṙí, ocuṙ bailci mic an
Iaṙla ḋo bṙiṙṙeḋ ḋuṙṁóṙ, ocuṙ an Mhiḋe uile ḋo
milleḋ eciṙ ċill ocuṙ cuaiċ, ocuṙ uilc imḋa ḋo ḋenum
ecoṙṙa; ocuṙ Maᵹ Nuaaḋ ḋo ᵹabáil leiṙin nᵹuiṙḋíṙ
hṙacṙanach, ocuṙ echca móṙa ḋo miuucceṙ mic an Iaṙla
ḋo ṁaṙbaḋ ann. O Conchobaiṙ ṙuaḋ .i. Caḋc buiḋe
mac Caṫail ṙuaiḋh ḋṙaᵹail ḃáṙ an ḃliaḋain ṙin, ocuṙ·
O Conchobaiṙ ḋo ᵹaiṙm ḋo Choiṙṙḋhelbach ṙuaḋ .i. ḋá
mac na ionaḋ. Ḃṙian mac Seain I Mhaoilṁuaiḋ ḋo
ṁaṙbaḋ aḃṙioll le cuiḋ ḋá ċineḋ ṙéin. O Gallċubaiṙ
.i. emmonn mac Eoin mic Cuaṫail ḋṙaᵹail ḃáṙ obuinn
in hoc anno. Coṙmac mac ṙeṙᵹail Mic in ḃaiṙḋ, ṙói
ṙe ḋán ocuṙ ḋuine ḋob ṙeṙṙ caimic ḋá ċineḋ ṙein ḋo
ċaoḃ ḋeiṙce ocuṙ ḋaonnachca, ḋṙaᵹail ḃáṙ ḋo ᵹaluṙ
obann iaṙ nonᵹaḋ ocuṙ naicṙiᵹe.

Ḳct. enaiṙ ṙoṙ ᴀoine; u. bliaḋna ḋhéc aṙ xxᵗ aṙ
.u. ceḋ aṙ mile. Commáṙ mac Iaṙla Ċille ḋaṙa ḋo
cenᵹal ṙe ᵹaoiḋelaiḃ ḋeiṙciṙc eṙenn an ḃliaḋain ṙi,
ocuṙ ó anaᵹhaiḋ an ᵹuiṙḋíṙ, caṙéiṙ a ṁaiṙéṙ ocuṙ a
ḃailce ḋo ḃuain ḋo mac an Iaṙla ḋon ᵹuiṙḋíṙ, ocuṙ ó

---

1 *The Foreigner.* The MS. has
anc aon mac ᵹoill, i.e. "the one son
of a Foreigner."

2 *By the Earl's son.* Archbishop
Alan was murdered by two of "Silken
Thomas's" servants, not by himself.

See the account of the murder in
Ware's *Annals of Ireland*, A.D. 1534;
Cox's *Hibernia Anglicana*, p. 234; and
Harris's ed. of Ware's *Bishops* (Works,
vol. i.), p. 347.

3 *Magh-Nuadhad.* Maynooth. In-

Albanachs, with one shot of an arrow, on Loch-Cuan. The Earl of Cill-dara, i.e. Garrett, son of Garrett, son of Thomas, went to Saxon-land, at the summons of the king of the Saxons; and the Earl was put to death—i.e. the Foreigner[1] of greatest account that was in Erinn in his own time; and the Earl's son, i.e. Thomas, ruined the king of the Saxon's people in Erinn with war; i.e. he demolished the residences of, and exacted their pledges from, all who were faithful to the king of the Saxons throughout Midhe. And the archbishop of Baile-atha-cliath was killed by the Earl's son[2] in this war. And a Saxon Justiciary came to Erinn from the king; and the majority of the towns of the Earl's son were demolished; and all Midhe was ruined both church and territory; and numerous injuries were committed between them. And Magh-Nuadhad[3] was taken by the Saxon Justiciary; and many eminent persons[4] of the people of the Earl's son were slain there. O'Conchobhair Ruadh, i.e. Tadhg Buidhe, the son of Cathal Ruadh, died this year, and his son Toirdhelbach Ruadh was proclaimed O'Conchobhair in his place. Brian, son of John O'Maelmhuaidh, was killed in treachery by some of his own sept. O'Gallchubhair, i.e. Edmond, son of John, son of Tuathal, died suddenly in hoc anno. Cormac, son of Ferghal Mac-in-Bhaird, an eminent poet, and the best man that came of his own kindred, as regards charity and humanity, died of a sudden illness, after unction and penitence.

The kalends of January on Friday; one thousand, five hundred, and thirty-five years. Thomas, son of the Earl of Cill-dara, leagued with the Gaeidhel of the south of Erinn this year, in opposition to the Justiciary, after his manors and towns had been taken from the Earl's son by

---

correctly written Ⅿaᵹ ⁊Ⅼuaⱦ. in the MS. The name of this place is also found written "Magh-Luadhad" in some of the more ancient tracts, and

also in the *Martyrology of Donegal,* and texts of comparatively modern date.
 [4] *Eminent persons.* eċⱦa móꞃa, lit. "great deeds."

réin ocur αραιϐe ϼο ϼαnṅ αιχe ϼιnnαϼϐαϼ αϼαn
Miϐe, ocur α χcur αnuchϲ ḟil mϐϼíαin ocur hi
Chonċoϐαιϼ ḟαιlχe; ocur coχαϼ móϼ mαιϲ αχá ϐenum
αιχe. Iϼ αnnϼιn ϲánιc ϼuine cumαchϲαch ϼo muinϲeϼ
ní Sαxϼαn α nɵϼιnṅ .ι. Loαϼϼ Lιonαϼϼ, ocur ϲανιc α
χcenϼ mιc αn Iαϼlα, ocur ϲuc ceιlχ uιme, ocur ϼo
χeαll ραϼϼún α huchϲ αn ϼιχ cuιχe, ocur ϼuc lαιϼ α
Sαϼϼαnαιϐ é. Χαϐϲαϼ mαc αn Iαϼlα, ocur cuιϼϲheϼ
α ϲuϼ αn ϼιχ é α mϐϼαιχϼenuϼ, ocur ϲánιc Loαϼϼ
Lιonαϼϼ α nɵϼιnn αϼíϼ ϲαϼ αιϼ, ocur ϼuαιϼ αn
χιuιϼϼíϼ ϼo ϐí αϐuϼ α nɵϼιnn báϼ .ι. Uιllíαm Sχemel·
ϲún; ocur χαϐuϼ Loαϼϼ Lιnαϼϼ ϼeϐmαnϲuϼ αn ϼιχ α
nɵϼιnn ċuιχe, ocur ϲuc clαιnn Iαϼlα móϼ Chιlle
ϼαϼα ċuιχe ϼοϼ α ιnchαιϐ ϼeιn .ι. clαnn Χéϼóιϼ mιc
Comáιϼ .ι. Sémuϼ ocur Olιueϼ, Seαn ocur Ριϼϲeϼϼ;
ocur ιαϼ mϐeϲ ϐóιϐ ϼοϼ ϲαοϐαϐ ocur ϼοϼ ιnchαιϐ
Loαιϼϼ Lιnαιϼϼ, ocur ϼιαϼ nα coιmιϼechϲ ϼéιn, ϼo χαϐαϐ
αnαοιneαchϲ leιϼ; ocur ϼo ċuιϼ ϼιnϼϼαιχeϼ ϼι Sαxαn·
íαϼ, ocur cuιϼϲeϼ α ϲuϼ αn ní íαϼ muϼ αραιϐe οιχϼι nα
hιαϼlαchϲα .ι. Comáϼϼ mαc αn Iαϼlα. Iαϼ mϐeιϲ
ιmοϼϼο ϲuιlleϼ ocur blιαϼαιn α lαιm ϐοιϐ ϼϼéιn
ocur ϼo Comáϼϼ α ϲuϼ αn ϼιχ ϼo cuιϼeϐ ċum báιϼ ιαϼ
αϐϼιαϐnuϼe luchϲα nα cαϲϼαch; ocur ní ϲánιc ϼo
χαllαιϐ ɵϼenn ϼιαm ϼeϼ α αοϼϼα ϼeιn ϼo buϐ móϼ ϼo
χníom ocur ϼéchϲ ϼo ϲαοϐ uαιϼιe ocur οιnιχ ocur
ċenϼuιϼ ϼeϐnα ιnά αn Comáϼϼ ϼιn mαc αn ιαϼlα; ocur
ní móϼ ϼenmοιϼ ϼα ϼϲánιc α nϼeιϼιϐ αιmϼιϼe ná α χιϼϼe
ϼo ϐí ϼlιochϲ nα hιαϼlαchϲα ϐá ϼχϼιοϼϼ α hɵϼιnn, ocur
ϲϼén nα hɵϼenn uιle αcα ϼe ϼαϐα ϼαιmϼιϼ ϼοιme ϼιn.
Muιϼceϼϲαch mαc ϼonnchαϼα, mαc Muϼchαϼα, ocur α
ϐιαϼϼ mαc .ι. Seαn χlαϼϼ ocur ϼeϼχαl, ϼo ṁαϼϐαϼ le
.h. nɵχϼα mϐuιϐe αϼ nά ċuϼ αmαϲ χο meαϐlαċ ϼo neοϐ

---

1 *Lord Leonard.* Leonard Lord Grey, Viscount Graney.

2 *Sgemeltún.* See p. 276, note 1.

3 *Calamity and loss.* The words ϼο χníom ocur ϼéchϲ literally mean "of action and deed," but are conventionally used to signify catastrophe, calamity, loss, &c.

A.D.
[1535.]

the Justiciary, and he himself, and his partizans, had been expelled from Meath, and driven to seek the protection of Síl-Briain and O'Conchobhair Failghe, when he waged a great, good war. Then it was that there came to Erinn a powerful man of the king of the Saxons' people, i.e. Lord Leonard;[1] and he went to meet the Earl's son, and practised deceit towards him, and promised him a pardon on the king's part; and he took him with him to Saxon-land. The Earl's son was apprehended, and placed in the king's tower in captivity; and Lord Leonard came back to Erinn. And the Justiciary who was here in Erinn died, i.e. William Sgemeltún,[2] and Lord Leonard assumed the king's government in Erinn; and he brought the sons of the great Earl of Cill-dara under his own guardianship, viz., the sons of Garrett, son of Thomas, viz., James, Oliver, John, and Richard. And after having been in the confidence, and under the guardianship, of Lord Leonard, and they in his own company, they were all at once apprehended by him; and he sent them to the king of the Saxons; and they were placed in the king's tower, where the heir to the earldom was, i.e. Thomas, the Earl's son. After they themselves and Thomas, moreover, had been more than a year in captivity in the king's tower, they were put to death in presence of the inhabitants of the city. And there never came, of the Foreigners of Erinn, a man of his own age whose death was a greater calamity and loss,[3] as regards nobility, and hospitality, and captainship, than this Thomas the Earl's son. And no greater sermon[4] occurred in latter times than the quickness with which the heirs of the earldom were exterminated out of Erinn, although they had the power of all Erinn for a long time previously. Muirchertach Mac Donnchadha, the son of Murchadh, and his two sons, viz., John Glas and Ferghal, were slain by O'hEghra

---

[4] *Sermon.* The corresponding word in the text is ꞃⱸⱥⱱⱼⱱ, into which form the English word "sermon" has been turned.

ꝺά ṁuınnꞇeꞃ ꞃeın α maıᵹ ımleaċ ın hoc αnno. Ɯac
8uıꞅne ḃάᵹuıne .ı. Ɯαolmuıꞃe, mac Neıʟʟ Ɯıc 8huıꞅ-
ne, ꝺo ṁαꞃbhαꝺ α bꞃıoll le nα ꝺeꞃbꞃαꞇhαıꞃ ꞃéın
.ı. Nıαll Ɯac 8uıꞅne lα ꞃéıle poıl ocuꞃ peꝺαıꞃ, α
nꝺoꞃuꞅ ċαıꞃléın Ɯıc 8huıꞅne ꞃéın .ı. Ꞃαċuın. Eıᵹnechꞩ-
ύn mac 'Oomnαıll hı 'Oomnαıll ꝺo ṁαꞃbαꝺ le clαınn
hı ḃhαıᵹıll muꞃ αn ceꝺnα ᵹo nemmαıċ. Ɯαoıleaċꞩ-
luınn mac Caıꞃbꞃe hı ḃıꞃn ꝺo ṁαꞃbαꝺ le clαınn
Chαꞇhαıl mıc Ꞃuαıꝺꞃı Ɯıc 'Oıαꞃmαꝺα, ocuꞃ ꞃα móꞃ αnꞇ
échꞇ é, oıꞃ ıꞃ ꞇeꞃc mά ꝺo ꞇí α neꞃuınn mac ꞇαoıꞃıᵹ α
ınṁe ꝺob ꞃeꞃꞃ α neᵹnα ocuꞃ α noınech ocuꞃ α hoıꞃꞃ-
ꝺeꞃcuꞃ ınάꞃꞃ. Conċobαꞃ mac Eoᵹαın mıc 'Ohonnchαꝺα,
ocuꞃ Ɑoꝺ mac αn ċαnάnαıᵹ ꝺo mαꞃbαꝺ le clαınn
Ꞇαıꝺᵹ mıc Ꞃuαıꝺꞃı Ɯıc 'Ohonnchαꝺα ó ċuıl 'Oeᵹhαıꝺ
α Cıll ꞃꞃαıꞃꞃ. Inᵹen hı Neıll .ı. 8ıuꞓαn ınᵹen Chuınn
mıc Enꞃí mıc Eoᵹαın, ben Ɯñαᵹnuꞃα 1 'Ohomnαıll,
ꝺꞃαᵹαıl ꞓάıꞃ α lάꞃ α hαoıꞃı ocuꞃ α hınṁe ocuꞃ α
maıꞓıuꞃα αn ꞓlıαꝺαın ꞃın, ocuꞃ α hαꝺlucαꝺ ᵹo honoꞃach
α maınıꞃꞇıꞃ 'Ohúın nα nᵹαll. Ɯαıꝺm moꞃ ꝺó ꞇαbαıꞃꞇ
ꝺo Ɯac Ɑṁlαoıꝓ αn ꞓlıαꝺαın ꞃı ꝺú ınαꞃ mαꞃbαꝺ
ꞇıᵹeꞃnα nα Claonᵹlαıꞃı ocuꞃ Ɯac ᵹıbún, ocuꞃ cóꞃuᵹαꝺ
móꞃ ꝺo ċloınn ꞇ8híꞇhαıꝺ, ocuꞃ mαꞃꞓꞇhαꞃ αnn ꞓóꞃ mac
Ɯαolmuıꞃe mıc ḃꞃıαın Ɯıc 8huıꞅne conꞃαbαl Ɯıc
Ɑṁlαıꝓ α ꞇoꞃach αn ımbuαlꞇα.

Ꞁcꞇꞇ. Enαıꞃ ꞃoꞃ ꞃαꞓαꞃn. 8e blıαꝺnα ꝺhéc αꞃ .xx. αꞃ
.u. ceꝺ αꞃ mıle αıꞃ ın Ꞇıᵹeꞃnα. ḃlıαꝺαın ᵹαlꞃαch eꞃlάn
αn blıαꝺαın ꞃın, ocuꞃ ıl ꞇeꝓmαnnα ınnꞇe .ı. plάıꝺ
coıꞇċenꝺ ocuꞃ ᵹαlαꞃ bꞃec, ocuꞃ plάıᵹ ꝓuınꝺech ocuꞃ

---

1 *Mac Suibhne Bághuine.* Mac
Suibhne (or Mac Swiney) of Tir-
Boghaine, now the barony of Banagh,
in the co. of Donegal. The name is also
written "Mac Suibhne Baghanagh."

2 *Wickedly.* ᵹo nemmαıċ ; lit.
"not goodly," the word nemmαıꞇ
being comp. of the neg. part. neın and
the adj. mαıꞇ, and the preposition ᵹo.

when placed before an adjective, having the same force as *ly* in English.

3 *Killed.* The *Annals of Connacht*
add that O'Birn was killed on "Mul-
lach-na-sithi."

4 *Sibhan;* i.e. Joan.

5 *Claen-glais;* now Clonlish, a district in the barony of Upper Connello,
co. Limerick, anciently the patrimony

Buidhe, in Magh-Imlech, in hoc anno, after having been A.D.
deceitfully betrayed by one of his own people. Mac [1535.]
Suibhne Bághuine,[1] i.e. Maelmuire, son of Niall Mac
Suibhne, was killed in treachery by his own brother, i.e.
Niall Mac Suibhne, on the day of the festival of Paul and
Peter, in the doorway of Mac Suibhne's own castle, i.e.
Rathain. Egnechán, son of Domhnall O'Domhnaill, was
in like manner wickedly[2] killed by the sons of O'Baighill.
Maelechlainn, son of Cairbre O'Birn, was killed[3] by the
sons of Cathal, son of Ruaidhri Mac Diarmada; and he
was a great loss, for it is doubtful if there was in Erinn
a better chieftain's son of his estate, in wisdom, bounty,
and excellence, than he. Conchobhar, son of Eoghan
Mac Donnchadha, and Aedh, son of the Cananach, were
killed by the sons of Tadhg, son of Ruaidhri Mac Donnchadha, from Cuil-Deghaidh, in Cill-Frais. O'Neill's
daughter, i.e. Sibhan,[4] daughter of Conn, son of Henry,
son of Eoghan, wife of Maghnus O'Domhnaill, died in the
middle of her age, estate, and good fortune, this year,
and was honourably buried in the monastery of Dun-na-
nGall. A great defeat was given by Mac Amhlaibh this
year, in which the lord of the Claen-glais,[5] and Mac
Gibun,[6] and a great body of the Clann-Sithidh, were slain;
and the son of Maelmuire, son of Brian Mac Suibhne,
Mac Amhlaibh's constable, was killed there also in the
beginning of the conflict.

The kalends of January on Saturday; the age of the [1536.]
Lord one thousand, five hundred, and thirty-six years.
This year was a sickly, unhealthy year, in which numerous
diseases, viz., a general plague, and small-pox, and a
flux-plague, and the bed-distemper,[7] prevailed excessively.

---

of a family called O'Coilen, or Collins,
but in the possession, at the date of
the event above referred to, of a branch
of the Fitzgeralds.

[6] *Mac Gibun*; i.e. FitzGibbon.

VOL. II.

[7] *Bed-distemper.* ᵹalaṗ na leap-
ṫa. Instead of this the Four Masters
make use of the word ṗiabṗaṗ,
"fever." It was probably some kind
of intermittent fever.

U

ζαλαp na Leapⰱa co himaipcech. Echꞇ ιp mó na ζach
eile echꞇ na aimpip peιn, ocup epⰱαⰅ ιp mó na ζach
epⰱαⰅ eli a nΕpinn ιpin mblíαⰅain pι, .ι. Copmac όζ mac
Copmaic mιc Thαιⰱc Mheζ Cappchaιζ .ι. aon poζa
Ζhaοιⰱιl Leιⰱι Moⰱα ΝuαⰅαⰅ, ⰅpαζαιL Ⰵáιp ιap mbpeιⰅ
ⰅuαⰅα ó Ⰵoman ocup ó Ⰵemun, eꞇ pepulꞇup epꞇ a ζcιll
Chpé. Mac ⰅáιⰒιⰅ .ι. Tomápp mac ⰅáιⰒιⰅ mιc Εmuιnn
Ⰵhec ιn hoc anno. Mac ΖοιpⰅelⰒ .ι. Sean ⰅuⰒ Ⰵhéc ιn
hoc anno. Tommápp .h. hUιζιnn, .ι. οιⰅe pep nΕpenn
ocup nΑlban pe Ⰵáιn, Ⰵhéc an ⰒLιαⰅain pι. Ο Cellaιζ
[Ⰵo mapⰱαⰅ] ιn hoc anno, ocup ⰅonnchαⰅ mac Εmuιnn
na ιonαⰒ ap Ⰵιp Mhaιne. Maιⰱe ιochꞇaιp Chonnachꞇ
.ι. Tαⰱc όζ mac TαιⰅζ mιc Αοⰱα, ocup Tαⰱc mac
Cαthaιl όιζ hι Conchoⰱαιp, ocup clann n⅄ⰅonnchαⰅα
ocup clann hι ⅄húⰒⰅα, Ⰵo ⰱul ap ꞇⰒlιchꞇ RιcaιpⰅ a
ⰱúpc ap cappuιnζ ιn eppuιc ⰱaιpéⰅ; ocup caopaιζeⰱⰱ
an ꞇιpe Ⰵo Ⰵul pompαⰱ a Ⰵcepmann ΟιpιⰅ, ocup anꞇ
eppuιc Ⰵá Lenmaιn ap an cepmann, ocup an ⰱaopaιζeⰱⰱ
Ⰵo ⰱaⰱaιpꞇ Ⰵo ⰅιnnpoιζeⰅ anꞇ pⱡúαιζ; ocup ζan aιpec
Ⰵo ⰱaⰱaιpꞇ uαchαιⰱ a nonóιp naοιm na neιmιⰱ ⰅóιⰒ.
Maιnιpⱡιp ⅄pomma Ⰵá eιⰱιαζap Ⰵo LopcuⰅ pan οιⰱⰱe
ιap collαⰅ Ⰵo ⰱáⰱ, ocup mópⱥn Ⰵo mⱨιlleⰒ ιnnꞇι. Peιⰱlιm
mac Peιⰱlιm hι Ruαιpc Ⰵpαζαl Ⰵáιp a nζeιⱨιl aζ
ⰱpιan Ο Ruαιpc, mac Εoζaιn mιc Thιζeppnáιn. Comⱨ-
opⰱα ⅄pommα Οιpⰱeαlαιζ .ι. CαthaL mac Seoιnín mιc
ⰱSheaιn hι Mhaoιlⱨoⰱéιpζe, pep beoⰱlupαⰱ ⰱuan
ⰱⱨnáιζ, ⰅpαζαιL Ⰵáιp an ⰒLιαⰅain pιn. Ο Conchoⰱαιp Ⰵo
ζaιpm Ⰵo TαιⰅζ όζ, mac TαιⰅζ mιc Αοⰱα mιc Thoιpp-
Ⰵelⰱαιζ ⰱappαιζ hι Chonchoⰱαιp; ocup níp Ⱂ́é pιn anꞇ
aιnm ba ζnαⰱ Leιpιn ꞇé ⰒuⰅ cιζeppna a nιochꞇap Chonnachꞇ Ⰵo ꞇpíol Conchoⰱαιp, achꞇ Mac ⅄omnαιll mιc

---

1 *Hoc.* ꞉c, MS.

2 *Thomas O'h Uiginn.* In the marg.
it is added that he was the son of
Domhnall, the son of Brian, the son
of Ferghal Ruadh O'hUiginn. This
name is now generally written Hig-
gins, without the O'.

3 *Herds.* caopaιζeⰱꞇ. This word
signifies the herds and flocks of a tribe,
as well as the armed persons driving
and guarding them.

4 *Druim-dhá-eithighar.* The name
of this place (Dromahaire, co. Leitrim) is written Druim-da-thiagar in

A calamity greater than all calamities in his own time, and a loss greater than all other losses, *occurred* in Erinn this year, viz., Cormac Og, the son of Cormac, son of Tadhg Mac Carthaigh, i.e. the choicest of the Gaeidhel of Leth-Modha-Nuadhadh, died after triumphing over the world and the devil, *et sepultus est in* Cill-Cré. Mac David, i.e. Thomas, son of David, son of Edmond, died in hoc[1] anno. Mac Goisdelbh, i.e. John Dubh, died in hoc anno. Thomas O'hUiginn,[2] i.e. the tutor of the men of Erinn and Alba in poetry, died this year. O'Cellaigh [was slain] in hoc anno; and Donnchadh, son of Edmond, *was appointed* in his place over Tir-Maine. The chieftains of Lower Connacht, viz., Tadhg Og, the son of Tadhg, son of Aedh, and Tadhg the son of Cathal Og O'Conchobhair, and the Clann-Donnchadha, and the sons of O'Dubhda, went against the descendants of Richard Burk, at the instigation of the Bishop Barrett. And the herds[3] of the country went before them to the termon of Oiremh; and the bishop followed them upon the termon, and brought the herds to the army; and restitution was not given by them in honour of saint or sanctuary. The monastery of Druim-dhá-eithighar[4] was burned in the night, after all had gone to sleep, and much was destroyed in it. Fedhlim, son of Fedhlim O'Ruairc, died whilst confined by[5] Brian O'Ruairc, the son of Eoghan, son of Tighernan. The comarb of Druim-Oirbhelaigh, i.e. Cathal, son of Seoinín, son of John O'Maelmocheirghe, a prosperous man of great wealth,[6] died this year. Tadhg Og, son of Tadhg, son of Aedh, son of Toirdhelbhach Carragh O'Conchobhair, was proclaimed the O'Conchobhair. And this was not the usual name of the person who was lord of Sil-Conchobhair in Lower Connacht, but whosoever of them was lord over Lower Connacht was usually called Mac Domhnaill Mic

---

the Annals of Connacht, and Druim-dhá-ethiar by the Four Masters.

[5] *Whilst confined by.* α ηϩeπínᴫ

αϩ; lit. "in gyves by."

[6] *Of great wealth.* buαn conάiϩ; lit. "of perpetual wealth."

Mhuιρčeρταιξ το ξαιρéι τοη τé bά τιξεριια αρ ιochταρ
Chonnacht τιб; acht chena ιρ τ̇ορμαιρ̇Lιuξατ α αιcme,
ocur το ᵭeρριρcnuξατ τοηα ριξuιб ροιme, το ρόιηe ριum
an claočLόб comanma ριη το ξαιρm б̇e. Ccτ Ua Conchobaιρ núa ριη, ocur mac Cathaιl όιξ hl Chonchobaιρ,
το τul αρ ριοбαl ιηηροιξετ α ξclaιηη Ξhοιρτeαlб, ocur
co ρucαταρ na ρ̇Lúaξα ριη α τιmčeαll chιlle ChoLmάιη
.ι. baιle mιc Ruξραιбι mιc Ξοιρτelб; ocur τάηιc ρeιη αρ
lάιm hl Conchobaιρ αρρ an mbaιle, maιlle ρe Luιρeč
coṁ̇ρomτα το б̇ι αιξe .ι. Lúιρech Mιc Ḟheoρuιρ. Ocur
τuc Ua Conchobaιρ an bράιξe ριη Leιρ co 8lιξech; ocur
ηι mορ το cρeαčuιб ρ̇ιαραταρ acht ριη αṁάιη. Ocur
ρuaιρ α lάη ṗuaρclαο αρρ ιη mbράιξιο ριη. Conchobaρ
ξαρб mac Cathaιl Mιc Ṫhιαρmαта το ṁαρbατ le mac
hl bιρη αρ an ξcοιll άιṁρéιб. O Ruaιρc το č̇αιρριηξ
το Ruaιορι mac Ταιбξ Mιc Ṫιαρmαта α τιmčell
č̇αιρléιη Chenτ̇moιξe, ocur an baιle το bριρρeб б̇όιб,
ocur na б̇αρτα το ṁαρbaб .ι. Cathal mac Coρmaιc όιξ,
ocur Ṗeρξal mac bριαιη, ocur αmбόι ann ό ριη αmač.
Ruaιορι na τculάη mac Ṫιαρmαта mιc Ruaιορι Mιc
Ṫιαρmαта, ocur clann Chathaιl mιc Ruaιορι Mιc
Ṫιαρmαта, το ιοηηαρbατ αρρ Maξ Luιρξ le Ruaιορι
mac Ταιбc Mιc Ṫιαρmατα, ocur cuιτ το chuρ α Τuaб̇-
ṁumaιη τιб, ocur cuιτ elι α τιρ Conaιll, τρe ṁαρbaτ
Mhaoιlρeačlaιηη hl bιρη το б̇όι na τeρб coṁταlτα αξ.
Rúaιορι Mac Ṫιαρmατα. Coξατ ρuč̇uιη ριρб̇uan
eιτιρ .h. nṪomnaιll ocur maιč̇ι ιochταιρ Connacht
acht bριαη O Ruaιρc αṁάιη, ξan α č̇οηξηum ρe nechταρ
б̇ιб an τan ρα. 8lúαξ mόρ le .h. nṪomnaιll .ι. Maξ
Uιбιρ ocur mac hl Neιll .ι. Nιαll όξ mac Ccιρτ, ocur
mac hl Raιξιllιξ .ι. Ccοб mac Mhaoιlṁόρбα, co néιρξe
αmač hl Raιξιllιξ; ocur ηι č̇άηιc clann hl Ṫomnaιll

---

1 *Proof.* coṁ̇ρoṁ, for coṁ-
ρ̇ρcmτα=comprobatus, MS. com-
ρατ̇ϊ., Ann. Connacht.

² *Coat of mail.* Lúιρech=lorica,
MS.

³ *The Coill-aimhréidh.* This name,
which signifies the "rough wood,"
would now be pronounced Kylavraig,
or Killavraig; but the place has not
been identified.

Muirchertaigh. Nevertheless, it was to exalt his family, and to excel the kings preceding him, that he was proclaimed by this change of name. This new O'Conchobhair, and the son of Cathal Og O'Conchobhair, went on an expedition into Clann-Goisdelbh ; and they brought their armies about Cill-Colmain, i.e. the town of the son of Rughraidhe Mac Goisdelbh ; and he himself came out of the town, into the hands of O'Conchobhair, bringing with him a proof[1] coat of mail[2] which he had, i.e. Mac Feorais's coat of mail. And O'Conchobhair carried this hostage with him to Sligech ; and they did not get many spoils except that alone. And he (*O'Conchobhair*) received his full ransom for this hostage. Conchobhar Garbh, son of Cathal Mac Diarmada, was slain by the son of O'Birn, in the Coill-aimhréidh.[3] O'Ruairc was brought by Ruaidhri, the son of Tadhg Mac Diarmada, to besiege the castle[4] of Cenn-maighe ; and they demolished the place, and killed the warders, viz., Cathal, son of Cormac Og, and Ferghal, son of Brian, and all who were there besides. Ruaidhri-na-ttulán, son of Diarmaid, son of Ruaidhri Mac Diarmada, and the sons of Cathal, son of Ruaidhri Mac Diarmada, were banished out of Magh-Luirg by Ruaidhri, son of Tadhg Mac Diarmada, (and some of them were sent to Tuadh-Mumha, and some more to Tir-Conaill), through the killing of Maelsechlainn O'Birn, who was the true foster-brother of Ruaidhri Mac Diarmada. A long, lasting, war between O'Domhnaill and the chiefs of Lower Connacht, except Brian O'Ruairc alone, who gave his assistance to neither of them this time. A great muster by O'Domhnaill, viz., Mag Uidhir, and the son of O'Neill, i.e. Niall Og, the son of Art, and the son of O'Raighilligh, i.e. Aedh son of Maelmordha, with the rising out of O'Raighilligh. And O'Domhnaill's own sons did not come there,

---

[4] *To besiege the castle.* The original of this clause is ᴅo ᴄᴀιρρᴎιᵹ ᴀ ᴛιmᴄᴇᴌᴌ ᴄᴀιρᴌᴇιn Chenᴠᴔᴎoιᵹe, the literal translation of which is "was drawn about the castle of Cenn-maighe."

αnn ɓuɓeiɲin; ocuɲ ɲo αnɲαc α cimceαll Maᵹnuɲα hi
Domnαill, oiɲ ní ćánic iɲin cɲom ɼocɲαiɓe ɼin, óiɲ ɒo
ɓí α neɼαoncα ɲe nα αchαiɲ. Ocuɲ cαnᵹαɒαɲ clαnn
cShuiɓne, ocuɲ O ɓaiᵹill, conα bɲiαnlαć áiᵹ ocuɲ
iɲᵹαile iɲin cinól ɼin hi Domnαill, αmαil bá ɓéɲ
ɒóiɓ. Ᵹluαiɲiɲ αn ɼlúαiᵹ ɲéncα ɼo ullαṁ ɼin αm ɒeoiᵹ
lαoi o áć Senαiᵹ, ᵹuɲ ᵹαɓαɒαɲ ɼoɲɼαɒ ocuɲ ɼié lonᵹ-
poɲc eiɒiɲ-ɓuiɓ ocuɲ Dɲoɓαoiɼ; ocuɲ cαɲéiɲ α coṁαlc-
uiɲ ɒo ćαiched ɓóiɓ, ɒo ćuiɲeɒαɲ lucht ɼoɲαiɲe ocuɲ
ɼuiɲecɲuiɲ ɒo ćoiṁéc αnc ɼlúαiᵹ αɲ ceiɼc αmmuiɲ
lonᵹpuiɲc ɒo ćαbαiɲc oɲɲα ɒo cɲíol Conchobαiɲ conα
cinól; óiɲ ɒo ɓαɒαɲ cɲuinn αn éin ionαɓ α Sliᵹech, ocuɲ
ᵹeαllαɒ buαilci αcα ɒ'Ohomnαill. Ocuɲ iɲɼé ɒo chúαiɒ
iɲin ɼoɲαiɲe αɲ cúɲ O ɓaiᵹill, oiɲ ɒo buɓ ɒóiᵹ lαiɼ co
bɼuiᵹheɓ ɼé ɒɲem éiᵹin ɒα lucht imɲeɲnα ocuɲ iomαɲ-
ɓáᵹᵹα, α niochcαɲ Chonnαcht, αᵹ ceαcht ɒo cαbαiɲc
αmuiɲ lonᵹpuiɲc αɲ αn ɼlúαiᵹ ɼin hi Dhomnαill.
Ocuɲ ɒo ćuαiɓ muinnceɲ αoɓα buiɓe hi Dhomnαill α
bɼoɲαiɲe muɲ αn ceɒnα; ocuɲ ɒo buαileɓ O ɓaiᵹill ocuɲ
iαɒ ɼein ɼá ćeli α ᵹcɲeαɲpuɲcαl nα mαiɒne moiće; ocuɲ
ɒo iunɼαiᵹ muinceɲ mic hi Dhoṁnαill α ᵹcoinne ocuɲ
α ᵹcomαiɲɼćiɲ hi ɓhαiᵹill conα ṁαɲcɼlúαiᵹ, α ɲicht
ɒɲoinᵹe éiᵹin ɒiochcαɲ Chonnαcht. Ni αɲ ɓuᵹα nα αɲ
ɓuαn ceiched ɒo ᵹαɓ O ɓaiᵹill ćuiᵹe α ionnɼoiᵹeɒ ɒα
eɲᵹcαiɲɒiɓ, oiɲ bá ɒeɲɓ ɒeimin leiɼ ᵹuɲαb íαɒ ɒo ɓói
ćuiᵹe. αcht chenα ɲucuɲɒαɲ O ɓaiᵹill bαnn ɒiocɼɲα
ɒeᵹćαɲαiɒ nα ᵹcoinne ocuɲ nα ᵹcomαiɲɼćiɲ, ocuɲ níɲ
αn αɲ α neinech ᵹαn ɒul inα meɼc ᵹo nemćoiméɒαch, ᵹo
bɼuαiɲ α oiᵹheɒ co cɲoćαṁαil cuɲαiɲɒech lé nα ɼioɲ
ćαiɲɒiɓ ɓuɓéin; ocuɲ iɼ lán ṁóɲ αn uiɲeɲbuɓ ɒo
ɓochcuiɓ ocuɲ ɒαiɓilᵹnechuiɓ, ɒαnbɼαnniɓ ocuɲ ɒollαṁ-
nαiɓ αnc écht ɼin .i. Níαll O ɓaiᵹhill. αcht chenα níɲ
coiɲmiɲc αnc αiɲɒ écht ɼin cɲiαll nα cinɒɲceɒαl αnc

---

1 *On the watch.* This second party
of watchers would seem to have proceeded to the same point to which
O'Baighill and his friends had gone,
and without the knowledge of
O'Baighill (or O'Boyle).

A.D.
[1536.]

but remained about Maghnus O'Domhnaill, (for he did not come in this great army, because he was in discord with his father). And the Clann-Súibhne, and O'Baighill, with their warlike and valorous bands, came also in this muster of O'Domhnaill, as was the custom with them. This charmed, ready, army moved late in the day from Ath-Senaigh, and occupied a resting place and encampment between Dubh and Drobhais. And after they had eaten their food, they sent watchers and sentinels to guard the army from the danger of a camp attack being made upon them by the Sil-Conchobhair, with their muster; for they were assembled in one place in Sligech, and had promised battle to O'Domhnaill. And the first who went on the watch was O'Baighill; for he thought that he might find some of his opponents and adversaries, in Lower Connacht, coming to make a camp attack on this army of O'Domhnaill. And Aedh Buidhe O'Domhnaill's people went on the watch[1] in like manner; and O'Baighill and they encountered each other in the twilight of the early morning. And the people of O'Domhnaill's son advanced against, and towards, O'Baighill with his cavalry, taking them for a party belonging to Lower Connacht. It was not with fear, nor with a desire to flee, that O'Baighill received this attack of his enemies, (for he was positively certain that it was they who were approaching him); but O'Baighill made a vehement, sudden, rush towards them, and to meet them; and he stayed not under their protection,[2] but went unguardedly amongst them, so that he received his death miserably, unfortunately, by his own true friends. And a very great loss to paupers and orphans, to the infirm and to professors, was this eminent man, i.e., Niall O'Baighill. This great calamity, however, did not prevent O'Domhnaill from attempting,

---

[2] *Stayed not under their protection.* In other words, O'Baighill (O'Boyle) did not seek quarter from his supposed enemies. The construction of this entry is altogether very loose and inelegant.

ḟlizeð ṙin um .h. nᴅoṁnaill, ocuṙ téiᴅ iaṙ tocht an
laoi ᴅá ionnṙoizeᴅ co ꝼinᴅíṙ, zuṙ ᵹaᵬ comnaiᵬe ocuṙ
comoiṙiṙeṁ iṙin maiᵹin ṙin zo heiṙᵹe ᵹṙeine iaṙ ná
ṁáṙach. Teiᴅ maṙcṙluaᵹh mic Cathail óiᵹ, .i. muinteṙ
Ɑiṙt, ó Shlizech ᴅinnṙaizheᴅ Ḃṙaᵹaᴅ Cuillíᴅh. ᵹaᵬuiᴅ
cuiᴅ ᴅo ṁaṙcṙluaiᵹ ant ṙluaiᵹ, ocuṙ tiaᵹuiᴅ a ᵹcóiṙ
iompṙuaᵹaᴅ ṙé ṙoile a mḃealaᵭ ᵭúin iaṙuinn. Maṙᵭ-
chaṙ maṙcach ᴅo muinᴄiṙ Ɑiṙt iṙin tachuṙ ṙin, ocuṙ
ᴅealaiziᴅ ṙe ᵭeli. Ɑnuiᴅ .h. ᴅomnaill na ṙoṙlonᵹṗoṙt
ṙéin an oiᵭᵭe ṙin, ocuṙ eiṙᵹiṙ iṙin maiᴅin aṙ ná maṙaᵭ,
ocuṙ téiᴅ co ꝼeṙṙat ṙanna an liaᵹáin ᴅo ᵭul taiṙiṙ
a Cúil Iṙṙa. ᴅo ᵬí O Conchobaiṙ cona ᵭinól a Slizech
aᵹ oṙᴅuᵹhaᴅ a muinᴄiṙe ᴅo ᵭul a ᵹcoinne hi ᴅhomnaill ᵹo ꝼeṙṙuiᴅ ṙanᴅa in liaᵹáin, maṙ aṙ maṙbaᵭ
Liaᵹán laoᵭṁiliᵭ ᴅo ꝼhoṁoṙchaib le Luᵹ Laṁṙaᴅa, aᵹ
teacht ᴅinnṙoizeᴅ ᵭaᵭa Moiᵹe Tuiṙeᴅ, maṙ a ṙaᵬaᴅaṙ
ꝼomoṙuiᵹ aᵹ ṙaizeᴅ a ᵹcíṙ ᵭána ꝼoṙ ꝼeṙuiᵬ Eṙenn ṙe
cian ᴅaimmṙiṙ ṙoime ṙin, coniᴅ uaᵭa ᴅo hainmniᵹheᴅ
an ꝼeṙṙat ṙin. Ocuṙ an ṙeᵭ ᴅo ᵬói an lán maṙa iṙin
bꝼeṙṙuiᴅ ᴅo ᵬí na ṙluaᵹa ṙin aᵹ bṙeiᵭ bṙeiᵭi aṙ a ᵭeli,
ocuṙ iṙṙí comaiṙle ᴅo ṙinne O Conchobaiṙ o nach ṙaiᵬe
coimlion ᴅaoiniᵭ ṙe .h. nᴅoṁnaill ᵹan tachuṙ ꝼṙiṙ aᵹ
an bꝼeṙṙuit, ocuṙ aṙ nᴅul ᴅO ᴅhomnaill a noṙᴅuᵹaᴅ,
ocuṙ aṙ ṙuiᵭiuᵹaᴅ a ᵹonnaᵭ móṙ ṙe hucht na ꝼeiṙṙte,
no ᵹu ṙaᵹaᴅ co neaṁṙuiṙiᵭe é a nionuᴅ eile. Teiᴅ
.h. ᴅoṁnaill taiṙ an bꝼeṙṙait iaṙ na ṙáᵹᵭáil ᵹan
ᵭoṙnaṁ ᵹan ᵭoᵭuᵹaᵭ, aᵹuṙ téiᴅ ᴅṙéam ᴅo maiᴄiᵬ
iochtaiṙ Chonnacht ᴅiaṙṙaᵭ iompṙuaᵹᵭa aṙ ṁuinnteṙ

---

1 *The army;* i.e. O'Domhnaill's
army.

2 *Conflict.* tochuṙ, MS., for tachuṙ. as in the Annals of Connacht,
and the Ann. Four Masters.

3 *Fersad-ranna-in-liagain;* lit. "the
pass of the promontory of the pillar
stone;" the name of a ford on the river
Gitley. The suggested derivation of

the name from Liagan, a man's name,
is entirely fanciful.

4 *Lugh Lamhfada.* "Lugh of the
long hand;" one of the Tuatha-de-
Danaan dynasty, whose reign is referred by O'Flaherty to A.M. 2764.
His exploits have been much celebrated by the Irish bards. See *Ogygia,*
p. 177.

and continuing, to pass that way; and after the approach of day he goes as far as Findir; and he rested and remained in that place until the rising of the sun on the morrow. The cavalry of Cathal Og's son, viz., Muinter-Airt, advance towards Braghad-Chuillidh. They meet some of the cavalry of the army,[1] and both parties proceed to attack each other in Belach-Dúin-iarainn. A horseman of Muinter-Airt is slain in this conflict,[2] and they separate from one another. O'Domhnaill remains in his own encampment that night; and he rises in the morning following, and goes to Fersad-ranna-in-liagain,[3] to go across it into Cuil-irra. O'Conchobhair was in Sligech, with his muster, arraying his people to go against O'Domhnaill to Fersad-ranna-in-liagain,[3] (where Liagán, a heroic warrior of the Fomorians, was killed by Lugh Lamhfada,[4] when coming to the battle of Magh-Tuiredh, where the Fomorians were imposing their tributes on the men of Erinn for a long time before that—so that it was from him this ford was named). And whilst the full tide was in the ford these armies were taking an estimate[5] of each other; and the resolution which O'Conchobhair adopted[6] was, since he had not as many men as O'Domhnaill, and as O'Domnaill had put his forces in order, and fixed his great gun[7] in front of the ford, not to oppose him at the ford, *but to wait* until he would find him unprepared in another place. O'Domhnaill goes across the ford, when he found it without defence, without protection; and a number of the chieftains of Lower Connacht go to demand battle from O'Domhnaill's people.

---

[5] *Taking an estimate.* The words ⲁᵹ bⲣeⲓⳅ bⲣeⲓⲧⲓ lit. signify "giving (or bearing) judgment."

[6] *The resolution which O'Conchobhair adopted.* ⲓⲣⲣⲓ comⲁⲓⲣⳑe ⲟⲟ ⲣⲩnne O Conchobⲁⲓⲣ. The literal translation of the original is "it is the counsel which O'Conchobhair made." The sentence has been partly transposed in the translation.

[7] *Great gun.* The text from the corresponding words down to the words ⳑe mⲩⲓnnⲧⲓⲣ ⲁn Ꝿⲩⲓⲣⲣⲧⲓⲣ in the entry under the year 1537 (see p. 306, note 1) has been written by the hand that copied the entries for 1466, &c.

1 Ὀhoṁnuιll. Ní híomċoṁαιρeach το ϝρeαȝραὸ αnτ ιαρατυϝ ϝιn αn ύαιϝ το ιοnnϝυιȝeαταϝ co meαnṁnaċ míċeιllιὸ α ċeιle. Mαρὸὡαρ euchτ αὸὡul ṁóρ το ċloιnn Ὀοnτchαιὸ αϝ αn ιοmϝυαȝαὸ ϝιn .ι. Mάοιleαch-luιnn mαc Cαιὸȝ meιc Ruαιὸϝι; αȝυϝ τυϝċυϝ το ȝοnτα ϝο mαϝὸὡὸ é. Mαϝὸὡυϝ mαϝcαċ eιle το ṁυιnnτeιϝ ι Ὀhoṁnuιll τυϝċαϝ το ȝα αnn .ι. 8emαϝ bαllαċ mαc Neιll ṁeιc 8eαin. Ὀeαlαιτ ϝé ϝοιle. Cέιτ O Ὀόm-nuιll α nτύτhαιὸ ϝlechτα ὁριαιn ι Chonċuὸαιϝ, αȝυϝ το bí τϝí hοιὸċe αιȝ mιlleὸ αϝὸα αȝυϝ αȝ lοϝȝυὸ ὡαιlτιὸ αȝαϝ ṁοnαιὸ. Ὀο bí O Conċuὸαιϝ αȝ ὁél αn τϝοιċιτ α ὡϝαϝlοnȝϝορτ. Cέιτ O Ὀοṁnuιll ταιϝ τϝαιȝ ϝíαϝ α τϝíϝ ϝhιαċϝαċ Mhύαιὸe, αȝυϝ mιllιὸ móϝαn αϝὸα αȝαϝ bαιleὸα, αȝυϝ τά ȝαċ eαϝnαιl mαιċeαϝα αϝċeαϝα ιnnτe, όιϝ το bí αn τíϝ αϝ α ȝcοmυϝ ϝéιn αchτ cυιτ τα cαιϝlénαιὸ; αȝυϝ το ϝυȝ αιϝ ṁόϝαn το ċαοϝυιὸeαchτ αn τíϝe τιmċeαll τϝleιὸe ȝαṁ. Cιαȝαιτ ταϝ Mύαιὸ ϝíαϝ αϝ ταϝϝυιnȝ ὡϝleαchτα Rιοcαιϝτ α ὁυϝc, αnτíαιȝ ċοτα το ċαοϝυιὸeαchτ ċloιnne ι Ὀhuὸτα. ȝαὸċυϝ ιnȝen ὁhαιċéιϝ α ὁυϝc leó .ι. beαn Θοȝhαιn ι Ὀhuὸτα mαιllι ϝe nα cϝeιċ. Ὀο bí τά ṁéτ τéταluιὸ αȝυϝ ταιϝιciὸ ϝúαιϝ O Ὀοṁnαιll, co τταὡαϝταοι mαϝτ nó ὸα mαϝτ αϝ αοn ὡοnn αnn, αȝυϝ nαċ ϝαȝȝċάοι ϝιn ϝéιn οϝϝα. Mαc Ὀιαϝmατα αȝυϝ clαnn Cαιὸȝ ṁeιc Ὀιαϝmατα αȝυϝ clαnn ṁeιc Ὀαιὸι το τeαchτ το ċοnȝnαṁ ϝé hιοchταϝ [Connαchτ] αnαȝαιὸ ι Ὀhoṁnαιll. Cϝιαllαιὸ O Ὀοṁnαιll ταϝ α αιϝ íαϝ nτénαṁ α ὡοϝȝα αȝυϝ α ὡυϝυιϝ ιϝιn τíϝ ϝιn αṁυιl bα lonn lαιϝ; αȝυϝ το bí α nυϝlαιṁe αȝ nα mαιthιὸ ϝιn ιοchταϝ Chonnαchτ ȝu ττιοὡϝατάοιϝ ταċυϝ τO Ὀhoṁnαιll αȝ τeαchτ ταιϝ α αιϝ ὸο, αȝυϝ ní ċυȝαταϝ αchτ líαṁαn ιοmϝύαȝαιτh, οιϝ níϝ ϝυιϝιὸ O Ὀοṁnαιll ό ὸο ϝάȝ τíϝ ϝhιαċϝαċ no co nτeαchαὸ co Ὀρύιm ċlιαὸ, αȝυϝ το bí α ȝcοιϝιċιὸ α ȝcοṁnαιὸe αϝ αn ȝcοṁϝατ ϝιn. Mαϝὸċυϝ mαϝcαċ το

---

1 *James Ballach*; i.e. James the Freckled [O'Domhnaill].

² *The strand.* The strand of Traigh-Eothuile, near Ballysadare. co. Sligo.

This demand had scarcely been responded to, when they proudly, furiously, attacked each other. A person of very great note of the Clann-Donnchaidh was killed in this conflict, i.e. Maelechlainn, the son of Tadhg, son of Ruaidhri; and by a shot of a gun he was killed. Another horseman of O'Domhnaill's people was killed there by a cast of a spear, i.e. James Ballach,[1] the son of Niall, son of John. They separate from each other. O'Domhnaill goes into the country of Brian O'Conchobhair's descendants, and was three nights destroying corn, and burning towns and moors. O'Conchobhair was at Bel-an-droichit in an encampment. O'Domhnaill goes across the strand[2] westwards to Tir-Fiachrach-Muaidhe, and destroys therein a great quantity of corn, and many towns, and much of every other kind of property; for the country was in their own power, except some of its castles; and he seized a great quantity of the herds of the country around Sliabh-Gamh. They proceed westwards across the Muaidh, at the invitation of the descendants of Richard Burk, in pursuit of some of the herds of the sons of O'Dubhda. The daughter of Walter Burk is seized by them, i.e. the wife of Eoghan O'Dubhda, together with his prey. So immense were the spoils and herds obtained by O'Domhnaill, that a beef, or two beeves, would be given there for one bonn,[3] and even this would not be got for them. Mac Diarmada, and the sons of Tadhg Mac Diarmada, and the sons of Mac David, went to assist those of Lower [Connacht] against O'Domhnaill. O'Domhnaill turns back, after accomplishing his expedition and journey into that country as he wished; and those chieftains of Lower Connacht were prepared to give battle to O'Domhnaill on his return home; but they only made a slight attack, for O'Domhnaill rested not from the time he left Tir-Fiachrach until he went to Druim-cliabh; and he was always in battle array during that time. A

---

[3] *Bonn.* A groat, or four-penny piece.

muinnẟin mic Caẟail óiᵹ 1 Chonċuẟaiṗ aṗ an íomṗuaᵹaẟ
ṗın aᵹ ẟul ẟaṗ ṗeṗṗaiẟ ṗanna ın Liaᵹaın ẟonẟ ṗLuaiᵹ
.ı. Ccoẟ mac ẟṗıaın ṁeıc Ccoẟa, ocuṗ mac ꞤNıc ꞂÐıaṗmaẟa ẟo ẟṗómLoẟ anẟ .ı. mac Eoᵹuın mıc Ꞇaıẟᵹ. Ꞇéıẟ
O ꞂÐoṁnaıLL ẟa ẟıᵹ ᵹan uṁla ᵹan oṗṗaım ẟṗaᵹaıL ó
ṁaıċıẟ ıochẟaıṗ Chonnachẟ ẟon ẟuL ṗa aṁuıL ba
neaṁᵹnáẟ. ꞤÐac ꞂÐonnchaẟa ẟo ᵹaıṗm ẟo ꞂÐhonẟchaẟ
ṁac Ꞇaıẟᵹ ṁeıc ꞂꞒuaıẟṗı meıc Conċuẟaıṗ ṁeıc Ꞇaıẟᵹ
ṁeıc· Ꞇomulẟuıᵹ meıc ꞤNuıṗᵹeaṗa meıc ꞂÐonchaẟa,
aᵹuṗ ᵹan ꞤNac ꞂÐonnchaẟa ṗéın ẟéᵹ, aᵹaṗ ṗé a néaṗṗ
a áoıṗı íaṗ na ẟaLLaẟ .ı. Eoᵹan mac ꞂÐonnchaẟa meıc
ꞤNuṗchaẟa; aᵹuṗ coᵹaẟ ac cLoınn Eoᵹhaın ṗe ꞤNac
n'Ꞃonnchaẟa ṗan aınm-ṗın, aᵹuṗ ᵹan ní ṗúaıċnıẟ ẟo
ṁılleẟ eaẟuṗṗa ṗóṗ. Ccn ᵹıoLLa ẟuẟ ṁac Ccoẟa mıc
ꞂꞒúaıẟṗı ẟaLLaıᵹ mıc 1 Chonċuẟaıṗ [ẟṗaᵹaıL ẟáıṗ an
ẟLıaẟaın ṗın. 8Lúaıᵹeẟ Le .ħ. Conchoẟaıṗ 8Lıᵹıᵹ ocuṗ
Le .ħ. ꞂꞒuaıṗc ocuṗ Le mac CaẟaıL óıc .ħ. Conchoẟaıṗ],
aṗ ẟaṗṗuınᵹ ꞤNıc ꞂÐıaṗmaẟa aᵹuṗ ċLoınne Ꞇaıẟᵹ ꞤNıc
ꞂÐıaṗmaẟa, aṗ Ꞇhóıṗṗẟealẟaċ ṗuaẟ anıṗna Ꞇúaẟaıẟ,
aᵹuṗ muınnẟıṗ Ccınlıᵹe ẟo ẟaẟuıṗc ẟṗaᵹaẟ ẟóıẟ aᵹuṗ
ᵹan a mılleẟ. ẟóıẟ eıẟıṗ ċıLL ıṗ ẟuaıẟ; aᵹaṗ a nẟol
aṗṗın a ꞤNaıneaċuıẟ, aᵹuṗ ᵹach aon ṗa caṗuıẟ ẟlla
Chonċuẟaıṗ ẟıẟ ẟo ṁılleẟ achẟ aṗaınıc mac 1 ꞂꞒuaıṗc,
óıṗ ní ẟo ṁılleẟ neaċ ẟo chuaıẟ, achẟ ẟá ṗeċuın
an bṗeẟṗaẟ ṗíoċchaın ẟo ẟénaṁ eıẟıṗ ꞤNac n'Ꞃıaṗ-
maẟa ᵹuna ẟṗaıẟṗıẟ aᵹuṗ O Cunċuẟuıṗ ṗuaẟ ᵹuna
ṗann coᵹaẟ ẟon ẟuL ṗın. ᵹaẟuıẟ an ṗLuaᵹ ṗın caıṗLén
an Ꞇuṗṗaıc aᵹuṗ bṗıṗıẟ é. Ꞇıᵹ ꞂÐonnchaẟ mac Emaınn
1 CheaLLaıᵹ ċuca ẟo ẟṗaᵹaıẟ ẟeaᵹla a ẟuẟhaıẟe ṗéın ẟo
ṁılleẟ. ꞆṗıaLLaıẟ an ṗLuaᵹ ṗın íaṗ nẟenaṁ a ẟẟuṗuıṗ

---

¹ *Aedh.* Hugh. A member of
the family of O'Conor Sligo.

² *In the decline of life.* α néaṗṗ
α áoıṗı; lit. "in the end of his age."
α néaṗṗ, for α n'ẟeṗıuẟ. See note
¹, p. 258 *supra*.

³ *O'Conchobhair.* The correspond-

ing portion enclosed within brackets
in the text, apparently omitted by the
scribe, has been supplied from the
Annals of Connacht.

⁴ *Toirdhelbhach Ruadh.* He was
the son of Tadhg Buidhe, son of Cathal Ruadh O'Conor.

horseman of the people of Cathal Og O'Conchobhair's son, i.e. Aedh, the son of Brian, son of Aedh,[1] was slain in that attack, whilst the army was going across Fersat-ranna-in-liagain, and the son of Mac Diarmada, i.e. the son of Eoghan, son of Tadhg, was severely wounded there. O'Domhnaill goes home without obtaining submission or homage from the chieftains of Lower Connacht on this occasion, as was unusual. Donnchadh, the son of Tadhg, son of Ruaidhri, son of Conchobhar, son of Tadhg, son of Tomaltach, son of Maurice, son of Donnchadh, was proclaimed Mac Donnchadha, though Mac Donnchadha himself, i.e. Eoghan, the son of Donnchadh, son of Murchadh, had not died; but he was in the decline of life,[2] after having been blinded; and Eoghan's sons waged a war with Mac Donnchadha concerning this title, but still nothing important was destroyed between them. The Gilla-dubh, son of Aedh, son of Ruaidhri Ballach, son of O'Conchobhair, [died this year. A hosting by O'Conchobhair Sligigh, and by O'Ruairc, and by the son of Cathal Og O'Conchobhair],[3] at the instance of Mac Diarmada. and the sons of Tadhg Mac Diarmada, against Toirdhelbhach Ruadh,[4] into the Tuatha; and Muinter-Ainlighe gave them hostages, on condition of not being injured by them both in church and territory.[5] And they went from thence[6] to the Mainechs,[7] and plundered every one of them who was the friend of O'Conchobhair, except those whom the son of O'Ruairc met; for it was not to injure any one he went, but[8] to see if he could make peace between Mac Diarmada, with his kinsmen, and O'Conchobhair Ruadh, with his allies. This army takes the castle of the Turrac, and demolishes it. Donnchadh, the son of Edmond O'Cellaigh, comes to them as a hostage, for fear his own country would be destroyed. This army proceeds, after

---

[5] *Both in church and territory ;* .e. in ecclesiastical and lay possessions. -

[6] *From thence.* αr rin ; repeated in MS.

[7] *Mainechs.* The inhabitants of Hy-Many, or O'Kelly's country, in the counties of Roscommon and Galway.

[8] *But.* αr rin. MS.. which is wrong.

aṁuil bá luinn leó, agus befur na bráigde sin co
Sligech .i. mac I Ccinlige agas mac I Cheallaig; agus
do teirid leo coṁla breac an caislein sin do
ξaḃudur cunn na cur se caislen Sligiξ. Sluaξ eile an
ḃliaξuin si leis an ngiḃdois tSaxanac annsa Muṁain
síar, dar gaḃ cassuic O gCoinneall agus dar ḃris
droiceat Murchaiḃ I Ḃriain; agus mas síos do bi
cuid do Dhonnchaḃ mac I Ḃriain andsna gníoṁaiḃ
sin. Ḣ.Ruairc do ξairm do Ḃrian mac Eoξain mic
Tigernáin. Caislen an caisce do leaξaḃ an Ḃliaξain
si lé .Ḣ.Rúairc. Mac Uilliam Cloinne Riocuird .i. Sean
ṁac Riocuird ṁic Emainn dég an Ḃliaξain si, agus
coξad mór eidir cloinn Riocuird san tiξerntus; agus
da mac Uilliam do ξairm irin tír .i. mac Uilliam
do ξairm do Risderd Bacach ṁac Uilliam, agus mac
Uilliam eile do ξairm dUillioc mac Riocuird óig; agus
Uillioc na cenn ac congnaṁ le Risdeard mbacach.
Donnchaḃ duḃ mac Concuḃair mic Ruaidri Buide, sear
saiḃreis agus tiξe oideḃ coitcinn, dragail bair ongca
agas aiṫriξe. Mag Fhlannchaiḃ taoireć Darτraiξe
.i. Feruḃac ṁac Uilliam, sξél mór don daonnacht
agus don eineć, dragail bair. O Raiξilliξ .i. Feargul
ṁac Seuin ṁeic Catail, sí .Ḣ. [nḂriuin] mḂreifne
agus Conmaicne, sear síal sisinneać soiξidneć, dég
íar comaoin agus ṫsacarbaic. Doṁnall mac Donnchaḃa I Cheallaig, cennsegna maiṫ agus tanuisde
O Maine o Charuiḃ gu Ξrein, agus mac a dearbraṫar
mailli sis .i. Eiξneaċan mac Maoileaċluinn mic
Donnchaḃa I Cheallaig, ammarḃuḃ aḃsill masaon lé

---

[1] *Justiciary.* giḃroir, for ξiusτir.
The use of aspirated ḃ (ḃ) for u is
rather frequent in the text of this
chronicle.

[2] *Bridge.* The Annals of Connacht
add that it was an Smainn, i.e. "on
the Shannon" (O'Brien's Bridge ?).

[3] *Brian.* He is called Brian "Ballach," or Brian "the Freckled," in the
Annals of Connacht.

[4] *Ulick-na-cenn;* i.e. Ulick of the
heads; so called from the number of
enemies' heads he had cut off. The
name is represented by na ceann in

accomplishing their expedition as they liked, and those
hostages are taken to Sligech, viz., the son of O'hAinlighe,
and the son of O'Cellaigh ; and they carry with them the
speckled door of the castle which they had taken, in order
to put it to the castle of Sligech.   Another hosting this
year by the Saxon Justiciary,[1] westwards into Mumha, on
which occasion he took Carraic-O'Goinnell, and broke
down Murchadh O'Briain's bridge[2] ; and if it be true,
Donnchadh, the son of O'Briain, had a share in these acts.
Brian,[3] the son of Eoghan, son of Tighernán, was proclaimed the O'Ruairc.   Caislen-an-cairthe was demolished
this year by O'Ruairc.   Mac William of Clann-Rickard,
i.e. John, the son of Rickard, son of Edmond, died this
year ; and a great war occurred amongst the Clann-
Rickard concerning the lordship ; and two Mac Williams
were proclaimed in the country, viz., Richard Bacagh, the
son of William, was proclaimed the Mac William, and
Ulick, the son of Rickard Og, was proclaimed another
Mac William ; and Ulick-na-cenn[4] sided with Richard
Bacagh.[5]   Donnchadh Dubh, the son of Conchobhar, son of
Ruaidhri Buidhe, a man of wealth, and keeper of a general
house of hospitality, died after unction and penitence.
Mac Flannchaidh, chieftain of Dartraighe, i.e. Feradach,
the son of William, a great loss to humanity and hospitality, died.   O'Raighilligh, i.e. Ferghal, the son of John,
son of Cathal, king of the Ui-[Briuin-]Breifne[6] and Conmaicne, a generous, truthful, charitable man, died after communion and sacrifice.[7]   Domhnall, the son of Donnchadh
O'Cellaigh, a good captain, and tanist of Ui-Maine from
Caradh to Grian, and his brother's son along with him, i.e.
Egnechan, the son of Maelechlainn, son of Donnchadh O'Cellaigh, were slain in treachery, together with Maelechlainn,

A.D.
[1536.]

the MS. ; the form in the text is supplied from the Annals of Connacht.
   [5] *Bacagh* ; i.e. "the Lame."
   [6] *Ui-[Briuin-] Breifne.*   This name
is written h·mbpeirtne in the MS.

Breifne O'Raighilligh, i.e. the present
co. of Cavan, is meant.
   [7] *After . . . . sacrifice.* ιαp
τραcαιþαιc MS. ρacaþþíc, Annals
of Connacht.

Maoileachuinn ṁac Uilliam ṁeic Maoileachuinn
1 Cheallaiġ ó ḟeḋuiḃ baile Cĉa luain, ap ḟupconġraḋ
ĉloinne Taiḃġ mic Donnchaḋa 1 Cheallaiġ .i. clann
depḃráĉap Doṁnaill buḃḃéin. Clann mic Uilliam
ĉloinne Riocuipo .i. Seun ouḃ aġup Rémonn puaḋ, eḋon
oíap mac Riocuipo mic Uillioġ, oo mapbaḋ lé cloinn
Ribcuipo óiġ mic Uilliġ puaiḋ ṁeic Uilliġ an ḟíona an
Cĉhaḋ opaoinín, ap mbpeiĉ aoĉópuiġechĉ ḟoppu a
haiĉle ĉpeaĉ an ĉípe oo ĉĝĝlomaḋ ḋóiḃ. Mac Ġoipoealḃ
.i. Seun mac an ġiolla ḋuiḃ, neaĉ oeipluicteĉ oaon-
nachĉaĉ oeiġ ĉennuippeġna, oo mapbaḋ oo ḟṕíappup
Ma[c] Ġoipoealḃ aġup oo ĉuio oo luchĉ Cĉipĉiġ in
hoc anno. O Conĉuḃuip Ḟhailġe .i. Ḃpian mac Caĉaip
oo oibeipĉ ap a ḋúĉhaiḋ, aġup a ĉaipléin uile
oo ḃpipeḋ, aġup mópan oa muinĉip oo mapḃuḋ innĉiḃ
leip an nġiḃpĉíp ĉpaxpanaĉ .i. loapo linapo; aġup ḟop
ĉpé ḟopmuĉ aġup ĉpeimḃeall oepḃráĉap 1 Chonĉuḃaip
ḟein .i. Caĉaip púaḋ, oo pinne pin uile.

|c[al]luinn ġénaip ḟop luan; bipeĉ ḟuippi; peachĉ
mbliaġna .x. ap ḟĉiĉ aġup cúiġ ceo aġup mile áoip
an Tiġepna. Taipech ṁuinnĉipe Cionaiĉ, .i. Taḃġ mac
Cĉoḋa mic Cĉoḋa mic Conĉḟnaṁa, [oḟaġail ḃaip in hoc
anno]. O Ġaġpa .i. Eoġan mac Diapmaĉa ṁeic Eoġuin,
ĉiġepna Chúil O Ḃḟinn, [ohec in hoc anno]. Mac
Uilliam Ḃupc .i. Teaboio mac Uillic mic Eumainn in
Cpipĉo quieuiĉ, aġup coġuḋ ḟa na inḃe oá éip. Sluaiġeḋ
leip [O Neill] .i. Conn O Heill, ap ĉpían Conġuil, oáp
ṁill aġup oap ĉpeaĉ mópan oon ĉíp, aġup mac 1 Néill
oo ġaḃail a mbél Ḟeippĉe ap oeipeḋ anĉ ḟluaiġ, aġup
O Néill oo ĉeachĉ oá ĉiġ iapuṁ; aġup ĉiġepna ĉpín
Conġuil .i. Hiall óġ mac Héill mic Cuinn oḟaġuil ḃáip

---

1 *Fedha.* The woods, or "Fews," a district near Athlone, in the present county of Roscommon, anciently the patrimony of the Naghten family.

² *Justiciary.* ġiḃpĉíp, MS.. for ġiupĉíp, or ġiúipĉíp, as the word is generally written in the text of this chronicle, which frequently has an aspirated b (ḃ) for u and ui.

the son of William, son of Maelechlainn O'Cellaigh, from the Fedha[1] of the town of Ath-Luain, at the instigation of the sons of Tadhg, son of Donnchadh O'Cellaigh, viz., the sons of Domhnall's own brother. The sons of Mac William of Clann-Rickard, viz., John Dubh and Redmond Ruadh, viz., the two sons of Rickard, son of Ulick, were slain in Achadh-drainín, by the sons of Rickard Og, son of Ulick Ruadh, son of Ulick-an-fhiona, who overtook them in pursuit, after they had collected the preys of the country. Mac Goisdelbh, i.e. John, son of the Gilla-dubh, a generous, humane man, and a good captain, was killed by Piers Mac Goisdelbh, and by some of the people of Airtech, in hoc anno. O'Conchobhair Failghe, i.e. Brian, the son of Cathair, was expelled from his country, and his castles were all demolished, and a great many of his people were killed in them, by the Saxon Justiciary,[2] i.e. Lord Leonard; and through the envy and malice of his own brother, i.e. Cathair Ruadh, moreover, he (*the Justiciary*) did all that.

The kalends of January on Monday; after a bissextile; [1537.] the age of the Lord one thousand, five hundred, and thirty-seven years. The chieftain of Muinter-Cinaith, i.e. Tadhg, the son of Aedh, son of Aedh Mac Consnamha, [died in hoc anno].[3] O'Gadhra, i.e. Eoghan, the son of Diarmaid, son of Eoghan, lord of Cúl-O'Finn, [died in hoc anno].[3] Mac William Burk, i.e. Tibbot, the son of Ulick, son of Edmond, in Christo quievit;[4] and a war took place respecting his property after him. A hosting by O'Neill, i.e. Conn O'Neill, to Trian-Conghail, when he destroyed and plundered a great part of the country; and O'Neill's son was taken prisoner at Bel-Ferste, in the rear of the army; and O'Neill returned home afterwards. And the lord of Trian-Conghail, i.e. Niall Og, the son of Niall, son of Conn, died suddenly about this time; and O'Neill

---

[3] *Anno.* The words enclosed within brackets in the text are added from the Annals of Connacht.

[4] *Quievit.* quiebit, MS.

VOL. II. x

ᵹu hobunn rón ám rin; aᵹur O Néill vo ḟilleḃ arír a
vtrían Conᵹuil. α ṁac vo bí a láiṁ vraxuil vó, aᵹur
ιmreruιn ra ếιᵹerncur ếrín Conᵹuil. Ϻαc 1 Ꞃαιᵹιlliᵹ .ι.
ḃrían ϻαc Ꝝerᵹuil, euchc mór aᵹur vuιne úarul maιế,
vo ϻαrbαḃ le muιnncιr an ᵹιuιrrcιr, αr ceáchc voιb
αr ếreιch a ccloιnv Ϻhαếᵹαṁnα. Ϻαc Ϻιc Shuιḃne
.ι. Ϻαelṁuιre vo ϻαrbαḃ le cloιnv Ϻurchαvα Ϻιc
Shuιḃne ra blιαḃoιn rιn. Coccαḃ ιvιr αeḃ ḃuιḃe Uα
ᴅomnαιll aᵹur Ϻαxnαrr O ᴅomnαιll aᵹur clanv 1,
ḃαeιḃιll, aᵹur cαιrlen ᴅúιn na ᵹαll vrαᵹhbαιl vαeḃ,
aᵹur a ḃeế na buαιḃrιuv mor a ccιr Conuιll; aᵹur cuιv
vo ḟlιochc ιn erbuιc 1 ccαlɫếuḃαιr vo ṁαrrαv le cloιnn
1 ḃαeιḃιll .ι. ϻαc Coιrrvhelbαιᵹ óιcc mιc ḃrιαιn, aᵹur
vιαrr ϻαc [Ɵoᵹαιn] ballαιᵹ mιế ḃrιαιn, co ccuιllev
mαιlle rιιu. Slυαιᵹeḃ larαn ᵹιuιrcιrr a nιb Ꝝαιlᵹe,
aᵹur cαιrlen ιn ᴅαιnᵹιn, .ι. ιnc en baιle vo bα vαιnᵹne
ιonαvh aᵹur orvuᵹhαv ι nƟιrιnn vo ḃrιrιoḃ vó, aᵹur
óchcα aᵹur eválα mórα vrαcchαιl annrιn ; aᵹur bαιlce
1 Conchobαιr uιle vo ḃeιế αr a comur, aᵹur ιn cιr
vo mιlleḃ .voιḃ. O ᴅomnαιll .ι. αev vub ϻαc αeḋα
ruαιḃ, mιc Néιll ᵹαιrb mιc Coιrrvhelbαιᵹ ιṅ ḟíonα,
cιᵹernα círe Conuιll aᵹur ιochcuιr Connachc, aᵹur
rer Ϻαnαế aᵹur ếιneoιl Ϻoáιn aᵹur lιnrι Ɵoᵹαιn,
aᵹur vo ếuιr a lán vo cιᵹernuruιḃ eιle ra rmachc, ϻαr
cá Ϻαᵹ luιrᵹ aᵹur mαếαιre Chonnachc, aᵹur Clann
Connmαιᵹ, aᵹur cír αmαlᵹαιv aᵹur Conmαιcne cúιle,
aᵹur ᵹoιrceαlbα aᵹur cúιl O rꝝιnn, ocur von cαeḃ ếoιr
ϻαr ιn cevnα .ι. clann αeḋα buιḃe αcur ιn Ꞃúcα, occur
oιrechc 1 Chαếáιn; or nι rαιḃe eιn cír αcα rιn nár

---

1 *People.* The original text from
this down to the year 1541 is in the
handwriting of Donnchadh Mac-in-
filedh (Mac Nilly). See note [7], p. 297.

2 *Aedh Buidhe*; i.e. "Yellow Hugh."
He was the son of Aedh Ruadh (or
Hugh Roe), the son of Niall Garbh
O'Donnell. The name Aedh is written
αeℸc in the MS.

3 *Sons of O'Baighill.* The Four
Masters say that they sided with
Aedh Buidhe O'Domhnaill.

4 *O'Gallchubhair.* O'Gallagher. 1
ccαlɫ., MS., the letters cc representing ᵹ.

5 *Of Eoghan.* Ɵoᵹαιn. Supplied
from the Annals of Connacht.

6 *Daingen.* Daingen-Ui-Failghe,

turned back into Trian-Conghail. He obtained his son, who was in captivity; and a dispute *occurred* regarding the lordship of Trian-Conghail. The son of O'Raighilligh, i.e. Brian, the son of Ferghal, a person much lamented, and a good gentleman, was slain by the Justiciary's people,[1] who had gone on a foray into Clann-Mathghamhna. The son of Mac Suibhne, i.e. Maelmuire, was slain this year by the sons of Murchadh Mac Suibhne. A war between Aedh Buidhe[2] O'Domhnaill and Maghnus O'Domhnaill, and the sons of O'Baighill;[3] and the castle of Dun-na-nGall was abandoned by Aedh. And there was great dissension in Tir-Conaill; and some of the descendants of the Bishop O'Gallchubhair,[4] viz., the son of Toirdhelbhach Og, son of Brian, and the two sons [of Eoghan][5] Ballach, son of Brian, and others along with them, were slain by the sons of O'Baighill. A hosting by the Justiciary into Ui-Failghe; and the castle of the Daingen,[6] i.e. the strongest and best fortified town in Erinn, was demolished by him; and many captives[7] and spoils were found there; and all O'Conchobhair's towns were in his power; and the country was destroyed by them. O'Domhnaill died, i.e. Aedh Dubh,[8] the son of Aedh Ruadh, son of Niall Garbh, son of Toirdhelbhach-an-fhina, lord of Tir-Conaill, and of Lower Connacht,[9] and Feara-Manach, and Cenel-Moain, and Inis-Eoghain. And he had placed many other lordships under his sway, such as Magh-Luirg, and Machaire-Connacht, and Clann-Conmaigh, and Tir-Amhalghaidh, and Conmaicne-Cuile, and Goisdelbha, and Cul-O'Finn; and on the eastern side,[10] in like manner, Clann-Aedha-Buidhe, and the Ruta, and Oirecht-Ui-Chathain; (for there was no country of these

---

or "the fastness [daingen=donjon, dungeon] of Offally;" now Philipstown, King's county.

[7] *Captives.* échta; lit. "deeds," but idiomatically signifying persons of great account.

[8] *Aedh Dubh.* Black Hugh. He

seems to have had a brother called Aedh Buidhe (Yellow Hugh). See note [2], last page.

[9] *Lower Connacht.* iochtuip Connacht. A line has been drawn through these words, as if to erase them.

[10] *Eastern side;* i.e. of Ireland.

cenꞁuicc co minic é, maille ꞃe cioꞃꞃ Ɥíoc co uṁal.
Accuꞃ ni héiꞍiꞃ a ꞃíom na a ꞃaiꞃneiꞃꞃ ꜰaċ aiꞍeꞃnaiꞍ
Ɥo cꞃechaib ocuꞃ Ɥo maꞇmannuiꞇ aꞃ a eꞃccaiꞍoiꞇ
conuicci ꞃin ; ocuꞃ Ɥo ꞃaeileꞇ ꜰuꞃ bé anꞇ Aeꞇ eanccach
Ɥo ꞇaiꞃnꜰeꞍaꞃ ꞃáiꞍi ocuꞃ ꞃiꞃꞃiꞇ é. Ocuꞃ ni ꞇanuic Ɥo
ꞃliochꞇ ꜰaeiꞍil ꜰlaiꞃꞃ na coimaimꞃiꞃ neaċ aꞃ mó Ɥo
ꞇinnlaic Ɥéiꜰꞃiꞇ ocuꞃ Ɥollamnaib ocuꞃ Ɥoꞃꞇꞇaiꞇ Ɥé
na anꞇ Aeꞇ ꞃin; ocuꞃ in cuiꜰeꞇ lá Ɥo mí luil ꞃuaiꞃ ꞃé
báꞃꞃ, aꞃ nꞍola naibiꞍ ꞃan ꟊꞃoinꞃiaꞃ a maineiꞃꞇiꞃ Ɥúin
na Ꜵall, Ɥa ꞇoil ocuꞃ Ɥa aenꞇaiꞇ ꞃéin maille ꞃéꞃún
maiꞇ; ocuꞃ ꞍaꞃꞍaein aꞃ aoi laiꞇi ꞃeachꞇmaine ꞇeꞃnó
on[ꞇ] ꞃaeċcal iaꞃ na onꜰaꞇ, occaꞃꞃ iaꞃ naiꞇꞃiꜰe Ɥo
molaꞇ na heꜰlaiꞃꞃe; ocuꞃ a mac .i. Maċcnuꞃ O Ɥom-
naill Ɥo ꞃiċcaꞇ na ionaꞍ Ɥo ċeꞇꞇ occuꞃꞍo ċoṁaiꞃle Chon-
allach acuꞃ comaꞃbaꞍ Coluim cille, aṁail ꞃa Ɥual Ɥó.
Sluaiꜰeꞇ laiꞃꞃ O nꞍomnaill .i. Maċcnuꞃ i niochꞇaꞃ
Connachꞇ, a mí ṁeaꞇoin ꞃoccmoiꞃ, Ɥaꞃ mill móꞃán
aꞃꞍa acuꞃ Ɥaꞃ loiꞃc accuꞃ Ɥaꞃ imꞇiꜰ ichꞇaꞃ Connachꞇ
.i. Ꞇíꞃ ꟊhiaċꞃach acuꞃ Caiꞃbꞃe, occuꞃ in Ɥá Luiꞇcne,
acuꞃ in CoꞃanꞍ, acuꞃ ꞇíꞃ Oilella ꞃoime anuaꞃꞃ. Ocuꞃ
ꜰaꞇꞇuꞃ baile 1 eꜰꞃa ꞃiaꞇuicc laiꞃꞃ Ɥon Ɥul ꞃin, acuꞃ
ꞇuc eineach ꞍO Oꜰꞃa ꞃéin aꞃ mbeiꞇ ꞃoꞃ a ċomuꞃ, cu
ꞇucc laiꞃꞃ a mbꞃaiꜰꞍenuꞃ é. Máꜰ UiꞍiꞃ .i. Cúꞇonnachꞇ
mac Conconnachꞇ mic ꞇhꞃiain, ꞇiꜰeꞃna ꞃeꞃ Manach,
ꞃeꞃ Ɥéꞃcaꞇ Ɥaennachꞇach, Ɥo bá mó clú láiṁe ocuꞃ
uaiꞃle ocuꞃ einech Ɥa Ɥꞇainic Ɥo ꞃliochꞇ na cColla ꞃe
cian Ɥaimꞃiꞃ, ocuꞃ Ɥo cuiꞃ o Chluain éiꞃ co Cael
uiꞃꜰi ꞃa uṁla ocuꞃ ꞃa ꞃmachꞇ; ocuꞃ Ɥo ba maiꞇ in

---

1 *Aedh Engach.* Aedh the Valiant.
The prophesied avenger of the wrongs
of Ireland. The Annals of Connacht
contain a much longer, and more ex-
travagant, eulogium on Aedh O'Domhnaill, in which it is stated that the four
elements were better represented in
him than in any other man, and that
as he was *not* the prophesied Aedh

Engach, that personage would never
come. See vol. i., p. 253.
² *Of Gaeidhel Glas.* ċcaeiꞍil
ꜰlaiꞃꞃ, MS.
³ *Orders;* i.e. Religious Orders.
⁴ *Northwards.* anuaꞃꞃ; literally
"down;" the words ꞃuaꞃ and anuaꞃ
("up" and "down") signifying rela-
tively "southwards" and "north-

that had not frequently recognized him, besides sub- missively paying tribute). And it is not possible to enumerate or relate all the depredations he committed, and all the defeats that he inflicted, on his enemies, up to that time. And it was thought that he was the Aedh Engach[1] whom prophets and wise men had foretold. And there came not, in his time, any one of the race of Gaeidhel Glas[2] that gave more to poets, professors, and the Orders[3] of God, than this Aedh. And the fifth day of the month of July he died, (after assuming the habit of Saint Francis in the monastery of Dun-na-nGall, with his own will and consent, for a good reason); and on Thursday, as regards the day of the week, he retired from the world, after he was anointed, and after doing penance according to the decision of the church. And his son, i.e. Maghnus O'Domhnaill, was made king in his place, with the permission and counsel of the Conallachs, and of the comarb of Colum Cille, as was his due. A hosting by O'Domhnaill, i.e. Maghnus, into Lower Connacht, in the middle month of Autumn, on which occasion he destroyed much corn, and burned and traversed Lower Connacht, viz., Tir-Fiachrach, and Cairbre, and the two Luighne, and the Corann, and Tir-Oilella, on his way northwards.[4] And O'hEghra Riabhach's town is taken by him on this occasion; and he gave protection to O'hEghra himself, on condition of submitting to his power, and carried him off in captivity. Mag Uidhir, i.e. Cuchonnacht, the son of Cuchonnacht, son of Brian, lord of Feara-Manach, a charitable, humane man, the most renowned for prowess, nobility, and hospitality, that had come of the race of the Collas[5] for a long while, and who placed from Cluain-Eois to Cael-uisce under obedience and government, (and this

wards." This entry would therefore seem to have been originally written by some person residing to the north of Cairbre (Carbury, co. Sligo).

[5] *The Collas.* Ancestors of the Oirghialla, or septs of Oriel, from which are descended the Maguires, O'Reillys, Mac Mahons, Mac Kennas, and their correlatives. See O'Fla- herty's *Ogygia*, p. 361.

ṗinachꞇ ṗin, oíṗ ní ꞇainic na ꝺuꞇhaiꝺ ṗéin ṗe ꞇṗeimṗe
ꝺaimṗiṗ ꞇiꝣeṗna ꝺob ṗeṗṗ ṗechꞇ ocuṗ ṗiacchail ocuṗ
aṗṗ mo ꝺo čoiṗc biꞇbenuičc occuṗ aeṗṗ uilc, ocuṗ ꝺo
čuiṗ na ꞇíṗꞇa na ṗuiꝺe co ṗocaiṗ ṗiꞇčanꞇa, ocuṗ aṗ mó
ꝺáṗ eiṗiꝺ ṗonuṗ ocuṗ ṗaiꞇṗeṗ ṗe a linn. α maṗbaꝺ
abṗioll a cCṗeačán ṗoṗ Loch Eṗne le ṗlicħꞇ Comáiṗṗ
Méꝣ Uiꝺiṗ ocuṗ le ṗlicħꞇ Coiṗṗꝺhelbaiꝣ Méiꝣ Uiꝺiṗ
an bliaꝺain ṗin; ocuṗ a aꝺlacaꝺ aṗ ꞇꞇúṗṗi nꝺaiminiṗ,
ocuṗ a čócbáil a ccionn aꞇhaiꝺ iaṗ ṗin leiṗ na bṗáicṗiꝺ
mionuṗa, ocuṗ a ꞇabaiṗꞇ co niainiṗꞇeṗ ꝺúin na ꝣall,
ocuṗ aṗaile. Mac αeꝺa mic Neill mic Cuinn mic
αeꝺa buiꝺe .i. Niall, aꝺbaṗ ꞇiꝣeṗna cṗin Concchail,
ocuṗ ṗeṗ ꝺénṁa uaiṗli ocuṗ einicch, ocuṗ leṗ coṗmuil
lenmain luiṗcc a ṗinnṗeṗ a cclú ocuṗ a ccaiꞇeṁ a leꞇ
le ꝺíl ꝺaṁ ocuṗ ꝺeoṗaiꝺ, éꝣeṗṗ ocuṗ aeṗṗ ealaꝺna,
ocuṗ aṗ einech ocuṗ aṗ uaiṗle; ammaṗbaꝺ le αlban-
chaiꝺ. O Conchobaiṗ Ṗailꝣe ꝺo ꝣabail a ꝺuꞇhaiꝺe ṗéin
ꝺo nemčoil in ꝣiuiṗꞇiṗṗ ocuṗ a bṗaicṗech ṗéin .i. clann
i Conchobaiṗ; occuṗ cuiꝺ ꝺa nꝺaeiniꝺ ꝺo buain ꝺíꝺ, ocuṗ
cṗeiṗie a číṗi ṗéin uile ꝺo ꝣabail ꝺó amail buꝺ cóiṗ.
baṗún ꝺealbna .i. Riṗꝺeṗꝺ mac Cṗiṗcoiṗ mic Comaiṗ,
ṗꝣiač ꝺiꝺin ocuṗ cliaꞇh ꝣaeiꞇe Ꝣhall ṗe ꝣaeiꝺheluiꝺ,
ṗiꝺiṗe cṗóꝺa coꝣčach, ꝺo čul ꝺeꝣ na baile ṗein ieṗ
mbuaiꝺh onꝣča ocuṗ aiꞇṗiꝺe; achꞇ ꝣeṗb iomꝺa ꝣuaṗ-
achꞇ ꝣliaꝺ aṗ aṗ ꞇeṗnó conuicce ṗin. Mac i Maeil-
eaclainn, .i. Sémuṗ mac Muṗchaꝺa, ꝺo maṗbaꝺ le
mac i Conchobaiṗ Ṗailꝣe, neach buꝺ mo clú ocuṗ
caiꞇṗeim na comaeiṗ ꝺo cinel Ṗhiachaiꝺ mic Néill.
Mac i Raiꝣilliꝣh .i. Caꞇaeiṗ moꝺaṗꝺa, mac Seáin
mic Caꞇail, ꝺo maṗbaꝺ a ꞇꞇóṗaiꝺhechꞇ le Saxančuiꝺ.

---

[1] *In despite.* ꝺo nemčoil, lit.
"with non-consent."

[2] *Dealbhna.* Delvin. The MS. has
ꝺealꝣα, which is wrong.

[3] *Wind-hurdle.* cliaꞇh ꝣaeiꞇe;
an epithet signifying shelter, or defence.

[4] *Warlike.* coꝣčach. The MS.
has coꝣčach, which is corrupt. The
correct form has been supplied from
the Ann. of Connacht.

[5] *His own place;* i.e. the castle of
Delvin, in the county of Westmeath.

[6] *Cenel-Fiachaidh-mic-Neill.* See

government was good, for there came not in his own country for a period of time a lord whose law and rule were better, and who more repressed thieves and evil-doers, and established the territories more quietly and peaceably, and in whose time happiness and wealth increased more), was this year slain in treachery at Creachán, on Loch-Erne, by the descendants of Thomas Mag Uidhir, and the descendants of Toirdhelbhach Mag Uidhir; and he was buried at first in Daimhinis, and was disinterred some time afterwards by the Friars Minors, and conveyed to the monastery of Dún-na-nGall, &c. The son of Aedh, son of Niall, son of Conn, son of Aedh Buidhe, i.e. Niall, heir to the sovereignty of Trian-Conghail, and a man who practised nobility and hospitality, and who was likely to follow in the footsteps of his ancestors in reputation and liberality, as regards rewarding the learned and destitute, poets and men of science, and in bounty and excellence, was killed by Albanachs. O'Conchobhair Failghe took possession of his own country, in despite[1] of the Justiciary, and of his own kinsmen, viz., the sons of O'Conchobhair; and he took some of their people from them, and assumed the supremacy of all his own country, as was right. The Baron of Dealbhna,[2] i.e. Richard, the son of Christopher, son of Thomas, the sheltering shield, and wind-hurdle,[3] of the Foreigners against the Gaeidhel, a brave, warlike[4] knight, died in his own place,[5] after the triumph of unction and penitence, although many were the dangers of battle from which he had escaped up to that time. The son of O'Maelechlainn, i.e. James, son of Murchadh, in his time the person of greatest fame and battle-career of the Cenel-Fiachaidh-mic-Neill,[6] was killed by the son of O'Conchobhair Failghe. The son of O'Raighilligh, i.e. Cathair Modardha,[7] the son of John, son of Cathal, was slain by Saxons,[8] in pursuit *of a prey.*

---

note [5], p. 500, vol. i. It has been considered necessary to alter the construction of this entry in the translation.

[7] *Cathair Modardha;* i.e. Cathair (or Charles) the Swarthy.

[8] *Saxons;* i.e. English.

Mac 1 Ꝺoċαрcαιᵹh .ı. Νιαll cαech, mac ᵹeрαιlc mιc
Ꝺoιɴɴαιll mιc Ƒeιlιm, ꝺo mαрbαꝺ α ɴᵹрeιρᵱ oιᵹċe le
ꝶuꝺрαιꝺhe mac Ƒeιlιm 1 Ꝺoċαрcαιᵹh, α mᵬαιle ɴα
ᵹcαɴαɴαch ꝼoρ ceρmαɴɴ Ꝺoιρı; ocuρ αꝺeριꝺ ɴαċ mαιꝉ
ꝼριoch é. O Ƒlαɴɴαcαιɴ Chuαιꝉ ρᾱcα ı. ᵹιollα 1ραe,
ocuρ α mαc, ꝺo mαрbαꝺ leιρ¹¹¹ ccuιꝺ oιle ꝺα cιɴeꝺ co
ɴemmαιch, ocuρ uιlc ιomᵬα ꝺo beꝉ ꝺα ɴꝺeɴαm α
ᵬꝼeρuιꝉ Mαɴαch α hαιcle bαιρρ Méιᵹ Uιᵬιρ. Cρeαċα
ocuρ loρcαꝺ ꝺo ꝺeɴαꝺ ꝺoɴ Cαlbαċ O Ꝺomɴαιll αρ
clαιɴɴ Ꝿmlαeιb, ocuρ cρech eιle ꝺo·ᵬeɴαm αρ O Cαċαιɴ
ꝺó.

ẛc. ιαɴαιρ ꝼoρ Mαιρc; ochc mbliαꝺɴα ꝺec αρ .xx.
αcuρ cuιᵹ ceꝺ αcuρ mιle αoιρρ ιɴ Cιᵹeρɴα. Coᵹαꝺ αρ
ɴeιρᵹe ecιρ Mac ɴ Ꝺιαρmαꝺα, .ı. Ꝿeꝺ mac Coρmαιc
Mιc Ꝺιαρmαꝺα, ocuρ ꝶuαιᵬρι mac Cαιᵬᵹ Mιc Ꝺιαρmαꝺα. ꝶuαιᵬρι ꝺo ᵹuιꝺe ꝺoιρꝼeoιρeꝺ αɴ bαιle, ocuρ
ꝼeolαꝺ ꝺꝼαᵹhαιl uαċα αρ αɴ mbαιle ꝺo ᵹαᵬᾱιl; ocuρ αρ
αmlαιꝺ ꝺo cumαꝺαρ ꝺó ceαchc ꝺocum ιɴ bαιle ραɴ
oιᵹċe, ocuρ ꝺρéιmeρeᵬα ꝺo ċuρ leιρ¹ɴ ccαρρuιc; ocuρ
ꝺo ċuαꝺαρ αρcceċ ocuρ ꝺo ᵹαᵬαꝺαρ Mac Ꝺιαρmαꝺα
ocuρ α mac .ı. Mαelρuαɴαιꝺh. Ocuρ ꝺo bᾱꝺαρ leꝉ
bliαᵹαιɴ α lαιm, ocuρ ꝺo cuαιꝺ ꝼoιρm ecoρρα, ocuρ αρí
ꝼoιρm ꝺo cuαιꝺ ecoρρα .ı. O Conchobαιρ ꝺoɴɴ ocuρ
O ᵬeιρɴ, ocuρ mαιꝉe ɴα cíρe mαιlle ꝼρuu; ocuρ αρ
αmlαιꝺ ꝺo ριɴɴeꝺαρ ρ¹¹ɴ leꝉ cιᵹeρɴαιρ, ocuρ αɴ cαρραιc
co ɴα ραeιρρ o Ꝿeꝺ Mac Ꝺιαρmαꝺα ꝺo ꝶuαιᵬρι Mαc
Ꝺιαρmαꝺα αρ ρeꝺ α beꝉα ρeιɴ. Mac 1 Ꝺomɴαιll .ı.
Ꝿeꝺ buιꝺe mac Ꝿeꝺα mιc Ꝿeꝺα ρuαιꝺ, ρ¹ꝺαmɴα cíρe
Conαιll, ɴeαċ lᾱɴ ꝺαιꝉɴe occuρ ꝺeιɴeαċ ocuρ ꝺeoluρ αɴ

· 1 *Well done.* ᵀɴαċ mαιꝉ ꝼριoꝉé; lit.
"that it was not found good;" i.e. that
the deed was not approved of. This
clause is not in the Annals of Connacht.

² *Wickedly.* co ɴemmαιch; lit.
unwell, MS.

³ *O'Cathain.* o ccαꝉαιɴ, MS., which
is corrupt, as the c should be aspirated,
and not doubled, or hardened, ac-

cording to the ordinary grammatical
rule. At the end of this entry the
scribe has added the note meιρı
Ꝺoɴɴchαꝺ mαc ιɴ ꝼιlιoꝺ ꝺo
ρᵱ¹ɴιoᵬ ιɴ leo beαc ρ¹ɴ, ocuρ αρ
ɴᾱᵲα ιɴ ceρꝺ ꝺαɴ α ꝼoᵹlαιm
αᵹαm, i.e., "I am Donnchadh Mac-
in-ihilidh (M'Nilly), who wrote this
little fragment, &c."

The son of O'Dochartaigh, i.e. Niall Caech, the son of Gerald, son of Domhnall, son of Felim, was killed in a nocturnal conflict by Rudhraidhe, the son of Felim O'Dochartaigh, in Baile-na-gcananach, in the termon of Doire; and they say that it was not well done.[1] O'Flannagain of Tuath-ratha, i.e. Gilla-Isa, and his son, were wickedly[2] slain by the rest of his tribe; and many evils were committed in Feara-Manach after Mag Uidhir's death. Depredations and burnings were committed by the Calbhach O'Domhnaill upon the Clann-Amhlaibh, and another depredation was committed by him upon O'Cathain.[3]

A.D.

[1537.]

The kalends of January on Tuesday; the age of the Lord one thousand, five hundred, and thirty-eight years. A war occurred[4] between Mac Diarmada, i.e. Aedh, the son of Cormac Mac Diarmada, and Ruaidhri the son of Tadhg Mac Diarmada. Ruaidhri solicited the doorkeepers of the place,[5] and obtained from them directions for taking it. And the plan they invented for him was, that he should go to the place in the night, and fix ladders to the Rock;[6] and they went in, and captured Mac Diarmada and his son, i.e. Maelruanaidh. And they were half a year in captivity, when an arrangement took place between them; and the persons who intervened[7] were O'Conchobhair Donn, and O'Beirn, and the principal men of the country along with them; and the arrangement they made was that half the lordship, and the Rock with its freedom, *should be given* by Aedh Mac Diarmada to Ruaidhri Mac Diarmada during his own life. The son of O'Domhnaill, i.e. Aedh Buidhe, son of Aedh,[8] son of Aedh Ruadh, royal heir of Tir-Conaill, a person full of knowledge,

[1538.]

---

[4] *Occurred.* aṅ neiṅge, lit. "after arising," MS.

[5-6] *The place—the Rock;* i.e. the Rock of Loch-Cé, Mac Dermot's principal residence in the county of Roscommon.

[7] *The persons who intervened.* The original text has aṙí ṗoiṅm ṫo cuaiṫ eṫoṅṙa, lit. "the form that went between them."

[8] *Aedh.* The Four Mast. call him Aedh Dubh (Black Hugh).

ealaḃanuiḃ, occuſ ꝺoḃ ꝼeꝛꝛ ꝺo ḃaꝛánꞇa ʟaime a
nᴣoꝛꞇaiḃ ᵹʟiaḃ ocuſ a mḃeꝛnaḃuiḃ baeḃail, ocuſ aꝛꝛ·
mó ꝺo ꝛaeileꝺ ꝺo ꝛochꞇain ꞇiᵹeꝛnaiꝛꝛ· a ꞇíꝛe ꝼein ꝺo
ꝛeiꝛ aiꝛᴣenaḃ ocuſ ꞇꝛéᵹᵹe ꞇiᵹeꝛna, ꝺa ꞇꞇucaḃ ꝺia
ꝛaeᵹal ꝺó, aꝛ ḃꝛaᵹail baiꝛꝛ in ḃliaḃain ꝛin ꝺo ᵹalaꝛ
aiꞇᵹeꝛꝛ a cciʟʟ O ꝺꞇónaiꝛ, ıeꝛ ccomaein [ocuſ] coꝛꝛ
Cꝛıꝛꞇ, ın aeine ıeꝛ ḃꝼéil ꝛáꝺꝛaıc. Nıaʟʟ mac Cuınn
mıc Ⱥıꝛꞇ 1 Neiʟʟ, mac ꝛíᵹ maıꞇ aꝛ aꝛaıḃe uaıꝛle ocuſ
eıneaꞇ, ꝺo maꝛḃaḃ le mac Neiʟʟ 1 Neiʟʟ aꝛ ᵹꝛeıꝛ oıᵹᴄeı
a ᵹcaıꝛlen na Omuıḃe, aꝛ ḃꝛaᵹhail ꝼeolꞇa coꝛa amach
aıꝛ o cııꝺ éıᵹın ꝺa muınꞇıꝛ ꝼéın; ocuſ Nıaʟʟ O Neiʟʟ
ꝺo ḃꝛıꝛıoḃ ın caıꝛlein na ꝺıaıḃ ꝛın, ocuſ beḃ anꝺıaıꝺ
[an] maꝛḃꞇa ꝛın aꝛ a mac ꝼeın. Mac Meᵹ Clanncaıᵹ,
aḃḃaꝛ ꞇaıꝛıᵹ Ɗaꝛꞇꝛaıḃe .ı. Caꞇaeıꝛ, mac Ꝼeꝛaꝺhaıᵹh
mıc Uıʟʟıam Meᵹ cClanncaıḃ, moꝛꞇuuꝛ eꝛꞇ a nꝺun
ᵹaıꝛḃꝛı a mı Maı. Sloıᵹheꝺ laꝛ O Ɗomnaiʟʟ .ı. Maᵹnuꝛ ı nıchꞇaꝛ Connachꞇ, ꝺaꝛ ᵹaḃaꝺ caıꝛlen Sliᵹıḃ
leıꝛ co áıꞇᵹꝛaꞇ, ꝺo bı ꝛa ꝼeol maıꞇ baꝛꝺaꝺ ocuſ
oꝛꝺonáıꝛ, ocuſ ꝺo bí aḃꝛaꝺ ꝛoıme ꝛın a ᵹaḃáıl ꝼe na
aꞇaıꝛ ᵹan ᵹaḃáıl; ocuſ aꝛ nᵹaḃáıl ın caıꝛlein ꝛın
ꞇéıꝺ O Ɗomnaiʟʟ a Moıᵹ Luıꝛᵹ, ocuſ miʟʟꞇeꝛ ın ꞇíꝛ
leıꝛ ᵹu ꝼéıꝛ; ocuſ ıaꝛ bꝛiʟʟeḃ ꞇaꝛ a aıꝛꝛ ꝺó, aꝛ
ꞇꞇeachꞇ ꞇimceʟʟ caıꝛlein 1 Ꝣaḃꝛa .ı. Ryaıḃꝛı mıc Céın,
maꝛḃꞇaꝛ mac maıꞇh 1 Ɗomnaiʟʟ co ꞇubuıꝛꞇech ꝺuꝛchoꝛ
ꝺo ᵹonna, .ı. Nıaʟʟ ᵹaꝛḃ, mac Maᵹnuꝛa mıc Ⱥeḃa
mıc Ⱥeḃa ꝛuaıꝺh; ocuſ ꞇánᵹaꝺaꝛ ꝼlán achꞇ ꝛın, ıaꝛ
miʟʟeḃ Moıᵹe Luıꝛᵹ ocuſ ıchꞇaıꝛ Connachꞇ achꞇ ın
cuıꝺ ꞇanuıc le umla ꝺocum 1 Ɗomnuıʟʟ ꝺıḃ, ocuſ ꝛuc

*   *   *   *   *   *   *

Ɗealb Muıꝛe ꝛo mıoꝛbuıleᵹ ꝺo bı a mbaıle Ⱥḃa
Cꝛuım, ꝺaꝛ cꝛeıꝺeꝺaꝛ Eıꝛennuıᵹ uıle le cıan ꝺaımꝛıꝛ
ꝛoıme ꝛın, ꝺo ꝼlánuıꝺheꝺ ꝺoıʟʟ ocuſ boḃaıꝛ ocuſ
bacaıᵹ, ocuſ ᵹaᵹ aınᵹeꝛ aꝛᵹena, ꝺo loꝛᵹaḃ le Saxanᵹuıḃ;

<hr />

1 *Surest hand.* ꝺoḃ ꝼeꝛꝛ ꝺo
baꝛánꞇa ʟaıme; lit. "the best
warrant of hand."

2 *O'Doṁnaill.* The contents of

three lines following this have been
erased. A corresponding blank occurs
in the Annals of Connacht.

bounty, and skill in sciences. and the surest hand[1] in fields of battle, and in gaps of danger, and who was most expected to reach the sovereignty of his own country, according to the characteristics and qualifications of a lord, if God would grant him life, died this year of a very short illness, in Cill-O'Tonair, after communion [and] the body of Christ, the Friday after the festival of Patrick. Niall, son of Conn, son of Art O'Neill, a good son of a king, who possessed nobility and hospitality, was killed by the son of Niall O'Neill in a nocturnal assault in the castle of the Omagh, after it had been betrayed to him by some of its own people ; and Niall O'Neill demolished the castle after that, and followed up this homicide against his own son. The son of Mac Clancaigh, heir to the lordship of Dartraighe, i.e. Cathair, son of Feradhach, son of William Mac Clancaigh, mortuus est in Dun-Gairbri, in the month of May. A hosting by O'Domhnaill, i.e. Maghnus, into Lower Connacht, on which occasion the castle of Sligech, which was well defended by warders and ordnance, and which his father had been for a long time previously trying to take, without success, was triumphantly captured by him. And after capturing the castle, O'Domhnaill goes into Magh-Luirg, and the country is entirely destroyed by him. And after he had turned back, whilst going round the castle of O'Gadhra, i.e. Ruaidhri the son of Cian, O'Domhnaill's good son, i.e. Niall Garbh, the son of Maghnus, son of Aedh, son of Aedh Ruadh, is unfortunately killed by a gun shot. And they came safely, with this exception, after destroying Magh-Luirg and Lower Connacht, save such of them as came with submission to O'Domhnaill[2]   *   *   *   *
*   *   *   *   *   *   *   *

The very miraculous image of Mary which was in the town of Ath-truim, in which all the people of Erinn believed for a long time previously, which healed the blind, and deaf, and lame, and every other ailment, was burnt

ocuꞃ an baċaꝇꝇ íoꞃa, ꝺo bi a mbaiꝇe Ǽa cꝇiaꞇh, aꝣ
ꝺénaṁ ꞃeaꞃꞇ ocuꞃ mioꞃbuiꝇe íomḃa í nɛiꞃínn o aimꞃiꞃ
ꝼꝑaꝺꞃaic ꝣuꞃ an ꞃé ꞃín, ocuꞃ ꝺo bi a ꝇaim Cꞃioꞃꞇ
ꞃéín, ꝺo ꝇoꞃcaḃ ꝇe Saxanchaib muꞃ ín ceꝺna; ocuꞃ ní
heaḃ aṁáín, acḣꞇ ní ꞃaiḃe cꞃoċ naoṁ na ꝺeaꝇb Muiꞃe,
ná íomáiꝣ oiꞃꝺꝺiꞃc í nɛiꞃínn, aꞃ anꝺeachaiꝺ a ccumachꞇa, ꝣan ꝇoꞃꝣaḃ, ocuꞃ ní mó ꝺo bí a ccumachꞇa aꞃ
oꞃꝺ ꝺona ꞃeachꞇ noꞃꝺuiḃ naꞃ ꞃꝣꞃiꞃioꝺaꞃ. Ocuꞃ ín
ꝑápa ocuꞃ ín eꝣꝇaiꞃ ꞇoiꞃ ocuꞃ aḃuꞃ ꝺo beꞇ a coinneꝇ-
báꞇhaꝺ na Saxanach ꞇꞃíꝺ ꞃín, ocuꞃ ꝣan ꞃuím na ꞇoꞃaḃ
ꝺo beꞇ aca ꞃan aiꞃ ꞃín, ocuꞃ aꞃaiꝇe; ocuꞃ ní ꝺeꞃb
ꝇiom naċ aꞃ an mbꝇiaꝺhaín am ꝺiaiꝺ ꞇüaꞃ aꞇá ꝇoꞃꝣaḃ
na míonn ꞃín. Ḃꞃían mac Eoꝣaín míc Conchobaiꞃ míc
Ruaiꝺꞃí buiḃe ꝺhec ín bꝇiaꝺaín ꞃe.

Jꞇ. Enáiꞃ ꞃoꞃ Céꝺaeín; naí mbꝇiaꝺna ꝺeꝣ aꞃ .xx.ᵗ
u. ceꝺ, miꝇe aeíꞃ ín Ꞇiꝣeꞃna. O Ḃꞃíaín, ꞃí Ꞇuaꝺmuman,
.í. Conchobaꞃ mac Ꞇoiꞃꞃꝺheꝇbaiꝣ míc Ꞇaiꝺꝣ, ꝺꞃaꝣáíꝇ
báíꞃꞃ ín bꝇiaꝺaín ꞃí íaꞃ ꞇꞃeímꞃí a ꝺꞇiꝣeꞃnuꞃ Ꞇüaꝺmu-
man, ocuꞃ ín ꞇíꞃ ꝣu ꞇoicꞇeċ ꞇꞃom conáíꝣ ꝇe na ꝇinn;
ocuꞃ Muꞃchaꝺ mac í Ḃꞃíaín, .í. mac Ꞇoiꞃꞃꝺheꝇbaiꝣ
míc Ꞇaiꝺꝣ, ꝺo ꞃíꝣaḃ na hínaꝺ amaíꝇ ꝺo ꞇuiꝇꝇ a haiꞃiꝇ-
ꝇeḃ ꞃeiꞃín coníꝣe ꞃín. O Ḃéiꝇꝇ .í. Conn ꝺo beiꞇ í nꝪun
na ꝣaꝇꝇ an bꝇiaꝺaín ꞃí ím cáiꞃꝣ, ocuꞃ caiꞇem ꞃocꞃach
onóꞃach ꝺo ꝺénaṁ ꝺꝇa Ꝺomnaiꝇꝇ ꝇe a ꝇinꝺ, amaíꝇ ꝺo
buꝺ cuꝣuiꝺ; ocuꞃ O Ḃéiꝇꝇ ocuꞃ O Ꝺomnaiꝇꝇ ꝺo ꝺenaṁ
caċ uiꝇe cenꝣaꝇ ꝺa ꝺaínꝣne ocuꞃ ꝺa ꞇaiꞃꞃꞃi annꞃín,
eꞇ ceꞇeꞃa.

Sꝇoiꝣeḃ ꝇeiꞃ O Ḃéiꝇꝇ .í. Conn. Sꝇóíꝣeḃ ꝇeiꞃ O nꝪom-
naiꝇꝇ .í. Maċcnuꞃ, ꝺo comaiꞃꝇe a ċéiꝇe ꞃa Miḃe, ocuꞃ
ín ꞇíꞃ ꝺo miꝇꝇeaḃ ocuꞃ ꝺo ꝇoꞃcaḃ ꝇeo co Ꞇemꞃaiꝣ,

---

1 *Saxons*; i.e. English.

2 *Bachall-Isa.* Staff of Jesus. For
some account, of this relic, see Todd's
Obits and Martyrology of Christ Church;
Introd., p. viii., *sq.*

3 *Abroad and at home.* ꞇoiꞃ ocuꞃ
aḃuꞃ, lit. "in the east and here."

4 *Should be.* aꞇá, i.e. "is." The
Four Masters record the events under
the year 1537; but Ware under 1538.
At the end of this entry Brian Mac
Dermot adds—Ꝺonnchaꝺ mac ín
ꝼiꝇeaꝺ ꝺo ꞃꝣꞃíḃ ꞃo ín ꝇuan an-
ꝺiaiꝺ Ꝺoṁnaiꝣ ꝑaꝺꞃaiꝣ aꞃ an

by Saxons;[1] and the Bachall-Isa,[2] which was in the town of Ath-cliath, working numerous prodigies and miracles in Erinn from the time of Saint Patrick to that date, and which had been in Christ's own hand, was burned by Saxons[1] in like manner; and not alone this, but there was not in Erinn a holy cross, or a figure of Mary, or an illustrious image, over which their power reached, that was not burned. And furthermore, there was not an Order of the seven Orders in their power that they did not destroy. And the pope, and the church abroad and at home,[2] were excommunicating the Saxons on account thereof; but they had neither respect nor regard for that, &c. (And I am not certain that it is not in the last year above the burning of those relics should be).[4] Brian, son of Eoghan, son of Conchobhar, son of Ruaidhri Buidhe, died this year.[5]

A.D.
[1538.]

The kalends of January·on Wednesday; the age of the Lord one thousand, five hundred, and thirty-nine years. O'Briain, king of Tuadh-Mumha, i.e. Conchobhar, the son of Toirdhelbhach, son of Tadhg, died this year, after having been a while in the sovereignty of Tuadh-Mumha; and the country was prosperous, very rich, during his time; and Murchadh, the son of O'Briain, i.e. the son of Toirdhelbhach, son of Tadhg, was made king in his place, as his own merits up to that time deserved. O'Neill, i.e. Conn, was in Dun-na-nGall this year about Easter, and a munificent, honorable, entertainment was provided by O'Domhnaill during his stay, as was becoming; and O'Neill and O'Domhnaill then concluded alliances of the most firm and friendly kind,[6] &c.

[1539.]

A hosting by O'Neill, i.e. Conn, and a hosting by O'Domhnaill, i.e. Maghnus, by mutual agreement, into Midhe; and the country was destroyed and burned by

---

scaiṗṙis; i.e. "Donnchadh Mac-in-filedh that wrote this, the Monday after Patrick's Sunday, on the Rock [of Loch-Cé];" which is followed by a brief observation in the handwriting of the scribe.

[5] *Year.* This event is added in the handwriting of Brian Mac Dermot.

[6] *Kind.* Here it is added in the hand of Donnchadh, son of Mac-in-filedh (Mac Nilly), that he wrote this part of the text.

ocur nap τιonóιlpeꝺ 5αoιꝺιl co 5αllαιb en pluαιχeꝺ αp
mó leιp mιlleꝺ .ꝺo mαιτep nα Mιꝺe nα ιn pluαιξιoꝺ
pιn, ocur ꝺop αιꝺble éꝺálα óιp ocur αιpccιꝺ ocur ûmα
ocur ιαpuιnn, ocur cαč uιle mαιτep αpčenα ; ocur co
áιpιꝺe ιn Umαmá ocur bαιle áτα pιpꝺιαꝺ ꝺo
lomαpcαιn leo, eτιp ιnnmαpp ocur upαꝺ ocur cαč uιle
mαιτep αpchenα. Ocur ιαp bpιllιoꝺ ꝺonα pluαꝺeꝺ pιn
ocur ιαꝺ lán ꝺuαιll ocur ꝺo ꝺιomup, ꝺo len ιn χιuιpτιp ιαꝺ .ι. loαpꝺ lιnαpꝺ lepτιnól nα mbαιlτιoꝺ móp,
ocur nα Mιꝺe eτιp cιll ocur τhuαιτh, ocur αpαιbe ꝺo
Sαxαnchαιb ι nEιpιnn, ocur αmbuι ꝺo coblαιξuιꝺ αp nα
cuαnταιꝺ cαčα ταob ꝺιb .ι. coblαč po móp ꝺo bí αp
Cαιplιnne co αιpιče. Ocur beιpιꝺ nα τιnóιlpιn ιn
χιuιpτιp αp αn pluαιχ 5αeιꝺhelαč ιn Oιpξιαlluιꝺ .ι. α
bpepnα ꝺo punnpαꝺ .ι. α mbeol áτα hOα ; ocur nι pαιnιc
leιpιn pluαꝺ 5αoιꝺhelαč ꝺul α nopꝺuchαꝺ αmαιl buꝺ
coιp, nα epmαpιn αp comαιple α nꝺeχ ꝺαeιne ꝺo ꝺenαm
le copnαm nα le coτhuχαꝺ, αchτ ιmτechτ co αnopꝺuιξče,
ocur mópán ꝺα néꝺáluιb péιn ocur ꝺéꝺαlαιb 5αll
ꝺpácbαιl αnꝺ pιn αχ pluαιχ ιn χιuιpτιpp; ocur cαιι α
becc ꝺechτuιb oιppꝺepcα ꝺpαcbαιl ꝺoιꝺ χe ꝺo ιmčιξpeꝺ
co αnopꝺuιξče ; conιꝺ é Mαolmuιpe mepceč mαc Eoιn
Mιc Shuιꝺne pcél αp mó po pácbαꝺ ꝺo Coñαllchαιb
áñn. Mαχ αconcupα .ι. Muιpcepταč ꝺo ξαbαιl le cuιꝺ
ꝺOιppcιαllαιb, ιαp nα bpαcbáιl co huαιτe αp nꝺeξáιl lé
α muιnτιp αp αn pιꝺbαl pιn ; ocur α beꝺ τámαll α lαιñ
cop ιopeαl, po conꝺepnαꝺ meαꝶαl pαιp ιαpum αp
comαιple coꝺα ꝺα cιneꝺ peιn, .ι. cenꝺαc ꝺo ξαbáιl ꝺo
cιnn α copα cum báιp, eτ ceτepα. Nιαll óc O ꝺαoιξιll
ꝺo mαpbαꝺ le Conchobαp mαc I ꝺαoιξιll, eτ ceτepα.

---

1 *Umamá.* ιñ Umαmá. The name
of this place is written nuαčonχbαιl
(i.e. nova habitatio) in the Annals of
the Four Masters. The place referred
to is now called Naván, to which name
the form in the text, allowing for the
attraction over of the *n* of the article
to the name Umama (=Numhama)

would be a nearer approach than the
form used by the Four Masters. The
name is omitted in the Annals of Connacht.

² *Lost.* ꝺpαcbαιl ; lit. "left."

³ *Maelmuire Mergech ;* i.e. Maelmuire "the Wrinkled."

⁴ *O'Baighill.* A note in the hand-

them' as far as Temhair. And the Gaeidhel mustered not against Foreigners any army by which more of the property of Midhe was destroyed than this army, or which had more prodigious spoils of gold, and silver, and copper, and iron, and of all other goods besides ; and particularly, the Umamá,[1] and the town of Ath-Firdiadh, were completely pillaged by them, both of treasures, apparel, and all other goods besides. And on the return of these armies, and they full of haughtiness and pride, the Justiciary, i.e. Lord Leonard, followed them with the entire muster of the large towns, and of Midhe, both ecclesiastical and lay, and all the Saxons that were in Erinn, and the fleets that were in the harbours on each side of them, i.e., at least a very large fleet which was on Cairlinne. And these musters of the Justiciary came up with the Gaeidhelic army in Oirghiall, i.e. exactly in Ferna, i.e. in Bel-atha-hOa. And the Gaeidhelic army had not succeeded in getting into proper array ; nor did they act on the counsel of their chieftains, to defend ' or sustain themselves; but they went away in a disorderly manner, and left a great quantity of their own spoils, and of the spoils of the Foreigners, to the Justiciary's army. And they lost[2] no men of note, although they went away in disorder; so that Maelmuire Mergech,[3] the son of John Mac Suibhne, was the person of greatest account lost there by the Conallachs. Mag Aenghusa, i.e. Muirchertach, was taken prisoner by some of the Oirghialla, he having been left, with a few attendants, after separating from his people on this march ; and he was secretly in captivity for a while, until treachery was afterwards practised upon him by the advice of some of his kindred, viz., to accept a reward in consideration of putting him to death, &c. Niall Og O'Baighill was killed by Conchobhar, the son of O'Baighill,[4] &c.

writing of Brian Mac Dermot inti- | was written by Donnchadh, son of mates that this part of the chronicle | Mac-in-fhiledh (or Mac Nilly).

Ịcṫ. Ɛnaiṗ ṗoṗ Ḋaṗḋaein, ḋa xxꞁᵗ bliaḋan ocuṗ cuig ceḋ, mile aoiṗ in Ṫigeṗna. Ḋiaṗṗ mac Uaiṫéiṗ mic Ṙiocaiṗḋ ḋo maṗbaḋ an bliaḋain ṗin .i. Ṙiṗḋeṗḋ ocuṗ Ṫomáṗ. Maineiṗṫiṗ Cluana ṗamṗaḋa ḋo ṫabaiṗṫ ḋona bṗáiṫṗiḃ bochṫa ḋe oṗṗeṗuanṗie in bliaḋain ṗin, aṗ ṗolaiṗem 1 Ḃṗiain ocuṗ maiṫe Ṫuaḋmumon, ocuṗ ḋo ċeṫ ocuṗ ḋo comaiṗle uachṫaṗán in ḋa oṗḋ ṗin .i. ṗan ṗṗoinṗiaṗ ocuṗ ḋe oṗṗeṗuanṗie. Saxanuiġh ḋo beiṫh a ḋibiṗṫ iaṗṗma na noṗḋ ṗin aṗ ṗuḋ Ɛiṗinn caċ áiṫ aṗ cuiṗṗeṫ a ccumachṫaṡ ocuṗ co aiṗiṫe mainiṗṫiṗ Muinechán ḋo milleḋ ḋoib, ocuṗ gaiṗḋian in baile maille moṗán ḋona bṗaiṫṗiḃ ḋo ḋiṫcennaḋ ḋoib. Caiṗlen Liaṫṗoma ḋo ḋenam in bliaḋain ṗi laṗ O Ṙuaiṗc .i. la Ḃṗian mac Ɛoġain 1 Ṙuaiṗc, ocuṗ moṗán coguiḋ cach ṫaob aiṗ .i. a Moiġ Luiṗcc ocuṗ a muinnṫiṗ Ɛolaiṗ, ocuṗ a mḂṗeiṫne 1 Ṙaigilliġh, ocuṗ a mac ṗéin ocuṗ cuiḋ ḋṗeṗuiḃ Ḃṗeiṫne a ccogaḋ ṗiṗṗ ṗoṗṗ; ocuṗ ḋo ṗinne in caiṗlen ṗe haimṗiṗ aṫġeiṗṗ, ocuṗ ḋo mill móṗán ṗa moiġ Luiṗc ocuṗ ṗan luchṫ cogaiḋ, eṫ ceṫeṗa. Ḋiaṗ mac 1 Ḃaoiġill .i. Niall ocuṗ Conchobaṗ ḋo coimċuiṫim in bliaḋain ṗi le céile .i. Niall ḋo ḋul ḋiaṗṗaḋ Conchobaiṗ a Luaċṗuṗ, ocuṗ cealc oiġċe ḋo ḋenaṁ ḋó a ḋṫempall Seancáin, ocuṗ Conchobaṗ ḋo ṫeachṫ aṗ ṗuḋ na ṫiṗe iaṗ na maṗaċ le na gnoṫhaiguiḃ ṗein, ocuṗ Niall co na muinṫeṗ ḋeiṗġe na ḋiaiḋ aṗin ṫempall. Ocuṗ oḋ ċonaiṗc Conchobaṗ ċuicce iaḋ beiṫ aṗ imḋechṫ [ḋo] ṫaṗ ṫṗáiġ Luacṗaiṗ ṗiaṗ; ocuṗ a muinṫeṗ ḋo ṗgaṗaḋ Leiṗ, ocuṗ Niall ḋa lenmain co ṗo ġéṗ ṗoim a cuiḋechṫa ṗein, ocuṗ bṗeṫh aṗ Conchobaṗ ḋa aimḋeoin, ocuṗ Conchobaṗ ḋṗuiṗech le Niall; a ccoimeṗcaṗ ann ṗin co beoḋa laiḋiṗ, ocuṗ bualaḋ a

¹ *By command.* aṗ ṗolaiṗem, MS., for aṗ ṗuṗaileṁ, as in the Annals of Connacht. The Four Mast. say aṗ ṗoṗconġṗa, which has very nearly the same meaning.

² *Was beheaded.* ḋo ḋiṫcennaḋ, for ḋo ḋicennaḋ, MS.

³ *Breifne.* This name, the etymology of which is rather uncertain, is corruptly written Ḃṗeiṫne in the MS.

The kalends of January on Thursday; the age of the A.D.
Lord one thousand, five hundred, and forty years. The [1540.]
two sons of Walter, son of Rickard, viz., Rickard and
Thomas, were slain this year. The monastery of Cluain-
ramhfhada was this year given to the Poor Friars De
Observantia, by command[1] of O'Briain and the nobles of
Tuadh-Mumha, and by the consent and advice of the
superiors of these two orders, viz., of Saint Francis and
De Observantia. The Saxons, wherever they established
their power throughout Erinn, were expelling the remainder of these orders; and they destroyed, especially,
the monastery of Muinechan ; and the guardian of the
place, together with several of the friars, was beheaded[2]
by them. The castle of Liath-truim was erected this
year by O'Ruairc, i.e. by Brian, the son of Eoghan
O'Ruairc, although great wars were waged against him
on all sides, viz., from Magh-Luirg, and from Muinter-
Eolais, and from Breifne[3]-O'Raighilligh ; and his own son,[4]
and some of the men of Breifne,[3] were at war with him also.
And he built the castle in a very short time, and destroyed
much throughout Magh-Luirg, and against the mili-
tants, &c. O'Baighill's two sons, viz., Niall and Conchobhar, fell by each other this year ;[5] viz., Niall went to seek
Conchobhar in Luachrus, and lay a night in wait for him
in Tempul-Sencháin ; and Conchobhar passed along the
country on the morrow, with his own servants, and Niall
and his people went after him from the church. And when
Conchobhar perceived them coming towards him, he was
proceeding westwards across the strand of Luachrus ; and
his people separated from him ; and Niall followed him
very quickly, in advance of his own company, and overtook Conchobhar against his will. And Conchobhar
waited for Niall ; and they then encountered each
other vigorously, strongly, and unsparingly struck each

---

[4] *His own son.* The Annals of Connacht give his name as Conn.

[5] *This year.* in bliaoain ri. Repeated in MS.

Dig   ʹᴸ   ᴮ

céile can coicill ɒoiꞃ, ocuꞃ Niall ɒo maꞃbaꞃ aꞃ in
laꞇaiꞃ ꞃin aꞃ ꞇúꞃ, ocuꞃ Conchobaꞃ ɒo beꞇ buailꞇe.
Ocuꞃ muinꞇeꞃ Neill ɒo ꞇeachꞇ aꞃ in laꞇaiꞃ, ocuꞃ
Conchobaꞃ ɒo ꞇuiꞇim leo; ocuꞃ niꞃ bo báꞃ iaꞃ
miolaoꞀuꞃ eꞇiꞃ, connaꞀ ꞃaiꞃe ɒa ꞃine ꞃein le ꞇꞃeiꞀꞃi
ꞃoime ꞃin ɒiaꞃ oꞇmacaem ɒo ba mó ꞃéchꞇ ináiɒ in
clann ꞃin 1 ꞃaoiᵹill. ꞃoꞃlonᵹꞃoꞃꞇ ɒlla ɒomnaill ꞃa
cꞃonnóic loꞀa ꞃeꞇa ꞃa ꞃaꞀꞃaɒ, aꞃ clainn 1 ɒomnaill
.i. ɒonnchaɒh ocuꞃ Ruɒꞃaiɒhe, ocuꞃ ꞃaoꞇaiꞃ iomɒa.
ɒo ɒénaꞀ Ꞁuca, ocuꞃ naꞃ buaiɒiᵹeꞃ in uaiꞃ ꞃin oꞃꞇa,
eꞇ ceꞇeꞃa. Clann Uilliam mic in eꞃbuiᵹ 1 ᵹallcaꞃaiꞃ,
.i. Aeɒ ᵹꞃuama ocuꞃ Uilliam óc, ɒo maꞃbaɒ le clainn
1 ꞃaoiᵹill .i. le ɒomnall ocuꞃ le Toiꞃꞃɒhelbach, a
nɒíᵹail maꞃbꞇa a naꞇaꞃ. Sloiᵹeɒ leiꞃ O ɒomnaill .i.
Maᵹnuꞃ a cciᵹeꞃ Connachꞇ in bliaɒain ꞃin, ɒia nɒea-
chaiɒ a Moiᵹ luiꞃc ocuꞃ a clainn Conmaiᵹ, ocuꞃ ɒaꞃ
mill ocuꞃ ɒaꞃ loiꞃᵹ na ꞇíꞃꞇa ꞃoime .i. Maᵹ luiꞃc ocuꞃ
clann Conmaiᵹ, ocuꞃ ɒaꞃ in Coꞃꞃꞃliabh, ocuꞃ ꞇoiᵹechꞇ
ꞃlán ieꞃ mbuaiɒ ccoꞃᵹaiꞃ. Sloiᵹeɒ eile laꞃ O ɒomnaill
in bliaɒain ceɒna ꞃa mac 1 lléill .i. Niall mac Aiꞃꞇ
óic, ꞇanaꞃꞇe ꞇíꞃ hEoᵹain, ocuꞃ ꞃa mac ɒomnaill na
hAlban .i. Colla mac Allurɒaiɒ, maille ꞃe móꞃán
Albanach; ocuꞃ a imꞇechꞇ aꞃ ꞇóꞃꞃ a ꞃeꞃuiꞃ Manach,
ocuꞃ móꞃán ɒo milleꞃ ꞃa ꞇíꞃ, ocuꞃ ᵹeallꞇa ɒꞃaᵹail ꞃe
na ꞃiaꞃ ieꞃaꞀ. Ocuꞃ ᵹaɒail ꞇꞃe Uꞃeiꞇne 1 Ruaiꞃc ocuꞃ
ꞃoime co Coꞃꞃliabh, ocuꞃ ꞃoꞃlonᵹꞃoꞃꞇ in Coꞃꞃꞃleiꞃe
ɒo ɒenaꞀ ɒo no cuꞃ ᵹeꞃꞃ ꞃé in Uealac buiꞇe; ocuꞃ
clanɒ Maolꞃuanaiɒ ɒo ꞇeachꞇ cuiᵹe na ɒiaiɒ ꞃin,
ocuꞃ bꞃaiᵹɒi ᵹill ɒo ꞇaꞃaiꞃꞇ ɒó le na bꞃeiꞇ ꞃein
oꞃin ꞃuaꞃ; ocuꞃ impo ꞃlán iaꞃum can ɒibail. Clann

---

1 *Death after cowardice.* The text
in the Annals of Connacht is a little
more explicit, in stating that "the
mutual fall of the pair" was not death
after cowardice.

2 *Aedh Gruama.* Aedh (or Hugh)
the Surly.

3 *O'Baighill.* O'Boyle. 1 ꞃaoiᵹill,
for 1 ꞃaoiᵹill, MS.

4 *Corr-sliabh.* The clause in the text,
ꞃoꞃlonᵹꞃoꞃꞇ in Coꞃꞃꞃleiꞃe ɒo
ɒenaꞀ ɒó, literally means "the encampment of the Corr-sliabh (Curlieu
Hills) was made by him."

other; and Niall was first slain on that spot, and Conchobhar was wounded. And Niall's people came on the ground, and Conchobhar fell by them. And it was not death after cowardice,[1] moreover, as there were no two young men of their own kindred, for a long period before that, of greater fame than these sons of O'Baighill. O'Domhnaill had an encampment about the crannóg of Loch-Betha, in the summer, against the sons of O'Domhnaill, viz., Donnchadh and Rudhraidhe; and great exertions were made against them, but they were not vanquished this time, &c. The sons of William, son of the Bishop O'Gallchubhair, viz., Aedh Gruama[2] and William Og, were slain by the sons of O'Baighill,[3] viz., by Domhnall and Toirdhelbhach, in revenge of the killing of their father. A hosting this year by O'Domhnaill, i.e. Maghnus, into the province of Connacht, when he went into Magh-Luirg and Clann-Conmhaigh, and when he destroyed and burned the districts before him, viz., Magh-Luirg and Claun-Conmhaigh; and *he returned* across the Corr-sliabh, and arrived safely, after gaining spoils. Another hosting by O'Domhnaill the same year, with the son of O'Neill, i.e. Niall, the son of Art Og, tanist of Tir-Eoghain, and with Mac Domhnaill of Alba, i.e. Colla the son of Alexander, accompanied by a great many Albanachs; and he went at first into Feara-Manach, and destroyed much in the country; and he afterwards received pledges of submission to him. And he proceeded through Breifne O'Ruairc, and on to Corr-sliabh; and he encamped in the Corr-sliabh,[4] until he cut down the Bealach-buidhe;[5] and the Clann-Maelruanaidh came to him afterwards, and gave him hostages for the observance of his own conditions from thenceforth. And he afterwards returned safely, without injury. The sons of O'Domhnaill, viz.,

---

[5] *Cut down the Bealach - buidhe.* The meaning is that O'Donnell cut down the obstructions to his passage through the Bealach-buidhe, or "Yellow Pass," a celebrated pass through the Curlieu mountains.

VOL. II.   Y 2

1 Ɗomnɑıⱡⱡ .ı. Ɗonnchɑꝺ cɑı<small>ᵱ</small>ḃᵱech ocuᵱ Séɑn ⱡuıᵱcc ꝺo
beꝥ ɑ ccoʒɑꝺ ɑᵱ O Ɗomnɑıⱡⱡ, ocuᵱ cᵱɑnꝺóc ⱡoꝼɑ ḃeꞇɑꝥ
ꝺo beꝥ ɑcɑ, ocuᵱ ıɑꝺ ɑc ḃuɑıꝺᵱeꝺ ın cıᵱe co móᵱ ɑıᵱꞇe;
ocuᵱ O Ɗomnɑıⱡⱡ ꝺɑ ʒɑḃɑıⱡ ɑᵱɑon; ocuᵱ ꝺo ʒɑḃɑꝺ
Eıʒnechɑn mɑc 1 Ɗomnɑıⱡⱡ ɑ[m]bɑıⱡe nɑ Conʒmɑⱡɑ,
ocuᵱ Seɑn O Ɗomnɑıⱡⱡ ꝺo cᵱochɑꝺ ꝺó, ocuᵱ Eıʒnechɑn
ocuᵱ Ɗonnchɑꝺ ꝺo coᵱ ɑ mḃᵱɑıʒꝺenuᵱ ᵱ̇ɑ ꝺɑoıᵱᵱı ocuᵱ
ᵱɑ ꝺocɑᵱ moᵱ; ocuᵱ cᵱɑnnóc ⱡoꝼɑ ḃeꞇɑꝥ ꝺo mıⱡⱡeꝺ
ꝺⱡⱡɑ Ɗomnɑıⱡⱡ. O Ɗoꝥɑᵱꞇɑıʒ .ı. ʒeᵱɑıⱡꞇ mɑc Ɗomnɑıⱡⱡ mıc Ƈeıⱡım, ᵱeᵱ cu ñuɑıᵱⱡe ocuᵱ co neınech ocuᵱ
co nꝺeıⱡḃ ᵱocᵱɑꝥ, ꝺᵱɑʒɑıⱡ bɑıᵱᵱ ın bⱡıɑꝺɑın ᵱın ıeᵱ
ʒcɑıꝥem ɑ ɑeıᵱı nɑꝺuᵱɑ ⱡe mɑıꝥ ocuᵱ ⱡe ꝺɑonɑchꞇ
conuıʒe ᵱın. O ḃɑeıʒıⱡⱡ ꝺo ꝺenɑ̃ ꝺo Ɗomnɑⱡⱡ mɑc
Néıⱡⱡ 1 ḃɑoıʒıⱡⱡ ın bⱡıɑꝺɑın ᵱın. In ʒıuıᵱꞇıᵱ ꝺo
bı ı nEıᵱınn .ı. ⱡoɑᵱꝺ ⱡınɑᵱꝺ ꝺo ꝺoⱡ ɑ Sɑᵱɑın ᵱɑ
ꝥuıᵱeꝺ ᵱıʒ Sɑᵱᵱɑn, ıɑᵱ mıⱡⱡeꝺ oᵱꝺ ocuᵱ oıᵱᵱıonn ocuᵱ
ᵯınn mıoᵱḃuıⱡıʒ Eıᵱenꝺ uıⱡe, ıeᵱ nꝺenɑ̃ oⱡc nıomꝺɑ
ᵱuꝺ ᵱɑꝺɑ ⱡe ɑ ınnıᵱın, ocuᵱ ʒıuıᵱꞇıᵱ eıⱡe ꝺo coᵱ nɑ
ınɑꝺ .ı. hɑnnꝺɑⱡın Sɑⱡeᵱꝺeᵱ. Rı ɑⱡbɑn ɑᵱ ccoᵱ
ʒɑᵱmɑ ɑᵱ mɑıꝥb nɑ coꝺɑ ɑbuᵱ ꝺɑⱡbɑnchɑıb, ocuᵱ
ꞇeɑchꞇ cuıʒe ɑᵱ ın ccuɑn ɑᵱɑıꝥe ᵱé; ocuᵱ ɑ ꝺꞇɑbɑıᵱꞇ
cuıʒe ᵱɑ ⱡuınʒ ɑᵱɑıꝥe ᵱéın, ocuᵱ ɑ nʒɑbɑıⱡ eꞇıᵱ ʒɑⱡⱡ
ocuᵱ ʒɑoıꝺheⱡ; ocuᵱ ɑ ʒoıⱡⱡ ꝺo ⱡeıʒen ɑmɑch ɑ ʒcıonn
ꞇɑmoıⱡⱡ nɑ ꝺıɑıꝺ ᵱoın, ocuᵱ mɑc Ϻıc Ɗomnɑıⱡⱡ .ı.
Semuᵱ ꝺo connᵯɑıⱡ ɑ ⱡɑıᵯ ꝺó, ocuᵱ ɑn méꝺ ᵱuɑıᵱ ɑᵱ
ᵱoʒnɑꝺ mɑıⱡⱡe ᵱᵱıᵱ ꝺɑ cıneꝺ ocuᵱ ꝺɑ ꝺɑeınıb ꝺo beꝥ ɑ
mḃᵱɑıʒꝺenuᵱ muᵱ [ɑn] ceꝺnɑ, ocuᵱ ꝺıbeᵱꞇ ón ᵱíʒ
ɑᵱ ɑᵱɑıꝥe ᵱɑ ᵱéıᵱ ɑcɑ ıeᵱɑᵯ. Seɑɑn mɑc Cuınn
1 Ɗomnɑıⱡⱡ ꝺo mɑᵱbɑꝺ ⱡe cⱡɑınn Ϻuᵱchɑꝺɑ mıc
Ϻıc Shuıꝥne nɑ ꞇꞇuɑꝥ ın hoc ɑnno. Ʋnɑ ınʒen
Ϻɑoⱡᵱuɑnɑıꝺ mıc Coᵱmɑıc Ϻıc Ɗıɑᵱmɑꝺɑ ꝺéʒ.

<small>1</small> *Donnchadh Cairbrech.* Donough
the Carbrian. So called from having
been fostered amongst the O'Conors of
Carbury, co. Sligo.

<small>2</small> *John of Lurg.* Apparently so
named from having been fostered by

the O'Muldoons of Lurg, in the present county of Fermanagh.

<small>3</small> *Egnechan.* Eıʒꝥ, MS.; cor-
rected from the Annals of Connacht.

<small>4</small> *Lord Leonard.* More correctly
Leonard, Lord Grey.

Donnchadh Cairbrech[1] and John of Lurg,[2] were warring
against O'Domhnaill; and they had the Crannóg of Loch-
Bethach, and were disturbing the country greatly from
it. And O'Domhnaill captured them both; and Egnechan,[3]
the son of O'Domhnaill, was captured in the town of the
Congmhail. And John O'Domhnaill was hanged by him;
and Egnechan[3] and Donnchadh were placed in confinement, under great bondage and hardship; and the crannóg
of Loch-Bethach was destroyed by O'Domhnaill. O'Dochartaigh, i.e. Gerald, the son of Domhnall, son of Felim,
a man of nobleness, hospitality, and graceful figure, died
this year, after spending his natural age up to that time
in *doing acts of* good and humanity. Domhnall, son of
Niall O'Baighill, was made *the* O'Baighill this year.
The Justiciary that was in Erinn, i.e. Lord Leonard,[4]
went to Saxon-land, at the summons of the king of the
Saxons, after destroying the orders, masses, and miraculous relics of all Erinn; after committing numerous evils
which it would be long to relate; and another Justiciary
was sent in his stead, i.e. Handalin Salesder.[5] The king
of Alba sent a summons to the chiefs of the Albanachs
who were here; and they went to him to the harbour
in which he was; and he brought them into the ship
in which he himself was, and took them prisoners, both
Foreigners and Gaeidhel. And he released his Foreigners
in a short time afterwards, and kept the son of Mac
Domhnaill, i.e. James, in confinement; and all he found
serving with him, of his kindred and people, were kept
in confinement in like manner; and all that were sub-
missive to them were afterwards exiled by the king.
John, the son of Conn O'Domhnaill, was slain by the
sons of Murchadh Mac Suibhne-na-ttuath in hoc anno.
Una, daughter of Maelruanaidh, son of Cormac[6] Mac
Diarmada, died. Tadhg, son of Brian, son of Maghnus

---

[5] *Handalin Salesder.* An attempt
at writing Anthony St. Leger.

[6] *Son of Cormac.* The name Το-

maltaιζ (gen. of Tomaltach), originally written in the text, instead of
Coρmαιc, has been expunged.

Caðc mac Ḃrιαιn mιc Maᵹnυrα Mιc Ḋιαrmαðα rυαιð
ðo ḃaċað rα ḃαnnα, ocυr é αr rlυαιᵹheð α ḃroċαιr
ι Rυαιrc. Cαιrm rᵹoιle ðo cαḃαιrc ðo Rυαιðrι
mac Cαιðc Mιc Ḋιαrmαðα ocυr ðα mnαeι rróᵹcα .ι.
ιnᵹen Mιc Uιllιαm, .ι. 8αðð α ḃúrc, ιnᵹen Rιoċαιrð
óιc, ben ðoḃ rerr ðα cιneð réιn nα ðo cιnneð eιle nα
coιmαιmrιr, ocυr nι rαιðι α ḃαrr αιce o Rυαιðrι, αr
ðáιl ιolmαeιneð ιṁ̇α ðéιᵹrιḃ ocυr ðollαmnαιḃ, ocυr
ðαorr cαcα elαðnα αrchenα; ocυr cánυιc ðocυm nα
ᵹαrmα rιn mac Ḋιαrmαðα .ι. Αϲoð mac Cormαιc mιc
Ḋιαrmαðα, ocυr O Ḃιrn .ι. Cαðc mac Cαιrḃrι, ocυr
O Flαnnαcαιn .ι. Emαnn [mac] Uιllιαm, ocυr Mac
Ḋιαrmαðα rυαð .ι. Caċαl [mac] Maᵹnυrα; ocυr clαnn
Ḃrιαιn mιc Maᵹnυrα. 8lιochc Conchoḃαιr mιc Rυαιðrι
bυιðe ðo cεαchc αnð .ι. Ferᵹαl mac Conchoḃαιr, ocυr
clαnn Ḋonnchαðα ðυιð mιc Conchoḃαιr .ι. Rυαιðrι
bυιðe ocυr Mαoιleċlαιnn ðonn ocυr Maᵹnυr cαoċ.
Cαnᵹαðαr αnn clαnn Conchoḃαιr óιc mιc Mυιrcherc-
αιᵹh .ι. Cαðc ocυr Ferċαl ocυr Ḃrιαn. Cαnυιc αnn
clαnn Chaċυιl mιc Αϲoðα, Αϲoð ocυr Ḋιαrmαιð. Cánαιc
clαnn Rυαιðrι ᵹlαιr mιc Ḃrιαιn cαoιc, Ḃrιαn cαoch ocυr
Αrc. Cαnᵹαðαr clαnn Uιllιαm ι Mαoιlenαιċc .ι. ιn
ᵹιollα ðυð ocυr Ḋιαrmαιð, Cαðc ocυr Mυιrᵹιor.
Cαnυιc αnn Comαlcaċ mac Αϲoðα mιc Conchoḃαιr.
Cαnυιc αnn cιᵹernα Αιrcιð, Caċαl mac Cαιðc óιc Mιc
Ḋιαrmαðα ᵹαll, co mαιðιð Αιrcιᵹ lαιrr. Cαnυιc Conn
mac Ḃrιαιn mιc Θoᵹαιn ι Rυαιrc, ocυr Comαlcaċ mac
Cαιðc Mιc Ḋιαrmαðα, ocυr Rυαιðrι nα ðcolán Mac
Ḋιαrmαðα, ocυr clαnð Caċαιl Mιc Ḋιαrmαðα, ocυr
mórán oιle naċ éιðιr ðιnnιrιn, oιr cánᵹαðαr éιxe ocυr
ollαmαn Eιrιonð co υcrαnrroρc eιnιᵹ ocυr enᵹnαmα
cúιceð Connαchc .ι. co cαιrιc Loċα cαomrrocαιᵹ Cé;
ocυr rυαραðαr caċ en ðreṁ αcα coιl α ṁenmαn ocυr α
hαιccencα réιn ðo réιr α υαιrle ocυr α eαlαðαn rα

<hr>

1 *Invitation.* cαιrm, for ᵹαιrm, MS.

2 *Brian Caech;* i.e. Brian the Blind [O'Conor].

3 *Son of Brian.* mac Ḃrιαιn, MS.

4 *Mac Diarmada.* Repeated in MS.

5 *For.* oι for oιr, MS.

A.D.

[1540.]

Mac Diarmada Ruadh, was drowned in the Banna, whilst on a hosting along with O'Ruairc. A school invitation[1] was given by Ruaidhri, son of Tadhg Mac Diarmada, and by his wedded wife, i.e. Mac William's daughter, i.e. Sadhbh Burk, daughter of Rickard Og, the best woman of her own kindred, or of any other family of her time, (and she had not the palm from Ruaidhri), for distributing various gifts to poets and ollamhs, and men of all other arts. And at this invitation Mac Diarmada came, i.e. Aedh, son of Cormac Mac Diarmada; and O'Birn, i.e. Tadhg son of Cairbre; and O'Flannagain, i.e. Edmond [son of] William; and Mac Diarmada Ruadh, i.e. Cathal, [son of] Maghnus; and the sons of Brian, son of Maghnus. The descendants of Conchobhar, son of Ruaidhri Buidhe, came there, viz., Ferghal son of Conchobhar, and the sons of Donnchadh Dubh, son of Conchobhar (viz., Ruaidhri Buidhe, and Maelechlainn Donn, and Maghnus Caech). The sons of Conchobhar Og, son of Muirchertach, viz., Tadhg, and Ferghal, and Brian, came there. Aedh and Diarmaid, the sons of Cathal, son of Aedh, came there. Brian Caech and Art, the sons of Ruaidhri Glas, son of Brian Caech,[2] came. The sons of William O'Maelenaigh came, viz., the Gilla-dubh and Diarmaid, Tadhg and Maurice. Tomáltach, son of Aedh, son of Conchobhar, came there. The lord of Airtech came there, i.e. Cathal, the son of Tadhg Og Mac Diarmada Gall, accompanied by the chiefs of Airtech. There came Conn, the son of Brian,[3] son of Eoghan O'Ruairc, and Tomaltach, the son of Tadhg Mac Diarmada, and Ruaidhri-na-dtolán Mac Diarmada,[4] and the sons of Cathal Mac Diarmada, and many more that cannot be mentioned; for[5] the poets and ollaves of Erinn came to the seat of the hospitality and generosity of the province of Connacht, i.e. to the Rock of the smooth-flowing Loch-Cé. And every one of them obtained the desire of his own mind and nature, according to his dignity and learning, on that illustrious, honourable

bͱéιʟ ͷαͱαιʟ oͷoͱαιξ ͱoιͷ .ι. ͱα ͷoʟʟαιc. Ocuͱ Ͳαbͱαͽ
cαč αθͷ ʟéιξͱιͱ ͱo beαͷͷαchͲ αͱ αͷͲαιͷ ͷα ͽeιͱι
ͽαeͷαchͲͷιͽͽ ͱιͷ α ͽͷbͱαͷͲαͱ ͱoͷͷαιͷͷ. Coͷͽ ͷαc
bͱͷαιͷ ͷιc Eoξαιͷ 1 Ruαιͱc ͽo ͷαͱbαͽ αͱͱιoʟʟ ʟe
cʟoιͷͷ ͷιc ͷαξͷͷͱα Cíͱe CuαͲhαιʟ, αͱ ͱuͱαιʟeͷͽ α
αͲαͱ ͱeιͷ, α ͽCαͷͷαιξ bó čαoιce, eͲ ceͲeͱα.

IcͲͲ. Eͷαιͱ ͱoͱ SαͲαͱͷ; bιͱιχ ͱuιͱͱe; bʟιαͽαιͷ ocuͱ
ͽα .χχͽ. ocuͱ cuιξ ceͽ αͱ ͷιʟe αoιͱ ιͷ Cιξeͱͷα; ocuͱ
ͽoιͷeͷͽ ͽeͱͷαιͱ α ͽͲúͱ ͷα bʟιαͽͷα ͱιͷ eͲιͱ ͱιoc
ocuͱ ͱͷeαchͲα, ͷαͱ ʟeιξ Ͳͱeαbαͽ ͽo ͽeͷαͷ ι ͷEιͱuιͷͷ.
CuαͲαʟ bαʟb ͷαc Seáͷ ͷιc Ruαιͽͱι 1 ξαʟʟcoͽαιͱ,
ͱαoι ͽuιͷe oιͱechͲα, ͽéξ. O Ͽoͷͷαιʟʟ ͽo ͽoʟ α cceͷͽ
ιͷ ξιuιͱͽιͱ coͷͷͱͽξe ιͷ Cαbαͷ, ocuͱ ceαͷξαʟ ocuͱ ͱιͲ ͽo
ͽeͷαͷ ͱe ceιʟι ͽoιb, ͷαιʟʟe ͱe oͷóιͱ ͷóιͱ ocuͱ ͱobe-
ͱeͷͱ ͽͱαξαιʟ ͽUα Ͽoͷͷαιʟʟ, eͲ ceͲeͱα. ͷαιͽͷ ͷóͱ
ͽo ͲαbαιͱͲ ͽo ͷαc Cιbιʟιͷ αͱ cʟoιͷͷ Cαͽα 1 Ͷéιʟʟ,
ͽú αͱ ͷαͱbαͽ Cαͷξuͱ ͷαc Ͽoͷͷchαͽα ͷιc ͷαoʟ-
ͷuιͱe ͷιc Shuιbͷe, ocuͱ ͷoͱáͷ ͽo ξαʟʟcʟαechαιb
Coͷαʟʟαch ͷαιʟʟe ͱͱιͱ; ocuͱ ͽo ͷαͱbαͽ ͷuͱ ιͷ ceͽͷα
cóͱuchαͽ ξαʟʟcʟαech ͽo cʟαιͷͷ Ͽoͷιͷuιʟʟ ξαʟʟcʟαeč,
ocuͱ α ʟáͷ eιʟe αͱ cαč Ͳαob ͷαč αιͱιͷͲeͱ αͷͱͱo; ocuͱ
ͷαc Uιbιʟιͷ ͽo ͽuʟ ͱʟuαξ ͱα ceͷͽ ξαιͱιͽ ͷα ͽιαιͽ
ͱιͷ αͱ cʟoιͷͷ Cαͽα 1 Ͷeιʟʟ, ocuͱ cʟαͷͷ Cαͽα .ι. Coͷͷ
ocuͱ Ͽoͷͷαʟʟ ͽo ͷαͱbαͽ ʟeιͱ. O Ceͱbαιʟʟ .ι. ͱeͱ
cαͷ αιͷͷ ͷαc ͷαoʟͱuαͷαιͽ ͽo ͷαͱbαͽ α bͱιoʟʟ ocuͱ
é ͽαʟʟ, ͱe cʟαͷͷ Ͽoͷͷchαͽα ͷιc Seáͷ 1 Ceͱbαιʟʟ,
ocuͱ ͱe ͷαc 1 ͷαoιʟͷuαιͽ .ι. Séαͷ ͷαc Ͽoͷͷαιʟʟ
čαcιč 1 ͷαoιʟͷuαιͽ; ocuͱ ξe ͽo bι ͱé ͽαʟʟ ͽιͱαͽαιͱc
αͷͷͱιͷ, ͽo ͱιͷͷe coͱͷαͷ ocuͱ cuͷξͷαͷ, ocuͱ ʟáͷ ͷαιͽ
ͽo cuαιͽ α ccʟú ocuͱ α ͷáιͱeͷͽ ͽó, αͱ ʟuchͲ ιͷ ͷαͱbͲα.

---

[1] *Instigation.* ͱuʟαιͱeͷͽ, for ͱuͱαιʟeͷͽ, MS.

[2] *Tamhnagh-bó-chaich.* This name
signifies "the tamhnagh (or 'fine
field') of the blind cow." The scribe,
Donough Mac-an-filedh, here adds the
memorandum ͷα Ͳαbͱαͽ αoͷ ͽα

ʟeιξͱo ͱo ξuͲh ιͷ ʟeιͲιͱ ͱιͷ, oιͱ
ͽo cͱαͱ ιͷ cuͱʟι αξαιͷ ʟe ιͷαͱ-
cαͽ ͷoͽͱαιͷe; i.e. "let no one who
reads this pronounce that letter [i.e.
the last letter in the word čαoιce,
which is redundant], for my pulse
shrank through excess of labour."

festival, i.e. at Christmas. And let every one who reads this give a blessing on the souls of the humane couple we have mentioned above. Conn, the son of Brian, son of Eoghan O'Ruaire, was killed in treachery by the sons of Mac Maghnusa of Tir-Tuathail, at the instigation[1] of his own father, in Tamhnagh-bó-chaich,[2] et cætera.

The kalends of January on Saturday; after a bissextile ;[3] the age of the Lord one thousand, five hundred, and forty-one years. Excessive bad weather in the beginning of this year, both frost and snow, which allowed no cultivation to be done in Erinn. Tuathal Balbh, the son of John, son of Ruaidhri O'Gallchubhair, a most eminent assembly man, died. O'Domhnaill went as far as the Cabhan to meet the Justiciary; and they concluded a compact and peace with each other; and O'Domhnaill received great honour and reverence, et cætera. A great defeat was given by Mac Aibhilin to the sons of Aedh O'Neill, in which Aenghus, son of Donnchadh, son of Maelmuire Mac[4] Suibhne, was killed, and a great number of the Conallian gallowglasses along with him; and a corps of gallowglasses of the Clann-Domhnaill Galloglaech, and a great many more on both sides not enumerated here, were slain in like manner. And Mac Uibhilin went with an army, a short time after that, against the sons of Aedh O'Neill; and the sons of Aedh O'Neill, viz., Conn and Domhnall, were killed by him. O'Cerbhaill, i.e. Fer-gan-ainm,[5] son of Maelruanaidh, was slain in treachery, (he being blind), by the sons of Donnchadh, son of John O'Cerbhaill, and by the son of O'Maelmhuaidh, i.e. John, the son of Domhnall Caech O'Maelmhuaidh; and though he was then blind, sightless, he performed acts of defence, assistance, and vigour against the slayers, which redounded to his fame and reputation.

---

[3] *Bissextile.* biṗix ṗuiṗṗe; lit. "a bissextile upon it," which is a very loose mode of expression.

[4] *Mac.* ṁc; repeated in MS.
[5] *Fer-gan-ainm*; lit., "man without [a] name," or Anonymous.

Dig. tiz - J D

Ⱥn cꞃɑnꝺóc oiꞃꞇeꞃɑċ ɑꞃ ʟoċ Ᵹ̇ꞁinne Ⱥʟʟáin ꝺo ᵹɑbɑıʟ ꝺo
cʟɑɴn ꝺomnɑıʟʟ mıc. ꝺonnchɑıꝺh ı Ꞃʋɑıꞃc ɑꞃ ꝺon-
chɑꝺh mɑc ꝺonnchɑıꝺh ı Ꞃʋɑıꞃc; ocʋꞃ ꝼɑ ceɴꝺ ᵹɑıꞃıꝺ
nɑ ꝺıɑıꞃ̆ ꞃın ꞇʋcɑꝺɑꞃ cʟɑnn ꝺonnchɑıꝺh ı Ꞃʋɑıꞃc .ı.
ꝺomnɑʟʟ ocʋꞃ ꝼeꞃ cɑn ɑınm ınnꞃɑıꝺıꞃ̆ ɑꞃ ın ccꞃɑnnóc,
ocʋꞃ ꝺo ʟoꞃᵹꞃɑꝺ ın bɑıʟe cɑn ꝼıoꞃꞃ. Ocʋꞃ moꞇhɑıᵹꞇeꞃ ıeꝺ
ocʋꞃ ʟenꞇʋꞃ ꝼɑ ʟoċ ıeꝺ, ocʋꞃ beıꞃıꝺ cʟɑnn ꝺomnɑıʟʟ
O Ꞃʋɑıꞃc oꞃꞃɑ. Ɱɑꞃbꞇɑꞃ ꝼeꞃ cɑn ɑınm mɑc ꝺonnchɑıꝺh ; ᵹɑbꞇɑꞃ ɑnꝺ ꝺomnɑʟʟ, ocʋꞃ cꞃoċꞇɑꞃ ıeꞃʋm ʟe
cʟɑnn ꝺomnɑıʟʟ ı Ꞃʋɑıꞃc. Sʟoıᵹeꝺ ʟɑꞃ O ꝺomnɑıʟʟ
.ı. Ɱɑᵹnʋꞃ mɑc Ⱥeꝺɑ ꝺʋıꞃ̆ mıc Ⱥeꝺɑ ꞃʋɑıꝺ̆, ɑᵹcoınne
ın ᵹıʋıꞃꞇıꞃ ɑ ꝺꞇıꞃ Ꞗoᵹɑın, ocʋꞃ ın ꞇíꞃ ꝺo ṁıʟʟeꝺ̆ ʟeo
ꝺon ꞇoıꞃᵹ ꞃın. In ᵹıʋıꞃꞇıꞃ ꝺımꝺechꞇ ɑꞃ ɑ ɑᵹɑıꝺ ꞃɑ
Ɱıꝺ̆e, ocʋꞃ O ꝺomnɑıʟʟ ꝺꞃıʟʟeꝺ ꞇɑꞃ ɑ ɑıꞃ co ꞇíꞃ
Connɑıʟʟ, ocʋꞃ ᵹɑn ꞇɑċɑꞃ nɑ ꞇeᵹmáıʟ ꝺꞃɑᵹɑıʟ ꝺo
ɑ[ᵹ] ᵹɑbáıʟ ꞇꞃe ꞇíꞃ Ꞗoᵹɑın ɑᵹ ꞇeɑchꞇ no ɑᵹ ımꞇeɑchꞇ ın
ʋɑıꞃ ꞃın. O ꝺomnɑıʟʟ ꝺo ꝺʋʟ ꝼɑ ceɴꝺ ᵹɑıꞃıꝺ nɑ
ꝺıɑıꝺ ꞃın ꝺon ꞇɑob ꞃoıꞃ ꝺo ʟoċ ɑ bꞃeꞃʋıꝺ̆ Ɱɑnɑch,
ocʋꞃ Çʋıʟ nɑ noıꞃeꞃ ocʋꞃ ɑn ꞇɑob ꞇoıꞃ ꝺo ʟoċ ꝺó
mıʟʟeꝺ̆ ʟeıꞃ ꝺo ꞇíꞃ ocʋꞃ ꝺo ʟoċ ꝺon ꝺoʟ ꞃın, oıꞃ ꝺo
báꝺɑꞃ bɑıꝺ ocʋꞃ ɑꞃꞇꞃʋıꝺ̆ɑıᵹe ɑc mıʟʟeꝺ̆ ı noıʟén, ocʋꞃ
ın ꞃʟʋɑᵹ̆ ɑc mıʟʟeꝺ̆ ın ꞇíꞃı, cʋꞃ ꝼáᵹɑıꝺ̆ ɑꞃ ꝺıoꞇ̆ ɑꞃbɑ co
móꞃ ın bʟıɑꝺɑın ꞃın ıɑꝺ. Sʟoıᵹeꝺ oıʟı ʟɑꞃ O nꝺomnɑıʟʟ .ı. Ɱɑᵹnʋꞃ ɑ bꞃeꞃʋıꝺ̆ Ɱɑnɑch, ꝺon ꞇɑob ꞇıɑꞃ
ꝺo ʟoċ Ꞗıꞃnı ; .ı. ꝺo ċʋıꞃ ɑ báıꝺ ocʋꞃ ɑ ɑꞃꞇ̆ꞃɑıꝺe ɑꞃ
ɑn ʟoċ, ocʋꞃ ꝺo ccɑꝺ̆ ꝼéın ɑ ꞃʟʋɑıᵹ̆ ꝺo ꞇıꞃ, co ꞃo
mıʟʟꞃeꝺ ɑccoınn ɑ ċéıʟe ꝺo ʟoċ ocʋꞃ ꝺo ꞇíꞃ, no co ꞃɑn-
cɑꝺɑꞃ Innıꞃ Sᵹéıċ̆ʟenꝺ ; ocʋꞃ ꝺo bꞃʋꞃıꝺɑꞃ ocʋꞃ ꝺo ʟeᵹ-
ɑꝺɑꞃ cɑıꞃʟen Innıꞃ Ceıċʟıonn ꝺon ꝺoʟ ꞃın ; ocʋꞃ ꞇɑn-
cɑꝺɑꞃ ꞃʟán ıɑꞃ ccoꞃᵹɑꞃ. ꝺomnɑʟʟ mɑc Ɲeıʟʟ ᵹɑıꞃm

---

1 *Glenn-Allain*. *Rectè* Glenn-Dallain (Dallan's Glen), now generally
called Glencar. It is a valley in the
parish of Killasnet, barony of Ross-
clogher, and co. of Leitrim.

2 *O'Ruairc*. The name is written
ouꞃ̅c̅ in the MS. ; the scribe adding the
characters ℓı(vel ı) over the ou, to

signify that the proper form was ı ꞃ̅c̅
(or ı Ꞃʋɑıꞃc). At the end of the entry
the scribe adds meıꞃı ꝺonꞇ̅.: "I am
Donnchadh." See note 1, p. 306 *supra*.

3 *The.* ın ; repeated in MS.

4 *The lake*; i.e. Loch-Erne.

5 *For.* oı for oıꞃ, MS.

6 *Inis-Sgeithlend—Inis-Ceithlionn.*

The eastern crannóg on the lake of Glenn-Alláin[1] was captured by the sons of Domhnall, son of Donnchadh O'Ruairc, against Donnchadh, son of Donnchadh O'Ruairc. And in a short time afterwards the sons of Donnchadh, viz., Domhnall and Fer-gan-ainm, made an attack on the crannóg, and secretly burned the place. And they are observed, and pursued into the lake; and the sons of Domhnall O'Ruairc[2] overtake them. Fer-gan-ainm, the son of Donnchadh, is slain; and Domhnall is taken prisoner there, and is afterwards hanged by the sons of Domhnall O'Ruairc. A hosting to Tir-Eoghain by O'Domhnaill, i.e. Maghnus, the son of Aedh Dubh, son of Aedh Ruadh, to meet the Justiciary; and the[3] country was ruined by them on this expedition. The Justiciary advanced into Midhe, and O'Domhnaill turned back to Tir-Conaill; and he received neither battle nor encounter this time whilst passing through Tir-Eoghain, in coming or going. O'Domhnaill went in a short time afterwards along the eastern side of the lake,[4] into Feara-Manach; and Cuil-na-noirer, and the eastern side of the lake, were destroyed by him, both country and lake, on this occasion; for[5] he had boats and vessels pillaging the islands, and the army destroying the country; so that he left them greatly in want of corn this year. Another hosting by O'Domhnaill, i.e. Maghnus, into Feara-Manach, along the western side of Loch-Erne; viz., he placed his boats and vessels on the lake, and he conducted his army by land, so that they conjointly destroyed both by lake and land, until they reached Inis-Sgéithlend.[6] And they broke and threw down the castle of Inis-Ceithlionn[6] on that occasion,[7] and returned safely in triumph. Domhnall, the son of Niall Garbh[8] O'Domhnaill, was killed by

---

Different forms of the name of the town at present called Enniskillen. The latter is the correct form.

[7] On that occasion. ᴅᴏ ᴅᴏʟ ꜱɪɴ, for ᴅᴏɴ ᴅᴏʟ ꜱɪɴ; lit. "on that going."

[8] Garbh. The MS. has ᵹᴀɪꜱᴍ for ᵹᴀɪꜱb; the sound of b when aspirated, as it should be here, being like that of aspirated m. The orthography is here very corrupt.

ı Ɗomnaıll ɖo maрбаɖ leıр O mƀaoıᵹıll ın blıaɖaın рı,
aр nɖol ɖo Ɗomnall ɖo conᵹnaɖ le Τoıррɖhelbach mac
ı ƀaoıᵹıll anaᵹhaıɖ ı ƀaoıcıll; ocuр рuaıᵹ ɖo ɫaƀaıрɫ
ɖO ƀaoıᵹıll ɖoıb aр ɫúр, ocuр O ƀaoıᵹıll ɖрılleɖ oррɫa
рan, ocuр рuaıᵹ ɖo ɫaƀaıрɫ ɖoıƀ, ócuр bрıрıoɖ oррɫa;
ocuр ın mac рın Neıll ı Ɗomnaıll ɖo maрбaɖ aр ın
рuaıᵹ рın. Mac ın ƀaıрɖ ɫíрı Conaıll .ı. Conchoбaр
рuaɖ mac Ꝼeрᵹaıl .ı. рaoı ꝼıр ɖána a bꝼocclaım ocuр
a bꝼeрachɫ ɖána, ocuр ꝼeр ɫıᵹe naoıɖıɖ ɖo commaıl
рuaр ɖa cac nɖae aрcena, ɖécc ın blıaɖaın рın. Ꝼanрı
buıɖe mac Ɗachɖı mıc Emaınn .ı. ɫıᵹeрna cloınɖe
Connmuıᵹ, ɖo maрбaɖ ɖo Τoıррɖealbach рuaɖ mac
Τaıɖᵹ buıɖe meıc Cachaıl рuaıɖ.

Ƙɫɫ. Θnaıр ꝼoр ɖómhnach; ɖa ɫlıaɖaın ocuр ɖa .xx.
ocuр cuıᵹ ceɖ ocuр mıle aoıр an Τıᵹeрna. Saɖɓ ınᵹen
Rıcaıрɖ oıᵹ mıc Uılleᵹ рuaıɖ mıc Uılleᵹ an ꝼına .ı.
ben рóрɖa Mhıc Ɗıaрmaɖa .ı. Ruaıɖрı mıc Τaıɖᵹ
mıc Ruaıɖрı óıᵹ mıc Ruaıɖрı coeıch, ocuр maɫhaıр a
claınne, ɖꝼaᵹaıl ɓaıꝼꝼ aр caıррıᵹ na рıᵹ .ı. Loıᵹꝼoрɫ
oınıᵹ ocuр oıррɖeрcuıр claınnı Maolрuanaıɖ; ocuр ıꝼ
ɫeрc ma ɖo ɫaınıc ɖıaрꝼma Uıllıam cuncuр рıam ben
a haoꝼꝼa ɖob ꝼeрр ınáрꝼ ɖꝼeıle ocuр ɖıonnрucuр, ɖo
connla ocuр ɖo cрaıɖɓɖıᵹe, ɖo ɖeıрc ocuр ɖo ɖeрlucaɖ.
Ɗaрɖaoın manɖáıl рuр ɖeᵹuıl a hanum ocuр a coрр рe
рoıle ıaр mƀúaıɖ onᵹɫa ocuр aıɫрıᵹe. Slóıᵹeɖ ɖo
ɖenum ɖo mac Uıllıam Chlaınne Rıcaıрɖ ꝼa macaıрe
Chonnachɫ, ocuр рo ɫaıррınᵹeɫ clann Τaıɖᵹ Mıc

---

¹ *O'Baighill.* O'Boyle; incorrectly
written ı ƀaoıcıɖ in the MS.

² *Year.* Here the scribe adds
meıрı Ɗonnchaɖ mac ın ꝼıleaɖ
ɖo ꝼᵹрıɓ ɖo ƀрıan mac Ɗıaрmaɖa рın; "I am Donnchadh Mac-
in-fhiledh, who wrote that for Brian
Mac Diarmada." The note is not in
the Ann. of Connacht.

³ *Cathal Ruadh;* i.e. Cathal the

Red; one of the sept of O'Conchobhair
Ruadh, or O'Conor Roe. This entry
ends at the top margin of fol. 91a.
The remainder of the page is occupied
by an entry relating to the year 1595,
in a contemporary handwriting, two
entries of events belonging to the year
1636, and one to 1648, the latter
written in 1652 by Maelruanaidh, son
of Aedh MacDermot. These entries are

O'Baighill this year, Domhnall having gone to assist A.D.
Toirdhelbhach, son of O'Baighill, against O'Baighill:[1] (they [1541.]
had first given an onset to O'Baighill; and O'Baighill
turned upon them and gave them an onset, and routed
them; and this son of Niall O'Domhnaill was slain in that
onset). Mac-in-Bhaird of Tir-Conaill, i.e. Conchobhar
Ruadh, the son of Ferghal, an eminent poet in learning
and poetry, and a man who maintained a house of
hospitality for all persons, died this year.[2] Henry Buidhe
Mac David, the son of Edmond, i.e. the lord of Clann-
Conmhaigh, was killed by Toirdhelbach Ruadh, the son
of Tadhg Buidhe, son of Cathal Ruadh.[3]

The kalends of January on Sunday; the age of the Lord [1542.]
one thousand, five hundred, and forty-two years. Sadhbh,
daughter of Rickard Og, son of Ulick Ruadh, son of
Ulick-an-fhina, i.e. the wedded wife of Mac Diarmada,
i.e. of Ruaidhri, the son of Tadhg, son of Ruaidhri Og,
son of Ruaidhri Caech, and his children's mother, died
on Carraig-na-righ, i.e. the abode of the hospitality and
dignity of the Clann-Maelruanaidh; and it is doubtful if
there ever came of the posterity of William the Conqueror,[4] a woman of her age better than she in hospitality
and worth, in prudence and piety, in charity and liberality.
On Maunday Thursday her soul and body separated from
each other, after the triumph of unction and penitence.[5]
A hosting was made by Mac William of Clann-Rickard
through[6] Machaire-Connacht; and the sons of Tadhg

---

printed at the end of the volume. In
the lower margin of the folio the name
of Ɖαϭɾὸҽ O Ɖυɩϭꬶҽɴɴɑɩɴ (David
O'Duigennain) appears in a reversed
form. The rest of the MS. is in the
handwriting of the scribe who copied
the portion containing the events from
1170 to 1257.

[4] *William the Conqueror;* i.e.
William Fitz Aldelm de Burgh.

[5] *Penitence.* Brian Mac Dermot
has added the marginal note "α
mbαɩʟҽ Ɑ̇ɫɑ ɴɑ ɾɩꬶ ꝺo cuɩɾҽαꝺh
í;" i.e. in the town of Ath-na-righ
[Athenry, county of Galway] she was
buried."

[6] *Through.* ꝓ., for ꝼα or ꝼo, against,
or about. This entry is not in the
Annals of Connacht.

 Diαrmαdα αtimcell Bhél átα uαchtαir e ; ocuy yo
bviyyedh αn bαile Leó don dol yin, ocuy yo mαrbαd
αnn cenn giomαnαch Mic Uilliαm, ocuy α gαlloglαeich
cúlcoimetα. Teid Mαc Uilliαm tαy yliαB yioy
don dol yin, ocuy tuc bráigde iochtαiy Chonnαcht
Lαiy don čuyyin .i. brαige Tαidg óig mic Tαidg mic
Αodα, ocuy bráigde Tαidg mic Cαthαil óig, ocuy
iochtαiy Chonnαcht; ocuy teydα Mαolmuiye mαc
Collα Mic Shuidne iyin mbrαigdenuy yin α gclαinn
Ricαiyd. O Cončobαy yuαd .i. Toiyydhelbαch· yuαd
mαc Tαidg Buidi do gαbáil Le Ruαidyi mαc Tαidg
Mic Diαrmαdα in hoc αnno. Comyoybα teymuinn
Mhég Crαid .i. Toiyydhelbαch mαc Αindyiαyyα Mhég
Crαid moytuuy eyt. Mαc Conmide .i. Byiαn doyču
mαc Solαim .i. yαoi ye dán ocuy ye yoglαim, ocuy yey
toictech tyoméonαig tige αoidhed coitčinn do čαč,
dhec do gαluy obαnn αidgeyy um féil Colυιm Chille
do yunnyαd. Coymαc mαc Diαrmαdα hi Chleiyig,
.i. αn brαthαiy minúy dob yoiyye egnαide nα αimyiy,
dhéc iyin féil Colυιm Cille cednα. Sloiged moy Leiy
O n'Domnαill .i. Mαgnuy mαc Αodα duid α niochtαy
Chonnαcht, gondeynα cyeču moyα αy Mαc n'Donn-
chαdα αn Choyuinn. Reitech dO Dhomnαill ocuy
diochtαy Connαcht ye yoile, ocuy yilled dUα Dhoṁnαill iαy mbuαid gcoyyαiy, ocuy íαy níoc α čioyyα yiy.
Slóiged ele Leiy O n'Domnαill ocuy Leiyin gCαlbαch
O n'Domnαill, ocuy Le hUα Ruαiyc .i. Byiαn mαc
Eogαin 1 Ruαiyc; ocuy dul doid yin uile αy Mαc
Uidilin. Dá čuid no tyi do denum dont yluαig ye
hucht nα bαnnα. Mαc Uidilín iliomαd dαoined don
tαod αyαill don Bhαnnα; gidedh čenα teid O Domn-
nαill ocuy O Ruαiyc tαy αn αduinn diα nαimbeoin.

<hr>

1 *The mountain*; i.e. Sliabh-Seghsa,
or the Corraliabh, between the counties
of Roscommon and Sligo.

2 *Aedh.* Hugh [O'Conor Sligo].

3 *In that captivity.* The Four
Masters, in their account of this ex-

pedition, state that Maelmuire Mac
Suibhne was one of the hostages
taken by Mac William.

4 *Mortuus est.* moytuy eytt, MS.

5 *The Festival of Colum Cille;* i.e.
the 9th of June.

Mac Diarmada brought him to invest Bel-átha-uachtair ; and the town was demolished by them on this occasion, and Mac William's chief hunter, and his rear guard of gallowglasses, were slain there.   Mac William goes down beyond the mountain[1] on that occasion ; and he brought the hostages of Lower Connacht with him on that journey, viz., the hostages of Tadhg Og, son of Tadhg, son of Aedh,[2] and the hostages of Tadhg, son of Cathal Og, and of Lower Connacht : and Maelmuire, the son of Colla Mac Suibhne, died whilst detained in that captivity[3] in Clann-Rickard.   O'Conchobhair Ruadh, i.e. Toirdhelbach Ruadh, the son of Tadhg Buidhe, was taken prisoner by Ruaidhri, son of Tadhg Mac Diarmada, in hoc anno. The comarb of Termon-MagCraith, i.e. Toirdhelbhach, the son of Andrias MagCraith, mortuus est.[4]   Mac Conmidhe, i.e. Brian Dorcha, son of Solomon, an eminent professor of poetry and literature, and a rich, opulent man, who kept a general house of hospitality for all, died of a sudden, brief illness, on the festival of Colum Cille[5] exactly. Cormac, the son of Diarmaid O'Clerigh, i.e. the most perfect,[6] learned, friar minor in his time, died on the same festival of Colum Cille.   A great hosting by O'Domhnaill, i.e. Maghnus, the son of Aedh Dubh, into Lower Connacht, when he committed great depredations upon Mac Donnchadha of the Corann.   O'Domhnaill and *the people* of Lower Connacht arranged with one another; and O'Domhnaill returned after gaining triumph, and after the payment to him of his rent.   Another hosting by O'Domhnaill, and by the Calbhach O'Domhnaill, and by O'Ruairc, i.e. Brian, the son of Eoghan O'Ruairc ; and all these went against Mac Uibhilín.   The army was divided into two or three parts in front of the Banna.   Mac Uibhilín, with a great number of men, was on the other side of the Banna; but nevertheless, O'Domhnaill and O'Ruairc go across the river in spite

---

* *Perfect.* ꝼoꞁꞃꞃe, for ꝼoꞁꞀbꞇꞁe, MS.

Αcht chena ϼo bαιϼheϼ Ϲαƀᵹ mac Ϭϼíαιn mιc Mhαᵹnuϼα Mιc'Ϭιαϼmαϼα ϼιιαιƀ, .ι. ϝeϼ α ϼeϼϼα ϼob αϼϼαchϼα ϼιϼϼϼeϼϲα α mαιƀ ocuϼ α lαιḣ ϼια čιnel ϝeιϼϼιn, ocuϼ ϼo ṁoϼán elι. Μí heιϼιϼ α ϼιιoιḣ no α áιϼeṁh α bϝuαιϼ Ϭ'Ϭomnαιll co nα ϼlúαιᵹ ϼαιϼᵹnιƀ ocuϼ ϼéϼαlαιb αϼ ϝeƀ αn ϼιϼe co huιlιƀι, ιαϼ mιlleϼ ṁoϼαιn nαch eιϼιϼ ϼαιϼeιḣ. Ϲαnιc Mαc Uιƀιlιn α ᵹcenn 1 'Ϭhomnαιll, ocuϼ ϼuc α ƀϼeƀ ϝéιn ϼechαιb ocuϼ ϼéϼeƀ ocuϼ ·ϼo Ƀuαιƀ ƀo, ocuϼ ϼo níαϼ ϼíƀ αϼϼ α hαιϲle, ocuϼ ϲιc Ϭ 'Ϭomnαιll ιαϼ mbúαιϼ ᵹcoϼϲαιϼ ϼon čuϼ ϼιn. Mαc Uιƀιlín .ι. Ꝛuᵹϼαιϼhe mαc Uαlϲαιϼ ϼo ƀul αϼ ϼιubαl cϼeιče αϼ Uα ᵹcαϲαιn. Cϼeƀ ṁóϼ ϼo ᵹlαcαϼ ƀó. Ϭ Cαϲán .ι. Μαᵹnuϼ mιαc 'Ϭonnchαϼα ϼo ƀϼeƀ oϼϼα α ϲoϼαιᵹechϲ, ocuϼ buαnnαƀα móϼα člαιnne Suιƀne mαιlle ϼιϼ. Ϭϼιϼϼeϼ ƀoιƀ αϼ Mαc Uιƀιlín ocuϼ αϼ Αlbαnchuιƀ bαϼαϼ mαιlle ϼιϼ, ιonnuϼ ᵹuϼ ϝáᵹbαϼ áϼ móϼ ϼαoιneƀ ϼιƀ ϝα mαc Αluϼϼαιnn Mιc 'Ϭomnαιll, ocuϼ ϝα mαc Mιc ϲSheαιn, ocuϼ ϝα ṁoϼán elι nαch αιϼιṁϲeϼ ϼo bαιϲheϼ ocuϼ ϼo mαϼbαϼ ϼιƀ. Μαolmuιϼe mαc Ϭoᵹαιn Mιc Shuιƀne ϼo ṁαϼbαϼ le clαιnn Μoelmuιϼι mιc Collα, ocuϼ . e αᵹ ιoƀlucαϼ člαιnnι 1 'Ϭhuƀϼα; ocuϼ ϝα cenn ϼαιƀι nα ƀιαιƀ ϼιn ιαϼ ϝeιn ϼιonnoϼbαϼ ocuϼ α mbαιlϲe ϼo Ƀϼιϼϼeƀ; ocuϼ ϝeϼ ϼιƀ ϝϼéιn ϼo mαϼbαϼ, ocuϼ moϼαn ϼα luchϲ lenṁunα. Ϝélιm ϼuƀ mαc Αoϼα hι Νeιll ϼo ṁαϼbαϼ ιn hoc αnno. Ϝeϼᵹαl mαc Ϸιlιϼ hι 'Ϭhuιƀᵹennαιn .ι. ϼoι Ϭϼenn ϼe ϼenčuϼ ϼhec. 'Ϭáιƀιƀ mαc Αƀϲαιϼɴ hι 'Ϭhuιƀᵹennáιn ϼhéc ιn hoc αnno. 1nᵹen mιc 'Ϭαƀι .ι. ben Ϲαιƀᵹ Μeιc 'Ϭιαϼmuϼα ϼhec; ocuϼ uαιϼhe ϼeϼϲα ϼlιochϲ ιnᵹeιne mιc 'Ϭαƀι, ocuϼ Sιuƀαn α hαιnm.

---

[1] *Returned.* ϲιc=ϼo-ιc, lit., comes.
[2] *Bonaghts.* Bodies of mercenaries.
[3] *Conveying.* αᵹ ιoƀlucαƀ. This entry is not very explicit. It does not appear whither the sons of O'Dubhda (or O'Dowd) were going.

[4] *They;* i.e. the sons of Maelmuire, son of Colla Mac Suibhne.
[5] *Hoc.* oc, MS.
[6] *Slicht-inghine-Mic-David;* lit."the posterity of Mac David's daughter." The word ϼlιochϲ is inaccurately

of them. Tadhg, the son of Brian, son of Maghnus Mac Diarmada Ruadh, i.e. the most famous, eminent man of his age, of his own tribe, and of many more, in goodness and in prowess, was drowned there. It is not possible to calculate or enumerate all the preys and spoils that O'Domhnaill and his army obtained throughout the entire country, after destroying much that cannot be reckoned. Mac Uibhilín came to meet O'Domhnaill, and gave him his own award of horses, and armour, and cows; and they forthwith concluded peace; and O'Domhnaill returned,[1] after gaining triumph on that occasion. Mac Uibhilín, i.e. Rughraidhe, the son of Walter, went on a predatory expedition against O'Catháin. He took a great prey. O'Catháin, i.e. Maghnus, the son of Donnchadh, along with whom were great bonaghts[2] of the Clann-Suibhne, overtook them in pursuit. They-defeated Mac Uibhilín and the Albanachs who were with him, so that a great many men of them were lost, including the son of Alexander Mac Domhnaill, and the son of Mac Shane, and many more of them that were drowned and killed, who are not enumerated. Maelmuire, the son of Eoghan Mac Suibhne, was killed by the sons of Maelmuire, the son of Colla, whilst he was conveying[3] the sons of O'Dubhda; and before the end of a quarter after that they[4] were themselves expelled, and their towns demolished; and one of themselves was killed, and several of their followers. Felim Dubh, the son of Aedh O'Neill, was killed in hoc[5] anno. Ferghal, son of Philip O'Duibhgennain, i.e. the sage of Erinn in history, died. David, son of Athairne O'Duibhgennain, died in hoc[5] anno. Mac David's daughter, i.e. the wife of Tadhg Mac Diarmada, died; (and from her the Slicht-inghine-Mic-David[6] were so called, and her name was Sibhán).[7]

A.D. [1542.]

---

written ꝛlıoꝛꞇ in the MS. This entry is added in the handwriting of Brian Mac Dermot, and is not con- | tained in the Annals of Connacht.
[7] *Sibhán*; pronounced *Shivawn*; Anglicé, Johanna.

ͳͽͳͳ. Ɛͷαιͱ ͱοͱ ͷuαͷ; ͳͱι bͷιαͻͷα οͨuͱ ͻá ͱͳͽͳͳ
οͨuͱ ͨuιͷ ͨͷͻ οͨuͱ mιͷͷ αοιͱ αͷ ͳιͷͽͷͷα. Ͳοmαιͱͷͷ
ͷα hƐͱͷͷͷ ͷͻιͱ ιαͱͷα οͨuͱ ͻαͱͷͷ, οͨuͱ uͱͷοͱ ͽαοιͻͷͷ
Ͳοͷͷαͨͳͳ [οͨuͱ] α ͷͽαιͷͷ αͱ αͷ ͽͨοmαιͱͷͷ ͱͷͷ .ι. αͷ ͻá
Ͷαͨ Ͷιͷͷιαm, οͨuͱ ͷα ͳͱι Ͷα Ͳοͷͨhοbαιͱ, οͨuͱ Ͷαͨ
Ͻιαͱͷαͻα .ι. Ͷuαιͻͱι mαͨ Ͳαιͻͽ Ͷιͨ Ͻιαͱͷαͻα.
ͷͷͳͽαιͷͷ Ͳhͷuαͷα ͱͷͷmαοιͷ, οͨuͱ ͷͷͳͽαιͷͷ Ͳhιͷͷͷ ͷα
mαͷαͨh ͻο ͽͷοͽαͨhαͻ ͻο Ͷuαιͻͱι Ͷαͨ Ͻιαͱͷαͻα αͱ
αͷ ͽͨοmαιͱͷͷ ͱͷͷ óͷ αιͱͻͷͱͱͽοb, οͨuͱ ó ͷα hͷͱͱͽο-
bαιͽ ͷͷι ͱο ͽαͻαͱ αͷͷ, οͨuͱ óͷ ͷͽιuιͱͻιͱͱ; οͨuͱ ͳuͨ
Ͷuαιͻͱι α ͷͷͳͽαιͷͷ ͱͷιͷ ͻοͷ ͷαιͷιͱͻιͱ ͻο ͱιͽιͱ αͱ
ͽͱαͽ ͻο Ͻhíα. Ͷαͨ Ͷιͨ Shuιͽͷͷ ͷͷáͷαͻ .ι. Ͷοͷͷ-
muιͱͷͷ mαͨ Ͻοmͷαιͷͷ óιͽ ͻο mαͱbαͻ ͷͷ ͨͷαιͷͷ Ͷιͨ
Shuιͽͷͷ ͷͷáͷαͻ, .ι. ͷͷ ͨͷαιͷͷ Ͳοιͱͱͻhͷͷbαιͽh mιͨ
Ͷuαιͻͱι mιͨ Ͷαοͷmuιͱι. Ͷαͨ Ͷιͨ Suιͽͷͷ ͳιͱͷͷ
bóͽαιͷͷ, .ι. Ɛοιͷ mαͨ Ͷͷιͷͷ, ͻͱαͽαιͷ ͽαιͱ α ͳúͱ α
αοιͱͱͷ οͨuͱ α ιͷͷͷͷ αͷ bͷιαͻαιͷ ͱͷ. Ͷαͨ ι ͷͷhαοιͽιͷͷ,
.ι. ͷͱιαͷ mαͨ Ͷͷιͷͷ mιͨ Ͳhοιͱͱͻͷͷbαιͽ, ͻο mαͱbαͻ α
bͱιοͷͷ ͷͷ ͨͷαιͷͷ Ͷͷιͷͷ οιͽ hι ͷͷhαοιͽιͷͷ, οͨuͱ ιαͻ
αͱ α ͷuιͷͷͷͳͷuͱ οͨuͱ αͱ α ͨuαͱuͱͻαιͷ ͱͷιͷ αιͽͷͷ.
Ɛαͱͱuͨ Ͷαͳα bοͽ .ι. Ɛmοͷͷ mαͨ ͷͱιαιͷ mιͨ ιͷ ͷͱͱuιͨ
ι Ͻhαͷͷͨubαιͱ ͻο óͽ αͱ bͱαͽαιͷ ͨοιͷͷͳιͷͷͷ mοιͱͷͷ α
ͳιmͨͷͷͷ α ͳιͽͷͱͷuιͱ. Ο Ͻοmͷαιͷͷ .ι. Ͷαͽͷuͱ ͻο ͽuͷ
ͻοͨum ͷα ͨοmαιͱͷͷ mοιͱͷͷ, οͨuͱ α bͱαιͳͱι ͻο ͽí α ͷαιm
αιͽͷͷ ͱͷ ͱαͻα ͱοιmͷͷ ͱͷͷ ͻο ͽͱͷιͽ ͷαιͱ ͻó, οͨuͱ α ͷͷιͽιοͷ
ͻο ͨοmαιͱͷͷ αͷ ͽιuιͱͻιͱ οͨuͱ Ͻhαͷͷ, οͨuͱ α ͳͷͷhͳ ͱο
ͱιͽ οͨuͱ ͱó ͱͷιͳͷͷh. Ͳοͷͷ Ο Ͻοmͷαιͷͷ ͻο ͽí α bͱαͻ
α ͷͽαͷͷοιb ͱοιmͷͷ ͱͷͷ ͻο ͱͷͻuͽαͻ ͱͷ hͶα ͷͻοmͷαιͷͷ
muͱ αͷ ͨͷοͷͷα; οͨuͱ Ͳοͷͷ ͻο ͽuͷ α Sαͽͱαͷαιͽ α ͨͷͷͷ
αͷ ͱιͽ ιαͱ ͱͷͷ, οͨuͱ Ο Ͻοmͷαιͷͷ ͻο ͱιͷͷͷͻ ͱͷáͷ αͱ
ͷͻͷͷum ͱοͨͱαιͻͷͷhͳα mοιͱͷͷ ͨαιͳmͷͷ ͻοͷͷ ͨhuͱ ͱͷͷ.
Ͷuιͱͽͷͱͱ mαͨ ͷαιͻíͷ hι Ͷαοͷͨοͷαιͱͷͷ .ι. ͱóι Ɛͱͷͷͷͷ

---

1 *His lordship*; i.e. the bishopric
of Raphoe. O'Gallchubhair's name
is not in the list of Bishops of Raphoe
published by Ware and Harris.

2 *Kinsmen*. The Four Masters

call them Egnechan and Donough
[O'Domhnaill].

3 *O'Maelconaire*. O'Mulconry. The
Maurice O'Mulconry whose obit is
here recorded made a copy of the old

The kalends of January on Monday ; the age of the
Lord one thousand, five hundred, and forty-three
years. The council of Erinn *met*, both earls and barons;
and the majority of the Gaeidhel [and] Foreigners of
Connacht were at this council, viz., the two Mac Williams,
and the three O'Conchobhairs, and Mac Diarmada, i.e.
Ruaidhri, the son of Tadhg Mac Diarmada. The half-
bally of Cluain-senmail, and the half-bally of Cill-na-
manach, were purchased by Ruaidhri Mac Diarmada, at
this council, from the archbishop and the other bishops
who were there, and from the Justiciary ; and Ruaidhri
gave its own half-bally again to the monastery, for love of
God. The son of Mac Suibhne Fánad, i.e. Maelmuire, the
son of Domhnall Og, was killed by the sons of *the previous*
Mac Suibhne Fánad, viz., the sons of Toirdhelbhach, son
of Ruaidhri, son of Maelmuire. The son of Mac Suibhne
of Tir-Bóghaine, i.e. John, the son of Niall, died in the
beginning of his age and estate, this year. The son of
O'Baighill, i.e. Brian, son of Niall, son of Toirdhelbhach,
was killed in treachery by the sons of Niall Og O'Baighill,
who were in his own friendship and pay. The Bishop of
Rath-both, i.e. Edmond, son of Brian, son of the Bishop
O'Gallchubhair, died after receiving great opposition
regarding his lordship.[1] O'Domhnaill, i.e. Maghnus, went
to the great council, and took with him his kinsmen[2]
whom he had in confinement for a long time previously ;
and he released them by the advice of the Justiciary and
the Foreigners ; and they returned in peace and amity.
Conn O'Domhnaill, who had been for a long time previously
in England, made peace with O'Domhnaill in like manner;
and Conn went afterwards to England, to meet the king;
and O'Domhnaill returned safely, after exercising great
hospitality on that occasion. Maurice, the son of Paidín
O'Maelconaire,[3] i.e. the sage of Erinn in history and

Book of Fenagh, in 1516, for Tadhg
O'Rody, comarb of Fenagh. A transcript of this curious MS., made by the

late Dr. O'Donovan from O'Mulconry's copy, is in the Library of the
Royal Irish Academy.

ɼe ɼenčuɼ ocuɼ ꝺɼɩɩᵹecht, ocuɼ ɼeɼ ᵹo ꝺcoɩce ocuɼ ᵹo
ꝺcɼom conách, ꝺhéc an blíaꝺaɩnɼɩ. Ꝛí Ꝏlban ꝺo ꝺol
ꝺhéc an blɩaꝺaɩn ɼɩ a cúɼ a oeɩɼɼɩ ocuɼ a ɩnṁe, aɼ
mbɼɩɼɼeꝺ ṁaꝺma moɩɼ aɼ Sacɼanachaɩꝩ ɼeɩṁe ɼɩn,
ocuɼ ᵹan oɩᵹ́ɼɩ ꝺ́áᵹbáɩl ɩna ꝺɩaɩꝺ achcmaꝺ aon lenam
ɩnᵹ́ɩne a ᵹcɩnn a hocht ɼeachcṁuɩne; ocuɼ ɼɩ Sacɼan
aɼ nᵹabaɩl neɩɼc aɼ Ꝏlbaɩn a haɩčle baɩɼɼ ɼɩᵹ Ꝏlban
ɼeɩn. Ɱac 1 Ꝺhočaɼcaɩᵹ́, .ɩ. Cačáɼ mac Ᵹeɼaɩlc mɩc
Ꝺomnaɩll mɩc Ƒelɩm, ꝺo ṁaɼbaꝺ le claɩnn 1 Ꝺhočaɼc-
αɩᵹ́ .ɩ. Ꝛuᵹɼaɩꝺɩ ocuɼ Sean, clann Ƒelɩm mɩc Conchobaɼɼ
čaɼɼaɩᵹ́; ocuɼ mac Ꝏoꝺa ᵹɼuamma h1 Ꝺočaɼcaɩᵹ́ ꝺo
maɼbaꝺ leɩɼɩn claɩnn ceꝺna ɼɩn 1 Ꝺhočaɼcaɩᵹ́. O Ꝺomn-
naɩll ꝺo ꝺul ɼlúaᵹ moɼ a nɩnɩɼ Eoᵹaɩn ꝺo ꝺɩᵹ́uɩl na
maɼꝩcha ɼɩn, ocuɼ mɩlleꝺ móɼ ꝺo ᵹenum ꝺo; ocuɼ
bɼaɩᵹ́ꝺe an čɩɼe ꝺ́aᵹaɩl ɩna ꝺɩaɩꝺ ɼɩn ꝺó. Slɩchc
Eoᵹaɩn Ɱɩc Suɩꝩne ocuɼ ɼlɩchc Coɼmaɩc Ɱɩc Ꝺonnchaꝺa ꝺo ꝺul aɼ ɼɩubal cɼeɩče aɼ O neᵹ́ɼa mbuɩꝺe.
O Conchobaɼɼ .ɩ. mac Ꞇaɩꝩᵹ́ mɩc Ꝏoꝺa ocuɼ O heᵹ́ɼa
ꝺo bɼeɩč oɼɼa, ocuɼ maɩče na claɩnnɩ Suɩꝩne ɼɩn ꝺo
ᵹabaɩl .ɩ. Ꝛuaɩꝺɼɩ mac Ꝺuꝩᵹaɩll, ocuɼ clann Ɱaol-
muɩɼe mɩc Eoᵹaɩn; ocuɼ maɼbcaɼ ann cuɩꝺ ꝺo ɼlɩchc
Coɼmaɩc ocuɼ ꝺo ṁuɩnncɩɼ claɩnnɩ Suɩꝩne. O Ɱaoɩl-
eačlaɩnn .ɩ. Ƒélɩm óᵹ ꝺo maɼbaꝺ le Ɱáᵹ Eočaᵹáɩn.
Ɱac Suɩꝩne na Ꞇúach ocuɼ a mac .ɩ. Ꝺɼɩan ꝺo ᵹabáɩl
le coꝩlač o ɩaɼcaɼ Connachc aɼ ɩnɼɼɩ mɩc Ꝺuɩɼn, ocuɼ
a mbɼeč leo allaɩṁ. Coᵹaꝺ moɼ ecɩɼ ṁáᵹ Uɩꝺɩɼ ocuɼ
ɼlɩchc Ꞇoɩɼɼꝺhelbaɩᵹ́ ṁéᵹ Uɩꝺɩɼ, ocuɼ ɼlɩchc Ꞇoɩɼɼ-
ꝺhelbaɩᵹ́ ꝺo ꝺul a cɩɼ Chonaɩll, ocuɼ mɩlleꝺ moɼ ꝺo
ᵹenuṁ aɼ ṁáᵹ Uɩꝺɩɼ a huchc h1 Ꝺhomnaɩll ꝺóɩꝩ.
Ɱáᵹ Uɩꝺɩɼ ꝺo ꝺul a ᵹcenꝺ 1 Ꝺomnaɩll aᵹcɩnn achaɩꝺ
ɩaɼ ɼɩn, ocuɼ ɼɩꝩ ꝺo ꝺenum ꝺó ɼɩɼ O nꝺomnaɩll; ocuɼ
Ɱáᵹ Uɩꝺɩɼ ꝺá čabaɩɼc ɼeɩn ocuɼ a čɩɼe ꝺO Ꝺhomnaɩll,
ocuɼ O Ꝺomnaɩll ꝺo čabaɩɼc Ꞇuač ɼáča ocuɼ ɩuɩɼᵹ ꝺo

---

¹ *Aedh Gruama*; i.e. Aedh (Hugh) the Surly.

² *Inis-mic-Duirn*; i.e. "the island of Dorn's son." The Four M. call it *Inis-mic-an-duirn*. It is now known as Rutland Island, and belongs to the parish of Templecrone, barony of Boylagh, co. Donegal.

A.D.
[1543.]

poetry, and a man of wealth and great prosperity, died this year. The king of Alba died this year, in the beginning of his age and estate, after having previously inflicted a great defeat on Saxons; and he left no heir behind him, except one infant daughter, in her eighth week; and the king of the Saxons assumed power over Alba after the death of the king of Alba himself. The son of O'Dochartaigh, i.e. Cathair, the son of Gerald, son of Domhnall, son of Felim, was slain by the sons of O'Dochartaigh, viz., Rudhraidhe and John, the sons of Felim, son of Conchobhar Carragh; and the son of Aedh Gruama[1] O'Dochartaigh was killed by the same sons of O'Dochartaigh. O'Domhnaill went with a large army to Inis-Eoghain, to avenge these homicides, and committed great destruction; and he afterwards obtained the hostages of the country. The descendants of Eoghan Mac Suibhne, and the descendants of Cormac Mac Dounchadha, went on a predatory march against O'hEghra Buidhe. O'Conchobhair (i.e. the son of Tadhg, son of Aedh) and O'hEghra overtook them, and the chiefs of those Clann-Suibhne were captured, viz., Ruaidhri, son of Dubhgall, and the sons of Maelmuire, son of Eoghan; and some of the descendants of Cormac, and of the Clann-Suibhne's people, were killed there. O'Maelechlainn, i.e. Felim Og, was killed by Mag Eochagáin. Mac Suibhne-na-Túath and his son, i.e. Brian, were taken prisoners by a fleet from the West of Connacht, on Inis-mic-Duirn,[2] and carried off in captivity. A great war between Mag Uidhir and the descendants of Toirdhelbhach Mag Uidhir; and the descendants of Toirdhelbhach went to Tir-Conaill, and committed great injuries on Mag Uidhir, in the interest of O'Domhnaill. Mag Uidhir went to meet O'Domhnaill some time after that, and made peace with O'Domhnaill; and Mag Uidhir delivered himself and his country to O'Domhnaill; and O'Domhnaill gave Tuath-rátha and Lurg, which were in his possession for

Mhág Uιδιρ, ocυγ ιαδ αιξе γе γαδα γειɱ γιn. Mac
Uιllιαm clαιnnι Rιcαιρδ, .ι. Uιlleξ na ξcenn mac
Rιcαιρδ, δγαξαιl bαιγγ án blιαδαιn γι, .ι. τιξεγna ξο
nδιomuγ ocυγ ξο nuαþαιγ, γο τγαοč ocυγ γο čοιγbιγ
moγan δο Ξhαοιδeαlαιδ γο ɱamuγ γειγγιn; ocυγ coξαδ
móγ aγ neιγξe a ξclαιnn Rιcαιρδ δία éιγ, .ι. Mac
Uιllιαm δο ξαιγm δο Uιlleξ mac Rιcαιρδ oιξ, ocυγ α
lαn δο čιγ ocυγ δο čοιcγιč na aξhαιδ le mac Mιc
Uιllιαm .ι. Tomáγ mac Uιlleξ na ξcenn. Ocυγ α τúγ na
blιαδna γιn δο čuαδαγ uγɱóγ uαιγlιδ Eγenn a Sαξγuιn
a ξcenδ čιnξ hαnδγαι; .ι. τéιδ O Neιll .ι. Conn mác
Cuιnn 1 Neιll, ocυγ mac Uιllιαm Chlαιnnι Rιcαιρδ .ι.
Uιlleξ na ξcenn, ocυγ Muγchαδ mac Tοιγγδhelbαιξ
1 bhγίαιn .ι. O bγίαιn, ocυγ na τγι hιαγlαδα .ι. ιαγlα
Deγmuman ocυγ ιαγlα Uγmuman ocυγ ιαγlα Cιlle
δαγα, ocυγ Donnchαδ mac Cončobαιγ 1 bγίαιn. ιαδγιn
uιle δγαξαιl onoγa moιγe on γί, ocυγ ιαγlα δο δenum
δO Neιll ocυγ δO bγίαιn ocυγ δUιlleξ na ξcenδ; ocυγ
cóιceδ na Ξαιllɱe δο δuαιn δUιlleξ na ξcenδ aγ an
ξcomαιγle γιn, ocυγ é γéιn δγαξαιl δáιγ a nδeγeδ na
blιαδna γιn. Maξnuγ mac Muιγcheγταιξ Mιc Dιαγ-
mαδa γuαιδ δhéc ιn hoc anno.

ǀctt. Enáιγ γoγ Mαιγτ; ceιτγι blιαδna ocυγ δα
γιchet ocυγ cuιξ ceδ ocυγ mιle αοιγ an Tιξεγna. ιαγlα
Deγmuman .ι. Semmuγ mac Seαιn δγαξαιl δáιγ ιαγ
bγαξαιl a lán δο čoξαδ ocυγ διmγεγuιn a τογach a
τιξεγnuιγ, ocυγ ιαγ coγξ a luchτ ιmγεγna ocυγ εγαοnτα
a čιγ ocυγ a coιξcγιč. Mac 1 Domnαιll .ι. an Calbach

---

a long time previously, to Mag Uidhir. Mac William of Clann-Rickard, i.e. Ulick-na-gcenn, son of Rickard, died this year, i.e. a haughty and proud lord, who reduced and subjected a great number of Gaeidhel under his own yoke. And a great war broke out in Clann-Rickard after him ; viz., Ulick, the son of Rickard Og,[1] was proclaimed the Mac William, and a great part of country and neighbourhood[2] was opposed to him, along with the son of Mac William, i.e. Thomas, the son of Ulick-na-gcenn. And in the beginning of this year the majority of the nobles of Erinn went[3] to Saxon-land to meet King Henry, viz., O'Neill went, (i.e. Conn, the son Conn O'Neill), and Mac William of Clann-Rickard (i.e. Ulick-na-gcenn), and Murchadh, the son of Toirdhelbhach O'Briain (i.e. the O'Briain), and the three Earls (viz., the Earl of Des-Mumha, the Earl of Ur-Mumha, and the Earl of Cill-dara), and Donnchadh, the son of Conchobhar O'Briain. All these obtained great honour from the King ; and O'Neill, O'Briain, and Ulick-na-gcenn, were made earls. And the province of the Gaillimh was taken[4] from Ulick-na-gcenn at that council ; and he himself died in the end of this year. Maghnus, son of Muirchertach Mac Diarmada Ruadh, died in hoc[5] anno.

The kalends of January on Tuesday ; the age of the [1544.] Lord one thousand, five hundred, and forty-four years. The Earl of Des-Mumha, i.e. James, the son of John, died after encountering[6] much war and contention in the beginning of his lordship, and after subduing his opponents and enemies in country[7] and neighbourhood. The son of O'Domhnaill, i.e. the Calbhach, went to meet

---

[3] *Went.* Ware (*Annals*), and also the Four Masters, have this entry under the year 1542, which is the proper date.

[4] *Taken.* This is not exactly correct. The first Earl of Clann-Rickard surrendered his vast estates into the hands of the king, who regranted them to him by letters patents bearing date the 1st of July, 1543.

[5] *Hoc.* oc, MS.

[6] *Encountering.* ιαρ βραgαιl; lit., "after getting."

[7] *Country;* i.e. his own district.

vo óul α zcenn αn ξιιιрvíр, ocυр cαιрτín no óó Sαzрαnαch zo nvαoιneó mopα vo ćαbαιрτ leιр α τιр Cho-
nαιll; ocυр vυl leo υm ćαιрlén Lιćbeр, ocυр bрαιξve
рlechτα Ccoóα hι ξhαllćυbαιр vo óí αz O n'Oomnαιll
рαvα реιṁιрιn vo óрeć υmon zcαιрlén vonα Sαcрαn-
αchαιó, .ι. Cαćαoιр mαc Cυαćαιl, ocυр Coιррvhelbαch
mαc felιm fιnn; ocυр mαрbταр Sαzрαnαch ιmon
mbαιlι von cev рzαταv, ocυр mαрóυιv nα Sαzрαnαιξ
Cαćαιр mαc Cυαćαιl ιnα ξlαррαιb рреιn; ocυр τυc
Ccoó O 'Oomnαιll ocυр αn ćυιv elι vo рlιchτ Ccoóα hι
ξhαllćυóαιр αn bαιle αр mαc felιm fιnn, ocυр αр mαc
elι Cυαćαιl vo óí α lαιm, ocυр рαξóιιιv nα Sαрαnαιξ
αn τíр αр níc ćυαрυрταιl ṁóιр vO 'Ohomnαιll рιú.
Mαc ι Néιll .ι. Nιαll mαc Ccιрτ óιz αр bрαzαιl óαιр αn
ólιάvαιn рι .ι. αnτ én mαc рιξ ιр mo vfυlαιnz vo óυαv
ocυр vo vochυр cozαιv eτιр ćιnel Eózαιn ocυр cιnél
Conαιll vá vταnιc vo рlιchτ Eozαιn mιc Heιll рιαm,
ocυр рoιvech vιnzṁálα vo рιξe ćιníl Eozαιn vá рoιchev
ι .ι. рер lán vαιćne ocυр veαlαvυιn leć рe léξτoрeαchτ
ocυр рe lιτιр zαoιóιlze, ocυр рe рonn beoιl ocυр lαιme.
Slυαιzev leιр O n'Oomnαιll von Rúτα zυр zαbαó
bαιlτι ιomóα vo ćαιрlénαιó ocυр vo cрαnnózαιó
lαιр ιnτe, ocυр zo bfυαιр eválα ιomóα; ocυр τoιξechτ
рlán voрιóιр. Mαc Sυιónι fάnαv .ι. Coιррvhelbαch
mαc Rυαιvрι mιc Mαolmυιрe .ι. рер lαn vo óeoóαchτ
ocυр vo cрoιóe, vo ṁαрbαv le clαιnn 'Oomnαιll óιz
Mιc Sυιбnι, ocυр τрιαр elι vo ćlαιnn τShυιónι vo
ćυιτιm mαιlle рιр; ocυр Mαc Sυιбnι vo ξαιрm vo
Rυαιvрι cαррαch mαc 'Oomnαιll óιz nα óιαιó. Cozαv
eτιр O n'Oomnαιll ocυр O Heιll αn blιαvαιn рι. Clαnn
'Oomnαιll .ι. Semυр ocυр Collα vo τeαchτ рechτ

---

¹ *Many.* mopα; lit. " great,"
MS.

² *To besiege.* υm; i.e. "about,"
or "around."

³ *Tuathal*; i.e. Tuathal O'Gallchubhair [or O'Gallagher)

⁴ *Felim Finn.* Felim the Fair.
Another member of the family of
O'Gallchubhair, or O'Gallagher.

⁵ *Died.* αр bрαzαιl óαιр; lit.
" after obtaining death."

⁶ *Expertness.* рonn. This word has

the Justiciary, and brought with him one or two Saxon captains, with many[1] men, to Tir-Conaill. And he went with them to besiege[2] the castle of Lithbher; and the hostages of Aedh O'Gallchubhair's descendants, whom O'Domhnaill had *in his power* for a long time previously, viz., Cathair, the son of Tuathal,[3] and Toirdhelbhach, son of Felim Finn,[4] were taken about the castle by the Saxons. And a Saxon is killed before the place at the first discharge, and the Saxons kill Cathair, son of Tuathal, in his own fetters; and Aedh O'Domhnaill, and the rest of the race of Aedh O'Gallchubhair, gave the place for the liberation of the son of Felim Finn, and of Tuathal's other son who was in confinement; and the Saxons leave the country, after the payment of great wages to them by O'Domhnaill. The son of O'Neill, i.e. Niall, son of Art Og, died[5] this year; i.e. the king's son who, of all that came previously of the race of Eoghan, son of Niall, had most experienced the success and misery of war between the Cenel-Eoghain and Cenel-Conaill; and a vessel worthy of the sovereignty of Cenel-Eoghain, if he attained it: i.e. a man full of knowledge and learning in regard to reading, and Gaeidhilic literature, and to expertness[6] of mouth and hand. A hosting by O'Domhnaill to the Rúta, when a great number[7] of castles and crannógs were taken by him in it; and he obtained numerous spoils, and came back safely. Mac Suibhne of Fánad, i.e. Toirdhelbhach, the son of Ruaidhri, son of Maelmuire, i.e. a man full of vigour and heart, was killed by the sons of Domhnall Og Mac Suibhne; and three more of the Clann-Suibhne fell with him; and Ruaidhri Carragh, the son of Domhnall Og, was proclaimed Mac Suibhne in succession to him. War between O'Domhnaill and O'Neill this year. The Clann-Domhnaill, viz., James

many other meanings, as "desire," "longing," "readiness," "harmony," "air," "land," &c.

[7] *Great number.* baιLτι ιοmὁά; lit., "numerous towns," or numerous places.

Clbanach α nθpinn ap ταιppinᵹ mic Uiδilín, ocuſ
milleⱱ mop ⱱo ᵹenim ap O ᵹCarháin ⱱo ⱱaoiniδ ocuſ
ⱱaipnéiſ. Mupchaⱱ mac Mic Shuiδni nα Túach, .i.
poi α neinech ocuſ α nuaipli, ⱱhec. ⱱonnchaⱱ mac
Mic Suibni α bpathaip eli ⱱhéc, ocuſ coᵹaⱱ mop iſ nα
Túathaiδ ⱱiα néiſ.

|Ctt. Enaip ſop Ceⱱaoin; cuiᵹ bliaⱱnα ocuſ ⱱá ſičet
ocuſ cuiᵹ ceⱱ ocuſ mile αoiſ an Tiᵹepnα. O Conchobaip 8liᵹiᵹ .i. Taⱱᵹ óᵹ mac Taiⱱᵹ mic Ccoⱱα ⱱo ṁapbaⱱ
le ſlichⱱ Copmaic mic Ruaiⱱpi Mic ⱱiapmaⱱα α nCcě
činn lačα, ocuſ ⱱo buⱱ ⱱepe ᵹaoiⱱeal ⱱob oippⱱepcα
α nenech ocuſ α nuaiple nápſ. Mac ᵹoipⱱealδ .i.
δhaiⱱep mac Uilliam Mic ᵹoipⱱealδ ⱱo δul ap ſiobal
ᵹo δun an ſeⱱáin ap clainn hi Conchobaip, ᵹo ᵹoipiⱱ
ⱱéiſ α nathap ⱱo ṁapbaⱱ. Clann i Conchobaip ⱱo
δpeč oppα, ocuſ cuiⱱ ⱱo člainn ⱱ8huiδne, α ⱱopaiᵹechⱱ.
Mac ᵹoipⱱealδ ocuſ α mac .i. Ruᵹpaiⱱe ⱱo ṁapbaⱱ,
ocuſ maiⱱm ⱱo ⱱabaiſc oppα; α púſcač nα ᵹaoiⱱi ſo
bpiſſeⱱ ſoppα. Sluaiᵹeⱱ leiſ O Ruaipc .i. δpian mac
Eoᵹain mic Tiᵹepnáin, no ᵹo paiiic ⱱun móp Mic
ſheoppuiſ, ocuſ ᵹuiſpo loiſc an baile co bſuaiſ bpáiᵹe;
ocuſ ⱱuc bpaiᵹⱱe Mic ⱱaiδíč člainni Connmaiⱱ, ocuſ
Mainech uile leiſ ⱱonc ſluaiᵹeⱱ ſin. δáiⱱep ſaⱱα
α δupc ⱱo ṁapbaⱱ α bſeall le ⱱomnall O bſhlaiⱱ-
bepraiᵹ .i. an mac ſiᵹ ⱱob uaiſle áppachtα α nupṁop
Epenn nα αimſiſ ſéin. Teaⱱóiⱱ ſiabach mac δháiⱱep
α δupc ⱱo mapbaⱱ le ſliochⱱ Uilleᵹ α δupc. Maoil-
ſechluinn ṁac δpíain hi Cheallaiᵹ ⱱo mapbaⱱ iſin

---

¹ *Wednesday. Rectè* Thursday; the
Dom. Let. being D. Mistakes of this
kind are frequent in the remainder of
the work.

² *Years.* Instead of the year 1545
the Dublin copies of the Annals of
Connacht have an entry belonging to
the year 1562, containing a bombastic
account of the death of Brian Ballagh
O'Rourke; after which occurs the following note, in the hand of the trans-

criber:—ιαſ nα ᵹpaiſneⱱ aſ lea-
δaſ αoſⱱα meaṁſuim, ocuſ ιαſ
nα chſiochnuᵹaⱱ an .xxix. lα ⱱon
míi Occobip, αoiſ an Tiᵹepnα
an ⱱan ſin 1764. Miſi Muiſiſ
O ᵹopṁain; i.e. "written out of an
old parchment book, and finished
the 29th day of the month of October,
the age of the Lord 1764. I am Maurice O'Gorman." See note ¹, p. 342.

* *Their father;* i.e. O'Conchobhair

and Colla, came to Erinn with a force of Albanachs, at the invitation of Mac Uibhilín; and they committed a great depredation upon O'Catháin, both in men and cattle. Murchadh, the son of Mac Suibhne-na-Túath, i.e. a most eminent man in hospitality and nobility, died. Donnchadh, son of Mac Suibhne, his other brother, died; and a great war *occurred* in the Túatha after them.

A.D [1544.]

The kalends of January on Wednesday;[1] the age of the Lord one thousand, five hundred, and forty-five years.[2] O'Conchobhair Sligigh, i.e. Tadhg Og, the son of Tadhg, son of Aedh, was slain by the posterity of Cormac, son of Ruaidhri Mac Diarmada, at Ath-chinn-locha; and there were few Gaeidhel more illustrious in bounty and nobility than he. Mac Goisdelbh, i.e. Walter, the son of William Mac Goisdelbh, went on an expedition to Bun-an-fhedáin, against the sons of O'Conchobhair, soon after their father[3] was killed. The sons of O'Conchobhair, and some of the Clann-Suibhne, overtook them in pursuit. Mac Goisdelbh and his son, i.e. Rughraidhe, were slain, and they[4] were routed: at Rúscach-na-gaithi[5] they were routed. A hosting by O'Ruairc, i.e. Brian, the son of Eoghan, son of Tighernan, until he reached Dun-mór-Mic-Feorais; and he burned the town until he received hostages; and he brought with him the hostages of Mac David of Clann-Connmhaigh, and of all the Mainechs,[6] on this occasion. Walter Fada[7] Burk, i.e. the noblest, bravest, son of a king in the greater part of Erinn in his own time, was killed in treachery by Domhnall O'Flaithbhertaigh. Tibbot Riabhach,[8] son of Walter Burk, was killed by the posterity of Ulick Burk. Maelsechlainn, the son of Brian O'Cellaigh, was killed in the Turrac by the sons

[1545.]

Sligigh, whose death is recorded in the preceding entry.

[4] *They*; i.e. Mac Goisdelbh's people.

[5] *Rúscach-na-gaithi.* The "*Ruscach* (or rough pasture) of the wind." There are many places in Ireland called *Rúscach* (or Rooskey).

[6] *Mainechs.* The people of Hy-Many, or O'Kelly's country.

[7] *Walter Fada*; i.e. Walter the Tall (or literally, the "Long").

[8] *Tibbot Riabhach.* Tibbot (or Theobald) the Swarthy.

Cuppac le · clainn Maoileĉlainn mic Uilliam hĺ
Cheallaiᵹ, ocuʃ le Moelʃuanaiᵭ mac Ruaiᵭʃi Mic
Ὀiaʃmaᵭa, ocuʃ an ᴄiʃ ᴅo cʃechaᴅ ᴅoiᵭ. Caᵭᵹ mac
Ruaiᵭʃi mic Coʃmaic Meic Ὀiaʃmaᵭa ᴅo ṁaʃᵭaᵭ le
cloinᴅ Eoᵹain Meic Ὀiaʃmaᵭa a ceʃᴄʃuin na capall,
ocuʃ ʃa coiʃ ᴅo Ὀia ʃin a ᴄuiᴄim, iʃ olc ᴅo ʃuaiʃ ʃe
O Conchobaiʃ Sliᵹiᵹ ᴅo maʃᵭaᵭ a ʃeall aᵹ ŒƐ ĉinn
Laĉa ʃuʃ Loĉ Ceaᴅ. ʃeʃᵹal mac Œoᵭ ṁeic Comal-
ᴄaiᵹ ᵭuiᵭe meic Coʃmaic óiᵹ ᴅhec. Bʃian mac
Maᵹnuʃa Meic Ὀiaʃmaᴅu ʃuaiᵭ ᴅhec aʃ Inᴅʃi na
ʃuaʃach, ocuʃ a aᵭnacail a mainiʃᴄiʃ na buille; ocuʃ·
ba moʃ inᴄ echᴄ ʃin.

ΙCᴄ. Enaiʃ ʃoʃ ᵭaʃᴅaoin; ʃe bliaᴅna ocuʃ ᴅá·
ʃiĉeᴄ ocuʃ .u. ceᴅ ocuʃ mile aoiʃ an Ciᵹeʃʃa. Bʃáiᵹᴅe
ĉlainni Maolʃuanaiᴅ ᴅo ᵭoiᵹeachᴄ o clainn Ricaiʃᴅ .i.
Bʃian mac Ruaiᵭʃi Mic Ὀiaʃmaᴅa ocuʃ Caᵭᵹ mac
Comalᴄaiᵹ Mic Ὀiaʃmaᴅa, ocuʃ ochᴄ bʃiĉiᴄ maʃᵹ ᴅo
ᵭul aʃᴅa. Comaʃ ʃaʃʃánᴄa mac Uilleᵹ na ᵹcenn, ocuʃ
Ὀonnchaᴅ ʃiabach mac Caiᵭᵹ ᵭuiᵭ hĺ Cheallaiᵹ ᴅo
ᵭul aʃ ʃiobal ᵹo Siol nŒnmchaᴅa, ocuʃ cʃeĉ moʃ ᴅo
ᵹlacaᴅ ᴅoiᵭ, ocuʃ ᴄoiʃ ᴄʃom ᴅo ᵭʃeiᵭ oʃʃa. Maʃᴄaʃ
Comaʃʃ ʃaʃʃánᴄa ᴅuʃchoʃ ᴅo ᵹunnai, ocuʃ ᴅo buᵭ
ᴅéchᴄaiᵭ moʃa a ʃine ᵭó. Bʃiʃᴄeʃ oʃʃa aʃʃ a haiᴄle,
ocuʃ benᴄaʃ a ᵹcʃeĉa ᵭiᵭ, ocuʃ ᴄiᵹ Ὀonnchaᴅ ʃiabach
ocuʃ uʃṁóʃ a ṁuinᴄiʃe aʃ éiᵹin. ʃeall ᴅo ᵭenum
ᴅo ĉlainn Œluʃᴅʃoinn Mic Cába aʃ O Ruaiʃc ina
ᵭaile ʃéin .i. an baile núa. Œn ʃeall ʃin ᴅʃilleᴅ
oʃʃa ʃʃéin, ocuʃ a maʃbaᴅ aʃoen .i. Sean ocuʃ
Maoilʃechlainn. Œnᴄ O Ruaiʃc ceᴅna ʃin .i. Bʃian
mac Eoᵹain ĺ Ruaiʃc ᴅo ᵭul aʃ ʃᵹeiṁliᵭ ᵹo Sliᵹech,

---

1 *Them.* The remaining entries for
this year are in the handwriting, and
very inaccurate orthography, of Brian
Mac Dermot.

ᵃ *Cartron-na-capall.* The "cartron
(or quarter) of the horses." This was
seemingly the name of some place in
the county of Roscommon. It is no
longer preserved.

ᵇ *Cormac Og.* Cormac the Younger.
Apparently a member of the Mac
Dermot family.

of Maelechlainn, son of William O'Cellaigh, and by Maelruanaidh, the son of Ruaidhri Mac Diarmada ; and the country was plundered by them.[1] Tadhg, son of Ruaidhri, son of Cormac Mac Diarmada, was killed by the sons of Eoghan Mac Diarmada, in Cartron-na-capall ;[2] and it was right of God that he should fall, for he acted badly in killing O'Conchobhair Sligigh, in treachery, at Ath-chinn-locha on Loch-Teched. Ferghal, the son of Aedh, son of Tomaltach Buidhe, son of Cormac Og,[3] died. Brian, the son of Maghnus Mac Diarmada Ruadh, died on Insi-na-suarach,[4] and was buried in the monastery of the Buill : and that was a great calamity.

The kalends of January on Thursday ; the age of the Lord one thousand, five hundred, and forty-six years. The hostages of the Clann-Maelruanaidh returned from Clann-Rickard, viz., Brian, the son of Ruaidhri Mac Diarmada, and Tadhg, the son of Tomaltach Mac Diarmada ; and eight score marks were paid for them. Thomas Farránta,[5] the son of Ulick-na-gcenn, and Donnchadh Riabhach, the son of Tadhg Dubh O'Cellaigh, went on an expedition to Sil-Anmchadha, and took a great prey ; and a heavy pursuing party overtook them. Thomas Far-ránta is killed by a shot of a gun: (and he was of the great notabilities of his sept). They are afterwards routed, and their preys are taken from them ; and Donnchadh Riabhach, and the majority of his people, escape with difficulty. Treachery was practised by the sons of Alexander Mac Caba against O'Ruairc, in his own town, i.e. the Baile-núa.[6] This treachery recoiled upon them-selves, and they were both slain, viz., John and Maelsech-lainn. The same O'Ruairc, i.e. Brian, the son of Eoghan O'Ruairc, went on a scouting party to Sligech ; and the

---

[4] *Insi-na-suarach.* This name would signify "the island of the paltry ob-jects." It was a second time written ınoᵱı na Suaᴄᵱach, but this form was afterwards expunged.

[5] *Thomas Farránta.* Thomas the Athletic, or Powerful.

[6] *Baile-núa ;* i.e. New-town ; a castle in the barony of Dromahaire, in the county of Leitrim.

ocuṗ mac h1 Raıᵹıllıᵹ, .ı. Toıṗṗohelbach mac Ferᵹaıl
h1 Raıᵹıllıᵹ, oo maṗbao oon ᵹeımlıuo ṗın le baṗoaıb
8lıᵹıᵹ. O Concuḃaıṗ oono .ı. Caṗbṗı mac Eoᵹaın caoıc
oṗaḃaıl ḃaıṗ.

Jctt. Enaıṗ ṗoṗ Ꝛoıne; ṗeacht mblıaona ocuṗ oá
ṗıcıt, cuıᵹ ceo ocuṗ mıle aoıṗ an Tıᵹeṗna. mac mıc
Oıaṗmaoa .ı. ḃṗıan mac Ruaıoṗı mıc Taıoᵹ oo lott le
8ıuṗtán mbuıoe mac 8eaın mıc Ḋáıteṗ mıc ᵹoıṗoealḃ;
ocuṗ ıṗ amlaıo oo ṗınneḃ ṗın .ı. 8ıuṗtán buıoe oo
ċoıᵹecht a maᵹ luıṗᵹ ocht noıolṁunıᵹ ḃéᵹ oıaṗṗao
ᵹaoa, ocuṗ ḃṗıan oo ḃualao uıme aon ṗeıṗeṗ aṁáın.
Oo tṗomloıtteo ḃṗıan; oe ṗın téıo an ḃuıoen ṗó láıṁ,
ocuṗ oo tṗomloıtteo an ᵹıolla ouḃ ṁáᵹ Pılıp le
ḃṗıan ṗéın. ᵹoṗt na tıᵹeḃ oo cṗeċaḃ ocuṗ oo loṗcao le
claınn Ruaıoṗı mıc Oıaṗmaoa ın ḃlıaoaın ṗı. Clann
Ruaıoṗı mıc Oıaṗmaoa muṗ an ceona, ocuṗ clann
mıc Ohaḃıᵹ oo ċul aṗ ṗıobal a ᵹCṗúċonn O maıne,
ocuṗ an tıṗ oo loṗcao ocuṗ oo cṗeċaḃ ḃóıḃ, ocuṗ
tóıṗ ṁóṗ oo ḃṗeıᵹ oṗṗa. Ro maṗbao leo hanṗaoı
mac 8eaın mıc Uıllıam mıc Emuınn, ocuṗ Uıllıam
caṗṗach mac Emuınn mıc Thommáıṗ, ocuṗ moṗán elı;
ocuṗ tanᵹaoaṗ ṗeın aṗ éıᵹın. Pṗınoṗa 8aᵹṗan ocuṗ
Eṗenn .ı. cınᵹ hanṗı oṗaᵹaıl ḃaıṗ, ocuṗ ıṗ oeımın naċ
tanıc a neıṗeoh aımṗıṗe ṗıᵹ oob ṗeṗṗ na ın ṗıᵹ ṗın,
ocuṗ oo ṗıᵹao a ınᵹen na ınaḃ .ı. cınᵹ maṗıa.

Jctt. Enaıṗ ṗoṗ ṗaċoṗn; ocht mblıaona ocuṗ oá ṗıcıt

---

1 *Died.* This entry is in the handwriting of Brian Mac Dermot, who
adds the note—ıṗ anoṗo aḃuṗ ıṗ
coıṗ baṗ Cınᵹ hanṗıᵹ oo ḃeıt, ("it
is here that the death of King Henry
should be,") in allusion to the entry of
the king's death under the year 1547.

² *Himself.* This entry concludes
folio 93 b of the MS. H. 1, 19, where
the scribe adds ṗcuıṗım oṗuacht,
" I desist, from cold."

³ *Cruthonn-O'Maine;* Cruthonn (or
Crumthann) of Hy-Many, a district
in the county of Galway, comprising
the barony of Killyan, and part of that
of Ballimoe. See the map prefixed to
O'Donovan's *Tribes and Customs of
Hy-Many.*

⁴ *Thomas;* i.e. Thomas O'Cellaigh
(or O'Kelly).

⁵ *Daughter.* a ınᵹen This mistake, as well as the very flattering

son of O'Raighilligh, i.e. Toirdhelbhach, the son of Ferghal O'Raighilligh, was killed on this scouting party by the warders of Sligech. O'Conchobhair Donn, i.e. Cairbre, the son of Eoghan Caech, died.[1] A.D. [1546.]

The kalends of January on Friday, (*rectè* Saturday); the age of the Lord one thousand, five hundred, and forty-seven years. The son of Mac Diarmada, i.e. Brian, son of Ruaidhri, son of Tadhg, was wounded by Jordan Buidhe, the son of John, son of Walter Mac Goisdelbh; and in this wise it was done: i.e. Jordan Buidhe came to Magh-Luirg, with eighteen followers, to seek stolen property, and Brian encountered him with only six men. Brian was heavily wounded, whereupon the band submitted; and the Gilla-dubh, son of Philip, was heavily wounded by Brian himself.[2] Gort-na-tighedh was plundered and burned by the sons of Ruaidhri Mac Diarmada, in hoc anno. The sons of Ruaidhri Mac Diarmada likewise, and the sons of Mac David, went on an expedition to Cruthonn-O'Maine,[3] and the country was burned and plundered by them; and a large pursuing party came up with them. Henry, the son of John, son of William, son of Edmond, and William Carragh, the son of Edmond, son of Thomas,[4] and many more, were slain by them; and they returned with difficulty themselves. The prince of the Saxons and of Erinn, i.e. King Henry, died; and it is certain that there came not in later times a better king than this king; and his daughter[5] was crowned in his place, i.e. King Mary.[6] [1547.]

The kalends of January on Saturday;[7] the age of the [1548.]

---

encomium passed upon King Henry VIII., attracted the attention of some reader, who has added the word "perperam" in the margin.

[6] *King Mary.* Cing Maria, MS. This entry is in the handwriting of Brian Mac Dermot. At the end he adds the note—Mesi Brian mac Diarmada do sgriḃ sin, ocus tabraḋ gaċ aon leig-ser sin bendacht ar uanmain. Is anosa ċallaind sin tall is coir bas a[n] riġ; i.e. "I am Brian Mac Diarmada who wrote that; and let every one who reads that give a blessing on my soul. It is in the other kalend yonder [i.e. under the year 1546] the death of the king [Henry VIII.] should be."

[7] *Saturday.* *Rectè* Sunday.

ocus cuig ced ocus mile aois an Tigerna. O Concobair donn .i. Diarmaid mac Cairbri mic Eogain ċaoiċ, ocus Mac Diarmada .i. Ruaidri mac Taiḋg Mic Diarmada, ocus Tomaltach mac Taiḋg Mic Diarmada, ocus clann Mic Diarmada, .i. Maolruanaid ocus Brian, iadsin uile ocus cuid do ġallóglaeċaiḃ clainni Suiḃni ocus ċlainni Duḃġaill, ocus morán do ḋaoinib eli nach áirimter sunn, do ḋul ar siobal sluaiged a gclainn Mhuiris, ocus Ricard mac Muiris do ṁarbad leó .i. ant ab óg, ocus caislén Mic Gerailt .i. an caislén caol do ġabáil, ocus ced no ḋo duine do ḃássugad etir an dá ḃaile sin; ocus tucadar a noei no a .x. do ceduiḃ bó ocus .x. neich leo; ocus tancodar fein slan. Loċ na cuanfadha do ġaḃail, ocus an tir do loscad, le hUa Ruairc ocus le Mac nDiarmada, an ṁí cedna. Aonġus ṁac Toirrdhelbaiġ mic Colla Mhég Dhoṁnaill do ṁarbad le Moelruanaid mac Ruaidri Mic Diarmada, ar Bealaċ an dairín, ocus tuc crech o ċlainn nDomnaill isin ló cedna. Mor ingen Maolruanáid meic Seain I Cerḃaill, in ben is ferr do ḃi a nen aimsir ria fein a nErinn .i. in ben do ḃí ag Iarla De[s]muman, dhec. Clond Taidg ḃuiḋe meic I Conchobair ḋuinn do ṁarḃaḋ a nUaran le sliocht Feilimi ċleiriġ I Chonchobair .i. Seain ocus Feilimi.

Kll. Enair for ḋoṁnach; noi mbliadna ocus dá ḟiċet, cuig ced ocus mile air an Tigerna. Aoḋ mac Cormaic mic Ruaidri mic Diarmada, ocus ab na Buille, ocus tigerna ċlainni Mhaolruanaid a naon persuin, dḟaġail ḃais comna ocus tsacarbuic iar nguasachtaiḃ iomḋa on ḟine féin ocus ó esgcairdib eli. Acht chena nir ḃó ró diamad leis tigernus Connacht, daiḋḃle a oiniġ ocus a uaisle, ocus do ṁéd a ṫiḋluicṫi ocus a ṫuarusdail; Dia ḋa ioc ren anmuin. Ruaidri

[1] *Caislén-cael;* "the narrow castle;" Castlekeel, bar. of Clanmorris, co. Mayo.

[2] *These two places.* There is some mistake here, as only one place is mentioned in the text.

[3] *Day.* The next two entries are in Brian Mac Dermot's hand.

[4] *Wife.* She was the wife of James, 15th Earl of Desmond. See Lodge's *Peerage of Ireland.*

Lord one thousand, five hundred, and forty-eight years. O'Conchobhair Donn, i.e. Diarmaid, the son of Cairbre, son of Eoghan Caech, and Mac Diarmada, i.e. Ruaidhri, the son of Tadhg Mac Diarmada, and Tomaltach, son of Tadhg Mac Diarmada, and the sons of Mac Diarmada, viz., Maelruanaidh and Brian—all these, and some of the gallowglasses of Clann-Suibhne and Clann-Dubhgall, and a great many other people who are not enumerated here, went on a hosting to Clann-Maurice ; and Rickard Mac Maurice i.e. the young abbot, was killed by them, and Fitz Gerald's castle, i.e. the Caislén-cael,' was taken ; and one or two hundred men were put to death between these two places.[2]   And they brought nine or ten hundred cows with them, and ten horses, and came safely themselves.   Loch-na-cuanfadha was occupied, and the country plundered, by O'Ruairc and Mac Diarmada, the same month.   Aenghus, son of Toirdhelbhach, son of Colla Mac Domhnaill, was killed by Maelruanaidh, the son of Ruaidhri Mac Diarmada, on Bealach-an-dairín ; and he brought a prey from the Clann-Domhnaill on the same day.[3] Mor, daughter of Maelruanaidh, son of John O'Cerbhaill, the best woman that was in Erinn in her own time, i.e. the Earl of Des-Mumha's wife,[4] died.   The sons of Tadhg Buidhe, son of O'Conchobhair Donn, were slain in Uaran by the descendants of Felimy Clerech O'Conchobhair, viz., John and Felimy.

The kalends of January on Sunday ;[5] the age of the [1549.] Lord one thousand, five hundred, and forty-nine years. Aedh, son of Cormac, son of Ruaidhri Mac Diarmada, abbot of the Buill, and lord of the Clann-Maelruanaidh, in one person, died after communion and sacrifice, after suffering numerous dangers from his own tribe, and from other enemies.   Nevertheless, it would not be too much if the lordship of Connacht belonged to him, from the extent of his bounty and nobility, and the amount of his gifts and wages.   May God repay it to his soul.

---

[5] *Sunday*. Should be Tuesday.

2 A.

mac Taiḋg mic Ruaiḋri oig Mic Diarmaḋa ḋo riġhaḋ
na ionaḋ; acht ger ṁór re hinnirin maiṫ Aoḋa nír ḃo
cloiċ an ionaḋ uiġe Ruaiḋri na ionaḋ. Ȝairm rȝoile
ḋo ṫabairt ḋo Mac Diarmaḋa .i. ḋo Ruaiḋri a noḋluic
na bliaḋna ra, ocur ni heiḋir a riom ina ro áiremh ar
ṫiḋluic ré ḋeiȝriḃ ocur ḋollamnaiḃ ocur ḋaoir ealaḋna
 Erenn, ocur ḋa ȝach ḋuine aipchena. Mac maiṫ ḋo
Mac Diarmaḋa .i. Maolruanaiḃ mac Ruaiḋri Mic
Diarmaḋa ḋo ṫabairt na ȝarma ceḋna, ocur ioliomaḋ
ḋo maiṫerr ant raoȝail ḋo rȝaoileḋ ar reruiḃ Erenn
ar lorg a athar. Ro ḋaingniȝ ocur ro ṫeȝroicraiḃ
an Ruaiḋri rin Mac Diarmaḋa ro na ṫiȝerntur ocur
ro na troim ċior moran ḋo na tirib a ȝcian ocur a
ḃroȝur, oir ḋo ḃen ré ḋa ceḋ ḃó ḋon ḋa Mhaȝ Raȝnaill,
ocur ceḋ ḃó ḋo Mac Donnchaḋa an Choruinn, ocur
tri riċit bo ḋUa Ȝhaḋra; ocht mba ocur ḋá riċet ḋUa
Ainliȝe, ocur ocht mba ocur ḋá riċet o Mac Oranáin;
ocur cetra ba riċeḋ o Ua Phlannaȝáin, ocur cetra ba
richet o Cruṫonn O Maine; ocur ceṫra ba richet ó
ṫrlicht Toirrḋhelbaiȝh ċarraiȝh 1 Conchobaip, ocur
riċe bert ḃuanḋachta ó ṫrlicht Taiḋg mic Oriain mic
Donnchaḋa, ocur riċe rȝillinn ḋo ċior ȝacha bliaḋna
maille ririn; ocur ciorr ar ṫrlicht Ruaiḋri Mic
Donnchaḋa a ȝcuil Deȝha; ocur ciorr ar ṫrlicht Aoḋa
buiḋe ocur ar rlicht Muirȝerra; ocur cirr ar rlicht
Ouḃȝaill ȝruama. Crecha móra ḋo ḋenum ḋo Mac
Diarmaḋa ar rlicht Donnchaḋa hi Cheallaiȝ, ocur a
ȝcuiḋ tire ḋo Lorcuḋ; ocur trí riċit bo ó Mac Ȝoir-
ḋealḃ an bliaḋain ceḋna. Crecha móra ó ċlainn Philip
ina raiḃe ḋa ceḋ ḋhéc bó ocur ḋeiċ neiċ ḋila maille

---

1 *School invitation.* An invitation
to an assembly where poets and learned men competed for prizes.

2 *Of Erinn.* eꞃ, MS.

3 *Twenty pair of bonaghtmen.* Ꝑiċe
beꞃt ḃuanḋachta. It is not quite
clear whether the word buanḋachta
should be rendered *bonaghtmen* (i.e.
military retainers) or translated

"reapers;" but the first is the more
probable meaning.

4 *Aedh Buidhe.* Aedh (or Hugh)
the Yellow; one of the family of Mac
Donnchadha, or Mac Donough.

5 *Slicht-Muirghesa;* i.e. "the descendants of Maurice," who was
also a member of the Mac Donough
family.

Ruaidhri, son of Tadhg, son of Ruaidhri Og Mac Diarmada, was made king in his place; and although Aedh's excellence was great, Ruaidhri in his place was not a stone in the place of an egg. A school invitation[1] was given by Mac Diarmada, i.e. Ruaidhri, at Christmas of this year; and it is not possible to count or over-reckon all that he gave to the poets, and professors, and learned men of Erinn,[2] and to all men besides. A good son of Mac Diarmada, i.e. Maelruanaidh, the son of Ruaidhri Mac Diarmada, gave the like invitation, and distributed much of the world's riches to the men of Erinn, after the example of his father. This Ruaidhri Mac Diarmada secured, and firmly established, many of the neighbouring and distant territories under his government and heavy tribute, for he exacted two hundred cows from the two Mag Raghnaills, and one hundred cows from Mac Donnchadha of the Corann, and sixty cows from O'Gadhra; forty-eight cows from O'hAinlighe, and forty-eight cows from Mac Branáin; and twenty-four cows from O'Flannagáin, and twenty-four cows from Cruthon-O'Maine; and twenty-four cows from the descendants of Toirdhelbhach Carragh O'Conchobhair; and twenty pair of bonaghtmen[3] from the descendants of Tadhg, son of Brian Mac Donnchadha, and twenty shillings rent every year therewith. And *he imposed* a tribute on the descendants of Ruaidhri Mac Donnchadha, in Cúil-Degha, and a tribute on the descendants of Aedh Buidhe,[4] and on the Slicht-Muirghesa,[5] and a tribute on the descendants of Dubhgall Gruama.[6] Great depredations were committed by Mac Diarmada on the descendants of Donnchadh O'Cellaigh; and he burned their portion of country. And *he took* three score cows from Mac Goisdelbh the same year, and great preys from Clann-Philip,[7] in which were twelve hundred cows, and ten saddle horses along with them;

---

[6] *Dubhgall Gruama.* "Dubhgall the Surly;" ancestor of the Mac Dubhgaill, or Mac Dowalls, of Connacht.

[7] *Clann-Philip;* i.e. the sons of Philip Mac Goisdelbh, or Mac Costelloe.

VOL. II.

2 A 2

pú; ocuʃ ιαʋʃιn uιle ʋo ξιιʋlucaʋ a nen lo ʋollam-
ιιαιξ ocuʃ ʋeʒʃιb epenn .ι. la ʃel 8ʋeʃαιn. Caʒhal óʒ
mac Coʃmαιc Meιc 'Ʋonnchαʋa ʋo maʃbaʋ le Mac
'Ʋonnchαʋa ιn Choʃαιnʋ, .ι. le Caιʃbʃe, aʃ 8ιξ ʃιαξαξ.
Caιʃlen ʋo ξenam a leιm na ʒιʃʃa ʋo clαιnn 'Ʋonnchαʋa ξuιξ mιc Conchobαιʃ, ocuʃ ʋo buξ maιξ ιn
conʒnam Ruαξʃι mac Cαιξʒ mιc 'Ʋιαʃmαʋa ocuʃ a
clann, .ι. Maolʃuanaιξ ocuʃ Ɓʃιan, ʋoξum ιn ξαιʃlein
ʃιn ʋo ξe[n]aṁ.

|Ctt. Enáιʃ ʃoʃ luan; x. mblιαʋna ocuʃ ʋa ʃιcheʒ,
.u. ceʋ ocuʃ mιle αιʃ an Cιʒeʃna. O Conchobαιʃ ʋonn
.ι. Ꙭoξ mac Ꙭoʒαιn ξaoιξ ʋαιξʃιoʒaʋ ʋιaʃla ξlαιnnι
Rιcαιʃʋ .ι. Rιcaʃʋ 8acʃanach, ocuʃ· cιʒeʃna ʋo ξenum
ʋo 'Ʋιαʃmαιʋ mac Caʃbʃι mιc Ꙭoʒαιn ξaoιξ.

|Ctt. Enαιʃ ʃoʃ ṁαιʃʒ; en blιαʋαιn ʋéʒ ocuʃ ʋá
ʃιcheʒ, ocuʃ cuιʒ ceʋ ocuʃ mιle, αιʃ an Cιʒeʃna. ιaʃla
ξlαιnnι Rιcαιʃʋ ʋo ξeachʒ co Roʃ Comáιn ʋιaʃʃaʋ
Roʃʃa Comáιn aʃ clαιnn Cαιξʒ ξuιξe hι Conchobαιʃ;
ocuʃ ní bʃuαιʃ an baιle; ocuʃ cειʋ ʃoιme co coʃuʃ Ꙭιlξe
cona ʃluαιʒ, muʃ aʃαιξe ʃoʃlonʒʃoʃʒ Mιc 'Ʋιαʃmαʋa .ι.
Ruαιʋʃι mιc Cαιξʒ Mιc 'Ʋιαʃmαʋa, ocuʃ ʃo leξnoιʒheʋ
an ʃlúαʒ ʃιn an ιaʃla aʃ ʃeʋh ʃoʃlonʒʃuιʃʒ Mιc 'Ʋιaʃ-
mαʋa ξá lo co noιξξe. Ꙭchʒ chena ιʃ ceʃc má ξo ξí
a nꙭʃιnn ʃoʃlonʒʃoʃʒ ιnaʃ lía ba ocuʃ eιξ, eιʋeξ ocuʃ
oʃʋanáʃʃ, ceol ocuʃ ʃιon, ιna ιn ʃoʃlonʒʃoʃʒ ʃιn Mιc
'Ʋιαʃmαʋa; óιʃ ní ʃaιξe ó Chul ṁaoιle co 8lιαξ ξuι-
ξιunn, na o ξel Ꙭξa hachαιʋh co 8ιonuιnn, aon ʋuιne
nach ʃαιξe ιʃιn bʃoʃlonʒʃoʃʒ ʃιn Mιc 'Ʋιαʃmαʋa.
ʃáʒξuʃ anʒ ιaʃla an ʃoʃlonʒʃoʃʒ aʃʃ a haιξle, ocuʃ
beʃιʃʃ Mac 'Ʋιαʃmαʋa allαιm leιʃ co clαιnn Conn-
mαιʋ, ocuʃ cέιʋ mac 'Ʋáξιξ .ι. Uιllec mac Comáιʃ ʋo

---

[1] *And.* The remainder of the sentence is interlined in a different
handwriting from that of the scribe.
The last entry for the year has been
added by Brian Mac Dermot.

[2] *Sith-riabhach.* The "swarthy

sith (pron. *shee*)," or fairy mound.
Now Sheerevagh, barony of Tirerrill,
co. Sligo.

[3] *Leim-na-girra;* "the leap of the
girr," (some kind of animal—a hare?).
This place has not yet been identified.

and[1] all these were given to the professors and poets of Erinn in one day, i.e. the day of Stephen's festival. Cathal Og, son of Cormac Mac Donnchadha, was killed by Mac Donnchadha of the Corann, i.e. by Cairbre, on Sith-riabhach.[2] A castle was erected in Leim-na-girra,[3] by the sons of Donnchadh Dubh, son of Conchobhar;[4] and Ruaidhri, the son of Tadhg Mac Diarmada, and his sons, viz., Maelruanaidh and Brian, were good assistance towards erecting that castle.

The kalends of January on Monday;[5] the age of the Lord one thousand, five hundred, and fifty years. O'Conchobhair Donn, i.e. Aedh, the son of Eoghan Caech, was deposed by the Earl of Clann-Rickard, i.e. Rickard Saxanach; and Diarmaid, the son of Cairbre, son of Eoghan Caech, was made lord.

The kalends of January on Tuesday;[6] the age of the Lord one thousand, five hundred, and fifty-one years. The Earl of Clann-Rickard went to Ros-Comáin, to demand Ros-Comain from the sons of Tadhg Buidhe O'Conchobhair; and he did not get the town. And he advances with his army to Tobur-Ailbhe, where the fortress of Mac Diarmada was, i.e. Ruaidhri, son of Tadhg Mac Diarmada; and this army of the Earl was distributed throughout Mac Diarmada's fortress during two days and a night. But truly, it is doubtful if there was in Erinn a fortress in which cows and horses, armour and ordnance, music and wine, were more plentiful than that fortress of Mac Diarmada; for there was not a man from Cúl-Mhaile to Sliabh-Badhun, nor from Bel-atha-hachaidh to the Sionainn, that was not in that fortress of Mac Diarmada. The Earl leaves the fortress soon after, and takes Mac Diarmada with him, in captivity, to Clann-Conmhaigh; and Mac David, i.e. Ulick, the son of Thomas, goes

---

[4] *Conchobhar;* i.e. Conchobhar Mac Diarmada, or Conor Mac Dermot.

[5] *Monday.* Rectè Wednesday; Dom. Let. E.

[6] *Tuesday.* This should be Thursday.

bráჳαιᵭ αрр, ocuſ ре̇ıᵭ̇ıჳᴄeр ჳαn ро ᵭ̇íჳᵬáıl ıαᵭ αроen·
Muılenn Ɑᵭαm ᵭo ჳαᵬαıl ᵭo mαc Mıc Ɔıαрmαᵭα ·ı·
ᵬрíαn mαc Ruαıᵭрı Mıc Ɔıαрmαᵭα; ocuſ cuıрıſ ᴄechᴄα
αр α ᵬрαıᵭ̇рechαıᵬ elı ·ı· Coрmαc ocuſ Mαolрuαnαıᵭ̃,
ocuſ ᵭo nıαᵭ cрeᴄ̃α móрα α ჳCoрαnn; ocuſ ᴄıc Coрmαc
ocuſ Mαolрuαnαıᵭ̃ lé nα neᵭáıl, ocuſ αnuſ ᵬрíαn ıſın
mbαıle· Ro ჳαᵬ̃ αn ſıαᵭ̃рuſ é; ᵭo nıαᵭ α ṁuınᴄıр
рeαchᴄ ჳcрeαᴄ̃α αn ſeᵭ̃ ᵭo ᵭ̃ı ſé ſeın nα luıᵭ̃e; ocuſ ᴄuc
Cαᵭ̃ჳ cαрραch mαc Mıc Ɔonnchαᵭα αn Choрuınn ceᵭ
mαрჳ αрр αn mbαıle ſın ᵭo clαınn Ruαıᵭрı Mıc Ɔıαрmαᵭα; ocuſ ᴄαnჳαᵭαр ſeın ſlαn eᵭαlαᴄ̃ αр· Loᴄ̃lαınn
mαc Pαıᵭın mıc Loᴄ̃lαınn mıc Mαoıleᴄ̃lαınn mıc Chαn-
αıᵭhe ·h· Mhαoılᴄ̃onαıрe ·ı· αрᵭ ollαm ᴄꞃıolα Muıрeᵭ̃-
αıჳ, ᵭꞃαჳαıl ᵬαıſ αn ᵬlıαᵭαın ſın, ocuſ α αᵬ̃lucαᵭ
α nOılſınn, ıαр mbꞃeıᴄ̃ ᵬuαıᵭe o ᵭ̃omαn ocuſ o ᵭ̃emαn·
O ᵬрıαın ᵭ̃éc ·ı· Muрchαᵭ mαc Coıррᵭheαlbαıჳ; ocuſ
ní ᴄαınıc ᵭo ᴄꞃlıochᴄ ᵬрíαın mıc Cınᵭeıᵭıჳ ſe ſαᵭα
ſıαm ſჳel buᵭ̃ mo nα he· Mαıᵭ̃m nα Muınᴄ̃ınᵭe
uαchᴄαıр ᵭo ᵭ̃αᵬαıрᴄ αр ᵭ̃Shıuрᴄαn mbuıᵭ̃e mαc Seαın
mıc Ꞷαᴄeıſ mıc ჳCoıрᵭeαlb, ſe ꞃlıochᴄ Muıрceрᴄαıჳ
Mıc Ɔıαрmαᵭα ꞃuαıᵭ̃, ᵭu αnᵭ αр ᴄuıᴄ ſıcheᵭ no ᵭo,
ocuſ ᵭo mαрbαᵭ̃ ın lα ſın Ɔoṁnαll O lαımın ocuſ
Cαᴄhαl O Mochαın le Sıuрᴄαn·

Ĵcᴄᴄ· Enαıр ſoр Ceᵭαoın; ᵭá blıαᵭαın ᵭ̃éc ocuſ ᵭá
ſıcheᵭ, ocuſ cuıჳ ceᵭ ocuſ mıle, αıſ αn Cıჳeрnα·
O Conchobαıр Slıჳıჳh ·ı· Cαᵭ̃ჳ mαc Cαᴄhαıl oıჳ hí
Conchobαıр, ᵭꞃαჳαıl ᵬ̃áıſſ; ocuſ αᵭeрαıᵭ αꞃoıle ჳuꞃαb
ᴄeрᴄ má ᵭ̃αınıc ᵭo ſlıchᴄ ᵬрıαın lαıჳnıჳ ᴄıჳeрnα ᵭob
ſeрꞃ ſéıle ocuſ ſoıჳıᵭe, ᵭeαlᵬ̃ ocuſ ᵭenum ınáꞃſ·
Ruჳрαıᵭ̃e mαc Cαıᵭ̃ჳ ᵬuıᵭ̃e mıc Cαᴄhαıl ꞃuαıᵭ̃ ᵭo
ṁαрbαᵭ̃ le Mαc Ɔıαрmαᵭα, ocuſ cαıſlén Culᴄ̃α ᵭo

---

¹ *In redemption of.* αꞃꞃ; lit., " out of," MS.

² *Spoils.* This sentence is in the handwriting of Brian Mac Dermot. The next entry has been added by the same person who wrote the ad-

dition to the text reierred to in note ¹, page 356. The remaining entries are in the handwriting of Brian Mac Dermot.

³ *Wednesday.* This should be Friday, the Dom. Lett. for the year

security for him; and they are both reconciled without injury. Muilenn-Adam was taken by the son of Mac Diarmada, (i.e. Brian, the son of Ruaidhri Mac Diarmada); and he sends messengers to his other brothers, viz., Cormac and Maelruanaidh, and they commit great depredations in Corann. And Cormac and Maelruanaidh return with their spoils, and Brian remains in the place. Fever seized him; and his people commit seven depredations whilst he himself was confined to bed. And Tadhg Carragh, son of Mac Donnchada of the Corann, gave one hundred marks, in redemption of[1] the place, to the sons of Ruaidhri Mac Diarmada; and they themselves came safely from it, laden with spoils.[2] Lochlainn, son of Paidin, son of Lochlainn, son of Maelechlainn, son of Tanaidhe O'Mael-chonaire, i.e. arch-ollamh of Sil-Muiredhaigh, died this year, and was buried in Oilfinn, after triumphing over the world and the devil. O'Briain died, i.e. Murchadh, the son of Toirdhelbhach; and there came not of the race of Brian, son of Cennedigh, for a long time previously, a person of greater account than he. The defeat of the upper Munchind was given to Jordan Buidhe, the son of John, son of Walter Mac Goisdelbh, by the descendants of Muirchertach Mac Diarmada Ruadh, in which a score or two fell; and Domhnall O'Laimhin, and Cathal O'Mochain, were killed on that day by Jordan.

The kalends of January on Wednesday;[3] the age of the Lord one thousand, five hundred, and fifty-two years. O'Conchobhair Sligigh i.e. Tadhg, son of Cathal Og O'Conchobhair, died; and some say that it is doubtful if there came of the race of Brian Laighnech a lord of better hospitality and charity, figure and form, than he. Rughraidhe, son of Tadhg Buidhe, son of Cathal Ruadh,[4] was killed by Mac Diarmada, and the castle of Tulach

---

1552 being CB. The criteria employed in this portion of the Chronicle are altogether wrong.

[4] *Cathal Ruadh.* Charles the Red. He was one of the sept of O'Conor Roe. See under A.D. 1553; p. 361.

bpippeꝺ., Uél na muilneꝺ ꝺo ꝺpippeꝺ, ocuр a ꝺapꝺa
ꝺo ṁapꝺaꝺ le Mac n'Ơiapmaꝺa ocuр le na člainn.
Ruaiꝺpi mac Ƒélim mic Mhaᵹnupa ꝺo puᵹhaꝺ a nionaꝺ
hi Conchobaip .i. Thaiꝺᵹ mic Cathail oiᵹ.   Clann
Ơonnchaꝺa. ꝺuiꝺ mic Conchobaip, .i. Ruaiꝺpi ꝺuiꝺe
ocuр Maoilečlainn ꝺonn, ꝺƒaᵹail ꝺáiр an ꝺliaꝺain ри.
Coᵹaꝺ móр ꝺo eipᵹe etip O Conchobaip .i. Ruaiꝺpi mac
Ƒélim mic Mhaᵹnupa, ocuр mac hi Conchobaip .i.
Ơomnall mac Thaiꝺᵹ mic Cathail óiᵹ; ocuр ꝺo ꝺaꝺap
clann Maolpuanaiꝺ ina ꝺá pann anaᵹhaiꝺ apoile
maille рир anꝺ ƒiol Conchobaip рin; .i. ꝺo ꝺi Mac
Ơiapmaꝺa ocuр a člann, ocuр Mac Ơonnchaꝺa čipé
hOilella, aᵹ mac hi Chonchobaip, aᵹ Ơoṁnall, ocuр ꝺo
ꝺi clann Eoᵹain Mic Ơiapmaꝺa ocuр Mac Ơonnchaꝺa
an Chopuinn aᵹ O Conchobaip; ocuр ni heiꝺip a рiom
iná áiperṁ ᵹach ap milleꝺ ap an ᵹcoᵹaꝺ рin.   Maolpuanaiꝺ mac Thaiꝺᵹ mic Eoᵹain ṁic Ơiapmaꝺa ꝺo
ṁapꝺaꝺ ꝺuрchoр ꝺo ᵹunna le cuiꝺ ꝺá čineꝺ ƒein .i.
рliochꝺ inᵹine Meᵹ Raᵹnaill.   Copmac cappaꝺ mac
Eoᵹain Mic Ơiapmaꝺa ꝺƒaᵹail ꝺaiр a ꝺiᵹ a muine ap
Coрррliaꝺ, ocuр ƒa móр in ƒeр millꝺe ocuр uilc ꝺo
ᵹenaṁ in ƒeр рin, oip ꝺo maрꝺ ре Ơiapmaiꝺ an
iniᵹ mac Ruaiꝺpi Meic Ơiapmaꝺa a ƒeall ap lioр
Αoꝺain.   Thaiꝺᵹ mac Thaiꝺᵹ mic Eoᵹain 1 Ruaipc ꝺo
maрꝺaꝺ a ƒeall a mꝺočaiᵹ 1 Ƒhialain ꝺon Ơauine mac
Ločluinꝺ.

Icꝺꝺ. Enaip foр ꝺaрꝺaoin; ꝺpi ꝺliaꝺna ꝺhéc ocuр ꝺa
ƒicheꝺ, ocuр cuiᵹ ceꝺ ocuр mile, aiр an Tiᵹeрna.
O Conchobaip рuaꝺ .i. Toippꝺhelbach рuaꝺ mac Thaiꝺᵹ
ꝺuiꝺe mic Cathail рuaiꝺ ꝺo ƒappainᵹ ꝺapaṁuin
Ơealꝺna ap Mhaᵹ Luipᵹ, ocuр cpecha nach eiꝺip ꝺo

---

[1] O'Conchobhair; i.e. O'Conor Sligo, whose death is the first entry under this year.

[2] Kindred. The remainder of the entries for this year are in Brian Mac Dermot's handwriting.

[3] Mag Raghnaill's daughter. She was the wife of Cathal Mac Diarmada.

[4] Tech-a-muine; "i.e. the house of the brake." The place has not been identified, as the name seems now altogether obsolete.

was demolished. Bél-na-muilnedh was demolished, and
its warders were slain, by Mac Diarmada and his sons.
Ruaidhri, son of Felim, son of Maghnus, was made king
in the place of O'Conchobhair,[1] i.e. Tadhg, son of Cathal
Og. The sons of Donnchadh Dubh, son of Conchobhar,
viz., Ruaidhri Buidhe and Maelechlainn Donn, died this
year. A great war broke out between O'Conchobhair,
i.e. Ruaidhri, son of Felim, son of Maghnus, and the son
of O'Conchobhair, i.e. Domhnall, the son of Tadhg, son
of Cathal Og; and the Clann-Maelruanaidh were in two
divisions, opposed to one another, with this Sil-Conchobhair, viz., Mac Diarmada and his sons, and Mac Donnchadha of Tir-Oilella, were with O'Conchobhair (i.e. with
Domhnall), and the sons of Eoghan Mac Diarmada, and
Mac Donnchadha of the Corann, with O'Conchobhair;
and it is not possible to calculate or over-reckon what
was destroyed in that war. Maelruanaidh, son of Tadhg,
son of Eoghan Mac Diarmada, was killed with a gun shot
by some of his own kindred,[2] viz., by the descendants of
Mag Raghnaill's daughter.[3] Cormac Carrach, son of
Eoghan Mac Diarmada, died in Tech-a-muine[4] on Corr-
sliabh : and this man was a great destroyer and evil-doer,
for he killed Diarmaid-an-enigh, the son of Ruaidhri Mac
Diarmada, in treachery, on Lis-Aedhain. Tadhg, the
son of Tadhg, son of Eoghan O'Ruairc, was slain in
treachery in Bothach-Ui-Fhialain,[5] by the Davine,[6] son of
Lochlainn.[7]

The kalends of January on Thursday ;[8] the age of the
Lord one thousand, five hundred, and fifty-three years.
O'Conchobhair Ruadh, i.e. Toirdhelbhach Ruadh, son of
Tadhg Buidhe, son of Cathal Ruadh, brought the Baron of
Delbhna upon Magh-Luirg; and innumerable preys, in

---

[5] *Bothach-Ui-Fhialain.* O'Fialain's
(O'Phelan's) bothy;" not identified.

[6] *Davine.* This name is probably
a phonetic form of ʋαıɼɧıɲ, which
signifies "little ox."

[7] *Son of Lochlainn.* mαc Loċluıʋ,

MS. Lochlainn was a Christian
name in the family of O'Ruairc; and
the person here alluded to was perhaps one of the sept.

[8] *Thursday.* This should be Sunday; Dom. Let. A.

ꞃíoṁ ⲇⲟ Ⳡeⲛum ⲁꞃ ꝑⳑⲓⳡⲧ Ⲙⲁⲟⳑꞃⲉⳑⳑⲁⲓⲛⲛ ⲇⲩⲓⲛⲛ, ⲇⲩ ⲓⲛⲁ
ꞃⲁⳠⲁⲇⲁꞃ ⲇⲁ ⲥⲉⲇ ⲇ⳵ⲉⲥ ⲃⲟ ⲩⲉⳑ ⲁⲙⲡⳑⲓⲩꞃ; ⲟⲓⳠⳠⲉ Ⳡⲉⳑⲉ ⲥꞃⲟⲓꞃ
ⲇⲟ ꞃⲓⲛⲛⲉⳠ ⲛⲁ ⲥꞃⲉⳡⲁ ꞃⲓⲛ.   Ⲙⲁⲟⳑꞃⲩⲁⲛⲁⲓⲇ ⲙⲁ⳼ Ꞃⲩⲁⲓⲇꞃⲓ
Ⲙⲓ⳼ Ⲇⲓⲁꞃⲙⲁⲇⲁ, .ⲓ. ⲁⲛ ⲙⲁ⳼ ꞃⲓ⳵ ⲇⲟⳠ ⲟⲓꞃꝑⲇⲉꞃ⳼ⲁ ⲇⳠⲉꞃ
ⲁⲟꞃꞃⲁ ⲇⲟⲓⲛⲉⳡ ⲟⲥⲩꞃ ⲇⲩⲁⲓꞃⳑⲉ ⲟⲥⲩꞃ ⲇⲟⲓꞃⳠⲉꞃⳡ, ⲇⲟ ⳝⲁꞃⳠⲁⲇ
ⲇⲩꞃⳡⲩꞃ ⲇⲟ ⳵ⲩⲛⲛⲁ ⳑⲉ ⲛⲁ Ⳡꞃⲁⳡⲁⲓꞃ Ⳡⲉⲓⲛ .ⲓ. ⲦⲁⳠ⳵ ⲙⲁ⳼
Ⲑⲟ⳵ⲁⲓⲛ Ⲙⲓ⳼ Ⲇⲓⲁꞃⲙⲁⲇⲁ, ⲓⲛ hoc anno.   Ⲁ⳼ⳡⲧ ⳡⲉⲛⲁ ⲛⲓꞃ
Ⳡⲟ ꞃó ⲙⲁⲓⳠ ⲇⲓⲁⲛ ⲇⲓⲛ⳵ⲛⲁⲇ ⲁⲛ ⲧé ꞃⲩꞃ ⲧⲟꞃⳡⲁⲓꞃ ⲁⲛⲛꞃⲓⲛ,
ⲟⲓꞃ ⲛⲓ ꞃⲁⲓⳠⲉ ⲁ ⳵ⲥⲟⲓ⳵ⲉⲇ Ⳡⲟⲛⲛⲁⳡⲧ ⲙⲁ⳼ ⲁⳡⲁꞃ ⲟⲥⲩꞃ
ⲙⲁⳡⲁꞃ ⲇⲟⳠ ꞃⲉꞃꞃ ⲟⳑⲇⲁꞃꞃ ⲓⲛ ⳵ⲁⳡ ⲩⲓⳑⲉ ⲙⲁⲓⳠ, ⲇⲟ ⲧꞃⲟⲓⲙⲉ
ⳠⲓⳠⳑⲩⲓ⳼Ⳡⲓ ⲟⲥⲩꞃ ⲧⲁⳠⲁꞃⲧⲁⲓꞃ ⲟⲥⲩꞃ ⲧⲓ⳵ⲉꞃⲛⲧⲩⲓꞃ, ⲇⳠⲉⳑⲉ ⲟⳡⲩꞃ
ⲇⲓⲟⳡⲧ, ⲇⲟⲓⲛⲉⳡ ⲟⲥⲩꞃ ⲇꞃⲟⲓ⳵ⲓⲇⲉ .ⲓ. Ꞃⲩⲁⲓⲇꞃⲓ ⲙⲁ⳼ ⲦⲁⲓⳠ⳵
ⲙⲓ⳼ Ꞃⲩⲁⲓⲇꞃⲓ óⲓ⳵, ⲟⲥⲩꞃ ЅⲁⳠⳠ ⲓⲛ⳵ⲉⲛ Ꞃⲓⲟⲥⲁⲓꞃⲇ óⲓ⳵ ⲙⲓ⳼
Ⳙⲓⳑⳑⲉ⳵ ꞃⲩⲁⲓⳠ ⲙⲓ⳼ Ⳙⲓⳑⳑⲉ⳵ ⲁⲛ Ⳡⲓⲟⲛⲁ.   Ⲁ⳼ⳡⲧ ⳡⲉⲛⲁ ⲇⲟ ⲛⲓ
Ⲙⲁ⳼ Ⲇⲓⲁꞃⲙⲁⲇⲁ ꞃⲓⳠ ⲁ hⲁⲓⳠⳑⲉ Ⳡⲁⲓꞃ ⲁ ⳟⲉⲓ⳼, ⲁⳡⲧ ⳵ⲉꞃ
Ⳡⲟⲓⳑⲓ⳵ ⳑⲁⲓꞃ ⲁ ⲇⲓ⳵hⲩⲓⲛ ⳑé ⲛⲁ ⳼ⲁꞃⲁⲓⲇ ⲟⲥⲩꞃ ⳑⲉ ⲛⲁ comꞠⲟⲓ⳵ꞃⲓⳠ
ꞃéⲓⲛ.   Ⲥꞃⲉⳡ ⲙⲟꞃ ⲇⲟ Ⳡⲉⲛⲩⲙ ⲇⲟ Ⳡꞃⲓⲁⲛ ⲙⲁ⳼ Ꞃⲩⲁⲓⲇꞃⲓ
Ⲙⲓ⳼ Ⲇⲓⲁꞃⲙⲁⲇⲁ ⲁꞃ ⲥⳑⲟⲓⲛⲛ Ⳑⲟⲉⲓꞃꞃⲓ⳵ ⲙⲓ⳼ ⲆhⲩⳠ⳵ⲁⲓⳑⳑ ⲁⲛ
ⲃⳑⲓⲁⲇⲁⲓⲛ ꞃⲓⲛ.   Ⲥꞃⲉ⳼ ⲉⳑⲓ ⳑⲉ Ѕⲓⲩꞃⲧⲁⲛ ⲙⲃⲩⲓⳠⲉ ⲙⲁ⳼ Ѕⲉⲁⲓⲛ
ⲙⲓ⳼ Ⳡhⲁⲓⲧⲉꞃ ó ⳼ⲩⲓⲇ ⲇⲟ ⳟⲩⲓⲛⲛⲧⲓꞃ ⲙⲓ⳼ Ⲙⲓ⳼ Ⲇⲓⲁꞃⲙⲁⲇⲁ .ⲓ.
Ⳡꞃⲓⲁⲛ, ⲟⲥⲩꞃ ⲛⲓꞃ ⲃⲟ ⳵ⲩⲓⲛ ⳵ⲁⲛ ⳼ⲩⲙⲁⲟⲓⲛ ꞃⲓⲛ.   Ⲟ Ⳡꞃⲓⲁⲛ ⲇ⳵ⲉⲥ
.ⲓ. Ⲇⲟⲛⲛⳡⲁⲇ ⲙⲁ⳼ Ⳡⲟⲛⳡⲟⲃⲁⲓꞃ .ⲓ. ꞃⲟ⳵ⲁ ⳵ⲁⲟⲓⲇⲉⳑ Ⲑꞃⲉⲛⲛ.
Ⳡⲓⲛ⳵ Ⲉⲇⲃⲟꞃⲇ .ⲓ. ꞃꞃⲓⲟⲛⲛꞃⲁ Ѕⲁ⳵ꞃⲁⲛ ⲟⲥⲩꞃ Ⲉꞃⲉⲛⲛ, [ⲇⲟ éⲥ]
ⲓⲁꞃ ⲙⲃⲉⲓⳠ ⲟⳡⲧ ⳑⲁ ⲟⲥⲩꞃ ⲟⳡⲧ ⲙí ⲟⲥⲩꞃ ꞃⲉ ⲃⳑⲓⲁⲇⲛⲁ ⲛⲁ
Ⳡⲓ⳵ⲉꞃⲛⲁ Ⳡⲟ, ⲟⲥⲩꞃ ⲁⲛ ꞃⲉⲓꞃꞃⲉⳠ ⳑⲁ ⲇⲟ ⲙí ⳟⲉⳠⲟⲓⲛ ⲧ꞉ⲁⲙ꞉ꞃⲁⳠ
ꞃⲩꞃ ⲇⲉⲁⳑⲁⲓ⳵ ⲁⲛⲁⲙ ⲟⲥⲩꞃ ⲥⲟꞃꞃ ꞃⲉ ꞃⲟⲓⳑⲉ ⲁⲓ⳵ⲉ; ⲟⲥⲩꞃ ꞃé
ⲃⳑⲓⲁⲇⲛⲁ ꞃⲟⲓⲙⲉ ꞃⲓⲛ ꞃⲩꞃ ⲧⲟꞃⳡⲁⲓꞃ ⲁ ⲁⳡⲁⲓꞃ .ⲓ. ⲥⲓⲛ⳵ hⲁⲛⲛ-
ꞃⲁⲟⲓ; ⲛⲁⲟⲓ ⲙⲃⳑⲓⲁⲇⲛⲁ ⲟⲥⲩꞃ ⲥⲉⲓⲧꞃⲓ ⲥⲉⲇ ó Ⳡⲁⲓⲛⲓⲥ ⲓⲁꞃⳑⲁ Ⲟ
Ѕⲇꞃⲁⲛ⳵ⲃⲟ ⳵ⲟ hⲈꞃⲓⲛⲛ, ⲟⲥⲩꞃ ⲟⳡⲧ ⲙⲃⳑⲓⲁⲇⲛⲁ ⲉⲇⲓꞃ ꞃⲓⲛ

1 *Posterity of Maelsechlainn Donn.*
A branch of the Mac Dermots of Moy-
Lurg.

2 *Hoc.* oc, MS.

3 *Killed.* ⲁ ⲇⲓ⳵ꞃ. (for ⲁ ⲇⲓ⳵hⲩⲓⲛ),
MS. This is not the way in which
the word ⲇⲓ⳵ⲩⲓⲛ is usually abbre-
viated; but the orthography of this
portion of the MS. is very loose.

4 *Jordan Buidhe;* i.e. Jordan the
Yellow [Mac Goisdelbh, or Mac Cos-
tello].

5 *A wound without retaliation.* ⳵ⲩⲓⲛ
⳵ⲁⲛ ⳼ⲩⲙⲁⲟⲓⲛ. This expression is
in the nature of a proverb. The
next entry is in the handwriting of
Brian Mac Dermot.

6 *Nine years.* This calculation is

which were twelve hundred cows, vel amplius, were taken from the posterity of Maelsechlainn Donn.[1] On the night of the festival of the Cross these depredations were committed. Maelruanaidh, the son of Ruaidhri Mac Diarmada, i.e. the most illustrious prince of his age for hospitality, nobility, and prowess, was killed with a gun shot by his own kinsman, i.e. Tadhg, the son of Eoghan Mac Diarmada, in hoc[2] anno. However, no good that the person then killed could do would be excessive, as there was not in the province of Connacht a son of a better father and mother in every good quality; for extent of munificence, generosity, and lordship; for hospitality, clemency, bounty, and charity—viz., Ruaidhri, son of Tadhg, son of Ruairdhri Og, and Sadhbh, the daughter of Rickard Og, son of Ulick Ruadh, son of Ulick-an fhina. Nevertheless, Mac Diarmada made peace soon after his son's death, though it grieved him that he should have been killed[3] by his own friends and relations. A great depredation was committed this year by Brian, the son of Ruaidhri Mac Diarmada, on the sons of Laisech Mac Dubhgaill. Another prey *was taken* by Jordan Buidhe,[4] the son of John, son of Walter, from the people of Mac Diarmada's son (i.e. Brian); and that was not a wound without retaliation.[5] O'Briain died, i.e. Donnchadh, the son of Conchobhar, i.e. the choice of the Gaeidhel of Erinn. King Edward, i.e. Prince of the Saxons and of Erinn, [died] after having been king six years, and eight months, and eight days; and the sixth day of July his soul and body separated from one another; and six years before that his father, i.e. King Henry, died. (Four hundred and nine years[6] since Earl Strongbow came to Erinn, and eight years[7] between that and his death: and it was

---

of course inaccurate, if based on the year of Edward's demise, as Strongbow (or the Earl O'Strangbo, as his name has been written by Brian Mac Dermot), came to Ireland in A.D. 1170.

But the writer probably reckoned from the year 1579, when he may have actually penned the entry.

[7] *Eight years;* ocht mbliadna; repeated in MS.

ocuṗ a éȝ; ocuṗ iṗṗé anc iaṗla ṗin cáinic le Ⴃiaṗmaiⴃ
ⴅac ⴅuṗċaⴃa ȝo ⴘeiṗinn, ocuṗ cuc ṗé a inȝen ocuṗ
cúiⴃ ⴃa ⴏuċaiⴃ ⴃó. Ⴅomalcaċ mac ⴅhaoilṗuanaiⴃ
meic Coṗmaic ⴅic Ⴃiaṗmaⴃa ⴃo maṗⴃaⴃ le clainn
Ⴄoȝain ⴅic Ⴃiaṗmaⴃa, ocuṗ le Ⴄiúṗcan mbuiⴃe mac
Ⴄeain meic Uaceṗ, a ṗeall aiṗ Luinȝ Ꞇiṗc[iȝ] uċclea-
ⴅain. Ⴅaⴃȝ mac Ruaiⴃṗi 1 Choṁⴃain, .i. ollam Ⴄṗenn
ocuṗ Ꞇlban ṗe ṗinm, ⴃeȝ. Inȝen 1 Ⴃomnaill .i. Ⴄiuan,
.i. in ben ⴃo ⴃí aȝ Ⴅaⴃȝ mac Caċail óiȝ, ⴃhec.

Ꞁcc. Ⴄnaiṗ ṗoṗ Ꞇóine; ceicṗi bliaⴃna ⴃhec ocuṗ ⴃá
ṗiċec, cuiȝ ceⴃ ocuṗ mile aoiṗ an Ⴅiȝeṗna. Cṗeċ
ṁóṗ ⴃo ⴃenum ⴃo clainn ⴅic Ⴃiaṗmaⴃa aṗ Ⴄiuṗcán
mbuiⴃi mac Ⴄeain mic ⴁhaiceṗ ⴅic Ȝoiṗⴃealⴃ. Ꞇl-
banaiȝ ocuṗ ȝallóȝlaeⴅ ⴃ ṗaṗⴃó ⴃon ⴕloinn ceⴃna ṗin
ⴅic Ⴃiaṗmaⴃa. Ⴃún Ⴄeill ocuṗ an Ȝṗainṗeċ ⴃeȝ ⴃo
cṗeⴅaⴃ ⴃo Choṗmac ⴅac Ⴃiaṗmaⴃa, ocuṗ ⴁṗían ⴃo
ⴃul aṗ ṗliċc Conċobaiṗ ⴅhéȝ Raȝnaill, ocuṗ cṗeⴅaⴃ
ocuṗ maṗbca ⴃo ȝenum ⴃó oṗṗa, ocuṗ an cíṗ ⴃo loṗcaⴃ
aċcmaⴃ beȝ. O ⴕlannaȝáin cona ċineⴃ ⴃo ⴅaⴃaiṗc
inṗṗoiȝeⴃ aṗ ⴁhṗían mac ⴅic Ⴃiaṗmaⴃa ṗiaṗ ȝo
hioṗⴅán, muṗ aṗaiⴃe cuiⴃ ⴃá ṁuinciṗ, ocuṗ ní ⴅaṗla
ⴃéⴃail ṗiú aċc míaṗṗa ocuṗ caiṗliṗṗ ⴁṗíain. Ⴅéiⴃ
na ṗȝéla ṗin ȝo ⴁṗían, ocuṗ ⴃo ⴃí ṗé ṗeⴃan cṗuinn aṗ
Ⴄȝiaⴅ na bṗeṗc mun am ṗin. Ro len Ⴅomalcaċ mac
Ⴅaiⴃȝ ⴅic Ⴃiaṗmaⴃa, ocuṗ ⴁṗían ocuṗ ṗliċc inȝine
ⴅhéȝ Raȝnuill na miaṗṗa ṗin, ocuṗ an caiṗliṗ; ocuṗ
cucaⴃaṗ ⴃá ṗiċic ⴃhec bó o ⴃel Ꞇⴅa ioṁⴃáin a
nⴃíȝuil na caiṗliṗṗi. Ro cṗeaⴅṗac muinceṗ ⴕhlanna-
ȝáin clainn an ṗeṗṗúin ⴅic ⴅhuiṗȝeṗṗa aṗ ⴃuaile

---

1 *Tomaltach.* This and the two following entries are in Brian Mac
Dermot's handwriting.

2 *Jordan Buidhe.* See note 4, p. 362.

3 *Lung - Airtigh - uchtleathain;* lit.,
"the *lung* (ship) of Airtech of the
wide breast;" now the river Lung,
which flows through the district of
Airtech [the parish of Tibohine, co.
Roscommon], and discharges itself
into Loch-Gara, co. Sligo. With
regard to the ancient limits of the
district of Airtech, see O'Donovan's
Four Mast., A.D. 1228, n. *.

this Earl that came to Erinn with Diarmaid Mac Murchadha, who gave him his daughter, and a part of his territory). Tomaltach,[1] the son of Maelruanaidh, son of Cormac Mac Diarmada, was killed by the sons of Eoghan Mac Diarmada, and by Jordan Buidhe,[2] son of John, son of Walter, in treachery, on Lung-Airtigh-uchtleathain.[3] Tadhg, son of Ruaidhri O'Comhdhain, i.e. the ollamh[4] of Erinn and Alba in music, died. O'Domhnaill's daughter, i.e. Sivan, i.e. the wife of Tadhg,[5] son of Cathal Og, died.

The kalends of January on Friday ;[6] the age of the Lord one thousand, five hundred, and fifty-four years. A great depredation was committed by the sons of Mac Diarmada on Jordan Buidhe,[2] the son of John, son of Walter Mac Goisdelbh. Albanachs and gallowglasses were retained by the same sons of Mac Diarmada. Dún-Neill and the Grainsech-beg were pillaged by Cormac Mac Diarmada; and Brian went against the descendants of Conchobhar Mag Raghnaill, and committed depredations and murders upon them, and burned nearly the entire country. O'Flannagáin, with his kindred, advanced against Brian, the son of Mac Diarmada, westwards to hIorchán, where some of his people were; but they got no spoils except Brian's dishes and chess-board.[7] The news of this reached Brian, who was with a compact band on Sgiath-na-bfert at that time. Tomaltach, the son of Tadhg Mac Diarmada, and Brian, and the descendants of Mag Raghnaill's daughter,[8] followed those dishes and the chess-board; and they brought twelve score cows from Bel-atha-Iomdháin, in retaliation for the chess-board. Muinter-Flannagáin preyed the sons of the Parson Mac Maurice on Buaile-ant-soilchéin, whilst they were under

---

[4] *Ollamh;* pron. *ollave;* i.e. chief doctor, or professor.

[5] *Tadhg;* i.e. Tadhg O'Conor Sligo. His death is the first entry under the year 1552.

[6] *Friday. Recte,* Monday.

[7] *Chess-board.* ᴄᴀɪᴘʟɪ‑; doubtless a corrupt form of the English word "tables," and usually signifying a backgammon (or chess) board.

[8] *Mac Raghnaill's daughter.* See note [3], p. 360.

αητ ϝοιλċéιη, οcυϝ ιαꝺ αϝ· cαḃυϝ hι Conchoḃαιϝ ḃυιηη
ḃοι ηα coṁḃαλτα αcα; οcυϝ ϝο ḃόι τϝι cεꝺ ḃó co ḃϝυιλ-
λιυḃ ιϝιη ϝϝειċ ϝιη cοηα ηꝺιολλ cαϝαλλ. Ταꝺ₅ mαc
Rυαιꝺϝι ḃυιḃε, οcυϝ Ḃϝιαη mαc Mαοιλϝεchλαιηη ꝺυιηꝺ,
ꝺο ṁαϝḃαḃ λειϝ Ο ϝλαηηα₅αιη, .ι. Εmαηꝺ mαc Uιλλιαm
ι ϝλαηηα₅αιηꝺ ꝺο ϝοιηꝺε αη mαϝḃαḃ. Ḃαιλε ηα hυαṁα
ꝺο ċιοηϝ₅ηα λε Ḃϝιαη mαc Rυαιꝺϝι Mιc Ꝺιαϝmαꝺα, ιαϝ
ηα ḃϝιϝεḃ ϝοιmε ϝιη ꝺΟ Ꝺοmηαιλλ, οιϝ ꝺο ḃαιη ϝε τϝι
cεαċϝυηα αϝ.

Ḳττ. Εηαιϝ ϝοϝ ϝαċοϝη; υ. ḃλιαꝺηα ꝺ‎héc οcυϝ ꝺá
ϝιċhετ, οcυϝ cυι₅ cεꝺ οcυϝ mιλε, αοιϝ αη Τι₅εϝηα.
Cλαηη Rυαιꝺϝι Mιc Ꝺιαϝmαꝺα ꝺο ḃυλ αϝ ιηηϝοι₅εꝺ α
₅Cϝυċοηη Ο Mαιηε, ϝλúα₅ ꝺοáιϝṁε, .ι. Coϝmαc οcυϝ
Ḃϝíαη, οcυϝ τυcαꝺαϝ cϝεċα móϝα λεο, οcυϝ ϝο λοιϝcτετ
αη τιϝ ₅ο hυιλιḃε; οcυϝ ταη₅οꝺαϝ ₅ο ϝυαϝαη Mhοι₅ε
hΟι α ḃϝοϝλοη₅ϝοϝτ αη α₅hαιꝺ ϝιη. Rο ₅αḃ ₅αλυϝ α
é₅α Coϝmαc mαc Rυαιꝺϝι mιc Ꝺιαϝmαꝺα αη οιḃċε ϝιη,
οcυϝ ϝυαιϝ ḃαϝϝ α ₅cιηη τϝεαchτṁυιηε αϝϝ α hαιċλε ;
οcυϝ ꝺο ḃυꝺ ꝺο ϝ₅έλαιḃ móϝα Connαchτ αη mαc ϝιη Mιc
Ꝺιαϝmαꝺα αλλειċ υαιϝλε οcυϝ ιηηϝοι₅τε, οιηι₅ οcυϝ οιϝ-
ḃεϝτα. Cαthαλ ό₅ mαc Εο₅αιη Mιc Ꝺιαϝmαꝺα ꝺϝα₅αιλ
ḃαιϝ, οcυϝ ꝺο ḃυꝺ móϝ αη ϝ₅ελ ϝιη. Co₅αꝺ ḃειϝ₅ε
ετιϝ ċλαιηη Εο₅αιη Mιc Ꝺιαϝmαꝺα οcυϝ Mαc Ꝺιαϝmαꝺα cοηα ċλαιηη. Mαιηιϝτιϝ ηα Ḃυιλλε ꝺο ₅αḃαιλ ꝺο
Ḃϝíαη mαc Mιc Ꝺιαϝmαꝺα αϝ cλαιηη Εο₅αιη, οcυϝ αḃ
ηα Ḃυιλλε ꝺο ₅αḃαιλ αηη .ι. Τοmαλταch mαc Εο₅αιη
Mιc Ꝺhιαϝmαꝺα. Ɲιϝ ḃο cιαη ꝺοιḃ ιαϝ ϝιη ₅υϝϝο
λοιϝcεꝺ αη ḃαιλε cεꝺηα αϝ Ḃϝíαη λε cλαιηη Εο₅αιη Mιc
Ꝺιαϝmαꝺα, οcυϝ ϝυιcϝατ ϝεαchτ ηειċ λεο. Τειꝺ Ḃϝíαη
ϝο ηα Rεηηαιḃ ꝺοϝιḃιϝ, οcυϝ τυc τϝι ϝιċιτ cαϝολλ λαιϝ,
οcυϝ ϝο ₅αḃ Mυιϝchεϝταch ο₅ Ο Mαοιλεηαι₅. Rο cϝεċ

---

¹ *Of horses.* capall=caballus,
Fr. cheval. The next entry is in
Brian Mac Dermot's hand.

² *Tadhg—Brian.* Members of the
Mac Dermot family.

³ *Out of it.* This entry is added at
the bottom of a page, in the hand of
Brian Mac Dermot, with the note

"cυιϝ ϝιη λειϝ αη cαλλαιηꝺ ϝιη
τυαϝ; "add this to that kalend
above" [i.e. the year 1554].

⁴ *The Rinns;* i.e. "the Points."
This name, formerly applied to a district containing 15 quarters of land,
is still preserved in that of Rinn, a
townland in the parish of Ardcarne,

the protection of O'Conchobhair Donn, who was their foster-brother; and there were three hundred cows, and more, in this prey, with a proportionate number of horses.[1] Tadhg,[2] the son of Ruaidhri Buidhe, and Brian,[2] son of Maelechlainn Donn, were killed by O'Flannagain; i.e. Edmond, the son of William O'Flannagain, that committed the homicides. Baile-na-huama was begun by Brian, the son of Ruaidhri Mac Diarmada, after it had previously been demolished by O'Domhnaill, for he took three quarters out of it.[3]

The kalends of January on Saturday; the age of the Lord one thousand, five hundred, and fifty-five years. The sons of Ruaidhri Mac Diarmada, viz., Cormac and Brian, went on an expedition into Cruthonn-O'Maine, with an immense army; and they brought large preys with them, and burned the country entirely. And they came to Fuaran-Maighe-hOi, where they encamped that night. His mortal illness seized Cormac, the son of Ruaidhri Mac Diarmada, that night, and he died in the course of a week afterwards: and this son of Mac Diarmada was of the celebrities of Connacht as regards nobility and daring, bounty and prowess. Cathal Og, the son of Eoghan Mac Diarmada, died; and that was a great calamity. A war broke out between the sons of Eoghan Mac Diarmada, and Mac Diarmada with his sons. The monastery of the Buill was taken by Brian, the son of Mac Diarmada, against the sons of Eoghan; and the abbot of the Buill was captured there, i.e. Tomaltach, the son of Eoghan Mac Diarmada. It was not long after that until the same place was burned against Brian, by the sons of Eoghan Mac Diarmada, who carried away seven horses. Brian went again towards the Rinns[4]; and he brought sixty horses[5] with him, and apprehended Muirchertach Og O'Maelenaigh. He plundered Coill-Feachtna in like

---

in the barony of Boyle, and county of Roscommon.

[5] *Horses.* capoll. See note [1], last page.

coill feachtna muη an ceona; ocuη τéιο Uηían mac
Eoζαιn Mιc Oιαηmαοα αη láιṁ Mιc Oιαηmαοα le na
ὃηειτ ηéιn οο ηιτ ocuη οο ηειτech, a hαιτle αη mιlleο
eτoηηα οιὃlιonαιὃ. O flannaζαιn οο ταιηηιnζ clαιnnι
Oιleηeη mιc an ιαηlα ocuη ṁιc hÍ feηζαιl ὃuιὃι .ι.
Loeιηech O feηζαιl. Cnτ ηochαιοe τηom ηιn οο τeachτ
aη Mac nOιαηmαοα, ocuη ηζemeαlτα οο leιζιon uαthα
no co ηαnζαοαη τochuη an cáḃα. Mac Oιαηmαοα ocuη
a mac .ι. Uηιan οο ὃειτh a noιηeητ Núὃαn mun αm ηιn.
Ζαὃáιl οóιὃ ocuη na hαιηζτe οο ὃuαιn amach οο c. neιὃιὃ
οóιὃ. Uηιηηeο aη an ηlúαζ aηη a hαιτle, acuη mαιὃm
οο ὃειτ οηηα ó ατ ṁαηὃτα Cathαιl ζο bél Cτα uachταιη;
áη οιáιηṁe οηáζὃáιl οóιὃ um mac Í feηζαιl .ι. Loαηηech,
ocuη um mac mαιτ Í fhlannaζαιn .ι. Emonn óζ mac
Emuιnn mιc Uιllιam Í fhlannaζáιn, ocuη um ceο
ηeη ζo ηuιllιuο mαιlle ηιú. Oοṁnαll mac Mhαoιl-
ηechluιnn hÍ Cheallαιζh οηαζαιl ὃáιη a ζcαιηlén an
ṁαζα,.ι. aon ηοζα ηleachτα Mαιne mιc Echach αlleιτ
oιnιζ ocuη aὃὃčloηηα, ocuη a áὃnocαl a Ροη Chomáιn.
Emonn buιὃe mac Τomaιη ὃαcαιζ a ὃuηc οο τuιτιm le
clαιnn Oιluéηuη a ὃúηc, ocuη Eoιn mac Ohuιηηιτ οο
τuιτιm mαιlle ηιη. 8ean ζlαηη mac hÍ Ohuὃοα
οηαζαιl ὃáιη an ὃlιαοαιn ηι. 8ean mac an ηηιόηα Mιc
Oháὃιτ οéζ. Mac Ζοιηοeαlὃ .ι. ηíαηuη οο ṁαηὃαο οο
τuιο οια ὃηáιτηιὃ ηηeιn a bηoll a ζcαιηlén Manuιnne.
Meαοhὃ ιnζen Oomnαιll mιc Eoζαιn Í Chončuὃαιη
οhec, ιn ben ι[η] ηeηη οο bιτ a nEηιnn na hamηιη ηeιn.
Cοὃ mac Eoζαιn mιc Conchuḃαιη mιc Ruαιοηι buιὃe
οhec.

Ktt. Enαιη ηoη Oomnach; ηé blιαοnα οhec
ocuη οα ηιcheτ .u. ceο ocuη mιle αιη an Τιζeηna.

---

1 *Oliver.* This was probably Oliver
Fitzgerald, fourth son of Gerald,
eighth Earl of Kildare, by his second
wife, and one of the five brothers
executed, with their nephew, Silken
Thomas, in 1536.

2 *Ath-marbtha-Cathail;* "the ford
of the killing of Cathal."

3 *Bel-útha-uachtair;* "the mouth
of upper ford." This was the name
of O'Flannagain's residence, in the co.
Roscommon.

manner; and Brian, son of Eoghan Mac Diarmada, placed himself in Mac Diarmada's hands, consenting to accept peace and an arrangement according to his own award, after all that had been destroyed between them both. O'Flannagain invited the sons of Oliver,[1] son of the Earl, and the son of O'Ferghail Buidhe, i.e. Laisech O'Ferghail. This heavy army went against Mac Diarmada; and they sent out scouting parties who went as far as Tochar-an-caba. Mac Diarmada and his son, i.e. Brian, were at Disert-Nuadhan at that time. They attacked, and recovered the herds of all kinds. The army was afterwards defeated, and routed from Athmarbtha-Cathail[2] to Bel-átha-uachtair.[3] They left a countless slaughter, including the son of O'Ferghail, i.e. Laisech, and the good son of O'Flannagain, i.e. Edmond Og, son of Edmond, son of William O'Flannagain, and more than one hundred men along with them. Domhnall, son of Maelsechlainn O'Cellaigh, i.e. the choicest of the race of Maine, son of Eochaidh, as regards bounty and renown, died in the castle of the Magh, and was interred in Ros-Comáin. Edmond Buidhe, the son of Thomas Bacagh Burk, fell by the sons of Oliver Burk; and John Mac Duibhsith fell along with him. John Glas, the son of O'Dubhda, died this year. John, son of the Prior Mac David, died. Mac Goisdelbh, i.e. Piers, was killed by some of his own kinsmen, in treachery, in the castle of Manuinn.[4] Medhbh, daughter of Domhnall, son of Eoghan O'Conchobhair, the best woman that was in Erinn in her own time, died. Aedh, son of Eoghan, son of Conchobhar, son of Ruaidhri Buidhe,[5] died.

The kalends of January on Sunday.[6] The age of the Lord one thousand, five hundred, and fifty-six years.

---

[4] *Manuinn.* Now Mannin, bar. of Costello, co. Mayo. The two following entries are in the handwriting of Brian Mac Dermot.

[5] *Ruaidhri Buidhe.* "Ruaidhri (or Rory) the Yellow;" one of the family of Mac Dermot.

[6] *Sunday. Recté* Wednesday.

O Conċubair donn .i. Diarmaid mac Cairbri, ocus mac Diarmada .i. Ruaidri, ocus Tomaltach Mac Diarmada, ocus Brian mac Mic Diarmada, do ḋul sluag mor ar an bPopal gcaoċ; ocus ni hétir a riom gach anderrnsat do creċaiḃ ocus do loiscṫib, ocus a tucsad dédail léo. An coimṫinól cedna do dul ar O Ruairc .i. Brian mac Eogain I Ruairc, ocus creċa mora do tabairt ó Mhullaċ Ṫuir, ocus o Ġlend buiḋi ḋoiḃ; ocus an Breifne do loscud co huiliḋi. Diarmaid O Maeilenaiġ dhéc in hoc anno. Forlungpor[t] do ġenaṁ [do] Doṁnall mac Taiḋg mic Cathail óig ar in Ġrainsiġ, ocus Semus mac Seain mic Ruaidri ocus a mac do tabairt ar an mbaile, ocus braiġde sleachta Briain do breṫ as in baile.

Kll. Enair for [Aoine]; seacht mbliadna dhéc ocus dá fichet, cuig céd ocus mile, ais an Tigerna. Brian mac Eogain mic Thaiḋg Mic Diarmada do ṁarbad le Mag Shaṁraḋain, ocus le cuid do ṡlicht Tomaltaiġ an oiniġ Mic Diarmada, do ṫairing ocus do ṫórcnaḋ a nionnsoiġed; ocus robud mór an sgél an té rus torchair annsin, óir is terc ma ḋo ḃói fer a aossa is mó ro ḟoirbir ocus ro ṫiḋluic deiceriḃ ocus dollamnaiḃ, ocus do lucht iarrata aṫċuinnge. Cogad mor deirġe etir O Ceallaiġ .i. Donnchad mac Emuinn ocus Brian mac Mhaoilsechlainn I Cheallaiġ, ocus ro ḟasdó Brían dolaiḃ .i. Risderd Usdár, cetra fichit giomanach. Ro loisced lios dá lon lais .i. baile I Cheallaiġ, ocus ro marbad a ċonsabal lais .i. mac Duḃġaill .i. Toirrdhealbach mac Loeiriġ Mic Duḃġaill, ocus ro milled an tir o Shuca co Sionuinn. Cuirir O Ceallaiġ tairing ar clainn Cathail mic Ruaidri Mic Diarmada,

[1] *Pobal-caech*; i.e. "populus cæcus;" otherwise written Pobal-in-chaich, or "populus cæci;" the name of a district lying around Clonbrock and Clogher, in the barony of Kilconnell, and county of Galway.

[2] *Hoc*. oc, MS.

[3] *Cathal Og*. O'Conor Sligo. This entry is in Brian Mac Dermot's handwriting.

[4] *James*. A member of the family O'Conor Sligo.

O'Conchobhair Donn, i.e. Diarmaid, the son of Cairbre, and Mac Diarmada, i.e. Ruaidhri, and Tomaltach Mac Diarmada, and Brian, son of Mac Diarmada, went with a great army upon the Pobal-caech,[1] and all the depredations and burnings they committed, and the spoils they brought with them, cannot be reckoned. The same assemblage went against O'Ruairc, i.e. Brian the son of Eoghan O'Ruairc, and brought great preys from Mullach-thuir, and from Glenn-buidhe; and they entirely burned the Breifne. Diarmaid O'Maelenaigh died in hoc[2] anno. An encampment was made [by] Domhnall, the son of Tadhg, son of Cathal Og,[3] against the Grainsech; and he brought James,[4] the son of John, son of Ruaidhri, and his son, out of the place; and he brought the hostages of the Slicht-Briain[5] out of the place.

The kalends of January on [Friday]; the age of the Lord one thousand, five hundred, and fifty-seven years. Brian, the son of Eoghan, son of Tadhg Mac Diarmada, was killed by Mag Samhradhain, and by some of the descendants of Tomaltach-an-einigh Mac Diarmada, who invited and procured their advance;[6] and the person who was then slain was a great loss, for there was hardly a man of his age who gave and presented more to poets and professors, and to persons soliciting requests. A great war arose between O'Cellaigh, i.e. Donnchadh son of Edmond, and Brian son of Maelsechlainn O'Cellaigh; and Brian retained a band, i.e. Richard Eustace and four score mercenaries. Lis-dá-lon, i.e. O'Cellaigh's residence, was burned by him,[7] and his constable, i.e. Mac Dubhgaill, i.e. Toirdhelbhach, the son of Laisech Mac Dubhgaill, was killed by him,[7] and the country from the Suca to the Sinainn was injured. O'Cellaigh sends an invitation to the sons of Cathal, son of Ruaidhri Mac

---

[5] *Slicht-Briain*; i.e. the descendants of Brian [O'Conor], the ancestor of sept of O'Conor Sligo.

[6] *Their advance*; i.e. the advance of Mag Samhradhain's forces.

[7] *By him*; i.e. by Brian O'Cellaigh.

VOL. II.

2 B 2

ocur ap Ruaιopι na ocυlán mac Oιapmaoa mιc
Oιapmaoa .ι. a bráιčpecha péιn, ocur cιзιο oon cιp
mapcplύaз móp. Ocur éιpξιp O Ceallaιξ ocur a mac .ι.
Cαoŏ a зcuιnne na peŏnach, ocur cιaξaιo an comŏáιl oo
čnoc an Oaιnзιn ocur oo ŏóchap na caĉalcaιξ. Ocur po
buaιleŏ bpιan O Ceallaιξ ocur ιao péιn pá čélι, ocur
cιιcaoap cpoιo oápoιle; ocur po bpιιppeŏ ap bhpíaιn,
ocur po mapbao Concobap O Nechcaιn ocur pιĉe ouιne
maιlle pιppιn; ocur po зabao Rιpoepo Upoap. Cpeĉ
móp oo ξenum oo bpιáιn mac Ruaιopι mιc Oιapmaoa
ap mac зoιpoealŏ, ocur Cυlaĉ ppuĉáιn oo Iopcaŏ.
Cóιp mop oo ŏpeŏ aιp, ocur a čochc plán éŏalaĉ aιp
eιзιn uacha. mac Oιapmaoa .ι. Ruaιopι oo ξaŏáιl oía
čapaιo péιn зo nemmaιŏ .ι. bpían mac Mhaoιleĉlaιnn
hι Cheallaιξ; ocur oo зabao ann Coιppohealbach
mac Eoзaιn mιc Oιapmaoa, ocur cuιo oιa mapcpluaιз
maιlle pιu. Ccchc chena nιp ŏó cpeĉ зan cóιp an
ξaŏáιl pιn mιc Oιapmaoa ó na čapuιo ocur ó na
mυιnncιp peιppιn. Ro len O Conchobaιp oonn ocur
mac Oáŏιŏ, ocur зalloзlaech claιnnι Ouŏξaιll, mac
Oιapmaoa зo maιnechaιŏ a зcιonn cpι noιŏĉe ιap
ná ξaŏáιl, ocur po ŏenpac app caιpplén nua Coŏ-
chaιξ hι Phallamuιn ap éιзιn hé; ocur oo pιnneoap
mapŏca oaur loιpĉι ann, ocur cιιcaoap cpíap bpáξao
ap mac Oιapmaoa oeзla a loιpĉe ιp ιn mbaιle; ocur
nι oépnaŏ a noepeŏ aιmpιpe cópaιξechc buŏ pepp
ιná an cópaιξechc pιn. In зιlla Coluιm O Cláŏaιξ .ι.
comapba Paopaιcc ap maξ Cóι .ι. pep coιccech cpom
ĉonáιξ cιξe aoιŏeŏ coιcĉιnn, ohec ιn hoc anno.

Ccll. Enaιp pop maιpc; ochc mblιaona ohec ocur oa

<hr />

1 *Ruaidhri-na-dtulán.* "Ruaidhri
(Rory) of the *tuláns*," (i.e. hillocks, or
mounds).

2 *Kinsmen.* bráιĉpecha. This word
is also used to signify "brothers."

3 *The Mainechs;* i.e. the inhabitants of Ui-Maine (O'Kelly's country),

in the counties of Galway and Roscommon.

4 *New castle.* Apparently the castle
of Milltown, in the parish of Dysart,
barony of Athlone, county of Roscommon, where Cobhthach O'Fallamhain
(pron. Covagh O'Fallon) lived in the

Diarmada, and to Ruaidhri-na-dtulán,[1] son of Diarmaid Mac Diarmada, i.e. his own kinsmen;[2] and they come into the country with a large force of cavalry. And O'Cellaigh and his son, i.e. Aedh, go to meet the force; and the whole assemblage proceeds by Cnoc-an-daingin, and by Bothar-na-tachaltaigh. And Brian O'Cellaigh and they met; and they gave battle to each other, and Brian was defeated; and Conchobhar O'Nechtain was killed, and twenty men along with him; and Richard Eustace was taken prisoner. A great depredation was committed by Brian, son of Ruaidhri Mac Diarmada, upon Mac Goisdelbh; and he burned Tulach-srutháin. A large pursuing band overtook him, and he escaped safely from them, by force, loaded with spoils. Mac Diarmada, i.e. Ruaidhri, was wickedly apprehended by his own friend, i.e. Brian, the son of Maelechlainn O'Cellaigh; and Toirdhelbhach, son of Eoghan Mac Diarmada, was taken prisoner there, and some of their cavalry along with them. This capture of Mac Diarmada, however, was not a depredation without pursuit on the part of his own friends and people. O'Conchobhair Donn, Mac David, and the gallowglasses of Clann-Dubhgaill, followed Mac Diarmada to the Mainechs,[3] before the end of three nights after his capture, and forcibly took him out of Cobhthach O'Fallamhain's new castle;[4] and they committed homicides and burnings there; and they gave three hostages for Mac Diarmada, through fear of his being burned in the place: and there was no pursuit conducted in later times better than that pursuit. The Gilla-Coluim O'Clabaigh, i.e. the comarb of Patrick on Magh-Ai,[5] i.e. a rich, opulent man, who kept a general house of hospitality, died in hoc anno.

The kalends of January on Tuesday;[6] the age of the [1558.]

---

year 1585. See O'Donovan's *Tribes and Customs of Hy-Many*, p. 19.

[5] *Magh-Ai*. The Four Mast., who have his obit under the year 1556, say that Gilla-Coluim O'Clabaigh was comarb (successor) of Patrick in

" Uaran-Maighc-hOi," i.e. Oran, barony of Ballymoe, co. Roscommon.

[6] *Tuesday*. This is wrong; for, as the Dominical Letter for the year is B, the first of January must have fallen on a Saturday.

ꝼιcheꞇ, ocuꞃ cuιꞅ ceꞇ ocuꞃ mιle, aιꞃ an Ꞇιꞅeꞃna. mac
Ɗιαꞃmαꞃα ocuꞃ a mac .ι. bꞃían ꞃo ꞅul aꞃ ιnꞃoιꞅeꞃ
aꞃ bꞃιán O Ceallαιꞡ. mac Ɗιαꞃmαꞃα ocuꞃ bun anꞇ
ꞃlúαιꞅ ꞃaιꞁuιn a mbaιle an ꞁuιlιnn. Ꞇeιꞃ bꞃían
ocuꞃ an čuιꞃ elι ꞃonꞇ ꞃlúαιꞡ ꞇaꞃ bꞃuιꞡél aꞃꞇeč, ocuꞃ
ꞇuc cꞃeč ocuꞃ ꞅꞃoιꞃ Choꞟchaιꞅh ꞁ ꝼhallαꞁaιn leιꞃ. Ɗo
chuaιꞃ ꞃuaꞃ a ꞇeιꞇheꞃ ocuꞃ ꞃo loιꞃc an ꞇíꞃ ꞅo huιlιꞟe
o bhꞃuιꞡél ꞃuaꞃ; ocuꞃ ꞇιꞅιꞃ ꞃ'lán éꞃalach. baιle hι
Choιnčenaιnn ꞃo čꞃečαꞟ ocuꞃ ꞃo loꞃcaꞃ le bꞃιan mac
Ɗιαꞃmαꞃα maꞃ an ceꞃna .ꞏ. an ꝼeꞃan.

Ｋꞇꞇ. enaιꞃ ꞃoꞃ Ceꞃaoιn; naoι mbliaꞃna ꞃhec ocuꞃ
ꞃa ꞃιcheꞇ ocuꞃ u. ceꞃ ocuꞃ mιle aιꞃ an Ꞇιꞅeꞃna. O
Conchobaιꞃ ꞃuaꞃ, .ι. Ꞇoιꞃꞃꞃhealbach ꞃuaꞃh mac Ꞇaιꞟꞅ
ꞟuιꞟe mιc Caꞇhaιl ꞃuaιꞃh, moꞃꞇuuꞃ eꞃꞇ; ocuꞃ ꞃo buꞏ
ꞃo ꞃꞅélaιꞟ moꞃa Θꞃenn na aιmꞃιꞃ é; ocuꞃ a mac .ι. ꝼé-
lιm ꞃuaꞃh ꞃo ꞃιꞅhaꞟ na ιonaꞟ aꞃ čluaιnꞇιꞟ člaιnιι
mιc ꝼhélιm. mac Ɗιαꞃmαꞃα ocuꞃ a mac, .ι. bꞃían, ꞃo
ꞟul aꞃ mac Ɗonnchaꞃα an Choꞃaιnn, ocuꞃ an ꞇιꞃ ꞃo
loꞃcaꞃ leó, ocuꞃ ꞇech a ꞇempla ꞃo čꞃečαꞟ. Clanιι
ꝼhιιαꞃach ꞃo čꞃečαꞟ ocuꞃ ꞃo loꞃcaꞃ le hO Conchobaιꞃ
nꞃonιι, ocuꞃ le bꞃían mac Ruaιꞃꞃι mιc Ɗιαꞃmαꞃα.
maιꞟm Ꜳa na beιꞇιꞡe allaníaꞃ ꞃo Lιoꞃꞃ ꞟallꞡaιle ꞃo
ꞇaꞟaιꞃꞇ le Ꞇomalꞇach mac Ꞇaιꞟꞅ mιc Ɗιαꞃmαꞃα,
ocuꞃ le bꞃían mac Ruaιꞃꞃι mιc Ɗιαꞃmαꞃα, ocuꞃ ꞃo
maꞃbaꞃ ann Θoιn mac mhaolmuꞃι ꞁιc Colla mιc
Shuιꞟne, ocuꞃ Colla mac Suιꞟne, ocuꞃ ꞃaoιne ιomꞟa elι;
ocuꞃ ꞇanꞅaꞃaꞃ ꝼeιn ꞃ'lán co néꞃáιl ιomꞟa leó, ocuꞃ
cꞃeč baιle na ꞅcloč acca; ocuꞃ aιꞃ O Chončuꞟaιꞃ
Slιꞅιꞡ .ι. Ruaιꞃꞃι mac ꝼeιꞟlιm mιc mιc maꞡnuꞃa, ocuꞃ
aꞃ mac Ɗonnchaꞃα ιn Choꞃaιnꞃ ꞇuꞅaꞟ an maoιꞃm ꞃιn·

---

¹ *Baile-an-mhuilinn.* "The town of
the mill," or Milltown. The place referred to is probably Milltown, in the
parish of Dysart, barony of Athlone,
co. Roscommon, O'Fallon's residence,
referred to in note ⁴, p. 372.

² *Wednesday.* The Dom. Letter

for the year 1559 being A, the first of
January fell on a Sunday.

³ *Cluainte;* i.e. "the plains;" the
name of a district in the barony and
county of Roscommon, the inheritance
of the sept of O'Conor Roe, which contained 72 quarters of land in the year

Lord one thousand, five hundred, and fifty-eight years.
Mac Diarmada and his son, i.e. Brian, went to make
an attack upon Brian O'Cellaigh. Mac Diarmada, and the
rear of the army, remained in Baile-an-mhuilinn.[1] Brian
and the rest of the army went in past Bruighél, and he
brought with him a prey, and Cobhthach O'Fallamhain's
stud of horses. He retreated upwards, and burned the
country entirely from Bruighél up; and he returned
safely, loaded with spoils. O'Conchenainn's town, i.e. the
Fedan, was plundered, and burned, by Brian Mac Diarmada in like manner.

The kalends of January on Wednesday;[2] the age of
the Lord one thousand, five hundred, and fifty-nine years.
O'Conchobhair Ruadh, i.e. Toirdhelbhach Ruadh, son of
Tadhg Buidhe, son of Cathal Ruadh, mortuus est; (and he
was of the celebrities of Erinn in his time); and his son,
i.e. Felim Ruadh, was made king in his stead over the
Cluainte[3] of the descendants of Felim's son. Mac Diarmada and his son, i.e. Brian, went against Mac Donnchadha
of the Corann; and the country was burned by them,
and Tech-a-templa was plundered. Clann-Fhuadach was
plundered and burned by O'Conchobhair Donn, and by
Brian son of Ruaidhri Mac Diarmada. The defeat of
Ath-na-beithighe, to the east of Lis-ballghaile, was given
by Tomaltach, son of Tadhg Mac Diarmada, and by
Brian, son of Ruaidhri Mac Diarmada; and John, son
of Maelmuire, son of Colla Mac Suibhne, and Colla Mac
Suibhne, and many other persons, were slain there; and
they came home safely themselves, with numerous spoils,
and having the plunder of Baile-na-gcloch: (and on
O'Conchobhair Sligigh, i.e. Ruaidhri, the son of Fedhlim,
grandson of Maghnus, and on Mac Donnchadha of the

1585. See the composition between
Sir John Perrott, Lord Deputy, and
the chieftains of Moylurg, &c., printed
for the first time in Hardiman's ed. of

O'Flaherty's *Iar Connaught*, p. 354,
where the district of *Cluainte*, or the
Clontics, is called by the alias name of
" Cowrine M'Brenan."

Mupchaoh gpánna, mac Ruaiopi Mic Suibne, ohec in hoc anno.

Ktt. Enaip pop bapoaoin; cpi pichic bliaoan ocup cuig ceo ocup mile aoip an Cigepna. Caög mac Opiain mic Eogain mic Cigepnain 1 Ruaipc oo bachao ap loc an Chlochaip, .i. pep a aopa ip mó oipbepc ocup oippoepcup, oinech ocup uaiple, oo plicht Cigepnain pe cian oaimpip poime, ocup aoöap píg Ua mOpiúin gan aéceo oíamao cian a pé. Felim puao O Conchobaip oo cpochao le Comalcach mac Caiög Mic Oiapma- oa, ocup le plicht Conchobaip mic Ruaiopi Guibe. Ruaiopi na oculán, mac Oiapmaoa an oinig mic Ruaiopi Mic Oiapmaoa, oçaöail Gáip an bliaoain pi; ocup oo buö mop an pgél pin .i. mac ingine hi Opíain, ocup an cé oo buo mó a méin ocup a méio, ocup a ngniom ocup a láioipecht, oa ocainic oo plicht Mhaoil- puanaio möip pe papa poime; ocup po haölucao a nochuplige a pen é .i. a mainipoip na Guille. Cpeé möp oo öenum oo plicht Felim pinn 1 Conchobaip ap Opían mac Ruaiopi Mic Oiapmaoa. Cpeaé eli le Opían péin o Shiupcan Guibe mac Seain mic Ohácep Mic goipoealö, ocup clann Hanpái hi gpáoaig oo mapbao leip. Cpeé eli le Opían ó cnoc na ríte, ocup cpeaé o muinncip Phlannagáin, ocup peacht neié. Ccé galloa oo bpippeo le hUa Conchobaip noonn, ocup lé Opían Mac nOiapmaoa. Maiöm áöbail a Cuaö- mumain ap Iapla Cuaömuman, ocup ap Iapla élainni Ricaipo, le hIapla Oepmuman, ocup le Caög mac Mupchaoa hi Ohpíain; ocup po mapbao annpin Emonn mac Ruaiöpi moip Mic Shuibne, ocup Emonn óg a mac, ocup Colla mac Mupchaoa mic Ruaiopi möip, ocup clann Mupchaoa Mic Shuibne, ocup conpabail Chúaé- muman go huiliöi; po pagbao nói mbpacacha oo

---

1 *Inflicted.* This clause, which is in the handwriting of Brian Mac Dermot, is transposed in the MS.

2 *Hoc.* oc, MS.

3 *Thursday.* *Recte* Monday ; the Dom. Lett. for the year being G F.

Corann, this defeat was inflicted).[1] Murchadh Gránna, son of Ruaidhri Mac Suibhne, died in hoc[2] anno. .

The kalends of January on Thursday ;[3] the age of the Lord one thousand, five hundred, and sixty years. Tadhg, the son of Brian, son of Eoghan, son of Tighernan O'Ruairc, was drowned on Loch-an-chlochair : i.e. the man of his age of greatest prowess, dignity, bounty and nobility, of the race of Tighernan for a long time previously, and the intended king of Ui-Briuin, without dispute, if his life was long. Felim Ruadh O'Conchobhair was hanged by Tomaltach, the son of Tadhg Mac Diarmada, and by the descendants of Conchobhar, son of Ruaidhri Buidhe. Ruaidhri-na-dtulán, son of Diarmaid-an-oinigh, son of Ruaidhri Mac Diarmada, died this year ; (and he was a great loss, i.e. the son of O'Briain's daughter, and the greatest in mien and size, in action and strength, that had come of the race of Maelruanaidh the Great for a long time before) ; and he was buried in the tomb of his ancestors, i.e. in the monastery of the Buill. A great depredation was committed by the descendants of Felim Finn O'Conchobhair upon Brian, son of Ruaidhri Mac Diarmada. Another prey *was taken* by Brian himself from Jordan Buidhe, the son of John, son of Walter Mac Goisdelbh ; and the sons of Henry O'Gradaigh were killed by him. Another prey *was taken* by Brian from Cnoc-na-síthe; and a prey, and seven horses, from Muinter-Flannagáin. Ath-gallda was demolished by O'Conchobh-air Donn, and by Brian Mac Diarmada. A prodigious victory in Tuadh-Mumha, over the Earl of Tuadh-Mumha, and over the Earl of Clann-Rickard, by the Earl of Des-Mumha, and by Tadhg, son of Murchadh O'Briain ; and Edmond, the son of Ruaidhri Mór Mac Suibhne, and his son Edmond Og, and Colla, son of Murchadh, son of Ruaidhri Mór, and the sons of Murchadh Mac Suibhne, and all the constables of Tuadh-Mumha, were slain there. Nine standards of the descendants of

ᴄᕒᴌɪᴄʜᴛ Oomnaιll ɴa máᵬmann, eᴄ aᴌɪɪ mulᴛɪ. ʜannᕒɪ
mac Uɪᴌᴌɪam meɪc ᴄomaɪᕒ mɪc Oaɪbɪᵬ mɪc Θmaɪɴo
ᴅʜéc; ocᴜᕒ ᕒa moᕒ ɪɴᴛ ecʜᴛ an mac ᕒɪɴ meɪc Oábɪᵬ a
ᴌeɪᵬ ᴜaɪᕒᴌe ocᴜᕒ ɪɴɪᵹ.

|ᴄᴛᴛ. Θɴáɪᕒ [ᕒoᕒ] ᴄᴄoɪne; bᴌɪaᴅaɪn ocᴜᕒ ᴛᕒɪ ᕒɪcʜɪᴛ,
.ᴜ. ceᴅ ocᴜᕒ mɪᴌe, aoɪᕒ an ᴄɪᵹeᕒɴa. ᴄaᵬᵹ mac ᴄaɪᕒ-
bᕒe ɪ ᵬɪᕒɴ .ɪ. O ᵬɪᕒɴ, ᴅᕒaᵹaɪᴌ ᵬáɪᕒ a ɴθᵬanach, ocᴜᕒ
ɪᕒ ᴛeᕒc ma ᵬo ᵬí a ɴθᕒɪɴɪɪ ᕒᵹéᴌ ᵬᴜᵬ mó ɪɴáᕒᕒ ᴅo
ᵬéɪᴅ ocᴜᕒ ᴅo ᵬaɪᕒɪ, ᴅo ᵬeɪᴌᵬ ocᴜᕒ ᴅo ᵬeᵹ cᴜma, ᴅeᵹɴa
ocᴜᕒ ᴅeaᴌaᵬᴜɪɴ, ᴅoɪɴecʜ ocᴜᕒ ᴅoɪᕒᕒᴅeᕒcᴜᕒ, ocᴜᕒ ɪɴ
ᵹacʜ ᴜɪᴌe ᵹɴé ᵬᴜᵬ coᕒmaɪᴌ ᴅo ᵬᴜɪɴe ᵬaɪᵬ; bennacʜᴛ
ᴌé ɴaɴaɪɴ. Maoɪᴌᕒecʜᴌaɪɴɴ mac ᴄᴜaᴛʜaɪᴌ ʜɪ Oʜomɴaᴌ-
ᴌaɪɴ ᴅʜéc .ɪ. oᴌᴌam ᴜᕒᵬóɪᕒ Connacʜᴛ ᕒe ᴅáɴ, ocᴜᕒ ᕒeᕒ
ᵬoɪᵹe aoɪᴅʜeᴅ ᴅo ᵹᕒéᕒᕒ. ᕒeᴌɪm bᴜɪᵬɪ mac ᴄaɪᕒbᕒɪ mɪc
ᴄᴄoᵬa mɪc ᕒʜeᴌɪm ᕒɪɴɴ ᴅo maᕒbaᵬ a ᴄᴜɪᴌᴌᕒcɪ ᴌe ᵬᕒɪaɴ
mac Rᴜaɪᴅᕒɪ ᵬɪc Oɪaᕒmaᴅa, ocᴜᕒ ᴌe cᴌaɪɴɴ ᴄomaᴌᴛaɪᵹ
Mɪc Oɪaᕒmaᴅa. Cᕒeᵬa móᕒaɪᵬᵬᴌe ᴌe Mac Oɪaᕒmaᴅa
.ɪ. Rᴜaɪᴅᕒɪ mac ᴄaɪᵬᵹ Mɪc Oɪaᕒmaᴅa, aᕒ Mac Oonn-
cʜaᴅa an Choᕒᴜɪɴɴ. ᵬᕒɪaɴ mac Mɪc Oɪaᕒmaᴅa ocᴜᕒ
cᴌaɴɴ ᴄomaᴌᴛaɪᵹ Mɪc Oɪaᕒmaᴅa, ocᴜᕒ a ᵹcᴜɪᴅ ᕒᴌᴜaᵹ,
ᴅo ᴅᴜᴌ ᵹo ᵬaɪᴌe an ᵬᴜᴛa, ocᴜᕒ aᕒ ɴᴅᴜᴌ ᕒóɴ mbaɪᴌe
ᵬoɪᵬ mac ᴄomaᴌᴛaɪᵹ Mɪc Oɪaᕒmaᴅa ᴅo ᵬaᕒbaᴅ
ᴅᴜᕒcʜoᕒ ᴅo ᵹᴜɴɴa .ɪ. Caᴛʜaᴌ Mac Oɪaᕒmaᴅa; ocᴜᕒ
maᕒᵬᴄᴜᕒ Θoᵹan mac aɪɪ ᕒɪᕒ ᵬoᕒᵬa Mɪc Oɪaᕒmaᴅa
ᕒᴜaɪᵬ ᴅaoɴ ᴜᕒcʜoᕒ ᴅo ᵬá ɪᕒɪɴ ᴌó ceᴅɴa. Sɪᴜᕒᴛáɴ bᴜɪᵬe
mac Seaɪɴ ᵬɪc ᵬʜaɪᴛeᕒ Mɪc ᵹoɪᕒᴅeaᴌb ᴅo ᵬaᕒbaᴅ ᴌe
cᴌaɪɴɴ Oáᵬɪᵬ ᵬáɪɴ a ᵬᴜᕒc a mbaɪᴌe ᴌoᵬa Oeaᴌa a ᴛíᕒ
ᴄᵬaᴌᵹaɪᴅ, ocᴜᕒ ᕒa hᴜaᕒaᴌ aɪᵬᴍɪᴌᴌᴛe an ᕒeᕒ ᕒɪɴ. ᴄᴄoᵬ
mac Θoᵹaɪɴ Mɪc Oɪaᕒmaᴅa ᴅo ᵬaᕒbaᴅ ᴅo ᕒᴌɪcʜᴛ ɪɴ-
ᵹɪɴe Mʜéᵹ Raᵹɴᴜɪᴌᴌ .ɪ. cᴌaɴɴ Caᴛʜaɪᴌ Mɪc Oɪaᕒmaᴅa
a ᵹcᴌᴜaɪɴ ɴᴅ móɴaᵬ. Maoɪᴌᕒecʜᴌᴜɪɴɴ, mac ᴄᴄoᵬa mɪc
ᴄʜaɪᵬᵹ mɪc ᴄomaᴌᴛaɪᵹ an oɪɴɪᵹ Mɪc Oɪaᕒmaᴅa, ᴅo

---

1 *Alii.* aᴌɪ, MS.
² *Henry.* This entry is added in the
handwriting of Brian Mac Dermot.

³ *Friday.* Should be Wednesday.
⁴ *Felim-Finn;* i.e. Felim the Fair
[O'Conor Roe].

A.D.
[1560]

[1561.]

Domhnall-na-madhmann were lost there, et alii[1] multi. Henry,[2] the son of William, son of Thomas, son of David, son of Edmond, died; and this son of Mac David was a great loss as regards nobility and hospitality.

The kalends of January [on] Friday;[3] the age of the Lord one thousand, five hundred, and sixty-one years. Tadhg, son of Cairbre O'Birn, i.e. *the* O'Birn, died in Echanagh; and it is questionable if there was in Erinn a person more celebrated than he for stature and beauty, form and stateliness, for wisdom and learning, for hospitality and dignity, and in every other quality incident to a good man : a blessing be with his soul. Maelsechlainn, son of Tuathal O'Domhnallain, died : i.e. the ollamh of the greater part of Connacht in poetry, and a man who always kept a guest-house. Felim Buidhe, the son of Cairbre, son of Aedh, son of Felim Finn,[4] was killed in Tuillsce by Brian, son of Ruaidhri Mac Diarmada, and by the sons of Tomaltach Mac Diarmada. Enormous depredations *were committed* by Mac Diarmada, i.e. Ruaidhri, the son of Tadhg Mac Diarmada, upon Mac Donnchadha of the Corann. Brian, the son of Mac Diarmada, and the sons of Tomaltach Mac Diarmada, and their army, went to Baile-an-mhúta; and after they had attacked the town the son of Tomaltach Mac Diarmada, i.e. Cathal Mac Diarmada, was killed by a gun shot; and Eoghan, son of the Ferdorcha Mac Diarmada Ruadh, was killed with one cast of a spear on the same day. Jordan Buidhe, the son John, son of Walter Mac Goisdelbh, was killed by the sons of David Bán Burk in Baile-Locha-Deala, in Tir-Amhalghaidh; and this man was noble, destructive. Aedh, the son of Eoghan Mac Diarmada, was killed by the descendants of Mag Raghnaill's daughter, viz., the sons of Cathal Mac Diarmada, in Cluain-na-mónadh. Maelsechlainn, the son of Aedh, son of Tadhg, son of Tomaltach-an-oinigh Mac Diarmada, was killed by the

ṁapbαꝺ le clαınn Ḟhıp ᵹαn αınm mıc Conchobαıp óıᵹ
Mıc Ꝺıαpmαꝺα, α popc Inıp Ꝺóıᵹpe. Ƿoplonᵹpopc
Mıc Ꝺıαpmαꝺα, .ı. Ruαıꝺpı mıc Cαıꝺᵹ Mıc Ꝺıαpmαꝺα,
ꝺo ꝺeıᵹ um Sᵹeıᵹín nα ᵹcenn, ocup um Ḟhuαpán
ṁoıᵹe hOı, αᵹ mılleꝺ nα ᵹcluαınceꝺ ocup Mhαınech,
o ꝺeαllcoıne co peıl Mıchıl, óıp níp pαᵹαıꝺ pé ceᵹ ᵹαn
Lopcαꝺ, ınα ᵹopc ᵹαn ᵹeppαꝺ, ó ᵹochup Choılle αn ᵹαıpп
co hOılpınn ꝺαp ꝺen pe plıchc Ꝺonnchαꝺα hı Cheαllαıᵹ,
nα pe plıchc Cαchαıl puαıꝺ I Conchobαıp; ocup nı
heıꝺıp α puoın ınα popoıllpıuᵹαꝺ ᵹαch αp ꝺen pé
ᵹαıpᵹnıꝺ ocup ꝺéꝺαlαıꝺ ꝺıꝺ; ocup nı poıꝺe α nepınn
poplonᵹpopc ınαp Líα eıᵹ ocup éıꝺeꝺ, peoıl ocup píon,
αop cıúıl ocup oıppıꝺıᵹ ocup eαlαꝺnα, ᵹαlloᵹlαech ocup
ᵹıomαnαıᵹ ocup Ɑlbαnαıᵹ, ınɑ ın poplonᵹpopc pın Mıc
Ꝺıαpmαꝺα Mαc Ꝺαꝺıᵹ ᵹlαınnı Connmαıꝺ, .ı. Uıll-
lıαm mαc Comáıp mıc Ꝺαꝺıᵹ mıc Emuınn, ꝺhec ın hoc
αnno; (α loc α Rop Chomαın). Mαoılpechluınn bαlꝺ
mαc Uıllıαm hı Cheαllαıᵹ, .ı. mαc ınᵹıne hı Ḃhpíαın,
ꝺo ṁαpbαꝺ ıpın Ƿúbαl ᵹcαoꝺ, ocup pα mop αnc échc.
Ꙇꙇαoıppe mαc Cıᵹpuαıꝺ, αnc αon ꝺuıne ıp bınꝺe ꝺo ꝺí α
nepınn, ꝺo ꝺαꝺαꝺ αp loᵹ Ꙅıle, ocup α ben, ınᵹen Mıc
Ꝺonnchαꝺαı ocup Ɑᵹαıpne mαc Mαᵹα ᵹlαıp; ocup pαo
mop ın pᵹél mαc I Ꝺuıꝺᵹeαnnαın. Mαıꝺm Slıᵹıᵹ ꝺo
ᵹαꝺαıpc αıp Cαchαl óᵹ Ꙇα Chonᵹubαıp ꝺO Ꝺoṁnαıll
.ı. ꝺⱭoꝺ mαc Mαᵹnuppα; ocup ꝺo mαpꝺαꝺ αnꝺpα
mαıꝺm pın αn Ꝺuꝺαlcαch mαc Cαıꝺp ın cpıuꝺαıp Meıc
Ꝺonnchαꝺα, ocup Eoᵹαn mαc Mαoılmuıpe Mıc Suıꝺne,

---

[1] *The Cluainte.* See note [3], page
374.

[2] *The Mainechs.* See note [3], page
372.

[8] *Tochar-choill-an-chairn.* "The
causeway of the cairn wood;" now
probably Togher, in the parish of
Taghmaconnell, barony of Athlone,
and county of Roscommon.

[4] *Hoc.* oc, MS.

[5] *Ros-Comain.* The clause within
parentheses is interlined in the original.

[6] *Pobal-caech.* See note [1], p. 370.
The remaining entries for this year
are in the handwriting of Brian Mac
Dermot.

[7] *Cithruadh.* This was apparently
the Cithruadh, son of Diarmaid Caech
Mac Firbisigh, who assisted in the

A.D.
[1561.]

sons of Fer-gan-ainm, son of Conchobhar Og Mac Diarmada, in Port-Inis-Doighre. Mac Diarmada, i.e. Ruaidhri, the son of Tadhg Mac Diarmada, had an encampment about Sgeithín-na-gcenn, and about Fuaran-Maighe-Ai, pillaging the Cluainte,[1] and the Mainechs,[2] from May day to Michaelmas, for he left not a house without burning, nor a corn field without cutting down, from Tochar-choill-an chairn[3] to Oilfinn, of all that belonged to the posterity of Donnchadh O'Cellaigh, or to the posterity of Cathal Ruadh O'Conchobhair; and it is not possible to reckon or over-explain all the plunder and spoils that he took from them; and there was not in Erinn a camp in which horses and armour, meat and wine, musicians, minstrels, and men of science, gallowglasses, mercenaries, and Albanachs, were more numerous than that camp of Mac Diarmada. Mac David of Clann-Connmhaigh, i.e., William, the son of Thomas, son of David, son of Edmond, died in hoc[4] anno : (he was wounded in Ros-Comain).[5] Maelsechlainn Balbh, the son of William O'Cellaigh, i.e. the son of O'Briain's daughter, was killed in the Pobal-caech;[6] and it was a great calamity. Naisse, the son of Cithruadh,[7] the most eminent musician that was in Erinn, was drowned on Loch-Gilè, and his wife, the daughter of Mac Donnchadha, and Athairne, the son of Matthew Glas;[8] and the son of O'Duibhgennain was a great loss. The defeat of Sligech was given to Cathal Og O'Conchobhair[9] by O'Domhnaill, i.e. by Aedh, son of Maghnus; and the Dubhaltach, son of Tadhg-in-triubhais[10] Mac Donnchadha, and Eoghan, son of Maelsechlainn Mac Suibhne, and

erection, in 1560, of the castle of Lecan, in Tireragh, co. Sligo. See O'Donovan's *Tribes and Customs of Hy-Fiachrach*, pp. 168, 169, and 408.

[8] *Matthew Glas* ; i.e. Matthew the Gray ; one of the family of O'Duibhgennain, or O'Duigenan.

[9] *Cathal Og O'Conchobhair* ; i.e. Charles the Younger O'Conor. He was *the* O'Conor Sligo at the time. The O' is represented by Uað (*recte* Ua) in the text.

[10] *Tadhg-in-triubhais.* "Tadhg (or Thaddeus) of the Trews."

ocuɼ Τοɩɼɼⱱeɑlbɑch cɑoᵭ mɑc Τoɩɼᵭeɑlᵬɑɩᵹ óɩᵹ, ocuɼ
Ɗuᵬᵹɑll mɑc Emɑɩnⱱ nɩc Ꞩhuɩᵬne, eꞇ ɑlɩɩ mulꞇɩ.

Ꝃꞇꞇ. Enɑɩɼ ɼoɼ ɼɑᵬoɼn ; ⱱɑ blɩɑⱱɑɩn ocuɼ ꞇɼɩ ɼɩchɩꞇ,
u. ceⱱ ocuɼ mɩle, ɑoɩɼ ɑn Τɩᵹeɼnɑ. Clɑnn Eoᵹɑɩn mɩc
Τɑɩᵬᵹ Ϻɩc Ɗɩɑɼmɑⱱɑ ⱱɼɑɼⱱóᵭ ᵭolɑɩⱱ ṁóɩɼ ɑnɑᵹhɑɩⱱ
Ϻɩc Ɗɩɑɼmɑⱱɑ .ɩ. Ꞃuɑɩⱱɼɩ, ᵹɑn ꝑɩɼ ⱱó ɼéɩn, óɩɼ ꞇucɑⱱɑɼ
clɑnn Ɑluɼⱱɩₐɩnn ᵹɑllⱱɑ Ϻhéᵹ Ɗhomnɑɩll ṁóɼɑ,
ocuɼ ᵬɼɩɑn éᵹ mɑc ᵬɼɩɑɩn ɑn ᵭoᵬlɑɩᵹ Ϻɩc Ꞩhuɩᵬnɩ,
ocuɼ ɼo ᵬɑⱱɑɼ ꞇɼɩ ceⱱ Ɑlbɑnɑch ocuɼ ᵹɑllóᵹlɑeᵭ. Ꞃo
ᵭɑɩɼɼnᵹeⱱɑɼ ɑn ⱱolɑɩᵭ ɼɩn ɑɼ Ϻɑc Ɗɩɑɼmɑⱱɑ, ocuɼ ɼo
loɩɼcꞇeꞇ ocuɼ ɼo cɼeᵭɼɑꞇ ɑɼ ᵬen ɼe ɼeɩcɼéɩⱱ Ϻɩc
Ɗɩɑɼmɑⱱɑ ⱱon ꞇɩɼ ; ocuɼ ɼo loɩɼcꞇeꞇ ɑn Lonᵹɼoɼꞇ co
huɩlɩᵬ, ocuɼ ᵬɑɩle nɑ huɑmɑ, ocuɼ ɑɼ ᵹɑch ꞇɑoᵬ ᵭé ;
ocuɼ ɼo mɑɼbɑⱱ Ϻuɼchɑⱱ mɑc ᵬɼɩɑɩn ᵭoeɩᵭ .ɩ. mɑɼcɑch
mɑɩᵭ ⱱo ṁuɩnnꞇeɼ Ϻɩc Ɗɩɑɼmɑⱱɑ leó ɩɼɩn Chlochɑɩɼ ;
ocuɼ nɩ heɩⱱɩɼ ɑ ɼɩom nɑ ɩnnɩɼɩn ᵹɑch ɑɼ mɩllɼeⱱ ⱱech-
ɑɩb ocuɼ ⱱo ᵬuɑɩᵬ, ⱱo ᵭɑɩɼlɩᵬ ocuɼ ⱱɑ ᵹɑch uɩle éⱱɑɩl
ɑɩɼchénɑ. Ꞃo ᵭóɩ ɑn ⱱolɑɩᵭ ɼɩn lá ocuɼ ɼeɑchꞇṁuɩn
ɑɼ ɼeᵬ ɑn ꞇɩɼe ɑᵹá mɩlleⱱ, ocuɼ Ϻɑc Ɗɩɑɼmɑⱱɑ ɑɼ
ɑn Cɑɩɼɼɩᵹ nɑ comnɑɩᵭe ɑɩ ɑn ᵬɼeᵭɼɩn. Ɑɼ moᵭuᵹhɑⱱ
ɑn ꞇɩɼe ⱱo ṁɩlleⱱ ⱱo Ϻɑc Ɗɩɑɼmɑⱱɑ .ɩ. ⱱo Ꞃuɑɩᵬɼɩ,
ɼo ᵭuɩɼ ꞇɑɩɼɼɩnᵹ ɑɼ Ɗoṁnɑll mɑc Ϻuɼchɑⱱɑ Ϻɩc
Ꞩuɩᵬnɩ, ocuɼ ɑɼ ꝑlɩchꞇ Emuɩnn Ϻɩc Ꞩhuɩᵬne ; ocuɼ ꞇuc
lɑɩɼ ꞇɑɼ Coɩɼɼɼlɩɑᵬ ᵬuᵭ ᵭuɑɩᵬ ɑ ꞇɼɩ no ɑ ceᵭɑɩɼ ⱱo ce-
ⱱɑɩᵬ Lúɩɼech, conɑ nⱱóɩol ᵹɩomɑnɑch léo. Ɗob é ɼɩɩ uɑɩɼ
ocuɼ ɑɩmɼɩɼ ɼo ᵬáⱱɑɼ clɑnn Eoᵹɑɩn Ϻɩc Ɗɩɑɼmɑⱱɑ
conɑ nⱱolɑɩᵭ ɑᵹ ɼɩlleᵬ ɑɼɼ ɑn ᵹcenn ꞇɩɑɼɼ ⱱon ꞇɩɼ ɩɑɼ
ɩnɩlleⱱ ṁoɼáɩn ɩnnꞇɩ, ocuɼ ⱱo ɼonɼɑꞇ ɩoɼnɑɩᵭe ᵬeᵹ ɑ
mbɑɩle ṁeɩc Ϻuɼchɑⱱɑ ; ɑchꞇ chenɑ ɼuc ɼᵹélɑ oɼɼɑ
ocuɼ ꞇɩɑᵹuɩⱱ ɑ noɼⱱuᵹɑⱱ. ᵬeɩɼɩⱱ ɼáɩɼꞇ ⱱo ꞇoɼɑch

---

1 *Toirdhelbhach Caech.* Toirdhelbhach (or Turlough) the Blind [Mac
Swiney].

2 *Saturday.* The Dom. Letter for
1562 being D, the first of January
fell on a Thursday.

3 *Mac Domhnaill.* This name is

followed by the word ṁóɩʋɑ, pl. of
moɼ "great ;" from which it would
seem that some other word had been
omitted.

4 *Brian-an-chobhlaigh;* pronounced
nearly *Brian an-kovley;* i.e. "Brian
of the Fleet."

Toirdhelbhach Caech,[1] son of Toirdhelbhach Og, and Dubhgall, son of Edmond Mac Suibhne, et alii multi, were slain in that defeat.

The kalends of January on Saturday ;[2] the age of the Lord one thousand, five hundred, and sixty-two years. The sons of Eoghan, son of Tadhg Mac Diarmada, retained a large band against Mac Diarmada, i.e. Ruaidhri, without his own knowledge; for they brought the sons of Alexander Gallda Mac Domhnaill,[3] and Brian Og, son of Brian-an-chobhlaigh[4] Mac Suibhne ; and there were three hundred Albanachs and gallowglasses. They brought this band against Mac Diarmada, and burned and pillaged all that belonged to Mac Diarmada's confidants[5] of the country ; and they burned the fortress[6] entirely, and Baile-na-huamha, and on every side of it. And Murchadh, the son of Brian Caech, i.e. a good horseman of Mac Diarmada's people, was killed by them in the Clochar ; and it is not possible to reckon or tell all the steeds, cows, horses, and property of every other kind they destroyed. This band was a week and a day going through the country, destroying it, and Mac Diarmada residing on the Rock[7] during that time. As soon as Mac Diarmada, i.e. Ruaidhri, perceived that they were wasting the country, he invited Domhnall, the son of Murchadh Mac Suibhne, and the descendants of Edmond Mac Suibhne ; and he took with him across Corr-sliabh, northwards, three or four hundred coats of mail, with their complement of mercenaries. This was the hour and time when the sons of Eoghan Mac Diarmada, with their band, were returning from the upper end of the country, after destroying much in it ; and they made a short stay in Baile-mic-Murchadha ;[8] but news reached them, and they went into array. A part of the

---

[5] *Confidants.* ꞃeꞁcꞃéꞁꝺ (= secret?), MS.

[6] *Fortress;* i.e. Mac Dermot's fortress, on the southern shore of Loch-Cé.

[7] *The Rock;* i.e. Mac Dermot's Rock, in Loch-Cé.

[8] *Baile-mic-Murchadha;* the town of Murchadh's son ; probably the Domhnall, son of Murchadh Mac Suibhne, mentioned a few lines before.

sluaig Mic Diarmada orra ag dul tar Cara an feḋa ḋóiḃ. Tomaltach mac Taiḋg Mic Diarmada, ocus Brían mac Mic Diarmada, do ċor greamma orra don taoḃ ṫall do ċaraiḃ, ocus briseḋ orra ass a haiṫle, ocus an maiḋm sin do ḃeiṫ orra no go rangadar Bratsliaḃ. Brian óg mac Bríain an ċaḃlaiġ Mic Suibni dḟágbail annsin, maille ré dá ced fer maroen ris. Mainistir na Búille do ġaḃáil do Mac Diarmada isin ló cedna don chur sin. Cluain Muireḋhaiġ do ḃriseḋ le Mac nDiarmada, .ocus Domnall mac Taiḋg óig ocus seiser dá ṁuintir do ṁarbaḋ innte. Mac Eochaid ocus O Fallaṁuin do creċaḋ le Tomaltach mac Taiḋg Mic Diarmada ocus le Brían Mac Diarmada. Mac Dabiṫ .i. Uilliam mac Tomais dhec, ocus Teaboid mac Uilleag do rigad na inaḋ, ocus a eg sa bliaġain cedna sin. Tomás óg mac Tomais mic Daibiṫ mic Emaind do rigad na ionad sin; ocus fa haṫbail na hechtta sin.

Kal. Enair for Domnach; tri bliadna ocus tri fiċit, cuig ced ocus mile air an Tigerna. Slicht Felim ċleiriġ, ocus slicht Donnchada ḋuiḃ mic Conchobair, do ḋul ar na puirlíniḃ, ocus ar nurnaide doiḃ ann slicht Cathail ruaid 1 Conchobair ocus muinter Fhlannagáin do ṫeacht futha, ocus briseḋ orra sios go Cill mic Coimsi. Dias mac Cairbri mic Bríain ruaid do ṁarbaḋ ann .i. Felim ocus Aoḋ, ocus Diarmaid mac Cairbri ċiottaiġ, ocus Brian mac Donnchada ḋuiḃ mic Conchobair, dfágbáil ann maille riú. Creċ ṁór do ḋenum do clainn Oilbérus a Burc a nAirtech, dú na raibe x. ced bó, ocus ro ṁillset muintir Briain Mic Diarmada go hiomarcach don ruathair. Mác 1 Chonċuḃair duind .i. Conn mac Diarmada mic Corbri do marbad le Brian O Ceallaiġ, a Cluain etir dá aṫ.

---

1 *Cara-an-fedha;* i.e. "the weir of the wood;" a weir on the Boyle river.

2 *Sunday.* Should be Friday.

3 *Felim Clerech;* i.e. Felim the Cleric [O'Conor].

van of Mac Diarmada's àrmy came up with them as they were going across Cara-an-fedha.[1] Tomaltach, the son of Tadhg Mac Diarmada, and Brian, the son of Mac Diarmada, hemmed them in on the other side of the weir; and they were subsequently routed; and this rout continued as far as Brad-sliabh. Brian Og, the son of Brian-an-chobhlaigh Mac Suibhne, was lost there, together with two hundred men. The monastery of the Buill was taken by Mac Diarmada òn the same day, on that occasion. Cluain-Muiredhaigh was demolished by Mac Diarmada; and Domhnall, son of Tadhg Og, and six of his people, were killed in it. Mac Eochaidh and O'Fallamhain were plundered by Tomaltach, son of Tadhg Mac Diarmada, and by Brian Mac Diarmada. Mac David, i.e. William, the son of Thomas, died; and Tibbot, son of Ulick, was inaugurated in his place; and he died in that same year. Thomas Og, the son of Thomas, son of David, son of Edmond, was inaugurated in his place; and those were prodigious calamities.

The kalends of January on Sunday;[2] the age of the Lord one thousand, five hundred, and sixty-three years. The descendants of Felim Clerech,[3] and the descendants of Donnchadh Dubh, son of Conchobhar, went upon the Publina; and whilst waiting there the descendants of Cathal Ruadh O'Conchobhair, and Muinter-Flannagáin, went against them, and they were routed down as far as Cill-Mic-Coimsi. The two sons of Cairbre, son of Brian Ruadh, were slain there, viz., Felim and Aedh; and Diarmaid, son of Cairbre Cittach, and Brian, the son of Donnchadh Dubh, son of Conchobhar, were lost there along with them. A great prey, in which there were ten hundred cows, was taken by the sons of Oliver Burk in Airtech; and they plundered Brian Mac Diarmada's people excessively in the foray. The son of O'Conchobhair Donn, i.e. Conn, the son of Diarmaid, son of Cairbre, was killed by Brian O'Cellaigh in Cluain-etir-dá-ath.

VOL. II. 2 C

Ιϲτt. Ɛnᴀɪρ ρορ Lᴜᴀn; ceɪτρᴜ blɪᴀᴅnᴀ ocᴜρ τρɪ ρɪᴄhɪτ, ᴜ. ceᴅ ocᴜρ mɪle ᴀoɪρ ᴀn Tɪᴈeρnᴀ. Coᴈᴀᴅ ᴅeɪρᴈe eτɪρ O Conchobᴀɪρ ρᴜᴀᴅ ocᴜρ Ⅿᴀc Ⅾɪᴀρmᴀᴅᴀ .ɪ. ℞ᴜᴀɪᴅρɪ. ℞oρ Chomᴀɪn ᴅo ᴈᴀᴃᴀɪl ᴅo ᴄlᴀnn Tᴀɪᴃᴈ óɪᴈ mɪc Thᴀɪᴃᴈ mɪc Thoɪρρᴅeᴀlbᴀɪᴈ 1 Conchobᴀɪρ ᴀρ O Conᴄoᴃᴀɪρ nᴅonn, ocᴜρ τᴜcᴀᴅᴀρ ᴀn bᴀɪle ɪᴀρ nᴀ ᴈᴀᴃᴀɪl ᴅo Conchobᴀɪρ ρᴜᴀᴅ .ɪ. Tᴀᴃᴈ óᴈ mᴀc Tᴀɪᴃᴈ ᴃᴜɪᴃe, ocᴜρ ρo mɪlleᴅ móρᴀn ᴀρ ρeᴃ Connᴀchτ ᴜɪle ɪomón nᴈᴀᴃᴀɪl ρɪn. Ƀρɪᴀn mᴀc ℞ᴜᴀɪᴅρɪ Ⅿɪc Ⅾɪᴀρmᴀᴅᴀ, ocᴜρ clᴀnn Tomᴀlτᴀɪᴈ Ⅿɪc Ⅾɪᴀρmᴀᴅᴀ, ᴅo ᴃᴜl ᴀ ᴈceᴀlᴈᴀᴃ ᴀ τɪmcell ℞oᴩᴩᴀ Comᴀɪn ᴅᴀoɪne ɪomᴃᴀ. Conᴄobᴀρ mᴀc hɪ Chonᴄobᴀɪρ ρᴜᴀɪᴅ ᴅeɪρᴈe ᴀmᴀᴄ ᴀρ ᴀn ᴈcᴜɪρτ ᴀn lᴀ ρɪn, ocᴜρ nᴀ ceᴀlᴈᴀ ρɪn ᴅeɪρᴈe ᴅᴜ ρeɪn ocᴜρ ᴅᴀ ᴍᴜɪnnτɪρ ᴀρ ᴈᴀch leɪᴃ, ocᴜρ ᴀ cᴜρ ᴅocᴜm nᴀ mᴀɪnɪρᴅρech, ocᴜρ ᴀ neɪch ᴅo bᴜᴀɪn ρe hᴜchτ ᴀn ᴅoρᴜɪρ ᴅɪᴃ, ocᴜρ ɪᴀᴅ ρéɪn ᴅo ᴃᴜl ᴅon ᴄloᴈᴀρρ. ᴀcchτ chenᴀ nɪρ ᴃo ᴅɪon ᴅóɪb ᴀnτ ɪonᴀᴃ ρɪn; ρo lenᴈᴀᴅ cᴀᴃ ɪᴀᴅ, ocᴜρ τᴀɪɪɪc Ⅾɪᴀ ρo ᴄenᴅ ᴀ ρᴀoᴈᴀl, oɪρ ᴈéρ ᴃᴀɪnᴈeɪɪ ᴀnτ ɪonᴀᴅ ρoɪ ᴀ ρᴀᴃᴀᴅᴀρ ᴅo benᴀᴃ ᴀ ᴈcɪɪɪ ᴜɪle ᴅɪᴃ. ℞o mᴀρbᴀᴅ Conchobᴀρ mᴀc Toɪρρᴅhelbᴀɪᴈ ρᴜᴀɪᴅ hɪ Conchobᴀɪρ ᴀɪɪρɪɪ, ·ocᴜρ ᴀon ᴅᴜɪɪɪe ᴅhec ᴅᴀ ᴍᴜɪnτɪρ mᴀɪlle ρɪρ; ocᴜρ ρo benᴀᴅ ᴅeɪᴄ neɪch ᴅɪρ. 8ᴀᴄᴀρn ᴅoᴍɪnᴀɪᴈ ρᴀᴅρᴀɪc ᴅo ρɪɪɪɪeᴃ nᴀ héchτᴀ ρɪn. Téɪᴅ Ƀρɪᴀn mᴀc Ⅿɪc Ⅾɪᴀρmᴀᴅᴀ ᴀn Lᴜᴀn ɪɪɪᴀ ᴃɪᴀɪᴃ ρɪɪ ᴀρ Ⅿᴀc nⅮonnchᴀᴅᴀ ᴀn Choρᴜɪnn, ᴈo bᴜn ᴀn ρeᴅᴀɪn, ocᴜρ ρo loɪρceᴅ ᴀn bᴀɪle ᴈo ᴅoρᴜρ lᴀɪρ; ocᴜρ τᴜc ᴅᴀ ceᴅ bó ᴀρρ, ocᴜρ ᴅo ρɪɪɪɪe mᴀρbᴅᴀ ᴀɪɪɪ. O Ɲeɪll .ɪ. 8eᴀn mᴀc Cᴜɪɪɪᴅ ᴅo τeᴀchτ ρlᴜᴀᴈ ᴅɪᴀɪρᴍe ᴈo ρɪɪɪe ᴈᴀll, ocᴜρ Ȝoɪll ᴅo cρᴜɪɪɪᴅᴀchᴀᴅ nᴀ ᴀᴈᴀɪᴅ, ocᴜρ ρᴜᴀɪᴈ ᴅo ᴃᴀᴃᴀɪρτ ᴅO Ɲeɪll ᴀρ nᴀ Ȝᴀlloɪb ᴅon τᴀoɪᴃ ᴀτᴜᴀɪᴃ ᴅᴀcρᴅ ᴍᴀᴄᴀ Ƀρeᴈe, ocᴜρ ᴀɪnnᴅρɪᴜ bᴜɪᴃe Ⅾɪᴜᴅ, ocᴜρ Ƀρᴜnᴀch ᴄɪlle ρᴀᴅρᴀɪᴈ, ocᴜρ ρe τɪᴈeρnᴀoɪ ᴅeᴈ mᴀρᴀoɪ

---

1 *The court.* O'Conor's chief residence in Roscommon.

2 *Patrick's Sunday;* i.e. the Sunday within the octave of St. Patrick's day (17th March).

3 *There.* The remaining entries for this year are in the handwriting of Brian Mac Dermot.

4 *Fell.* ᴈo ᴅτᴜɪτɪɪɪ, MS., which is corrupt.

The kalends of January on Monday, (*rectè* Saturday) ; the age of the Lord one thousand, five hundred, and sixty-four years. A war arose between O'Conchobhair Ruadh and Mac Diarmada, i.e. Ruaidhri. Ros-Comain was taken by the sons of Tadhg Og, son of Tadhg, son of Toirdhelbhach O'Conchobhair, from O'Conchobhair Donn ; and they gave the town, after taking it, to O'Conchobhair Ruadh, i.e. Tadhg Og, son of Tadhg Buidhe ; and much was destroyed throughout all Connacht on account of this capture. Brian, son of Ruaidhri Mac Diarmada, and the sons of Tomaltach Mac Diarmada, with many men, went into ambush around Ros-Comain. Conchobhar, the son of O'Conchobhair Ruadh, went out from the court[1] that day, and the ambuscaders attacked himself and his people on all sides ; and they were driven to the monastery, and their horses were taken from them before the door ; and they themselves went into the belfry. But this place was no defence to them. All followed them, and God decreed the termination of their lives ; for, though strong the place in which they were, their heads were taken off them all. Conchobhar, son of Toirdhelbhach Ruadh O'Conchobhair, was killed there, and eleven of his people along with him ; and ten horses were taken from them. On the Saturday of Patrick's Sunday[2] these deeds were committed. Brian, the son of Mac Diarmada, went on the Monday after against Mac Donnchadha of the Corann, to Bun-an-fedhain ; and the place was burned to the door by him ; and he brought two hundred cows out of it, and committed homicides there.[3] O'Neill, i.e. John, son of Conn, came with a countless host to Finè-Gall ; and the Foreigners mustered against him ; and O'Neill gave an onset to the Foreigners on the northern side of Ard-Macha-Brege ; and Andrew Buidhe Tuit, and Brown of Cill-Patraic, and sixteen of the principal lords of the Foreigners along with them, fell[4] there. Hubert, son of Fergus, son

ʃiu do maiṫniḃ Ʒall do tuitim and. hoiberd mac
Ferʒuʃa mic Emuind, tiʒearna claindi Conchobair,
dhec; ocuʃ annʃa ċallaind ʃo ʃum ata bar hoiberd
mic Ferʒuʃa.

Ktt. Enair ʃor ṁairt; cuiʒ bliadna ocuʃ tri ʃichit,
cuiʒ cet ocuʃ mile aoiʃ an Tiʒerna. Maiḋm ʒlenna
ʃeirʒ le hO lleill .i. Sean mac Cuinn hl Neill, ar
ċlainn Mic Dhomnaill na hCClban, inar ṫuitʃed diar
mac Mic Domnaill .i. Sémuʃ ocuʃ CCluʃʃann uaiḃʃech,
et alii multi. O Conchobair donn ocuʃ Oʃían mac
Ruaidʃi Mic Diarmada do dol ʒo Moiʒ ʃinn a ṫiʃ
Mhaine, ocuʃ ʃiċe ced bo do ṫabairt dóiḃ ó CCʃd na
ʒclog ocuʃ ó tochuʃ ċoille an ċaiʃn; ocuʃ ʃo loiʃʒʃet
an tiʃ ʒo huiliʒi; ocuʃ ʃo benaḋ ʃeʃ bʃattaiʒe
Oʃíain Mic Diarmada díḃ .i. Conn mac Oʃíain ċoeich.
Cʃeċ ṁóʃ le clainn Tomaltaiʒ Mic Diarmada ó Ua
Conchobair ʃuaḋ, do ʃliaḃ Oaḋna. Ro ḋói neʃt clainni
Taidʒ Mic Diarmada aʃ ʃeḋ uʃṁóiʃ Chonnacht i. o
ḃaile CCḋa an ʃiʒ co ʃó Dʃoḃaoiʃ, diomad a nech
ocuʃ a néidiʒ, a ndoine ocuʃ a mindile, ocuʃ do tʃeiʃʃi
a ʒcaʃad in ʒach ionad. Dun ʒaʃ do ṫionnʃcna le
Oʃían mac Ruaidʃi Mic Diarmada do toil Mic
Diarmada ʒall ocuʃ a ċineḋ ʒo huiliʒi. CCn Diudach
.i. Ricaʃd Diúid dhec, ocuʃ ba móʃ an ʃʒél ʃin.
O Raʒallaiʒ .i. Maolmóʃḋa mac Seain mic Cathail,
ant oen duine iʃ ʃeʃʃ taʃis dá ċineḋ ʃein ʃiam, ocuʃ
iʃ ainminic táinic do ʃlicht Ʒaoidel ʒláiʃ nech ba
ʃeʃʃ máʃ do ʃeiʃ aiċni ocuʃ eóluiʃ ċáiʒ aiʃ, .i. ʃeʃ
dáʃ ṫoiʃḃiʃ Día na ʃuḃáilċe co hiomlán aʃ túʃ .i.
búaiḋ ndealḃa ocuʃ ndénmuʃa, búaid ninnʃcni ocuʃ
nuʃlaḃʃa, búaid naiċni ocuʃ neoluʃa, búaid ceille
ocuʃ comaiʃle, búaid noiniʒ ocuʃ nenʒnuma; ocuʃ

---

1 *Kalends under;* i.e. under the year 1565.
2 *Should be.* ата, lit. "is," MS.
3 *Glenn-sheisg.* The Four Masters incorrectly write the name "Glenn-taisi." See O'Donovan's ed., note x, A.D. 1566. Glenshesk is the name of a valley near Ballycastle, co. Antrim.

i.

of Edmond, lord of Clann-Conchobhair, died; (and in these kalends under[1] the death of Hubert, son of Fergus, should be[2]).

The kalends of January on Tuesday (*recte* Monday); the age of the Lord one thousand, five hundred, and sixty-five years. The victory of Glenn-sheisg[3] by O'Neill, i.e. John, son of Conn O'Neill, over the sons of Mac Domhnaill of Alba, in which fell Mac Domhnaill's two sons, viz., James and Alexander Uaibhrech,[4] et alii[5] multi. O'Conchobhair Donn, and Brian, the son of Ruaidhri Mac Diarmada, went to Magh-Finn in Tir-Maine, and brought two thousand cows from Ard-na-clog and from Tochur-choille-an-chairn; and they burned the country entirely; and Brian Mac Diarmada's standard bearer was taken from them, i.e. Conn, the son of Brian Caech. A great prey *was taken* by the sons of Tomaltach Mac Diarmada from O'Conchobhair Ruadh, from Sliabh-Badhna. The sway of the sons of Tadhg Mac Diarmada was over the greater part of Connacht, viz., from the town of Ath-an-righ as far as Drobhais, owing to the quantity of their horses and armour, of their men and flocks, and the power of their friends in every place. Dun-gar was commenced by Brian, the son of Ruaidhri Mac Diarmada, with the consent of Mac Diarmada Gall, and of all his kindred. The Tuit, i.e. Richard Tuit, died; and that was a great calamity. O'Raghallaigh,i.e. Maelmordha, son of John, son of Cathal, the best man that ever came of his own sept,. and thaṅ whom there seldom came of the race of Gaeidhel Glas a better person, according to the information and knowledge of all regarding him—i.e. a man to whom God granted all the virtues at first, viz., the palm of figure and shape, the palm of speech and eloquence, the palm of knowledge and learning, the palm of sense and counsel,[6] the palm of bounty and prowess; (and it would not be

---

[4] *Alexander Uaibhrech.* Alexander the Haughty, the son of John Cahánagh Mac Donnell.

[5] *Alii.* aʟı, MS.

[6] *Of Sense and counsel.* ʒceıʟʟe ocuʀ ʒcomaıpʟo, MS.

nipb ingnað ṙað ðo ḃeið a coinlenmain ṗip na
mbuaðpin, gup toghað ðo ðpuim na naðḃap pin na
aipðpí ap 1ð Raȝallaiȝ é, gup iompuip ḃáp paip ocup
é a láiṁ ag Ȝalloiḃ.

Ḱtt. Enáip pop Ceðaoin; pe bliaðna ocup tpi picheð,
ocup .u. ceð ocup mile, aip an Tiȝepna. Coinaltach
mac Caiðg mic Ruaiðpi óig mic Ruaiðpi ðaoiḃ Mic
Ðiapmaða ðo ðul a gclainn Coinmaið, ocup a mac
mapóen pip .i. Maolpuanaið; ocup ap nðol ðon típ
ðóiḃ po ðaiðiṁiȝpet ó poile .i. po an Comaltach a nÐún
Iomðan, ocup teið Maolpuanaið .i. a mac go Cill
beȝnað allapteð ðo Ȝeiṁip, ocup uathað ðá ðeȝ
muinntep maille pip. Ap ðtopnað ðo Mhaolpuanaið
ocup ðá ṁuinntep ap an bpion puapaðap ipin mbaile,
guppat mepcða meðopðaoin íað, ni po aipiȝpet aon ni
gunðo tuiplingpet a neptaipðe ap na ðoipppiḃ acu .i.
Ðpían mac Maoilpechlainn hi Cheallaiȝ, cona pianlað
áiȝ ocup iopȝaile na pořaip. Ro éipiȝ Maolpuanaið
co na uathað ðeȝ ðaoineḃ, ocup po bpipp pop a ðiðbað
aiḃ, ocup po imðiȝ ap eiȝin oppa ðo nept a laime, no
gup ðeȝlaiȝ a ṁuinntip pip o iomað anbṗopluinn
ocup o mepuȝhað na meipce; gup po mapbað Maolpuanaið ann .i. pep a aoppa ðob áppachta a nuaiple
ocup a noinech ocup a noippðeppcup, ocup ip mo ðo
ðuip ap ollaṁnaiḃ ocup ap aoip ealaðna na aimpip;
ocup ðo mapbað ann maille pip Ðiapmaið piabach

---

1 *Foreigners.* The construction of
this sentence is very faulty. Brian
Mac Dermot adds a marginal note in
the following words:—O Ðoinnaill
.i. an Calbach mac Maȝnuip mic
Coða ðuiḃ hi Ðomnaill, ocup
Maȝ Uiðip .i. Sean mac Concon-
nacht, ðpaȝail ḃaip aȝȝaipið an
aon nin; ocup ni paiḃe ðo Ȝhaoi-
ðealaiḃ Epenn ðip ðo buð mó ðo
pȝeluiḃ iná iatt: i.e. "O'Domhnaill,
viz., the Calbhach, son of Maghnus,
son of Aedh Dubh O'Domhnaill, and

Mag Uidhir, i.e. John, the son of
Cuconnacht, died within a brief period,
in the same month; and there were not
of the Gaeidhel of Erinn two persons
of greater account than they."

2 *People.* muinntep. This is the
last word of the text on fol. 97a, on
the lower margin of which Brian
Mac Dermot has added the following
entry:—"Maiðm ðo tuḃaipt ap
muinntip inn Iapla .i. Riocaipð
Saȝpanach, ðo Mupchað na
ðtuað, ðu ann ap Luipuið Eniann

wonderful that luck should attend the man of these virtues; and for these reasons he was elected chief king over the Ui-Raighilligh)—was put to death whilst detained in captivity by Foreigners.[1]

The kalends of January on Wednesday, (*recte* Tuesday); the age of the Lord one thousand, five hundred, and sixty-six years. Tomaltach, the son of Tadhg, son of Ruaidhri Og, son of Ruaidhri Caech Mac Diarmada, went to Clann-Connmhaigh, accompanied by his son, i.e. Maelruanaidh; and on going into the country they separated from one another, viz., Tomaltach remained in Dun-Iomdhain, and Maelruanaidh, i.e. his son, went to Cill-Begnad, on the inner side of Geimhis, accompanied by a few of his chief people.[2] When Maelruanaidh and his people applied themselves to[3] the wine which they found in the place, so that they were confused, intoxicated, they observed nothing until their enemies, viz., Brian, son of Maelsechlainn O'Cellaigh, with his band of valour and conflict, appeared[4] at the doors close by them. Maelruanaidh arose, with his few good men, and defeated his enemies; and he escaped from them forcibly, by the strength of his hand, until his people separated from him, being oppressed by superior force, and through the confusion of intoxication, so that Maelruanaidh was killed there; i.e. the most distinguished man of his age in nobility, bounty, and excellence, and who conferred most on professors and men of science in his time. And there were slain along with him Diarmaid Riabhach, the

---

óg mac Emainn mic Uilleag, ocuf tri ced maraon rir, taob tiar don Gallin. Do marbad and Ereihon mac Emainn Meaic Suibne, ocuf Domnall óg Mac Suibne, et alii multi;" i.e. "a defeat was given to the people of the Earl (i.e. Rickard Saxanach), by Murchadh-na-tuath, in which Edmond Og, son of Edmond, son of Ulick, was slain, and three hundred along with him, to the west of the Gaillimh. Eremhon, the son of Edmond Mac Suibhne, and Domhhall Og Mac Suibhne, were slain there, et alii multi." This battle is not noticed in the other Irish annals.

[3] *Applied themselves to.* The actual meaning of the original is "had fallen upon."

[4] *Appeared.* guppo tuirplingret; lit. "alighted."

mac Cathail mic Aoḋa, ocuſ Emonn an ṁaċaıre mac
Maoılꝛechlaınn ouınn mic Oonnchaoa ouıḃ, .ı. ꝼeꝛ a
aoꝛꝛa ıſ mó oo oeꝛluıc oo ḃáıṁ ocuſ oo ḃeúꝛaıxıḃ na
aımꝼıꝛ ꝼéın oo mac ſıꝛ Lenṁuna, ocuſ Eoxan mac an
ḃaıꝛo .ı. maoꝛ Mıc Oıaꝛmaoa; ocuſ ꝛo benaḋ eıch ocuſ
éoalaċa ıomḋa oıḃ ann. Comalcach mac Caıḋx Mıc
Oıaꝛmaoa ꝼéın oꝛaxaıl báıſ aċxaıꝛıo an ꝛeıꝛeḋ lá
ohéc a haıċle ḃáıſ a mıc ; ocuſ aoeꝛaıo aꝛoıle xuꝛab
oo ċuma a mıc ocuſ a muınceꝛı coꝛċaıꝛ ; oé Oomnaıx
ocuſ lá ꝼélı ſan Seaın aꝛ aon lá, ıſ ann coꝛċꝛaoaꝛ
na cꝛuım échca ſın. Ꝼeꝛ xan aınm mac Ḃꝛíaın Mıc
Oıaꝛmaoa ꝛuaıḋ oꝛaxaıl ḃáıſ an Ḃlıaoaın ſı .ı. ꝛóı
ḋuıne ın xach uıle ṁaıċ. Cꝛeċ ṁóꝛ le Mac Oıaꝛmaoa
.ı. Ruaıoꝛı, ocuſ le na mac .ı. Ḃꝛían, ó Ḃꝛían mac Maoılꝛechlaınn hı Cheallaıx; ocuſ ꝛo ꝼáxḃaoaꝛ maꝛcach
maıċ oía muınncıꝛ ıꝛın Cuıꝛꝛech mbuıoı ouꝛchuꝛ oo
xunna .ı. Ꝼelım mac Ḃꝛíaın ċoeıch; ocuſ ꝛo haḋluıceo
Oomnach na Cꝛınóıoı é a maınıſoıꝛ na Cꝛınóıoe ꝼeın.
Ḃꝛıan mac Mhaoılꝛechlaınn hı Cheallaıx .ı. ꝛoxa
ḋuıne uaſaıl a xcennuſ ꝛeḋna ocuſ a cꝛeċaıꝛechc,
ocuſ ꝼeꝛ íꝼlıxċı a eꝛcaꝛao, ohéc ın hoc anno. Cꝛeċ
ṁóꝛ le Ḃꝛıan mac Mıc Oıaꝛmaoa ó Aċ líax an
Ḃlıaoaın ſı. Clann Ouḃxoıll meıc Oonnchaıḋ ċaım,
ocuſ clann xıolla eꝛbuıx mıc Ouḃxoıll mıc Aıllın, oo
maꝛḃaḋ le ıaꝛla cloınoe Rıocaıꝛo ; .ı. le Rıcaꝛo
Saxꝛanach cuxaḋ ın maıḋm ſın, ocuſ oo cuıc ano ochc
xceo Albanaċ; ocuſ aıꝛ Rıꝛoeꝛc ınn ıáꝛaıno oo cuxaḋ
an maıḋm ſın a Cluaın í ax cꝛaıx ḃaın na neanıxeoh ;
ocuſ ꝛa haḋḃal oıḃ Albanaċ anoꝛın.

Ictt. Enaıꝛ ꝼoꝛ Aoıne ; bıꝛex ꝛuıꝛꝛe ; ꝛeachc
mblıaona ocuſ cꝛı ꝛıchec, cuıx ceo ocuſ mıle, aıſ ın
Cıxeꝛna. Maıḋm Ꝼeıꝛꝛce móıꝛe óꝛ Loċ na Súılıoe

---

1 *Hoc. oc,* MS.

2 *Richard-an-iarainn.* " Richard
of the Iron ;" familiarly called " Iron
Dick." This entry is in the hand of

Brian Mac Dermot, who writes the
name of this celebrated personage
Rıꝛoeꝛc aınn ıaꝛaıno.

A.D.
[1566.]

son of Cathal, son of Aedh, and Edmond-an-Mhachaire, son of Maelsechlainn Donn, son of Donnchadh Dubh, (i.e. the man of his age who gave the most to guests and exiles in his own time, the son of a faithful pair), and Eoghan Mac-an-bhaird, i.e. Mac Diarmada's steward; and numerous horses and spoils were taken from them there. Tomaltach, the son of Tadhg Mac Diarmada, died himself soon after, the sixteenth day after his son's death; and some say that it was of grief for his son, and for his people, he died. On Sunday, which was the day of Saint John's festival, these heavy losses occurred. Fer-gan-ainm, the son of Brian Mac Diarmada Ruadh, died this year; i.e. an eminent man in every kind of good. A great prey *was taken* by Mac Diarmada, i.e. Ruaidhri, and by his son, i.e. Brian, from Brian son of Maelsechlainn O'Cellaigh; and they lost a good horseman of their people in the Cuirrech-buidhe, from a gunshot, i.e. Felim, the son of Brian Caech; and he was buried on Trinity Sunday in the monastery of the Trinity. Brian, the son of Maelsechlainn O'Cellaigh, i.e. a choice gentleman in captainship and depredation, and the humbler of his enemies, died in hoc[1] anno. A great prey *was taken* by Brian, the son of Mac Diarmada, from Ath-liag, this year. The sons of Dubhgall, son of Donnchadh Cam, and the sons of Gilla-esbuig, son of Dubhgall Mac Ailin, were slain by the Earl of Clann-Rickard; i.e. by Rickard Saxanagh this defeat was given; and eight hundred Albanachs fell there; and on Richard-an-iarainn[2] this defeat was inflicted, in Cluain-I, at Traigh-bhan-na-neanighedh;[3] and the destruction of Albanachs there was prodigious.

The kalends of January on Friday;[4] after a bissextile; the age of the Lord one thousand, five hundred, and sixty-seven years. The victory of Fersad-mór, above

[1567.]

---

[3] *Traigh-bhan-na-neanighedh.* "The White Strand of the *ennuchs* (or swamps)." It is still called the White Strand, and is about three miles to the west of Galway.

[4] *Friday.* Should be Wednesday.

αρ O Néill .ι. αρ Shean mac Cuinn hι Neill, le hUα
n'Oomnaill .ι. Ccoɓ mac Maᵹhaιr mιc Ccoɓa hι 'Ohomn-
naιll; acur ní heιoιr α rιom ιná ιnnιrιn αρ ráᵹbao
ocur αρ báιcheo ann. O Néill .ι. an Sean ceona rιn
mac Cuinn .ι. cιᵹerna an Cóιᵹeo Ullcaιᵹ, ocur αɓɓαr
rí Erenn ᵹan rrerrαbrα, ocur an rer αr mó ro cιɓ-
luιc ocur ro cóιrɓιr α nErιnn, oo ṁαrbαo α ɓrιoll
oCClbanachaιɓ, ιαr ná ɓul uαchαo oαoιneɓ αρ α nιon-
chaιb rειn ιnα brorlonᵹrpuιrc cuca. Mac 'Oιαrmαoα
.ι. Ruaιorι mac Caιɓᵹ Mιc 'Oιαrmαoα oo ᵹαɓáιl oo
muιncιr Phlannaᵹáιn, ocur αoεrαιo αroιle ᵹurαb αρ
rιc oo rιnneɓ. an ᵹnιomrιn. Muιncεr Phlannaᵹáιn oíα
rεcαoαɓ oO Conchobaιr ruaɓ, ocur O Conchobaιr oα
rεcαoαɓ oo Murchαo mac Caιɓᵹ mιc 'Ooṁnaιll hι
Perᵹaιl, ᵹo claιnn Ccṁlαoιɓ, oια cóιmeo. Nír ruιlnᵹεo
na ᵹnιoma rιn le mac Mιc 'Oιαrmαoα .ι. le Orían mac
Ruaιorι Mιc 'Oιαrmαoα; .ι. ro ᵹαɓ ror buaιɓreɓ ocur
ror bιcṁεrcαo α ɓιɓɓαιoιb, ocur αᵹ roᵹuιl ᵹo rír
αrrachcα ror α ercaιroιɓ, αnoιαιɓ α αchαr, ᵹurrur
creɓ ocur ᵹurrur loιrc Muιncεr Phlannaᵹáιn ᵹo
hιomlán, ocur na Cluaιncι co huιlιɓι; oιr ιn ro ráᵹαιb
ᵹorc ᵹan ᵹerrαɓ ιná cεɓ ᵹan lorcαo αρ rlιαɓ báɓna
ιná αρ ᵹach caoɓ ɓe. Ccr mιlleɓ ocur αρ mórαrᵹuιn
na ᵹcrιoc ocur na ᵹcιnneoac rιn oo mac Mιc 'Oιαrmαoα, ro cαιrrιnᵹ mac hι Ruaιrc .ι. Orían mac Oríaιn
mιc Eoᵹaιn hι Ruaιrc laιr αρ clαιnn Ccṁlαoιɓ. Ro
loιrceo ocur ro creɓαo an cír uιle léo, ocur ro mαrbαo
Cachal mac Caιɓᵹ mιc 'Ooṁnaιll hι Perᵹaιl leιr, ocur
mac mιc I Perᵹaιl ɓuιɓe, ocur morán elι maιlle rú.
Ro rιllrεc ιαr mbuaιɓ corcαιr. Ccᵹcιonn αɓᵹoιrιo na
ɓιαιɓ rιn cαnιc Q Raιᵹιllιᵹ .ι. Ccoɓ mac Maolṁórɓα
I Raιᵹιllιᵹ, αρ ιonnroιᵹeo αρ O mOιrn co hUα mOrιúιn
na Sιonna. Ro creɓ ocur rò loιrc an cír, ocur ro

---

¹ *During peace;* i.e. whilst peace | captors. The words of the text, αρ
existed between Mac Dermot and his | rιc, lit. mean "upon peace."

Loch-na-Suilidhe, over O'Neill, i.e. over John son of Conn O'Neill, by O'Domhnaill, i.e. Aedh, son of Maghnus, son of Aedh O'Domhnaill; and it is not possible to reckon, or tell, all that were lost and drowned there. O'Neill, i.e. the same John, son of Conn, i.e. lord of the Ultonian province, and royal heir of Erinn without dispute, and the man who gave and presented most in Erinn, was killed in treachery by Albanachs, after he had gone to them to their camp, under their own protection, accompanied by a few men. Mac Diarmada, i.e. Ruaidhri, the son of Tadhg Mac Diarmada, was taken prisoner by Muinter-Flannagain; (and some say that it was during peace[1] this act was done). Muinter-Flannagain transferred him to O'Conchobhair Ruadh, and O'Conchobhair sent him to Murchadh, son of Tadhg, son of Domhnall O'Ferghail, to Clann-Amhlaibh, to be detained. These acts were not endured by Mac Diarmada, i.e. by Brian, son of Ruaidhri Mac Diarmada: i.e., he began to disturb and confound his enemies, and boldly to plunder his adversaries, on account of his father, so that he preyed and burned Muinter-Flannagain[2] entirely, and the Cluainte altogether; for he left neither a corn-field without cutting, nor a house without burning, on Sliabh-Bádhna, or on either side of it. After the destruction and pillage of these districts and septs, by the son of Mac Diarmada, he brought the son of O'Ruairc, i.e. Brian, the son of Brian, son of Eoghan O'Ruairc, with him against Clann-Amhlaibh. The entire country was burned and plundered by them; and Cathal, the son of Tadhg, son of Domhnall O'Ferghail, was killed by him,[3] and the grandson of O'Ferghail Buidhe, and many more along with them. They returned with triumph. In the course of a short time after that O'Raighilligh, i.e. Aedh, the son of Maelmordha O'Raighilligh, came on an expedition against O'Birn, to Ui-Briuin-na-Sinna. He

---

[2] *Muinter-Flannagain;* i.e. the territory of Muinter-Flannagain, in the county of Roscommon.

[3] *By him:* i.e., by Brian, son of Ruaidhri Mac Diarmada, or Rory Mac Dermot.

ṁarḃsat cuid dá daoineḃ. Rug Brían mac I Ruairc ocus Brían mac Mic Diarmada á toraiġecht air, ocus ro lensat co Móin lesc é. Do benaḋ a ċreċa dO Raiġilliġ annsin, ocus do benad ced ech maille rú, ocus cuid ṁór dá ndaoineḃ. Mac Diarmada dfuaslucad dia mac fein .i. Brían, deis ar milled na ṫimċeall isin mbliadain cedna, oir tuc sé tri ced bó ass, ocus síṫ síḃruiḋṫi, ocus do buḋ dairnéis na gCluainti fein leṫ an fuasluicṫi sin. Feall do ḋenaṁ do Maiġistir Framsa, ocus do Macomais ocus do Saxsanachaib, air Muircertach O Morḋa ocus air a muinntir; ocus ase inaḋ andernaḋ in feall sin a raiṫ mor ṁullaidh Maisden; ocus do marḃaḋ andsin Muircertach, ocus ceiṫre ḋuine dhec ocus tri fichid; ocus ni dernaḋ a nErinn riam gnim buḋ grane na sin. Maġnus mac Cormaic mic Domnaill ṁaoil I Laimin, .i. feaḋmanntaċ Ruaidri Mic Diarmada, do marbad le sliocht Eogain Mic Diarmada, ocus le sliocht Cormaic Mic Diarmada, a feall ar an Moloig. Cormac mac Taiḋg Mic Diarmada .i. mac Táiḋg mic Ruaidri, do marbad do Cathal mac Maoilruanaiḋ Mic Diarmada. Droichett aṫa Luain for Sinuinn do ḋenum isin mbliadain sin leisin mbainrigan Shaxanach, ocus sir hanrai Sidneiġ na ġiuisdis a nErinn, ocus Eilísdabed ainm na banrigana sin. O Conċuḃair Sligiġ do dul go Saxsanaiḃ .i. Doṁnall.

Kl. Enair for [Dardain]; ocht mbliadna ocus tri fichit, cuig ced ocus mile, ais an Tigerna. Bliadain ḟuar ainfinech esbadach an ḃliadain si, ocus as beg ant ingnad sin, oir is innti adbaṫ Mac Diarmada .i. Ruaiḋri mac Taiḋg mic Ruaidri óig .i. rí ṁoiġe Luirg

---

1 *Brian.* The rest of the entries for this year have been transposed in the MS., as appears from the context, and also from a brief marginal note in the handwriting of Brian Mac Dermot. The liberty has been taken of placing them in their proper order above.

2 *Framsa.* Framsa is by mistake for Fransa, i.e. Francis Cosby.

3 *Macomas.* This is evidently corrupt. The name intended was probably mac Thomais, or the "son of Thomas." The Annalist Dowling, who, like the Four M., records this trans-

plundered and burned the country; and they killed a number of his people. Brian, the son of O'Ruairc, and Brian son of Mac Diarmada, overtook him in pursuit, and followed him as far as Móin-lesc. His preys were there taken from O'Raighilligh ; and one hundred horses were taken along with them, and a large number of his men. Mac Diarmada was ransomed by his own son, i.e. Brian,[1] after all that had been destroyed on his account in the same year; for he gave three hundred cows as his ransom, and a firm peace; (and the half of this ransom was of the cattle of the Cluainte alone). Treachery was committed by Master Framsa,[2] and by Macomas,[3] and the Saxons, on Muirchertach O'Mordha, and on his people; (and the place where this treachery was committed was in the great rath of Mullagh-Maisten); and Muirchertach and seventy-four men were slain there; and no uglier deed than that was ever committed in Erinn. Maghnus,[4] the son of Cormac, son of Domhnaill Mael O'Laimhin, i.e. Ruaidhri Mac Diarmada's servant, was killed by the descendants of Eoghan[5] Mac Diarmada, and the descendants of Cormac Mac Diarmada, in treachery, on the Molog. Cormac, the son of Tadhg Mac Diarmada, (i.e. the son of Tadhg, son of Ruaidhri), was killed by Cathal, son of Maelruanaidh Mac Diarmada. The bridge[6] of Ath-Luain, over the Sinainn, was constructed in this year by the Saxon queen ; (and Sir Henry Sidney was Justiciary in Erinn, and Elizabeth was the name of this queen). O'Conchobhair Sligigh went to Saxon-land, i.e. Domhnall.

The kalends of January on [Thursday] ; the age of the Lord one thousand, five hundred, and sixty-eight years. A cold, stormy, year of scarcity was this year ; and this is little wonder, for it was in it Mac Diarmada died, i.e. Ruaidhri, the son of Tadhg, son of Ruaidhri Og, i.e. king

---

action under the year 1577, mentions Robert Harpoll as Cosby's associate.

[4] *Maghnus.* This entry is added in the lower margin, in Brian Mac Dermot's handwriting.

[5] *Eoghan.* oeoᵹ, MS.

[6] *Bridge.* This entry, and the following, are added in the handwriting of Brian Mac Dermot, who spells Elizabeth "Eilíroaben."

ocuſ Ɑiſtiᵹ ocuſ tiſe Ṫuaṫail, ocuſ aiſotiᵹeſna aſ
cſiċ ċlainni Ṁhaolſuanaiƀ ᵹo huilⅰƀⅰ, ocuſ aſaill ᵭo
cſiochaiƀ ocuſ ᵭo caom ṫuaṫaiƀ Connachⱅ, a ᵹcill
ocuſ a ⱅuaiṫ; ſí ſo ċaiṫ ocuſ ſo ċoſſuin Cſuaċan co
na caoiⱅoiſeſaiƀ, ocuſ cúiᵹeᵭ Connachⱅ aiſchena; ſⅰ
nach bſuaiſ aon ſí ᵭá ᵭⱅaniſ ᵭa aicme ſoime ſiam, ᵹo
Ṁaolſuanaiƀ móſ, oiſeᵭ inⱞe ocuſ aſᵭ ſlaiṫiſ ſiſ a
ⱅuaiṫ ocuſ a neᵹluiſ; conaƀ ᵭia ⱞolaƀ a haiṫlⅰ a ƀáiſ
ſo ſaiƀ an ſilⅰ ná ſecail ſe, ᵭſoillſiuᵹhaᵭ a einiᵹ
ocuſ a aiṫne ocuſ a eſlabſa ſaiſ, conebiſⱅ,

ᵹeᵹ ioṫmaſ ſineⱞna na néiᵹiuſ ocuſ na ᵭollaman,
Cſaoƀ cumſa ċnuaiſſ na ᵹcliaſ ocuſ na ᵹceſſbach,
Ꝺóſſ ᵭiona na ᵭᵭáⱞ ocuſ na ᵭᵭeoſaiᵭ,
Ɓile buaᵭa buan ſoſcaiᵭ na mbſuᵹhaiᵭ ocuſ na mbiaⱅⱅach.

Inᵭeoin ſoſaiſ an enᵹnuma ocuſ an einiᵹ; ſéiᵹe ſoſóſ-
ƀa na ſéle, an ſlaiṫ ſial ſoiſᵹliᵭi ſiſeolaċ; colaⱞan
coſanⱅa ciſⱅ ocuſ cóſa clainni Ṁhaolſuanaiƀ ᵭo ſeiſ
a ſoċaiſ ocuſ a ſenleabaſ. Coſmac ua Cuinn cet
caⱅhaiᵹ ᵭſioſ ocuſ ᵭeoluſ ocuſ ᵭealaƀnachaiƀ;
Cuċulainn cſiċe Connachⱅ ſe coſnum ocuſ ſe caⱅ-
ƀuaᵭha aſ ƀⅰƀbaᵭaiƀ, ocuſ aſ ƀⅰċ ᵭanaſaiƀ; Ꝣuaiſe
ᵭuaſſach ᵭeᵹ oiniᵹ ⱅſlechⱅa Ṁuiſeᵹhaiᵹh ⱞuilleċain;
Laoċ Liaⱅⱞuine leiċe Cuinn aſ ſéile, aſ ſiſinne, aſ
oinech; ſeſ ᵭo coiméᵭ a ċlú ocuſ a ainm, ocuſ a
áiſeⱞ, a ᵭeiſc ocuſ a ƀaonnachⱅ ocuſ a ƀeᵹaiṫne, o
aoiſ naoiƀenⱅachⱅ ᵹo hioⱞⱞaiƀ a éᵹa, ocuſ a nam
an éᵹai ſeiſſin, ᵹan aoiſ ᵹan iⱅᵭeſᵹaᵭ, ᵹan éᵹnach

---

[1] *He said.* The name of the composer of the enconiums which follow
is not given. They were probably
the effusions of some member of the
O'Duigenan family of poets and
chroniclers. In addition to the ex-
travagant laudations which encumber
the text, the margin of the MS. con-
tains thirteen lines of epithets of a
like character, which it has not been
considered necessary to print.

[2] *Cormac Ua Cuinn-cet-chathaigh ;*

i.e., " Cormac, grandson of Conn of
the hundred battles."

[3] *Pirates.* ᵭanaſaiƀ; dative plu-
ral of ᵭanaſ. The name of *Danar*,
originally applied by the Irish to the
Danes, was at a later period applied
to pirates, ruffians, and desperadoes
generally. See Todd's ed of *Cogadh
Gaedhel re Gallaibh*, Introd., pp. xxx.,
xxxi., and cxc.

[4] *Guaire.* Guaire Aidhne, king of
Connacht (ob. A.D. 662); a prince

of Magh-Luirg, and Airtech, and Tir-Tuathail, and chief lord over the whole territory of Clann-Maelruanaidh, and some more of the districts and fair territories of Connacht, both ecclesiastical and lay ; a king who spent and defended Cruachan with its fair borders, and the rest of the province of Connacht ; a king compared to whom no king that came of his sept before him, up to Maelruanaidh Mór, obtained as much wealth and high sovereignty in territory and in church. And hence it was to praise him after his death the poet uttered these words, to illustrate his bounty, his intelligence, and his generosity, when he said,[1]

The productive vine branch of the poets and doctors ;
The fragrant fruit tree of the learned and gamesters ;
The sheltering tree of guests and strangers ;
The triumphant ever-shady tree of the brughaidhs and biatachs ;

the generating furnace of prowess and honour ; the golden ridge-pole of generosity ; the bounteous, decisive, truly-learned prince ; the defensive column of the right and justice of the Clann-Maelruanaidh, in accordance with their privileges and old books ; a Cormac Ua Cuinn-cet-chathaigh[2] in knowledge, skill, and sciences ; the Cuchullainn of the territory of Connacht in contending against, and triumphing over, enemies and pirates ;[3] the rewarding, generous, Guaire[4] of the race of Muiredhach Muillethain ; the Laech-Liathmhaine[5] of Leth-Cuinn for generosity, truth, and bounty ; a man who preserved his fame, his name, his repute, his charity, his humanity, and his good intelligence, from the age of infancy to the time of his death, and even at the hour of death, free from

whose generosity obtained for him the name of " Guaire the Hospitable."

[5] Laech - Liathmhaine. " Hero of Liathmhain." The name of this person was Cuan Mac Cailchin. His fort of Liathmhain, or Cloch-Liathmhaine, is no longer in existence ; but the name is preserved in that of the townland of Cloghleafin, in the barony of Condons and Clongibbons, co. Cork.

ᵹαn eᵽcuιne, ᵹαn oιᵽbιᵽe ᵹαn άτιompάᵭ, ᵽo ᴄαιᴇ̆ α ᵽιᵹꞙ
ocuᵽ α ᵱo ꝼⱡαιᴄ̆eᵽ, α ᵱαιᵭᵭᵽeᵽ ocuᵽ α ᵱιoᵱ ιnᵯe, ᴅo ᵽéιᵱ
ᵯenmαn α ᵯóᵱ cᵽoιᵭe ᵭuᵭéιn. Cchᴄ chenα, ᵹeᵽ ᵭάᵭᵭαⱡ
ᵱe ᵱαιᵽnéιᵽ ocuᵽ ᵹeᵽ ⱡιonmαᵽ ᵱe ⱡάnᵽoιⱡⱡᵱιuᵹαᴅ, ocuᵽ
ᵹιᵭ nάᵱ ᵭéιᴅιᵱ α ᵱíom ᵱe nα ᵱo eoⱡchαιb ᴄᵱeιᵽᵱι α
ᴇ̆ιᵹeᵽnαιᵽ αᵱ nα cᵱιochαιb ocuᵽ αᵱ nα cαomᴇ̆uαᴄhαιb
αᵱ ᵱeᵭ uᵽᵯóιᵱ Chonnαchᴄ α cιⱡⱡ ocuᵽ α ᴄuαιᴇ̆, nι ᵱo
ᵱάᵹαιᵭ ⱡuαᴄ̈ én ᵭuιnn ᴅoιᵹ̈ᵽechᴄ, αchᴄ αᵯάιn ᵱo ᴇ̆uιⱡⱡ
bennαchᴄαιn ocuᵽ buιᴅechuᵽ éᵱⱡoᵯ ocuᵽ eᵹoιⱡᵽech,
ᵱιⱡeᵭ ocuᵽ oⱡⱡαmαn, ᵭochᴄ ocuᵽ ᵭαιnᴄᵱeαᵭᴄαch, ᵭeoᵱαιᵭ
ocuᵽ ᵭíⱡⱡechᴄαᵭ, αnᵭᵱαnn ocuᵽ oιⱡιᴇ̆ᵱech, αoᵽᵱα mαᵽᴄᵱα
ocuᵽ móᵽᵹαⱡαιᵱ, αoιᴅheᴅ ocuᵽ ιonnoᵱᵱᴄαch, ᵭó ᵱéιn ocuᵽ
ᴅά ιαᵱᵱmα ocuᵽ ᴅά oιᵹᵽeᴅhαιb. ꝼuαιᵽ ᵱóᵱ ᴄαbαᵽᴄuᵽ
ocuᵽ ᴄιᵭⱡucαᵭ ᴄᵱomαᵭbαιⱡ on Cᵱιnóιᴅ ᴇ̆oᵹhαιᴅe ᴄᵱe
ᵱeᵽᵱαnαιᵹ .ι. ᵹαⱡαᵱ ᵹαn αccαιᵽ ᵹαn αnbᵱoᵱⱡonn, ᵹαn
ᵹuαιᵱᵱ ᵹαn ᵹᵱάιn, α ᴄ̈ιαⱡⱡ ocuᵽ α ᴄ̆uιmne, α ᵱeᵽᵱún
ocuᵽ α ᵱoᴇ̆uιcᵽι ᵱéιn αᵱ α ᴄ̆ommuᵽ, ᵹo bᵱuαιᵱ αιᴇ̆ᵱιᵹꞙ
ιoᵭαn ocuᵽ αιᴇ̆ᵱechuᵽ αᵭbαιⱡ ιnα ᴄ̆ιonαιᴅ, ιαᵱ ᵹcαιᴇ̆eᵯ
ochᴄᵯoᵭα bⱡιαᵭαn αchᴄmαᴅ ᵱuαιⱡⱡ, ocuᵽ ᴄᵱί ᵱιᴄ̈ιᴅ
bⱡιαᴅαn ᴅιᵭᵱιn nα αb αᵱ oιⱡén nα Cᵱιnóιᴅe ᵱoᵱ ⱡoᴄ̆ Cé
ocuᵽ ᵱoᵱ ⱡoᴄ̆ uαchᴄαιᵱ, ocuᵽ bⱡιαᵭuιn ιᵱ ⱡuᵹα nó ᵱιᴄ̈e nα
αιᵱᴅᴄιᵹeᵽᵱα αᵱ cᵱιochαιb cⱡαιnnι Mhαoⱡᵱuαnαιᴅh ᵹo
huιⱡιᵭι, ocuᵽ ⱡeᴇ̆ ᵹαch αon ᵭⱡιαᴅnα ᵭιᵭᵱιn α bᵱoᵱⱡonᵹꞷ
ᵱoᵱᴄ αᵱ mαᴄ̆αιᵱe Chonnαchᴄ, ᴅαιᵯᵭeoιn moᵱάιn ᴅo
Ᵹhαⱡⱡoιb ocuᵽ ᴅo Ᵹhαoιᵭeαⱡαιb Eᵱenn ocuᵽ ᵹαch comꞷ
αᵱᵱαn άιᵱchenα; nó ᵹomαᴅ ᴅά ᵭⱡιαᴅαιn ocuᵽ ᴅά ᵱιᴄ̈eᴄ
ᵱo ᴄαιᴇ̆ Mαc Ꝺιαᵱmαᴅα αᵱ αn oᵱᴅuᵹαᴅᵱιn; ocuᵽ ιᵱᵱé

1 *From satire.* Here begins the fragment in the British Museum MS., Clar. 45, which has hitherto passed for a *portion* of the MS. H.1.19; but as the contents of the four first pages of the Brit. Mus. fragment are also contained in the MS. H. 1. 19, it is plain that the former cannot be a part of the latter. It is rather a portion of another copy of the same annals, made about the same time as the

MS. H. 1. 19, and seemingly belonging to the same owner, namely, Brian Mac Dermot, chief of Moylurg. This fragment is indicated by the title " Clar." in the following notes. Its relation to the MS. H. 1. 19 forms the subject of some observations in the Introduction.

2 *Guests and exiles.* αoιᴅeᵭ ocuᵽ ιoιnαᵱᴄach, Clar., where the words are transposed.

satire[1] or reproach, censure or malediction, rebuke or envy; who spent his sovereignty and great lordship, his wealth and large property, according to the desire of his own great heart. But, though it would be excessive to relate, and copious to completely illustrate, and though the most learned could not calculate, the power of his sovereignty over the districts and fair territories throughout the greater part of Connacht, both ecclesiastical and lay, he left not the value of one groat of inheritance; but he earned the blessing of patrons and ecclesiastics, poets and doctors, the poor and widows, strangers and orphans, the infirm and pilgrims, martyrs, and victims of heavy sickness, guests and exiles,[2] for himself, and for his posterity, and heirs. He obtained, moreover, prodigious bounty and gifts from the elect Trinity, viz., illness without pain, without oppression, without anguish, without horror, and the command of his own sense, memory, reason, and understanding, until he experienced pure penance, and great penitence for his faults, after spending nearly[3] eighty years. And three score years[4] of this period he was abbot in Trinity-Island on Loch-Cé, and on Loch-uachtair, and nineteen years chief lord over all the territories of the Clann-Maelruanaidh;[5] and the half of every year of these he spent in an encampment on Machaire-Connacht, in despite of many of the Foreigners and Gaeidhel of Erinn, and of all other neighbours; (or it was[6] forty-two years, perhaps, Mac Diarmada spent in that manner); and the

---

[3] *Nearly.* achtmaꝺ ꞃuaill, "but little," Clar. ꞃuall, MS.

[4] *Three score years.* · tꞃí ꞃíceꝺ bliaꝺan. Doubtless a mistake for tꞃí bliaꝺna ꞃíceꝺ, "twenty-three years."

[5] *Of the Clann - Maelruanaidh.* Clainni Ⱳhaolꞃuanaꞇꝺh, MS. Cloinne Ⱳaolꞃ, Clar. The Clar. fragment adds, "amail aꞃoubꞃamaꞃ naꞃnꝺiaꞇꝺ; ocuꞃ iꞃꞃé an Ruaiꝺꞃi ꞃin ꞃóꞃ ꞃo ċait ꝺá

bliaꝺain ocuꞃ ꝺá ꞃícet, &c.;" "as we have said further on [lit. 'after us']; and it was this Ruaidhri that spent two score and two years," &c. See next note.

[6] *Or it was.* The original of the clause in parenthesis is given in slightly altered phraseology in the Clar. fragment, where the clause is also a little transposed. The construction of the entire entry is very loose and inaccurate in style.

ιοναͻ ιναμbιͻ α ͷοͷlonͻ̇ͷoͷτ αͷ αν b̷ͷeͻͷιη ͻ̇ο̇ ͻναͼhαͼ
.ι. um ͷͻeιͼín να ͻͻ̇cenͻ ocuͷ um ͷ̇ναͷάν νͻ̇αͷ, ocuͷ
um ιοмαιͷe μοιͻ̇e hΟι, ocuͷ αͷ ͻαch ͼαοͻ̇ ͻ̇ιͻ̇. αchͼ
chena ͷͻ̇ιοͷμuιͷ αν ͼeιͻ̇m ͼαͷ nach ͻͼίαͻ̇αͷ, ocuͷ αͷ
nach eιͻιͷ ιοмͻ̇αbάιl ͷαιͷ, co b̷ͷuαιͷ bαͷͷ comna ιαͷ
ναιͷͷͷenn ocuͷ ιαͷ bͷͷοιͻ̇eͷͼ, ͻͻαͷͻαοιν manͻάιl αͷ
caιͷͷιͻ̇ Ϻιc ͻιαͷμαͻα, ocuͷ ͻ̇uͷͷuͷ άͻ̇lύcαͻ̇ α coͷͷ ͻ̇ο
huαͷαl onoͷach α ναͻ̇ͻ̇α να ναom ocuͷ α νιομͻ̇ha να
néͷlum .ι. ͷoͷ oιlén να Ͳͷίnόιͻe, αмαιl ͷo oͷͻαιͻ̇
ͷeιν α chuͷ α ναͻ̇lucαͻ να ναb ͷoιмe, ͻo αͻ̇μάιl ocuͷ
ͻo ͷ̇οιllͷιuͻ̇αͻ α eͻ̇να ocuͷ α eoluιͷ, ocuͷ ͻo ͻ̇ιulͼαͻ̇αͻ
ͻον ͻιομuͷ, ocuͷ ͻo μ̇ͻ̇ͻ̇uͻ̇αͻ onόͷα να heͻ̇luιͷι να
ͻ̇ιαιͻ̇. Ꞃo αͷͻ̇nám α anum ίαͷͷιν αͷ αν ͻ̇caιͷc ͻ̇coιͼ-
ͼιnn ͻ̇αν ͼ̇ͷιͼ̇ ͻ̇αν ͷ̇οιͷͼenͻ ιν ͷécula ͷeculoͷum αмen;
conιͻ̇ ͻό ͷo ͷάιͻ̇ αͻ̇ͼ uͼ̇ͻαͷ αν ͷανιι,

> Ochͼ mblιαͻνα ͷeͷcu ͻeͷͻ̇ ͻ̇αm,
> Cuιͻ̇ ceͻ ιͷ mίle blιαͻαν,
> Ο ͻ̇eιν Cͷιͷͼ, οιͷιͷ ͷαͻα,
> ͻ̇άͷͷ Ꞃuαιͻ̇ͷί Ϻιc ͻιαͷμαͻα.

αchͼ chéna, ͻo ͷιͻ̇neͻ̇ cͷuιͼ ͻ̇αν ͼ̇éιͷ ocuͷ ceαll ͻ̇αν
αbαͻ, ocuͷ ͼíͷ ͻ̇αν ͼιͻ̇eͷna, ͻo ͼ̇íͷ Ϻιc ͻιαͷμαͻα
αhαιͼ̇le ͻ̇άιͷ Ꞃuαιͻ̇ͷί Ϻιc ͻιαͷμαͻα, όιͷ ͼανͻ̇αͻαͷ
uιlc ιομͻ̇α ιαͷ να éͻ̇ .ι. ͻίͼ̇ ocuͷ ͻιlͻ̇enͻ Chlαιννι
Ϻhαolͷuαναιͻ̇ ͷo να νeͷͼ conuιͻ̇e ͷιν. Ꞃo мαοlαͻ̇ α
menmα ocuͷ α мeιͷnech; ͷo bochͼαιͻ̇heͻ α bͷuͻ̇hαͻα
ocuͷ α bιαͼͼαιͻ̇̇ ocuͷ α bαινͼͷeαͻ̇ͼhαιͻ̇h; ͷo hιονͷ̇αͷ-
bαͻ α héͷloιm ocuͷ α hollαмαιν ocuͷ α hoιͷͼ̇ιννιͻ̇̇; ͷo

---

1 *Was wont to be.* ιναμbιͻ̇, MS.
αμboιͻ̇, Clar.

² *Near.* um. ιm, Clar.

³ *After mass.* ιαͷ ναιͷͷͷenn.
ιαͷ ναιͷͷͷιοnn, Clar.

⁴ *Thursday.* The page of the MS.
H. 1. 19 (fol. 97 b) containing the rest
of the entries for this year is a good
deal injured, and some words have

consequently been supplied from the
Clar. fragment.

⁵ *Of the patrons.* να néͷlum;
supplied from Clar.

⁶ *In the sepulchre.* α ναͻ̇lucαͻ.
α νιομͻ̇hα, Clar.

⁷ *His wisdom and knowledge.* α
eͻ̇να ocuͷ α eoluιͷ; supplied from
Clar.

place in which his fortified camp was wont to be[1] during that time was near[2] Sceithin-na-cend, and near[2] Fuaran-Gar, and near[2] Imaire-Maighe-hAi, and on each side of them. But the disease from which there is no escape, and which cannot be avoided, attacked him, and he died after communion, after mass,[3] and after precept, on Maunday Thursday,[4] on Carraig-Mic-Diarmada; and his body was nobly, honourably, interred in the abode of the saints, and the bed of the patrons,[5] i.e. in Trinity-Island, as he himself had ordered that he should be buried in the sepulchre[6] of the preceding abbots, to exhibit, and manifest, his wisdom and knowledge,[7] and to renounce pride, and to magnify the honour of the church after him. His[8] soul afterwards journeyed to the general Pasch without end or limit, in sæcula sæculorum.[9] Amen. It was for him, therefore, the author[10] composed the stanza,

" Sixty-eight years, certain to me,
Five hundred, and a thousand years,
From the birth of Christ, a long record,
To the death of Ruaidhri MacDiarmada."

Moreover, Mac Diarmada's country was made a harp without a céis,[11] and a church without an abbot, after the death of Ruaidhri Mac Diarmada, for numerous evils[12] came after his decease, viz., the ruin and destruction of the power which the Clann-Maelruanaidh possessed up to that time. Their ardour and spirit were blunted; their[13] brughaidhs,[14] and biatachs,[15] and widows, were impoverished; their[13] patrons, and professors, and airchinnechs

---

[8] *His.* α. Omitted in Clar.

[9] *Sæculorum.* ſecloꞃum, MS. and Clar.

[10] *Author.* uċꝺaꞃ uᵹꝺaꞃ, Clar.

[11] *Céis.* A céis (pron. *kaysh*) is explained in *Lebar na hUidhre* as "a small harp which accompanied a large one." See O'Donovan's *Supplement to O'Reilly's Dictionary,* v. *céis.*

[12] *Numerous evils.* uiⱡc iomꝺa; supplied from Clar.

[13] *Their.* The chronicler is here speaking of MacDermot's country; and for "their" we should probably translate "its."

[14] *Brughaidhs.* Extensive farmers.

[15] *Biatachs.* Another class of landholders.

muṡhaiṡeḃ ocur ro marḃaḋ morán ḋá macaiḃ riṡ ocur ḋeṡḃaoiniḃ. Ro rárr coṡaḋ coicċenn eṫir Ṡhalloiḃ ocur Ṡhaoiḃealaiḃ, Ӑlbanċaiḃ ocur 8aχanaiḃ, riol Conchobair ocur clainn Maolruanaiṡ, ṫaoirriṡ ocur ṫúaċha, ṫaréir an aro rlaċa. Ro rárroiṡeḋ maṡ luirṡ ocur maṡ Ӑoi ocur Ӑirṫech, ocur ṫúaċha Connachṫ co huilíḃe o loċ Ӑillinne ṡo Camrruċán. Ro rárr, imorro, ruachṫ ocur rirṡorṫa, ṡoiḋ ocur eiṡion, rlaḋ ocur ráruṡaḋ, inḋliṡeḋ ocur éḋualanṡ, reċnoin na ṡcrioċ ocur na ṡcennaḋach. Ro hionnarḃaḋ ocur ro heirréiḋheḋ iaḋ uile eṫir raor ocur ḋaor a ṡcríochaiḃ ciana comaiṡṫecha .i. a ṫír Ӑṁalṡaiḃ ocur a ṫir Ṗiacraċ, a niochṫar Connachṫ ocur a Mainechaiḃ, a clann Connmaiḃ ocur a clann Ricairo. Ӑraill eli .i. Ṫoirrohealbach mac Eoṡain Mic Ḋiarmaḋa ḋo rioṡaḋ ina ionaḋ, ḋo ċoil ċille ocur ṫuaiċi, eṡlairi ocur ollaman. Cunḋaoir ċlainni Ricairo .i. Mairṡréṡ, inṡen Ḋonnchaḋa mic Conchobair hi Ḃriain .i. an ben ir rerr ḋo ḃói a nErinn ina haimrir réin, ḋhéc an ḃliaḋain rin. O Concuḃair 8liṡiṡ .i. Ḋomnall ḋo ċeachṫ a 8aχranaiḃ, ocur raiṫenṫ ḋo ċaḃairṫ leir ar a ḋuchaiḋ o in banriṡan.

Ịctt. Enair. Noi mbliaḋna ocur ṫri riċiṫ, cuiṡ ceḋ ocur mile, aoir an Ṫiṡerna. Creċa aiḃḃle oirroerca ḋo ḋenum ḋO Ruairc .i. Maṡnur mac Ḃriain mic Eoṡain hi Ruairc, ocur ḋo Mháṡ Uiḃir .i. Cuconnachṫ oṡ mac Conconnachṫ, ar Mac Ḋiarmaḋa .i. Ṫoirrohealbach Mac Ḋiarmaḋa, ... cuiṡ mile bó cona nḋiol

---

[1] *Annihilated and slain.* The order in Clar. is ro marḃaḋ ocur ro muṡaiḋheḋ, "were slain and annihilated."

[2] *After.* ṫaréir. ḋéir, MS.

[3] *Entirely.* co huilíḃe. Omitted in Clar.

[4] *Moreover.* imorro. Omitted in Clar.

[5] *Famine.* rirṡorṫa. riorṡorṫa, Clar.

[6] *Violence.* eiṡion; eṡen, Clar.

[7] *Foreign.* coṁaiṡṫiḃ, Clar.

[8] *This year.* The phraseology of this entry is different in Clar., but the difference is not important. The next entry, which is not in Clar., is in the handwriting of Brian Mac Dermot.

[9] *January.* There is a blank space in the MS. for the day of the week. In Clar. ḋarḋaoin, "Thursday," has been written in the margin, and then

were expelled, and many of their princes and nobles were annihilated and slain.[1] A general war broke out between Foreigners and Gaeidhel, Albanachs and Saxanachs, the Sil-Conchobhair and Clann-Maelruanaidh, chieftains and people, after[2] the high prince. Magh-Luirg, and Magh-Ai, and Airtech, and the districts of Connacht from Loch-Aillinne to Cam-sruthan, were entirely[3] wasted. Moreover,[4] cold and famine[5], theft and violence,[6] rapine and desecration, illegality and oppression, grew throughout the districts and tribes. They were all banished and driven, both high and low, to distant, foreign[7] territories, viz., to Tir-Amhalghaidh, and to Tir-Fiachrach, to Lower Connacht, to the Mainechs, to Clann-Connmhaigh, and to Clann-Rickard. Another person, i.e. Toirdhelbhach, the son of Eoghan Mac Diarmada, was made king in his place, with the consent of the church and laity, of ecclesiastics and ollamhs. The countess of Clann-Rickard, i.e., Margaret, the daughter of Donnchadh, son of Conchobhar O'Briain, i.e. the best woman that was in Erinn in her own time, died this year.[8] O'Conchobhair Sligigh, i.e. Domhnall, came from England, and brought with him a patent for his country from the queen.

The kalends of January.[9] The age of the Lord one thousand, five hundred, and sixty-nine years. Enormous, splendid, depredations were committed by O'Ruairc,[10] i.e. Maghnus, the son of Brian, son of Eoghan O'Ruairc, and by Mag Uidhir,[11] i.e. Cuchonnacht Og, son of Cuchonnacht, upon Mac Diarmada, i.e. Toirdelbhach Mac Diarmada, *when they carried off*[12] five thousand cows, with a

---

expunged, the criteria bτ̃ bιτ̃ αοιη (for bliαdαιn bιτec̄ ςοιηe, signifying "a year [after] bissextile, Friday,") being added. But this is incorrect, as the first of January occurred on a Sunday in the year 1569.

[10] *O'Ruairc.* Uα Ruαιτc, Clar., which omits the pedigree above given of the person referred to.

[11] *Mag Uidhir.* His Christian name, and that of his father, are omitted in Clar.

[12] *When they carried off.* The corresponding words are obliterated in the MS. They are omitted in Clar., which also wants the additional words cuις ιnιle bó coηα ηδιοl cαpαll ocuτ̃ dα ςαch eudáιl eli.

capall ocus da gach edáil eli, ionnus gur milled ocus gur mórḃuaiḋred. Connacht ocus Maġ Luirg go huiliḋe don creich sin, ler marbaḋ dá noireṁnaiḃ ocus da nardtreaḃṫachaiḃ, ocus dá lucht foġanta. Creċa móra eli do ḋenum do Mac Diarmada ar O Rúairc mar an cedna. Morán uilc do ḋenum an ḃliadain sin a nErinn, ocus a Connachta go háiriġṫi. Ross Chomain do tabairt dO Chonċuḃair dond don ġiusdis, ocus ase Diarmaid mac Cairbre meic Eogain ċaoich int O Conċuḃair, ocus sir Hanriġ Sinie ainm in giusdis.

Kal. Enáir; deiċ mbliadna ocus tri fiċit, ocus coig ced ocus mile, aois an Tigerna. Cogaḋ mor deirġe etir ċlainn Mic Diarmada .i. clann Ruaidri mic Taiḋg Mic Diarmada, ocus Mac Diarmada .i. Toirrdhelbach mac Eogain Mic Diarmada cona ḃraiṫrechaib, gur fassaighed na tíreċi ocus na treaḃa, na híaṫa ocus na haicmeḋa na coṁgar. Ro ḟórsodar clann Eogain Mic Diarmada tri ced Albanach anaghaiḋ ċlainni Ruaidri Mic Diarmada; ocus do cuireḋ clann Ruaidri aran tír go cloinn Connmaiḋ, ocus go Mainechaiḃ. Ro milled morán a muiġ Luirg leis na hAlbanachuiḃ sin a cill ocus a tuaiṫ; ocus an la deiġenach taréis a naimsire do taḃairt dona hAlbanachuiḃ sin, tánic Brían mac Ruaidri mic Diarmada cona braiṫriḃ .i. clann Tomaltaiġ mic Taidg mic Diarmada, ar cloinn Connmaiḋ dréchain an tíre, ocus ro leigsed sgeimealta uatha fo na nesgcairdiḃ ar gclos Albanach dimṫeacht; ocus ro marbad leo Díarmaid riabach mac Eogain mic Taiḋg [Mic] Diarmada don reim sin; ocus ro buḋ mor an sgél ante dororċuir and .i. an mac

1 *Connacht*. Omitted in Clar.

2 *Ploughmen*. oireṁnaib; dat. pl. of oireṁ.

3 *O'Ruairc*. See note 10, p. 405.

4 *Name*. This entry, (which is not in Clar.), is in the handwriting of Brian Mac Dermot, who adds mesi Brian, "I am Brian."

5 *Brothers*. This clause is a little different in Clar., where the brothers are also called the sons of Eoghan, son of Tadhg Mac Diarmada.

proportionate quantity of horses, and of all other kinds of spoil, so that all Connacht[1] and Magh-Luirg were injured, and greatly disturbed, by this depredation, through the number of ploughmen,[2] great farmers, and servants that were slain. Other great depredations were committed by MacDiarmada upon O'Ruairc[3] in like manner. Numerous injuries were committed this year in Erinn, and particularly in Connacht. Ros-Comain was given by O'Conchobhair to the Justiciary; and Diarmaid, son of Cairbre, son of Eoghan Caech, was the O'Conchobhair; and Sir Henry Sidney was the Justiciary's name.[4]

The kalends of January. The age of the Lord one thousand, five hundred, and seventy years. A great war broke out between the descendants of Mac Diarmada, viz., the sons of Ruaidhri, son of Tadhg Mac Diarmada, and Mac Diarmada, i.e. Toirdelbhach, the son of Eoghan Mac Diarmada, with his brothers,[5] so that the territories and houses, the lands and septs, in their neighbourhood were wasted. The sons of Eoghan Mac Diarmada retained three hundred[6] Albanachs against the sons of Ruaidhri Mac Diarmada; and the sons of Ruaidhri were driven out of the country, to Clann-Connmhaigh, and to the Mainechs. Much was destroyed in Magh-Luirg by those Albanachs, in church and territory. And on the last day, after those Albanachs had completed their period of service, Brian, the son of Ruaidhri Mac Diarmada, with his kinsmen, (viz., the sons of Tomaltach, son of Tadhg Mac Diarmada), came out of Clann-Connmhaigh to view the country; and they sent skirmishing parties against their enemies, on hearing that the Albanachs had departed; and Diarmaid Riabhach, the son of Eoghan, son of Tadhg [Mac][7] Diarmada, was killed by them in that incursion; and a great loss[8] was the person

---

[6] *Three hundred.* τρι ceo. Supplied from Clar. The MS. H. 1, 19 has αιbαnαιɡ mopα ("great Albanachs," i.e. a large number of Albanachs). The next page of the MS. (II. 1. 19) is almost entirely obliterated, and the remaining entries for this year are therefore taken from the Clar. fragment.

[7] *Mac.* Omitted in MS., and also in Clar.

[8] *Loss.* ρceλ; lit. "story."

rig [vob fepp] vuruñop vια coιppṁne ṛeιpιn, voιnech
ocuṛ voιpbepc [ocuṛ] voιppvepcuṛ. 'Oo pιξnevap nα
hCClbanaιξ pιn po ḃaoι ap ṛaṛvóḃ aξ claιnn Eoξaιn
mιc 'Oιapmava cpeḃa mópa α moιξ Luιpξ ιpιn ló cévnα
.ι. an cpeṛ lá vo cṛampaḃ. Iι pṛéιpιvenṛ .ι. Evḃapv
ṛecón vo ḃoιξechc α Connachcaιḃ aṁ ṛampaḃ pιn,
ocuṛ apmáιl na baιnpιξnα leιṛ, maιlle ṛe héṛξe amaḃ
Connachc an ṁéιv ṛα huṁal vó ḃιḃ .ι. ιapla claιnnι
Rιcaιpv ocuṛ ṛlιchc Uιlleξ an ṛιonα uιle, ocuṛ ṛιoḃ
ξCeallaιξ ocuṛ clann 'Ooṁnaιll anc ṛleιḃe ṛuaιḃ, ocuṛ
caιpcín Coιléιṛ ocuṛ Paιvṛιcín Cιompóξ, ocuṛ eιpξe
amaḃ na ξaιllṁe, ocuṛ mopán ele naḃ poιḃ lιnn váιpeṁ ;
ocuṛ cιaξaιv pιn uιle vo ξaḃáιl ḃaιṛléιn Spuḃpα. mac
Uιllιam α Ḃúpc cona bpaιḃpιḃ ocuṛ cona ḃoṁṛoξuṛ,
ocuṛ clann Oιlḃépuṛ α Ḃúpc, vo cpuιnnιuξhav ṛlúaιξ
ṁoιp vCClbanachuιḃ,

```
   *       *       *       *       *       *
       *       *       *       *       *       *
   *       *       *       *       *       *
       *       *       *       *       *       *
   *       *       *       *       *       *
       *       *       *       *       *       *
```

ǀctt. Enaιṛ. En blιαvaιn vhec ocuṛ cṛι pιcheτ, u. cev
ocuṛ mιle, aιṛ an Tιξeṛnα. Ppeιṛιvenṛ ḃoιξιv Connachc
α mbaιle CCḃα Luaιn an canṛα. O Conchobaιṛ voιnn .ι.
'Oιapmaιv mac Caιṛbpι mιc Eoξaιn ḃoeιch hI Conchobaιṛ
vo vul na ḃenn, ocuṛ α ξaḃaιl leιṛιn ppeιṛιvenṛ ap α
ιochc ṛeιn. CC mac ṛéιn .ι. CCoḃ O Conḃobaιṛ, ocuṛ CCoḃ
mac hI Chonchobaιṛ ṛuaιḃ, ocuṛ apoιle vo ḃaomιḃ

---

¹ *The best.* vob ṛepp, Omitted
in MS. and Clar.

² *And.* The character representing
ocuṛ is also omitted in the MS., and
in Clar.

³ *Sliabh-ruadh.* This is the name
of a mountain near Blesinton, county
Wicklow. The Clann-Domhnaill of
Sliabh-ruadh, one of the septs of the

Mac Donnells of Leinster, were seated
in the present bar. of Talbotstown, co.
Wicklow ; their possessions, called the
Clandonnell's country, lying along
the mountain of Sliabh-ruadh. See
O'Donovan's ed. of the Four Mast.,
A.D. 1570, note ʲ.

⁴ *Patrickin ;* i.e. "little Patrick."

⁵ *Albanachs.* This word concludes

who fell there, i.e. by far [the best[1]] prince of his own A.D
immediate kindred, in hospitality, energy, [and[2]] dignity. [1570.]
Those Albanachs, who had been retained by the sons of
Eoghan Mac Diarmada, committed great depredations in
Magh-Luirg on the same day, i.e. the third day of summer. The President, i.e. Edward Fitton, came into Connacht this year, accompanied by the Queen's forces, together with the rising out of Connacht, (as many of them
as were obedient to him), viz., the Earl of Clann-Rickard,
and all the race of Ulick-an-fhiona, and the Sil-Cellaigh,
and the Clann-Domhnaill of Sliabh-ruadh,[3] and Captain
Collier, and Patrickin[4] Cusack, and the rising out of
Gaillimh, and many more that we cannot enumerate ;
and all these went to take the castle of Sruthair. Mac
William Burk, with his kinsmen and relatives, and the
sons of Oliver Burk, assembled a large army of Albanachs,[5]

* * * *

* * * * *

* * * *

* * * * *

* * * * *

The kalends[6] of January. The age of the Lord one [1571.]
thousand, five hundred and seventy-one years. The
President[7] of the province of Connacht was in the
town of Ath-Luain at this time. O'Conchobhair
Donn, i.e. Diarmaid, the son of Cairbre, son of Eoghan
Caech O'Conchobhair, went to meet him ; and he was
taken prisoner by the President whilst under his own
guarantee.[8] His own son, i.e. Aedh O'Conchobhair, and
Aedh, the son of O'Conchobhair Ruadh, and other choice

---

fol. 27b in the Clar. fragment, where
a deficiency occurs. The next entry in
it belongs to 1577. See note¹, p. 414
infra.

⁶ Kalends. The events of this year
(1571) are contained in the MS. H. 1,
19, fol. 98 b, the date "1561" appear-
ing over the entries ; but this date has

been properly corrected to 1571. The
Clar. fragment has no notice of the
events of this year.

⁷ President. Sir Edward Fitton.

⁸ Under his own guarantee. ⲁⲣ ⲁ
ιосҺτ ⲣⲉⲓⲛ ; i.e. under his (Sir Edward Fitton's) own assurance of protection.

τoξτa, το δul ξo baιle Ccτa Luaιn luchτ appτpaιξ.
O Conchobaιp τp[   ] a τιξ ópτa allamuιξ .τon
čuιpτ τóιδ. Τucpaτ O Conchobaιp ap aτhaιτ ó Ζhalloιδ
leo. Ccp τeachτ h1 Conchobaιp ó Ζhalloιδ amlaιδ pιn
po papτó achτ ceτ Ccbanach, ocup po cenξaιl pe peιn
ocup clann Θoξaιn mιc Τιapmaτa pe čelι. Τιaξaιτ ap
pιobal plúaιξeτ a nuachτap Connachτ. Loιpcιτ an
popul coeč ocup Cpúτon, ocup ceτpoma[   ], ocup
τucaτap cpeča mópa leo, ocup τanξaτap plan. Ccn
ppeιpιτenp τo τeachτ ap mačaιpe Connachτ pluaξ mop.
δaιle an τopaιp ocup an [caιplen pιa]bach το ξaδáιl
leιp, ocup po bpιp an caιplén pιabach, ocup po pιll
ap aιpp íappιn. O Conchobaιp τonn ocup a Ccbanaιξ
το δeč a maδ Luιpξ na ξcoιnne aξ τoξbáιl bepτeñ pop
ξač [leιč], ocup ap maξ Luιpξ co haιpιξčι, oιp το δóι
ceτ Mιc Τιapmaτa aca čuιce. Ní paιδe δpιan mac
Ruaιτpι, ιna a δpaιδpech, ocup OConchobaιp τén pξél
mun am pιn, ocup ní paιδe a pιp aξ δpιan, O Conchobaιp
το δeιč a nanbpač το no ξup τepδ peιn a anbpač .ι.
ξuppo ξaδ Τιapmaιτ mac Ruaιτpι mιc Τιapmaτa, ocup
Τomalτach oξ mac Τomalταιξ mιc Τιapmaτa, íap
čaobaδ ṁuιnτepι h1 Conchobaιp δóιδ, ocup ξup benaτ a
neιč ocup a neιτιξe τιδ. Ro eloδ Τomalτach oξ a ξcιonn
aτhaιτ ιappιn; po benaδ puaplucaτ app Τιapmaιτ. Cc
ξpoιδ ocup cuιτ τa čaopaιξečτ το δuaιn το δpían mac
Τιapmaτa τona hCclbanchaιb pιn h1 Conchobaιp ιna
διaιδ. Ro δóι δpían peιn ιna luιδι a τιnnep ap an
bpeδ pιn uιle. 1ap neιpξe app a luιδe δó po δen ba
ocup eιč τO Conchobaιp. Ro mapbaτ póp le δpían τon
čoξaτ pιn mac Conchobaιp mιc Caτaoιp h1 Conchobaιp,
ocup ceτpop΄τa muιnτιp maιlle pιp. Ṗoplonξpopτ το
δenum το [δpιan] mac Τιapmaτa, ocup το claιnn
Τomalταιξ mιc Τιapmaτa, um páč δhpénuιnn, ocup ópιn
co Camppučan. Cpeča mópa το δenum ap ab na δuιlle
τoιδ, ocup cpeč elι ap Mac Τonnchaτa an Chopuιnn.

---

1 Cethroma[   ]. The second member of this name is obliterated.

men, went to the town of Ath-Luain, a ship's company.
O'Conchobhair [   ] a hotel for them outside the
court. They brought O'Conchobhair by stealth from the
Foreigners. After O'Conchobhair had thus come from the
Foreigners, he retained 800 Albanachs, and he and the sons
of Eoghan Mac Diarmada combined together. They went
on an expedition to Upper Connacht. They burned the
Pobal-caech, and Crúthonn, and Cethroma[1][   ]; and
they brought great preys with them, and returned safely.
The President came upon Machaire-Connacht, with a great
army. Baile-an-tobair, and the [Caislen-ria]bhach, were
taken by him; and he broke down the Caislen-riabhach,
and turned back afterwards. O'Conchobhair Donn, and
his Albanachs, were in Magh-Luirg before them, levying
tributes on every [side], and on Magh-Luirg especially, for
they had Mac Diarmada's permission thereto. Brian
son of Ruaidhri was not, nor were his kinsmen, acting
with O'Conchobhair about that time; and Brian did not
know that O'Conchobhair was acting treacherously, until
he himself proved his treachery, i.e. until he apprehended
Diarmaid, son of Ruaidhri Mac Diarmada, and Tomaltach
Og, son of Tomaltach Mac Diarmada, after they had sided
with O'Conchobhair's people, and until their horses and
armour were taken from them. Tomaltach Og escaped
in the course of some time after that. A ransom was
exacted from Diarmaid. His stud, and some of his herds,
were afterwards taken from Brian Mac Diarmada, by those
Albanachs of O'Conchobhair. Brian himself was lying in
pain during all that time. On his recovery, he took cows
and horses from O'Conchobhair. The son of Conchobhar,
son of Cathair O'Conchobhair, and four of his people,
were killed by Brian, moreover, in that war. An encampment was made by [Brian] Mac Diarmada, and by the
sons of Tomaltach Mac Diarmada, about Rath-Brenainn,
and from that to Cam-sruthan. They committed great
depredations upon the abbot of the Buill, and another

Inιr Ḟloιnn umoρρo, ocur inιr mιc Ḋáḃíḋ, ϫo Lorcaϫ leo ιrιn bliaϫaιn ceϫna. Ɑn ρρeιrιϫenr ϫo ceacht co Rorr Chomáιn, ocur a ḃeιḃ reacht reachtṁuιne na comnaιϫe innte. Ɑ ḟιlleϫ car aιr ϫorιḃιr, ocur ρo raʒaιb braιʒϫe. Ɑn ρρeιrιϫenr ϫo ḃeacht a Connachtaιb ϫorιḃιr arṁáιl ṁóρ ϫo ṁuιntιr na baιnrιʒna, ocur ϫul ϫoιb a ʒclaιnn Rιcaιrϫ. Iarla claιnnι Rιcaιrϫ ocur an rluaʒ ʒall rιn ϫo ḃul a ʒCúιlecha, ocur a ḃo no trι ϫo ḃaιlτιb caιrlen ϫo ʒaḃaιl ϫoιḃ. O Ḋomnaιll, .ι. Ɑoḃ mac Maʒnuιr hI Ḋomnaιll, ϫo ḃeacht a nιochtαr Connacht, ocur clann Eoʒaιn mιc Ḋιarmaϫa ϫo ḃul na ḃuιnne co Ḃaιle erra ϫara, ocur cenʒal re roιle ḃóιḃ anaʒhaιϫ a nercaραϫ ϫιḃlιonaιḃ. O Ḋomnaιll ϫo ḟιllιuϫ a nUlltóιb ϫorιḃιr. [Cuιϫ] mor ϫια muιnntιr [ϫo] ḃeacht le claιnn Eoʒaιn, maιlle re na nϫaoιnιb réιn, ocur ρo ιnnroιʒret rorlonʒρort Ḃríaιn mιc Ḋιarmaϫa a ʒclaιnn Raʒartaιʒ, ocur ρo ḃenaϫar rιḃe ceϫ ʒo bḟuιllιuϫ ϫo ḃuaιḃ, cona nϫιϫl ϫo ḃaιrlιb ϫe, ocur τanʒoϫar rlán. Ɑn ρρeιrιϫenr ϫo ḃeḃ a ʒCuιlech mun am rιn. Ceachta ϫo ϫol na ḃenϫ ó Ḃríaιn ϫo ḃorráoιϫ na nʒnιom rιn rιr. Nιr raιllιʒheϫ na rʒela rιn Larιn ρρeιrιϫenr cona Ʒhalloιb, oιr nι ϫernaτ oιrιrιom ιna comnaιḃe no ʒo ταnιc a ʒclaιnn Chonnmaιϫh. Ceιϫ Ḃríaιn mac Ḋιarmaϫa ocur clann Comaltaιʒ mιc Ḋιarmaϫa na ḃoιnne a claιnn Chonnmaιϫh, ocur ϫo leιʒ re Ḃrιan roιme ar aιr a maιϫ Luιrʒ, ϫo braḃ Mιc Ḋιarmaϫa ocur Ɑlbanach, ocur ϫo roιʒne reιn coṁnaιϫe na ḃeoιḃ a ʒclaιnn Connmaιϫh an aʒhaιϫ rιn; ocur ρo ʒaḃrat ιonaϫ coιnne re roιle ar na ṁárach a Ráḃ na ʒcléιrech. Ϫo rreaʒraϫar antιonaϫ coιnne rιn leḃ ar leḃ, ocur ρo ḃóι Mac Ḋιarmaϫa ocur a ḃlann, ocur Caϫʒ mac Caḃaιl mιc Ḋιarmaϫa a ʒCluaιn na cea[   ] a nuachtar tíre. Ɑcht chena nιrι raιllιʒheϫ le Ḃríaιn cona braιḃrιḃ an taιrrιnʒ rιn, oιr ρo τreoraιʒret an rlúaʒ ϫaon uιʒe o re[   ] maḃaιre Connacht co bealaḃ [na nur] ṁoιnte or cιonn

A.D.
[1571.]

depredation upon Mac Donnchadha of the Corann. Inis-Floinn, moreover, and Inis-Mic-David, were burned by them in the same year. The President came to Ros-Comain, and was seven weeks residing in it. He turned back again, and left hostages. The President came to Connacht again, with a large armament of the queen's people; and they went into Clann-Rickard. The Earl of Clann-Rickard, and this army of Foreigners, went into Cuilecha, and took two or three castellated towns. O'Domhnaill, i.e. Aedh, son of Maghnus O'Domhnaill, came to Lower Connacht; and the sons of Eoghan Mac Diarmada went to meet him to Baile-esa-dara, and they combined together against their enemies. O'Domhnaill returned again to Ulster. A large [number] of his people went with Eoghan's sons, along with their own people; and they attacked Brian Mac Diarmada's residence in Clann-Faghartaigh; and they took from him two thousand cows, and more, with a proportionate number of horses, and returned safely. The President was this time in Cuilecha. Messengers went to meet him from Brian, to complain to him of those deeds. These reports were not neglected by the President, with his Foreigners, for he made no stay, or delay, until he came into Clann-Connmhaidh. Brian Mac Miarmada, and the sons of Tomaltach Mac Diarmada, went to meet him in Clann-Connmhaidh; and he sent Brian on before him again to Magh-Luirg, to watch Mac Diarmada and the Albanachs, and he himself remained after him in Clann-Connmhaidh that night; and they appointed to meet each other on the morrow at Rath-na-cleirech. This appointment was observed on both sides; and Mac Diarmada and his sons, and Tadhg, son of Cathal Mac Diarmada, were in Cluain-na-cea[ ] in Uachtar-tírè. This invitation was not neglected by Brian and his kinsmen, for they guided the army, in one march, from the [   ] of Machaire-Connacht to Bealach[-na-nur]-mhointe

ᴏṗoıčıᴅ mıc Ꮇꭒanaıẋ. Ꭰo ṗóɴṗaᴅ beẋan ṗcıṗaᴅ ocꭒṗ
comnaıᴆe anɴṗın. Ꮯeıᴅ ḃṗían ocꭒṗ Sean mac Ꮯomaıṗ
mıc Rıcaıṗᴅ [   ], ṗo ᴆóı na ṗıṗṗıam mꭒn
am ṗın, ocꭒṗ ṗeᴆan ᴅona Ꙅaoıᴆelaıḃ maılle ṗꭒ́, ṗíaṗ.
na Ꙅalloıḃ aṗ ınṗoıẋeᴅ na ḃꭒılle.

     *   *   *   *   *

    *   *   *   *   *   *

   *   *   *   *   *   *

Ꮇac hı Ꙅhaᴅṗa, .ı. Cıan mac Ꭰıaṗmaᴅa mıc Ꮛoẋaın
lıı Ꙅhaᴅṗa, ᴅhec. O Conchobaıṗ ᴅonn ocꭒṗ O Conchobaıṗ ṗꭒaᴅh, ocꭒṗ ṗlıchᴅ Ꮯoıṗṗᴅhelbaıẋ laıẋnıẋ meẋ
Ꭰhoṁnaıll, ᴅo ᴆꭒl aṗ ıonnṗoıẋeᴅ aṗ Ꮇac Ꭰonnchaᴆa
an Choṗꭒınn, ocꭒṗ cṗeᴆa moṗa ᴅo ᴆenam ᴆóıḃ. Cachal
oẋ mac hı Conchobaıṗ Slıẋıᴅh ocꭒṗ ᴔlbanaıẋ ᴅıa len-
maın a ẋcoıṗṗṗlıaḃ ocꭒṗ ᴅṗe maẋ lꭒıṗẋ, ocꭒṗ aṗṗın co
Ꮯꭒıllṗcı, ocꭒṗ ẋan bṗeᴆ oṗṗa no co ṗanẋoᴅaṗ Cločan
na ṗıẋṗaıᴆı. Ḃeẋan ẋṗeamma ᴅo beıᴆ ᴅo maṗcṗlꭒaẋ na
ᴅóṗa oṗṗa anɴṗın. Ꝑılleᴅ oṗṗa ᴅo ᴆꭒn na ṗeᴆna, ocꭒṗ
Rꭒaıᴅṗı ẋlaṗṗ, mac ḃṗıaın ᴆoeıᴆ mıc Rꭒaıᴅṗı ẋlaıṗ,
ᴅo ᴆꭒıᴅım ᴅen bꭒılle ẋa le ḃṗıan mac hı Ꝑhlannaẋaın,
ocꭒṗ a ṗochᴅaın ṗeın ṗᴅan cona cṗeᴆaıᴆ. O Conchobaıṗ
Slıẋıẋ ocꭒṗ ḃṗıan mac Ꭰıaṗmaᴅa ᴅo ᴆꭒl a ẋcenᴅ
caıṗᴅín Ꮇaılbıe .ı. ᴅıẋeṗna Chonnachᴅ ó Ꙅhalloıb, aṗ
na ṗaẋaıl ᴅóıᴆ a Roṗ Comaın, ocꭒṗ ṗa ṗoṗᴆaoılıᴆ an
caıṗᴅín ṗompꭒ ᴅıᴆlıonaıᴆ; ocꭒṗ ṗo ıaṗṗaᴅaṗ ṗlꭒaıẋ
ṗaıṗ ᴅo bꭒaın bꭒna Ꭰṗoᴆoeıṗ ᴅO Ꭰhoṁnaıll. Ro
ṗaẋᴆaᴅaṗ an ṗlꭒaẋ benᴅa nanᴅıaıᴆ. Ꮯeıᴅ O Conchobaıṗ
ᴅıa ᴆaıle ṗeın, ocꭒṗ ṗo ṗaẋꭒıᴆ ḃṗıan ṗe haẋaıᴅ anᴅ
ṗlꭒaıẋ ᴅo ᴆaıṗṗınẋ ᴆꭒıẋe. ıaṗ ᴅınól a ṗlꭒaıẋ ımoṗṗa
ᴅon caıṗᴅín, ṗo ẋlꭒaıṗ ṗonṁe an ceᴅ lá no co ṗáınıc cꭒıl
Ceṗṗṗa an uchᴅ ḃhuılle, ocꭒṗ ᴅeıᴅ aṗ na ṁaṗach ᴅaṗ

---

[1] *Buill.* This is the last legible | but one of the MS.), begins, also
word in fol. 98 *b*; but it is plain | imperfectly, with entries of events
that the entries for the year 1571 did | belonging to the year 1577; of which
not end here. The next page of the | it contains several that are not
MS. H. 1, 19, (which is the last page | to be found in the Clar. fragment.

above Droichet-Mic-Muanaigh. They made a short rest and stay there. Brian, and John the son of Thomas, son of Rickard [   ], who was sheriff at that time, accompanied by a band of the Gaeidhel, went before the Foreigners, to attack the Buill.[1]

*   *   *   *   *

*   *   *   *   *   *

*   *   *   *   *

*   *   *   *   *   *

The son of O'Gadhra, i.e. Cian, the son of Diarmaid, son of Eoghan O'Gadhra, died. O'Conchobhair Donn, and O'Conchobhair Ruadh, and the descendants óf Toirdhelbhach Laighnech Mac Domhnaill, went on a foray against Mac Donnchadha of the Corann, and committed great depredations. Cathal Og, the son of O'Conchobhair Sligigh, and Albanachs, pursued them into Corr-sliabh, and through Magh-Luirg, and from that to Tuilsce; but they did not overtake them until they reached Clochan-na-righraidhi, where the cavalry of the pursuers had them a little in check. The rear of the army turned back upón them, and Ruaidhri Glas, son of Brian Caech, son of Ruaidhri Glas, was slain with one blow of a lance, by Brian, son of O'Flannagain; and they arrived safely themselves, with their preys. O'Conchobhair Sligigh, and ·Brian MacDiarmada, went to meet Captain[2] Malbie, the lord of Connacht on the part of the Foreigners, on their finding him in Roscomain; and the captain welcomed them both; and they asked him for an army to take Bun-Drobhais from O'Domhnaill. They left the army to be assembled after them. O'Conchobhair went to his own place, and left Brian for the purpose of drawing the army to him. After his army had been mustered by the captain, moreover, he advanced the first day until he reached Cuil-Cesra, in front of Buill, and went on the

---

The hiatus in this latter manuscript, which' begins under the year 1570 (see note 5, p. 408) terminates with

the word "ρετιοech," fifth line from bottom, p. 416.

[2] *Captain.* caιρín, MS.

Coipprliab buðčuaið no ʒo panic baile an ṁúta. Tanic
O Conchobaip Sliʒiʒ ocur mac Uilliam burc čuca
annrin, ocur maiči Connacht uile acht O Ruaipc aṁáin,
ocur a coimčinél. Tiaʒaið pompu ʒo bun Opoðoeir arr
a haičle. Ro ʒabað an baile ʒan ṗuipech leo. Ro
mapbað mac Cathail čleipiʒ ðén upchup ʒa ðo mac
1 Domnaill .i. Coð oʒ mac Coða ðuið 1 Dhomnaill. Ro
Loitteð ocur ro mapbað ochtap ðo Sacranchaib imon
mbaile rih, ocur ro raʒaið an caiptin an baile aʒ
O Conchobaip ðon ðul rin. Clann Ouiṗṗiʒ na hCCLban
.i. Domnall óʒ ocur Ṗepðopča, cona mbraičrið, ocur
cona coimčinel CCLbanach ocur Erennach, ðo ðul ap
O Conchobaip nðonn ap riobal innroiʒeð, ocur crech ðo
buain ðe ðoið. O Conchobaip rein, ocur rirpriam rorra
Comáin, ðo ðreč orra beʒan ðaoineð. Ṗilleð orra
ðCCLbanchaib, ðcur [   ] ðo maičið člainni Suiðne
ðo ṁarbað ann .i. Coð mac Mhaolmuire, ocur Maolmuire mac Toirpðhelbaiʒ čoič, [   ] mac Ruaiðri
ðuið mic Maolmuiri Mic Shuiðni. Sloiʒeað le hUa
nDomnaill .i. Coð mac Maʒnura [   ] a niochtap
Connacht. Creča mora ðo ʒenum ðo a ttir Oillella,
ocur milleð mor tiʒheð ocur arðonna ðo ðenum ðO
Domnaill ðont rloiʒeð rin a tír Oilella, ocur a Luiʒni
ocur a ʒCairbri. Sippiam čunðae Sliʒiʒ, .i. Rirðepð
mac Teaboið buiðe meʒ Seoinin, ðo ṁarbað a Sliʒech
le hUa nDomnaill aʒ rilleð ðont rloiʒeð rin, ocur a
imteacht rein rlán. Ṗeitiðech an ṁuilinn čirr .i.
ʒeroið ðhec. ·Ṗorlonʒpopt ðo ðenuṁ ðO Dhoṁnaill
ro ðun Opoðoeir. O Conchobaip Sliʒiʒ ðo čairpinʒ
čaiptin čuiʒið Connacht ʒo rluaʒ mór ʒall ocur
ʒaoiðel maille rir, map ataið riol Conchobaip ocur

---

1 *Petidech*. Petit, or Petty. The
Clar. fragment recommences with
this name, after the termination of the
hiatus beginning under the year 1570,
referred to in note 5, p. 408 *supra*.
The text from this down to the word

ʒulloiḃ, line 1., page 420, has been
taken from the MS. H. 1, 19, the
phraseology of which is here almost
identical with that of the Clar. fragment.

2 *Garrett*. ʒeroið. This name

morrow across Corr-sliabh, northwards, until he reached Baile-an-mhúta. O'Conchobhair Sligigh, and Mac William Burk, came to them then, and all the nobles of Connacht, except O'Ruairc alone, and his kindred. They afterwards proceeded on to Bun-Drobhais. The place was captured by them without delay. The son of Cathal Clerech was killed with one cast of a spear by O'Domhnaill's son, i.e. Aedh Og, son of Aedh Dubh O'Domhnaill. Eight of the Saxons were wounded and slain about that place; and the captain left the place to O'Conchobhair on that occasion. The Clann-Duibhsith of Alba, viz., Domhnall Og and Ferdorcha, with their brethren and kindred of Alba and Erinn, went on an expedition against O'Conchobhair Donn, and took a prey from him. O'Conchobhair himself, and the sheriff of Ros-Comain, overtook them, with a few men. The Albanachs turned upon them, and [
     ] of the chieftains of Clann-Suibhne were slain there, viz., Aedh, son of Maelmuire; and Maelmuire, son of Toirdhelbhach Caech, [   ], son of Ruaidhri Dubh, the son of Maelmuire Mac Suibhne. A hosting by O'Domhnaill, i.e. Aedh, son of Maghnus [   ], into Lower Connacht. Great preys were taken by him in Tir-Oilella; and a great destruction of houses, and corn-fields, was committed by O'Domhnaill on that hosting in Tir-Oilella, and in Luighne, and in Cairbre. The sheriff of the county of Sligech, i.e. Richard, son of Tibbot Buidhe Mac Seoinin, was killed in Sligech by O'Domhnaill, when returning from that hosting; and he departed safely himself. Petidech[1] of the Muilenn-cerr, i.e. Garrett,[2] died. A fortified camp was established by O'Domhnaill against Bun-Drobhais. O'Conchobhair Sligigh brought[3] the captain[4] of the province of Connacht, together with a large army of Foreigners and Gaeidhel,

is added in the margin, in Clar., in the handwriting of Brian Mac Dermot.

[3] Brought. ᵭᴏ ʈᴀɩᴘᴘɩᴨʒ; lit. "drew."

[4] *Captain.* Captain Malbie is meant. The word captain is frequently written cᴀɩᴘᴨ in the text, the ᴛ being omitted.

clann MaolpuαnαιɃ ocuʃ ʃιl ʒCeallαιʒ. Cιcιɒʃιn
uιle co maιnιʃɒιʃ na Ƀuιlle a nuchc CoιʃʃʃleιɃ.
CιαʒαιɃ caʃ ʃlιαɃ ʃίoʃ aʃ na Ƀaʃach, ocuʃ ʃo ʒαbαɒ
cuιl Ɒeʒhαιɒ leo.   αʃʃιn co Ƀaιle an cocαιʃ ɒóιɃ, ocuʃ
ʃo ʒαƀʃαc e maʃ an ceɒna.   αʃʃιn co bun ⱰʃoɃaoιʃ
ɒoιɃ, ocuʃ ʃo anʃαc ceιcʃι lo con oιɃče αʒ cuʃ čoʃɒuιʃ
ann ιαʃ [n-αčċuʃ] 1 Ɒhoɱnαιll. Ro ʃιllʃec co 8lιʒech
ιαʃʃιn, ocuʃ ɒo ʃeιɃιʒʃec ʃe hUα Ruaιʃc. Ro cʃečʃαɒ
cuιɒ ɒo čloιnn Ɒιαʃmαɒα ʃuaιɒ na ʒcoιllce, αʒ ʃιlleɒ
caʃanaιʃ ɒoιɃ.   Cιcιɒ a maʒ Luιʃʒ aʃʃ a haιčle.   Ƀaιle
na huamα ɒo cαbαιʃc aʃ ιαʃʃachc ɒon čaιʃcιn ɒo
Ɓʃιαn mac Ɒιαʃmαɒα.   αn caιʃcιn ɒa ʃαʒbαιl αʒ
Goιn oɒhaʃ ɱαιʒ Néιll ʃe haʒhaιɒ čoʒαιɒ αlbanach.
Uαιčne mac αoɃα 1 Ɒhιomuʃαιʒ ɒo maʃbαɒ le cuιɒ ɒo
ʃιl MoʃɃα a bʃιoll.   Caιʃcιn hαʃanc ocuʃ mac
maιʒιʃcιʃ Fʃaɱʃα ɒo ʒαƀαιl ɒo RuʒʃαιɃι oʒ O MoʃɃα.
1onnʃoιʒeɒ ʃoʃlonʒpuιʃc ɒo čαbαιʃc ɒo 8αʒʃanchαιb
aʃ RuʒʃαɃ oʒ, ocuʃ bʃeιč aʃ Choʃmac mac h1 Conchobαιʃ ʃaιlʒιʒ ιʃιn ʃoʃlonʒpoʃc ʃιn.   Ɒιαʃʃ člaιnnι
RuʒʃoιɃe oιʒ, ocuʃ a Ƀen .ι. ιnʒen αoɃα mιc 8eαιn mιc
Remuιnn, ocuʃ Coʃmac O Conchobαιʃ, ɒo maʃbαɃ ιʃιn
Ƀʃoʃlonʒpoʃc le 8αʒʃanchαιb, ocuʃ caιʃcιn hαʃanc
ɒo Ƀʃeιč leo ɒoιɃ ocuʃ e lečmaʃb.   Feʃɒoʃčα mac
ⱰhuιɃʃιč .ι. ʃoʒα a čιnιɃ ʃeιn ɒuaιʃle ocuʃ ɒuʃʃaɒuʃ,
ɒo maʃbαɒ le hGoιn oɒhaʃ ɱαιʒ Neιll, ocuʃ cʃeč ɱoʃ
ɒo čαbαιʃc leιʃ ɒo.   Ƀaιle an muca ɒo ʒαƀαιl ɒo
8αʃʃanchαιb a Ƀʃιoll, ocuʃ Mac Ɒonnchαɒα ɒo ʒαƀαιl
leo ann .ι.   αoɃ mac Caιʃbʃι mιc CαιɃʒ, cιʒeʃna an
Ƀaιle ʃeιn, ocuʃ Coʃmac mac CαιɃʒ an cʃιuɃαιʃ .ι.
Mac Ɒonnchαɒα cιʃe hOιlella.   8ean ʃαlač mac

---

1 *Sil-Conchobhair.* The Clar. fragment specifies the Irish chieftains
who formed part of this army, as
O'Conchobhair Ruadh, the son of
O'Conchobhair Donn, Aedh O'Cellaigh, and Brian Mac Diarmada.

2 *Coillte.* Coillte-Conchobhair, in
the north of the county of Roscommon.

3 *Magh-Luirg.* It is stated in the
Clar. frag. that they rested one night
at Baile-an-dúin, on their return.

4 *Master Francis.* maιʒιʃcιʃ
Fʃaɱʃα; i.e. Francis Cosby, the
person engaged in the horrid massacre
of Mullach-Maisten, or Mullaghmast.
See under the year 1567.

such as the Sil-Conchobhair,[1] the Clann-Maelruanaidh, and Sil-Cellaigh. All these came to the monastery of the Buill, in front of Corr-sliabh. They went down across the mountain, on the morrow, and Cuil-Deghaidh was taken by them. From thence they went to Baile-an-tochair, and they took it likewise. They proceeded from thence to Bun-Drobhais, and they remained four days and nights feasting there, after [the expulsion] of O'Domhnaill. They returned to Sligech afterwards, and arranged with O'Ruairc. They plundered some of Clann-Diarmada Ruadh of the Coillte,[2] when returning. They came after this to Magh-Luirg.[3] Baile-na-huama was given as a loan to the captain, by Brian Mac Diarmada. The captain left it to John Odhar Mac Neill, for the purpose of warring against Albanachs. Uaithne, son of Aedh O'Dimusaigh, was killed by some of the Sil-Mordha in treachery. Captain Harant, and the son of Master Francis,[4] were captured by Rughraidhe Og O'Mordha, A camp assault was made by Saxons upon Rughraidhe Og, and they captured Cormac, the son of O'Conchobhair Failghe, in that camp. Rughraidhe Og's two sons, and his wife, i.e. the daughter of Aedh,[5] son of John, son of Redmond, and Cormac O'Conchobhair, were slain in the camp by Saxons; and they carried off Captain[6] Harant with them, and he half dead.[7] Ferdorcha Mac Duibhsith, i.e. the choice of his own kindred for nobility and guarantee, was killed by John Odhar Mac Neill, who carried off a great prey. Baile-an-muta was taken by Saxons in treachery; and Mac Donnchadha[8] was captured by them there, i.e. Aedh, son of Cairbre, son of Tadhg,[9] the lord of the place itself, and Cormac, son of Tadhg-an-triubhais, i.e. Mac Donnchadha of Tir-Oilella. John Salach, son of

---

[5] *Aedh* ; i.e., Aedh (or Hugh) O'Byrne, the father of the celebrated Fiagh Mac Hugh.

[6] *Captain.* caιpιn, MS.

[7] *Half dead.* The Clar. frag. states that the son of Master Francis (the son of Francis Cosby, called Alexan-

der by O'Sullivan) was killed by Rughraidhe Og, who escaped himself.

[6] *Mac Donnchadha.* Mac Donough of Corann.

[9] *Tadhg.* This Tadhg was the son of Ruaidhri Mac Donough, according to the Clar. fragment.

VOL. II.

2 E 2

Ἀοᵫ mɩc Seɑɩɴ mɩc Remuɩɴɴ ꞅo [mɑpᵬɑᵬ] le ɔɑlloɩᵬ.
Conchoɓɑp cɑppɑᵬ mɑc 1 Chɑᵬɑɩɴ ꞅo mɑpᵬɑᵬ leɩp
OCɑᵬɑɩɴ. ᵬɑɩle ɑɴ muꞇɑ ꞅo ᵹɑᵬɑɩl le pḷochꞇ Ꞇo-
mɑlꞇɑɩᵹ Meɩc ꞅoɴɴchɑꞅɑ, ocuṗ le pḷochꞇ ꞅuᵬᵹoɩll
ᵹpuɑmᵹɑ eɩp Sɑᵹpɑɴɑchɑɩᵬ. Ceɴꞅ mɑɩɴꞅꞅpeɑᵬ ɴɑ
Ꞇpɩɴoɩꞅe, ocuṗ oɓɑɩp ɓɑᵹᵬuɩɴ ꞅuɴɑ ᵹɑp, ꞅo ᵬeᵬ ɑp
puᵬɑl ɑɴɑoɩɴṗechꞇ eɩᵹ ᵬpɩɑɴ mɑc Ruɑᵬpɩ Meɩc ꞅɩɑp-
mɑꞅɑ, oɩp ꞅoɓ e ɩɴ ᵬpɩɑɴ pɩɴ uɑchꞇɑpɑɴ ɴɑ mɑɩɴꞅꞅpeᵬ,
ocuṗ ꞇɩᵹepɴɑ ɴɑ cɑppᵹe. Ꞇɑᵬᵹ mɑc Mupchɑꞅɑ meɩc
Ꞇoɩpᵬeɑlɓɑɩᵹ 1 ᵬhpɩɑɩɴ, ocuṗ Ꞇoɩpᵬeɑlɓɑᵬ mɑc meɩc
Mɑᵬᵹɑɴɴɑ, ꞅpɑᵹɑɩl ᵬɑɩp ɑ ɴꞅeɩpeᵬ ɴɑ ɓlɩɑꞅɴɑpɑ; ocuṗ
ɴɩ poɩᵬe ɑ ɴⴹɩpɩɴɴ ɴɑ ɴɑmpɩp peɩɴ pleɑpᵹɑɩᵬ ɓuᵬ mo
ɩɴ pᵹel ɴɑ ɩɑꞅ ɑɴꞅ ᵹɑᵬ uɩle ᵬɑɩl. Robepꞇ Sɑᵬuɩp .ɩ.
puᵬpɩppɩɑm ᵬuɩɴꞅɑe Slɩᵹɩᵹ ꞅo ṁɑpᵬɑᵬ, ocuṗ peɩppep
ꞅɑ ṁuɩɴɴꞇɩp mɑpɑoɴ pɩp, le Mɑc ꞅoɴɴchɑꞅɑ ɩɴ
Chopɑɩɴꞅ. ⴹumɑɴꞅ mɑc Mupchɑꞅɑ 1 ꞅepᵹɑɩl ocuṗ
Conchoɓɑp oᵹ Mɑᵹ Rɑɴɑɩll ꞅpɑᵹɑɩl ᵬɑɩp.

Ⱪcꞇꞇ. ⴹɴɑɩp pop ᵬeɩꞅɩɴ, ocuṗ ɑpɩ ɑoɩp ɩɴ Ꞇɩᵹepɴɑ ɩɴ
ꞇɑɴpɑ ochꞇ mɓlɩɑꞅɴɑ ꞅeᵹ ocuṗ ꞇpɩ pɩᵬeꞇ, cuɩᵹ ceꞅ ocuṗ
mɩle. Mɑc 1 Néɩll ꞅo ṁɑpᵬɑᵬ ꞅɑoɴ upchop ꞅo ᵹɑ le
mɑc 1 ᵹɑllᵬoᵬɑɩp .ɩ. ⴹɴpɩ O Neɩll, ocuṗ pɑo mop·ɩɴꞇ
eɑᵬꞇ pɩɴ mɑc Ꞇoɩpᵬeɑlᵬɑɩᵹ Loɩɴɩᵹ mɩc Neɩll ᵬoɴɑllɑɩᵹ.
Uɑpɑl pɑᵹɑpꞇ oɩleɩɴ ɴɑ Ꞇpɩɴoɩꞅe .ɩ. Seɑɴ ɓuɩᵬe O
Se[p]ᵹoɩꞅ ꞅo ᵬɑꞅhɑꞅ ɑp loᵬ Ce lɑ cɑɩᵹ. Ꞇɩᵹepɴɑ Luᵬɑ
.ɩ. Cpɩᵹꞅoɩp pluɩɴᵹceꞅ ꞅo le[ɴ]ṁuɩɴ Meᵹ Mɑᵬᵹuɴɑ ɑ
ꞇopɑɩᵹechꞇ, ocuṗ ɑ cpeᵬ poɩme. Mɑᵹ Mɑᵬuɴɑ ꞅo ᵬɑᵬ-
ɑɩpꞇ puɑᵹɑ ꞅoɩᵬ, ocuṗ ꞇɩᵹepɴɑ Luᵬɑ, ocuṗ mɑc Meᵹ
Ἀoɴᵹɑppɑ .ɩ. ᵬpɩɑɴ, ꞅo ṁɑpᵬɑᵬ ꞅoɴ puɑɩᵹ pɩɴ, ocuṗ
cuɩᵹpep mɑpcɑᵬ mɑpɑoɴ pɩu; ocuṗ pɑ mop ɩɴꞇ eᵬꞇ pɩɴ
ꞅo poɩɴɴe ɩɴ lɑ pɩɴ. Seɑᵬɑɴ mɑc ꞅoɴɴchɑꞅɑ meᵹ Uɩꞅɩp
ꞅo ᵬpochɑꞅ le ɴɑ ꞅepᵬpɑɩꞇhpɩᵬ peɩɴ .ɩ. le ᵬpɩɑɴ ocuṗ

---

1 *Foreigners.* ᵹɑlloɩᵬ. This is
the last word legible in the MS. II. 1,
19, the page which follows (the final
one) being totally defaced. The remainder of the text is therefore
altogether taken from the Clar.
fragment, in which this entry, and

the three next, are added in the handwriting of Brian Mac Dermot.

2 *Against.* eɩp (for ɑpɩ); lit. "upon."

3 *By.* eɩᵹ; which is corrupt. The
more usual form is ɑc or ɑᵹ.

4 *The Rock;* i.e. Mac Dermot's
Rock, in Loᴄh-Cé.

Aedh, son of John, son of Redmond, [was killed] by Foreigners.[1] Conchobhar Carragh, the son of O'Cathain, was killed by O'Cathain. Baile-an-muta was taken by the descendants of Tomaltach Mac Donnchadha, and by the descendants of Dubhgall Gruamach, against[2] Saxons. The head (roof?) of the monastery of the Trinity, and the erection of the bawn of Dun-gar, were in progress at the same time by[3] Brian, the son of Ruaidhri Mac Diarmada; for this Brian was the superior of the monastery, and lord of the Rock.[4] Tadhg, the son of Murchadh, son of Toirdhelbhach O'Briain, and Toirdhelbhach, son of Mac Mathghamhna, died at the close of this year; and there were not in Erinn, in their own time, two youths of greater account than they in every way. Robert Savage, i.e. the sub-sheriff of the county of Sligo, was killed, and six of his people along with him, by Mac Donnchadha of the Corann. Edmond, son of Murchadh O'Ferghail, and Conchobhar Og MagRanaill, died.[5]

The kalends[6] of January on Wednesday; and the age of the Lord at this time is one thousand, five hundred, and seventy-eight years. O'Neill's son, i.e. Henry O'Neill, was killed with one cast of a spear by O'Gallchubhair's son; and he was a great loss, that son of Toirdhelbhach, the son of Niall Conallagh. The chief priest of Trinity-Island, i.e. John Buidhe O'Sergoid, was drowned in Loch-Cé on Easter-day. The Lord of Louth, i.e. Christopher Plunket, followed Mac Mathguna[7] in pursuit, who had his prey before him. Mac Mathuna[8] gave them an onset; and the Lord of Louth, and MagAenghusa, i.e. Brian, were killed in that onset, and five horsemen along with them : and that was a great deed he performed that day. John, the son of Donnchadh Mag Uidhir, was hanged by

---

[5] *Died.* The writer, who adds meṙ bṙuan mac Oιaṙmaυa, "I am Brian Mac Dermot," had written part of another entry, which was afterwards expunged.

[6] *Kalends.* The entries for this year are all in the handwriting, and incorrect orthography, of Brian Mac Dermot.

[7-8] *Mac Mathguna—Mac Mathuna.* Corrupt forms of the name of Mac Mathghamhna, now Mac Mahon.

Le Ɔonnchaⱱ óᵹ, aⱂ ⲧeᵹaⱂᵹ Meᵹ Uⲓⱱⲓⱂ .ⲓ. Cuconnachⲧ.
Sⲓaⱂⱂⲓaⲧ connⱱaⱱe Muⲓᵹe ⱱeó ⱱo ṁaⱂⱱaⱱ Le Emaⲛⲛ
a Ꝺuⱂc, mac Ⲧomaⲓⱂ ⲓⲛ maⲓⱅⲓⱂe .ⲓ. Muⲓlⲓⱂⱂe mac Uaⲧeⱂ;
ocuⱂ ⱂa moⱂ ⲓⲛ ⱂᵹeal ⱂⲓⲛ; ocuⱂ a caⲓⱂlen na hⲈⲓlle ⱱo
ⱂoⲓⲛⱱe ⲓⲛⲧ eⲉⱅ ⱂⲓⲛ. O Conchobaⲓⱂ Slⲓᵹⲓᵹ .ⲓ. Ɔoṁⲛall
mac Ⲧaⲓⱱᵹ meⲓc Caⱅhaⲓl oⲓᵹ, ocuⱂ mac mⲓc Ɔhⲓaⱂmaⱱa
.ⲓ. Ꝺⱂⲓaⲛ mac Ruaⲓⱱⱂⲓ mⲓc Ɔhⲓaⱂmaⱱa, ⱱo ⱱul ᵹo baⲓle
Aⱅa clⲓaⱅ aⲓⱂ ⲓⲛ coṁaⲓⱂle moⲓⱂ, ocuⱂ ⱱeⲓⱅ ⱱoⲓⱱ cuⲓᵹ
ⱂeⱅⲧmaⲓⲛe aⱂ ⲓⲛ ᵹcuⲓⱂⲧ ⱂⲓⲛ, ocuⱂ onoⲓⱂ moⱂ ⱱⱂaᵹaⲓl
ⱱoⲓⱱ o coṁaⲓⱂle na hⲈⱂeⲛⲛ, ocuⱂ a ⲧeachⲧ ⱂlaⲛ. Lⲓaⱅⱂouⲓm muⲓⲛⲛⲧⲓⱂe hⲞⲓlaⲓⱂ ⱱo ᵹaⱱaⲓl Le Saxanachaⲓb aⱂ
Ꝺⱂⲓaⲛ mac Ꝺⱂⲓaⲓⲛ ⲓ Ruaⲓⱂc, ocuⱂ cuⲓᵹⱂⲓⱂ ⱱeᵹ ⱱo maⱂ-
ⱱaⱱ ⲓⲛⲛⲧe, ocuⱂ ⲓumaⱱ ⱱa ᵹach uⲓle éⱱaⲓl ⱱo ⱱⱂeⱅ eⱂⲧe.
Mac ⲓ Ruaⲓⱂc .ⲓ. Ꝺⱂⲓaⲛ ⱱo ⱱul a ᵹceⲛⱱ ⲓⲛ·ᵹⲓuⱂⲧⲓⱂ, ocuⱂ
ⱂéuⱱ ⱱó ⱂe ᵹalloⲓb, ocuⱂ a baⲓle ⱱⱂaᵹaⲓl ⱱó.ⲓ. Lⲓaⱅⱂouⲓm
Ruⱱⱂⲓᵹ oᵹ O Moⱂᵹa ⱱo ṁaⱂⱱuⱱ Le Ꝺⱂⲓaⲛ oᵹ mac ᵹⲓolla-
phaⱱoⱂaⲓᵹ ocuⱂ Le ᵹalloⲓb, ocuⱂ nⲓ ⱂoⲓⱱe a nⲈⲓⱂⲓⲛⲛ ⱂeⱂ
mⲓllⲧe eⲓⱂ ᵹhallⲓⱅ ⱱuⱱ mo na ⲓⲛ ⱂeⱂ ⱂⲓⲛ; ocuⱂ ⱂa ⱂo
ṁoⱂ ⲓⲛⲧ eaⲉⱅ he. Ꝺuⲛ Ɔⱂoⱱuⲓⱂ ⱱo ⱅaⱱaⲓⱂⲧ ⱱo Uaⱱ
Ɔomⲛaⲓll ⱱon ᵹⲓuⱂⲧⲓⱂ, ocuⱂ ⱱa ceⱱ ⱱeᵹ maⱂᵹ ⱱo ⱱuaⲓⲛ
ⱱe aⱂ uel amplⲓuⱂ; ocuⱂ aⱱeⲓⱂmúⲓⱱ ᵹuⱂab olc ⱱo ⱂⱂⲓ
baⲓle ⱂleaⲉⱅa Ꝺⱂⲓaⲓⲛ Luⲓᵹⲛⲓᵹ ⱱo ⱂeⲓc ⱂⲓⱂ O n'Ɔomⲛaⲓll
ⱱa Leⲓᵹeⱱ ⲓⲛⲛ eᵹla ⱱuⲓⲛⲛ a ⲓⲛⱱⲓⱂⲓⲛ. Rⲓᵹⲧeᵹh moⱂ
na caⱂⱂᵹe ⱱo ⲧⲓⲛⲛⱂᵹna ⱱo Ꝺⱂⲓaⲛ mac Ruaⲓⱱⱂⲓ Meⲓc
Ɔⲓaⱂmaⱱa, ocuⱂ ⱱoⱅⲓ ⱂⲓⲛ ocuⱂ ceⲛⲛ maⲓⲛⲓⱅⲧⱂech na
Ⲧⱂⲓⲛoⲓⱱe, ocuⱂ baⱱuan Ɔuⲛa ᵹaⱂ aⱂ ⱂⲓuⱱal anaoⲓⲛⱂeⲉⱅ
aⲓᵹe; ocuⱂ nⲓ ⱂoⲓⱱe ⲧⲓᵹeⱂⲛuⱂ na ⲧaⲛⲓⲓⱂⲧechⲧ aⲓᵹe an
uaⲓⱂ ⱂⲓⲛ. Uaⱂal ⱂaᵹaⱂⲧ Ꝺhaⲓle na cⲓlle a cloⲓⲛⱱ

---

1 *Magh-eó.* "Plain of the Yew;"
now Mayo. The name is corruptly
written Muⲓᵹe [nom. Maᵹ] ⱱeo by
Mac Dermot.

2 *Caislen-na-hEille.* The "castle of
the Eill," now the Neale, in the bar.
of Kilmaine, co. Mayo.

3 *Muinter-Eolais.* The form of the
name in the text, "Liatrouim muinntire Oilias," is very corrupt. But the

same may be said generally of Brian
Mac Dermot's orthography.

4 *O'Mordha.* O'More. O Moⱂᵹa
in the text; which is incorrect.

5 *Against.* eⲓⱂ (*rectè* aⱂ); lit.
"upon."

6 *O'Domhnaill.* This name is also
written corruptly Uaⱱ Ɔomⲛaⲓll.

7 *Brian Luighnech's descendants;*
i.e. the sept of O'Conor Sligo.

his own brothers, viz., by Brian and Donnchadh Og, through the advice of Mag Uidhir, i.e. Cuconnacht. The sheriff of the county of Magh-eó,[1] i.e. Meiler, the son of Walter, was killed by Edmond Burk, son of Thomas-an-Machaire ; (and that was a great calamity ; and in Caislen-na-hEille[2] he committed that deed): O'Conchobhair Sligigh, i.e. Domhnall, the son of Tadhg, son of Cathal Og, and Mac Diarmada's son, i.e. Brian, the son of Ruaidhri Mac Diarmada, went to Baile-atha-cliath, to the great council; and they were five weeks at that court, and received great honour from the council of Erinn ; and they returned safely. Liatruim of Muinter-Eolais[3] was taken by Saxons against Brian, the son of Brian O'Ruairc; and fifteen men were killed in it ; and a great quantity of all kinds of spoil was taken out of it. The son of O'Ruairc, i.e. Brian, went to meet the Justiciary ; and he made peace with the Foreigners, and obtained his town, i.e. Liatruim. Ruaidhri Og O'Mordha[4] was killed by Brian Og MacGillapatraic, and by the Foreigners ; and there was not in Erinn a greater destroyer against[5] Foreigners than that man ; and he was a very great loss. Bun-Drobhais was given to O'Domhnaill[6] by the Justiciary, who exacted twelve hundred marks from him for it, vel amplius ; and we would say that it was wrong to sell the residence of Brian Luighnech's descendants[7] to O'Domhnaill, if fear allowed us to say it. The great, regal, house of the Rock was begun by Brian, the son of Ruaidhri Mac Diarmada; and he had this work, and the head (roof?) of the monastery of the Trinity, and the bawn[8] of Dun-gar, in progress together ; and he had neither lordship nor tanistship[9] at that time. The chief priest of Baile-na-cille in Clann-Connmhaigh, i.e. Tadhg

---

[8] *Bawn.* baḃuan. A very corrupt form of the word, which is also incorrectly written baġóun under the year 1577.

[9] *Tanistship.* τanuirτechτ. This is also bad orthography, the correct form of the word being τanairτechτ. Under the previous year Brian Mac Dermot is said to have been lord of the district, and abbot of Trinity Island, when the "head" of the monastery was in process of construction.

Chonɒmuіᵹ ɒpαᵹαιl ᵬαιp, .ι. Ϲαᵬᵹ Ο Ϲοnαιpe, ecιp ɒα ḟeιl
Ⅿuιpe pαn οᵬpuɲ. Ⅿαc 1 Conchoᵬαιp ᵬuιnn .ι. Ϲαᵬᵹ
ᵬuιᵭe mαc Conchoᵬαιp 1 Chončuᵬαιp, οcuɲ α ᵭιαɲ mαc
.ι. Ḟeιlιm οcuɲ ιn Ɒuᵬαlⲧαch, ɒο ṁαpᵬαᵭ le Ϲοmαɲ
Ⅱɒιɲ α pιoll eιp cαιppeαll nα hΟιlιᵭe, αp ᵬpu čuppαιᵭ
čιnɒ eιⲧⲧe. Ɒolᵬ mαc Ɒuᵬᵭαιᵹ 1 Ɒhuιᵬᵹennαιn .ι.
Ο Ɒuιᵬᵹennαιn ɒpαᵹαιl ᵬαιp. Ⅿαᵹ [Ḟ]lαnnčαιᵭ .ι.
Cαⲧhαl ɒuᵬ ɒpαᵹαιl ᵬαιp.

Ⅼⲧⲧ. Ɛnαιp pοp ᵬαpɒαοιn ; nοι mᵬlιαɒnα ɒhec οcuɲ
ⲧpι pιcheⲧ, οcuɲ u. ceɒ οcuɲ mιle αιɲ αn Ϲιᵹepnα. Seαn
Ο Ⅿαοlṁοčeιpᵹe .ι. comᵬopᵬα ɒpοmα Οιpᵹιαllα .ι. pόι
Ɛpenn α nοιnech čιᵹe αοιɒheɒ coιⲧčιnn ɒpepαιᵬ Ɛpenn
οcuɲ αn ɒοmαιn, αn ṁeιɒ no pοιcheɒ é ᵭιᵬ, ɒhéc.
Ο ᵹαɒpα .ι. Ɒιαpmαιɒ mαc Ɛoᵹαιn h1 ᵹhαɒpα, οcuɲ αn
ᵹιllα ɒuᵬ ṁάιᵹ Phιlιp .ι. ⲧιᵹepnα nα Ⅼιⲧpι, ɒhec α nαοn
ṁί οcuɲ αn comαpᵬα. Cpečα mοpαιᵬᵬle ɒο ᵹenum α
mαᵹ Ⅼuιpᵹ αp Ⅰhpίαn mαc Ɍuαιɒpι Ⅿιc Ɒιαpmαɒα ɒο
člοιnn Ɒonnchαɒα Ⅿhéᵹ Ⅱιᵭιp, .ι. ɒια čαιpɒιᵬ ᵬunαιᵭ
peιpιn, οcuɲ ɒ ⅭⅬbαnchαιᵬ .ι. Ɛoιn mαc ⅭⅭonᵹupα mιc
ᵹιlle epᵹαιb ᵬάιn ṁéᵹ Ɒοṁnαιll, οcuɲ ɒο člαιnn
Ɒuιppίč. ⅭⅭoᵬ mαc Seαn mιc Ɍemuιnn [ο] ᵹlιοnn
Ⅿαlupα ɒο éc ιn hoc αnnο; οcuɲ ɒο buᵬ ɒο pᵹélαιb
ṁopα Ɛpenn ɒό αlleιᵭ uαιple οcuɲ eιnιᵹ. Ɍolonɒ
Ⅰupⲧαιɲ ɒpαᵹαιl ᵬαιp mup αn ceɒnα, οcuɲ pα ɒéchⲧuιᵬ
mόpα čοιceɒ Ⅼαιᵹen αn ɒιαp pιn. Ɛoιn οᵬαp ṁαιᵹ Neιll
ɒο ṁαpbαɒ lα člαιnn Ɛoᵹαιn Ⅿιc Ɒιαpmαɒα α lαⲧhαιᵹ
ᵬpenɒpumαι α nuchⲧ Chοιppɲleιᵬ, οcuɲ mόpαn ɒα muιn-
ⲧep ɒο mαpbαɒ α ⲧοιp αn lοι ceɒnα lα ᵹαllοιb Ɍoppα
Comάιn αp mαčαιpe Connαchⲧ. Sαᵬb ιnᵹen Ϲomαιpɲ mιc

1 *Two festivals of Mary;* i.e. the
festivals of the Assumption and Nati-
vity, or the 15th of August and 8th
of September.

² *In the autumn.* pαn οᵬpuɲ;
οᵬpuɲ being a wrong form of the word
pοᵹṁαp.

³ *Udis.* This name is written Uidir,
or Odis, under the year 1581.

⁴ *Died.* The writer adds mepι
Ⅰpιαn, "I am Brian." This is the
conclusion of the second folio of the
Clar. fragment (fol. 28 of the vol.),
both of which folios are paper. The
four succeeding leaves are vellum, not
so thick as the vellum in the MS. H.
1, 19, and not ruled for writing as the
vellum in the latter MS. ia.

O'Tonaire, died between the two festivals of Mary[1] in the autumn.[2] The son of O'Conchobhair Donn, i.e. Tadhg Buidhe, the son of Conchobhar O'Conchobhair, and his two sons, viz., Felim and the Dubhaltach, were killed by Thomas Udis,[3] in treachery, on Caisel-na-hOilidhe, on the margin of Curragh-cinn-eite. Dolbh, the son of Dubhtach O'Duibhgennain, i.e., *the chief* O'Duibhgennain, died. Mac [F]lannchaidh, i.e. Cathal Dubh, died.[4]

The kalends[5] of January on Thursday; the age of the Lord one thousand, five hundred, and seventy-nine years. John O'Maelmocheirghe, i.e. comarb of Druim-Oirghialla,[6] the most eminent man in Erinn for keeping a general house of hospitality for the men of Erinn, and of the world, (as many of them as he could supply), died. O'Gadhra, i.e. Diarmaid, the son of Eoghan O'Gadhra, and the Gilla-dubh MacPhilip, i.e. the lord of the Leitir,. died in the same month as the comarb. Immense depredations were committed in Magh-Luirg, upon Brian, son of Ruaidhri Mac Diarmada, by the sons of Donnchadh Mag Uidhir, viz., by his own relatives, and by Albanachs, viz., John, the son of Aenghus, son of Gilla-espuig Bán Mac Domhnaill, and the Clann-Duibhsith. Aedh,[7] the son of John, son of Redmond, [from] Glenn-Malura, died in hoc anno; and he was of the great woes[8] of Erinn, as regards nobility and bounty. Roland Eustace died likewise : and these two were of the great losses of the province of Laighen. John Odhar Mac Neill was killed by the sons of Eoghan Mac Diarmada, in Lathach-Brendruma, in front of Corr-sliabh ; and several of his people were slain in the beginning of the same day, by the Foreigners of Ros-Comain, on Machaire-Connacht. Sadhbh, daughter of Thomas, son of Richard Og Burk, i.e.,

---

[5] *Kalends*. This part of the Clar. fragment has been written by the scribe who copied the portion of the MS. H, 1, 19, containing the events of 1568, &c.

[6] *Druim-Oirghialla*. The correct form is Druim-Oirbhelaigh, as the name is elsewhere written.

[7] *Aedh*; i.e., Aedh (or Hugh) O'Byrne.

[8] *Woes*. ᴅᴏ ᵊ̃ᴜᴜᴀɪᴃ ; lit. " of stories."

Ricaro óig a bupc, .i. ben poroa Catéc mic Uilliam
h1 Cheallaig, .i. an ben rob ferr ocur rob foigroige
na haimrir rein, moptua erc, ocur a haonacal a
Cill Conaill. Mac Muirir ruié mic 1apla Ohermuman ro toigecht 1 nErinn irin mbliaoain rin,
ocur began Spainoec maille rir. Do gaérat run in
óir irin Mumain; ocur o ro cuala giuirvir na hErenn
rin ro tinoil rluag mor .i. 1apla Chilli rapa ocur
caircín Malbie .i. tigerna toiged Connacht mun am
rin, ocur morán ro Ghaoioelaib Connacht, ocur coiged
Laigen cona armáil, ocur morán ro Mhuimnechaib.
Orro cuala, imorro, clann 1aplai Oerrmuman .i. Sean
mac Semuir, ocur Sémur na tinól a brathair eli,
Semur mac Muirir ruié ro toigecht co hErinn, ocur
na Sbainnig maille rir, ro togbovar comruarma
cogaio rria Galloib Muman, ocur ro marbao rreiri-
vemr va toiged Muman, ocur ochtor vo maitib na
ngall maille rir ina noirecht rein. Semur mac
Muirir ruié vo teacht ar riubal a gcrié élainni
Uilliam. Clann Uilliam na Siuire .i. 1arrma an 1apta
ruaio vo breié rair. Tacar rria poile tóié. Mac
Muirir ruié vo tuicim ann, ocur triar vo élainn
Uilliam vo tuicim rir. Acht chena ra mor vo aurob
mara ocur tíre ruair conuigi rin recnóin na Spainne
ocur na Fraince, ac venum invill ar a ercairoib, ocur
ra mor vo gaircio ocur vo gniom vílmuintir vo rigne
irna coicrichaib rin, tar cenn a crice ocur an érevmn.
Ceio in giuirvir an tinól aibail rin aouéromar von
Mhumain, ocur ni heivir a ríom no áireim gach ar
milleo irin Mumain von vol rin vo bailtib, ocur var-
éonnuib, ocur vairmeir. Int erruc.h.hElibe .i. rói egnai
ocur crabaio in vomuin uile, ocur mac h1 Ruairc .i.
Connbrator mac Briain mic Eogain h1 Ruairc, vo
toigecht arran voman anoir tarir a leigti ocur a
turair. Giuirvir na hErenn vo breié orra, ocur a

the wedded wife of Tadhg, son of William O'Cellaigh, i.e., the best and most patient woman in her own time, mortua est; and she was buried in Cill-Conaill. The son of Maurice Dubh, son of the Earl of Des-Mumha, came to Erinn in this year, and a few Spaniards along with him. They occupied Dun-in-óir in Mumha; and when the Justiciary of Erinn heard this he assembled a large army, viz., the Earl of Cill-dara, and Captain Malbie, i.e. the governor of the province of Connacht at that time, and a great number of the Gaeidhel of Connacht, and the province of Laighen, with its armament, and a great number of Muimhnechs. When the sons of the Earl of Des-Mumha, viz., John, the son of James, and Shemus-na-tinol,[1] his other brother, heard that James, the son of Maurice Dubh, had come to Erinn, accompanied by the Spaniards, they raised an insurrection of war against the Foreigners of Mumha; and the president of the two provinces of Mumha, and eight of the principal Foreigners along with him, were killed in their own territory. James, the son of Maurice Dubh, went on an expedition into the country of Clann-William. The Clann-William of the Suir, i.e. the posterity of the Red Earl, overtook him. They fought with each other. The son of Maurice Dubh fell there; and three of the Clann-William fell with him. And he endured much hardship by sea and land up to that time, throughout Spain and France, making preparations against his enemies, and performed great bravery, and warlike deeds, in those foreign countries, for the sake of his own land, and of the faith. The Justiciary went to Mumha, with this large army which we have mentioned, and it is not possible to reckon or calculate the towns, corn-fields, and property, destroyed in Mumha on that occasion. The Bishop O'hElidhe, i.e. the paragon of learning and piety of the whole world, and the son of O'Ruairc, i.e. Connbrathar, the son of Brian, son of Eoghan O'Ruairc, came from the east, after their education and tour. The Justiciary of Erinn

ʒcρochατ αραοɴ ταρ ραρυʒατ Τé οcυρ ταοιɴe; οcυρ
bα τρυαᵹ αɴ ʒɴιοm ριɴ .ι. eρρυc οɴóραch αρτcραιᵬτech,
οcυρ bράτhαιρ mιοɴúρ τᵹυιʟ úαρυιʟ, το ᵬáρρυʒατ mαρ
ɴáρ čυbαιτ. Ἀchτ čeɴα το ροιᵹɴe Τíα ριρτ ριαᵬɴαch
ροʟʟυρ αρ αɴ ɴʒιυιρτíρ .ι. ρο ʒαᵬ τοιʒʰ α čeɴτ αɴ ʟα ρο
cροchατ αɴ τιαρ ριɴ, οcúρ ɴí ρο ᵬeαʟαιʒ αɴ τοιᵹ ριɴ ρριρ
cο bᵹυαιρ bαρρ τι α cιɴɴ ᵬeʒαιɴ αιmρeιι. Cαᵬʒ mαc
Cυιɴɴ čιοταιᵹ mιc Ἀοτα mιc Θοʒαιɴ τheʒ. Rιρτéρτ
Uρτáιρ οcυρ Rιρτeρτ Òρíρ, cο ɴιmατ ρʟυαιʒ mαιʟʟe ρριú,
το ᵬυʟ αρ ριυbαʟ αρ cʟαιɴɴ ιɴ ιαρʟα ιɴα ɴταιɴʒɴιᵬιᵬ
ρρeιɴ. Cʟαɴɴ ιɴ ιαρʟα οcυρ ταοιɴe mιc Mυιριρ τυιᵬ, α
hαιčʟe α ᵬáιρ ρéιɴ, το ᵬρeιᵬ ρορρα. Ἰɴ τá Rιρτeρτ ριɴ
το mαρᵬαᵬ, οcυρ τá ceτ eʟι mαιʟʟe ρριυ, υeʟ αmρʟιυρ.
Rιρτeρτ Τοmɴαʟʟ τραᵹαιʟ ᵬáιρ; οcυρ ρá móρ αɴ τιᵬ
το ʒοeιτeʟαιb Θρeɴɴ ɴα τρι Rιρτeρτ ριɴ το mαρčαιɴ.
Cρeιριρéιρ ɴα hΘρeɴɴ .ι. Θτbορτ ριτóɴ, τραᵹαιʟ ᵬáιρ α
mbαιʟe Ἀᵬα cʟιαᵬ αɴ ʟα τeιᵹιοɴαch το mι meᵬοιɴ ιɴτ
ραᵯραᵬ, οcυρ ɴí čáɴιc ρe ρατα το ᵹαʟʟοιb 8αχαɴ ρᵹéʟ
τιτ mó ιɴáρρ, αʟʟeᵬ υαιρʟe οcυρ οιρρτeρcυιρ. Ϻαc
Τοɴɴchατα ᵬíρe hΟιʟeʟʟα το ᵯαρbατ ʟe Ϻαοʟρυαɴαιᵬ
mαc Cαϧhαιʟ mιc Θοʒαιɴ mιc Τοɴɴchατα, οcυρ αɴ
τιρ.cο hιmbᵹeρɴech ɴα τeοιᵬ eτιρ cʟαιɴɴ ɴΤοɴɴchατα.
Ο Òριαιɴ .ι. Τοᵯɴαʟʟ mαc Choɴčυᵬαιρ ι Òριαιɴ τραᵹαιʟ
ᵬαιρ, οcυρ ρα mορ ιɴ ρᵹeʟ ριɴ. Οɴορρα ιɴʒeɴ
Τοɴɴchατα mιc Choɴčυbαιρ ι Òριαιɴ τραᵹαιʟ ᵬαιρ. .
Cοmαρ mαc ιɴ ᵬαρυιɴ Νυιɴτρeɴτ τeʒ. Ϻαιρʒρeʒ
ιɴʒeɴ Òριαιɴ meιc Τιαρmατα ρυαιᵬ, αɴ beɴ το ᵬι αᵹ
Cαϧhαʟ mαc Θοʒαιɴ meιc Τοɴɴchατα, τeʒ. Rιᵹ ρορ-
τιᵹeʟ το mαρᵬαᵬ ʟeιρ αɴ Cυρcαč α cαᵬ, οcυρ τα ριcheτ
mιʟe ρeρ mαραοɴ ριρ, οcυρ ʟα ʟυɴαρα τυʒαᵬ ιɴ cαᵬ ριɴ.
Rιᵹ ɴα Ρeιρρe το τeαchτ αρ ιɴ Cυρcαč ρʟυαᵹ τιαιρme,

<hr />

1 *Tadhg.* One of the family of
O'Conor. This entry is added in the
'handwriting of Brian Mac Dermot.

2 *Citach;* i.e. left-handed.

3 *Bris.* The name of this officer
was Price.

4 *Earl.* The Earl of Desmond.

5 *Richard, son of Domhnall.* The
names "Richard Domhnall," are
both written in the nom. case in
the MS., and it is to be apprehended
that there is some omission, which

apprehended them; and they were both hanged, to the profanation of God and men. And that was a pitiful deed, i.e., to put an honourable, most pious bishop, and a friar minor of noble blood, to death in an unbecoming manner. But God performed a plain, manifest miracle on the Justiciary; i.e. a burning attacked his head the day these two were hanged, and this burning did not leave him until he died of it in the course of a short time. Tadhg,[1] the son of Conn Citach,[2] son of Aedh, son of Eoghan, died. Richard Eustace, and Richard Bris,[3] accompanied by a large army, went on an expedition against the sons of the Earl,[4] into their own fastnesses. The Earl's sons, and the people of Maurice Dubh's son, after his own death, overtook them. These two Richards were slain, and two hundred persons along with them, vel amplius. Richard, *son of* Domhnall,[5] died; and the existence of these three Richards was a great injury to the Gaeidhel of Erinn. The treasurer of Erinn, i.e. Edward Fitton, died in Baile-atha-cliath, the last day of the middle month of summer; and there came not of the Saxon Foreigners, for a long time, one more to be lamented than he, as regards nobility and dignity. Mac Donnchadha of Tir-Oilella was killed by Maelruanaidh, the son of Cathal, son of Eoghan Mac Donnchadha; and the country was in a disturbed condition after him, between the Clann-Donnchadha. O'Briain,[6] i.e. Domhnall, son of Conchobhar O'Briain, died; and that was a great calamity. Honora, daughter of Donnchadh, son of Conchobhar O'Briain, died. Thomas, son of the Baron Nugent, died. Margaret, daughter of Brian Mac Diarmada Ruadh, the wife of Cathal, son of Eoghan Mac Donn-chadha, died. The king of Portugal was killed by the Turk[7] in a battle, and forty thousand men along with him; and on Lammas Day this battle was given. The king of Persia went against the Turk,[7] with a countless

---

renders it difficult to identify the person meant.

⁶ *O'Briain.* The remaining entries

for this year are in the handwriting of Brian Mac Dermot

⁷ *Turk.* Ⲧⲩⲣⲁⲥ̇, Clar.

anoíξail a čαραυ ριξ ρορτιξel υo τιιτ leiρ, ocuρ υo cuιρeὄ cač eτoρρα, ocuρ υo τιιτ ριče mιle υo mιιιιnτιρ ιn Τυρcαιὄ, ocuρ υo čéρnαιξ ριξ nα Τυρcαč αριn cač ρlαn ταρéιρ a mιιnnτeρι υo ṁαρὄαὄ. Υonn Seon Ccuρυρe .ι. υeρβραčαίρ cιnξ Ριlιρ ριξ nα Sbαιnne, ιnτ αon ὄιιne ιιαραl ιρ ρeρρ ταιnιc ρ'αn Cριορυαοιξeαchτ ριαιn, υραξαιl βαιρ ιn cιιξeυ lá υon céυ mí υon ρoξmαρ. Oιξρe cιnξ Ριlιρ υραξαιl βαιρ ιn υαρα mι. Maoιὄm αn αοιιαιξ ὄeξ υo čαὄαιρτ αρ Shemuρ nα τιnol, ocuρ αρ ὄSeαn mαc Semαιρ, le cαρτιn Malbιe, υú ατορčιιιρ Eoξαn mαc Emαιnυ meιc Sιčhιξ, ocuρ mοιρρ'eιρρeρ υα čeιneὄ υυαιρ'le člαιnυe Sιčιξ, ocuρ ριcheυ no υo mαραon ριιι.

Ιcτ. Eιιαιρ ρορ Ccoιne, ocuρ υob e αoιρ ιn Τιξeρnα .ι. M. ocuρ cuιcc ceυ ocuρ ceὄρα .xx. Mαc Ιllιlιαm Ουρcc .ι. Seὄán mαc Oιlbeρuρ, cenυ ιιαιρlι ocuρ oιmιξ ocuρ oιρρυeρcαιρ coιccιὄ Connαchτ, υo éucc ιρ'ιn blιαυαιn ρe. Ιnτ eρbucc a Ουρc, .ι. Rolonτ mαc Remαιnυ υo éuξ, ceιυ ecαιlρeč Connαchτ. Maιυm ξlenυα Moluρα υo ταβ- αιρττ αρ Saxαnchαιb, ιnαρ bαραιξheυ .ιx. cαιρτιn, ocuρ ceυ mαιllι ριρ'ιn cαιρτίn αcα, υo clqιnn Roloιn lúρττάρ ocuρ υρ'ιαchα mαc Ccυhα mιc Seὄαιn mιc Remαιnυ. Eoξhαn mαc Ρelιm ριιαιὄ mιc Ccιρττ mιc Ccoὄα hΙ Νéιll, υιαρbα coṁαιnm ριιαč αn αιρξιυ, υρ'αξαιl bαιρ a mbαιlι Ccéα clιαč. Maolριιαυαιξ mαc Cαčαιl mιc Eoξαιṅ mιc Υonnchαυα, αυbορ ριξυαṁnα O nOιlelα ξαn ιmρeραιn, υραξάιl bαιρ a Cul nιαeιle, ιαρ mbρeιč bιιαυα o υomαn ocuρ o υeαmon; ocuρ ρα ρcel ρočαιρ ocuρ ρuιlbιρeαchτα υια eρccαιρυιὄ ιn bάρ ρ'ιn mιc Mιc Υonnchαυα, ocuρ ρά mαnα mορčuṁαὄ υια cαιρυιb. Ουιlι Loča Rιαč υo ξαρ'αιl υo cloιnυ αn ιαρlα αρ

1 *Between them.* αυoρρα, Clar., which is corrupt. The correct form of the word is eτoρρα.

2 *Of the Turks.* Τυρcαιč, Clar., in mistake for Τυρcαč.

3 *Month.* The word lα (day) was first written, but subsequently expunged by the writer, who added meρι Ουιαn, "I am Brian."

4 *Kalends.* The handwriting here seems the same as that in the specimen page prefixed to vol. i.

army, to avenge his friend the king of Portugal, who had
fallen by him; and a battle was fought between them,[1]
and twenty thousand of the Turk's people fell; and the
king of the Turks[2] escaped safely from the battle, after
his people had been slain. Don John of Austria, i.e. the
brother of king Philip, king of Spain, the best nobleman
that ever came into Christendom, died the fifth day of
the first month of autumn. The heir of king Philip died
the second month.[3] The defeat of Aenagh-beg was given
to Shemus-na-tinol, and to John son of Shemus, by Captain Malbie, in which Eoghan, the son of Edmond Mac
Sithigh, and seven of his kindred, of the noblest of the
Clann-Sithigh, were slain, and one or two score along
with them.

The kalends[4] of January on Friday; and the age of the [1580.]
Lord was one thousand, and five hundred, and eighty.
Mac William Burk, i.e. John,[5] the son of Oliver, head of
the nobility, honour, and dignity of the province of
Connacht, died in this year. The Bishop Burk,[6] i.e.
Roland, son of Redmond, head of the ecclesiastics of
Connacht, died. The defeat of Glenn-Malura, in which
nine captains were slain, and one hundred men along with
each captain, was inflicted on Saxons by the sons of
Roland Eustace, and by Fiacha, son of Aedh, son of John,
son of Redmond. Eoghan, son of Felim Ruadh, son of
Art, son of Aedh O'Neill, who was called Fuath-an-airgid.[7]
died in Baile-atha-cliath. Maelruanaidh, son of Cathal,
son of Eoghan Mac Donnchadha, undisputed royal heir
of Ui-nOilella, died in Cul-mhaile, after triumphing over
the world and the devil; and this death of the son of
Mac Donnchadha was happy, joyful, news to his enemies,
and the cause of great sorrow to his friends. Baile-
Locha-Riach was taken by the sons of the Earl[8] from

---

[5] *John.* Corruptly written Seóán
in the text.
[6] *Bishop Burk.* Bishop of Clonfert.

[7] *Fuath-an-airgid*; lit., "hate of
money."
[8] *Earl*; i.e. of Clann-Rickard.

Saxanchaib. Mopán millti do denaṁ do Ḃpian
O Ruaipc ap muiᵹ Luipᵹ, ocuy Ḃpian Mac Diapmada
do denaṁ ın cedna ap éiᵹepncup hI Ruaipc. Mac
Uilliam do ᵹaipm do Ripdepd an iapainn. Séumay na
cınól, mac iapla Deymuman, do bápuᵹhad don ᵹiúiydiy
a Copcaiḃ. Aé yceiddın do ᵹabáil don ᵹiúiydiy cedna,
ocuy baypda do cop ann. Cappuicc an puill do ᵹabail
don fiop cedna, ocuy apoiḃe and do mapḃaḃ, ocuy an
baile do bpippeḃ. O Ḃıpn .ı. Cadᵹ occ mac Caidᵹ I Ḃeıpn
dpaᵹail ḃaıy a mí ṁapda, ocuy ya mop ınc eéc yın.
Mouḃda Dioluin, ben I Fhepᵹail, dhec. Sbaınıoh do
coachc ᵹo hEıpınn a cuıᵹ no yé do ćeduiḃ ᵹo Dun án
oıp, ocuy a cuıcım uıle leıy ın ᵹiuıydiy. Royya mac
Condla Meᵹ Eochaᵹaın do mapḃaḃ le na depḃpachaıp
yeın ᵹo nemmaıé, ocuy ba mop ınc eéc yın. Cadᵹ
yıaḃach O Duḃda do cuıcım do ḃaypcaıylein Conchobaıp, ocuy a mapḃaḃ ᵹo cımpeıydeaé. Loch an yᵹuıp
do ᵹabaıl le Cachal duḃ mac Ḃpíaın Mıc Diapmada,
ocuy Maoılyeélaınn mac Meᵹ Ranaıll do mapḃaḃ and.
Cpeé do ᵹenaṁ do Ḃpían Mac Diapmada aıp Maᵹ
Ranaıll, ocuy loyᵹaḃ yóp.

Ictt. Enaıp yop ḋoṁnaé, ocuy ıyı aeıy an Cıᵹepna ın
can yo blıadaın ocuy cedpa .xx. ocuy cuıᵹ ced ocuy
mıle. Iapla Cuaḃmuṁan .ı. Concuḃap mac Donnchada
I Ḃpıaın, dhéc an blıadhaın yı. Máoıleélaınn mac ın
aba I Cheallaıᵹ, ocuy Seaan mac Uıllíam oıᵹ mıc
Uıllıam mıc Concuḃaıp, ocuy Diapmaıd O Maınnín, do
ṁapbad le Domnall mac an aba I Cheallaıᵹh .ı. a
depḃpachaıp yeın, ocuy le hEmann dopéa mac Domnaıll Mıc Shuıḃne. Cpeaé do ḋénaṁ do Sharanchaıb
ap Cadᵹ mac Eoᵹaın Mıc Diapmada. ᵹepaılc mac
Oıleyeıp mıc an Iapla dhéc. Domnall mac ın ᵹılla

---

¹ *Richard-an-iarainn.* "Richard
of the Iron," or Iron Dick.

² *Ath-sceittin.* This is a corrupt
form of the Irish name of Askeaton
(county Limerick). The correct form

is ey ᵹeıḃcınne, or the "cataract of
Gebhtinne."

³ *Man.* The remainder of the entries
for this year are in the handwriting
of Brian Mac Dermot.

A.D.
[1580.]

Saxons. Great injuries were committed by Brian O'Ruairc on Magh-Luirg; and Brian Mac Diarmada committed the like on O'Ruairc's lordship. Richard-an-iarainn[1] was proclaimed Mac William. Shemus-na-tinol, son of the Earl of Des-Mumha, was put to death in Corcach by the Justiciary. Ath-sceittin[2] was taken by the same Justiciary, who placed warders therein. Carraic-an-phuill was taken by the same man ;[3] and all who were there were killed, and the place was demolished. O'Birn, i.e. Tadhg Og, son of Tadhg O'Birn, died in the month of March : and that was a great calamity. Maude Dillon, O'Ferghail's wife, died. Spaniards came to Erinn, five or six hundred, to Dun-anoir[4]; and they all fell by the Justiciary. Rossa, son of Connla Mac Eochagain, was wickedly killed by his own brother ; and that was a great calamity.[5] Tadhg Riabhach O'Dubhda fell[6] from the top of Caislen-Conchobhair, and was unfortunately killed. Loch-an-scuir was taken by Cathal Dubh, son of Brian Mac Diarmada ; and Maelsechlainn, son of MagRanaill, was killed there. A depredation was committed by Brian Mac Diarmada upon MagRanaill, and burnings besides.

[1581.]

The kalends of January on Sunday ; and the age of the Lord at this time is one thousand, five hundred, and eighty-one years. The Earl of Tuadh-Mumha, i.e. Conchobhar, son of Donnchadh O'Briain, died this year. Maelechlainn, son of the Abbot O'Cellaigh, and John, the son of William Og, son of William, son of Conchobhar, and Diarmaid O'Mainnin, were killed by Domhnall, son of the Abbot O'Cellaigh, i.e. his own brother, and by Edmond Dorcha, the son of Domhnall Mac Suibhne. A depredation was committed by Saxons upon Tadhg, the son of Eoghan Mac Diarmada. Gerald, son of Oliver, son of the Earl,[7] died. Domhnall, son of the Gilla-dubh, son of Eoghan

---

[4] *Dun-an-oir.* Gold-fort. Corruptly written Ðuan an oip, in Clar.
[5] *Calamity.* eċt. eṗċṫ, Clar.

[6] *Fell.* ɔo ɔtuitim, Clar.
[7] *Son of the Earl;* i.e. the son of Gerald, 8th Earl of Kildare.

VOL. II.   2 ғ

duib mic Eoghain caoié, o Letpup, opaxail ðaip co
ceimpepceach a Slizech, ocup a aðnacal ann. Coððach
puað Maz [S]ampaðain on Lepgain opaxail ðaip in
bliaoain pi. baile an cobaip oo bi az Saxanchaib oo
cabuipc oon Oubalcach mac Cuachail 1 Concubaip.
Caoz oz mac Cacuil oiz hi Concubaip oo mapbao le
hCClbanchaib an bliaoain cecna. Semup mac Uaceip
Nuinnpenn, o ðún uabuip, opazhail ðaip an bliaohain
pe. CCilin mac bpiain Mic Suiðne .i. conpabal 1 Concubaip ðuinn oéz. CCn Calðac mac Oomnaill mic Caioz
mic Cachail oiz hi Concubaip, oizpe Slizioh ocup
ichcaip Connacc zan impepain, opazail ðaip in aoine
ioip oa cáipc na bliaona po, ocup ip oo pzélaib mopa
na hEipenn anc én mac pin Oomnaill 1 Concubaip ocup
Moipe inzine 1 Ruaipc; ocup ni cáinic oo plichc bpiain
Luizniz piam pep a aopa buo mo oo pcel ná é, ocup
ni ooiz co cicpa; ocup oo cpáið in pzel pin cpoiðeða
Connachc, ocup co haipiðe oo cpáið pe éizep ocup
ollumhain cuizeo Connachc, ocup oo compoinn pe mo
cpoiðe péin na oa cuio. Uch, uch, ip cpuaz map caim
a noeoiz mo ceile ocup mo companaiz, ocup an ci ba
coca ocup oo ba caipipi lem ap bið. Mipi bpian mac
Oiapmaoa oo pzpið pin ap cappuiz Mic Oiapmaoa,
ocup ip pamalca me anoip pe hOilioll olom anoiaið a
cloinne, ap na mapbao a bpocaip CCipc einpip mic
Cuinn ceo cachaiz a cac muiže Mucpuime le Mac Con
mac Maicniað mic Luizeð, no pe Oeipope capeip cloinne
hUipnech oo mapbao a ðpeall a nEamuin Maca, le
Concubap mac Pachcna pachaiz, mic Roza puaið mic
Ruðpaiohe. Oip acáim zu oubac oobponach oibpa-
zoioeð oomenmnach, a nouðaize ocup a noozaillpi; ocup
ní hecip a píom na a innipin map acáim aniu anoiaið

---

1 *Brian Mac Diarmada*. This
entry, which professes to have been
made by Brian Mac Dermot, does not
appear to be in his own handwriting.
It would rather seem to be a transcript

made from Brian's autograph, by the
person who has copied the brief entry
in deeper coloured ink represented on
the specimen page prefixed to vol. i.

Caech, from Lethrus, died unfortunately in Sligech, and was interred there. Cobhthach Ruadh Mag Samhradhain, from the Lergan, died this year. Baile-an-tobair, which the Saxons had, was given to the Dubhaltach, son of Tuathal O'Conchobair. Tadhg Og, son of Cathal Og O'Conchobhair, was killed by Albanachs the same year. James, the son of Walter Nugent, from Dun-uabhair, died this year. Ailín, the son of Brian Mac Suibhne, i.e., O'Conchobhair Donn's constable, died. The Calbhach, son of Domhnall, son of Tadhg, son of Cathal Og O'Conchobhair, the undisputed heir of Sligech and Lower Connacht, died the Friday between the two Easters of this year; and the death of this only son of Domhnall O'Conchobhair, and of Mor, daughter of O'Ruairc, is one of the great woes of Erinn; and there never came of the race of Brian Luighnech a man of his years a greater loss than he, and it is not likely that there will come. And this loss has grieved the hearts of Connacht, and it has especially grieved the 'poets and doctors of the province of Connacht; and it has divided my own heart into two parts. Alas! alas! wretched is my condition, after my comrade and companion, and the person who was the choicest and dearest to me in the world. I am Brian Mac Diarmada,[1] who wrote this on Carraig-Mic-Diarmada; and I am now to be compared to Oilill Olum[2] after his sons, when they had been slain along with Art Enfhir, son of Conn Céd-chathach, in the battle of Magh-Mucraimhe, by Maccon, the son of Macniadh, son of Lughaidh; or to Deirdre, after the sons of Uisnech had been killed in treachery in Emhain-Macha, by Conchobhar, the son of Fachtna Fathach, son of Rossa Ruadh, son of Rudhraidhe; for I am sad, sorrowful, distressed, dispirited, in grief and anguish. And it is not possible to reckon or describe how I am this day, after the

---

[1] *Oilill Olum.* A king of Munster, who lived in the third century, and whose grief for the loss of his sons, slain in the battle of *Magh-Mucraimhe,* forms the subject of a very ancient poem alleged to have been composed by himself, and contained in the *Book of Leinster,* fol. 105, b 2.

mo companaiʒ το δul uaim .1. an Calbach, ocuʃ an la
τειʒenač το ṁi ṁáʃτa το liaδlaiceδ a 8liʒech é. Ƒeʃ
caoʒaτ O Ɔuiδʒennáin .1. mac Ƒeʃʒail mic Ρilip τʃaʒail
δáiʃ a ʒcluain 1 Ḃʃáoin. Ḃʃian caoč O Coinneaʒain,
ʃaoi cleiʃiʒ ocuʃ ʃeʃ τiʒe aoiδeδ coiτčinn, τʃaʒail
δáiʃ, ocuʃ iʃi ʃoiṁ annlaicτe το čoʒ ʃe ʃein τó .1. a
aδlucaδ aʒ τuṁa Ḃaile an τobaiʃ, ocuʃ iʃé ṁeʃmaoiτ
nach o τʃoch cʃeiτeṁ το ʃinne Ḃʃian caoč an τoʒa
ʃin, achτ maʃ nač bʃacaiδ ʃé ʃeiʃδíʃ Ɔe τa τénaṁ a
néin eaʒlaiʃ na ƒochaiʃ ʃan aimʃiʃ ʃi. O Ceʃbaill, .1.
Uilliam oδaʃ mac ƒiʃi ʒan ainm mic Maolʃuanaiδ mic
8eain 1 Ceʃδuill, το maʃbaτ le ʃil Cončubaiʃ ƒailʒe
aʒ τeachτ o Ḃaile áτa cliaδ το. Τomaʃ anτ ʃléiδe mac
Riʃτoeʃτ Mic ʒoiʃτoelδ τʃaʒail δáiʃ. Mac 1aʃla Čloinne
Ricaiʃτο, .1. Uilliam Ḃuʃc, το δul ʒo ʒailliṁ το δénaṁ
ʃíδe ʃe ʒalluiδ, aʃ coʃ ocuʃ aʃ ʃlanaiδ in maoʃa ocuʃ
an baile moiʃ aʃčena; ocuʃ το bí ʃoiṁe aʃτiʒ ʃeʃ uilc
ocuʃ uʃδuiδe το δénaṁ aʃ cloinn Ricaiʃτο .1. Uilliam
oʒ Maiʃτín, ocuʃ τa δanna ʃaiʒτiuiʃ maʃaen ʃiʃ; ocuʃ
τaʃeiʃ mic an 1aʃla το δul aʃτeaʒ το ƒeaτl Uilliam
oʒ Maiʃτín ocuʃ na 8aʃanaiʒ aiʃ, ocuʃ το ʒabατaʃ
é ʃein, ocuʃ το cʃočaδ ʃeʃ ocuʃ ochτaʃ τa ṁuinnτiʃ,
ocuʃ το cuiʃeδ e ʃein a ʃʃiʃún το neaṁτoil an ṁéʃa
ocuʃ an baile ṁoiʃ. Ocuʃ ni ʃaτa na τiaiδ ʃin an úaiʃ
το cʃočaδ mac an 1aʃla ocuʃ Τoiʃʃτoelbach mac Ɔonn-
caiδ hi Ḃʃiain; ocuʃ iʃ Ɔaʃτáoin áluinn το cʃochaτ
mac an 1aʃla, ocuʃ aʃ na ṁáʃuč το cʃochaδ mac hi
Ḃʃíain. Aʃ τʃuiτim ʃíʒ Ƒoiʃτenʒél annʃa cač ʃo ʃéṁ-
ʃáiδʃem, το čuiʃ cinʒ Ρilip .1. ʃí na 8báinne a oiτe ʃein.
ocuʃ aʃmáil maʃaon ʃiʃ ʒu Liʃbúinn, ocuʃ ni ʃaiδe

---

1 *At the mound.* aʒ τuṁa. The
chronicler doubtless meant "in the
mound" E. This entry is not contained in any other Irish chronicles of
the period. It is of some interest in
connexion with the subject of interments in pagan tumuli.

2 *Want of religion;* τʃoch
cʃeiτeṁ; lit. "bad faith."

3 *Because.* náʃ, Clar.

4 *Corpus Christi.* τaʃτáoin
áluinn; lit., "beautiful Thursday."
The Four Masters state that Turlough

departure of my companion from me, i.e. the Calbhach: and the last day of the month of March he was interred in Sligech. Fer-caogad O'Duibhgennain, i.e. the son of Ferghal, son of Philip, died in Cluain-Ui-Brian. Brian Caech O'Coinnegain, an eminent cleric, and keeper of a general house of guests, died; and the place of sepulture which he selected for himself was, i.e. to be buried at the mound[1] of Baile-an-tobair. And we think that it was not through want of religion[2] Brian Caech made this selection, but because[3] he saw not the service of God practised in any church near him at that time. O'Cerbhaill, i.e. William Odhar, the son of Fer-gan-ainm, son of Maelruanaidh, son of John O'Cerbhaill, was killed by the Sil-Conchobhair-Failghe, as he was coming from Baile-átha-cliath. Thomas-ant-sleibhe, son of Richard Mac Goisdelbh, died. The Earl of Clann-Rickard's son, i.e. William Burk, went to Gaillimh to make peace with the Foreigners, on the engagement and guarantees of the Mayor, and of the town besides; and there was within before him a perpetrator of injury and destruction upon the Clann-Rickard, i.e. William Og Martin, and two bands of soldiers along with him. And after the Earl's son went in, William Martin and the Saxons acted treacherously towards him; and they apprehended himself; and nine of his people were hanged, and he himself was put in prison, in despite of the mayor, and of the town. And not long after that the Earl's son, and Toirdhelbhach, the son of Donnchadh O'Briain, were hanged; and on Corpus Christi[4] the Earl's son was hanged, and O'Briain's son was hanged on the morrow. After the fall of the king of Portugal in the battle we have before mentioned,[5] king Philip, i.e. the king of Spain, sent his own guardian, with an army, to Lisbon; and

---

O'Brien was hanged on the 26th of May, which day coincided with Corpus Christi in the year 1581, and

William Burk on Saturday, "the third day after."
[4] *Mentioned.* See above; p. 421.

oıჳͱe aͱ ͱıჳ ʆoıͱͼeͷჳél αͼͼ ͼeͱbͱáͼαıͱ bαͱͽαıͱͽ,
ocuͱ ͽoͷͷ Ͱͼ(ͷͷͼαıͷe bα hαıͷm ͽó ; ocuͱ ͽo cuıͱeͽ
cαͼ ıͽıͱ ͽoͷͷ Ͱͼ(ͷͷͼαıͷe ocuͱ ͽıúıce o ͽαͷbͷıჳe .ı.
oıͽe ͱıჳ ͷα 8bάıͷͷe ; ocuͱ ͽo bͱıͱeͽ ıͷ cαͼ αͱ ͽhoͷͷ
Ͱͼ(ͷͷͼαıͷe, ocuͱ ͽo mαͱbαͽ αͼͱí ͷó α ceͼαıͱ ͽo ͷͱıͷͼıͽ
ͱeͱ ͱα ͽoͷ Ͱͼ(ͷͷͼıͷe ; ocuͱ ͽo ımͼıჳ ͱé ͱéıͷ αͱαͷ
cαͼ ; ocuͱ ͽo ჳαͽuͽ ͷıͱͽͷͷͷ αıͱ ; ocuͱ ͼαıͷıc cıͷჳ ʆıͷıͱ
ჳu ͷıͱbúıͷͷ, ocuͱ αͼα ıͷ ͼαͼαıͱ αıჳe ocuͱ α ͱıჳαcͽͼ.
Ͱͱmάıͷ ͷͷoͱ Ͱͼ(bαͷuch ͽo ͼuͱ ͽo cαıͱͼαeıͷ ͷαͷbıe
α ͷıchͼαͱ Coͷͷαcͽͼ .ı. cͷαͷͷ ͽomͷαıͷͷ bαͷͷαıჳ ͷhéჳ
ͽomͷαıͷͷ. O Coͷͼuͽαıͱ 8ͷıჳıჳ ocuͱ Cαͼαͷ oჳ O Coͷͼuͽαıͱ ͽo ͼuıͷͷıuჳαͽ ͱomͱα, ͷíoͷ α ͼͼıͷóıͷ ͽo ͷαͱͼ-
ͱͷúαჳ ocuͱ ͽo ჳαͷͷoჳͷαchαıͷ ocuͱ ͽo ჳímάͷͼαıͽ ; ocuͱ
ͷα Ͱͼ(bαͷαıჳ ͽo beͼ α ჳCoͱͱαͷͷ αჳ ͷoͼ ͷα bͱıͽͷαch
α bͱoͱͷoͷჳͱoͱͼ, ocuͱ ıαͽ ͱéıͷ ocuͱ O Coͷcuͱαıͱ ͽo beͼ
αͱ αͽuıͽ α ͼéıͷe ; ocuͱ ͽo cuıͱeͽαͱ ͷα Ͱͼ(ͷbαͷuıჳ ͱჳıαͼ
ͼαͱ ͷoͱჳ oͱͱͼα oͷ ͷoch ͱuαͱ ͽocum chúıͷe O bͷıͷͷ, ͷo
ჳu ͱαͷჳαͽαͱ móıͷ ıͷ ͽoıͱe ͽαͱαıჳ ; ocuͱ ͽo ͼuıͱͷıͷჳ
Cαͼαͷ óჳ αͱ αͷ móͷαıჳ ͱıͷ, ocuͱ ͷα mαıͼe ͱıͷ mαͱαoͷ
ͱıͱ .ı. ͷαoͷͱúαͷαıͽ mαc Coıͱͽeͷbαıჳ ͷıc ͽhíαͱmıͽα,
ocuͱ ͷαoͷmóͱͱα mαc ͷαoıͷmuıͱe ͷıc 8uıͽͷe, ocuͱ
O hͽͽͱα buıͽe .ı. Coͷͷ mαc ͱuαıͽͱı hı Eαͽͱα, ocuͱ
mαc Comαͷͼαıჳ (.ı. Comαͷͼαch óჳ) mıc ͷαoͷͱúαͷαıͽ
ͷıc ͽíαͱmαͽα, ocuͱ mαc bͱíαıͷ mıc Θıͱeͷͷóıͷ ͷıc
8uıͽͷe ; ocuͱ ͽo ͱάჳbαͽ Cαͼαͷ óჳ O Coͷcuͱαıͱ ocuͱ
ͷα mαıͼe ͱıͷ uıͷe αͱαoͷ ͱıͱ, ocuͱ moͱάͷ eıͷe ͷαͼ άıͱ-
eͷͼαͱ αͷͷͱo, ͷe Ͱͼ(ͷbαͷͼαıͽ αͷ ͷά ͱıͷ ; ocuͱ ıͱ móͱ
αͷ ͽıͼ ocuͱ αͷ ͽıͷჳeͷͷ ͽo ჳαoıͽeͷαıͽ Θıͱeͷͽ, ocuͱ ჳu
hαıͱıͼhe ͽo ჳαoıͽeαͷαıͽ ͼuıჳıͽ Coͷͷαcͽͼ, ıͷ bαͱ ͱıͷ
Cαͼuıͷ ı Coͷcuͱαıͱ. Ͱαͽ mαc ͽıαͱmαͽα mıc Cαıͱbͱe
hı Coͷchuͱαıͱ .ı. mαc hı Coͷchoͱαıͱ ͽuıͷͷ, ocuͱ αͽͽuͱ
hı Coͷchoͱαıͱ, ͽo αͷocoͷ αͷͷ ; α ͽͱeıͼ α ͷαım αͱͱ αͷ

---

¹ *Duke of Alva.* ͽıúıce u ͽαͷ-
ͽuıჳe (Duke O'Dalbhaigh), Clar.

² *Executed a retreat.* ͽo cuıͱeͽαͱ . . . ͱჳıαͼ ͼαͱ ͷoͱჳ

oͱͱͼα ; lit., " they placed a shield
across the track upon them.".

³ *Móin-in-daire-daraigh ;* i.e. " the
bog of the oak wood." See Index.

the king of Portugal had no heir except a bastard brother, whose name was Don Antoine. And a battle was fought between Don Antoine and the Duke of Alva,[1] the king of Spain's guardian, and the battle was gained against Don Antoine; and three or four thousand men were slain under Don Antoine, but he escaped himself from the battle; and Lisbon was taken against him. And king Philip came to Lisbon; and he has the city and the kingdom. A great army of Albanachs was sent by Captain Malbie to Lower Connacht, viz., the sons of Domhnall Ballagh Mac Domhnaill. O'Conchobhair Sligigh, and Cathal Og O'Conchobhair, mustered before them all their force of cavalry, gallowglasses, and servants. And the Albanachs were in Corrann, at Loch-na-fidhnach, in an encampment; and they and O'Conchobhair were face to face. And the Albanachs' executed a retreat[2] from the lake up to Cul-O'Finn, until they reached Móin-in-daire-daraigh.[3] And Cathal Og arrived on this bog, and these other chieftains along with him, viz., Maelruanaidh, son of Toirdhelbhach Mac Diarmada; and Maelmóra, son of Maelmuire Mac Suibhne; and O'hEdhra Buidhe, i.e. Conn, son of Ruaidhri O'hEdhra; and the son of Tomaltach (i.e. Tomaltach Og), son of Maelruanaidh Mac Diarmada; and the son of Brian, son of Eremhon Mac Suibhne. And Cathal Og O'Conchobhair, and all these chieftains along with him, and many more who are not enumerated here, were killed by Albanachs on that day. And this death of Cathal O'Conchobhair is a great loss and destruction to the Gaeidhel of Erinn, and especially to the Gaeidhel of the province of Connacht. Aedh, son of Diarmaid, son of Cairbre O'Conchobhair, i.e. the son of O'Conchobhair Donn,[4] the intended O'Conchobhair,[5]

---

[4] *Donn.* This concludes fol. 30 b of the Clar. fragment, the succeeding three pages of which are in the handwriting of the scribe who copied the earlier portion of the MS H. 1. 19.

[5] *Intended O'Conchobhair.* aῦbaη h1 Conchobaiη; i.e. the *materies* of the O'Conchobhair, or the intended chief of the sept of O'Conchobhair Donn.

maiom ṁ ṙın. Caıṗlén ṁaıᵹe hı Ᵹhaᵹṗa ᴅo loṙcuᴅ
ᴅ℃lbanċhaıb ıṙın ló ceᴅna, ocuṗ Ᵽıaṗmaıᴅ óᵹ mac
Ceın hı Ᵹhaᵹṗa ᴅo ᵬáṙṙuᵹaᴅ ann, ocuṗ Taᵬᵹ ṁáᵹ
Ruaıᴅṗı, eᴛ alıı mulᴛı. baıle ṁá hı Ruaıṗe, ocuṗ
Ᵽṗuım ᵬá eıᵬıáṗ .ı. lonᵹṗoṗᴛ ᵹnaᴛaċh hı Ruaıṗe, ᴅo
coımbṗıṙṙeᵬ a noen aımṗıṗ le .h. Rúaıṗe ṙcın ᴅeᵹla
Shaᴁanaċh ᴅo ṙuıᵬe ıoınᴛa. Sluaıᵹeᴅ la caıṗᴛın
maılbıe .ı. ᴛıᵹeṗna ᵬóıᵹeᴅ Connaċhᴛ ᵹo hıochᴛaṗ Chon-
naċhᴛ, ᵹo ṙaıᵬe ᴛṗı hoıᵬᵬe a Slıᵹech ocuṗ ᴅá oıᵬᵬe a
n'Ᵽṗuın ᵬá eıᵬıáṗ; ocuṗ bṗaıᵹᴅe hı Conchobaıṗ Slıᵹıᵹ
ocuṗ ıchᴛaıṗ Connaċhᴛ ᴅo ᵬabaıṗᴛ laıṗ ᴅon ᴅol ṙın ᴅó.
Sloıᵹeᴅ elı laṙan caıṗᴛín ceᴅna ṙın a n℃llᴛoıb no ᵹo
ṙanıc leıᴛᵬıṗ, ocuṗ ᴅo bṗıṙṙeᵬ an baıle ṙın laıṗ. ℃nᴛ
Sṙaıᴛ ᵬán ᴅo bṗıṙṙeᵬ la .h. Neıll ᴅeᵹla Saṙanach ᴅo
ṙuıᵬe ann; ᴅṙıṗᴛachᴛ hı Ᵽhomnaıll ᴅo ᵬuaᴅaṗ na
Saᴁanaıᵹ ṙın a n℃llᴛoıb ᴅon ᵬula ṙın. maıᵬm la .h.
Neıll ṙoṗ .h. n'Ᵽomnaıll ıṙın mblıaᴅaın ceᴅna ṙın,
ᴅú anᴅoṗchaıṗ mac Suıᵬne báᵹanach ocuṗ a ᴅıaṗṗ
mac, ocuṗ ᴅıaṗ mac ℃oᵬa mıc Neıll óıᵹ, ocuṗ Hıall
moᴅaṗṗᵬa mac Néıll óıᵹ, ocuṗ ınaṗ ᵹabaᵬ mac Suıᵬne
na ᴛuaᵬ ocuṗ mac muṗchaᴅa maıll mıc Shuıᵬne, ocuṗ
ınaṗ maṗbaᴅ ᴅá ceᴅ no ᴛṗí ᵹo ᴛuıll.eᵬ; ocuṗ bá ᴅoáı-
ṙıṁ aṗ ᵬuıᴛ ıṙın maıᵬm ṙın la .h. Neıll, ocuṗ ıṗ ṁealᴛ
ṙe ṙíom ıaᴅ ᵬóṙṙ. Toıṙṗᴅhealbach luınech mac Heıll
Chonallaıᵹ anᴛ .h. Heıll ṙın. ℃chᴛ chena ṙa haᵬbaıl
ṙe ınnıṙın uılc ocuṗ éᵹaoıne na blıaᴅna ṙın a ṙann na
hEoṗṗa uıle, ocuṗ a nEṙınn co háıṙıᵬe. mac Ᵽıaṗmaᴅa
ᵹall .ı. Eoᵹan caoᵬ mac Caᴛhaıl mıc Thaıᵬᵹ óıᵹ ᴅhéc
ın lá ṙía bṙeıl muıṗe móṗ. bṗıan mac Ᵹıllaᵬaᴅṗaıc,
.ı. mac Ᵹıllaᴅaᴅṗaıc, ᴅhec a mbaıle áᵬa clıaᵬ, ocuṗ ṙé
a laım aᵹ an nᵹıuıṙᴅíṙ; ocuṗ ᴅo buᵬ ᴅéchᴛuıᵬ móṙa
Eṗenn ᴅó. Sıṙṙıam ᵬunᴅáᵬ Slıᵹıᵹ .ı. bṙıan mac Taıᵬᵹ

---

1 Alii. alı, Clar.

2 O'Ruairc's new town. A place
situated near the village of Druim-
dha-eithiar, Dromahaire, in the county
of Leitrim.

3 The Mac Gilla-Patraic. A brief
marginal note, in a handwriting not
unlike that of Sir James Ware, adds
" Baro de Upper Ossory. Br. McGil-
patrick obiit Dublini in carcere."

was saved there, and was borne off a prisoner from this defeat. The castle of Magh-O'Gadhra was burned by the Albanachs on the same day; and Diarmaid Og, son of Cian O'Gadhra, was put to death there, and Tadhg, the son of Ruaidhri, et alii[1] multi. O'Ruaire's new town,[2] and Druim-dhá-eithiar, i.e., O'Ruaire's usual residence, were broken down at the same time by O'Ruairc himself, for fear the Saxons would occupy them. A hosting by Captain Malbie, i.e., the governor of the province of Connacht, to Lower Connacht; and he was three nights in Sligech, and two nights in Druim-dhá-eithiar; and he brought with him the hostages of O'Conchobhair Sligigh, and of Lower Connacht, on that occasion. Another hosting by the same Captain to Ulster, as far as Leithbhir; and that town was demolished by him. The Srath-bán was broken down by O'Neill, for fear the Saxons would occupy it. (In aid of O'Domhnaill these Saxons went to Ulster on that occasion.) A victory by O'Neill over O'Domhnaill in the same year, in which fell Mac Suibhne Bághanagh, and his two sons, and the two sons of Aedh, son of Niall Og, and Niall Modardha, son of Niall Og; and in which Mac Suibhne-na-tuath, and the son of Murchadh Mall Mac Suibhne, were taken prisoners; and in which two or three hundred, and more, were slain. And it would be difficult to count all that fell in that victory by O'Neill, and also tedious to enumerate them. The O'Neill referred to was Toirdhelbhach Luinech, son of Niall Conallach. But truly, the evils and lamentations of that year throughout all Europe, and in Erinn especially, would be excessive to relate. Mac Diarmada Gall, i.e. Eoghan Caech, the son of Cathal, son of Tadhg Og, died the day before the great festival of Mary. Brian Mac Gilla-Patraic, i.e. the Mac Gilla-Patraic,[3] died in Baile-átha-cliath, whilst imprisoned by the Justiciary; and he was one of the most lamented of Erinn. The sheriff of the county of Sligo, i.e. Brian, the son of Tadhg, son of Brian, son of Eoghan

mic ḃріαιn mic Eoʒαιn ʜı Ruαιрc, ɒo ṫuʟ αр ınnроıʒeɒ
co ḃрeιррne ʜı Ruαιрc, ocuр Eрenɒuıẋ ocuр ɒрonʒ ɒo
Sʜαcрαnchαıb ɒo ṫuʟ ʟαıр. Cрeṫ ṁóр ɒo ṫαbαıрc ɒo
nα Sαроnchαıb ʟeo, ocuр bрeıṫ αр nα ʒαoıɒeʟαıṫ αр
ɒeрeṫ nα nʒαʟʟ, ocuр bрıррeṫ αр nα ʒαoıɒeʟαıṫ, ocuр
mαрbαɒ móр ɒo ṫenum оррα. Pрıóıр Ḃαıʟe Œṫα αn ріẋ
.ı. Uıʟʟıαm .ʜ. Cınαoṫα moрcuuр eрc. Œрmáıʟ ṁóр ɒo
ṫuʟ ó ṫıʒeрnα ṫúıʒıɒ Chonnαchc .ı. cαıрcín Mαıʟbıe, α
mıchcoр Chonnαchc рe hαʒhαıɒ ṫoʒαıɒ αn cuαıрceрc ocuр
ʜı Ruαıрc; ocuр ıррíαɒ рo ɒob рeрр ɒon αрmáıʟ̇ın, ɒíαр
mαc Ɒomnαıʟʟ Ḃαʟʟαıẋ mıc Ɒomnαıʟʟ ɒŒʟbαnchαıb,
ocuр Comáр Oıɒıр .ı. cαıрcın uαррαʟ ɒo Shαррαnchαıṫ,
ocuр Uıʟʟıαm Cʟıṫṫαрɒ, ocuр cαıр[c]ín Moрnα, ocuр
рıррıαm ṫunɒαe Sʟıʒıʒh .ı. ḃрıαn mαc Cαıṫc ʜı Ruαıрc;
ocuр α cúıʒ no α рé ɒo ceɒuıṫ Œʟbαnαch mαıʟʟe рe
cʟoınn Ɒomnαıʟʟ Ḃαʟʟαıẋ mıc Ɒhoṁnαıʟʟ; ocuр ınαmbóı
ɒo Shαʒрαnchαıb mαıʟʟe ррір nα cαıрcínıṫ рın ɒo
ṫuʟ α connɒáe Sʟıcıʒh uıʟe. ʜ.Conchobαıр Sʟıʒıẋ ɒıα
ʟeṫhαɒ αр αn connɒáe. Ʒαıріɒ ınα ṫıαıṫ рın αn cαn ɒo
ẋuıṫ .ʜ.Conchobαıр Sʟıcıẋ αmbóı ɒo ṫαıрcínıb Sαcрαn-
αch αnnрın ɒoṫum α mbeıṫ αр αon рṫéʟ ррір рeın.
Mαıṫe ocuр moрuαıрʟe ıochcαıр Connαchc uıʟe, mαıʟʟe
рe .ʜ.Conchobαıр Sʟıʒıẋ ocuр рір nα Sαрαnchαıb рın,
ɒınnрαıʒeɒ Œʟbαnαch ocuр cʟαınne Ɒomnαıʟʟ Ḃαʟʟαıẋ,
ocuр Œʟuрɒαıр mαc Ɒomnαıʟʟ Ḃαʟʟαıẋ Mıc Ɒomnαıʟʟ.
.ı. αn mαc Œʟbαnαch ıр ɒóṫuıррıɒı Ḃαрαṁʟαıɒe, ocuр
ɒob oıрbeрcαıẋı uррαṁαncα, cáııc α Connαchcuıṫ рe
cıαn ɒαımрıр, ɒo ṁαрbαṫ αnn α ınbun αn рeɒáın ʟα
.ʜ. Conchobαıр Sʟıʒıẋ ocuр ʟá Sαрαnchαıb, α nɒıẋuıʟ
Chαchαıʟ óıʒ ʜı Conchobαıр, ocuр α nɒıẋuıʟ αр mαрbαṫ
mαıʟʟe ррір ʒαıріɒ роıme рın. Œchc chenα coрcрαɒαр
ceɒ no ṫó ʒo cuıʟʟeṫ ɒonα hŒʟbαnchαıb ɒon bрeıрріm
рın, ın ʒαch ıonαɒ αmbáɒαр αр рeɒı nα conɒáe; ocuр
рo ımṫıẋ Ɒomnαʟʟ ʒoрm mαc Ɒomnαıʟʟ Ḃαʟʟαıẋ αрр

---

1 *Were killed.* The literal transla-
tion of the words of the text, mαрbαɒ | móр ɒo ṫenum оррα, is " a great
| killing was committed on them."

A.D.

[1581.]

O'Ruairc, went upon an expedition to Breifne-Ui-Ruairc, and Irishmen, and a number of Saxons, went with him. The Saxons brought a great prey with them; and the Gaeidhel were caught in the rear of the Foreigners; and the Gaeidhel were routed, and a great many of them were killed.[1] The prior of the town of Ath-an-righ, i.e., William O'Cinaedha, mortuus est. A great army was sent to Lower Connacht by the governor of the province of Connacht, i.e. Captain Malbie, to take part in the war between the North and O'Ruairc; and the best in this army were the two sons of Domhnall Ballagh Mac Domhnaill, of the Albanachs, and Thomas Odis, an eminent captain of the Saxons, and William Clifford, and Captain Morna, and the sheriff of the county of Sligech, i.e. Brian, the son of Tadhg O'Ruairc. And there were five or six hundred Albanachs with the sons of Domhnall Ballagh Mac Domhnaill. And all the Saxons that were along with these captains went into the county of Sligech. O'Conchobhair Sligigh spread them over the county. Soon after that O'Conchobhair Sligigh entreated all the Saxon captains that were there to join him.[2] The chieftains and nobles of all Lower Connacht, along with O'Conchobhair Sligigh and those Saxons, attacked the Albanachs, and the sons of Domhnall Ballagh; and Alasdar, the son of Domhnall Ballagh Mac Domhnaill, i.e., the most hopefully regarded, and bravely distinguished, son of an Albanach that had come into Connacht for a long time, was killed there at Bun-an-fedáin, by O'Conchobhair Sligigh and the Saxons, in revenge of Cathal Og O'Conchobhair, and in revenge of the persons slain along with him a short time before that. In fine, one or two hundred of the Albanachs, and more, were slain in that defeat, wherever they were throughout the county. And Domhnall Gorm, son of Domhnall Ballagh, escaped

---

[2] *To join him.* The words of the text, a mbeiṫ aꞃ aon ꞃéil ꞃꞃiꞃ rein, actually mean "that they would be in the same account with himself."

an sgathad sin, ocus ni heidir a ríoṁ iná roáireṁ ar benaḋ amaċ annsin dechaib ocus déideḋ, darmoiḃ ocus dordonár, ocus da gach édail eli airchena; ocus ge deruid aroile gurab olc do friṫ an gniom sin ní héidir a raḋ naċ maiṫ fuair .h. Conchobair a ċuid féin de, óir nír ḟuaradar a ḟolta friu iar tuitim a ḋerbráthar ocus a ċónsopal ocus a ḋaoineḋ maiṫi roime sin friú, ocus gan síṫ iná geallaḋ etorra ina ḋiaiḋ; oir is annsa Cedaoin ria nDardaoin álainn ċuirp Chrisd torċuir Cathal óg conamḃói maille fris, ocus eidir Nolluic ocus féil Brígdi torċradar Albanaiċ ocus mac Domnaill Ḃallaiġ inn, giḋ nár ḃéruic i naghaid aroile iad. Maiḋm adḃal mór do ṫabairt dIarla Dhesmuman ar Iarla Urṁuman ocus ar tSharanchaib, du atorcradar tri ced go tuilled do Ghalloib ocus do Ghaoidelaiḃ, etir marcsluaig ocus glaslaiṫ, ocus inar benaḋ imad édála ḋíḃ. Caor ṫinntiġ do ṫoiġecht co caislen nua tslechta Bresail hI Cheallaiġ, ocus Sean ruaḋ mac an ḟileḋ do ṁarbaḋ ḋi, ocus eiċ ocus airnéis do ṁarbaḋ ann. Bend ṫempuill ċille O Sgóra do brisseḋ ḋi. Ruaidri mac Enna hI Uiginn dhec a suiḋe bḟhínain; ocus a aḋlucad a cluain Senṁaoil. Geróid clapach .i. duine uasal do Gheraltachuiḃ, ocus fer milltí morain, do ḃássugad la Saranchaib. Maġnus mac an persúin mic Mhuirġersa dhec a nerr a aoisi ar loch Lábáin, iar ndenum maiṫiusa móire do ḋeirc ocus do ḋaondacht ṫiġe aoidhed conuige sin, ocus [a] aḋnacul a

---

[1] *Right.* Gurab olc do friṫ. These words signify literally, "that it was found evil;" but idiomatically convey the meaning assigned to them in the translation.

[2] *Was not justified.* The original of this expression. naċ maiṫ fuair .h. Conchobair a ċuid féin de, literally rendered, would be "that O'Conchobhair did not find his own share of it good"; but the translation represents the idiomatic signification.

[3] *Dardain-álainn.* "Beautiful Thursday;" i.e. Corpus Christi.

[4] *An eric for each other;* i.e. the death of the Albanachs, or men of Scotland, and of Alexander Mac Domhnaill, the son of Domhnall Ballagh, was not a sufficient *eric*, or compensation, for the death of Cathal Og O'Conchobhair and his companions, who had been previously slain by the Albanachs, as related at p. 439.

[5] *Fell upon.* do ṫoiġecht co; lit.,

from this destruction. And the quantity of horses taken there, and of coats of mail, arms, and ordnance, and of all other spoils besides, cannot be calculated or over-reckoned. And though some say that this deed was not right,[1] it cannot be said that O'Conchobhair was not justified[2] in his own share of it, for his anger against them had not cooled since the fall of his brother, and his constable, and his good men, by them before that ; and there was neither peace nor promise between them afterwards ; for it was on the Wednesday before Dardain-álainn[3] of Corpus Christi that Cathal Og fell, with those who were along with him ; and between Christmas and Brigid's festival the Albanachs, and the son of Domhnall Ballagh, were slain ; although they were not an eric for each other.[4] A prodigious defeat was given by the Earl of Des-Mumha to the Earl of Ur-Mumha, and to Saxons, in which fell three hundred and more of the Foreigners and Gaeidhel, both cavalry and infantry, and in which numerous spoils were taken from them. A fiery bolt fell upon[5] the new castle[6] of the race of Bresal O'Cellaigh ; and John Ruadh Mac-an-fhiledh[7] was killed by it ; and horses and cattle were killed there. The pinnacle of the church of Cill-O'Scoba was broken by it. Ruaidhri, the son of Enna O'hUiginn, died in Suidhe-Fínáin, and was buried in Cluain-Senmhail. Gerald Clabach,[8] i.e. a gentleman of the Geraldines, and a destroyer of much, was put to death by Saxons. Maghnus, son of the Parson MacMuirghesa, died in the end of his age,[9] on Loch-Labain, after doing great good by charity and humanity, keeping a house for guests, up to that time ;

"came to." The particle no is erroneously repeated.

[6] *The new castle.* The reference in the next sentence to the church of Cill-O'Scoba (Killoscobe), in the barony of Tiaquin, county Galway, suggests that the "new castle" was in the same barony.

[7] *Mac-an-fhiledh;* "son of the poet;" a name now written M'Aneely, and M'Nilly.

[8] *Gerald Clabach;* i.e. Gerald the thick-lipped. The Four Masters state that a Gerald, son of John, son of Edmond, son of Thomas [Fitzgerald] of Claenghlais (Clonlish, co. Limerick), died in 1582 "by the sword, or a natural death."

[9] *In the end of his age;* i.e. after having completed the ordinary term of human life.

cluᴀın ꝼeıṁᴀoıl. Cʟᴀnn ᴄ8heᴀın mıc Cuınn mıc Gnꝛı hı
Heıll ᴅo ᴄoᴄhᴄ aꝛ ınnꝛaıᴣe a mᴮꝛeꝛnı hı ꝛaıᴣıllıᴣ.
Pıʟıp mᴀc ᴀoᴅᴀ hı ꝛaıᴣıllıᴣ .ı. mᴀc hı ꝛaıᴣıllıᴣ ᴄo na
ᴮꝛaıᴄꝛechuıᴮ ocuꝛ co na ʟuchᴄ ʟenmᴀnᴀ ᴅo ᴮꝛeıᴄ oꝛꝛa,
ocuꝛ 8eᴀn óᴣ mᴀc hı Heıll ᴅo ṁaꝛbᴀᴅ ann, ocuꝛ mᴀc
eʟı hı Heıll ᴅo ᴣabáıl, ocuꝛ ceᴄꝛáꝛ ᴅá mᴀꝛcrʟúaıᴣ mᴀıᴄ
ᴅo mᴀꝛbᴀᴅ ᴀnn ᴮóꝛ. ınᴣen hı ᴅomnᴀıll .ı. ᴍᴀıꝛᴣꝛéᴣ
ınᴣen ᴀoᴅᴀ ᴅuıᴮ mıc ᴀoᴅᴀ ꝛuᴀıᴅ, ocuꝛ ben ᴍhᴀoıl-
ṁóꝛᴅᴀ mıc 8eᴀın mıc Cᴀᴄhᴀıl hı ꝛaıᴣıllıᴣ, oouꝛ an ᴮen
bá mó cʟú ocuꝛ oıꝛꝛᴅeꝛcuꝛ ı nGꝛınn ınᴀ hᴀımꝛıꝛ ꝼeın,
ᴅhéc ıꝛın Chaᴮán ın hoc anno. Ochᴄ noıᴣhꝛeᴅha ᴅéᴣ ᴅo
ṁᴀıᴄıᴮ ᴣall na ᴍıᴅhe ᴅo chuꝛ ᴅoᴄum báıꝛ a mbaıle
ᴀᴄᴀ clıaᴄ ᴅo ᴣıuıꝛᴅíꝛ na hGꝛenn ın bʟıᴀᴅaın ꝛın.

Ktt. Gnᴀıꝛ ꝼoꝛ Luᴀn ; anno ᴅomını ᴍ°.ccccc°. ochᴄ-
ṁoᴅa aꝛ ᴅhá ᴮlıᴀᴅaın. ᴍaᴣ ꟼhlanᴅchaıᴅ .ı. Cᴀᴄhᴀl
óᴣ mᴀc Cᴀᴄhᴀıl ᴅuıᴮ ᴅo ṁaꝛbᴀᴅ ᴅıa ᴮeꝛbꝛaᴄhaıꝛ ꝼéın
.ı. ᴅo Chaᴅᴣ óᴣ mᴀc Cᴀᴄhᴀıl ᴅuıᴮ, ocuꝛ ᴄıᴣeꝛna ᴅo
ᴮenum ᴅe ꝼeın na ıonaᴅ an bʟıᴀᴅaın ꝛın. 8éᴀn mᴀc
ıaꝛla ᴅeꝛmumᴀn .ı. an mᴀc ıaꝛla ᴅob ꝼeꝛꝛ oınech
ocuꝛ uᴀıꝛle ocuꝛ oıꝛꝛᴅeꝛcuꝛ ᴅá ᴄáınıc ᴅo ᴣheꝛalᴄ-
achuıᴮ ꝛıaṁ, ocuꝛ ᴣan oıᴣꝛechᴄ aıᴣe achᴄ a ᴣnıom
ꝼeıꝛꝛın, ᴅo mᴀꝛbᴀᴅ le 8axuıᴮ a mí ᴣenáıꝛ na bʟıᴀᴅna
ꝛın. Clᴀnn an ᴣıllᴀ ᴅuıᴮ ᴍıc ᴣoıꝛᴅeaʟᴮ, .ı. an ᴣıllᴀ
ᴅuıᴮ óᴣ ocuꝛ Eᴣnechán, ᴅo ṁaꝛbᴀᴅ la ᴍac ᴅonnchaᴅa
an Choꝛuınn peꝛ ᴅolum. ᴅıuıqı o ᴅalᴮuıᴣhe .ı. oıᴅe
ᴄınᴣ Pıʟıp ꝛíᴣ na 8paınne, ᴅo óᴣ ıaꝛ mᴮꝛıꝛꝛeᴅ aꝛ
ṁoꝛán ᴅo ᴄaᴄhaıᴮ ocuꝛ ᴅo ᴄoıṁᴄeᴣṁalaıᴮ a huchᴄ a
ᴅalᴄa, ocuꝛ ᴅꝼeaᴮuꝛ a ʟaıṁe conuıᴣıꝛın, ocuꝛ ıaꝛ bꝼoꝛ-
bᴀᴅ ꝛé ꝼıᴄeᴄ bʟıᴀᴅan ᴅaoıꝛ. Uıllíam mᴀc an ᴮaꝛúın
ᴅealᴮna ᴅo ᴅul ᴣo hᴀlbaın aꝛ ınnᴀꝛᴮᴀᴅ o 8aᴣꝛanaıᴮ.
ᴮaınꝼeıꝛ ꝛıᴣᴅa ꝛoṁóꝛ ᴄıᴣeꝛna na caıꝛꝛᴣe ocuꝛ a

---

1 *Alva.* Written in the Irish form
o ᴅalᴮuıᴣhe (O'Dalbhaighe; pron.
O'Dalwy) in the text.

2 *Saxons;* i.e. English. This concludes fol. 31b of the Clar. fragment.

3 *Lord.* ᴄıᴣe; most likely a mistake for ᴄıᴣeꝛna, Ciar. Pro-

fessor O'Curry, in his copy of the
Clar. fragment made for the library
of Trinity College, Dublin, questions
whether the remaining transactions
of this year should not be added to
the events of 1578. But they properly belong to the year 1582.

and he was buried in Cluain-Senmhail. The sons of
John, son of Conn, son of Henry O'Neill, went on a foray
into Breifne-O'Raighilligh.   Philip, son of Aedh O'Raighilligh, i.e., son of the O'Raighilligh, with his kinsmen and
followers, came up with them ; and John Og, the son of
O'Neill, was killed there, and O'Neill's other son was taken
prisoner; and four of his good cavalry were killed there
also.   O'Domhnaill's daughter, i.e. Margaret, daughter of
Aedh Dubh, son of Aedh Ruadh, and wife of Maelmordha,
son of John, son of Cathal O'Raighilligh,—and the most
famous and worthy woman in Erinn in her own time,
—died in the Cabhán in hoc anno.   Eighteen heirs of
the nobles of the Foreigners of Midhe were put to death
in Baile-atha-cliath, by the Justiciary of Erinn, that year.

The kalends of January on Monday ; anno Domini one
thousand, five hundred, and eighty-two years.   Mag
Flannchaidh, i.e. Cathal Og, son of Cathal Dubh, was killed
by his own brother, i.e. by Tadhg Og, son of Cathal Dubh,
who was made lord in his place this year.   John, son of
the Earl of Des-Mumha, i.e., the best Earl's son for bounty,
nobility, and dignity, that ever came of the Geraldines, though he had no inheritance but his own energy,
was killed by Saxons in the month of January of this
year.   The sons of the Gilla-dubh Mac Goisdelbh, viz., the
Gilla-dubh Og, and Egnechán, were slain by Mac Donnchadha of the Corann, per dolum.   The Duke of Alva,[1]
the guardian of king Philip, king of Spain, died after
gaining many battles and conflicts on the part of his
ward, and by the excellence of his hand, up to that time,
and after completing six score years of age.   William,
son of the baron of Delbhna, went to Alba, having been
exiled by the Saxons.[2]

The great, regal, wedding feast of the lord[3] of the Rock,

The execution of the "eighteen heirs
of the Foreigners of Midhe," recorded
above under the year 1581, is referred
to a little lower down (see note 6, p.
449); and the entry regarding the

sons of Walter Fada Burk (p. 451)
is contained in the Ann. F. Mast.
at 1582, which disposes of the sug-
gestion that the events belong to
1578.

ṁna, .i. Meaṫú inṫen Domnaill hí Conchobaiṗ.i.inṫen hí
Conchobaiṗ Sliṫiṫ, do ṫenum a coiṁnénecht do Uhṗian
mac Ruaiṗṗi Mic Diaṗmada, dú iṁaṗ bṗonnaṫ ocuṗ
iṁaṗ biéṗṫaoileṫ ilimad da ṫach cenél cṗuiṫ ocuṗ dá
ṫach aṗnáil innṁuiṗ ocuṗ édala, do ṗéiṗ a náilṫiṗ, dá
ṫach aon dṗeṗuiṫ Eṗenn ocuṗ Alban dá tánic da hiaṗ-
ṗad aṗ ṗeṫ na bliadna ṗin. Uaṗun Dealṫna do ṫeiṫ a
láiṁ aṫ Saxanchaib in Uliaduin ṗin, ocuṗ moṗán dá
ṫíṗ do ṁilleṫ. Seiṗion dṗóṫṗa do ṫaiṗtín Roṗṗa Comáin in tan ṗin .i. caiṗtín Pṗaṗaṗdún, ocuṗ maiṫe na
conndae do ṫul dodom na comṫála ṗin. A ndul ṫo toṗ
na nṫáinneṫh, ocuṗ ṫioṗdáil an tuiṗ do ṫuitim ṗútha
ocuṗ an caiṗtín ṗein conambói do ṫaoiniṫ malle ṗṗiṗ
dont ṗoiléṗ [   ] Oṗlannaṫáin .i. Toiṗṗdealb-
ach ant ṗleiṫe mac Uilliám hí Ṗlannaṫáin, ocuṗ a
ṫáṗṗ do teacht don eṗcuṗ ṗin. O Ruaiṗc do denum
cṗeiṫe aṗ muinteṗ Aiṗt, ocuṗ bṗaiṫde do buain eide
ṫo. Cṗeṫ eli do ṫenum dont ṗiṗṗiam O Ruaiṗc ocuṗ
do Shaxanchaib maille ṗṗiṗ aṗ ṫlainn Mic Thiṫeṗnáin
na Ưneiṗṗne, aṫ Loṫ Roda, ocuṗ a mṅá do bṗeiṫ ambṗoid
uatha. O Dúṫda .i. Cathal duṫ mac Conṫobaiṗ hí
Dhuṫda .i. aonṗoṫa tṗleṫta Dháṫi mic Ṗiacṗach, do
hec in hoc anno. Emonn .h. Dúṫda do ṗíṫad na ionaṫ.
Niculáṗ mac Cṗiṗdóiṗ mic an ṫaṗúin do chuṗ dodum
báiṗ iṗin muilénd ceṗṗ, ocuṗ Niculáṗ Ciṁṗóṫ do chuṗ
dodum báiṗ maṗaon [ṗṗiṗ], ocuṗ Seon Ciṁṗóṫ do ṫuiṗ
ant aimleṗ ṗeṗ milled aṗaiṫ dóiṫṗedaib maiṫi ṫlainni
ṫall aṗ na mbáṗṗuṫad ṗoime ṗin. Clann mic Ṫilla
Padṗaic .i. Domnall ocuṗ Cellaṫ do ṁaṗṫad do mac
hí Mhaoilṁuaiṫ .i. do Dhomnall mac Teṗóid hí
Mhaoilṁuaiṫ, a bṗioll ina ṫiṫ ṗein, ocuṗ do maṗṫaṫ

---

1 *His wife*; i.e. the wife of Brian
Mac Dermot.

2 *Prapasdún*. Brabazon.

3 *Tor-na-ngainnedh*; "the tower
of the narrow passages;" apparently a

tower attached to the Castle of Roscommon.

4 *O'Flannagain*. This entry is im-
perfect; some clauses before the name
of O'Flannagain, enumerating the

A.D.
[1582.]

and of his wife,[1] i.e., Medhbh, the daughter of Domhnall O'Conchobhair, i.e.. daughter of O'Conchobhair Sligigh, was celebrated together by Brian. son of Ruaidhri Mac Diarmada, at which large quantities of all kinds of stock, and of all descriptions of treasure and valuables, were presented and dispensed, according to their wish, to every one of the men of Erinn and Alba that came to solicit them during that year. The Baron of Delbhna was detained a prisoner by the Saxons this year; and a great part of his country was destroyed. A session was proclaimed by the captain of Ros-Comain at that time, i.e. Captain Prapasdún;[2] and the principal men of the county went to that meeting. They went to Tor-na-ngainnedh,[3] and the joisting of the tower fell under them, and the captain himself, and all the people that were with him, *were precipitated* to the cellar. . . . . O'Flannagain,[4] i.e., Toirdhelbhach-ant-sleibhe, son of William O'Flannagain; and his death resulted from that fall. O'Ruairc committed a depredation upon Muinter-Airt, and exacted hostages from them. Another depredation was committed by the Sheriff O'Ruairc, and by the Saxons along with him, upon the sons of Mac Tighernain of the Breifne, at Loch-Roda; and their women were borne off captives from them. O'Dubhda, i.e., Cathal Dubh, son of Conchobhar O'Dubhda, i.e., the choicest of the race of Dathi, son of Fiachra, died in hoc anno. Edmond O'Dubhda was inaugurated in his place. Nicholas, son of Christopher, son of the Baron,[5] was put to death in Múilenn-cerr, and Nicholas Cusack was put to death along [with him]; and it was John Cusack that made the false charge on which all the good heirs of the Foreigners were put to death before that.[6] The sons of Mac Gilla-Patraic, viz., Domhnall and Cellach, were killed by the son of O'Maelmhuaidh, i.e., Domhnall, son of Tibbot O'Maelmhuaidh, in treachery, in his own

persons injured, being obviously omit- ted, although no sign of an omission appears in the MS. There is no reference to the incident in any of the other chronicles of the period.

[5] *The Báron*; the Baron of Delbhna, or Delvin.

[6] *Before that.* See the last entry under the year 1581, and page 446 note [3].

'Oomnall ɼein co oíúıt̃ nα ᵭeᵹhαıᵭ ɼın α n'Oúɼṁαᵹ Choluım chılle ᵭo ɼíl Conchobαıɼ ɼαıⅼᵹe. 'Oα mαc Ruᵹnαıᵭe óıᵹ hı Ⅿhoɼᵭα ᵭo chuɼ ᵭoᵭum bάıɼ Le ᵹαⅼⅼoıᵭ, ocuɼ mαc ɼeıᵭlımıᵭ hı Cuαthαıⅼ ᵭo ᵭάɼuᵹαᵭ mαılle ɼɼıú. Clαnn Uάıteɼ ɼαᵭα ᵭo ᵭuⅼ αɼ ɼıobαⅼ ınnɼoıᵹeᵭ α tíɼ Cⅿhαⅼᵹαıᵭ, ocuɼ cɼech ᵭo ᵭenum ᵭóıᵭ. Cⅽoɼ óᵹ tɼlechtα Rıcαıɼᵭ α ḃúɼc ᵭo ᵭɼeıt̃ α toɼαıᵹecht oɼɼα, ᵭcuɼ cuɼ ᵭucα ᵭóıᵭ. ɼıⅼleᵭ ᵭo clαınn Uαıteɼ ɼαᵭα ɼɼıu, ocuɼ bɼıɼɼeᵭ αɼ αn tóɼαᵭ ɼe hımαᵭ nα Lάṁ αᵹ mάm αn ᵹαıɼ α nᵹlenᵭ ᵭuıᵭ, ᵭon tαoıᵭ óteɼɼ ᵭo Neıṁɼınn. Rıcαɼᵭ mαc Emuınn mıc Uılleᵹ ó t̃αıɼLén αn ḃhαɼɼαıᵹ ᵭo mαɼbαᵭ αnn, ocuɼ Emonn αlⅼtα mαc Rıɼᵭeɼᵭ mıc Oılbeɼuɼ ᵭo mαɼbαᵭ αnn ɼóɼ. Cⅿéɼuɼ mαc 'Oάᵭıt̃ ᵭαıñ, ocuɼ Oılbéɼuɼ mαc Seαın mıc 'Oάᵭıt̃ ᵭάın ᵭo t̃ɼomⅼoc αñn, ocuɼ cuıᵭ ṁóɼ ᵭά Lucht Lenmαnα mαılle ɼɼıú. Ḃɼıαn mαc Eoᵹαın ṁαoıl hı 'Ohomnαlⅼάın, .ı. ɼóı Eɼenn ɼe ᵭάn ocuɼ ɼe ɼoᵹluım ᵭɼeɼ αoɼα ɼéın, ᵭɼαᵹbάıl αnn, ocuɼ ɼleıᵹαch eαⅼαᵭnα ᵭo muınntıɼ 'Ohάⅼαıᵹ mάılle ɼɼıɼ; ocuɼ αn t̃ɼeαch ᵭo ᵭɼeıt̃ Leó ᵭóıᵭ ıαɼɼın. Cɼıṁt̃hαnn mαc Ⅿuɼchαᵭα mıc Ⅿuıɼıɼ Cαomάın ᵭo mαɼbαᵭ Le ᵹαⅼⅼαıᵭ. Ⅿαc 'Oıαɼmαᵭα ɼuαᵭ, .ı. Cαᵭᵹ mαc Conchobαıɼ óıᵹ mıc Ⅿuıɼceɼtαıᵹ, ᵭɼαᵹαıl ᵭάıɼ ıɲ cet̃ɼomαᵭ Lά αnᵭıαıᵭ ɼéıle Ḃɼenuınn αɼ ınnɼı αchαıᵭ ın t̃αıɼt̃e, ocuɼ α αᵭlucαᵭ α mαınıɼtıɼ nα ḃúıⅼⅼe. Cαıɼtín Ⅿαcαɼoɼt ᵭo ṁαɼbαᵭ Lα Cαthαⅼ mαc hı Conᵭobαıɼ. Ⅿαc Cⅽılın nα hCⅽlbαn ᵭéᵹ ın blıαᵭαın ɼın. Ⅿαc Uılⅼıαm búɼc, .ı. Rıɼᵭeɼᵭ αn ıαɼαınn mαc 'Oαbı mıc Emαınn mıc Uılleᵹ, ᵭɼαᵹαıl

---

1 *Walter Fada;* i.e. Walter the Tall, son of David Burk. See note ², p. 446.

² *Was killed.* The words ᵭo mαɼbαᵭ, omitted by the scribe, have been added in the margin by Brian Mac Dermot.

³ *Innsi-achaidh-in-chairthe;* "the island of the pillar-stone field."

⁴ *Macafort.* This appears to be an attempt at writing the name of Mac-worth. See Hamilton's *Calendar of State Papers relating to Ireland,* vol. II., p. 371; and the *Calendar of the Carew MSS.,* vol. II., p. 328.

⁵ *O'Conchobhair.* This concludes the text of fol. 32a of the Clar. fragment, in the lower margin of which occurs the memorandum: "honest, good, hospitable Robert Ware, esq., of

house; and Domhnall himself was killed soon after that, in Durmhagh of Colum-Cille, by the Sil-Conchobhair-Failghc. The two sons of Rudhraidhe Og O'Mordha were put to death by Foreigners, and the son of Fedhlimidh O'Tuathail was put to death along with them. The sons of Walter Fada[1] went on an expedition into Tir Amhal-ghaidh, and committed a depredation. The young men of the posterity of Rickard Burk overtook them in pursuit, and set upon them. The sons of Walter Fada turned against them, and the pursuers were routed by superior numbers, at Mám-an-ghair in Glenn-dubh, on the southern side of Neimhfin. Rickard, son of Edmond, son of Ulick, of Caislen-an-Bharraigh, was killed there; and Edmond Allta, the son of Richard, son of Oliver, was also killed there. Ambrose, son of David Bán, and Oliver, son of John, son of David Bán, and a great many of their follow-ers along with them, were severely wounded there. Brian, son of Eoghan Mael O'Domhnallain, i.e., the most eminent man in Erinn, of his own age, in poetry and learning, was lost there, together with a graduate in science of Muinter-Dalaigh. And the prey was afterwards carried off by them. Crimhthann, son of Murchadh, son of Maurice Caomain, was killed[2] by foreigners. Mac Diarmada Ruadh, i.e., Tadhg, the son of Conchobhar Og, son of Muirchertach, died the fourth day after the festival of Brenainn, on Innsi-achaidh-in-chairthe,[3] and was interred in the monastery of the Buill. Captain Macafort[4] was killed by Cathal, the son of O'Conchobhair.[5] MacAilin[6] of Alba died this year. Mac William Burk, i.e., Richard-an-iarainn, son of David, son of Edmond, son of Ulick, died the third

---

Stephens Greene. James Magrath is his servant for ever to comand." The rest of the fragment consists of paper.

[6] MacAilin; "son of Ailen." This

VOL. II.

is the correct form of the name now incorrectly written Mac Callum, or Campbell. The handwriting of this part of the fragment, which is on paper, is very rude.

2 G 2

báp in ·tper lá ɗon caipg in bliaɗain pi. Maipi a
ɓupc ingen Oileuepiip, ben an abaiɗ caoich, ɗhec. Ɗa
banna Saxanaɕ ɗo muinntep Iapla Ipmuman ɗo mapbaɗ
le hIapla Ɗepmuman in bliaɗain pi. Mac Uilliam ɗo
gaipm ɗo Ripɗepɗ mac Oiluepiip in bliaɗain ceɗna.
O Ragallaig .i. Cloɗ conallaɕ ɗég. Cloɗ mac Peɗlimiɗ
bacaig Ui Neill, ocup ɗa cétt Saxanaig ɗo Saxanchaib
mapaon pip, ɗo mapbaɗ pa Rúttai le Samaiple mbuiɗe
Mac Ɗomnuill ocup le na ɕineɕ. Ɗubpaiɕ ɗo tinnpgna
le bpian mac bpiain mic Eogain Ui Ruaipc. Mac Ui
Concobaip ɗuinn .i. Toippɗelbach mac Ɗiapmaɗa mic
Caipbpi ɗég, ocup a aɗnacal a ttempall ɗúiña na
Rorhanach; ocup ɗo bí pin ap échtaiɓ mopa Epenn ɗo
mac pig. Eppog Saxanach ɗo bi a nOilpinn ɗég a mi
meɗoin int pampaɗ. Tomap Septap a ainm; ocup a
cill Liathain ɗo puaip bap. bpian mac Pip gan ainm
mic Concobaip óig Mic Ɗiapmaɗa ɗég. Taɗg mac
Maoileɕlainn mic hoibepɗ Meg Ragnaill ɗo mapbaɗ
le bpian mac Ruaiɗpi Mic Ɗiapmaɗai, ap Cnoc na
capaɗ laiñ pe caipel tobaip int pepbain. Ingen Ui
Concobaip ɗuinn, .i. Meɗb ingen Concobaip mic Eogain
caoich, ɗhec. Semup Nuinnpenɗ mac Cpipɗopai mic in
bapuin, ocup Emann mac in bapuin Nuinnpenn, ɗo
tuitim pe ɕeili, ocup peipep no cuigep mapaon piu.
Concuɓap mac Copmaic mic I. Concubaip .i. mac Ui
Concobaip Pailgi, ocup Taɗg mac gilla Pattpaicc I
Concobaip, ɗo ɗol hi ccómpacc pe [ɕeili] a nClɕ cliaɕ,
ocup Concobap ɗo tuitim pa compac pin. Cathal mac
Maoileɕlainn oig Meg Ragnaill ɗeg. Ɗiapmaiɗ mac
Meg Cappchaig moip ɗo ɗol ap cpeich, ocup banna

1 *The Blind Abbot.* William Burk,
who had himself proclaimed Mac
William in 1598, after the death of
Richard, son of Oliver Burk, but
died soon after in distress, and in exile
from his district.

2 *Aedh Conallagh.* "Aedh (or Hugh)

the Conallian;" so called from having
been fostered by the O'Donnells in
Tir-Conaill.

3 *Saxons of the Saxons;* i.e. genuine
Englishmen.

4 *Dumha - na - Romhanach;* i.e.,
"the mound of the Romans," called

day of the Easter, this year. Mary Burk, daughter of Oliver, wife of the Blind Abbot,[1] died. Two Saxon bands of the Earl of Ur-Mumha's people were killed this year by the Earl of Des-Mumha. Richard, son of Oliver, was proclaimed Mac William the same year. O'Raighilligh, i.e., Aedh Conallagh,[2] died. Aedh, son of Fedhlimidh Bacagh O'Neill, and two hundred Saxons of the Saxons[3] along with him, were slain in the Ruta by Somhairle Buidhe Mac Domhnaill, and by his kindred. Dubhrath was begun by Brian, son of Brian, son of Eoghan O'Ruairc. The son of O'Conchobhair Donn, i.e., Toirdhelbhach, son of Diarmaid, son of Cairbre, died, and was buried in the church. of Dumha-na-Romhanach ;[4] and he was one of the most lamented princes of Erinn. A Saxon bishop who was in Oilfinn died in the middle month of the summer: his name was Thomas Chester; and in Cill-Liathain he died.[5] Brian, the son of Fer-gan-ainm,[6] son of Conchobhar Og Mac Diarmada, died. Tadhg, son of Maelechlainn, son of Hubert Mag Raghnaill, was killed by Brian, son of Ruaidhri Mac Diarmada, on Cnoc-na-carad, close to Caisel-tobair-ind-serbhain. O'Conchobhair Donn's daughter, i.e., Medhbh, daughter of Conchobhar, son of Eoghan Caech, died. James Nugent, son of Christopher, son of the Baron, and Edmond, son of the Baron Nugent, fell by each other, and six persons, or five, along with them. Conchobhar, the son of Cormac, son of O'Conchobhair, i.e., son of O'Conchobhair Failghe, and Tadhg, son of Gilla-Patraic[7] O'Conchobhair, went to fight[8] with [one other], in Ath-cliath, and Conchobhar fell in that fight. Cathal, son of Maelechlainn Og Mag Raghnaill, died. Diarmaid, son of Mac Carthaigh Mor, accompanied by a band of soldiers, went on a

---

also Rath-na-Romhanach; in Kilmore parish, county of Roscommon.

[5] *Died.* Ware (*Bishops*) refers his death to the year 1584.

[6] *Fer-gan-ainm*; "vir sine nomine;" rather a curious Christian name.

[7] *Son of Gilla-Patraic.* mac ᵹιⱡⱡa mic ᵹιⱡⱡaιpaccpaιcc, Clar.

[8] *To fight.* This is the earliest account recorded of a duel in Ireland according to the English mode of trial by combat, or wager of battle.

ᵱaιᵹoιuᵽ laιᵽ,aᵽ O Súιllemáιn. Oomnall O Suιllemaιn
ᴅo bᵽeιᴄh oᵽᵽℸaι, ocuᵽ maιᴆm ᴅo ᴄabaιᵽᴄ aᵽ Oιaᵽmaιᴅ,
ocuᵽ e ᵱéιn ocuᵽ a Saxanuιᵹ ᴅo ᴄιιᴄιm, eᴄ alιι mulᴄι.
((Coᴆ ᴅuᴆ mac Ⅲuᵽchaᴅa Uí ᵱlaιᴄbeᵽᴄuιᵹ, ocuᵽ Uιᵽᴅιuι
Ⅲáιᵹ Ooᵯnaιll, ᴅo ᵹabaιl aᵱᵱeall lé Sean mac an
Iaᵽla Rιcaᵽᴅaιᵹ, .ι. Rιcaᵽᴅ Saxanać, ocuᵽ ιaᴅ ac ᵱιlleᴆ
oιι ceᵽoιċ naoιm, ocuᵽ ᴄιιcc ᵱe ιaᴅ ᴅo caιᵽᴅaén Ⅲalbιe
ᴅo bι oᵽ cιιnn Connachᴄ; ocuᵽ nι ᵱaᴅa ᴅo leιcc Oιa
ocuᵽ ιn cᵽoċ naom ᵱιn ᵱe Sean. Cᵽeċa moᵽa ᴅo ᴅénam
ᴅo cloιnn an ιaᵽla Rιcaᵽᴅaιᵹ .ι. Uιlleᵹ ocuᵽ Sean, aᵽ
ᵱlιchᴄ Uιlleᵹ a buᵽc, ocuᵽ aᵽ muιnnᴄιᵽ Uιᵹιnn ιn
ᴄeᵽmuinn. ᵱell ᵹᵽanna ᴅo ᴅenam ᴅUιlleᵹ mac ιn
Iaᵽla, ocuᵽ ᴅo Rémann mac Uιlleᵹ na ᵹcenᴅ, ocuᵽ ᴅo
Remunn mac an eᵽbuιᵹ, aᵽ Sean mac an Iaᵽla, oιᵽ
ᴄuᵹaᴄaᵽ an ᴅa Rémann cuιᵱeᴆ ᴅo, ocuᵽ ᵱuᵹaᴄaᵽ co bél
aᴄha ᵱιnnᴄuιnn é, ocuᵽ ᴅo ᴄaιᵽᵱuᵹeᴄaᵽ ιnᴄ Iaᵽla .ι.
Uιlleᵹ aᵽᴄeach aιᵽ, ocuᵽ ᴅo maᵽbaᴅ e a ᵱιnᵹuιl, ocuᵽ
Goιn mac Ccoᴅa Ⅲιc Suιᴆne, ocuᵽ Sean mac bᵽιaιn
mιc ᵹιllacellaιᵹ, ocuᵽ ᵱιnᵹιn buιᴆe mac Ⅲaoιlᴄιιle,
aᴆbaᵽ maιċ leᵹa, maᵽaon ᵱιᵽ; ocuᵽ o ᴅo maᵽbaᴅ
Naoιᵱι mac Uιᵱnech a ᵱell an Gᵯuιn Ⅲacha nι ᴅeᵽnaᴅ
a leιᴄheιᴄ ᵱι ᴅᵱιnᵹuιl; ocuᵽ nιᵽ maᵽbaᴅ ᵱeᵽ a aoιᵱι
ᵱeιn ᴅo mac ᵹoιll buᴅ ιno ᵱᵹel na he. Caιᵽᴅen Ⅲalbιe
ocuᵽ a ᵱaιbι ᴅo ᵹallaιb a Connachᴄuιb ᴅo ᴅul a cloιnn
Rιcaιᵽᴅ ᵱa ᴄoιchιm na ᵱellι ᵱιιn, ocuᵽ anᴄ aonmaᴅ la
.x. ᴅo Nouιmbιᵽ ᴅo ᵱonaᴅ ιn ᵹnιm ᵱιn. Soιbaᵽᴅ Iaᵽla
chιllι ᴅaᵽa ᴅéᵹ .ι. Ⅲaιlιᵽ huᵱe, a ᴄᴄoᵽach na blιaᴅna ᵱo. Gᵽbaᵹoιᴅechᴄ Oιleᵱιnn ᴅo ᴄabaιᵽᴄ ᴅCcιnᴅᵽιu
O Cᵽaιᴆéιn ᴅo comaιᵱle na hGᵽenᴅ a nCccᴄh clιaᴄh.
Iaᵽla Oeᵽmuman ᵱe nabaᵽℸaι ᵹeᵱóιᴅ na ᵱecaιᴅhe ᴅo

---

¹ *Alii.* alι, Clar.

² *Ulick-na-gcenn.* "Ulick of the
heads." He was son to the first Earl
of Clann-Rickard.

³ *Naiss.* One of the three sons of
Uisnech, whose murder by king Conor

Mac Nessa, in the first century of the
Christian era, forms one of the "three
sorrowful stories of Erinn," and the
subject of Moore's beautiful song,
"Avenging and bright fall the swift
sword of Erin." See the *Transactions*

predatory expedition against O'Suillebhain. Domhnall
O'Suillebhain overtook them, and defeated Diarmaid; and
he and his Saxons fell, et alii multi.[1] Aedh Dubh, the
son of Murchadh O'Flaithbhertaigh, and Justin Mac
Domhnaill, were apprehended, in treachery, by John, son of
the Earl of Clann-Rickard, i.e., Richard Saxanach, as they
were returning from the Holy Cross; and he delivered
them to Captain Malbie, who was over Connacht: and
not long did God and the Holy Cross let that go *unpunished* with John. Great depredations were committed
by the sons of the Earl of Clann-Rickard, viz., Ulick and
John, upon the descendants of Ulick Burk, and upon
Muinter-Uiginn of the Termon. An ugly treachery was
practised by Ulick, the son of the Earl, and by Redmond,
son of Ulick-na-gcenn,[2] and by Redmond, the bishop's son,
on the Earl's son John; for the two Redmonds gave him
an invitation; and they took him to Bél-atha-Finntainn,
and drew the Earl, i.e., Ulick, upon him; and he was slain
in fratricide; and John, the son of Aedh Mac Suibhne,
and John, the son of Brian Mac Gilla-Cellaigh, and
Finghin Buidhe Mac Maeltuile, the good material of a
physician, were killed along with him. And the like of
this fratricide was not committed since Naise,[3] son of
Uisnech, was killed in treachery in Emhain-Macha; and
no Foreigner's son of his own age was slain who was more
lamented than he. Captain Malbie, and all the Foreigners
that were in Connacht, went to Clann-Rickard on the
report of this treachery; and on the 11th day of November
this deed was committed. The Earl of Cill-dara's steward,
i.e., Meiler Husè, died in the beginning of this year. The
bishopric of Oilfinn was given to Andrew O'Craidhén, by
the Council of Erinn at Ath-cliath. The Earl of Des-
Mumha, usually called Geróid-na-secaidhe,[4] was killed by

---

of the Gaelic Society, Dublin, 1808;
and the *Atlantis*, vol. vi., p. 377. The
event has also been versified by Dr.
Samuel Ferguson: *Lays of the Western
Gael*, London, 1867.

[4] *Geróid-na-secaidhe.* "Garrett of
the excursions." The circumstances
attending his death are related at
much greater length in the Annals
of the Four Masters.

mapbaṫ le bapṫaiḃ caiṗlein na Ⅿaingi, ocuṗ a cenn
ṫo cuṗ co Saxanaiṫ; ocuṗ in paiḃi a nepinn echṫ naṗ
commoṗ ṗin ṫuaiṗle ocuṗ ṫoineć ocuṗ ṫo cumachṫiṅ,
ocuṗ iṗ mo leṗ ṫuiṫ ṫi Saxanchaiḃ, ocuṗ ṫo cuiṗ coṗṫuṗ
aṗ in mḃaṅṗigan. Sili ingen 1 Ḋomnaill ṫég, an ben ṫo
ḃi ag Ṫaṫg og mac Ṫaiṫg mic Ccéṫa. Peṗ gan egla mac
Ⅿaoilmuiṗi Ⅿeg Shuiṫne ṫeg. Peaṗ gan egla mac
Ḋomnaill mic Peiṫlimiṫ mic Ṫoiṗṗṫealḃaig caṗṗaiṫ
1 Concuḃaiṗ ṫég. Saṗṗanuṫ ṫo ṗinṫi a ṫṫuillṗi ocuṗ
a gcluain Ⅿuiṗeṫuiṫ, ocuṗ a gcaṗṗṗṫ Ḋoiṗen, ocuṗ a
ḃfeṗann na ṫaṗać, ocuṗ an 1mliuch móṗ, ocuṗ an
Uaṗán, ocuṗ a gcluain Ọ gCaṗinacain, ocuṗ ṗa
ḃfoṫannuṫ, ocuṗ ṫiṫeṗ ṫo ṫenaṁ ṫóiṫ ṗna áiṫiṫ ṗin.
Ọ gallcaḃaiṗ ṫo maṗbaṫ leiṗ Ọ Héill. Ⅿag Ccoṫa in
Ⅿóinṫiṫ, .i. Séan, ṫo maṗbaṫ le muinṫiṗ na héilli.
Uilliam Ḃúṗc mac Ⅿaoiliṗ ḃáin ṫég. Oṗláim moiṫi
luiṗg ṫo ṫaḃaiṗṫ ṫo Ḃṗian mac Ruaiṫṗi Ⅿic Ṫiaṗmaṫa
in ḃliaṫain ṗin. Ⅽn cuać ṫo gaiṗm aṫhaiṫ nollag ag
aṗṫ mic Gṗaini, a ḃṗiaṫnaiṗi Roiḃeṗṫ Ḋilmain ocuṗ
Ṫiaṗmaṫa meg Ḋuiṫ, ocuṗ ṗa móṗ anṫ ingnaṫ ṗin.
1aṗla Ọ Suṗaic .i. Ṫomaṗ in uiṗṫi, ocuṗ ṫo ḃi ṗe na
giuiṗṫiṗ ṗaṫa ṫaimṗiṗ aṗ Eiṗinn, ocuṗ a heg ṗa
cinciṗ.

Ⅼct. ṗoṗ Ⅽeṫṫain; aoiṗṗ in Ṫiṫeṗinai in ṫan ṗa mile
ḃliaṫan ocuṗ cuic ceṫ, ceṫṗi ḃlaṫnai ocuṗ ceṫṗi .xx. Peṗ
ṫogḃala ciṗṗai na ḃaṅṗiṫhina a Connachṫoiṫ ṫo ég in
ḃliaṫain ṗi; Ⅽnṫune Piṫon a ainm. Ḋomnall glaṗṗ
mac Ṫaiṫg ṗuaiṫ hi Ⅽiṗṫ, ocuṗ Eoin mag Caṗinaic .i.
ṗaccaṗṫ ṫempaill Eoin, ṫṗi la ṗ́na ṗeil Ḃeṗaiṫ a ég.
Ⅿaiṗgṗecc ingen Ⅿic Ḋonnchaṫa, ben Ui Ḋuiḃgenṫain,

---

¹ *Cost.* In the margin (p. 33) the
scribe has added the memorandum
na ṫaḃaiṗ guṫ oṗm a ṗṗ a leṫṫe
ṗin, ocuṗ naṗ ṗuiṗiṫ me ṗe ṫech-
ṫuṫaṫ ṫo ṫaḃaiṗṫ aiṗṗin, ocuṗ go
cuiṗṗiṫeṗ o . . . . .; i.e., "do
not reproach me, O man who may read
this, for I have not waited to give it

proper arrangement, and that . . .
will be placed" . . .

² *Tadhg Og.* "Tadhg the Younger."
He was one of the family of O'Conor
Sligo.

³ *Fer-gan-egla*; lit., "man without
fear."

⁴ *Sussex.* The scribe writes the

the warders of Caislen-na-Maingi, and his head was sent to Saxon-land; and there was no one in Erinn whose equal he was not in nobility, honour, and powers, and by whom more Saxons fell, and who put the queen to greater cost.[1] Síle, daughter of O'Domhnaill, the wife of Tadhg Og,[2] son of Tadhg, son of Aedh, died. Fer-gan-egla,[3] the son of Maelmuire Mac Suibhne, died. Fer-gan-egla, the son of Domhnall, son of Fedhlimidh, son of Toirdhelbhach Carragh O'Conchobhair, died. Saxons established themselves in Tuillsce, and in Cluain-Muiredhaigh, and in Cairge-Doiren, and in Ferann-na-darach, and in Imlech-mór, and in Uaran, and in Cluain-O'Gormacain, and in the Fothannadh; and they erected houses in those places. O'Gallchubhair was killed by O'Neill. Mac Aedha of the Mointech, i.e., John, was killed by the people of the Eill. William Burk, the son of Meiler Bán, died. The possession of Magh-Luirg was this year given to Brian, son of Ruaidhri Mac Diarmada. The cuckoo called on Christmas night, at Ard-mic-Grainni, in the presence of Robert Dillon and Diarmaid MacDuibh; and that was a great wonder. The Earl of Sussex,[4] i.e., Thomas-in-uisgi,[5] who was for a long time Justiciary over Erinn, died at Whitsuntide.

The kalends of January on Wednesday; the age of the Lord at this time being one thousand, five hundred, and eighty-four[6] years. The receiver of the queen's rents in Connacht died this year; his name was Anthony Fitton. Domhnall Glas, son of Tadhg Ruadh O'hAirt, and John Mac Carmaic, i.e. the priest of Tempul-Eoin,[7] died three days before the festival of Berach.[8] Margaret, daughter of Mac Donnchadha, the wife of O'Duibhgennain, died.

---

name O Suṛaic, as if it was that of an Irishman.

[5] *Thomas-in-uisgi.* "Thomas of the water."

[6] *Eighty-four.* The transactions of the year 1583 have been omitted.

[7] *Tempul-Eoin.* "John's church;" St. John's, near Athlone, county of Roscommon.

[8] *Berach.* St. Berach, patron of Termonbarry, co. Roscommon, whose festival is kept on February 15.

ꝺeꞡ· Ḃꞃꞁαn mac Ꝺoɴncháꝺ méꞡ Uꞁꝺꞁꞃ ocuꞃ Ꝺómnαll óꞡ
O Ꝺoḃoꞁlén ꝺecc. Ꞁn Ꝡꞁllαe ꞡlαꞃꞃ ꞃuαꝺ mac Ɱαolꞃuα-
nαꞁꝺ ꞃꞁnꝺ ꝺeꞡ; α mꞁ Ꝑeḃꞃαꞁ ꝺó eꞡαꞇꞇαꞃ ꞃꞁn. Ɱαc Uꞁ
Ꝡαllꞔuꞁbαꞁꞃ .ꞁ. ꞁn ꞃeꞃ ꝺoꞃꞔα mac Ꞓoꞡαꞁn ꝺo mαꞃbαꝺ le
Ɱαnαcháꞁb co ꞇꞁmꞃꞁꞃꞇech. 8ꞁꞃ Ꞁꞁꞁcαlαꞃꞃ Ɱαlbꞁc ꝺo
bꞁ nα cαꞁꝺꞁn oꞃ cꞁnꝺ Connαchꞇ ꝺeꞡ ꞁn ꞇꞃeꞃꞃ lα ꝺo mí
Ɱαꞃꞇα, ocuꞃ nꞁ ꞇαꞁꞁc α nꞂꞃꞁnn α comαꞁmꞃꞁꞃ ꞃꞃꞁꞃ nα
ꞡo menꞁc ꞃꞁαm ꝺo Ꝡαlloꞁb, ꝺuꞁne uαꞃαl buꝺ ꞃeꞃꞃ ꞁnα
ꞃe, ocuꞃ ꝺo cuꞁꞃ ꞃe cuꞁcceꝺ Connαchꞇ uꞁlꞁ ꞃo ꝺoeꞁꞃꞃꞁ;
ocuꞃ nꞁ ꞃeꞇuꞃ α ꞃꞁn no α áꞁꞃemh ꞡαch αꞃ mꞁll ꞁn ꞃeꞃ
ꞃꞁn αꞃ ꞃéꝺ Ꞃꞃeꞁnn ; ocuꞃ ꝺo ꞃꞁnne ꞃé moꞃαn oꞁbꞃeꞔ αꞃ
cuꞁꞃꞇ bαꞁle αꞇhα luαꞁn ocuꞃ ꞃoꞃꞃα Commαꞁn ꝺo ꞃunn-
ꞃαꝺ· Cꞃech moꞃ ꝺo ꝺenαṁ ꝺAꞔeꝺ ꞃuαꝺh mac Ꞁ Ꝺomnαꞁll,
ocuꞃ ꝺU Ꝡαllꞔoḃαꞁꞃ, αꞃ mac Ꞇαꞁꝺꞡ Ꞁ Ꞃuαꞁꞃc α ꞡCnoc
nα ꞡαoꞁꞔe. Ɱαc 8αṁꞃαꞁꝺáꞁn .ꞁ. Ḃꞃꞁαn óc mac Ḃꞃꞁαn
ꝺéꞡ ꞁn blꞁαꝺαꞁn ꞃꞁn. Cꞁll Ɱꞁꝺáꞁn ꝺo loꞃꞡαꝺ ꞁn blꞁαꝺαꞁn
ꞃꞁn. Ɱαc ꞁn ꞃꞁleꝺ ꝺeꞡ ꞁn blꞁαꝺαꞁn ꞃꞁn .ꞁ. Ꝡꞁllα Cꞃꞁoꞃꞇ
mac 8éꞃꞃαꞁꝺ· Ɱαc ꞁn eꞃbαꞁꞡ α ḃúꞃc, .ꞁ. Ꞃemαnꝺ, ꝺo
mαꞃbαꝺ le Ꝺꞁαꞃmαꞁꝺ ꞃꞁαbαch mac Aꞔeꝺα mꞁc Ꝺonn-
cháꝺ, α nꝺꞁoꞡuꞁl 8eáꞁn α ḃuꞃc. Ꞁnꞡeꞁn mꞁc Ꝺꞁαꞃmαꝺα .ꞁ.
8αꝺḃ ꞁnꞡen Ꞓoꞡαꞁn, ꞁn ben ꝺo bꞁ αc O Ꝡαḃꞃα .ꞁ. Ꝺꞁαꞃmαꞁꝺ
mαc Ꞓoꞡhαꞁn Ꞁ Ꝡαḃꞃα, ꝺéꞡ. Ꞁn ꞡꞁuꞃꞇꞁꞃ .ꞁ. 8emuꞃ Ꝺuꝺαl
ꝺeꞡ ꞁn blꞁαꝺαꞁn ꞃꞁn. Cαꞇαl mac Ꞃuꝺꞃαꞁꝺꞁ mꞁc Ꞁꞃ
Ɱꞁcc Ꞃαꝺꞁꞁll ꝺeꞡ ꞁn blꞁαꝺαꞁn ꞃꞁn lα ꞃéꞁlꞁ Ḃꞃenuꞁꞁn.
Ꞓáꞃboc ꝺo ꝺenαṁ ꝺo 8éαn mac 8emαꞁꞃ α lꞁnꞃꞁ α
nOꞁlꞃꞁnn ꞁn blꞁαꝺαꞁn ꞃꞁn, ocuꞃ Aꞁnꝺꞃꞁu O Cꞃꞁꝺαꞁn
ꝺo cuꞃ αꞃ ccúl. O Ꞃαꝺαllαꞁꞡh ꝺo ꝺenαmh ꝺo 8eαn
mαc Aꞔeꝺαe conαllαꞡ ꝺo Ꝡαlloꞁb, αꞃ belαꞁb clαꞁnꞁꞁ
Ɱαoꞁlmoꞃꝺαꞁ Uꞁ Ꞃαꞁꞡꞁllꞁꞡ ꝺo buꝺ ꞃꞁn[e] ꞁnαꞃ e, ocuꞃ
ꝺo mꞁlleꞇαꞃ clαnn Ɱαoꞁlmoꞃꝺαꞁ ꞁn ꞇꞁꞃ uꞁlꞁ ꞇꞃꞁꝺ
ꞃꞁn. Ꝡꞁuꞃꞇꞁꞃꞃ ꝺo ꞇeαchꞇ co hꞂꞃꞁnn αꞃ blꞁαꝺαꞁn ceꝺnα,

---

1 *The Gilla-glas-ruadh;* i.e., the
"gray-red gillie," or "fellow."

2 *Manachs;* i.e. the Feara-Manach,
or the people of Fermanagh. The

orig. has mancachaꞁb, which is
corrupt.

3 *And.* ocuꞃ oꞁꞃ, "and because,"
Clar.

4 *O'Cridhain.* The name is written

Brian, son of Donnchadh MagUidhir, and Domhnall Og O'Dobhailen, died. The Gilla-glas-ruadh,[1] son of Maelruan-aidh Finn, died: in the month of February they died. The son of O'Gallchubhair, i.e., the Ferdorcha, son of Eoghan, was accidentally killed by the Manachs.[2] Sir Nicholas Malbie, who had been captain over Connacht, died the third day of the month of March; and there came not to Erinn in his own time, nor often before, a better gentleman of the Foreigners than he; and[3] he placed all Connacht under bondage. And it is not possible to count or reckon all that this man destroyed throughout Erinn; and he executed many works, especially on the courts of the towns of Ath-Luain and Ros-Comain. A great depredation was committed by Aedh Ruadh, the son of O'Domhnaill, and by O'Gallchubhair, on the son of Tadhg O'Ruairc, in Cnoc-na-gaithe. Mac Samhradhain, i.e., Brian Og, son of Brian, died this year. Cill-Midain was burned this year. Mac-in-fhiledh died this year, i.e., Gilla-Christ, son of Jeffrey. The son of the Bishop Burk, i.e., Red-mond, was killed by Diarmaid Riabhach, son of Aedh, son of Donnchadh, in revenge of John Burk. The daughter of Mac Diarmada, i.e., Sadhbh, daughter of Eoghan, the wife of O'Gadhra, i.e., Diarmaid, son of Eoghan O'Gadhra, died. The Justiciary, i.e., James Dowdall, died this year. Cathal, the son of Ruaidhri, son of Ir Mag Raghnaill, died this year on the day of Brenainn's festival. John, son of James Lynch, was made bishop in Oilfinn this year, and Andrew O'Cridhain[4] was removed.[5] John, son of Aedh Conallach, was made the O'Raighilligh by the Foreigners, in presence of the sons of Maelmordha O'Raighilligh, who were senior to him; and the sons of Maelmordha destroyed the entire country through that. A Justiciary came to Erinn the same year, whose name was

O'Craidhén (or O'Crean) under the year 1582, when he is stated to have been appointed by the Council of Ireland. See p. 455. There is no mention of this person in Ware's list of Bishops.

[5] *Removed.* vo ċuꞃ aꞃ ccúl; lit., " was put back."

rip Seon Pipoiɔ a ainm. Ꞇɩꝫepna ɔo ꞇeachꞇ apConnach-
ꞇuɩp mapaon pip; Rɩpɔepɔ Ƀɩnꝫɩam a ainm. Ꞇeachꞇ
ɔo na ꝫalloɩb pin ap ꞇeachꞇ a nꝪpinn co popp Commaɩn,
ocup Ccoɔ mac Uɩ Concobaɩp ɔuinn ɔo ꝫapaɩl ɔoɩb;
ocup ɔo peɓɩꝫeꞇap a capaɩɔ é co haɩꞇꝫepp .ɩ. O Concobaɩp Slɩꝫɩꝝ ocup Ƀpian mac Ruaɩɔpi Mɩc Ɗɩapmaɔa,
ocup Ꞇomalꞇaꞇ oꝫ mac Ꞇomalꞇaɩꝝ Mɩc Ɗɩapmaɔa;
ocup ɩp amlaiɔ ɔo peɩɔɩꝫeꞇap é, ꞇpi mɩlɩ punꞇ ɔo pꝫpi-
baɔ ap an ꞇpiúp a mbannaɩɔhɩb pe hanamain a pɩꞇ ɔo,
ocup Ƀpian mac Ɗomnaɩll Mɩc Suɩbni, conpabla ɔa
muɩnnꞇep, ɔpaꝫbaɩl a pop Commaɩn an ɩapnac ap Ccoɔh.
Ɗul ɔona ꝫalloɩb pin co ꝫaɩllɩm, ocup mac Uɩllɩam ɔo
ꞇeachꞇ na ꝫeenɔ, ocup bpaɩꝫɔɩ ɔo buaɩn ɔo mac Uɩllɩam
ocup ɔa cineɓ. Ccppin ɔoɩb co Luɩmnech. Sluaɩꝫeɔ le
Rɩpɔepɔ Ƀɩnꝫɩam .ɩ. lepin ꞇɩꝫepna pin cuɩꝫeɔ Connachꞇ,
a nɩchꞇap Connachꞇ, ɔap ben bpáɩꝫɩ ɔUa Ruaɩpc, ocup
ɔap ꝫab Ƀaɩlɩ ɩn múꞇa, ocup ɔap cpech ɩn Copann, ocup
ɔa puꝫ Caꞇhal oꝫ mac Caꞇhaɩl ɔuɩɓ mɩc Ɗonnchaɩɓ lepp
ɔo bpáꝫaɔ ꞇapeɩp ap mɩlleɓ a Copaɩnn; ocup Ccoɔ mac
Caɩpbpi meɩꝫ Ɗonnchaɩɓ pa ꞇɩꝫepna ap Copann ɩn uaɩp
pin. In ꝫiuɩpɔɩp ɔo ɔola a nUllꞇuɩb .ɩ. pip Seon Pipóiɔ,
ocup mac Uɩ Ꞁéɩll .ɩ. Ꞇoɩppɔelbaɩch Luɩmɩꝝ, ɔo ꞇabaɩpꞇ
laɩp ɔo bpaꝫaɔ. Ꝫɩpe uɩle ap na ꝫabáɩl le ꝫallaɩbh
ɩn blɩaɔhaɩn pin, ɩnnup ccup cuɩppeꞇ oɩnech ocup uaɩple
pep nꝪpinn ap ꝫcul. Ccꞇɩaꞇpo ꞇɩꝫepnaɓa Connachꞇ ɩn
blɩaɔaɩn pi .ɩ. Ɗonnchaɔ mac Concopaɩp mɩc Ɗonn-
chaɔa ɩna ɩapla ap Ꞇuaɔmumaɩn, ocup Uɩlleꝫ mac
Rɩcaɩpɔ Saꞇanaɩꝝ na ɩapla ap cloinn Rɩcaɩpɔ, ocup
Ccoɔ mac ƊonnchaɔaUɩ Cellaɩꝝ ap ꞇíp Maɩne; hoɩbepɔ
buɩɔɩ mac Uɩllɩam mɩc Ꞇomáɩpp ap cloɩnn Connmaɩɔ;
Ɗɩapmaɔ mac Caɩpppi Uɩ Concobaɩp ap cloinn Ꞇoɩpp-
ɔelbaɩꝝ. Ꞇaɔꝫ óꝫ mac Ꞇaɩɔꝫ buɩɔe ap cloinn mɩc
Ꝉelɩm. Ƀpian mac Ruaɩɔpi Mɩc Ɗɩapmaɔa ap maꝫ

---

[1] *Clann-Toirdhelbhaigh.* This was
the tribe name of the sept of O'Conor
Donn.

[2] *Descendants of Felim's son;* i.e.,
the sept of O'Conchobhair Ruadh, or
O'Conor Roe.

Sir John Perrot. A governor of Connacht came with him, whose name was Richard Bingham. These Foreigners came to Ros-Comain, on their arrival in Erinn, and Aedh, son of O'Conchobhair Donn, was made prisoner by them ; and his friends, viz., O'Conchobhair Sligigh, and Brian, son of Ruaidhri Mac Diarmada, and Tomaltach Og, son of Tomaltach Mac Diarmada, released him quickly ; and the way they released him was, the three gave bonds for three thousand pounds to guarantee his continuing in peace ; and Brian son of Domhnall Mac Suibhne, a constable of his people, was left in Ros-Comain, in irons, as security for Aedh. These Foreigners went to Gaillimh, and Mac William came to meet them ; and hostages were exacted from Mac William, and from his kindred. From thence they went to Luimnech. A hosting by Richard Bingham, i.e., by that lord of the province of Connacht, to Lower Connacht, on which occasion he exacted hostages from O'Ruairc, and took Baile-in-mhúta, and plundered the Corann, and carried off Cathal Og, son of Cathal Dubh Mac Donnchadha, as a hostage, after all that was destroyed in Corann ; and the lord over Corann at that time was Aedh, son of Cairbre Mac Donnchadha. The Justiciary, i.e., Sir John Perrot, went to Ulster, and brought the son of O'Neill, i.e.; of Toirdhelbhach Luinech, as a hostage with him. All Erinn was occupied by the Foreigners this year, so that they put back the honour and nobility of the men of Erinn. These are the lords of Connacht in this year ; viz., Donnchadh, son of Conchobhar, son of Donnchadh, is Earl over Tuadh-Mumha ; and Ulick, son of Rickard Saxanach, is Earl over Clann-Rickard ; and Aedh, son of Donnchadh O'Cellaigh, over Tir-Maine ; Hubert Buidhe, son of William, son of Thomas, over the Clann-Connmaigh ; Diarmaid, son of Cairbre O'Conchobhair, over the Clann-Toirdhelbhaigh ;[1] Tadhg Og, son of Tadhg Buidhe, over the descendants of Felim's son ;[2] Brian, son of Ruaidhri Mac Diarmada, over

Luιρ̃. bριαɴ mαc bριαιɴ Uí Ruαιρc αρ ιɴ mbρeρ̃ɴe,
ocuρ 'Oomɴαll mαc Cαιϑ̃ mιc Cαϑαιl óιϑ̃ αρ ιcϑαρ
Coɴɴαcϑ; Rιρϑeρϑ mαc Olιueρuρ α buρc αρ cριch
clαιɴɴι hUιllιαm; ocuρ ɴι heιϑιρ α ριm ɴo α αιροιm
ɴo α ρ̃αιρɴeιρ cech αɴϑeρρɴαϑαρ ϑ̃oιll ϑolcαιb ocuρ
ϑαιɴleϑϑρom αρ ɴα ρeραιb ριɴ. Œɴ ρeρϑoρchα mαc
Muιρϑ̃eρα αρ ϑιρ Œιlιllα; Œoϑ mαc Cαιρbρι αρ ιɴ
cCoραɴɴ; Coρmαc O heϑ̃ρα αρ Luιϑ̃ɴe buιϑe. ρeρϑ̃αl
cαρραch αρ Luιϑ̃ɴe ριαbαch; Emαɴ O 'Ouϑϑα αρ ϑιρ
ριαč̃ρach Muαιϑ̃ι. Œcριɴ ϑιϑ̃eρɴαϑα ιɴ cuιϑ̃ιϑ ιɴ ϑαɴρα.
Cαϑ̃ϑ̃ mαc Œoϑ̃αϑ̃αιɴ, ollαm̃ ρlechϑα Rιcαιρϑ oιϑ̃ α buρc
ρe ρeιɴechuρ, ϑeϑ̃ ιɴ blιαϑαιɴ ρι. Mαc Mιc Coɴρɴαmα,
.ι. Coιρρϑelbach óϑ̃ mαc Coιρρϑelbαιϑ̃, ϑeϑ̃. Uιllιαm
cαoch mαc 'Ooɴɴchαϑα ι Cellαιϑ̃ ϑo cρochαϑ leριɴ
ɴϑ̃uιbeρɴoιρ ι ɴϑ̃αιllιm. M̃αc 8ιuρϑαιɴ bαιle αϑhα
leč̃αιɴ, .ι. Comαρρ ϑub, ϑeϑ̃. Ocuρ αϑαιϑ ρo ρα hαιρϑ
ϑιϑ̃eρɴαϑα αρ Ullϑoιb ιɴ ϑαɴ ροιɴ, .ι. Coιρρϑelbach
Luιɴιoch αρ ϑιρ Eoϑ̃αιɴ, ocuρ Œoϑ mαc Mαϑ̃ɴuρα Uι
'Oomɴαιll αρ ϑιρ Coɴuιll; Coɴɴ mαc Neιll oιcc αρ
clαιɴɴ Œoϑα buιϑe; αɴ ρeρ ϑoρchα mαc 'Oomɴαιll óιϑ̃
ɴα Mαϑ̃ Œoɴϑ̃uρα αρ ιϑ̃ Ec̃hαch. Œρϑ mαc bριαιɴ ɴα
mocheρϑ̃ι αρ Oιρϑ̃ιαllαιb. Cucoɴɴαcϑ oϑ̃ mαc Coɴ-
coɴɴαcϑ αρ ρeρuιb Mαɴαch. Ruαιϑρι mαc Mαϑ̃ɴuρα
ι Cαč̃αιɴ oρ cιɴɴ οιρecl̃ϑα ι Cαϑ̃hαιɴ. Mαϑhα mαc
Mαοιleč̃lαιɴɴ ριαbαιϑ̃ mιc Mαolϑuιlι ϑeϑ̃. 8αϑb ιɴϑ̃eɴ
Uι 'Ouιbϑ̃eɴϑαιɴ, beɴ ϑ̃ιllαcoluιm mιc Mαolmuιρe
mιc bριαιɴ óιϑ̃, ϑeϑ̃. Mαc Eochαϑu .ι. ρeρ ϑ̃αɴ αιɴm
Mαc Eochαϑα, ollαm̃ Lαιϑ̃eɴ ιɴ ρeρ ϑ̃αɴ αιɴm ριɴ, ϑeϑ̃.

---

1 *Men.* This clause seems misplaced,
and should apparently come in after
the enumeration of the chieftains of
Connacht, which is continued, and
concluded, in the sentence immediately following.

2 *Maurice*; i.e., Maurice Mac Donnchadha, or Mac Donough.

3 *Cairbre.* Also a Mac Donough.

4 *Luighne Buidhe*; i.e., the part of
Luighne (Leyny, co. Sligo) belonging
to O'hEghra Buidhe, or O'Hara the
Yellow.

5 *Luighne-Riabhach.* The part of
Luighne belonging to O'Hara Riabhach (O'Hara the Swarthy).

6 *These.* It would seem that the
enumeration of the Ulster chieftains,

Magh-Luirg; Brian, son of Brian O'Ruairc, over the Breifne; Domhnall, son of Tadhg, son of Cathal Og, over Lower Connacht; and Richard, son of Oliver Burk, over the territory of Clann-William. And it is impossible to count, or reckon, or relate, all the injuries and oppressions the Foreigners committed upon these men.[1] The Ferdorcha, son of Maurice,[2] is over Tir-Ailella; Aedh, son of Cairbre,[3] over the Corann; Cormac O'hEghra over Luighne-Buidhe;[4] Ferghal Carragh over Luighne-Riabhach;[5] Edmond O'Dubhda over Tir-Fiachrach-Muaidhe. Those are the lords of the province at this time. Tadhg Mac Aedhgain, the ollamh in Fenechas of the descendants of Rickard Og Burk, died this year. The son of Mac Consnamha, i.e., Toirdhelbhach Og, son of Toirdhelbhach, died. William Caech, son of Donnchadh O'Cellaigh, was hanged by the governor in Gaillimh. Mac Jordan of Baile-atha-lethain, i.e., Thomas Dubh, died. And these[6] were the chief lords over the Ulidians at that time, viz., Toirdhelbhach Luighnech over Tir-Eoghain, and Aedh, son of Maghnus O'Domhnaill, over Tir-Conaill; Conn, son of Niall Og, over Clann-Aedha-Buidhe; the Ferdorcha, son of Domhnall Og, was Mag Aenghusa over Ui-Echach; Art, son of Brian-na-mocherghi,[7] over Oirghialla; Cuconnacht Og, son of Cuconnacht,[8] over Feara-Manach; Ruaidhri, son of Maghnus O'Cathain, over Oirecht-Ui-Cathain. Matthew, son of Maelechlainn Riabhach Mac Maeltuile, died. Sadhbh, daughter of O'Duibhgennain, wife of Gillacoluim,[9] son of Maelmuire, son of Brian Og, died. MacEochadha, i.e., Fer-gan-ainm MacEochadha, (this Fer-gan-ainm was ollamh of Laighen), died. A

---

here commenced, should follow immediately after the completion of the list of Connacht lords given above.

[7] *Brian-na-mocherghi.* "Brian of the early rising;" a chieftain of the sept of Mac Mahon of Oriel.

[8] *Cuconnacht.* Chief of the family of Mac Uidhir, or Maguire.

[9] *Gillacoluim.* One of the Mac Swine clan. The name Gillacoluim signifies the "gillie" of Colum, or St. Colum-Cille.

Danna Saxranač ꝺo marbaꝺ ra Ruta ro cloinꝺ
'Doṁnaill na hCClban, ocur ꝺo baineaꝺar ꝺın Lırre
ꝺo Saxranaib, ocur ꝺo marbaꝺar aroıꞗe anꝺ.

Ktt. 1anaır ror CCoıne, ocur arı aoır ın Tıƶerna ın
taı ra cuıƶ bliaꝺna ocur cetra rıchet, cccc. ocur
mıle. Mac Taıꞇƶ 1 Ruaırc. ı. Bman, ocur cınꝺ ꝺo cloınꝺ
tȘıꞇıƶ ꝺo bı ar rarꝺo aıƶe, ꝺo'ꝺuɫ ar rıuꞇaɫ ınnrıꞇe
aır Maƶ [ꝼ]Lanꝺchaıꝺh, ocur creacha mora ꝺo ƶɫacaꝺ
ꝺoıꞗ la rele Sꝺeaꞗaın. Maƶ [ꝼ]Lanꝺchaıꝺh ocur mac
1 Ruaırc. .ı. Tıƶernan mac Bríaın 1 Ruaırc ꝺo breꞇ
orrꞇa, ocur tacar ꝺo ꞇaꞗaırc ꝺa ꞇele ꝺoıꞗ; ocur
Maƶnur oƶ Maƶ 'Duꞗaın ꝺo marbaꝺ a torač ın tachaır
rın. Ƒır Breırne ocur 'Dartraoı ꝺo breꞇ orra na
ꝺıaıꝺ rın, ocur cur ꝺoıꞗ ꝺoꞇum na reaꝺna rın, ocur
brıreꝺh ar mac Taıꞇƶ 1 Ruaırc ocur ar a muınꝺtır,
ocur Eoƶan mac Sıthıꝺ mac Toırrꞗeaɫbaıƶ mıc Emaınꝺ
mıc Sıchıꝺ ꝺo marbaꝺ, ocur ꝺa rícheꝺ maraon rır ar
a[ı] Lachaır rın. 'Do ƶaꞗaꝺ mac Taıꝺƶ 1 Ruaırc ocur
Maƶnur oƶ O Curnın, ocur ꝺo cuıreꝺh ar Loꞇ na cuɫa
ıaꝺ ro ıarnach; ocur ꝺo marꞗaꝺar clann Tıƶernaın
ıaꝺ ƶo hoɫc; ocur ar maƶ hOıɫꞇear tuƶuꝺ ın maoıꞗm
rın. 1n ƶuıꞗernoır, .ı. tıƶerna Connacht, ꝺo teacht
Lucht ꝺa arrꞇrač o baıle CCꞇa Luaın ƶo carraıƶ Meıc
'Dıarmaꝺu, aoıꞇce cınꝺ ın ꝺa la ꝺhec ƶo nonoır moır
ocur noırrꝺıꝺ naꞗbaıl a tıƶh Bríaın Mıc 'Dıarmaꝺu, ꝺo
rıll re tar aır ꝺoꞇum [a] aıtte reın. Toırrꞗeaɫbach
mac an aba Meƶ Urꝺır ꝺo marbaꝺ le Maƶ Maꞇ-
ƶamna. Uıllıam mꝼc ın barun Uınnrenn ꝺo teacht
ƶo hErınn tarer a ruaır re ꝺaıro ar reꝺ an ꝺomaın
raır, ar raƶhaıl a rairꝺın ꝺo on mbanrıƶan. Clann
báıter raꝺa a Bure ꝺo ƶabaıl ꝺon ƶıınꞗernoır co nem-
maıch, ocur a ccur ro ıernach co baıle atha Luaın.

Saxon band was slain in the Ruta, by the Clann-Domhnaill of Alba ; and they took Dun-Lipsi[1] from the Saxons, and killed all who were there.

The kalends of January on Friday ; and the age of the Lord at this time is one thousand, five hundred, and eighty-five years. The son of Tadhg O'Ruairc, i.e., Brian, and some of the Clann-Sithigh whom he had retained, went on a foray against Mag [F]lannchaidh ; and they captured great preys, on Stephen's festival. Mag [F]lannchaidh, and the son of O'Ruairc, i.e., Tighernan,[2] son of Brian O'Ruairc, overtook them ; and they attacked each other ; and Maghnus Og Mac Dubhain was killed in the beginning of that attack.[3] The men of Breifne and Dartrai came up with them after that, and attacked the band ; and a victory was gained over the son of Tadhg O'Ruairc, and over his people ; and Eoghan Mac Sithigh, son of Toirdhelbhach, son of Edmond Mac Sithigh, was killed, and two score along with him, on that field. The son of Tadhg O'Ruairc, and Maghnus Og O'Curnin, were captured, and placed in irons on Loch-na-cula; and the sons of Tighernan wickedly slew them. And on Magh-Oilches this defeat was given. The governor, i.e., the lord of Connacht, with two boats' crews, came from the town of Ath-Luain to Carraig-Mic-Diarmada. The night before[4] the twelfth day, *spent* with great honour and excessive enjoyment in Brian Mac Diarmada's house, he returned back to his own place. Toirdhelbhach Mac-an-aba Mag Uidhir was killed by Mac Mathghamhna. William, son of the Baron Nugent, came to Erinn,[5] after all the hardship he encountered throughout the world eastwards, on receiving a pardon from the queen. The sons of Walter Fada Burk were wickedly taken prisoners by the governor, and sent in irons to the town of Ath-Luain. Gormlaith

A.D.

[1584.]

[1585.]

some words. But the entry is still sufficiently intelligible.

[5] *Erinn.* The remaining entries for this year, with the exception of those

indicated in note [1], p. 468, are written in the same hand as that in which the events for 1584 are written.

ȝαɼmluιɓ ιnȝen ɓɼιαιn mιc Θoȝαιn Uι Ruαιɼc ꝺeȝ
cαoιcɓιȝιɼ ɼe mbelltuιne ; ocuɼ ꝺo buꝺ ꝺo bαιnéchtuιɓ
mαιcɮ Θɼenn ꝺι. Cɼechα moɼα ꝺo ꝺenαɱ αɼ CClbαn-
chαιb ιɼnα ȝlιnnιɓ le Sαxαnchαιb. Roιɼι ιnȝen 1 Neιll
ꝺéȝ .ι. ιn ɓen ꝺo bι αȝ Conn mαc ιn cαlbαιȝ Uι ꝺomnαιll.
ꝺomnαll ȝoɼm, mαc ꝺomnαιll bαllαιȝ meȝ ꝺomnαιll,
ꝺo mαɼbαꝺ ιɼ nα ȝlιnnιb le Comáɼɼ Uꝺιɼ ; cαιɼꝺιn
Sαxαnαch αn Comáɼɼ ɼιn. CClbαnoιȝ ꝺo αɮɮuɼ α
hΘɼιnn ꝺo Sαxαnchαιɓ. Fιɼ Θɼenn uιle, ꝺo neoch ꝺoɓ
ιnαιɼιɱ ꝺιb, ꝺo ꝺol ȝo bαιle CCthα clιαth ꝺocum αctα
ραιɼlιmιnc. Mαc Uí Mαoιlmuαιꝺ, ocuɼ Θmαnn ꝺoɼchα
mαc ꝺomnαιll mιc Muɼchαꝺα mιc 8uιɓne, ocuɼ ꝺαoιne
ιnꝺα oιle, ꝺo cɼochαꝺ αɼ αn αctα ραιɼlιmιnc ɼιn.
Mαιche Θɼenn ꝺo ɮeαcht ɼlán on comαιɼle ɼιn CCthα
clιαc ȝαn cαɼbα. ɓelȝι Θɼenn ꝺo ɼeιɓιoȝαꝺ, ꝺo neoch
bα ꝺαιnȝen ꝺιb, le Sαxαnchαιb. ꝺoeιɼɼíɼ moɼ ꝺo cuɼ
αɼ Connαchtuιb ꝺo Sαxαnchuιb .ι. uιnȝι ꝺóɼ ɼα ceɮɼαm-
αιn ιcιɼ cιll ocuɼ thuαιtl, ocuɼ cιȝeɼnuɼ ȝαch uιle
cιȝeɼnα ȝαιꝺeαlαch ꝺιɼɼleȝhαꝺ ꝺoιb. 8eαn nα Muαιꝺι
.ι. cιȝeɼnα ɮlαιnnι mιc nΘoȝαιn, ɼeɼ oιnιȝ ocuɼ cιȝι
nαoιɓeɓ co moɼ, ꝺo éȝ. Comáɼɼ mαc ɓαιceɼ Huιnn-
ɼenn o cιȝ Munnα ꝺeȝ. Conn mαc CCιɼc oιȝ mιc Neιll
Conαllαιȝ Uι Neιll ꝺo mαɼbαꝺ le hCCoꝺ mαc Concon-
nαcht Meȝ Uιꝺιɼ .ι. mαc Meȝ Uιꝺιɼ. Felιm ꝺub mαc
Neιll mιc Cuιnn ꝺo mαɼbαꝺ le 8eαn mαc Meȝ Uιꝺιɼ.
1αɼlα Cιlle ꝺαɼα, .ι. Ȝeɼoιꝺ oȝ mαc Ȝeɼoιꝺ mιc Ȝeɼoιꝺ,
ꝺéȝ α Sαxαnαιɓ. ꝺomnαll óȝ mαc ꝺuιɓɼιche ꝺo mαɼbαꝺ α nꝺαɼcɼαιɓe Meȝ Flαnnchαιɓ le cecheɼnn cιȝι
nα bαnɼιȝhαn. Flιuchαꝺ αɼ ɼeɓ nα blιαꝺnα ɼα. Mαc
Uιllιαm ɓuɼc ꝺeȝ .ι. Rιꝺeɼꝺ mαc Oιlueɼuɼ. CCncuιɼbια

---

1 *Udis;* i.e., Wodehouse.

2 *Act of Parliament.* The chronicler meant a "Session" of Parliament,
holden by Sir John Perrot.

3 *An ounce of gold.* The rent re-
served to the crown, by the composi-

tions entered into between Sir John
Perrot and the chieftains of Connacht,
was 10*s.* annually out of every quarter
of land. See Hardiman's ed. of O'Flaherty's *Iar Connacht*, App., p. 299, sq.

4 *Shane-na-Muaidhe.* "John of the

daughter of Brian, son of Eoghan O'Ruairc, died a fortnight before May-day; and she was one of the best lamented women of Erinn. Great depredations were committed upon Albanachs, in the Glenns, by Saxons. Rose, daughter of O'Neill, died—i.e., the wife of Conn, son of the Calbhagh O'Domhnaill. Domhnall Gorm, the son of Domhnall Ballagh MacDomhnaill, was killed in the Glenns by Thomas Udis[1]: (this Thomas was a Saxon captain). Albanachs were expelled from Erinn by Saxons. The men of all Erinn—such of them as were of any account—went to Baile-atha-cliath to an Act of Parliament.[2] The son of O'Maelmhuaidh, and Edmond Dorcha, son of Domhnall, son of Murchadh Mac Suibhne, and several other persons, were hanged at this Act of Parliament.[2] The nobles of Erinn came safely from that Council of Ath-cliath, without profit. The passes of Erinn—such of them as were secure—were levelled by Saxons. A great tribute was imposed on Connacht by Saxons, i.e., an ounce of gold[3] on every quarter, both ecclesiastical and lay; and the sovereignty of each Gaeidhelic lord was lowered by them. Shane-na-Muaidhe,[4] i.e. the lord of Clann-mic-nEoghain, a man of great hospitality, and much celebrated for keeping a guest house, died. Thomas, son of Walter Nugent, from Tech-Munna, died. Conn, son of Art Og, son of Niall Conallagh O'Neill, was killed by Aedh, son of Cuconnacht Mag Uidhir, i.e., the son of the Mag Uidhir. Felim Dubh, son of Niall, son of Conn,[5] was killed by John, the son of Mag Uidhir. The Earl of Cill-dara, i.e. Garrett Og, son of Garrett, son of Garrett, died in Saxon-land. Domhnall Og Mac Duibhsithe was killed in Dartraighe-Mic-Flannchaidh, by the kerne of the queen's house. Wet weather during all this year. Mac William Burk[6] died, i.e. Richard,

---

Muaidh (or river Moy)". One of the O'Kellys of Hy-Many.

[5] Conn; i.e. Conn O'Neill.

[6] Mac William Burk. He was Mac William Iochtar, or the Lower; i.e., the northern Mac William.

ꝺαꝛ comαɩɲm Ɑɲbuɩꝛꝺ α pleɲꝺꝛuꞃ ꝺo ᵹαbαɩɫ ɫe cɩɲᵹ
ꞅɩɫɩꝺ .ɩ. ɫe ꝛɩᵹ ɲα 8pαɩɲe, αꝛ pɫémeɲɲcαɩꝺ ocuꞃ αꝛ
8αxαɲcαɩꝺ, ocuꞃ ɩmαꝛcαꝺ ꝺoeɲe ꝺo mαꝛbαꝺ ɩɩɲcɩ.
Ꝋ ɦɑɩɲɫɩꝺe ꝺαꝛαb comαɩɲm Ꞇαꝺᵹ bαɫɫαcɦ ꝺeᵹ. Cɫe-
meɲꞃ mαc 8emuɩꞃ 8ᵹeꝛαɩꞇ ꝺeᵹ; uαꝛꝺɩαɲ ɲα Ᵹαɩɫɫue.
1αꝛɫα óᵹ Cɦɩɫɫe ꝺαꝛα ꝺo ꞇoɩꞅeαcɦꞇ α ɲƐɩꝛɩɲɲ, .ɩ. ɦαɲɲꝛɩ
ɲα ꞇuαcɦ mαc Ᵹeꝛoɩꝺ mɩc Ᵹeꝛoɩꝺ mɩc Ᵹeꝛoɩꝺ, ꞅα čuɱ-
αcɦꞇα moꝛα oɲ mbαɲꝛɩᵹαɩɲ, ocuꞃ bαꝛuɲ Ꝺeαɫꞃɲα ꝺo
ꞇeαcɦꞇ mαꝛαoɲ ꝛɩꞃ, ocuꞃ cuɱαcɦꞇα α ꝺuꞇαɩꝺe ꞅeɩɲ
ɫeɩꞃ; ocuꞃ ɩɲꞇ 1αꝛɫα óᵹ ꞃɩɲ ꝺo čαbαɩꝛꞇ čuɩꝛꝛ α αčαꝛ ɫαɩꞃ
ocuꞃ α ꝺeꝛbꝛαꞇαꝛ ꝺocum Ɛɩꝛeɩɲɲ, ocuꞃ α ɲαꝺɫocαꝺ ꞅα
ꝺɩꝺɩɲ Ꝺe ocuꞃ ꝺꝛɩꝺe α Cɩɫɫ ꝺαꝛα. Muꝛcαꝺ mαc 1
Ceɩɲɲeɩꝺ[ɩᵹ] ꝺɦec. ꞅɩɲꝺꞇαɲ mαc 1ɫɫαɩɲꝺ mɩc Ꝺubꞇαɩᵹ
1 Mɦαoɩɫcoɲαɩꝛe, .ɩ. αꝺbαꝛ oɫɫumαɲ čꞃɩoɫ Muɩꝛeꝺαɩᵹ,
ꝺɦec. Ɑɫαꝛꞇαꝛ mαc 8omαɩꝛɫe buɩꝺe ɱeᵹ Ꝺoɱɲαɩɫɫ
ꝺo mαꝛbαꝺ ꝛe 8αᵹꝛαɲαɩꝺ, ocuꞃ ꝛɩcɦeꝺ ꝺα muɩɲꞇɩꝛ
ꞅαꝛɩꞃ; ocuꞃ ꝺo ꝛɩᵹuꝺ α ceαɲɲ ᵹo bαɩɫe Ɑčα cɫɩαč.

|ɕꞇ. ꞅoꝛ 8αꞇαꝛɲɲ; αoɩꞃ ɩɲ Ꞇɩᵹeꝛɲαɩ mɩɫe bɫɩαꝺαɲ
ocuꞃ cuɩcc ceꝺ, ocuꞃ ceꞇꝛα ꝛɩcɦeꝺ ocuꞃ ꝛe bɫɩαꝺɲα.
ꝺꝛɩeɲ mαc Ceɩɲ Uí Ɛᵹꝛα ꝺo čuꝛ ꝺočum bαɩꝛꞃ α ɲᵹαɩɫ-
ɫɩɱ αꝛ ꞅuɫαɩꝛɩm ꞇɩᵹeꝛɲα cuɩᵹɩꝺ Coɲɲαcɦꞇ, .ɩ. Rɩꞃꝺeꝛꝺ
ꝺɩɲᵹɩem; ocuꞃ ꞅα moꝛ ɩɲꞇ écɦꞇ αɲ mαc ꞃɩɲ Ceɩɲ Uí
Ɛᵹꝛα α ɫeč uαɩꝛɫe ocuꞃ oɩɲɩᵹɦ. Ꞇomαꞃꞃ ꝛuαꝺ, mαc
Rɩocαɩꝛꝺ mɩc 8eαɩɲ ɩɲ ꞇeꝛmuɩɲɲ, ꝺo mαꝛbαꝺ αꞅꞅeαɫɫ
ꝺo 8αxαɲcαɩꝺ, ocuꞃ ꞅα moꝛ ɩɲꞇ écɦꞇ ɩɲ mαc ꞃɩɲ mɩc
Uɩɫɫɩαm. Mαc mɩc Ᵹoɩꝛꝺeɫb, .ɩ. Uɩɫɫɩem mαc ꝺɩeꝛαꝛꞃα,
ꝺo cꝛocαꝺ ɫe ꝛɩꝛꝛɩem coɲꝺαe Roꝛꝛα Commαɩɲ, αꝛ
ꝺumα ɲα Róɱαɲαcɦ. Mαc Mαᵹɲuꝛα ꞇɩꝛɩ Ꞇuαꞇαɩɫ
ꝺo cꝛocαꝺ ɫeꝛɩɲ ꝛɩꝛꝛɩem ceꝺɲα; Ꞇoɩꝛꝛꝺeɫbαcɦ buɩꝺɩ
α comαɩɲm, ocuꞃ αꝛ Cꝛuαcαɲ ꝺo cꝛocαꝺ é; ocuꞃ ɲíꝛ.
ꞅecαꝺ ꝺoɲ ꝛαꝛꝺúɲ ꝺo bɩ αɩᵹɩ ꝺó; ocuꞃ αɲ ꞇꝛeꝛꝛ ɫá ꝺo

---

1 *Henry-na-tuadh*; i.e., Henry of
the [battle-]axes. This entry, and
the remaining ones for this year, are in
the handwriting of Brian Mac Dermot.

2 *Brother*; i.e., Gerald, Lord Offaly,
eldest son of Gerald, eleventh Earl of
Kildare.

3 *Of God.* Ꝺɩα, Clar. The proper genit. form has been substituted.

4 *Died.* ꝺ, for ꝺɦec or ꝺo ɦec,
Clar.

5 *Mac Domhnuill.* ɱeᵹ Coɱɲαɩɫɫ
(which is a mistake for ɱeᵹ Ꝺoɱɲαɩɫɫ), Clar.

ɩ

son of Oliver. The city which is called Antwerp, in Flanders, was taken by king Philip, i.e. the king of Spain, from the Flemings and Saxons ; and a great number of men were slain in it. O'hAinlidhe, whose name was Tadhg Ballagh, died. Clemens, son of James Skerritt, died; .i.e., the warden of the Gaillimh. The young Earl of Cill-dara, i.e., Henry-na-tuadh,[1] the son of Garrett, son of Garrett, son of Garrett, came to Erinn with great powers from the queen ; and the Baron of Delbhna came with him, having the supremacy of his own country. And this young Earl brought the bodies of his father and brother[2] with him to Erinn ; and they were interred under the protection of God[3] and Brigid, in Cill-dara. Murchadh, son of O'Ceinned[igh], died. Fintan, son of Illann, son of Dubhthach O'Maelconaire, i.e., intended ollave of Sil-Muiredhaigh, died.[4] Alaster, son of Somhairle Buidhe MacDomhnaill,[5] was killed by the Saxons, and twenty of his people along with him ; and his head was taken to Baile-atha-cliath.

The kalends on Saturday ; the age of the Lord one thousand, five hundred, and eighty-six years. Brian, son of Cian O'hEghra, was put to death in Gaillimh, at the command[6] of the governor of the province of Connacht, i.e., Richard Bingham ; and that son of Cian O'hEghra was greatly lamented in respect of nobility and hospitality. Thomas Ruadh, the son of Rickard, son of Shane-in-termuinn,[7] was killed in treachery by Saxons ; and that son of Mac William was greatly lamented. The son of Mac Goisdelbh, i.e., William, son of Piers, was hanged by the sheriff of the county of Ros-Comain, on Dumha-na-Romhanach. Mac Maghnusa of Tir-Tuathail was hanged by the same sheriff: (his name was Toirdhelbhach Buidhe; and on Cruachan he was hanged ; and the pardon which he[8] had for him was not regarded ; and the third day of

---

[6] *Command.* ꝑuꝉaιꝑιm, for ꝑuꝃ-aιꝉeιn, Clar.

[7] *Shane-in-termuinn.* John of the Termon, i.e., of the Termon of Balla.

in Mayo. He was one of the Burks of Lower Connacht.

[8] *He;* i.e., the sheriff, whose name was Richard Mapother.

Mαρτα το ριnneᵬ αn ʒnim ρin. Cluαin Ꝺubαin το
ʒαbαil τon ʒuбеρnoiρ, ocuρ Mαᵹʒαmαin mαc αn еρbuιcc
Uι Ꝺριαin, ocuρ [α] bαρτα-uιle, το cuρ τocum bαiρρ αnn,
ocuρ αn bαιle το bρiρеᵬ; ocuρ ρα moρ inτ echτ ρin το
τoeb uαιρle ocuρ oinιʒh.·· Siρuιle inʒen mιc Ꝺαbι τeʒ;
ocuρ το buτ moρ in ρʒel ρin. Oιlueρuρ mαc Sеαin mιc
Ꝺαᵬí báin α Ꝺuρc, ocuρ Toмαρρ mαc Ꝺαbι bαin, το
cρochατ lеiρin nʒuιбеρnoiρ. Ccn ʒuιбеρnoiρ το τol
ρluαᵹ τiαρṁe ατimchell Cαιρlen nα cαιllιᵹi, ocuρ cuιτ
το ρlιchτ Uιlleʒ α Ꝺuρc ocuρ το ρlιchτ Emuιnn α Ꝺuρc
το bеᵬ iρin cαιρlen, ocuρ αn ʒuιбеρnoiρ τinnρoιʒeτ áн
bαιle luchτ α το no α τρι το báτuιb; ocuρ το cuιρeταρ
τocum in bαιle, ocuρ το mαρbατ τα xxет το muιnnτιρ
in ʒuιбеρnoiρ, ocuρ το hobρατ é ρein τρáʒbáιl; ocuρ
το imᵬeτταρ nα bαρτα nα τiαιᵬ ρin, ocuρ nι τeρnαᵬ
τíʒᵬαιl τoιb. O hCCiρτ ·ı. Ꝼelim mαc Uιllιαm Uι CCiρτ
τeʒ αιτʒι cαρʒ, ocuρ α ατnαccατ α Slιʒeᵬ τiα Luαin.
Ꞃicαρτ oʒ, mαc Ꞃicαιρτ mιc Sеαin αn τeρmuιnn; το
cρochατ τon ʒuιбеρnoiρ iρin cρich, ocuρ ρα huαραl
τoennαchταch τeʒoιnιᵹ in ρeρ ρin, τρι hoιτᵬe ρᵬ ʒcαιρʒ.
Ꝺα mαc Ꝺαιτeρ ρατα α Ꝺuρc, ·ı. Mαoιlιρ ocuρ Teboιτ,
το cρochατ τon ʒuιбеρnoiρ α ρoρρ Commαin αρ mbеᵬ
bliαταin α lαiṁ τoιb, ocuρ α nαᵬnαcατ α ρoιlιʒ Tem-
puιll αn αιᵹnéιn ιτιρ cαιρʒ ocuρ belltuιne; ocuρ το
bαταρ ρin αρ échτuιᵬ moρα Eρenn το Ꝃαlloιb αρ en
αιmριρ ρiú. Mαc Uí Ꝺoṁnαιll, ·ı. Mαʒnuρ oʒ mαc
Mαʒnuρα Uι Ꝺoṁnαιll, το mαρbατ le cuιτ το ρlιchτ
Ꝺonnchατα Uι Ꝃαllᵬubαιρ. Mαc Suιbne bαᵹαnαᵬ, ·ı.
Ꝺριαn bαcαch, το mαρbατ le nα bραιτριb ρein. Ꝃiuιρτιρ
mαιth τobι ρατα ρoρ Eρinn τeʒ α Sαxαnαιᵬ ·ı. hαnρι
Siτnιe. Coʒαᵬ moρ ιτιρ cinʒ Ꝑιlιb ρι nα Spαinne ocuρ

1 _Governor._ Sir Richard Bingham.

2 _Bishop O'Briain._ This was Toirdhelbhach (or, as Ware writes it,
Terence) O'Brien, bishop of Killaloe,
whose death is entered in the Annals of
the Four Masters, under the year 1569.

3 _Rickard Og._ "Rickard the Young;"
commonly called _Fal fo Erinn,_ or the
"hedge of Erinn." See the _Miscellany
of the Celtic Society,_ pp. 195–6, where
he is called the "Pall" (and also the
"Perall") of Ireland.

the month of March this deed was committed.) Cluain-Dubhain was taken by the governor;[1] and Mathgamhain, son of the Bishop O'Briain,[2] and all the warders, were put to death there; and the place was demolished. And that was a great loss in respect of nobility and hospitality. Cecilia, daughter of Mac David, died; and that was a great calamity. Oliver, son of John, son of David Bán Burk, and Thomas, son of David Bán, were hanged by the governor. The governor went with a numerous army about Caislen-na-caillighe; and some of the posterity of Ulick Burk, and of the posterity of Edmond Burk, were in the castle; and the governor advanced towards the place with a force of two or three boats. And they attacked the place; and forty of the governor's people were slain; and he himself was nearly lost there. And the warders subsequently departed; and no harm was done to them. O'hAirt, i.e., Felim, the son of William O'hAirt, died on Easter night, and was buried in Sligech on Monday. Rickard Og,[3] son of Rickard, son of Shane-in-termuinn,[4] was hanged by the governor, in the district, three nights before Easter: and he was a noble, humane, most hospitable man. The two sons of Walter Fada Burk, viz., Meiler and Tibbot, were hanged by the governor in Ros-Comain, after having been a year in confinement; and they were interred in the cemetery of Tempul-an-aighnéin between Easter and May-day. And those were amongst the most lamented of the Foreigners of Erinn in their time. The son of O'Domhnaill, i.e., Maghnus Og, the son of Maghnus O'Domhnaill, was killed by some of the posterity of Donnchadh O'Gallchubhair. Mac Suibhne Baghanach, i.e., Brian Bacach,[5] was killed by his own kinsmen. A good Justiciary who was a long time over Erinn died in Saxon-land, i.e., Henry Sidney. A great war between king Philip, king of Spain, and the

---

[4] *Shane-in-termuinn.* See note [7], page 469.

[5] *Brian Bacach;* i.e. Brian the Lame.

ρριηηρα Saxanač .ı. Eλıroabéτ, ρα Plóηoρuρ. O hEτρα
ρıabach .ı. Ρερ̃al caρρach oeσ. O Ruaηaoa .ı. Seaη,
ηo Cαonξuρ, mac Ruaıoρı oıξ, oo maρbαo le Seaη
mac Uı Cαnluaıη. Cαn ξuıbeρηoıρ ocuρ ıaρla claıηηı
Rıcaıρo, ocuρ ıaρla Ζuaomuman, ocuρ ρluaξa moρa
maılle ρıu, ocuρ ρoρloηξρoρτ oo oeηam ıρıη Ζόčaıρ
ocuρ a mbaıle ıη Rooba ooıb, ocuρ oo cρόčaταρ τρuıρ
leηab oo bı a laım acu ρeıη ρe ρaoa ρoıme ρıη .ı. mάč
an abao caoıch, ocuρ mac Maoılıρ mıc baıτeρ ρaoa,
ocuρ mac Seaıη a buρc, a Roρρ moρ; ocuρ oo buo τρuaıξ
ıη ξηım ρıη cρochao ηa leηab ηeımčıηταč. Ocuρ Eoξaη
mac Oomηaıll an coξaıo Uı Plaıčbeρταıξ oo maρbao
ρeρ oolum, ocuρ moράη oa muıηητıρ oo cρochao ocuρ
oo maρbao ooıb; ocuρ τuξαταρ an ρluaξ oo ρoıηηe ηα
ξηıma ρıη τρı mıle bo ρıú, ocuρ oo cρechaταρ Cıaρρaıoe
co huılıoı. Claηη τ8emuıρ meξ Oomηaıll oo τeachτ
a ηEρıηη, mıle co leč Cαlbaηach, ocuρ oo mılleταρ
moρaη a ηUılltoıb; ocuρ τeachτ ooıb co cıll Roηaıη a
cρıch Coηηachτ, ocuρ oo baoaρ cőıce oıξče ıηητe, ocuρ
oo bı ıη ξuıbeρηóıρ a mbél ıη άča ρaoa, ρluaξ oıάıρımh
oo maıčb Coηηachτ ocuρ oo Saxaηčuıb ηa ρochaıρ.
Ocuρ oo čuıρeoaρ Cαlbaηuıξ ρcıač ταρ loρcc oρča
oocum Cuılmıuıηe, ocuρ ταηξaoaρ cuıo oo cloıηη
Uıllıem ηa ξcoıηηe; ocuρ oo ıoηρaıξeoaρ oρočao ıη
čıllıη¹; ocuρ o ρo cualaoaρ Saxaηuıb Cαlbaηuıb oo oul
ταρρa ρíoρ oo leηaoaρ ıeo, ocuρ oo buaıleb ρa ceıle
ıao aξ oρočao ıη cıllıη, ocuρ τucaoaρ ταčaρ τeηo oa
čéıle aηη, ocuρ oo maρbao a cúıξ ηo ρé oeachaıb an
ξoıbeρηóρa, ocuρ oo ımoeoaρ Cαlbaηuıb ξaη oıbáıl
oocum Sléıbe oam, ocuρ ρucaoaρ cρech leo ξu Cαρo ηα
ρıα. Oála ıη ξuıbeρηoρa, oo loηηuıoeb ocuρ oo
láıηρeρ̃uıoeb leıρρ ρa Cαlbaηcuıb oımoechτ uao, ocuρ
oo léıξρo aρaıbı aξa oeıρξe amach . ξaoıoheluıb uao,
ocuρ oo ρıll ρé ρuaρρ oocum an caıρleıη móıρ; ocuρ

¹*Droiched-in-chillin*; i.e. "the bridge
of the little *kill* (or church)". This
appears to have been the name of a
bridge over the river Owenmore, at
Cul-mhaine, or Collooney, barony of
Tirerrill, co. Sligo.

ԇ

prince of the Saxons, i.e., Elizabeth, regarding Flanders. O'hEghra Riabhach, i.e., Ferghal Carragh, died. O'Ruanadha, i.e., John (or Aenghus), son of Ruaidhri Og, was killed by John, the son of O'hAnluain. The governor, and the Earl of Clann-Rickard, and the Earl of Tuadh-Mumha, accompanied by large armies, established a camp in the Tochar, and in Baile-in-Rodba; and they hanged three children in Ross-mor, whom they themselves had in their hands for a long time before that, viz., the son of the Blind Abbot, and the son of Meiler, son of Walter Fada, and the son of John Burk : and that was a pitiful deed—the hanging of the innocent children. And they killed Eoghan, the son of Domhnall-an-chogaidh O'Flaithbhertaigh, per dolum, and killed and hanged several of his people. And the army that committed those deeds brought three thousand cows with them, and entirely plundered Ciarraidhe. The sons of James Mac Domhnaill came to Erinn, *with* fifteen hundred Albanachs; and they destroyed much in Uladh. And they went to Cill-Ronain in the territory of Connacht, and were five nights in it; and the governor was at Bel-an-atha-fada, a numerous host of the chieftains of Connacht, and of Saxons, being with him. And the Albanachs retreated to Cul-mhaine; and some of the Clann-William came to meet them; and they advanced to Droiched-in-chillín.[1] And when the Saxons heard that the Albanachs had gone past them down, they followed them; and they encountered one another at Droiched-in-chillín, and delivered a vigorous battle to each other there; and five or six of the governor's horses were killed; and the Albanachs departed uninjured to Sliabh-damh, and carried a prey with them to Ard-na-riadh. As regards the governor, he was rendered furious and fully angry at the escape of the Albanachs from him, and he permitted all the "rising out" of the Gaeidhil that he had to depart, and returned southwards towards the Caislén-mór.[2] And two Saxon

---

[2] *Caislén-mór;* "the great castle," i.e. Castlemore-Costello.

ρucαδαρ αιρ αηηριη δα bαηηα Shαxαηαch cαηιιιc on
Illumαιη, ocuρ δο bι ρε αηηριη ρεαchc mbαηηα δοη
αρmáιl δοb ρερρ αρ bιch ; ocuρ ρο Len ιεδ ζu huαραl
αρραchcα áηccρεηcα co ραιηιc Ccρδ na ρια. Ocuρ ιη
ιιαιρ δο conncαδαρ Cclbαηιιιδ čuca ιαδ δο ειρζιοδαρ
αmαch αραn mbαιlι α ζcοιηηε ocuρ α ζcοmδáιl na ηζαll,
ocuρ cucαδαρ ρραρα διαηα διρζαιρε δα ηαρmαιb
διοbραιcι αηαζhαιδ na ηζαll, ocuρ δο δí δο δοηuρ αρ
Cclbαηcuιδ ηαρ Loιcεδαρ διιηε na each δοη ρραρ ριη,
ocuρ ζuρ ζαbαδαρ ραοη mαδmα ocuρ cειčmε δοcum na
Illuαιδι, ocuρ ζuρ mαρbαδ ocuρ ζuρ báchαδ .xx. cεδ no
αmρlιuρ. Ծο mαρbαδ αηη δα mαc Sémαιρ mιcc
Ծοmηαιll .ι. Ծomnαll ζορm ocuρ Cclυρδαρ, ocuρ δο
mαρbαδ αηη ζιοllα ερbιιc mαc Ծubζαιll mιc Ծοηηchαιδ čαιm mιc Ccιlín, ocuρ δο mαρbαδ εmαηη cíocαραč
mαc Ծαιbí báιn α ύúρc, ocuρ Cαčαοιρ mαc Ծοmnαιll
mιc Ծοηηcαιδ ρuαιδ Illεζ Ծοmnαιll, ocuρ mοράη οιlε
nαch ρέδmuιδ δαιρεm αρ α méδ ; ocuρ α ηCcρδ na ρια
cucαδ αηc áρ ριη ρεαchcmuιη ρε bρειl Illιčεοιl. Ocuρ
cucαδ cαch α bρlόηδρuρ an lá ριη εcιρ cιηζ ριlιρ
ocuρ bαηριζαη Sαxαn. ριlιρ mαc ριρ hCcnριζ δο
mαρbαδ αηδρα cαch ριη, ocuρ mοραη ειlε. Sρuč na
Sιοηηα δο ριllεαδ cαραιρ δοčum Loča ριζ, ocuρ α
δειč cειčρε huαιρε ριchεδ αρ an ορδuδ ριη α ριαδnuιρε
αροιδε an αč Luαιη uιlε. Ծροιčεδ ύhαιlε αρρα δαρα
δο čριčnu[ζα]δ Le O Cončubαιρ Slιζιζ. Illuιρζερ mαc
Illuιρcερcαιζ mιc Ծοηηchαιδ δhεc. In ζζορlοζαč
δhεc. Ccoδ mαc εοζαιη mιc Shuιδηε .ι. conραbαl
cLοιηδε Rιcαιρc δhεc, ocuρ buδ mορ ιηc εαčc ριη.
ύριαη bραchαch mαc Illιc Ծοηηchαιδ ιη Choραιηη
δhεc αρ ιη Illαιζιιι. Cοmαρ mαc ι ρLοιηδ δο cροcαδ
α Rορα Chomαιη δα lα ρια. ρειl Cαchcριηα. Illαc

---

1 *The.* nα; repeated in Clar.

² *Son of Domhnall.* Illαc Conαιll,
"son of Conall," Clar. But this is a
mistake, arising from the aspiration

of the first letter of the name "Domhnaill," which is hardly sounded in the
pronunciation of the name, and the
attraction over of the c of *Mac.*

companies that came from Mumha overtook him there; and he had then seven companies of the best army in the world ; and he followed them nobly, valiantly, vigorously, until he reached Ard-na-riadh. And when the Albanachs saw them approaching they advanced from the town to meet and encounter the Foreigners, and discharged vehement, furious, showers from their firearms against the[1] Foreigners ; and such was the misfortune of the Albanachs, that they wounded neither man nor horse with that discharge, and that they commenced a movement of rout and flight towards the Muaidh, and that twenty hundred, or more, were killed and drowned. James Mac Domhnaill's two sons were killed there, viz., Domhnall Gorm and Alaster ; and Gilla-espuig, son of Dubhghall, son of Donnchadh Cam MacAilin, was slain there ; and Edmond Kiocarach, son of David Bán Burk, and Cathair, son of Domhnall,[2] son of Donnchadh Ruadh Mac Domhnaill, were slain there, and many more whom we cannot reckon, from their number. And in Ard-na-riadh this slaughter was given, a week before the festival of Michael. And a battle was fought in Flanders on that day,[3] between king Philip and the queen of the Saxons. Philip, the son of Sir Henry, was slain in that battle, and several others. The stream of the Sionainn turned back to Loch-Righ ; and it was twenty-four hours in that order, in the presence[4] of all who were in Ath-Luain. The bridge of Baile-esa-dara was finished by O'Conchobhair Sligigh. Maurice, the son of Muirchertach Mac Donnchaidh, died. The Scurlock died. Aedh, the son of Eoghan Mac Suibhne, i.e., the constable of Clann-Rickard, died ; and that was a great calamity. Brian Brathach,[5] son of Mac Donnchaidh of the Corann, died on the Maighin. Thomas, son of O'Floinn, was hanged in Ros-Comain, two days before the festival of Catherine. Mac Diarmada Ruadh

[2] *Day.* The next eight entries are in the handwriting of Brian Mac Dermot.

[4] *In the presence.* α ꝥ⁊ᴜᴉꝛᴇ, Clar.
[5] *Brathach ;* i.e., treacherous. ᴣꝛᴀᴄh, Clar.

Ⴑιαρмαⴇα ⴐυαⴆ ⴆhec .ι. Ⴑⴐⴐⴁαl mac Conchobaⴐ óⴆ
meic Muⴐⴐⴐⴀⴐⴇⴐⴇⴐ. Ⴄⴅⴅⴅⴅ Ⴅⴅⴅⴅ

Ⴄⴆⴕⴀⴈ Ⴇⴅⴅⴅⴅⴅⴅⴅⴅⴅ, αⴈ ⴅⴅⴅⴅ ⴐⴐ ⴐⴐⴐⴐ
ⴆⴆ ⴆⴐ α ⴈⴄⴐⴐⴈⴈ, ⴆⴄⴅ. ⴐⴀⴐⴅⴀ ⴐ ⴅⴅⴅⴅⴐ ⴆⴐ ⴆⴅⴅ ⴐⴅⴅⴅⴆⴆ
ⴆⴐⴀⴐⴐⴐ ⴆⴐ ⴅⴅⴅⴅⴆⴐⴆ ⴅⴅ ⴑⴅⴅⴅⴅⴈⴈⴅⴐⴐⴅ ⴅⴐ ⴑⴅⴅⴈⴆⴅⴐⴐⴈⴈⴈⴐⴈ.
Rι ⴈα Ⴑⴕⴀⴐⴈⴈⴄ ⴆⴅ ⴆⴅⴈαⴈ αⴐⴈαⴅα αⴈαⴆⴀⴐⴆ ⴈα ⴀⴐⴐⴈ-
ⴈⴈⴈⴀⴈα ⴐⴈⴈ, ⴅⴅⴐⴕ ⴅⴀⴅ ⴆⴅ ⴅⴀⴅⴅ ⴅⴅⴐⴐⴅ, ⴅⴅⴐⴕ ⴈⴐⴈⴈⴅⴆ ⴆⴅ
ⴈⴈⴐⴅⴈ ⴆⴅ ⴅⴅⴅⴅⴈⴈ ⴅⴅⴅⴅⴐⴅⴅ ⴅⴐ ⴆⴅⴅⴈ ⴅⴅⴅⴅ. Ⴈⴅⴅⴐⴈⴅⴆ
mac Uι Ⴈⴈⴈⴈⴅⴐⴆⴐⴆ ⴆⴅ ⴅⴅⴅⴅⴈⴈ ⴅⴅⴐ Ⴍ ⴆⴈⴅⴐⴅⴅⴅⴅⴈ .ι. ⴈⴈ
Ⴈⴅⴅⴅⴅⴀⴈ. Ⴈⴅⴅⴈ ⴅⴈ ⴅⴅⴐⴅⴐ Ⴈⴅⴅⴅ ⴅⴈ ⴐⴐⴅⴅⴅⴈ, .ι. Ⴈⴐⴐⴐⴐ
mac Ⴈⴅⴅⴐⴐⴅⴆⴆ, ⴆⴅ ⴆⴅⴈⴈ ⴆⴅⴆ. Uⴐⴈⴅⴅⴅⴐ Ⴍ Ⴈⴅⴐⴐⴅⴅⴆ, .ι. ⴐⴅⴈ
ⴐⴐⴅⴅⴅⴐⴐ ⴆⴅⴐ ⴐⴅⴐⴐ ⴆⴅ ⴆⴐ α ⴈⴄⴐⴐⴈⴈ ⴆⴅ ⴐⴅⴐⴈⴅⴈⴅⴐⴆⴆ,
ⴆⴐⴀⴆⴐⴀⴐⴅ ⴆⴀⴐⴐ αⴐ αⴈ Ⴈⴅⴅⴅⴈⴈ. Ⴈⴈ ⴆⴅⴅⴅ ⴆⴅ ⴆⴐ α
ⴈUⴅⴅⴅⴐⴐⴆ ⴐⴅ ⴐⴅⴐⴐⴐⴈⴈⴅ ⴆⴐⴀⴆⴅⴐⴅ ⴆⴀⴐⴐ, .ι. Ⴈⴅⴆⴈⴐⴐ mac
Ⴑⴐⴅⴅⴅ. Uⴐⴈⴅⴅⴅⴐ ⴆⴐⴐⴅ mac Ⴄⴈⴅⴐⴈⴈ ⴅ ⴅⴐⴐⴅⴐ ⴅⴈⴅⴐⴈⴈⴅ
ⴐUⴐⴈⴅⴅⴅⴐⴀⴈ ⴆⴅⴆ; ⴅⴐⴆⴐⴐ αⴈ ⴐⴀⴐⴐⴀ ⴐⴐⴅⴐⴆⴐ αⴈⴅ Uⴐⴈⴅⴅⴅⴐⴀ
ⴐⴐⴈ, ⴅⴅⴐⴕ ⴆⴀ ⴈⴅⴐ αⴈⴅ ⴅⴅⴐⴅ ⴐⴐⴈ. Ⴈⴅⴐⴐⴅⴈ ⴈⴅⴐ Ⴈⴅⴅⴅ
ⴆⴈⴅⴐⴆⴅⴅⴐⴐ, ⴅⴅⴐⴕ ⴅⴅⴅⴅ ⴅⴐⴆⴅⴐⴈⴅⴐ ⴐⴈ ⴅⴐⴐⴅ, ⴆⴅ ⴅⴅⴅⴀⴐⴐⴅ
ⴆⴅ Ⴈⴅⴅⴅⴅⴐⴆ Ⴑⴐⴅⴅⴐⴈ ⴆⴅ Ⴈⴅⴅ ⴆⴅⴐⴆⴅⴅⴅⴐ .ι Ⴑⴅⴅⴈ mac ⴐⴈ
ⴆⴐⴅⴅⴅ ⴆⴅⴐⴆ meⴐⴅ ⴐⴅⴐⴆⴅⴐⴆ. Ⴍ ⴆⴅⴆⴐⴅ ⴆⴅ ⴅⴀⴆⴅⴐⴐⴅ ⴅⴅⴐⴆ
ⴈⴆⴅⴐⴅⴅ ⴈα ⴐⴅⴈⴆ, ⴅⴅⴐⴕ ⴅⴅⴐⴐⴅⴈ Ⴑⴅⴐⴐⴅ ⴈⴅⴐⴐ, ⴆⴅⴈ ⴐⴐⴐ
ⴅⴅⴆⴈⴅ. Ⴍⴐⴅⴅⴅⴐⴈ Ⴍ ⴆⴅⴆⴐⴅ ⴅⴅⴆ ⴐⴐⴈ ⴅⴅⴆⴅ.

Ⴈⴅ. ⴐⴅⴐ Ⴑⴅⴐⴐⴈⴅⴅⴈ; αⴅⴐⴐ ⴐⴈ Ⴇⴐⴆⴅⴐⴈⴅ mⴐⴅⴅ ⴆⴅⴐⴅⴆⴅⴈ
ⴅⴅⴐⴕ ⴅⴅⴐⴅⴅ ⴅⴅⴆ, ⴅⴅⴐⴕ ⴅⴅⴅⴐⴅ xxⁱᶜ ⴅⴅⴐⴕ ⴐⴅⴅⴅⴅⴅ mⴆⴅⴐⴅⴆⴈⴅ.
Ⴈⴈ ⴆⴅⴈⴐⴐⴆⴅⴈ Ⴈⴈⴆⴅⴈⴈⴅⴅ ⴆⴅ ⴆⴐ α Ⴑⴅⴐⴈ ⴐⴅ ⴐⴅⴅⴅ ⴐⴅⴐⴈⴅ
ⴐⴐⴈ αⴆ ⴆⴅⴈⴐⴐⴆⴅⴈ ⴅⴑⴅⴅⴅⴈ ⴆⴅ ⴅⴅⴐ ⴆⴅⴅⴅⴈ· ⴆⴅⴐⴐ ⴆⴅⴈ ⴆⴅⴐⴈ-
ⴐⴐⴆⴅⴅⴈ ⴅⴑⴅⴅⴅⴅⴈⴅⴆ, ⴅⴅⴐⴕ ⴐⴐ ⴐⴅⴐⴆⴐ α ⴐⴅⴈⴈ Ⴄⴅⴐⴐⴅ ⴆⴅⴈ
ⴆⴅⴆ ⴆⴐⴅⴆⴅ ⴐⴈⴅⴐ ⴐ. Ⴈⴈⴅ ⴅⴅⴐⴅⴅⴅⴆ Ⴑⴅ ⴆⴅ ⴐⴅⴐⴐⴅ ⴆⴅ
ⴅⴅⴐⴐⴅⴆ ⴆⴅⴅⴅⴈ ⴆⴅⴐⴐ ⴐ. Ⴈⴅⴅⴅ Ⴑⴅⴅⴐⴅⴅⴈⴈ Ⴍ Ⴑⴅⴅⴅⴅⴐⴅⴅ, .ι.
Ⴑⴅⴅⴈ ⴆⴅⴐⴆⴐ, ⴆⴅⴆ. Ⴑⴐⴐ Uⴐⴈⴅⴅⴅⴐ Ⴑⴆⴅⴅⴈⴈⴐⴈ, ⴐⴆⴐⴐⴅ ⴅⴅⴐⴅⴅ
ⴆⴅ ⴅⴅⴐⴐⴅⴆ ⴆⴅⴈⴐⴐⴆⴅⴈ ⴅⴑⴅⴅⴅⴈ ⴐⴅ ⴐⴅⴆⴅⴐⴆ ⴅⴅⴆⴅⴐⴆ ⴅⴅ Ⴑⴅⴅⴈ-
ⴆⴐⴐ, ⴆⴅ ⴆⴅⴅ αⴈⴅⴆⴅⴐⴆ ά ⴐⴐⴈⴈⴐⴐ ⴐⴅⴐⴈ ⴆⴅ ⴅⴅⴈⴆⴈⴅⴅ Ⴑⴅ
ⴐⴐⴆ ⴈⴅ Ⴑⴅⴅⴐⴈⴈⴅ, ⴅⴅⴐⴕ αⴐⴅ Ⴑⴐⴈ ⴆⴅ ⴆⴅⴐⴈⴐⴆ ⴆⴅ ⴅⴅⴅⴅⴐⴆ Ⴑⴅⴐⴐ
ⴐⴅ ⴅⴅⴆ .x. ⴆⴅ Ⴑⴅⴅⴅⴈⴅⴅⴐⴆ, ⴅⴅⴐⴕ ⴆⴄⴐⴐⴅⴈⴈⴅⴐⴆ, ⴅⴅⴐⴕ
ⴆⴈⴅⴅⴅⴐⴈⴅⴐⴆ. Ⴈⴅⴅⴐⴅⴅⴅⴐⴈⴈ mⴅⴅ Ⴈⴅⴅⴐⴐⴐⴅⴅⴈⴅⴆ mⴐⴅ

---

1 *Ultach;* i.e. the Ultonian. His real
name was Donlevy. The remainder
of this entry, and the seven succeeding

entries, are in a different handwriting
from that of Brian Mac Dermot.

2 *The great castle.* Castlemore, or

died, i.e., Ferghal, son of Conchobhar Og, son of Muirchertach. Eoghan Ultach,[1] the best leech that was in Erinn,
died. The Earl of Leicester went to Flanders with a numerous army, to assist the Flemings. The king of Spain
assembled an army against that army ; and a battle was
fought between them, and several thousands fell between
them on each side. Murchadh, the son of O'Ceinnédigh,
fell by O'Cerbhaill, i.e., the Calbhach. Mac-an-bhaird of
Cuil-an-ûrtain, i.e., Maurice, the son of Laisech, died.
William O'Cernaigh, i.e., an old friar, the best preacher
that was in Erinn, died on the Maighin. The blind man
who was prophesying in Ulster, i.e., Maghnus Mac Sithe,
died. William Burk, son of Edmond, from the territory
of Clann-William, died : (this William was the Red Earl's
heir; and he was much lamented). The great castle[2] of
Mac Goisdelbh, and half the lordship of the country,
were given to Tibbot Dillon by Mac Goisdelbh, i.e., John,
son of the Gilla-dubh,[3] son of Hubert. O'Gadhra gave
five towns in his division, and the castle of Daire-mór, to
the same man. (Oilillin O'Gadhra that gave those away.)

The kalends on Sunday ; the age of the Lord one
thousand, five hundred, and eighty-seven years. The
queen of Alba, who had been imprisoned for a long time
previously by the queen of the Saxons, was put to death
by the Saxon queen ; and there was not in any part of
Europe a woman more beautiful than she. The eighth
day of February she was put to death. The son of
Lochlainn O'Lugaill died, i.e., John Buidhe. Sir William
Stanley, an illustrious knight whom the queen of the
Saxons sent to the war to Flanders, went against his own
prince, to aid the king of Spain ; and the number of men
that went with him was 1,600, of Saxons, Irishmen,
and Albanachs. Maelechlainn, the son of Maelruanaidh

Castlemore-Costelloe, co. Mayo. The
remaining entries are in Brian Mac
Dermot's handwriting.

[3] *Gilla-dubh.* This name signifies
"the Black gillie," or " Black fellow."
ᵹαᪿᪿα óuıᵬ, Clar.

Ὀιαρμαὸα mιc Seαιn ὀeᵹ. Ꝃᵹ mορ αρ ceᵵραιb nα
blιαὸnα ᵗα, ocuᵗ ρο ὸιᵵ αρᵬα ιιιnꞇι beoᵗ. ᵬαιꞇeᵗ
ᵗιαbαch mαc Mᵘιᵗιᵗ mιc ᵬαιꞇeᵗ mιc αn 1αᵗlα, ocuᵗ
clαnn ᵬᵗιαιn mιc Cαᵵαoιᵗ mιc Ƈιᵗꞇ mιc Ὀιαρμαὸα
Lαιmὸeᵗᵹ, ὸο ὸol αᵗ cᵗeιch αᵗ boᵗὸ Leᵵlιnne ιn
ὀᵗoιchιὸ, ocuᵗ cᵗech ὸo ὸenαιῆ ὸoιb; ocuᵗ ꞇoιᵗ ὸo
bᵗeιᵵ oᵗᵗα .ι. mαc mαᵗuᵗcαιl αn 1ᵬαιᵗ ocuᵗ αᵗmαιl
mαᵗαon.ᵗιᵗ. ᵬαιꞇeᵗ ᵗιαbαch ocuᵗ α mᵘιnnꞇeᵗ ὀᵗιlleὸ
oᵗᵗα, ocuᵗ mαc αn mαᵗuᵗcαιl ocuᵗ ceꞇᵗαᵗ αᵗ ꭕꭕιꞇ ὸα
mᵘιnnꞇιᵗ ὸo mαᵗbαὸ αᵗ ιn lαᵵαιᵗ ᵗιn; ocuᵗ ᵗα moᵗ
ιnꞇ echꞇ ὸo ꞇoeb ιn mιc ᵗιn αn mαᵗuᵗcαιl. Cαᵵαl
mαc Coιᵗᵗὸelbαᵹ mιc Ὀιαρμαὸα ὸo ᵹαbαιl, ocuᵗ α
bᵗeᵵ co ᵗoᵗ Comαιn ᵗα ὸαoιᵗᵗι. Mαc Ὀonnchαιὸ αn
Coᵗαιnn ὸeᵹ .ι. Ƈoὸ mαc Cαιᵗbᵗι. Ꞃo ὸιᵹbαιl bιὸ αn
Ꝃᵗιnn αn blιαὸαιn ᵗι. Ꝕoᵗꞇ ὸo ὸenαm ὸo cαιᵗὸιn
Ꝣᵗάιιn αᵗ ὸᵗoιcheꞇ mιc Mαonαᵹ, ocuᵗ ᵗoᵗꞇ oιle ὸo
ὸenαm α n'Ὀᵗuιm ὸὸ mαιᵹιᵗꞇιᵗ Leᵹιnn. Mαc ᵁι
Coⱼcenuιnn .ι. Mᵘιᵗᵗceᵗꞇαch mαc Cαᵵαιl ὸeᵹ. Ὀιαᵗ
mαc Ꝃoᵹάιn ᵗᵘαιὸ mιc Coᵗmαιc ὸo cᵗochαὸ α cnoc ιn
bιcαιᵗᵗe le cαιᵗὸιn Ꝣᵗαιὸιn, ocuᵗ le Seoιᵗᵗι mαc Ꝕιꞇαιᵗ
Ꝑᵘιnᵗᵗenn, ᵗeᵗ ὸolum; ocuᵗ αn Ὀubαlꞇαch mαιᵹ
Ꞃιαbαιᵹ ὸo cᵗochαὸ mαᵗ ιn ceὸnα. ᵬᵗιαn bαllαch
mαc αn cαlbαιᵹh mιc Cαιὸᵹ buιὸι ᵁι Concobαιᵗ, ocuᵗ
Ὀunαὸαch mαc Ὀubᵹιιll αᵗ ᵗeᵗιon ὸo cᵗochαὸ α mι
meὸoιn ꞇᵗαmᵗαὸ α ᵗoᵗ Comαιn. Seᵗιon ὸo ὸenαm α
Slιᵹech ὸo Seoιᵗᵗι ᵬιnᵹιαm ocuᵗ ὸon ᵹιuιᵗꞇιᵗ Ὀιlmαιn,
ocuᵗ ὸo mαιᵹιᵗꞇιᵗ Comαᵗꞇun, ocuᵗ connὸαe Slιᵹιᵹ
ὸo ꞇeαchꞇ ὸocum nα comὸαlα ᵗιι, ocuᵗ Ꝑelιm mαc

1 *Walter Riabhach;* i.e., Walter the
Swarthy. A member of the Fitzgerald family, and the son-in-law of
Fiach MacHugh, the active chief of
the O'Byrne sept of Wicklow.

2 *Diarmaid Laimhderg.* Dermot of
the Red Hand, of the family of
Kavanagh, or Mac Murrough. He was
king of Leinster, and died in 1417.

3 *Leithglinn-in-droichid;* "the glen-
side of the bridge;" now Leighlin
Bridge, co. Carlow.

4 *The Ibhar;* i.e., the yew; the old
name of Newry, co. Louth. The
Marshal referred to was Sir Nicholas
Bagenal, whose son was Sir Dudley
Bagenal.

5 *Captain Grain.* Apparently the

Mac Diarmada, the son of John, died. Great mortality amongst the cattle of this year; and there was also great destruction of corn in it. Walter Riabhach,[1] the son of Maurice, son of Walter, son of the Earl, and the sons of Brian, son of Cathair, son of Art, son of Diarmaid Laimhderg,[2] went on a predatory expedition on the borders of Leithglinn-in-droichid,[3] and committed a depredation; and a pursuing band overtook them, viz., the son of the Marshal of the Ibhar,[4] accompanied by an armament. Walter Riabhach and his people turned upon them; and the Marshal's son, and twenty-four of his people, were slain on that field; and great was the woe on account of that son of the Marshal. Cathal, the son of Toirdhelbhach Mac Diarmada, was apprehended, and taken to Ros-Comain in bondage. MacDonnchaidh of the Corann died, i.e., Aedh, the son of Cairbre. Great destruction of food in Erinn this year. A residence was erected by Captain Grain[5] on Droichet-mic-Maenaigh, and another residence in Druim by Master Leighinn. The son of O'Concenainn, i.e., Muirchertach, son of Cathal, died. The two sons of Eoghan Ruadh, son of Cormac, were hanged at Cnoc-in-bicaire by Captain Graidhin,[6] and by George, son of Peter Nugent, per dolum; and the Dubhaltach Mac Riabhaigh was hanged in like manner. Brian Ballagh, son of the Calbhagh, son of Tadhg Buidhe O'Conchobhair, and Dunadach Mac Dubhgaill, were hanged at a session, in the middle month of summer, in Ros-Comain. A session was held in Sligech by George Bingham, and by the Justice Dillon,[7] and by Master Comartun;[8] and *the inhabitants of* the county of Sligech

---

person called " Graidhin " in the second next entry, and the same as Captain Gilbert Grayne, slain in 1593 by Brian O'Ruairc, according to the Four Masters, and Docwra's "*Relation.*"

⁶ *Graidhin.* See preceding note.

⁷ *Justice Dillon.* Thomas Dillon, the chief justice of the province of Connacht.

⁸ *Comartun.* Garrett Comberford, or Comerford, attorney-general of the same province.

Ꝺonnchaꞓ oıȝ Uı Ɑıꞃꞇ ꝺo cꞃochaꝺ aɴɴꞃıɴ, ocuꞃ
Emaɴɴ mac EꞋꞃı. Ɑɴ ȝuıbeꞃɴoıꞃ ꝺo ꝺol a Ꞩaxaɴaıb.
Ꞇoıꞃꞃꝺelbach mac Uı Ꞓꞃoıɴ ꝺo cꞃochaꝺ le Ꞩaxaɴchaıb,
ocuꞃ é Ꞌꞃaꞃıu ꞃeıɴ a ꞃeꞃbıꞃ ɴa baꞃꞃıȝɴα. Caıꞃꞃꞃı mac
Ɑꝺꝺa meȝ Ꝺonnchaꞓ .ı. mac mıc Ꝺonnchaꞓ, ꝺéȝ.
Ȝıllacoluım Uα hUıȝıɴɴ, mac ꝳaoılmuıꞃe mıc Ꞓꞃıαıɴ
óıȝ Uı Uıȝıɴ, ꝺeȝ ꞇꞃı hoıꝺꞃı ꞃe luȝɴαꞃαꝺ. ꝳαc
ȝıuıꞃꞇıꞃ ɴα heꞃeɴɴ ꝺeȝ; ꞃıꞃ ꞃeoɴ Pıꞃoıꝺ aıɴm ıɴ
ȝıuıꞃꞇıꞃ ꞃıɴ. Concobaꞃ mac Eɴɴa Uı Uıȝıɴ ꝺeȝ;
ꞃúoı ꞃe ꝺaɴ aɴ Concobaꞃ ꞃıɴ, ocuꞃ a αꝺɴacαꝺ a caıꞃıll
ɴα heılıꝺı aꞃ ꝳaꞓaıꞃe ɴα ɴaıleꞓ. Cıꞇh cloıchꞃɴeach-
ꞇa ꝺo ꞓuꞃ a machaıꞃe Connachꞇ a ccıɴɴ ꞇꞃeachꞇ-
muıɴe ıaꞃ luȝɴαꞃαꝺ, ocuꞃ ɴıꞃ mo mıɴ uball ɴα ȝach
cloch ꝺonꞇ ꞃɴeachꞇa ꞃıɴ, ocuꞃ aꞃꞓaꞃ ımꝺa ꝺo mılleꞓ
ꝺo. O Concobaıꞃ ꝺonn .ı. Ꝺıaꞃmaıꝺ mac Caıꞃꞃꞃı mıc
Eoȝaıɴ caoıch Uı Concobaıꞃ, aɴ ꞃeꞃ ıꞃ mó ꞃo ꞇꞃaocꞋı
ocuꞃ ꞃo ꞓuıꞃɴ ꝺıa ɴaımꝺıb, ocuꞃ ıꞃ mo ꞃo ꞃoȝhaıl ocuꞃ
ꞃo αꝺmıll ꝺa eꞃcaıꞃꝺıꞓ ıɴ ȝach aıꞃꝺ, aɴꞇ aoɴ ꝺuıɴe
uaꞃal ıꞃ ꞃeꞃꞃ ꞇaɴıc ꝺo ꞃlıchꞇ Ꞇoıꞃꞃꝺelbaıȝ moıꞃ Uı
Concobaıꞃ ꞃe cıaɴ ꝺaımꞃıꞃ ꝺéȝ, ocuꞃ a αꝺɴacαꝺ α
mꞓaıle aɴ ꞇoꞃaıꞃ ꞃa ꝺıꝺeɴ Ꝺe ocuꞃ Ꞓꞃıȝꝺı, aɴ ꞇꞃeꞃ la
ꞃe ceꝺ ꞃeıl ꝳuıꞃı, aꞃ mꞓeꞓ cuıȝ blıaꝺɴa .x. aꞃ ꞃıcheꝺ
a ꞇıȝeꞃɴuꞃ ꝺó. Ꞇoıꞃꞃꝺelbach mac Ɑꝺꝺa Uı Ꞓaoıȝıll,
ocuꞃ Ɑꝺꝺ óȝ mac Ɑꝺꝺa buıꝺı Uı Ꝺomɴaıll, ocuꞃ
moıꞃꞃeꞃıoꞃ ꝺa muıɴɴꞇıꞃ, ꝺo maꞃbaꝺ le claıɴɴ Neıll
ꞃuaꞓ Uı Ꞓaoıȝıll. CeꞇꞇacꞋ mac Ꞇoıꞃꞃꝺelbaıȝ Uı
Ruaıꞃc ocuꞃ ꝳaꞓȝamaıɴ mac Cαbα, ocuꞃ ꞇꞃıuꞃ ɴo
ceꞓꞃaꞃ maꞃaoɴ ꞃıu, ꝺo maꞃbaꝺ ocuꞃ ꞃıaꝺ a ꞃoꞓaıꞃ
Ꝺoꝳɴaıll Uı Ruaıꞃc, le cloıɴɴ Ꞓꞃıaıɴ mıc Eoȝaıɴ Uı
Ruaıꞃꞓ .ı. Ꞇıȝeꞃɴaɴ ocuꞃ Ꝺomɴall; ocuꞃ aȝ Raıch
ȝıaíɴ ꝺo ꞃoɴaꝺ ıɴ maꞃbaꝺ ꞃıɴ; ocuꞃ ꝺo ımꞇhıȝ mac
Ꞇaıꝺȝ Uı Ruaıꞃc .ı. Ꝺomɴall ꝺo ꞃıꞇh ocuꞃ aꞃ éıȝıɴ.
O Ꝺubꝺa .ı. Emuɴɴ mac Eoȝaıɴ Uı Ꝺubꝺa ꝺeȝ. Ꞩıꞃ
Rıꞃꝺeꞃꝺ Ꞓıɴȝıam ꝺo ꞓuꞃ ꝺoɴ baꞃꞃıȝaɴ co Plonꝺꞃuꞃ,

---

[1] *His.* ꝺıα; "of his;" repeated in the MS. | [2] *Of God.* Ꝺıα, MS.

came to that assembly; and Felim, son of Donnchadh Og O'hAirt, was hanged there, and Edmond, son of Henry. The governor went to Saxon-land. Toirdhelbhach, son of O'Briain, was hanged by Saxons, and he along with themselves, in the queen's service. Cairbre, son of Aedh Mac Donnchaidh, i.e., son of *the* Mac Donnchaidh, died. Gilla-Coluim O'hUiginn, the son of Maelmuire, son of Brian Og O'hUiginn, died three nights before Lammas. The son of the Justiciary of Erinn died: this Justiciary's name *was* Sir John Perrot. Conchobhar, son of Enna O'hUiginn, died: a most eminent poet was this Conchobhar; and he was interred in Caisel-na-heilidhi, on Machaire-na-nailech. A shower of hail fell in Machaire-Connacht within a week after Lammas, and a small apple was not bigger than each stone of that snow ; and it destroyed much corn. O'Conchobhair Donn, i.e., Diarmaid, son of Cairbre, son of Eoghan Caech O'Conchobhair, the man who subdued and humbled his[1] enemies the most, and who plundered and destroyed his adversaries the most in every quarter, the best gentleman that came of the race of Toirdhelbhach Mór O'Conchobhair for a long time, died ; and he was interred in Baile-in-tobair, under the protection of God[2] and Brigid, the third day before the first festival of Mary, after he had been thirty-five years in sovereignty. Toirdhelbhach, son of Aedh O'Baighill, and Aedh Og, son of Aedh Buidhe O'Domhnaill, and seven of their people, were slain by the sons of Niall Ruadh O'Baighill. Cedach, son of Toirdhelbhach O'Ruairc, and Mathghamhain Mac Caba, and three or four along with them, were slain whilst in the company of Domhnall O'Ruairc, by the sons of Brian, the son of Eoghan O'Ruairc., viz., Tighernan and Domhnall : and at Rath-Giain this killing was done ; and the son of Tadhg O'Ruairc, i.e., Domhnall, escaped by running, and with difficulty. O'Dubhda, i.e., Edmond, the son of Eoghan O'Dubhda, died. Sir Richard Bingham was sent by the queen to Flanders; and his brother, i e.,

ocur a ɒepⱱpaċaip .i. 8eoipɼi ɒo ɼaʒbail ina inaɒ oɼ
cinn Connachɔ. Єoʒan mac Ruaiɒɼi mic Ƒelim mic
Maʒnuɼa ɒeʒ caoicip ɼia ɼamhain, ocur a aⱱnacaɒ a
8liʒech. Ccoⱱ ɼuaⱱ mac Ui ɒomnaill .i. mac Ccoɒa
mic Maʒnuɼa, ocur mac mic 8uibne Ƒanaɔ, ocur mac
Єoʒain mic 8eain mic Coɼbmaic buiɒi Ui ʒallⱱobaip,
ɒo ʒabail aɼ cuan ɼaɔha Maolain ɒo luinʒ 8axanaⱱ,
aɼ nɒol ɒól ɼina inɔi ɒoib, ocur a mbɼeⱱ co baile
Ccɔha cliaɔh. Mac Ui Ƒeɼʒail bain .i. Ɔaɒʒ oʒ ɒéʒ.
ɒomnall mac ⱱaoɔʒalaiʒ Mic Ccoɒaʒain ɒeʒ. inʒen
ⱱɼiain mic ɒiaɼmaɒa ɼuaiɒ, ben oiɼⱱiiniʒ ⱱaile na
cclepech .i. Caɔhal, ɒhec. Ccn ɼinaɼcal Ui muiʒ
Caille ocur Ƥaɒɒɼiʒin mac mic Muiɼip, ocur Ƥaɒɒ-
ɼicin Cunɒun, ocur ɒonnchaɒ mac Coɼbmaic Meʒ
Caɼɼɔhaiʒ, ɒo ʒabail a nCcɔh cliaⱱ ɒo comaiɼle na
hЄɼenn peɼ ɒolum. Poɼɔ ɒo ɒenam a ccluain Єoaiɼ
a hOiɼʒiallaiⱱ ɒo ɼiɼ hanɼai ɒiuic, ɒo ɼiɒiɼe ɼaxanach.
Cumeⱱa mac mic Conmaɼa ɼinn ocur a ben, inʒen
meʒ Ƥiaɼuiɼ, ɒɼaʒbail baiɼ an aoin ɼeachɔmuin,

ƙcɫ. ɼoɼ Luaii; aoiɼ in Ɔiʒeɼna mile bliaɒan, ocur
cuiʒ ceɒ ocur ceɔɼa ɼicheɒ ocur ochɔ mbliaɒna. O
Conchobaiɼ 8liʒiʒ .i. ɒomnall mac Ɔaɒʒ mic Caɔhail
oiʒ, ɼoʒa ʒaoiɒel Єɼenn, ɒeʒ aiɒʒi noɒlaʒ beʒ a
8liʒech, ocur a aɒnacaɒ innɔi. Ccoɒ mac in calbaiʒ
Ui ɒomnaill, ocur ɼeɼ ocur ochɔaɼ maɼaon ɼiɼ, ɒo
maɼbaɒ a ɼeall a ʒcɼannoiʒ Muiʒi ʒaiblin le hinʒen
ɔ8emaiɼ meʒ ɒomnaill, le mnaoi Ui ɒomnaill.
Maɔha ɼuaⱱ O Luinin, .i. ɼaoi ɼe ɼenⱱuɼ, ɒeʒ an
bliaɒain ceɒna. ⱱaiɔeɼ mac Riɼɒeɼɒ mic Ricaiɼɒ
oiʒ a ⱱuɼɼ ɒéʒ. ʒiuiɼɔiɼ nua ɒo ɔeachɔ co hЄɼinn .i.

---

1 *Eoghan.* He was of the family of
O'Conor Sligo. His death is not recorded by the Four Masters.

2 *O'Domhnaill.* The Four Masters
state that this Aedh (or Hugh) was
really the son of the Dean O'Gallagher,

although then usually called the son
of Calvagh O'Donnell.

3 *Crannog of Magh-gaibhlin.* Magh-
gaibhlin, now Mongavlin, is a townland in the parish of Taughboyne, co.
Donegal. The "crannog" is not now

George, was left in his place over Connacht. Eoghan,[1]
the son of Ruaidhri, son of Felim, son of Maghnus, died a
fortnight before Allhallowtide, and was buried in Sligech.
Aedh Ruadh, the son of O'Domhnaill, i.e., the son of Aedh,
son of Maghnus, and the son of Mac Suibhne Fanad,
and the son of Eughan, son of John, the son of Cormac
Buidhe O'Gallchubhair, were taken prisoners in the
harbour of Rath-Maelain, by a Saxon ship, after they
had gone to drink wine in it; and they were carried
off to Baile-atha-cliath. The son of O'Ferghail Bán, i.e.,
Tadhg Og, died. Domhnall, the son of Baethghalach
MacAedhagain, died. The daughter of Brian Mac
Diarmada Ruadh, wife of the Airchinnech of Baile-na-
clerech, i.e., Cathal, died. The Seneschal of Ui-mic-Caille,
and Patrickin, son of Fitz-Maurice, and Patrickin Condon,
and Donnchadh, son of Cormac Mac Carthaigh, were taken
prisoners in Ath-cliath, by the council of Erinn, per dolum.
A residence was erected at Cluain-Eois in Oirghialla, by
Sir Henry Duke, a Saxon knight. Cumedha, the son of
Mac Conmara Finn, and his wife, the daughter of Mac
Piers, died in one week.

The kalends on Monday; the age of the-Lord one
thousand, five hundred, and eighty-eight years. O'Conchobhair Sligigh, i.e., Domhnall, the son of Tadhg, son of
Cathal Og, the choice of the Gaeidhel of Erinn, died
on Little Christmas night in Sligech, and was buried
in it. Aedh, son of the Calbhach O'Domhnaill,[2] and
nine men along with him, were slain in treachery in
the crannog of Magh-gaibhlín,[3] by the daughter of James
Mac Domhnaill, the wife of O'Domhnaill.[4] Matthew Ruadh
O'Luinin, i.e., an eminent antiquary, died the same year.
Walter, son of Richard, son of Rickard Og Burk, died. A
new Justiciary came to Erinn, i.e., William FitzWilliam,

A.D.
———
[1587.]

[1588.]

---

traceable; nor is there any water in
the locality in which such a structure
could have existed, with the exception of the waters of Lough Foyle, on
the margin of. which Mongavlin is

situated, and in which the crannog
must have been.
[4] *O'Domhnaill;* i.e., Aedh, son of
Maghnus O'Domhnaill, or Manus
O'Donnell.

Uıllıam Ƒaoıuıllıam, ocuṗ nı ṗaıbı ṗıcɧ ınɑ ṗoınenn a
nЄṗınn ınɑ coṗaıꝺ ṗeın o ꝺo ꞇanıc. Єaṗṗacc mɑl-
laıᵹꞇı heṗeᵹꝺɑ ꝺo beꝺ a nOılṗınn, ocuṗ ꝺo ṗınne Ꝺıɑ
ṗeṗꞇɑ ṗele aıṗ; ocuṗ aṗı áıꞇ a ṗaıꝺı a ꞇıᵹeꝺaṗ a
nᵹṗaınṗıᵹ ın Macɧaıṗe ṗıabaıᵹ; ocuṗ ꝺo cuıṗeꝺ cıcɧ
ṗnecɧꞇɑ ꝺó, ocuṗ nıṗ mó ṗıaꝺ uꝺall na ᵹacɧ clocɧ ꝺe ;
ocuṗ nıṗ ṗaᵹbaꝺ ᵹṗaınne na baıle, ocuṗ ıṗ ṗe ṗluaṗꝺıb
ꝺo cuıṗꞇı an ṗnecɧꞇɑ ṗın o na ꞇıᵹꞇıb; ocuṗ aṗ a mí
meꝺoın ꞇṗampaꝺ ꝺo cuıṗeꝺ an cıoꞇ ṗın. O Ƒallamaın
.ı. Coꝺꞇacɧ O Ƒallamaın ꝺeᵹ, ocuṗ a mac Remann
ꝺoıṗneꝺ na ınaꝺ. Ꞁean mac Ꞇomaıṗ mıc Ꝺabı mıc
Єmuınn .ı. ṗaccaṗꞇ uaṗal onoṗaꝺ ꝺeᵹ. Ꙟlac Uı Raıᵹıllıᵹh .ı. Єmann mac Ꙟlaoılmoṗꝺa ꝺo ꞇeacɧꞇ aṗ
cṗeıcɧ aṗ Ꝺṗıan mac Ƒeṗᵹaıl oıᵹ Uı Raıᵹıllıᵹh, ocuṗ
cṗecɧa ꝺo ᵹlacaꝺ ꝺó; ocuṗ mac Ƒeṗᵹaıl oıᵹ ꝺo bṗeꝺ
oṗṗa, ocuṗ Ꞁean oᵹ mac Ꞁeaın mıc Ꞇoıṗṗꝺelbaıᵹ Uı
Raıᵹıllıᵹh, ocuṗ ꞇṗoıꝺ ꝺo ꞇabaıṗꞇ ꝺa cɧele ꝺoıb, ocuṗ
an cṗecɧ ꝺo ꝺuaın ꝺЄmann ocuṗ ṗıcɧe ꝺa muınnꞇıṗ ꝺo
maṗbaꝺ, ocuṗ Ꞁean oᵹ mac Ꞁeaın mıc Ꞇoıṗṗꝺelbaıᵹ ꝺo
maṗbaꝺ le hЄmann. Ⱥn Ꝺubalꞇacɧ mac Remuınn
Uı Ƒallamaın ꝺo maṗbaꝺ le Remann mac Coꝺꞇaıᵹ ı
Ƒallamaın. Ᵹılla na naom mac Iṗıaıl Uı Uıᵹınn
ꝺéᵹ. Ꙟlac mıc Ꝺıaṗmaꝺa .ı. Caꞇal mac Ꞇoıṗṗꝺelbaıᵹ,
ocuṗ mac ı Choncubaıṗ ṗuaıꝺ .ı. Ceꝺaꝺ, ocuṗ mac Ꙟlıc
Conꞇıaṗa ꝺo cṗocaꝺ, ocuṗ mac Ƒeıꝺlım buıꝺı .ı. Ꝺonn-
cɧaꝺ, ꝺo cṗocaꝺ maṗaon ṗıu a nᵹaıllım. Ꙟlac mıc
Ᵹoıṗꝺelba ꝺéᵹ .ı. Єmann. Ꙟlac ı Ꙟlaoılconaıṗı ꝺéᵹ
[.ı.] Ꞁenčán. Ꝑılıb O hЄınıꝺ ꝺécc .ı. ꝺuıne ṗoıꝺınn ꝺo
bı a noṗınm. Ꝺomnall mac ı Ꝺomnaıll, ocuṗ ṗlıocɧꞇ
Ⱥoꝺa ı Ᵹallcobaıṗ, ꝺo ꝺul aṗ ṗıubal ınṗuıꝺıꝺ aṗ
cloınn Cuınn mıc ın calbaıᵹ, ocuṗ ꝺo maṗbaꝺ leo ın
calbaꝺ óᵹ mac Cuınn mıc ın calbaıᵹ, ocuṗ ṗucaꝺaṗ

---

1 *Bishop.* John Lynch, who was
appointed in 1583, and resigned the
see in 1611; and who is said, according to Harris (Ware's *Works*, vol. i.,
p. 634), to have "lived a concealed,
and died a Public Papist."

2 *Great miracles.* ṗeṗꞇɑ ṗele.
Probably a mistake for ṗeṗꞇɑ ṗıleꝺ,
"poet-miracles." See under the year
1024; vol. i., p. 27.

3 *Edmond;* i.e. Edmond Burk.

4 *Felim Buidhe.* Felim the Yellow:

and there was neither peace nor quietness in Erinn, in his own party, since he came. There was a wicked, heretical, bishop[1] in Oilfinn; and God performed great miracles[2] upon him. And his place of residence was in the Grainsech of Machaire-riabhach; and a shower of snow was shed for him, and a wild apple was not larger than each stone of it; and not a grain was left in his town; and it was with shovels the snow was removed from the houses; and it was in the middle month of summer that shower fell. O'Fallamhain, i.e., Cobhthach O'Fallamhain, died; and his son Redmond was ordained in his place. John, son of Thomas, son of David, son of Edmond,[3] i.e., a noble, honourable priest, died. The son of O'Raighilligh, i.e., Edmond, son of Maelmordha, came on a predatory incursion against Brian, son of Ferghal Og O'Raighilligh, and took preys; and the son of Ferghal Og, and John Og, son of John, son of Toirdhelbhach O'Raighilligh, overtook them; and they gave battle to each other; and the prey was taken from Edmond, and twenty of his people were slain; and John Og, son of John, son of Toirdhelbhach, was killed by Edmond. The Dubhaltach, son of Redmond O'Fallamhain, was killed by Redmond, the son of Cobhthach O'Fallamhain. Gilla-na-naemh, son of Irial O'hUiginn, died. The son of Mac Diarmada, i.e., Cathal, son of Toirdhelbhach, and the son of O'Conchobhair Ruadh, i.e., Cedach, and the son of Mac Conmara, were hanged in Gaillimh; and the son of Felim Buidhe,[4] i.e., Donnchadh, was hanged along with them. The son of Mac Goisdelbh died, i.e., Edmond. The son of O'Maelconaire died, [i.e.] Senchán. Philip O'hEinidh died, i.e., a most·excellent man, who had been in Normandy(?). Domhnall, son of O'Domhnaill, and the posterity of Aedh O'Gallchubhair, went on an expedition against the sons of Conn, son of the Calbhach;[5] and the Calbhach Og, son[6] of Conn, son of the Calbhach, was slain by them;

---

the son of Felim Finn, or Felim the Fair, grandson of Turlough Roe, and ancestor of the sept of O'Conor Roe.

[5] *Calbhach*; i.e., the Calbhach (or Calvagh) O'Donnell.

[6] *Son.* m̅c.; repeated in Clar.

ʟeo τορáɴ ɒo buαɪɓ ocuρ ɒo cαɪρʟɪɓ. O ᴅoĉαρταɪᵹ ocuρ O ᵹαʟʟcobαɪρ ɒo ᵹαbαɪʟ ɒoɴ ᵹuɪρτɪρ, ocuρ α mbρeĉ co αĉh cʟɪαĉ. ꝑeʟɪm occ mαc Concobαɪρ mɪc Τoɪρρɒeʟbαɪᵹ ρuαɪɒ, ocuρ αɴ Cαʟbαĉ mαc Cuɪɴɴ mɪc ꝑeʟɪm ρuαɪɒ, ɒo ɒoʟ co ραɴɴ mɪc Uɪʟʟɪαm buρc, ocuρ muɪɴɴτeρ αɴτ ρɪρρɪαm ɒo mαρbαɒ ρeρ ɒoʟum. Uɪρɒɪuɴ mαc Mαoʟmuɪρe mɪc ꝑeʟɪm meᵹ ᴅomɴαɪʟʟ ɒo cρochαɒ ʟeρρɪɴ ɴᵹuɪbeρɴoɪρ. Sbαɪɴɴɪᵹ ɒo τeαchτ co hꝦɪɴɴ ʟoɪɴᵹeρ αɓbαɪʟ moρ, ocuρ ɒo bαɪcheɓ α hochτ ɴo α ɴαoɪ ɒo ɴα ʟoɴᵹαɪb ρɪɴ α Mumhαɪɴ ocuρ α Coɴɴαchτuɪb, ocuρ αɴ méɒ ɴαρ bαɪch αɴ muɪρ ɒo ʟuchτ ɴα ʟoɴᵹ ρɪɴ ɒo bαɪcheɒ, ɒo mαρɓαταρ Sαχαɴαɪᵹ ɪαɒ; ocuρ ɴɪ heɪɒɪρ α ρɪḿ ɴo α ɪɴɴɪρɪɴ ᵹαĉ αρ bαɪcheɒ ocuρ ᵹαch αρ mαρbαɒ ραɴ ʟoɪɴᵹeρ ρɪɴ αρ α méɒ, ocuρ ᵹαch α ρρɪch ɒoɴ eɒáɪʟ, ɒóρ ocuρ ɒαɪρᵹeɒ ocuρ ɒα ᵹαch mαɪcheρ αρceɴα. Sʟɪᵹech ɒo buαɪɴ ɒo ᴅoɴɴchαɒ mαc Cαĉhαɪʟ oɪᵹ Uí Concobαɪρ ɒoɴ ᵹuɪbeρɴoɪρ, ocuρ mαc Cαĉhαɪʟ oɪcc ɒo ɒoʟ α ccoραɪɒ co Sαχαɴαɪɓ. O hꝦɪɓɪɴ ɒéᵹ .ɪ. Ꝇoᵹαɴ mαɴɴταch O hꝦɪɴ. Ceτταch mαc bρɪαɪɴ mɪc ᴅɪαρmαɒα ρuαɪɓ ɒeᵹ. ɪαρʟα o ʟeρταρ .ɪ. ρρɪɴρα ρo chumαchταch ɒo muɪɴɴτɪρ bαɴρɪᵹαɴ Sαχαɴ ɒeᵹ. Cαɪρɒɪɴ Coɪʟéρ ɒeᵹ. Sʟuαɪᵹeɒ Ꝧeɴɴ uɪʟe αchτ cuɪᵹeɒ Uʟαɒ ɴαmα ɒo τeαchτ α Coɴɴαchτuɪɓ ʟe ρɪρ Uɪʟʟɪαm ꝑαoɪuɪʟʟɪαm .ɪ. ᵹuɪρτɪρ ɴα hꝦeɴɴ, ocuρ ᵹαɴ eɴ ρeɒ mαɪĉeρα ɒo ɒeɴαm ɒo, αchτ αραɪbɪ o αĉh ʟuαɪɴ co hꝦɪρɴe ɒo mɪʟʟeɓ ɒo, ocuρ mαc Uɪ ᴅoĉαρταɪᵹ .ɪ. Caĉαoɪρ, ɒo mαρbαɒ ʟe Sαχαɴchαɪb. Mαɪᵹ Ꝧochαᵹαɪɴ .ɪ. Coɴɴʟα mαɪᵹ Ꝧochαᵹαɪɴ, ρeρ uαραʟ ɒeᵹoɪɴɪᵹ, ɒéᵹ. Mαc Τɪᵹeρɴαɪɴ ɴα bρeρɴe .ɪ. ꝑeρᵹαʟ ɒecc. Mαc Suɪɓɴe chɪρe bαᵹuɪɴe, .ɪ. Nɪαʟʟ meɪρᵹeαch mαc Mαoɪʟmuɪρe,

---

1 *O'Dochartaigh.* John Og, son of John, son of Felim O'Doherty.

2 *O'Gallchubhair.* This was Sir John O'Gallagher, the son of Tuathal Balbh, whom Ware (*Annals*) incorrectly calls Sir Owen MacToole, and Cox (*Hib. Anglic.*) Sir Owen O'Toole.

3 *Toirdhelbhach Ruadh.* Turlough Roe; one of the sept of O'Conchobhair Ruadh, or O'Conor Roe.

4 *Felim Ruadh.* Another member of the last named sept.

5 *Justin.* Uɪρɒɪuɴ. This name is written " Euston " by Cox, and " Ewster " in Docwra's *Relation;* (*Miscell. of Celtic Soc.*; Dublin, 1849, p. 202).

6 *Nine.* This is only half the number officially reported as lost by Mr. Geoffrey Fenton, Irish Secretary of

A.D.
[1588.]

and they carried away with them a great number of cows and horses. O'Dochartaigh[1] and O'Gallchubhair[2] were apprehended by the Justiciary, and taken to Ath-cliath. Felim Og, son of Conchobhar, son of Toirdhelbhach Ruadh,[3] and the Calbhach, son of Conn, son of Felim Ruadh,[4] went to Mac William Burk's division; and they killed the sheriff's people, per dolum. Justin,[5] the son of Maelmuire, son of Felim Mac Domhnaill, was hanged by the governor. Spaniards came to Erinn, a very great fleet; and eight or nine[6] of those ships were wrecked in Mumha and Connacht; and Saxons killed all who were not drowned of the crews of those ships that were wrecked; and it is not possible to reckon or tell all that were drowned, and all that were slain in that fleet, on account of their number, and the quantity of the spoils got, of gold and silver, and of every kind of treasure besides. Sligech was taken from Donnchadh, son of Cathal Og O'Conchobhair, by the governor; and the son of Cathal Og went to complain to Saxon-land. O'hEidhin died, i.e., Eoghan Manntach O'hEidhin. Cedach, son of Brian Mac Diarmada Ruadh, died. The Earl of Leicester, i.e., a very powerful prince of the queen of the Saxons' people, died. Captain Collier died. The hosting of all Erinn, except the province of Ulster alone, went to Connacht with Sir William FitzWilliam, i.e., the Justiciary of Erinn; and he effected not a particle of good, but injured all that was from Ath-Luain to Erne; and the son of O'Dochartaigh, i.e., Cathair, was killed by Saxons. Mag Eochagain, i.e., Connla Mag Eochagain a noble, very hospitable man, died.[7] Mac Tighernain of the Breifne, i.e., Ferghal, died. Mac Suibhne of Tir-Baghuine, i.e., Niall

State at the time. See the extract from his report published by Dr. O'Donovan, in his ed. of the Annals of the Four Mast., under the year 1588.

[7] *Died.* The remaining entries for this year, and the earlier ones under the next, are in the handwriting of Brian Mac Dermot.

no marbad re Donnchad noub mac Maoilmuire
meirzzib meic Suibne pen dolum. Mairzpeg ni Cuai-
peil in ben do bí az Ziollacollium O Chlabbuiz dhec;
ocur ni faceman a cill piam ben bub peapp. Seatan
mac Maoilpe ban iñic Uilliam bupc, mic Ricaipd oiz,
no marbad re Uilliam Caiz a Slizech zo timpipteaċ.
Cpeċa mora do denam dlloċ mac in ċalbaiz 1 Domnaill poime e pein do marbad, ocur do mac 1 Neill
ap tip lloba, du ano apoibe tpi mili bo. Hi tainic re
eian daimpip a nEipinn piam coñmaiċ na bliadna po
do fazaman; ap búb mó bia ocur topad. feall
zpanna do denaiñ do piz fpanz, oip do marbad re
duice maiċ da muintip pein pep dolum. Do baiched
bpian mac in pepruin ocur llpiap mac in pepruin,
ocur Copmac O hllipp, annpa loinzeap Sbaineaċ pin
tainic zo Caipbpi.

Kt. ianaip pop Cédaoin, ocur aoir in Cizepna naoi
mbliadna ocur seatpa pichẹd ccccc. mile. Siappuim
conndae Muizẹ nEo .i. mazirtip bpun, ocur Domnall O
Dalaiz do dul ap riubal zo hIoppar. Mopcpeċa ocur
marbta do denam doib pep dolum. Ripdeapt mac
deamain in chopain, ocur Uatẹp mac Ricaipd meic
Seain in Cepmuinn, do bpeaiċ oppẹa; ocur do badar
Saxpanaiz tpi cẹd darmail, ocur do ċuadar do bualad
a ċele, ocur do bpipead aip Sazpanchaib, ocur do
marbud Domnall O Dalaiz ocur mazirtip bpun .i.
in riappiam, ocur maiċe a poibe papu uile, ocur do
tuzad in maidm oppẹa zo happaċta uapal tpe mip-
buile De atap. Cadz mac Kuaidpi meic Conchobaip
.i. duine uapal do tpliċt fepzail meic Diapmada,
dhec. Cathal mac Duoizip .i. pazapt llċanaiz dhec.

---

¹ O'Clabbaigh. O ċlabbaiz, Clar.
² Duke. The Duke of Guise.
³ Per. peap, Clar.
⁴ Demhan-in-chorain, "the demon
of the reaping hook," otherwise called

"Devil's hook." This was Rickard
Burk, son of Rickard, son of Rickard,
son of William, son of Edmond, son of
Rickard Burk, surnamed "O'Cuairsce,"
or "of the crooked shield."

Meirgech, son of Maelmuire, was killed by Donnchadh Dubh, the son of Maelmuire Meirgech Mac Suibhne, per dolum. Margaret Ni Cuareil, the wife of Gilla-Coluim O'Clabbaigh,[1] died; and we never saw a better woman in a cemetery. John, the son of Meiler Ban MacWilliam Burk, son of Rickard Og, was unfortunately slain in Sligech by William Taig. Great preys were taken by Aedh, son of the Calbhach O'Domhnall, before he himself was killed, and by the son of O'Neill, in Tir-Aedha, in which there were three thousand cows. There came not for a long time in Erinn so good a year as this as regards the harvest; it was the most plentiful in food and produce. An ugly treachery was committed by the king of France, for he killed a good duke[2] of his own family, per dolum. Brian Mac-in-Persuin, and Andrew Mac-in-Persuin, and Cormac O'hAirt, were drowned in that Spanish fleet which came to Cairbre.

The kalends of January on Wednesday, and the age of the Lord one thousand, five hundred, and eighty-nine years. The sheriff of the county of Magh-Eo, i.e., Master Browne, and Domhnall O'Dalaigh, went on an expedition to Irrus. They committed numerous depredations and homicides, per[3] dolum. Richard, the son of Demhan-inchorain,[4] and Walter, the son of Rickard, son of Shane-antermuin,[5] overtook them; and the Saxons were three hundred in number; and they proceeded to attack one another, and the Saxons were defeated, and Domhnall O'Dalaigh, and Master Brown, i.e., the sheriff, and all the principal persons who were along with them, were slain; and this victory was nobly, valorously, gained over them through the miracle of God the Father. Tadhg, son of Ruaidhri, son of Conchobhar, i.e., an excellent man of the posterity of Ferghal Mac Diarmada, died. Cathal Mac Daighir, i.e., priest of Achanach, died.

---

[5] *Shane-an-termuin.* Shane, or John (Burk), of the termon; i.e., of the termon of Balla, county of Mayo.

O Neill, .i. Toirdealbach luineac, do teacht ar tarraing Neill garb mic Coind meic an Chalbuig 1
Domnaill, ar Eogan mac in decanaig 1 Ghallcubair,
ocur do gclagadar cred mor; agur do rig orra
muintter Ghallcubair ocur caid do clainn tSuibne,
ocur do cuireadar cugad go maic no go rangadar int
ineoh andaroibe O Neill. An uair do connairc
O Neill a muinntir da randtu do rill anagaid na
tora, ocur do brir orrea, ocur do marbad andrin
Maolmuire mac Emaind do conrabluib na Muman,
ocur riched maraon rir. Do rill O Neill rlan edalach.
Maidm do eadairt air Roibend mac hanrig duib
Dil111 a nOirgeallaib meg Matgamna, ocur e a dul
na errarrim ar Mag Uidir; ocur do gabub e rein ocur
do marbad a muinntir; ocur Brian mac Aoda oig
meg Matgamna cig in maoidm rin. Cland Murchada
na tuach mic Taidg 1 Flatbertaig do dul ar riubal
innruige go Conmaicne, ocur crea mora do gclagad
doib. Saxanaig do breit orrea da danda do glere
glanrluaig, ocur dol do bualad a cele doib; ocur
brirad ar muinntir Flatbertaig, ocur Tadg O Flatbertaig mac [M]urchada, ocur Arun mac Murchada,
ocur Tadg og O Flatbertaig, ocur ced maraon rir do
marbad; ocur do gcrodad Emann O Flaithbertaig,
mac Murchada na tuat do di a laim a ngaillim an
cedaoin eidir da eairg; ocur de racirin carga do
tugad an maoim ag Cairlen an eatirea a gCuileca;
ocur ra haubad na hechta rin. Ocur do brirdar clann
Uilliam a coirlen, ocur do loirgidar a tige ocur a
narbinna; ocur do brirdar baile Aea leeair, ocur
orin riar go rairrge. An Copinn ocur tir Oilella do
crechad do clom 1 Ruairc .i. Eoghan ocur Brian og.

1 *O'Flaithbhertaigh.* The text from | of the chronicle including the entries
this down to the beginning of the para- | for the years 1462 and 1463, &c.
graph on p. 494 is in the handwriting | ² *The two Easters.* Easter Sunday
of the person who copied the portion | and Low Sunday.

O'Neill, i.e., Toirdhelbhach Luinech, came upon the invitation of Niall Garbh, son of Conn, son of the Calbhach O'Domhnaill, against Eoghan, son of the Dean O'Gallchubhair; and they obtained a great prey; and Muinter-Gallchubhair, and some of the Clann-Suibhne, overtook them, and attacked them bravely until they came to the place where O'Neill was. When O'Neill saw his people eagerly sought after, he turned against the pursuers, and defeated them; and Maelmuire, son of Edmond, one of the constables of Mumha, was slain there, and twenty men along with him. O'Neill returned safe, enriched with spoils. A defeat was given to Robert, son of Henry Dubh Dillon, in Oirghiall-Mic-Mathghamhna, whilst going as sheriff against Mag Uidhir; and he was taken prisoner himself, and his people were slain; and it was Brian, son of Aedh Og Mac Mathghamhna, that gave that defeat. The sons of Murchadh-na-tuadh, son of Tadhg O'Flaithbhertaigh, went upon an expedition to Conmaicne, and took great preys. Saxons overtook them—two bands of choice troops; and they proceeded to attack each other; and Muinter-Flaithbhertaigh were defeated, and Tadhg O'Flaithbhertaigh,[1] the son of Murchadh, and Urun, son of Murchadh, and Tadhg Og O'Flaithbhertaigh, and one hundred along with them, were slain; and Edmond O'Flaithbhertaigh, the son of Murchadh-na-tuadh, who was imprisoned in Gallimh, was hanged on Wednesday between the two Easters;[2] and on Easter Saturday the defeat was given, at Caislen-an-chathirtha in Cuilecha; and those were prodigious events. And the Clann-William broke down their castles, and burned their houses and corn crops; and they demolished Baile-átha-lethair,[3] and from thence westwards to the sea. The Corann and Tir-Oilella were plundered by the sons of O'Ruairc, viz., Eoghan and Brian Og. Tir-Fiachrach was plundered by

---

[3] *Baile-atha-lethair.* Apparently for Baile-atha-lethain, "the town of the | wide ford." There is a place so called in the bar. of Gallen, co. Mayo.

Cír Fhíapač τo čpechaὅ τO Ruaipc pen o Iαrſuιᵹ ſαoιp. Mac 1 Ruaipc .ı. Eoᵹhan τo ὅul ᵹo maċaιpe Chonnachτ ᵹonτechaιὅ pe ᵹo cıll Colltoᵹ, ocup clann 1 Cončaὅaıp pнaıὅ mαpαon ſpıp; ocup ᵹαn cpech τo ᵹlαcaὅ τóıὅ τo ὅıč mαpcpluαιᵹ, ocup pılleὅ cαp a нαıp τoıὅ ᵹo pαnᵹαταp bočαp pen nτo[m]нuıᵹ. Sıαppıum na cunnταe τo ὅpeıč oppα .ı. Ruıpceıpc Máпúcαp, ocup clann n'Ouᵹαıll τo ὅpeıč oppα αннpιn ocup banna pαoιτιτúp. Αn τα ſeὅuın pιn τo ὅul αn opτuᵹaὅ αp cuιnнe a čeıle, ocup bpιpeὅh αp Sαxιnachαιb, ocup an bpıpeὅh pιn τo ὅeč oppa ᵹo cαıpıll Mıaὅαčáın, ocup a nτpuma ocup a mbpαcač τo ὅúaιn τıὅ, ocup τpem ὅıαıpeннe ὅoſαıpнeıpı τo muιnnčep na Sαxαnač τſαᵹὅáıl ıpın cpep ceᵹнalač cpenὅopb pιn. baıle an τoıpe, ocup Lıač cpuιm, ocup cluaın Muıpe ocup baıle na nᵹıolla τo Lopᵹuὅ ὅóıὅ. Αpc mac Ruαıὅpí ᵹlαıp .ı. pep bpαcαıᵹ bpıaın нıc 'Oıαpmατα τſαὅuıl ὅáıp αn blıaὅαıн pιn. O Cončoὅaıp pнaὅ ocup Comalcach óᵹ Mac 'Oıαpmατα, ocup Ruαıὅpí caoč Mac 'Oıαpmατα τo ᵹαὅáıl pep τolum, ocup a ᵹcup ᵹo pop Chumáın po ὅαoíppı нóıp. Αop óᵹ ſleačτα Sheoun a búpc τo čeἐč ᵹo Copunn, ocup cpeč τo ᵹlαcaὅ ὅóıὅ. Cóıp τo ὅpeıč oppa; cup čum a čeıle ὅóıὅ; pılleὅ ὅóıὅ αp an cópατ, ocup Copmac O Ruαnαıὅ τo нαpbaὅ, ocup τaoıne ele nach αıpmeτ. Maᵹ Uıτıp .ı. Cučonnacht oᵹ mac Conconnachc, pᵹel buὅ mo a ὅeᵹuıὅ ὅEıpınn τſαὅuıl ὅáıp. Αılınopα ınᵹen ıαplα 'Oepнumhan τo ὅul τhec, beн 1 Ruaıpc .ı. bpıan mac bpıaın 1 Ruaıpc. Αpe bα cıαᵹpnna ón mbαнnpıoᵹhan αp čoıᵹeὅ Chonnacht an uaıp pın .ı. pıp Ruıpceıpc bınnᵹem, ocup an нeıτ nαp čpoč pe τo claın Uıllıαm τo čuıp pe αᵹ coᵹατ αp an mbαнpıoᵹhan íατ, ocup clann n'Oonнaıll mαp an ceτnα; ocup τo čuıp pe pлıočτ Coppὅelbaıᵹ

<hr />

[1] *With him.* pпeıp, Clar.
[2] *Bothar-Scndomhnaigh*; the "road
of Sen-domhnach," or of the "old
dominica," now known as Shankill, a

A.D.
[1589.]

O'Ruairc himself, from Iascagh eastwards. The son of O'Ruairc, i.e., Eoghan, went to Machaire-Connacht, until he went to Cill-Toltog, and the sons of O'Conchobhair Ruadh along with him;[1] and they took no prey, for want of cavalry. And they turned back until they came to Bothar-Sendomhnaigh.[2] The sheriff of the county, i.e., Richard Mapother, and the Clann-Dubhgaill, and a band of soldiers, came up with them then. These two bodies went into array against one another, and the Saxons were routed; and this rout continued to Caisel-Miadhachain; and their drums and standard were taken from them; and a countless, indescribable, number of the Saxons' people were lost in that fierce, mutual, conflict. Baile-an-doire, and Liath-truim, and Cluain-Muire, and Baile-na-ngiolla were burned by them. Art, the son of Ruaidhri Glas, i.e., Brian Mac Diarmada's standard bearer, died this year. O'Conchobhair Ruadh, and Tomaltach Og Mac Diarmada, and Ruaidhri Caech Mac Diarmada, were taken prisoners, per dolum, and sent to Ros-Comain under great bondage. The young men of the posterity of John Burk came to Corann, and took a prey. A pursuing party overtook them. They approached each other. They turned upon the pursuers, and killed Cormac O'Ruanaidh, and others who are not enumerated. Mag Uidhir,[3] i.e. Cuchonnacht[4] Og, son of Cuchonnacht, almost the greatest loss to Erinn, died. Ailenora, the Earl of Des-Mumha's daughter, died; (the wife of O'Ruairc, i.e., of Brian, son of Brian O'Ruairc).

The person who was governor from the queen over the province of Connacht this time was Sir Richard Bingham, and all of the Clann-William whom he did not hang, he set at war with the queen; and the Clann-Domhnaill in like manner; and he set the posterity of Toirdhelbhach

---

very old church in the parish of the same name, barony of Boyle, and county of Roscommon.

[3] *Mag Uidhir.* Mᴀ5 Uıbıη, Clar.
[4] *Cuchonnacht.* Cuᴀᴅ́connᴀċᴄ, Clar.

τuınn 1 Chonċαḃαıp ocuſ ſlıoċὃ Ꮯoḃα mıc ſeıὃılım,
ocuſ muınnτeſ ſhlαnnıgάın, ocuſ O Ruαıſc ocuſ mαg
[ſ]lαnnchαıὃ, ocuſ ſlıoċὃ Ꮻoꝝhαın mıc ᴅıαſmαᴅα
αg cogαὃ αſ ſen ocuſ αſ αn mbαnſıoꝝhαn. Ocuſ ᴅo
ſunne bſeıᴅ ſlαταċ ſαıſτhıeċ ᴅo ċoıꝝeὃ Chonnαchτ,
ocuſ ᴅo ċuıſ ſe ſlıoċὃ Ꮟſıαın Lαoıὃnıꝝ ocuſ muınnτeſ
Ꮯıſτ ſαn ċogαὃ ſın, αn ṁeᴅ nαſ ċſoċ ſe ὃıὃ.

Mαſ ᴅo ċuαlαıꝝ gıuſτıſ nα hꝶſenn ınτ olc ſın ᴅo
ċuſ αſ Connαchτ ᴅo Ꮟıngαmαchαıb, ταınıc ſe go ſeıſꝝ
moıſ ocuſ go lonᴅuſ nαὃḃαıl go ſαınıc gαıllım, ocuſ
nı ċuꝝ ſe ᴅo ſluαꝝ leıſ αchτ ceᴅ mαſcαch ocuſ
ceᴅ coıſſıꝝe; ocuſ ᴅo αn ın guıbeſnoıſ α nαċ Luαın α
ſτuıᴅeſ mαſ ᴅo mıllſeαᴅh αn cuıᴅ nα αſ mıll ſe ᴅo
cuıgeᴅh Conαchτ. Ꞇαngαᴅαſ clαnn Uıllıαm go Ꝛαıllım,
ocuſ Muſchαᴅ O Ꝼlαċḃeαſταıꝝ, ocuſ ᴅo ſonnαᴅαſ ſıċ
ſıſın gıuıſτıſ, ocuſ ᴅo ċuıſeᴅαſ α ınbſαıꝝᴅe α lαım
muınᴅτıſe nα Ꝛαıllὃe. Uıllıαm Ꞇαıċ ocuſ cuıgeαſ αſ
ſıcheᴅ ſoıᴅıuſ, ocuſ cuıgeαſ mαſcαċ, ᴅo ᴅul ᴅoċum
ın beαlıꝝ buıὃe αſ Coſſſlıabh ᴅoıὃ. Mαc 1 Ruαıſc
ocuſ ſlıochτ Ꮻoꝝαın meıc ᴅıαſmαᴅα, ocuſ cuıᴅ ᴅo
clαınn ᴅonnchαıὃ, ᴅo ὃeıċ ſumſu αſ ın mbeαlαch,
ocuſ α ᴅo no τſı ᴅo ceαᴅuıὃ; ocuſ ᴅo eıſgeαᴅαſ ſın
ᴅonα Ꝛαlloıb, ocuſ ᴅo bſıſeαᴅαſ oſſἔα, ocuſ ᴅo
mαſbαᴅ αnᴅſın ceαċſα αſ ſıċıᴅ, ocuſ ᴅo bαıneᴅh
.x. neıċ ocuſ τſı bαıſıll ſıonα ᴅıὃ; ocuſ ᴅo ımıꝝ
Uıllıαm Ꞇαıꝝ. Mαg Mαċgαṁnα .ı. Roſſα buıὃe mαc
Ꮯıſτ mαoıl ᴅhec; ocuſ ſα moſ ınτ echτ ſın. Ꮟſıαın
mαc Ꮯoḃα oıg ᴅo ſıgαᴅ nα ınαὃ. Mαıꝝıſτıſ 8τſαınſe
ocuſ ſſımſαıꝝ Ꮯſᴅα mαċα, ocuſ αn gıuıſτıſ ᴅıluın,
ᴅo ᴅul go hαċ Cılle ſſαnαın αſ huchτ ın gıuıſτıſ,
ᴅo ὃenαṁ ſıċe ſe mαc 1 Ruαıſc; ocuſ ᴅo ſoınneαᴅαſ
ſıċ ſe ċele ſα ċoſᴅıα. Ꞃıſᴅeαſᴅ mαc Uατeſ mıc

¹ When. Brian MacDermot's handwriting recommences with the corresponding word in the text.

² Taith. Written "Taigh" in the
next sentence, and also elsewhere.
³ Of Eoghan. Ꮻαoꝝ, Clar.

A.D.
[1589.]

Donn O'Conchobhair, and the posterity of Aedh, son of Felim, and Muinter-Flannagain, and O'Ruairc, and Mac [F]lannchaidh, and the posterity of Eoghan Mac Diarmada, at war with himself and the queen. And he made a bare, polished, garment of the province of Connacht. (And he drove the posterity of Brian Laighnech, and Muinter-Airt, into that war—all of them that he did not hang).

When[1] the Justiciary of Erinn heard of that evil being inflicted on Connacht by the Binghams, he came with great anger and terrible fury, until he arrived at Gaillimh; and he brought with him no army, save 100 horse, and 100 foot. And the governor remained in Ath-Luain, studying how he might ruin the portion that he had not ruined of the province of Connacht. The Clann-William came to Gaillimh, and Murchadh O'Flaithbhertaigh; and they made peace with the Justiciary, and placed their hostages in the hands of the people of Gaillimh. William Taith,[2] and twenty-five soldiers, and five horsemen, went to the Bealach-buidhe on the Corr-sliabh. The son of O'Ruairc, and the posterity of Eoghan[3] Mac Diarmada, and some of the Clann-Donnchaidh, were before them on the pass, with two or three hundred persons; and they rose up against the Foreigners, and routed them; and twenty-four were then slain, and ten horses and three barrels of wine were taken from them; and William Taigh departed. Mac Mathghamhna, i.e., Rossa Buidhe, the son of Art Mael, died; and that was a great calamity. Brian, son of Aedh Og, was ordained in his place. Master Strange,[4] and the primate of Ard-Macha, and Justice Dillon, went to Ath-Cille-Sranain, on the part[5] of the Justiciary, to make peace with the son of O'Ruairc; and they cordially concluded peace with each other.

---

[4] *Master Strange.* Sir Thomas Le Strange appointed deputy-governor of Connacht, by Queen Elizabeth, in 1588, during the absence of Sir Richard Bingham in the Low Countries.

[5] *On the part.* ар huaṗ, for aр huachт (*recte* a huchт), Clar.

Seain mic Oliuepup a ḃupc vo mapbav vupċap vo
ṡunna a culaiᵹ Ccoṫa, ocuṛ ṛa mop inc echc ṛin.
Seaċan ṛuav mac Loċlainn mic Phavin .i. mac 1
Maoilċonṛe vhec, ocuṛ ṛa mop [in]c echc ṛin a leiṫ
vaonachca ocuṛ ealaṫna. Siupcan mac Comaiṛ na
capall vhec an iapnaċ anvṛan Eill aᵹ Saxṛanachaiḃ.
Cuiᵹaṫ Connachc uile ó aċ Luain ᵹo hEiṛne ṛa en olc
o aṛaonca Ᵹall ocuṛ Ᵹaoiveal ṛe ċele. Vaioᵹṛe
O Duiḃᵹenain, voine ṛo ḃinv ṛuilcuiṛ, vhec. Ᵹiollapav-
ṛaiᵹ oᵹ mac Ᵹillapavṛaiᵹ mic Ḟiliṛ meic Coiṛḃealb-
aiᵹ meᵹ Uiṫiṛ, ocuṛ ṛeaṛ ocuṛ ochcaṛ maṛaon ṛiṛ, vo
maṛbav ṛe Conchobaṛ oᵹ mac Conchobaiṛ ṛuaiv meᵹ
Uiṫiṛ, aṛ ceachc voiḃ le Donvchav óᵹ mac Donnchava
meᵹ Uiṫiṛ aiṛ Conchobaṛ oᵹ, vo ṫenaiḣ ᵹclaᵹaċaṛ aiṛ;
ocuṛ vo baineaṫ ṛichev no ṫo eċ viḃ, ocuṛ vo loiceaṫ ṛe
ṛiṛ ṫeᵹ aṛ ṛichev vo vaoinuiḃ Donnchava óiᵹ, ocuṛ vo
biṫ ṛiuṫal cṛi mile aiṛ. Ccoṫ mac Conchobaiṛ oiᵹ
mic Muiṛceṛcaiᵹ meic Diaṛmava ṛuaiṫ vheᵹ, ocuṛ va
mop in ṛᵹeal ṛin a leaṫ laime ocuṛ vaonachca; ocuṛ
cṛi ṛia cev ḟeil muiṛe ṛa ṛomaṛ veᵹ ṛe; ocuṛ vo
cuiṛeaṫ e a maiṛiṛcin na Ḃuile; ocuṛ vo maṛbav a mac
ṛoime ṛin ṛe ṛliochc Eoᵹain meic Diaṛmava .i. Ṛeaṛ-
vopċa mac Ccoṫa; ocuṛ Eoᵹan mac Ṛuaṫṛi mic in
ᵹiolla ṫuiṫ meic Diaṛmava ṛuaiṫ vo maṛb é. Sluaᵹ
Saxṛanaċ vo ċuṛ von ᵹuiḃeṛnoiṛ ᵹo hichcaṛ Connachc,
ocuṛ cuᵹavaṛ laṁ aṛ O n'Duḃva vo ċṛeachav, ocuṛ ni
aṛ eiṛiᵹ ṛin voiḃ ce vo ċuavaṛ ᵹo Cill ᵹlaiṛ ocuṛ ᵹo
heiṛᵹiṛ oḃuinn; cunᵹavaṛ caṛ a naiṛ ᵹo cuil cnam
ocuṛ vo ṁilleavaṛ anvṛin moṛan biṫ ocuṛ eviᵹ; ocuṛ
vo ċuavaṛ aṛṛin ᵹo ᵹleann Dallain, ocuṛ ni ṫṛuaṛavaṛ
evail na aṁancuṛ anvṛin. Ocuṛ vo ṛoinvevaṛ in
cṛeaṛ ṛiuṫal aṛ ċṛliochc Eoᵹain meic Diaṛmava;
ocuṛ ce vo ċuavaṛ ᵹo ciṛ Cuaṫil ocuṛ ᵹo coillciḃ

---

¹ *Thomas-na-capall.* Thomas "of
the horses," a nickname frequently
applied to freebooters.

² *Ferdorcha.* This name literally
signifies "dark man."

³ *Tried.* cuᵹavaṛ laṁ; lit.,
"they gave a hand."

⁴ *Coille-Conchobhair*; "the woods
of Conchobhar," a district in the north
of the co. Roscommon.

Richard, son of Walter, son of John, son of Oliver Burk, was killed by a gunshot in Tulach-Aedha; and that was a great calamity. John Ruadh, son of Lochlainn, son of Paidin, i.e., the son of O'Maelconaire, died; and that was a great calamity as regards humanity and science. Jordan, son of Thomas-na-capall,[1] died *whilst confined* in irons, in the Eill, by Saxons. The entire province of Connacht, from Ath-Luain to Erne, was under one evil, from the dissensions of Foreigners and Gaeidhel with each other. Daighre O'Duibhgennain, a most affable, musical man, died. Gilla-Patraic Og, son of Gilla-Patraic, son of Philip, son of Toirdhelbhach MagUidhir, and nine men along with him, were slain by Conchobhar Og, the son of Conchobhar Ruadh MagUidhir, on their coming with Donnchadh Og, son of Donnchadh MagUidhir, against Conchobhar Og, to take a prey from him; and a score or two of horses were taken from them; and thirty-six of Donnchadh Og's men were wounded, and he was pursued three miles. Aedh, son of Conchobhar Og, son of Muirchertach MacDiarmada Ruadh, died; and he was much to be lamented as regards prowess and humanity; and three days before the festival of Mary in the autumn he died; and he was buried in the monastery of the Buill; and his son, i.e., Ferdorcha,[2] the son of Aedh, was killed before that by the posterity of Eoghan Mac Diarmada; (and Eoghan, son of Ruaidhri, son of the Gilla-dubh Mac Diarmada Ruadh, that killed him). A Saxon army was sent by the governor to Lower Connacht; and they tried[3] to plunder O'Dubhda, but did not succeed, although they went to Cill-glas, and to Esker-abhann. They returned back to Cuil-cnamh, and destroyed much food and clothing there; and they went from thence to Glenn-Dallain, and they found neither spoils nor adventure there. And they made the third expedition against the posterity of Eoghan Mac Diarmada; and though they went to Tir-Tuathail, and to Coillte-Conchobhair,[4] and

Conchobaıp, ocuʏ ταp ʋpoıʒeτ mıc Mαonαıʒ ʏuαp, nı αp
eıpıʒ άϸ nα αṁαnτup ϸoıϸ; ocuʏ ʋo bύʋ coıp ʋo Όıα ʒαn
éʋαıl ʋpαʒαıl ʋoıϸ; ʏıublαıʒϊe ʏɘıłłe ʋo poınʋeαʋαp.
8eon bınʒαm cenʋ ınτ ʏłuαıʒ ʏın .ı. ʋepϸpατhαıp ın
ʒıubepnoıp; ocuʏ nı ϊαınıc α Connαchτα ʏıαṁ coṁołc α
poıϸe αp ın ʏłuαʒ ʏın, oıp nı poıϸe ʋuıne ʏα ʋomαn ʋα
ʏαϸαʋαp ʋıłeαp α ccıłł nα τuαıτh. 8en bαʋun 8łıʒıʒ
ocuʏ Όpoım nα ʏʒołb ʋo łopʒαϸ ʋo muınnτıp Ɑıpτ.
bpıαn mαc Ɑoϸα óıʒ meʒ Mαϊʒαmnα, ocuʏ Ɑoϸ puαʋ
mαc Ɑıpτ ṁαoıl, ʋo ʋul ʒo bαıle Ɑϊα cłıαϊ, ʋoϊom bpeϊe
ın ʒıuıʏτıp ocuʏ nα comαpłe ʏα τıʒepnuʏ Oıpʒeαłł
meʒ Mαϊʒαmnα; ocuʏ ʋo puʒαʋαp nα mαıϊe ʏın ın
τıʒepnuʏ ʋɑoϸ puαϸ mαc Ɑıpτ mαoıl, ocuʏ ʋo ϊuıp ın
ʒıuıʏτıp ʏe bαnʋα łe Ɑoϸ puαϸ, ocuʏ ʋo ʒoıp ʏe τıʒepnα
ʋe. Όo ımϊıʒ mαc Ɑoϸα oıʒ αṁpeıʒ ʋα ʋuϊαıʒ ʏeın ʒo
Όαpτpαoı, ocuʏ ʋo ʏαʒ ʏe ın τíp ocuʏ ʋo puʒ α cαopıʒ-
αchτ łeıp ʏo nα ʋαınʒnıϊuıϸ, ocuʏ ʋo ʏαʒ ʏe Ruʋpαıʒ
α ʋepbpıαϊαıp α bαpʋαϊτ Όαpτpαoı. Ocuʏ ʋo ʒαϸ eαpτın
Płüınceτ ʋoϊum α τípe, ocuʏ ʋo ϊpıol ʏe ʒo poıϸ ʏı
ʏαłαṁ; ocuʏ ʋo eıpıʒ Ruʒpıʒ ʋoıϸ ocuʏ ʋo ϊuıp ʏe
ϊucu, ocuʏ ʋo bpıʏ oppϊα, ocuʏ ʋo mαpbαʋ ın cuıʋ
bα mo ʋα bαnnα [αıp] cαpτın Płüınceτ. Όo mıłłeαϸ
ın τıp eατoppα .ı. mαc Ɑoϸα óıʒ ocuʏ mαc Ɑıpτ mαoıl.
Mαc 1 Neıłł .ı. Conn mαc 8eαın ʋo łeıʒeαn αp bpαıʒ-
ʋenuʏ ʋO Neıłł ın błıαʒαın ʏe, ocuʏ cpeϊα mopα ʋo
ϸenαm αp ıαpłα Ułłαϸ .ʋo ʏʏeın ocuʏ ʋα bpατpıb.
Uıłc mopα α nUłłτoıb ocuʏ Connαchτα ın błıαʒαın ʏe.
Όon hɑnτuıne ʋepϸpατhαıp píʒ Popτınʒeαł, ʋo ϸí αp
ınnαpbαʋ ʏάϊpé bαnpıʒαn 8αxpαn .ı. Ełıʏʋαbeʋ, o ʋo
mαpʋαʋ pıʒ Popτıʒeαł α cαϊh łeıp ın Τupʒαch, ocuʏ ʋo
ınʋαpb pıʒ nα 8bαınne ʋon hɑnτuıne αn uαıp ʏın, ocuʏ
ʋo ϸαın ʏé ın pıʒeαchτ ocuʏ cαϊαıp łıópbuınne ʋe, ocuʏ
ʋo ṁαpb ʏé α ʋαoıne uıłe; ocuʏ ατα ʏé ʏαpıʏ ın

---

1 *Expeditions.* ʏuıϸłαıʒϊɘ, Clar.
2 *To whom they were faithful.* ʋα
ʏαϸαʋαp ʋıłeαʏ; repeated in Clar.

3 *Bawn.* bαnu, for bαnun, (*recte*
bαʋun), Clar.
4 *Regarding.* ʏαϊ for ʏα, Clar.

upwards past Droichet-mic-Maenaigh, they met neither good fortune nor adventure. And it was right of God that they should not get spoils: treacherous expeditions[1] they performed. John Bingham was the head of that army, i.e., the governor's brother; and there never came into Connacht such wicked people as were in that army; for there was not a man in the world to whom they were faithful,[2] in church or territory. The old bawn[3] of Sligech, and Druim-na-scolb, were burned by Muinter-Airt. Brian, the son of Aedh Og Mac Mathghamhna, and Aedh Ruadh, the son of Art Mael, went to Baile-atha-cliath, to obtain the decision of the Justiciary and council regarding[4] the lordship of Oirghiall-Mic-Mathghamhna ; and those nobles gave the lordship to Aedh Ruadh, the son of Art Mael ; and the Justiciary sent six companies with Aedh Ruadh, and proclaimed him lord. The son of Aedh Og went discontented[5] to his own country, to Dartrai ; and he left the district, and carried off his creaghts towards the fastnesses ; and he left his brother Rudhraighe in the wardship of Dartrai. And Captain Plunket proceeded to his country, thinking that it was unoccupied ; and Rudhraighe rose against them ; and he attacked them, and routed them ; and the greater number of Captain Plunket's band were slain. The country was ruined between them, i.e., *between* the son of Aedh Og and the son of Art Mael. The son of O'Neill, i.e., Conn, son of John, was released from confinement by O'Neill this year ; and great depredations were committed upon the Earl of Ulster by himself and his brothers. Great injuries *were committed* in Ulster and Connacht this year. Don Antonio, the king of Portugal's brother, was in exile, residing with the queen of the Saxons, i.e., Elizabeth, since the king of Portugal was slain in battle by the Turk, (when the king of Spain banished Don Antonio, and took from him the sovereignty, and the city of Lisbon,

---

[5] *Discontented.* airíṗeiṡ ; lit., "uneasy," Clar.

mbanpiʒhan o ṙin; ocuṛ ᴅo ċuiṛ ṛi aṛmail Leiṛ ᴅoċum
a ᴅuċhaiᴅe .i. cuiʒ mili ᴅheʒ, ocuṛ cuiʒ mile ᴅhec eile,
ınann ṛin ocuṛ .x. mile ṛicheᴅ. Ocuṛ ᴅo ċuaᴅaṛ ʒo
Lioṛbuinᴅ, ocuṛ ᴅo maṛbaᴅaṛ moṛan ᴅaoineᴅh, ocuṛ ᴅo
Loiṛʒeaᴅaṛ aṛoiᴆe on ṗṛim ċaᴆṛuiʒ amach aṛ ʒaċ
ταοᴆ ᴅı. 'Oo ṗuʒaᴅaṛ 8bainniʒh oṛṛéa, ocuṛ ᴅo τuiτ
meiᴅ aᴆṛiᴆe ᴅo milτibh aτoṛṛa, ocuṛ ᴅo τuiτ ochτ mile
ᴅhec ᴅo ᴆṛaxṛanaib ann. Ocuṛ iṛ ıaᴅ ṛo anmanṅa na
haṛmala ᴅo ċuiṛ ın banṛiʒan le ᴅon hℂnτuine .i. ṛiṛ
8eon Noṛaiṛ ocuṛ ıaṛla o Ḃṛeauiʒ, ocuṛ ṛiṛ Ḟṛamṛa
'Oṛach, ocuṛ ᴅeiċ mile ṛicheᴅ maṛaon ṛıu; ocuṛ ᴅo
maṛbaᴅ ᴅiᴆ ṛin ochτ mile ᴅeʒ a Liṛbuin. Ni ṛeṛ ᴅuin
ᴅiᴆ 8bainech. Ṛiʒ Ḟṛanʒ ᴅo maṛbaᴅ ᴅo bṛaᴆaiṛ ṗeṛ
ᴅolum, oiṛ ᴅo búᴆ coiṛ ᴅo 'Oia ṛin; ᴅo ṛinne ṛe ṛein
ṛeall, oiṛ ᴅo maṛb ṛe ᴅuice o Cuibeṛ.

In ʒıuiṛτıṛ ᴅo ᴆeachτ ʒo ʒaıLLuıᴆ .i. UilLiam Ḟaoı-
uilLiam, ocuṛ τanıc mac UilLiam ocuṛ Muṛchaᴅ na τuaᴆ
na cenᴅ, ocuṛ ᴅo ṛoinᴅeᴅaṛ ṛiᴆ ṛiṛ; ocuṛ ᴅo ċuaıᴅ ın
ʒıuiṛτıṛ aṛṛın ʒo 8liʒech, aʒuṛ τaıñıc ṛe aṛṛın ʒo ṛoṛa
Chomain, ocuṛ ᴅo ṛoinᴅne ṛiᴆ ṛe Connachτuıᴆ uile;
ocuṛ ᴅo ċuaıᴆ aṛṛın a nUllτoib, ocuṛ ᴅo ċuaıᴆ moṛan
ᴅo maıᴆuıᴆ Θṛenn Leiṛ, ocuṛ ᴅo ṛoinᴅe ṛiᴆ eτiṛ clanna
NeilL. Inᴅṛaoıʒe Laoı ᴅo τabaıṛτ ᴅℂoᴆ ṛuaᴅ mac
ℂıṛτ ṁaoıl Meʒ Maʒamna aṛ Ḃṛian mac ℂoᴆa óıʒ
Meʒ Maʒamna, ocuṛ ṛe ṛıoṛ ᴅhec ᴅa muınnτıṛ ᴅo
maṛbaᴅ aıṛ an Laᴆaıṛ ṛın. Ṛuaᴆṛı caoċ mac Τaıᴅʒ
meıc Τomalτaıʒ mıc 'Oiaṛmaᴅa, ocuṛ clann Maoıl-
ṛuanaıᴅ mıc Τomalτaıʒ, ocuṛ clann 1 Conċuᴆaiṛ ṛuaıʒ,
ᴅo bualuᴆ ṛa ċele an aṛᴅ mıc nΘoʒain anᴅṛan aoıᴆċe,
ocuṛ ᴅo maṛbaᴅ anᴅṛin mac 1 Ḟhlanaʒain .i. Θmann
mac Ḃṛiain, ocuṛ ᴅo maṛbaᴅ ᴅon τaoıᴆ aᴆuṛ mac meıc
'Oiaṛmaᴅa ṛuaıᴆ .i. 8ean mac Τaıᴅʒ mıc Chonċubaıṛ

---

1 *Essex.* The scribe seems to have
entirely misunderstood this name,
which he strangely represents by
o Ḃṛeauiʒ. This sentence and the
next are misplaced in the MS., in
which they follow the entry of the
murder now placed after them in the
text.

and killed all his people ; and he has been with the
queen ever since). And she sent an armament with him to his country, viz., fifteen thousand, and fifteen thousand more—which is equal to thirty thousand. And they went to Lisbon ; and they killed many men, and burned all that was outside the capital on each side. The Spaniards came up with them, and some thousands fell between them ; and eighteen thousand Saxons fell there. (And these are the names of the commanders the queen sent with Don Antonio, viz., Sir John Norreys, and the Earl of Essex,[1] and Sir Francis Drake ; and thirty thousand were along with them ; and eighteen thousand of these were slain at Lisbon. We know not the loss of the Spaniards.) The king of France was killed by a friar, per dolum ; but this was just of God, because he himself had committed treachery, for he killed the Duke of Guise.[2] The Justiciary i.e., William FitzWilliam, came to Gaillimh ; and Mac William, and Murchadh-na-tuadh, came to meet him, and they made peace with him. And the Justiciary went from thence to Sligech ; and he came from thence to Ros-Comain, and concluded peace with all Connacht. And he went from thence to Ulster ; and a great many of the chieftains of Erinn went with him ; and he concluded peace between the Clanna-Neill. A day attack was made by Aedh Ruadh, son of Art Mael Mac Mathghamhna, on Brian, the son of Aedh Og Mac Mathghamhna ; and sixteen men of his people were slain on that field. Ruaidhri Caech, the son of Tadhg, son of Tomaltach Mac Diarmada, and the sons of Maelruanaidh son of Tomaltach, and the sons of O'Conchobhair Ruadh, encountered each other at Ard-mic-nEoghain in the night ; and O'Flannagain's son, i.e., Edmond, son of Brian, was killed there ; and the son of Mac Diarmada Ruadh, i.e.,

---

[2] *Guise.* The scribe's attempt at writing this name is hardly more successful than the endeavour to write that of the Earl of Essex. It is not easy to discover the name of Guise under the form o Cuɩbeɼ.

oιz mιc Mαιρcερταιξ. 1nτ εαρρος mαzz Conzαιlε .ι.
ιn zιllα zlαp ohεc αnoρnα cεαlluιổ bεzα, αzup pα moρ
ιnτ εchτ pιn α lειổ ιιιξ ocup oαonαchτα. Toιρổεαlbαch
O Ốριαιn, .ι. mαc Tαιổz mιc Conchobαιρ 1 Ốριαιn, ohεc.
Connoαοιp Tuαmumαn .ι. ιnzεn mιc 1 Ốριαιn Ccραổ,
ocup Unα α hαιnm, ohεc. Ốριαιn mαc Mαοιlρuαnαιổ
mειc Fερzαιl, .ι. ιn clειρεch oob fεpp oo bιổ αn Eριnn,
oo héz pεổτmαιn pια pαmuιn αp αn nZpαιnpιξ moιρ,
ocup bα hαổbαιl ιnτ εchτ pιn α lειổ oαonαchτα ocup
εαlεαổnα. Cρεαchα moρα oo ổεnαm oo ιαρlα Uluoh
αp U Cαổαιn, ocup αn cεonα oo ổεnαm oo cloιno τ8εαιn
1 Nειll, ocup oo mαc Toιρoεαlbαιξ luιnιξ .ι. mαc
1 Nειll, αp Coρmαc mαc ιn ổαρuιn, ou αno αροιổε oά
cεo ohεz bo. Moραn oo cαοριαchτ 1 Nειll oo oul α
Fεαρmαnαổ α τεchεo, ocup mαp oo ổuαlαιξ αnτ ιαρlα
α bραổαιρ oo cρεổαổ oo lεn pε cαοριαchτ 1 Nειll zo
Fεαρmαnαổ, ocup oo puz pε pιchεo cεo bo lειp. Oo
puιno ιnτ ιαρlα nα cρεαổα, ocup oo ραnιc pε cεo bo ε
pειn; ocup oo lεαnαoup oρonz oo mαρερluαξ 1 Nειll
ιnτ ιαρlα αp α oροιιιm, ocup oo puz pιαo ιn pε cεo bo
pιn uαổα. Mαc Tomαlταιξ mιc Oιαρmαoα .ι. Tomαl-
ταch óz oo pέổuổα oo Ốριαn mαc Oιαρmuoα ocup oo
mαc Oάbιổ αp pιιpιιι nα bαnριzαn. Mαc Fερzαιl οιz
1 Rαιξιllιξ .ι. Ốριαn oo mαρbαo α pεαll oo ổpιαρριαm
nα Ốρεpnε .ι. Eουổαρo hoιρεαbεαρτ, ocup α muιξε
ổhρεcριξε oo pοιnoεαổ ιn mαρbαo pιn; ocup pα hαổbαιl ιnτ εchτ pιn α lειổ ειnιξ ocup uαιplε. Fιαchρα
mαc Ohαhí 1 Ouổoα ohεc. Oonnchαo zραnα mαc
Uιllιαm οιz mιc Uιllιαm mιc Conchobαιρ .ι. τιzερnα
Coιllεαổ ιn bozαιoh ohεc. Mαc Oιαρmαoα Ruαổ .ι.

¹ On this side; i.e., on the side of
the Mac Dermots.

² Gilla-glas; i.e. the "grey fellow."
His name was Domhnall Mac Conghaile (or Magonigle, as the name is
now written). He was bishop of
Raphoe, and assisted at the Council

of Trent, in 1563. See Harris's ed.
of Ware's Works, vol. 1, p. 275.

³ Earl of Ulster. The Earl of
Tir-Eoghain, or Tyrone.

⁴ The Baron's son. Son to Matthew,
Baron of Dungannon, and brother of
Hugh O'Neill, Earl of Tyrone. Cor-

A.D.
[1589.]

John, son of Tadhg, son of Conchobhar Og, son of Muirchertach, was slain on this side.[1] The Bishop Mac Conghaile, i.e., the Gilla-glas,[2] died in the Cella-bega ; and that was a woeful event in respect of bounty and humanity. Toirdhelbhach O'Briain, i.e., the son of Tadhg, son of Conchobhar O'Briain, died. The countess of Tuadh-Mumha, i.e., the daughter of Mac-I-Briain-Aradh, (and her name was Una), died. Brian, son of Maelruanaidh, son of Ferghal, i.e , the best cleric that was in Erinn, died a week before Allhallowtide, in the Grainsech-mór ; and that was a prodigious calamity in respect of humanity and learning. Great depredations were committed by the Earl of Ulster[3] upon O'Cathain ; and similar preys, in which were 1,200 cows, were taken by the sons of John O'Neill, and by the son of Toirdhelbhach Luinech, i.e., the son of O'Neill, from Cormac, the Baron's son.[4] A great portion of O'Neill's creaghts went into Feara-Manach, to escape; and when the Earl heard that his brother had been plundered, he followed O'Neill's creaghts to Feara-Manach, and carried off two thousand cows. The Earl divided the preys, and six hundred cows fell to his own share. And a party of O'Neill's cavalry followed after the Earl, and they carried off those six hundred cows from him. The son of Tomaltach Mac Diarmada, i.e., Tomaltach Og, was liberated by Brian Mac Diarmada, and by Mac David, from the queen's prison. The son of Ferghal Og O'Raighilligh, i.e., Brian, was killed in treachery by the sheriff of the Breifne, i.e., Edward Herbert; and in Magh-Brecraighe that homicide was committed; and that was a prodigious calamity in respect of bounty and nobility. Fiachra, son of David Dubh O'Dubhda, died. Donnchadh Grana, son of William Og, son of William, son of Conchobhar, i.e., the lord of Coill-in-bogaidh,[5] died. Mac Diarmada Ruadh, i.e., Maurice, son

---

mac was generally known as "Cormac Mac Baron."

[5] *Coill-in-bogaidh.* The "wood of the bog" (or "beggy land").

Muiɼɼeɼ mac Conchobaiɼ oiʒ mic Muiɼceɼταiʒ ᴅhec a
τoɼach ın ʒeımpıʒ. Maʒnuɼ mac Coınᴅ mic ın calbaiʒ
1 ᴅomnaıll ᴅo maɼbaᴅ ɼe ɼlıochτ Coɼmaıc buıᴅe
1 ʒhallcubaıɼ. 1nʒen 1 Falluın .ı. 8ıle ınʒen Coᴆuıʒ, ın
ben ᴅo ᴆıᴆ aʒ Ceᴅach mac ᴅomnaıll 1 Ceallaıʒ, ᴅhec.
ᴆɼıɼeaᴆ coınᴅe ᴅo ᴆabaıɼτ aɼ Tomalτach óʒ· mac
Tomalτaıʒ mıc ᴅıaɼmaᴅa, ᴅo claınn 1 Conchobaıɼ
ɼuaıᴆ ocuɼ ᴅO Flannaʒaın, .ı. ᴆɼıan mac Emaınn, aʒ
Cɼᴅ ın čomla, ocuɼ ᴅo maɼbaᴅ annɼın ᴆɼıan mac
Eoʒaın ʒɼanna, ocuɼ ᴅonnchaᴅ ᴅuᴆ mac ᴅonnchaᴅa
ʒɼana, ocuɼ ᴅuᴆʒall mac ʒıollaɼamaıɼ, τɼı ɼeachτ-
muıne ɼıa nollaıʒ. Taɼeıɼ ɼıʒ Fɼanʒ ᴅo maɼbaᴅ ᴅon
ᴆɼaċhaıɼ ᴅaɼ čomaınm 8ečaɼım, aᴅubaıɼτ ɼıʒ ᴅa
Naᴆaɼɼa ʒo mbeaᴆ ɼıʒeachτ na Fɼanʒe aıʒe ɼeın, ocuɼ
aᴅubaıɼτ ɼɼıanɼa Fɼemuınnτe ᴅaaɼ čomaınm ᴅuıᴆce
8aue ʒo mbeaᴆ ɼıʒechτ na Fɼanʒe aıʒe ɼeın. ᴅo cuıɼ
banɼıʒan 8axɼan ᴅeıč mılı ɼeɼ ᴅo čoᴊnam le ɼıʒ ᴅa
Naᴆaɼɼa. ᴅo čuıɼ cınʒ Fılıp ıumaᴅ ᴅaoıneaᴅ ᴅo
conʒnam le ɼɼınɼa Feɼmuınτe, ocuɼ ᴅo cuıɼeᴅh caᴆ
eıᴅıɼ na ɼıʒuıᴆ ɼın, ocuɼ ᴅo τuıτ ɼeachτ mıle ɼıcheᴅ
aτoɼɼa.

Eoʒan mac ᴆɼıaın mıc ᴆɼıaın mıc Eoʒaın 1 Ruaıɼc,
ɼeɼ a oıɼɼe ıɼ ɼeɼɼ τanıc ᴅo τɼlıochτ Cοᴆa Fınᴅ ɼe
ɼaᴅa, ᴅhec ın τɼeaɼ la ᴅon noᴅlaıʒ. Mac mıc
ʒoıɼᴅealb .ı. Uıllıam caoch mac 8ıuɼτaın mıc 8eaın
ᴆuıᴆ, ocuɼ Uıllıam mac 8eaın mıc Maoılɼe ɼuaıᴆ, ᴅo
maɼbaᴅ aɼ 8lıaᴆ muıɼe le ᴅonnchaᴅ mac Emaınᴅ
boᴅaıɼ 1 Ceallaıʒ, ɼeᴄτmuın ɼıa noᴅlaıc. 1n ʒıuıɼτıɼ
ᴅo τeachτ ʒo ʒaıllım ɼluaʒ ᴅıᴄaıɼme caoıcıɼ ɼıa
noᴅlaıʒ, ᴅo ᴆenaᴊ ɼıᴄe ɼe claınn Uıllıam ocuɼ ɼe
claınn ᴅomnaıll. Mac 1 lleıll .ı. Cοᴆ ʒeımleaᴄ mac
8eaın ᴅo ʒaᴆaıl ɼe 8eaan mac Meʒ Uıᴅıɼ a ɼeall a

---

1 *Conference.* The expression bɼıɼeᴅ | made by one party on another, whilst
coınne "breach of conference" was | engaged in a conference for the ar-
used to signify a treacherous attack | rangement of mutual differences.

of Conchobhar Og, son of Muirchertach, died in the beginning of the winter. Maghnus, son of Conn, son of the Calbhach O'Domhnaill, was killed by the posterity of Cormac Buidhe O'Gallchubhair. O'Fallon's daughter, i.e., Celia, daughter of Cobhthach, the wife of Cedach, son of Domhnall O'Cellaigh, died. A breach of conference[1] was committed upon Tomaltach Og, son of Tomaltach Mac Diarmada, by the sons of O'Conchobhair Ruadh, and by O'Flannagain (i.e., Brian, son of Edmond), at Ard-inchomla; and Brian, son of Eoghan Grana, and Donnchadh Dubh, son of Donnchadh Grana, and Dubhgall, son of Gillasamhais, were slain there, three weeks before Christmas. After the murder of the king of France by the friar whose name was James, the king of Navarre said that he himself should have the kingdom of France; and the prince of Piedmont, who was called Duke of Savoy, said that he should have the kingdom of France himself. The queen of the Saxons sent ten thousand men to assist[2] the king of Navarre. King Philip sent many men to assist the prince of Piedmont; and a battle was fought between these kings, and twenty-seven thousand fell between them.

Eoghan, son of Brian, son of Brian, son of Eoghan O'Ruairc, the best man of his years that had come of the race of Aedh Finn for a long time, died the third day of Christmas. The son of Mac Goisdelbh, i.e., William Caech, son of Jordan, son of John Dubh, and William, son of John, son of Meiler Ruadh, were slain on Sliabh-Muire by Donnchadh, son of Edmond Bodhar O'Cellaigh, a week before Christmas. The Justiciary came to Gaillimh, with a numerous[3] army, a fortnight before Christmas, to make peace with the Clann-William and Clann-Domhnaill. O'Neill's son, i.e. Aedh Geimhlech, son of John, was taken prisoner[4] by John, the son of Mag Uidhir, in treachery, in the house

---

[1] *To assist.* oo comnam. This is bad orthography. The proper form is oo congnam.

[2] *Numerous.* oitaipihe, for oi-aipihe, lit. "innumerable," Clar.

[3] *Taken prisoner.* oo gaubail, *ib.*

τιζ mαpcαιξ το muιηητιp Mαζ Uιτιp. Cαιηιc ιαpλα
ťιpe hEoζαιη ζo pepuιჄ Mαηαᵭ, ocup το ζαჄ pe Mαζ
Uιτιp, ocup το mαpbατ ochταp τα muιητιp, ocup το
puζ ιητ ιαpλα λειp CcoჄ O Ńειλλ; ocup το τuζ pe ρᵭe
eᵭ το ᵭ8heᵭαη Mαζ Uιτιp το ᵭιητ α τpoᵭ pepbιppe;
ocup τoᵭum α ṁιλλτe το puζ pe CcoჄ O Ńειλλ λειp.
Mαoλpechλαιηη oζ mαc Copmαιc mειc Ⴐοηηchατα,
αჄჄαp pιξ O ηOιλιoλλα, τeζ α ηeppαᵭ ηα bλιατηα pα,
ocup pα αჄჄαλ ιητ echτ pιη mαc ιηζιηe Mιc Ⴐιαpmατα
α λειᵭ uαιpλe ocup ιηιξ.

ǀᴄτɬ. ιαηαιp pop Ⴐepταoιη, ocup αppι αoιp ιη Cιζepηα
τειᵭ mbλιατηα ocup cειᵭpe pιcheτ .ccccc. oζup mιλe.
O Ceαλλαιξ .ι. CcoჄ mαc Ⴐοηηchατα mιc Emαιητ ǀ
Cheαλλαιξ, ocup pα uαpαλ αppαchτα ιη peαp pιη, ocup
αη ceυ λα τοη bλιατuιη το puαιp bαp .ι. λα ηoτλαιc
beζ, ocup το cuιpeατh e α cιλλ pιητbuιჄe, eτ bα
hαჄbαιλ ιητ echτ pιη. Ιη ζιuιpτιp το pαζჄαιλ ηα
Ⴔαιλλme τpι pechτmuιηe ιαp ηoτλαιζ, ocup ηι αp pαζ
pe pιᵭ ηα pocpαchτ α ConnαchτuιჄ τοη τuλ pιη; ocup
το αη ιη ζuιჄepηoιp α ηᏃαιλλιm το ζeηαṁ ζcoζαιτ eιp
cλαιηη Uιλλιαm. Cλαηη mειc Uιλλιαm το τeαchτ ζo
hCcιpτeαch, ocup αp α ჄpιλλeჄ τοιჄ ταp α ηαιp τuζαταp
pζαᵭαჄ τοη Ⴤeαηη pατα, ocup το mαpbατ αητpιη
Ccηητuιηe mαᵭ Uατep cαoιᵭ mιc Cοmαιp τuιჄ mιc
Shιupταιη, ocup τιoλuηαᵭ eιλe, ocup το λoιpζeαჄ ιη
bαιλe o cαιpλeη αmαᵭ. Mαc ǀ Ńειλλ .ι. CcoჄ ζeιmλech
mαc Seαιη mιc Coιητ, ιαp ηα ζαჄαιλ α peαλλ το ťpeααη
mαc Mαζ Uιτιp, ocup α ᵭαჄαιpτ τCcoჄ O Ńειλλ .ι. ιαpλα
τιpe hEoζαιη; ocup το cpoᵭ ιητ ιαpλα ιη mαc pιη ǀ Ńειλλ
το ηemᵭoιλ αpoιbe α τιp Eoζαιη uιλe, ocup pα αჄჄαιλ

---

¹ *Cill-Finnbhuidhe.* Killinvoy, bar.
of Athlone, co. Roscommon. This
concludes fol. 39b of the Clar. fragment. Prof. O'Curry has added a
pencil note at the head of the next
folio (40) in the following words:—

"Note—This folio is not consecutive
to any of the other folios." But this
is a mistake, into which O'Curry
seems to have been led by observing
that the greater part of the last line
on fol. 39b was left blank; for it is

of a horseman of Mag Uidhir's people. The Earl of Tir- A.D.
Eoghain came to Feara-Manach, and apprehended Mag [1589.]
Uidhir; and eight of his people were slain; and the Earl
took Aedh O'Neill with him; and he gave twenty horses
to John Mag Uidhir, in reward for his evil service. And
it was with a view to his destruction he took Aedh O'Neill
with him.   Maelsechlainn Og, the son of Cormac Mac
Donnchadha, intended king of Ui-nOilella, died in the
spring of this year; and this son of Mac Diarmada's
daughter was very much lamented in respect of nobility
and bounty.

The kalends of January on Thursday; and the age of [1590.]
the Lord is one thousand, five hundred, and ninety years.
O'Cellaigh, i.e., Aedh, son of Donnchadh, son of Edmond
O'Cellaigh, *died*; and he was a noble, brave man; and
the first day of the year he died, i.e., Little Christmas
day; and he was buried in Cill-Finnbhuidhe,[1] and that
was a prodigious calamity.

The Justiciary left Gaillimh three weeks after Christmas; and he left neither peace nor quietness in Connacht
on that occasion. And the governor remained in Gaillimh,
to make war on the Clann-William. Mac William's
sons went to Airtech;[2] and when they were turning back,
they made an attack upon the Benn-fada, and Anthony,
son of Walter Caech, son of Thomas Dubh, son of Jordan,
was killed there, and another soldier; and the town was
burned from the castle out. O'Neill's son, i.e., Aedh
Geimhlech, son of John, son of Conn, after having been
treacherously apprehended by John, the son of Mag
Uidhir, was surrendered to Aedh O'Neill, i.e., the Earl of
Tir-Eoghain;[3] and the Earl hanged this son of O'Neill in
despite of all who were[4] in Tir-Eoghain; and that was[4] a

---

certain that the first line of fol. 40 is a
continuation of the entry of Aedh (or
Hugh) O'Cellaigh's death, and that
the remaining entries belong to the
year 1590.

[2] *Airtech*. hCCirceah, Clar.
[3] *Of Tir-Eoghain*. cine hoóg,
Clar.
[4] *Was*. ract for ra, Clar. This
is very corrupt orthography.

ιnc eċc ριn. Conn mac Neιll óιʒ, cιʒepnα clαιnne
Ccoδα buιδe, ɒhec. Mαc mιc Ɒomnαιll nα hCClbαn,
Sαmαιρle buιδe, ɒhec. Ůριαn cαρραċ mαc Coρmαιc
ɒhec. Seαn mαc Ůριαιn mιc Felιm bαcαιʒ 1 Neιll ɒo
mαρbαɒ le mαc Sαmαιρle buιδe, ocuρ bα hαδbαιl nα
hecħcα ριn. Mαc Mιc Ɒιαρmαɒα .ι. Mαolρuαnαιδ
mαc CCoδα Mιc Ɒιαρmαɒα, ɒo mαρbαɒ ρe Comαlcαch
mαc Cαιδʒ mιc Eoʒαιn Mιc Ɒιαρmαɒα, ocuρ ρe
Ruαδριʒ cαoċ mαc Eoʒαιn mιc Cαιδʒ mιc Ruαδρι Mιc
Ɒιαρmαɒα, αnɒ¡α Chαlαδ α ρeαll, ocuρ ρα cρuαʒ ιn
ʒnιαm ριn. Sιρ Rιρɒeαρc ɒo ɒul ρluαʒ ɒιαρme αρ
clαιnn Uιllιαm no ʒo ραιnιc ρlιαδ ɒo CCoδα. Cuιɒ ɒo
clαιnn Uιllιαm ocuρ ɒo clαιnn Ɒomnαιll ɒo eιρʒe ɒoιδ,
ocuρ cρoιɒ ɒo ċαδαιρc ɒα celι ɒoιδ, ocuρ beʒαn mαρδċα
ɒo δenαm αcαρρuδ αιρ ʒαch cαoιδ. In ʒuιδeαρnoιρ
ɒo ɒul ʒo Ůαιle αρρα cαoραch, ocuρ ρoρlonʒρoρc ɒo
δenαm ɒo αnɒ, ocuρ ɒul αρριn ɒo ɒon Lαʒαn. Mαc
Uιllιαm ocuρ α ċιneαδ, ocuρ clαnn Ɒomnαιll, ɒo beιċ
α δρορlonʒρoρc ρe cαoιδ ιnc ρluαιʒ ʒαll ριn. Cuιɒ co
ceιριnɒ ιnc ρluαιʒ ɒo ceαchc ɒo loρʒuδ αρδα Uαceρ α
δuρc, ocuρ ɒo ρuʒ oρρα mαc Uιllιαm ocuρ Uαceρ cιcαċ,
ocuρ ɒo mαρbαɒ ɒιαρ ɒon ċeιριnɒ ; ocuρ ɒo Ůuαιl neαch
αcuραn mαc Uιllιαm ɒo Ůuιle αρ α ċoιρ, ocuρ ɒo ben ρe
α coρ ɒe; ocuρ Uιllιαm cαoċ mαc Ɒαδι mιc Emαιnɒ ιn
mαc Uιllιαm ριn. Ɒo ʒαδ ιn ʒuιδeαρnoιρ ρuαρ cαρ
αιρ ʒo ραιnιc Conmαιcne cuιle, ocuρ cαnʒαɒαρ clαnɒ
Uιllιαm ocuρ clαnɒ Ɒomnαιll nα ceαnn, ocuρ cuʒαɒαρ

---

1 *Cormac*, Cormac O'Neill.

2 *Sir Richard.*, Sir Richard Bingham.

3 *Sides.* After this follows a clause
in these words: "ocuρ muρ ɒo ċun-
cαɒαρ ιn ρluαʒ ċuʒuδ ρῑρ
muιnncιρ cιρe hCClhαlʒαoιδ, ɒo
loιρʒeαɒαρ mαιnιρcιρ nα mαιʒne
⟨cuρ mαιnιρcιρ Rαċα αbραċnα,
ocuρ mαιnιρcιρ Roρ ρeιρce, ocuρ

ɒo bριρeɒαρ α cαιρlenα, ocuρ ɒo
loιρʒeαɒαρ 'α cιʒe ocuρ α cuιɒ
αρδα; i.e. "and as the army saw
coming down towards them the
people of Tir-Amhalghaidh, they
burned the monastery of the Maighin
(Moyne), and the monastery of Rath-
Abrathua (Rathbran ?), and the
monastery of Ros-Seirce; *and they
broke down their castles, and burned*

terrible calamity. Conn, the son of Niall Og, lord of Clann-Aedha-Buidhe, died. The son of Mac Domhnaill of Alba, Somhairle Buidhe, died. Brian Carragh, son of Cormac,[1] died. John, son of Brian, son of Felim Bacagh O'Neill, was killed by the son of Somhairle Buidhe; and those were great calamities. Mac Diarmada's son, i.e., Maelruanaidh, son of Aedh Mac Diarmada, was killed by Tomaltach, son of Tadhg, son of Eoghan Mac Diarmada, and by Ruaidhri Caech, son of Eoghan, son of Tadhg, son of Ruaidhri Mac Diarmada, in the Caladh, in treachery; and that was a pitiful deed. Sir Richard[2] went with an immense army against the Clann-William, until he arrived at Sliabh-bo-Aedha. Some of the Clann-William and Clann-Domhnaill opposed them; and they gave battle to each other, and a few persons were slain between them on both sides.[3] The governor went to Baile-assa-caerach,[4] and established a camp there; and he went from thence to the Lagan. Mac William and his kindred, and the Clann-Domhnaill, were encamped by the side of this army of Foreigners. Some of the kerne of the army went to burn Walter Burk's corn; and Mac William and Walter Cittach came up with them, and two of the kerne were slain; and some one of them struck Mac William a blow on the foot, and cut off his foot;[5] and this Mac William was William Caech, son of David, son of Edmond. The governor went up[6] again until he reached Conmaicne-Cuile; and the Clann-William and Clann-Domhnaill

their houses and their share of corn." A pen has been drawn through all this, with the exception of that portion represented by italics in the translation.

[4] Baile-assa-caerach; the "town of the cascade of the sheep," now Ballysakeery, in the parish of the same name, barony of Tirawley, co. Mayo. O'Donovan writes the name Baile-easa-caoile, in his ed. of Hy-Fiachrach; Topog. Index.

[5] Foot. The words "ocuṗ ṗo euṡ mac Uilliam, ocuṗ ṗa moṗ inṫ echṫ ṗin a leiṫ iniṡ ocuṗ uaiṗle," ("and Mac William died; and that was a great calamity in respect of honour and nobility"), follow; but a pen has been drawn through them.

[6] Up; i.e., southwards.

bpaıᵹꝺꝺ ꝺon ᵹuıbepnoıp, ocup ꞇαınıc ꞇap aıp ᵹo aꞇ
Luaın. O Conchobaıp ꝺonn ꝺo Leıᵹen app a bpaıᵹ-
ꝺenup. 1nꞇ O Conchobaıp pın ocup Seon ꝺınᵹam ꝺo
ꝺul a muıᵹe Luıpᵹ, ocup ꝺpıan mac Ꝺıapmaꝺa ꝺo
ᵹabaıl ꝺoıꝺ ᵹo peallꞇach. Sıop ꞇomap Sꞇpaıpe ꝺhec
a nᵹaıllım, ocup ꝺoꝺ mop ınꞇ echꞇ pın, oıp nı poıꝺe a
Connachꞇ mac ᵹoıll ꝺuꝺ mo ꝺo pᵹel ꝺo Connachꞇ na
e. 1n pluaᵹ pın po ba meapa ıochꞇ ocup conᵹeall ꝺo
ꞇí ap peaꝺ Epenn, pe ap ᵹaбaꝺ ꝺpıan mac Ꝺıapmaꝺa
mapꞇ ınıꝺe; ꝺo puᵹaꝺap é an oıꞿe pın ᵹo baıle
ꞇomalꞇaıᵹ oıᵹ meıc ꞇomalꞇaıᵹ Mıc Ꝺıapmaꝺa, ocup
ꝺo ꙮıllaꝺap mopan pan ꝺaıle pın ꝺaap comaınm
ꝺaıle ın coıllın; ocup ꝺo puᵹaꝺap ꝺpıan pıu ap na
maıpeaꞿ, ocup ꝺo cuıpeꝺap mapcꞇpluaᵹ leıp co pop
Chomaın; ocup ceꝺaoıne ın luaꞇpıꝺhe pın ꝺo ꞇunꝺ-
paꝺ. Ocup ꝺo ꞿuaꝺap an aoıꝺꞿe pın ᵹo hᲚıpꞇech,
ocup ꝺo ꞿpeꞿpıaꝺ plıochꞇ ın peppuın mıc Muıpᵹepa,
ocup mac Ruaıꝺpı 1 Uıᵹınꝺ; ocup ꝺo mapб O Conchobaıp ꝺonn Caꞇhal mac Eoᵹaın mıc an pıleaꝺ pe na
laım ppeın ᵹan aꝺbap ap bıꞿ, ocup nı ap mapbaꝺ pe
cıan ꝺaımpıp a macapamla peın ꝺechꞇ ꝺuꝺ mó
na Caꞇhal mac ın pıleaꝺ. Nı beᵹ pın, achꞇ benꝺachꞇ
ap anmaın. Ꝺıapmaıꝺ ꝺall mac Ruaıꝺpı mıc ꞇaıꝺᵹ
Mıc Ꝺıapmaꝺa ꝺhec, ocup ꝺoꝺ uapal ꝺeıᵹeınıᵹ ꝺaon-
achꞇaꞿ ın pep pın; ocup ın ceꝺ Ꝺepꝺaoın ꝺon copᵹap
ꞇeapꞇa Ꝺıapmaıꝺ, ocup ꞇepꞇa maıᵹıpꞇıp Sꞇpaınpe,
ocup ꝺo mapbaꝺ Caꞇhal mac ın pıleaꝺ. ᲚL Lıop a
ᵹcoıpce a ꞇıᵹ ꝺaoıꝺın ꝺo poınꝺe an mapbaꝺ pın an
cuıᵹeaꝺ la ꝺoꝺ ꙮapꞇa. Ꝺıapmaıꝺ mac Caꞇhaıl mıc
Caꞇhaıl puaıꝺ 1 Conchobaıp, .ı. bıocaıpe ꞇempoıl an
aoıꝺneın, ocup ꝺo ꞇí a paꝺ poıme pın na ppıoıp ap
bpaꞇhpaıb poppa Chomaın, ꝺhec a pop Chomaın; ocup
pa maıꞿ ın ꝺuıne ın Ꝺıapmaıꝺ pın mac Caꞇhaıl puaıꝺ
beıᵹ meıc Caꞇhaıl puaıꝺ eıle. Mac 1 Ruaıpc ꝺo
ꝺul ap pıuꝺal ınnpuıᵹe a Copann, ocup cpeꞿ ꝺo ᵹclacaꝺ

came to meet him, and delivered hostages to the governor, who came back to Ath-Luain. O'Conchobhair Donn was liberated from his imprisonment. This O'Conchobair, and John Bingham, went to Magh-Luirg, and treacherously apprehended Brian Mac Diarmada. Sir Thomas Strange died in Gaillimh ; and that was a great calamity; for there was not in Connacht a Foreigner more to be deplored by Connacht than he. This army, the worst as to honour and troth that was in all Erinn, by whom Brian Mac Diarmada was apprehended on Shrove-Tuesday, carried him off that night to the town of Tomaltach Og, son of Tomaltach Mac Diarmada; and they destroyed much in that town, the name of which was Baile-in-coillin. And they carried Brian away with them, on the morrow, and sent a cavalry escort with him to Ros-Comain. And that was Ash-Wednesday particularly. And they went that night to Airtech ; and they plundered the descendants of the Parson MacMuirghesa, and the son of Ruaidhri O'hUiginn. And O'Conchobhair Donn killed Cathal, son of Eoghan Mac-in-fhiledh, with his own hand, without any cause whatever ; and there was not slain for a long time one like himself who was more to be lamented than Cathal Mac-in-fhiledh. That is enough[1] ; but a blessing upon his soul. Diarmaid Dall, son of Ruaidhri, son of Tadhg Mac Diarmada, died ; and he was a noble, honourable, humane man : and the first Thursday of Lent Diarmaid died, and Master Strange died, and Cathal Mac-in-fhiledh was killed. (In Lis-an-coirce, in Tech-Baithin, that murder was committed, the fifth day of March.) Diarmaid, son of Cathal, son of Cathal Ruadh O'Conchobhair, i.e., vicar of Tempul-an-aidhnein, and who had been for a long time before that prior over the Friars of Ros-Comain, died in Ros-Comain : and a good man was that Diarmaid, son of Cathal Ruadh Beg, son of another Cathal Ruadh. The son of O'Ruairc went on an expedition into Corann, and took a prey. George Bingham and

---

[1] *Enough*; ni beg ṙin, lit., "that is not little."

το. Seoιρρə bιηζαm ocuρ Ccoτ mυρ το τρετ oρρα α τοριζεchτ. Pιlleατh αρ αη τοιρ, ocuρ .x. αρ ριcheτ το mαρbατ τιτ, ocuρ Ccoτ mυρ το loτ. bαρτα Sαxριnατ το ραξταιl α n'Oun ζαρ ιη lα το mαρbατ Cατhαl mαc ιη ριleατ. Sluαξəτ ατbαιl moρ το cuρ τοη ζuιbeρnoιρ αιρ O Ruαιρc ζο mυιηητιρ Θolιρ α τορατ ιη mαρτα, ocuρ το ρuζαταρ αρ τειτ cəτ bo; ocuρ το τιτuρ αη αοιτcə ριη α mαοταιl; ocuρ το cuατταρ ζο Lιατριιm αρ να ṁαιρeαch, ocuρ το τιταρ τα αοιτcə αηηριη; αρ ριη τοιτ ζο Pιoνατ, ocuρ το bαταρ τρι αοιcə αητ; αρ ριη τοιτ ζο τρυιm Oιριαlαιξ, ocuρ το bατuρ cειτρι αοιτcə αηη; ocuρ το τuζαταρ bραιξτe cιoноιl Luαchαιn ocuρ τeαllαιξ Choηcο leo, ocuρ το loιρζeαταρ ρορmορ ιη τιρə. Cαρτεη ζροιη το loτ, ocuρ τιαρ ηο τριuρ τα mυιηητιρ το ṁαρbατ, ocuρ cəταρ το mυιηητιρ 1 Ruαιρc το τuιτιm leιρ ριη τατcuρ ριη. Τανιc bραιξe o τοṁαρbα Pιoτναch, ocuρ bραιξe o τοṁαρbα τρυmα Oιριαllαιξ, ocuρ ταηζαταρ ρeρ ocuρ ochταρ o mυιηητιρ Θoιlαιρ eτιρ cιll ocuρ τuαιξ, το bραιξτοιτ le Sαζραναchαιb τοη τul ριη. Ιη bρeρnə το loρζατ τοητ ρluαζατ ριη. Seoιη mαc Θoζαιη 1 Chραoιeoιη, ιη mαc cennιξe ιρ Luτα ιρ olc το bιτ α ηΘριηη, τhec α Slιζech, ocuρ bα moρ ιητ echτ ριη. bαρτα ραζραναch το τuρ α mbαιle 1 bιρη, ocuρ e ρeιη το τρeτατ. mυιξe Luιρξ uιle ocuρ Ccιρτeατ το ṁιlleτ τoνα ρluαιξτuιτ ριη; ocuρ ριlleατ ταρ α ναιρ τoιbh, ocuρ το αη α τo ηo τρι το cετuιb ρə hατταιξ coζαιτ 1 Ruαιρc; ocuρ mαc Ταιτξ 1 Ruαιρc, ocuρ mαc Ccoτα ζαllτα 1 Ruαιρc, το ζcoηζnαm αcu ριη αναζhαιτ 1 Ruαιρc. Porloηζρορτ 1 Ruαιρc το beαιτ α n[O]αρτραοιτ, ocuρ bριαη mαc bριαιη mιc Θoζαιη 1 Ruαιρξ ιητ O Ruαιρc ριη. mαc Τοmαlταιξ mιc

Hugh Mus[1] overtook them in pursuit. They turned upon the pursuers, and killed thirty of them; and Hugh Mus was wounded. Saxon warders were left in Dun-gar the day that Cathal Mac-in-fhiledh was killed. An immense army was sent by the governor against O'Ruairc, to Muinter-Eolais, in the beginning of March; and they captured ten hundred cows. And they were that night in Maethail; and they went to Liatruim on the morrow, and were two nights there. From thence they went to Fidhnacha, and they were three nights there; from thence to Druim-Oiriallaigh, and they were four nights there. And they brought with them the pledges of Cenel-Luachain and Tellach-Choncho,[2] and burned the greater part of the country. Captain Grain was wounded, and two or three of his people were killed; and four of O'Ruairc's people fell by him in that conflict. Pledges from the comarb of Fidhnacha, and pledges from the comarb of Druim-Oiriallaigh, and nine pledges from Muinter-Eolais, both church and territory, came with the Saxons on that occasion. The Breifne was burned on that hosting. John, son of Eoghan O'Craidhen, the least wicked merchant that was in Erinn, died in Sligech; and that was a great cause of lamentation. Saxon warders were placed in O'Birn's town;[3] and he himself was plundered. All Magh-Luirg, and Airtech, were injured by those armies. And they turned back; and two or three hundred of them remained to take part in the war against O'Ruairc; and the son of Tadhg O'Ruairc, and the son of Aedh Galldha O'Ruairc, were assisting them against O'Ruairc. O'Ruairc's encampment was in Dartraighe; and this O'Ruairc was Brian, the son of Brian, son of Eoghan O'Ruairc.[4] The son of Tomaltach, son of Maurice, son of

A.D. [1590.]

the scribe adds the following note: mep̄i b̄ḟuan vo ṫsp̄ib̄ p̄in an maip̄c p̄oime cevaoine in bp̄aiċ, ocup̄ me a l̄aim a p̄op̄ Chomain a pṁiṫp̄un an p̄eċh p̄in p̄aċ bp̄oiv, o cevaoine in l̄uaiċhp̄iv ꝺo p̄oiꝽe p̄in;" "I, Brian, wrote that, the Tuesday before Spy-Wednesday, and I in confinement in Ros-Comain, in prison, during that period, from Ash-Wednesday to that time." *See* page 511.

Muiɼʓeɼα mic Ꞇomaltaiʓh Mic Ꞁiaɼmαꝺα ɼuaiꝺ .i.
Emann, ocuɼ CαꞇhaƖ óʓ mαc CαꞇhaiƖ mic Mαʄnuaɼα
Meic Ꞁiaɼmαꝺα ɼuaiꝺ, ꝺo maɼbaꝺ Ɩe ꞀomnαƖƖ nα
cαpaƖƖ maiʓ ꞀomnaiƖƖ.

Ɓɼaiʓꝺe ꝺo ɓí α Ɩaiɯ́ α mɓaiƖe in ɯ́uꞇꞇa, ocuɼ ꝺo
ꞇionʓαꝺαɼ in baiƖe ꝺo ʓabaiƖ .i. ꝻeiꝺƖim oʓ mαc
Mαʄnuɼα mic Ꞃuαʄɼaiꝺe, ocuɼ ꝻeiꝺƖim ꝺαɼꞇiʄαꞓ mαc
ΑꞼꝺfα meic Conchobaiɼ oiʓ i hΑꞼiɼꞇ; ocuɼ ꝺo maɼbaꝺ
annɼin iαꝺ, ocuɼ ni αɼ ʓαꝺαꝺαɼ in baiƖe.

8Ɩuαʄ 8αʓɼαnαꞓ ꝺo ɓuƖ ʓo Ꞁαɼꞇꞇɼαoiꝺ. O Ꞃuαiɼc
ocuɼ Mαʓ Lαnnchαiꝺh ꝺo ɓeiꞓ α ɓꞅoɼƖonʓɼoɼꞇ ɼompu
ꞅα ꞇiɼ, ocuɼ αɼ ɓꞅαʓbaiƖ ꞅoɼƖonʓɼuiɼꞇ i Ꞃuαiɼc ꝺo
Mαʓ Lαnnchαiꝺh ꝺo buaiƖeꝺ α naimꝺe uime .i. MαoiƖ-
ɼeachƖαinn Mαʓ Lαnnchαiꝺh ocuɼ ꝺɼem eƖe ꝺonꞇ
ɼƖuαʓαꝺ ꞅα Mαʓ Lαnnchαiꝺh, ocuɼ ꝺo maɼbαꝺαɼ e
ocuɼ ochꞇαɼ maɼαon ɼiꞅ; ocuɼ ꝺo cuiɼeαꝺ α cenn ʓo
hαꞓ Luαin.

---

¹ *Attempted.* ꝺo ꞇionʓαꝺαɼ, Clar.,
which is corrupt. ꝺo ꞇionɼʓnαꝺαɼ
would be more correct.

² *Dartighach.* *Recte,* "Dartraigh-
ech," or the **Dartrian**; a name applied
to **Fedhlim** from his having been
fostered by the **Mac Clancys** of Dartry,
co. Leitrim.

Tomaltach Mac Diarmada Ruadh, i.e., Edmond, and Cathal A.D.
Og, son of Cathal, son of Maghnus Mac Diarmada Ruadh, [1590.]
were killed by Domhnall na-capall Mac Domhnaill.

Hostages who were imprisoned in Baile-in-mhuta attempted[1] to take the place, viz., Fedhlim Og, son of Maghnus, son of Rughraidhe, and Fedhlim Dartighach,[2] son of Aedh, son of Conchobhar Og O'hAirt ; and they were slain there, and did not take the place. A Saxon army went to Dartraighe. O'Ruairc and Mac Flannchaidh were in a fortified camp in the district before them. And when Mag Flannchaidh was leaving O'Ruairc's camp, his enemies encountered him, viz., Maelsechlainn Mag Flannchaidh, and another part of the army under Mag Flannchaidh. And they killed him, and eight persons along with him ; and his head was sent to Ath-Luain.[3]

---

[3] *Ath-Luain.* This concludes the Irish text of the Clar. fragment, which terminates on folio 40 b.

The next few entries, which belong to a later period than is embraced by the chronicle, are copied from memoranda added by different hands in the MS. H., 1, 19.

Cnno Domini 1595. Seóinne óṡ bionṡam do manbad a Sliṡech ne hUillioc a búnc mac Remund na nṡúab, ocup an baile do ċabainc dO Dhoṁnuill .i. dClod núad mac Cloda mic Maṡnuip; ocup ip món do leapuiṡ aṁ manbad pin pa pepuib Condachc, [don] ṁeide dib do bí an dibepc.

ḱcḃ. Cnaip 1599. bennṁuṁan oṡ ni Dhuibṡennain, inṡen Pháidín mic Mhaoileċlainn mic Dubċaiṡ óiṡ mic Dubċaiṡ ṁóip, do ċóṡbáil an lechca do ċlochaib pnoiṡce acá óp up cobaip ṁóip na Sṡpíne, pe hanam a pip popca .i. an biocaipe ṁac Doṁnaill, ocup Coṡan mac Doṁnaill ainm in biocaipe pin péin; ocup Maipe inṡen Caióṡ óaill Uí Uiṡinn do bpeic in bliaóain péṁpáici pi; ocup bennaċc Dé pop na hanmannaib pin.

ḱcḃ. Cnaip. Cn bliaóain po dáoip an Tiṡepna anno Domini, Mile ocup pe ceud ocup dá bliaóain deuṡ. Maoileoin Uá Daluiṡ déucc lá peile na manb; ocup a adnacal in inip Muipeóhaiṡ, iap mbpeich búaide ó domhan ocup ó óeṁan; ocup ṡaċ aon da leiṡpió po ċabpad bennachc ap a anmuin.

ḱcḃ. Cnaip pop doṁnach, Cnno Domini 1636. bpian oṡ mac bpiain mic Ruaidpi mic Caióṡ mic Ruaidpi óiṡ, .i. ciaṡepna muiṡhe Luipṡ ocup Cipciṡ ocup cípe Tuachail, pep a aoipi ocup inme acup a apd ciṡepnuip aṡ pepp cainic do ṡaoidealaib iapcaip Coppa pé linn pein, oip app e ap mo po ciodlaic ocup po coipbip do ollamnaib ocup deiṡpib ocup daoip ealadna, do cuipib, do cliapuib ocup do coicepiochaib, do endṡaib, do ipipib, ocup d'iodanopduib, do bochcaib, do baincpeabachaib ocup beiṡionnmupuib, do dupaib, do dallaib ocup do deiblennaib de, do poiṡníb, do pioṡnaib ocup po ṡalṡadaib; do uaiplib, do oippdib ocup do adbail penoipib; pep conṡmala ṡach copa, ṡach cipc ocup ṡaċ caoinbep, pep dicuipce ṡac uilc, ṡaċ eṡcopa ocup ṡaċ aidmillci; pep cennpaiṡci na ccoipcech, ocup na ccoilleched; pep metaiṡce ṡach maiciupa ocup ṡach mopcoiċe, ṡo niomad dpiop ocup

---

1 _Redmond-na-Scuab._ "Redmond of the brooms." This entry is written on fol. 90 a, after the record of the transactions of the year 1541.

2 _Benmumhan._ A name signifying "Woman of Munster." This entry has been added on fol. 74 a, after the events of the year 1496.

Anno Domini 1595. George Og Bingham was killed in Sligech, by Ulick Burk, son of Redmond na-scúab,[1] and the town was given to O'Domhnaill, i.e., to Aedh Ruadh, son of Aedh, son of Maghnus. And that killing was of great service to the men of Connacht, such of them as were in exile.

A.D. [1595.]

The kalends of January, 1599. Benmumhan[2] Og Ni Duibh-gennain, daughter of Maelechlainn, son of Dubhthach Og, son of Dubhthach Mór, erected the tomb of hewn stones which is over the edge of the great well of the Scrin, for the soul of her husband, i.e., the Vicar MacDomhnaill; and Eoghan MacDomhnaill was that same vicar's name. And Mary, daughter of Tadhg Dall O'hUiginn, was born the aforesaid year. And God's blessing on those souls.

[1599.]

The kalends of January, this year of the age of the Lord, one thousand, six hundred, and twelve years. Maeleoin O'Dalaigh died on the festival day of the dead,[3] and was interred in Inis-Muiredhaigh, after bearing triumph from the world and the devil; and let every one who reads this give a blessing on his soul.

[1612.]

The kalends of January on Sunday; anno Domini 1636. Brian Og, son of Brian, son of Ruaidhri, son of Tadhg, son of Ruaidhri Og,[4] i.e., lord of Magh-Luirg, and Airtech, and Tir-Tuathail, the best man of his age, and estate, and high lordship, that came of the Gaeidhel of the West of Europe in his own time; for it was he that presented and dispensed most to ollaves and poets, and to men of science; to visitors, companies, and strangers; to innocent, devout persons, and to pure orders; to paupers, to widows, and people of little property; to the deaf and blind, and the poor of God; to chiefs, princes, and great champions; to nobles, minstrels, and to great seniors; the maintainer of every sort of right, justice, and good custom; the expeller of every evil, wrong, and injury; the subduer of the sinful and iniqui-tous; the augmenter of every good, and of every great property; possessed of a great deal of knowledge, wisdom, and learning, of

[1636.]

---

[3] *Dead.* All Souls' day. This memorandum has been written at the top of fol. 31 *b*.

[4] *Ruaidhri Og.* Rory the younger;

of the family of Mac Dermot. This entry occupies the greater part of fol. 90 *a* and *b*. The writer's name appears at the end of it.

veoluiŗ ocuŗ vŗoȝlaṁ, vo ȝaoiŗ, vo ȝoil ocuŗ vo ȝaiŗciv, vo
bŗut vo bŗiȝ ocuŗ vo buantoiŗbiŗt; ŗeŗ aŗ mo ŗo cennaiȝ
vo vuantaib, vo vŗechtaib, ocuŗ vo veȝ moltuib ina coimŗe
ŗein; ŗeŗ ŗuillinȝa na nainveŗ, na nvilocht, ocuŗ na nvil-
leactaib; ŗeŗ tiȝe aoiveo coitcinn va ȝaċ luiŗȝ no lenŗav é
an aimŗiŗ a neŗbava ocuŗ a navbail uiŗeŗbai; ocuŗ aŗ
coŗmail ȝo bŗuaiŗ luac a vaonnachta ocuŗ a veȝ cŗoive on
tŗinoiv tŗe peŗŗannaiȝ, oiŗ avbeŗ ȝach voctuiŗ ocuŗ ȝach
viavaiŗe an tan aŗ eatal an beta ȝuŗab amlaiv an baŗ, ocuŗ
mav maiṫ ocuŗ mav anvocc an baŗ ȝo bŗuiȝe an ŗocŗaiȝ tall
amail aŗ techva vo. Iaŗ nvul ȝo hatt luain vo, ait aŗab-
avaŗ maite Connacht aŗ a cionn aȝ cuŗ a ccomaiŗle um
comoiŗcill plantaŗion, ȝalaŗ a eȝa va ȝabail iŗin baile ŗin
.i. viŗinteŗia, ocuŗ ŗuaiŗ baŗ ant octmav la ŗiċit vo mi
Ianuaŗi, via Satain vo ŗunnŗavh, iaŗ mbuaiv onȝta ocuŗ
aitŗiȝe, ocuŗ iaŗ mbŗeṫ buaive o vomun ocuŗ o veamun, ocuŗ
aŗ lamaib ilimav oŗv ocuŗ eȝailŗech, ocuŗ iaŗ nȝlacav
aibive ŗanct Voimnic uime, ocuŗ iaŗ mbeṫ tŗi bliavna veȝ
ocuŗ ŗiċe ocuŗ ŗaiṫe a ttiȝeŗnuŗ a tiŗe ocuŗ a talman ŗein va
ttoil ocuŗ va naonta buvvein, ocuŗ iaŗ mbeiṫ tŗi bliavna
veȝ ocuŗ va ŗiċit vaoiŗ vó an tan avbaṫ; ocuŗ a avlacav ȝo
huaŗal onoŗaċ a ccluain inic Noiŗ ŗo oiven De ocuŗ Ciaŗain,
la ŗeil bŗiȝvi; ocuŗ ŗo havnaċt, vin, ŗice tiaȝeŗna va cineṫ
ŗan ŗoilicŗin ŗoime.

Iaŗla antŗom .i. Raȝnall aŗannac, cenn oiniȝ ocuŗ oiŗ-
beŗtuiŗ a tiŗe ocuŗ a talman ŗein, vŗaȝail baiŗ an bliavain
ceona. Siŗ Seon Cinȝ .i. ŗen ŗioiŗe vo comaiŗle na hEŗenn,
moŗtuuŗ. Maoilechlainn O Ceallaiȝ .i. mac I Ceallaiȝ,
aon ŗoȝa a tiŗe veȝ in hoc anno. Aŗ móŗ aŗ vaoinib an
bliavain ŗi laŗin mbolȝach biȝ.

Avṫ mac bŗiain mic Ruaivŗi mic Viaŗmava véaȝ a
nȝŗánŗȝ na manaċ, an cetŗuiṁa la véȝ vo mí Máŗta 1648.
Maolŗuanaiv mac Avṫa mic Viaŗmava ŗo ȝŗŗiob an
beȝan ŗin, 1652.

---

¹ *Council.* This "council" was the
Inquisition held by direction of Straf-
ford, to find the king's title to the
whole of the county Roscommon.

² *Him.* Two stanzas are here
added, containing a few chronological
data, which are not worth printing.

acuteness, bravery, and valour; of energy, vigour, and constant bounty; the man who purchased the most of odes, and poems, and good eulogies, in his own time; the supporter of the maidens, innocents, and orphans; a man who kept a general guest-house for all who frequented it in the time of their want and great destitution. And it is likely that he obtained the reward of his humanity, and of his good heart, from the Tri-personal Trinity; for every doctor and divine says that when the life is pure, so is the death; and if the death is good and pure, that one will obtain the suitable reward beyond. After going to Ath-Luain, where the chieftains of Connacht were be-fore him, holding council[1] in expectation of a plantation, his mortal illness, dysentery, seized him, and he died the 28th day of January, that is to say, Saturday, after the triumph of unction and penitence, and after obtaining victory over the world and the devil, and from the hands of very many orders and ecclesi-astics; and after assuming the habit of St. Dominic; and after having been thirty-three years and a quarter in the sovereignty of his own country and land, by their own will and consent; having been fifty-three years of age when he died. And he was interred nobly, honourably, in Cluain-mic-Nois, under the protection of God and Ciaran, on the festival day of Brigid. (And twenty lords of his kindred were interred, moreover, in that cemetery before him.[2])

The Earl of Antrim, i.e., Raghnall Arannach,[3] head of the honour and valour of his own country, and land, died the same year. Sir John King, i.e., an old knight of the Council of Erinn, mortuus. Maelechlainn O'Cellaigh, i.e., the son of O'Cellaigh, the elect of his country, died in hoc anno. Great mortality amongst people this year, from the small-pox.

Aedh, son of Brian, son of Ruaidhri Mac Diarmada, died in Grainsech-na-manach, the fourth day of the month of March,[4] 1648.

---

[3] *Raghnall Arannach.* Raghnall (or Randall) of Aran.

[4] *March.* The writer adds Ⅲ ꜵⱶ-ꞃuꜵnꜵıꝺ ·mꜵc Ꜷoꝺꜵ mıc Ⅾıꜵꞃ-mꜵꝺꜵ ꞃo ꞃcꞃıoꝺ ꜵn ꝺeꝵꜵn ꞃın,

1652; i.e., "Maelruanaidh, son of Aedh Mac Diarmada, wrote that little portion, 1652." The name Ⅾꜵıꝺꞃꝺe Ó Ⅾuıꝉꝵennꜵın is also written, re-versed, on the lower margin of the page.

INDEX.

INDEX.

Ath-Slisen, or Ath-Slision (now *Bellaslishen* Bridge, on the River Uair, near Elphin, co. Roscommon), i. 497, 549.

Ath-tighe-an-Mesiagh (*Attymass*, bar. of Gallen, co. Mayo), i. 279.

Ath-truim (*Trim*, co. Meath), ii. 159; burned, i. 125; image of the Virgin Mary at, ii. 143, 315.

Attymass; *see* Ath-tighe-an-Mesaigh.

Aughrim; *see* Echdruim-Ui-Maine.

Aulb, David, i. 459.

Austria, Don John of, ii. 431.

B.

Babylon, the soldan of, i. 523.

Bac, a district in the bar. of Tirawly, co. Mayo, i. 279.

Bachalls (*croziers*), i. 147, 267.

Bachal-Iosa, or Bachall-Isa (the Staff of Jesus), i 15, 89, 103, ii. 317; profanation of, i. 67.

Badhna, or Slieve Bawne, co. Roscommon, i. 419.

Badlaigh (Badley), Philip, i. 58, n. 4.

Bagenal, Sir Dudley, slain, ii. 479.

——— Sir Nicholas, ii. 478, n. 4.

Baile-an-chlair (*Clare-Galway*, barony of Clare, co. Galway), ii. 171.

Baile-an-doire (*Ballinderry*, bar. of Ballintober South, co. Roscommon), ii. 493.

Baile-an-dúin (*Ballindoon*, bar. of Tirerrill, co. Sligo), ii. 213, 418 n.⁵; demolished, *ib.* 9; the monastery of, *ib.* 207.

Baile-an-mhuilinn, co. Roscommon, ii. 375.

Baile-an-muta, or Baile-in-mhuta (*Ballymote*, bar. of Corran, co. Sligo), i. 633, 653, ii. 379, 415, 515; taken by English, *ib.* 419, 461; taken from the English, *ib.* 421. *See* Ath-cliath-in-Chorainn.

Baile-an-tobair; *see* Baile-in-tobair.

Baile-an-tochair (*Ballintogher*, bar. of Tirerrill, co. Sligo), ii. 419.

Baile-assa-caerach (*Ballysakeery*), ii. 509.

Baile-átha-cliath, or Ath-cliath (*Dublin*), ii. 437, 441, 447, 469, 483, 499; Luke, Arch-

Baile-atha-cliath—*cont.* bishop, i. 409; parliaments at, ii. 423, 467; *see* Ath-cliath.

Baile-Atha-lethain; (*Ath-lethan*, or Ballylahan, co. of Mayo), burned, i. 585, ii. 463; *see* Ath-lethan.

Baile-atha-lethair, demolished, ii. 491.

Baile-atha-tidh (*Malahide*, co. Dublin), ii. 51.

Baile-choillte-foghair (*Castlefore*, co. Leitrim), ii. 131.

Baile-esa-dara (*Ballysadare*, co. Sligo), ii. 413; the bridge of, *ib.* 475. *See* Es-dara.

Baile-in-coillin (*Ballinkillen*, co. Roscommon), ii. 511.

Baile-in-mhuta; *see* Baile-an-muta, and Ath-cliath-in-Chorainn.

Baile-in-Rodba (*Ballinrobe*, co. Mayo), ii. 473.

Baile-in tobair, or Baile-tobair-Brighde (*Ballintober*, bar. of Castlereagh, co. Roscommon), i. 559, 651, ii. 23, 49, 59, 129, 257, 435; burned, i. 567, ii. 271; taken by Sir Edward Fitton, ii. 411; the mound of, *ib.* 437; interments in, *ib.* 481.

Baile-Locha-Deala (*Ballyloughdalla;* par. of Ballysakeery, bar. of Tirawley, co. Sligo), ii. 379.

Baile-Locha-Dechair (*Ballaghdacker*, bar. of Killian, co. Galway), ii. 15.

Baile-Locha-Mesca, or Loch-Mesc Castle, bar. of Kilmaine, co. Mayo, i. 469, ii. 143.

Baile-Locha-Riach (*Loughrea*, co. Galway), ii. 431.

Baile-mic-Dubhda (*Ballymacooda*, bar. of Islands. co. Clare), ii. 247.

Baile-mic-Murchadha (*Ballymacmurragh*, par. of Tibohine, bar. of Frenchpark, co. Roscommon), ii. 383.

Baile-mór-O'Floinn (*Ballymore*, co. Roscommon), i. 575.

Baile-na-brághad (*Braid*, bar. of Omagh, co. Tyrone). ii. 257.

Baile-na-cille in Clann-Connmhaigh (*Ballynakill*, bar. of Ballymoe, co. Galway), ii. 423.

Baile-na-clerech (bar. of Boyle, co. Roscommon), the herenagh of, ii. 483.

2 M

2 M 2

Burk—*cont.*

—— Sir Edmond, died, ii. 23.

—— Sir Edmond Albanach, i.e. MacWilliam, died, ii. 51.

—— Edmond Allta, son of Richard, son of Oliver, killed, ii. 451.

—— Edmond Buidhe, son of Thomas Bacagh, slain, ii. 369.

—— Edmond Kiocarach, son of David Bán, slain, ii. 475.

—— Edmond Og, son of Edmond, son of Ulick, slain, ii. 391, *note.*

—— Edmond, son of the Earl of Ulster, drowned, i. 627.

—— Edmond, the posterity of, ii. 471.

—— Edmond MacWilliam, i. 623, 625, 627, 629, 631, 637, 639, 641.

—— Edmond MacWilliam, died ii. 165.

—— Edmond, son of Thomas-an-Machaire, ii. 423.

—— Edmond, son of Ulick, died, ii. 133.

—— Edmond, son of William, son of Richard, slain, ii. 13.

—— Henry, son of Ulick, son of Richard, died, ii. 21.

—— Henry, son of William, son of Thomas, son of David, ii. 379.

—— Hubert, i. 637.

—— Hubert, the son of, slain, i. 637.

—— Hubert, died, ii. 11.

—— Hubert, son of David Donn MacWilliam, i. 645.

—— Hubert, son of Edmond, son of Hubert, slain, i. 91.

—— Hubert, son of Fergus, son of Edmond, died, ii. 387-9.

—— Hubert Buidhe, son of William, son of Thomas, chief of Clann-Connmhaigh, ii. 461.

—— Johanna, daughter of MacDavid, died, ii. 387.

—— Sir John, son of the Red Earl, i. 607.

—— John, died, ii. 59.

—— John, killed, ii. 207.

—— John, the descendants of, ii. 279, 493.

—— John, son of Edmond, son of Hubert, son of Sir David, ii. 121.

Burk—*cont.*

—— John Buidhe, son of Seoinin, slain, ii. 107.

—— John MacWilliam, son of Oliver, died, ii. 431.

—— John Ruadh MacDavid, i. 651.

—— John, son of Meiler Ban, slain, ii. 489.

—— John, son of Richard Saxanach Earl of Clann-Rickard, ii. 453.

—— John Dubh, son of Rickard, son of, Ulick, slain, ii. 305.

—— John, son of Thomas, son of David, son of Edmond, died, ii. 485.

—— John, son of Thomas, son of Rickard, ii. 415.

—— John (son of Walter Fada?), the son of, hanged, ii. 473.

—— Margaret, daughter of Walter, died, ii. 27.

—— Mary, daughter of Oliver, wife of the Blind Abbot, died, ii. 453.

—— MacDavid ; *see* MacDavid Burk.

—— MacWilliams, i. 332, 407, 417, 421, 423, 435, 441, 443, 445, 447, 457, 549, 551, 553 ; ii. 3, 7, 13, 85, 149, 171, 179, 183, 273, 433 ; *see* under "Ulster, Earl of."

—— MacWilliam Iochtar, ii. 65 ; *see* under MacWilliam Burk.

—— Meiler, killed, ii. 57.

—— Meiler, son of Walter, sheriff of Mayo, killed, ii. 423.

—— Meiler, son of Walter Fada, hanged by Bingham, ii. 471.

—— Meiler, son of Walter Fada, the son of, hanged, ii. 473.

—— Oliver, the sons of, ii. 369, 385, 409.

—— Oliver, son of John, son of David Bán, severely wounded, ii. 451.

—— Oliver, son of John, son of David Bán, hanged, ii. 471.

—— Redmond, son of the Bishop, ii. 455.

—— Redmond, son of the Bishop, killed, ii. 459.

—— Redmond, son of Ulick-na-gcenn, ii. 455.

—— Redmond Ruadh, son of Rickard, son of Ulick, slain, ii. 305.

—— Richard, slain, ii. 55.

—— Richard, died, ii. 129.

—— Richard, ii. 169.

Cronan, abbot of Dunkeld, slain, i. 47.

Crops, good, i. 403, 405.

Cros-Doire-chaein, in the parish of Kilronan, co. Roscommon, i. 409.

Cros-Maeilina (*Crossmolina*), co. Mayo, ii. 259.

Cros-Maighe-Croin (*Crossmacrin*, bar. of Athenry, co. Galway), ii. 169.

Cros-na-riagh (a cross at Londonderry, at which people were hanged), i. 199.

Crossa-Brighde (*Brigid's crosses*), at Armagh, i. 181.

Cross-Caibhenaigh (*Crosscaranagh*, bar. of Dungannon, co. Tyrone), ii. 199.

Cross, the Holy, ii. 189.

Cruachan (*Rathcroghan*, co. Roscommon), i. 475, 497; ii. 399.

Cruachan (*Croghan*, barony of Boyle, co. Roscommon), i. 575, 577; ii. 179.

Cruach, Cruach-Patraic, or Cruachan-Aighle (*Croagh-Patrick* mountain, co. Mayo), i. 269; ii. 7; persons killed by lightning upon, i. 103.

Cruachan-Gaileng (*Croaghan*, a district in the bar. of Gallen, co. Mayo), ii. 221.

Cruachan-O'Cúbhrán (now *Croaghan*, near Killashandra, co. Cavan), i. 417.

Cruimther-Fraech, i. 188, n. 3.

Crumhthonn, Cruthonn, or Cruthonn-O'Maine (*Cruffon*, co. Galway), i. 435; ii. 351, 355, 367, 411.

Cuailgne, *recté* Cuailnge (*Cooley*, a mountainous district in the north of the co. Louth), i. 45, 131.

Cuana; *see* Conrad.

Cuan MacCailchin, ii. 399, n. s.

Cuan-Sligigh, ii. 197.

Cuchiche, son of Eignechan, king of Cenel-Enna, died, i. 39.

Cuchullain, i. 199; ii. 399.

Cu-Cuailgne, the son of, died, i. 29.

Cúdhniligh, royal heir of Caisel, slain, i. 41.

—— son of Cenneidigh, one of Brian Borumha's guards, slain, i. 13.

Cuil-Brighdin, MacBrady's country, in the co. Cavan, i. 653; ii. 141.

Cuil-Cernadha; *see* Cul-Cernadha.

Cuil-cnamh (a district comprising the par. of Dromard, bar. of Tireragh, co. Sligo), i. 215; ii. 497.

Cuil-Ceara, in front of Boyle, co. Roscommon, ii. 415.

Cuil-an-tuaisceirt ("the corner of the North"; the north-east liberties of Coleraine), i. 147.

Cúil-an-úrtain (*Cooloorta*, bar. of Tiaquin, co. Galway), ii. 477.

Cuil-Deghaidh, bar. of Tirerrill, co. Sligo, ii. 289, 355, 419.

Cuilecha, a name for the present barony of Kilmaine, co. Mayo, ii. 413, 491; and *see* Conmaicne-Cuile-Tolaidh.

Cuilend, son of Dergan, drowned, i. 55.

Cuilen-tragh, Queen's co., the castle of, ii. 219.

Cuil-irra (a district comprising the parishes of Killaspugbrone, and Kilmacnowen, bar. of Carbury, co. Sligo), i. 373, ii. 297.

Cuil-na-noirer (the bar. of *Coole*, co. Fermanagh), ii. 223, 331.

Cuil-O'Guaire (*Coologe*, in the barony of Tullyhaw, co. Cavan), i. 521.

Cuil-Rathain; *see* Cul-Rathain.

Cul-Cernadha (*Coolcarney*, a district comprising the parishes of Kilgarvan and Attymas, bar. of Gallen, co. Mayo), i. 279; ii. 141.

Cuinnche (*Quin*, bar. of Bunratty, co. of Clare), i. 483.

Cuirrech-buidhe (*Curraghboy*, bar. of Athlone, co. Roscommon), ii. 393.

Cuirrech-Liffe (the *Curragh of Kildare*), the battle of, i. 319.

Cuirrech-O'Guanradh, co. Roscommon, ii.199.

Cuirrin-Connachtach (*Curreen*, near Lanesborough, co. Roscommon), i. 363.

Cuisín, David, slain, i. 467.

—— David, son of Richard, i. 409.

—— Richard, i. 421.

Culbháthar (pron. *Coolwar*), co. Roscommon, i. 573.

Cul-maile, Cúl-Mhaine, or Cúl-Mhaile (*Collooney*, co. Sligo), i. 651; ii. 67, 357, 431; battle near, ii. 473; the castle of, ii. 225, 259, 267.

Cúil-mhic-an-tréin (*Castleforward*, bar. of Raphoe, co. Donegal), the castle of, ii. 269.

De Marisco ; *see* Fitz-Geoffroi.

Demhan-in-chorain, ("Devil's hook "), one of the Burks of Mayo, ii. 489.

De Montfort, Simon, i. 457.

—— Simon the younger, i. 453.

De Netterville, Lucas, Primate of Ireland, i. 263.

Derbhorcaill, wife of Tighernan O'Ruairc, goes on a pilgrimage, i. 173 ; dies, i. 187.

De Ridelisford, Piers, i. 405.

—— Walter, i. 321.

Dermhagh (*Durrow*, King's co.), the stone church of, i. 19; burnt with its books, i. 81. *See* Durmhagh.

De Rokeby, Thomas, Justiciary of Ireland, died, ii. 15.

Derranc ; *see* Doirén.

Derg-bruach (now *Gransha*, or *Grange*, par. of Clondermot, co. Londonderry), i. 199.

Derry (or *Doire*, q. v.; *Londonderry*); abbots or comarbs of, i. 27, 151, 153.

   Bishops of, viz. :—

     Mac Oirechtaigh, Henry, i. 519.

     O'Cerbhallain, Florence, i. 305, 395.

     O'Cerbhallain, Florence, i. 509.

     O'Cerbhallain, Fogartach, i. 175.

     O'Cerbhallain, Gilla-an-Choimdedh, i. 485.

     O'Cobhthaigh, Muiredhach, i. 149.

     O'Fallamhain, Domhnall, ii. 201.

     O'Murray, Amhlaibh, i. 171.

     O'Neill, Hugh, i. 597.

     Weston, Nicholas, ii. 177, 183.

   See also under "Cenel-Eoghain, bishops of."

Derrybrusk ; *see* Airech-Brosca.

Derrymore ; *see* Daire-mór.

Derrypatrick ; *see* Daire-Patraic.

De Salerna, Walter, Archbishop of Tuam, died, i. 427.

Desertcreaght ; *see* Disert-dá-chrich.

Des-Mumha (*Desmond*), i. 163 ; invaded, i. 439, 443 ; ii. 209; given to MacCarthy, ii. 109; plundered, ii. 113, 115; the English of, ii. 281, 283, 285, 385 ; the hostages of, slain, ii. 117, 119; the men of, ii. 135, 233.

—— Garrett, or Gerald, fifth Earl of, ii. 43.

—— Garrett, sixteenth Earl of, ii. 377, 453; slain, ii. 455.

Des Mumha—*cont.*

—— James, seventh Earl of, ii. 165–7.

—— James, eleventh Earl of, died, ii. 269.

—— James, fifteenth Earl of, ii. 343; the sons of, ii. 429.

—— James, son of the Earl of, ii. 223.

—— John, son of the Earl of, ii. 209, 221, 223.

—— Maurice, first Earl of, ii. 11.

—— Maurice, tenth Earl of, ii. 187.

—— Thomas, sixth Earl of, ii. 137.

—— Thomas, son of James, son of Garrett, fourth Earl of, ii. 167, 169.

—— Mor, wife to the fifteenth Earl of, ii. 353.

—— Shemus-na-tinol, son of the fifteenth Earl of, hanged, ii. 433.

—— Sibhan, daughter of the Earl of, ii. 135.

—— Countess of, ii. 75.

—— Earls of, ii. 17, 101, 445.

—— Kings or chiefs of (all of the family of MacCarthy), i. 117, 237, 241, 271, 307, 439, 521, 525, 531 ; ii. 19, 73, 227.

—— Royal heirs of, i. 523.

—— Tanist of, ii. 175.

De Valle ; *see* Wale.

Devenish Island ; *see* Daimhinis.

De Verdun, John, i. 421, 437, 441, 447.

Devine ; *see* O'Doimhín.

Diarmaid, son of Enna, king of Laighen, killed, i. 85.

Diarmaid, son of Mael-na-mbó, king of Laighen, i. 55; slain, i. 67.

Diarmaid, son of Simon-na-tragha, i. 539.

Diganway, in Wales ; *see* Engannoc.

Dillon, Dabac, son of Ulick of Umhall, died, ii. 9.

—— Edmond, son of Thomas, son of Garrett, died, ii. 187.

—— Justice, ii. 479, 495.

—— Maude, wife of O'Ferghail, died, ii. 433.

—— Robert, ii. 457.

—— Robert, son of Henry Dubh, sheriff of Fermanagh, ii. 491.

—— Tibbot, ii. 477.

Dilmhain ; *see* Dillon.

Diseases, ii. 109.

Disert-dá-chrich (*Desertcreaght*, bar. of Dungannon, co. Tyrone), battle of, i. 487.

r

2 o

2 o 2

J.

M.

r

586 INDEX.

MacDomhnaill (MacDonnell)—cont.

ander, son of Domhnall, son of John of Ilay, died, ii. 175.

—— James, ii. 325.

—— James, ii. 345.

—— James; arrival in Ireland of the sons of, ii. 473.

—— James; the daughter of, ii. 483.

—— James, son of John Cathanach, slain, ii. 389.

——John, son of Aenghus, son of Gillaespuig Bán, ii. 425.

—— John Cathánach, hanged, ii. 201; the sons of, ii. 247.

—— John Dubh; the son of, ii. 249.

—— John Mór, king of Insi-Gall, hanged ii. 201.

—— Justin, taken prisoner, ii. 455.

—— Justin, son of Maelmuire, son of Felim, hanged, ii. 487.

—— Raghnall, son of Alexander, ii. 83.

—— Somhairle, or Sorley, son of John Dubh, constable of Ulster, ii. 29.

—— Somhairle, eric for the death of, ii. 89.

—— Somhairle Buidhe, or Sorley Boy, ii. 453.

—— Somhairle Buidhe, died, ii. 509.

—— Somhairle Buidhe, son of Marcus, slain, ii. 87.

—— Toirdhelbhach, or Turlough, ii. 33.

—— Toirdhelbhach, ii. 149, 151.

—— Toirdhelbhach Luighnech; the descendants of, ii. 415.

—— Toirdhelbhach Og; the son of, killed, ii. 219.

MacDomhnaill Gallóglaech, or MacDonnell of the Gallowglasses, ii. 247.

—— Colla, son of Colla, constable of Tyrone, died, ii. 273.

MacDomhnaill mic Muirchertaigh, the title of the chief of the O'Conors of Carbury, co. Sligo, ii. 291.

MacDonlevy; see MacDuinnsleibhe.

MacDonnchadha, or MacDonnchaidh (MacDonough), Aedh, son of the Cananach, killed, ii. 289.

MacDonchadha (MacDonough)—cont.

—— Aedh, son of Cairbre, lord of Corann, ii. 461-3; died, ii. 479.

—— Aedh, son of Cairbre, son of Tadhg, lord of Corann, ii. 419-21.

—— Aedh Buidhe; the descendants of, ii. 855.

—— Aine, daughter of, died, ii. 63.

—— Bebhinn, wife of Tomaltach, ii. 37.

—— Brian, son of Maelruanaidh, chief of Corann, died, ii. 199.

—— Brian, son of Tadhg, i. 609; slain, i. 611.

—— Brian, son of Tadhg, lord of Corann, slain, ii. 173.

—— Brian, son of Tomaltach, slain, i. 609.

—— Brian, royal heir of Tir-Oilella, slain, ii. 21.

—— Brian Brathach, son of, died. ii. 475.

—— Cairbre, lord of Corann, ii. 355.

—— Cairbre, the son of, died, ii. 481.

—— Cathal, slain, ii. 25.

—— Cathal, died, ii. 107.

—— Cathal, died, ii. 131.

—— Cathal, son of Eoghan; the wife of, ii. 429.

—— Cathal Cairbrech, slain, ii. 61.

—— Cathal Clerech, the son of, ii. 5.

—— Cathal Og, son of Cathal Dubh, taken prisoner by Bingham, ii. 461.

—— Cathal Og. son of Cormac, killed, ii. 355.

—— Catherine, daughter of Maelechlainn, son of Maurice, drowned, ii. 143.

—— Conchobhar, ii. 67, 69.

—— Conchobhar, king of Tir-Oilella, ii. 129.

—— Conchobhar, son of Eoghan, slain, ii. 289.

—— Conchobhar, son of Maurice, died, ii. 9.

—— Conchobhar, son of Ruaidhri, killed, ii. 207.

—— Conchobhar, son of Tadhg, slain, i. 587.

—— Conchobhar Carrach, i. 385.

—— Cormac, ii. 39.

—— Cormac, ii. 259.

—— Cormac; the sons of, ii. 255.

O'Connmachaiu, i. 603.

O'Connorchi, Christian, bishop of Lismore, i. 175.

O'Conolly; *see* O'Conghaile.

O'Conor, or Ua Conchobhair; *see* O'Conchobhair.

O'Conroi, Gilla-na-naingel, killed, i. 481.

O'Corcrain, or Ua Corcrain, Diarmaid, vision of, i. 9.

O'Cormacán, Maelpetair, master of Ros-Comain, died, i. 319.

O'Craidhén, O'Croidhén, or O'Cridhain (*O'Crean*), Andrew, bishop of Elphin, ii. 455, 459.

—— Domhnall, died, ii. 207.

—— John, son of Eoghan, died, ii. 513.

O'Crean; *see* O'Craidhén, and O'Crechain.

O'Crechain (*O'Crean*), Macleoin, died, i. 861.

O'Crichain, or Ua Crichain, royal heir of Fernmhagh, i. 103.

—— Cathal, i. 25.

—— Cathalan, king of Fernmhagh, i. 27; killed, i. 29.

—— Cumhidhe, king of Fernmhagh, and his son, slain, i. 131.

—— Domhnall, king of Ui-Fiachrach of Ardsratha, slain, i. 69.

—— Niall, king of Ui-Fiachrach of Ardsratha, slain, i. 127.

O'Criodachain, Catherine, daughter of, died, ii. 227.

O'Croidhén; *see* O'Craidhén.

O'Cuairsceith; *see* under Burk.

O'Cuanna, Diarmaid, great priest of Elphin, i. 381.

—— Madadhan, i. 83.

—— Mathghamhain, king of Claenghlais, killed, i. 453.

O'Cuilin, Gillacoimdedh, provost of Inis-Mic-Nerin, in Loch-Cé, died, i. 333.

O'Cuill (*O'Quill*) Cennfaeladh, poet, died, i. 49.

—— Cennfaeladh, died, ii. 207.

O Cuindlis, Domhnall, a historian, slain, i. 643.

O'Cuinn (*O'Quin*), Aedh, slain, i. 207.

—— Amhlaibh, slays Ruaidhri O'Flaherty, i. 209.

O'Cuinn (*O'Quin*)—*cont.*

—— Ámhlaibh, son of Diarmaid, slain, i. 407

—— Cairbre, chief of Muinter-Gillgan, died, ii. 25.

—— Cathal, chief of Muinter-Gillgan, slain, ii. 13.

—— Conghalach, king-chieftain of Magh-Lughach, slain, i. 259.

—— Cuchonnacht, chief of Muinter-Gillgan, i. 635.

—— Diarmaid, i. 51.

—— Diarmaid, slain, i. 407.

—— Diarmaid, chief of Muinter-Gillgan, died, i. 319.

—— Dubhthemhrach, daughter of, i. 309.

—— Etain, queen of Munster, died, i. 181.

—— Gilla-Beraigh, slain, i. 435.

—— Gilla-na-naemh, chieftain of Muinter-Gillgan, died, i. 451.

—— Gormghal, chief of Muinter-Gillgan, taken prisoner, i. 207.

—— Sitric, i. 197.

—— Sitric, chief of Muinter-Gillgan, slain, i. 163.

—— Thomas, a Friar Minor, elected bishop of Elphin, i. 367.

—— Thomas, bishop of Cluain-mic-Nois, i. 403; died, i. 483.

O'Cuirc (*O'Quirk*), Cennedigh, king of Muscraidhe, i. 45.

—— Domhnall, king of Muscraidhe, slain, i. 45.

—— Gillabrighde, king of Muscraidhe-Breoghain, i. 87.

O'Cuirnin, Cairbre, slain, ii. 67.

—— Cathal, ollave of Breifne, died, ii. 139.

—— Conchobhar Carrach, ollave of the Breifne, died, ii. 199.

—— Conla, slain, ii. 131.

—— Cormac, died, ii. 89.

—— Diarmaid, son of Muirchertach, slain, ii. 131.

—— Domhnall Glas, died, ii. 231.

—— Domhnall Ruadh, son of Sigradh, died, ii. 89.

—— Ferccirtne, ii. 231.

—— John, slain, ii. 131; the son of, *ib.*

2 T

2 T 2

2 X

S.

2 x 2

Sil-Muiredhaigh—*cont.*

bishops of (*see* under Ailfinn, or Elphin); O'Cillin, vice-abbot of, i. 175; the men of, i. 411, 445, 639; expelled from Connacht, i. 79; return to Connacht, i. 81; defeated by the Conmaicne, i. 99; defeat the men of Thomond, i. 81; and the Conmaicne, i. 101; and the Ui-Maine, i. 137; submit to Cathal Carrach O'Conor, i. 213; invite the aid of the Aedh O'Neill, i. 273; the hostages of, i. 295, 499, 569; the chieftains of, i. 483; ii. 57; ollaves or poets of, ii. 109, 359, 469; the district of, i. 387, 389, 581; divided between O'Conor Donn and O'Conor Roe, ii. 63.

Simnel, Lambert, ii. 232, n.

Simon-na-tragha ("Simon of the Strand"), i. 539.

——, Diarmaid, son of, i. 571.

Sinainn, Sinuinn, or Sionainn (the river *Shannon*), i. 145, 387, 419, 463, 465, 503, 533, 577; ii. 271, 357, 371; dried up, i. 399; one of the bridges of, ii. 211; reflux of the waters of, ii. 475.

Sinnach (*Fox*, or *O'Catharnaigh*), i. 175.

—— Bebhinn, wife of, ii. 27.

—— Donnchadh, lord of Muinter-Tadhgain, died, ii. 91.

—— Muirchertach, king of Feara-Tethbha, died, ii. 45.

—— Niall, king of Feara-Tethbha, slain, i. 587.

—— Ruaidhri, died, i. 497.

—— the wife of, ii. 87.

—— the name of, i. 404, n. ³. *See* Fox.

Siograd (or Sigurd) Donn, son of Lothar, i. 5, 11.

Siograd Finn, son of Lothar, i. 5, 11.

Sith-riabhach (*Sheerevagh*, bar. of Tirerrill, co. Sligo), ii. 355.

Sitrec, or Sitric, son of Amhlaibh, king of the Foreigners (Danes), blinds Braen, king of Leinster, i. 19; defeated by Ughaire, king of Leinster, i. 21; goes to Rome, i. 29; kills Raghnall, king of Waterford, i. 37; plunders Ard-Brecain, *ib.*; defeats the Conaille and others, i. 35; slain, i. 67.

Sitrec, or Sitric—*cont.*

—— son of Conrach, son of Eoghan, slain, i. 89.

—— son of Imhar, king of Port-Lairge, slain, i. 23.

Skeffington, William, Justiciary of Ireland, ii. 277, 285, 287.

Skerritt, Clemens, son of James, warden of Galway, died, ii. 469.

Skye, Isle of; *see* Sciadh.

Slaine, or Slane, co. Meath, the castle of, i. 153; the baron of, ii. 189; death of Christopher Fleming, baron of, ii. 227.

Sleimhin, or Sleimhne (*Slevin*), the sons of, i. 164, n. ¹.

—— Master, i. 293.

Sliabh-an-iarainn, or Slieve-an-erin, a mountain in the co. Leitrim, i. 301, 303, 350, n. ⁴.

Sliabh-Badhna, or Slieve-Bawne, a mountain in the n. e. of the co. Roscommon, ii. 357, 389, 395.

Sliabh-Betha (*Slieve Beagh*, between the counties of Monaghan and Tyrone), ii. 201.

Sliabh-Bladhma (*Slieve Bloom*, Queen's Co.), kings of, i.e. kings of Ossory, q. v.

Sliabh-bo-Aedha, a mountain in the bar. of Tirawley, co. Mayo, ii. 509.

Sliabh-Bregh (*Slieve Brey*), co. Louth, i. 565.

Sliabh-Corran. co. Leitrim, ii. 71.

Sliabh-Crot (*Mount-Grud*, co. Tipperary), battle of, i. 55.

Sliabh-dha-en, bar. of Tirerrill, co. Sligo, i. 543.

Sliabh-Damh, or Sliabh-Gamh (the *Ox Mountains*, co. Sligo), i. 493, 577; ii. 299, 473.

Sliabh-Elpa, or the Alps, i. 111.

Sliabh-Fuaid ("*Fuad's* mountain," or the *Fews* mountains, co. Armagh), i. 25, 71, 85, 99, 271.

Sliabh-Guaire, or Sliabh-Gorey, a mountainous district in the bar. of Clankee, co. Cavan, i. 53.

Sliabh-Lugha (a territory in the co. Mayo containing so much of the bar. of Costello as is included in the diocese of Achonry),

DUBLIN: Printed by ALEXANDER THOM, 87 & 88, Abbey-street,
For Her Majesty's Stationery Office.

ImTheStory.com

Personalized Classic Books in many genre's

Unique gift for kids, partners, friends, colleagues

Customize:

- Character Names
- Upload your own front/back cover images (optional)
- Inscribe a personal message/dedication on the
  inside page (optional)

Customize many titles Including
- Alice in Wonderland
- Romeo and Juliet
- The Wizard of Oz
- A Christmas Carol
- Dracula
- Dr. Jekyll & Mr. Hyde
- And more...

CPSIA information can be obtained
at www.ICGtesting.com
Printed in the USA
LVOW04s0749120216

474635LV00017B/462/P

9 781314 125122